ADVERTISING &
Fourth Canadian Edition
PROMOTION

AN INTEGRATED MARKETING COMMUNICATIONS PERSPECTIVE

GEORGE E. BELCH
San Diego State University

MICHAEL A. BELCH
San Diego State University

MICHAEL A. GUOLLA
University of Ottawa

McGraw-Hill
Ryerson
Connect. Learn. Succeed.

Dedicated to my wonderful family,
Teresa, Louise, Daniel, and Nicholas.

Advertising and Promotion
Fourth Canadian Edition

ISBN-13: 978-0-07-007338-8
ISBN-10: 0-07-007338-4

1 2 3 4 5 6 7 8 9 10   TCP   1 9 8 7 6 5 4 3 2 1 0

Printed and bound in Canada

Care has been taken to trace ownership of copyright material contained in this text; however, the publisher will welcome any information that enables them to rectify any reference or credit for subsequent editions.

Vice President, Editor-in-Chief: Joanna Cotton
Executive Sponsoring Editor: Leanna MacLean
Executive Marketing Manager: Joy Armitage Taylor
Developmental Editor: Rachel Horner
Senior Editorial Associate: Stephanie Hess/Erin Catto
Permissions Editor: Tracy Leonard
Supervising Editor: Graeme Powell
Copy Editor: Kelli Howey
Production Coordinator: Lena Keating
Cover Design: Brett Miller
Cover Image: Philippe Colombi/Getty Images RF
Page Layout: Bookman
Printer: Transcontinental Printing Group

Library and Archives Canada Cataloguing in Publication

Belch, George E. (George Eugene)
   Advertising & promotion : an integrated marketing communications perspective / George E. Belch, Michael A. Belch, Michael A. Guolla. — 4th Canadian ed.

Includes bibliographical references and index.
ISBN 978-0-07-007338-8

   1. Advertising—Textbooks.   2. Sales promotion—Textbooks.   3. Communication in marketing—Textbooks.   I. Belch, Michael A   II. Guolla, Michael Angelo   III. Title.
IV. Title: Advertising and promotion.

HF5823.B38 2011   659.1   C2010-905566-7

BRIEF CONTENTS

Preface   viii

PART 1
UNDERSTANDING INTEGRATED MARKETING COMMUNICATIONS   2

CHAPTER 1
Integrated Marketing Communications   2

CHAPTER 2
Organizing for Integrated Marketing
Communications   34

CHAPTER 3
Consumer Behaviour and Target Audience
Decisions   62

CHAPTER 4
Communication Response Models   94

PART 2
ARTICULATE THE MESSAGE   122

CHAPTER 5
Objectives for the IMC Plan   122

CHAPTER 6
Brand Positioning Strategy Decisions   148

CHAPTER 7
Creative Strategy Decisions   176

CHAPTER 8
Creative Tactics Decisions   216

CHAPTER 9
Measuring the Effectiveness of the Promotional
Message   246

PART 3
DELIVER THE MESSAGE   274

CHAPTER 10
Media Planning and Budgeting for IMC   274

CHAPTER 11
Broadcast Media   318

CHAPTER 12
Print Media   348

CHAPTER 13
Out-of-Home and Support Media   382

PART 4
STRENGTHEN THE MESSAGE   416

CHAPTER 14
Sales Promotion   416

CHAPTER 15
Public Relations   458

CHAPTER 16
Direct Marketing   486

CHAPTER 17
Internet Media   506

PART 5
ADVERTISING AND SOCIETY   542

CHAPTER 18
Regulatory, Ethical, Social, and Economic
Issues for IMC   542

Endnotes   576

Credits and Acknowledgments   593

Name and Company Index   595

Subject Index   600

CONTENTS

Preface   viii

PART 1
UNDERSTANDING INTEGRATED MARKETING COMMUNICATIONS

CHAPTER 1
Integrated Marketing Communications   2

Marketing Communication   4
  Marketing   4
  Communicating Product   5
  Communicating Price   7
  Communicating Distribution   9
The Promotional Mix   9
  Advertising   9
  Sales Promotion   12
  Public Relations   12
  Direct Marketing   13
  Internet Marketing   14
  Personal Selling   15
  Participants in the Promotional Process   15
Integrated Marketing Communications   16
  The Evolution of IMC   17
  A Renewed Perspective of IMC   17
  Importance of IMC   19
Integrated Marketing Communications Planning   23
  Review the Marketing Plan   23
  Assess the Marketing Communications Situation   25
  Determine IMC Plan Objectives   28
  Develop IMC Programs   28
  Implement and Control the IMC Plan   29
IMC Planning: Organization of Text   30
Chapter Objectives and Summary   32
Key Terms   33
Discussion Questions   33

CHAPTER 2
Organizing for Integrated Marketing
Communications   34

Organizing for Advertising and Promotion in the Firm   36
  The Centralized System   36
  The Decentralized System   37
Advertising Agencies   38
  Advertising Agency Decision   38
  Advertising Agency Industry   41
  Full-Service Advertising Agencies   42
  Other Types of Agencies and Services   46
Agency Compensation and Evaluation   47
  Commissions from Media   47
  Fee Arrangement   49
  Cost-Plus Agreement   50
  Incentive-Based Compensation   50
  Evaluation of Agencies   51
  Reasons for Agencies Losing Clients   52
Specialized Services   54
  Sales Promotion Agencies   54
  Public Relations Firms   55
  Direct-Response Agencies   55
  Interactive Agencies   56
IMC Planning: Agency Relationships   56

Integrated IMC Services   56
Agency–Client Responsibility   57
Agency–Client Partnership   58
Chapter Objectives and Summary   60
Key Terms   61
Discussion Questions   61

CHAPTER 3
Consumer Behaviour and Target Audience Decisions   62

Consumer Decision-Making Process   64
  Need Recognition   64
  Consumer Motivation   66
  Information Search   68
  Perception   69
  Alternative Evaluation   71
  Attitudes   72
  Purchase Decision   73
  Integration Processes   74
  Postpurchase Evaluation   74
  Satisfaction   75
Variations in Consumer Decision Making   76
  Types of Decision Making   76
  Group Decision Making   77
Target Audience Decision   78
  Marketing Planning Process   78
  Market Segmentation   80
  Target Market Selection   85
  Target Audience Options   86
IMC Planning: Target Audience Profile   89
  Profile for Messages   89
  Profile for Media   90
  Profile for IMC Tools   91
Chapter Objectives and Summary   92
Key Terms   93
Discussion Questions   93

CHAPTER 4
Communication Response Models   94

A Basic Model of Communication   96
  Overview of the Model   96
  Source/Encoding   96
  Message   97
  Channel   99
  Receiver/Decoding   100
  Noise   101
  Response/Feedback   101
  Summary of the Model   102
The Response Process   103
  Traditional Response Hierarchy Models   103
  Implications of the Traditional Hierarchy Models   104
  Alternative Response Hierarchies   106
  Implications of the Alternative Response Models   108
Cognitive Processing of Communications   110
  The Cognitive Response Approach   110
  The Elaboration Likelihood Model   112
IMC Planning: Response Model for Decision Making   115
  Does Advertising Work?   115
  Managerial Approach   117
Chapter Objectives and Summary   120
Key Terms   121
Discussion Questions   121

iv

PART 2
ARTICULATE THE MESSAGE

CHAPTER 5

Objectives for the IMC Plan 122

Objective Setting 124
  Value of Objectives 124
  Marketing Objectives 125
  Sales Objective Debate 126
  Behavioural Objectives 126
  Communication Objectives 128

From Communication Response Models to
Communication Objectives 129
  Defining Advertising Goals for Measured Results 129
  Comprehensive Response Model Applications 131

Setting IMC Objectives 134
  Options for Behavioural Objectives 134
  Options for Communication Objectives 138

IMC Planning: Objectives for Buyer Decision Stages 142

Chapter Objectives and Summary 146

Key Terms 147

Discussion Questions 147

CHAPTER 6

Brand Positioning Strategy Decisions 148

Positioning 150
  Market Positioning Strategy 150
  Brand Positioning Strategy 152
  Brand Positioning Strategy Decision Process 154

Brand Positioning Strategy Decisions 158
  Market Definition 158
  Differential Advantage 159
  Target Audience Brand Attitude 162
  Consumer Purchase Motive 165

Brand Repositioning Strategy 167
  Market Definition 167
  Differential Advantage 168
  New Target Audience 168
  Purchase Motivation 171

IMC Planning: Brand Positioning Extensions 172
  Multiple Target Audiences 172
  Buyer Decision Stages 173
  Corporate Brands 173

Chapter Objectives and Summary 174

Key Terms 175

Discussion Questions 175

CHAPTER 7

Creative Strategy Decisions 176

Advertising Creativity 178
  Definition of Advertising Creativity 178
  Importance of Advertising Creativity 179

Planning Creative Strategy 181
  Creative Challenge 182
  Creative Process 183
  Account Planning 183
  Research in the Creative Process 184
  Copy Platform 186

Creative Theme 187
  Origin of Creative Theme 187
  Creative Theme Consistency 191
  Canadian Creative Themes 193

Message Appeals 195
  Rational Appeals 196

  Emotional Appeals 199
  Fear Appeals 200
  Humour Appeals 201
  Combined Rational and Emotional Appeals 203

Source Characteristics 205
  Source Credibility 205
  Source Attractiveness 206

IMC Planning: Message and Source Combinations 212

Chapter Objectives and Summary 214

Key Terms 215

Discussion Questions 215

CHAPTER 8

Creative Tactics Decisions 216

Creative Execution Style 218
  Straight Sell 218
  Scientific/Technical Evidence 218
  Demonstration 218
  Comparison 219
  Testimonial 219
  Slice of Life 220
  Animation 220
  Personality Symbol 221
  Imagery 221
  Dramatization 223
  Humour 224

Message Structure 224
  Order of Presentation 224
  Conclusion Drawing 225
  Message Sidedness 226
  Verbal versus Visual Messages 226

Design Elements for IMC Tools 227
  Design for Print Messages 228
  Design for Video Messages 231
  Design for Audio Messages 234

Frameworks for Creative Tactics 235
  The FCB Planning Model 235
  The R&P Planning Model 236

IMC Planning: Guidelines for Creative Evaluation 241

Chapter Objectives and Summary 244

Key Terms 245

Discussion Questions 245

CHAPTER 9

Measuring the Effectiveness of the Promotional
Message 246

The Measuring Effectiveness Debate 248
  Reasons for Measuring Effectiveness 248
  Reasons for Not Measuring Effectiveness 248

Decisions for Measuring Effectiveness 250
  What to Test 250
  When to Test 251
  Where to Test 252

Methods of Measuring Effectiveness 253
  Concept Generation and Testing 253
  Rough Art, Copy, and Commercial Testing 254
  Pretesting of Finished Ads 257
  Market Testing of Ads 263

IMC Planning: Program for Measuring Effectiveness 268
  Criteria for Effective Research 269
  Guidelines for Effective Testing 270

Chapter Objectives and Summary 272

Key Terms 273

Discussion Questions 273

v

Contents

PART 3

DELIVER THE MESSAGE

CHAPTER 10
Media Planning and Budgeting for IMC 274

Media Planning 276
  Overview 276
  Media Plan 279
  Media Planning Challenges 280
Media Strategy Decisions 283
  The Media Mix 283
  Target Audience Coverage 285
  Geographic Coverage 287
  Scheduling 289
  Reach versus Frequency 290
Media Tactics Decisions 294
  Media Vehicle 294
  Relative Cost Estimates 296
  Blocking Chart 299
Budget Setting 300
  Overview 300
  Theoretical Approaches in Budget Setting 302
  Managerial Approaches in Budget Setting 305
IMC Planning: Budget Allocation 311
  IMC Tools 312
  Market Share Goals 313
  Client/Agency Policies 314
  Organizational Characteristics 315
Chapter Objectives and Summary 316
Key Terms 317
Discussion Questions 317

CHAPTER 11
Broadcast Media 318

Television 320
  Strengths of Television 320
  Limitations of Television 322
  Buying Television Advertising Time 326
  Types of Television Advertising 326
  Time Periods and Programs 329
  Specialty Television Advertising 330
  Measuring the Television Audience 334
Radio 336
  Strengths of Radio 338
  Limitations of Radio 339
  Buying Radio Time 341
  Time Classifications 341
  Measuring the Radio Audience 342
IMC Planning: Strategic Use of Broadcast Media 343
  Television 343
  Radio 344
Chapter Objectives and Summary 346
Key Terms 347
Discussion Questions 347

CHAPTER 12
Print Media 348

Evaluation of Magazines 350
  Classifications of Magazines 350
  Foreign Publications 354
  Strengths of Magazines 355
  Limitations of Magazines 361
Buying Magazine Advertising Space 363
  Magazine Circulation and Readership 363
  Magazine Audience Measurement—PMB 364
  Magazine Advertising Rates 365

Evaluation of Newspapers 365
  Types of Newspapers 365
  Types of Newspaper Advertising 367
  Strengths of Newspapers 368
  Limitations of Newspapers 371
Buying Newspaper Advertising Space 372
  Newspaper Circulation and Readership 372
  Daily Newspaper Audience Measurement 374
  Newspaper Advertising Rates 376
IMC Planning: Strategic Use of Print Media 377
  Magazines 377
  Newspapers 379
Chapter Objectives and Summary 380
Key Terms 381
Discussion Questions 381

CHAPTER 13
Out-of-Home and Support Media 382

Outdoor Media 384
  Outdoor Media Options 384
  Audience Measurement 387
  Strengths of Outdoor Media 391
  Limitations of Outdoor Media 392
Transit Media 393
  Transit Media Options 393
  Strengths of Transit Media 395
  Limitations of Transit Media 396
Place-Based Media 397
  Place-Based Media Options 397
  Strengths of Place-Based Media 399
  Limitations of Place-Based Media 400
Promotional Products 401
  Strengths of Promotional Products 403
  Limitations of Promotional Products 404
  Promotional Products Research 404
Product Placement 405
  Product Placement Decisions 405
  Strengths of Product Placement 408
  Limitations of Product Placement 409
  Audience Measurement for Product Placement 410
IMC Planning: Strategic Use of Out-of-Home and
  Support Media 410
  Out-of-Home Media 411
  Support Media 412
Chapter Objectives and Summary 414
Key Terms 414
Discussion Questions 415

PART 4

STRENGTHEN THE MESSAGE

CHAPTER 14
Sales Promotion 416

Sales Promotion Planning 418
  Characteristics of Sales Promotion 418
  Types of Sales Promotion 418
  Growth of Sales Promotion 420
Sales Promotion Plan 423
  Objectives of Consumer Sales Promotion 423
  Consumer Sales Promotion Strategy Decisions 425
  Consumer Sales Promotion Tactics Decisions 428
Consumer Sales Promotion Strategy Options 428
  Sampling 429
  Coupons 431
  Premiums 435

Contests and Sweepstakes   437
Refunds and Rebates   439
Bonus Packs   440
Price-Off Deals   440
Frequency Programs   441
Event Marketing   442
Trade Sales Promotion   **444**
Objectives of Trade Sales Promotion   444
Trade Sales Promotion Strategy Options   445
IMC Planning: Strategic Use of Sales Promotion   **451**
Budget Allocation   451
Creative Themes   452
Media Support   452
Brand Equity   453
Measuring Sales Promotion Effectiveness   455
Chapter Objectives and Summary   456
Key Terms   457
Discussion Questions   457

CHAPTER 15
Public Relations   458

Public Relations   460
The Traditional Definition of PR   460
The New Role of PR   460
Publicity   461
Public Relations Plan   462
Situation Analysis   463
Determine Relevant Target Audiences   464
Behavioural Objectives   466
Communication Objectives   466
Strategy   467
Tactics   468
Public Relations Effectiveness   468
Media Publicity   469
Media Options   470
Strengths of Media Publicity   471
Limitations of Media Publicity   473
Corporate Advertising   473
Corporate Reputation   473
Image Advertising   475
Cause-Related Advertising   476
Sponsorship   479
IMC Planning: Strategic Use of PR   482
Chapter Objectives and Summary   484
Key Terms   485
Discussion Questions   485

CHAPTER 16
Direct Marketing   486

Direct Marketing   488
Defining Direct Marketing   488
Developing a Database   489
Direct-Marketing Plan   492
Target Audiences for Direct Marketing   492
Direct-Marketing Objectives   493
Direct-Response Media   494
Direct-Marketing Effectiveness   499
Evaluation of Direct Marketing   499
Strengths of Direct Marketing   499
Limitations of Direct Marketing   500
IMC Planning: Strategic Use of Direct Marketing   501
Decision-Making Process   501
Direct Marketing and IMC Tools   502
Chapter Objectives and Summary   503
Key Terms   504
Discussion Questions   504

CHAPTER 17
Internet Media   506

Internet Communication   508
Internet Users   508
Website Communication   511
Website Communication Objectives   511
Website Strategy   513
Internet Media Options   516
Methods of Reaching Target Audiences   516
Advertising   517
Sales Promotion   526
Public Relations   527
Direct Marketing   529
Measuring Internet Effectiveness   533
Audience Measures   533
Exposure and Processing Measures   534
Communication Effects Measures   534
Measures of Behaviour   536
Sources of Measurement Data   536
Evaluation of Internet Media   536
Strengths of Internet Media   536
Limitations of Internet Media   537
IMC Planning: Strategic Use of Internet Media   538
Chapter Objectives and Summary   540
Key Terms   541
Discussion Questions   541

PART 5

ADVERTISING AND SOCIETY

CHAPTER 18
Regulatory, Ethical, Social, and Economic Issues
for IMC   542
Advertising Regulation in Canada   544
Canadian Radio-television and
    Telecommunications Commission (CRTC)   545
Competition Act   546
Regulation of Tobacco Advertising   546
Regulations on Advertising to Children   547
Advertising Standards Council (ASC)   547
Ethical Effects of Advertising   555
Advertising as Untruthful or Deceptive   555
Advertising as Offensive or in Bad Taste   557
Advertising and Children   559
Social Effects of Advertising   560
Advertising Encourages Materialism   561
Advertising Makes People Buy Things They
    Don't Need   562
Advertising and Stereotyping   563
Advertising and the Media   566
Advertising and Social Benefit   568
Economic Effects of Advertising   568
Effects on Consumer Choice   569
Effects on Competition   569
Effects on Product Costs and Prices   570
Summarizing Economic Effects   571
Chapter Objectives and Summary   574
Key Terms   575
Discussion Questions   575

Endnotes   576

Credits and Acknowledgments   593

Name and Company Index   595

Subject Index   600

PREFACE

ADVERTISING & PROMOTION

Most people are influenced to some degree by advertising and other forms of promotion, even though they might not admit it or realize it. Organizations in both the private and public sectors frequently demonstrate that communicating effectively and efficiently with their target audiences is critical to their success. Advertising and other types of promotional messages known as marketing communication are used to sell goods and services as well as to promote causes and individuals, and to influence attitudes and behaviour to resolve societal problems. In fact, it would be rare to find any organization that doesn't do any form of communication to achieve its objectives and marketing communication plays a critical role in those objectives.

For decades, the advertising strategy for a national brand involved one or two commercials run on network television, a few print ads placed in general interest magazines, and sales promotion support such as coupons or premium offers. However, in today's world there are myriad media outlets—print, radio, specialty TV channels, out-of-home—competing for consumers' attention. Marketers also communicate with their customers and potential customers, along with various stakeholders through additional means like events, sponsorships, and public relations. Finally, Internet media as an advertising vehicle and as a tool for other communication purposes extends a manager's options considerably. Innovative digital applications including informational and transformational websites, social media, podcasting, and mobile media, to name a few, intensify the marketing communication presence considerably.

This text introduces students to the field of advertising and promotion. Currently, marketers and their agencies approach advertising and promotion from an integrated marketing communications (IMC) perspective, which calls for a "big picture" approach to planning promotion programs and coordinating the various communication functions. To understand the role of advertising and promotion in today's business world, one must recognize how a firm can use all the promotional tools to communicate.

OVERVIEW OF THE FOURTH CANADIAN EDITION

- **A Continued Focus on IMC** This edition approaches advertising and promotion from an integrated marketing communications perspective to attain communication and behavioural objectives for multiple target audiences. The importance of specific communication objectives for each target audience and the importance of unique messages that resonate for each target audience are developed in many chapters. This approach helps establish a unique brand position for each target audience while maintaining the overall market position of the brand.

- **Canadian Examples** Updated statistical information presented in tables, charts, and figures appears throughout the text. Many new Canadian examples and ads are featured to give a comprehensive look at the most innovative marketing communication occurring in our country.

- **Clear Decision Focus** Chapter 1 summarizes a planning framework and identifies the content of an IMC plan. This framework is followed closely throughout the text as major parts are organized and given a title that corresponds to the steps in the IMC plan. A distinction is made between the type of decisions that an advertiser makes versus the information used to formulate the decision. This approach makes it easier for students to understand the key decisions that need to be made for a successful IMC plan.

- **Internet Focus** This revision focused on updating Internet media or tools throughout the text where it appeared most relevant. The majority of the opening vignettes and chapter perspectives highlight the use of websites or other digital tools. As part of this, the Internet chapter is almost completely re-written, with 35 academic references and 33 trade references added.

- **Current in Theory and Practice** Extensive updating of the academic references from the *Journal of Advertising* and the *Journal of Advertising Research* have been made for this edition. Over 100 new journal citations have been interspersed throughout the material and 300 additional trade references were added from sources such as *Marketing Magazine, Strategy*, the *National Post, The Globe and Mail*, and others.

ORGANIZATION OF THIS TEXT

This book is divided into five major parts. In Part 1, "Understanding Integrated Marketing Communications," we provide background in the areas of IMC planning, consumer behaviour, and communication. Chapter 1 provides an overview of advertising and promotion and an IMC planning model shows the steps in the promotional planning process. This model provides a framework for developing the IMC program and is followed throughout the text. In Chapter 2, we describe how firms organize for advertising and promotion and examine the role of ad agencies and other firms that deliver promotional services. Chapter 3 explains how managers can use an understanding of buyer behaviour to develop effective communication that is directed to specific target audiences. Chapter 4 examines communication theories and models of how consumers respond to advertising messages and other forms of marketing communication.

In Part 2, "Articulate the Message," we consider how firms develop objectives for their IMC programs and how to translate those objectives into meaningful messages. Chapter 5 stresses the importance of knowing what to expect from advertising and promotion, the different types of communication objectives, characteristics of good objectives, and problems in setting objectives. Chapter 6 explores various ways advertisers try to position their brands through effective communication. Chapter 7 discusses the planning and development of the creative strategy and advertising campaign. In Chapter 8 we turn our attention to ways to execute the creative strategy and some criteria for evaluating creative work. Chapter 9 discusses ways to measure the effectiveness of promotional messages from an IMC program, including methods for pretesting and posttesting advertising messages and campaigns.

In Part 3, "Deliver the Message," we explore the various ways of getting the message to the target audience. Chapters 10 through 13 cover media strategy and planning and advertising media. Chapter 10 introduces the key principles of media planning and strategy, and examines how a media plan is developed for all IMC tools. We have also included methods for determining and allocating the promotional budget into this chapter across all IMC tools.

Chapter 11 discusses the strengths and limitations of broadcast media, as well as issues regarding the purchase of radio and TV time and audience measurement. Chapter 12 considers the same issues for the print media (magazines and newspapers). Chapter 13 examines the role of out-of-home and support media.

In Part 4, "Strengthen the Message," we continue the IMC emphasis by examining other promotional tools. Chapter 14 examines the area of sales promotion, including both consumer promotions and programs targeted to the trade (retailers, wholesalers, and other intermediaries). Chapter 15 covers the role of public relations in IMC. Chapter 16 looks at direct marketing and the importance of databases allowing companies to communicate directly with target audiences through various media. Chapter 17 describes how Internet media deliver promotional messages and other IMC tools.

The text concludes with Part 5, "Advertising and Society," and contains Chapter 18, which discusses the regulatory, social, ethical, and economic issues for advertising and promotion.

CHAPTER FEATURES

The following features in each chapter enhance students' understanding of the material as well as their reading enjoyment.

Chapter Objectives

Objectives are provided at the beginning of each chapter to identify the major areas and points covered in the chapter and guide the learning effort. The objectives are restated at the conclusion of each chapter to guide the chapter summary.

■ CHAPTER OBJECTIVES

1 To examine the importance of marketing communication within the marketing mix.

2 To highlight the elements of the promotional mix: advertising, sales promotion, public relations, direct marketing, Internet marketing, and personal selling.

3 To introduce the concept of integrated marketing communications (IMC) by considering its evolution, renewed perspective, and importance.

4 To summarize a model of the IMC planning process and to examine the steps in developing a marketing communications program.

ix

Chapter Opening Vignettes

Each chapter begins with a new vignette that describes an exciting example of the effective use of integrated marketing communications by a company or ad agency, bringing current industry issues into focus, as they pertain to the chapter.

DORITOS FINDS A WINNER

Seeking a new and innovative way to reach teens and young adults (i.e., ages 13–24) with its marketing communication, Doritos decided to let potential customers reach out to the brand by producing their own 30-second video message to launch a new flavour of the popular snack product. The "Become a Doritos Guru" contest, promoted on TV, social media, MuchMusic, and Doritos packaging, invited Canadians to develop their own vision of the brand with the chance to receive a financial prize of $25,000 and 1% of sales, see the ad on national TV, and experience the thrill of having their ad disseminated throughout the digital world. The grand launch, which occurred during the Super Bowl telecast, urged consumers to visit the website DoritosGuru.ca.

Doritos worked with a variety of marketing communication agencies including BBDO Toronto (creative), Capital C (packaging and point-of-purchase display), Proximity (digital media), Fleishman-Hillard (public relations), and OMD Canada (media placement). Together, these experts conceived a concept where contestants would post their entry to DoritosGuru.ca, Facebook, or YouTube, allowing viewers to vote on the one they liked best to identify the five semi-finalists. Research indicated that Millennials, the target audience, relate to brands differently than other consumers, so Doritos maker

The contest obtained 30,000 Facebook fans, 1.5 million visitors to the YouTube channel, 2,100 video submissions (surpassing the number received in a similar campaign conducted in the United States a year previously), and 589,000 votes. A judging panel that included Toronto Raptor Chris Bosh viewed the top five and selected as the winner a team headed by Ryan Coopersmith, which branded the new chip "Scream Cheese." The ad showed a number of people screaming while doing everyday activities (e.g., work, movie, dinnertime), and ended with "What are you screaming about?" Cooper-

IMC, Ethical, and Global Perspectives

These boxed items feature descriptions of interesting issues related to the chapter material or the practical application of integrated marketing communications and ethical and global marketing.

IMC PERSPECTIVE 16-1
Dove and the Shoppers Drug Mart Double Loyalty Club

With just over 10 million members, Shoppers Drug Mart isn't the only one happy about the success of its Shoppers Optimum loyalty program. Marketers often see sales of their brands spike when they invest in a Shoppers Optimum promotion since participating consumers receive bonus points toward in-store discounts. Now, Unilever—one of the drugstore chain's largest vendors—has upped the ante, running a loyalty initiative specifically for Dove that exists within the Shoppers Optimum program. Called Dove Optimum Rewards, membership gives consumers the opportunity to earn double the points when they buy two or more different Dove products. "We've created a club within a club," says Gabriel Verkade, retail activation manager of national accounts at Toronto-based Unilever.

Dove Optimum Rewards is the first vendor program of its kind for Shoppers Drug Mart. As the loyalty segment matures, experts suggest this is just the start of what they're calling "loyalty program guardians," where marketers ranging from retailers to hotels create new and innovative partnerships with vendors. Before Shoppers Drug Mart partnered with Dove, rival packaged goods companies had approached the retailer about creating a vendor subprogram within Shoppers Optimum. Ultimately, Shoppers Drug Mart chose Dove because the brand ties nicely into the retailer's identity, focusing on health, beauty, and convenience, and had many SKUs to drive sales.

The four-week introductory campaign for Dove Optimum Rewards included a permission-based e-mail to one million Shoppers Optimum members, as well as to the permission-based e-mail lists of Chatelaine and mochasofa.ca; a national two-page flyer delivered to 4.4 million homes; an ad in Glow magazine; and signage, posters, and header cards in more than 974 Shoppers Drug Mart and Quebec-based Pharmaprix®) stores. The advertising included a coupon which, when scanned at the checkout, signed up Shoppers Optimum members to

the Dove program. Shoppers Optimum members can also register online at www.shoppersdrugmart.ca/dove. Once registered, Shoppers Optimum card holders are automatically tagged as Dove Optimum Rewards members—in other words, no need for customers to carry yet another loyalty card.

Unilever aims to do more than just encourage trial among customers who typically purchase only a single Dove product. Unilever ultimately wants to develop a relationship with these customers through the new Dove Optimum database. Because strict privacy regulations mean Shoppers Drug Mart doesn't give vendors access to its Shoppers Optimum database—which includes everything from the typical amount of a member's shopping basket to their demographic profile. But, the Shoppers Drug Mart/Unilever partnership does give Unilever access to information about the Dove Optimum Rewards members and the ability to work with Shoppers to better target them.

For Dove, the challenge is keeping the Dove Optimum Rewards program top of mind so that consumers realize that it is, in fact, a club within a club. "Once they are enrolled, our challenge is reminding them that they have joined an additional program and of the value they are receiving from it," says Verkade. That might mean a combination of direct mail, flyers, and e-mail or promotions on existing or new products, but also more value-added, enriched content, such as a booklet about beauty tips or information on managing sensitive skin.

Source: Chris Daniels, "The Layered Look," Marketing Magazine, March 26, 2007.

Questions
1. Explain how Dove's relationship to the Shoppers Optimum program works.
2. What concerns would you have about this joint promotion?

IMC Planning

Each chapter includes an IMC Planning section illustrating how chapter content relates to integrated marketing communication. It provides guidance on how a manager can use the conceptual material to make better practical decisions.

IMC PLANNING: RESPONSE MODEL FOR DECISION MAKING

In this final section we attempt to reconcile the models presented in this chapter by summarizing the academic perspective and by presenting the most relevant response model for managerial decision making. The first section concludes that traditional communication response models based on a hierarchy or adaptation of a hierarchy are limited in their ability to explain how advertising works. The subsequent section summarizes another part of the Rossiter and Percy perspective that is managerially oriented and will be used to set communication objectives and plan for creative messages in subsequent chapters.

Key Terms

Important terms are highlighted in boldface and listed at the end of each chapter with a page reference. These terms help call students' attention to important ideas, concepts, and definitions and help them review their learning progress.

KEY TERMS

account executive, 46 · advertising manager, 36 · brand manager, 37 · centralized system, 36 · commission system, 47 · copywriters, 42 · cost-plus system, 50 · creative boutique, 46 · decentralized system, 37 · departmental system, 46 · direct-response agencies, 55 · fee-commission combination, 49 · financial audit, 51 · fixed-fee method, 49 · full-service agency, 42 · group system, 46 · incentive-based system, 50 · in-house agency, 38 · interactive agencies, 50 · media buying services, 47 · negotiated commission, 49 · public relations firm, 55 · qualitative audit, 51 · sales promotion agency, 54 · superagencies, 41

Chapter Summaries

These heavily revised synopses serve as a quick review of important topics covered to illustrate how the learning objectives have been achieved, providing a more thorough approach for reviewing chapter content.

CHAPTER OBJECTIVES AND SUMMARY

1 To understand how companies organize for advertising and other aspects of integrated marketing communications.

Companies use two basic systems, centralized and decentralized, to organize internally for advertising and promotion. The marketing communication managers within a centralized system are responsible for planning and budgeting of the IMC plan, administering and executing all communication, coordinating with other departments such as market research, and coordinating with outside agencies for additional expertise and resources. In contrast, the decision-maker for a decentralized system, such as brand manager, has profit and loss responsibility for all aspects of the brand and the scope of activities becomes more extensive, going beyond what the advertising or communication manager is responsible for in a centralized system.

2 To examine methods for selecting, compensating, and evaluating advertising agencies.

Firms have to decide whether they

have the disadvantage of less experience, objectivity, and flexibility.

Many firms use advertising agencies to help develop and execute their programs. These agencies may take on a variety of forms, including full-service agencies, creative boutiques, and media buying services. The first offers the client a full range of services (including creative, account, marketing, and financial and management services); the other two specialize in creative services and media buying, respectively.

Agencies are compensated through commission systems, and fee- and cost-based systems. Recently, the emphasis on agency accountability has increased. Agencies are being evaluated on both financial and qualitative aspects, and some clients are using incentive-based compensation systems that tie agency compensation to performance measures such as sales and market share.

3 To explain the role and functions of specialized marketing communications

firms, and interactive agencies. Contracting out work to a specialized agency can enhance the creativity of the overall IMC plan with experts from specific fields. Moreover, while it may be more costly or time-consuming working with other specialists, these organizations may reach the target audience more precisely thus yielding a favourable ROI. A marketer must decide whether to use a different specialist for each promotional function or have all of its integrated marketing communications done by one advertising agency that offers all of these services under one roof. This latter idea allows an account team to know and control all aspects of the communication.

4 To examine perspectives on the use of integrated services and responsibilities of advertisers versus agencies.

Recent studies have found that most marketers believe it is their responsibility, not the ad agency's, to set strategy for and coordinate IMC campaigns. The lack of a broad perspective and specialized skills in non-advertising areas

Discussion Questions

Questions at the end of each chapter give students an opportunity to test their understanding of the material and to apply it. These questions can also serve as a basis for class discussion or assignments.

DISCUSSION QUESTIONS

1. What are some of the specific responsibilities and duties of an advertising manager under a centralized advertising department structure? Why is an advertising manager needed if a company uses an outside agency?

2. Discuss the pros and cons of using an in-house advertising agency. What are some of the reasons why companies might change from using an in-house agency and hire an outside agency?

3. Discuss the functions a full-service advertising agency performs for its clients. Might any one of these functions be more important than another?

4. Discuss some of the reasons why traditional advertising agencies have been developing more IMC capabilities. What changes might these agencies have to make to improve their service?

5. Why might a company choose to use a creative boutique rather than a larger full-service agency?

6. Why are marketers likely to use a media buying service to handle their media planning and buying versus the media department of an agency?

7. Discuss the methods by which advertising agencies are compensated. What factors will determine the type of compensation arrangement a company uses with an agency?

8. Why are companies moving away from the traditional commission system and using

incentive-based compensation for their agencies? Why might an agency be reluctant to accept an incentive-based compensation system?

9. Discuss the reasons why marketers often choose to switch advertising agencies. Find an example of a company that has recently changed advertising agencies and analyze the reasons given for the change.

10. Discuss the reasons why a company might want to have all its integrated marketing communication activities performed by a single agency versus having several different agencies that specialize in various areas of IMC, like public relations, direct marketing, sales promotion, and Internet marketing.

SUPPORT MATERIAL

With this support package, you and your students receive everything from the basic supplements to the latest in educational technologies. Check it out for yourself.

LECTURE PREPARATION, ASSESSMENT, AND PRESENTATION TOOLS

The following tools are available online to support instructors (www.mcgrawhillconnect.ca):

- *Instructor's Manual.* The Instructor's Manual includes Chapter Overviews, Chapter Objectives, Chapter and Lecture Outlines, Teaching Suggestions, Answers to Discussion Questions, and Additional Discussion Questions and Answers (not shown in text).

- *PowerPoint® Presentation and Digital Assets.* These incorporate a high-quality photo and art program, including figure slides, product shots, and advertisements.

- *Computerized Test Bank.* This test bank contains over 3,000 questions categorized by topic and level of learning (definitional, conceptual, or application). The instructor-friendly format

allows easy selection of questions from any part of the text, boxed materials, and cases. The program allows you to select any of the questions, make changes if desired, or add new questions—and quickly print out a finished set customized to your course.

- *Video Case Studies.* A unique series of contemporary advertising cases is available on *Connect*.

ONLINE TECHNOLOGY

connect™

McGraw-Hill *Connect* is an online teaching and learning platform developed and supported in Canada for Canadian institutions, their faculty, and students. *Connect* was inspired by multiple student and instructor research initiatives, including a quantitative usage and attitude study that captured insights from more than 1,400 students across Canada.

Connect embraces diverse study behaviours and preferences with breakthrough features that help students master course content and achieve better results. The powerful course management tool in *Connect* also offers a wide range of exclusive features that help instructors spend less time managing and more time teaching.

Interactive and Searchable eBook

- Interactive view is searchable and features a digital toolbox with highlighting and sticky note features

- Seamless book view is also available

Flexible Study Plan Options

Students succeed when they're given individualized attention. With *Connect*, all your students can receive comprehensive, customized feedback that dynamically provides help where they need it most.

- Students complete pre- and post-assessments that identify knowledge gaps and point them to concepts they need to learn.

- *Connect* provides students the option to work through recommended learning exercises and create their own personalized study plan using multiple sources of content, including a searchable eBook, multiple-choice and true/false quizzes, interactivities, personal notes, videos, and more.

- Using the copy, paste, highlight, and sticky note features, students collect, organize, and customize their study plan content to suit their study style. The result is higher levels of engagement and improved learning outcomes.

Step-by-Step Assignment Builder

- Create and deliver assignments easily with chapter-by-chapter questions and test bank material to assign online.

- Streamline lesson planning, student progress reporting, and assignment grading to make classroom management more efficient than ever.

- Go paperless with the eBook and online submission and grading of student assignments.

Personalized Teaching Plan

- Prepare your course plan within *Connect* using the searchable eBook and the full collection of teaching resources included with *Connect*.

- Personalize your plan using the copy, paste, highlight, and sticky note features to collect and organize plan content and teaching materials along with all your assessment and grading resources.

- Share your plan with associates and save for subsequent course requirements.

At-a-Glance Grade Book

- Automatically score assignments, giving students immediate feedback on their work and side-by-side comparisons with correct answers.

- Access and review each response; manually change grades or leave comments for students to review.

- Easily export grade reports into Learning Management Systems such as Blackboard, Desire2Learn, Moodle, and WebCT.

Turnkey Instructor Setup

- The *Connect* development team and customer service groups are located in our Canadian offices and work closely together to provide expert technical support for both instructors and students.

- Available turnkey programs to help instructors easily set up their course with ongoing support.

Accessible for Students

- Online access to *Connect* with eBook is included with all *Connect* printed textbooks—no extra charge to the student.

- Students also have the option to purchase a separate PIN code that provides online access to *Connect* with eBook only.

SUPERIOR SERVICE

Service takes on a whole new meaning with McGraw-Hill Ryerson and *Advertising & Promotion*. More than just bringing you the textbook, we have consistently raised the bar in terms of innovation and educational research—both in marketing and in education in general. These investments in learning and the education community have helped us to understand the needs of students and educators across the country, and allowed us to foster the growth of truly innovative, integrated learning.

Integrated Learning

Your Integrated Learning Sales Specialist is a McGraw-Hill Ryerson representative who has the experience, product knowledge, training, and support to help you assess and integrate any of our products, technology, and services into your course for optimum teaching and learning performance. Whether it's using our test bank software, helping your students improve their grades, or putting your entire course online, your *i*Learning Sales Specialist is there to help you do it. Contact your local *i*Learning Sales Specialist today to learn how to maximize all of McGraw-Hill Ryerson's resources!

iLearning Services Program

McGraw-Hill Ryerson offers a unique *i*Services package designed for Canadian faculty. Our mission is to equip providers of higher education with superior tools and resources required for excellence in teaching. For additional information, visit www.mcgrawhill.ca/highereducation/iservices.

Teaching, Learning & Technology Conference Series

Teaching & Learning Conference Series

The educational environment has changed tremendously in recent years, and McGraw-Hill Ryerson continues to be committed to helping you acquire the skills you need to succeed in this new milieu. Our innovative Teaching, Learning & Technology Conference Series brings faculty together from across Canada with 3M Teaching Excellence award winners to share teaching and learning best practices in a collaborative and stimulating environment.

ACKNOWLEDGEMENTS

Many colleagues provided detailed and thoughtful reviews that helped immensely. I would like to thank the following reviewers who provided valuable feedback to guide the content of the fourth Canadian edition: Mary Ann Cipriano and Harold Simpkins, Concordia University; Deepa Acharya, Mount Royal University; Mary Sharon Dellar, McGill University; Malcolm Howe, Niagara College; Vern Kennedy, Centennial College; Richard Patterson, York University; Sameer Deshpande, University of Lethbridge; and Janice Shearer, Mohawk College.

I would also like to acknowledge the cooperation I received from many people in the business, advertising, and media communities. The fourth Canadian edition contains several additional ads, illustrations, charts, and tables published by advertisers and/or their agencies, various trade sources, and other advertising and industry organizations. Many individuals provided materials and gave permission to use them. A special thanks to all of you for helping us teach students with up-to-date examples and information. A marketing book cannot exist without the assistance of marketing people!

A successful book like this is the result of a great deal of work on the part of a publisher. Various individuals at McGraw-Hill Ryerson have been involved with this project over the past 18 months. My sponsoring editor, Leanna Maclean, encouraged a complete revision to keep the book up to date. A special thanks goes to Rachel Horner, my developmental editor, for her tremendous and time-consuming effort and high expectations to stay on schedule and to produce a solid manuscript. I want to acknowledge the outstanding work of Tracy Leonard for obtaining permissions for the Canadian content that appears throughout the book. I'd also like to recognize Kelli Howey for her splendid editing and attention to detail that improved the text immensely. Thank you to Graeme Powell for managing the production process. Thanks to the other members of the production team for all of their hard work on this edition.

Many thanks to my current and previous students who have given me the opportunity to develop my ideas. It is very gratifying to know that you enjoy my teaching and are using your newfound knowledge in the business world.

On a personal note, my children, Louise, Daniel, and Nicholas, have been very supportive during this time-consuming and hectic process of working on the text. Their interest and encouragement have been very inspiring. All my love and gratitude goes to my wife, Teresa, who has helped me tremendously during this and all my academic pursuits.

Michael Guolla

ABOUT THE AUTHOR

Michael Guolla is an assistant professor at the Telfer School of Management of the University of Ottawa. He completed his Ph.D. in Business Administration with a concentration in Marketing at the University of Michigan (Ann Arbor) and received his Honours in Business Administration from the Richard Ivey School of Business at the University of Western Ontario. Dr. Guolla has published articles in academic journals, proceedings of scholarly conferences, and management journals.

INTEGRATED MARKETING COMMUNICATIONS

■ CHAPTER OBJECTIVES

1 To examine the importance of marketing communication within the marketing mix.

2 To highlight the elements of the promotional mix: advertising, sales promotion, public relations, direct marketing, Internet marketing, and personal selling.

3 To introduce the concept of integrated marketing communications (IMC) by considering its evolution, renewed perspective, and importance.

4 To summarize a model of the IMC planning process and to examine the steps in developing a marketing communications program.

DORITOS FINDS A WINNER

Seeking a new and innovative way to reach teens and young adults (i.e., ages 13–24) with its marketing communication, Doritos decided to let potential customers reach out to the brand by producing their own 30-second video message to launch a new flavour of the popular snack product. The "Become a Doritos Guru" contest, promoted on TV, social media, MuchMusic, and Doritos packaging, invited Canadians to develop their own vision of the brand with the chance to receive a financial prize of $25,000 and 1% of sales, see the ad on national TV, and experience the thrill of having their ad disseminated throughout the digital world. The grand launch, which occurred during the Super Bowl telecast, urged consumers to visit the website DoritosGuru.ca.

Doritos worked with a variety of marketing communication agencies including BBDO Toronto (creative), Capital C (packaging and point-of-purchase display), Proximity (digital media), Fleishman-Hillard (public relations), and OMD Canada (media placement). Together, these experts conceived a concept where contestants would post their entry to DoritosGuru.ca, Facebook, or YouTube, allowing viewers to vote on the one they liked best to identify the five semi-finalists. Research indicated that Millennials, the target audience, relate to brands differently than other consumers, so Doritos maker Frito-Lay needed to hand them a "blank canvas" to help create the new brand identity. The target audience involved themselves in activities such as watching and sharing online videos, voting in contests, and communicating via social media, and the digital side of the campaign appeared to be a hit during the planning stages as all parties participated to fit the elements together.

Although the digital part of the contest appeared to be a noteworthy characteristic of the 11-week campaign, according to Tony Matta, VP Marketing for Frito-Lay, "If you can create something that's a big enough story, people are going to want to have conversations about it regardless of how you put it into market." And in this case, the story was the opportunity to put one's creative stamp on the Doritos brand. As leader of 14 different Frito-Lay brands, Matta encouraged big ideas along with new media to foster dialogue with consumers.

The contest obtained 30,000 Facebook fans, 1.5 million visitors to the YouTube channel, 2,100 video submissions (surpassing the number received in a similar campaign conducted in the United States a year previously), and 589,000 votes. A judging panel that included Toronto Raptor Chris Bosh viewed the top five and selected as the winner a team headed by Ryan Coopersmith, which branded the new chip "Scream Cheese." The ad showed a number of people screaming while doing everyday activities (e.g., work, movie, dinnertime), and ended with "What are you screaming about?" Coopersmith's team planned to use the winnings to finance their own feature film. Marketing commentators agreed that this campaign is an example where the media execution made sense and the user-generated content helped establish the brand successfully.

Sources: Emily Wexler, "Frito Lay Canada's Tony Matta: Raising the Stakes," *Strategy,* December 2009, p. 30; Calvin Leung, "Social Media," *Canadian Business Magazine,* June 15, 2009; Matt Semansky, "Montreal Filmmaker Achieves Doritos Guru Status," *Marketing Magazine,* May 4, 2009; Jeromy Lloyd, "Doritos Unveils Consumer-Generated Brand Launch," *Marketing Magazine,* February 13, 2009; Jonathan Paul, "The Doritos Guru Chips In," *Strategy,* April 2009, p. 30; Jennifer Wells, "It's Crunch Time," *The Globe and Mail,* February 13, 2009, p. B7.

QUESTIONS:

1. Why would consumers be motivated to participate in the contest?
2. Do the results highlighted indicate a successful or unsuccessful campaign?

As the opening vignette illustrates, companies use many tools such as advertising, websites, direct marketing, sales promotion, public relations, and event sponsorship to communicate something about their products, prices, or availability. In fact, finding the right combination of marketing communication tools is a critical decision for small and large firms, private and public organizations, and those that market goods, services, or ideas. In response, many companies use *integrated marketing communications* to link or connect their promotional tools and communicate with their current and prospective customers. Companies develop their marketing communication plans such that each promotional tool retains its unique communication effect and that the combination of promotional tools contributes to the overall communication effect of the brand or organization.

This opening chapter sets the direction for the entire book as it highlights the marketing context for advertising and promotion and introduces the topic of marketing communication. It briefly describes the different promotional or marketing communication tools available for marketers. Next, we develop the idea of integrated marketing communications and indicate why it is so important. We then identify the content of an integrated marketing communications (IMC) plan as a way of orienting the perspective and organization of this text.

MARKETING COMMUNICATION

In this opening section we briefly identify the role of marketing communication within an organization's overall marketing effort. We begin by reviewing the definition of marketing to understand the importance of marketing communication to convey value to consumers. We then explore some examples of the content of marketing communication plans to illustrate their many different purposes.

Exhibit 1-1 This Patak's ad attempts to show and explain how consumers would enjoy the taste.

MARKETING

Historically, the American Marketing Association (AMA), the organization that represents marketing professionals in the United States and Canada, defined marketing as *the process of planning and executing the conception, pricing, promotion, and distribution of ideas, goods, and services to create exchanges that satisfy individual and organizational objectives.*[1] This definition focused on **exchange** as a central concept in marketing and the use of the basic marketing activities to create and sustain relationships with customers.[2] For exchange to occur there must be two or more parties with something of value to one another, a desire and ability to give up that something to the other party, and a way to *communicate* with each other. Marketing communication plays an important role in the exchange process by informing consumers of an organization's product and convincing them of its ability to satisfy their needs or wants. Exhibit 1-1 conveys how the Patak's Taste of India brand provides satisfaction.

The marketing function in an organization facilitates the exchange process by examining the needs and wants of consumers, developing a product or service that satisfies these needs, offering it at a

Product Decisions	Price Decisions	Distribution Decisions
Product Type	Price Level	Channel Type
Features or Attributes/Benefits	Price Policy	Channel Policy
Corporate Name/Identification	Discount	Type of Intermediary or Reseller
Brand Name/Identification	Allowance	Type of Location/Store
Package Design	Flexibility	Service Level

FIGURE 1–1

Examples of typical marketing decisions

certain price, making it available through a particular place or channel of distribution, and developing a program of promotion or communication. These four Ps—product, price, place (distribution), and promotion (marketing communication)—are elements of the **marketing mix**. The basic task of marketing is combining these four elements into a marketing program to facilitate the potential for exchange with consumers in the marketplace. The remainder of this section will illustrate how the marketing mix decisions of product, price, and distribution (Figure 1-1) are often the content of the primary message of marketing communication.

COMMUNICATING PRODUCT

An organization exists because it offers a product to consumers, generally in exchange for money. This offering may come in the form of a physical good (such as a soft drink, pair of jeans, or car), a service (banking, air travel, or legal assistance), a cause (United Way, March of Dimes), an idea (don't drink and drive), or even a person (a political candidate). The product is anything that can be marketed and that, when used or supported, gives satisfaction to the individual. And these different product types are not always independent. When eating at a restaurant, consumers enjoy the food itself but also value the service of not having to prepare the meal, or the opportunity to eat food they may not have the culinary skill to make. Thus, whatever the product type, marketing communication attempts to show how consumers can receive value through the product offering.

Every product has fairly obvious features or attributes that characterize what it is. A chocolate bar can have varying types of chocolate (e.g., milk, dark) and different kinds of ingredients (e.g., nuts, wafers). Thus, marketing communication can take the simple role of identifying the ingredients or composition of a good. For example, ads for Rice Krispies cereal reminded consumers that each "krisp" contained a single grain of rice, while ads for Shreddies cereal highlighted its unique diamond shape. Notice how the Montblanc ad in Exhibit 1-2 conveys attributes of the watch regarding the steel, crystal, and silver. Moreover, organizations often use marketing communication to educate consumers on how the services are delivered. For instance, many WestJet ads demonstrate the personal attentiveness the airline's staff provide to customers, while many Keg Steakhouse ads focus on the ambiance of the restaurant as well as the food.

A product does not comprise only physical characteristics. Consumers typically view a product as a bundle of benefits signifying what the attributes can do. Benefits can be functional (the performance of the product), experiential (what it feels like to use the product), and/or psychological (feelings such as self-esteem or

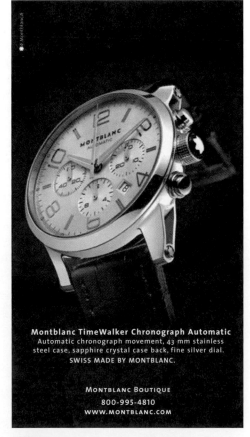

Montblanc TimeWalker Chronograph Automatic
Automatic chronograph movement, 43 mm stainless steel case, sapphire crystal case back, fine silver dial.
SWISS MADE BY MONTBLANC.

MONTBLANC BOUTIQUE
800-995-4810
WWW.MONTBLANC.COM

Exhibit 1-2 Quality attributes are identified for Montblanc watches.

5

status that result from owning a particular brand). Advertising and other marketing communication tools draw attention toward these benefits. Managers often have to decide which benefits to emphasize or how to portray the benefits in a message, and the best way to deliver that message. BMW's latest advertising emphasizes the joy of driving a BMW vehicle (i.e., experiential benefit) by showing an "expression of joy." A recent print ad did not show the product, but rather depicted the car's tire marks in colour as if they were painted upon a canvas.[3]

The term **product symbolism** refers to what a product or brand means to consumers and what they experience in purchasing and using it.[4] For products with strong symbolic features, the social and psychological meaning may be more important than functional utility.[5] For example, designer clothing such as Versace, Gucci, and Prada is often purchased on the basis of its symbolic meaning. Marketing communication plays an important role in developing and maintaining the symbolism of these brands (Exhibit 1-3).

A brand or corporate name and its identification through its logo, symbol, or trademark represent critical product decisions. Marketers use brand names that can communicate product concepts clearly, such as Air Canada (airlines) and Seadoo (water craft). The importance of selecting an appropriate visual representation of the brand can be seen every day when we look at virtually any automobile and notice the symbol used to convey the brand or company. One primary purpose of marketing communication is to present the brand and its identification in favourable locations, situations, or time frames that allow consumers to think or feel more positively toward the brand. The identification of a logo in an ad is critical, as evidenced by a legal challenge Molson-Coors filed against Labatt in which the company suggested the stylized mountaintop shown in a Kokanee ad appeared too similar to the logo used by Coors Light.[6]

Brand identification and the symbolism of the brand is often reinforced by the tagline or slogan appearing in any form of marketing communication. IKEA's latest slogan encapsulates the essence of the brand magnificently with "Any space can be beautiful." Some executives suggest that the tagline is still very relevant since it "communicates a brand position or brand benefit." For example, Swiss Chalet returned to a previously successful tagline, "Always so good for so little," after making many changes the past few years. Harvey's has reminded us often over the years of the beauty of its hamburgers. Firms that offer many types of goods and services use an audio logo as one way of connecting brand messages across multiple media and IMC tools, much like a visual logo. For example, the Rogers audio logo can be heard for many of its services, including wireless and cable. Continuity and consistency in the promotional message across IMC tools—television, radio, wireless, interactive displays, Internet, podcasts—makes simple reminders a key part of the brand experience.[7]

Packaging provides functional benefits such as economy, protection, and storage. These aspects can be the main purpose for marketing communication; however, marketing communication is generally responsible for conveying the brand through

Exhibit 1-3
This ad for Joe's Jeans conveys symbolic meaning through the use of sexuality.

its packaging. Since the package can be associated so closely with the brand by giving it a distinctive look, its symbolism and image become the focal point. For example, the main message of an ad can be to show the packaging of the product, since this influences consumer choice as in the case of perfume (Exhibit 1-4).

Finally, a very important role of advertising for a brand is creating and maintaining **brand equity**, which can be thought of as an intangible asset of added value or goodwill that results from the favourable image, impressions of differentiation, and/or strength of consumer attachment to a company name, brand name, or trademark.[8] Brand equity allows a brand to earn greater sales volume and/or higher margins than it could without the name, providing the company with a competitive advantage (Exhibit 1-5). Conceptually, IMC planning and resulting decisions are expected to strongly generate brand equity.[9] Figure 1-2 highlights the top 10 most valuable Canadian brands, while Figure 1-3 identifies the most iconic Canadian brands as compiled by Brand Finance Canada.[10]

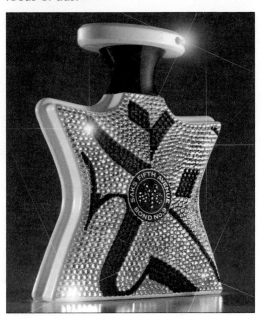

Exhibit 1-4 Showing packaging is often a focus of ads.

COMMUNICATING PRICE

The *price* refers to what the consumer must give up to purchase a product. Price is usually expressed in dollar amount exchanged for an item; however, the true cost of a product to the consumer includes time, mental activity, and behavioural effort.[11] Price planning involves decisions concerning the level, policy, adjustments through discounts or allowances, and flexibility when facing competition. Moreover, it also signals the economic cost to consumers for all product benefits combined.

Marketing communication plays a key role in reinforcing a consumer's belief that the product's benefit or quality accurately reflects the price. The relationship among price, product quality, and advertising was examined in one study using information on 227 consumer businesses from the PIMS (Profit Impact of Marketing Strategies)

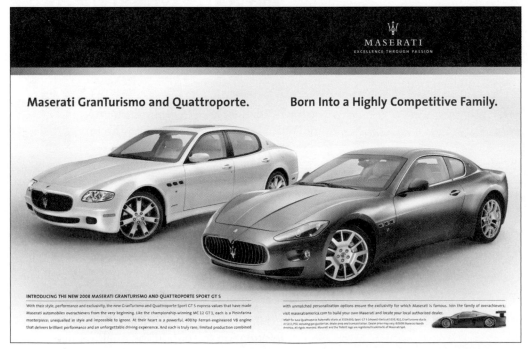

Exhibit 1–5
This Maserati ad contributes to its brand equity.

FIGURE 1–2

The top 10 most valuable Canadian brands

Rank 2009	Rank 2007	Brand	Parent Company
1	1	RBC	Royal Bank of Canada
2	18	BlackBerry	Research In Motion
3	2	TD	TD Bank Financial Group
4	3	Manulife	Manulife Financial Corp
5	4	Bell	BCE Inc.
6	6	Scotiabank	Bank of Nova Scotia
7	7	Loblaws	Loblaw Companies Ltd.
8	15	Bombardier	Bombardier Inc.
9	8	BMO	Bank Of Montreal
10	5	CIBC	Canadian Imperial Bank Of Commerce

Source: Brand Finance Canada, Canada's Most Valuable Brands 2009, p. 19. http://www.brandfinance.com/Uploads/pdfs/BrandFinanceCanadaMostValuableBrands2009.pdf

project of the Strategic Planning Institute.[12] The study concluded that pricing and advertising strategies go together. High relative ad expenditures should accompany premium prices, and low relative ad expenditures should be tailored to low prices.

Price is often a key aspect of the product conveyed. For example, car dealerships focus on price and various discounts and allowances offered in many aspects of their marketing communication. Internet ads focus on price or offers that attempt to influence consumer price beliefs. A main purpose of the Rogers ad in Exhibit 1-6 is to communicate the price of the phone. Research concludes that price comparison advertising plays a key role in consumers' reference price for products when determining

FIGURE 1–3   The most iconic Canadian brands

1	Canada Post
2	Canadian Tire
3	Tim Hortons
4	CBC
5	Air Canada
6	Toronto Maple Leafs
7	Montreal Canadiens
8	Petro-Canada
9	VIA Rail
10	CN Tower

Source: Brand Finance Canada, Canada's Most Valuable Brands 2009, p. 22. http://www.brandfinance.com/Uploads/pdfs/BrandFinanceCanadaMostValuableBrands2009.pdf

Exhibit 1-6 Some ads feature price information to support the quality claim.

the value of a product. Other research finds that communicating price information is critical for influencing consumers who are in the process of deciding to buy a product.[13]

COMMUNICATING DISTRIBUTION

A firm can have an excellent product at a great price, but it will be of little value unless it is available where the customer wants it, when the customer wants it, and with the proper support and service. Marketing channels, the "place" element of the marketing mix, are "sets of interdependent organizations involved in the process of making a product or service available for use or consumption."[14] Most consumer product companies distribute through **indirect channels**, usually using a network of wholesalers and/or retailers. A company can choose not to use any channel intermediaries and sell to its customers through **direct channels** such as the Internet.

In either case, marketing communication often provides information as to where a product can be purchased. For example, since most sporting goods companies have different quality and price levels, they might be inclined to communicate which brands and models are at different types of retailers. Alternatively, different kinds or levels of service might be available in various locations of the distribution network and this could be the focus of marketing communication. For instance, some locations for cosmetics products offer customized beautifying services, while others can be close to self-serve. Extensive marketing communication occurs in order to direct consumers to organizational websites for online purchases.

THE PROMOTIONAL MIX

Promotion is the coordination of all seller-initiated efforts to set up channels of information and persuasion to sell goods and services or promote an idea.[15] While implicit communication occurs through the other elements of the marketing mix, most of an organization's communication with the marketplace occurs as part of a carefully planned and controlled promotional program. The basic tools an organization uses in a promotional program are referred to as the **promotional mix** (Figure 1-4). While either term is suitable, promotion or marketing communication, many marketers use the latter since the tools are often connected. For example, a television commercial can direct viewers to a website. Or a brand may use the same type of message in its radio and print ads. We now review the definition of each of the tools and summarize their roles more clearly.

ADVERTISING

Advertising is defined as any paid form of nonpersonal communication about an organization, product, service, or idea by an identified sponsor.[16] The *paid* aspect of this definition reflects the fact that the space or time for an advertising message

FIGURE 1–4 Tools of the promotional mix

generally must be bought. An occasional exception to this is the public service announcement (PSA), whose advertising space or time is donated by the media.

The *nonpersonal* component means advertising involves mass media (e.g., TV, radio, magazines, newspapers) that can transmit a message to large groups of individuals, often at the same time. The nonpersonal nature of advertising means there is generally no opportunity for immediate feedback from the message recipient (except in direct-response advertising). Therefore, before the message is sent, the advertiser must consider how the audience will interpret and respond to it.

Canadian advertisers spend more than $14 billion annually to reach their audiences, and there are several reasons why advertising is such an important part of many marketers' promotional mixes. First, it can be a very cost-efficient method for communicating with large audiences. For example, during a television season, prime-time network television reached 85 percent of Canadians on a daily basis. The most-watched TV show each week attracts an audience of about 3 million English-speaking viewers. The average top 10 show audience is about 2.4 million viewers, while the average audience for the top 11 to 20 shows is about 1.7 million viewers.[17] A recent study quotes media experts who estimate the cost per thousand reached at $25 for a top 10 show and $20 for a top 11–20 show. To reach an audience for Canadian-produced television shows cost $16 per thousand; specialty channel audiences cost $8 per thousand.[18]

Second, assuming that a majority of the viewers actually watched the ad, paid attention during the airing, and remember something about the message, then advertising can be seen as a very cost-effective form of marketing communication for many brands.

Third, advertising is also a valuable tool for building company or brand equity as it is a powerful way to provide consumers with information as well as to influence their perceptions. Advertising can be used to create favourable and unique images and associations for a brand, which can be very important for companies selling products or services that are difficult to differentiate on the basis of functional attributes. Brand image and brand reputation play an important role in the purchase of many goods and services, and advertising remains a recommended approach to build a brand.[19]

Fourth, increasingly advertising in media such as television, print, and outdoor is employed to encourage consumers to interact with the brand online. For example, a Broil King campaign created the fictitious journalist Rob Liking, who interviewed people grilling on their barbeques. Executives identified research showing that consumers researched their purchase online prior to a store visit, thus leading to a primary objective of influencing consumers' behaviour in the form of visiting the company's website.[20]

Finally, advertising is a flexible tool that can be used for many industries (e.g., cars or soft drinks), situations (e.g., new products or established products), channel members (e.g., consumers or retailers), and target audiences (e.g., new customers or loyal customers). For example, the new campaign for American Express tries to attract customers of other credit cards with its message, "Impossible? Nah. Does that sound like the service you get from your card?"[21] Furthermore, marketers advertise to the consumer market with national and retail/local advertising, which may stimulate primary or selective demand. For other markets, they use business-to-business (Exhibit 1-7), professional, and trade advertising. Figure 1-5 describes the most common types of advertising.

Exhibit 1-7 Business-to-business marketers use advertising to build awareness and brand identity.

ADVERTISING TO CONSUMER MARKETS

National Advertising

Advertising done by large companies on a nationwide basis or in most regions of the country. Most of the ads for well-known companies and brands that are seen on prime-time TV or in other major national or regional media are examples of national advertising. The goals of national advertisers are to inform or remind consumers of the company or brand and its features, benefits, advantages, or uses and to create or reinforce its image so that consumers will be predisposed to purchase it.

Retail/Local Advertising

Advertising done by retailers or local merchants to encourage consumers to shop at a specific store, use a local service, or patronize a particular establishment. Retail or local advertising tends to emphasize specific partronage motives such as price, hours of operation, service, atmosphere, image, or merchandise assortment. Retailers are concerned with building store traffic, so their promotions often take the form of direct action advertising designed to produce immediate store traffic and sales.

Primary versus Selective Demand Advertising

Primary demand advertising is designed to stimulate demand for the general product class or entire industry. Selective demand advertising focuses on creating demand for a specific company's brands. Most advertising for various products and services is concerned with stimuluating selective demand and emphasizes reasons for purchasing a particular brand.

An advertiser might concentrate on stimulating primary demand when, for example, its brand dominates a market and will benefit the most from overall market growth. Primary demand advertising is often used as part of a promotional strategy to help a new product gain market acceptance, since the challenge is to sell customers on the product concept as much as to sell a particular brand. Industry trade associations also try to stimulate primary demand for their members' products, among them cotton, milk, orange juice, pork, and beef.

ADVERTISING TO BUSINESS AND PROFESSIONAL MARKETS

Business-to-Business Advertising

Advertising targeted at individuals who buy or influence the purchase of industrial goods or services for their companies. Industrial goods are products that either become a physical part of another product (raw material or component parts), are used in manufacturing other goods (machinery), or are used to help a company conduct its business (e.g., office supplies, computers). Business services such as insurance, travel services, and health care are also included in this category.

Professional Advertising

Advertising targeted to professionals such as doctors, lawyers, dentists, engineers, or professors to encourage them to use a company's product in their business operations. It might also be used to encourage professionals to recommend or specify the use of a company's product by end-users.

Trade Advertising

Advertising targeted to marketing channel members such as wholesalers, distributors, and retailers. The goal is to encourage channel members to stock, promote, and resell the manufacturer's branded products to their customers.

FIGURE   1–5

Classifications of advertising

SALES PROMOTION

Sales promotion is defined as marketing activities that provide extra value or incentives to the sales force, distributors, or the ultimate consumer and can influence their behaviour and stimulate sales. Sales promotion is generally broken into two major categories: consumer-oriented and trade-oriented activities.

Consumer sales promotion is targeted to the ultimate user of a product or service and includes couponing, sampling, premiums, rebates, contests, sweepstakes, and various point-of-purchase materials. Exhibit 1-8 is an example of a coupon offer within an ad. These promotional tools encourage consumers to make an immediate purchase, participate in brand activity, or be more engaged with the organization's marketing communication. *Trade sales promotion* is targeted toward marketing intermediaries such as wholesalers, distributors, and retailers. Promotional and merchandising allowances, price deals, sales contests, and trade shows are some of the promotional tools used to encourage the trade to stock and promote a company's products.

Promotion and *sales promotion* create confusion sometimes. On the one hand, promotion is an element of marketing by which firms communicate with their customers; it is a term that is synonymous with all the marketing communication tools outlined in Figure 1-4. On the other hand, practitioners often use the term "sales promotion" to mean the incentives directed toward either consumers or the trade to influence their behaviour and stimulate sales. We follow this distinction and use promotion in the broader sense to refer to the marketing communication activities of an organization.

PUBLIC RELATIONS

When an organization systematically plans and distributes information in an attempt to control and manage its image, it is engaging in public relations (PR). **Public relations** is defined as "the management function which evaluates public attitudes, identifies the policies and procedures of an individual or organization with the public interest, and executes a program of action to earn public understanding and acceptance."[22] Public relations uses a variety of tools—including special publications, participation in community activities, fundraising, sponsorship of special events, and various public affairs activities—to enhance an organization's image. Many organizations make PR an integral part of their predetermined marketing and promotional strategies. Exhibit 1-9 shows how sponsorship activities are part of a PR strategy. PR is now recognized as a communications tool that uses and supports advertising and sales promotion.[23] For example, Cisco and the CBC, two key drivers of the "One Million Acts of Green" program, recruited Tim Hortons to their cause through the promotion of a 10-cent discount for each hot drink purchased and consumed with a reusable travel mug.[24]

Publicity refers to nonpersonal communications regarding an organization, product, service, or idea not directly paid for or run under identified sponsorship. The message reaches the public in the form

Exhibit 1-8 Dole combines its sales promotion with its advertising.

of a news story, editorial, or announcement about an organization and/or its products and services. Like advertising, publicity involves nonpersonal communication to a mass audience, but unlike advertising, publicity is not directly paid for by the company. The company or organization attempts to get the media to cover or run a favourable story on a product, service, cause, or event. Tools used to gain publicity include news releases, press conferences, feature articles, and audio-visual media.

An advantage of publicity over other forms of promotion is its credibility. Consumers generally tend to be less skeptical toward favourable information about a product or service when it comes from a source they perceive as unbiased. For example, the success (or failure) of a new movie is often determined by the reviews it receives from film critics, who are viewed by many moviegoers as objective evaluators. Another advantage of publicity is its low cost, since the company is not paying for time or space in a mass medium such as TV, radio, or newspapers. While an organization may incur some costs in developing publicity items or maintaining a staff to do so, these expenses will be far less than those for the other promotional programs.

DIRECT MARKETING

Direct marketing occurs when organizations communicate directly with target audiences to generate a response and/or a transaction. Direct marketing includes telemarketing and call centres, direct mail, mail-order catalogues, and direct-response ads in various broadcast and print media. The availability of credit cards, toll-free phone numbers, and reliable delivery services has facilitated the purchase of products from direct marketing tools. This evolution has made shopping more convenient for consumers and has led to the tremendous growth of direct marketing. Traditionally, direct marketing has not been considered a part of the promotional mix since it had distinct objectives, strategies, and tactics. However, we view direct marketing as an important component of a firm's marketing communication program since it is connected to many other communication tools.

Direct-marketing tools are used by companies that distribute their products to consumers directly and by companies that distribute their products through traditional distribution channels or their own sales force. In order to communicate directly, companies develop and maintain databases containing the addresses and/or phone numbers of present and prospective customers. They use telemarketing to call customers directly and attempt to sell products and services or qualify them as sales leads. Call centres are used to respond to customer inquiries or concerns. Marketers also send out direct-mail pieces ranging from simple letters and flyers to detailed brochures, catalogues, and DVDs to give potential customers information about their products or services. Direct-marketing techniques are also used to distribute product samples and other promotional items. In addition, marketers use **direct-response advertising**, whereby a product is promoted through an ad (e.g., television or print) that encourages the consumer to purchase directly from the manufacturer (Exhibit 1-10).

Exhibit 1-9 Jackson-Triggs supports the Toronto International Film Festival, which gives the brand added prestige.

13

Exhibit 1-10 Dell uses direct-response advertising to promote its products.

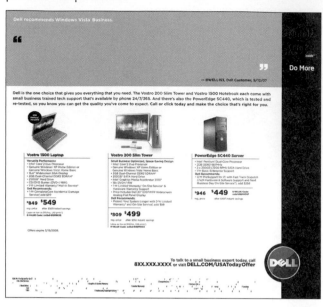

INTERNET MARKETING

We are currently experiencing a dynamic change in marketing through interactive media, delivered via the Internet. **Interactive media** allow for a back-and-forth flow of information whereby users can participate in and modify the form and content of the information they receive instantly. Unlike traditional forms of marketing communication such as advertising, which are one-way in nature, these new media allow users to perform a variety of functions such as receiving and altering information and images, making inquiries, responding to questions, and, of course, making purchases.

Many firms have developed websites to promote their products by providing current and potential customers with information. Other firms develop websites to entertain or communicate more emotionally with their clientele. In fact, as part of a complete IMC program that included advertising, sales promotion, events, and public relations, Guinness beer used the Internet to help initiate the Guinness Party of Canada, a pseudo-political organization dedicated to making St. Patrick's Day a national holiday. Interested drinkers could join via the website and keep track of the results of Guinness's efforts.[25]

As this example illustrates, the Internet is a medium that can be used to execute all the elements of the promotional mix. In addition to advertising on the Web, marketers offer sales promotion incentives such as coupons, contests, and sweepstakes online, and they use the Internet to conduct direct marketing, personal selling, and public relations activities more effectively and efficiently. For example, Exhibit 1-11 shows how consumers can interact with Sharp's Aquos brand on the internet.

Exhibit 1-11
Sharp's campaign for the new Aquos TV creatively integrated the use of advertising and the internet.

Social media avenues like Facebook and YouTube are ways for marketers to reach consumers with print and video ads, respectively. Each also allows brands to establish groups (Facebook) or channels (YouTube) for all kinds of marketing communication activities such as simple ads and sophisticated sales promotions. With imagination and creativity, all aspects of marketing communication are adapted in these new opportunities. Moreover, the interactive features of new media allow for extended communication among members, thereby providing a powerful means of additional communication.

Access to websites, social media, and other interactive experiences and their resulting marketing communication sponsorship (i.e., ads) has been made easier and more prevalent with the development of wireless mobile media devices. In essence, these smart portable devices and their accompanying applications are opening the door for marketers to adapt and invent ways of implementing marketing communication. For example, while walking down the street a person could receive a message with an incentive to turn back and eat at a restaurant he just passed by.

PERSONAL SELLING

The final promotional mix element is **personal selling**, a form of person-to-person communication in which a seller attempts to assist and/or persuade prospective buyers to purchase the company's product or service or to act on an idea. Personal selling involves direct contact between buyer and seller, either face-to-face or through some form of telecommunications such as a telephone. This interaction gives the marketer communication flexibility; the seller can see or hear the potential buyer's reactions and tailor the message to the customer's specific needs or situation. In this book, we do not devote material to personal selling as many decisions pertaining to this topic are the responsibility of a sales manager.

15

PARTICIPANTS IN THE PROMOTIONAL PROCESS

Thus far we have identified the major promotional tools that marketers use. To understand the context in which promotional decisions are made, we identify the participants of the promotional process (Figure 1-6). Overall, there are five major groups: the advertiser (or client), advertising agencies, media organizations, specialized marketing communication services, and collateral services. Each group has specific roles in the promotional process.

The advertisers, or **clients**, have the products, services, or causes to be marketed, and they provide the funds that pay for advertising and promotions. The advertisers also assume major responsibility for developing the marketing program and making

FIGURE 1–6   Participants in the promotional process

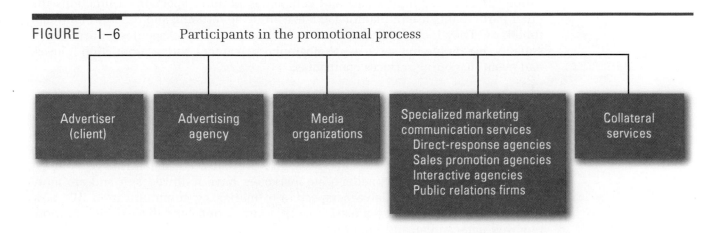

Exhibit 1-12 *National Geographic* promotes its value to advertisers.

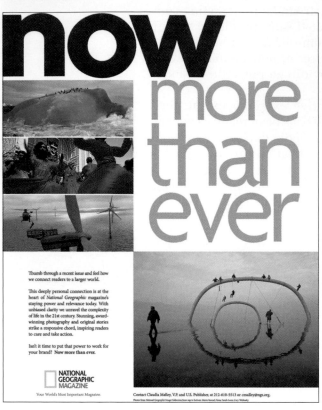

the final decisions regarding the advertising and promotional program to be employed. The organization may perform most of these efforts itself, either through its own advertising department or by setting up an in-house agency.

However, many organizations use an **advertising agency**, an outside firm that specializes in the creation, production, and/or placement of promotional messages. The agency may also provide other services like research to facilitate the promotional process. Many large advertisers retain the services of a number of agencies, particularly when they have multiple products. Often, an ad agency will act as a partner with an advertiser and assume more responsibility for developing the marketing and promotional programs.

The primary function of **media organizations** is to provide information or entertainment to their subscribers, viewers, or readers. But from the perspective of the promotional planner, the purpose of media is to provide an environment for the firm's marketing communication message. The media must have editorial or program content that attracts consumers so advertisers and their agencies will want to buy time or space with them. While the media perform many other functions that help advertisers understand their markets and their customers, a medium's primary objective is to sell itself as a way for companies to effectively reach their target audiences with their messages (Exhibit 1-12).

Specialized marketing communication services include direct marketing agencies, sales promotion agencies, interactive agencies, and public relations firms. These organizations provide services in their areas of expertise. A direct-response agency develops and implements direct-marketing programs, while sales promotion agencies develop contests and sweepstakes, premium offers, or sampling programs. Interactive agencies are being retained to develop websites for the Internet. Public relations firms are used to generate and manage publicity for a company and its products and services as well as to focus on its relationships with its relevant publics.

Other firms provide **collateral services**, the wide range of support functions used by advertisers, agencies, media organizations, and specialized marketing communication firms. These individuals and companies perform specialized functions the other participants use in planning and executing advertising and other promotional functions. They include marketing research companies, package design firms, consultants, media buying services, photographers, printers, video production houses, and event marketing services companies.

INTEGRATED MARKETING COMMUNICATIONS

Most large companies recognize that the wide range of promotional tools must be coordinated to communicate effectively and present a consistent image to target audiences. In turn, even smaller-scale marketers have followed suit and are moving to a more comprehensive perspective of marketing communication. We now turn to the topic of integrated marketing communications and discuss its evolution, renewed perspective, and importance.

THE EVOLUTION OF IMC

During the 1980s, many companies moved toward the process of **integrated marketing communications (IMC)** as the need for strategic planning and integration of their promotional tools intensified. Marketers subsequently asked their agencies to coordinate the use of more promotional tools rather than rely primarily on media advertising. Companies also looked beyond traditional advertising agencies and employed other promotional specialists to develop and implement various components of their promotional plans. A task force from the American Association of Advertising Agencies (the "4As") developed one of the first definitions of integrated marketing communications that focuses on the process of using all forms of promotion to achieve maximum communications impact:

> a concept of marketing communications planning that recognizes the added value of a comprehensive plan that evaluates the strategic roles of a variety of communication disciplines—for example, general advertising, direct response, sales promotion, and public relations—and combines these disciplines to provide clarity, consistency, and maximum communications impact.[26]

In the 1990s, companies saw IMC as a way to coordinate and manage their marketing communication programs to ensure customers received a consistent message about the company and/or its brands. IMC represented an improvement over the traditional method of treating the promotional tools as virtually separate activities. At this point, agencies devoted a considerable amount of time to IMC planning for their clients.[27] More recently, IMC has been challenged on the basis that it focuses primarily on the tactical coordination of various communication tools with the goal of making them look and sound alike.[28] It has been criticized as an "inside-out" marketing approach that is a relatively simple matter of bundling promotional mix elements together so they have one look and speak with one voice.[29] As IMC continues to evolve, both academics as well as practitioners see the need for a renewed perspective that views the discipline from a more strategic perspective. IMC Perspective 1-1 describes how Loblaw has adapted recently.

A RENEWED PERSPECTIVE OF IMC

A renewed understanding of IMC involves more than just coordinating the various elements of a company's marketing and communications programs into a "one look, one voice" approach. As IMC evolves, it is viewed as a business process that helps companies identify the most appropriate and effective methods for communicating and building relationships. Don Schultz of Northwestern University developed an appropriate definition of IMC, as follows:

> Integrated marketing communication is a strategic business process used to plan, develop, execute and evaluate coordinated, measurable, persuasive brand communications programs over time with consumers, customers, prospects, employees, associates and other targeted relevant external and internal audiences. The goal is to generate both short-term financial returns and build long-term brand and shareholder value.[30]

This definition views IMC as an ongoing strategic business process rather than just tactical integration of various communication activities. It also recognizes that there are a number of relevant audiences that require specific communication programs. Finally, Schultz notes that this definition reflects the increasing emphasis that is being placed on the demand for accountability and measurement of the *outcomes* of marketing communication programs as well as marketing in general. Building on this idea, a newer perspective suggests that IMC has four general characteristics[31]:

1. Unified communication for consistent message and image.
2. Differentiated communication to multiple customer groups.

No-Name Advertising Returns

Canadians shopping for groceries have lots of choice among national/regional brands and store brands, leading to diffuse beliefs. For example, 60 percent believe that store brands are just as good as brand-name products, although 40 percent believe the latter are more innovative. Furthermore, store brands accounted for 50 percent of all food items for two-thirds of a sample of households surveyed, and virtually every single household uses a store brand. And Loblaw is the clear leader in developing store brands with its President's Choice (PC) offerings—including PC Green, PC Organics, PC Blue Menu, No Name, and Club Pack—which are distributed to its many store banners (Loblaws, Zehrs, No Frills). In fact, President's Choice is Canada's second strongest food brand behind Kraft.

Senior VP Craig Hutchinson, who is responsible for all the brands, continually makes decisions for a variety of marketing communication tools. According to Hutchinson, "I probably have, right now, nine different TV commercials—six PC, three Joe Fresh. I've probably got eight different radio scripts on the go, six or seven different major in-store events, and we're working on healthy and lawn and garden Insider's Reports." Much of these activities are a throwback to Loblaw's previous glory as it revives programs with the goal of being more market-oriented once again.

For example, one ad compared a basket of No Name goods with national brand goods to illustrate a savings of 26 percent. The ad featured executive chairman Galen Weston and copied a similar ad Loblaw used in the 1980s when then-president Dave Nichol, inventor of the PC brand and whose signature adorns the brand's imagery, starred in the commercials. A money-back guarantee attached to the ad offered consumers reassurance that the invigorated No Name brand would meet expectations. (One critic felt that having Mr. Weston appear in the No Name ad took away the credibility he carried while promoting the PC brand and the Loblaws grocery store.)

In other ads the new No Name packaging, which copies the original packaging of the past, became the focal point, with a black text message upon a bright yellow background. One text read, "We don't have a single item under $2, we have 300." No Name's return to the past shows how important advertising is in allowing consumers to understand the discount brand's distinctiveness. More recent packaging competed with national brands by showing food content. Although discounted by 25 percent, the imagery did not support the lower, more economical cost. The No Name ads are inexpensive to produce, so many different executions are possible to help consumers readily identify the products at the store.

Sources: Carey Toane, "Loblaw's Craig Hutchinson: Back to the Future," *Strategy*, December 2009, p. 27; Robert Levy, "Private Label's Big Push," *Marketing Magazine*, March 23, 2009; "Store Brands Enjoy Recessionary Growth," *Marketing Magazine*, August 18, 2009; Hollie Shaw, "No Name Returns to No Frills, *National Post*, Friday, January 22, 2010.

Questions:

1. Why is it a good idea to focus on packaging in the ads for No Name?
2. Do you agree with the idea of reissuing old commercials?

---

3. Database-centred communication for tangible results.
4. Relationships fostering communication with existing customers.

Many companies are realizing that communicating effectively with customers and other stakeholders involves more than just the tactical use of the traditional marketing communication tools. These firms, along with many advertising agencies, are embracing IMC and incorporating it into their marketing and business practices. In fact, it is hypothesized that IMC is now critically connected to a firm's market and brand orientation.[32] Some research reports higher use of IMC leading to higher levels of sales, market share, and profits.[33] Some academics and practitioners have questioned whether IMC is just another "management fashion" whose influence will be transitory.[34] Critics of IMC argue that it merely reinvents and renames existing ideas and concepts and that it questions its significance for marketing and advertising thought and practice.[35]

In contrast, Procter & Gamble (P&G) overhauled its marketing and organizational operations, which had enormous implications for how P&G makes its promotional decisions with an IMC perspective. The change originated when managers decided to focus on when the consumer chooses to buy and use the product as the central drive for all decisions. Marketers in Canada work on multi-functional teams to customize worldwide product launches for local success. This has resulted in P&G Canada typically using the original TV creative, but augmenting the campaign with more targeted IMC tools. From an agency perspective, P&G partnered with diverse types of agencies and employed multiple parties to execute new brand initiatives. Furthermore, P&G expected strategic communication planning from its agencies, which were immersed in their client's newfound customer-centric direction. Innovative communication practices resulted from these internal and external developments. The Canadian campaign for Cover Girl Outlast Lipstick featured motion-sensitive ads in bars and restaurants in Toronto. Old Spice dance events, known as "Red Zone after hours," occurred at Canadian bars and included an online contest, out-of-home media, and a televised competition.[36]

While the debate over the value and relevance of IMC is likely to continue, proponents of the concept far outnumber the critics. IMC is proving to be a permanent change that offers significant value to marketers in the rapidly changing communications environment they face in the new millennium. IMC has been described as one of the "new-generation" marketing approaches being used by companies to better focus their efforts in acquiring, retaining, and developing relationships with customers and other stakeholders.[37] Some scholars have stated that IMC is undoubtedly the major communications development of the last decade of the 20th century.[38] We will now discuss some reasons regarding the importance of IMC.

IMPORTANCE OF IMC

A successful IMC program requires that a firm find the right combination of promotional tools, define their role and the extent to which they can or should be used, and coordinate their use. This perspective becomes important for organizations because of the many audiences it communicates with, the vast number of messages consumers receive from many brands, the emergence of strong marketing relationships, consumer adoption of technology and media, and improved managerial planning.

Audience Contacts   The promotional mix elements are the major tools that marketers use to communicate with current and/or prospective customers as well as other relevant audiences such as employees, suppliers, community, and government. Many companies are taking an *audience contact* perspective in developing their IMC programs whereby they consider all the potential ways of reaching their target audience and presenting the message of the company or brand in a favourable manner. In terms of customers, for example, marketers identify how their loyal buyers interact with a company or brand. This contact can range from simply seeing or hearing an ad for a brand to actually having the opportunity to use or experience a brand at a company-sponsored event. Moreover, this idea can be extended to non-customers and all other potential audiences the company or brand may choose to target its marketing communication.

Figure 1-7 shows the various ways by which target audiences can come into contact with a company or brand. Marketers must determine how valuable each contact tool is for communicating with their target audience and how they can be combined to form an effective IMC program. This is generally done by starting with the target audience and determining which IMC tools will be most effective in reaching, informing, and persuading them and ultimately influencing their behaviour. It is the

FIGURE 1–7   IMC audience contact tools

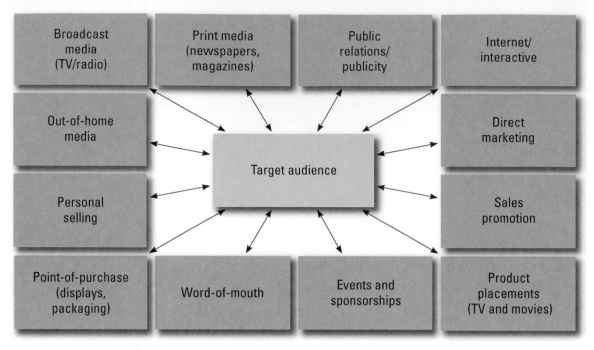

responsibility of those involved in the marketing communication process to determine how the various contact tools will be used to reach the target audience and help achieve the company's marketing objectives. IMC Perspective 1-2 shows how Nissan reaches many target audiences.

Consumer's Point of View   It is important for marketers to keep concepts distinct to communicate with colleagues within the organization or other organizations when making decisions. For example, when planning a sales promotion, it is useful to refer to it as a sales promotion so that everyone involved can discuss its merits appropriately and allocate the sales promotion expenditure within the correct budget. What is the right sales promotion (e.g., coupon versus bonus pack)? Is the incentive strong enough to encourage the target audience to switch to our brand? Consumers, on the other hand, receive many exposures from many different brands, each using many different promotional tools. In fact, consumers receive so many exposures that they have the habit of often referring to any promotional tool as "advertising." Given this situation, the need for planning with an IMC perspective becomes imperative. All the elements of the promotional campaign have to be carefully linked in some manner so that the message is clear and does not misrepresent the brand.

L'Oréal Canada built its Maybelline and L'Oréal Paris brands through innovative use of advertising, sales promotion, sponsorship, public relations, and Internet marketing. Faced with constraints of key marketing activities decided at the brand headquarters in Paris, New York, and Tokyo, L'Oréal Canada created a Canadian identity for its primary consumer brands. Maybelline sponsored the hit Quebec television reality show *Star Académie* and tweaked its famous slogan to fit the show's "star" theme, allowed its makeup artists to interact with the public on the Internet, organized autograph sessions in shopping malls with contestants who had been eliminated, and continued its advertising message on other media like radio. L'Oréal Paris also sponsored the hit show *Canadian Idol.* In addition to regular commercials and a highlighted presence on the website for *Canadian Idol,* the show

Nissan's Many Messages

As one of the finalists for *Strategy* magazine's Marketer of the Year, Nissan's VP of Sales and Marketing Jeff Parent took an innovative approach for marketing communication through specialized and customized messages to multiple groups as they increased market share to a record high of 5.6 percent.

In Quebec, Toyota, Honda, and Mazda outsold Nissan as the brand languished with less advertising support resulting in weaker awareness. To address this problem, Nissan launched the "Gros Bon Sens" (Big Common Sense) campaign to counter the belief that Nissan sold more expensive cars. This message fit well with the Quebec market since consumers purchase a higher percentage of small, less expensive cars; Nissan concentrated the message with the Sentra and Versa models.

The Gros Bons Sens concept manifested with an approachable, everyday kind of guy who represented the average consumer Nissan targeted. In the TV ads the character advised Nissan engineers and design personnel on how to improve their car initially, and then moved on to other aspects of buying and enjoying a Nissan product. Retail-oriented ads in newspapers and online ensured the affordability message existed so the overall price/quality message resonated across all media. The next phase moved to an actual common-sense manual so that consumers could purchase a Nissan with confidence. Additional support exposure occurred through magazines and billboards. Overall sales grew by 24 percent, with market share growing a full percentage point with unit sales of over 28,000. Brand attitudinal measures scored higher as well, indicating favourable response to the message.

In other parts of Canada, Nissan highlighted the enjoyment consumers experience with their vehicles with the message, "Best part of your day." Ads showed people struggling with day-to-day activities only to find their day brighten once they began to use or drive their Rogue, Versa, or Sentra. Consumers found comfort, convenience, and excitement depending upon the situation represented. Later in the campaign, a website (Bestpartofyourday.ca) provided enjoyable content and applications to carry on with the emotional boost felt from the commercials. For example, consumers could make bumper stickers, or use the excuse generator to avoid going to work.

To reach another group, Nissan leveraged its CFL sponsorship with an online experience (Nissanarmchairhero. com) where consumers could design their own football play for five participating teams. Users voted on the best play, with the winners receiving Grey Cup tickets. Each winner for the Toronto and Edmonton teams received the opportunity to see their play practised by the professional team and see their play in the team's official playbook; pretty good real-world brand experience that digital could not provide.

Sources: Jonathan Paul, "Nissan's Jeff Parent: No Guts, No Glory," *Strategy*, December 2009, p. 34; Jeromy Lloyd, "Nissan Gives Football Fans a Chance to Play with the CFL," *Marketing Magazine*, August 21, 2009; Jeromy Lloyd, "Nissan Canada Launches New Site to Make Car Buyers Smile," *Marketing Magazine*, August 21, 2009; Kristin Laird, "TV Ads Show How Nissan Spices Up the Mundane," *Marketing Magazine*, July 15, 2009; cassies.ca.

Question:

1. Why does Nissan take so many different approaches to its marketing communication?

---

featured sponsorship announcements and on-air promotions that linked consumers to interactive, stylish fun on the L'Oréal Paris website. L'Oréal Canada received positive publicity for its interactive campaign in honour of International Women's Day that provided needed money for the Canadian Women's Foundation's Economic Development Fund. Promotional support for other fashion and arts events permitted L'Oréal Canada to keep its profile high. And to help facilitate these media, L'Oréal Canada worked with pharmacy retailers to deliver contest promotions and much-needed communication at the point of sale. Collectively, L'Oréal Canada's success indicates the importance of a well planned communications strategy that carefully considers the consumer's response to many tools.[39]

Relationship Marketing   Many marketers seek more than a one-time exchange or transaction with customers and concentrate on developing and sustaining *relationships* with their customers. This has led to a new emphasis on **relationship marketing**, which involves creating, maintaining, and enhancing long-term relationships with individual customers as well as other stakeholders for mutual benefit.[40] The banking industry has been very successful with building relationships; the extensive personal and financial information banks have access to allows them to offer products and services in a timely manner as people's financial needs change. This is enhanced through services provided by financial advisers and wealth managers.

This relationship focus is generally more profitable since it is often more cost-effective to retain customers than to acquire new ones. Furthermore, these retained customers tend to buy more products or expand their purchases to other products that an organization offers. Marketers are giving more strategic importance in their plans to the *lifetime value* of a customer because studies have shown that reducing customer defections by just 5 percent can increase future profit by as much as 30 to 90 percent.[41] Recently, the AMA adopted a revised and more strategic definition of **marketing**, which is as follows:

> Marketing is an organizational function and a set of processes for creating, communicating and delivering value to customers and for managing customer relationships in ways that benefit the organization and its stakeholders.[42]

In order to facilitate the relationship, companies build databases containing customer names; geographic, demographic, and psychographic profiles; purchase patterns; media preferences; credit ratings; and other characteristics. Marketers use this information to target consumers through a variety of IMC tools thereby enhancing the relationship. With so many tools, and since their customers are involved so closely with the firm, the need for consistency and coordination becomes even more critical.[43]

Consumer Adoption of Technology and Media The expanded use of integrated marketing communications is more critical due to consumer adoption of technology and media. For example, cable television and digital satellite systems have vastly expanded the number of channels available to households. As a result, audiences are more fragmented and television advertising reaches smaller and more selective audiences. This requires brands to ensure their messages are attended to in other media or other IMC tools. Thus, the more selective television ad might direct the viewer to seek out the brand's website for a coupon or sample, or to read about its charitable sponsorship activities.

Online services provide information and entertainment as well as the opportunity to shop for and order a vast array of products. Marketers are responding by developing websites where they can advertise their products and services interactively as well as transact sales. New applications for advertising on the Internet are invented each year, allowing marketers greater opportunity to reach particular audiences. For instance, some brands have initiated "sponsored groups" on Facebook where consumers can join and receive brand messages and promotional offerings like contests and samples. Toyota created the F1 Canada group and offered desktop wallpapers and ringtones for its 3,000 members. Other applications included targeted banner ads based on consumer profile variables like demographics, psychographics, and media consumption preferences. Telus experimented with a virtual-reality world that 120,000 of its 1.2 million customers experienced; word of the new venture spread through blogs and newspaper articles. With essentially no monetary investment in the venture, the media exposure Telus received helped convey it as a technologically advanced company. More importantly, Telus ultimately planned some promotions to customers based on the behaviours exemplified in the simulated game.[44]

Planning Efficiency and Effectiveness   A final reason for IMC importance is that marketers understand the value of strategically integrating the various communication functions rather than having them operate autonomously. By coordinating their marketing communications efforts, companies can avoid duplication, take advantage of synergy among various promotional tools, and develop more efficient and effective marketing communications programs. Advocates of IMC argue that it is one of the easiest ways for a company to maximize the return on its investment in marketing and promotion.[45] Empirical research supports this contention as strong IMC performance leads to stronger market performance.[46] Exhibit 1-13 shows a marketing effort where planning is paramount.

INTEGRATED MARKETING COMMUNICATIONS PLANNING

In developing an IMC strategy, a company combines the promotional mix elements, balancing the strengths and limitations of each, to produce an effective program for marketing communication. **IMC management** involves the process of planning, executing, evaluating, and controlling the use of promotional mix elements to communicate effectively with target audiences. The marketer decides which promotional tools to use and how to combine them to achieve IMC objectives. Furthermore, the marketer decides on the role and function of the specific elements of the promotional mix, develops strategies for each element, and implements the plan. The resulting **IMC plan** provides the framework for developing, implementing, and controlling the organization's IMC program. A model of the IMC planning process is shown in Figure 1-8. The remainder of this chapter presents a brief overview of the steps involved.

REVIEW THE MARKETING PLAN

The first step in the IMC planning process is to review the marketing plan and objectives. Before developing an IMC plan, marketers must understand where the company (or the brand) has been, its current position in the market, where it intends to go, and how it plans to get there. Most of this information should be contained in the **marketing plan**, a written document that describes the overall marketing strategy and programs developed for an organization, a particular product line, or a brand. Marketing plans can take several forms but generally include five basic parts:

- A detailed situation analysis that consists of an internal marketing audit and review and an external analysis of the market, company, consumer, competition, and macro-environment.
- Specific marketing objectives that provide direction, a time frame for marketing activities, and a mechanism for measuring performance.
- A marketing strategy and program that includes selection of target market(s) and decisions and plans for the four elements of the marketing mix.

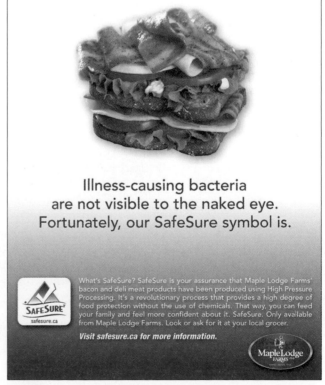

Illness-causing bacteria are not visible to the naked eye. Fortunately, our SafeSure symbol is.

SafeSure²
safesure.ca

What's SafeSure? SafeSure is your assurance that Maple Lodge Farms' bacon and deli meat products have been produced using High Pressure Processing. It's a revolutionary process that provides a high degree of food protection without the use of chemicals. That way, you can feed your family and feel more confident about it. SafeSure. Only available from Maple Lodge Farms. Look or ask for it at your local grocer.

Visit safesure.ca for more information.

MapleLodge
FARMS

Exhibit 1-13   Maple Lodge reassures consumers about the safety of its meat products with its new symbol.

FIGURE   1–8   An integrated marketing communications planning model

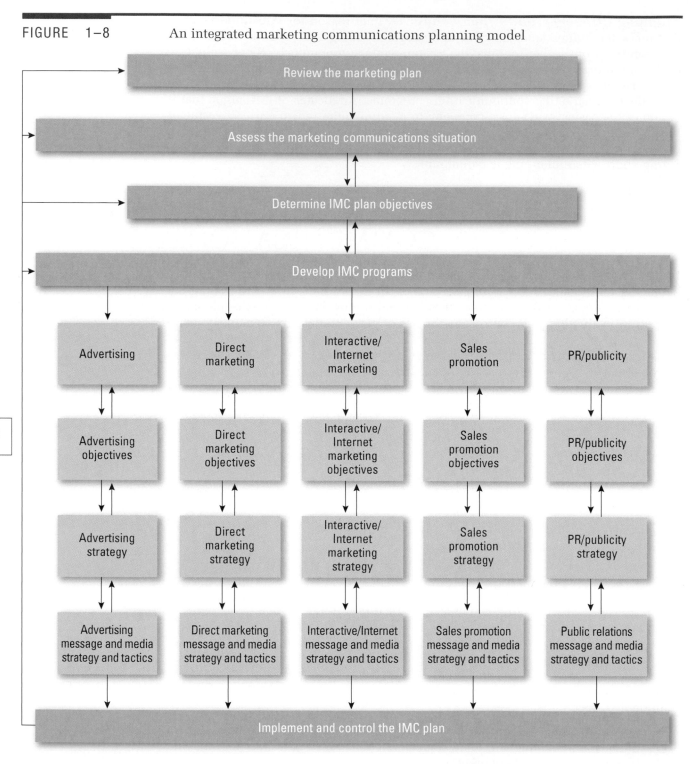

- A program for implementing the marketing strategy, including determining specific tasks to be performed and responsibilities.
- A process for monitoring and evaluating performance and providing feedback so that proper control can be maintained and any necessary changes can be made in the overall marketing strategy or tactics.

Promotional planners focus on information in the marketing plan that is relevant to the IMC strategy since they must know the roles advertising and other promotional mix elements will play in the overall marketing program. The promotional

Review the Marketing Plan
Focus on market company, consumer, competitive, and environmental information
Examine marketing objectives, strategy, and programs
Understand role of promotion within marketing plan

Assess the Marketing Communications Situation
Internal analysis
   Relative strengths and weaknesses of products/services
   Previous promotional programs
   Brand image
   Promotional organization and capabilities
External analysis
   Customer behaviour analysis
   Competitive analysis
   Environmental analysis

Determine IMC Plan Objectives
Establish IMC communication objectives
Establish IMC behaviour objectives

Develop IMC Programs
For advertising, sales promotion, public relations, direct marketing, and Internet marketing:
   Set specific communication and behaviour objectives for each IMC tool
   Determine budget requirements
   Develop relevant message strategy and tactics
   Select suitable media strategy and tactics
Investigate integration options across all five programs

Implement and Control the IMC Plan
Design all promotional materials internally or with agencies and buy media space/time
Measure promotional program results/effectiveness and make adjustments

FIGURE 1–8
(concluded)

An integrated marketing communications planning model

25

plan is developed similarly to the marketing plan and often uses its detailed information. However, some IMC strategy decisions require more comprehensive or specific information, or more detailed analysis and specific consideration of existing information, therefore requiring a situation analysis for marketing communication.

ASSESS THE MARKETING COMMUNICATIONS SITUATION

In the IMC program, the situation analysis focuses on those factors that are relevant to development of a promotional strategy. Like the overall marketing situation analysis, the promotional program situation analysis includes both an internal and an external analysis.

Internal Analysis The **internal analysis** assesses relevant areas of the product offering and the firm itself. The internal analysis assesses the relative strengths and limitations of the product; the product's unique selling points, attributes, or benefits; its packaging, price, and design; and so on. This information is important to the creative personnel who must develop the brand's advertising message.

Since the firm is planning a new promotional plan, it is imperative that a review of the firm's previous promotional programs is undertaken. Specifically, the objectives, budgets, strategies, and tactics of all promotional mix elements should be closely

Exhibit 1-14 Starbucks has a very strong brand image and reputation as a socially responsible company.

examined to understand the strengths and limitations. Furthermore, if the firm has utilized marketing research to track the results of previous programs, this information needs to be examined closely.

Another aspect of the internal analysis is assessing the strengths and limitations of the firm or the brand from an image perspective. Often the image the firm brings to the market will have a significant impact on the way it can advertise and promote itself as well as its products and services. Companies or brands that are new to the market or those for whom perceptions are negative may have to concentrate on their images, not just the benefits or attributes of the specific product or service. On the other hand, a firm with a strong image is already a step ahead when it comes to marketing its products. For example, Starbucks has an outstanding image that is a result of the quality of its coffee and other products as well as its reputation as a socially responsible company. The company is recognized as a good citizen in its dealings with communities, employees, suppliers, and the environment. Starbucks recognizes that being recognized as a socially responsible company is an important part of its tremendous growth and success. The company publishes a Corporate Social Responsibility Annual Report each year that describes its social, environmental, and economic impacts on the communities in which it does business (Exhibit 1-14).

Reviewing the capabilities of the firm and its ability to develop and implement a successful promotional program, and the organization of the promotional department, the analysis may indicate the firm is not fully capable of planning and implementing the promotional program. If this is the case, it would be wise to look for assistance from an advertising agency or some other promotional facilitator. If the organization is already using an ad agency, the focus will be on the quality of the agency's work and the results achieved by past and/or current campaigns.

Figure 1-9 is a checklist of some of the areas one might consider when performing analyses for promotional planning purposes. Addressing internal areas may require information the company does not have available internally and must gather as part of the external analysis.

External Analysis The **external analysis** focuses on factors such as characteristics of the firm's customers, market segments, competitors, and environment as shown in Figure 1-9. An important part of the external analysis is a detailed consideration of customers' characteristics and buying patterns, their decision processes, and factors influencing their purchase decisions. Attention must also be given to consumers' perceptions and attitudes, lifestyles, and criteria for making purchase decisions. Often, marketing research studies are needed to answer some of these questions. A key element of the external analysis is an assessment of the market. The attractiveness of various market segments must be evaluated and the segments

FIGURE 1−9 Areas covered in the situation analysis

Internal Factors	External Factors
Assessment of firm's promotional organization and capabilities	**Customer behaviour analysis**
Organization of promotional department	Who buys our product or service?
Capability of firm to develop and execute promotional programs	Who makes the decision to buy the product?
	Who influences the decision to buy the product?
Determination of role and function of ad agency and other promotional facilitators	How is the purchase decision made? Who assumes what role?
Assessment of firm's previous promotional programs	What does the customer buy? What needs must be satisfied?
Promotional objectives	Why do customers buy a particular brand?
Promotional budgets and allocations	Where do they go or look to buy the product or service?
Promotional mix strategies and programs	When do they buy? Any seasonality factors?
Results of promotional programs	What are customers' attitudes toward our product/service?
Assessment of firm or brand image	What social factors might influence the purchase decision?
Assessment of relative strengths and weaknesses of product/service	Do the customers' lifestyles influence their purchase decisions?
	Do demographic factors influence the purchase decision?
What are its key attributes and benefits?	**Competitive analysis**
Does it have any unique selling points?	Who are our direct and indirect competitors?
Are the package and label consistent with the brand image?	What key benefits and positioning are used by our competitors?
	What is our position relative to the competition?
	How big are competitors' promotion budgets?
	What promotion strategies are competitors using?
	Environmental analysis
	Are there any current trends or developments that might affect the promotional program?

to target identified. Exhibit 1-15 shows ads from a campaign for Tourism Kelowna, where a good consumer understanding is important.

The external phase of the promotional program situation analysis also includes an in-depth examination of both direct and indirect competitors. While competitors were analyzed in the overall marketing situation analysis, even more attention is devoted to promotional aspects at this phase. Focus is on the firm's primary

Exhibit 1-15 Tourism Kelowna's ads have visuals that encourage visits from across Canada.

competitors: their specific strengths and limitations; their segmentation, targeting, and positioning strategies; and the promotional strategies they employ. The size and allocation of their promotional budgets, their media strategies, and the messages they are sending to the marketplace should all be considered.

DETERMINE IMC PLAN OBJECTIVES

An important part of this stage of the promotional planning process is establishing relevant and appropriate objectives. In this text, we stress the importance of distinguishing among different types of objectives that are generally decided during the planning of different strategies. **Marketing objectives** refer to what is to be accomplished by the overall marketing program. They are often stated in terms of sales, market share, or profitability and are determined when the marketing plan is constructed.

Communication objectives refer to what the firm seeks to accomplish with its IMC program. They are often stated in terms of the nature of the message to be communicated or what specific communication effects are to be achieved, such as awareness. The promotional planner must think about the process consumers will go through in responding to marketing communications. **Behavioural objectives** in terms of trial purchase or repeat purchase, among others, may be defined along with the communication objectives. Communication and behavioural objectives should be the guiding force for the IMC strategy and for each promotional tool. The importance of setting objectives is seen in the Heart & Stroke ad shown in Exhibit 1-16.

While determining these objectives, two questions are asked to tentatively set the budget: What will the promotional program cost? and How will these monies be allocated? Ideally, the amount a firm spends on promotion should be determined by what must be accomplished to achieve communication and behavioural objectives. In reality, promotional budgets are often determined using a more simplistic approach, but in either case more detailed and finalized budgets occur once specific promotional mix strategies are developed.

Exhibit 1-16 The Heart & Stroke Foundation logo is a sign of healthy food choices.

DEVELOP IMC PROGRAMS

Developing the IMC program is generally the most involved and detailed step. Since each promotional mix element has certain strengths and limitations, decisions have to be made regarding the role and importance of each element and their coordination with one another. As Figure 1-8 shows, each promotional mix element has its own set of objectives and a budget and strategy for meeting them. Decisions must be made and activities performed to implement the promotional programs and evaluate performance to make any necessary changes.

For example, the advertising program will have its own set of objectives, usually involving the communication of some message or appeal to a target audience. A budget will be determined, providing the advertising manager and the agency with some idea of how much money is available for developing the ad campaign and purchasing media to disseminate the ad message.

Two important aspects of the advertising program are development of the message and the media strategy. Message development, often referred to as *creative strategy,* involves determining the basic message the advertiser wishes to convey to the target audience. This process, along with the ads that result, is to many students the most fascinating aspect of promotion. *Media strategy* involves determining which communication channels will be used to deliver the advertising message to the target audience. Decisions must be made regarding which types of media will be used (e.g., newspapers, magazines, radio, TV, billboards) as well as specific media selections (e.g., a particular magazine or TV program). This task requires careful evaluation of the media options' strengths and limitations, costs, and ability to deliver the message effectively to the target audiences. A similar process takes place for the other elements of the IMC program as objectives are set, an overall strategy is developed, and message and media strategies are determined.

Alternatively, if a firm considers using multiple tools for its complete plan it must decide which ones best fit together to solve a particular marketing communication problem. For example, in its first major promotional campaign in many years, Melitta Coffee increased its budget substantially and selected three IMC tools (Figure 1-10).[47] In addition, an IMC plan might evolve from an initial plan from one tool used, especially advertising. For example, Visa's "Win what you buy" sales promotion built upon the same message of "disappearing debt" conveyed in the television and print ads.[48]

IMPLEMENT AND CONTROL THE IMC PLAN

Once the message and media strategies have been determined, steps must be taken to implement them. Most large companies hire advertising agencies to plan and produce their messages and to evaluate and purchase the media that will carry their ads. However, most agencies work very closely with their clients as they develop the ads and select media, because it is the advertiser that ultimately approves (and pays for) the creative work and media plan. While the marketer's advertising agencies may be used to perform some of the other IMC functions, they may also hire other communication specialists.

It is important to determine how well the promotional program is meeting communication and behavioural objectives and helping the firm accomplish its overall

Budget:	$1.8 million (previous year $50,000)
Target:	Women 25–54
Advertising Message:	Everyday indulgence
Advertising Media:	Radio (Vancouver, Calgary, Toronto, Montreal) Television (Prime, Deja View, Mystery, Cool TV, W) Print (*Canadian Living, Coup de Pouce, Canadian Grocer*) March to May, and September to December
Sales Promotion:	Product placement on *Me, My House and I* Contest supported by *Spectacular Spas* television show and newspaper Gift Basket giveaway June to August
Internet:	MochaSofa/Mokasofa.com

FIGURE 1–10

Melitta Coffee campaign

marketing objectives. The promotional planner wants to know not only how well the promotional program is doing but also why. For example, problems with the advertising program may lie in the nature of the message or in a media plan that does not reach the target market effectively. The manager must know the reasons for the results in order to take the right steps to correct the program.

This final stage of the process is designed to provide managers with continual feedback concerning the effectiveness of the promotional program, which in turn can be used as input into the planning process. As Figure 1-8 shows, information on the results achieved by the promotional program is used in subsequent promotional planning and strategy development.

IMC PLANNING: ORGANIZATION OF TEXT

The purpose of this book is to provide a thorough understanding of the field of advertising and other elements of a firm's promotional mix and show how they are combined to form an integrated marketing communications program. The previous section developed the perspective for IMC planning, and we continue with this idea of an IMC planning section to conclude each chapter throughout the text. Its purpose is to relate the specific chapter material to the overall direction of an IMC plan. The final section of this chapter establishes this approach by illustrating how the entire book is organized around the IMC planning perspective. The book is organized around five major parts to facilitate this goal.

Part I, "Understanding Integrated Marketing Communications," comprises four chapters. This initial chapter introduces the basic tools of IMC and how they relate to marketing. The chapter also gives a brief description of IMC and the content of a promotional plan. We discuss how firms organize for IMC and make decisions regarding ad agencies and other firms that provide marketing and promotional services in Chapter 2. To plan, develop, and implement an effective IMC program, those involved must understand consumer behaviour and the communications process. We focus on consumer behaviour and the target audience decision, and summarize various communication response models in Chapters 3 and 4, respectively. Combined, these two chapters establish a conceptual foundation for developing the subsequent set of decisions of an IMC plan.

The heart of marketing communication lies in what we are trying to say. Part II, "Articulate the Message," concerns a number of decisions firms make to put together a persuasive message. Chapter 5 explains how to set IMC objectives to achieve the desired effects. Perhaps the most exciting aspects of IMC are discussed in Chapters 6, 7, and 8, where we illustrate the brand positioning strategy, creative strategy, and creative tactics decisions that result in vibrant and exciting ads. Chapter 9 examines how to measure advertising effectiveness, which also sets the stage for understanding how to assess the effects of all IMC tools.

Part III, "Deliver the Message," explores the key media strategy and media tactics decisions in Chapter 10 and the six traditional media choices (i.e., television, radio, magazines, newspapers, out-of-home, and support) within Chapters 11, 12, and 13. Collectively, Parts II and III provide a foundation for the IMC program. As all other IMC tools share this message and media characteristic, the general ideas can be applied throughout the IMC plan.

Our interest turns to the other areas of the promotional mix—sales promotion, public relations, direct marketing, and Internet marketing—in Part IV, "Strengthen the Message." Each tool is explored in its own chapter and related to communication objectives as done in Part III. The book concludes with Part V, "Advertising and Society," which examines advertising regulation and the ethical, social, and economic effects on an organization's advertising and promotional program.

CHAPTER OBJECTIVES AND SUMMARY

1 To examine the importance of marketing communication within the marketing mix.

The basic task of marketing is to combine the four controllable elements, known as the marketing mix, into a comprehensive program that facilitates exchange with a group of customers. The elements of the marketing mix are the product, price, place (distribution), and promotion (market communication). Advertising and other forms of promotion are an integral part of the marketing process in most organizations since these tools communicate the value consumers receive within the exchange. Marketing communication conveys many aspects of the product including attributes, benefits, symbolic meaning, and brand identity with the hopes of building brand equity. Providing price and distribution information are two other important roles of marketing communication so that value is perceived by both customers and non-customers.

2 To highlight the elements of the promotional mix: advertising, sales promotion, public relations, direct marketing, Internet marketing, and personal selling.

Promotion is accomplished through a promotional mix that includes advertising, sales promotion, public relations, direct marketing, Internet marketing, and personal selling. The inherent advantages and disadvantages of each of these promotional mix elements influence the roles they play in the overall marketing program. In developing the promotional program, the manager must decide which tools to use and how to combine them

to achieve the organization's objectives. Many organizations assist promotional managers in developing or implementing their plans including advertising agencies, media organizations, and specialized communication services firms like direct-response agencies, sales promotion agencies, interactive agencies, and public relations firms.

3 To introduce the concept of integrated marketing communications (IMC) by considering its evolution, renewed perspective, and importance.

Historically, companies used mass-media advertising extensively in their promotional plans. Eventually, companies linked their promotional tools to achieve a more efficient and effective communication program. Managers referred to this practice as integrated marketing communications (IMC). Today, IMC is viewed as a strategic and comprehensive planning perspective for all facets of an organization's marketing communication.

An IMC perspective is an important direction for decision making for a number of reasons. Most organizations need to communicate with multiple target audiences requiring decisions on the consistency or uniqueness of messages to each member. When planning for IMC, managers have to consider how each promotional tool will communicate the brand effectively depending on who is receiving the brand message. The emergence of IMC has become even more important for organizations that communicate with some messages to current customers and with other messages to prospective customers.

An IMC perspective also starts with the consumer's point of view in that much marketing communication is perceived as being very similar to or at least labelled as advertising. Moreover, an IMC perspective for promotional planning has become critical as audiences receive messages from competing brands across different IMC tools.

A movement toward building long-term relationships through strategies like relationship marketing has altered the communication perspective of many promotional planners. Customized communication to individual customers via extensive databases to enhance the lifetime value of customers makes IMC more critical.

Increased consumer adoption of technology and media allows marketers far-reaching avenues for communication that makes paramount the need to consider each tool's effects. Finally, the advantages of taking an IMC perspective are increasingly viewed as being a very effective way of planning for promotion that can lead to greater efficiencies.

4 To summarize a model of the IMC planning process and to examine the steps in developing a marketing communications program.

IMC management involves coordinating the promotional mix elements to develop an integrated program of effective marketing communication. The model of the IMC planning process in Figure 1-8 contains a number of steps: a review of the marketing plan; a marketing communication situation analysis; determining

IMC plan objectives; development of IMC programs; and implementation and control of the overall program. This model is consistent with the more general marketing planning model, but is more specific to the context of marketing communication. It shows that individual marketing communication tools can be recommended to achieve multiple objectives so that the completely coordinated or integrated plan can build brand equity across multiple target audiences.

KEY TERMS

advertising, **9**
advertising agency, **16**
behavioural objectives, **28**
brand equity, **7**
clients, **15**
collateral services, **16**
communication objectives, **28**
direct channels, **9**
direct marketing, **13**

direct-response advertising, **13**
exchange, **4**
external analysis, **26**
IMC management, **23**
IMC plan, **23**
indirect channels, **9**
integrated marketing communications (IMC), **17**

interactive media, **14**
internal analysis, **25**
marketing, **22**
marketing mix, **5**
marketing objectives, **28**
marketing plan, **23**
media organizations, **16**
personal selling, **15**
product symbolism, **6**
promotion, **9**

promotional mix, **9**
public relations, **12**
publicity, **12**
relationship marketing, **22**
sales promotion, **12**
specialized marketing communication services, **16**

DISCUSSION QUESTIONS

1. Discuss how integrated marketing communications differs from traditional advertising and promotion. What are some of the reasons why more marketers are taking an IMC perspective to their advertising and promotion programs?

2. Why would brands combine their advertising message and sales promotion offer in the same print ad?

3. Sports sponsorship, a public relations tool, continues to grow at an increasing degree in the IMC plans of major brands. Explain how this is a good investment of marketing resources.

4. Will newer direct media like e-mail and smartphones eventually replace direct mail in the future?

5. Describe how the Internet can be used to execute the IMC tools identified in this chapter.

6. Discuss the role IMC plays in the brand-building process. How are marketers changing the ways they go about building strong brands?

7. What are contact tools? Select a company or brand and discuss the contact tools that marketers can use to reach consumers of this product.

8. Discuss the role IMC plays in relationship marketing. How might the customization of advertising and other forms of marketing communication be possible?

9. Why is it important for those who work in the field of advertising and promotion to understand and appreciate all various IMC tools, not just the area in which they specialize?

10. What parts of the IMC planning model are similar to and different from a marketing planning model?

2 ORGANIZING FOR INTEGRATED MARKETING COMMUNICATIONS

■ **CHAPTER OBJECTIVES**

1 To understand how companies organize for advertising and other aspects of integrated marketing communications.

2 To examine methods for selecting, compensating, and evaluating advertising agencies.

3 To explain the role and functions of specialized marketing communications organizations.

4 To examine perspectives on the use of integrated services and responsibilities of advertisers versus agencies.

AGENCY OF THE YEAR FOR DDB

Strategy magazine named DDB its Agency of the Year for 2009, a deserving honour when looking at the awards it received and the creativity of its work for clients like Subaru, the BC Dairy Foundation, and the Canadian Tourism Commission. Led by Frank Palmer, the agency faced considerable disruption in personnel for a variety of reasons, yet somehow managed to come out on top with its affiliated agencies Tribal, Karacters, and Kidthink.

In Subaru, DDB scored with its spots for the Outback, Forester, and Legacy brands. One spot begins as an infomercial for the ubiquitous Snuggie (a blanket with sleeves); after 11 seconds, the scene quickly changes via a crowbar prying the ad away from the screen, revealing an intervening man who is outdoors with his Outback. The super suggests, "Maybe you should get out more" to its target—owners of small SUVs who live in cities and appreciate the outdoors. DDB saw that Subaru, with only 2 percent market share, needed a surprise in its message and the approach certainly worked, with a 200 percent sales increase. For the Forester, DDB featured "sexy" sumo wrestlers in a campaign that won the "Best of the Best" award and numerous other gold awards from the Canadian Marketing Association. This sporting imagery improved sales by more than 100 percent. Finally, respect and social approval worked as the message to attract potential owners of the Legacy sedan. Creative Director Andrew Simon noted that, "Sedan ownership comes with some baggage, so although you're getting a great value and vehicle you know that you're compromising on the cool factor."

For the BC Dairy Foundation, DDM invented a number of quirky scenarios reflecting competitive situations that teens experience in life. Each concluded with the vanquished participant saying "Must drink more milk," implying that milk would give more energy and reverse the outcome. With the goal of increasing consumption among teens who understood the health benefits of milk, the campaign proved successful with a 3 percent growth in volume. Moreover, spillover to user-generated executions on YouTube enabled milk to take a central role in teen life once again.

"Locals know" became the theme for a campaign for the Canadian Tourism Commission to increase the amount of domestic travel—in other words, to encourage Canadians to visit Canada instead of international destinations. DDB put together the message and visuals to show the country's unique and exotic places that only "locals" know about. A number of print images and TV ads asked, "Where is this?" in reference to unexpected Canadian geography such as sand dunes, a volcano, and tropical blue water. Viewers went to the website to find out the answer, upload vacation pictures, or talk about different locations. Forbes cited the campaign as one of the top 10 in the world, 450,000 visited the website, and follow-up research found 22 percent booked a domestic trip in response to the ads.

Sources: Carey Toane, "AOY Gold: DDB Rules the Roost," *Strategy*, November 2009; Kristin Laird, "Subaru Pulls Off Snuggie Ad for Outback Spot," *Marketing Magazine*, November 17, 2009; Kristin Laird, "Subaru Restores Steve's Respect," *Marketing Magazine*, September 16, 2009; Jeromy Lloyd, "Subaru's Sumo Take Top Prize at CMAS," *Marketing Magazine*, November 30, 2009.

QUESTION:

1. In what way is each of the campaigns creative?

Developing and implementing an integrated marketing communications program is usually a complex and detailed process involving the efforts of many individuals from both the marketing firm and the advertising and other types of agencies. To manage this process, firms ensure that they are organized internally and have strong relationships with advertising agencies and other communication specialists. Overall, this chapter describes organizational characteristics for those who are unfamiliar and may want to work in the field of marketing communication.

This chapter indentifies how companies organize internally for advertising and promotion. For many companies, marketing communication is planned and executed by an outside agency with IMC capabilities. Thus, we will examine the characteristics of a full-service agency and its client relationship. We also summarize the role of specialized marketing communications organizations such as direct-response, sales promotion, and interactive agencies and public relations firms. The chapter concludes with a discussion of whether marketers are best served by using the integrated services of one large agency or the separate services of a variety of communications specialists.

ORGANIZING FOR ADVERTISING AND PROMOTION IN THE FIRM

Marketing personnel have the most direct relationship with advertising and are often involved in many aspects of the decision process, such as providing input to the campaign plan, agency selection, and evaluation of proposed programs. Top management is usually interested in how the advertising program represents the firm, and may be involved for major expenditures or significant changes in the strategy. While many people both inside and outside the organization participate in the process, direct responsibility for administering the program must be assumed by an advertising or communications manager operating under a marketing director. An alternative used by many large multiproduct firms is a decentralized marketing (brand management) system.

THE CENTRALIZED SYSTEM

Marketing activities are divided along functional lines in the **centralized system**, with advertising placed alongside other marketing functions such as sales, marketing research, and product planning, as shown in Figure 2-1. A centralized system is used when companies have few divisions, product or service lines, or brands to advertise. The **advertising manager** is responsible for all promotions activities

FIGURE 2–1   The advertising department under a centralized system

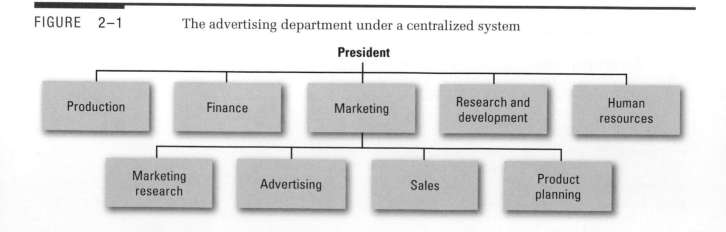

except sales. The advertising manager controls the entire promotions operation, including budgeting, coordinating the creation and production of ads, planning media schedules, and monitoring and administering the sales promotions programs for all the company's products or services. Basic functions the manager and staff perform include the following.

Planning and Budgeting   The advertising department is responsible for developing advertising and promotions plans that will be approved by management and recommending a promotions program based on the overall marketing plan, objectives, and budget. Formal plans are submitted annually or when a program is being changed significantly, as when a new campaign is developed. While the advertising department develops the promotional budget, the final decision on allocating funds is usually made by top management.

Administration and Execution   The manager must organize the advertising department and supervise and control its activities. The manager also supervises the execution of the plan by subordinates and/or the advertising agency. This requires working with such departments as production, media, art, copy, and sales promotion. If an outside agency is used, the advertising department is relieved of much of the responsibility for execution; however, it must review and approve the agency's plans.

Coordination with Other Departments   The manager must coordinate the advertising department's activities with those of other departments, particularly those involving other marketing functions. For example, the advertising department must communicate with marketing research and/or sales to determine which product features are important to customers and should be emphasized in the company's communications. Research may also provide profiles of product users and nonusers for the media department before it selects broadcast or print media. The advertising department may also be responsible for preparing material for the sales force, such as sales promotion tools, advertising materials, and point-of-purchase displays.

Coordination with Outside Agencies and Services   Many companies have an advertising department but still use many outside services. For example, companies may develop their advertising programs in-house while employing media buying services to place their ads and/or use collateral services agencies to develop brochures, point-of-purchase materials, and so on. The department serves as liaison between the company and any outside service providers and also determines which ones to use. Once outside services are retained, the manager will work with other marketing managers to coordinate their efforts and evaluate their performances.

THE DECENTRALIZED SYSTEM

Corporations with multiple divisions and many different products generally have a **decentralized system**, with separate manufacturing, research and development, sales, and marketing departments for various divisions, product lines, or businesses. Companies usually assign each product to a **brand manager** who is responsible for the total management of the brand, including planning, budgeting, sales, and profit performance. (The term *product manager* is also used to describe this position.) The brand manager, who may have one or more assistant brand managers, is responsible for the planning, implementation, and control of the marketing program.[1]

Under this system, the responsibilities and functions associated with advertising and promotions are transferred to the brand manager, who works closely with the outside advertising agency and other marketing communications specialists as they develop the promotional program.[2] In a multiproduct firm, each brand may have its

 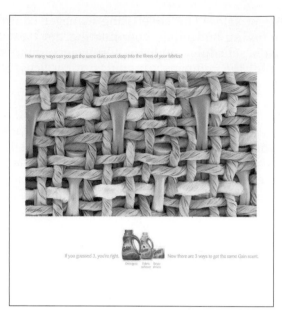

Exhibit 2-1   Many of Procter & Gamble's brands compete against each other.

own ad agency and may compete against other brands within the company, not just against outside competitors. For example, Exhibit 2-1 shows ads for Tide and Gain, which are both Procter & Gamble products that compete for a share of the laundry detergent market.

As shown in Figure 2-2, the advertising department is part of marketing services and provides support for the brand managers. The role of marketing services is to assist the brand managers in planning and coordinating the integrated marketing communications program. In some companies, the marketing services group may include sales promotion. The brand managers may work with sales promotion people to develop budgets, define strategies, and implement tactical executions for both trade and consumer promotions. Marketing services may also provide other types of support services, such as package design and merchandising.

ADVERTISING AGENCIES

The use of an advertising agency is unique for each advertiser as there are many different types. In this section we provide a general overview; we review the advertising agency decision, describe the activities of a full-service agency, highlight the agency industry, and identify other types of agencies.

ADVERTISING AGENCY DECISION

Irrespective of whether an advertiser uses a centralized or decentralized organizational structure, there remains the choice of whether a firm will have its own in-house agency or whether it will employ an external advertising agency. We now briefly discuss the relative merits and concerns of both options.

In-House Agency   An **in-house agency** is an advertising agency that is set up, owned, and operated by the advertiser. Some in-house agencies are little more than advertising departments, but in other companies they are given a separate identity and are responsible for the expenditure of large sums of advertising dollars.

FIGURE   2–2   A decentralized brand management system

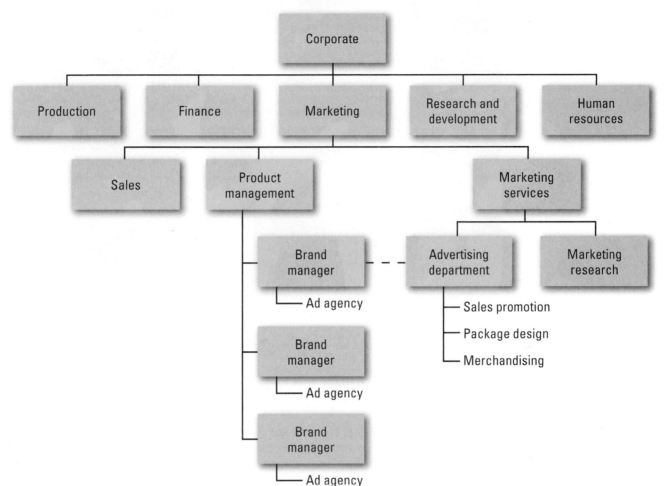

Research finds that about half of all companies use an in-house agency and that the likelihood of this occurring decreases with larger advertising budgets but increases with advertising intensity (i.e., advertising/sales ratio), technological intensity, and for creative industries.[3] Many companies use in-house agencies exclusively; others combine in-house efforts with those of outside agencies. For example, Benetton handles most of its advertising in-house, but the company does use an outside agency for some of its creative work (Exhibit 2-2).

A major reason for using an in-house agency is to reduce advertising and promotion costs. Companies with very large advertising budgets pay a substantial amount to outside agencies. An in-house agency can also provide related work—such as sales presentations and sales force materials, package design, and public relations—at a lower cost than outside agencies. A study by M. Louise Ripley found that creative and media services were the most likely functions to be performed outside, while merchandising and sales promotion were the most likely to be performed in-house.[4]

Saving money is not the only reason why companies use in-house agencies. Time savings, bad experiences with outside agencies, and the increased knowledge and understanding of the market that come from working on advertising and promotion for the product or service day by day are also reasons. Companies can also maintain tighter control over the process and more easily coordinate promotions with the firm's overall marketing program.[5]

Exhibit 2-2
Benetton's in-house agency works with outside agencies to develop ads.

40

A limitation of an in-house agency is that personnel may grow stale while working on the same product line in comparison to an outside agency where creative specialists design campaigns for variety of products. Furthermore, changes in an in-house agency could be slow or disruptive compared to the flexibility of hiring a new outside agency.

Advertising Agency   Many major companies use an advertising agency to assist them in developing, preparing, and executing their promotional programs. An ad agency is a service organization that specializes in planning and executing advertising programs for its clients. Probably the main reason why outside agencies are used is that they provide the client with the services of highly skilled individuals who are specialists in their chosen fields. An advertising agency's staff may include artists, writers, media analysts, researchers, and others with specific skills, knowledge, and experience who can help market the client's products or services. Many agencies specialize in a particular type of business and use their knowledge of the industry to assist their clients.

An outside agency can also provide an objective viewpoint of the market and its business that is not subject to internal company policies, biases, or other limitations. The agency can draw on the broad range of experience it has gained while working on a diverse set of marketing problems for various clients. For example, an ad agency that is handling a travel-related account may have individuals who have worked with airlines, cruise ship companies, travel agencies, hotels, and other travel-related industries. The agency may have experience in this area or may even have previously worked on the advertising account of one of the client's competitors. Thus, the agency can provide the client with insight into the industry (and, in some cases, the competition).

The Institute of Communications and Advertising offers a comprehensive document that acts as a guide for selecting the most appropriate agency. Using a "best practices" approach, the steps in the search process are carefully diagrammed and explained so that both clients and agencies could benefit. If all the steps are adhered, selecting the right agency could range from 8 to 16 weeks. In the end, the client and agency form a partnership where the responsibilities of each are recorded and agreed upon with the intention of a positive working relationship.

ADVERTISING AGENCY INDUSTRY

The Canadian advertising agency industry is similar to that in other countries—there is a combination of domestic firms and international organizations, especially from the United States. The strong presence of international ad agencies in Canada reflects a global trend of large agencies merged with or acquired by other agencies and support organizations. These **superagencies** now provide clients with integrated marketing communications services worldwide. Many mid-size agencies were acquired by or forged alliances with larger agencies because clients wanted an agency with international marketing communication capabilities, and their alignment with larger organizations permitted access to a network of agencies around the world. Currently, most major agencies offer specialized services in areas of interactive communications, direct marketing, and sales promotion so that they can offer their clients an ever-broader range of IMC services.[6] Global advertising campaigns are facilitated by using larger international agencies (Exhibit 2-3).

Figure 2-3 summarizes the "agency family tree" produced by *Marketing Magazine*.[7] The tree identifies all the major players on the Canadian advertising scene. (Note that the original tree spanned eight pages; we retained the scope of the diagram and acknowledge some missing information or lack of detail to fit this broad array of information in a single table.) The idea of the superagency is readily observed—we see two major Canadian firms, Cossette and MDC, along with their full agency and other businesses that cater to all marketing communication services. As expected, two major players exist based in New York, Omnicom and Interpublic; each one includes famous advertising agencies recognized for their creative talent. Canadian affiliates of these large agencies are responsible for country-based marketing communication activities that are part of the worldwide campaigns. For example, BBDO Proximity of Toronto developed an Internet application to promote the Gillette Fusion brand in Canada (Exhibit 2-4). Additionally, the table includes two major European conglomerates that own established American advertising greats like Ogilvy & Mather, JWT, and Leo Burnett. IMC Perspective 2-1 highlights the accomplishments of some Canadian agencies.

Exhibit 2-3 TAG Heuer uses a global campaign featuring different celebrity ambassadors for various countries.

FIGURE   2–3   A summary of the "agency family tree" produced by *Marketing Magazine*.

	Full Service	Public Relations	Digital & Direct	Sales Promotion	Media Buying	Design	Other
Cossette (Quebec City)	Cossette	Optimum Rocket XL	Blitz Direct Bloom Digital Fjord Interactive	Strateco-Blitz	Cossette	Identica Koo Creative	Altius Sport Fusion Alliance Magnet Search Nucleus
MDC (Toronto)	Zig Allard Johnson	Veritas	Henderson Bas	6 Degrees		Bruce Mau	Bryan Mills Iradesso Northstar
Omnicomm (New York)	DDB Anderson DDB DDB Echology BBDO DAS	DDB PR Porter Noveli Ketchum Fleishman-Hillard	Tribal DDB Rapp Radar Critcal Mass		OMD	Karacters Interbrand	Kidthink TBWA Radiate
Interpublic (New York)	MacLaren McCann Lowe Roche Draft FCB	CMG	MacLaren MRM Rivet	MacLaren Momentum Segal	MediaBrands	CMG	CMG
WPP (London)	Grey Ogilvy & Mather JWT Young & Rubicam	Hill & Knowlton Res Publica	OgilvyOne RMG Connect Wunderman	OgilvyAction	GroupM	JWT Sauce Sudler & Hennessy	Kantar Redworks Ethos
Publicis (Paris)	Publicis Saatchi & Saatchi Leo Burnett	MS&L	Publicis		Zenith Starcom	Publicis	Publicis

42

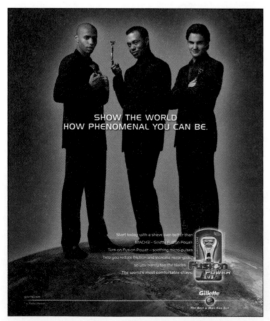

SHOW THE WORLD
HOW PHENOMENAL YOU CAN BE.

Exhibit 2-4 Agencies often customize global campaigns for local markets.

FULL-SERVICE ADVERTISING AGENCIES

The services offered and functions performed vary depending upon the size of the agency. A **full-service agency** offers its clients a complete range of marketing, communications, and promotions services including planning, creating, and producing the advertising; performing research; and selecting media. A full-service agency may also offer nonadvertising services, such as strategic market planning; sales promotions, direct marketing, and interactive capabilities; package design; and public relations and publicity. The full-service agency is made up of departments that provide the activities needed to perform the various advertising functions and serve the client, as shown in Figure 2-4. In this section we summarize these main characteristics.

Creative Services   The creative services department is responsible for the creation and execution of advertisements. The individuals who conceive the ideas for the ads and write the headlines, subheads, and body copy (the words constituting the message) are known as **copywriters**. They may also be involved in determining the basic appeal or theme of the ad

A pair of agencies, Ogilvy and Taxi, performed well, just behind ultimate winner DDB, for *Strategy*'s Agency of the Year Award. Together, the two runners-up represent creators of the best advertising in the country for 2009.

Strategy recognized Ogilvy for its works with Cisco, Cogeco, Hellman's, Dove, and Shreddies. For Cisco, Ogilvy created "One Million Acts of Green" as an initiative for consumers to record their ideas online concerning little changes in all of our behaviour that could have a dramatic effect for the environment. With the assistance of notable personalities and partners, visitors identified a total of 1.74 million acts resulting in 6.9 brand exposures and 200 media reports for publicity. Ogilvy orchestrated an exclusive launch event for IT professionals as part of a launch for Toronto Hydro Telecom's effort to attract business for its 100-percent-owned, network-based fibre-optic Internet service. The Hellman's campaign highlighted the Canadian ingredients in the product by drawing attention to all the non-Canadian food in our food chain in a three-minute online video. Supported with TV and media stories, the YouTube video attracted 50,000 viewers and the PR garnered 18 million impressions. For Dove, the agency executed an online game to fit with the target of women in their twenties for the new Go Fresh product line. The game simulated the romantic comedy adventures of a woman where the users decided the outcome of each stage of the story. Directed to the site by movie trailers, TV, and blogs, about a quarter million viewers explored the story for an average of five minutes, resulting in sales nearly 50 percent above target. And after the initial success of Diamond Shreddies in 2008, Ogilvy extended the idea with an opportunity for consumers to vote on which version they liked best, all due to the complaints Kraft-Post received from withdrawing the original Shreddies off the market.

Taxi looked good for *Strategy* because of the agency's effort on the Canadian Tire, Dairy Farmers of Canada, Viagra, Carling, and Reitmans accounts. Taxi moved Canadian Tire in a new direction with the "For the Days Like Today" campaign, designed to show how the established retailer plays an important role in the lives of Canadian families. Their inaugural Canadian Cheese Rolling Festival at Whistler's multimedia and a website showing video of the festival's activities helped spur sales growth of cheese in B.C. by 2.5 percent. Taxi maintained Viagra's rising image with a new take on why men would need the product. This time, the ED prescription medication acted as an alternative to strolling, antiquing, and reading; all in jest, of course. Carling beer, around since 1840, used its rich heritage to show a number of executions where its drinkers have always made "Great Beer Decisions." Finally, Taxi helped Reitmans refine its long-lasting message of its women's clothing being "Designed for Real Life" with a humorous comparison to high fashion.

Carey Toane, "AOY Finalist: Ogilvy Shines Bright," *Strategy,* November 2009, p. 7; Carey Toane, "AOY Finalist: Taxi Ranks High," *Strategy,* November 2009, p. 6; Carey Toane, "AOY Bronze: Zigg Ideas, Zig Changes," *Strategy,* November 2009, p. 4.

Question:

1. Do you agree that the marketing communication identified by the agencies is worth recognition?

campaign and often prepare a rough initial visual layout of the print ad or television commercial.

While copywriters are responsible for what the message says, the *art department* is responsible for how the ad looks. For print ads, the art director and graphic designers prepare *layouts*, which are drawings that show what the ad will look like and from which the final artwork will be produced. For TV commercials, the layout is known as a *storyboard*, a sequence of frames or panels that depict the commercial in still form.

Members of the creative department work together to develop ads that will communicate the key points determined to be the basis of the creative strategy for the client's product or service. Writers and artists generally work under the direction of the agency's creative director, who oversees all the advertising produced by the organization. The director sets the creative philosophy of the department and may even become directly involved in creating ads for the agency's largest clients.

FIGURE 2—4 Full-service agency organizational chart

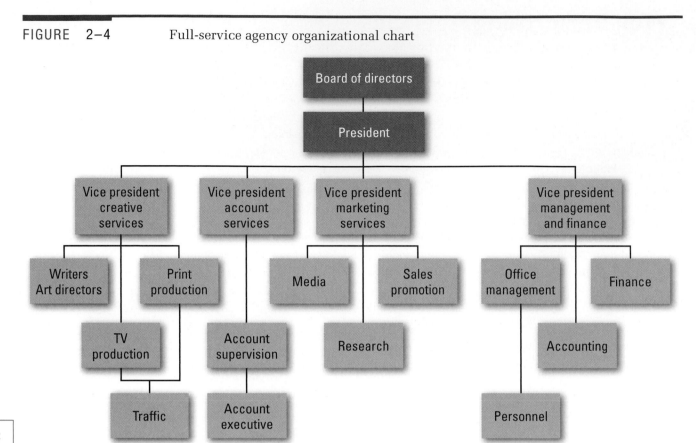

Once the copy, layout, illustrations, and mechanical specifications have been completed and approved, the ad is turned over to the *production department*. Most agencies do not actually produce finished ads; they hire printers, engravers, photographers, typographers, and other suppliers to complete the finished product. For broadcast production, the approved storyboard must be turned into a finished commercial. The production department may supervise the casting of people to appear in the ad and the setting for the scenes as well as choose an independent production studio. The department may hire an outside director to turn the creative concept into a commercial. Copywriters, art directors, account managers, people from research and planning, and representatives from the client side may all participate in production decisions, particularly when large sums of money are involved.

Creating an advertisement often involves many people and takes several months. In large agencies with many clients, coordinating the creative and production processes can be a major problem. A *traffic department* coordinates all phases of production to see that the ads are completed on time and that all deadlines for submitting the ads to the media are met. The traffic department may be located in the creative services area of the agency, or be part of media or account management, or be separate.

Marketing Services These services delivered by an advertising agency vary; they can be found in one department or, increasingly in larger firms, separated into two or three others with corresponding vice presidents or directors. For example, a firm might have a vice president for strategy and research, and another for media planning.

Most full-service agencies maintain a *research department* whose function is to gather, analyze, and interpret information that will be useful in developing advertising for their clients. This can be done through primary research—where a study is designed, executed, and interpreted by the research department—or through the use of secondary (previously published) sources of information. Sometimes the research department acquires studies conducted by independent syndicated research firms or consultants. The research staff then interpret these reports and pass on the information to other agency personnel working on that account. The research department may also design and conduct research to pretest the effectiveness of advertising the agency is considering. For example, copy testing is often conducted to determine how messages developed by the creative specialists are likely to be interpreted by the receiving audience.

In many large agencies, the marketing services or strategic planning department may include *account planners,* who gather information that is relevant to the client's product or service and that can be used in the development of the creative strategy as well as other aspects of the IMC campaign. Account planners work with the client as well as other agency personnel including the account executives, creative team members, media specialists, and research department personnel to collect information that can be helpful in gaining a better understanding of the client's target audience and the best ways to communicate with them. They gather and organize information about consumers as well as developments in the marketplace that can be used to prepare the *creative brief,* which is a document that the agency's creative department uses to guide the development of advertising ideas and concepts. Account planners may also be involved in assessing consumers' reactions to the advertising and other elements of the IMC program and providing the creative staff as well as other agency personnel with feedback regarding performance. Account planning is a very important function in many agencies because it provides the creative team, as well as other agency personnel, with more insight into consumers and how to use advertising and other IMC tools to communicate with them.[8] However, the account planning function has also become more demanding as the number of marketing communication channels and ways of contacting consumers has increased. Account planners interact with individuals from a variety of marketing communication disciplines and have to keep up with developments that are occurring in all of these areas.

The *media department* of an agency analyzes, selects, and contracts for space or time in the media that will be used to deliver the client's advertising message. The media department is expected to develop a media plan that will reach the target audience and effectively communicate the message. Since most of the client's ad budget is spent on media time and/or space, this department must develop a plan that both communicates with the right audience and is cost-effective.

Media specialists must know what audiences the media reach, their rates, and how well they match the client's target audience. The media department reviews information on demographics, magazine and newspaper readership, radio listenership, and consumers' TV viewing patterns to develop an effective media plan. The media buyer implements the media plan by purchasing the actual time and space. The media department is becoming an increasingly important part of the agency business as many large advertisers consolidate their media buying with one or a few agencies to save money and improve media efficiency. An agency's strategic ability to negotiate prices and effectively use the vast array of media vehicles available is becoming as important as its ability to create ads.

Some agencies offer additional marketing services to their clients to assist in other promotional areas. An agency may have a sales promotion department, or merchandising department, that specializes in developing contests, premiums, promotions, point-of-sale materials, and other sales materials. It may have direct-marketing specialists and package designers, as well as a PR/publicity department. Many agencies have developed interactive media departments to create websites or develop social media and e-mail campaigns for their clients. As shown in Figure 2-4, these other services could be independent firms owned by the agency.

Account Services Account services, or account management, is the link between the ad agency and its clients. Depending on the size of the client and its advertising budget, one or more account executives serve as liaison. The **account executive** is responsible for understanding the advertiser's marketing and promotions needs and interpreting them to agency personnel. He or she coordinates agency efforts in planning, creating, and producing ads. The account executive also presents agency recommendations and obtains client approval. As the focal point of agency–client relationships, the account executive must know a great deal about the client's business and be able to communicate this to specialists in the agency working on the account. The ideal account executive has a strong marketing background as well as a thorough understanding of all phases of the advertising process.

To provide superior service for its accounts, many agencies use the **group system**, in which individuals from each department work together in groups to service particular accounts. In contrast to the **departmental system** we have been discussing thus far, each group is headed by an account executive or supervisor and has one or more media people, including media planners and buyers; a creative team, which includes copywriters, art directors, artists, and production personnel; and one or more account executives. The group may also include individuals from other departments such as marketing research, direct marketing, or sales promotion. The size and composition of the group varies depending on the client's billings and the importance of the account to the agency. For very important accounts, the group members may be assigned exclusively to one client. In some agencies, they may serve a number of smaller clients. Many agencies prefer the group system because employees become very knowledgeable about the client's business and there is continuity in servicing the account.

OTHER TYPES OF AGENCIES AND SERVICES

Many advertisers, including some large companies, are not interested in paying for the services of a full-service agency but are interested in some of the specific services agencies have to offer. Over the past few decades, alternatives to full-service agencies have evolved, including creative boutiques and media buying services.

Creative Boutiques A **creative boutique** is an agency that provides only creative services. These specialized agencies have creative personnel but do not have media, research, or account planning capabilities. Creative boutiques have developed in response to some companies' desires to use only the creative services of an outside agency while managing the other functions internally. While most creative boutiques work directly for companies, full-service agencies often subcontract work to creative boutiques when they are very busy or want to avoid adding full-time employees to their payrolls. Many creative boutiques have been formed by members of the creative departments of full-service agencies who leave the firm and take with them clients who want to retain their creative talents. Exhibit 2-5 highlights an example of Canada's most successful creative boutiques.

One area where Canadian agencies have worked with specialized creative firms is in the development of messages targeted to specific ethnic markets. It is very expensive and difficult for large agencies to be set up for each ethnic community that it may try to reach in a campaign, so they rely on specialists who have the expertise. With tremendous growth in the numbers of Chinese immigrants in Toronto and Vancouver, firms such as Ford have used tailored messages and ethnic media to influence the attitudes of this target audience, which has very different beliefs than other consumers because of its heritage. Ford could not succeed in establishing a unique brand position with this target audience without the assistance of those more familiar. One trade-off that advertisers need in order to make this work is to put the media savings from lower-cost publications or TV programming into the production of appropriate creative messages.[9]

Media Buying Services **Media buying services** are independent companies that specialize in the buying of media, particularly radio and television time. The task of purchasing advertising media has grown more complex as specialized media proliferate, so media buying services have found a niche by specializing in the analysis and purchase of advertising time and space. Agencies and clients usually develop their own media strategies and hire the buying service to execute them. Some media buying services do help advertisers plan their media strategies. Because media buying services purchase such large amounts of time and space, they receive large discounts and can save the small agency or client money on media purchases. IMC Perspective 2-2 describes a prominent Canadian media agency.

Media buying services have been experiencing strong growth in recent years as clients seek alternatives to full-service agency relationships. Many companies have been unbundling agency services and consolidating media buying to get more clout from their advertising budgets. As noted earlier, many of the major agencies have formed independent media services companies that handle the media planning and buying for their clients and also offer their services separately to companies interested in a more specialized or consolidated

Exhibit 2-5 An example of Rethink's creative talent.

approach to media planning, research, and/or buying. The rise of the independent media-buying services, operating outside the structure of the traditional ad agency media department, and the divestment of these departments from the agency system are two of the most significant developments that have occurred in the advertising industry in recent years. Exhibit 2-6 shows how Initiative, which is one of the largest media specialist companies, promotes its services.

AGENCY COMPENSATION AND EVALUATION

Agencies use a variety of compensation methods depending on the type and amount of service they provide to their clients. We review a number of methods, because there is no one method of compensation to which everyone subscribes. We also examine the related topic of performance evaluation and explore reasons why clients switch agencies.

COMMISSIONS FROM MEDIA

The historical method of compensating agencies is through a **commission system**, where the agency receives a specified commission (usually 15 percent) from the media on any advertising time or space it purchases for its client. This system

Strategy magazine recognized Starcom MediaVest Group (SMG) as the Media Agency of the Year for 2009 after a run of successful media placements for brands such as Tassimo, Swiffer, Pogo, Johnnie Walker, and Special K. SMG's experienced media agency leader, CEO Lauren Richards—famous for overseeing many campaigns while previously at Cossette, such as the launch of McDonald's pizza—transformed the company into a worldwide innovator in marrying media and creative strategies.

Tassimo, a single-serving coffee brewer, married an ad page and an editorial page with a kitchen scene within an issue of *Style at Home* with a mostly translucent overlay page so that a picture of the product appeared along with the message, "All this kitchen needs is a countertop café." Nine different executions for a variety of kitchen styles appeared across different magazines. Sales increased 22 percent and brand attitudinal and intention measures grew by 40 percent. A repeat of the ad and content idea occurred with Swiffer. A makeover of the month article in *Canadian House & Home* showed a laundry room with a dirty floor, with the subsequent page showing the same room with a clean floor and the Swiffer and a message: "Swiffer gives cleaning a whole new meaning."

SMG revived Pogo with the "Be proud of your wiener" campaign, which included street events where teenage boys hung out along with a challenge to see who could hold his Pogo in the air the longest, and quick seven-second ads on youth TV channels leading to increased awareness of 300 percent for Pogo in the frozen food category. In targeting Johnnie Walker scotch to Chinese-Canadians, SMG distributed 100,000 greeting posters to interested visitors at the Pacific Mall, located in the Toronto CMA. People placed the posters, produced by world-famous calligrapher guan Sui Sheng, in the homes or offices to Chinese tradition. Along with other creative messaging, sales for the Blue Label version increased by 258 percent, while the Black Label increased by 19 percent.

Special K started its new plan to build a relationship with women aged 25 to 49 seeking help for weight management shortly after New Year's during heightened resolution intention time. SMG established a Special K Diet and Fitness channel on the Yahoo.ca portal that provided information and linked those interested to the Yahoo group. A mass media blitz initiated visits to the portal rather than advertising a website address, with the group gaining 400 percent new members and 100 percent growth in visits to SpecialK.ca. Sales and brand measures both increased sufficiently.

Sources: Chris Powell, "The Art of Innovation," *Marketing Magazine,* March 23, 2009; Kristin Laird, "Starcom MediaVest Group," *Marketing Magazine*, November 9, 2009; Jonathan Paul, "Starcom MediaVest Group Breaks Ground," *Strategy*, November 29, p. 12; Melita Kuburas, "Starcom MediaVest Group's Brian Chan: Building New Connections," *Strategy*, June 2009, p. 26.

Question:

1. Explain why a media agency is so critical for advertising.

Exhibit 2-6 Initiative is one of the leading media specialist companies.

provides a simple method of determining payments, as shown in the following example.

Assume an agency prepares a full-page magazine ad and arranges to place the ad on the back cover of a magazine at a cost of $100,000. The agency places the order for the space and delivers the ad to the magazine. Once the ad is run, the magazine will bill the agency for $100,000, less the 15 percent ($15,000) commission. The media will also offer a 2 percent cash discount for early payment, which the agency may pass along to the client. The agency will bill the client $100,000 less the 2 percent cash discount on the net amount, or a total of $98,300, as shown in Figure 2-5. The $15,000 commission represents the agency's compensation for its services.

Media Bills Agency		Agency Bills Advertiser	
Costs for magazine space	$100,000	Costs for magazine space	$100,000
Less 15% commission	–15,000	Less 2% cash discount	–1,700
Cost of media space	$ 85,000	Advertiser pays agency	$ 98,300
Less 2% cash discount	–1,700		
Agency pays media	$ 83,300	Agency income	$ 15,000

FIGURE 2–5

Example of commission system payment

The commission system to compensate agencies has been quite controversial despite its prevalent use for decades. Critics argue that the commission system encourages agencies to recommend high-priced media to increase their commission level. Another concern regarding the commission system is that it ties agency compensation to media costs, allowing the agency to be disproportionately rewarded. Critics of the system have argued that it provides an incentive for agencies to recommend mass-media advertising when other forms of communication such as direct marketing or public relations might do a better job.[10]

Defenders of the commission system argue that it is easy to administer and it keeps the emphasis in agency competition on non-price factors such as the quality of the advertising developed. Proponents argue that agency services are proportional to the size of the commission, since more time and effort are devoted to the large accounts that generate high revenue for the agency. They also say the system is more flexible than it appears because agencies often perform other services for large clients at no extra charge, justifying such actions by the large commission they receive.

A study of agency compensation conducted by the Association of Canadian Advertisers (ACA) indicates that agency compensation based on the traditional 15 percent commission is becoming rare.[11] The survey found that the commission model was one of many approaches used and that no one model stood out as being the very best. In fact, a trend toward so many other models implies that the 15 percent commission is on a significant decline. Many advertisers have gone to a **negotiated commission** system to compensate their agencies. In this system, commissions average 8 to 10 percent, and are based on a sliding scale that becomes lower as clients' media expenditures increase. Agencies are also relying less on media commissions for their income as their clients expand their integrated marketing communications programs to include other forms of promotion and cut back on mass-media advertising. The percentage of agency income from media commissions is declining, and a greater percentage is coming through other methods such as fees and performance incentives.

FEE ARRANGEMENT

There are two basic types of fee arrangement systems. In the straight or **fixed-fee method**, the agency charges a basic monthly fee for all of its services and credits to the client any media commissions earned. Agency and client agree on the specific work to be done and the amount the agency will be paid for it. Sometimes agencies are compensated through a **fee–commission combination**, in which the media commissions received by the agency are credited against the fee. If the commissions are less than the agreed-on fee, the client must make up the difference. If the agency does much work for the client in noncommissionable media, the fee may be charged over and above the commissions received.

49

Both types of fee arrangements require that the agency carefully assess its costs of serving the client for the specified period, or for the project, plus its desired profit margin. To avoid any later disagreement, a fee arrangement should specify exactly what services the agency is expected to perform for the client. A recent interview of four agency executives suggests that the fee arrangement is becoming the more accepted method of compensation in Canada.[12]

COST-PLUS AGREEMENT

Under a **cost-plus system**, the client agrees to pay the agency a fee based on the costs of its work plus some agreed-on profit margin (often a percentage of total costs). This system requires that the agency keep detailed records of the costs it incurs in working on the client's account. Direct costs (personnel time and out-of-pocket expenses) plus an allocation for overhead and a markup for profits determines the amount the agency bills the client. An agency can add a markup of percentage charges to various services the agency purchases from outside providers (e.g., market research, artwork, printing, photography).

Fee agreements and cost-plus systems are commonly used in conjunction with a commission system. The fee-based system can be advantageous to both the client and the agency, depending on the size of the client, advertising budget, media used, and services required. Many clients prefer fee or cost-plus systems because they receive a detailed breakdown of where and how their advertising and promotion dollars are being spent. However, these arrangements can be difficult for the agency, as they require careful cost accounting and may be difficult to estimate when bidding for an advertiser's business. Agencies are also reluctant to let clients see their internal cost figures.

INCENTIVE-BASED COMPENSATION

Clients expect accountability from their agencies and link agency compensation to performance through some type of **incentive-based system**. The basic idea is that the agency's ultimate compensation level will depend on how well it meets predetermined performance goals. In Canada, the Performance by Results (PBR) system, initiated by the Institute of Communications and Advertising, highlights the importance of clearly identifying the objectives of the promotional plan and measuring the performance of the plan based on these objectives. PBR defines an advertising remuneration process where the basic advertising agency fee is adjusted by a reward based on the degree of achieving mutually agreed upon objectives between the client and the agency. Overall, the remuneration is a part of a system of linking performance, its measurement, and reward within the client–agency relationship, something that has been characteristic of supply relationships in other industries. The benefits of the PBR system are:

Greater efficiency and accountability	Stronger mutual understanding
Achievement of cost efficiencies	Improved retention of creative talent
Higher productivity	Increased agency strategic input
Fewer barriers of self-interest	Improved client–agency communication

Performance measures are a key element of the PBR system and the study highlights three general groups that should comprise the evaluation: overall business performance, marketing communication effectiveness, and agency process evaluation. Business measures include sales, market share, profitability, and margins. Marketing communication effectiveness measures include brand awareness, brand image ratings, and likability of advertising. This group also includes four objectives that are more behavioural: intent to purchase, trial, repeat purchase, and brand loyalty. The final group concerns the various services the agency provides and its overall management process.

The PBR system recognizes that there is no standard formula in applying these measures. The relative importance of each measure needs to be investigated for each brand and its marketing situation. Furthermore, the measures should take into account the role of promotion in the marketing mix and how promotion contributes to business results for the brand and within the product category or industry. In addition, the PBR system provides the following suggestions. Objectives can be short term and long term. An appropriate number of objectives should be used to focus the organization. The objectives should be consistent with other performance measures used in the organization. Objectives should be periodically re-evaluated by the client and the agency. Although some of these recommendations may be intuitive, the Canadian PBR is the most thorough published examination of the PBR system in the world. Another remarkable achievement for our marketing communication industry![13]

Over the past five years, about one-third of all Canadian marketers compensated their agencies with some form of payment by results. However, this overall figure varies depending upon the size of the communications budget. A total of 58 percent of firms spending more than $100 million use incentives, compared to only 18 percent of firms spending less than $15 million. Moreover, about two-thirds of clients compensating their agencies in this manner report improved performance. Larger firms, like Unilever, for example, employ this compensation method for all of their service agencies including sales promotion and public relations.[14]

EVALUATION OF AGENCIES

Regular reviews of the agency's performance are necessary. The agency evaluation process usually involves two types of assessments, one financial and operational and the other more qualitative. The **financial audit** focuses on how the agency conducts its business. It is designed to verify costs and expenses, the number of personnel hours charged to an account, and payments to media and outside suppliers. The **qualitative audit** focuses on the agency's efforts in planning, developing, and implementing the client's advertising programs and considers the results achieved. Sometimes it may appear that an evaluation is not required when the advertiser publicly praises its agency (Exhibit 2-7).

The agency evaluation is often done on a subjective, informal basis, particularly in smaller companies where ad budgets are low or advertising is not seen as the most critical factor in the firm's marketing performance. Some companies have developed formal, systematic evaluation systems, particularly when budgets are large and the advertising function receives much emphasis. As advertising costs continue to rise, the top management of these companies wants to be sure money is being spent efficiently and effectively.

As part of its mandate as an industry resource, the Institute of Communications and Advertising provides a Guide to Best Practice that includes information to facilitate agency evaluation (the

THE BOOK OF *e* BUSINESS

"IF IT DOESN'T SELL, IT ISN'T CREATIVE."
–David Ogilvy

Touffou – the Ogilvy castle. "Just throw those Clios and Lions in the basement."

WE WOULD LIKE to congratulate Ogilvy & Mather for this year's Grand EFFIE–winning e-business Infrastructure campaign and the Silver-winning "Easy to Buy" campaign. The work was impressive. The numbers, staggering. Your friends and partners at IBM thank you for a year of incredible success.

IBM.

IBM is a registered trademark of International Business Machines Corp. in the United States and/or other countries. © 2002 IBM Corporation. All rights reserved.

Exhibit 2-7 IBM congratulates its agency for developing an award-winning campaign.

Guide and the PBR study are both available at www.ica-ad.com). The document provides guidelines on the client–agency relationship and includes many forms that can be used as a basis for evaluating an agency in all areas of performance such as account management, creative, planning and research, production, media planning and buying, budget and financial, agency management, direct marketing, interactive marketing, and public relations.

One example of a formal agency evaluation system is that used by Whirlpool, which markets a variety of consumer products. Whirlpool management meets once a year with the company's agencies to review their performance. Whirlpool managers complete an advertising agency performance evaluation, part of which is shown in Figure 2-6. These reports are compiled and reviewed with the agency at each annual meeting. Whirlpool's evaluation process covers six areas of performance. The company and the agency develop an action plan to correct areas of deficiency.

REASONS FOR AGENCIES LOSING CLIENTS

The evaluation process described above provides valuable feedback to both the agency and the client, such as indicating changes that need to be made by the

FIGURE 2–6   Whirlpool's ad agency performance evaluation.

CREATIVE SERVICES

Always	Often	Occasionally	Seldom	Never	NA	Marks Scored
4	3	2	1	0		

1. Agency produces fresh ideas and original approaches
2. Agency accurately interprets facts, strategies and objectives into usable advertisements and plans
3. Creative group is knowledgeable about company's products, markets and strategies
4. Creative group is concerned with good advertising communications and develops campaigns and ads that exhibit this concern
5. Creative group produces on time
6. Creative group performs well under pressure
7. Creative group operates in a businesslike manner to control production costs and other creative charges
8. Agency presentations are well organized with sufficient examples of proposed executions
9. Creative group participates in major campaign presentations
10. Agency presents ideas and executions not requested but felt to be good opportunities
11. Agency willingly accepts ideas generated by other locations/agency offices vs. being over-protective of its own creative product
12. Other areas not mentioned
13. Agency demonstrates commitment to client's business
14. Agency creative proposals are relevant and properly fulfill creative brief

Value—(marks)

Rating:	Excellent	90–100%	Total marks scored
	Good	80–89%	
	Average	70–79%	Total possible marks
	Fair	60–69%	
	Poor	below 60%	Score

ACCOUNT REPRESENTATION & SERVICE

Always	Often	Occasionally	Seldom	Never	NA	Marks Scored
4	3	2	1	0		

1. Account representatives act with personal initiative
2. Account representatives anticipate needs in advance of direction by client (ie: are proactive)
3. Account group takes direction well
4. Agency is able to demonstrate results of programs implemented
5. Account representatives function strategically rather than as creative advisors only
6. Account representatives are knowledgeable about competitive programs and share this information along with their recommendations in a timely manner
7. Account representatives respond to client requests in a timely fashion
8. Account group operates in a business-like manner to control costs
9. Agency recommendations are founded on sound reasoning and supported factually, and appropriately fit within budget constraints
10. Agency is able to advise the client on trends and developments in technology
11. Account representatives demonstrate a high degree of professionalism in both written and oral communication
12. Agency presents ideas and executions not requested by felt to be good opportunities
13. Agency makes reasoned recommendations on allocation of budgets
14. Agency demonstrates commitment to client's business
15. There is a positive social relationship between client and agency

Value—(marks)

Rating:	Excellent	90–100%	Total marks scored
	Good	80–89%	
	Average	70–79%	Total possible marks
	Fair	60–69%	
	Poor	below 60%	Score

agency and/or the client to improve performance and make the relationship more productive. Many agencies have had very long-lasting relationships with their clients (see Exhibit 2-8); however, long-term relationships are becoming less common.

Agency-of-record (AOR) is the term used to describe those situations where a client works with a primary agency for a number of years. It is the very foundation on which the advertising agency business exists—a service provider whose foremost interest is in building the client's brand. In some instances, the AOR will subcontract work to other specialized agencies; however, the AOR will have considerable responsibility given its designation with the client. A recent trend is that some advertisers do not have a specific AOR, but work with different agencies at once, or in succession, depending upon their communication needs. In essence, agencies engage in project-like work for a client by developing a short campaign or performing creative work only. For example, a client can contract the creative work to an agency but rely on its own market research resources. Advertisers believe they are saving money, finding the best ideas for an assignment, and putting pressure on agencies to perform. Critics believe this allows marketing investments to gravitate away from advertising and limit brand development, minimizes consistency across multiple campaigns, or constrains creativity to position the brand effectively.[15]

Exhibit 2-8 Young & Rubicam has been the agency for Dr Pepper for more than three decades.

While the debate continues, many Canadian campaigns such as Coors, Shoppers Drug Mart, Mr. Sub, Budget, Apple, and WestJet are the result of project work. In some cases, the brand had an AOR status but the client decided to use a smaller or different agency for a particular assignment. Advertisers cite the need to remain flexible and the desire to test out new agencies for future relationships. In fact, a considerable amount of the project work went to smaller independent agencies or creative boutiques, which suggests longer-term relationships could be in the future.[16]

There are a number of reasons why clients switch agencies.[17] Some of the more common reasons for agencies to lose clients are as follows:

- *Poor performance or service.* The client becomes dissatisfied with the quality of the advertising and/or the service provided by the agency.
- *Poor communication.* The client and agency personnel fail to develop or maintain the level of communication necessary to sustain a favourable working relationship.
- *Unrealistic demands by the client.* The client places demands on the agency that exceed the amount of compensation received and reduce the account's profitability.
- *Personality conflicts.* People working on the account on the client and agency sides do not have enough rapport to work well together.
- *Personnel changes.* A change in personnel at either the agency or the advertiser can create problems. New managers may wish to use an agency with which they have established ties. Agency personnel often take accounts with them when they switch agencies or start their own.
- *Changes in size of the client or agency.* The client may outgrow the agency or decide it needs a larger agency to handle its business. If the agency gets too large, the client may represent too small a percentage of its business to command attention.
- *Conflicts of interest.* A conflict may develop when an agency merges with another agency or when a client is part of an acquisition or merger.

53

- *Changes in the client's corporate and/or marketing strategy.* A client may change its marketing strategy and think a new agency is needed to carry out the new program.
- *Declining sales.* When sales of the client's product or service are stagnant or declining, advertising may be seen as contributing to the problem. One recent study reports that a decline of market share in the immediate two quarters precedes an agency firing.[18]
- *Conflicting compensation philosophies.* Disagreement may develop over the level or method of compensation. As more companies move toward incentive-based compensation systems, disagreement over compensation is becoming more commonplace.
- *Changes in policies.* Policy changes may result when either party reevaluates the importance of the relationship, the agency acquires a new (and larger) client, or either side undergoes a merger or acquisition.

If the agency recognizes these warning signs, it can try to adapt its programs and policies to make sure the client is satisfied. Some of the situations discussed here are unavoidable, and others are beyond the agency's control. But to maintain the account, problems within the agency's control must be addressed. Losing a major client can have a disastrous effect on a smaller agency, such that it could in fact go under as many of the staff leave for greener pastures. However, in the case of Grip Limited, the loss of Bell—accounting for one-quarter of revenue—allowed the upstart agency established with the help of Labatt to forge on and reinvent itself with a stronger focus toward interactive media and a more diversified client base.[19]

SPECIALIZED SERVICES

Many companies assign the development and implementation of their promotional programs to an advertising agency. But several other types of organizations provide specialized services that complement the efforts of ad agencies. Sales promotion agencies, public relations firms, and direct-response agencies are important to marketers in developing and executing IMC programs. Let us examine the functions these organizations perform.

SALES PROMOTION AGENCIES

Developing and managing sales promotion programs such as contests, sweepstakes, refunds and rebates, premium and incentive offers, and sampling programs is a complex task. Most companies use a **sales promotion agency** to develop and administer these programs. Some large ad agencies have created their own sales promotion department or acquired a sales promotion firm (refer to Figure 2-3). However, most sales promotion agencies are independent companies that specialize in providing the services needed to plan, develop, and execute a variety of sales promotion programs.

Sales promotion agencies often work in conjunction with the client's advertising and/or direct-response agencies to coordinate their efforts with the advertising and direct-marketing programs. Services provided by large sales promotion agencies include promotional planning, creative, research, tie-in coordination, fulfillment, premium design and manufacturing, catalogue production, and contest/sweepstakes management. Many sales promotion agencies are also developing direct/database marketing and telemarketing to expand their integrated marketing services capabilities. Sales promotion agencies are generally compensated on a fee basis.

PUBLIC RELATIONS FIRMS

Many large companies use both an advertising agency and a PR firm. The **public relations firm** develops and implements programs to manage the organization's publicity, image, and affairs with consumers and other relevant publics, including employees, suppliers, shareholders, government, labour groups, citizen action groups, and the general public. The PR firm analyzes the relationships between the client and these various publics, determines how the client's policies and actions relate to and affect these publics, develops PR strategies and programs, implements these programs using various public relations tools, and evaluates their effectiveness.

The activities of a public relations firm include planning the PR strategy and program, generating publicity, conducting lobbying and public affairs efforts, becoming involved in community activities and events, preparing news releases and other communications, conducting research, promoting and managing special events, and managing crises. As companies adopt an IMC approach to promotional planning, they are coordinating their PR activities with advertising and other promotional areas. Many companies are integrating public relations and publicity into the marketing communications mix to increase message credibility and save media costs.[20]

DIRECT-RESPONSE AGENCIES

One of the fastest-growing areas of IMC is direct marketing, where companies communicate with consumers through telemarketing, direct mail, television, the Internet, and other forms of direct-response advertising. As this industry has grown, numerous direct-response agencies have evolved that offer companies their specialized skills in both consumer and business markets. Many of the top direct-marketing agencies are subsidiaries of large agency holding companies (refer to Figure 2-3). However, there are also a number of independent direct-marketing agencies including those that serve large companies as well as smaller firms that handle the needs of local companies (Exhibit 2-9).

Direct-response agencies provide a variety of services, including database management, direct mail, research, media services, and creative and production capabilities. While direct mail is their primary weapon, many direct-response agencies are expanding their services to include such areas as infomercial production and database management. Database development and management is becoming one of the most important services provided by direct-response agencies. Many companies are using database marketing to pinpoint new customers and build relationships and loyalty among existing customers.[21]

A typical direct-response agency is divided into three main departments: account management, creative, and media. Some agencies also have a department whose function is to develop and manage databases for their clients. The account managers work with their clients to plan direct-marketing programs and determine their role in the overall integrated marketing communications process. The creative department consists of copywriters, artists, and producers. Creative is responsible for developing the direct-response message, while the media department is concerned with its placement.

Exhibit 2-9 Protocol promotes its direct-marketing services.

Exhibit 2-10 Agency.com developed online promotions for British Airways.

INTERACTIVE AGENCIES

Many marketers are using **interactive agencies** that specialize in the development and strategic use of various interactive marketing tools such as websites for the Internet, banner ads, text messages, search engines, social media applications, e-mail campaigns, and kiosks. The development of successful interactive marketing programs requires expertise in technology as well as areas such as creative website design, database marketing, digital media, and customer relationship management. Many traditional advertising agencies have established interactive capabilities, ranging from a few specialists within the agency to an entire interactive division (see Figure 2-3).

While many agencies have developed or are developing interactive capabilities, a number of marketers are turning to more specialized interactive agencies to develop websites and interactive media. They feel these companies have more expertise in designing and developing websites as well as managing and supporting them. Interactive agencies range from smaller companies that specialize in website design and creation to full-service interactive agencies that provide all the elements needed for a successful Internet/interactive marketing program. These services include strategic consulting regarding the use of the Internet and online branding, technical knowledge, systems integration, and the development of electronic commerce capabilities. For example, Agency.com developed the website and online promotions that support the global brand positioning strategy for British Airways (Exhibit 2-10).

IMC PLANNING: AGENCY RELATIONSHIPS

Currently, marketers can choose from a variety of organizations to assist them in planning, developing, and implementing an integrated marketing communications program. Companies must decide whether to use specialized organizations for each marketing communications function or consolidate them with a large advertising agency that offers all of these services. In this final section, we discuss whether an advertiser would want to use an integrated services agency, assess the agency–client responsibilities for IMC, and summarize the current situation regarding the agency–client relationship in the context of an IMC environment.

INTEGRATED IMC SERVICES

It has been argued that the concept of integrated marketing is nothing new, particularly in smaller companies and communication agencies that have been coordinating a variety of promotional tools for years. Larger advertising agencies have been trying to gain more of their clients' promotional business for more than 20 years. However, in the past, the various services were run as separate profit centres. Each was motivated to push its own expertise and pursue its own goals rather than develop truly integrated marketing programs. Moreover, the creative specialists in many agencies resisted becoming involved in sales promotion or direct marketing. They preferred to concentrate on developing magazine ads or television commercials rather than designing coupons or direct-mail pieces.

Proponents of the integrated marketing services agency (the one-stop shop) contend that past problems are being solved and the various individuals in the agencies and subsidiaries are learning to work together to deliver a consistent message to the client's customers. They argue that maintaining control of the entire promotional process achieves greater synergy among each of the communications program elements. They also note that it is more convenient for the client to coordinate all of its marketing efforts—media advertising, direct mail, special events, sales promotions, and public relations—through one agency. An agency with integrated marketing capabilities can create a single image for the product or service and address everyone, from wholesalers to consumers, with one voice.

But not everyone wants to turn the entire IMC program over to one agency. Opponents say the providers become involved in political wrangling over budgets, do not communicate with each other as well and as often as they should, and do not achieve synergy. They also claim that agencies' efforts to control all aspects of the promotional program are nothing more than an attempt to hold on to business that might otherwise be lost to independent providers. They note that synergy and economies of scale, while nice in theory, have been difficult to achieve, and competition and conflict among agency subsidiaries has been a major problem.[22] Many companies use a variety of vendors for communication functions, choosing the specialist they believe is best suited for each promotional task, be it advertising, sales promotion, or public relations.

Compounding these concerns is the opinion that advertising agencies are neither sufficiently staffed to ensure complete integration, nor fully cognizant of multiple target audiences. Advertising agency personnel are trained in particular aspects of the process and are less inclined to consider many marketing variables in their decisions. Furthermore, they tend to consider only the end user or consumer rather than all the parties in the marketing process who are connected to the results of the communications plan. It is recommended that marketers ensure the agencies consider the needs of all (e.g., customer service staff, sales representatives, distributors, and retailers) in their communication plans.[23]

AGENCY–CLIENT RESPONSIBILITY

Surveys of advertisers and agency executives have shown that both groups believe integrated marketing is important to their organizations' success and that it will be even more important in the future.[24] However, marketers and agency executives have very different opinions regarding who should be in charge of the integrated marketing communications process. Many advertisers prefer to set strategy for and coordinate their own IMC campaigns, but most agency executives see this as their domain.

While agency executives believe their shops are capable of handling the various elements an integrated campaign requires, many marketers, particularly larger firms, disagree. Marketing executives say the biggest obstacle to implementing IMC is the lack of people with the broad perspective and skills to make it work. Agencies are felt to lack expertise in database marketing, marketing research, and information technology. Internal turf battles, agency egos, and fear of budget reductions are also cited as major barriers to successful integrated marketing campaigns.[25]

Many ad agencies are adding more resources to offer their clients a full line of services. They are expanding their agencies' capabilities in interactive and multimedia advertising, database management, direct marketing, public relations, and sales promotion. However, many marketers still want to set the strategy for their IMC campaigns and seek specialized expertise, more quality and creativity, and greater control and cost efficiency by using multiple providers.

Most marketers do recognize that ad agencies will no longer stick primarily to advertising and will continue to expand their IMC capabilities. There is an opportunity for agencies to broaden their services beyond advertising—but they will have to develop true expertise in a variety of integrated marketing communications areas. They will also have to create organizational structures that make it possible for individuals with expertise in a variety of communications areas to work well together both internally and externally. One thing is certain: as companies continue to shift their promotional dollars away from media advertising to other IMC tools, agencies will continue to explore ways to keep these monies under their roofs.

AGENCY–CLIENT PARTNERSHIP

In a series of interviews, an executive from each of BMO Financial Group, Levi Strauss & Co., Nestlé Canada, and Moosehead Breweries offered his or her opinion on broad questions surrounding agency–client relations. What do marketers (i.e., clients) want from their agency partners? Are agencies meeting these needs? What can marketers do to forge stronger relations with agency partners?[26]

The needs of marketers are broad and varied, including more integrated plans using a range of communication tools, constant messages across many tools, greater understanding of the marketer's brand, overall good quality, more precise measurement of communication effects, insight into market positioning strategies, and, of course, very creative ads.

Agencies appear to be performing very well in some areas, but there is room for improvement. While attempts at integration have increased, individuals may be biased toward one tool versus another. Improved creative planning has emerged; however, concern regarding full accountability currently exists. Agencies offer greater services with larger multinationals, although this has not always been completely beneficial for clients. The creative planning process has become very efficient, but the process has not changed significantly to reflect evolution of IMC. Although measurement of communication effects is recognized as a priority, there remains a need to find innovative ways to know whether communication dollars have been invested properly. Finally, clients prefer to have more strategic thinking along with the outstanding creative ads that agencies continue to deliver.

Marketers believe they can help agencies within the relationship by being better clients through good personnel, clear decision making, sufficient budgets and lead times, and solid market research. In addition, clients should provide clear direction of their needs at the start of the creative process and involve the agency completely. This also includes sharing sensitive and confidential information so the agency understands the client's business, marketing, and market positioning objectives. In the end, the agency and client must be viewed as one team, not two organizations.

Some of these and other findings emerged from a recent survey of agencies and clients conducted in both Canada and the U.S. In partnership, *Marketing Magazine* and *Brandweek* administered more than 10,000 addressed e-mail questionnaires. A highlight of this research is that it tried to obtain a balanced perspective on many advertising industry issues by having an independent research organization—rather than industry associations—design the study and collect the data.[27]

A survey of the marketers reported the following:

- Forty-five percent maintained a primary relationship with an ad agency, while many preferred working on a project basis or with multiple specialty agencies.
- Agencies from all disciplines were used: advertising (79 percent), public relations (59 percent), direct marketing (54 percent), sales promotion (54 percent), events (46 percent), and interactive marketing (46 percent).
- Clients valued creativity, strategic insights, and excellence in execution fairly equally.

- Agencies tended to have poor performance in multidisciplined thinking (31 percent), strategic depth (30 percent), creative breadth (26 percent), and resource availability (26 percent).
- Additional services deemed important were independent ROI audits and training of agency staff with respect to marketing versus advertising only.

A survey of the agencies revealed a few noteworthy facts:

- About half focused on multiple disciplines while the other half specialized in one.
- Agencies tended to have one or two dominant clients and only one-third had 15 or more clients.
- Business of the AOR and the project was split roughly equally.
- Approximately 60 percent of all relationships lasted three years or more.
- Agencies viewed client relationships, client loyalty, and strategic involvement as more important factors compared to profits or performance-based rewards.

In reviewing the two perspectives of the agency–client relationship, some issues for future collaboration appear relevant. Some divergence on the type of partnership between agency and client is emerging. A different view regarding performance-based remuneration is a challenge for agreement. Long-term relationships appear to be more difficult to maintain. The degree to which claimed and actual integration across disciplines occurs is at odds. The ability of agencies to deliver independent marketing ideas and focus on ROI may be a limitation that clients will desire with increased frequency.

CHAPTER OBJECTIVES AND SUMMARY

1 To understand how companies organize for advertising and other aspects of integrated marketing communications.

Companies use two basic systems, centralized and decentralized, to organize internally for advertising and promotion. The marketing communication managers within a centralized system are responsible for planning and budgeting of the IMC plan, administering and executing all communication, coordinating with other departments such as market research, and coordinating with outside agencies for additional expertise and resources. In contrast, the decision-maker for a decentralized system, such as brand manager, has profit and loss responsibility for all aspects of the brand and the scope of activities becomes more extensive, going beyond what the advertising or communication manager is responsible for in a centralized system.

2 To examine methods for selecting, compensating, and evaluating advertising agencies.

Firms have to decide whether they will hire an external advertising agency or use an in-house service to create their ads and purchase media. In-house agencies, while offering the advantages of cost savings, control, and increased coordination,

have the disadvantage of less experience, objectivity, and flexibility.

Many firms use advertising agencies to help develop and execute their programs. These agencies may take on a variety of forms, including full-service agencies, creative boutiques, and media buying services. The first offers the client a full range of services (including creative, account, marketing, and financial and management services); the other two specialize in creative services and media buying, respectively.

Agencies are compensated through commission systems, and fee- and cost-based systems. Recently, the emphasis on agency accountability has increased. Agencies are being evaluated on both financial and qualitative aspects, and some clients are using incentive-based compensation systems that tie agency compensation to performance measures such as sales and market share.

3 To explain the role and functions of specialized marketing communications organizations.

In addition to using ad agencies, marketers use the services of other marketing communication specialists, including direct marketing agencies, sales promotion agencies, public relations

firms, and interactive agencies. Contracting out work to a specialized agency can enhance the creativity of the overall IMC plan with experts from specific fields. Moreover, while it may be more costly or time-consuming working with other specialists, these organizations may reach the target audience more precisely thus yielding a favourable ROI. A marketer must decide whether to use a different specialist for each promotional function or have all of its integrated marketing communications done by an advertising agency that offers all of these services under one roof. This latter idea allows an account team to know and control all aspects of the communication.

4 To examine perspectives on the use of integrated services and responsibilities of advertisers versus agencies.

Recent studies have found that most marketers believe it is their responsibility, not the ad agency's, to set strategy for and coordinate IMC campaigns. The lack of a broad perspective and specialized skills in non-advertising areas is seen as the major barrier to agencies' increased involvement in integrated marketing communications. Some recent surveys suggest that the individual perspectives of clients and agencies will continue to adapt as the growth of IMC evolves.

KEY TERMS

account executive, **46**

advertising manager, **36**

brand manager, **37**

centralized system, **36**

commission system, **47**

copywriters, **42**

cost-plus system, **50**

creative boutique, **46**

decentralized system, **37**

departmental system, **46**

direct-response agencies, **55**

fee-commission combination, **49**

financial audit, **51**

fixed-fee method, **49**

full-service agency, **42**

group system, **46**

incentive-based system, **50**

in-house agency, **38**

interactive agencies, **56**

media buying services, **47**

negotiated commission, **49**

public relations firm, **55**

qualitative audit, **51**

sales promotion agency, **54**

superagencies, **41**

DISCUSSION QUESTIONS

1. What are some of the specific responsibilities and duties of an advertising manager under a centralized advertising department structure? Why is an advertising manager needed if a company uses an outside agency?

2. Discuss the pros and cons of using an in-house advertising agency. What are some of the reasons why companies might change from using an in-house agency and hire an outside agency?

3. Discuss the functions a full-service advertising agency performs for its clients. Might any one of these functions be more important than another?

4. Discuss some of the reasons why traditional advertising agencies have been developing more IMC capabilities. What changes might these agencies have to make to improve their service?

5. Why might a company choose to use a creative boutique rather than a larger full-service agency?

6. Why are marketers likely to use a media buying service to handle their media planning and buying versus the media department of an agency?

7. Discuss the methods by which advertising agencies are compensated. What factors will determine the type of compensation arrangement a company uses with an agency?

8. Why are companies moving away from the traditional commission system and using

incentive-based compensation for their agencies? Why might an agency be reluctant to accept an incentive-based compensation system?

9. Discuss the reasons why marketers often choose to switch advertising agencies. Find an example of a company that has recently changed advertising agencies and analyze the reasons given for the change.

10. Discuss the reasons why a company might want to have all its integrated marketing communication activities performed by a single agency versus having these activities performed by several different agencies that specialize in various areas of IMC, like public relations, direct marketing, sales promotion, and Internet marketing.

CONSUMER BEHAVIOUR AND TARGET AUDIENCE DECISIONS

■ CHAPTER OBJECTIVES

1 To understand the consumer decision-making process and how it relates to marketing communication.

2 To understand internal psychological processes, their influence on consumer decision making, and implications for marketing communication.

3 To identify how the consumer decision-making process varies for different types of purchases and the effects on marketing communication.

4 To understand the similarities and differences of target market and target audience.

5 To understand the options for making a target audience decision for marketing communication.

MARKETING COMMUNICATION INNOVATION AT KRAFT

Kraft, the large consumer packaged goods firm—maker of brands such as Delissio pizza, Cracker Barrel cheese, and Kool-Aid drink crystals—proved to everyone that the giant could be entrepreneurial and innovative with its marketing communication. Although directed by the U.S. head office for some of its marketing, Kraft Canada found opportunities to show consumers a new side of brands such as Shreddies cereal, Maxwell House coffee, Premium Plus and Ritz crackers, Kraft Peanut Butter, and, of course, Kraft Dinner—and was recognized as marketer of the year by *Marketing Magazine*.

Shreddies captured imaginations with a new angle on the historical brand, presenting the legendary square turned 45 degrees so that it became a diamond—and, voila, Kraft launched the "new" Diamond Shreddies cereal. While some loved the concept—Shreddies received the Grand Clio award and a Cassie award—others felt the campaign's humour was too far-fetched and insulted consumers' intelligence. In either case, the objective of getting people to talk about a brand after it had been on the market for so many years worked.

For Maxwell House, Kraft stripped down the production of its TV ads and plainly showed the product, thus saving a couple of hundred thousand dollars per execution. The message mentioned this, and asked where the savings should be donated. Viewers responded with ideas on the Maxwell House website, and money eventually went toward Habitat for Humanity, children's music programs, and guide dog training—certainly good deeds reinforcing the tagline, "Brew Some Good."

Down the cracker aisle, a young boy left a trail of Ritz to woo a young gal, while Premium Plus fell into various bowls of soup as the song "Raise a Little Hell" played. One creative director commented, "What they've been able to do—which is fantastic—is take some of these older brands and contemporize them without alienating their traditional customer base."

A couple of cuddly bears often represented Kraft's peanut butter, and the pair came to life as part of the multimedia "Spread the Feeling" campaign, where the two mascots appeared at Ontario Place and gave out hugs while Kraft donated a jar of peanut butter to the food bank for every hug given. Kraft discovered how much their product meant to consumers in their research and decided to go beyond their traditional TV ads and into the above event, a website (Spreadthefeeling.ca), newspaper, radio, and e-mail.

Kraft Dinner, also known as KD, appeals to many different groups and allowed the brand to move in multiple directions while still retaining the essence of "Gotta Be KD." It targeted children with a unique animated TV ad and targeted moms with key nutritional messages in magazines. For teens, Kraft created a website (Unikd.com) that let teens hang out and talk about the product, post content, and enter contests.

Sources: Matt Semansky, "The Best of '08 Marketers: Kraft Canada," *Marketing Magazine*, November 24, 2008; Matt Semansky, "2008 Marketer of the Year: Quality Kraft-Manship," *Marketing Magazine*, December 8, 2008; Emily Wexler, "Kraft's Domenic Borrelli: Krafting Icons," *Strategy*, April 2009, p. 25.

QUESTIONS:

1. How does such varied creativity help Kraft?
2. Would it be possible for Kraft to have a similar creative message for all of its products?

The brands described in the opening vignette reveal that the development of effective marketing communication programs begins with understanding why consumers behave as they do. This understanding helps marketers know how to encourage new consumers to buy a product (e.g., Shreddies, Maxwell House), what to emphasize in communications to specific audiences (e.g., Ritz and Premium Plus), and which types of IMC tools might be used (e.g., Kraft Peanut Butter, Kraft Dinner). These types of communication problems or opportunities, and others, can be addressed with a thorough understanding of consumer behaviour.

It is beyond the scope of this text to examine consumer behaviour in depth. However, promotional planners need a basic understanding of consumer decision making, factors that influence it, and how this knowledge can be used in developing promotional strategies and programs. This chapter addresses these topics and concludes with a summary of the options a promotional planner has for the initial decision: the target audience for an ad or promotional campaign.

CONSUMER DECISION-MAKING PROCESS

Consumer behaviour is the process and activities people engage in when searching for, selecting, purchasing, using, evaluating, and disposing of products and services so as to satisfy their needs and desires. The conceptual model in Figure 3-1 will be used as a framework for analyzing the consumer decision-making process. We will discuss what occurs at each of the five stages of this process model and how advertising and promotion can be used to influence decision making. The model views the consumer as a problem solver and information processor who engages in mental processes to evaluate alternative brands and determine the degree to which they might satisfy needs or purchase motives, which is a form of cognitive learning.[1] Other perspectives regarding how consumers acquire the knowledge and experience they use in making purchase decisions exist; however, this model is the most widely accepted and managerially useful.

NEED RECOGNITION

The first stage in the consumer decision-making process is **need recognition**, which occurs when the consumer perceives a need and becomes motivated to enter a decision-making process to resolve the felt need. Marketers are required to know the specific needs consumers are attempting to satisfy and how they translate into purchase criteria. This information allows marketers to accurately portray the need in promotional messages or place messages in an appropriate location.

FIGURE 3–1　　A basic model of consumer decision making

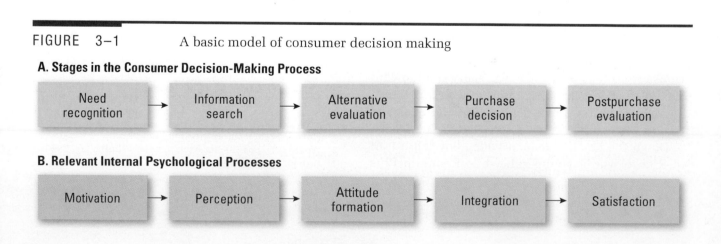

A. Stages in the Consumer Decision-Making Process

Need recognition → Information search → Alternative evaluation → Purchase decision → Postpurchase evaluation

B. Relevant Internal Psychological Processes

Motivation → Perception → Attitude formation → Integration → Satisfaction

Need recognition is caused by a difference between the consumer's *ideal state* and *actual state*. A discrepancy exists between what the consumer wants the situation to be like and what the situation is really like. A goal exists for the consumer, and this goal may be the attainment of a more positive situation from a neutral state. Or, the goal could be a shift from a negative situation, and the consumer wishes to be at a neutral state. The sources of need recognition can be internal or external, may be very simple or very complex, and arise from changes in the consumer's current and/or desired state.

Out of Stock Need recognition occurs when consumers use up their existing supply of a product and must replenish their stock. The purchase decision is usually simple and routine and is often resolved by choosing a familiar brand or one to which the consumer feels loyal.

Dissatisfaction Need recognition is created by the consumer's dissatisfaction with the current state of affairs and/or the product or service being used. For example, a consumer may think her ski boots are no longer comfortable or stylish enough. Advertising may be used to help consumers recognize when they have a need to make a purchase. The Oral B ad shown in Exhibit 3-1 helps users realize that some toothbrushes are superior.

Exhibit 3-1 Oral B identifies reasons why consumers might be dissatisfied with their current toothbrushes in this ad.

New Needs/Wants Changes in consumers' lives often result in new needs and wants. For example, changes in one's financial situation, employment status, or lifestyle may create new needs. Graduates from college or university may need a wardrobe change when starting a new professional career. Not all product purchases are based on needs. Some products or services sought by consumers are not essential but are nonetheless desired. A **want** has been defined as a felt need that is shaped by a person's knowledge, culture, and personality.[2] Many advertised products satisfy consumer wants rather than their basic needs.

Related Products/Purchases Need recognition can also be stimulated by the purchase of a product. For example, the purchase of a new camera may lead to the recognition of a need for accessories, such as additional lenses or a carrying case. The purchase of a personal computer may prompt the need for software programs or upgrades.

Marketer-Induced Need Recognition Some marketers' actions encourage consumers to be less content with their current state or situation. Ads for personal hygiene products may be designed to create insecurities that consumers can resolve through the use of these products. Marketers change fashions and clothing designs and create perceptions among consumers that their wardrobes are out of style. Marketers also take advantage of consumers' tendency toward *novelty-seeking behaviour*, which leads them to try different brands. Consumers often try new products or brands even when they are basically satisfied with their regular brand. Marketers encourage brand switching by using advertising and sales promotion techniques that encourage consumers to reconsider their current consumption habits. The Palm ad in Exhibit 3-2 demonstrates the need for a device that can e-mail, text, browse, and talk.

New Products Need recognition can also occur when innovative products are introduced. For example, the Moen ad shown in Exhibit 3-3 explains the product's improved features. Marketers' attempts to create need recognition among consumers are not always successful. Consumers may not see a need for the product the marketer is selling. A main reason why many consumers were initially reluctant to purchase a personal computer was that they failed to see how it fulfilled their needs. One way PC manufacturers successfully activated need recognition was by stressing how a computer helps children improve their academic skills and do better in school.

CONSUMER MOTIVATION

While need recognition is often a basic, simple process, the way a consumer perceives a purchase situation and becomes motivated to resolve it will influence the remainder of the decision process. For example, one consumer may perceive the need to purchase a new watch from a functional perspective and focus on reliable, low-priced alternatives. Another consumer may see the purchase of a watch as more of a fashion statement and focus on the design and image of various brands. To better understand the reasons underlying consumer purchases, marketers devote considerable attention to examining **motives**—that is, those factors that compel a consumer to take a particular action.

66

Exhibit 3-2 Palm introduces new product to help consumers communicate better.

Exhibit 3-3 Moen highlights the design features of its new faucets.

One of the most popular approaches to understanding consumer motivations is based on the classic theory of human motivation popularized many years ago by psychologist Abraham Maslow.[3] His **hierarchy of needs** theory postulates five basic levels of human needs, arranged in a hierarchy based on their importance. As shown in Figure 3-2, the five needs are (1) *physiological*—the basic level of primary needs for things required to sustain life, such as food, shelter, clothing, and sex; (2) *safety*—the need for security and safety from physical harm; (3) *social/ love and belonging*—the desire to have satisfying relationships with others and feel a sense of love, affection, belonging, and acceptance; (4) *esteem*—the need to feel a sense of accomplishment and gain recognition, status, and respect from others; and (5) *self-actualization*—the need for self-fulfillment and a desire to real-ize one's own potential. For example, Columbia Sportswear Company focuses on the importance of personal protection when marketing its clothing and equipment (Exhibit 3-4).

According to Maslow's theory, the lower-level physiological and safety needs must be satisfied before the higher-order needs become meaningful. Once these basic needs are satisfied, the individual moves on to attempting to satisfy higher-order needs such as self-esteem. In reality, it is unlikely that people move through the needs hierarchy in a stairstep manner. Lower-level needs are an ongoing source of motivation for consumer purchase behaviour. However, since basic physiological needs are met in most developed countries, marketers often sell products that fill basic physiological needs by appealing to consumers' higher-level needs.

While Maslow's needs hierarchy has flaws, it offers a framework for marketers to use in determining what needs their products and services satisfy. Advertising cam-paigns can be designed to show how a brand fulfills these needs for one or multiple segments of consumers. For example, a young single person may be attempting to satisfy social or self-esteem needs in purchasing a car, while a family with children will focus more on safety needs. The Porsche ad in Exhibit 3-5 appears to address self-actualization.

67

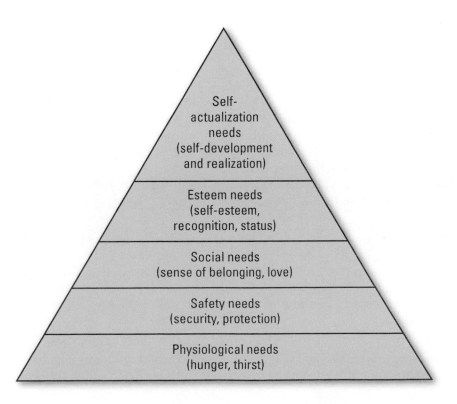

FIGURE   3–2

Maslow's hierarchy of needs

Exhibit 3-4 Columbia shows the importance of the protection features of its outerwear.

Exhibit 3-5 Porsche uses an appeal to self-actualization.

INFORMATION SEARCH

The second stage in the consumer decision-making process is *information search*. Once consumers perceive a need that can be satisfied by the purchase of a product, they begin to search for information needed to make a purchase decision. The initial search effort often consists of an attempt to scan information stored in memory to recall past experiences and/or knowledge regarding various purchase alternatives.[4] This information retrieval is referred to as **internal search**. For many routine, repetitive purchases, previously acquired information that is stored in memory (such as past performance or outcomes from using a brand) is sufficient for comparing alternatives and making a choice.

If the internal search does not yield enough information, the consumer will seek additional information by engaging in **external search**. External sources of information include:

- *Personal sources* (e.g., friends, relatives, or co-workers, face-to-face or via social media),
- *Marketer-controlled sources* (e.g., advertising, salespeople, or displays and Internet),
- *Public sources* (e.g., articles in print media, reports on TV, Internet discussion boards),
- *Personal experience* (e.g., actually handling, examining, or testing the product).

Determining how much and which sources of external information to use involves several factors, including the importance of the purchase decision, the effort needed to acquire information, the amount of relevant past experience, the degree of perceived risk associated with the purchase, and the time available. For example, the selection of a movie to see on a Friday night might entail simply talking to a friend or checking the movie guide in the daily newspaper. A more complex purchase such as a new car might use a number of information sources—perhaps a review of *Road & Track*, *Motor Trend*, or *Consumer Reports*; discussion with family members and friends; and test-driving of cars. At this point in the purchase decision, the information-providing aspects of advertising are extremely important.

The Internet influences consumers' external search patterns significantly for many products. For the travel industry, 60 percent indicated in 2006 that the Internet is very or extremely important for making travel plans, compared to one-third in 2002. TNS Canadian Facts research also noted that website satisfaction reached 36 percent, compared with 27 percent previously. The type of information sought involved significant moves from simple things like researching the weather or the destination to more complex comparisons of travel costs and accommodations.[5] The growth of mobile devices allows consumers to search for any information at any time while shopping; 21 percent of all Canadians use a smartphone. While this is lower than other countries, and Canadians are reluctant to spend more for their devices, clearly some consumers are relying on the mobile tools for product information purposes.[6]

PERCEPTION

Knowledge of how consumers acquire and use information from external sources is important to marketers in formulating communication strategies. Marketers are particularly interested in (1) how consumers sense external information, (2) how they attend to various sources of information, (3) how this information is interpreted and given meaning, and (4) how the information is retained. These four processes are all part of **perception**, the process by which an individual receives, attends to, interprets, and stores information to create a meaningful picture of the world.[7] Perception is an individual process; it depends on internal factors such as a person's beliefs, experiences, needs, moods, and expectations. The perceptual process is also influenced by the characteristics of a stimulus (such as its size, colour, and intensity) and the context in which it is seen or heard. Selectivity occurs throughout the four stages of the consumer's perceptual process. Perception may be viewed as a filtering process in which internal and external factors influence what is received and how it is processed and interpreted. The sheer number and complexity of the marketing stimuli a person is exposed to in any given day requires that this filtering occur. **Selective perception** may occur within all four stages of the perceptual process, as shown in Figure 3-3.

Sensation   **Sensation** is the immediate, direct response of the senses (taste, smell, sight, touch, and hearing) to a stimulus such as an ad, package, brand name, or point-of-purchase display. Perception uses these senses to create a representation of the stimulus. Marketers plan certain marketing stimuli to achieve consumers' physiological reactions. For example, the visual elements of an ad must be designed so that consumers sense their existence. This is one reason why many TV ads start

FIGURE   3–3   The selective perception process

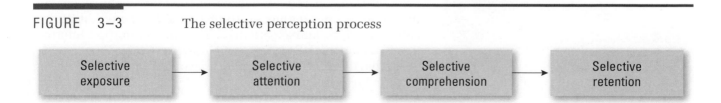

| Selective exposure | → | Selective attention | → | Selective comprehension | → | Selective retention |

with a particular sound effect or visual movement. The ping of an e-mail message from a favourite brand of shoes is also now used for sensation purposes.

Marketers try to increase the level of sensory input so that their advertising messages will get noticed. For example, marketers of colognes and perfumes often use strong visuals as well as scent strips to appeal to multiple senses and attract the attention of magazine readers. **Selective exposure** occurs as consumers choose whether or not to make themselves available to information. For example, a viewer of a television show may change channels or leave the room during commercial breaks. A non-user of perfume might decide to not open the scented strip to sample the aroma. Or, the smartphone user can decide to simply delete an unwanted e-mail message from an unfamiliar brand.

Selecting Information An individual's perceptual processes usually focus on elements of the environment that are relevant to his or her needs and tune out irrelevant stimuli. In a marketing communication context, two people may perceive the same stimuli (e.g., Intenet banner ad, sample offer) in very different ways because they select and attend to messages differently. Determinants of whether marketing communication stimuli will be attended to and how they will be interpreted include internal psychological factors such as the consumer's personality, needs, motives, expectations, and experiences.

Selective attention occurs when the consumer chooses to focus attention on certain stimuli while excluding others. One study of selective attention estimates the typical consumer is exposed to nearly 1,500 ads per day yet perceives only 76 of these messages.[8] Other estimates range as high as 3,000 exposures per day. This means advertisers must make considerable effort to get their messages noticed. Advertisers often use the creative aspects of their ads to gain consumers' attention. For example, some advertisers set their ads off from others by showing their products with vibrant colours (Exhibit 3-6). Marketers also place ads in certain times or locations so that consumers will notice them more easily. For example, a consumer may pay more attention to a commercial that is heard while alone at home than to one heard in the presence of friends, at work, or anywhere distractions may be present. If advertisers can isolate a particular time when the listener is likely to be attentive, they will probably earn his or her undivided attention.

Interpreting the Information Once a consumer selects and attends to a stimulus, the perceptual process focuses on organizing, categorizing, and interpreting the incoming information. This stage of the perceptual process is very individualized and is influenced by internal psychological factors. The interpretation and meaning an individual assigns to an incoming stimulus also depend in part on the nature of the stimulus. For example, many ads are objective, and their message is clear and straightforward. Other ads are more ambiguous, and their meaning is strongly influenced by the consumer's individual interpretation.

Even if the consumer does notice the advertiser's message, there is no guarantee it will be interpreted in the intended manner. Consumers may engage in **selective comprehension**, interpreting information on the basis of their own attitudes, beliefs, motives, and experiences. They often interpret information in a manner that supports their own position. For example, an ad that disparages a consumer's favourite brand may be seen as biased or untruthful, and its claims may not be accepted.

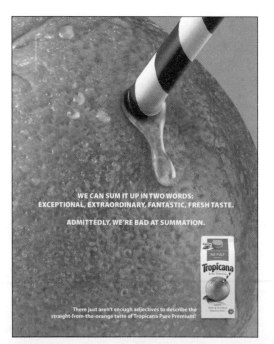

WE CAN SUM IT UP IN TWO WORDS:
EXCEPTIONAL, EXTRAORDINARY, FANTASTIC, FRESH TASTE.

ADMITTEDLY, WE'RE BAD AT SUMMATION.

Tropicana
PURE PREMIUM

There just aren't enough adjectives to describe the straight-from-the-orange taste of Tropicana Pure Premium!

Exhibit 3-6 Tropicana uses colour to focus attention on orange juice.

Retaining the Information   The final stage of the perceptual process involves the storage of the information in short-term or long-term memory. Consumers may make mental notes or focus on some aspect of an advertising message to ensure that they will not forget, thus permitting easy retrieval during the information search stage. **Selective retention** means consumers do not remember all the information they see, hear, or read even after attending to and comprehending it. Advertisers attempt to make sure information will be retained in the consumer's memory so that it will be available when it is time to make a purchase. **Mnemonics** such as symbols, rhymes, associations, and images that assist in the learning and memory process are helpful. Many advertisers use telephone numbers that spell out the company name and are easy to remember. Energizer put pictures of its pink bunny on packages to remind consumers at the point of purchase of its creative advertising.

Subliminal Perception   Advertisers know consumers use selective perception to filter out irrelevant or unwanted advertising messages, so they employ various creative tactics to get their messages noticed. One controversial tactic advertisers have been accused of using is appealing to consumers' subconscious. **Subliminal perception** refers to the ability to perceive a stimulus that is below the level of consciousness. Psychologists generally agree it is possible to perceive something without any knowledge of having seen it. The possibility of using hidden persuaders such as subliminal audio messages or visual cues to influence consumers might be intriguing to advertisers but would not be welcomed by consumers. The idea of marketers influencing consumers at a subconscious level has strong ethical implications. The use of subliminal techniques is *not* a creative tactic we would recommend to advertisers.

ALTERNATIVE EVALUATION

After acquiring information during the information search stage of the decision-making process, the consumer moves to alternative evaluation. In this stage, the consumer compares the various brands he or she has identified as being capable of solving the consumption problem and satisfying the needs or motives that initiated the decision process. The brands identified as purchase options to be considered during this stage are referred to as the consumer's *evoked set*.

The evoked set is generally only a subset of all the brands of which the consumer is aware. The consumer reduces the number of brands to be reviewed during the alternative evaluation stage to a manageable level. The exact size of the evoked set varies from one consumer to another and depends on such factors as the importance of the purchase and the amount of time and energy the consumer wants to spend comparing alternatives.

The goal of most advertising and promotional strategies is to increase the likelihood that a brand will be included in the consumer's evoked set and considered during alternative evaluation. Marketers use advertising to create *top-of-mind awareness* among consumers so that their brands are part of the evoked set of their target audiences. Popular brands with large advertising budgets use *reminder advertising* to maintain high awareness levels and increase the likelihood they will be considered by consumers in the market for the product. Marketers of new brands or those with a low market share need to gain awareness among consumers and break into their evoked sets.

Once consumers have identified an evoked set and have a list of alternatives, they must evaluate the various brands. This involves comparing the choice alternatives on specific criteria important to the consumer. **Evaluative criteria** are the attributes of a product that are used to compare different alternatives. Evaluative criteria can be objective or subjective. For example, in buying an automobile, consumers use

71

objective attributes such as price, warranty, and fuel economy as well as subjective attributes such as image or styling.

Many marketers view their products as *bundles of attributes*, but consumers also tend to think about products or services in terms of their *consequences* or bundles of benefits. J. Paul Peter and Jerry Olson define consequences as specific events or outcomes that consumers experience when they purchase and/or consume a product.[9] **Functional benefits** are concrete outcomes of product usage that are tangible and directly related to product performance. The taste of a soft drink or a potato chip, the acceleration of a car, and the clarity of a fax transmission are examples of functional consequences. Experiential benefits are related to how a product makes the consumer feel while consuming the product. These emotions can be feelings of happiness or joy, for example, as seen by some car ads illustrating consumers enjoying the drive in a particular brand. Psychological benefits can refer to the status a consumer encounters when associated with a brand.

Marketers should distinguish between product attributes and benefits, because the importance and meaning consumers assign to an attribute are usually determined by its consequences for them. Moreover, advertisers must be sure consumers understand the link between a particular attribute and a benefit. For example, the Cashmere ad in Exhibit 3-7 focuses on the extraordinary softness of its tissue. Product attributes and the benefits consumers think they will experience from a particular brand are very important, for they are often the basis on which consumers form attitudes and decide among various choice alternatives.

ATTITUDES

Attitudes represent one of the most heavily studied concepts in consumer behaviour. According to Gordon Allport's classic definition, "attitudes are learned predispositions to respond to an object."[10] More recent perspectives view attitudes as a summary construct that represents an individual's overall feelings toward or evaluation of an object.[11] Consumers hold attitudes toward a variety of objects that are important to marketers, including individuals (endorsers like Sidney Crosby), brands (Cheerios), companies (Microsoft), product categories (beef, pork, tuna), retail stores (The Bay, Sears), or even advertisements.

Attitudes are important to marketers because they theoretically summarize a consumer's evaluation of an object (or brand or company) and represent positive or negative feelings and behavioural tendencies. Marketers' keen interest in attitudes is based on the assumption that they are related to consumers' purchase behaviour. Considerable evidence supports the basic assumption of a relationship between attitudes and behaviour.[12] The attitude–behaviour link does not always hold; many other factors can affect behaviour.[13] But attitudes are very important to marketers. Advertising and promotion are used to create favourable attitudes toward new products/services or brands, reinforce existing favourable attitudes, and/or change negative attitudes. IMC Perspective 3-1 illustrates how advertising influences attitudes.

72

Exhibit 3-7 Cashmere's campaign conveys the softness of its product.

Advertising Meaningful Brands

How brands become and stay relevant for consumers in their purchasing and postpurchase experiences is foremost on the minds of promotion decision makers because consumers' experiences with marketing communication tend to play a role in their resulting brand impressions. Here, we profile four consumers and four brands—Converse, American Eagle, West49, and Joshua Perets—to illustrate this significant connection.

Converse, the all-time favourite basketball shoe from decades past, continues to reinvent itself to appeal to new groups of youth. A recent campaign promoted the shoes and a fashion tie-in with clothes designer John Varvatos. Ads in music and fashion magazines featuring new and old musical artists communicated the image along with ongoing in-store displays and signage. Our consumer Mohammed discovered the brand while seeing people wear the original "Chucks" on TV shows and movies and in TV ads and out-of-home (e.g., malls and outdoors). He believes that the brand is original and it makes him feel unique and stylish; the star logo suggests to him fame and popularity.

American Eagle, a casual clothing store for 15- to 25-year-old guys and gals, is a favourite for Feroz, who sees the brand as having a cool image. He believes those wearing the brand "exude a fresh aura," and that it is a brand for those who want to look cool and respectable. Furthermore, the brand's logo looks strong, confident, and mean! Interestingly, the ads make Feroz feel jealous because the models are very good looking and are well dressed. In general, he likes preppy brands since they make him look and feel good.

West49, a skate, board, and surf clothing retailer, sells popular styles like Billabong, Burton, DC, Hurley,

Quiksilver, and the West49 brand to 10- to 18-year-olds. Mass media ads include spots on MTV and MuchMusic along with radio and outdoor ads. Jordan discovered the brand while shopping at a mall with friends; he liked the West49 store the best because the clothes looked so nice. The brand appeals to him because his friends can't make fun of him wearing the clothes when they wear the same brand. The logo suggests that he step 49 feet west and there will be a nice store to buy clothes. He sees the brand when out of home and visits the website to see new arrivals.

Joshua Perets offers trendy streetwear to females aged 8 to 18 and reaches them with radio and transit ads and website promotions such as tickets to a Jonas Brothers 3D concert movie. For Kanol, the brand is for young females who want to stand out; she likes the brand because "it's flashy and has lots of bright colours." The logo means puppy love to her and she sees the brand everywhere since all the girls at school have something from it. The brand appeals to Kanol since it fits with her "street chic" image, which includes brands such as Baby Phat and Joshua Perets.

Sources: Carey Toane, "Converse: How It Maintains Timeless Cool," *Strategy*, April 2009, p. 54; Carey Toane, "American Eagle: What the Label Says About the Folks That Wear It," *Strategy*, April 2009, p. 49; Carey Toane, "West49: The Tween POV on Canada's Favourite Boarder Brand," *Strategy*, April 2009, p. 56; Carey Toane, "Joshua Perets: Why Quebec Teens Love Their JP," *Strategy*, April 2009, p. 52.

Question:

1. How does advertising influence these consumers to like their brands?

PURCHASE DECISION

At some point in the buying process, the consumer must stop searching for and evaluating information about alternative brands in the evoked set and make a *purchase decision*. As an outcome of the alternative evaluation stage, the consumer may develop a **purchase intention** or predisposition to buy a certain brand. Purchase intentions are generally based on a matching of purchase motives with attributes or characteristics of brands under consideration. Their formation involves many of the personal subprocesses discussed in this chapter, including motivation, perception, and attitude formation.

A purchase decision is not the same as an actual purchase. Once a consumer chooses which brand to buy, he or she must still implement the decision and make the actual purchase. Additional decisions may be needed, such as when to buy, where to buy, and how much money to spend. Often, there is a time delay between the formation of a purchase intention or decision and the actual purchase, particularly for highly involved and complex purchases such as automobiles, personal computers, and consumer durables.

For nondurable products, which include many low-involvement items such as consumer packaged goods, the time between the decision and the actual purchase may be short as it occurs while in the store or while planning at home. Before leaving home, the consumer may make a shopping list that includes specific brand names because the consumer has developed **brand loyalty**—a preference for a particular brand that results in its repeated purchase. Marketers strive to develop and maintain brand loyalty among consumers. They use reminder advertising to keep their brand names in front of consumers, maintain prominent shelf positions and displays in stores, and run periodic promotions to deter consumers from switching brands. Maintaining consumers' brand loyalty is not easy. Competitors use many techniques to encourage consumers to try their brands, among them new product introductions and free samples. Marketers must continually battle to maintain their loyal consumers while replacing those who switch brands.

INTEGRATION PROCESSES

A key part of the purchase decision stage is the way consumers combine information about the characteristics of brands. **Integration processes** are the way product knowledge, meanings, and beliefs are combined to evaluate two or more alternatives.[14] Analysis of the integration process focuses on the different types of *decision rules* or strategies consumers use to decide among purchase alternatives.

Consumers often make purchase selections by using formal integration strategies or decision rules that require examination and comparison of alternatives on specific attributes. This process involves a very deliberate evaluation of the alternatives, attribute by attribute. When consumers apply such formal decision rules, marketers need to know which attributes are being considered so as to provide the information the consumers require.

Sometimes consumers make their purchase decisions using more simplified decision rules known as **heuristics**. Heuristics are easy to use and are highly adaptive to specific environmental situations (such as a retail store).[15] For familiar products that are purchased frequently, consumers may use price-based heuristics (buy the least expensive brand) or promotion-based heuristics (choose the brand for a price reduction through a coupon, rebate, or special deal).

One type of heuristic is the **affect referral decision rule**,[16] in which consumers make a selection on the basis of an overall impression or summary evaluation of the various alternatives under consideration. This decision rule suggests that consumers have affective impressions of brands stored in memory that can be accessed at the time of purchase. Marketers selling familiar and popular brands may appeal to an affect referral rule by stressing overall affective feelings or impressions about their products. Market leaders, whose products enjoy strong overall brand images, often use ads that promote the brand as the best overall (Exhibit 3-8).

POSTPURCHASE EVALUATION

The consumer decision process does not end with the purchase. After consumption, the consumer assesses the level of performance of the product or service. The postpurchase evaluation process is important because the feedback acquired from actual use of a product will influence the likelihood of future purchases. Positive performance means the brand is retained in the evoked set and increases the likelihood it will be purchased again. Unfavourable outcomes may lead the consumer to form negative attitudes toward the brand, lessening the likelihood it will be purchased again or even eliminating it from the consumer's evoked set.

Consumers engage in a number of activities during the postpurchase evaluation process. They may seek out reassurance and opinions from others to confirm the wisdom of their purchase decision, lower their attitudes or opinions of the unchosen alternative, deny or distort any information that does not support the choice they made, or look for information that does support their choice. An important source of supportive information is advertising; consumers tend to be more attentive to advertising for the brand they have chosen.[17] Thus, it may be important for companies to advertise to reinforce consumer decisions to purchase their brands.

SATISFACTION

The most significant psychological concept during the postpurchase evaluation process is satisfaction. A leading expert in satisfaction research has recently defined **satisfaction** as a judgment that consumers make with respect to the pleasurable level of consumption-related fulfillment.[18] The notion of fulfillment implies that a consumer's goal has been achieved (i.e., needs met), and that the fulfillment is "judged with reference to a standard." Thus, consumers make a comparison between the consumption outcome and some other referent.

Consumers can make many comparisons. One is to compare the level of product performance to the expectations of the product that consumers had prior to purchase. Satisfaction can occur when the consumer's expectations are either met or exceeded, whereas dissatisfaction results when performance is below expectations. Consumers can also compare the product performance to some absolute standard of quality to perceive satisfaction or dissatisfaction.

Exhibit 3-8 Market leaders such as Labatt can appeal to consumer affect.

Another aspect of satisfaction is **cognitive dissonance**, a feeling of psychological tension or postpurchase doubt that a consumer experiences after making a difficult purchase choice. Dissonance is more likely to occur in important decisions where the consumer must choose among close alternatives (especially if the unchosen alternative has unique or desirable features that the selected alternative does not have).

Marketers must recognize the importance of the postpurchase evaluation stage. Dissatisfied consumers not only are unlikely to repurchase the marketer's product but also may spread negative word-of-mouth information that deters others from purchasing the product or service. The best guarantee of favourable postpurchase evaluations is to provide consumers with a quality product or service that always meets their expectations. Marketers must be sure their advertising and other forms of promotion do not create unreasonable expectations their products cannot meet.

Marketers have come to realize that postpurchase communication is also important. Some companies send follow-up letters and brochures to reassure buyers and reinforce the wisdom of their decision. Many companies have set up toll-free numbers for consumers to call if they need information or have a question or complaint regarding a product. Marketers also offer liberal return and refund policies and extended warranties and guarantees to ensure customer satisfaction. Some have used customers' postpurchase dissatisfaction as an opportunity for gaining new business.

75

VARIATIONS IN CONSUMER DECISION MAKING

We have reviewed the consumer decision-making process with respect to individual purchases. However, variations in this process arise depending upon the type of purchase and whether the individual is making the decision with other people. We now discuss these two variations in the consumer decision-making process.

TYPES OF DECISION MAKING

The general model of consumer decision making is a useful description; however, consumers do not always engage in all five steps of the purchase decision process or proceed in the sequence presented. They may minimize or even skip one or more stages if they have previous experience in purchasing the product or service or if the decision is of low personal, social, or economic significance. To develop effective promotional decisions, marketers need to understand the type of problem-solving processes their target consumers use to make purchase decisions.[19]

Many purchase decisions consumers make are based on a habit known as **routine problem solving** or routine response behaviour. For many low-priced, frequently purchased products, the decision process consists of little more than recognizing the need, engaging in a quick internal search, and making the purchase. The consumer spends little or no effort engaging in external search or alternative evaluation.

Marketers of products characterized by a routine response purchase process need to get and/or keep their brands in the consumer's evoked set and avoid anything that may result in their removal from consideration. Established brands that have strong market share position are likely to be in the evoked set of most consumers. Marketers of these brands want consumers to follow a routine choice process and continue to purchase their products and use relevant IMC tools to maintain high levels of brand awareness. Alternatively, marketers of new brands or those with a low market share face a different challenge. They must find ways to disrupt consumers' routine choice processes and get them to consider their brand by using IMC tools that encourage consumers to reconsider their habit or routine choice and switch brands. The Sun-Rype ad in Exhibit 3-9 tries this approach.

A more complicated decision-making process occurs when consumers have limited experience in purchasing a particular product or service and little or no knowledge of the brands available and/or the criteria to use in making a purchase decision. Consumers learn what attributes or criteria should be used in making a purchase decision and how the various alternatives perform on these dimensions. For products or services characterized by **limited problem solving** or **extended problem solving** marketers should make information available that will help consumers make a decision. Advertising that provides consumers with detailed information about a brand and how it can satisfy their purchase motives and goals is important. Marketers may also want to give consumers information through other ways (e.g., displays, brochures, salespeople).

It's like nectar of the gods. Assuming you worship raspberries.

Exhibit 3-9 The visual in Sun-Rype's ad invites consumers to reconsider their beverage choice.

76

GROUP DECISION MAKING

A group has been defined as "two or more individuals who share a set of norms, values, or beliefs and have certain implicitly or explicitly defined relationships to one another such that their behavior is interdependent."[20] Groups are one of the primary factors influencing learning and socialization, and group situations constitute many of our purchase decisions. For example, a woman's purchase of a dress for a party might be influenced by the type of party and who is attending.

A **reference group** is "a group whose presumed perspectives or values are being used by an individual as the basis for his or her judgments, opinions, and actions." Consumers use reference groups as a guide to specific behaviours, even when the groups are not present.[21] In the party example, peers—although not present—provided a standard of dress that referred the woman to her clothing selection. Likewise, friends, family, and co-workers, or even a group to which she aspires, may serve as referents, and consumption patterns will typically conform to the expectations of the groups that are most important to her.

Marketers use reference group influences in developing advertisements and promotional strategies. The images in Exhibit 3-10 is an example of an *aspirational* reference group (to which we might like to belong). In some cases marketers use *disassociative* groups (to which we do not wish to belong), such as in ads related to drinking and driving.

In some instances, the group may be involved more directly than just as a referent. Family members may serve as referents to each other, or they may actually be involved in the purchase decision process—acting as an individual buying unit. As shown in Figure 3-4, family members may assume a variety of roles in the decision-making process.[22] As the example indicates, there can be group interaction at every stage of the consumer decision-making process since various members take on a role. The ad in Exhibit 3-11 highlights different roles.

Exhibit 3-10   A reference group is shown in the images of this website message.

Exhibit 3-11   Ads for Kinder Surprise target the purchaser.

FIGURE 3–4

Roles in the family decision-making process

The initiator. The person responsible for initiating the purchase decision process; for example, the mother who determines she needs a new car.

The information provider. The individual responsible for gathering information to be used in making the decision; for example, the teenage car buff who knows where to find product information in specific magazines or collects it from dealers.

The influencer. The person who exerts influence as to what criteria will be used in the selection process. All members of the family may be involved. The mother may have her criteria, whereas others may each have their own input.

The decision maker(s). That person(s) who actually makes the decision. In our example, it may be the mother alone or in combination with another family member.

The purchasing agent. That individual who performs the physical act of making the purchase. In the case of a car, a husband and wife may decide to choose it together and sign the purchase agreement.

The consumer. The actual user of the product. In the case of a family car, all family members are consumers. For a private car, only the mother might be the consumer.

Each role has implications for marketers. First, the advertiser must determine who is responsible for the various roles in the decision-making process so that messages can be targeted at that person (or those people). These roles will also dictate media strategies, since the appropriate magazines, newspapers, or TV or radio stations must be used. Second, understanding the decision-making process and the use of information by individual family members is critical to the design of messages and choice of promotional program elements. In general, to create an effective promotional program, a marketer must have an overall understanding of how the decision process works and the role that each group member plays.

78

TARGET AUDIENCE DECISION

We reviewed the consumer decision-making process since marketers need to thoroughly understand the behaviour they are trying to influence through their promotional plans. Marketers also try to understand consumers as much as possible since an IMC plan, IMC program (e.g., advertising campaign), or ad is directed to a particular target audience or multiple target audiences, which is usually a primary decision made prior to any other communication decision. The direction of the target audience decision is derived from the segmentation and target market decisions of the marketing plan. In this section, we review the marketing process to understand the context of promotional planning. Next, we summarize approaches for market segmentation and identify how it is used for target market selection. Finally, we explore how these marketing decisions provide direction for identifying options for the target audience decision.

MARKETING PLANNING PROCESS

The process of developing and implementing marketing and promotion decisions is summarized in Figure 3-5. The target market is the focus of the firm's marketing effort, and specific sales, market share, and profitability objectives are set according to where the company wants to be and what it hopes to accomplish in this market. The method by which marketers do this involves three basic steps: segment the market, select a target market, and determine the market positioning strategy of one's product or service. The selection of the target market (or markets) in which the firm will compete is an important part of its marketing strategy and has direct implications for its advertising and promotional efforts. Specific communication

FIGURE   3–5   Marketing and promotions process model

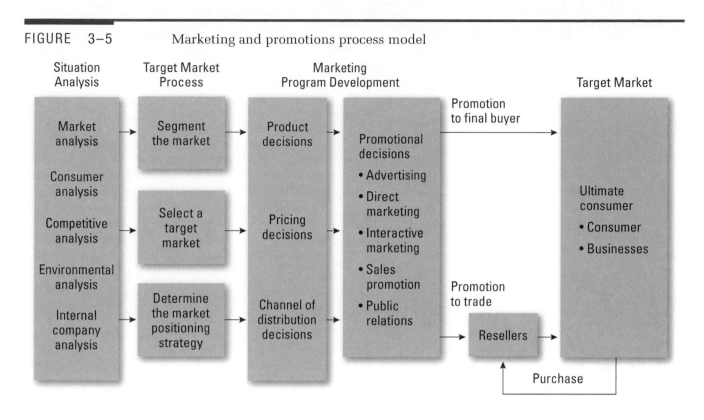

objectives are derived and the promotional mix strategies are developed to achieve these objectives. Thus, different objectives may be established, different budgets may be used, and the promotional mix strategies may vary, depending on the market selected.

As we introduced this section, we used the terms target market and target audience. We concur with a recent perspective that suggests promotional planners should make a careful distinction between these concepts since an advertising plan or IMC plan is one part of the overall marketing plan.[23] The **target market** is the group of consumers toward which an overall marketing program is directed. The **target audience** is a group of consumers toward which the advertising campaign, for example, is directed. Conceptually, these targets are interdependent but their distinction allows promotional planners the ability to make more effective communication decisions with enhanced precision.

The difference between target audience and target market can be seen when firms develop selective promotional programs beyond their normal target market. For example, tea represents the fourth most consumed drink after coffee, milk, and tap water. With many types of tea and different kinds of tea drinkers, tea brands need to approach specific audiences with their communication efforts. The health benefits perceived with tea have recently attracted many young Canadian consumers toward specialty teas. In particular, sales for green, red, and white teas rose substantially in 2006; however, herbal and black tea dropped slightly. Although the main tea consumer is women over 40, according to Twinings tea, the well-established brand developed its latest campaign toward newer consumers (i.e., younger) with a strong emphasis to teach the less experienced more about tea and the various types. Its communication consisted of door-hangers and samples to specific locations and displays for select retailers.[24]

The difference between target audience and target market can also be seen when firms develop promotional programs that fit with an established target market that has a new cohort of consumers every couple of years. This occurs with products like Pogo (a wiener covered with a bread substance on a stick), which has a clear demographic target market of teenage boys. Yet these boys grow older, so every

Targeting with Advertising

Ongoing IMC programs, advertising campaigns, specific IMC tools, and individual messages all have at least one thing in common: there is a specific target for whom the marketing communication is directed, as seen in the following snippets from Bud Light Lime, Heinz, Pepsi, Burger King, and Halo.

Labatt introduced Bud Light Lime in Canada after fans of five different "Bring It to Canada" Facebook groups requested the new flavour due to its popularity south of the border. The launch here featured a half-human-half-lime character named Limey, a "lime invasion" YouTube video message, street events of people dancing, and a branded Facebook page. Loyal customers (presumably, those who had visited the U.S. and tried the beer) asking for the product was a great way to start the new brand—and, curiously, follow-up research indicated that it attracted women who previously enjoyed white wine!

To mark its 100th anniversary, Heinz replayed its most memorable ads to rekindle the emotions its loyal customers feel toward its ketchup brand. In fact, customers ask Heinz for copies of the ads and encourage the company to keep replaying popular ones that are 20 and 30 years old. As part of the nostalgia trip, Heinz ran a contest where entrants explained why they are the biggest ketchup fan of all time and included media in a PR baking event.

Marketing communication focusing on the logo redesign for Pepsi aimed to "reacquaint Canadians with the brand" (i.e., to recapture lost customers). With an emphasis on positive emotions surrounding the brand, the English Canadian campaign directed messages with a "Joy It Forward" initiative. In Quebec, the emotional trigger worked with the cultural history of the province and how the brand is a part of it.

Burger King, perennially in battle with other fast-food restaurants, advertised and promoted its sandwiches under the King Deal banner, which offers a discounted combo every day of the week. Its bold attempt to switch consumers for their daily or weekly fix resulted in double sales growth compared to its arch rivals.

The popular Xbox 360 game Halo took a new tack to attract new users to the latest edition. In addition to encouraging Xbox 360 Halo users to buy another version, Microsoft spent considerable effort to influence PC-based gamers that Halo is an excellent game for their preferred platform. Internet advertising on gaming sites attracted 59,000 users to the Xbox site, representing a click-through ratio of 1.3 percent. The campaign also included video clips of the game, a contest, a sample re-skin unit for gamers to appreciate, and information found in blogs and forums. According to the agency, "Our strategy was to create mass awareness and excitement by leveraging the Halo reputation and also outlining Halo Wars' differentiating factor as the first-ever strategy game created exclusively for the Xbox 30 console."

Sources: Kristin Laird, "Bud Light Limes Up for Canada," *Marketing Magazine*, May 22, 2009; Melita Kuburas, "M2 Universal's Ryan Mensezes: Going After Gamers," *Strategy*, June 2009, p. 23; Kristin Laird, "Heinz Relives the Past for 100th Anniversary," *Marketing Magazine*, May 19, 2009; Jonathan Paul, "Pepsi Joys It Forward," *Strategy*, July 2009, p. 15; Jonathan Paul, "Burger King's Angry, and Amping Up Value," *Strategy*, September 2009, p. 8.

Question:

1. Identify the segmentation variable used in the above examples to identify the target audience.

few years there is a whole new group of teenage boys that Pogo directs marketing communication toward, and is therefore a new target audience (i.e., unaware, or unfamiliar with the brand experience). Its most recent venture included Pogothons, street events, short flash TV ads of eight seconds, stickers delivered in skateboard parks, and so on, all with the intention to encourage website visits so that the new users—a new audience—could relate to the brand.[25] IMC Perspective 3-2 shows the target audience of the advertising for some popular brands.

MARKET SEGMENTATION

To identify a target market, the marketer identifies the specific needs of groups of people (or segments), selects one or more of these segments as a target, and develops marketing programs directed to each. This approach has found increased applicability in marketing for a number of reasons, including changes in the market (consumers are more diverse in their needs, attitudes, and lifestyles); increased use of segmentation by competitors; and the fact that more managers are trained in segmentation and realize the advantages associated with this strategy. The remainder of this section discusses different ways to segment the market (Figure 3-6). Marketers may use one of the segmentation variables or a combination of approaches for both marketing and marketing communication decisions. The Gap serves consumers looking for a store with a certain image, yet the ad in Exhibit 3-12 appeals to couples for online shopping.

FIGURE 3–6 Examples of market segmentation variables

Main Dimension	Segmentation Variables	Typical Breakdowns
Geographic	Region	West, Central, East
	City size	Under 10,000; 10,000–24,999; 25,000–49,999; 50,000–99,999; 100,000–249,999; 250,000–499,999; 500,000–999,999; 1,000,000 or more
	Metropolitan area	Census Metropolitan Area (CMA); etc.
	Density	Urban; suburban; small town; rural
Demographic	Gender	Male; female
	Age	Under 6 yrs; 6–11 yrs; 12–17 yrs; 18–24 yrs; 25–34yrs; 35–44yrs; 45–54 yrs; 55–64 yrs; 65–74 yrs; 75 yrs plus
	Race	Asian; Black; Hispanic; Indian; White/Caucasian; etc.
	Life stage	Infant; preschool; child; youth; collegiate; adult; senior
	Birth era	Baby boomer (1949–1964); Generation X (1965–1976); baby boomlet/Generation Y (1977–present)
	Household size	1; 2; 3–4; 5 or more
	Residence tenure	Own home; rent home
	Marital status	Never married; married; separated; divorced; widowed
Socioeconomic	Income	<$15,000; $15,000–$24,999; $25,000– $34,999; $35,000–$49,999; $50,000–$74,999; $75,000+
	Education	Some high school or less; high school graduate; some college or university; university/college graduate; etc.
	Occupation	Managerial and professional specialty; technical, sales, and administrative support; service; farming, forestry, and fishing; etc.
Psychographic	Values	Actualizers; fulfilleds; achievers; experiencers; believers; strivers; makers; strugglers
	Lifestyle	Activities, interests, opinions
	Personality	Gregarious; compulsive; introverted; aggressive; ambitious; etc.
	Culture	Ethnic; social
	Social class	Low middle class; upper middle class; etc
Behaviour	Brand Loyalty	Completely loyal; partially loyal; not loyal
	User status	Nonuser; ex-user; first-time user; regular user
	Usage rate	Light user; medium user; heavy user
	Situation	Usage situation; purchase situation
	Benefits sought	Quality; service; price/value; convenience; prestige

81

Exhibit 3-12 Gap appeals to couples and builds its brand image with this ad.

Geographic Segmentation In the **geographic segmentation** approach, markets are divided into different geographic units. These units may include nations, provinces, states, counties, or even neighbourhoods. Consumers often have different buying habits depending on where they reside. To address this, advertisers might use different IMC tools or advertising messages.

Demographic Segmentation Dividing the market on the basis of demographic variables such as gender, age, marital status, household size, and socioeconomic variables like income, education, and occupation is called **demographic segmentation**. For example, the Alberta Securities Commission targeted young adults aged 24–35 who had very little knowledge of investing and had a perceived need for financial advice as indicated by market research. Print and radio ads directed interested consumers to an education link on the Commission's website. A second phase of the advertising message featured links on Web portals that also highlighted a contest.[26] While a demographic is a common method of segmenting markets, it is important to recognize that other factors may be the underlying basis for homogeneity and/or consumer behaviour. The astute marketer will identify additional approaches for segmenting and will recognize the limitations of demographics.

Psychographic Segmentation Dividing the market on the basis of values and lifestyle, personality, culture, and social class is referred to as **psychographic segmentation**. Each of these variables can be the basis for segmentation.

Values and Lifestyle The determination of lifestyles is usually based on an analysis of the activities, interests, and opinions (AIOs) of consumers that are obtained via surveys. These lifestyles are then correlated with the consumers' product, brand, and/or media usage. For many products and/or services, lifestyles may be the best discriminator between use and nonuse, accounting for differences in food, clothing, and car selections, among numerous other consumer behaviours.[27] Notice how the ad for Maybelline in Exhibit 3-13 reflects the life of the target audience member. Taken from another perspective, our activities, interests, and opinions are reflective of our individual values. We highlight two major approaches that have developed these forms of segmentation with proprietary research methods.

Psychographic segmentation occurred with the advent of the values and lifestyles (VALS) program now offered by Strategic Business Insights. Developed in the late 1970s and refined a decade later, VALS is a method for applying segmentation based on values. The underlying premise of VALS is that psychological

Exhibit 3-13 The target audience's lifestyle is reflected in this Maybelline ad.

traits and demographics are better predictors of behaviour than demographics alone. The VALS approach combines an estimate of the resources the consumer can draw on (education, income, health, energy level, self-confidence, and degree of consumerism) along with their motivation to identify eight different types of people to understand their consumption behaviour. This U.S. invention is now adapted to other cultures such as Japan, the U.K., and Latin America.

PRIZM$_{NE}$, developed by Claritas, is another American lifestyle segmentation approach that has been adapted for the Canadian market through the two divisions of the research firm Environics (Research Group & Analytics). PRIZM C2 associates the lifestyle questions asked on the survey with demographic data from the federal government's Census. The analysis provides 66 different lifestyle segments and 18 social groups based on whether the respondent is a pre-boomer, boomer, or post-boomer. PRIZM C2 claims that the segmentation system is useful for communication decisions like target audience profiling and media planning, and many other marketing strategy decisions for virtually all industries. The data from the different lifestyle segments can also be aligned with other data sources such as media consumption and geography to allow more precise targeting for various marketing decisions.

Personality Borrowing from psychological theory, we are interested in consumers' personality traits—the relatively enduring characteristics of one's personality that lead people to respond in a reasonably consistent manner. Characteristics like social orientation (introvert versus extrovert), innovativeness (degree a person likes to try new things), materialism (emphasis placed on product ownership), and self-consciousness (projection of personal image to others) are examples of personality traits used to describe a group of consumers more precisely.[28]

Culture The broadest and most abstract of the external factors that influence consumer behaviour is **culture**, or the complexity of learned meanings, values, norms, and customs shared by members of a society. Cultural norms and values offer direction and guidance to members of a society in all aspects of their lives, including their consumption behaviour. Marketers must also be aware of changes that may be occurring in a particular culture since it could be the basis for effective segmentation.

While marketers recognize that culture exerts a demonstrable influence on consumers, they often find it difficult to respond to cultural differences in different markets. The subtleties of various cultures are often difficult to understand and appreciate, but marketers must understand the cultural context in which consumer purchase decisions are made and adapt their advertising and promotional programs accordingly. For example, Bell Mobility rang in the Chinese New Year early in 2004 with an advertising and promotion campaign directed to Asian customers in Western Canada, the first of many specific communication efforts to appeal to a large group of potential customers. To resonate with the people of this culture more significantly, Bell Mobility introduced new creative messages to celebrate the Year of the Monkey. It also edited existing television ads to include scenes reflecting Asian lifestyles more accurately while also translating ads into Cantonese and Mandarin.[29]

Within a given culture are generally found smaller groups or segments whose beliefs, values, norms, and patterns of behaviour set them apart from the larger cultural mainstream. These **subcultures** may be based on age, geographic, religious, racial, and/or ethnic differences. A number of subcultures exist within Canada. These racial/ethnic subcultures are important to marketers because of their size, growth, purchasing power, and distinct purchasing patterns. Other types of subcultures are also targeted through promotional communication. For example, many major brands including Honda Civic, Radio Shack, Adidas Canada, and Athletes World target those within the hip-hop culture. The firms have included the hip-hop culture in their television ads and marketing events.[30]

83

Social Class   Virtually all societies exhibit some form of stratification whereby individuals can be assigned to a specific social category on the basis of criteria important to members of that society. **Social class** refers to relatively homogeneous divisions in a society into which people sharing similar lifestyles, values, norms, interests, and behaviours can be grouped. While a number of methods for determining social class exist, class structures in Canada are usually based on occupational status, educational attainment, and income. For example, sociologists generally agree there are three broad levels of social classes in North America: the upper (14 percent), middle (70 percent), and lower (16 percent) classes.[31]

Social class is an important concept to marketers, since consumers within each social stratum often have similar values, lifestyles, and buying behaviour. Thus, the various social class groups provide a natural basis for market segmentation. Consumers in the different social classes differ in the degree to which they use various products and services and in their leisure activities, shopping patterns, and media habits. Marketers respond to these differences through their products and service offerings, the media strategies they use to reach different social classes, and the types of advertising messages they develop. With smaller Canadian households (2.5 persons) and rising disposable household income, marketers of premium products find that the middle-class consumers behave as upper-class consumers for selective purchases. A sizable group of middle-class consumers who cannot afford premium or luxury goods for all their purchases are "trading up" for items such as clothing, home furnishings, or alcohol.[32]

Behaviouristic Segmentation   Dividing consumers into groups according to different actions that consumers engage in is known as **behaviouristic segmentation**. Consumer behaviour is looked at in terms of brand loyalty, user status, usage rate, situation, and benefits sought.

Loyalty   The degree of loyalty to the brand is a variable used considerably in marketing as programs are developed to retain current customers or attract consumers who purchase other brands. Loyalty status is often combined with demographic and/or psychographic criteria to develop profiles of audiences for specific communication. We will have more to say on this idea, because it is a critical variable in designing promotional messages. Its importance is easily seen; current brand users obviously are aware of the brand and have considerably stronger product knowledge, and they have some regular or irregular interaction with the brand. For example, loyal users of Nike shoes might be more likely to look at the Nike website to see the latest brands.

User Status   In the case of usage, the marketer assumes that non-purchasers of a brand or product who have the same characteristics as purchasers hold greater potential for adoption than nonusers with different characteristics. A profile (demographic or psychographic) of the user is developed, which serves as the basis for promotional strategies designed to attract new users. For example, teenagers share certain similarities in their consumption behaviours. Those who do not currently own, say, an iPod are more likely to be potential buyers than people in other age groups. In this case, the new users may view this purchase decision as a new experience requiring comparison shopping with limited problem-solving activities and are therefore more involved while reading ads or looking at websites or talking to friends online.

Usage Rate   Another factor related to the previous two concerns how much of a product category is consumed. Most product categories and most consumers can be classified along the lines of light, medium, or heavy usage. With these groups in mind, and demographic or psychographic variables, advertisers can direct messages more appropriately. For example, men tend to consume fewer cosmetic products than women (yes, men's skin care is a big business), so ads can be designed to move the many light users to more medium users.

Situation   Another way of viewing behaviouristic segmentation is to examine the situation in which consumers plan to use the product or brand since it directly affects their perceptions, preferences, and purchasing behaviours.[33] Two types of **situations** may be relevant: the specific usage situation and the purchase situation. *Usage situation* refers to the circumstance in which the product will be used. For example, purchases made for private consumption may be thought of differently from those that will be obvious to the public. Furthermore, purchases made for oneself versus for others as gifts offer another way to view consumer markets. The *purchase situation* more directly involves the environment operating at the time of the purchase. Time constraints, store environments, and other factors guide consumers' behaviour, which opens the door for inventive ways of segmenting the market.

Benefit Segmentation   In purchasing products, consumers are generally trying to satisfy specific needs and/or wants. They are looking for products that provide specific benefits to satisfy these needs. The grouping of consumers on the basis of attributes sought in a product is known as **benefit segmentation** and is widely used. Consider the purchase of a wristwatch. While someone might buy a watch for particular benefits such as accuracy, water resistance, or stylishness, others may seek a different set of benefits. Watches are commonly given as gifts for birthdays, Christmas, and graduation. Certainly some of the same benefits are considered in the purchase of a gift, but the benefits the purchaser derives are different from those the user will obtain. Ads that portray watches as good gifts stress different criteria to consider in the purchase decision. Another example of benefit segmentation can be seen in the ads for NY Fries, where potato flavour and taste are important (Exhibit 3-14).

Exhibit 3-14   NY Fries reminds consumers of the benefit of authentic potato flavour.

TARGET MARKET SELECTION

As we have seen, a number of alternative segmentation approaches may be used. Each time a specific segment is identified, additional information is gathered to help the marketer understand this group. For example, once a specific segment is identified on the basis of benefits sought, the marketer will examine lifestyle characteristics and demographics to help characterize this group and to further its understanding of this market. Behaviouristic segmentation criteria will also be examined. In the purchase of ski boots, for example, specific benefits may be sought—flexibility or stiffness—depending on the type of skiing the buyer does. All this information will be combined to provide a complete profile of the skier.

Promotional planners will refer to the segmentation approach used in the marketing plan. The market segmentation may be based on demographics so the target market could be men ages 18–24 or women 25–44. And, it may be incumbent upon the promotional planner to perform additional research to develop a more complete profile. Alternatively, the market segmentation used in the marketing plan could employ one variable as a starting point and offer additional variables to further define the target market, as seen in the ski boots example. Recently, Marks Work Wearhouse entered the market of premium women's wear with its Ispiri brand; the new brand, aimed at working mothers between 30 and 40, is a step up from its Denver Hayes line introduced a decade ago and a step down from high-designer clothes.[34]

The promotional planner must consider whether the target segment is substantial enough to support individualized strategies. Can it be reached with a communications program? For example, Chapter 10 identifies instances where no media can be used to reach some targeted groups. Or the promotions manager may identify a number of segments but be unable to develop the required programs to reach them. For example, the firm may have insufficient funds to develop the required advertising campaign. The more marketers segment the market, the more precise is their understanding of it. But the more the market becomes divided, the fewer consumers are in each segment. Thus, a key decision involves how far one should go in the segmentation process. Another issue arises as to which segmentation variable is used first and which others are used as additional profile variables. The answer to this question is the art of marketing: the insight promotional planners see in the information to understand their target market and target audience options.

TARGET AUDIENCE OPTIONS

We now turn to the Rossiter and Percy (R&P) perspective of identifying and selecting the target audience for promotional communication.[35] R&P state that the primary and most logical factor for initially defining a target audience is the current behaviour of consumers. This factor is critical since it is the individual decision of each customer to purchase a brand that dictates a firm's total sales. Furthermore, this behaviour is a manifestation of a consumer's attitude toward the brand. Thus, in setting the direction for any IMC plan or component of an IMC plan (i.e., advertising), the manager must have a clear idea of the customer status of the target audience. Essentially, this decision hinges on a key question: Is the marketing communication directed toward customer groups or non-customer groups?

Customer Groups Promotional planners have the opportunity to direct marketing communication to **brand-loyal customers** who regularly buy their firm's products. Recent marketing strategies (i.e., relationship marketing, discussed in Chapter 1) and communication strategies regularly focus on a firm's current customers to ensure that customers maintain their current purchasing and consumption behaviour. As we noted in Chapter 1, it is generally very profitable to maintain a stable core of current customers. From a communication standpoint, it suggests that we do not have to advertise as often or we do not have to have as many sales promotions. However, we still see campaigns directed toward current loyal customers. For example, The Movie Network ran an eight-week television, radio, and outdoor campaign that was entirely devoted to its current subscribers base.[36]

To put this idea into another context we highlight the fact that one-third of all Canadians do not drink beer at all and that 74 percent of all Canadian beer drinkers claim they are loyal to their favourite beer.[37] This raises the question as to whether beer company ads should target their loyal customers and ensure future purchases by strengthening the loyalty with relevant messages, or target the remaining customers who claim they are not loyal to a specific beer.

Favourable brand switchers are a second customer group highlighted by R&P. These customers buy the promotional planner's brand but also buy other brands within a given relevant time period for the product category. For some product categories, consumers habitually purchase from a few favourites or those brands within their evoked set. These types of purchases may occur for many reasons. Consumers often face different purchase situations (e.g., own purchase versus gift). Sometimes certain moods influence brand choice. Whatever the motivation or external influencing factor, consumers adjust their purchases accordingly. While a promotional planner would undoubtedly strive to have all customers be truly loyal, favourable brand switchers are an important source of purchases and are loyal to a degree. For these reasons, marketers would like to communicate directly with these consumers so that their brand remains in the evoked set. Alternatively, continued communication may influence stronger loyalty in the future. Butter is always competing with margarine for increased loyalty (Exhibit 3-15).

The importance of varying degrees of loyalty within a brand's customer base is the topic of recent research. In a study of the cola market, the authors provide a decision-making framework for measuring varying degrees of customer loyalty and link these customers to varying levels of ROI. The conclusions suggest that customer groups with different loyalty levels are predicated upon their beliefs toward the brand on the more salient attributes.[38]

Returning to our beer example, it turns out that Canadian beer drinkers may not be strongly aligned to one beer, as 30 to 40 percent will switch brands if a promotional offer coincides with an advertising message.[39] In reality, it appears many Canadian beer drinkers are loyal to their favourite beer to a degree, but they will also include it along with other brands. This implies that a brand manager for beer (e.g., Molson Canadian) is faced with the task of communicating to favourable brand switchers, a group of consumers who are habitually buying their brand and a few others (e.g., Labatt Blue). In turn, another brand manager (e.g., Labatt Blue) could be faced with the same task of communicating to favourable brand switchers who consume an entirely different group of beer brands (e.g., Lakeport, Steamwhistle).

Non-Customer Groups   Communication directed to non-customers is the focus of much advertising and promotion. R&P identify three key groups: *new category users*, *other brand switchers*, and *other brand loyals*. These consumers are more difficult to attract as they do not currently purchase the promotional planner's brand.

New category users, as the name implies, are those customers that are not purchasing within a product category. For example, after graduating from college or university many young adults begin to enter numerous categories partly because they have the income but also because they are at a stage of their life when new or latent needs emerge. Advertisers attempt to court this target audience since many of these consumers are potentially ready to make a purchase. Later on in life consumers face different needs and move into a product category, as shown

87

Exhibit 3-15
Butter advertises to avoid switching to substitute products.

Natural selection. Butter.

QUALITY MILK

Exhibit 3-16 Toyota suggests the need for a minivan in many of its recent print ads.

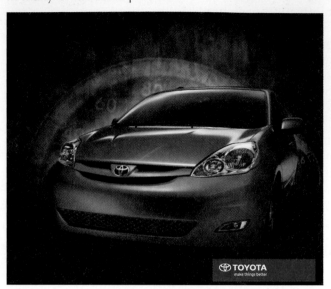

in Exhibit 3-16. Marketers believe that steady communication may entice these customers to their brand when the time comes for these consumers to actually purchase. Capital One, a financial services organization, attracted as new customers new Canadians (i.e., recent immigrants) who had not fully developed their credit history and who had minimal or no purchases with respect to banking products and services. To attract those who did not have a credit card Capital One used "take-one" pads on signage of street cars that passed through Chinatown in Toronto, pre-movie ads shown before Bollywood films, and point-of-purchase ads in ethnic grocery stores.[40]

New category users also appear when brands try to attract new customers who might not perceive the product category as relevant for fulfilling their needs. Most people have entertainment needs that can be satisfied in many ways (e.g., dancing at club, watching a movie at theatre). Young people typically do not see the arts, such as ballet, as potentially fulfilling their entertainment needs, so the National Ballet of Canada faced an interesting communication challenge to attract new young consumers to its production of *The Seagull*. The solution involved distributing an actual origami gull—5,000 of them, in fact—in Toronto bars, restaurants, and coffee shops. The unfolded gull displayed a flyer with key information and an opportunity to win tickets to the production.[41]

Other brand switchers are like the switchers in the customer group in that they purchase a few different brands within a category. However, from a promotional planner's perspective, they are fundamentally different because they are not purchasing their brand. This is a challenging target audience, as the brand needs to break into consumers' evoked set and within the brands that these consumers are currently purchasing. It's a formidable task, but still the focus of a considerable amount of advertising and promotion. (Exhibit 3-17 is an ad to attract drinkers of other brands of beer.)

For example, Coffee Crisp recently started advertising on television after a 10-year hiatus. As the brand manager noted, "Because Coffee Crisp hasn't been advertised for so many years, we haven't brought in a new generation of Coffee Crisp consumers." Naturally, many young consumers were eating other brands of chocolate bars, so Coffee Crisp faced the challenge of appealing to these other brand switchers with a taste alternative. Research showed that Coffee Crisp "owned" the coffee association in the chocolate bar market, and with a generation of young coffee drinkers that frequent cafés the brand had a good opportunity to improve sales with its new ads. In fact, the room for growth is impressive—the famous bar, which once was ranked number one or two in Canada, had fallen to number five with a lack of advertising for so many years.[42]

R&P's final group for target audience selection includes **other brand loyals**. As this label implies, these consumers purchase only one other brand. For example, Porter Airlines attempts to draw from Air Canada's customers (Exhibit 3-18). It is difficult to say how much in advertising and promotion expenditure is directed to these types of consumers across many industries. Logically, it would be very difficult to break

Exhibit 3-17 Grolsch plays on its name to attract new customers.

Exhibit 3-18 Porter Airlines' "rules" campaign sways Air Canada customers.

Exhibit 3-19 Danone challenges new users to try its brand of yogurt.

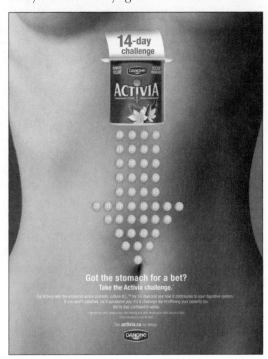

the strongly held behaviours in which these consumers currently engage. Nevertheless, this is still a potential target to which a firm may wish to deliver some form of advertising and promotion. The yogurt ad in Exhibit 3-19 shows a strong message to encourage non-users to switch.

IMC PLANNING: TARGET AUDIENCE PROFILE

According to R&P, after prioritizing the target audience in terms of customer groups other segmentation variables like lifestyle or demographics are used to develop a complete target audience profile. A complete profile of the target audience beyond the initial behavioural variable is necessary for direction of the remaining decisions in the promotional plan. Creative decisions involving the main message to be communicated require appropriate content so that consumers will attend to and understand the message. Effective media decisions require the promotional planner to match the consumer characteristics of the specific media with a complete target audience profile. Finally, more information about the target audience allows greater precision when assessing and choosing IMC tools to deliver the message. We now explore the planning implications of these three ideas.

PROFILE FOR MESSAGES

In later chapters we will identify different aspects of constructing the main message a promotional planner would want to develop for its advertising or sales promotion or any other IMC tool like the Internet or public relations. For the message to be completely understood, the content of the message must be consistent with the background or experiences of the intended audience. For example, if the ad uses language or references to a lifestyle that is unfamiliar to the target audience, there is less likelihood of it influencing in the direction intended. Thus, a complete profile of the target audience will be useful when finalizing the body copy in a print ad or the scenes in a television commercial.

Many companies target a younger demographic. We may read in the press or in marketing trade publications that a firm is targeting an 18- to 24-year-old demographic. While this may be true, often there is an inherent behavioural variable implied. Sometimes it is more like a new category user, since young adults start to consume new categories of products as they mature. Other times, it is more like favourable brand switchers in an attempt to make these consumers exhibit stronger loyalty. Thus, a communication message has to resonate with the target audience based on their current behaviour, whether they buy the brand or not, and another variable like demographics.

One clever ad by Tide detergent illustrates this point from the other direction. The ad shows a child sitting in a highchair who has just finished eating a bowl of spaghetti. The picture clearly shows the child's face and the child is naturally very messy. The headline reads, "The day I switched to Tide," and there is no other text in the ad. It appears that this message is targeted toward other brand switchers or other brand loyals who are at a particular stage of the family life cycle. The ad represents the significant decision they undertook to finally stop consuming a current brand and move on to a presumably better brand. Had the ad shown an alternative picture, the additional profile variable would have been considerably different. For instance, the image of a young woman wearing athletic clothing who observes a stain or that the colours of her clothing are fading too quickly suggests an active lifestyle. This illustrates that any marketing segmentation variable can be used to further profile the behavioural variable.

PROFILE FOR MEDIA

Later in this text, we will also identify the different media decisions. For example, the promotional planner could select television or radio to deliver its message, or the promotional planner might consider newspapers or magazines or a multitude of other media. Each medium offers many avenues that also must be considered. For instance, would the promotional planner place the television commercial on a TSN sports event during the day, or on a CTV drama in the evening? A detailed profile of the target audience allows the message to be more precisely delivered in a medium that has a higher proportion of the target audience.

Some contend that the advent of many different television channels leading to greater audience fragmentation has led to television being less efficient, since an advertiser is required to place a commercial on more than one station to reach a larger audience. In contrast, the detailed target audience profile for media helps a promotional planner move toward greater effectiveness. With the possibility of offering a more customized message to different audiences, promotional planners can have one type of commercial oriented toward younger non-customers on one channel and another message to older current customers on a different channel. Or, with the extensive number of new television channels in languages other than the two official languages, advertisers can provide more customized messages on the respective channels. For example, the OpenRoad Auto Group brand of car dealerships selling Toyota, Lexus, Honda, Acura, Hyundai, and Audi vehicles has successfully used different combinations of media to effectively reach the Vancouver resident with a Chinese background.[43]

Moving toward more interactive media for the purposes of building and maintaining relationships, brands could use certain kinds of media and media vehicles to communicate with different segments based on unique relationship variables that are within the firm's database.[44] This would allow more accurate exposure and more customized messages depending upon where the customer is within the relationship.

PROFILE FOR IMC TOOLS

Similarly, in a later part of the book we investigate the decisions involved for other IMC tools like sales promotion, public relations, direct marketing, and the Internet. Each of these represents additional avenues for reaching target audiences, and each represents a tool with a greater opportunity for building the brand. Like media, there is also the possibility of more closely aligning the use of a tool with a promotional planner's target audience, provided sufficient profiling is done.

Western Union created cultural events for Toronto, Vancouver, and Winnipeg residents with Filipino heritage to encourage usage when sending money to their previous country. This idea arose after research indicated an interest in entertainment, in particular performers and celebrities from the former country. Ethnically based media advertising supported this effort to convince these consumers that the brand was not an overpriced, indifferent global company.[45]

From another angle, Canadian Tire—historically geared for men—continues to evolve with a greater emphasis toward women. Altering its product offerings and store design was just one step, as it offers a substantially different set of communications directed to women with a stylish-home kind of lifestyle. Its television advertising featured creative messages more fitting for women, placed on specialty channels. Canadian Tire featured print advertising in stylish publications like *Wish*, *Style at Home*, and *Canadian House & Home*. Store displays appeared more inspiring and less informational, also to fit with this newfound audience.[46]

CHAPTER OBJECTIVES AND SUMMARY

1 To understand the consumer decision-making process and how it relates to marketing communication.

This chapter briefly reviewed the field of consumer behaviour and examined its relevance to promotional strategy. Consumer behaviour is best viewed as the process and activities that people engage in when searching for, selecting, purchasing, using, evaluating, and disposing of products and services to satisfy their needs and desires.

A five-stage model of the consumer decision-making process consists of need recognition, information search, alternative evaluation, purchase, and postpurchase evaluation. The decision process model views consumer behaviour primarily from a cognitive orientation. Marketing communication plays a role in every stage as marketers adjust their messages and media along with IMC tools to influence appropriately so that consumers move from one stage to the other.

2 To understand internal psychological processes, their influence on consumer decision making, and implications for marketing communication.

Internal psychological processes that influence the consumer decision-making process include motivation, perception, attitude formation and change, integration processes, and satisfaction. Each of these are areas in which advertising attempts to influence. Most advertising reflects a particular purchase motive. Certain elements of an ad are designed to attract attention or ensure that that the target audience retains the information or symbolic message. The body copy in a print ad, for example, can be written to influence the receiver's attitude, and allows certain ways of integrating the information. Finally, some advertising is designed to suggest to consumers that they made the correct purchase so they feel satisfied.

3 To identify how the consumer decision-making process varies for different types of purchases and the effects on marketing communication.

Consumer decision making is classified along a continuum from routine problem solving to extended problem solving. Consumers generally spend more time and effort as they move from routine to extended problem solving. Different types of marketing communication are more relevant than others depending upon the type of behaviour expected. Consumer decision making moves from an individual decision to a group decision, and once again marketing communication must adjust its message, media, or IMC tool accordingly.

4 To understand the similarities and differences of target market and target audience.

This chapter also investigated how promotional planners make a target audience decision for any aspect of an IMC plan. To understand the context of this decision, the chapter examined the role of promotion in the overall marketing process, as shown in Figure 3-5. The process includes a situation analysis, target market process, and marketing program development all directed toward a prescribed target market.

One of the key aspects pertains to the target marketing process, which includes segmenting the market, selecting a target market, and determining the market positioning strategy, as this process gives direction to the target audience decision. Accordingly, we reviewed how marketing planners and promotional planners segment the market, and explained how each made the target market and target audience decision, respectively.

5 To understand the options for making a target audience decision for marketing communication.

Finally, the chapter concluded by identifying a model to profile a target audience by considering the current purchase behaviour of the target audience with respect to the promotional planner's brand as the primary segmentation variable. Promotional messages can be directed to current customers, such as brand-loyal or favourable brand switchers. Alternatively, promotional messages could be targeted to non-customers, like new category users, other brand switchers, or other brand loyals. Other variables to more accurately define the audience in terms of lifestyle or psychographics became relevant after this initial direction became finalized. This descriptive profile becomes useful for all facets of the promotional plan (i.e., message, media, IMC tools).

KEY TERMS

affect referral decision rule, *74*

behaviouristic segmentation, *84*

benefit segmentation, *85*

brand loyalty, *74*

brand-loyal customers, *86*

cognitive dissonance, *75*

consumer behaviour, *64*

culture, *83*

demographic segmentation, *82*

evaluative criteria, *71*

extended problem solving, *76*

external search, *68*

favourable brand switchers, *86*

functional benefits, *72*

geographic segmentation, *82*

heuristics, *74*

hierarchy of needs, *67*

integration processes, *74*

internal search, *68*

limited problem solving, *76*

mnemonics, *71*

motives, *66*

need recognition, *64*

new category users, *87*

other brand loyals, *88*

other brand switchers, *88*

perception, *69*

psychographic segmentation, *82*

purchase intention, *73*

reference group, *77*

routine problem solving, *76*

satisfaction, *75*

selective attention, *70*

selective comprehension, *70*

selective exposure, *70*

selective perception, *69*

selective retention, *71*

sensation, *69*

situations, *85*

social class, *84*

subcultures, *83*

subliminal perception, *71*

target audience, *79*

target market, *79*

want, *65*

DISCUSSION QUESTIONS

1. Why is using the consumer decision-making model important for planning marketing communication?

2. Explain how consumers might engage in each of the processes of selective perception described in the chapter. Provide examples.

3. Explain the difference between functional and experiential benefits. Why might the messages recommended in an IMC plan focus on each separately or together?

4. After buying a new car, a customer receives many pieces of direct mail such as a driving magazine or information on automobile care from the manufacturer. Explain why this is effective or ineffective communication.

5. In the text it was indicated that families may influence the consumer decision-making process. Describe how various family members may assume the different roles described in Figure 3-4. Also explain how these roles might change depending upon the product under consideration.

6. Which segmentation variables are more useful or appropriate for profiling a target market? Similarly, which are more useful or appropriate for profiling the target audience?

7. In what way are French-speaking and English-speaking consumers the same target market for a brand but different target audiences?

8. In what situations is the target audience and the target market the same? In what situations is the size of the target audience larger or smaller than the target market?

9. When defining a target audience for communications, why is it a good idea to use consumer behaviour with respect to your brand as the primary variable before using other variables such as demographics or lifestyle?

10. How is it possible for a brand to communicate to both customers and non-customers in an IMC plan?

COMMUNICATION RESPONSE MODELS

■ CHAPTER OBJECTIVES

1 To understand the basic elements of the communication process and the role of marketing communication.

2 To summarize traditional communication response models and alternative response hierarchies.

3 To analyze the response processes of receivers of marketing communication through two models of cognitive processing.

4 To summarize an integrative communication response model from a theoretical and managerial perspective.

DAS AUTO BY VOLKSWAGEN

What happened to the Sunday Drive?

What is a "Very Volkswagen" ad? Decades ago, unique advertising for the Beetle paved the way for small cars to take hold in North America. Rather than looking at the size as a negative, the ad used humour to show the benefits of driving a pint-sized vehicle. And somehow, through all these years, that irreverence remained and still guides what we see in today's ads ending with "Das Auto," which means "the car" in German. Internationally, VW won the 2009 Advertiser of the Year at Cannes.

And in Canada, the advertising and the messaging for the sales promotion "Autobahn for All" spurred VW to improve sales and market share during 2009. Much of the adverting executions we see in Canadian media are developed here; however, the Ajax-based firm deploys locally whatever creative appeals from international markets. In turn, some Canadian ads are picked up abroad.

The Montreal-based agency Palm + Havas created numerous spots featuring many of the VW brands, each with a signature "Very Volkswagen" feel. For example, a spot for the new VW Routan showed a group of depressed hippies longing for the '60s, and their classic ride becoming brighter when they see the new van riding down their street. An ad for the TDI Clean Diesel shows an athletic woman running on the beach toward an environment-loving man, whereupon they embrace and a message of bringing power and the environment together resonates.

Digitally, many new activities including a new website, new dealer websites, and exclusive ads to support online TV shows on CTV.ca continue the "Very Volkswagen" idea. On Sympatico.ca, VW implemented mini webisodes that featured some of its own personnel and those from its agency in a spoof where an agency tries to develop jingles for VW with obvious difficulty (off tune, wrong message) to illustrate the humour.

More recently, VW promoted the Golf with the suggestion "Anyone for a Sunday Drive?" Prompted by the notion that people have lost the desire to take the car out for a spin, the ads encourage consumers to visit a nearby town or the countryside—while riding in a VW, of course. In particular, executives believe the Golf is a very fun car to drive, and the campaign appealed to those who really enjoy driving a car. The multimedia campaign (TV, newspaper, radio) also included a website (vwsundaydrive.ca) where consumers could mix music with driving scenes. Feels "Very VW."

Sources: Press release obtained on Stockhouse.com, "Volkswagen Canada Reinvents the Sunday Drive," June 8, 2010; Garine Tcholakian, "Volkswagen Webisodes to Air on Sympatico.ca," *Media in Canada*, October 5, 2009; Emily Wexler, "Volkswagen Canada: Defying Das Odds," *Strategy*, June 2009, p. 13.

QUESTIONS:

1. How is the style of the VW message understood by consumers?
2. Why is it important for consumers to like VW ads?

An organization's IMC strategy is implemented through the communication tools and messages it sends to current or prospective customers as well as other relevant publics. Organizations communicate in many ways, such as through advertisements, websites, press releases, sales promotion, and visual images. Those involved in the planning of an IMC program need to understand how consumers will perceive and interpret their messages and how these reactions will shape consumers' responses to the company and/or its product or service.

This chapter takes a historical perspective to illustrate how academics and practitioners have evolved in their thinking to understand how persuasion works in the context of marketing communication. We begin with a basic model to illustrate the complexity of the communication process. Next, we examine the response process of consumers that is explained by traditional models, alternative hierarchies, and cognitive processing of communication. Finally, we summarize with a framework that illustrates an IMC planning perspective.

A BASIC MODEL OF COMMUNICATION

Communication has been defined as the passing of information, the exchange of ideas, or the process of establishing a commonness or oneness of thought between a sender and a receiver.[1] These definitions suggest that for communication to occur, there must be some common thinking between two parties and information must be passed from one person to another (or from one group to another). This section elaborates on this idea by introducing a model of communication and discussing its elements.

OVERVIEW OF THE MODEL

The communication process is often very complex. Success depends on such factors as the nature of the message, the audience's interpretation of it, and the environment in which it is received. The receiver's perception of the source and the medium used to transmit the message may also affect the ability to communicate, as do many other factors. Words, pictures, sounds, and colours may have different meanings to different audiences, and people's perceptions and interpretations of them vary. Marketers must understand the meanings that words and symbols take on and how they influence consumers' interpretation of products and messages.

Over the years, a basic model of the communication process has evolved, as shown in Figure 4-1.[2] Two elements represent the major participants in the communication process: the sender and the receiver. Another two are the major communication tools: message and channel. Four others are the major communication functions and processes: encoding, decoding, response, and feedback. The last element, noise, refers to any extraneous factors in the system that can interfere with the process and work against effective communication.

SOURCE/ENCODING

The sender, or **source**, of a communication is the person or organization that has information to share with another person or group of people. The source may be an individual (say, a salesperson or hired spokesperson, such as a celebrity who appears in a company's advertisements) or a nonpersonal entity (such as the brand or organization itself). Because the receiver's perceptions of the source influence how the communication is received, marketers must be careful to select a communicator the receiver believes is knowledgeable and trustworthy or with whom the receiver can identify or relate in some manner.

FIGURE 4–1   A model of the communication process

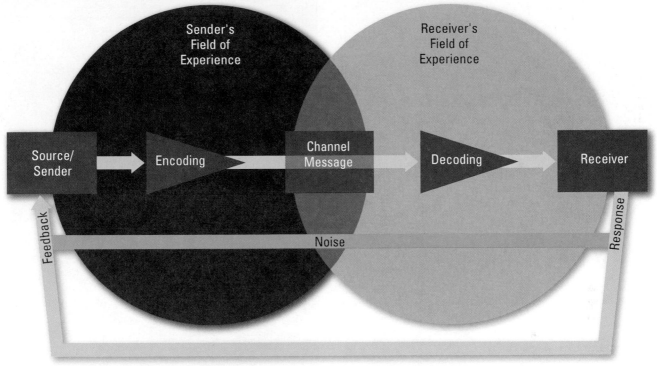

   The communication process begins when the source selects words, symbols, pictures, and the like to represent the message that will be delivered to the receiver(s). This process, known as **encoding**, involves putting thoughts, ideas, or information into a symbolic form. The sender's goal is to encode the message in such a way that it will be understood by the receiver. This means using words, signs, or symbols that are familiar to the target audience. The Nestea ad in Exhibit 4-1 is constructed to allow multiple meanings for the receiver. Many companies also have highly recognizable symbols—such as McDonald's golden arches, Nike's swoosh, or the Coca-Cola trademark. So when these symbols are shown in a message, consumers instantly understand the brand that is associated with the message.

MESSAGE

The encoding process leads to development of a **message** that contains the information or meaning the source hopes to convey. The message may be verbal or nonverbal, oral or written, or symbolic. Messages must be put into a transmittable form that is appropriate for the channel of communication being used. In advertising, this may range from simply writing some words or copy that will be read as a radio message to producing an expensive television commercial. For many products, it is not the actual words of the message that determine its communication effectiveness but rather the impression or image the ad creates. Notice how the Coach ad shown in Exhibit 4-2 uses only a picture to deliver its message. However, the brand name and picture help communicate a feeling of eloquence and the classic design of its handbag.

   To better understand the symbolic meaning conveyed in a communication, advertising and marketing researchers focus on **semiotics**, which studies the nature of meaning and asks how our reality—words, gestures, myths, signs, symbols,

Exhibit 4-1 The many elements in this ad require extensive decoding by consumers.

Exhibit 4-2 The image projected by an ad often communicates more than words.

products/services, theories—acquires meaning.[3] Semiotics is important in marketing communication because products and brands acquire meaning through the way they are advertised, and consumers use products and brands to express their social identities. However, some experts question whether social scientists read too much into advertising messages and are overly intellectual in interpreting them. In defence, the meaning of an advertising message or other form of marketing communication lies not in the message but with the people who see and interpret it, because consumers behave on the basis of meanings they ascribe to marketplace stimuli. Thus, marketers must consider the meanings consumers attach to signs and symbols. Semiotics may be helpful in analyzing how various aspects of the marketing program—such as advertising messages, packaging, brand names, and even the nonverbal communications of salespeople (gestures, mode of dress)—are interpreted by receivers.[4]

Marketers may also use individuals trained in related fields such as cultural anthropology to better understand the conscious and subconscious meanings that nonverbal signs and symbols in their ads transmit to consumers. For example, the European-based company Unilever used a technique from cultural anthropology called *ethnography* to observe young males between the ages of 18 and 22 and their friends in their everyday environs to learn more about their likes, dislikes, activities, and decision making. They analyzed video recordings of 28 young men to gain insights through the participants' own descriptions of their activities while being observed in everyday facets of their lives. Afterward, Unilever executives and their agencies met to understand the participant's mating life—that is, what he is about, why he does what he does, what excites him, and what he fears. Not surprisingly, much of the young men's lives focused on sex. Their interest was not just dating: They preferred to go to parties with other male friends and "hook up." Relationships were avoided whenever possible, as were the words *boyfriend* and *girlfriend.* They just wanted to have sex. The anthropologists even typed the males into groups based upon their characteristics into classifications such as "pimp daddy," "player," "sweetheart," and "shy guy."

Unilever developed an IMC campaign theme based on these interpretations—"Wear this deodorant and you'll pick up chicks!" Simply put, using Axe products (deodorant, body spray, shower gel, and more) will help you in your mating attempts. The television commercials focus on spontaneous sexual encounters and the need to be ready at any time, while protected (and enhanced) by Axe. The Axe man is always ready. The commercials have won the Gold Lion—the top award given at the Cannes Film Festival for international advertising quality—two of the past four years, and 10 times overall. The advertising campaign theme extended to many other IMC activities throughout the world. Overall results are staggering, suggesting that in this case ethnography and IMC produced a winning combination.[5] (See Exhibit 4-3.)

Exhibit 4-3 Ethnography helped Unilever develop the Axe ads.

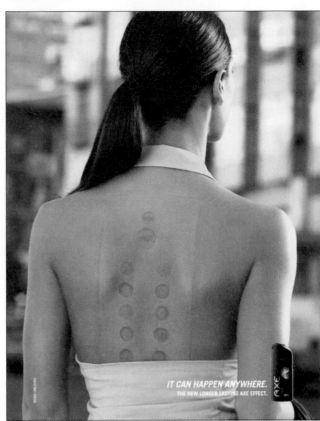

IT CAN HAPPEN ANYWHERE.
THE NEW LONGER LASTING AXE EFFECT.

99

CHANNEL

The **channel** is how the communication travels from the source or sender to the receiver. At the broadest level, channels of communication are of two types, personal and nonpersonal. *Personal channels* of communication are direct interpersonal (face-to-face) contact with target individuals or groups. Salespeople serve as personal channels of communication when they deliver their sales message to a buyer or potential customer. Social channels of communication such as friends, neighbours, associates, co-workers, or family members are also personal channels. They often represent *word-of-mouth communication*, a powerful source of information for consumers.[6] Companies attempt to generate positive word-of-mouth for their brands. Knowing that the average consumer often listens to what others say about a brand, marketers will target specific groups of influential consumers such as trendsetters or loyal customers.

A study conducted by David Godes and Dina Mayzlin on the effects of a word-of-mouth campaign for a chain store examined the characteristics of the most successful "agents" so that firms could better understand at whom they should target their buzz marketing efforts.[7] They found that agents who were not loyal customers of the store were more effective at generating sales through word of mouth than were loyal customers. The explanation offered for these somewhat counterintuitive findings is that loyal customers have already told their friends and acquaintances about a product and are already generating positive word of mouth. On the other hand, nonloyal customers may be more responsive to buzz marketing campaigns designed to encourage them to spread the word about a product. Other studies find that post-campaign word-of-mouth contributes to strengthening profitability through customer lifetime value calculations and that advertising does lead to a measurable link enhanced word-of-mouth communication.[8]

Nonpersonal channels of communication are those that carry a message without interpersonal contact between sender and receiver. Nonpersonal channels are generally referred to as the **mass media** or mass communications, since the message is sent to many individuals at one time. For example, a TV commercial broadcast on a prime-time show may be seen by a million households in a given evening. Nonpersonal channels of communication consist of two major types, print and broadcast. Print media include newspapers, magazines, direct mail, and billboards; broadcast media include radio and television.

The technical capabilities of the Internet allow innovative marketers to use it as a personal channel and a non-personal channel with both print and broadcast characteristics. From a personal perspective, consumers communicate about brands with social media and use the networking features to send ads, links, and so on to whomever they choose. It is also a nonpersonal channel as major TV stations like CTV stream live sports broadcasts online, while CBC offers shows online that cannot fit on the regular TV schedule.[9]

The wide acceptance of the Internet can be seen in its recent competition with TV for audience share. For Canada's broadcasters, the Internet began as a dumping ground of sorts—a place to show old and cancelled programs and video clips, and to advertise their main network offerings. That practice has all but disappeared in the quest for eyeballs and supplementary advertising. Canada's broadcasters now view their online sites as mini-networks—places to air original content, bonus material, and special events. CTV Television is perhaps farthest along toward the fully digital world; its seven-channel CTV Broadband Network currently offers a couple thousand hours of full-length programming, plus live streams from sources such as CTV Newsnet.

© 2009 Porsche Cars Canada Ltd. Porsche recommends seatbelt usage and observance of all traffic laws at all times.

For more information visit www.porsche.ca

Hopefully, you'll run into your ex.

The new Boxster is here.

PORSCHE

Exhibit 4-4 Porsche attracts an audience from a niche market with its ads.

RECEIVER/DECODING

The **receiver** is the person(s) with whom the sender shares thoughts or information. Generally, receivers are the consumers in the target market or audience who read, hear, and/or see the marketer's message. The target audience may consist of individuals, groups, niche markets, market segments, or a general public or mass audience as discussed in the previous chapter. The ad in Exhibit 4-4 targets a small group of drivers who can afford the price of a Porsche.

Decoding is the process of transforming the sender's message back into thought. This process is heavily influenced by the receiver's frame of reference or **field of experience**, which refers to the experiences, perceptions, attitudes, and values he or she brings to the communication situation. For effective communication to occur, the message decoding process of the receiver must match the encoding of the sender. Simply put, this means the receiver understands and correctly interprets what the source is trying to communicate. As Figure 4-1 showed, the source and the receiver each have a frame of reference (the circle around each) that they bring to the communication situation. Effective communication is more likely when there is some *common ground* (i.e., overlap of circles) between the two parties. The more knowledge the sender has about the receivers, the better the sender can understand their needs, empathize with them, and communicate effectively.

Advertisers invest in research to understand the frames of reference of the target audiences and pre-test messages to make sure consumers understand and decode them in the manner the advertiser intended prior to the launch. Exhibit 4-5 shows an ad where various ways of decoding might occur.

While this notion of common ground between sender and receiver may sound basic, it often causes great difficulty in the advertising communications process. Marketing and advertising people often have very different fields of experience from the target audience with whom they must communicate. For example, many advertising and marketing people are university-educated and work and/or reside in large urban areas. Yet they are attempting to develop messages that will effectively communicate with consumers who have never attended university, work in blue-collar occupations, and live in rural areas or small towns.

NOISE

Throughout the communication process, the message is subject to extraneous factors that can distort or interfere with its reception. This unplanned distortion or interference is known as **noise**. Errors or problems that occur during message encoding or distractions at the point of reception are examples of noise. Perhaps the foremost distraction is advertising clutter, whereby the receiver is confronted with many competing messages. Noise may also occur because the fields of experience of the sender and receiver don't overlap. Lack of common ground may result in improper encoding of the message—using a sign, symbol, or words that are unfamiliar or have different meaning to the receiver.

Exhibit 4-5 The Senses ad allows for many interpretations in decoding.

feed your perspective

sen5es

at the SoHo Metropolitan Hotel

101

RESPONSE/FEEDBACK

The receiver's set of reactions after seeing, hearing, or reading the message is known as a **response**. Receivers' responses can range from nonobservable actions such as storing information in memory to immediate action such as visiting the brand's Facebook page after seeing an ad. Marketers are very interested in **feedback**, that part of the receiver's response that is communicated back to the sender. Feedback closes the loop in the communication flow and lets the sender monitor how the intended message is being decoded and received. While the ultimate form of feedback occurs through sales, it is often hard to show a direct relationship between marketing communication and purchase behaviour. So marketers use other methods to obtain feedback, among them customer inquiries, store visits, engagement with promotions, and visits to websites. With Coca-Cola's sponsorship of the torch relay for the 2010 Olympics, the popular brand could gauge the success of the message that encouraged Canadians to sign up for a chance to carry the torch at icoke.ca.[10] With research-based information like this, advertisers can determine reasons for success or failure in the communication process and make adjustments. IMC Perspective 4-1 shows ways the Internet allows for greater customer feedback.

Domestic Advertising Playbook

A few years ago, the Canadian Football League (CFL) established its own profile despite the overwhelming popularity of alternatives with the idea of affordability, authenticity, and accessibility. And with the advent of digital technology and the continuation and establishment of multiple promotional activities, the CFL stayed in the forefront of sports marketing in Canada. According to a CFL vice president, the league plans to "amplify people's sense of belonging by making them a part of it, bringing the brand closer to them."

A revamped website (CFL.ca) led the way, with links to all the team websites and extensive video offerings with a big screen feature along with social media links. Visits and page views shot up 33 percent and 20 percent, respectively. The CFL jumped on the Twitter and Facebook wave, with the former used for live game events and the latter used to set up them up. Even the league commissioner used Twitter to keep in touch with fans to support his usual phone calls thanking them for their support.

The CFL historically employed and continued to use numerous promotional activities even with the growth of digital media. For example, for many years the CFL supported the "Making a Connection" program intended to improve the cardiovascular health of its fans by having them use the website to develop a personalized exercise regime. Associated promotion included a contest to win tickets, a workout with a trainer and CFL players, gym memberships, and a home gym.

Tie-ins with other brands kept the CFL top of mind and helped promote Nissan, Tums, and Future Shop. Nissan sponsored the CFL and promoted an online experience (Nissanarmchairhero.com), where consumers designed their own football play for five participating teams. The support of Tums involved numerous fronts. Consumers entered a "Take a Time Out with Tums" contest by entering a PIN located on specially marked packages with the chance to win a travel voucher and autographed CFL merchandise. Information of the promotion occurred through direct mail and in-store display and coincided with sampling.

Continuing with fan participation, the CFL and Future Shop encouraged fan voting for the league's all-star teams. One ad had football players dressed as Future Shop employees, boasting about their accomplishments after being approached by a customer. The reason why the Future Shop works with the CFL is summed up nicely by a senior marketing manager: "Our customers are huge CFL fans. They love football and they love the Canadian Football League, so it's something that they're actively participating."

Sources: Jonathan Paul, "The Canadian Football League: Being the Brand," *Strategy*, October 2009, p. 25; Kristin Laird, "Tums, CFL Contest Kicks Off," *Marketing Magazine*, May 28, 2009; Matt Semansky, "Future Shop Turns Out the CFL Fan Vote," *Marketing Magazine*, September 2009; Eve Lazarus, "CFL Puts Fans' Hearts into the Game," *Marketing Magazine*, June 27, 2009; Jeromy Lloyd, "Nissan Gives Football Fans a Chance to Play with the CFL," *Marketing Magazine*, August 21, 2009.

Questions:

1. Why are the IMC tools effective in this example?

SUMMARY OF THE MODEL

The model has stood the test of time for more than 50 years to describe how advertising communicates through traditional media. Practitioners are debating how new digital channels and social media are affecting their marketing communication decisions. They appear to conclude that despite the revolution of new communication occurring, the fundamental tenets of a consistent brand strategy and understanding how that message is delivered through the new avenues is still a critical perspective.[11]

We can still conclude that successful communication is accomplished when the marketer selects an appropriate source, develops an effective message or appeal that is encoded properly, and then selects the channels or media that will best reach the target audience so that the message can be effectively decoded and delivered. So whether we are talking about delivering a message on television or through social media, the general communication principles are important to consider for effective decisions. Since these decisions must consider how the target audience will respond to the promotional message, the remainder of this chapter examines the process by which consumers respond to marketing communication.

THE RESPONSE PROCESS

An important aspect of developing effective communication programs involves understanding the *response process* the receiver may go through in moving toward a specific behaviour and how the promotional efforts of the marketer influence consumer responses. To explain the response process we now review two types of response hierarchy models—traditional and alternative.

TRADITIONAL RESPONSE HIERARCHY MODELS

A number of models have been developed to depict the process a consumer may pass through in moving from a state of not being aware of a company, product, or brand to actual purchase behaviour. Figure 4-2 shows four of the best-known response models, which are known as hierarchy models since there is a prescribed order or defined steps the receiver experiences. While these response models may appear similar, they were developed for different reasons.

The **AIDA model** was developed to represent the steps a salesperson must take a customer through in the personal selling process.[12] The salesperson must first get the customer's attention and then arouse some interest in the company's product or service. Strong levels of interest should create desire to own or use the product. The action step in the AIDA model involves getting the customer to make a purchase commitment and closing the sale. To the marketer, this is the most important step in the selling process, but it can also be the most difficult. Companies train their sales

FIGURE 4–2 Models of the response process

Stages	Models			
	AIDA model	Hierarchy of effects model	Innovation adoption model	Information processing model
Cognitive stage	Attention	Awareness	Awareness	Presentation
				Attention
		Knowledge		Comprehension
Affective stage	Interest	Liking	Interest	Yielding
		Preference		
	Desire	Conviction	Evaluation	Retention
Behavioural stage			Trial	
	Action	Purchase	Adoption	Behaviour

Exhibit 4-6 Sampling or demonstration programs encourage trials of new products, such as disposable contact lenses.

reps in closing techniques to help them complete the selling process.

Perhaps the best known of these response hierarchies is the model developed by Robert Lavidge and Gary Steiner as a method for setting and measuring advertising objectives.[13] Their **hierarchy of effects model** assumes a consumer passes through a series of steps in sequential order from initial awareness of a product or service to actual purchase. A basic premise of this model is that advertising effects occur over a period of time. Advertising communication may not lead to immediate behavioural response or purchase; rather, a series of effects must occur, with each step fulfilled before the consumer can move to the next stage in the hierarchy. As we will see in Chapter 5, the hierarchy of effects model has become the foundation for objective setting and measurement of advertising effects in many companies.

The **innovation adoption model** evolved from work on the diffusion of innovations.[14] The model represents the process a consumer experiences when adopting a new product or service. Like the other models, it says consumers must be moved through a series of steps before taking the action of adopting a new product. The steps preceding adoption are awareness, interest, evaluation, and trial. The challenge facing companies introducing new products is to create awareness and interest among consumers and then get them to evaluate the product favourably. The best way to evaluate a new product is through actual use so that performance can be judged. Marketers often encourage trial by using demonstration or sampling programs or allowing consumers to use a product with minimal commitment (Exhibit 4-6). After trial, consumers either adopt the product or reject it.

The final hierarchy model shown in Figure 4-2 is the **information processing model** of advertising effects, developed by William McGuire.[15] This model assumes the receiver in a persuasive communication situation like advertising is an information processor or problem solver. McGuire suggests the series of steps a receiver goes through in being persuaded constitutes a response hierarchy. The steps of this model are similar to the hierarchy of effects sequence; attention and comprehension are similar to awareness and knowledge, and yielding is synonymous with liking. McGuire's model includes a step not found in the other models: retention, or the receiver's ability to retain that portion of the comprehended information that he or she accepts as valid or relevant. This step is important since most promotional campaigns are designed not to motivate consumers to take immediate action but rather to provide information they will use later when making a purchase decision.

IMPLICATIONS OF THE TRADITIONAL HIERARCHY MODELS

As shown in Figure 4-2, the four models presented all view the response process as consisting of movement through a sequence of three basic stages even though the specific steps may be unique or defined with some variation. The *cognitive stage* represents what the receiver knows or perceives about the particular product or brand. This stage includes awareness that the brand exists and knowledge, information, or comprehension about its attributes, characteristics, or benefits. The *affective stage* refers to the receiver's feelings or affect level (like or dislike) for the particular brand. This stage also includes stronger levels of affect such as desire, preference, or conviction. The *conative* or *behavioural stage* refers to the consumer's action toward the brand: trial, purchase, adoption, or rejection.

The hierarchy models of communication response are useful for promotional planners to make specific marketing communication decisions for each stage. Potential buyers may be at different stages in the hierarchy, so the advertiser will face different sets of communication problems. For example, a company introducing an innovative product like the Hitachi plasma high-definition television (HDTV) may use media advertising to make people aware of the product along with its features and benefits (Exhibit 4-7). Hitachi provides product information in its ads but also encourages consumers to visit retail stores as well as its website to learn more about its television. Consumers who visit the Hitachi website or go to the retail store for a product demonstration will progress through the response hierarchy and move closer to purchase than those who only see an ad. In contrast, marketers of a mature brand that enjoys customer loyalty may need only supportive or reminder advertising to reinforce positive perceptions and maintain the awareness level for the brand.

The hierarchy models can also be useful as intermediate measures of communication effectiveness that could guide future communication decisions. The marketer needs to know where audience members are on the response hierarchy. For example, research may reveal that one target segment has low awareness of the advertiser's brand, whereas another is aware of the brand and its various attributes but has a low level of liking or brand preference. For the first segment of the market, the communication task involves increasing the awareness level for the brand. The number of ads may be increased, or a product sampling program may be used. For the second segment, where awareness is already high but liking and preference are low, the advertiser must determine the reason for the negative feelings and then attempt to address this problem in future advertising.

Finally, all four models assume a similar ordering of the three stages. Cognitive development precedes affective reactions, which precede behaviour. One might assume that consumers become aware of and knowledgeable about a brand, develop feelings toward it, form a desire or preference, and then make a purchase. While this logical progression is often accurate, the response sequence does not always operate this way. Over the past few decades, considerable research in marketing, social psychology, and communications has led to questioning of the traditional cognitive → affective → behavioural sequence leading to other configurations of the response hierarchy.

Exhibit 4-7
Advertising for innovative new products such as HDTV must make consumers aware of their features and benefits.

ALTERNATIVE RESPONSE HIERARCHIES

Michael Ray has developed a model of information processing that identifies three alternative orderings of the three stages based on perceived product differentiation and product involvement.[16] Figure 4-3 identifies the alternative response hierarchies as the standard learning, dissonance/attribution, and low-involvement models.[17]

The Standard Learning Hierarchy In many purchase situations, the consumer will go through the response process in the sequence depicted by the traditional communication models. Ray terms this a **standard learning model**, which consists of a learn → feel → do sequence. Information and knowledge acquired or *learned* about the various brands are the basis for developing affect, or *feelings,* that guide what the consumer will do (e.g., actual trial or purchase). In this hierarchy, the consumer is viewed as an active participant in the communication process who gathers information through active learning.

Ray suggests the standard learning hierarchy is likely when the consumer is highly involved in the purchase process and there is much differentiation among competing brands. High-involvement purchase decisions such as those for industrial products and services and consumer durables like personal computers, printers, cameras, appliances, and cars are areas where a standard learning hierarchy response process is likely. Ads for products and services in these areas are usually very detailed and provide customers with information that can be used to evaluate brands and help them make a purchase decision (Exhibit 4-8).

The Dissonance/Attribution Hierarchy A second response hierarchy proposed by Ray involves situations where consumers first behave, then develop attitudes or feelings as a result of that behaviour, and then learn or process information that supports the behaviour. This **dissonance/attribution model**, or do → feel → learn, occurs in situations where consumers must choose between two alternatives that are similar in quality but are complex and may have hidden or unknown attributes. The consumer may purchase the product on the basis of a recommendation by some nonmedia source and then attempt to support the decision by developing a positive attitude toward the brand and perhaps even developing negative feelings toward the rejected alternative(s). This reduces any *postpurchase dissonance* (as

FIGURE 4–3

Alternative response hierarchies

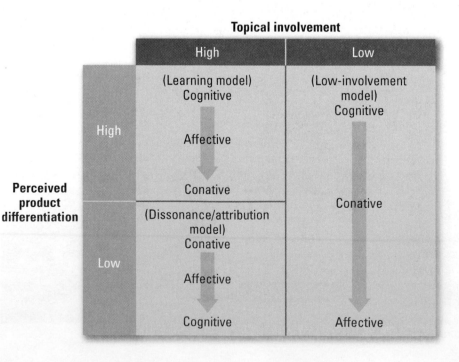

Exhibit 4-8 Ads for high-involvement products provide consumers with information to help them evaluate brands.

Exhibit 4-9 This ad reinforces the wisdom of the decision to use a Visa credit card.

discussed in Chapter 3) the consumer may experience resulting from doubt over the purchase. The *selective perception* (as discussed in Chapter 3) the consumer engages in supports the reasons (i.e., attributions) for brand choice. According to this model, attitudes develop *after* purchase, as does learning from the mass media. Ray suggests that in these situations the main effect of the mass media is not the promotion of original choice behaviour and attitude change but rather the reduction of dissonance by reinforcing the wisdom of the purchase or providing supportive information. For example, the ad shown in Exhibit 4-9 reinforces the consumer's decision to use a Visa credit card by providing reassurance regarding the layers of security the company provides to its cardholders.

Some marketers resist this view of the response hierarchy because they can't accept the notion that the mass media have no effect on the consumer's initial purchase decision. But the model doesn't claim the mass media have no effect—just that their major impact occurs after the purchase has been made. Marketing communications planners must be aware of the need for advertising and promotion efforts, not just to encourage brand selection but also to reinforce choices and ensure that a purchase pattern will continue. For example, one study found that advertising can lessen the negative effects of an unfavourable trial experience on brand evaluations when the ad is processed before the trial. However, when a negative trial experience precedes exposure to an ad, cognitive evaluations of the ad are more negative.[18] More recent research has also shown that advertising can affect consumers' objective sensory interpretation of their experiences with a brand and what they remember about it.[19]

The Low-Involvement Hierarchy Perhaps the most intriguing of the three response hierarchies proposed by Ray is the **low-involvement hierarchy**, in which the receiver is viewed as passing from cognition to behaviour to attitude change. This learn → do → feel sequence is thought to characterize situations of low consumer involvement in the purchase process. Ray suggests this hierarchy tends to occur when involvement in the purchase decision is low, there are minimal differences among brand alternatives, and mass-media (especially broadcast) advertising is important.

The notion of a low-involvement hierarchy is based in large part on Herbert Krugman's theory explaining the effects of television advertising.[20] Krugman wanted to find out why TV advertising produced a strong effect on brand awareness and recall but little change in consumers' attitudes toward the product. He hypothesized that TV is basically a low-involvement medium and the viewer's perceptual defences are reduced or even absent during commercials. In a low-involvement situation, the consumer does not compare the message with previously acquired beliefs, needs, or past experiences. The commercial results in subtle changes in the consumer's knowledge structure, particularly with repeated exposure. This change in the consumer's knowledge does not result in attitude change but is related to learning something about the advertised brand, such as a brand name, ad theme, or slogan. According to Krugman, when the consumer enters a purchase situation, this information may be sufficient to trigger a purchase. The consumer will then form an attitude toward the purchased brand as a result of experience with it.

In the low-involvement hierarchy, the consumer engages in passive learning and random information catching rather than active information seeking. The advertiser must recognize that a passive, uninterested consumer may focus more on nonmessage elements such as music, characters, symbols, and slogans or jingles than actual message content. The advertiser might capitalize on this situation by developing a catchy jingle that is stored in the consumer's mind without any active cognitive processing and becomes salient when he or she enters the actual purchase situation.

Advertisers of low-involvement products also repeat simple product claims such as a key copy point or distinctive product benefit. A study by Scott Hawkins and Stephen Hoch found that under low-involvement conditions, repetition of simple product claims increased consumers' memory of and belief in those claims.[21] They concluded that advertisers of low-involvement products might find it more profitable to pursue a heavy repetition strategy than to reach larger audiences with lengthy, more detailed messages. For example, Heinz has dominated the ketchup market by repeatedly telling consumers that its brand is the thickest and richest. Heinz has used a variety of advertising campaigns over the years, but they all repeat the same basic message and focus on the consistent quality of the brand (Exhibit 4-10).

Exhibit 4-10 Advertising promoting taste quality has helped Heinz dominate the ketchup market.

IMPLICATIONS OF THE ALTERNATIVE RESPONSE MODELS

A review of the alternative response models shows that the traditional standard learning model does not always apply. The notion of a highly involved consumer who engages in active information processing and learning and acts on the basis of higher-order beliefs and a well-formed attitude may be inappropriate for some types of purchases. Sometimes consumers make a purchase decision on the basis of general awareness

Wonderful, Wonderful, Cover Girl

With market share dropping due to increased distribution of high-end cosmetic brands, especially at Shoppers Drug Mart's new beauty boutique, the mainstream brand Cover Girl found itself in a precarious market position in late 2007, when the current brand manager Fiona Stevenson took charge. In fact, high-end labels (e.g., Lancôme, Clinique) garnered a quarter of the cosmetic dollar sales in Shoppers, more than Procter & Gamble's Cover Girl and rival L'Oréal. The turnaround moved overall market share up incrementally three years in a row, allowing Drew Barrymore's favourite brand to reach 17 percent.

Enter the Shade Brigade, a street team that went to high-traffic areas and helped the target select the right shade for her complexion and skin tone. After the consultation, the consumer was given a coupon indicating the correct shade to facilitate her purchase at a retail location. For those not reached by the team, in-store shade selectors assisted in decision making or acted as a key selling tool for beauty consultants, such as the ones in Shoppers.

Although Cover Girl relied on U.S. creative for TV and print for all its different cosmetic products and also received support from product placement on American TV shows like *America's Next Top Model*, the Canadian launch of LashBlast mascara worked at the retail level with unique creative at various points in the store—such as displays, shelf, and cash checkout messages designed to coincide with a consumer's retail visit. Depending on the consumer, the next (or previous) step in the decision-making process included visiting a website (Covergirl.ca) that featured a uniquely created Canadian design. The helpful nature of other marketing communication activities carried over to the site, which provided information about sampling events and interactive elements to assist in colour selection. Consumers interested in more experiences signed up to receive a newsletter containing Canadian content, like articles about *Canada's Next Top Model*, which Cover Girl sponsored. Cover Girl continued to innovate in its marketing communication with a domination plan in Toronto and Montreal subway stations, wrapping material around turnstiles to give the effect of a giant mascara brush to support the LashBlast brand.

Key influencers are not forgotten by Cover Girl; beauty editors and bloggers received customized kits. These individuals often receive product packages, but Cover Girl attracted their attention and interest by offering insight to spokesperson Drew Barrymore in an execution for TRUblend Microminerals, and presenting kits for Exact Eyelights mascara that fit the exact eye colour of the recipients. The results speak for themselves, as Cover Girl measured a greater share of voice in the influencers' recommendations.

Sources: Emily Wexler, "Fiona Stevenson: P&G's Cover Girl Blasts the Competition," *Strategy*, October 2009, p. 12; Kristin Laird, "TV Viewers Don't Want Product Placement Interruptions," *Marketing Magazine*, November 13, 2009; Kristin Laird, "Cover Girl Puts Giant Mascara Wands Underground," *Marketing Magazine*, February 2, 2010.

Question:

1. Why are the IMC tools effective in this example?

resulting from repetitive exposure to advertising, and attitude development occurs after the purchase, if at all. The role of advertising and other forms of promotion may be to induce trial, so consumers can develop brand preferences primarily on the basis of their direct experience with the product.

From a promotional planning perspective, it is important that marketers examine the communication situation for their product or service and determine which type of response process is most likely to occur. They should analyze involvement levels and product/service differentiation as well as consumers' use of various information sources and their levels of experience with the product or service. Once the manager has determined which response sequence is most likely to operate, the integrated marketing communications program can be designed to influence the response process in favour of the company's product or service. IMC Perspective 4-2 illustrates how Cover Girl adapted its marketing communication efforts to influence the involvement of its target audience.

COGNITIVE PROCESSING OF COMMUNICATIONS

For many years, research on the previous response models centred around identifying relationships between specific controllable variables (such as source and message factors) and outcome or response variables (such as attention, comprehension, attitudes, and purchase intentions). This approach appeared limited since it did not explain what caused the reactions.[22] In response, researchers attempted to understand the nature of cognitive reactions to persuasive messages. This section reviews two widely accepted approaches for understanding consumers' cognitive processing of advertising messages.

THE COGNITIVE RESPONSE APPROACH

One of the most widely used methods for examining consumers' cognitive processing of advertising messages is assessment of their **cognitive responses**, the thoughts that occur to them while reading, viewing, and/or hearing a communication.[23] These thoughts are generally measured by having consumers write down or verbally report their reactions to a message. The assumption is that these thoughts reflect the recipient's cognitive processes or reactions and help shape ultimate acceptance or rejection of the message.

The cognitive response approach has been used in research by both academicians and advertising practitioners. Its focus has been to determine the types of responses evoked by an advertising message and how these responses relate to attitudes toward the ad, brand attitudes, and purchase intentions. Figure 4-4 depicts the three basic categories of cognitive responses researchers have identified—product/message, source-oriented, and ad execution thoughts—and how they may relate to attitudes and intentions.

Product/Message Thoughts The first category of thoughts comprises those directed at the product or service and/or the claims being made in the communication. Much attention has focused on two particular types of responses: counterarguments and support arguments.

Counterarguments are thoughts the recipient has that are opposed to the position taken in the message. For example, consider the ad for Ultra Tide shown in

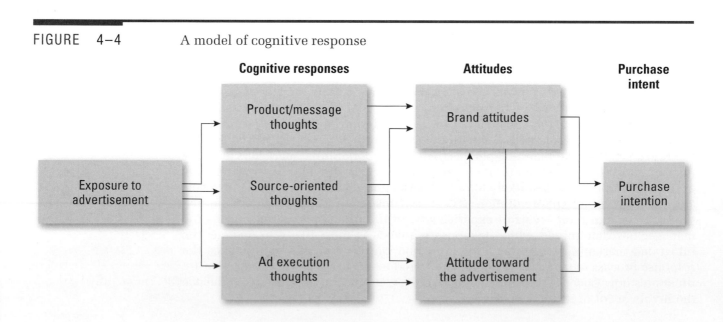

FIGURE   4–4   A model of cognitive response

Exhibit 4-11. A consumer may express disbelief or disapproval of a claim made in an ad—"I don't believe that any detergent could get that stain out!" Other consumers who see this ad may generate **support arguments**, or thoughts that affirm the claims made in the message—"Ultra Tide looks like a really good product—I think I'll try it."

The likelihood of counterarguing is greater when the message makes claims that oppose the receiver's beliefs. For example, a consumer viewing a commercial that attacks a favourite brand is likely to engage in counterarguing. Counterarguments relate negatively to message acceptance; the more the receiver counterargues, the less likely he or she is to accept the position advocated in the message.[24] Support arguments, on the other hand, relate positively to message acceptance. Thus, the marketer should develop ads or other promotional messages that minimize counterarguing and encourage support arguments.

Source-Oriented Thoughts A second category of cognitive responses is directed at the source of the communication. One of the most important types of responses in this category is **source derogations**, or negative thoughts about the spokesperson or organization making the claims. Such thoughts generally lead to a reduction in message acceptance. If consumers find a particular spokesperson annoying or untrustworthy, they are less likely to accept what this source has to say.

Source-related thoughts are not always negative. Receivers who react favourably to the source generate favourable thoughts, or **source bolsters**. In general, most advertisers attempt to hire spokespeople their target audience likes so as to carry this effect over to the message. (Considerations involved in choosing an appropriate source or spokesperson will be discussed in Chapter 7.) How might consumers react to the model in Exhibit 4-12?

Ad Execution Thoughts The third category of cognitive responses shown in Figure 4-4 consists of the individual's thoughts about the ad itself. Many of the thoughts receivers have when reading or viewing an ad do not concern the product and/or message claims directly. Rather, they are affective reactions representing the consumer's feelings toward the ad.[25] These thoughts may include reactions to ad execution factors such as the creativity of the ad, the quality of the visual effects, colours, and voice tones. **Ad execution-related thoughts** can be either favourable or unfavourable.[26] They are important because of their effect on attitudes toward the advertisement as well as the brand.

Attitude to Ad Consumers' affective reactions to ads are an effect of cognitive responses, something not included in the previous models. **Attitude toward the ad** (A → ad) represents the receivers' favourable or unfavourable feelings toward the ad.[27] Advertisers are interested in consumers' reactions to the ad because they know that affective reactions are an important determinant of advertising effectiveness, since these reactions

Exhibit 4-11 Consumers often generate support arguments in response to ads for quality products.

111

Exhibit 4-12 The source in this ad could elicit both types of source thoughts.

may be transferred to the brand itself or directly influence purchase intentions. One study found that people who enjoy a commercial are twice as likely as those who are neutral toward it to be convinced that the brand is the best.[28] Another study finds that those with more positive attitudes toward advertising in general result in stronger persuasion levels.[29]

Consumers' feelings about the ad may be just as important as their attitudes toward the brand (if not more so) in determining an ad's effectiveness.[30] The importance of affective reactions and feelings generated by the ad depend on several factors, among them the nature of the ad and the type of processing engaged in by the receiver.[31] Many advertisers now use emotional ads designed to evoke feelings and affective reactions as the basis of their creative strategy. The success of this strategy depends in part on the consumers' involvement with the brand and their likelihood of attending to and processing the message.

THE ELABORATION LIKELIHOOD MODEL

Differences in the ways consumers process and respond to persuasive messages are addressed in the simplified **elaboration likelihood model (ELM)** of persuasion, shown in Figure 4-5.[32] The ELM was devised by Richard Petty and John Cacioppo to explain the process by which persuasive communications (such as ads) lead to persuasion by influencing *attitudes.* According to this model, the attitude formation or change process depends on the amount and nature of *elaboration,* or processing, of relevant information that occurs in response to a persuasive message. High elaboration means the receiver engages in careful consideration, thinking, and evaluation of the information or arguments contained in the message. Low elaboration occurs when the receiver does not engage in active information processing or thinking but rather makes inferences about the position being advocated in the message on the basis of simple positive or negative cues.

112

FIGURE 4–5

Simplified
elaboration likelihood
model of persuasion

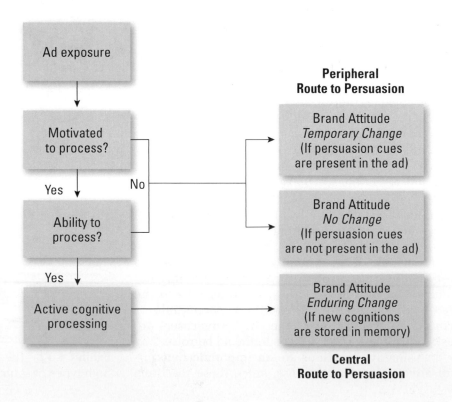

The ELM shows that elaboration likelihood is a function of two elements, motivation and ability to process the message. *Motivation* to process the message depends on such factors as involvement, personal relevance, and individuals' needs and arousal levels. *Ability* depends on the individual's knowledge, intellectual capacity, and opportunity to process the message.

Central Route   Under the **central route to persuasion**, the receiver is viewed as a very active, involved participant in the communication process who has high ability and motivation to attend, comprehend, and evaluate messages. When central processing of an advertising message occurs, the consumer pays close attention to message content and scrutinizes the message arguments. A high level of cognitive response activity or processing occurs, and the ad's ability to persuade the receiver depends primarily on the receiver's evaluation of the quality of the arguments presented. Predominantly favourable cognitive responses (support arguments and source bolsters) lead to favourable changes in cognitive structure, which lead to positive attitude change, or persuasion. Conversely, if the cognitive processing is predominantly unfavourable and results in counterarguments and/or source derogations, the changes in cognitive structure are unfavourable resulting in negative attitude change. Attitude change that occurs through central processing is relatively enduring and should resist subsequent efforts to change it.

Peripheral Route   Under the **peripheral route to persuasion**, the receiver is viewed as lacking the motivation or ability to process information and is not likely to engage in detailed cognitive processing. Rather than evaluating the information presented in the message, the receiver relies on peripheral cues that may be incidental to the main arguments. The receiver's reaction to the message depends on how he or she evaluates these peripheral cues.

The consumer may use several types of peripheral cues or cognitive shortcuts rather than carefully evaluating the message arguments presented in an advertisement.[33] Favourable attitudes may be formed if the endorser in the ad is viewed as attractive and/or likable, or if the consumer likes certain executional aspects of the ad such as the way it is made, the music, or the imagery. Notice how the ad in Exhibit 4-13 contains positive peripheral cues contained in the excellent visual imagery. These cues might help consumers form a positive attitude toward the brand even if they do not process the message portion of the ad.

Peripheral cues can also lead to rejection of a message. For example, ads that advocate extreme positions, use endorsers who are not well liked or have credibility problems, or are not executed well (such as low-budget ads for local retailers) may be rejected without any consideration of their information or message arguments. As shown in Figure 4-5, the ELM views attitudes resulting from peripheral processing as temporary. Therefore, favourable attitudes must be maintained by continual exposure to the peripheral cues, such as through repetitive advertising.

Exhibit 4–13   The colourful imagery of the spices in this ad acts as a peripheral cue.

113

Exhibit 4-14 Lancôme associates its brand with moisture.

Explanation for ELM One reason for explaining how the peripheral route to persuasion works lies in the idea of **classical conditioning**. Classical conditioning assumes that learning is an *associative process* with an already existing relationship between a stimulus and a response. This process is transferred to a **conditioned stimulus** that elicits a **conditioned response** resembling the original unconditioned reaction. Two factors are important for learning to occur through the associative process. The first is contiguity, which means the unconditioned stimulus and conditioned stimulus must be close in time and space. The other important principle is *repetition,* or the frequency of the association. The more often the unconditioned and conditioned stimuli occur together, the stronger the association between them will be.

Buyers can be conditioned to form favourable impressions and images of various brands through the associative process. Advertisers strive to associate their products and services with perceptions, images, and emotions known to evoke positive reactions from consumers. Many products are promoted through image advertising, in which the brand is shown with an unconditioned stimulus that elicits pleasant feelings. When the brand is presented simultaneously with this unconditioned stimulus, the brand itself becomes a conditioned stimulus that elicits the same favourable response. The ad for Lancôme in Exhibit 4-14 shows an application of this strategy. Notice how this ad associates Lancôme's moisture with the freshness of a rose.

Classical conditioning can also associate a product with a favourable emotional state. A study by Gerald Gorn used this approach to examine how background music in ads influences product choice.[34] He found that subjects were more likely to choose a product when it was presented against a background of music they liked rather than music they disliked. These results suggest the emotions generated by a commercial are important because they may become associated with the advertised product through classical conditioning. Kellaris and colleagues also showed that music that was congruent with the message enhanced both ad recall and recognition.[35]

Implications of the ELM The ELM has important implications for marketing communication since the most effective type of message depends on the route to persuasion the target audience follows. If the involvement level of the target audience is high, the message should contain strong arguments that are difficult for the receiver to refute or counterargue. If the involvement level of the target audience is low, peripheral cues such as music or images may be more important than detailed message arguments. Therefore, marketers of low-involvement products often rely on creative tactics that emphasize peripheral cues and use repetitive advertising to create and maintain favourable attitudes toward their brand.

An interesting test of the ELM showed that the effectiveness of a celebrity endorser in an ad depends on the receiver's involvement level.[36] When involvement was low, a celebrity endorser had a significant effect on attitudes. When the receiver's involvement was high, however, the use of a celebrity had no effect on brand attitudes; the quality of the arguments used in the ad was more important. The explanation given for these findings was that a celebrity may serve as a peripheral cue in the low-involvement situation, allowing the receiver to develop favourable attitudes based on feelings toward the source rather than engaging in extensive processing of the message. A highly involved consumer, however, engages in more detailed central processing of the message content. The quality of the message claims becomes more important than the identity of the endorser.

IMC PLANNING: RESPONSE MODEL FOR DECISION MAKING

In this final section we attempt to reconcile the models presented in this chapter by summarizing the academic perspective and by presenting the most relevant response model for managerial decision making. The first section concludes that traditional communication response models based on a hierarchy or adaptation of a hierarchy are limited in their ability to explain how advertising works. The subsequent section summarizes another part of the Rossiter and Percy perspective that is managerially oriented and will be used to set communication objectives and plan for creative messages in subsequent chapters.

DOES ADVERTISING WORK?

Vakratsas and Ambler reviewed more than 250 journal articles and books in an effort to better understand how advertising works.[37] They concluded that although hierarchy models have been actively employed for nearly 100 years, there is little support for the temporal sequence of the hierarchy of effects and that the models exclude product category and brand experiences. They identify three critical intermediate effects between advertising and purchase (Figure 4-6) of the consumers' response process. These include *cognition*, the "thinking" dimension of a person's response; *affect*, the "feeling" dimension; and *experience*, which is a feedback dimension based on the outcomes of product purchasing and usage.

The authors conclude that these three responses to advertising are mediated or filtered by factors such as motivation and ability to process information, which can radically alter or change the individual's response to advertising. They suggest that the effects of advertising should be evaluated using the cognition, affect, and experience dimensions, with some intermediate variables being more important than others depending on factors such as the product category, stage of the product life cycle, target audience, competition, and impact of other marketing-mix components.

Other researchers have been critical of the hierarchy models as well. For example, Hall argues that advertisers need to move away from explicit and implicit reliance on hierarchical models of advertising effects and develop models that place affect and experience at the centre of the advertising process.[38] The implication of these criticisms is that marketers should focus on cognition, affect, and experience as critical variables that advertising may influence. However, they should not assume a particular sequence of responses but, rather, engage in research and analysis to better understand how advertising and other forms of promotion may affect these intermediate variables in various product/market situations.

William Weilbacher has noted that marketing communications programs include more than just advertising.[39] Consumers are continually immersed in brand-sponsored communications, and he argues that hierarchy models must move

FIGURE 4–6

A framework for
studying how
advertising works

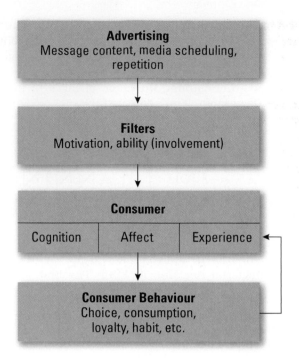

beyond just explaining the effects of advertising and consider how, and with what effects, consumers synthesize information from all the various integrated marketing communications activities for a brand. Others have been equally critical by offering their own interpretations to go beyond the idea of a hierarchy.[40]

Despite these concerns, many believe that hierarchical models are of value to advertising practice and research. For example, Thomas Barry contends that despite their limitations, hierarchical models do help predict behaviour. He notes that these models also provide insight into whether advertising strategies need to focus on impacting cognition, affect, and/or behaviour based on audience or segmentation experiences and that they provide valuable planning, training, and conceptual frameworks.[41]

Based on this theoretical debate regarding the exactness of how advertising works, we suggest a few conclusions that are relevant for managers in making advertising and promotion decisions. After all, academics will continue this investigation while managers still need to make decisions.

First, it appears that managers should consider and plan for both the cognitive and the affective responses of the receiver when the latter is processing advertising or any promotional message. Receivers typically have both cognitive and emotional reactions to the messages they see all around them every day.

Second, managers are undoubtedly concerned with the resulting effects of the advertising or promotional message for a time period after the receiver has received and processed the message. As suggested in many of the models, managers want to know if their messages are improving awareness or attitudes.

Finally, the primary characteristic that influences communication success appears to be the receiver's previous brand experience. This implies managers should be cognizant of to whom exactly they are directing their message. As discussed in Chapter 3, the manager needs a detailed profile of the target audience to have some understanding to gauge communication success. Thus, managers require a decision framework that addresses these points, which is the topic of the next section.

MANAGERIAL APPROACH

We introduced the Rossiter and Percy (R&P) perspective in Chapter 3 when identifying options for the target audience decision. This perspective suggests promotional planners initially consider the message as being directed to either customers purchasing their brand or non-customers who have not purchased their brand. This managerial view starts with the consumer and is based on the consumer's previous brand experience and degree of brand loyalty, two critical factors that influence how motivated or involved the audience would be when responding to promotional messages.

A continuation of the R&P perspective is a communication response model that takes a managerial view by identifying the responses in terms of the promotional manager's brand for any type of marketing communication decision. Figure 4-7 shows the initial processing stage, which highlights the immediate responses to any advertising message while receiving the ad exposure. This implies the psychological experiences that occur in the target audience's mind while watching a television commercial, for example. Communication effects refer to the lasting brand impressions that remain with the target audience after the target audience processes the message. This implies the target audience's memory of the brand that results after watching the television commercial. We now explore the planning implication of this perspective.

Processing of Messages   This notion of processing is consistent with all the features of the previous models discussed. After attending to the ad, the target audience may have low or high involvement in terms of how much thought regarding the brand's benefit claims is generated while receiving the message. For example, as the ELM indicated, highly involved target audiences are more likely to engage in active cognitive responses. In addition, affect, or emotional responses, will influence and be generated as a result of these cognitive responses. Furthermore, pleasant or unpleasant emotional responses may occur while attending to the execution

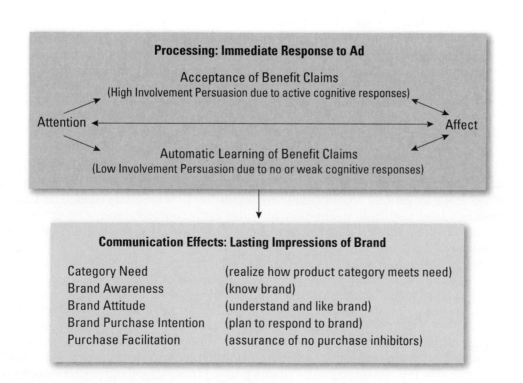

FIGURE   4–7

Planning for processing and communication effects

variables (e.g., music) of the message, and positive (or negative) emotional responses may focus greater (or less) attention to the message.

From an IMC planning perspective, managers need to design brand messages with the understanding of the target audience. For instance, to attract new customers, the manager may consider brand messages that will support high-involvement processing. And, as we will see in the media chapters and the chapters relating to other communication tools, the manager may consider more involving avenues for delivering the message.

Alternatively, companies often have programs to both attract and retain customers. This could require promotional planners to strategically evaluate the balance of their messages. Should messages that attempt to generate high involvement be primary or secondary in the overall message strategy? Analytical questions such as this emerge by considering the processing stage as a key precursor to planning for the communication effects stage.

Communication Effects of Messages Figure 4-7 also distinguishes the brand communication effects that are established more permanently in the target audience's memory. Overall, R&P summarize five **communication effects** for the target audience.

- *Category need:* Target audience's perception of requiring a specific product category to satisfy a particular need.
- *Brand awareness:* Target audience's ability to recognize and/or recall the brand within the product category in sufficient detail to make a purchase.
- *Brand attitude:* Target audience's overall evaluation of the brand in relation to its ability to satisfy the reason why they want it.
- *Brand purchase intention:* Target audience's self-instruction to respond (purchase; purchase-related action) to the brand.
- *Purchase facilitation:* Target audience's perception that a marketing factor could affect their purchase or use of the brand.

Three important planning implications are realized with the R&P model. First, there is an obvious and clear connection to the target audience's purchase of the promotional manager's particular brand. This is apparent with its reference to the brand in three communication effects. It is also seen in the connection to category need, which addresses the underlying reason why the target audience is motivated to buy the promotional manager's brand, and where the target audience understands the brand fits in the market in relation to other brands. Moreover, it is observed with the link to purchase facilitation, which highlights the importance of communicating information to make sure the promotional manager's brand is purchased by the target audience.

Second, the R&P model uses brand attitude as a central communication effect. Note that the other models viewed the entire process (i.e., cognition, affect, behaviour) as reflecting an attitude, and that some models argued consumers experienced various steps in various orders depending upon the purchase situation. The target audience's brand attitude evaluation includes both cognitive and affective components, acknowledging that each aspect is relevant for planning for all purchase situations.

Third, the R&P model can be applied for all aspects of an IMC program. It can guide individual television ads, as previously suggested, and it can be used for any ad in any media environment. For example, promotional planners can consider this model for print ads or video-type ads placed on the Internet. Moreover, the model can be used for planning any IMC tool. In another direction, the communication effects can be used to assess the target audience's reaction to an overall advertising campaign consisting of many different types of media. An entire and comprehensive IMC program can be planned using these target audience responses.

And, finally, planners can use the same effects whether planning for one or multiple target audiences.

The R&P model and some of the other communication response models will be revisited in the next chapter. Promotional planners use a communication response model to determine the communication objectives for advertising and other promotional tools. It is important to base marketing communication decisions on a model and translate them into specific objectives since promotional planners need clear guidance for the remaining marketing communication decisions.

CHAPTER OBJECTIVES AND SUMMARY

1 To understand the basic elements of the communication process and the role of marketing communication.

The function of all elements of the promotional mix is to communicate, so promotional planners must understand the communication process. This process can be very complex; successful marketing communication depends on a number of factors, including the nature of the message, the audience's interpretation of it, and the environment in which it is received. For effective communication to occur, the sender must encode a message in such a way that it will be decoded by the receiver in the intended manner. Feedback from the receiver helps the sender determine whether proper decoding has occurred or whether noise has interfered with the communication process.

2 To summarize traditional communication response models and alternative response hierarchies.

Promotional planning begins with the receiver or target audience, as marketers must understand how the audience is likely to respond to sources of communication or types of messages. Traditional response models provide an initial understanding of this process; however limitations of these models led to more comprehensive approaches. Alternative response hierarchies imply modification of the traditional models due to the target audience's involvement and perceived product differentiation. Different orderings of the traditional response hierarchy include the standard learning, dissonance/attribution, and low-involvement models. The alternative response hierarchy postulated different ordering of cognition, affect, and behaviour depending upon the involvement and differentiation.

3 To analyze the response processes of receivers of marketing communication through two models of cognitive processing.

The cognitive processing of communication revealed two models: the cognitive response approach and the elaboration likelihood model. The former examines the thoughts evoked by a message in terms of product/message thoughts, source-oriented thoughts, and ad execution thoughts and how they shape the receiver's ultimate acceptance or rejection of the communication by influencing brand attitude and attitude to the ad. The elaboration likelihood model of attitude formation and change recognizes two forms of message processing, the central and peripheral routes to persuasion, which are a function of the receiver's motivation and ability to process a message. The model postulates that each route leads to varying degrees of attitude change.

4 To summarize an integrative communication response model from a theoretical and managerial perspective.

Theoretical research concludes that there are three critical intermediate effects between advertising and purchase including cognition, affect, and experience. Those responsible for planning the IMC program should learn as much as possible about their target audience and how it may respond to advertising and other forms of marketing communications. A managerial view of the response process provides direction for understanding how promotional planners should determine their brands' communication strategies. The model suggests both cognitive and emotional processing responses are critical during the initial stages of receiving the message, and the lasting brand communication effects can be construed along a more managerial friendly approach.

KEY TERMS

ad execution-related thoughts, *111*
AIDA model, *103*
attitude toward the ad, *111*
central route to persuasion, *113*
channel, *99*
classical conditioning, *114*
cognitive responses, *110*
communication, *96*
communication effects, *118*

conditioned response, *114*
conditioned stimulus, *114*
counterarguments, *110*
decoding, *100*
dissonance/attribution model, *106*
elaboration likelihood model (ELM), *112*
encoding, *97*
feedback, *101*
field of experience, *100*

hierarchy of effects model, *104*
information processing model, *104*
innovation adoption model, *104*
low-involvement hierarchy, *108*
mass media, *100*
message, *97*
noise, *101*

peripheral route to persuasion, *113*
receiver, *100*
response, *101*
semiotics, *97*
source, *96*
source bolsters, *111*
source derogations, *111*
standard learning model, *106*
support arguments, *111*

DISCUSSION QUESTIONS

1. Discuss the various elements of the communications process. Find an example of an advertising campaign being used by a company and analyze this campaign in terms of these elements of the communications model.

2. Discuss how semiotics can be of value to the field of integrated marketing communications. Select a marketing stimulus such as an advertisement, package, or other relevant marketing symbol and conduct a semiotic analysis of it.

3. Explain why the four response models of Figure 4-2 are limited in planning for an IMC campaign.

4. How do the response models in Chapter 4 relate to the consumer decision-making process described in Chapter 3?

5. What are the key differences between traditional response models and alternative response hierarchies?

6. Assume that you are the marketing communications manager for a brand of paper towels. Discuss how the low-involvement hierarchy could be of value in developing an advertising and promotion strategy for this brand.

7. Find an example of a print ad and evaluate it using the cognitive response model shown in Figure 4-4. Identify the specific types of cognitive responses that the ad might elicit from consumers and discuss why they might occur.

8. Explain what is meant by a central versus peripheral route to persuasion and the factors that would determine when each might be used by consumers in response to an advertisement.

9. Select an ad you think would be processed by a central route to persuasion and one where you think peripheral processing would occur. Show the ads to several people and ask them to write down the thoughts they have about each ad. Analyze their thoughts using the cognitive response categories discussed in the chapter.

10. Why do cognition and affect components for both processing and communication effects exist in the R&P model?

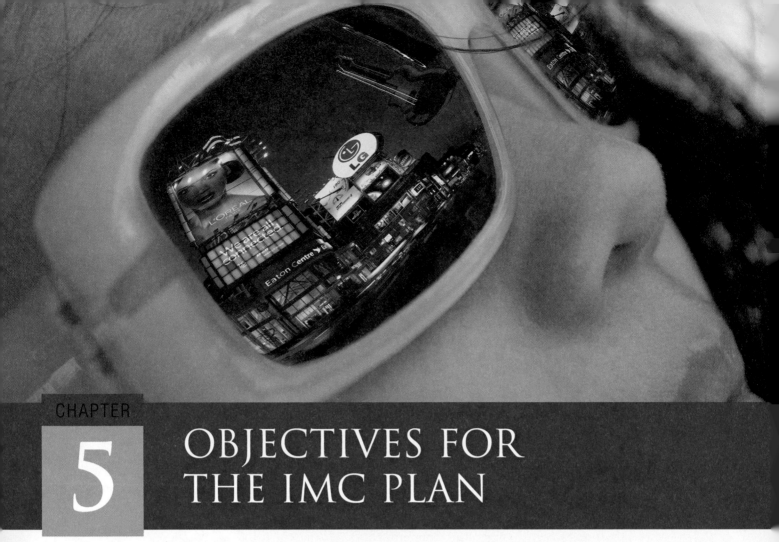

OBJECTIVES FOR
THE IMC PLAN

■ CHAPTER OBJECTIVES

1 To recognize the value of setting specific objectives for advertising and promotion.

2 To know the differences among marketing, behavioural, and communication objectives and the issues regarding the use of each.

3 To know the historical approaches for setting communication objectives for advertising.

4 To understand a comprehensive framework for setting communication and behavioural objectives for all aspects of the IMC plan.

DAVID SUZUKI LEADS US WITH POWERWISE

"David Suzuki?" And so starts one of the ads sponsored by PowerWise, the brand behind the provincial government's attempt to encourage the people of Ontario to consume less electricity. In this particular execution, David explains to the homeowner, Bob, that his basement beer fridge uses lots of electricity that costs about $150 per year to operate. Bob quickly concludes that saving electricity means more beer and he humorously dashes throughout the house shutting off the TV, radio, and hair dryer (all, of course, while his family members are using the items). This "Basement" ad and many other ads ended with the message "You Have the Power" and included a visual of the website address (Powerwise.ca).

Other spots with David Suzuki reflected different areas where electricity consumption could be reduced. In "Penguin," Suzuki suggests to the homeowner—surrounded by penguins in his cold house—that if we all increased our air conditioning temperature by one degree we could power 38,000 homes. In "Basketball," Suzuki tosses a basketball and pokes his head through a hole he saws in the homeowner's kitchen wall, encouraging the couple to use caulking to minimize the cold air coming through the tiny holes around the house that add up to a large hole the size of a basketball.

Other executions looked at the social acceptance of using clotheslines instead of dryers, the influence children have to get their parents to conserve, the effects of moving to CFC light bulbs, and the need for consumers to visit the website. In another direction, some messages included the web address for the Ontario Power Authority (everykilowatt counts.ca) to support their campaign as well.

A number of website video illustrations by David Suzuki clearly taught consumers how to use less electricity or showed them how to change their behaviour for less electricity consumption. The website also allowed consumers to join and submit their own electricity saving tip, and provided extensive resources so that consumers could make necessary adaptations.

Commenting on the campaign, two advertising executives agreed that David Suzuki was the perfect spokesperson for the initiative given his lifetime experiences and achievements, and that the ads portrayed him as very human and approachable. They did have concerns about the TV ad regarding how consumers could make a clear conclusion about conserving electricity and whether it supported sufficient consumer action to take the next step, such as visiting the website. Finally, the "You Have the Power" message implied that consumers had the power to save electricity, but unfortunately implied that the people of Ontario had limitless electrical power.

Sources: Jonathan Paul, "PowerWise: Amp Up the Action," *Strategy*, May 2009, p. 20; Powerwise.ca/features/video. Chris Powell, "Camwest Moves Marketing Ventures into Broadcast Sales," *Marketing Magazine*, October 23, 2008.

QUESTION:

1. Do you agree with the analysis of the campaign from the experts?

Complex marketing situations, conflicting perspectives regarding what advertising and other promotional mix elements are expected to accomplish, and uncertainty over resources make the setting of marketing communication objectives "a job of creating order out of chaos."[1] While the task of setting objectives can be complex and difficult, it must be done properly, because specific goals and objectives are the foundation on which all marketing communication decisions are made and provide a standard against which performance can be measured.

This chapter examines the purpose of objectives and the role they play in guiding the development, implementation, and evaluation of an IMC program. First, we distinguish between marketing, behavioural, and communication objectives. Then we consider the approaches of setting objectives for marketing communication based on the response models discussed in Chapter 4. We then present a comprehensive approach for setting behavioural and communication objectives for each element of the IMC plan and for the overall IMC plan that we will be consistently referring to in the remaining parts of the book.

OBJECTIVE SETTING

Setting specific objectives should be an integral part of the planning process. However, many companies either fail to use specific marketing communication objectives or set ones that are inadequate for guiding the development of the promotional plan or measuring its effectiveness. This section discusses the value of objectives and distinguishes between marketing, behavioural, and communication objectives for optimal IMC planning.

VALUE OF OBJECTIVES

Perhaps one reason why many companies fail to set specific objectives for their integrated marketing communications programs is that they don't recognize the value of doing so. Advertising and promotional objectives are needed for several reasons, including the functions they serve in communications, planning and decision making, and measurement and evaluation of results.

Communications Specific objectives for the IMC program facilitate coordination of the groups working on the campaign. Many people are involved in the planning and development of an IMC program including client personnel and contracted agencies. The program must be coordinated within the company, inside the ad agency, and between the two. Any other parties involved, such as public relations and/or sales promotion firms, research specialists, or media buying services, must know what the company hopes to accomplish through its marketing communication program. Potential problems can be avoided if all parties have written approved objectives to guide their actions and serve as a common base for discussing issues related to the promotional program. For example, the ad and Ford's involvement with the cause shown in Exhibit 5-1 was dependent upon all participants understanding Ford's objectives.

Planning and Decision Making Specific promotional objectives also guide development of the integrated marketing communications plan. All phases of a firm's promotional strategy should be based on the established objectives, including budgeting, creative, and media decisions as well as supportive programs such as direct marketing, public relations/publicity, sales promotion, and/or reseller support. Meaningful objectives can also be a useful guide for decision making. Promotional planners are often faced with a number of strategic and tactical options in terms of choosing creative options, selecting media, and allocating the budget among various elements of the promotional mix. Choices should be made based on how well a particular strategy matches the firm's promotional objectives.

Measurement and Evaluation of Results An important reason for setting specific objectives is that they provide a benchmark against which the success or failure of the promotional campaign can be measured. Without specific objectives, it is extremely difficult to determine what the firm's advertising and promotion efforts accomplished. One characteristic of good objectives is that they are measurable; they specify a method and criteria for determining how well the promotional program is working. By setting specific and meaningful objectives, the promotional planner provides measures that can be used to evaluate the effectiveness of the marketing communications program. Most organizations are concerned about the return on their promotional investment, and comparing actual performance against measurable objectives is the best way to determine whether the return justifies the expense.

MARKETING OBJECTIVES

Marketing objectives are generally stated in the firm's marketing plan and are statements of what is to be accomplished by the overall marketing program within a given time period. Marketing objectives are usually defined in terms of specific,

Exhibit 5-1 The objective of this ad is to demonstrate Ford's support for a cause.

TIED TO THE CAUSE

measurable outcomes such as sales volume, market share, profit, or return on investment. Good marketing objectives are quantifiable; they delineate the target market and note the time frame for accomplishing the goal (often one year). For example, a copy-machine company may have as its marketing objective "to increase sales by 10 percent in the small-business segment of the market during the next 12 months." To be effective, objectives must also be realistic and attainable.

The choice of the type of marketing objective is likely a function of market conditions. A company with a very high market share may seek to increase its sales volume by stimulating growth in the product category. It might accomplish this by increasing consumption by current users or encouraging nonusers to buy the product. A firm in a fast-growing market may have market share as its marketing objective since this reflects that it is growing more quickly than its direct competitors. In mature markets with limited growth, firms tend to focus on profit as the key marketing objective. Finally, a firm that faces unique consumer preferences across various geographic markets (i.e., Ontario versus Quebec) may in fact have a unique marketing objective for each region.

Once the marketing communication manager has reviewed the marketing plan, he or she should understand the marketing objectives of the marketing program, how it intends to get there, and the role advertising and promotion will play. Marketing goals defined in terms of sales, profit, or market share increases are usually not appropriate promotional objectives. They are objectives for the entire marketing program, and achieving them depends on the proper coordination and execution of all the marketing mix elements, including not just promotion but also product planning and production, pricing, and distribution. Alternatively, many promotional

Exhibit 5-2 Shell's objectives for this ad may be broader than an increase in sales.

The distinction between repeat purchase versus trial purchase behaviour is critical as it provides direction for the communication objectives which subsequently provide guidance for message development. For example, increasing the repeat purchasing rate of brand loyals might have a message reminding these customers of the previous enjoyable consumption experiences, while a message to encourage trial from other brand switchers might require a comparative message to these non-customers showing the benefits of the competing brands. In both of these cases, the communication objective is substantially different and is entirely derived from the target audience and the behavioural objective.

COMMUNICATION OBJECTIVES

Communication objectives are statements of what the IMC tools will accomplish, and are usually based on one or more of the consumer response models discussed in Chapter 4. We can speak of communication objectives on three levels depending upon the decision at hand. There are communication objectives for the overall IMC plan. We can also speak of communication objectives for individual IMC tools (i.e., advertising). Often, as was shown in Chapter 1, these communication objectives are referred to as objectives for the particular tool (i.e., advertising objectives). When working in this field, marketers may use either of these terms depending upon their background or company practices. Finally, we can also use the concept of communication objectives for individual elements of a communication tool. When we design an individual print ad, we want to make sure it achieves the communication objectives we set for it. For example, Shell had a very specific objective for the ad shown in Exhibit 5-2, which is quite unique.

Irrespective of whether we are speaking of communication objectives for the IMC plan, a particular tool, or a specific ad, the communication objectives should be based on the particular communication tasks required to deliver the appropriate messages to the specific target audience at a relevant point within the target audience's purchase decision-making process and consumption experience.

Managers must be able to translate a general marketing objective into a behavioural objective and specific communication objectives. Some guidance in doing this may be available from the situation analysis of the marketing plan, which includes the following:

- The market segments the firm wants to target and the target audiences (customer status, demographics, psychographics, and purchase motives) that the firm wishes to communicate with.
- The product's main features, attributes, benefits, uses, and applications.
- The company's and competitors' brands (sales and market share in various segments, market positioning, competitive strategies, promotional expenditures, creative and media strategies, and tactics).

After reviewing all the information, the promotional planner should see how integrated marketing communication fits into the marketing program and what the firm hopes to achieve through advertising and other promotional elements. The importance of setting communication objectives for a promotional plan is seen in Dove's famous Campaign for Real Beauty. Clearly the whole IMC campaign had certain esteem objectives. The advertising contributed to these IMC objectives, but also had more specific emotional effects. Finally, the sponsorship activities achieved its own behavioural change objective.

FROM COMMUNICATION RESPONSE MODELS TO COMMUNICATION OBJECTIVES

Over the years, a number of methods have been developed for deciding upon communication objectives for advertising, related tools, and complete IMC plans. We review two approaches from a historical perspective in this section. We begin with the DAGMAR model, which provided guidance for setting advertising objectives. Next, we consider Lavidge and Steiner's hierarchy of effects model discussed in Chapter 4.

DEFINING ADVERTISING GOALS FOR MEASURED RESULTS

In 1961, Russell Colley prepared a report for the Association of National Advertisers titled Defining Advertising Goals for Measured Advertising Results—**DAGMAR**,[5] a model for setting advertising objectives and measuring the results of an ad campaign. The major contribution of the DAGMAR model is its conclusion that communication effects are the logical basis for advertising goals and objectives against which success or failure should be measured.

Under the DAGMAR approach, an advertising goal involves a communication task that is specific and measurable. A **communication task**, as opposed to a marketing task, can be performed by, and attributed to, advertising rather than to a combination of several marketing factors. Colley proposed that the communication task be based on a hierarchical model of the communication process with four stages:

- Awareness—making the consumer aware of the existence of the brand or company.
- Comprehension—developing an understanding of what the product is and what it will do for the consumer.
- Conviction—developing a mental disposition in the consumer to buy the product.
- Action—getting the consumer to purchase the product.

DAGMAR emphasized the value of using communication-based rather than sales-based objectives to measure advertising effectiveness and encouraged the measurement of stages in the response hierarchy to assess a campaign's impact. Colley's work improved the advertising and promotional planning process by providing a better understanding of the goals and objectives toward which planners' efforts should be directed. Many promotional planners use the general idea of this model as a basis for setting objectives and assessing the effectiveness of their promotional campaigns.

A second major contribution of DAGMAR to the advertising planning process was its definition of what constitutes a good objective. Colley argued that advertising objectives should specify a target audience, be stated in terms of concrete and measurable communication tasks, indicate a benchmark starting point and the degree of change sought, and specify a time period for accomplishing the objective(s).

Target Audience An important characteristic of good objectives is a well-defined target audience. The primary target audience for a company's product or service is described in the situation analysis. It may be based on descriptive variables such as geography, demographics, and psychographics (on which advertising media selection decisions are based) as well as on behavioural variables such as customer status (i.e., brand-loyal users), usage rate, or benefits sought. This step is critical since the communication effect has to be interpreted from the perspective of the intended receiver.

Concrete, Measurable Tasks The communication task specified in the objective should be a precise statement of what appeal or message the advertiser wants to communicate to the target audience. Advertisers generally use a copy platform to describe their basic message that should be specific and clear enough to guide the creative specialists who develop the advertising message. According to DAGMAR, the objective must also be measurable to determine whether the intended message has been communicated properly.

Benchmark and Degree of Change Sought To set objectives, one must know the target audience's present status concerning response hierarchy variables (e.g., awareness) and then determine the degree to which consumers must be changed by the advertising campaign. Determining the target audience's present position regarding the response stages requires **benchmark measures**. Often a marketing research study must be conducted to determine prevailing levels of the response hierarchy. In the case of a new product or service, the starting conditions are generally at or near zero for all the variables, so no initial research is needed. Exhibit 5-3 shows an ad for Herbal Essences that is probably attempting to establish a positive attitude toward the brand's new Hydralicious formulation.

Establishing benchmark measures gives the promotional planner a basis for determining what communication tasks need to be accomplished and for specifying particular objectives. For example, a preliminary study for a brand may reveal that awareness is high but consumer perceptions and attitudes are negative. The objective for the advertising campaign must then be to change the target audience's perceptions of and attitudes toward the brand.

Quantitative benchmarks not only are valuable in establishing communications goals and objectives but also are essential for determining campaign success. Objectives provide the standard against which the success or failure of a campaign is measured. An ad campaign that results in a 90-percent awareness level for a brand among its target audience cannot really be judged effective unless one knows what percentage of the consumers were aware of the brand before the campaign began. A 70-percent pre-campaign awareness level would lead to a different interpretation of the campaign's success than would a 30-percent level.

Specified Time Period A final consideration in setting advertising objectives is specifying the time period in which they must be accomplished. Appropriate time periods can range from a few days to a year or more. Most ad campaigns specify time periods from a few months to a year, depending on the situation facing the advertiser and the type of response being sought. For example, awareness levels for a brand can be created

130

Exhibit 5-3 A new Herbal Essences shampoo colourfully informs consumers of its moisturizing feature.

How Green Was My Advertising?

Research by environmental marketing firm TerraChoice finds that only 2 percent of consumer products make legitimate environmental claims. This leading consulting organization suggests that the majority commit at least one of the "seven sins of greenwashing" by misleading consumers about the environmental benefits of the brand or the activities of the company. The research sample included big box stores carrying four product categories (toys, baby, cosmetic, cleaning) representing a total of 2,219 "green" products in the U.S., Canada, U.K., and Australia.

These results came shortly after Advertising Standards Canada's advisory that "green" claims should be consistent with its guidelines for accuracy and clarity for any and all product claims. For example, in applying this part of the code, the advisory identifies key guideline questions such as the following: Does the environmental benefit claimed for the product appear to be supported by science-based evidence? Echoing this concern are the results of a study by BrandSpark that found 63 percent of consumers are trying to buy products that are as natural as possible and 51 percent are willing to pay more for products that are environmentally friendly. And, notably, 83 percent agree that some companies are exploiting environmentally friendly claims for marketing purposes.

Despite this challenge, commentators on the subject believe that marketers can and should place emphasis on convincing consumers to buy smarter, rather than simply more. One advertising firm, Change, sees green messages as critical for brands: "Our entire pitch at Change is that green is a brand differentiator and an advantage over your competitors."

And firms appear to be listening to this message— like Walmart: "We aren't positioning ourself as scientific experts, what we're doing is making it easier for consumers to find those products that have been third-party certified," commented a spokesperson. To execute these programs, Walmart used a variety of marketing communication tools including in-store signage, flyers, demonstrations, and some mass media. Some other firms have also moved to the "green side":

- Lavo's La Parisienne brand of coldwater detergent used four TV commercials to communicate the benefits of its biodegradable, phosphate-free cleaning product.
- Toyota Canada considers the environmental impact of its product from conception to disposal and communicates its activities with advertising, supporting it with the "Make Things Better" positioning.
- Canada's largest banks established the RBC Water Project, a 10-year, $50 million program for water conservation, protection, and accessibility. Extensive print and TV ads along with in-branch signage communicate RBC's commitment.

Sources: Matt Semansky, "An Inconvenient Paradox," *Marketing Magazine*, April 20, 2009; Rebecca Harris et al., "Green Leaders," *Marketing Magazine*, April 20, 2009; Kristin Laird, "Just 2% of Green Claims Completely Legitimate: Study," *Marketing Magazine*, April 17, 2009; "Less Plastic, More Green," *Marketing Magazine*, February 23, 2009; Brian Dunn, "La Parisienne Touts Green Washing," *Marketing Magazine*, March 24, 2009; Kristin Laird, "Wal-Mart Promotes Earth Month," *Marketing Magazine*, April 13, 2009.

Question:

1. How can advertisers persuade consumers to spend more for products that are less harmful to the environment?

---

or increased fairly quickly through an intensive media schedule of widespread, repetitive advertising to the target audience. Repositioning of a product requires a change in consumers' perceptions and takes much more time. IMC Perspective 5-2 highlights the challenges of getting consumers to accept "green" advertising claims.

COMPREHENSIVE RESPONSE MODEL APPLICATIONS

DAGMAR inspired more involved or comprehensive response models for setting communication objectives. Many in advertising prefer the Lavidge and Steiner hierarchy of effects model, as it is more specific and provides a better way to establish and measure results.[6] This particular hierarchical model has been used as a basis for analyzing the communication response processes of consumers and has been the foremost application for setting communication objectives for many years.

Figure 5-2 shows the steps in the Lavidge and Steiner hierarchy of effects model as the consumer moves from awareness to purchase, along with examples of types of promotion or advertising relevant to each step. Recall from Chapter 4 that consumers pass through three successive stages: cognitive, affective, and behavioural. As consumers proceed through the three stages, they move closer to making a purchase. Consumers are not expected to respond immediately; rather, advertisers realize they must provide relevant information and create favourable predispositions toward the brand before purchase behaviour will occur. For example, the ad for Philips in Exhibit 5-4 is designed to inform consumers of the company's focus on technology, which makes sense and is simple. While there is no call for immediate action, the ad creates favourable impressions about the company by creating a distinct image. Consumers will consider this image when they enter the market for products in this category.

Setting communication objectives with a model like this is similar to the way a pyramid is built, by first accomplishing lower-level objectives such as awareness and knowledge or comprehension.[7] Subsequent tasks involve moving consumers who are aware of or knowledgeable about the product or service to higher levels in the pyramid (Figure 5-3). The initial stages, at the base of the pyramid, are easier to accomplish than those toward the top, such as trial and repurchase or regular

FIGURE 5–2

132

Communication effects hierarchy

Related behavioural dimensions	Movement toward purchase	Example of types of promotion or advertising relevant to various steps
Conative The realm of motives. Ads stimulate or direct desires.	Purchase	Point-of-purchase Retail store ads Deals "Last-chance" offers Price appeals Testimonials
	Conviction	
Affective The realm of emotions. Ads change attitudes and feelings.	Preference	Competitive ads Argumentative copy
	Liking	"Image" copy Status, glamour appeals
Cognitive The realm of thoughts. Ads provide information and facts.	Knowledge	Announcements Descriptive copy Classified ads Slogans Jingles Skywriting
	Awareness	Teaser campaigns

use. Thus, the percentage of prospective customers will decline as they move up the pyramid. Figure 5-4 shows how a company introducing a new brand of shampoo targeted at 18- to 34-year-old females might set its IMC objectives using the communications effects pyramid.

The communication effects pyramid can also be used to determine promotional objectives for an established brand. The promotional planner must determine where the target audience lies with respect to the various blocks in the pyramid. If awareness levels for a brand and knowledge of its features and benefits are low, the communication objective should be to increase them. If these blocks of the pyramid are already in place, but liking or preference is low, the advertising goal may be to change the target audience's image of the brand and move consumers through to purchase.

Even though comprehensive response models have been used to set communication objectives for many years, research shows that its acceptance has been limited over time. A 1969 study showed that most advertising agencies did not state appropriate objectives for determining advertising success.[8] Another more recent study found that most advertisers in their sample did not set concrete advertising objectives, specify objective tasks, measure results in terms of stages of a hierarchy of effects, or match objectives to evaluation measures.[9] The authors concluded: "Advertising practitioners have only partially adopted the concepts and standards of objective setting and evaluation set forth 25 years ago."[10] Finally, another recent study measured the attitudes of chairs, presidents, and other senior

Exhibit 5-4 Philips creates an image for its products.

© 2005 Philips Electronics North America Corporation.

Things start uncomplicated. Why change them?

Life is complicated enough. Technology shouldn't add to the problem. So Philips is committed to making technology that makes sense. Technology that's as simple as the box it comes in. Technology that's easy to use. Technology designed around the way you live and work. In other words, technology that's pure simplicity.

Join us on our journey at www.philips.com/simplicity

PHILIPS
sense and simplicity

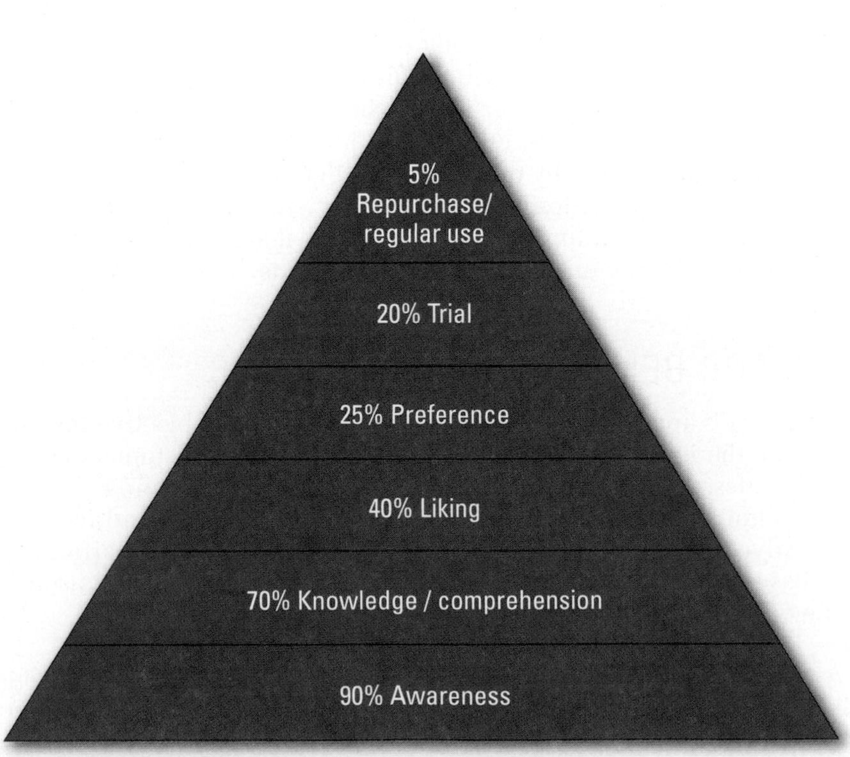

FIGURE 5–3

Communication effects pyramid

5% Repurchase/ regular use

20% Trial

25% Preference

40% Liking

70% Knowledge / comprehension

90% Awareness

FIGURE 5–4

Setting objectives
using the
communications
effects pyramid

Product: Backstage Shampoo

Time period: Six months

Objective 1: Create awareness among 90 percent of target audience. Use repetitive advertising in newspapers, magazines, TV and radio programs. Simple message.

Objective 2: Create interest in the brand among 70 percent of target audience. Communicate information about the features and benefits of the brand—i.e., that it contains no soap and improves the texture of the hair.

Objective 3: Create positive feelings about the brand among 40 percent and preference among 25 percent of the target audience. Create favourable attitudes by conveying information, promotions, sampling, etc.

Objective 4: Obtain trial among 20 percent of the target audience. Use sampling and cents-off coupons along with advertising and promotions.

Objective 5: Develop and maintain regular use of Backstage Shampoo among 5 percent of the target audience. Use continued reinforcement advertising, fewer coupons and promotions.

managers of business-to-business advertising companies; more than half of the 427 respondents said they did not know whether their advertising was working and fewer than 10 percent thought it was working well.[11] Cleary, the evidence suggests a newer perspective with a stronger managerial point of view for enhanced adoption.

SETTING IMC OBJECTIVES

We now turn to the Rossiter and Percy (R&P) perspective, which promotional planners should consider when setting behavioural and communication objectives. We introduced their ideas in Chapter 3 when discussing the guidelines for target audience identification and selection, and in Chapter 4 when summarizing communication response models. We include the R&P perspective here since it attempts to resolve the limitations of other approaches for objective setting and provides guidelines for creative tactics (i.e., Chapter 8). The R&P perspective has three distinguishing characteristics. First, it provides guidelines for behavioural objectives that are not specified completely in other approaches. This step is critical for linking a marketing objective (i.e., sales) to communication objectives. Second, it is consistent with the DAGMAR model by making a direct connection between the purchase decision and the communication task required for each target audience. Finally, it provides guidelines for communication objectives that are more managerially useful that do not completely rely on a set hierarchy of effects.

OPTIONS FOR BEHAVIOURAL OBJECTIVES

A key part of R&P's approach is to have a clear behavioural objective for each target audience since the individual purchasing behaviour of all customers adds up to a firm's overall sales. As suggested earlier, the link between marketing objectives (i.e., sales) and communication objectives (i.e., attitude toward the brand) is behavioural objectives. Advertising and promotion can focus on influencing a particular form of behaviour based on the nature of the advertising message or IMC tool used. We now discuss the options a manager has for behavioural objectives.

Trial A **brand trial purchase** is defined as a consumer's first purchase of a brand. For example, the purchase of most everyday products (e.g., soft drink or snack food) occurred many years ago and it is probably difficult to remember when one made their first purchase. However, these firms continue to have a **brand trial objective** to some degree as consumers enter the market when they attain a certain age or have income (i.e., allowance from parents). In fact, a brand trial objective is a behavioural objective for almost all firms, but it is not necessarily the primary behavioural objective for all campaigns or all communication tools. Brand trial also emerges once again for brand extensions.

Alternatively, it is quite unlikely that consumers continue to purchase the same brand of soft drink as the first trial purchase. In fact, many people consume more than one brand of soft drink, and for whatever reason stop purchasing their initial brand. Many brand managers are faced with this dilemma of trying to re-capture past customers who have not purchased the brand for a period of time (e.g., perhaps a year). The manager of such a brand would like these past customers to have a new trial experience of the brand. Thus, a **brand re-trial purchase** is defined as a consumer's first purchase of a brand after some time delay. The length of the delay to focus on when setting a **brand re-trial objective** is a decision the promotion manager makes. It depends upon the purchase frequency of the product, among other factors observed from the situation analysis.

A manager may plan for a brand trial or brand re-trial objective when consumers are purchasing another brand. A **brand-switching purchase** is defined as a consumer's purchase toward a brand from some other competing brand. A brand-switching purchase occurs whereby the consumer makes a re-trial purchase of a brand and leaves the new favourite. A brand-switching purchase also occurs when the consumer makes a trial purchase of a brand from a competing brand. Thus, brand trial or brand re-trial objectives are also known as **brand-switching objectives**.

Now let's put the trial purchase in another perspective: consider the purchase of a smart phone, which many young adults currently own. The smart phone is a different kind of product and likely a somewhat involved purchase for many consumers. Despite this, phone companies and service providers had trial objectives as they attempted to attract consumers who did not own such technology. While this is obviously a brand trial purchase, it is also something broader. A **category trial purchase** is defined as a consumer's first purchase in a product category that the consumer has not purchased in previously. Marketers of new products, like the smart phone, have a dual challenge of attaining both **category trial objectives** and brand trial objectives.

Brand trial is also possible in situations where a "purchase" does not occur. Each year, Canadian Blood Services recruits new donors, people who have never given blood. Its latest campaign tried to move the number of new donors from 85,000 to 90,000 with the message, "What If You Needed Blood?" The approach tried to affect the complacency people generally have with giving blood by getting them to think that at some point in their life they may in fact need blood and should be part of the solution.[12]

Repeat Purchase   In the age of relationship marketing and a focus on customer retention, this form of purchase behaviour is most critical. A **repeat purchase** is defined as a consumer's continued purchase of a brand within a specified time period. Again, the time factor is at the discretion of the marketer, and once again it is contingent upon purchase frequency of the product or other factors derived from the situation analysis.

Firms can have a **repeat-purchase objective** in many situations. As noted above, marketers desire to have a stable core of customers that remain loyal to the brand. Many firms communicate with these consumers to maintain their positive attitude toward the brand. For example, some argue that most of Coca-Cola's advertising and promotions is directed toward its repeat customers. In many product categories, a group of consumers habitually consume two or three brands continuously. For instance, of 15 purchases, 10 consecutive purchases might be of the brand with the remaining five purchases spread across two other brands. This is another situation where a marketer may emphasize a repeat-purchase objective in its communication plan. While this type of consumer does not purchase the brand for every single occasion, the consumer is a consistent contributor to the firm's sales and a marketer would want to communicate appropriately to repeat purchasers to ensure future sales.

The repeat-purchase objective is pervasive for most organizations. Thus, we identify three alternatives to guide managers in setting their behavioural objectives for IMC: how often to purchase, how much to purchase, and when to purchase.

The first alternative concerns the rate, or how often to purchase the brand. This implies that a marketer may set an objective pertaining to consumers purchasing its brand every week instead of every two weeks. This example shows an option where a manager may want to increase the rate of purchase from a "half" product per week to "one" product per week. A second managerial option is to maintain the rate of purchase. While this is a more conservative objective, it is still a viable option in very competitive environments. Finally, a manager may want to decrease the rate of purchase. This option may be viable in unique situations of high demand or with products that have potentially negative consequences (i.e., alcohol).

The amount or how much to purchase each occasion is the second alternative. As this alternative implies, a marketer may set an objective where consumers purchase two products per occasion versus one per occasion. As above, this option is to increase the amount per occasion, but a marketer could still evaluate whether to maintain or decrease the amount per occasion.

The final alternative is the timing, or when to purchase. Certain products are seasonal, have a peak in their sales, or can be easily stored. Marketers may have a behavioural objective to influence when consumers will make the purchase. For example, Wendy's restaurant advertises on television in the evening and communicates the fact that its drive-through service stays open late, thus prompting consumers to purchase at a certain time of day. Consistent with the other two alternatives, we can conceive three options: maintain, accelerate, and delay. Exhibit 5-5 encourages consumers to purchase now rather than later.

An evolution in its message from "Perspective Is Everything" to "Don't Miss a Day" signals how *The Globe and Mail* newspaper specified its repeat-purchase objectives over time. Faced with competition from other newspapers, the "perspective" message conveyed one aspect of quality in an attempt to maintain its readership. Recognizing that some readers may not purchase or read its newspaper every day, *The Globe and Mail* focused its message on increasing the frequency of reading the newspaper in its more recent "day" message.[13]

Exhibit 5-5 LG encourages consumers to upgrade their appliances by focusing on product design.

Purchase-Related Behaviour Often, communication is designed to encourage a consumer to progress through the decision-making process more smoothly. For example, most people find it imperative to visit a car dealership prior to buying a car. So the focus of some parts of an IMC plan is to have consumers take action that will lead them one step closer to the final destination of a purchase. **Purchase-related behaviour** is an action consumers take that will lead to a higher probability of purchasing the brand. Many types of purchase-related action exist, but in general most concern the consumer seeking some amount of information (e.g., visit a website) about the brand or some kind of experience with the brand (e.g., participate in an event, watch a demonstration, consume a sample). For some ads, brand would determine the number of website visits expected. Accordingly, marketers can have many purchase-related behaviour objectives to know whether enough of the target audience is involved or engaged with the brand during the decision-making process. For example, the firm can track the number of sales inquiries or requests for samples, or demonstrations to gauge how well it is performing for the objective.

Repeat Consumption   Thus far we have considered repeat purchase as a behavioural objective. Related to this is repeat consumption as a behavioural objective. **Repeat consumption** is defined as the continued consumption of the brand once purchased. Marketers may have a **repeat-consumption objective** when communicating with their current customers who have previously purchased the brand and have the product at their home or work. Some communication has an objective of modifying how often to consume the brand, how much to consume each occasion, and when to consume.

To give an idea of a repeat-consumption objective in action, we will cite two common approaches. Often, food and drink products advertise certain television commercials that show consumption visuals that may prompt consumers to snack or have another beverage. Also, research suggests that for these kinds of product categories that have a well established market leader, a consumption intention is a better predictor of advertising success since goods are already in stock and a repeat purchase will not occur until the inventory is depleted.[14] The Kit-Kat ad in Exhibit 5-6 reinforces continued consumption when its customers "Take a break." Another approach is to show consumers how to enjoy the product for other uses, or in new or alternative situations.

Milk faces a unique problem of 100-percent trial and 99-percent household penetration, yet its consumption continues to decline. The B.C. Dairy Foundation identified teens and young adults as an audience for a campaign to maintain consumption since research indicated that consumption levels dropped off during the ages of 16–23. Since many of these people still lived at home, the print and television messages "Don't take your body for granted" and "What would life be like without a body?" tried to ensure that this age group would not stop consuming

137

Exhibit 5-6
Kit-Kat associated with a situational use to increase repeat purchases.

milk prior to moving out on their own. Exciting outdoor events geared toward this audience attempted to make drinking milk as "cool" as any other beverage![15] Next door, the Prairie Milk Marketing Partnership, representing the remaining western provinces, used mass, social, and location media to reach teens and increased sales by 18 percent through increased consumption once teens understood the health benefits of milk.[16]

The Canadian Tourism Commission (CTC) and Toyota presented an interesting example of a campaign designed to increase repeat consumption. This dual-branded message encouraged Canadians to "drive the world's greatest country" in a series of newspaper, television, and radio ads followed by a second wave of Internet and dealer promotions. Since it was assumed that most Canadians had previously taken a road vacation to see various Canadian sites, this campaign attempted to capitalize on the growing trend of domestic travel.[17] More recently, the CTC activated Canadians once again with a message "Locals Know." Showing Canadians its unique geography encouraged them to visit their own country for their summer vacation plans. Using a similar media strategy, the campaign implied that Canadians could have a unique and fantastic experience in their own country, just like they might experience abroad.[18]

The type of purchase and consumption behaviour that firms may try to influence is quite varied. If a firm has multiple target audiences to reach, quite likely it will have to carefully specify the type of behaviour associated with each target audience so that it can develop the most appropriate message and select the most relevant IMC tool. To assist a manager in making these subsequent decisions, it is important to set clear communication objectives.

OPTIONS FOR COMMUNICATION OBJECTIVES

Earlier in this chapter we saw how communication response hierarchy models can be used to formulate communication objectives. The R&P approach is similar since it translates their perspective of communication effects into clear options for managers to set communication objectives. In fact, it offers a number of options for each of the five communication objectives that can be applied to one target audience or multiple target audiences.

These options for communication objectives can be viewed as a universal framework for (i) a specific communication like one print ad or television commercial, (ii) a specific campaign like advertising or sponsorship, and (iii) a complete IMC program that includes all promotional tools. It should be noted that the characteristics of good objectives still retain the characteristics set forth earlier (i.e., specific benchmark with the degree of change sought within a specified time period). Furthermore, the framework is flexible enough to apply the various communication objectives to each stage of the buyer decision-making process. We now turn to summarizing the various options for each communication objective and show this application to the buyer decision process.

Category Need **Category need** pertains to whether the target audience believes that purchasing within a particular product category will fulfill the consumer's need. Before describing the three options available for managers, it is useful to understand what we mean by category. Smartphones are a clear product for which some people are consumers and some are not. A phone company may try to build demand by convincing new users of the benefits of owning a smart phone versus not owning one. This type of message is likely to be different than the type of message used to convince a current user to switch to another brand when the technology improves with new features. In this example, it is a question of whether the target audience believes their communication needs would be more fulfilled with the product or without it. Exhibit 5-7 identifies how this type of watch can fulfill the need for status.

Another example of category need occurs with transportation. When thinking about buying a "car" upon graduation, a student's choice may in fact be a truck or a sports utility vehicle. In a broad sense, all vehicles can be used for transportation, but consumers have particular needs that are satisfied more easily with some types or categories of vehicles versus others. A marketer for SUVs may try to communicate in a way so that a target audience will feel the need for an SUV more strongly than the need for a sporty sub-compact, which might be the initial category of product that young consumers would gravitate toward. In this example, it is a question of which distinct yet related category fulfills the target audience's need more completely.

A car purchase is certainly not restricted to one's first purchase, and category need is a communication objective managers need to consider as an option when marketing to current car owners. For example, 64 percent of all Canadian minivan owners who bought a new vehicle purchased another minivan in 2000; however, this dropped to 48 percent in 2003. In contrast, corresponding numbers rose for large SUVs (e.g., 28 percent to 38 percent) and small cars (e.g., 49 percent to 63 percent). Research suggests consumers "wanted something different" as the most heavily cited reason for changing the type of vehicle.[19] It appears that astute marketers anticipate changing needs and adjust their advertising accordingly and introduce category need as an objective when it is appropriate even in existing markets.

We can describe category need in another perspective. Sticking with the transportation theme, public transit services illustrate their benefits by comparing themselves to the limitations of commuting with a car. Recent television ads in Montreal featured the message "Discover Public Transit" by demonstrating how one could not travel quickly on the highways. The irony of the ad existed in its use of "car-like" visuals—travelling freely at great speed—but then coming to a sudden stop due to traffic. Outdoor signs supported the message at precisely the time when drivers would be experiencing the problem and possibly considering an alternative.[20]

In either of these situations or others, a manager has three options with respect to the category need objective:

- *Category need is omitted.* If the need is quite apparent, then it does not need to be the focus of a particular message or campaign.
- *Category need is reminded.* One obvious example of this is reminder advertising, where the brand is featured in the message and the need for the product is implicitly communicated or clearly illustrated. Often, the reminder option of category need is the focus of campaigns for lapsed users. For example, the ad for Dairyland Milk 2 Go products in Exhibit 5-8 reminds consumers that it is a convenient drink when away from home, like soft drinks or sport drinks.
- *Category need is emphasized* (that is, "sold"). The above two examples (that is, smartphones and vehicles) show two situations where we actively attempt to persuade the target audience to believe that the product category will fulfill a particular need.

The Swiss Water Decaffeinated Coffee Company required category need as its communication objective as it faced the difficult task of explaining that its process

Exhibit 5-7 Eli Manning's status is conveyed in this Citizen watch ad.

139

Exhibit 5-8 This ad for Dairyland Milk 2 Go products is part of a campaign designed to increase sales and market share.

for decaffeinating coffee used water instead of chemicals. Known as the Swiss Water Process, brand-name coffees use this approach and highlight the fact on their packages much like the famous "Intel Inside" or the VQA designation on Canadian wines indicating an adherence to quality production. Swiss Water used the message "Decaf without the chemistry" to highlight the difference, yet not scare the target audience toward other products like decaffeinated tea.[21] Thus, a category need objective is usually imperative when competing technologies or substitute products emerge on the market thus creating two subcategories instead of one general category.

Brand Awareness **Brand awareness** is a universal communication objective. This means that every single point of communication should contribute to a target audience's understanding and knowledge of the brand name. This understanding and knowledge should go even further such that the target audience knows the category that the brand typically competes in when the consumer is in position to make a purchase or some other related action. This stronger interpretation of awareness is important for the brand to be considered in the decision-making process.

Essentially, there are two types of brand awareness:

- *Brand awareness through recognition.* If the target audience makes a choice at the point of purchase, then simple recognition of past brand messages can be sufficient for brand consideration or purchase.
- *Brand awareness through recall.* If the target audience feels the need for a product but needs to remember what brands to consider away from the point of purchase, then recall becomes the focus of the campaign.

Naturally, if both forms of brand awareness are relevant, then a manager may have both as awareness objectives.

Brand recall is often referred to as unaided brand awareness when measuring. After its launch in western Canada in 2001, Bell had achieved only 10 percent unaided brand recall. What this means is that when people are thinking about buying a cell phone service, only one in 10 will think of Bell. Obviously, this reduces Bell's chances of having many consumers enter Bell stores or call to enquire about its services.[22]

Bell Mobility's continued expansion westward included enhanced network and call centre investments along with more intense distribution of Bell World locations and other retail outlets. As expected, brand awareness remained an important communication objective in 2003 when it also launched its new "Making It Simple" campaign. With an eye to new customers in the 18–34 age range and an emphasis on quality and innovation, Bell Mobility improved its awareness to 27 percent.[23]

In defining brand awareness we must be careful in distinguishing it from advertising awareness, which concerns itself with whether consumers are aware of a brand's television or print ads. While there is some logical connection between the two, they are not identical. For example, one study pegged Ford's unaided brand awareness at 78 percent but its unaided advertising awareness at 57 percent. Four other major car firms, GM, Chrysler, Toyota, and Honda, also showed a consistent 20-percent difference between the two types of awareness.[24]

Brand Attitude   **Brand attitude** is another universal communication objective. Like brand awareness, every aspect of a firm's IMC program or any particular element, such as a television commercial, should contribute to some aspect of the overall evaluation of the brand from the perspective of the target audience. A logical conclusion to this point is that there should be no such thing as an "awareness campaign," as the campaign should surely influence brand awareness and some aspect of brand attitude.

Since brand attitude is such an important communication objective, prior understanding of the existing brand attitude is a critical guide for each option:

- *Brand attitude is established.* A new target audience that has no awareness and therefore no prior attitude toward the brand generally requires extensive communication so that an attitude is created or established. The Sonicare ad in Exhibit 5-9 needs to establish a favourable brand attitude with its new teeth cleaning features.
- *Brand attitude is maintained.* Often, advertising is performed so that existing attitude levels will remain constant in order to ensure future sales. Stopping communication is one reason for declining sales that have been seen in many examples over time. In contrast, many major advertisers (e.g., Coca-Cola) consistently follow this approach to maintain sales.
- *Brand attitude is increased.* Target audiences who are familiar with the brand and moderately favourable toward the brand can be

influenced. For example, we can increase their brand attitude by getting the target audience to believe that the brand delivers better performance on a particular attribute or benefit. The beef ad in Exhibit 5-10 tries to increase consumers' already favourable attitude toward this source of nourishment.

- *Brand attitude is modified.* Similar to the previous option, if the target audience is moderately favourable, we still seek to improve their attitude. However, we modify the brand attitude if no increase is possible. In this option, marketers use a different point of reference in communicating the benefits. Typically, marketers focus on a new consumer motive for purchasing the brand that the target audience will be receptive toward. The tea ad in Exhibit 5-11 attempts to influence attitudes in a new direction.
- *Brand attitude is changed.* Negative attitudes are difficult to influence, but in some communication situations the marketer is faced with the challenge of changing the brand attitude for a target audience.

Brand Purchase Intention   There are two fairly simple options for **brand purchase intention** here:

- *Brand purchase intention is assumed.* In situations (i.e., low involvement) where the strength of an intention to purchase is consistent (i.e., highly correlated) with brand attitude, a marketer is not required to include this objective.
- *Brand purchase intention is generated.* In contrast, managers need the target audience to have a plan to purchase a brand in situations of high involvement.

Exhibit 5-9   A strong basis for differentiation could establish a clear brand attitude.

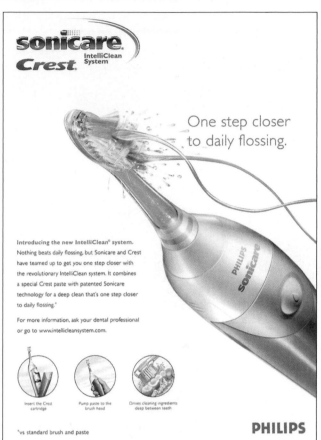

141

Exhibit 5-10 Canadian Beef reinforces the belief that its product is a source of protein.

Exhibit 5-11 Nestea provides new reasons for consuming its product.

Brand Purchase Facilitation   A proactive interpretation of marketing communication pervades **brand purchase facilitation** by these two options:

- *Purchase facilitation is included.* If the target audience believes that some aspect of the marketing mix is weak or problematic (i.e., availability at certain types of stores), then the marketer should take this into account when designing ads, and offer reassurance, explanation, or information.
- *Purchase facilitation is omitted.* Naturally, this is not a focus of the ad if there are no perceived problems.

IMC PLANNING: OBJECTIVES FOR BUYER DECISION STAGES

In Chapter 3, we presented a model of consumer decision making that showed the stages typically experienced when making a purchase. We outlined several steps: need recognition, information search, alternative evaluation, purchase decision, and postpurchase evaluation. One important role of marketing communications is to help the target audience move through these stages. Marketers require specific communication tools and messages that will resonate with each target audience as they proceed through these stages. We assess this decision-making process for each target audience and make a conclusion as to which communication objectives are most relevant for each stage. Figure 5-5 illustrates how this works.

The analysis occurs in the first six rows, where the marketer includes the target audience information and makes a conclusion on the key communication objectives that need to be attained so that the target audience will continue to the next stage. We have addressed some of these ideas already. The first question (Who?) looks at the key participants in the decision. We highlighted these roles in Chapter 3. The next three questions are descriptors of where, when, and how the shopping behaviour will occur. This is based on market research, managerial experience, flashes of inspiration, and assumptions. The key point is that we need to make clear the behaviour that we are trying to influence.

After summarizing these questions, we determine which communication objectives are necessary to ensure that the consumer continues through all stages. For example, what aspect of brand attitude needs to be addressed at the need-recognition stage versus the alternative-evaluation stage? Is recall an awareness objective at the need-recognition stage and recognition an awareness objective at the purchase-decision stage? We also need to determine the most relevant behavioural objective. For example, we may wish to encourage phone enquiries at the information search stage. Or perhaps we may desire Internet visits to compare brands at the alternative evaluation stage.

Once this assessment has been done, then the marketer can outline preliminary options concerning the types of messages and communication tools that would be most useful. Returning to the first question above, a marketer may decide to have a fun television commercial (e.g., communication tool option) that emphasizes the

FIGURE 5-5   Assessing the consumer decision-making process

Analysis and Conclusions	Need Recognition	Information Search	Alternative Evaluation	Purchase Decision	Postpurchase Evaluation
Who? (roles)					
Where? (location)					
When? (time, timing)					
How? (shopping behaviour)					
Why? (key motivator)					
Communication Objectives					
Behavioural Objectives					
Message Options					
Communication Tool Options					

emotional attachment (e.g., brand attitude) to the product. It should be noted that when identifying some options, the marketer has not fully committed or recommended that this is exactly the plan, but rather that this is the template of analysis for making the final decision.

The Rogers@Home "Download Rigor Mortis" IMC campaign is an excellent example of these concepts. In the spring and fall of 2000, Rogers put together a campaign to attract new users for its high-speed cable Internet service. It featured the humorous result of consumers requiring medical attention after experiencing rigor mortis when they waited for Internet downloads to occur through regular phone lines. The campaign included TV, print, radio, billboards, Web, and direct mail, and resulted in 100,000 new subscribers. As one Rogers executive noted, "I don't think any one piece works entirely on its own. That's what is nice about integrated campaigns; each piece layered on helps build it."

We can now surmise how each IMC tool played a key role in achieving key communication objectives at each stage of the decision-making process. TV worked well at the need-recognition stage, as it generated initial awareness and allowed consumers to easily see the benefit of a new type of Internet service for them (i.e., category need) and understand that Rogers could deliver the key attribute of speed (i.e., brand attitude). Print and Web enhanced the belief that Rogers could deliver the complete service package, as they contained more information (i.e., brand attitude) that consumers would be seeking at the information-search stage. Radio and posters likely reminded consumers to seek additional information (i.e., purchase facilitation) by phoning the company or visiting the website, if the consumer had not done so previously when in the purchase-intention stage. Direct mail encouraged consumers to act (i.e., purchase decision).[25]

The rest of this book focuses on how to make IMC plan decisions that are based on the target audience, behaviour objectives, and communication objectives established at the start of the plan. Chapters 6–9 focus on the message, while Chapters 10–17 focus on the communication tools. As we noted at the start of this chapter, content of this framework becomes the key criteria for making all promotional decisions and the criteria by which the results are measured. While all firms may not be able to afford comprehensive studies to assess communication effects, they would benefit from the use of the framework because it provides disciplined thinking before investing in promotion.

CHAPTER OBJECTIVES AND SUMMARY

1 To recognize the value of setting specific objectives for advertising and promotion.

This chapter examined the role of objectives in the planning and evaluation of the IMC. Specific objectives are needed to guide the development of the promotional program, as well as to provide a benchmark against which performance can be measured and evaluated. Objectives serve important functions as a communications device, as a guide to planning and decision making for all aspects of the IMC program, and for measurement and evaluation.

2 To know the differences among marketing, behavioural, and communication objectives and the issues regarding the use of each.

Objectives for IMC evolve from the organization's overall marketing plan and are based on the roles various promotional mix elements play in the marketing program. Many managers use sales or a related measure such as market share as the basis for setting objectives. However, many promotional planners believe the communication role of advertising and other promotional mix elements is not directly connected or associated with sales-based objectives. They use communication-based objectives like those in the response hierarchy as the basis for setting goals. The implication of these models suggest the importance of setting specific behavioural objectives such as trial or repeat purchase and appropriate communication objectives to direct the IMC strategy so that it contributes to the attainment of marketing objectives.

3 To know the historical approaches for setting communication objectives for advertising.

Historically, considerable emphasis in setting objectives concerned traditional advertising-based views of marketing communication. This originated from an application of basic response models like DAGMAR and the hierarchy of effects. DAGMAR established the principle that objectives should specify a target audience, be stated in concrete and measurable communication tasks, indicate a benchmark starting point and the degree of change sought, and specify a time period for accomplishing the objectives. As an extension of this idea, the principles of the hierarchy of effects model, used in setting advertising objectives, could be applied to other elements in the promotional mix. The hierarchy of effects model suggested that unique promotional tools could be implemented in different stages of the response hierarchy. Managers would determine the location of a particular audience in the hierarchy and make appropriated decisions to move them closer to a trial and repeat purchase.

4 To understand a comprehensive framework for setting communication and behavioural objectives for all aspects of the IMC plan.

We presented a comprehensive framework for setting behavioural and communication objectives for many IMC planning purposes, IMC plans, individual IMC tools (i.e., advertising), and specific elements (i.e., direct mail offer with coupon). Both types of objectives need to be established for any individual communication

element, ranging from an activity at a sponsorship event to what is portrayed in a point-of-sale display. In short, all target audience contact points play a role in fulfilling IMC plan objectives and their expenditures can be accountable through achievement of their mandate. Advertising, and any other tool, requires particular objectives to enhance its effect in the overall plan. Finally, the complete plan requires direction through behavioural and communication objectives so that all tools and elements communicate accurately.

The framework identified options for behavioural objectives to guide the achievement of marketing objectives and to provide direction to form communication objectives. Behavioural objectives included brand trial, brand re-trial, brand-switching, category trial, repeat purchase, purchase-related behaviour, and repeat consumption. The framework also presented many options for setting communication objectives in terms of category need (i.e., omit, remind, emphasize), brand awareness (i.e., recognition and/or recall), brand attitude (i.e., establish, maintain, increase, modify, change), brand purchase intention (assume, generate), and brand purchase facilitation (omit, include). The end result provides managers with the ability to construct a multitude of IMC plans.

The framework was then linked to the buyer decision-making model to see the connection between a consumer's behaviour and a particular brand's objectives. This application implies that as a consumer's decision-making progressed, managers can consider how objectives evolve at each stage in order to adjust the message, media, or IMC tool employed to communicate.

KEY TERMS

benchmark measures, *130*

brand attitude, *141*

brand awareness, *140*

brand purchase
facilitation, *142*

brand purchase
intention, *141*

brand re-trial objective, *135*

brand re-trial purchase, *135*

brand-switching
objective, *135*

brand-switching
purchase, *135*

brand trial objective, *135*

brand trial purchase, *134*

carryover effect, *126*

category need, *138*

category trial objective, *135*

category trial purchase, *135*

communication
objectives, *128*

communication task, *129*

DAGMAR, *129*

marketing objectives, *125*

purchase-related
behaviour, *137*

repeat consumption, *137*

repeat-consumption
objective, *137*

repeat purchase, *135*

repeat-purchase
objective, *135*

DISCUSSION QUESTIONS

1. Discuss the value of setting objectives for the integrated marketing communications program. What important functions do objectives serve?

2. In meeting with your new boss, she informs you that the only goal of advertising and promotion is to generate sales. Present your argument as to why communications objectives must also be considered.

3. What are some of the problems associated with using sales objectives as the only measure of advertising performance? Can you think of any situation where it may be the best and only measure?

4. What are the strengths and weaknesses of using traditional hierarchy models for setting communication objectives?

5. Some claim that promotion is all about communication, so we should focus only on communication objectives and not worry about behavioural objectives. Convince them otherwise.

6. If a firm cannot afford large market research studies to quantitatively assess whether communication objectives have been achieved, why should the firm bother setting communication objectives?

7. How is the framework discussed in the last section similar to and different from setting communications objectives based on the traditional hierarchy models?

8. In what situations would brand awareness be the only communication objective for an advertising campaign?

9. A firm is running a campaign with advertising, sales promotion, and public relations. Why might it have different communication objectives for each IMC tool?

10. Find a print ad and explain what its communication objectives are. Look at the company's website and determine whether the communication objectives are similar or different.

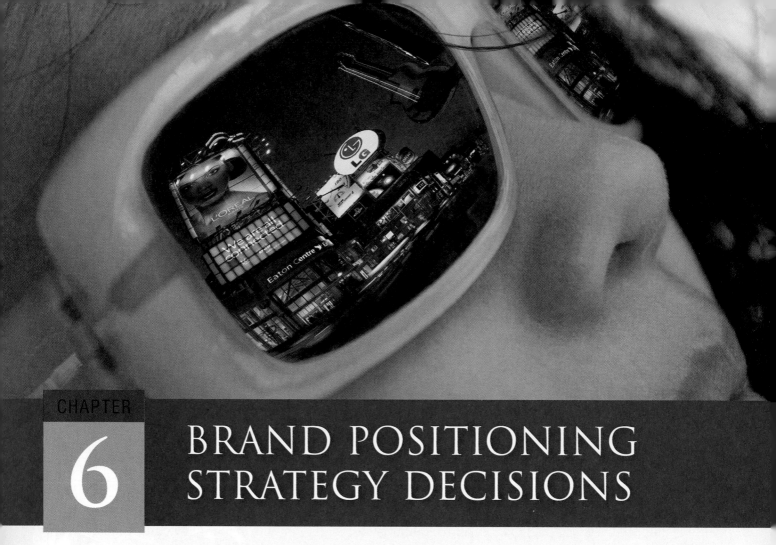

BRAND POSITIONING STRATEGY DECISIONS

■ CHAPTER OBJECTIVES

1 To review the concepts of market positioning strategy and market position.

2 To apply the positioning concept in an advertising context by defining brand positioning strategy and brand position.

3 To illustrate how to formulate the brand positioning strategy decisions.

4 To summarize various brand repositioning strategy opportunities.

A BATTLE OF ADVERTISING CLAIMS AMONG TELCOS

For the most part, advertising claims by brands are not controversial—but every once in a while a battle ensues that leaves advertising experts scratching their heads, wondering "What the heck is going on?"

The most recent battle by Canadian telecommunications firms started in mid 2009, when Rogers asked consumers to take the "Rogers home phone challenge." Using a dual-coloured couch as a visual—red for Rogers and blue for Bell—the ads claimed price was the only difference in the services with quality being equal. Rogers entered the home phone market, a traditional Bell strength, in 2005 and intended the ad as a suggestion for consumers to comparison shop.

Bell shot back with the same imagery, and extended its end of the couch to defend the price claim. It also promoted its 3G network and HD channels and moved to defend its price and quality position with its own blue couch, with five blue cushions and one red cushion. The message was, "Get more than Rogers for less than Rogers." According to a Bell senior VP, "It wasn't our preference to engage the marketing communication this way, but given the opportunity from Rogers we would've been remiss not to exploit the opportunity."

Commenting from the sidelines, two marketing executives proclaimed the battle counterproductive for brand positioning. For example, one executive felt that both brands used the same strategy and that the ultimate result would be consumer confusion. The other executive suggested that consumers would benefit by actually starting to consider whether they get value for their money and admired Bell for aggressively defending its home turf.

Despite this foray, a new battle emerged in the courts at the end of 2009 when Telus sued Rogers for the latter's claims of its wireless service having "The fastest and most reliable network" and "Canada's fastest network: Two times faster than any other." Telus cited a technological upgrade that it and Bell established, making their network

superior: "In light of our recent launch of Canada's largest 3G+ network, Rogers has no network advantage and should not be misleading Canadians with a false claim of superiority."

A few weeks later a judge agreed, and ordered Rogers to remove the "fastest" and "most reliable" claims on all of its marketing communication. As a result, Rogers discarded approximately $3 million worth of promotional material already produced and erected. Rogers switched its claim to "Canada's reliable network," dropping the word "most." At the same time, Rogers sued Bell for the latter's inaccurate claim of the "Largest, fastest and most reliable" and "The best and most powerful" network—and subsequently won a week later.

Sources: Hollie Shaw, "Duelling Couches," *National Post*, July 24, 2009, p. FP10; Jonathan Paul, "Bell & Rogers: Couch Wars," *Strategy*, September 2009, p. 24; Scott Deveua, "Telus Sues Rogers Over 'Fast' Claims," *National Post*, November 19, 2009, p. FP1; Simon Houpt, "Telus, B.C. Judge on Same Wavelength," *The Globe and Mail*, November 25, 2009, p. B1; Simon Houpt, "B.C. Judge Tells Rogers: Tear Down Those Billboards," *The Globe and Mail*, December 1, 2009, p. B1; Simon Houpt, "Rogers Suit Turns the Tables on Competition," *The Globe and Mail*, December 2, 2009, p. B1.

QUESTION

1. What is your opinion regarding these competing advertising claims and court battles?

As the opening vignette implies, advertising and all IMC tools that occur within a marketing strategy have a significant contribution toward the overall positioning of the product to selected target markets, or what is known as a market positioning strategy. However, advertising and all promotional activities have their own unique communication objectives to persuade a particular target audience. In this sense, we can examine how various promotional tools and the whole promotional program influences the positioning of a brand to a designated target audience, or what is known as a brand positioning strategy.

Our investigation in this chapter—to understand positioning for both marketing strategy and marketing communication—is consistent with the distinction between target market and target audience (Chapter 3) and the importance of linking communication objectives and strategy with the marketing objectives and strategy (Chapter 5). First, we review market positioning strategy, define brand positioning strategy, and subsequently describe the brand positioning strategy decision process. We then define and illustrate the four decisions for developing a comprehensive brand positioning strategy. Finally, we explore opportunities for changing the brand positioning strategy, known as repositioning.

POSITIONING

In this section, we distinguish between positioning within the marketing strategy and positioning with marketing communication. We also highlight the difference between the decision a manager makes in terms of a positioning strategy and the resulting effects in terms of the position in which the target market or target audience perceives the firm or brand to be competing. We end the section with an overview of the decision-making process for a brand positioning strategy.

Exhibit 6-1   Coach is just one of many companies competing in the luxury goods market.

MARKET POSITIONING STRATEGY

Any organization that wants to exchange its products or services in the marketplace successfully should have a **strategic marketing plan** to guide the allocation of its resources. A strategic marketing plan usually evolves from an organization's overall corporate strategy and serves as a guide for specific marketing programs and policies. In Chapter 1 we emphasized the importance of promotional planners using the marketing plan as a key information source to plan for marketing communication decisions. In particular, those creating ads should be familiar with their client's or organization's market positioning strategy since it gives direction for how a brand should be positioned in the promotional program.

Positioning has been defined as "the art and science of fitting the product or service to one or more segments of the broad market in such a way as to set it meaningfully apart from competition."[1] A **market positioning strategy** concerns the final decision of the market(s) in which firms wish to compete, combined with the specific elements of the marketing mix that are designed to fulfill the respective needs of the market(s). For example, Coach now competes in the luxury goods market with its stylish products (Exhibit 6-1). Happy Planet drinks originally competed only in the healthy drink category, but now compete against Red Bull in the energy drink category.[2]

Typically, firms write a market positioning strategy statement in their marketing plan to accurately communicate this decision. This statement provides direction for each of the four areas of decision within the marketing program development phase: product, price, distribution, and marketing communication. For example, different market segments in the personal computer (PC) industry include the home, education, science, and business markets. These segments can be even further divided. The business market consists of both small companies and large corporations; the education market can range from elementary schools to colleges and universities. A company that is marketing its products in the PC industry must decide in which particular market segment or segments it wishes to compete. This decision depends on the amount and nature of competition the brand will face in a particular market.

While developing its market positioning strategy, the firm may consider many combinations of product attributes with varying price levels across different retail outlets. Alternatively, it could evaluate narrow product choices with very wide distribution and a mass advertising appeal. As these examples suggest, a firm considers as many feasible options as possible so that it does not miss a market opportunity. At this stage, the firm uses its market research and experience wisely to put together a "package of benefits" or "value offering" that will be acceptable to the target market selected.

Once the marketing programs are developed and implemented, organizations may find results at, above, or below expectations. For example, sales or market share objectives may or may not be obtained. The reactions of consumers may be very close to what the firm intended, or they could be quite different. We define this response to be the **market position** of a firm. This distinction signifies that it is not the current or past strategic plans of the marketing managers, but rather the intended or unintended consumer beliefs of the organization's marketing efforts.

To expand on these ideas, we will use the Canadian airline industry as an example. As of 2001, Air Canada represented essentially the country's only full-service national airline. While it has had various ad campaigns over the years, it has always attempted to maintain this full-service position. WestJet, previously a small regional discount carrier, purchased larger, newer jets so that it could offer services for cross-country routes.[3] Advertising maintained its discount market position throughout the country. We illustrate this situation with a simple market position diagram, recognizing that alternative interpretations may be feasible (Figure 6-1). We graph two axes, full and limited service versus high and low price, and locate WestJet$_1$ and Air Canada at opposite ends of the spectrum given the history of each organization's

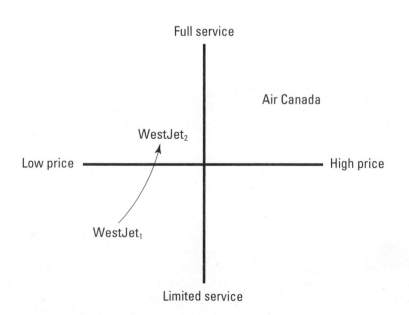

FIGURE   6–1

Hypothetical illustration of market position of airlines

marketing activities. While these initial market positioning strategies appear as suitable attempts to successfully deliver needed airline services, time would tell whether consumers truly believed that each occupies the intended market space and has the correct market position in terms of consumers' perceptions.

Over the next few years, WestJet experienced substantial success in the market; however, it realized that consumers in general perceived a discount or low-cost airline to offer a "no-frills" or "bring your own seatbelt" kind of flight experience. Alternatively, it appeared that WestJet offered greater service than perceived—in other words, WestJet needed to improve its market position by moving from the bottom left of Figure 6-1 to somewhere closer to the horizontal line or even above it. This problem was one of two things that prompted the successful "WestJetters Are Owners" campaign. From an overall marketing standpoint, the campaign represented a new market positioning strategy. And the results materialized, as four key measures of airline stature improved an average of 8 percent in a few short months.[4]

More recently, WestJet added more Canadian routes, extended service to international destinations, improved in-flight service elements, and developed joint-venture initiatives with other international carriers. As one industry analyst commented, WestJet "has morphed itself into more of a mainline carrier."[5] Figure 6-1 also shows a hypothetical illustration of where the brand may be located with Westjet$_2$. With its extended service area and increased amenities, consumers might conclude that it is more of a full-service airline as it could meet multiple air travel needs. They may also conclude that its prices are slightly higher given the improved delivery. In turn, Air Canada continues to reinforce its significant position in the airline travel market as it overhauls the interior of its jets and attempts to deliver superior service interactions with its staff and customers while serving 31 million passengers a year.[6]

A limitation of perceptual maps for understanding market position is highlighted with the placement of Porter airlines. This new airline would be considered limited-service as it serves very few markets compared to the other two competitors. However, for the cities it does serve, consumers might respond with very high levels of service in terms of attentiveness of the staff and Porter's refined travel style as demonstrated in Exhibit 6-2.[7] In conclusion, the market position is entirely dependent upon clearly identifying and accurately defining the criteria for the two axes, and suggests that multiple diagrams may be necessary for some multifaceted customer experiences like air travel.

porter
flying refined

Breeze into the Windy City.
Only Porter offers up to 6 daily non-stops between Toronto City Airport and Chicago's downtown Midway Airport.

Book online, call 1-888-619-8622 or contact your travel agent.

Sign up for VIPorter frequent flyer program
www.flyporter.com

Exhibit 6-2 Porter's entry to the airline market resulted in different ad campaigns.

BRAND POSITIONING STRATEGY

Because promotion is so visible, it is tempting to believe that it alone defines the market positioning strategy. While this may be true in some situations, in most cases, advertising and IMC campaigns typically focus on a particular message that helps consumers understand the product in comparison to other brands *within* a specific product market or category. Furthermore, most ads or other IMC tools speak to a very specific target audience. A bank can have a direct-mail piece to a current customer to obtain a mortgage renewal and focus the message on the ease of continuity and the good follow-up service. Or it may run a TV ad with a message of attractive interest rates and specialized options that may attract customers from competing banks. These examples identify different target audiences with different competitive reference points and suggest the need to use the positioning concept appropriately in a marketing communication context that is distinct from positioning in a marketing strategy context. This notion of positioning in marketing communication is the subject of a new direction in the marketing literature,[8] and the topic to which we now turn.

Many advertising practitioners consider positioning the most important decision in establishing a brand in the marketplace. David Aaker and John Myers note that the term "position" has been used to indicate the brand's or product's image in the marketplace.[9] Jack Trout and Al Ries suggest that this brand image must contrast with that of competitors: "In today's marketplace, the competitors' image is just as important as your own. Sometimes more important."[10] Thus, a **brand positioning strategy**, as used in this text, relates to the intended image of the product or brand relative to a competing brand for a given competitive space as defined by certain product market or category characteristics. The brand positioning strategy is a key decision prior to determining the most effective selling message of advertising or other IMC tools. The ad in Exhibit 6-3 targets consumers who drink bottled water and might enjoy carbonation.

Now consider consumer reactions to having seen television commercials or any other communication for any type of product or service. What do consumers think about the brand, having experienced the message? Do they have positive or negative feelings for the brand? What unique attributes or benefits come to mind when considering the brand? All of these questions pertain to the reactions consumers have to promotions, and constitute what we will refer to as the **brand position**. We need to distinguish between what the firm plans to do with its image versus what the actual image of the brand is, since both occur at different points in time and reside in different locations. The brand positioning strategy is a part of the overall advertising or IMC plan, while the brand position exists within the target audience.

Let us return to our airline example. In the course of developing its discount market positioning strategy, WestJet has a number of options to communicate, of which we will highlight a couple. It could encourage those who never or rarely travel to consider flying since it is now so affordable. Or it may try to convince those who buy the cheapest economy-class tickets (i.e., red-eye flights back east) to buy a WestJet ticket and travel at a more civilized time of the day. In either case, there is a distinct brand positioning strategy decision made to reach each unique target audience. Accordingly, each target audience will have its own unique brand position based on its experiences with the ads and the service.

We continue this idea with a more competitive angle since Air Canada has entered the discount market with Tango. Both WestJet and Tango will compete to be the leader in the discount market, and WestJet may need some elements of its IMC plan to encourage WestJet customers not to switch to Tango or to switch Tango customers to WestJet. These are just a few examples of how WestJet could be using a brand positioning strategy to speak with unique target audiences who are a part of the overall target market and may be receptive to the overall market positioning strategy.

We now return to our brand position (i.e., consumer perceptions) diagram, whereby WestJet and Tango are competing on certain **salient attributes**. Figure 6-2 shows two axes on which the companies *may* compete: frequency of flights and number of cities serviced. We can also surmise that the airlines *may* be competing

Exhibit 6-3 Pepsi's Sparkling Aquafina targets a new audience.

153

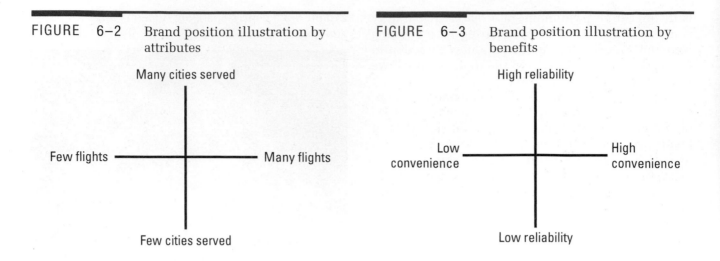

FIGURE 6–2 Brand position illustration by attributes

FIGURE 6–3 Brand position illustration by benefits

on certain **salient benefits** (Figure 6-3) of reliability (i.e., on-time departures, no mechanical delays) and convenience (i.e., check-in, ticket purchase).

The "WestJetters Are Owners" campaign addressed another concern. Focusing its message on superior customer service during the whole pre-flight, flight, post-flight experience allowed WestJet to attract dissatisfied Air Canada travellers who had possibly received poorer service. Preliminary research suggested that this target audience existed in sufficient numbers to ensure financial viability of the marketing communication investment. Follow-up research indicated that two measures of travel experience improved by 9 percent, and a third improved by 20 percent.[11] An extension of this message is the new Care-antee, where WestJet employees—who are also owners—offer their own personal guarantee of quality service with care. Ads are shown on TV and are available on the WestJet channel distributed via YouTube.[12]

Two important implications arise from this example. The first concerns how the campaign contributed to both market position and the brand position for a specific target audience. The campaign allowed WestJet to establish an improved market position by indicating that it did not offer a discount experience. In this respect it inched closer to being a "full-fledged" airline. And, as established in the previous paragraph, the campaign also focused on a salient benefit that would be critical for motivating dissatisfied Air Canada passengers to switch. The second implication concerns how the salient consumer benefits for positioning evolve over time or differ across various target audiences. As WestJet became more established, the dynamics of how it could compete allowed it to compete on superior customer service.

BRAND POSITIONING STRATEGY DECISION PROCESS

We present a five-step process for making the brand positioning strategy, adapted from other sources.[13] Chapter 1 briefly outlined this process, but we investigate the actual steps in more detail here to fully understand the brand positioning strategy decisions.

Develop a Market Partition A useful approach for defining the market is to make it consistent with how consumers make a purchase decision. It is suggested that promotional planners view the market broadly as a general product category and subsequently divide the market into various sub-categories until consumers perceive brands as being relatively similar. The criteria for market partitioning include the type of product, end benefit, usage situation, and brand name. Figures 6-4 to 6-7 show a basic partition of the car market for each of these four approaches,

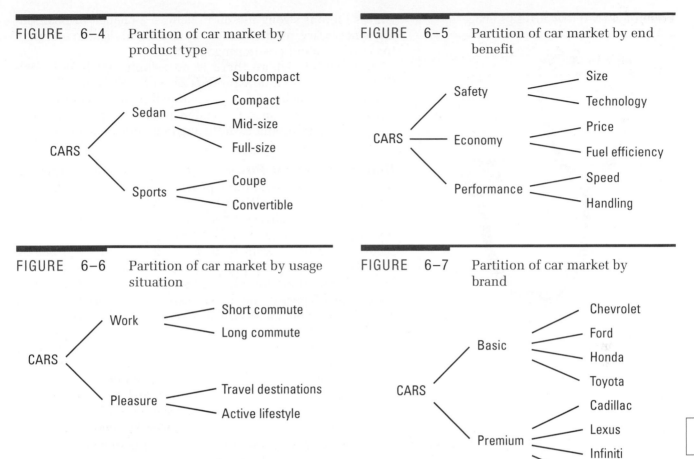

FIGURE 6-4 Partition of car market by product type

FIGURE 6-5 Partition of car market by end benefit

FIGURE 6-6 Partition of car market by usage situation

FIGURE 6-7 Partition of car market by brand

and these simple illustrations can be expanded or altered to the decision maker's requirements. This task is important for establishing the initial parameters for identifying the most important competitors to determine a unique positioning strategy that can be communicated.

Assess Competitors' Position Once we define the competitors through the market partition, we must determine how consumers perceive them by assessing their respective brand positions. To do so, we rely on new or existing consumer research. Oftentimes the research is a survey, indicating how consumers perceive the key brands on the more relevant and important attributes and benefits that consumers use when evaluating a brand. The data from these types of surveys are used to formulate the brand position maps shown previously in Figures 6-2 and 6-3.

Sometimes, preliminary consumer research may be necessary to ensure that promotional planners do not overlook key aspects some competitors may be communicating to establish a differential brand position. For example, cars compete on numerous attributes and benefits, and over time newer product characteristics may become important and need to be added to usual competitive profiles to accurately assess the brand positions.

Assess Brand Position Consumer research for the promotional planner's brand, either existing or new, is used to assess how consumers currently perceive the brand. This research would be compared with the previously determined brand positioning strategy (e.g., last year, or the prior two to four years). If current efforts are not working it may be time to consider an alternative strategy (Exhibit 6-4).

Exhibit 6-4 V-8 revitalizes its image.

Listen to your heart. Just one 12 oz. bottle of Low Sodium V8® 100% vegetable juice holds 3 servings of heart-healthy vegetables*, brimming with antioxidants and potassium. All that with no cholesterol and 0g saturated fat. And in case you need another reason, we're certified by the American Heart Association. Could've had a V8.

©2007 CSC Brands, LP. *1 serving of vegetables = 1/2 cup

Unless there is strong reason to believe a change in positioning is necessary, promotional planners are advised to maintain the current brand positioning strategy.

In situations where there is no established brand position, such as with a new product or where there has been no advertising for many years, promotional planners could assess characteristics that may be related to the corporate brand or complementary products in the organization's portfolio.

Determine Brand Positioning Strategy Going through the first three steps should provide direction for where to establish a brand position; however, planners will often be faced with alternatives to select from. Toyota previously positioned its trucks and SUVs as recreational, with messages like "I don't want to work all day," and "You belong outside." Promotional planners considered three positioning strategies along the idea of "tough." The first involved a "work-tough" positioning by showing the Tacoma at work on Canadian oil fields and farms. A second, "recreation-tough," would show the Tacoma engaged in off-road activities. Finally, "international-tough" intended to demonstrate the Tacoma's use throughout the world. The final choice won as the planners used live footage of Toyota trucks involved in delivering aid during international disasters to create the launch TV ad that carried the tagline "Never Quit."[14]

As this example suggests, the content of the brand positioning strategy decision is quite involved and oftentimes managers are faced with either performing research to make the final decision or using subjective judgments based on experience. To understand how to make this decision, the remainder of this chapter will present a structure and summarize the parts for a well-developed brand positioning strategy. It is at this point in the process that the promotional planner will construct a detailed description by writing a brand positioning strategy statement. In making the decision, planners will assess the degree to which the brand positioning strategy will be strong enough in the face of competition. They also will consider whether there are sufficient resources to establish the brand position over time since it requires substantial investment in media or other IMC tools for sufficient consumers in the target audience to receive and retain the message.

Implement Brand Positioning Strategy The brand positioning strategy decisions are an important requirement for setting the overall strategy for advertising. From this direction, the content of the advertising message, its creative strategy, and tactics can be formulated. Thus, the next step is to ensure that the creativity and the content of the message persuades the target audience appropriately and is consistent with the brand positioning strategy. We illustrate this connection between strategy and the creativity and content of the message in the context of advertising since it is so pervasive and familiar. Many of the uniquely Canadian examples cited used advertising along with other tools and communicated a consistent brand positioning strategy. The decisions are consistent with other promotional communication tools. For example, prior to launching a public relations or publicity campaign, a marketer would specify the positioning of its brand to its intended target audience before deciding upon the exact content of its message and how he or she would creatively present it. IMC Perspective 6-1 summarizes how a few beer companies implemented their brand positioning strategy.

Positioning for a Few Beers

For some consumer products, like beer, advertising and promotion play a central role in the brand positioning since the product and distribution seldom or infrequently change after the product launch. In fact, many beers advertise using an authentic recipe from centuries ago! Recently, a number of beers such as Carlsberg, Grolsch, and Rickard's have extended or revised their messages to give consumers a unique or new perspective for their brands.

Carlsberg claims to be "probably the best beer in the world" as part of its worldwide messaging, and in Canada it customized this positioning with a contest to find "probably the best mate in the world." The target of males aged 24–30 entered online by completing a quiz and entry form and uploading a photo. A selection of 30 winners received a mobile phone to video-record their "best mate" skills, and the ultimate winner won a trip to Las Vegas. As suggested by the agency, "When you get back to the audience that we're talking to, it really is about their entourage, the guys they hang out with." With extensive mass, digital, and social media, the campaign expected to confirm Carlsberg as a social beer.

In Canada, Grolsch claims an "independent positioning" observed by its tagline "Itself. Since 1615." Using extensive print media, Grolsch's messages offered witty and clever sayings or stories to distinguish it from other generic beers. For example, in one ad the copy explored the experience of holding the heavier bottle, hearing the swing-top opening, and tasting the beer. A marketing manager commented, "If you look at Grolsch, we believe it's a brand that looks like nothing else, feels like nothing else—it's a big, hefty bottle with a unique feel to it—it's got a distinctive sound when it pops open, and it's a refreshingly hoppy beer."

Rickard's recently moved from a "Pint of Glory" to a "Pint of Delicious." Although the ad retains the same routine of a man in a pub ordering a draught beer with something to it, the positioning moves in a new direction to signify the unique taste. After clever comments about the beer from three barflies, the bartender offers the full glass to the new patron with, "Take the best day or your life, and put it your mouth." The insight for the use of "delicious" emerged from consumer research that mentioned the flavour of Rickard's as one reason for its enjoyment. "Consumers have always seen Rickard's as something different than their usual choices. Our goal is to bring the enthusiasm that people have for the flavour varieties to like in a way that reflects the distinctiveness for its taste," commented a VP from the agency.

Sources: Matt Semansky, "Grolsch Promises Feast for Senses," *Marketing Magazine*, May 21, 2009; Kristin Laird, "Carlsberg Looking for Best Mates," *Marketing Magazine*, April 15, 2009; Kristin Laird, "Molson Begins Delicious Campaign for Rickard's," *Marketing Magazine*, December 15, 2009; Matt Semansky, "Moosehead Takes Slow Paddle in Cracked Canoe," *Marketing Magazine*, April 22, 2009.

Questions

1. Why are these advertising claims so important for marketing these brands of beer?

Monitor Brand Positioning Strategy Once a brand position has been established, we want to monitor how well it is being maintained. Tracking studies measure the image of the brand over time. Changes in consumers' perceptions can be determined, with any slippage immediately noted and reacted to. In the Toyota example, key communication effects improved substantially during the first seven months indicating strong positioning. Brand awareness gained from 83 percent to 95 percent, advertising awareness rose from 5 percent to 19 percent, and purchase intention increased from 22 percent to 40 percent. Many consumer perception ratings rose significantly that surpassed competitors. For example, more than 70 percent of the consumers surveyed rated the Tacoma as high quality, dependable, well-built, and trusted. Sales nearly doubled in a year, with market share moving to the 14 percent to 16 percent range. These remarkable results occurred with Chevrolet re-branding its S-10 to Colorado and the Dodge Dakota and Ford Ranger spending more money on advertising than the Tacoma.[15]

BRAND POSITIONING STRATEGY DECISIONS

The essence of positioning the brand in the context of advertising is to clearly indicate where the brand is competing, with whom it is competing, how it is competing, and finally why consumers will purchase the brand. Each of these questions must be addressed through four decisions within the brand positioning strategy: market definition, differential advantage, target audience brand attitude, and consumer purchase motive.

MARKET DEFINITION

A primary decision for positioning is how the promotional planners define the market and where they intend for the brand to compete with its benefit claims. The market partition illustrations showed that brands compete against other brands on end benefits, brand name, usage situation, and product category. One purpose of advertising is to contribute to developing a perceived advantage over competing brands within the competitive space. Thus, each of these offer tremendous opportunity to communicate benefit claims and establish a perceived differential advantage.

Positioning by End Benefit A common approach to positioning is setting the brand apart from competitors on the basis of the specific characteristics or benefits offered. Sometimes a product may be positioned on more than one product benefit. Marketers attempt to identify salient attributes (those that are important to consumers and are the basis for making a purchase decision).

For example, the focus of the Harvey's advertising message "Long Live the Grill" emphasizes an attribute regarding how the chain cooks its hamburgers. Consequently, many consumers can easily interpret a benefit of good taste or better flavour compared with other fast food retailers.[16] Advertisers require good research and reasons for justifying this kind of positioning recommendation, because moving toward a specific attribute like this precludes messages regarding other attributes and benefits. Becel's health focus has been portrayed in different ways over the years (Exhibit 6-5).

Selecting the right benefit is a very basic but critical decision, and one that is often determined too quickly or without sufficient research. Research for Schick's Intuition razor for women, a one-step lather and shave design, revealed that women perceived "easy to use" as being much different from "convenient" despite these two usage benefits appearing very similar. This discovery created a substantially different positioning and gave the creative specialists different focus.

While we refer to benefits in this discussion, often marketers will make a direct link between a particular attribute and the derived benefit, or they may highlight the attribute and allow the target audience to interpret the benefit. Again, research for Schick's Quattro for women indicated indifference regarding the engineered four blades, but a distinct desire to know that the brand produced a truly long-lasting shave.[17] This approach is often done in the car

Exhibit 6-5 Becel's health claims remain strong with product extensions.

158

market and is how the Lexus IS F competed in performance by showing extensive visuals of the engine in many forms of digital media.[18]

Positioning by Brand Name Marketers often use price/quality characteristics to position their brands. One way they do it is with ads that reflect the image of a high-quality brand where cost, while not irrelevant, is considered secondary to the quality benefits derived from using the brand. Premium brands positioned at the high end of the market use this approach to positioning.

Another way to use price/quality characteristics for positioning is to focus on the quality or value offered by the brand at a very competitive price. For example, the Lands' End ad shown in Exhibit 6-6 uses this strategy by suggesting that quality can be affordable. Remember that although price is an important consideration, the product quality must be comparable to, or even better than, competing brands for the positioning strategy to be effective.

Positioning by Usage Situation Another way to communicate a specific image or position for a brand is to associate it with a specific use. For example, Black & Decker introduced the SnakeLight as an innovative solution to the problem of trying to hold a flashlight while working. A TV commercial showed various uses for the product, while creative packaging and in-store displays were used to communicate the uses. While this strategy is often used to enter a market based on a particular use, it is also an effective way to expand the situational usage of a product. For example, Nutella advertised and promoted its hazelnut spread as a nutritious part of a wholesome breakfast since it contained protein. While previously viewed more as a chocolate treat, the association of breakfast provided a new usage approach for the brand.[19] Finally, empirical research suggests that marketing communication plays a strong role in consumers adopting new uses.[20]

Positioning by Product Category Often, the competition for a product comes from outside the product category. For example, airlines know that while they compete with other airlines, trains and buses are also viable alternatives. Via Rail has positioned itself as an alternative to airplanes, citing cost savings, enjoyment, and other advantages (Exhibit 6-7). Many margarines position themselves against butter. Rather than positioning against another brand, an alternative strategy is to position the brand against another product category.

DIFFERENTIAL ADVANTAGE

Brand benefit claims embodied in the positioning and represented in the ads contribute to the differential advantage for a brand. While it is generally

Exhibit 6-6 Lands' End positions its brand as having high quality for the right price.

Exhibit 6-7 Via competes with other forms of transportation.

expected that a brand positioning strategy should take a differential positioning approach and have a product benefit focus, we highlight some situations where brands do not follow this pattern.

Differential vs. Central Positioning In the previous section, we mentioned the importance of advertising contributing to the perceived differential advantage for the brand. This is true for most brands. For example, Reitmans, a women's clothing retailer, distances itself from other high-fashion stores with its many campaigns that reinforce its positioning, "Designed for real life."[21] However, market circumstances allow brands to claim a central position within the product category. A central brand positioning strategy is possible when the brand can claim and deliver on the most salient benefits. This may be a function of the brand being the market share leader, achieving success during the growth stage of the product life cycle, or having unique brand characteristics that essentially define the category. A new brand of subcompact car illustrates one successful central positioning strategy.

After a successful launch in Canada, Toyota changed its entry into the subcompact car market from the Echo to the Yaris due to a change in international strategy. The problem appeared particularly vexing because the switch from Tercel to Echo had occurred just a few years previously. Moreover, the Echo sedan and hatchback established a 42-percent market share, so the change could have emerged as a significant risk for Toyota. The task seemed even more challenging when promotional planners acknowledged that the Yaris had improved styling, a higher price, and no advantageous standard features in a category that consumers perceived as an economic compromise with a rational purchase process. Finally, Toyota's research indicated a trend of its customers getting older, so a younger-oriented positioning also appeared necessary.

The solution emerged in the form of "Uncle Yaris," a fictional character to reflect the lifestyle associated with the brand and act as an adviser to young people without the stigma of the message coming from one's parents. The promotional planners decided to move away from the idea of a subcompact car specifically and let its advertising act as a leader to attract consumers through its innovative creativity. It appears that the Yaris planners envisioned a market partition along the end benefit "fun to drive"—a more emotional criterion for purchase. Follow-up research indicated sales far superior to the Echo launch, a younger clientele, and a solid position as category leader with the consumer perception of being a fun car.[22]

Achieving central positioning in a category through advertising is not an easy task for most promotional planners. The Yaris example demonstrates that a market leader—or one of the market leaders—can attempt this position in mature product categories. It should be noted that the subcompact market recently appeared in transition for a period as five-door hatchback vehicles and small cars in general made a comeback thanks to rising gasoline costs. In this sense, the market segment undertook renewed growth as consumers switched from other preferences and first-time buyers considered small cars more frequently.

In another market context, being the first brand in a product category is a good start, but research suggests it is not a guarantee; in some categories the second and third entries after the initial pioneer have also established strong positions. Yves Rocher, a pioneer in the plant-based skin care category, lost its dominance as other brands claimed these ingredients important in their ads (e.g., Aveeno). So the French brand ensured that its advertising, and all other marketing offers (e.g., store, spa, information lab) reflected its botanical roots to re-confirm its central position.[23] Finally, sometimes brands attempt to take a central position in a subcategory, as seen in Exhibit 6-8.

Brand Benefit vs. User Positioning We have thus far implied that most positioning decisions involve unique and differential benefit claims that the brand can deliver. The market partition and competitive analysis gives promotional planners

Exhibit 6-8 Lipton tries to establish itself in the carbonated green tea category.

Exhibit 6-9 Valvoline positions by product user.

the opportunity to identify and determine the most important ones to claim in advertising. For example, Lay's potato chip ads extol the virtues of using 100 percent Canadian potatoes.[24] The premise of the strategy focused on getting back to the core of the product, presumably to differentiate from other snacks with less pure ingredients. Again, while this is true for many product categories and brands, some situations allow for a user positioning. This was the previous approach for Lay's that challenged consumers to eat only one chip. Often, a brand is positioned by association with a particular user or group of users. An example is the Valvoline ad shown in Exhibit 6-9. This campaign emphasizes identification or association with a specific group, in this case car enthusiasts. A user brand positioning strategy occurs in situations where the individual is motivated for social or individual reasons and the ads emphasize how good the consumer feels while using the brand (Exhibit 6-10).

CIBC emphasized a user positioning in a campaign to offer its customers additional products and services with the "It's worth a talk" message. Each execution focuses on a key financial planning issue, like: "How can I pay less tax?" and "Is there an easier way to understand my financial picture?" These kinds of questions intend to spark interest in customers to forge a stronger relationship with themselves and CIBC's financial advisers.[25] And higher-education institutions have entered into advertising for new students each year: Brock University's creative and daring visual effort, with a focus on how students can study what they desire, is again representative of a user positioning.[26] The new marketing

Exhibit 6-10 Positioning that focuses on the product user.

Nissan Thinks Outside the Box with Its Cube

Positioning is a tricky decision when launching a new brand and a new product format. With that in mind, Nissan took one of its greatest risks ever with the Cube, a small car with its own flair and personality. According to a Nissan VP, "Instead of telling people what this car was, we asked people who we thought would be predisposed to liking it what it should be. We wanted to harness the creative minds in Canada to an idea and see what they could come up with." Nissan and its agency, Capital C, arrived at a unique contest to award 50 winners a new vehicle. Through social media, Nissan invited various artistic people to enter the contest online (at hypercube.ca), with the top 500 subsequently asked to audition over a period of six weeks. Their task involved a demonstration of their creativity and social media networking ability, with the winners determined by an independent judging panel and online votes.

Nissan received 7,000 entries, representing a variety of consumer variables including those from teens not yet of legal driving age. As one Nissan executive commented, "Even in traditional launches, you have your target demographic but when you go back and analyze who's actually purchased the vehicle, it's often very different from that." The contest yielded 117,000 website visits, a quarter-million votes, 1.4 million views of the 50 finalists' web pages, and extensive press coverage throughout the three-month effort. Winners got their new Cube and blogged about their experiences (cubecommunity.ca) with the vehicle for the next 12 months.

Even with all the successful metrics and additional brand exposure through blogging, Nissan endured criticism over how it handled the judging. Some griped about winners not meeting the contest criteria; one social media effort landed on the issue of a social connection between a member of the judging panel and a winner. Because the nature of the contest fixated on social groups Nissan expected some conflict, and judges did excuse themselves for all conflicts except the one in question. Beyond this, some also criticized Nissan for "pre-identifying" the winners based on a comment from one executive; "The Cube is a quirky, function-follows-form kind of car. It is not for everybody, and it is not meant to be. The person getting out of there will have dreadlocks and a courier bag, or they will have their modeling portfolio under their arm; they are not giving in. They are pursuing their creative dreams."

After the successful beginning and negative reactions, a question remained regarding the next step as suggested by the VP, "Is there ever an appropriate time for me to put this car on television now?" And, indeed, by the end of 2009 the next step included extensive product placement on the new show *Crash and Burn*, where the main character drove the Cube as his work vehicle and mobile office. The deal also involved on-air billboards and TV ads during the show along with print and radio ads.

Sources: Jonathan Paul, "Nissan's Hypercube: A Convincing Social Test Drive," *Strategy*, October 2009, p. 26; Matt Semansky, "Controversy Cubed," *Marketing Magazine*, August 6, 2009; Matt Semansky, "Nissan Auditions the Cube Via Social Media Campaign," *Marketing Magazine*, March 19, 2009; Matt Semansky, "Nissan Rewards Top Cubists," *Marketing Magazine*, August 6, 2009.

Question:

1. In what ways did Nissan actually position the new Cube?

communication for the Nissan Cube raises interesting questions regarding the first two positioning decisions, as seen in IMC Perspective 6-2.

TARGET AUDIENCE BRAND ATTITUDE

Previously in this chapter we identified the concepts of salient attributes or salient benefits. This notion is based on the idea that consumers may hold a number of different beliefs about brands in any product or service category. However, not all of these beliefs are activated in forming an attitude. Beliefs concerning specific attributes or benefits that are activated and form the basis of an attitude are referred to as **salient beliefs**. Marketers should identify these salient beliefs and understand how the saliency varies among different target audiences, over time, and across different consumption situations. Marketers can use a specific model to develop persuasive brand positioning strategies since it guides which attributes and benefits to empha-size in advertising.

Brand Attitude Model Consumer researchers and marketing practitioners use multiattribute attitude models to study consumer attitudes.[27] A **multiattribute atti-tude model** views an attitude object, such as a product or brand, as possessing a number of attributes that provide the basis on which consumers form their attitudes. According to this model, consumers have beliefs about specific brand attributes and attach different levels of importance to these attributes. Using this approach, an attitude toward a particular brand can be represented as

$$A_B = \sum_{i=1}^{n} B_i \times E_i$$

where A_B = attitude toward a brand
B_i = beliefs about the brand's performance on attribute i
E_i = importance attached to attribute i
n = number of attributes considered

For example, a consumer may have beliefs (B_i) about various brands of toothpaste on certain attributes. One brand may be perceived as having fluoride and thus pre-venting cavities, tasting good, and helping control tartar buildup. Another brand may not be perceived as having these attributes, but consumers may believe it per-forms well on other attributes such as freshening breath and whitening teeth.

To predict attitudes, one must know how much importance consumers attach to each of these attributes (E_i). For example, parents purchasing toothpaste for their children may prefer a brand that performs well on cavity prevention, a preference that leads to a more favourable attitude toward the first brand. Teenagers and young adults may prefer a brand that freshens their breath and makes their teeth white and thus prefer the second brand.

Brand Attitude Persuasion Multiattribute models help marketers diagnose the beliefs that underlie consumers' evaluations of a brand and the importance of various attributes or benefits allow-ing marketers to develop communication strategies, like maintaining attitudes of current customers or changing attitudes of non-customers. A recent study demonstrated that research examining attribute ratings of these two groups provided important guid-ance for improving the marketing communication strategy for a European telecommunications firm.[28] Thus, the multiattribute model shows how marketers can persuade attitudes of varying target audiences.

Influence Attribute Belief The first strategy is to identify an attribute or benefit that is important and communicate how well the brand performs. In situations where consumers do not perceive the mar-keter's brand as possessing an important attribute or the belief strength is low, advertising strategies may be targeted at changing the belief rating; this approach appears to be relevant for Cashmere in Exhibit 6-11. Even when belief strength is high, advertising may be used to increase the rating of a brand on an important attribute. The Harvey's campaign for grill-cooked hamburgers illustrates

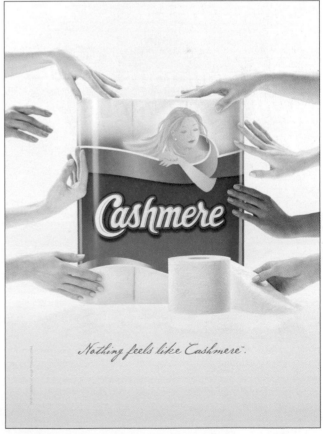

Exhibit 6-11 Cashmere associates its brand name with the attributes of its namesake to convey softness.

163

this approach. Other quick-service food retailers focused on fast drive-through or convenient locations, along with enhanced menus with healthier foods. Harvey's appeared disadvantaged in comparison and faced declining sales and a reduced number of franchises. The grill attribute positioning conjured both functional benefits (e.g., fresh, natural, healthy) and emotional benefits (e.g., outdoor BBQ, male bonding). The positioning succeeded, with unaided awareness moving from 13 percent to 22 percent, key brand attitude measures improving, purchase intention rising from 21 percent to 38 percent, and negative sales growth of 3 percent reversed to positive growth of 2 percent.[29]

Influence Attribute Importance Marketers attempt to influence consumer attitudes by changing the relative importance of a particular attribute. This second strategy involves getting consumers to attach more importance to the attribute in forming their attitude toward the brand. Marketers using this strategy want to increase the importance of an attribute their particular brand has. The print ads for Jergens Ultra Care moisturizer highlight the importance to a woman of regularly applying lotion all over her body. The positioning was intended to demonstrate that moisturizing was as important as all the other beauty activities that women engage in every day. The main message suggested that women "Take care of what you wear every day" with a visual showing the lotion on a woman's body, and obviously associated a woman's skin with her wardrobe. The positioning was initiated in Quebec as the brand underachieved significantly compared to other parts of Canada. Research indicated that women from Quebec did not separate beauty and skin care from health. This insight suggested that new users could be attracted to the brand if the ads conveyed the sensuality of moisturized skin. A 50 percent increase in sales in Quebec allowed the brand's positioning to be extended in English rather than continuing with the planned U.S. ads.[30]

Add New Attribute Belief The third strategy for influencing consumer attitudes is to add or emphasize a new attribute that consumers can use in evaluating a brand. Marketers do this by focusing on additional benefits or consequences associated with using the brand that have not been communicated previously. Exhibit 6-12 is an ad for Mott's Fruitsations, with enhanced nutrients for bone health. Wonder+, a line extension of the famous Wonder bread, needed to communicate that it had the same great taste as the original, but that it had the nutrition of whole wheat bread. The new brand attempted to influence lapsed users of Wonder bread due to the perception that white bread was no longer healthy. Yet at the same time, managers knew that the message had to reinforce the attitude of loyal customers. Adding the health benefit worked, with clever imagery of twins eating both types of bread and believing that they both taste the same, yet one is now whole wheat. The positioning of this advertising produced significant gains for all communication effects and sales.

Influence Attribute Belief of Competitor Brand A final strategy marketers use is to change consumer beliefs about the attributes of competing brands or product categories. This strategy has become much more common with the increase in comparative

Exhibit 6-12 Mott's highlights the importance of strong bones via its Fruitsations brand.

advertising, where marketers compare their brands to competitors' on specific product attributes. An example of this is the comparative ad shown in Exhibit 6-13.

CONSUMER PURCHASE MOTIVE

Since positioning involves presenting the brand's benefit claims to a target audience, the portrayal of the benefits influences how consumers will respond to the brand's delivery and whether the target audience perceives them as important. The portrayal of benefits is reflected by the purchase motivation associated with the brand. Thus, the purchase motivation of the target audience is another important decision for the brand positioning strategy.

Importance of Purchase Motives   As we suggested with the Harvey's attribute positioning, given the content of the ad, the underlying reason for enjoying a grilled hamburger appears to be the taste sensation. However, another perspective is that it could reflect healthier eating compared to fried hamburgers, since less fat is retained in the meat and consequently less fat is consumed, so consumers can feel better about their dietary choices. This connection between the cooking attribute and healthier eating could have been communicated with some subtle changes in the ads of the current campaign. Thus, the attribute positioning still requires the right kind of motivation or reason for purchase demonstrated in the ad to be completely successful.

Keep in mind that the reasons for the Harvey's hamburger purchase are quite distinct: the sensory enjoyment of the hamburger versus the individual accomplishment of eating properly. We highlight these two ideas since they are two of eight basic consumer purchase motives that are more managerially useful to guide the brand positioning strategy decision within Rossiter and Percy's framework we have discussed previously. Figure 6-8 summarizes these motives into two types consistent with psychological theory.

Informational motives are negatively based since the consumer perceives their current consumption situation as some kind of deficit in which the purchase of the product would minimize the shortfall and bring the consumer a neutral or normal state. Exhibit 6-14 suggests an informational motive for non-users. **Transformational motives** imply consumers perceive their consumption situation as requiring some improvement from a neutral state. Negative- and positive-oriented motives are consistent with psychological theories of motivation and are similar to Maslow's theory—however, there is no implied hierarchy.

Exhibit 6-13   Influencing beliefs of competitor brand.

Exhibit 6-14   Ad implies incomplete satisfaction of competing brands.

165

Informational Motives	**Transformational Motives**
Problem removal	Sensory gratification
Problem avoidance	Intellectual stimulation or mastery
Incomplete satisfaction	Social approval
Mixed approach-avoidance	
Normal depletion	

FIGURE   6–8

Eight basic consumer purchase motives

Informational Motives   Problem-removal motives reflect consumption situations where consumers perceive a problem, for example dandruff, and seek a product that resolves the problem, like anti-dandruff shampoo. Many products in this category have emphasized this motive in their ads while attempting to highlight a unique attribute or benefit positioning. However, more recent ads for Head & Shoulders in Canada have mentioned the problem while emphasizing how good one's hair feels after using their anti-dandruff shampoo, thus reflecting a different primary motive beyond the initial problem removal. This is the reason for connecting the purchase motive shown in the ad to the brand positioning strategy—it identifies the particular way to communicate effectively with a target audience that the brand has profiled in great detail.

Problem avoidance motives occur when consumers anticipate a problem if they do not take some preemptive action through the purchase of a product. Listerine successfully illustrated a problem avoidance motive in its ad messages by colourfully showing how mouthwash superheroes fight germs that cause bad breath. While a positioning by use may be operational, the underlying reason for purchase more precisely defines the overall strategy.

Incomplete satisfaction motives are based on the consumer perceptions that they are not fully satisfied with their current brand choice and are seeking a better product. Canadian food retailer New York Fries, with 180 outlets in Canada, Australia, and the Middle East, emphasized fresh-cut potatoes and cooked-to-order in a new "Authentically New York" ad message.[31] A positioning on quality, directed toward teens and young adults who purchase high volumes of quick-service food, resonates with those who are not completely satisfied with french fries from multiple competing outlets. From another perspective, we can see ads that indicate an incomplete satisfaction motive yet have a positioning-by-competitor focus. For example, Bell Mobility ran ads inviting Fido users to switch their cell phone provider.[32]

Mixed approach-avoidance motives are active for consumers in purchase situations where they enjoy some elements of a product but dislike other parts and are seeking alternative solutions. WestJet proclaimed itself a low-fare leader in its initial advertising messages. As it developed its service, it also evolved the message to show that it flew more destinations with fun and friendly service.[33] It appears WestJet employed a price/quality brand positioning strategy and its ability to find a competitive niche against Air Canada suggests a mixed approach-avoidance motive, where some consumers liked Air Canada but were seeking a more affordable alternative that had reasonably comparable service levels.

Consumers regularly require a product because they have none on hand, and so normal depletion as a reason for purchase is an almost-everyday situation; however, it is not a viable option for a primary brand positioning strategy. A message focusing on a reminder purchase when a consumer does not have the product is featured in seasonal purchases. For example, gardening products in the spring and school supplies in the fall are two obvious ad messages we commonly see. In essence, a normal depletion motive is not a long-term strategy; however, it is useful for short-term situations and reaching particular target audiences at a particular point in time to maximize total sales during a year.

Transformational Motives   As the term implies, sensory gratification motives are predicated on the product providing a positive experience via one of the five senses. The ad for Nestlé Mousse conveys the sensual enjoyment of eating this unique chocolate experience (Exhibit 6-15). Clearly, this is a valuable approach for many types of products, but it is important to focus on the right aspect with the right reference point. In Alberta consumers were encouraged to attend horse racing for reasons similar to going to the movies—for the entertainment value—demonstrating a brand repositioning strategy or perhaps positioning by product class to non-users and indicating a sensory gratification motive. Small newspaper ads designed like movie ads and placed in the entertainment section (versus the sports section, to reach current users) provided an entertainment alternative and increased awareness and attendance.[34]

Intellectual stimulation or mastery is an individual motive linked to some element of self-improvement through the purchase of a particular product. Working with its Canadian agency, US Organic Orange Growers sought to develop the Canadian market with the same message—"Grown in the U.S.A."—that worked well south of the border. Research indicated that Canadians knew that most oranges originated from the U.S., in addition to a few other countries; they perceived this attribute with less importance compared to the fact that organic oranges contained 30 percent more vitamin C.[35] Appealing with a health attribute brand positioning strategy, we surmise that improved diet indicates an intellectual stimulation motive as consumers demonstrated their concern for well-being and heightened involvement in their nourishment needs.

Personal recognition is suggested with the social approval motive, whereby consumers are motivated to purchase certain products or brands because consumers aspire to be accepted in certain social groups. An anti-smoking message by the Nova Scotia Office of Health Promotion illustrates a social approval motive within the context of positioning toward the product user. The characters from the Canadian cult film *Fubar* provided great tongue-in-cheek reasons to smoke by emphasizing the benefits of body odour and emphysema. The campaign thus positioned non-smoking to non-users of tobacco as something socially desirable.[36]

Exhibit 6-15 Nestlé conveys the sensual enjoyment of chocolate consumption.

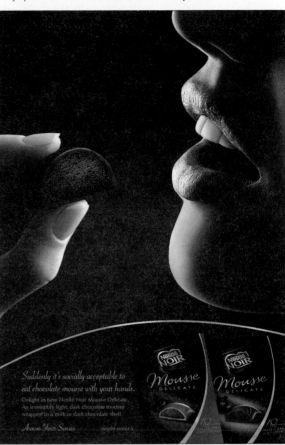

BRAND REPOSITIONING STRATEGY

The brand positioning strategy may have to be changed due to factors found in situation analysis. For example, marketing objectives such as sales or share may be below forecast, or advertising claims from competitors may threaten the current strategy. Developing a new brand positioning strategy is referred to as repositioning. This is often difficult to achieve because of established attitudes to the brand. The options for altering the brand positioning strategy typically focus on the same four topics previously defined: market definition, differential advantage, target audience, and a salient motive. (Further details of the examples provided in this section can be found in the case studies available on Cassies.ca.)

MARKET DEFINITION

McCain's Crescendo Rising Crust Pizza experienced weak results after battling with Kraft's Delissio for five years. Despite McCain introducing the first product and establishing the frozen pizza category, Kraft outsold McCain by a four to one margin in the $400-million market due to heavier retail and advertising expenditures.[37] The initial message from both brands positioned the products against pizza ordered from a restaurant (i.e., pizzeria) and delivered or picked up from the location. For example, McCain claimed, "Who can tell it from takeout?" while Kraft exclaimed,

167

"It's not delivery, it's Delissio!" Clearly, both brands defined the market in terms of a store purchase for home preparation versus a restaurant takeout/delivery purchase, thus exhibiting a product category positioning.

McCain repositioned Crescendo on the key benefit of a "rising crust," distancing it from the established product category positioning that Kraft owned. The rising crust claim implied quality, freshness, and taste. The repositioning also featured a change in target audience to teens who recommended or influenced the pizza purchase to their parents, who did the shopping and paid for the groceries. The "Tan Lines" campaign, with the tagline "Nothing rises like Crescendo," carried out this positioning as oblivious teens got slight tan lines on their faces while they watched the crust rise as it baked.

Media included television and billboards, while teens with makeup tan lines offered coupons and buttons at street promotional events. Impressive results emerged as sales rose 34 percent, market share increased 8 percent, and some research reported increased awareness. Finally, the campaign garnered publicity as it was spoofed on *Air Farce* and *This Hour Has 22 Minutes,* satirized by Aislin in a *Montreal Gazette* cartoon, and featured in a newspaper article that jokingly questioned scientists as to whether one could get tan lines through an oven door.

DIFFERENTIAL ADVANTAGE

As discussed earlier, determining the differential advantage concerned a differential versus central positioning, and product benefits versus user positioning. RBC's "First for You" campaign, launched in 2004, appears to have repositioned the brand on both accounts. RBC looked to have an overall campaign for each of its three business lines—personal banking, corporate, and institutional—with the goal of increasing the number of products purchased by its current customers from its current 2.46.

Previous messages focused on benefits of RBC's products and services with an emphasis on differentiation. Instead, the new campaign emphasized the innovativeness of the organization over time through things like sports sponsorship, personal services, and credit card rewards with the intention to convey RBC as the market leader in the banking industry. In other words, the brand moved from a differentiated positioning strategy to a central positioning strategy. Depicting a customer representing the letter "I" in the word "first" and emphasizing their satisfaction in selecting RBC contributed to a shift from a product benefit positioning strategy to a user positioning strategy.

The launch featured multiple media, and over the course of the first two years RBC ran 19 TV ads, 140 print ads, and 30 posters. The campaign also included events, direct, Internet, and corporate communication. Total spending amounted to $26 million annually, about the same as previous years. Results for RBC imply the new positioning is headed in the right direction. Some awareness, attitudinal, and brand equity measures suggest RBC is in the top 20 percent for all financial ads. Products per customer rose, suggesting a strong ROI for the advertising investment.[38]

NEW TARGET AUDIENCE

As we saw in Chapter 3, organizations target advertising messages to both customers, such as brand loyals and favourable brand switchers, and non-customers, such as new category users, other brand switchers, and other brand loyals. We now illustrate various repositioning strategies for each of these target audiences.

Brand-Loyal Customers Gatorade experienced a decline in the sports drink market for the first time in 20 years during 2004. Faced with competition within its category from Powerade, and pressure from emerging product categories such as energy drinks and new formats for water (enhanced, flavoured), Gatorade saw its share slip from 73 percent to 68 percent. Although the efficacy of Gatorade for hydration is scientifically established, regulations do not allow this benefit claim to be communicated in broadcast media. Finally, despite an established brand position as "the" sports drink for all male athletes who play their best at all times and desire maximum performance, Gatorade required a new approach to maintain its past success.

Consumer insight suggested that Canadian sports people enjoyed playing and watching many sports despite being overwhelmingly passionate about hockey. This differed significantly from American male athletes and indicated an opportunity to associate a unique consumption experience for the new flavour, X-Factor. A key execution in this reformulated strategy showed the many sports in which Gatorade might be consumed in a montage of scenes moving from the letter A to the letter X, ending with a product shot of the new entrant. For example, for the letter B, the visual showed an overhead picture of a hockey net, which outlines the letter.

The positioning established important effectiveness measures as "level of enjoyment" and "relevance" hit levels well beyond average—as did purchase intention. Sales and share improved while Powerade's sales declined, giving some indication that Gatorade had regained some of its loyal customers with a new image. Gatorade is an example of a brand where much of its marketing communication reinforces its positioning with its loyal customers (see Exhibit 6-16).[39]

Favourable Brand Switcher Customers For the 2005 model year, Toyota had its hands full in the compact car category as the well-established Corolla attempted to defend its share against a new model from Honda Civic and more recent models from Mazda, Pontiac, and Chevrolet, along with newer Korean brands offering very good value. In 2004, the Civic led the category with 46,000 units sold; Corolla and Mazda were close behind.

Research indicated that among various key benefits 56 percent of consumers believed the Corolla to be reliable and dependable, compared to the 34 percent of consumers believing compact cars could deliver reliability or dependability. This fit well with the psychographic profile of Corolla buyers, who tended to balance form and function when buying almost anything, and to whom minimizing risk when buying something like a car appeared very important. So while the positioning on reliability to compact consumers in the market during 2005 may have seemed kind of boring, the resulting message of "One thing you can count on" hit the mark just right. By May 2006 Corolla edged ahead of the Honda Civic, even while spending less than half as much money on communication.[40]

New Category Users With 3 percent of the juice drink market, Five Alive faced the task of growing beyond its predominant sales to mothers aged 25–54 purchasing mostly for their children. The new target audience identified young adults 25–34, of which one-third were regular users despite awareness at 72 percent. In particular, the brand focused on a psychographic group labelled "experiencers," who desired to try new experiences in all facets of life (e.g., social and leisure activities) just prior to moving on to "family life" in a few years. In addition, the five fruit juices provided a unique drink for this lifestyle that appeared healthier than pop or iced

Exhibit 6-16 Gatorade targets different audiences with unique messages.

tea and easier to consume than 100-percent juice. Although Five Alive could not claim "Five Alive makes you feel alive" due to legal regulations, it could claim that "Five Alive captures the spirit of feeling alive." Thus, the ads communicated the positioning of the five fruit flavours as a unique characteristic of the brand.

Over five years, Five Alive employed many TV and out-of-home ads to produce impressive results. Brand and advertising awareness and attitudinal measures increased substantially. For instance, ad awareness improved from 44 percent to 82 percent despite actually lowering the amount of money spent on advertising over time. Purchase intentions rose from 30 percent to 38 percent and trial rates improved from 70 percent to 75 percent. By the end of five years sales had nearly doubled to $40 million while the category shrank by 4 percent, allowing Five Alive to move market share from 2.5 percent to 5.2 percent.[41]

Other Brand Loyals Scotiabank tackled the problem of attracting non-customers after spending considerable time building loyalty among its own customers. Many consumers of other banks believed that switching banks would not be worth the effort, with an attitude that "all banks are the same." Since the four other major banks attained about 30 percent household penetration each, Scotiabank envisioned an opportunity to move beyond its level of 19 percent. Research indicated a prevailing theme of some consumers needing banking services to help manage their money more effectively on a month-to-month basis. Many experienced frustration while working hard and making sufficient income, yet feeling like they did not have sufficient resources.

Scotiabank's positioning on enhanced financial service, encapsulated by the phrase "You're richer than you think," allowed the brand to connect with consumers dissatisfied with their experiences at other banks. The ads to support this positioning clearly showed how Scotiabank would help consumers find money they did not know they had by managing their loans and financing more effectively. IMC tools employed to support this innovative brand positioning strategy included TV and magazine ads, branch point-of-sale, direct mail, Internet, permission-based e-mail, and financial seminars.

The new positioning appeared promising for Scotiabank after 18 months; brand awareness increased from 36 percent to 56 percent, and unaided TV advertising awareness moved from 6 percent to 22 percent while aided grew from 15 percent to 39 percent. Scotiabank noted stronger brand associations, and purchase intentions grew to 33 percent from 24 percent. Finally, business results improved—$40 million profit with a 38 percent increase in new customers per month.[42]

Other Brand Switchers With share dwindling to below 5 percent because of lagging product innovation and weak advertising expenditure, Juicy Fruit managers determined that the chewing gum brand required a radical change in the positioning strategy with respect to its target audience. Its historical target of reasonably loyal adults aged 18–34 who comprised half the brand's sales would be teens who accounted for only 6 percent of sales. Moreover, teens represented the heaviest users and exhibited fickle preferences across brands due to their impulse purchase habits, whereby 84 percent purchased chewing gum weekly.

Preliminary qualitative research produced the concept of "sweet." The meaning to teens implied both "cool" and "don't take things too seriously." To establish this positioning, it meant Juicy Fruit had to literally destroy the old positioning to show "cool" things to teens with the iconic smashing guitar scenes in the TV ads. Sweet described the brand's classic fruit flavour, so the double meaning appeared as another catchy way to reinvent Juicy Fruit's old image. Sweet also allowed Juicy Fruit to have an overall positioning for all its product formats (i.e., sugar free, blue, red).

Overall market share more than doubled to almost 11 percent by the end of 2004 and returned the brand to profitability. Awareness undoubtedly improved, but critical brand image statistics supported the idea that Juicy Fruit had established a new brand position with teens. A tracking study suggested stronger attitudes toward Juicy Fruit compared to Dentyne Ice and Trident for characteristics like "fun," "cool," and "brand I can relate to." Teen consumption shifted from the initial 6 percent of sales to 19 percent.[43]

PURCHASE MOTIVATION

A brand repositioning strategy through consumer purchase motivation implies a shift from one type of motive to another. The most significant shift would be moving from an informational motive to a transformational motive or vice versa. We present two examples to show successful repositioning through a new consumer purchase motivation.

Problem–Solution   Moores Clothing for Men found great success by altering the purchase motive conveyed in its ads. Originally named Moores: The Suit People, an entry-level retailer, its initial advertising employed the line "Well Made. Well Priced. Well Dressed." Although quality perceptions grew, because of the "high-end" look of some of its ads consumers became confused as to whether the brand represented a discount clothing store or a fashion store. The new positioning clearly showed men with various wardrobe problems like *suit too tight* or *suit out of style,* and offered Moores as a solution (see Exhibit 6-17). This positioning connected with a group of men who wore business clothes for work yet preferred not to wear such clothes and would rather spend their disposable income on other life purchases. For this target audience, shopping was a necessary activity rather than entertaining or adventurous. Moores certainly carved out a niche with this positioning, as sales growth reversed from 4.5 percent to 6.5 percent.[44]

Intellectual Stimulation   Listerine's established position as a mouthwash that "kills germs that cause bad breath" had run its course as consumers became more proactive in their oral health instead of relying completely on their dentist. From a competitive standpoint, consumers believed the brand to be "old," "serious," and "authoritarian," and Listerine fell behind the market leader Scope and private-label brands as consumers did not perceive much difference. As part of the increased awareness and behaviour change for oral health, consumers became more concerned about the health of their gums. Listerine's clinical research proved that it could be effective against gingivitis, but the connection for this gum disease and mouthwash appeared to be very distant in the eyes of consumers. Listerine targeted "therapy seekers," those consumers who actively managed their health including their oral health. They appeared receptive to an empowering message oriented to their personal decision to be a healthier person.

The creative to support this positioning emerged as "Listerine: The action hero for your gums." Over the course of six years, the new positioning allowed Listerine to grow remarkably. In the first three years, Listerine improved its key brand image ratings—such as helps fight gingivitis, promotes healthy mouth, and kills germs—from an average of about 50 percent to 80 percent. Purchase intention and usage

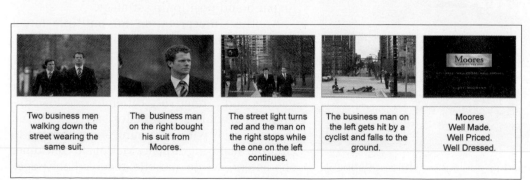

Exhibit 6-17
Moores's repositioning introduced a purchase motive not seen for clothes.

rates improved by about 10 percent each as well. Awareness of the ads showed strong numbers, and many consumers could link the ads to the brand. These numbers remained very strong for the remaining three years and showed continued modest gains. Finally, Listerine moved its market share from 39 percent to 52 percent, while Scope's declined from 28 percent to 20 percent.[45]

IMC PLANNING: BRAND POSITIONING EXTENSIONS

From an IMC planning perspective, we can extend or adapt the concepts encompassing the brand positioning strategy decisions in three directions: multiple target audiences, buyer decision stages, and corporate brands. The idea is to work with the general model for the positioning decisions and modify it for different parts of the IMC plan.

MULTIPLE TARGET AUDIENCES

Throughout this chapter we have examined the brand positioning strategy for a single target audience of end users. Many organizations target multiple audiences for their marketing communication for many reasons. For example, in Chapter 3 we outlined different customer and non-customer groups; brands in fact do have the opportunity to invest in marketing communication devoted to each group. This raises the question as to whether the brand should develop exactly the same positioning strategy for each target audience, or whether some variation should exist. The new marketing strategy by Mark's has led to new target audiences for marketing communication (Exhibit 6-18). And, if variation is necessary, what aspects of the brand positioning strategy need to be customized? A number of the examples in Chapter 3 implied this issue; however, after describing positioning strategy, we need to return to the opportunity for promotional planners to fully consider their options.

Although promotional planners could consider customizing all four brand positioning strategy decisions, the first two, market definition and differential advantage, would likely remain relatively constant across customer and non-customer groups. The specific messages to influence brand attitude and the purchase motive communicated offer greater opportunity for getting the right message at the right time. One IMC tool to execute this customized brand positioning strategy is the Internet. For example, automobile advertisers might consider consumers who visit websites to gather information while searching for a vehicle as more likely to be brand switchers, and will include messages that position the brand against its strongest competitor on specific benefits and portray those benefits along the lines of the target audience having some dissatisfaction with their current brand. While this is just one example, promotional planners can look at all advertising options and all IMC tools for opportunities to deliver a more specific message to a particular target audience that reinforces a particular brand positioning strategy.

Another interpretation for multiple target audiences involves group decision making, another topic introduced in Chapter 3. For example, in traditional family situations an advertiser may attempt one brand positioning strategy for parents and a relatively different one for children. McDonald's has historically employed this approach with communication directed to children featuring Ronald McDonald and other characters, while parents received messages of the special time they could enjoy with their

Exhibit 6-18   Mark's revised its audiences while updating its marketing strategy.

172

family. Additionally, considering a husband and wife scenario, automobile brands can use print ads to emphasize certain car features that appeal to men in magazines where men represent a higher proportion of the audience, and similarly for women.

BUYER DECISION STAGES

In the IMC planning section of Chapter 5 we noted that marketers could consider message and communication tool options for each stage of the consumer decision-making process. Various message options can be discerned from the brand positioning strategy decisions outlined in this chapter. First, promotional planners can decide which part of the brand positioning strategy would be most relevant or effective at each stage. Market definition and differential advantage may be more appropriate at the pre-purchase stage or need-recognition stage. For example, the marketing for the Mini in Canada used television advertising to signal that it competed against two markets: regular compact cars like Honda Civic, and other smaller sports cars like the BMW 3 Series. It also emphasized its advantage of being small in size, but not *too* small.

In contrast, Internet microsites (mini.ca/experiment, mini.ca/choice, mini.ca/family, mini.ca/date) offered positioning on specific benefits with a transformational motive for consumers actively searching for information about the new brand. In fact, the Internet microsites facilitated customer relationships by inviting prospects to register. Mini reported an average response rate of 20 percent for each of the four sites. The brand positioning strategies along buyer decision stages also illustrated the second option. Specifically, promotional planners can use different IMC tools to communicate certain elements of the brand positioning strategy. Finally, promotional planners can use various media to convey specific attributes that are not in other media. For example, Mini used billboards to communicate its British heritage and speed, and magazines to illustrate its safety.

CORPORATE BRANDS

Thus far we have defined brand positioning strategy and illustrated examples where the brand is at the product level. For instance, our initial brand positioning strategy example involved WestJet and how its communication intended to establish an enhanced brand position among dissatisfied Air Canada customers. Corporate brands are also part of integrated marketing communications and are the focus of the public relations topics in Chapter 15. In this context, corporate brands often have varied target audiences, for example investors or members of a particular community.

Given the broader scope of the corporate brand, the initial positioning decision for market definition would concern brand name in most cases. Establishing a differential advantage from a corporate brand entails both differential and central positioning. For example, corporate brand-building activities for Honda suggest that it attempted to establish a central positioning concerning environmental responsibility. This would coincide with its marketing activities of introducing the first hybrid vehicle. Again, the organization-wide communication would imply that most corporate brand positioning would focus on brand benefit positioning over user positioning; however, recent "green marketing" efforts by companies suggest potential for the latter with an appropriate message that signifies altruistic feelings upon the target audience.

All marketing communication decisions are or should be designed to influence target audience attitudes, so corporate brand attitude persuasion is entirely relevant. For example, organizations often involve themselves in various sponsorship activities to signal that they are socially responsible, a key attribute to communicate to the general public or to future employees or other stakeholders. Finally, most corporate brand communication is intended along the lines of transformational motives; the clearest examples are television commercials with triumphant music and everlasting positive images.

CHAPTER OBJECTIVES AND SUMMARY

1 To review the concepts of market positioning strategy and market position.

The strategic marketing plan describes all marketing decisions including promotion and the supporting analysis and justification. It typically includes the market positioning strategy, which summarizes the markets the organization is competing in (i.e., target market) and how the marketing mix fulfills the needs of this market. The resulting consumer perception as to where the consumer believes the organization to be competing is known as the market position. Oftentimes, market research illuminates where consumers perceive an organization with respect to its competitors, which can be graphed on a market position diagram or perceptual map. Promotional planners rely on this document for all decisions including the overall IMC direction, creative strategy, and creative tactics for advertising or any other IMC tool such as sales promotion, public relations, direct, or Internet.

2 To apply the positioning concept in an advertising context by defining brand positioning strategy and brand position.

For many communication problems or opportunities, promotional messages are directed to target audiences. These audiences are a subset of the target market or an entirely different group depending upon the communications situation. As discussed in Chapter 3, promotional planners require a detailed profile of the target audience with most appropriate segmentation variables, including whether the target is a customer or non-customer. Advertising or any other promotional message is guided by the brand positioning strategy that specifies how it is intended to influence its target audience with a given product category or product market. The resulting target audience perception as to what the brand offers is known as the brand position. The flexibility of influencing a target audience's brand position through many IMC tools allows promotional managers to plan for unique brand positions for multiple target audiences.

3 To illustrate how to formulate the brand positioning strategy decisions.

The process for developing a brand positioning strategy in the context of marketing communications is similar to developing a positioning strategy for the overall marketing. However, it differs by evaluating or integrating very micro-level aspects of consumer behaviour in its planning by closely considering the nature of the purchase decision. The direction of the decisions is much different, with the goal of finding the most appropriate message, media, or IMC tool versus determining optimal product design features.

The brand positioning strategy comprises four decisions: market definition, differential advantage, target audience brand attitude, and consumer purchase motive. The market definition decision allows the promotional planner to consider whether to define the market in which the brand is competing by benefits, brand name, usage situation, or product category. Differential advantage decisions include whether the brand takes a differential or central positioning and whether the brand focuses its positioning on its benefit claims or the user. Target audience attitude decisions consider how the message is expected to persuade existing beliefs to the desired beliefs about the brand. Finally, promotional planners decide what type of purchase motive should be associated with the brand.

4 To summarize various brand repositioning strategy opportunities.

In some communication situations—such as new competitors, changing consumer tastes, or poor brand performance—promotion planners need to reposition their brand. The repositioning can follow the same decisions as described above, where the promotional planner can consider an alternative market definition, communicate a new differential advantage, emphasize different benefit claims, or focus on another motivational option. Promotional planners can consider altering one or all four of these decisions to achieve moderate or very significant change in the current brand position.

KEY TERMS

brand position, *153*

brand positioning strategy, *153*

informational motive, *165*

market position, *151*

market positioning strategy, *150*

multiattribute attitude model, *163*

positioning, *150*

salient attributes, *153*

salient beliefs, *162*

salient benefits, *154*

strategic marketing plan, *150*

transformational motive, *165*

DISCUSSION QUESTIONS

1. Establishing brand image is often difficult for new companies. Explain what these companies must do to establish a strong brand image.

2. Describe how the market positioning strategy adopted for a brand would need to be supported by all other elements of the marketing mix.

3. What is meant by brand positioning strategy? How is it similar to or different from a market positioning strategy?

4. Why is it useful to distinguish between brand positioning strategy and brand position?

5. Develop a market position for chocolate bars.

6. How do major chocolate bar brands define their market?

7. Explain why a central positioning is feasible. Do any brands currently use this approach in their communications?

8. Why is the brand model important for brand positioning strategy?

9. What problem would a brand encounter if it communicated with an incorrect motive?

10. What factors would lead a marketer to the use of a repositioning strategy?

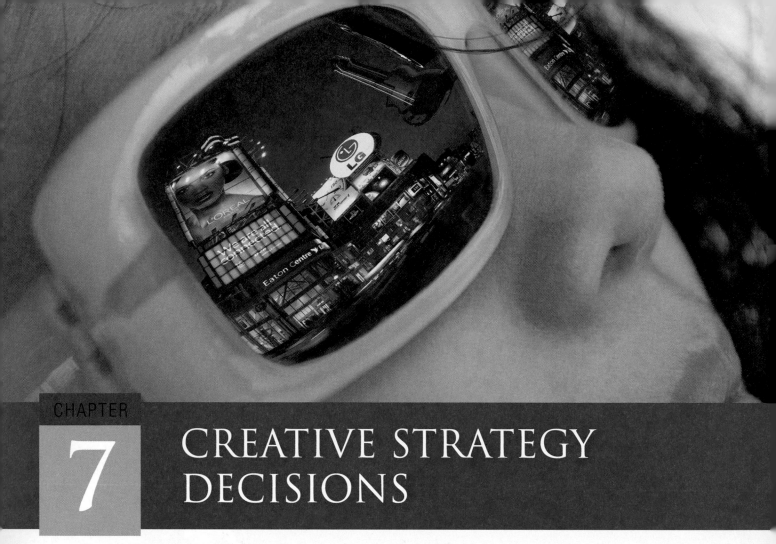

CREATIVE STRATEGY DECISIONS

■ CHAPTER OBJECTIVES

1   To explore the creative strategy planning process.

2   To identify three key decisions that comprise a creative strategy: creative theme, message appeal, and message source.

3   To explore various approaches used for determining the creative theme that forms the basis of an advertising campaign.

4   To summarize the different types of message appeals that advertisers use to persuade their target audience.

5   To highlight the source or communicator options a marketer has for a promotional message.

THE SOUL OF KIA

Kia Canada's "Peer into Your Soul" campaign launched the new urban crossover passenger car to unsuspecting TV viewers with three unbranded teaser ads over the course of three weeks. For 15 seconds, viewers watched mysterious characters staring back toward them and then saw the web address Peerintoasoul.ca—inviting enough curiosity for 180,000 visits before three branded ads for the Kia Soul appeared on TV. Explains the creative director of the campaign, "We decided to do something that would not only intrigue people on TV, but that would drive them to the Web and create a lot of curiosity and excitement around what this might be." Picking up on the idea that people often stare into new cars parked on the street, Kia emulated this little nugget of consumer behaviour in the ads.

The three following executions spoofed different types of films. A "buddy" movie is seen in "Well," where a guy stuck in a well has his friend run for help only to get distracted by Kia's new vehicle. In a gangster style, "Mob" shows a couple of tough guys letting their hostage get away while they peer into a Soul. Finally, a horror flick emerges with "Cabin," as the intended victims awaken to find their would-be attacker fell asleep after staring at the uniquely styled car. Quoting the senior art director, "To speak to a hip urban target you have to communicate in a language they can relate to. In this case, we appropriated current influential film genres to entertain and involve an audience that typically reject corporate messaging."

In addition to the TV and website ads, Kia hooked up with the popular TV show *24*. Wireless customers received teaser ads and exclusive *24*

content during the run-up to the start of the final season of the espionage thriller. A spy-based online game continued the theme at Winyoursoul.com, where one lucky person could be the victor and get a new vehicle. The game featured puzzles and activities along with Kia content as users could feel like Jack Bauer on a mission.

Print, radio, out-of-home, and point-of-purchase media complemented the initial communication and all emphasized the look of the car. Events at auto shows and dealerships invited interested drivers to peer into a Soul as well. According to the creative director, "Generally people buy cars or are interested in cars for the very first time on an emotional level. Looks are what disarms and seduces a potential car buyer."

Sources: Garine Tcholakian, "Kia Gets Soul-ful," *Media in Canada*, February 9, 2009; Jonathan Paul, "Kia Incites Vehicular Voyeurism," *Strategy*, March 2009, p. 16; Kristin Laird, "Kia Bares Its Soul," *Marketing Magazine*, February 10, 2009.

QUESTIONS:

1. What are the quotes from the executives really saying?
2. Why are the film and TV show connections for the theme fitting for this brand?

An important part of an IMC program is the advertising message. From the marketer's perspective, the advertising message is a way to tell consumers how the product can solve a problem or help satisfy desires or achieve goals. Advertising messages can also create images or associations and establish a brand position as well as transform the experience of buying and/or using a product. Advertising messages are crucial to the success of the firm's promotional effort since they play a leading role in the IMC program or are adapted to other IMC tools. While most students may not ever design ads, everyone involved in marketing or promotion should understand the strategic decisions that underlie the development of advertising messages.

It is easy to see many ways to convey an advertising message while watching commercials on TV or the Internet or perusing print ads in a magazine or at out-of-home locations. Underlying these messages is a **creative strategy** that determines *what* the advertising message will communicate and **creative tactics** for *how* the message will be executed. In this chapter, we focus on three creative strategy decisions. First, we describe approaches to determine the idea of the creative theme, which provides direction for attention-getting, distinctive, and memorable messages. Second, we identify the message appeals that advertisers use to persuade consumers. Third, we focus on the key source characteristics that advertisers typically use to gain attention and alter consumers' attitudes. Prior to these decisions, we explore the process of planning for creative strategy. We also conclude with our IMC planning perspective.

ADVERTISING CREATIVITY

Upon determining the direction for the communications program, the advertising agency or the department in the organization responsible for developing ads focuses on finding an appropriate creative approach to communicate a message that reinforces the brand positioning strategy. Good advertising creativity can often be central to determining the success of a product as it clearly contributes to a strong brand position with its intended target audience. The essence of advertising is its creativity, and we now provide a working definition and indicate its importance.

DEFINITION OF ADVERTISING CREATIVITY

For many students, as well as many advertising and marketing practitioners, the most interesting aspect of advertising is the creative side. We have all at one time or another been intrigued by an ad and admired the creative insight that went into it. A great ad is a joy to behold and often an epic to create, as the cost of producing a TV commercial can exceed $1 million. Conceiving an ad is such an exciting and enticing activity that a contest searching for the next top ad executive is operated each year for university students by the DeGroote School of Business at McMaster University.[1] Many companies see money spent on advertising and other forms of marketing communication as good brand investment. They realize that the manner in which the advertising message is developed and executed is often critical to the success of the promotional program, which in turn can influence the effectiveness of the entire marketing program (Exhibit 7-1).

Creativity is probably one of the most commonly used terms in advertising. Ads are often called creative. The people who develop ads and commercials are known as creative specialists. These specialists work for ad agencies that develop ad campaigns or for marketers that handle their own advertising without the help of an agency. Perhaps so much attention is focused on the concept of creativity because many people view the specific challenge given to those who develop an advertising message as being creative. It is their job to turn all of the information regarding product features and benefits, marketing plans, consumer research, and communication objectives into a creative concept that will bring the advertising message to life. This begs the question: What is meant by *creativity* in advertising?

Advertising creativity is the ability to generate fresh, unique, and appropriate ideas that can be used as effective solutions to marketing communication issues (e.g., problem or opportunity). To be *appropriate* and *effective*, a creative idea must be relevant to the target audience.[2] Relevance, as an important characteristic of creativity, has to instantly capture the target audience's attention and generate critical brand associations through specific cognitive and emotional responses. The relevance is even more critical when an advertiser takes into account the selective attention of the target audience. Moreover, the creativity has to crystallize the brand so that it is understood by the target audience, which is also experiencing selective comprehension when faced with many competing promotional messages. Extending this further, the relevance of the creativity to the target audience is critical to establishing an important link to the brand, its benefits, and why the target audience would purchase it. In other words, relevance clearly supports the brand positioning strategy.

Exhibit 7-1 Excellent advertising helps create an image for BMW automobiles.

Advertising creativity is not the exclusive domain of creative specialists, as creative thinking occurs from everyone involved in the promotional planning process. Agency people, such as account executives, media planners, researchers, and attorneys, as well as those on the client side, such as marketing and brand managers, must all seek creative solutions to problems encountered in planning, developing, and executing an advertising campaign. For example, the original creative strategy for Absolut vodka plays off the distinctive shape of its bottle and depicts it with visual puns and witty headlines that play off the Absolut name. The agency and client customized the advertising campaign by tailoring the print ads for each magazine. The agency's creative and media departments jointly selected magazines to appeal to the readers of each publication. Although Absolut moved on from this campaign it remains a significant example. Its unique creativity stood the test of time for over 20 years. The working relationship of creative specialists and others demonstrated a model for working effectively. Strong results continued for many years until the brand found sales lagging a few years ago and switched direction.

IMPORTANCE OF ADVERTISING CREATIVITY

Perspectives on what constitutes creativity in advertising differ. At one extreme are people who argue that advertising is creative only if it sells the product. An advertising message's or campaign's impact on sales counts more than whether it is innovative. At the other end of the continuum are those who judge the creativity of an ad in terms of its artistic or aesthetic value and originality. They contend creative ads can break through the competitive clutter, grab the consumer's attention, and have a positive communication effect. Both perspectives indicate the importance of advertising creativity as it either presents a good public exposure or contributes to a brand positioning strategy and ultimately sales.

The growth of brands has highlighted the importance of advertising creativity leading to renewed investigations.[3] Surveyed executives believe creativity has improved in recent decades compared to the origin of modern-day advertising during the 1960s.[4] The Leo Burnett agency and *Contagious Magazine* conduct worldwide research to uncover the success of the most creative advertising in traditional and newer evolving media, while others present new or reconfigured ideas to define creativity.[5] In general, creative advertising messages help focus the receiver's attention allowing deeper processing and stronger recall and recognition.[6]

Perspectives on advertising creativity often depend on one's role. A study by Elizabeth Hirschman examined the perceptions of various individuals involved in the creation and production of TV commercials, including management types (brand managers and account executives) and creatives (art director, copywriter, commercial director, and producer).[7] She found that product managers and account executives view ads as promotional tools whose primary purpose is to communicate favourable impressions to the marketplace. They believe a commercial should be evaluated in terms of whether it fulfills the client's marketing and communicative objectives. The perspective of those on the creative side was much more self-serving, as Hirschman noted:

> In direct contrast to this client orientation, the art director, copywriter, and commercial director viewed the advertisement as a communication vehicle for promoting their own aesthetic viewpoints and personal career objectives. Both the copywriter and art director made this point explicitly, noting that a desirable commercial from their standpoint was one which communicated their unique creative talents and thereby permitted them to obtain "better" jobs at an increased salary.[8]

What constitutes creativity in advertising is probably somewhere between the two extremes. To break through the clutter and make an impression on the target audience an ad often must be unique and entertaining, as seen in the Nintendo ad (Exhibit 7-2). Research has shown that a major determinant of whether a commercial will be successful in changing brand preferences is its "likability," or the viewer's overall reaction.[9] Advertising messages that are well designed and executed and generate emotional responses can create positive feelings that are transferred to the product or service being advertised.[10] Creative specialists believe this occurs if they are given considerable latitude in developing advertising messages, but purely creative ads might fail to communicate a relevant product message. In an attempt to resolve this discussion, research findings suggest that very creative advertising messages have additional positive brand communication effects (i.e., brand quality, brand interest) beyond recall and likability.[11] However, the issue becomes less clear as one study finds that the creative specialists themselves can disagree on the merits of creativity. A survey of art directors and copy writers finds that the former are more concerned with visual creativity while the latter more strongly believe in message delivery.[12] Finally, in the age of consumer-generated "advertising" messages, another study finds that perceptions of creativity differ among advertising professionals, students, and the general public.[13] Thus, it appears everyone must keep a balanced perspective on the creativity of advertising messages. IMC Perspective 7-1 demonstrates the importance of advertising creativity.

Exhibit 7-2 Nintendo placed a creative ad in a women's magazine to attract new users.

What's up with all the animals on TV, online, on bill-boards, and in so many advertising spaces? Despite the frenzy, Telus leads the way with its distinct approach of introducing a new cast of characters with each season, campaign, or new product. And in some cases, the more memorable—and, dare we say, famous—ones reappear to star once again or come together en masse all in one ad.

The nature inspiration began in the late 1990s when a member of the agency Taxi watched a documentary about insects and discovered that the music and camera work made the insects' activities appear almost human. Set against the simplistic white background, the "Future is friendly" message established a unique identity for Telus (named Clearnet at the time).

For a few years, we saw exotic birds (e.g., macaws), other insects, colourful frogs, and lizards—until Telus took over, and began with a "disco duck" to celebrate the millennium and then moved on to penguins, monkeys, pot-bellied pigs, iguanas, bunnies, meerkats, hedgehogs, prairie dogs, fish, and back to exotic birds (flamingos, pea-cocks) once again. A VP for Telus commented, "Nature has universal appeal. You can talk to any age from seven to 77. And it allows you to do metaphors."

Pygmy goats danced to the hit "Jump Around" and a couple of other songs in more recent incarnations to mar-ket Web-enabled phones and services, but the reprised Hazina the hippo represented the biggest hit for 2009. Initially introduced during Christmas 2005, Hazina made another appearance four years later, and in early 2009 she and her bunny friend moved about the screen symbol-izing the size and speed of Telus's network. "We thought we would continue with the hippo because of consumer likability but we wanted to add the speed factor," com-mented a Telus VP. In another execution, Hazina's mother and brother frolicked in water—with the picture actually in a handset to give the screen a life-like feel.

According to experts, the characteristics associated with animals through stories (e.g., cunning fox) act as a quick and simple reference that transfers to the adver-tised product. Furthermore, the feeling associated with the animal may also transfer to the product, so if someone likes Hazina they are more likely to feel more positivity toward Telus.

The animal theme worked with so many consumer products and services, Telus extended the idea to other markets. To attract small and medium businesses in need of wireless communication, Telus used poster ads with magnetized butterflies attached that allowed potential customers to take one. The gift included a tag that directed recipients to a website (Telustalksbusiness.com) to seek additional information.

Sources: Simon Houpt, "How Nature Can Nurture Our Brand Appre-ciation," *The Globe and Mail*, October 2, 2009, p. B5; Kristin Laird, "Telus Sponsoring Cheap Tuesdays at Cineplex," *Marketing Maga-zine*, September 10, 2009; Kristin Laird, "Hippos Make Telus Big and Fast," *Marketing Magazine*, March 5, 2009; Kristin Laird, "Telus Sponsoring Cheap Tuesdays at Cineplex," *Marketing Magazine*, Sep-tember 10, 2009.

Question

1. For how much longer can Telus continue with this advertising theme?

Another perspective on the issue of creativity is that some Canadian creative people believe that advertising should play an important role in society and be financially accountable. Advertising can have subtle flair and finesse reflecting current social trends and enhance the collective intelligence of society while still cleverly indicating a motive for purchase to ensure a positive investment from a business standpoint.[14] Whether all marketers and agencies agree with this perspec-tive, it still highlights the inherent tension between creativity and financial results.

PLANNING CREATIVE STRATEGY

Creative specialists must take all the research, creative briefs, strategy statements, communications objectives, and other input and transform them into an advertis-ing message. Their job is to write copy, design layouts and illustrations, or produce commercials that effectively communicate the central theme on which the campaign is based. Rather than simply stating the features or benefits of a product or service, they must put the advertising message into a form that will engage the audience's interest and make the ads memorable.[15] In this section, we describe the creative challenge, illustrate the creative process, summarize the job of an account planner, identify forms of research for creative decision making, and summarize the end result—the copy platform—when planning for creative promotional communication.

CREATIVE CHALLENGE

The job of the creative team is challenging because every marketing situation is different and each campaign or advertisement may require a different creative approach. Numerous guidelines have been developed for creating effective advertising.[16] Creative people follow proven formulas when creating ads because clients can feel uncomfortable with advertising that is too different. Bill Tragos, former chair of TBWA, the advertising agency noted for its excellent creative work for Absolut vodka, Evian, and many other clients, says, "Very few clients realize that the reason that their work is so bad is that they are the ones who commandeered it and directed it to be that way. I think that at least 50 percent of an agency's successful work resides in the client."[17] Decades later, empirical research supports this practitioner's point of view.[18]

Many creative people say it is important for clients to take some risks if they want breakthrough advertising that gets noticed. One client taking a risk is Marriott International, as observed in the advertising for its Residence Inn chain. A highly evocative campaign showcases Residence Inn's new "Innfusion" décor, which redefines the extended-stay experience with distinctive zones that meet the living needs of the extended-stay guest—cooking, dining, working, relaxing, and sleeping. The ads use theatrical performers to show guests how to master—not just survive—a long trip. In one spot showcasing Residence's in-room grocery service, a performer flips upside down, lands on the kitchen counter, and balances an apple on her toes (Exhibit 7-3). In other ads a trapeze artist glides across the chain's newly designed rooms, a plate spinner twirls four plates to highlight the full kitchen in each unit, and a fire breather/juggler performs at an outdoor fire pit to showcase the new look of Residence properties. The television spots are part of an integrated campaign that includes print and online components such as a website (Masterthelongtrip.com) that engages visitors with a virtual tour of the new Residence Inn designs.[19]

One agency that has been successful in getting its clients to take risks is Rethink, best known for its excellent creative work for Playland, Science World, A&W, and Solo Mobile. The agency's founders believe a key element in its success has been a steadfast belief in taking risks when most agencies and their clients have been retrenching and becoming more conservative. The agency can develop great advertising partly because its clients are willing to take risks and agree with the agency's approach of

GROCERY DELIVERY
ONE OF MANY FEATURES DESIGNED TO KEEP YOU BALANCED
MASTER THE LONG TRIP™
RESIDENCEINN.COM

Residence Inn
Marriott

Exhibit 7-3 Residence Inn takes a very creative approach with its new ads.

listening to their client and arriving at a creative solution for their marketing communication problem or opportunity.

Not all agree that advertising has to be risky to be effective, however. Many marketing managers are more comfortable with advertising that simply communicates product or service features and benefits and gives the consumer a reason to buy. They see their ad campaigns as multimillion-dollar investments whose goal is to sell the product rather than finance the whims of their agency's creative staff. They argue that some creative people have lost sight of advertising's bottom line: Does it sell?

CREATIVE PROCESS

Some advertising people say creativity in advertising is best viewed as a process and creative success is most likely when some organized approach is followed. One of the most popular approaches to creativity in advertising was developed by James Webb Young, a former creative vice president at the J. Walter Thompson agency. Young said, "The production of ideas is just as definite a process as the production of Fords; the production of ideas, too, runs an assembly line; in this production the mind follows an operative technique which can be learned and controlled; and that its effective use is just as much a matter of practice in the technique as in the effective use of any tool."[20] Working from a sociological view, Young's process of creativity follows a four-stage approach:

- *Preparation.* Read background information regarding the problem.
- *Incubation.* Get away and let ideas develop.
- *Illumination.* See the light or solution.
- *Verification.* Refine the idea and see if it is an appropriate solution.

Models of the creative process such as Young's are valuable to those working in the creative area of advertising, since they offer an organized way to approach an advertising problem. These models do not say much about how this information will be synthesized and used by the creative specialist because this part of the process is unique to the individual. A recent investigation along these lines reveals four invidual factors: orientation toward the creative work, approach to the communication problems, mindscribing (i.e., free-flow thinking), and heuristics (i.e., quick creative decision rules).[21]

ACCOUNT PLANNING

To facilitate the creative process many agencies use **account planning**, which involves conducting research and gathering all relevant information about a client's product or service, brand, and consumers in the target audience. Jon Steel, a former vice president and director of account planning, has written an excellent book on the process titled *Truth, Lies & Advertising: The Art of Account Planning.*[22] He notes that the account planner's job is to provide the key decision makers with all the information they require to make an intelligent decision. According to Steel, "Planners may have to work very hard to influence the way that the advertising turns out, carefully laying out a strategic foundation with the client, handing over tidbits of information to creative people when, in their judgment, that information will have the greatest impact, giving feedback on ideas, and hopefully adding some ideas of their own."

Account planning plays an important role during creative strategy development by driving the process from the customers' point of view. Planners will work with the client as well as other agency personnel, such as the creative team and media specialists. They discuss how the knowledge and information they have gathered

183

can be used in the development of the creative strategy as well as other aspects of the advertising campaign. Account planners are usually responsible for all the research (both qualitative and quantitative) conducted during the creative strategy development process. In the following section we examine how various types of research and information can provide input to the creative process of advertising.

RESEARCH IN THE CREATIVE PROCESS

The creative specialist first learns as much as possible about the product, the target audience, the competition, and any other relevant **research**. Much of this information would come from the marketing plan and advertising plan developed by the client. Alternatively, good clients will give proper direction for their agency by constructing a client brief that recapitulates their internal documents and adds additional information which would give the creative specialist an idea as to the direction of the brand positioning strategy. The Institute of Communications and Advertising produces a best practices document that shows brand managers how to construct a client brief that serves the needs of both parties, thus encouraging more creative marketing communication.

From this, the creative specialist can acquire additional background information in numerous ways. Some informal fact-finding techniques have been noted by Sandra Moriarty:

* Read anything related to the product or market.
* Talk to people (e.g., marketing personnel, designers, engineers, consumers).
* Visit stores and malls.
* Use the product or service and become familiar with it.
* Work in and learn about the business.[23]

Creative people use both general and product-specific preplanning input. **General preplanning input** can include books, periodicals, trade publications, scholarly journals, pictures, and clipping services, which gather and organize magazine and newspaper articles on the product, the market, and the competition, including the latter's ads. Another useful general preplanning input concerns market trends and developments. Information is available from a variety of sources, including local, provincial, and federal governments, secondary research suppliers, and industry trade associations, as well as advertising and media organizations that publish research reports and newsletters. Those involved in developing creative strategy can also gather relevant and timely information by reading Canadian publications like *Marketing Magazine* or *Strategy,* and American publications like *Adweek, Advertising Age,* and *Brand Week.*

In addition to getting general background research, creative people receive **product/service-specific preplanning input**. This information generally comes in the form of specific studies conducted on the product/service and/or the target audience. Quantitative consumer research includes attitude studies, market structure, and positioning studies such as perceptual mapping and psychographic or lifestyle profiles. As noted in Chapter 3, some agencies or affiliated research companies conduct psychographic studies annually and construct detailed psychographic or lifestyle profiles of product or service users. Dove conducted one of the more significant research studies prior to launching the "Campaign for Real Beauty." The research involved numerous personal interviews and sampled women from many countries regarding their attitudes toward beauty with a survey methodology.

Qualitative research is used to gain insight into the underlying causes of consumer behaviour. Methods employed include in-depth interviews, projective techniques, association tests, and focus groups in which consumers are encouraged to bring out associations related to products and brands (see Figure 7-1). This research is often referred to as motivation research. In general, motivation research is considered

In-depth interviews

Face-to-face situations in which an interviewer asks a consumer to talk freely in an unstructured interview using specific questions designed to obtain insights into his or her motives, ideas, or opinions.

Projective techniques

Efforts designed to gain insights into consumers' values, motives, attitudes, or needs that are difficult to express or identify by having them project these internal states upon some external object.

Association tests

A technique in which an individual is asked to respond with the first thing that comes to mind when he or she is presented with a stimulus; the stimulus may be a word, picture, ad, and so on.

Focus groups

A small number of people with similar backgrounds and/or interests who are brought together to discuss a particular product, idea, or issue.

FIGURE   7–1

Some of the marketing research methods employed to probe the mind of the consumer

important in assessing how and why consumers buy. Focus groups and in-depth interviews are valuable methods for gaining insights into consumers' feelings, and projective techniques are often the only way to get around stereotypical or socially desirable responses.

Focus groups are a prevalent research tool at this stage of the creative process. Focus groups are a research method whereby consumers (usually 10 to 12 people) from the target audience are led through a discussion regarding a particular topic. Focus groups give insight as to why and how consumers use a product, what is important to them in choosing a particular brand, what they like and don't like about various products, and any special needs they might have that aren't being satisfied. A focus group session might also include a discussion of types of ad appeals to use or evaluate the advertising of various companies. Focus group interviews bring the creative people and others involved in creative strategy development into contact with the customers. Listening to a focus group gives copywriters, art directors, and other creative specialists a better sense of who the target audience is, what the audience is like, and who the creatives need to write, design, or direct to in creating an advertising message.

Since motivation research studies typically use so few participants, there is also concern that they really discover the idiosyncrasies of only a few individuals and their findings are not generalizable to the whole population. Still, it is difficult to ignore motivation research in furthering our understanding of consumer behaviour. Its insights can often be used as a basis for advertising messages aimed at buyers' deeply rooted feelings, hopes, aspirations, and fears.

Toward the end of the creative process, members of the target audience may be asked to evaluate rough creative layouts and to indicate what meaning they get from the ad, what they think of its execution, or how they react to a slogan or theme. The creative team can gain insight into how a TV commercial might communicate its message by having members of the target audience evaluate the ad in storyboard form. A **storyboard** is a series of drawings used to present the visual plan or layout of a proposed commercial. It contains a series of sketches of key frames or scenes along with the copy or audio portion for each scene (Exhibit 7-4).

Exhibit 7-4
Marketers can gain insight into consumers' reactions to a commercial by showing them a storyboard.

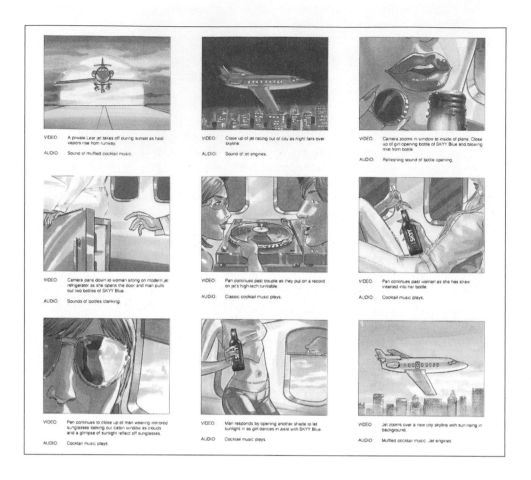

Evaluating a commercial in storyboard form can be difficult because storyboards are too abstract for many consumers to understand. To make the creative layout more realistic and easier to evaluate, the agency may produce an **animatic,** a videotape of the storyboard along with an audio soundtrack. Storyboards and animatics are useful for research purposes as well as for presenting the creative idea to other agency personnel or to the client for discussion and approval. At this stage of the process, the creative team is attempting to find the best creative strategy before moving ahead with the actual production of the ad. The process may conclude with more formal, extensive pretesting of the ad before a final decision is made. Pretesting and related procedures are examined in detail in Chapter 9.

COPY PLATFORM

The end result of the creative process is the written document referred to as copy platform. It specifies the basic elements of the creative strategy and other relevant information. The **copy platform** may have other names, depending upon the firm. Essentially, it is a plan that summarizes the entire creative approach that is agreed upon by the creative team and the marketing managers. Figure 7-2 shows a sample copy-platform outline. Just as there are different names for the copy platform, there are variations in the outline and format used and in the level of detail included.

The first three sections are derived from the marketing plan and prior communication between the creative specialists and brand managers. The planning framework of this text, shown in Chapter 1, also supports all sections of this copy platform illustration. Chapter 1 highlighted the importance of the marketing plan for promotional planning, which should provide sufficient background on the nature of the communication problem or opportunity. Chapter 3 described important aspects of

1. Basic problem or opportunity the advertising must address
2. Target audience(s) and behaviour objective(s)
3. Communication objectives
4. Brand positioning strategy statement
5. Creative strategy (creative theme, message appeal, source characteristic)
6. Supporting information and requirements

FIGURE 7–2

Copy-platform
outline

consumer behaviour along with options for target audience selection and guidelines for a target audience profile. Combined, Chapters 4 and 5 explained the usefulness of response models and communication objectives that guide remaining decisions. The previous chapter indicated different brand positioning options that creative specialists might propose as communication solutions. The rest of this chapter describes the creative strategy decisions that the creative specialists typically recommend. Finally, copy platforms may also include supporting information and requirements that should appear in any message to ensure uniformity across the ads used in a campaign.

At times, creative specialists experience communication problems among the participants of the creative process. Part of the problem is attributed to creative personnel not actually writing a copy platform. The creative process may be initially described in a series of notes or sketches, and as it evolves through the stages of the creative process some of the original participants may not be aware of all the changes. Alternatively, the lack of full description leads to misunderstanding of how the sequence of events, for example, would occur in a television commercial. And while it is important to have a written copy platform, it should be brief enough so that all participants could read it quickly and easily and still demonstrate the creativity of the advertising. In the end we can say that the copy platform should (1) be objective, (2) have proper vocabulary, spelling, and grammar, (3) demonstrate logical thinking, (4) be both creative and brief, (5) have specific recommendations, and (6) be viewed as a firm agreement.[24]

CREATIVE THEME

Most ads are part of a series of messages of an **advertising campaign,** which is a set of interrelated and coordinated marketing communication activities that centre on a single **creative theme** that appears in different media across a specified time period. Determining the unifying theme around which the campaign will be built is a critical part of the creative process as it often sets the tone for other forms of marketing communication that will be used, such as sales promotion or digital applications. Furthermore, the creative theme should be a strong idea since it represents the central message of a marketing communication program, reflects the market positioning strategy, and directly communicates the brand positioning strategy to its intended target audience. In this section, we cover three related decisions that comprise the creative theme. First, we discuss various ways to determine the creative theme. Next, we explore the issue of consistency of the creative theme across many parts of the promotional program. We conclude by exploring the importance of unique Canadian creative advertising and its success.

ORIGIN OF CREATIVE THEME

The creative team is provided with the challenge of deciding upon the strong or "big" idea of the creative theme that attracts the consumer's attention, gets a response, and sets the advertiser's product or service apart from the competition. Well-known adman John O'Toole describes the *big idea* as "that flash of insight that synthesizes the purpose of the strategy, joins the product benefit with consumer desire in a fresh, involving way, brings the subject to life, and makes the reader or audience stop, look, and listen."[25] It is difficult to pinpoint the inspiration for a big idea or to teach advertising people how to find one. However, the following approaches can guide the creative team's search for a creative theme.

- Using a unique selling proposition.
- Creating a brand image.
- Finding the inherent drama.
- Positioning.

Unique Selling Proposition The concept of the **unique selling proposition (USP)** was developed by Rosser Reeves, former chair of the Ted Bates agency, and is described in his influential book *Reality in Advertising.* Reeves noted three characteristics of unique selling propositions:

- Each advertisement must make a proposition to the consumer. Not just words, not just product puffery, not just show-window advertising. Each advertisement must say to each reader: "Buy this product and you will get this benefit."
- The proposition must be one that the competition either cannot or does not offer. It must be unique either in the brand or in the claim.
- The proposition must be strong enough to move the mass millions, that is, pull over new customers to your brand.[26]

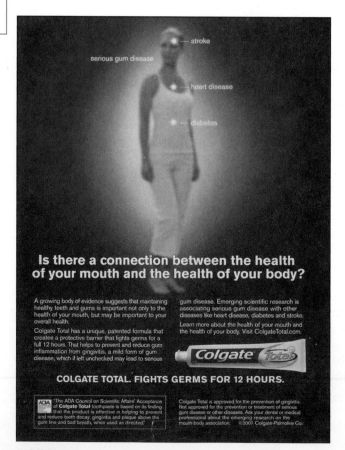

Is there a connection between the health of your mouth and the health of your body?

A growing body of evidence suggests that maintaining healthy teeth and gums is important not only to the health of your mouth, but may be important to your overall health.

Colgate Total has a unique, patented formula that creates a protective barrier that fights germs for a full 12 hours. That helps to prevent and reduce gum inflammation from gingivitis, a mild form of gum disease, which if left unchecked may lead to serious

gum disease. Emerging scientific research is associating serious gum disease with other diseases like heart disease, diabetes and stroke.

Learn more about the health of your mouth and the health of your body. Visit ColgateTotal.com.

COLGATE TOTAL. FIGHTS GERMS FOR 12 HOURS.

Exhibit 7-5 This Colgate Total ad uses a unique selling proposition.

Reeves said the attribute claim or benefit that forms the basis of the USP should dominate the ad and be emphasized through repetitive advertising. An example of advertising based on a USP is the campaign for Colgate Total toothpaste (Exhibit 7-5). The brand has a unique, patented formula that creates a protective barrier that fights germs for 12 hours, which helps reduce and prevent gum disease.

For Reeves's approach to work, there must be a truly unique product or service attribute, benefit, or inherent advantage that can be used in the claim. The approach may require considerable research on the product and consumers, not only to determine the USP but also to document the claim.

Creating a Brand Image In many product and service categories, competing brands are so similar that it is very difficult to communicate a unique attribute or benefit. Many of the packaged-goods products that account for most of the advertising dollars spent are difficult to differentiate on a functional or performance basis. The creative theme used to communicate these products is based on the development of a strong, memorable identity for the brand through **image advertising.**

David Ogilvy popularized the idea of brand image in his famous book *Confessions of an Advertising Man.* Ogilvy said that with image advertising, "every advertisement should be thought of as a contribution to the complex symbol which is the brand image." He argued that the image or personality of the brand is particularly important when brands are similar. The key to successful image advertising is developing an image that will appeal to product users. For example, in 2005 Reebok initiated a $50-million global ad campaign using the "I am what I am" theme, which uses image advertising to promote the athletic shoe company as the brand for young consumers.[27] The campaign is designed to create an image for Reebok as a brand that is about being yourself rather than trying to become something you are not. The ads feature a variety of celebrity personalities including NHL star Sidney Crosby, tennis star Andy Roddick, and film star Lucy Liu. The image-oriented ads feature a portrait of the celebrity next to a visual symbol of an aspect of the star's private life and a quote about his or her life (see Exhibit 7-6).

Image development often occurs through literary devices such as metaphors or analogies. This involves both visual and copy elements of an ad that allow consumers to interpret the message by transferring meaning from another aspect to the brand. These metaphors can be concrete (e.g., direct, obvious) or abstract (e.g., indirect, interpretive). Selecting the right metaphor is sometimes difficult as some consumers have difficulty discovering the references.[28]

Exhibit 7-6 Reebok's "I am what I am" campaign creates an image of the brand as about being yourself.

Finding the Inherent Drama   Another approach to determining the creative theme is finding the **inherent drama** or characteristic of the product that makes the consumer purchase it. The inherent drama approach expresses the advertising philosophy of Leo Burnett, founder of the Leo Burnett Agency in Chicago. Burnett said inherent drama "is often hard to find but it is always there, and once found it is the most interesting and believable of all advertising appeals."[29] He believed advertising should be based on a foundation of consumer benefits with an emphasis on the dramatic element in expressing those benefits.

Burnett advocated a down-home type of advertising that presents the message in a warm and realistic way. Some of the more famous ads developed by his agency using the inherent drama approach are for McDonald's fast food, Maytag appliances, Kellogg's cereals, and Hallmark cards. Notice how the Hallmark commercial shown in Exhibit 7-7 uses this approach to deliver a poignant message.

Positioning   Since advertising helps establish or maintain the brand position, it can also be the source of the creative theme. Positioning is often the basis of a firm's creative strategy when it has multiple brands competing in the same market. For example, Procter & Gamble markets many brands of laundry detergent—and positions each one differently. Positioning is done for companies as well as for brands. For example, the ad shown in Exhibit 7-8 is part of "the other IBM" campaign that is designed to position the company as a provider of business consulting and more than just a technology provider. The integrated campaign, which includes print ads, television and online ads, sponsorships, and a micro website, is designed to reveal a side of IBM that has been largely unknown to many potential business consulting and services clients.[30]

Trout and Ries originally described positioning as the image consumers had of the brand in relation to competing brands in the product or service category, but the concept has been expanded beyond direct competitive positioning.[31] As discussed in Chapter 6, products can be positioned on the basis of end benefit, brand name,

Exhibit 7-7
This Hallmark
commercial uses
an inherent drama
approach.

Exhibit 7-8
This ad is part of
a campaign that
positions IBM as a
provider of business
consulting and
services.

usage situation, or product category. Any of these can spark a theme that becomes the basis of the creative strategy and results in the brand's occupying a particular place in the minds of the target audience. Since brand positioning can be done on the basis of a distinctive attribute, the positioning and unique selling proposition approaches can overlap.

Molson Export returned to its well-established position as an authentic beer in Quebec as the origin for a clever theme. Research indicated that consumers young and old alike still perceived Export as having a strong 100-year history and associated it with classic beer-drinking moments, even though the brand had inconsistent advertising and weak marketing support in recent years. The slogan captured the essence of the repositioning: "Molson Ex. Today's beer since 1903." The first few executions of the creative strategy showed the progression and similarity of Export consumption since its inception. For example, the first spot, "Evolution," says it all as a number of scenes depicted people bringing cases of Export to various parties over the course of time. Using the computer morphing techniques, the images also showed how the labels of the brand had changed.[32]

CREATIVE THEME CONSISTENCY

Consistency in promotional creativity is generally regarded as a key success factor so that the target audience retains the brand position. We explore examples of consistency in the creative theme across time, creative execution, advertising media, promotional tools, and products. The essential point is that when the target audience is exposed to a series of messages across different contexts, the creative theme should not change such that there is a clear reinforcement of the brand positioning strategy. Deviation of the theme allows the possibility that the target audience will process the message alternatively and arrive at a different interpretation of the brand.

Consistency across Time Advertising or communication plans are generally done on an annual basis, thus the creative theme is often short-term in nature. However, the creative themes are usually developed with the intention of being used for a longer time period. While some marketers change their campaign themes often, a successful creative theme may last for years. A consistent creative theme across time builds on the established awareness of the brand's current customers by encouraging continued processing of future advertising messages. Moreover, the familiarity of the creative theme is recognizable to a brand's non-customers when they may be entering the product category or considering switching their purchases. Nissan's campaign, employed for almost 10 years, uses a combination of emotional and product-focused ads designed to strengthen its image while showing its product line all under the "Shift" umbrella tagline (Exhibit 7-9).

Pepsi-Cola's campaign in Quebec has starred comedian Claude Meunier for more than 16 years. The campaign is a unique creative strategy for Pepsi from a worldwide perspective, and it is the longest running campaign and celebrity endorsement in the history of the brand. In fact, the relationship is so established that Meunier writes many of the spots and creates the characters he portrays.[33]

Exhibit 7-9 In Nissan's new ads, the cars are once again the stars.

Despite this consistent creative theme, Pepsi introduced Patrick, Etienne, Paco, Sebastien, and Ivon (first letters spell PEPSI) in a TV ad as five guys who really, really like Pepsi to continue with its advertising theme of humour, entertainment, and youthful energy. However, this deviation was not the end of Meunier, as Pepsi planned on his continued participation.[34]

After its initial launch, Koodo revised its creative theme but retained many characteristics so that the campaigns appeared continuous. They retained the same "fun, quirky and colourful characters"; however, they are no longer in spandex urging consumers to lose their bloated bills from other providers. Rather, the new characters articulate clever words like, "textelation," "contractophobe," "fee-ectomy," and "bigbillification." The freshened campaign intended to keep the brand distinct from the campaign theme, as the message to consumers of other brands is to switch to this new discount provider.[35]

Consistency across Executions As we noted above, an advertising campaign features a series of creative executions over time and it is important that marketers ensure that all ads feature a similar "look and feel." Exactly what this entails is a matter of interpretation, but most advertisers and consumers would say they recognize it when they see it. For example, many would say that the creative theme for Absolut vodka is consistent in all its print ads even though we see the distinctive bottle in many different types of scenes or situations that fit with the specific target audience of each magazine the ads are placed in.

Kraft Canada has used the same creative theme of an angel consuming Philadelphia cream cheese in the clouds of heaven throughout all of its television executions. This creative approach for communicating the brand's benefits has served it well as a distinctive presentation that is recognizable and consistent with positioning the brand as a tasty and healthy food product.[36]

Consistency across Media Often a successful creative theme is one that is amenable to more than one media. For instance, the essence of creativity in a print ad is still captured in a follow-up radio ad. Or, the big idea found in a TV commercial transfers to an outdoor billboard. In both cases, the creativity of the initial media is seen in a supportive media—one less central to the primary media, yet still important to continue exposing a similar idea to the target audience. Interestingly, this idea is difficult to convey with visual creative themes moving to radio. For quite some time, listeners heard a "friendly thought" from Telus that differed significantly from the nature theme portrayed in all visual media.

Consistency across Promotional Tools Using the advertising creative theme across the various promotional tools is an issue to be resolved. The argument for the same look and feel is pervasive. For example, Telus Mobility keeps its nature theme in all of its communications—from TV ads to promotional displays to its website and finally all of its public relations and publicity. Actions such as this support the notion that the creative theme for the integrated marketing communication must support the broad market positioning and all brand positioning strategies for its many target audiences. This is also evident with Bud Light, which created the character Budd Light who appeared in all TV ads and was featured at promotional events. Representing the number-five beer in Canada, the fictional spokesperson embodies the spirit of the brand as he "Keeps the good times going." This uniquely Canadian theme works with target of fun-loving young men, yet spills over to women as well through other promotional activities like a contest to win a Caribbean cruise.[37]

Consistency across Products The same kind of use of a consistent theme across all IMC tools is evident in RBC Financial Group's "First" campaign; the theme pervades all of RBC's tools for all its products and services. And so the campaign's consistent theme works on multiple levels. It is positioning the overall firm as an innovative and forward-looking organization, yet the campaign adapts well to a variety of purchase and consumption situations for credit or investment products that can be also adjusted depending on whether the target audience is a loyal customer or a potential one that RBC Financial Group is attempting to switch. Consistency is also evident with RBC's message of "create" and their use of the financial adviser Arbie (i.e., R.B., for Royal Bank) who appears in messages across all IMC tools and products. Arbie is especially prominent in public relations activities, like the Olympic sponsorship, and for corporate advocacy issues such as water conservation.[38] Similarly, for its consumer products Knorr has used a very similar design and colour scheme for all its product advertising (Exhibit 7-10).

CANADIAN CREATIVE THEMES

We now present ideas regarding creative themes used in Canadian advertising and promotional communication. We begin with a perspective that supports the importance for unique ways of speaking to Canadian consumers. Since many brands are part of a North American or international marketing strategy, there is a tendency to standardize the message. As further evidence of the importance for Canadian creativity in communication, we highlight recent success stories.

Exhibit 7-10 Colourful ads are often used in Knorr's product advertising.

Importance of Canadian Creative Themes The need for unique creative advertising can be found in the divergence of values between Canadians and Americans. Decades of consumer research by Environics researcher Michael Adams suggests that while the citizens of North America share similar aspects of society, the underlying values are quite distinct.[39] For example, in 1992, 17 percent of Canadians and 34 percent of Americans agreed that "a widely advertised product is probably a good product"; however, in 2000 the percentage for Canadians had remained unchanged while the percentage for Americans had risen to 44 percent.[40] Statistics such as these have led to a profound conclusion:

> Canadians operate by a fundamentally different set of social values than Americans do, and marketers need to be sensitive to these differences. Americans are much more outer-directed, risk-taking, and yet are more concerned with maintaining social order and tradition. In contrast, Canadians are more inner-directed, more security-seeking, and yet are more socially liberal and tolerant of individual diversity. Americans celebrate those who have lived the American Dream—working hard, taking chances and striking it rich—so visual markers of success such as expensive cars, homes and vacations become important indicators of one's status on the social hierarchy. Canadians, on the other hand, believe in greater interdependence, achieving equitable balances, and the "fair" distribution of the wealth of the nation—the Canadian Dream is a strong social safety net. As a result, Canadians are more suspicious of wealth, are less trusting of business and are more skeptical of advertising.[41]

These unique Canadian values influence the motivation for consumption—Canadians buy products for what they can do for us versus what they say about us. Canadians favour experiences over possessions and are less inclined toward conspicuous consumption. For example, Canadians are more likely to believe that a car is basic transportation versus a statement of personal style or image. Therefore, certain types of advertising messages are more palatable for Canadians since the underlying reasons for purchase are more accurately reflected in the dialogue of a commercial or the body copy of a print ad produced by Canadian advertisers.

In fact, one author believes that Canada is truly in an advertising renaissance where agencies are consistently producing world-calibre creative campaigns.[42] Furthermore, the distinctiveness of Canadians derived from this data may be strong evidence for allowing Canadian managers more latitude in developing unique creative messages.[43]

Putting together a creative for Canada can be met with some obstacles. Canadian managers who market U.S. brands in Canada often feel the pressure to run the same campaign in Canada that is being run in the U.S. While this obviously saves on production costs of new ads, it can be more than offset with lower sales due to messages not resonating with Canadian culture. Sometimes firms need to perform specific market research to demonstrate that a unique creative is warranted for the Canadian market. For example, Lever Pond's of Canada felt the U.S. creative for Degree deodorant featuring CEOs and race car drivers would not be acceptable to Canadian consumers. Research was done, a discussion ensued with U.S. managers, and finally a humorous campaign looked at stressful situations where the dryness benefit of the product could be understood. Ironically, the ads in the U.S. barely registered with consumers in follow-up research while the Canadian campaign tested above average.[44]

Successful Canadian Creative Themes Historically and recently, insightful and innovative Canadian creative themes demonstrate effective advertising and promotional communication. We take this time to identify the Canadian organizations that recognize creative themes that have been truly outstanding. Specifically, we summarize the CASSIES, the Marketing Awards, the Bessies, and the Extra Awards. We also highlight Canada's performance at the prestigious Cannes competition held in France.

Exhibit 7-11 Sumo wrestlers reminded consumers that Subaru is an automaker from Japan.

CASSIES Awarded by the Institute of Communication and Advertising (ICA), the Association of Quebec Advertising Agencies, and Publicité Club de Montréal, this recognition is perhaps the most significant in Canada as it identifies Canadian advertising success stories. Initiated in Canada in 1993, the award is based on a similar idea started during the 1980s in the United Kingdom. Originally awarded every second year from 1993 until 2001, the CASSIES are now an annual event.

The CASSIES award recognizes advertising and promotional campaigns that document a direct cause and effect relationship between the campaign and communication and business results. Entrants have to submit the details of their campaign in the form of a business case that summarizes the performance of the brand prior to the campaign and indicates the degree to which the performance has improved. The website, Cassies.ca, provides the complete entry requirements, identifies the winners, and contains the actual case history submitted. Subaru won in 2009 when it showed sumo wrestlers in its new Forester ads to remind consumers that it was a Japanese brand (Exhibit 7-11).

The Grand Prix is the single most prestigious award presented. It has been won by seven firms since its inception: Pepsi in Quebec (1993), Listerine in Quebec (1995), Chrysler minivan (1997), Sunlight laundry detergent (1999), Molson Canadian (2001), Diet Pepsi (2002), Familiprix (2003), the Quebec Federation of Milk Producers (2006), Dove (2007), and Shreddies (2009).

Trade Magazines   Two awards given out annually, sponsored by different trade magazines—*Strategy* and *Marketing Magazine*—identify the top Canadian creative communication launched each year in a number of categories. For example, there is an overall winner for best multimedia campaign, a winner for best single ad and campaign across all major media, and awards for non-traditional media, point-of-purchase, and public service announcements.

Bessies   These awards are given by the Television Bureau of Canada (TVB), an organization whose members comprise television stations, networks, and specialty services. The TVB promotes the use of television as an effective medium and has an important role as an information resource for its members. The Bessies recognize the best in English TV advertising each year and have been doing so since the early 1960s, shortly after the invention of television (an equivalent award for French TV advertising is awarded at La Fête de la Pub).

Extra Awards   The Canadian Newspaper Association is similar to the TVB but for daily newspapers. Its Extra Awards recognize outstanding creative advertising in this medium by giving ads a gold, silver, bronze, or merit award in nine product categories and types of ads (i.e., local ad, local campaign, national campaign, small-space ad).

Cannes   On a global level, the Cannes International Advertising Film Festival is widely considered the most prestigious advertising award competition. The Cannes competition receives entries from agencies around the world hoping to win Lions (the name of the award) in each of the major categories: television; print and poster; online (cyber) advertising; media buying and planning; and direct. Canada has done fabulously at Cannes competitions over the past decade, winning an average of about seven Lions per year.

In the past, some questioned the overall effectiveness of Canadian creativity due to the nature of our culture to not take risks and the fact that many of the brands advertised are part of American or other global brands. However, others contend the increased presence of Canadians in attendance and on the juries of all five categories bodes well for future Canuck creative advertising and our recognition on the international stage. In fact, some argue that countries that have emerged recently with stronger advertising is a result of their advertisers taking the competition more seriously by sending a large contingent of committed creative specialists who learn considerably from international counterparts.[45] IMC Perspective 7-2 strolls down memory lane by identifying some defining moments for Canadian creativity.

MESSAGE APPEALS

The **message appeal** refers to the approach used to influence consumers' attitude toward the product, service, or cause. A message appeal can also be viewed as "something that moves people, speaks to their wants or needs, and excites their interest."[46] As this suggests, the message appeal is an important creative strategy decision since it has an important role with influencing the target audience's attitude toward the brand. Hundreds of different appeals can be used as the basis for advertising messages. We concentrate on five broad appeals: rational appeals,

To mark its 20th anniversary, *Strategy* asked various experts their opinion on the transformation that has occurred in the world of marketing communication during that time. As backdrop, Hugh Dow of Mediabrands noted how much the media landscape had transformed in five ways: agencies moved from media departments to independent media agencies, media vehicles reach smaller niches offering even greater creative opportunities, consumers became leaders instead of followers with brand marketing communication, global advertising agencies emerged and relied on sophisticated market research to support international IMC initiatives, and in Canada we adapted to the most advanced broadcast measurement system in the world.

Frank Palmer of DDB focused on a number of topics: procurement specialists influenced agency selection decisions toward the lowest-cost provider, agencies neglected the development of creative talent, agencies relied on the glory of winning awards at the expense of results, and global brands centralized their advertising agencies and left Canadian firms behind. Echoing these thoughts, a voice from the academic world highlighted the reworking of the agency; creative and media grew in importance compared to account and strategy; global firms, small creative shops (e.g., Rethink), and specialty firms (e.g., Armstrong) all emerged; and new models of client relations (e.g., Grip) took hold.

Meanwhile, Nancy Vonk of Ogilvy Mather reminded us of the most innovative creative work. She noted billboard ads for McDonald's and the Weather Network as two clever messages. The word "pizza," written with two golden arches angled just right to form two zeds, instantly told consumers the hamburger giant now sold a new product. Images pointing to the sky with messages like, "Told you so" certified the Weather Network's prediction ability. The fictitious Bud Light Institute demonstrated its inventiveness by "advertising" for employees and discovering ways to allow men to get more free time to drink the beer (e.g., inventing 24-hour online shopping). Mini won digital awards three out of four years with its interactive and engaging mini-sites; each execution conveyed the humour and fun driving experience of the re-born classic from the past. The initial version featured four different driving experiences with animation and a soothing calm voice guiding users through the different stages. Dove's "Evolution" film, made in Canada and seen around the world, epitomized the trend toward social messages associated with a brand, video messages disseminated electronically, and a brand's support of a particular cause. Finally, in Vonk's list of most creative campaigns, Taxi stood out as the visionary with seven significant achievements all in the latter third of the two decades.

Sources: Hugh Dow, "Beyond Transformation: 20 Years of Media," *Strategy*, December 2009, p. 16; Nancy Vonk, "Five Canadian Creative Game-Changers," *Strategy*, December 2009, p. 14; Frank Palmer, "Frank's Big Five: The Ad Biz Revolution," *Strategy*, December 2009, p. 18; Ken Wong, "20-Year Review: The Marketer's View," *Strategy*, December 2009, p. 12.

Question:

1. With so much change and turmoil in the industry, how is it that creative advertising continues to be developed?

emotional appeals, fear appeals, humour appeals, and combined rational and emotional appeals. In this section, we focus on ways to use these appeals as part of a creative strategy and consider how they can be combined in developing the advertising message.

RATIONAL APPEALS

Rational appeals focus on the consumer's practical, functional, or utilitarian need for the product or service and emphasize features of a product or service and/or the benefits or reasons for owning or using a particular brand. The content of these messages emphasizes facts, learning, and the logic of persuasion.[47] Rational-based appeals tend to be informative, and advertisers using them generally attempt to convince consumers that their product or service has a particular attribute(s) or provides a specific benefit that satisfies their needs. Their objective is to persuade the target audience to buy the brand because it is the best available or does a better job of meeting consumers' needs. For example, Atkins uses a rational appeal to promote the nutritional benefits of its Advantage Bars in the ad shown in Exhibit 7-12. Weilbacher[48] identified several types of advertising appeals that fall under the category of rational approaches, among them feature, comparative, favourable price, news, and product/service popularity appeals. We also include reminder appeals in this list.

Ads that use a *feature appeal* focus on the dominant traits of the product or service. These ads tend to be highly informative and present the customer with a number of important product attributes or features that will lead to favourable attitudes and can be used as the basis for a rational purchase decision. Technical and high-involvement products often use message appeal. Exhibit 7-13 shows an ad for a Cobra golf club that focuses on the features and benefits of the club's technology.

A *comparative appeal* is the practice of either directly or indirectly naming competitors in an ad and comparing one or more specific attributes. Audi is one car brand that uses comparative ads to show that its automobile is more stylish (see Exhibit 7-14).[49] Some studies show that recall is higher for comparative than noncomparative messages, but comparative ads are generally not more effective for other response variables, such as brand attitudes or purchase intentions.[50] Advertisers must also consider how comparative messages affect credibility. Users of the brand being attacked in a comparative message may be especially skeptical about the advertiser's claims.

Exhibit 7-12   A rational appeal is used to promote the nutritional benefits of Advantage bars.

Exhibit 7-13   Cobra Golf uses a feature appeal to promote its clubs.

Exhibit 7-14 Audi's stylish cars offer the opportunity to use comparative ads.

Comparative appeals may be particularly useful for new brands, since they allow a new market entrant to position itself directly against the more established brands and to promote its distinctive advantages. Direct comparisons can help position a new brand in the evoked, or choice, set of brands the customer may be considering.

Comparative appeals are often used for brands with a small market share. They compare themselves to an established market leader in hopes of creating an association and tapping into the leader's market. Market leaders, on the other hand, often hesitate to use comparison ads, as most believe they have little to gain by featuring competitors' products in their ads.

A *favourable price appeal* makes the price offer the dominant point of the message. Price appeal advertising is used most often by retailers to announce sales, special offers, or low everyday prices. Price appeal ads are often used by national advertisers during recessionary times. Many fast-food chains have made price an important part of their marketing strategy through promotional deals and "value menus" or lower overall prices, and their advertising strategy is designed to communicate this. Many other types of advertisers use price appeals as well.

News appeals are those in which some type of news or announcement about the product, service, or company dominates the ad. This type of appeal can be used for a new product or service or to inform consumers of significant modifications or improvements. This appeal works best when a company has important news it wants to communicate to its target market. Exhibit 7-15 shows an ad using a news appeal that was run by Boeing to announce the first flight of the company's new Boeing 777-200LR Worldliner, which is the world's longest-range commercial airplane. The ad was run a few days after the inaugural flight to create interest and excitement in the new plane, which can connect any two cities in the world with nonstop service.

Product/service popularity appeals stress the popularity of a product or service by pointing out the number of consumers who use the brand, the number who have switched to it, the number of experts who recommend it, or its leadership position in the market. The main point of this advertising appeal is that the wide use of the brand proves its quality or value and other customers should consider using it. The ad for Neutrogena's Healthy Skin Anti-Wrinkle cream shown in Exhibit 7-16 uses a product popularity appeal by noting that it is the brand most recommended by dermatologists as well as the sales leader in the category.

A *reminder appeal* has the objective of building brand awareness and/or keeping the brand name in front of consumers. Well-known brands and market leaders often use a reminder appeal, which is often referred to as reminder advertising. Products and services that have a seasonal

FIRST FLIGHT AND ALREADY MILES AHEAD.

BOEING

Exhibit 7-15 Boeing uses a news appeal to promote its 777-200LR Worldliner.

pattern to their consumption also use reminder advertising, particularly around the appropriate period. For example, marketers of candy products often increase their media budgets and run reminder advertising around Halloween, Valentine's Day, Christmas, and Easter.

EMOTIONAL APPEALS

Emotional appeals relate to the customer's social and/or psychological needs for purchasing a product or service. Many of consumers' motives for their purchase decisions are emotional, and their feelings about a brand can be more important than knowledge of its features or attributes. Advertisers for many products and services view rational-based appeals as dull. Many advertisers believe appeals to consumers' emotions work better at selling brands that do not differ markedly from competing brands, since rational differentiation of them is difficult.[51]

The choice between rational or emotional appeal is a challenge and careful consideration must take place to ensure the advertising resonates with the target audience and evokes relevant processing responses connected to the purchase decision or consumption experience. For example, Gaz Métro, the largest natural gas provider in Quebec, repositioned itself to expand sales in the residential market after well establishing itself in the industrial, institutional, and commercial sectors. Faced with strong electric power competition from Hydro Quebec, Gaz Métro needed to educate and reassure consumers that natural gas was a secure alternative to electricity when consumers were renovating or upgrading their household energy requirements. While some might have expected Gaz Métro to use a rational argument, it instead used an emotional appeal that showed how comfortable one's home would feel with the seductive blue flame of natural gas in a stunning visually oriented television commercial.[52]

Many feelings or needs can serve as the basis for advertising appeals designed to influence consumers on an emotional level, as shown in Figure 7-3. These appeals are based on the psychological states or feelings directed to the self (such as pleasure or excitement), as well as those with a more social orientation (such as status or recognition).

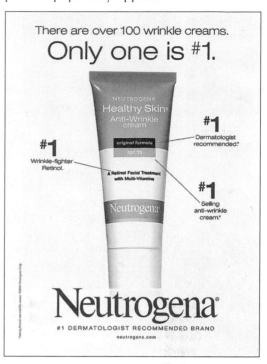

Exhibit 7-16 This Neutrogena ad uses a product popularity appeal.

Personal States or Feelings		Social-Based Feelings
Safety	Arousal/stimulation	Recognition
Security	Sorrow/grief	Status
Fear	Pride	Respect
Love	Achievement/accomplishment	Involvement
Affection	Self-esteem	Embarrassment
Happiness	Actualization	Affiliation/belonging
Joy	Pleasure	Rejection
Nostalgia	Ambition	Acceptance
Sentiment	Comfort	Approval
Excitement		

FIGURE 7-3

Bases for emotional appeals

Advertisers can use emotional appeals in many ways in their creative strategy. Kamp and MacInnis note that commercials often rely on the concept of *emotional integration*, whereby they portray the characters in the ad as experiencing an emotional benefit or outcome from using a product or service.[53] Ads using lifestyle, humour, sex, and other appeals that are very entertaining, arousing, upbeat, and/or exciting can affect the emotions of consumers and put them in a favourable frame of mind. For example, Second Clothing, a Montreal-based premium denim brand, demonstrated the feeling women have when first trying on a pair of yoga jeans. With very sensual images, sexy music, and the sound of an amorous woman "cooing," one presumes the experience lives ups to the tagline "Feel Good. Real Good."[54]

Marketers use emotional appeals in hopes that the positive feeling they evoke will transfer to the brand and/or company. Research shows that positive mood states and feelings created by advertising can have a favourable effect on consumers' evaluations of a brand.[55] Studies also show that emotional advertising is better remembered than nonemotional messages.[56]

Mercedes-Benz Canada successfully used an emotional appeal in its first Canadian-made television commercial. Preliminary research indicated that many potential buyers had a very positive attitude toward Mercedes-Benz but delayed purchasing for various reasons. Brand associations of Mercedes-Benz being "older money and prestige," and "distancing and intimidating," along with consumers feeling they had not "arrived yet" led to a sizable target audience of young consumers who have never bought previously. Enter the positioning message "Mercedes-Benz. You're Ready" along with "The Story of Raymond," which traces the life of one who delays buying ice cream as a boy and throughout much of his adult life. At the conclusion, we see a few shots of the car and realize the creative is a metaphor for desiring a Mercedes-Benz yet postponing the purchase. Subsequent research revealed outstanding levels for emotions, entertainment value, and consumer understanding of the key message. In fact, Mercedes-Benz received e-mail and telephone responses from consumers saying the ad spurred them to purchase.[57]

FEAR APPEALS

Fear is an emotional response to a threat that expresses, or at least implies, some sort of danger. Ads sometimes use **fear appeals** to invoke this emotional response and arouse individuals to take steps to remove the threat. Some, like anti-smoking ads, stress physical danger that can occur if behaviours are not altered. Others—like those for deodorant, mouthwash, or dandruff shampoos—threaten disapproval or social rejection.

Before deciding to use a fear appeal–based message strategy, the advertiser should consider how fear operates, what level to use, and how different target audiences may respond. One theory suggests that the relationship between the level of fear in a message and acceptance or persuasion is curvilinear, as shown in Figure 7-4.[58] This means that message acceptance increases as the amount of fear used rises—to a point. Beyond that point, acceptance decreases as the level of fear rises.

This relationship between fear and persuasion can be explained by the fact that fear appeals have both facilitating and inhibiting effects.[59] A low level of fear can have facilitating effects; it attracts attention and interest in the message and may motivate the receiver to act to resolve the threat. Thus, increasing the level of fear in a message from low to moderate can result in increased persuasion. High levels of fear, however, can produce inhibiting effects; the receiver may emotionally block the message by tuning it out, perceiving it selectively, or denying its arguments outright. Figure 7-4 illustrates how these two countereffects operate to produce the curvilinear relationship between fear and persuasion.

A recent study by Anand Keller and Block provides support for this perspective on how fear operates.[60] Their study indicated that a communication using a

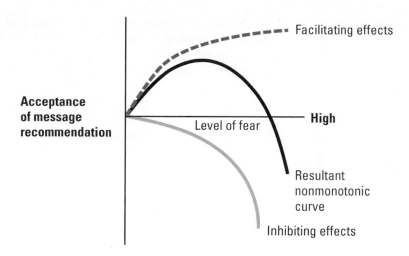

FIGURE 7–4

Relationship between
fear levels and
message acceptance

low level of fear may be ineffective because it results in insufficient motivation to elaborate on the harmful consequences of engaging in the destructive behaviour (smoking). However, an appeal arousing high levels of fear was ineffective because it resulted in too much elaboration on the harmful consequences. This led to defensive tendencies such as message avoidance and interfered with processing of recommended solutions to the problem.

Another approach to the curvilinear explanation of fear is the protection motivation model.[61] According to this theory, four cognitive appraisal processes mediate the individual's response to the threat: appraising (1) the information available regarding the severity of the perceived threat, (2) the perceived probability that the threat will occur, (3) the perceived ability of a coping behaviour to remove the threat, and (4) the individual's perceived ability to carry out the coping behaviour. This model suggests that ads using fear appeals should give the target audience information about the severity of the threat, the probability of its occurrence, the effectiveness of a coping response, and the ease with which the response can be implemented.[62]

In reviewing research on fear appeals, Herbert Rotfeld has argued that some of the studies may be confusing different types of threats and the level of potential harm portrayed in the message with fear, which is an emotional response.[63] He concludes that the relationship between the emotional responses of fear or arousal and persuasion is not curvilinear but rather is monotonic and positive, meaning that higher levels of fear do result in greater persuasion. However, Rotfeld notes that not all fear messages are equally effective, because different people fear different things. Thus they will respond differently to the same threat, so the strongest threats are not always the most persuasive. This suggests that marketers using fear appeals must consider the emotional responses generated by the message and how they will affect reactions to the message.

HUMOUR APPEALS

Humorous ads are often the best known and best remembered of all advertising messages. Humour is usually presented through radio and TV commercials as these media lend themselves to the execution of humorous messages. However, humour is occasionally used in print ads as well (Exhibit 7-17). Oftentimes humour is used since it fits so well with certain products like food, beverages, and household goods; however, some advertisers are moving toward using it for personal care products that might have used a fear appeal in the past, which shows that the context and audience dictate the suitability of its use. For example, a maker for incontinence products paired up with Just for Laughs by suggesting that it was okay to laugh since their product

Exhibit 7-17 Altoids uses humour and facts in its ads.

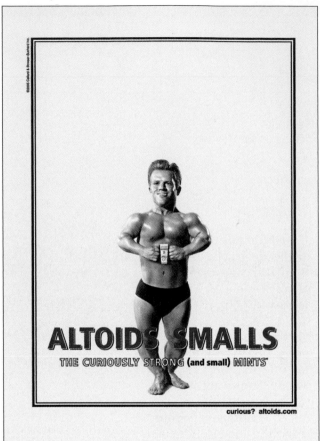

ALTOIDS SMALLS
THE CURIOUSLY STRONG (and small) MINTS

curious? altoids.com

202

would work. Winners of a contest would go to a Just for Laughs festival in Toronto, Montreal, or Chicago.[64]

Advertisers use **humour appeals** for many reasons. Humorous messages attract and hold consumers' attention. They enhance effectiveness by putting consumers in a positive mood, increasing their liking of the ad itself and their feeling toward the product or service. And humour can distract the receiver from counterarguing against the message.[65] Critics argue that funny ads draw people to the humorous situation but distract them from the brand and its attributes. Also, effective humour can be difficult to produce and some attempts are too subtle for mass audiences.

Clearly, there are valid reasons both for and against the use of humour in advertising. Not every product or service lends itself to a humorous approach.[66] A number of studies have found that the effectiveness of humour depends on several factors, including the type of product and audience characteristics.[67] For example, humour has been more prevalent and more effective with low-involvement, feeling products than high-involvement, thinking products.[68] An interesting study surveyed the research and creative directors of the top 150 advertising agencies.[69] They were asked to name which communications objectives are facilitated through the appropriate situational use of humour in terms of media, product, and audience factors. The general conclusions of this study are shown in Figure 7-5.

FIGURE 7–5

Conclusions of the humour study

- Humour does aid awareness and attention, which are the objectives best achieved by its use.
- Humour may harm recall and comprehension in general.
- Humour may aid name and simple copy registration.
- Humour may harm complex copy registration.
- Humour may aid retention.
- Humour does not aid persuasion in general.
- Humour may aid persuasion to switch brands.
- Humour creates a positive mood that enhances persuasion.
- Humour does not aid source credibility.
- Humour is generally not very effective in bringing about action/sales.
- Creatives are more positive on the use of humour to fulfill all the above objectives than research directors are.
- Radio and TV are the best media in which to use humour; direct mail and newspapers are least suited.
- Consumer nondurables and business services are best suited to humour; corporate advertising and industrial products are least suited.
- Humour should be related to the product.
- Humour should not be used with sensitive goods or services.
- Audiences that are younger, better educated, upscale, male, and professional are best suited to humour; older, less educated, and downscale groups are least suited to humour appeals.

COMBINED RATIONAL AND EMOTIONAL APPEALS

In many advertising situations, the decision facing the creative specialist is not whether to choose an emotional or a rational appeal but rather determining how to combine the two approaches. As noted copywriters David Ogilvy and Joel Raphaelson have stated:

> Few purchases of any kind are made for entirely rational reasons. Even a purely functional product such as laundry detergent may offer what is now called an emotional benefit—say, the satisfaction of seeing one's children in bright clean clothes. In some product categories the rational element is small. These include soft drinks, beer, cosmetics, certain personal care products, and most old-fashioned products. And who hasn't experienced the surge of joy that accompanies the purchase of a new car?[70]

Exhibit 7-18 Advertising for personal computers appeals rationally and emotionally.

Consumer purchase decisions are often made on the basis of both emotional and rational motives, and attention must be given to both elements in developing effective advertising. For example, ads in the personal computer market highlight the functional performance and the experience of the user-friendly style and design (Exhibit 7-18).

Advertising researchers and agencies have given considerable thought to the relationship between rational and emotional motives in consumer decision making and how advertising influences both. McCann-Erickson Worldwide, in conjunction with advertising professor Michael Ray, developed a proprietary research technique known as *emotional bonding*. This technique evaluates how consumers feel about brands and the nature of any emotional rapport they have with a brand compared to the ideal emotional state they associate with the product category.[71]

The basic concept of emotional bonding is that consumers develop three levels of relationships with brands, as shown in Figure 7-6. The most basic relationship indicates how consumers *think* about brands in respect to product benefits. This occurs, for the most part, through a rational learning process and can be measured by how

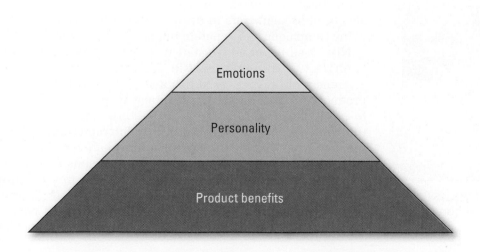

FIGURE 7–6

Levels of relationships with brands

well advertising communicates product information. Consumers at this stage are not very brand loyal, and brand switching is common.

At the next stage, the consumer assigns a *personality* to a brand. For example, a brand may be thought of as self-assured, aggressive, and adventurous, as opposed to compliant and timid. The consumer's judgment of the brand has moved beyond its attributes or delivery of product/service benefits. In most instances, consumers judge the personality of a brand on the basis of an assessment of overt or covert cues found in its advertising.

McCann-Erickson researchers believe the strongest relationship that develops between a brand and the consumer is based on feelings or emotional attachments to the brand. Consumers develop *emotional bonds* with certain brands, which result in positive psychological movement toward them. The marketer's goal is to develop the greatest emotional linkage between its brand and the consumer. McCann-Erickson believes advertising can develop and enrich emotional bonding between consumers and brands. McCann and its subsidiary agencies use emotional bonding research to provide strategic input into the creative process and determine how well advertising is communicating with consumers. McCann-Erickson used emotional bonding research as the basis for the "Priceless" campaign for MasterCard International, which has been extremely successful. When the agency took over the account in the late 1990s, MasterCard had become the third card in the consumer's wallet, behind Visa and American Express. The challenge was to reposition the brand and create an emotional bond between consumers and MasterCard while retaining the brand's functional appeal. The idea behind the campaign is that good spenders use credit cards to acquire things that are important to them and enrich their daily lives. The creative execution involved showing a shopping list of items that could be purchased for a certain dollar amount and one key item that could not and thus was deemed "Priceless." The tagline "There are some things money can't buy. For everything else there's MasterCard," positions the card as the way to pay for everything that matters. An entire integrated marketing campaign has been built around the "Priceless" campaign theme that includes sponsorships with Major League Baseball, the National Hockey League, and the PGA golf tour. Contests and sweepstakes have also been part of the campaign. The campaign now runs in 80 countries and has won numerous creative awards. Exhibit 7-19 shows one of the print ads from the campaign.

A unique example of combining rational and emotional appeals is the use of **teaser advertising.** Advertisers introducing a new product often use teaser advertising, which is designed to build curiosity, interest, and/or excitement about a product or brand by talking about it but not actually showing it. Teasers, or *mystery ads* as they are sometimes called, are also used by marketers to draw attention to upcoming advertising campaigns and generate interest and publicity for them.

Nike used teaser ads to start its campaign for its successful "RunTO 10K" running event in Toronto. Looking to generate awareness of the race, establish a stronger link between Nike products and running, and encourage average or non-runners to participate (register online or in-store, and actually run), the creative featured "Running Guy," who represented all novice runners determined to complete the challenge despite not being in the best of shape. Messages at various out-of-home locations and in newspapers such as "10 km to a collapsed lung" and "10 km to the fetal position" preceded "Running Guy," thus provoking curiosity and introducing his persona. The campaign garnered significant media publicity, especially

204

Exhibit 7-19 MasterCard's "Priceless" campaign creates an emotional bond with consumers.

with "Running Guy" participating in the morning show of a radio station consistent with the target audience. In total, 7,500 runners finished the challenge, which easily surpassed the per capita participation rate of other major international cities.[72]

SOURCE CHARACTERISTICS

The third creative strategy decision is the source of the message appeal. We use the term **source** to mean the person involved in communicating a marketing message, either directly or indirectly. A *direct source* is a spokesperson who delivers a message and/or demonstrates a product or service. An *indirect source (e.g., model)* doesn't actually deliver a message but draws attention to and/or enhances the appearance of the ad. Some ads use neither a direct nor an indirect source; the source is the brand or organization with the message to communicate. Since most research focuses on individuals as a message source, our examination follows this approach. Companies carefully select individuals to deliver their advertising messages due to the costs involved and the fit with their brand positioning strategy. To understand this decision we rely on a model that identifies three basic source attributes: credibility, attractiveness, and power.[73] This section looks at the first two characteristics in the context of advertising. Source power is omitted, as compliance is not really possible in most promotional communication.

SOURCE CREDIBILITY

Credibility is the extent to which the recipient sees the source as having relevant knowledge, skill, or experience and trusts the source to give unbiased, objective information implying two important dimensions to credibility, expertise and trustworthiness. A communicator seen as knowledgeable—someone with expertise—is more persuasive than one with less expertise. But the source also has to be trustworthy—honest, ethical, and believable. The influence of a knowledgeable source will be lessened if audience members think he or she is biased or has underlying personal motives for advocating a position (such as being paid to endorse a product).

One of the most reliable effects found in communications research is that expert and/or trustworthy sources are more persuasive than sources who are less expert or trustworthy.[74] Information from a credible source influences beliefs, opinions, attitudes, and/or behaviour through a process known as **internalization,** which occurs when the receiver adopts the opinion of the credible communicator since he or she believes information from this source is accurate. Once the receiver internalizes an opinion or attitude, it becomes integrated into his or her belief system and may be maintained even after the source of the message is forgotten.

Expertise Because attitudes and opinions developed through an internalization process become part of the individual's belief system, marketers want to use communicators with expertise. Spokespeople are often chosen because of their knowledge or experience with a particular product or service. Endorsements from individuals or groups recognized as experts, such as doctors or dentists, are also common in advertising (Exhibit 7-20). The importance of using expert sources was shown in a study by Roobina Ohanian, who found that the perceived expertise of celebrity endorsers was

Exhibit 7-20 Dove promotes the fact that it is recommended by experts in skin care.

more important in explaining purchase intentions than their attractiveness or trustworthiness. She suggests that celebrity spokespeople are most effective when they are knowledgeable, experienced, and qualified to talk about the product they are endorsing.[75]

Trustworthiness While expertise is important, the target audience must also find the source (e.g., celebrities or other figures) to have a trustworthy image. For some brands, options for selecting a trustworthy spokesperson may be limited. Alternatively, trustworthy public figures hesitate to endorse products because of the potential impact on their reputation and image.

A way of finding an appropriate trustworthy source is to use the company president or chief executive officer as a spokesperson in the firm's advertising. The use of this source is the ultimate expression of the company's commitment to quality and customer service. Some research suggests the use of a company president or CEO can improve attitudes and increase the likelihood that consumers will inquire about the company's product or service.[76] Companies are likely to continue using their top executives in their advertising, particularly when they have celebrity value that helps enhance the firms' image. However, there is a risk if CEO spokespeople become very popular and get more attention than their company's product/service or advertising message. Perhaps the most prolific corporate leader acting as the advertising spokesperson is Frank D'Angelo, who promotes his beer and energy drink brands. Loblaws recently returned to using its president in advertising, something the retailer originated during the 1970s. Owners or presidents of small or local businesses also rely on this approach for source trustworthiness.

Limitations of Credible Sources Several studies have shown that a high-credibility source is not always an asset, nor is a low-credibility source always a liability. High- and low-credibility sources are equally effective when they are arguing for a position opposing their own best interest.[77] A very credible source is more effective when message recipients are not in favour of the position advocated in the message.[78] However, a very credible source is less important when the audience has a neutral position, and such a source may even be less effective than a moderately credible source when the receiver's initial attitude is favourable.[79]

Another reason why a low-credibility source may be as effective as a high-credibility source is the **sleeper effect**, whereby the persuasiveness of a message increases with the passage of time. The immediate impact of a persuasive message may be inhibited because of its association with a low-credibility source. But with time, the association of the message with the source diminishes and the receiver's attention focuses more on favourable information in the message, resulting in more support arguing. However, many studies have failed to demonstrate the presence of a sleeper effect.[80] Many advertisers hesitate to count on the sleeper effect, since exposure to a credible source is a more reliable strategy.[81]

SOURCE ATTRACTIVENESS

A source characteristic frequently used by advertisers is **attractiveness**, which encompasses similarity, familiarity, and likability.[82] *Similarity* is a supposed resemblance between the source and the receiver of the message. *Likability* is an affection for the source as a result of physical appearance, behaviour, or other personal traits. Even when the sources are not famous, consumers often admire their physical appearance, talent, and/or personality. *Familiarity* refers to knowledge of the source through exposure. We describe these three characteristics and see how they operate via celebrity endorsers and decorative models in this section.

Source attractiveness leads to persuasion through a process of **identification**, whereby the receiver is motivated to seek some type of relationship with the source and thus adopts similar beliefs, attitudes, preferences, or behaviour. Maintaining this position depends on the source's continued support for the position as well as the receiver's continued identification with the source. If the source changes position, the receiver may also change. Unlike internalization, identification does not usually integrate information from an attractive source into the receiver's belief system. The receiver may maintain the attitudinal position or behaviour only as long as it is supported by the source or the source remains attractive. Exhibit 7-21 is an ad where source attractiveness may be working effectively.

Similarity Research findings suggest that people are more likely to be influenced by a message coming from someone with whom they feel a sense of similarity.[83] If the communicator and receiver have similar needs, goals, interests, and lifestyles, the position advocated by the source is better understood and received. Similarity can be used to create a situation where the consumer feels empathy for the person shown in the commercial. In a slice-of-life commercial, the advertiser usually starts by presenting a predicament with the hope of getting the consumer to think, "I can see myself in that situation." This can help establish a bond of similarity between the communicator and the receiver, increasing the source's level of persuasiveness. Many companies feel that the best way to connect with consumers is by using regular-looking, everyday people with whom the average person can easily identify.

Exhibit 7-21 The model in this Tropez ad is an example of source attractiveness.

The characters for A&W have been around longer than the two guys debating whether PC or Mac is the better device, and their success may be attributed to the fact that they appear to be everyday guys (Exhibit 7-22). The A&W manager represents the typical man trying to do a good job every day, while the younger Gen-Y slacker is along to resonate with today's youth in a humorous way.[84] The men's clothing retailer Harry Rosen returned to its roots of using regular businessmen for its print ads recently after using more famous names the past 15 years. Moving from very familiar faces from the entertainment, sports, and business fields toward the more similar everyday manager gives a fresh look to the largely rational messages located in many newspapers.[85]

Likability As noted in the above definition, a likable source in an ad is derived from virtually any characteristics the advertiser would like to draw attention toward in the message. Presumably, promotional planners would select a characteristic that reinforces the brand. For example, a facial skin care brand would select a person who has a very good complexion so that physical characteristic would be noticed and associated with Jergens. Oftentimes beverage brands will use likable sources with personality characteristics that emerge in the story of the ad to develop the brand personality.

One requirement for a national campaign with an identifiable and likable spokesperson who actually speaks in the ads is that the person has to be fluent in both official languages. Danone did this with actress Sophie Lorain, who convincingly played a strong central character in its commercials. She demonstrated that Danone was for women who wanted to include yogurt as a healthy part of their

Exhibit 7-22 This Apple ad is an example of source likability.

208

busy everyday lives. Lorain had previously been the spokesperson in the Quebec ads for two years when Danone tested her in an English ad. While the language was a necessary requirement for success, Danone executives believed that Lorain's character (i.e., likability, similarity) communicated the brand benefits effectively, which was the primary concern.[86]

Familiarity Familiarity through exposure from some other context can provide a strong source. Essentially, advertisers hope the characteristics associated with the source from which the audience knows the original context carries over to the brand. This connection is often reinforced with the creative theme of the ad, so the two strategic variables work in tandem. In fact, the connection can be quite surprising and very effective in some circumstances, especially for the British Columbia Automobile Association (BCAA). Three television commercials advertised its new Premier Membership with three former B.C. premiers, Dave Barrett, Bill Vander Zalm, and Glen Clark, each who faced varying political fortunes while leading Canada's westernmost province. Seeking to stay ahead of new competitive entrants in the roadside assistance market, BCAA sought to retain its market leadership position through higher sales growth while maintaining its reputation for strong products and excellent customer service. The answer of a risky creative that captured former premiers in humorous, self-deprecating situations that poked fun at themselves seemed the best bet to break through clutter and clearly identify the brand name Premier. Each "actor" agreed to waive his fee in lieu of a donation to his favourite charity. Initial sales in the spring topped 2,000 and BCAA looked to up that to 10,000 by the end of 2004.[87]

Celebrity Endorsers Advertisers recognize the value of using spokespeople who are admired: TV and movie stars, athletes, musicians, and other popular public figures (Exhibit 7-23). Why do companies spend huge sums to have celebrities appear in their ads and endorse their products? These celebrities are clearly very likable due to their professional achievements, are generally very familiar given the exposure in various media, and are often physically attractive as well. Through their accomplishments and image, the celebrities help draw consumer attention to advertising messages in a very cluttered media environment. Marketers think a popular celebrity will favourably influence consumers' feelings, attitudes, and purchase behaviour. When selecting a celebrity, marketers consider their congruence with the audience, credibility, profession, popularity, and obtainability—and, given the financial investments involved, are encouraged to follow a clear and formal process to avoid any problems.[88] Finally, marketers believe celebrities can enhance the target audience's perceptions of the product in terms of image and/or performance. For example, a well-known athlete like Sidney Crosby may convince potential buyers that the product will enhance their own performance (see Exhibit 7-24).

A number of factors must be considered when a company decides to use a celebrity spokesperson, including the dangers of overshadowing the product and being overexposed, and the target audience's receptivity.

Exhibit 7-23 Maria Sharapova has endorsement contracts with a number of companies including Nike, Canon, Motorola, and Tag Heuer.

Exhibit 7-24 Sidney Crosby is featured at this Gatorade promotional event.

Overshadowing the Product How will the celebrity affect the target audience's processing of the advertising message? Consumers may focus their attention on the celebrity and fail to notice the brand. Advertisers should select a celebrity spokesperson who will attract attention and enhance the sales message, yet not overshadow the brand. For example, Chrysler Corp. chose singer Celine Dion to appear in ads for various brands including the Pacifica sport wagon, Crossfire sports coupe, and Town & Country minivan, and also signed on as the sponsor of her Las Vegas show "A New Day." She starred in a number of lavish TV commercials that were part of Chrysler's "Drive & Love" campaign, which was developed to give Chrysler a more upscale image and help achieve a premium positioning for the brand. However, it was believed that her celebrity persona overshadowed the products and the campaign did more to sell her than the cars.[89]

Overexposure Consumers are often skeptical of endorsements because they know the celebrities are being paid.[90] This problem is particularly pronounced when a celebrity endorses too many products or companies and becomes overexposed. Advertisers can protect themselves against overexposure with an exclusivity clause limiting the number of products a celebrity can endorse. However, such clauses are usually expensive, and most celebrities agree not to endorse similar products anyway. Many celebrities try to earn as much endorsement money as possible, yet they must be careful not to damage their credibility by endorsing too many products.

Target Audience's Receptivity One of the most important considerations in choosing a celebrity endorser is how well the individual matches with and is received by the advertiser's target audience. Consumers who are particularly knowledgeable about a product or service or have strongly established attitudes may be less influenced by a celebrity than those with little knowledge or neutral attitudes. One study found that college-age students were more likely to have a positive attitude toward a product endorsed by a celebrity than were older consumers.[91] The teenage market has generally been very receptive to celebrity endorsers, as evidenced by the frequent use of entertainers and athletes in ads targeted to this group for products such as apparel, cosmetics, and beverages. However, many marketers are finding that teenage consumers are more skeptical and cynical toward the use of celebrity endorsers and respond better to ads using humour, irony, and unvarnished truth. Some marketers targeting teenagers have responded to this by no longer using celebrities in their campaigns or by poking fun at their use.

The Meaning of Celebrity Endorsers Advertisers must try to match the product or company's image, the characteristics of the target audience, and the personality of the celebrity.[92] The image that celebrities project to consumers can be just as important as their ability to attract attention. An interesting perspective on celebrity endorsement was developed by Grant McCracken.[93] He argues that credibility and attractiveness don't sufficiently explain how and why celebrity endorsements work and offers a model based on meaning transfer (Figure 7-7).

According to this model, a celebrity's effectiveness as an endorser depends on the culturally acquired meanings he or she brings to the endorsement process. Each celebrity contains many meanings, including status, class, gender, and age as well as personality and lifestyle. In explaining stage 1 of the meaning transfer process, McCracken notes:

> Celebrities draw these powerful meanings from the roles they assume in their television, movie, military, athletic, and other careers. Each new dramatic role brings the celebrity into contact with a range of objects, persons, and contexts. Out of these objects, persons, and contexts are transferred meanings that then reside in the celebrity.[94]

For example, cyclist Lance Armstrong has developed a very favourable image as a fierce competitor and an All-American superhero by winning the gruelling Tour

FIGURE 7–7   Meaning movement and the endorsement process

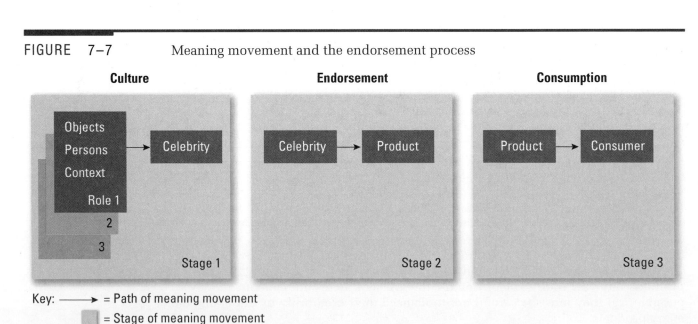

Key: ——▶ = Path of meaning movement
    ▨ = Stage of meaning movement

de France cycling race four times after overcoming a life-threatening form of testicular cancer. McCracken suggests celebrity endorsers bring their meanings and image into the ad and transfer them to the product they are endorsing (stage 2 of the model in Figure 7-7). For example, PowerBar, the leading brand of energy performance bars, takes advantage of Armstrong's image as a competitor and champion with great determination in ads such as the one shown in Exhibit 7-25. He is also an effective endorser for the product since he competes in a demanding sport where the benefits of sustained energy are very important.

In the final stage of McCracken's model, the meanings the celebrity has given to the product are transferred to the consumer. By using Armstrong in its ads, PowerBar hopes to enhance its image as a product that can provide extra energy to athletes and enhance their performance. McCracken notes that this final stage is complicated and difficult to achieve. The way consumers take possession of the meaning the celebrity has transferred to a product is probably the least understood part of the process.

The meaning transfer model has implications for using celebrity endorsers. Marketers must first decide on the image or symbolic meanings important to the target audience and then determine which celebrity best represents the meaning or image to be projected. An advertising campaign must be designed that captures that meaning in the product and moves it to the consumer. Marketing and advertising personnel often rely on intuition in choosing celebrity endorsers for their companies or products, but some companies conduct research studies to determine consumers' perceptions of celebrities' meaning. Marketers may also pretest ads to determine whether they transfer the proper meaning to the product. When celebrity endorsers are used, the marketer should track the campaign's effectiveness by assessing whether the celebrity continues to communicate the proper meaning to the target audience.

Finally, studies have shown that advertising and marketing managers take many factors into account when choosing a celebrity endorser.[95] Among the most important factors are the celebrity's match with the target audience and the product/service or brand, the overall image of the celebrity, the cost of acquiring the celebrity, trustworthiness, the risk of controversy, and the celebrity's familiarity and likability among the target audience. Going in the opposite direction, Steve Nash, two-time MVP of the NBA, acts a spokesperson for brands that support his charitable causes like the Steve Nash Foundation that provides funds to children for health and education.[96]

Decorative Models   Advertisers often draw attention to their ads by featuring a physically attractive person who serves as a passive or decorative model rather than as an active communicator. Research suggests that physically attractive communicators generally have a positive impact and generate more favourable evaluations of both ads and products than less attractive models.[97] The gender appropriateness of the model for the product being advertised and his or her relevance to the product are also important considerations.[98] Products such as cosmetics or fashionable clothing are likely to benefit from the use of an attractive model, since physical appearance is very relevant in marketing these items.

Some models draw attention to the ad but not to the product or message. Studies show that an attractive model facilitates recognition of the ad but does not

Exhibit 7-25   Cyclist Lance Armstrong helps position PowerBar as a product that provides energy to athletes.

Exhibit 7-26 Dove's "Campaign for Real Beauty" uses everyday women rather than supermodels in its ads.

campaignforrealbeauty.com *Dove*

Let's face it, firming the thighs of a size 2 supermodel is no challenge. Real women have real curves. And according to women who tried new Dove Firming, it left their skin feeling firmer in just one week. What better way to celebrate the curves you were born with? New Dove Firming. Lotion, Cream and Body Wash. For beautifully firm skin.

enhance copy readership or message recall. Thus, advertisers must ensure that the consumer's attention will go beyond the model to the product and advertising message.[99] Marketers must also consider whether the use of highly attractive models might negatively impact advertising effectiveness. Some recent studies have shown that some women experience negative feelings when comparing themselves with beautiful models used in ads and the images of physical perfection they represent.[100]

Some companies have developed marketing campaigns that undermine the traditional approach to beauty care advertising by telling women, as well as young girls, that they're beautiful just the way they are. For example, Unilever's Dove brand has long eschewed the use of supermodels in its ads and used everyday women and girls who resemble its typical consumers. The company recently developed an interesting global integrated marketing campaign designed to appeal to everyday women.[101] The "Campaign for Real Beauty" includes magazine ads, extensive public relations, and a website (Campaignforrealbeauty.ca) where women can discuss beauty-related issues (Exhibit 7-26). Dove has taken a social advocacy approach in the campaign, which it proclaims "aims to change the status quo and offer in its place a broader, healthier, more democratic view of beauty."[102]

IMC PLANNING: MESSAGE AND SOURCE COMBINATIONS

As noted at the outset of this chapter, the creative strategy comprises decisions regarding the creative theme, message appeal, and source characteristics. In the creative theme section, we noted that promotional planners determine the degree to which there is creative consistency across time, executions, media, promotional tools, and products. In this IMC planning section, we present a table that allows promotional planners to consider various combinations of message and source decisions.

Figure 7-8 presents a table summarizing the possible combinations of all message and source decisions. Essentially any ad or IMC tool has one of these 15 combinations. Promotional planners can consider using certain combinations for certain parts of the IMC plan. For example, a brand may select a more credible source with a rational appeal for its print communication and possibly consider a familiar source with an emotional appeal for its television commercials. As noted in the creative consistency section, Telus has used a different message appeal and source on television and radio. Television ads feature likable critters with emotional appeals, while radio ads feature a trustworthy source with rational appeals.

	Rational Appeal	Emotional Appeal	Combined Appeal
Credible			
Trustworthy			
Similar			
Likable			
Familiar			

FIGURE 7–8

Possible
combinations
for message and
source decisions

While a number of combinations exist—and we have shown two examples where
brands have adapted the source and message across IMC tools or media—promotional planners can certainly decide to keep the same source and message appeal
for all their tools and media.

CHAPTER OBJECTIVES AND SUMMARY

1 To explore the creative strategy planning process.

The creative development and execution of the advertising message are a crucial part of a firm's integrated marketing communications program. The creative specialist or team is responsible for developing an effective way to communicate the marketer's message to both customers and non-customers and reinforce the brand positioning strategy. Marketers often turn to ad agencies to develop, prepare, and implement their creative strategy since these agencies are specialists in the creative function of advertising.

The challenge facing the writers, artists, and others who develop ads is to be creative and come up with fresh, unique, and appropriate ideas that can be used as solutions to marketing communication problems. Creativity in advertising is a process of several stages, including preparation, incubation, illumination, and verification. Various sources of information are available to help the creative specialists determine the best creative strategy.

Creative strategy is guided by marketing goals and objectives and is based on a number of factors, including the basic problem the advertising must address, the target audience, behavioural and communication objectives the message seeks to accomplish, and key benefits the advertiser wants to communicate as reflected in the brand positioning strategy. These factors and the creative strategy decisions are generally stated in a copy platform, which is a work plan used to guide development of the ad campaign.

2 To identify three key decisions that comprise a creative strategy: creative theme, message appeal, and message source.

The inherent creativity of advertising messages makes describing the content quite perplexing. This chapter suggests a trio of key decisions to summarize or identify a creative strategy to keep planning simplified. The creative theme acts as a brand story to give it uniqueness compared to competitors. A message appeal reveals the intended persuasion of the brand. Finally, the message source is the approach to deliver the message appeal.

3 To explore various approaches used for determining the creative theme that forms the basis of an advertising campaign.

An important part of creative strategy is determining the creative theme of the campaign. Often, a big idea strikes the creative specialist while embarking upon the creative process which becomes the genesis of the creative theme. There are several approaches to discover this big idea, including using a unique selling proposition, creating a brand image, looking for inherent drama in the brand, and positioning. In general, the creative theme guides much of the advertising campaign or IMC program. Consistency, originality, and its ability to effectively communicate are three key strengths of a good creative.

4 To summarize the different types of message appeals that

advertisers use to persuade their target audience.

A message appeal, the second decision of the creative strategy, is the central message used in the ad to elicit cognitive and emotional processing responses and communication effects from the target audience. Appeals can be broken into two broad groups, rational and emotional. Rational appeals focus on consumers' practical, functional, or utilitarian need for the product or service. Emotional appeals relate to social and/or psychological reasons for purchasing a product or service. Numerous types of appeals are available to advertisers within each group, and it is important for the client to clearly specify its intended message as accurately as possible.

5 To highlight the source or communicator options a marketer has for a promotional message.

Selection of the appropriate source or communicator to deliver a message is the third creative strategy decision. Three important attributes are source credibility, attractiveness, and power. Marketers enhance message effectiveness by hiring communicators who are experts in a particular area and/or have a trustworthy image. The use of celebrities to deliver advertising messages has become very popular; advertisers hope they will catch the receivers' attention and influence their attitudes or behaviour through an identification process. The chapter discusses the meaning a celebrity brings to the endorsement process and the importance of matching the image of the celebrity with that of the company or brand.

KEY TERMS

account planning, *183*
advertising campaign, *187*
advertising creativity, *179*
animatic, *186*
attractiveness, *206*
creative strategy, *178*
creative tactics, *178*
creative theme, *187*

copy platform, *186*
credibility, *205*
emotional appeal, *199*
fear appeal, *200*
focus groups, *185*
general preplanning
    input, *184*
humour appeal, *202*

identification, *206*
image advertising, *188*
inherent drama, *189*
internalization, *205*
message appeal, *195*
product/service-specific
    preplanning input, *184*
rational appeal, *196*

research, *184*
sleeper effect, *206*
source, *205*
storyboard, *185*
teaser advertising, *204*
unique selling proposition
    (USP), *188*

DISCUSSION QUESTIONS

1. Television commercials can use unusual creativity that has very little to do with the product being advertised. Explain why creative specialists would recommend such ads and why the brand managers would approve the production and placement.

2. Assume you have been assigned to work on the advertising campaign for a new brand of bottled water. Describe the types of general and product-specific preplanning input you might evaluate.

3. What is your opinion of advertising awards, such as the Cannes Lions, that are based solely on creativity? If you were a marketer looking for an agency, would you take these creative awards into consideration in your agency evaluation process? Why or why not?

4. Find an example of a print ad that you think is very creative and an ad you feel is dull and boring. Evaluate each ad from a creative perspective. What makes one ad creative and the other bland?

5. Find an example of an ad or campaign that you think reflects one of the approaches used to develop a creative theme such as unique selling proposition, brand image, inherent drama, or positioning. Discuss how the creative theme is used in this ad or campaign.

6. Discuss the pros and cons of using a comparative advertising appeal for the following products: beer, cellphones, furniture, airlines.

7. Assume that you have been asked to consult for a government agency that wants to use a fear appeal to encourage college and university students not to drink and drive. Explain how fear appeals might affect persuasion and what factors should be considered in developing the ads.

8. It has been observed that Canadian advertisers use fewer celebrity endorsers compared to American advertisers. Do you agree with this? If it is true, what is the explanation?

9. Find a celebrity who is currently appearing in ads for a particular company or brand and analyze and use McCracken's meaning transfer model (shown in Figure 7-7) to analyze the use of the celebrity as a spokesperson.

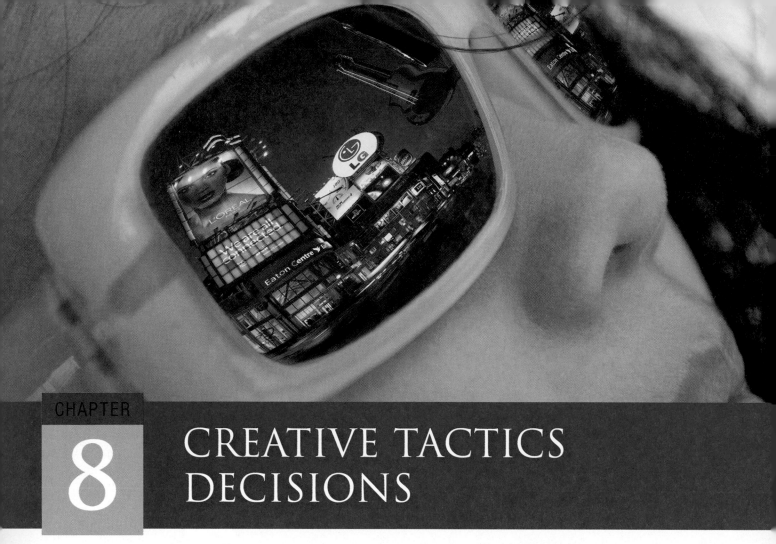

CREATIVE TACTICS DECISIONS

■ CHAPTER OBJECTIVES

1 To identify three key decisions for creative tactics: execution style, message structure, and design elements.

2 To analyze the creative execution styles that advertisers can use and the situations where they are most appropriate.

3 To examine different types of message structures that can be used to develop a promotional message.

4 To analyze design elements involved in the creation of print advertising and TV commercials.

5 To understand a planning model for making creative tactics decisions.

6 To consider how clients evaluate the creative work of their agencies and discuss guidelines for the evaluation and approval process.

MICROSOFT'S ADVERTISING CREATIVITY

With Microsoft entering many markets with its Bing search engine, Xbox gaming stations, and all sorts of Internet applications, a core business remains with Windows. During the launch of Windows 7, Microsoft began advertising for just the second time in the 20-year life of the operating system (with Windows 95 being the first time). While this might appear surprising, the brand and the technology sector often relied on public relations, especially through the trade and trade publications. And the message was not so much about the operating system but rather the Windows PC and how it benefits consumers versus other alternatives—hence the "I'm a PC" campaign that emerged for the consumer market.

Across the many markets for this product, the advertising took many formats with multiple executions. For example, Microsoft sponsored house parties where consumers would host friends and they would all explore the features of the new operating system. They filmed one such party, and found the resulting video distributed across the Internet. American-produced TV ads, later shown worldwide, had users self-identify themselves with the campaign's catchphrase, "I'm a PC." Another version filmed potential buyers as they made their PC decision over Mac under the guise of a market research study, only to find out at the conclusion that their story would be the content of an ad. Some, like four-year-old Kylie and college student Lauren, became the darlings of the campaign with their on-air cuteness and personality, respectively. Lauren concluded that, "I'm just not cool enough to be a Mac person."

To influence business and IT decision makers in the business market, the catchphrase "It's Everybody's Business" drove the campaign for Microsoft to claim it delivers quality information technology goods and services so that their customers' businesses can thrive. The execution for these ads featured animation of the CEOs of the Microsoft customers. With an interview format and all sorts of technological sketches to go along with the CEO images, the campaign went global with key executives from many countries.

In Canada, WestJet Airlines CEO Sean Durfy answered the question, "So, Durf, how do you keep the vision alive?" by talking about the growth of the company through technology, highlighting the accomplishments of WestJet employees and how they use and rely on technology to perform their jobs. A perfect message for both parties ensued, with WestJet endorsing Microsoft and once again identifying the importance of its employees (i.e., owners) when delivering airline services.

Sources: Christopher Loudon, "Ballmer's Battle Plan: The Full Transcript," *Marketing Magazine*, November 9, 2009; Jennifer Wells, "So, How Does Microsoft Keep the Vision Alive?" *The Globe and Mail*, January 16, 2009, p. B5; "PC Puts Another Chink in Mac's Cool Armour," *Marketing Magazine*, March 27, 2009; "Microsoft's House Party Video Becomes Viral Hit (Or Miss), *Marketing Magazine*, October 1, 2009.

QUESTIONS:

1. Why is Microsoft using different type of ads for its consumer and business markets?
2. Why is an animated TV commercial a good execution and media for IT professionals in Canada?

In the previous chapter, we identified and described the three creative strategy decisions. This chapter focuses on the three main creative tactics decisions. It examines various execution styles that can be used to develop the ad, the important message structure choices available, and the elements involved in the design and production of effective advertising messages. We also present a framework for guiding the creative tactics decisions. We conclude by presenting some guidelines marketers can use to evaluate the creative recommendations they need to approve to effectively communicate their brand positioning strategy.

CREATIVE EXECUTION STYLE

Once the message appeal has been determined, the creative specialist or team decides the creative tactics. One critical creative tactic is the **creative execution style**, which is the way a message appeal is presented. While it is obviously important for an ad to have a meaningful message appeal to communicate to the consumer, the manner in which the ad is executed is also important. We now identify 11 commonly seen execution styles and provide examples of each. Many of these can be combined to present the message appeal.

STRAIGHT SELL

One of the most basic types of creative executions is the straight sell. This type of ad relies on a straightforward presentation of information concerning the product or service. This execution is often used with rational appeals, where the focus of the message is the product and its specific attributes and/or benefits. Straight-sell executions are commonly used in print ads. A picture of the product or service occupies part of the ad, and the factual copy takes up the rest of the space. They are also used in TV advertising, with an announcer generally delivering the sales message while the product/service is shown on the screen. Ads for high-involvement consumer products as well as industrial and other business-to-business products generally use this format. The ad for the Hitachi line form series plasma TV shown in Exhibit 8-1 is part of a campaign that uses a straight-sell execution style.

SCIENTIFIC/TECHNICAL EVIDENCE

In a variation of the straight sell, scientific or technical evidence is presented in the ad. Advertisers often cite technical information, results of scientific or laboratory studies, or endorsements by scientific bodies or agencies to support their advertising claims. The ad for Eagle One's NanoWax shown in Exhibit 8-2 positions the brand as the most technologically advanced car wax available and uses scientific evidence to support this claim.

Exhibit 8-1 Hitachi uses a straight-sell execution style in this ad.

DEMONSTRATION

Demonstration is designed to illustrate the key advantages of the product by showing it in actual use or in some staged situation. Demonstration executions can be very effective in convincing consumers of a product's utility or quality and of the benefits of owning or using the brand. TV is particularly well suited for demonstration executions, since the benefits or advantages of the product can be shown right on the screen. Although perhaps a little less dramatic than TV, demonstration ads can also work in print. The Mentadent toothpaste ad shown in Exhibit 8-3 uses this style to demonstrate how the brand's "liquid calcium" technology replenishes the surface enamel to whiten teeth.

COMPARISON

A comparison execution style, direct, indirect, and visual, is popular among advertisers. Direct brand comparisons are the basis for advertising executions to communicate a competitive advantage or to position a new or lesser-known brand with industry leaders. For example, computer manufacturers use direct comparisons to demonstrate superior performance claims. Although previous research found little support for the effectiveness of comparative ads, one study found positive result for the situation where a challenger brand compares itself to a category leader.[1] One unusual indirect comparison execution style occurred with ads for the Subaru Outback that compared life outdoors with the car against life indoors with a Snuggie blanket. The ad begins as a Snuggie ad that becomes a Subaru ad after a virile man uses a crowbar to symbolically pry the television screen so that the viewer can see the car in the wilderness. Although a tactical consideration, this element clearly reinforces the brand positioning in terms of the target, motive, and key benefits the car offers.[2] Finally, a visual comparison, instead of a brand comparison, can be used to convey particular product characteristics as seen in the colourful ad for Q HorsePower motor oil found in Exhibit 8-4.

Exhibit 8-2 This ad uses scientific evidence to promote Eagle One NanoWax.

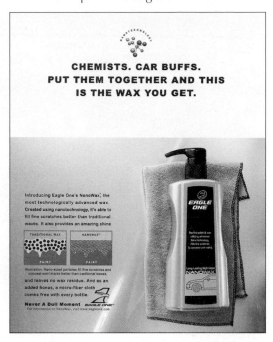

TESTIMONIAL

Many advertisers prefer to have their messages presented by way of a testimonial, where a person praises the product or service on the basis of his or her personal experience with it. Testimonial executions can have ordinary satisfied customers discuss their own experiences with the brand and the benefits of using it. This approach can be very effective when the person delivering the testimonial is someone with whom the target audience can identify or who has an interesting story to tell. The testimonial must be based on actual use of the product or service to avoid legal problems, and the spokesperson must be credible. Testimonials can be particularly effective when they come from a recognizable or popular person.

Toyota dealers in western Canada used actual customers to communicate their product's quality and dependability. Among the four spots initially produced, in one a country veterinarian drove his 13-year-old Toyota 4Runner with 742,000 km; in another, a travelling salesman complained that the odometer of his Corolla only had six digits. All ads were based on actual customer experiences, and although the campaign was a risky departure the initial results appeared promising for a regional launch prior to the spring buying season.[3]

Exhibit 8-3 This ad uses demonstration execution to explain the benefits of Mentadent.

Exhibit 8-4 A visual comparison in this ad shows how fast the Ferrari travels with this brand of motor oil.

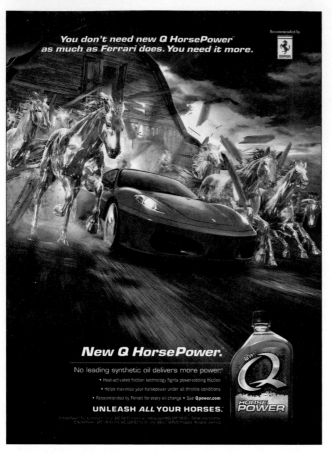

SLICE OF LIFE

A widely used advertising format, particularly for packaged-goods products, is the slice-of-life execution. Slice-of-life executions are often criticized for being unrealistic and irritating to watch because they are often used to remind consumers of problems of a personal nature, such as dandruff, bad breath, body odour, and laundry or cleaning problems. Often these ads come across as contrived, silly, phony, or even offensive to consumers. However, many advertisers still prefer this style because they believe it is effective at presenting a situation to which most consumers can relate and at registering the product feature or benefit.

Execution is critical in using the technique effectively, as these ads are designed to be dramatizations of a supposedly real-life situation that consumers might encounter. Getting viewers to identify with the situation and/or characters depicted in the ad can be very challenging. Since the success of slice-of-life ads often depends on how well the actors execute their roles, professional actors are often used to achieve credibility and to ensure that the commercial is of high quality. Smaller companies and local advertisers often do not have ad budgets large enough to hire the talent or to pay for the production quality needed to effectively create slice-of-life spots. Thus, this execution technique is more likely to be used by companies with ad budgets that are large enough to fund the use of professional talent and production of quality commercials.

Often marketers use the slice-of-life approach since it effectively addresses a problem or issue and offers a solution. For example, Listerine used a slice-of-life commercial effectively to introduce a new Natural Citrus flavour of its popular mouthwash.[4] The spot was designed to address the problem that some consumers have with the intense taste of the original flavour of the product. The spot opens with a mother returning home from the store with two surprises: Danish and Listerine. However, when her husband and two kids see the mouthwash they run and hide. The mother then tells them it is Natural Citrus Listerine, which tastes less intense. The humorous spot ends with the father coming out of a kitchen cupboard and pots and pans dangling as one of the boys climbs down from the top of the kitchen island and the voiceover says, "You can handle it. Germs can't" (see Exhibit 8-5).

ANIMATION

With animation, scenes are drawn by artists or created on the computer, and cartoons, puppets, or other types of fictional characters may be used. Cartoon animation is especially popular for commercials targeted at children for products like toys

Exhibit 8-5 Listerine uses a slice-of-life execution to introduce a new flavour.

and cereal. Bits & Bites, a snack food directed to adults, used animation in its long-standing television commercial. The ad featured a neighbourly man talking about the product while standing behind a fence. First conceived in the 1970s, the light-hearted commercial ran for decades due to favourable market research results. Faced with increased competition from a variety of snack foods, Kraft refreshed the graphics by brightening the colour and adding more detail to the drawings, and developed new versions of the ad by having three different "blooper out-takes" (i.e., line flubs, staging collapses, and character mishaps).[5] RBC moved to numerous animated ads on TV and other media with its news spokesperson Arbie. The friendly financial adviser finds himself in all sorts of situations showing how helpful RBC can be for consumers who want to create various things in their lives.

PERSONALITY SYMBOL

Another type of advertising execution involves developing a central character or personality symbol that can deliver the advertising message and with which the product or service can be identified (see Exhibit 8-6). This character can be a person, like the Maytag repairman, who sits anxiously by the phone but is never needed because the company's appliances are so reliable. A recent study finds positive brand attitude effects through the use of spokes-characters.[6] Sometimes the personality symbols get a change; executives rebranded the iconic Ronald McDonald as "an ambassador for a balanced active lifestyle." Three versions of a TV spot called "Active Ronald, You and I" played on Teletoon and YTV in Canada, depicting Ronald changing from his clown suit into a track suit and kicking soccer balls, riding snowboards, and running and jumping his way around town. The two-minute, 30-second, and 15-second ads encouraged kids to get up off the couch and get moving.

Canadian brands have been at the forefront in developing and nurturing a personality. Kool-Aid's "Face" icon and the three-dimensional Kool-Aid pitcher provide an instantly recognizable character. In fact the personality, established in Canada, has been used in campaigns in the U.S. and Mexico. The American headquarters for Clorox invented the Man from Glad personality about 40 years ago; he has not been seen in ads south of the border for 20 years while continuously appearing in Canadian spots. Captain High Liner has been extolling the virtues of his brand of frozen fish products for over 25 years in Canada. A&W has used two types of personalities over the years, a person dressed as a bear and many family members to represent the different names of their burger products. Over time, however, some personalities are changed or possibly retired. The St-Hubert chicken has been updated many times over the last 50 years, but executives are uncertain of its future since research indicates that it does not quite fit the new restaurant format and décor.[7]

Photography by Ondrea Barbe.

Exhibit 8-6 The Aussie Roo became part of the brand's identity after the initial launch campaign.

IMAGERY

Some ads contain little or no information about the brand or company and are almost totally visual.

Acceptable Advertising Styles

What we can and cannot say or show in an advertising execution is governed by laws and social acceptability. Federal laws governed by various government departments enforce some regulations, while the self-regulating body Advertising Standards Canada (ASC) administers other aspects. And while these control mechanisms are in place, critics of advertising continue to find problems—such as continued sexual innuendo, and in some cases pornographic references or descriptions, in recent ads for fast-food restaurants.

Social acceptability is certainly a moving target; for instance, finding an ad for condoms was unlikely 20 years ago. Yet with growing awareness for sexual health and heightened public discourse regarding sexual pleasure, these ads are as common as many other products. And with that occurring as a backdrop, Trojan condoms of Canada executed an award-winning animated website that placed users at a street corner to decide whether to visit the safe or the sensual side. With either route selected, the visitor entered locations for educational or titillating explanations and demonstrations for the product's attributes and benefits. While we see a variety of executions on the Internet due to its more private message reception for the user, other more public media like TV and print continue to face strong guidelines or stringent expectations on acceptability, as seen in recent trends and examples.

In response to numerous complaints regarding unsafe driving in automobile ads, ASC issued an advisory to fully explain the safety code within the specifics of ads for this product category. The result is a clearer direction as to the acceptable scenes and behaviours that can be shown in a car ad. Volkswagen welcomed the new approach after receiving notification from the self-regulating body that recommended VW stop showing an ad where a driver avoided obstacles on the road to demonstrate the handling

of the vehicle when unexpected road conditions occurred. "We felt it was a really good spot to raise awareness and depict active safety features, yet the consumer found it depicted unsafe driving," commented one VW director.

Messages for prescription drugs sold in Canada face the difficult challenge of communicating to consumers the benefits of a branded drug without directly or explicitly identifying what it is. These regulations differ from those in the U.S., so Canadian consumers experience both types of prescription drug messages. Despite this brand/message constraint, agencies like Taxi, for example, have managed to successfully develop creative messages for products like Viagra that have won Cannes awards and been picked up for airing in other countries.

Even though we can find an isolated example of success like Viagra, numerous other drugs are not supported by direct-to-consumer advertising. In response, media companies challenged the drug advertising regulations as a way of increasing the number of advertisers and advertising revenue. For example, U.S. advertising totalled $38 billion, while Canada's chipped in only $200 million over the same 10-year time period ending in 2006. In response, one health research expert noted that authorities from most industrial nations agree that direct-to-consumer advertising is not appropriate.

Sources: Simon Houpt, "No Car Chases, Please. We're Canadian," *The Globe and Mail*, October 28, 2009; Susan Krashinsky, "Drug Marketers Try to Cut Through the Wombleminki," *The Globe and Mail*, July 10, 2009, p. B4; Misty Harris, "Burger Porn; Sex Sells— And the Recession Made Them Do It," *National Post*, September 11, 2009, FP10.

Question:

1. Do you agree that advertising messages should be regulated or controlled?

These advertisements use imagery executions whereby the ad consists primarily of visual elements such as pictures, illustrations, and/or symbols rather than information. An imagery execution is used when the goal is to encourage consumers to associate the brand with the symbols, characters, and/or situation shown in the ad. Imagery ads are often the basis for emotional appeals that are used to advertise products or services where differentiation based on physical characteristics is difficult.

An imagery execution may be based on *usage imagery* by showing how a brand is used or performs and the situations in which it is used. For example, advertising for trucks and SUVs often shows the vehicles navigating tough terrain or in challenging situations such as towing a heavy load. Notice how the clever Jeep ad shown in Exhibit 8-7 uses only the image of the vehicle on the bottom of a snowboard to associate the vehicle with the outdoors and adventuresome activities. This type of execution can also be based on *user imagery*, where the focus is on the type of person who uses the brand. Ads for cosmetics often use very attractive models in the hope of getting consumers to associate the model's physical attractiveness with the brand (see Exhibit 8-8). Most Nike ads have very little copy and rely primarily on images of athletes achieving success by using the company's products. Image executions rely heavily on visual elements such as photography, colour, tonality, and design to communicate the desired image to the consumer. Marketers who rely on image executions have to be sure that the usage or user imagery with which they associate their brand evokes the right feelings and reactions from the target audience.

DRAMATIZATION

Another execution technique particularly well suited to television is dramatization, where the focus is on telling a short story with the product as the star. Dramatization is akin to slice-of-life execution, but it uses more excitement and suspense in telling the story. The purpose of using drama is to draw the viewer into the action it portrays. Advocates of drama note that when it is successful, the audience becomes lost in the story and experiences the concerns and feelings of the characters.[8]

Exhibit 8-7 This ad associates the Jeep Wrangler with images of the outdoors and adventure.

Exhibit 8-8 This Bebe ad uses an attractive model to create a favourable image for the brand.

Exhibit 8-9 This Golf Pride ad uses a humour execution style to communicate an important product benefit.

No More Snowmen

The eraser will not make an 8 go away. But you can avoid blow-up holes altogether by regripping with Golf Pride, the grip 8 out of 10 tour pros insist on. Regripping will give you the confidence and control to play your best. See how new grips can save you strokes at golfpride.com.

Golf Pride

Although we typically see dramatization used in television or radio ads, because they have audio capabilities, it is possible to use this execution style in print. Good Year Tires conveyed the drama of driving in bad winter snow conditions with an effective newspaper ad that showed a car skidding through the weather page! Designed to evoke the worst type of January weather, the fall campaign reminded consumers the importance of purchasing new snow tires before it was too late.[9]

HUMOUR

Like comparisons, humour was discussed in Chapter 7 as a type of message appeal, but this technique can also be used as a way of presenting other message appeals. Humorous executions are particularly well suited to television or radio, although some print ads attempt to use this style.

The Golf Pride ad in Exhibit 8-9 uses a humour execution style for a mostly rational message appeal. The snowman represents a score of 8 on a hole that golfers want to avoid. The visual attracts the audience's attention, and the copy explains how Golf Pride can improve performance with new grips.

224

MESSAGE STRUCTURE

Marketing communication usually consists of a number of message points that the communicator wants to convey as advertising messages have an important information provision characteristic. Extensive research has been conducted on how the structure of an advertising message can influence its persuasive effectiveness, including order of presentation, conclusion drawing, message sidedness, and verbal versus visual message characteristics. These first three message structure points mostly focus on the written words of a print ad or the announcer in a TV or radio commercial, while the last addresses the importance of visuals to deliver the message.

ORDER OF PRESENTATION

A basic consideration in the design of a persuasive message is the arguments' order of presentation. Should the most important message points be placed at the beginning of the message, in the middle, or at the end? Research on learning and memory generally indicates that items presented first and last are remembered better than those presented in the middle (see Figure 8-1).[10] This suggests that a communicator's strongest arguments should be presented early or late in the message but never in the middle.

Presenting the strongest arguments at the beginning of the message assumes a **primacy effect** is operating, whereby information presented first is most effective. Putting the strong points at the end assumes a **recency effect**, whereby the last arguments presented are most persuasive.

Whether to place the strongest selling points at the beginning or the end of the message depends on several factors. If the target audience is opposed to the communicator's

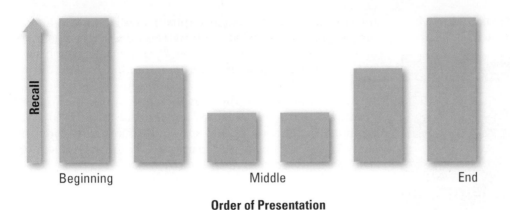

FIGURE 8–1

Ad message recall as
a function of order of
presentation

position, presenting strong points first can reduce the level of counterarguing. Putting weak arguments first might lead to such a high level of counterarguing that strong arguments that followed would not be believed. Strong arguments work best at the beginning of the message if the audience is not interested in the topic, so they can arouse interest in the message. When the target audience is predisposed toward the communicator's position or is highly interested in the issue or product, strong arguments can be saved for the end of the message. This may result in a more favourable opinion as well as better retention of the information.

The order of presentation can be critical when a long, detailed message with many arguments is being presented. For short communications, such as a 15- or 30-second TV or radio commercial, the order may be less critical. However, many product and service messages are received by consumers with low involvement and minimal interest. Thus, an advertiser may want to present the brand name and key selling points early in the message and repeat them at the end to enhance recall and retention. One study strongly concludes that the brand name should be identified at the start of a TV ad to enhance its persuasive ability.[11]

CONCLUSION DRAWING

Marketing communicators must decide whether their messages should explicitly draw a firm conclusion or allow receivers to draw their own conclusions. Research suggests that, in general, messages with explicit conclusions are more easily understood and effective in influencing attitudes. However, other studies have shown that the effectiveness of conclusion drawing may depend on the target audience, the type of issue or topic, and the nature of the situation.[12]

More highly educated people prefer to draw their own conclusions and may be annoyed at an attempt to explain the obvious or to draw an inference for them. But stating the conclusion may be necessary for a less educated audience, who may not draw any conclusion or may make an incorrect inference from the message. Marketers must also consider the audience's level of involvement in the topic. For highly personal or ego-involving issues, message recipients may want to make up their own minds and resent any attempts by the communicator to draw a conclusion. One study found that open-ended ads (without explicit conclusions) were more effective than closed-ended arguments that did include a specific conclusion—but only for involved audiences.[13]

Whether to draw a conclusion for the audience also depends on the complexity of the topic. Even a highly educated audience may need assistance if its knowledge level in a particular area is low. Does the marketer want the message to trigger immediate action or a more long-term effect? If immediate action is an objective, the message should draw a definite conclusion. When immediate impact is not

Exhibit 8-10 This Silk ad makes effective use of an open-ended approach.

How did you know you liked water before you tried it?

All natural, lactose free, high in protein, with a surprisingly good taste. *Don't be so stubborn.*

226

the objective and repeated exposure will give the audience members opportunities to draw their own conclusions, an open-ended message may be used. Drawing a conclusion in a message may make sure the target audience gets the point the marketer intended. But many advertisers believe that letting customers draw their own conclusions reinforces the points being made in the message. The ad for Silk Soymilk in Exhibit 8-10 is a very good example of an open-ended message. The question in the headline encourages consumers to be open to the idea of drinking soymilk.

MESSAGE SIDEDNESS

Another message structure decision facing the marketer involves message sidedness. A **one-sided message** mentions only positive attributes or benefits. A **two-sided message** presents both good and bad points. One-sided messages are most effective when the target audience already holds a favourable opinion about the topic. They also work better with a less educated audience.[14]

Two-sided messages are more effective when the target audience holds an opposing opinion or is highly educated. Two-sided messages may enhance the credibility of the source.[15] A better-educated audience usually knows there are opposing arguments, so a communicator who presents both sides of an issue is likely to be seen as less biased and more objective.

Most advertisers use one-sided messages. They are concerned about the negative effects of acknowledging a weakness in their brand or don't want to say anything positive about their competitors. There are exceptions, however. Sometimes advertisers compare brands on several attributes and do not show their product as being the best on every one.

In some situations, marketers may focus on a negative attribute as a way of enhancing overall perceptions of the product. For example, W.K. Buckley Limited has become one of the leading brands of cough syrup by using a blunt two-sided slogan: "Buckley's Mixture. It tastes awful. And it works."[16] Ads for the brand poke fun at the cough syrup's terrible taste but also suggest that the taste is a reason why the product is effective (Exhibit 8-11). They have used this slogan for many years and have built the brand from 2 percent to now 16 percent market share. It helps that this slogan is a bit of truth in advertising that consumers certainly appreciate.[17]

A special type of two-sided message is known as a **refutation**. The communicator presents both sides of an issue and then refutes the opposing viewpoint. Since this tends to "inoculate" the target audience against a competitor's counterclaims, they are more effective than one-sided messages in making consumers resistant to an opposing message.[18] Refutational messages may be useful when marketers wish to build attitudes that resist change and must defend against attacks or criticism of their products or the company. Market leaders, who are often the target of comparative messages, may find that acknowledging competitors' claims and then refuting them can help build resistant attitudes and customer loyalty.

VERBAL VERSUS VISUAL MESSAGES

Thus far our discussion has focused on the information, or verbal, portion of the message. However, the nonverbal, visual elements of an ad are also very important.

Many ads provide minimal amounts of information and rely on visual elements to communicate. Pictures are commonly used in advertising to convey information or reinforce copy or message claims.

Both the verbal and visual portions of an ad influence the way the advertising message is processed.[19] Consumers may develop images or impressions based on visual elements such as an illustration in an ad or the scenes in a TV commercial. In some cases, the visual portion of an ad may reduce its persuasiveness, since the processing stimulated by the picture may be less controlled and consequently less favourable than that stimulated by words.[20]

Pictures affect the way consumers process accompanying copy. A recent study showed that when verbal information was low in imagery value, the use of pictures providing examples increased both immediate and delayed recall of product attributes.[21] However, when the verbal information was already high in imagery value, the addition of pictures did not increase recall. Advertisers often design ads where the visual image supports the verbal appeal to create a compelling impression in the consumer's mind.

Sometimes advertisers use a different approach; they design ads in which the visual portion is incongruent with or contradicts the verbal information presented. The logic behind this strategy is that the use of an unexpected picture or visual image will grab consumers' attention and get them to engage in more effortful or elaborative processing.[22] A number of studies have shown that the use of a visual that is inconsistent with the verbal content leads to more recall and greater processing of the information presented.[23]

The "Deflate the Elephant" ads by the Liquor Control Board of Ontario designed to prevent drinking and driving used the visual of an elephant appearing in social gatherings to symbolize the awkwardness people experience when they feel compelled to speak to someone who has consumed too much alcohol. While most people in the over-35 target know they should not drink and drive, once in a while they slip up and drink more than planned. Their sober friends know they should speak up but suffer in a social grey zone of not knowing what to say. Hence, the elephant becomes a handy reference to give people courage and address the situation with some light-hearted humour.[24]

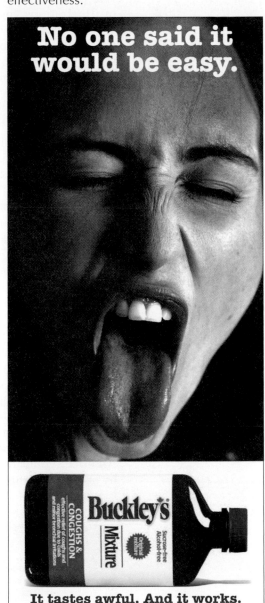

Exhibit 8-11 Buckley's cough syrup uses a two-sided message to promote the product's effectiveness.

227

DESIGN ELEMENTS FOR IMC TOOLS

The design and production of advertising messages involves a number of activities, among them writing copy, developing illustrations and other visual elements of the ad, and bringing all of the pieces together to create an effective message. In this section, we examine the verbal and visual elements of an ad and discuss tactical considerations in creating print, video, and audio messages. We use general terminology of print, video, and audio as these basic design elements can be applied to any print, video, or audio media distributed through advertising or other IMC tools.

DESIGN FOR PRINT MESSAGES

The basic elements of a print message are the headline, the body copy, the visual or illustrations, and the layout. The headline and body copy are the responsibility of the copywriters; artists, often working under the direction of an art director, are responsible for the visual presentation. Art directors also work with the copywriters to develop a layout, or arrangement of the above elements. We briefly examine the three design elements and explain how they are coordinated. These elements pertain to virtually all print messages that can be found in any media.

Headlines   The **headline** is the words in the leading position of the ad—the words that will be read first or are positioned to draw the most attention.[25] Headlines are usually set in larger, darker type and are often set apart from the body copy or text portion of the ad to give them prominence. Most advertising people consider the headline the most important part of a print ad.

The most important function of a headline is attracting readers' attention and interesting them in the rest of the message. While the visual portion of an ad is obviously important, the headline often shoulders most of the responsibility of attracting readers' attention. Research has shown the headline is generally the first thing people look at in a print ad, followed by the illustration. Only 20 percent of readers go beyond the headline and read the body copy.[26] So in addition to attracting attention, the headline must give the reader good reason to read the copy portion of the ad, which contains more detailed and persuasive information about the product or service. To do this, the headline must put forth the main theme, appeal, or proposition of the ad in a few words. Some print ads contain little if any body copy, so the headline must work with the illustration to communicate the entire advertising message.

Headlines also perform a segmentation function by engaging the attention and interest of consumers who are most likely to buy a particular product or service (see Exhibit 8-12). Advertisers begin the segmentation process by choosing to advertise in certain media vehicles (e.g., fashion magazine, national newspaper, out-of-home). An effective headline goes even further in selecting good prospects for the product by addressing their specific needs, wants, or interests.

228

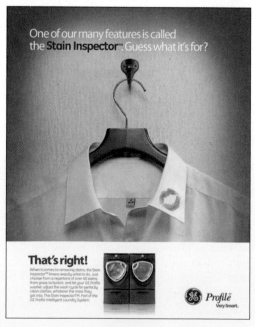

Exhibit 8-12   GE innovates with headlines by asking a question after stating a product fact.

Types of Headlines There are numerous headline possibilities. The type used depends on several factors, including the creative strategy, the particular advertising situation (e.g., product type, media vehicle(s) being used, timeliness), and its relationship to other elements of the ad, such as the illustration or body copy. Headlines can be categorized as direct and indirect. **Direct headlines** are straightforward and informative in terms of the message they are presenting and the target audience they are directed toward. Common types of direct headlines include those offering a specific benefit, making a promise, or announcing a reason why the reader should be interested in the product or service.

Indirect headlines are not straightforward about identifying the product or service or getting to the point. But they are often more effective at attracting readers' attention and interest because they provoke curiosity and lure readers into the body copy to learn an answer or get an explanation. Techniques for writing indirect headlines include using questions, provocations, how-to statements, and challenges.

Indirect headlines rely on their ability to generate curiosity or intrigue so as to motivate readers to become involved with the ad and read the body copy to find out the point of the message. This can be risky if the headline is not provocative enough to get the readers' interest. Advertisers deal with this problem by using a visual appeal that helps attract attention and offers another reason for reading more of the message. For example, the ad for the Volkswagen Jetta shown in Exhibit 8-13 uses an indirect headline that might create curiosity among readers and encourage them to read further. The copy below explains how the headline refers to awards the Jetta has won and its new features like an extra large trunk. The visual element supports the theme by highlighting the improved design.

Exhibit 8-13 This ad uses an indirect headline and strong visual image that motivate consumers to read the copy.

While many ads have only one headline, it is also common to see print ads containing the main head and one or more secondary heads, or **subheads**. Subheads are usually smaller than the main headline but larger than the body copy. They may appear above or below the main headline or within the body copy. Subheads are often used to enhance the readability of the message by breaking up large amounts of body copy and highlighting key sales points. Their content reinforces the headline and advertising slogan or theme.

Body Copy The main text portion of a print ad is referred to as the **body copy** (or sometimes just *copy*). While the body copy is usually the heart of the advertising message, getting the target audience to read it is often difficult. The copywriter faces a dilemma: The body copy must be long enough to communicate the advertiser's message yet short enough to hold readers' interest.

Body copy content often flows from the points made in the headline or various subheads, but the specific content depends on the type of advertising appeal and/ or execution style being used. For example, straight-sell copy that presents relevant information, product features and benefits, or competitive advantages is often used with the various types of rational appeals discussed earlier in the chapter. Emotional appeals often use narrative copy that tells a story or provides an interesting account of a problem or situation involving the product. Advertising body copy can be written to go along with any message appeal or execution style. Furthermore, copywriters select body copy that is appropriate for the creative strategy (i.e., theme, message appeal, source) and supports the creative tactics like the message structure and other design elements.

An interesting example of the use of long copy occurred with Rogers (AT&T) Wireless. Borrowing from the idea that a picture is worth a thousand words, the poster ads extolled upon the attributes and benefits of picture messaging with a small photo of the product and exactly one thousand words! To garner attention and full processing of the copy, the ads involved the reader in personally relevant conversations that the target audience would be familiar with, such as a woman talking to her man-friend about which shoes to wear to her high-school reunion, and a man talking to his buddy about his golfing triumphs. The entertaining dialogue provided a quick and enjoyable read, giving the feeling that one was actually experiencing the conversation.[27]

Visual The third major element of a print ad is the visual. The illustration is often a dominant part of a print ad and plays an important role in determining its effectiveness. The visual portion of an ad must attract attention, communicate an idea or image, and work in a synergistic fashion with the headline and body copy to produce an effective message. In some print ads, the visual portion of the ad is essentially the message and thus must convey a strong and meaningful image. The ad for Olay Ribbons body wash shown in Exhibit 8-14 contains important visual elements. The stunning colours of the water presumably attract the attention of women interested in such a product. In addition, the water conveys the clean and rejuvenating experience of using a body wash product. The prominent placement of the product package and ribbon signify the brand's unique characteristic and effect of the mica minerals that give a shimmering feel, which are reinforced with the shimmering light off the water.

Many decisions have to be made regarding the visual portion of the ad: what identification marks should be included (brand name, company or trade name, trademarks, logos); whether to use photos or hand-drawn or painted illustrations; what colours to use (or even perhaps black and white or just a splash of colour); and what the focus of the visual should be. Even the number of pages of visual ads is critical, as in the case of fashion products or automobiles. One study finds that advertisers should use fewer pages (e.g., 4 to 6) versus longer pages (e.g., 8 to 10) and insert the ads more frequently.[28]

Layout While each individual element of a print ad is important, the key factor is how these elements are blended into a finished advertisement. A **layout** is the physical arrangement of the various parts of the ad, including the headline, subheads, body copy, illustrations, and any identifying marks. The layout shows where each part of the ad will be placed and gives guidelines to the people working on the ad. For example, the layout helps the copywriter determine how much space he or she has to work with and how much copy should be written. The layout can also guide the art director in determining the

Exhibit 8-14 The visual background of this Olay ad allows the brand to stand out and reinforce its characteristics.

size and type of photos. Many layouts are standard poster format shown in a portrait orientation, although landscape formats occur in some circumstances. Sometimes there are vertical or horizontal splits, with the latter being a separation between the visual and body copy as shown in Exhibits 8-12 and 8-13. For enhanced creativity, ads with multiple visuals are uniquely placed throughout the ad along with the body copy as shown in Exhibit 8-3. An optimal layout is an artistic expression of the brand as it achieves balance among the space, visuals, and colours.

DESIGN FOR VIDEO MESSAGES

Video messages contain the elements of sight, sound, and motion, which can be combined to create a variety of advertising appeals and executions. Video messages occur in more instances beyond television, as they are seen at theatres, online, and in stores or other place-based locations. In most of these instances, the viewer does not control the rate at which the message is presented, so there is no opportunity to review points of interest or reread things that are not communicated clearly. As with any form of advertising, one of the first goals in creating video messages is to get viewers' attention and then maintain it. This can be particularly challenging because of the clutter and because people often view these messages while doing other things. Creating and producing commercials that break through the clutter and communicate effectively is a detailed and expensive process. On a cost-per-minute basis, commercials are the most expensive productions seen on television. Getting the video and audio elements to work together to create the right impact and communicate the advertiser's message requires careful planning.

Video The video elements of a commercial are what the consumer sees on the screen. The visual portion generally dominates the presentation, so it must attract viewers' attention and communicate an idea, message, and/or image. A number of visual elements may have to be coordinated to produce a successful ad. Decisions have to be made regarding the product, the presenter, action sequences, demonstrations, and the like, as well as the setting(s), the talent or characters who will appear in the commercial, and such other factors as lighting, graphics, colour, and identifying symbols. Many video messages cost a small fortune in production costs to get the product and actors looking just right, and sometimes unusual or unique video is used as seen in the following examples.

Attempting to attract new users of a younger demographic, Becel margarine used a new filming technique called Dogme that featured a 35-mm camera, no lighting, no sets, all shot on location, natural sounds, and natural actors (no wardrobe or make-up). Becel was placed in places to remind customers of the alternative, which was both a healthier way to live and a key reinforcement of Becel's positioning (e.g., Becel placed between elevator doors so consumers had to use the stairs).[29] Carrying on with this idea and with the growth of consumer generated ads, some brands moved toward using reality-type filming of actual customers in purchase and consumption situations. Production costs are notably less and the reality style is fashionably accepted by viewers.[30] Kokanee's new campaign after retiring its park ranger featured a point-of-view style that followed a man's everyday activities like personal care, sports, and meeting women at a party while drinking the beer.[31]

Audio The audio element of a video message includes voices, music, and sound effects. Voices are used in different ways. They may be heard through the direct presentation of a spokesperson or as a conversation among various people appearing in the script. A common method for presenting the audio is through a **voiceover**, where the message is delivered or action on the screen is narrated or described by an announcer who is not visible.

231

Music is also an important element and can play a variety of roles.[32] Music provides a pleasant background or helps create the appropriate mood. Advertisers often use **needledrop**, which Linda Scott describes as follows:

> Needledrop is an occupational term common to advertising agencies and the music industry. It refers to music that is prefabricated, multipurpose, and highly conventional. It is, in that sense, the musical equivalent of stock photos, clip art, or canned copy. Needledrop is an inexpensive substitute for original music; paid for on a one-time basis, it is dropped into a commercial or film when a particular normative effect is desired.[33]

Music can be a central element as it is used to get attention, break through the advertising clutter, communicate a key selling point, help establish an image or position, or add feeling.[34] For example, music can work through a classical conditioning process to create positive emotions that become associated with the advertised product or service. Music can also create a positive mood that makes the consumer more receptive toward the advertising message.[35]

Sometimes, marketers creatively use music that previously existed. PEI tourism organizations asked Stompin' Tom Connors to re-record his song "Dial an Island" in a television ad that encouraged Canadians to call the toll-free phone number for information. With visuals of old home movies, the lyrics to the song along with a bouncing ball made music an integral part of the message to suggest PEI as a holiday option.[36] Delissio used the old tune "Hit the Road, Jack" to wrap up the ad for its new garlic bread pizza. After a teenager greets her date at the door, who is either Dracula or a goth, he turns into a bat and flies away once he hears about and smells the new ingredient.[37]

Often music is composed specifically for a campaign. Musicians and composers participate early on in the process of developing the ad; alternatively, the creative specialists who produce the ad look for very specific types of music to support the visuals. For example, the original musical score for the Canadian launch of the Mini was written after filming the ad. The visuals and the musical request led to a very unique sound that contributed to the brand positioning strategy in such a way that people thought it was previously recorded. In fact some in the industry believe that custom-written music is the best since it almost always works.[38]

Another memorable musical element is a **jingle**, a catchy song about a product or service that delivers the advertising theme and a simple message. For example, "Black's is photography" and "You always have time for Tim Hortons" are two retail jingles that have stood the test of time. Tim Hortons moved to a new jingle "Always Fresh. Always Tim Hortons" while Swiss Chalet reverted to a previous one, "Always so good for so little," after trying four different ones in the past 10 years.[39] Sometimes, jingles simply identify a brand and appear at the end of the message. Jingles are often composed by companies that specialize in writing music for advertising. These jingle houses work with the creative team to determine the role music will play in the commercial and the message that needs to be communicated.

Production of Video Messages Advertisers recognize that they need to do more than talk about, demonstrate, or compare their products or services. Their messages have to break through the clutter and grab viewers' attention; they must often appeal to emotional, as well as rational, buying motives. Video messages are often an entertainment medium, and many advertisers recognize that these ads are most successful when they entertain as well as inform. Many of the most popular advertising campaigns are characterized by ads with strong entertainment value.

The elements are brought together in a **script**, a written version of a message that provides a detailed description of its video and audio content. The script shows the

For the 2009 Super Bowl, Labatt experimented with two interactive Budweiser TV ads for the Quebec market. Labatt handles the marketing for Anheuser-Busch InBev beer products in Canada. Like most marketers, Labatt tested new technologies to find innovative ways to advertise that go beyond mass media. As one manager put it, "We're definitely trying to change our mindset to use mass TV in a more efficient and effective way. Digital extensions pick up where mass media leave off." Viewers who watched the game on RDS could use their remote to access links embedded in the ad in order to watch or bookmark a three-minute mini documentary about the ad.

Creative Super Bowl ads often make a big splash, with pre-game hype in the U.S. for newly launched ads. In Canada, we see American ads if the brand purchases air time on Canadian stations, otherwise we are shut out and see the Canadian ads for that brand, ads for other brands that are part of existing advertising campaigns, or Super Bowl ads based on Canadian creative. Recent digital connections with Super Bowl ads include online display ads, sponsorship of Super Bowl–related websites, or commercials on video hosting sites. This latest Canadian opportunity extends the exposure time, and hopefully longer and deeper processing with the brand's message.

Executed by Etc.tv, Labatt paid for the interactive ads based on the number of unique visitors, and the click-through rates produced five times the average rate. "Given the size of the audience, given the product, we expected a lift because there are more there than just football fans, it's a cultural phenomenon," commented a VP from the agency. The link located at the bottom left corner while the Budweiser ad played attracted people to watch the extended version of the ad while the game occurred shortly thereafter. The majority of those watching viewed the extended video in HD.

Etc.tv of Montreal is a leading firm in developing interactive TV ads, and offers its service for two million households in Quebec with plans to develop the market throughout Canada. The Budweiser ad represented the first Super Bowl ad with a digital link to access the video-on-demand features of today's television technology. According to Etc.tv, "This is a way of reaching the right consumer at the right time with the right message, and it resonates with the digital consumer's desire to get the information they want, when they want it."

Sources: Emily Steel, "Labatt Brews Up Interactive Super Bowl Ads," *The Globe and Mail*, January 28, 2009, p. B11; Kirstin Laird, "On-Demand Bud Ads Score During Super Bowl," *Marketing Magazine*, February 4, 2009; "Interactive TV Sets Record in Super Bowl," broadcastermagazine, February 3, 2009; www.etc.tv.

Question:

1. When someone clicks on an interactive TV ad, is this experience like watching a TV ad, or like watching the brand's video message on a video-hosting website?

audio elements—the copy to be spoken by voices, the music, and sound effects. The video portion of the script provides the visual plan—camera actions and angles, scenes, transitions, and other important descriptions. The script also shows how the video corresponds to the audio portion of the commercial.

Once the basic script has been conceived, the writer and art director get together to produce a storyboard, a series of drawings used to present the visual plan or layout. The storyboard contains still drawings of the video scenes and descriptions of the audio that accompanies each scene. Like layouts for print ads, storyboards provide those involved in the production and approval with a good approximation of what the final commercial will look like. In some cases an animatic (actual video of the storyboard along with the soundtrack) may be produced if a more finished form is needed for client presentations or pretesting. Once the storyboard or animatic is approved, it is ready to move to the production phase, which involves three stages as shown in Figure 8-2. Before the final production process begins, the client must usually review and approve the creative strategy and tactics that will be used for the advertising message.

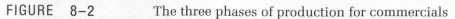

FIGURE   8–2   The three phases of production for commercials

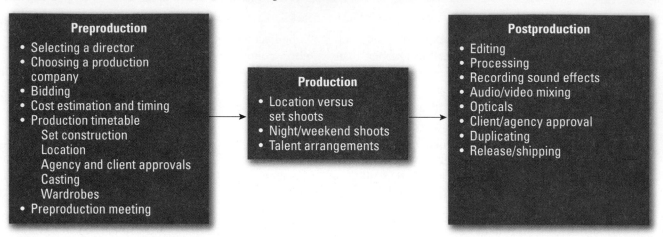

DESIGN FOR AUDIO MESSAGES

Audio messages are mostly delivered through radio, and that is the context for most of the design guidelines; however, recent digital opportunities make audio messages more prevalent. For example, audio messages can be included in podcasts, and certainly any ad on the Internet (e.g., banner, pop-up) could have an audio equivalent. Imagine listening to an ad while reading the online newspaper. The key elements of an audio message are similar to the audio of video messages, so we concentrate on the verbal and sound elements.

Verbal   Historically, radio has been referred to as the theatre of the mind; the voice(s) speaking to us in these audio messages offer a description or story, like the body copy of a print ad, that allows a visual to take hold. The talking can take many forms—straight announcer, dialogue between two actors, announcer/actor, customer interview—while following any of the executional styles identified earlier in the chapter. Depending on which format is used, a script is written that will attract attention in the opening, communicate the brand's attribute or benefits, and wrap up with a close that includes some kind of call to action, like a store visit, phone number, or website address. The dialogue of the script is critical, much like the voice-over in a video message, but the illuminating words support the theatre idea to maximize the amount of processing time of the message.

Sound   Audio messages naturally rely on sound due to the lack of a visual. Brands employ unique sound effects to allow the visual to take hold in the receiver's mind. Alternatively, the unique voices of the speakers help create a personality to allow the visual to take hold even more. As seen with video messages, music becomes a key component for audio messages on a number of fronts such as attracting attention or supporting the message and reinforcing the positioning. Moreover, as seen with video messages, jingles become even more critical as they fit with the format of listening to music. Audio logos are used significantly with audio messages, and are usually the same ones. Astral Media, owner of many different radio formats, uses 11 different versions of its audio logo to fit the genre of music played on the respective station. For example, a guitar riff plays the logo on a rock station followed by the common ending "You're listening to an Astral Media radio station."[40]

234

FRAMEWORKS FOR CREATIVE TACTICS

In this section, we present two planning models that guide the decision for selecting the most appropriate creative tactics. Each model builds on a perspective of the consumer response processes that we described in Chapter 4. We discuss the models from a historical perspective to explain how the more recent model is an improvement over the initial model.

THE FCB PLANNING MODEL

An interesting approach to analyzing the communication situation comes from the work of Richard Vaughn of the Foote, Cone & Belding advertising agency. Vaughn and his associates developed an advertising planning model by building on traditional response theories such as the hierarchy of effects model and its variants and research on high and low involvement.[41] They added the dimension of thinking versus feeling processing at each involvement level by bringing in theories regarding brain specialization. The right/left brain theory suggests the left side of the brain is more capable of rational, cognitive thinking, while the right side is more visual and emotional and engages more in the affective (feeling) functions. Their model, which became known as the FCB grid, delineates four primary advertising planning quadrants—informative, affective, habit formation, and satisfaction—along with the most appropriate variant of the alternative response hierarchies (Figure 8-3).

Vaughn suggests that the *informative strategy* is for highly involving products where rational thinking and economic considerations prevail and the standard

	Thinking	Feeling
High involvement	**1. Informative (thinker)** Car–house–furnishings. model: Learn–feel–do **Possible implications** Media: Long copy format Reflective vehicles Creative: Specific information Demonstration	**2. Affective (feeling)** Jewellery–cosmetics–fashion apparel. model: Feel–learn–do **Possible implications** Media: Large space Image specials Creative: Executional Impact
Low involvement	**3. Habit formation (doer)** Food–household items model: Do–learn–feel **Possible implications** Media: Small space ads 10-second I.D.s Radio; POS Creative: Reminder	**4. Self-satisfaction (reactor)** Liquor–candy model: Do–feel–learn **Possible implications** Media: Billboards Newspapers POS Creative: Attention

FIGURE 8–3

The Foote, Cone, and Belding (FCB) grid

learning hierarchy is the appropriate response model. The *affective strategy* is for highly involving/feeling purchases. For these types of products, advertising should stress psychological and emotional motives such as building self-esteem or enhancing one's ego or self-image. The *habit formation strategy* is for low-involvement/ thinking products with such routinized behaviour patterns that learning occurs most often after a trial purchase. The response process for these products is consistent with a behaviouristic learning-by-doing model known as operant conditioning. The *self-satisfaction strategy* is for low-involvement/feeling products where appeals to sensory pleasures and social motives are important. Vaughn acknowledges that some minimal level of awareness (passive learning) may precede purchase of both types of low-involvement products, but deeper, active learning is not necessary.

The FCB grid provides a useful way for those involved in the advertising planning process, such as creative specialists, to analyze consumer–product relationships and develop appropriate promotional strategies. Consumer research can be used to determine how consumers perceive products or brands on the involvement and thinking/feeling dimensions.[42] This information can then be used to develop effective creative options such as using rational versus emotional appeals, increasing involvement levels, or even getting consumers to evaluate a think-type product on the basis of feelings. Although the FCB model did not explicitly give detailed suggestions for all quadrants, Vaughn concluded that the four responses guide the content of how messages could be executed by suggesting possible implications.

THE R&P PLANNING MODEL

We highlighted the Rossiter and Percy (R&P) perspective in Chapter 5 when discussing objectives for the IMC plan. Another part of their framework concerns recommendations for creative tactics so that the appropriate communication effects will occur with the target audience while they are processing the message. On the surface, their planning model appears similar to the FCB planning model as both represent consumer attitudes and explain how marketers use creative tactics to influence attitudes. However, we will discuss four improvements as we explain the R&P model.

Brand Awareness Tactics   The first improvement is that the R&P model argues that brand awareness is a necessary precursor to brand attitude. According to R&P, both brand awareness and brand attitude are universal communication objectives for all circumstances (i.e., one ad, ad campaign, IMC plan). In this view, all marketing communication should strive to achieve awareness in order to make brand attitude operational. R&P have three suggestions for awareness:

- *Match* the brand stimuli and the type of response behaviour of the target audience so that understanding of the brand in a category is unambiguous.
- *Use* a unique brand execution style to connect the brand to the category.
- *Maximize* brand contact time in the exposure to reinforce name and category connection.

For awareness to be fully established, the target audience needs to understand the context (brand, behaviour, category) as this is a clue as to how or why the brand exists. If the context is not clear, then the target audience has trouble remembering when it comes time to purchase. A unique execution style helps cut through the clutter. The connection to the category and sufficient exposure is required to make sure that the message is retained. For example, TV ads can sometimes show the package or brand name for too short a time for target audiences to fully grasp where the brand competes in the market.

We also noted that R&P suggest that awareness can be achieved via recognition and/or recall. R&P have two suggestions for recognition that require less media frequency as consumers need only to be familiar with the brand stimuli at the point of purchase:

- The brand package and name should have sufficient exposure in terms of time or size depending on the media.
- Category need should be mentioned or identified.

Since recall is a more difficult mental task, R&P have six suggestions for this aspect of awareness. Recall also requires high levels of frequency since the brand has to be remembered prior to being at the point of purchase:

- The brand and the category need should be connected in the primary benefit claim.
- The primary benefit claim should be short to be easily understood.
- Within an exposure, the primary benefit claim should be repeated often.
- The message should have or imply a clear personal reference.
- A bizarre or unusual execution style can be used if it is consistent with the brand attitude objective.
- A jingle or similar "memory" tactics should be included.

We have many more specific recommendations for recall since it is a much more difficult mental task for consumers. Advertisers have to help their target audience know their brand prior to purchasing. The ad in Exhibit 8-15 follows many guidelines for improving recall. Thus, careful attention has to be put on all three creative tactics decisions to ensure the target audience can retrieve the brand name from long-term memory when the need to purchase a product category arises.

Exhibit 8-15 Kelowna's ad uses key brand recall guidelines to encourage extended visits.

Brand Attitude Grid Tactics   The R&P view of consumer attitudes is also framed as a matrix, with the dimensions of involvement and motivation. For each of these dimensions, R&P argue that their view is a more accurate representation of attitude for planning purposes than the FCB model, and the use of these two concepts represents the second and third improvements.

Low-involvement decision Informational motivation	Low-involvement decision Transformational motivation
High-involvement decision Informational motivation	High-involvement decision Transformational motivation

The involvement dimension is similar to the FCB model, from low involvement to high involvement. However, R&P argue that theirs is specific to the brand as the target audience makes a purchase decision. Further, the high- and low-involvement levels are also consistent with the central and peripheral routes to persuasion. More precisely, R&P interpret involvement as the degree of risk perceived by the target audience (i.e., new category user or loyal customer) in choosing a particular brand for the next purchase occasion. One extension of this idea, not fully developed by R&P, is that the concept can extend to purchase-related behaviour that we discussed in Chapter 5. For example, how much risk does a person buying a car for the first time take in deciding to visit a particular dealer for a test drive?

The motivation dimension is a continuum from negative motive, or informational-based attitude, to positive motive, or transformational-based attitude. The historical interpretation of an informational-based attitude implies that it is based on careful reasoning that results from the cognitive responses that the target audience has while experiencing advertising messages. This purely cognitive orientation is also the foundation of the "think" dimension of the FCB model. However, R&P argue that this is too limiting as attitude is based on both cognition and affect. Accordingly, they suggest that creative tactics for this side of the matrix should account for the benefit claims (i.e., cognition) and the emotional portrayal of the motive (i.e., affect). Thus, in order for it to be an informational-based attitude, the emphasis of the benefit claim is stronger than the emotional portrayal of the negative motive.

The notion of transformational-based attitude is partly based on the idea of a transformational ad defined as, "one which associates the experience of using (consuming) the advertised brand with a unique set of psychological characteristics which would not typically be associated with the brand experience to the same degree without exposure to the advertisement."[43] This type of advertising is often used by companies in the travel industry to help consumers envision the experience or feeling they might have when they take a trip such as a cruise or visit a particular destination. Image advertising, which is designed to give a company or brand a unique association or personality, is often transformational in nature. It is designed to create a certain feeling or mood that is activated when a consumer uses a particular product or service. For example, the Lambesis agency has created a unique image for Skyy Vodka by creating ads that associate the brand with cinematic-based cocktail moments (see Exhibit 8-16).

Just like the informational-based attitude is not purely cognitive, the transformational-based attitude is not purely based on emotion but includes some cognitive elements. Intuitively, this makes a lot of sense as some ads with a very strong fear appeal often leave us thinking. Overall, the emphasis of the emotional portrayal is stronger than the benefit claim for transformational-based attitude. Providing information in transformational ads is part of the Fresh Air campaign for Newfoundland and Labrador. Much of the message involved breathtaking views of the landscape and a humorous way of conveying the clean air one can breathe along the coastline. Another key component included travel logistics and accommodation information.[44]

The fourth improvement of the R&P model is that its guidelines for creative tactics balance elements in the ad for both cognitive and emotional responses that contribute to both aspects of brand attitude. On the emotional side, we are concerned with how the motive is portrayed or conveyed in the ad. To consider this, we have three characteristics: its authenticity, or how real it appears to the target audience; whether the target audience likes the ad; and finally, the target audience's reaction to the execution style. On the informational side, we are concerned with the brand's message with respect to the benefit claims. We also have three characteristics to consider: the number, the intensity, and the repetition of the claims.

While the guidelines for all six characteristics may be a function of all three creative tactics decisions, we can make a stronger connection for some. The authenticity and whether

Exhibit 8–16 Advertising for Skyy vodka uses a cinematic theme to create an image for the brand.

the target audience likes the ad are typically associated with the design elements of the ad. Quite obviously, there is a direct connection between the execution style of the framework and that particular creative tactic decision discussed in this chapter. The benefit claims are mostly a function of the message structure since the latter concerns the details of explaining the product's benefits. It is also a function of the relative balance between a verbal and visual message. We now turn our attention to creative tactics recommendations for the four brand attitude cells.

Low Involvement–Informational Creative Tactics   Ads designed to influence target audiences' attitudes based on low involvement–informational persuasion should have a very obvious benefit claim with an unusual execution style. New York Fries has used this idea in many of its recent ad campaigns (Exhibit 8-17). Since the intention is to persuade the target audience so that they automatically learn the connection among the brand, its category, and the benefit, consumer acceptance or rejection of the message is not a factor. Further, the emotion demonstrated in the ad and whether the target audience likes the ad are not necessary as the message is intended to make a creative link among the brand, category, and benefit.

Low Involvement–Informational

Emotional portrayal of motive

Authenticity	Not necessary
Like ad	Not necessary
Execution style	Unusual, problem-solution format

Benefit claim of brand message

Number of benefits	One or two, or one clear group
Intensity of benefit claim	State extremely
Repetition of benefit claim	Few required for reminder

Low Involvement–Transformational Creative Tactics   Three emotional portrayal guidelines are critical for this type of attitude. These points are consistent with transformational ads described above. For example, the representation of the consumption of the brand in the drama or story of the ad must "ring true" with the target audience such that it is perceived as a very enjoyable ad. This characteristic is demonstrated in the BMO ad (Exhibit 8-18). In a low-involvement situation, some benefit claims are still included but may be indirectly communicated through the story or emotion surrounding the story. Actual acceptance of the benefit claim is not a requirement; however, rejection of the overall message can lead to a reduction in the attitude of the target audience.

Low Involvement–Transformational

Emotional portrayal of motive

Authenticity	Key element and is the single benefit
Like ad	Necessary
Execution style	Unique to the brand

Benefit claim of brand message

Number of benefits	One or two, or one clear group
Intensity of benefit claim	Imply extremely by association
Repetition of benefit claim	Many exposures to buildup before trial purchase and reinforce attitude after trial

Exhibit 8-17 This ad contains low involvement-informational creative tactics.

Exhibit 8-18 The passion of Toronto FC fans is uniquely conveyed in this BMO sponsorship ad.

240

High Involvement–Informational Creative Tactics This side of the model illustrates the importance of information as high involvement implies the requirement of considerable and accurate benefit claims. Many benefits can be claimed here but they must be organized and presented in a manner that respects the current attitude of the target audience. Since this is an informational-based attitude, the emotional portrayal is important but not the primary consideration. Furthermore, the high-involvement characteristic means that the target audience has to accept the benefit claims. Rejection of the benefit claims may not result in any negative change in attitude if the copy respected the prior attitude of the target audience.

High Involvement–Informational

Emotional portrayal of motive	
Authenticity	Key element early in product life cycle and declines as product reaches later stages
Like ad	Not necessary
Execution style	Unusual
Benefit claim of brand message	
Number of benefits	Overall claim to summarize multiple (no more than seven) benefits
Intensity of benefit claim	Initial attitude is key reference point
	Very accurate claim; cannot over-claim or under-claim
	Comparative or refutation messages are strong options
Repetition of benefit claim	Many claims within an exposure

High Involvement–Transformational Creative Tactics Persuasion through this type of attitude formation requires strong emphasis of the emotion. A positive attitude toward the ad leads to a positive brand attitude. Likewise, the target audience must truly relate to the execution style and feel like the ad supports their lifestyle. Nutella captures this point with the ad in Exhibit 8-19. The end result is that if the target audience rejects the message because the emotion is not accurate, then the persuasion will not work and may even cause significant attitude reduction. The remaining guidelines illustrate that considerable information is required similar to what is seen for the high involvement—informational attitude. Once again this implies that acceptance of the benefit claims is critical for the attitude to take hold with the target audience.

Exhibit 8-19 Nutella's ad accurately conveys the lifestyle of those consuming the product.

High Involvement–Transformational

Emotional portrayal of motive

Authenticity	Paramount; must reflect lifestyle of target audience
Like ad	Necessary
Execution style	Unique; target audience must identify with product, people, or consumption situation shown

Benefit claim of brand message

Number of benefits	Acceptable number to provide key information
Intensity of benefit claim	Very accurate claim; may over-claim but do not under-claim
Repetition of benefit claim	Many are required to support informational message

241

IMC PLANNING: GUIDELINES FOR CREATIVE EVALUATION

While the creative specialists have much responsibility for determining the message appeal and execution style to be used in a campaign, the marketer must evaluate and approve the creative approach before any ads are produced. A number of people may be involved in evaluating the creative recommendation, including the advertising or communications manager, product or brand managers, marketing director or vice president, representatives from the legal department, and sometimes even the president or chief executive officer (CEO) of the company or the board of directors.

In situations where an advertising agency is used, top management is involved in selecting an ad agency and must approve the theme and creative strategy for the campaign. Evaluation and approval of individual ads proposed by the agency is often the responsibility of advertising and product managers. The account executive and a member of the creative team present the creative concept to the client's advertising and product managers for their approval before beginning production. A careful evaluation should be made before the ad actually enters production, since this stage requires considerable time and money as suppliers are hired to perform the various functions required to produce the actual ad. Basic criteria for evaluating the creative approach focus on a number of questions requiring managerial judgment:

- *Is the creative approach consistent with the brand's marketing and advertising objectives?* One of the most important factors the advertiser must consider is whether the creative strategy and tactics recommended by the agency are consistent with the marketing strategy for the brand and the role advertising and promotion have been assigned in the overall marketing program (i.e., brand image, marketing positioning strategy).
- *Is the creative approach consistent with the communication objectives?* The creative strategy and tactics must meet the established communication objectives. Creative specialists can lose sight of what the advertising message is supposed to be and come up with an approach that fails to execute the advertising strategy. Individuals responsible for approving the ad should ask the creative specialists to explain how the creative strategy and tactics achieve the creative and communications objectives.
- *Is the creative approach appropriate for the target audience?* Generally, much time has been spent defining, locating, and attempting to understand the target audience for the advertiser's product or service. Careful consideration should be given to whether the creative strategy and tactics recommended will appeal to, be understood by, and communicate effectively with the target audience. This involves studying all elements of the ad and how the audience will respond to them. Advertisers do not want to approve advertising that they believe will receive a negative reaction from the target audience.
- *Does the creative approach communicate a clear and convincing message to the customer?* Most ads are supposed to communicate a message that will help sell the brand. Many ads fail to communicate a clear and convincing message that motivates consumers to use a brand. While creativity is important in advertising, it is also important that the advertising communicate information attributes, features and benefits, and/or images that give consumers a reason to buy the brand.

- *Does the creative approach keep from overwhelming the message?* A criticism of advertising is an emphasis of the creative approach that overshadows the advertiser's message. Many creative, entertaining commercials have failed to register the brand name and/or selling points effectively. With advertising clutter, it may be necessary to use a novel creative approach to gain the receiver's attention. However, the creative approach cannot inhibit or limit message delivery to the target audience.
- *Is the creative approach appropriate for the media environment in which it is likely to be seen?* Each media vehicle has its own specific climate that results from the nature of its editorial content, the type of reader or viewer it attracts, and the nature of the ads it contains. Consideration should be given to how well the ad fits into the media environment in which it will be shown.
- *Is the ad truthful and tasteful?* Marketers should consider whether an ad is truthful, as well as whether it might offend consumers. The ultimate responsibility for determining whether an ad deceives or offends the target audience lies with the client. It is the job of the advertising or brand manager to evaluate the approach against company standards. The firm's legal department may review the ad to determine whether the creative appeal, message content, or execution could cause any problems for the company.

The advertising manager, brand manager, or other personnel on the client side can use these basic guidelines in reviewing, evaluating, and approving the ideas offered by the creative specialists. There may be other factors specific to the firm's advertising and marketing situation. Also, there may be situations where it is acceptable to deviate from the standards the firm usually uses in judging creative output. As we shall see in the next chapter, the client may want to move beyond these subjective criteria and use more sophisticated pretesting research using quantitative and qualitative methods to determine the effectiveness of a particular approach suggested by the creative specialists.

CHAPTER OBJECTIVES AND SUMMARY

1 To identify three key decisions for creative tactics: execution style, message structure, and design elements.

In this chapter, we examined how the advertising message is implemented and executed. Once the creative strategy that will guide the ad campaign has been determined, attention turns to the specific creative tactics that will enhance the cognitive and emotional processing of the message. This chapter summarizes three critical creative tactics decisions: execution style, message structure, and design elements. The latter topic concerns the details for producing either print, video, or audio ads that can be delivered through a variety of media. The initial two are also relevant for executing a creative strategy and can be adapted for any of the three delivery approaches.

2 To analyze the creative execution styles that advertisers can use and the situations where they are most appropriate.

The creative execution style is the way the advertising appeal is presented in the message. A number of common execution techniques were examined in the chapter, along with considerations for their use. The most appropriate style is a matter of balancing uniqueness in the market versus effective communication to achieve the stated objectives. A number of standard approaches are available, like straight-sell, slice-of-life, testimonial, drama, humour, and

imagery—all of which can be put in TV commercials, print ads, and radio spots and are now being developed for online video, banner ads, and podcast sponsorships.

3 To examine different types of message structures that can be used to develop a promotional message.

The design of the advertising message is a critical part of the communication process and is the second creative tactic discussed. There are various options regarding the message structure, including order of presentation of message arguments, conclusion drawing, message sidedness, refutation, and verbal versus visual traits. How these elements are constructed has important implications for enhancing the processing of the message and whether communication effects are achieved with the target audience.

4 To analyze design elements involved in the creation of print advertising and TV commercials.

Attention was also given to tactical issues involved in creating print, video, and audio messages. The elements of a print ad include headlines, body copy, illustrations, and layout. We also examined the video and audio elements of video messages and considerations involved in the planning and production of commercials. Together, these showed some of the important design decisions that have to be made to complete the creative approach.

Finally, we highlighted a couple key factors in the development of audio messages.

5 To understand a planning model for making creative tactics decisions.

We presented a framework for creative specialists and marketers to help them make the appropriate decisions for the creative tactics. The framework uses the target audience's attitude as the key factor when deciding upon the correct execution style, message structure, and design. These three characteristics ensure that both cognitive and emotional aspects of processing and attitude formation are addressed in the receiver of the message. The model is a like a list to double check and know whether the creative execution results have characteristics that influence the target audience's attitude in the way expected.

6 To consider how clients evaluate the creative work of their agencies and discuss guidelines for the evaluation and approval process.

Creative specialists are responsible for determining the creative strategy and tactics from the marketer's input. However, the client must review, evaluate, and approve the creative approach before any ads are produced or run. A number of criteria can be used by advertising, product or brand managers, and others involved in the promotional process to evaluate the advertising messages before approving final production.

KEY TERMS

body copy, *229*
creative execution style, *218*
direct headlines, *229*
headline, *228*
high-involvement
 decision, *237*

indirect headlines, *229*
informational motivation, *237*
jingles, *232*
layout, *230*
low-involvement
 decision, *237*

needledrop, *232*
one-sided message, *226*
primacy effect, *224*
recency effect, *224*
refutation, *226*
script, *232*

subheads, *229*
transformational
 motivation, *237*
two-sided message, *226*
voiceover, *231*

DISCUSSION QUESTIONS

1. Discuss the difference between a message appeal and a creative execution style. Why is it important to make this distinction?

2. Explain how the dramatization advertising execution technique could be used for the following products: beer, cellphones, furniture, airlines.

3. Discuss the use of the slice-of-life execution style. For what types of products might this approach work best?

4. Explain how a humour execution style differs from a humour message appeal.

5. What is transformational advertising? Why is it an important option for advertisers?

6. What is meant by a one-sided versus two-sided message? Discuss some the reasons marketers may or may not want to use a two-sided message.

7. Discuss the role of headlines and subheads in print advertisements. Would you say that headlines are more important for processing (i.e., gaining attention) or establishing a communication effect (i.e., awareness)?

8. Discuss the role of music in advertising. Why might companies such as Microsoft, Cadillac, and Nike pay large sums of money for the rights to use popular songs in their commercials?

9. What are the similarities and differences of creative tactics across the four cells of the R&P planning model?

10. Explain how the guidelines for creative evaluation can be applied to ads seen on the Internet.

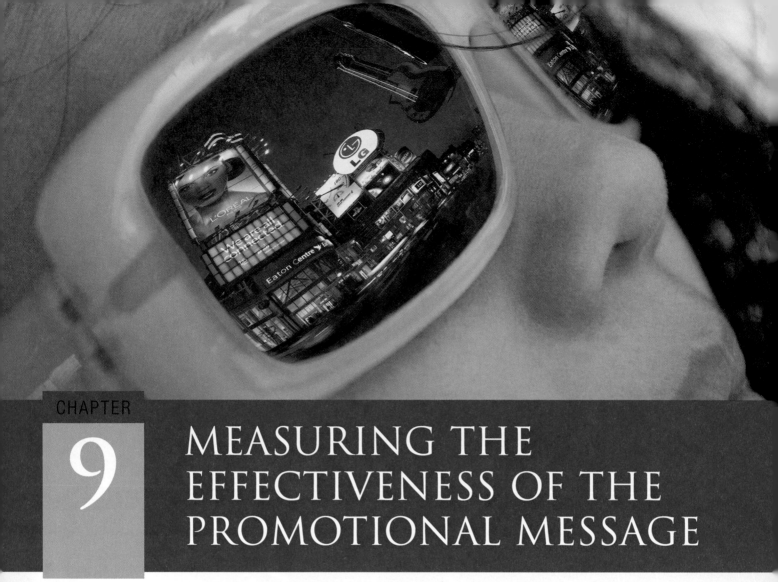

MEASURING THE EFFECTIVENESS OF THE PROMOTIONAL MESSAGE

■ CHAPTER OBJECTIVES

1 To understand reasons for measuring promotional program effectiveness.

2 To know the various measures used in assessing promotional program effectiveness.

3 To evaluate alternative methods for measuring promotional program effectiveness.

4 To understand the requirements of proper effectiveness research.

EMOTIONALLY INVOLVED RESEARCHERS MEASURE AD EFFECTIVENESS

Imagine sitting in an office wondering how consumers would react to new ads shown as storyboards developed by an advertising agency. Or perhaps consider whether the completed print ads should be placed in magazines for the next campaign. For that matter, if managers are wondering about *any* message to be delivered across any or multiple media, how or what evaluation should be implemented to ensure success? Although many standard or traditional approaches for promotional effectiveness exist, new methods continue to emerge.

One promising development is a method allowing researchers to get a better read on consumer emotions. Many approaches toward effectiveness tend to measure consumer knowledge in terms of brand recall or recognition, advertising recall or recognition, and rational thoughts connected to the brand. Typically, consumers have difficulty expressing their emotional attachment to a brand as they often convey their brand usage in relation to product attributes or benefits.

This dilemma led Ipsos-ASI to innovate with a measurement tool designed to gauge consumers' emotional reactions to an ad by asking three questions: How do you feel toward the ad? What feeling is the advertiser trying to get across? and What emotions do you associate with being a brand user? Consumers selected their emotional response from a group of facial illustrations that exhibited many emotions.

Their research also identified 11 personality traits that could be used to assess brands. Some of these traits include social, outgoing, extroverted; emotional, touching, sensitive; reserved, quiet, introverted; and spontaneous, creative, impulsive. Finally, building on existing motivation research,

their investigation examined 11 different motivators for purchasing a brand, such as self-sufficient, independent, autonomous; experience personal success or achievement; and pleasurable sensuous feeling. Overall, these measures have allowed Ipsos-ASI to distinguish between categories like cars or beer, and brands such as Ford and Audi or Budweiser and Heineken.

New advances for measuring audience involvement with marketing communication messages gained ground as well. In fact, the notion of measuring involvement recently expanded to all marketing communication points beyond television. Working together, many agency and research firms explore varying approaches to understand the degree of consumer reaction to marketing messages. For example, MediaCom's new measurement tool attempts to measure the depth of involvement with the message. The Media Company's new research method looks to understand the amount of involvement of people who are actually exposed to an advertising message on television. Finally, Carat Canada's research indicated that mothers with children were less involved when receiving messages with their children versus without their children.

Sources: Paul Brent, "The New Tools of Engagement," *Marketing Magazine,* August 14, 2006; Pattie Summerfield, "Getting to Engagement," *Strategy,* June 2006; Rebecca Harris, "Measuring Emotions," *Marketing Magazine,* September 25, 2006; John Hallward, "The Creators of Motivation: Advancement in the Exploration of Emotions," *Ipsos-ASI,* June 2004.

QUESTIONS

1. Why are advertisers so concerned with measuring emotions and involvement?
2. Should promotional planners measure these two variables for other IMC tools, such as sales promotions or direct response?

Measuring the effectiveness of the promotional program is critical since it allows the marketing manager to assess the performance of specific program elements and provide input into the next period's situation analysis. We are concerned with evaluative research to measure the effectiveness of advertising and promotion and/or to assess various strategies and tactics before implementing them. This is not to be confused with planning research used to develop the promotional program, although the two can (and should) be used together.

In this chapter, we explore the measuring effectiveness debate. Next we examine key research decisions for evaluative research. Finally, we summarize research methods and conclude with our IMC planning perspective. Our primary focus is measuring the effects of advertising, because it is well established and other aspects of marketing communication have an advertisement-like message. Thus, most research techniques can be applied or have been adapted for other IMC tools. We highlight methods of measuring effectiveness for these tools in their respective chapters.

THE MEASURING EFFECTIVENESS DEBATE

Employees are generally given objectives to accomplish, and their job evaluations are based on their ability to achieve these objectives. Advertising and promotion should be held to the same standard where its performance is measured against the objectives established in the promotional plan as indicated in Chapter 5. Although this may appear logical, some consider it debatable.

REASONS FOR MEASURING EFFECTIVENESS

Assessing the effectiveness of ads both before they are implemented and after the final versions have been completed and fielded offers a number of advantages.

Avoiding Costly Mistakes Total advertising topped $14 billion in 2008, and any brand's advertising budget is often a substantial expenditure. Thus, if a program is not achieving its objectives, the marketing manager needs information to know how or where to spend money more effectively. The opportunity loss due to poor marketing communication is just as important. If the advertising and promotions program is not accomplishing its objectives, the potential gain that could result from an effective program is not realized, thereby minimizing the firm's return on its marketing investment. For example, one mass merchant discovered that promoting Tide detergent generated more cross-selling opportunities than did promotions of nonpremium brands (Exhibit 9-1). At the same time, promotions of motor oil had no cross-selling impact.[1]

Evaluating Alternative Strategies Typically, a firm has a number of strategies under consideration such as which medium should be used or whether one message is more effective than another. Or the decision may be between two promotional program elements: should money be spent on sponsorships or on advertising? One retailer found that advertising do-it-yourself products on

Exhibit 9-1 Tide has been shown to be an effective promotional draw.

the radio was effective in rural areas but not in urban locales.[2] Companies often test alternate versions of their advertising in different cities to determine which ad communicates most effectively. Thus, research may be designed to help the manager determine which strategy is most likely to be effective.

Increasing Advertising Efficiency   The expression "can't see the forest for the trees" pertains here since advertisers get so close to the project they sometimes lose sight of their objectives. They may use technical jargon that not everyone is familiar with. Or the creative department may get too creative or too sophisticated and lose the meaning that needs to be communicated. How many times have you seen an ad and asked yourself what it was trying to say, or how often have you seen an ad that you really like but you can't remember the brand name? Conducting research helps companies develop more efficient and effective communications. An increasing number of clients are demanding accountability for their promotional programs and putting more pressure on the agencies to produce.

REASONS FOR NOT MEASURING EFFECTIVENESS

Companies give a number of reasons for not measuring the effectiveness of advertising and promotions strategies.

Cost   A frequently cited reason for not testing is the expense; good research can be expensive in terms of both time and money. Many managers decide that time is critical and they must implement the program while the opportunity is available. Many believe the monies spent on research could be better spent on improved production of the ad, additional media buys, and the like. While the first argument may have some merit, the second does not. Imagine the results of a poor campaign or the incentive program did not motivate the target audience; money would be wasted if the effects could do more harm than good. Spending more money to buy media does not remedy a poor message or substitute for an improper promotional mix. For example, one firm watched its test-market sales for a new brand of beer fall short of expectations. As a solution, the firm purchased all the TV time available that matched its target audience. After two months, sales failed to improve resulting in cancellation of the test market. Analysis showed the problem occurred with the message that communicated no reason to buy. Preliminary research would have identified the problem earlier, saving money and the brand.

Research Problems   A second reason cited for not measuring effectiveness is that it is difficult to isolate the effects of promotional elements. Each variable in the marketing mix affects the success of a product or service. Because it is rarely possible to measure the contribution of each marketing element directly, some managers become frustrated and decide not to test at all. This argument also suffers from weak logic. While we agree that it is not always possible to determine the dollar amount of sales contributed by promotions, research can provide useful results. Communications effectiveness can be measured and may carry over to sales.

Disagreement on What to Test   The objectives sought in the promotional program may differ by industry, by stage of the product life cycle, or even for different people within the firm. The sales manager may want to see the impact of promotions on sales, top management may wish to know the impact on corporate image, and those involved in the creative process may wish to assess recall and/or recognition of the ad. Lack of agreement on what to test often results in no testing, but there is little rationale for this position. With the proper design, many or even all of the above might be measured. Since every promotional element is designed to accomplish its own objectives, research can be used to measure its effectiveness in doing so.

Objections of Creative Specialists An age-old industry debate is that the creative department does not want its work to be tested and many agencies are reluctant to submit their work for testing. Ad agencies' creative departments argue that tests are not true measures of the creativity and effectiveness of ads; applying measures stifles their creativity; and the more creative the ad, the more likely it is to be successful. They want permission to be creative without any limiting guidelines. At the same time, the marketing manager is ultimately responsible for the success of the product or brand. Given the substantial sums being allocated to advertising and promotion, it is the manager's right, and responsibility, to know how well a specific program, or a specific ad, will perform in the market.

DECISIONS FOR MEASURING EFFECTIVENESS

We now identify some broad issues for measuring the communication effects of advertising. This section considers what elements to evaluate, as well as when and where such evaluations should occur. We cover the issue of how to measure in the next section.

WHAT TO TEST

The focus of the testing is mostly on the creative strategy and creative tactics decisions that the advertiser makes while putting a campaign together. In the beer example discussed earlier, the message never provided a reason for consumers to try the new product. In other instances, the message may not be strong enough to pull readers into the ad by attracting their attention, or it may not be clear enough to help them evaluate the product. Sometimes the message is memorable but doesn't achieve the other goals set by management. One study showed that 7 of the 25 products that scored highest on interest and memorability in Video Storyboard Tests' ad test had flat or declining sales.[3] As these few examples show, many of the creative strategy and creative tactics decisions regarding the message can be tested.

Creative Strategy Decisions The primary creative strategy decision—the creative theme—can be tested. When a company decides to change its theme or is planning to launch an unusual attention-getting approach, it may want to see the reactions of the target audience prior to investing in the media placement. Similarly, different message appeals can be tested (i.e., rational versus emotional), or different versions of one appeal can be tested. Finally, another important question is whether the spokesperson being used is effective and how the target audience will respond to him or her. A product spokesperson may be an excellent source initially but, owing to a variety of reasons, may lose impact over time in terms of attractiveness or likeability. Thus, all major creative strategy decisions can be tested.

Creative Tactics Decisions Different execution styles displayed on storyboards can be presented to members of the target audience in focus groups for their reaction. The message structure can be looked at, such as reading the body copy in an interview or some other method. Specific design elements, such as the music in a television ad or the headline of a print ad, can also be the focus of research. Overall, advertisers use a variety of research methods to test essentially any creative tactic that they are unsure about or that requires confirmation.

Other Promotional Tools Many of the other tools we will discuss in this book have an associated creative or message. Many sales promotions have a visual as well as some advertising-like message that reinforces the brand position in the target

250

audience's mind. Similarly, firms use many creative tactics to gain the attention of media personnel so that their story will get picked up by the media in order to get publicity exposure. Thus, while we have examined the creative in the context of advertising in the book, as we noted previously, all the decisions are relevant in the other promotional tools, and as expected the same research is possible if the advertiser believes it necessary. We review a few specifics in each of the subsequent chapters to measure the effectiveness of other promotional tools.

WHEN TO TEST

Virtually all test measures can be classified according to when they are conducted. **Pretests** are measures taken before the campaign is implemented; **posttests** occur after the ad or commercial has been in the field. A variety of pretests and posttests are available to the marketer, each with its own methodology designed to measure some aspect of the advertising program. Figure 9-1 classifies these testing methods.

Pretesting   Pretests may occur at a number of points, from as early on as idea generation to rough execution to testing the final version before implementing it. In addition, testing could occur at more than one point in time. For example, concept testing may take place at the earliest development of the ad or commercial, when little more than an idea, basic concept, or positioning statement is under consideration. Later on in the process, layouts of the ad campaign that include headlines, some body copy, and rough illustrations are tested along with storyboards and animatics for proposed TV commercials.

The methodologies employed to conduct pretests vary. In focus groups, participants freely discuss the meanings they get from the ads, consider the relative advantages of alternatives, and even suggest improvements or additional themes. In addition to or instead of the focus groups, consumers are asked to evaluate the ad on a series of rating scales. In-home interviews, mall intercept, or laboratory methods may be used to gather the data.

Pretests	Lab	Field
Concept	Concept tests	
Rough/copy/commercial	Rough tests Consumer juries	Comprehension and reaction tests
Finished print ads	Portfolio Readability	Dummy advertising vehicles
Finished TV ads	Theatre Physiological	On-air

Posttests		
Finished print ads in magazines		Inquiry tests Recognition tests Recall tests Tracking studies
Finished TV ads on-air		Recall tests Comprehensive measures Test marketing Single-source Tracking studies

FIGURE   9–1

Classification of testing methods

The advantage of pretesting is that feedback is relatively inexpensive. Any problems with the concept or the way it is to be delivered are identified before large amounts of money are spent in development. Sometimes more than one version of the ad is evaluated to determine which is most likely to be effective. A study of 4,637 on-air commercials designed to build normative intelligence conducted by McCollum Spielman Worldwide (MSW) found that only 19 percent were considered outstanding or really good. Nearly twice as many (34 percent) were failures. On the other hand, of those spots that were pretested before the final form was aired, the share of good to outstanding rose to 37 percent, while the failure rate fell to 9 percent.[4]

The disadvantage is that mock-ups, storyboards, or animatics may not communicate nearly as effectively as the final product. The mood-enhancing and/or emotional aspects of the message are very difficult to communicate in this format. Another disadvantage is time delays. Many marketers believe being first in the market offers them a distinct advantage over competitors, so they forgo research to save time and ensure this position.

Posttesting   In contrast to pretesting, posttesting occurs after placing the marketing communication in a media like broadcast or print, or another communication tool if needed. Posttesting is designed to (1) determine if the campaign is accomplishing the objectives sought and (2) serve as input into the next period's situation analysis. An excellent example of using research to guide future advertising strategies is reflected in an experiment conducted in the U.S. by Lowes, a home improvement retailer. In a study designed to test 36 different versions of covers for its catalogues (which are sent to between 30 and 40 million homes per year), the company determined that by putting more products on the covers, using real pictures rather than cartoons, and reducing the size of the catalogue, the catalogues were more effective. Other tests varying the number of TV spots, newspaper ads, and sports sponsorships led to increases in advertising spending and affirmation of the company's sponsorship of NASCAR auto racing.[5] A variety of posttest measures are available, most of which involve survey research methods.

WHERE TO TEST

In addition to when to test, decisions must be made as to *where.* These tests may take place in either laboratory or field settings.

Laboratory Tests   In **laboratory tests**, people are brought to a particular location where they are shown ads and/or commercials. The testers either ask questions about them or measure participants' responses by other methods—for example, pupil dilation, eye tracking, or galvanic skin response.

The major advantage of the lab setting is the *control* it affords the researcher. Changes in copy, illustration, formats, colours, and the like can be manipulated inexpensively and the differential impact of each assessed. This makes it much easier for the researcher to isolate the contribution of each factor.

The major disadvantage is the lack of *realism.* Perhaps the greatest effect of this lack of realism is a **testing bias**. When people are brought into a lab (even if it has been designed to look like a living room), they may scrutinize the ads much more closely than they would at home. A second problem with this lack of realism is that it cannot duplicate the natural viewing situation, complete with the distractions or comforts of home. Looking at ads in a lab setting may not be the same as viewing at home; however some testing techniques have made progress in correcting this deficiency. Overall, however, the control offered by this method probably outweighs the disadvantages, which accounts for the frequent use of lab methods.

Field Tests **Field tests** are tests of the ad or commercial under natural viewing situations, complete with the realism of noise, distractions, and the comforts of home. Field tests take into account the effects of repetition, program content, and even the presence of competitive messages.

The major disadvantage of field tests is the lack of control. It may be impossible to isolate causes of viewers' evaluations. If atypical events occur during the test, they may bias the results. Competitors may attempt to sabotage the research. And field tests usually take more time and money to conduct, so the results are not available to be acted on quickly. Thus, realism is gained at the expense of other important factors. It is up to the researcher to determine which trade-offs to make.

METHODS OF MEASURING EFFECTIVENESS

Testing may occur at various points throughout the development of an ad or a campaign: (1) concept generation research, (2) rough, prefinished art, copy, and/or commercial testing, (3) finished art or commercial pretesting, and (4) market testing of ads or commercials (posttesting). In this section, we describe various methods used for each of these four stages.

CONCEPT GENERATION AND TESTING

Figure 9-2 describes the process involved in advertising **concept testing**, which is conducted very early in the campaign development process in order to explore the targeted consumer's response to a potential ad or campaign or have the consumer evaluate advertising alternatives. Positioning statements, copy, headlines, and/or illustrations may all be under scrutiny. The material to be evaluated may be just a headline or a rough sketch of the ad. The colours used, typeface, package designs, and even point-of-purchase materials may be evaluated.

One of the more commonly used methods for concept testing is focus groups, which usually consist of 8 to 10 people in the target audience for the product. Companies have tested everything from product concepts to advertising concepts using focus groups. For most companies, the focus group is the first step in the research process. The number of focus groups used varies depending on group consensus, strength of response, and/or the degree to which participants like or dislike the concepts. In general, about 10 are usually needed to test a concept sufficiently.

While focus groups continue to be a favourite of marketers, they are often overused. The methodology is attractive in that results are easily obtained, directly observable, and immediate. A variety of issues can be examined, and consumers are free to go into depth in areas they consider important. Also, focus groups don't require quantitative analysis. Unfortunately, many managers are uncertain about research methods that require statistics, and focus groups, being qualitative

Objective:	Explores consumers' responses to various ad concepts as expressed in words, pictures, or symbols.
Method:	Alternative concepts are exposed to consumers who match the characteristics of the target audience. Reactions and evaluations of each are sought through a variety of methods, including focus groups, direct questioning, and survey completion. Sample sizes vary depending on the number of concepts to be presented and the consensus of responses.
Output:	Qualitative and/or quantitative data evaluating and comparing alternative concepts.

FIGURE 9–2

Concept testing

in nature, don't demand much skill in interpretation. Weaknesses with focus groups are shown in Figure 9-3. Clearly, there are appropriate and inappropriate circumstances for employing this methodology.

Another way to gather consumers' opinions of concepts is mall intercepts, where consumers in shopping malls are approached and asked to evaluate rough ads and/or copy. Rather than participating in a group discussion, individuals assess the ads via questionnaires, rating scales, and/or rankings. New technologies allow for concept testing over the Internet, where advertisers can show concepts simultaneously to consumers throughout Canada, garnering feedback and analyzing the results almost instantaneously. IMC Perspective 9-1 highlights recent trends in communication research done through the Internet.

ROUGH ART, COPY, AND COMMERCIAL TESTING

Because of the high cost associated with the production of an ad or commercial, advertisers are increasingly spending more on testing a rendering of the final ad at early stages. Slides of the artwork posted on a screen or animatic and photomatic **rough tests** may be used at this stage. (See Figure 9-4 for an explanation of terminology.) Because such tests can be conducted for about $3,000 to $5,000, research at this stage is becoming ever more popular.

But cost is only one factor. The test is of little value if it does not provide relevant, accurate information. Rough tests must indicate how the finished commercial

FIGURE 9–3

Weaknesses associated with focus group research

- The results are not quantifiable.
- Sample sizes are too small to generalize to larger populations.
- Group influences may bias participants' responses.
- One or two members of the group may steer the conversation or dominate the discussion.
- Consumers become instant "experts."
- Members may not represent the target market. (Are focus group participants a certain type of person?)
- Results may be taken to be more representative and/or definitive than they really are.

FIGURE 9–4

Rough testing terminology

A rough commercial is an unfinished execution that may fall into three broad categories:

Animatic Rough
Succession of drawings/cartoons
Rendered artwork
Still frames
Simulated movement: Panning/zooming of frame/rapid sequence

Photomatic Rough
Succession of photographs
Real people/scenery
Still frames
Simulated movements: Panning/zooming of frame/rapid sequence

Live-Action Rough
Live motion
Stand-in/nonunion talent
Nonunion crew
Limited props/minimal opticals
Location settings

A Finished Commercial Uses
Live motion/animation
Highly paid union talent
Full union crew
Exotic props/studio sets/special effects

Advertising Research Adopts the Internet

The Internet is reinventing market research by making it cheaper, more engaging, and more creative. Consider the experience of a large U.S. retailer client that pretested a major television campaign before taking it to air. Using its own nationwide panel of about 30,000 customers, this retailer carefully selected a sub-sample of 1,000 and conducted an online poll that involved respondents viewing several versions of the TV campaign and completing a short questionnaire. The study was completed in 48 hours and cost $3,000—about the same as a conventional focus group with 12 participants. Ten years ago the only viable method for gauging the views of a large group of respondents to stimuli such as an ad campaign was through shopping mall interviews or by mailing out test videos. Using either method, a study on the scale undertaken by the U.S. retail client would have taken weeks to complete and cost $50,000 to $100,000.

Technology is rapidly changing roles and relationships for the three principal players in market research: marketers, researchers, and respondents. On the client side, corporate research departments—which were sometimes ignored during the 1980s and '90s—are on the ascendancy. That's because the new speed, cost, and quality equation allows for more timely and relevant research than was ever possible before. Marketer-side researchers can respond within hours to C-suite requests for information on everything from new concepts to competitive threats, thus making research part of the fast-moving decision cycle of most large companies.

The second role transformation associated with the current technological revolution involves companies and researchers on the "supply" side of the research industry. Here the story is about the re-emergence of small and mid-size consultancies—because, in the new era, size is becoming increasingly irrelevant. Previously, smaller research companies lacked the resources and infrastructure necessary to undertake large, complex research missions. But now the same dynamic that is liberating marketers is providing highly creative researchers with a changing environment for their practices. With market research, as with so many other areas touched by the Internet, small is once again beautiful.

The third, and in many respects most important, role change occurring today involves respondents: the men and women who participate in market research surveys, focus groups, and market simulations. Historically, the market research industry grew on the fertile ground of citizen and consumer civility. Millions of people have answered the questions and responded to the pokes and prods of researchers because answering the questions of strangers on the other end of the phone line was considered a polite and socially acceptable thing to do. Across North America and increasingly around the world, respondent engagement has become a huge threat to the market research industry as non-cooperation rates often exceed 80 percent. In many respects the Internet can be a convivial tool for collecting opinions as respondents can choose the time and place for completing a survey. And because the high cost of call centre distribution has been eliminated, it's economically feasible to provide a small incentive to encourage participation.

Another significant change the Internet promises for respondents concerns the ability of this technology to make the survey experience itself much more pleasant. Most online surveys are little more than telephone scripts that have been placed on a screen. But that's starting to change as 3D animation, simulated shopping experiences, and online shopping games find traction. It's all about visuals and engagement—a phenomenon that will only accelerate as more households move to high-speed Internet connections.

Source: Angus Reid, "Market Research Liberated," *Marketing Magazine*, September 25, 2006.

Question

1. Will assessing consumer reaction to advertising using market research over the Internet improve the quality of information in the future?

would perform. Some studies have demonstrated that these testing methods are reliable and the results typically correlate well with the finished ad.[6] Most of the tests conducted at the rough stage involve lab settings. Popular tests include comprehension and reaction tests and consumer juries.

Comprehension and Reaction Tests One key concern for the advertiser is whether the ad or commercial conveys the meaning intended. The second concern is the reaction the ad generates. Obviously, the advertiser does not want an ad that evokes a negative reaction or offends someone. **Comprehension and reaction tests** are designed to assess these responses. Tests of comprehension and reaction employ no one standard procedure. Personal interviews, group interviews, and focus groups have all been used for this purpose, and sample sizes vary according to the needs of the client; they typically range from 50 to 200 respondents.

Consumer Juries This method uses consumers representative of the target audiences to evaluate the probable success of an ad. **Consumer juries** may be asked to rate a selection of layouts or copy versions presented in pasteups on separate sheets. The objectives sought and methods employed in consumer juries are shown in Figure 9-5.[7] Sample questions asked of jurists are shown in Figure 9-6.

While the jury method offers the advantages of control and cost effectiveness, serious flaws in the methodology limit its usefulness:

- *The consumer may become a self-appointed expert.* One jury method benefit is the objectivity and involvement that the targeted consumer can bring to the evaluation process. However, knowing they are being asked to critique ads, participants sometimes become more expert in their evaluations by paying more attention and being more critical than usual. The result may be a less than objective evaluation or an evaluation on elements other than those intended.
- *The number of ads that can be evaluated is limited.* Whether order of merit or paired comparison methods are used, the ranking procedure becomes tedious as the number of alternatives increases. Consider the ranking of 10 ads. While

---

FIGURE 9–5

Consumer juries

Objective:	Potential viewers (consumers) are asked to evaluate ads and give their reactions to and evaluation of them. When two or more ads are tested, viewers are usually asked to rate or rank order the ads according to their preferences.
Method:	Respondents are asked to view ads and rate them according to either (1) the order of merit method or (2) the paired comparison method. In the former, the respondent is asked to view the ads, then rank them from one to *n* according to their perceived merit. In the latter, ads are compared only two at a time. Each ad is compared to every other ad in the group, and the winner is listed. The best ad is that which wins the most times. Consumer juries typically employ 50 to 100 participants.
Output:	An overall reaction to each ad under construction as well as a rank ordering of the ads based on the viewers' perceptions.

FIGURE 9–6

Questions asked in a consumer jury test

1. Which of these ads would you most likely read if you saw it in a magazine?
2. Which of these headlines would interest you the most in reading the ad further?
3. Which ad convinces you most of the quality or superiority of the product?
4. Which layout do you think would be most effective in causing you to buy?
5. Which ad did you like best?
6. Which ad did you find most interesting?

the top two and the bottom two may very well reveal differences, those ranked in the middle may not yield much useful information. In the paired comparison method, 15 evaluations are required for six alternatives. As the number of ads increases, the task becomes even more unmanageable.

- *A halo effect is possible.* Sometimes participants rate an ad as good (bad) on all characteristics because they like (dislike) a few and overlook specific weaknesses (strengths). This tendency, called the **halo effect**, distorts the ratings and defeats the ability to control for specific components.
- *Preferences for specific types of advertising may overshadow objectivity.* Ads that involve emotions or pictures may receive higher ratings or rankings than those employing copy, facts, and/or rational criteria. Even though the latter are often more effective in the marketplace, they may be judged less favourably by jurists who prefer emotional appeals.

Some of the problems noted here can be remedied by the use of ratings scales instead of rankings, but ratings are not always valid either. Thus, while consumer juries have been used for years, questions of bias have led researchers to doubt their validity.

PRETESTING OF FINISHED ADS

At this stage, a finished advertisement or commercial is used; since it has not been presented to the market, changes can still be made. Many researchers believe testing the ad in final form provides better information. Several test procedures are available for print and broadcast ads, including both laboratory and field methodologies. Print methods include portfolio tests, analyses of readability, and dummy advertising vehicles. Broadcast tests include theatre tests and on-air tests. Both print and broadcast may use physiological measures.

Pretesting Finished Print Messages A number of methods for pretesting finished print ads are available. One is described in Figure 9-7. The most common of these methods are portfolio tests, readability tests, and dummy advertising vehicles.

Portfolio Tests **Portfolio tests** are a laboratory methodology designed to expose a group of respondents to a portfolio consisting of both control and test ads. Respondents are then asked what information they recall from the ads. The assumption is that the ads that yield the highest recall are the most effective.

While portfolio tests offer the opportunity to compare alternative ads directly, a number of weaknesses limit their applicability:

- Factors other than advertising creativity and/or presentation may affect recall. Interest in the product or product category, the fact that respondents know they are participating in a test, or interviewer instructions (among others) may account for more differences than the ad itself.

Objective:	Tests recall and readers' impressions of print ads.
Method:	Mall intercepts in two or more cities are used to screen respondents and have them take home "test magazines" for reading. Participants are phoned the next day to determine opinions of the ads, recall of ad contents, and other questions of interest to the sponsor. Approximately 225 people constitute the sample.
Output:	Scores reported include related recall of copy and visual elements, sales messages, and other nonspecific elements. Both quantitative (table) scores and verbatim responses are reported.

FIGURE 9-7

Diagnostic Research Inc.'s print test

257

- Recall may not be the best test. Some researchers argue that for certain types of products (those of low involvement) ability to recognize the ad when shown may be a better measure than recall.

One way to determine the validity of the portfolio method is to correlate its results with readership scores once the ad is placed in the field. Whether such validity tests are being conducted or not is not readily known, although the portfolio method remains popular in the industry.

Readability Tests The communication efficiency of the body copy in a print ad can be tested with the **Flesch formula** to assess its readability by determining the average number of syllables per 100 words. Human interest appeal of the material, length of sentences, and familiarity with certain words are also considered and correlated with the educational background of target audiences. Test results are compared to previously established norms for various target audiences. The test suggests that copy is best comprehended when sentences are short, words are concrete and familiar, and personal references are drawn.

This method eliminates many of the interviewee biases associated with other tests and avoids gross errors in understanding. The norms offer an attractive standard for comparison. Disadvantages are also inherent, however. The copy may become too mechanical, and direct input from the receiver is not available. Without this input, contributing elements like creativity cannot be addressed. To be effective, this test should be used only in conjunction with other pretesting methods.

Dummy Advertising Vehicles In an improvement on the portfolio test, ads are placed in "dummy" magazines developed by an agency or research firm. The magazines contain regular editorial features of interest to the reader, as well as the test ads, and are distributed to a *random sample* of homes in predetermined geographic areas. Readers are told the magazine publisher is interested in evaluations of editorial content and asked to read the magazines as they normally would. Then they are interviewed on their reactions to both editorial content and ads. Recall, readership, and interest-generating capabilities of the ad are assessed.

The advantage of this method is that it provides a more natural setting than the portfolio test. Readership occurs in the participant's own home, the test more closely approximates a natural reading situation, and the reader may go back to the magazine, as people typically do. However, the testing effect is not eliminated, and product interest may still bias the results.

Diagnostic Measures While all previously described methods are available, the most popular form of print ad pretesting involves a series of measures that account for the shortcomings of each of the other methods. The tests can be used for rough and/or finished ads and are most commonly conducted in the respondents' homes enabling the researcher to collect multiple measures from many samples. For example, Millward-Brown's link copy test includes measures of emotional responses to ads, assessing metrics such as enjoyment, engagement, likes, and dislikes to address overall emotional response. Ipsos-ASI's methodology also offers multiple measures, as shown in Figure 9-8.

Pretesting Finished Broadcast Ads A variety of methods for pretesting broadcast ads are available. The most popular are theatre tests, on-air tests, and physiological measures.

Theatre Tests In the past, one of the most popular laboratory methods for pretesting finished commercials was **theatre testing**. Participants are invited by telephone, mall intercepts, and/or tickets in the mail to view pilots of proposed TV programs. In some instances, the show is actually being tested, but more commonly a standard program

Objective:	To assist advertisers in copy testing of print advertisements to determine (1) main idea communication, (2) likes and dislikes, (3) believability, (4) ad attribute ratings, (5) overall likability, and (6) brand attribute ratings.
Method:	Tests are conducted in current issues of newsstand magazines. The recall measure consists of 150 responses. Diagnostic measures range from 105 to 150 responses. Highly targeted audiences are available through a version known as the Targeted Print Test.
Output:	Standard scores and specific diagnostics.

FIGURE 9–8

Ipsos-ASI's
Next*Print

is used so that audience responses can be compared with normative responses established by previous viewers. Sample sizes range from 250 to 600 participants.

On entering the theatre, viewers are told a drawing will be held for gifts and asked to complete a product preference questionnaire asking which products they would prefer if they win. This form also requests demographic data. Participants may be seated in specific locations in the theatre to allow observation by age, sex, and so on. They view the program and commercials, and a form asking for evaluations is distributed. Participants are then asked to complete a second form for a drawing so that changes in product preference can be noted. In addition to product/brand preference, the form may request other information:

- Interest in and reaction to the commercial.
- Overall reaction to the commercial as measured by an adjective checklist.
- Recall of various aspects of the commercial.
- Interest in the brand under consideration.
- Continuous (frame-by-frame) reactions throughout the commercial.

The methods of theatre testing operations vary, though all measure brand preference changes. For example, many of the services now use videotaped programs with the commercials embedded for viewing in one's office rather than in a theatre. Others establish viewing rooms in malls and/or hotel conference rooms. Some do not take all the measures listed here; others ask the consumers to turn dials or push buttons on a keypad to provide the continual responses. An example of one methodology is shown in Figure 9-9.

Those opposed to theatre tests cite a number of disadvantages. First, they say the environment is too artificial. The lab setting is bad enough, but asking respondents to turn dials or, as one service does, wiring people for physiological responses takes them too far from a natural viewing situation. Second, the contrived measure of brand preference change seems too phony to believe. Critics contend that participants will see through it and make changes just because they think they are supposed to. Finally, the group effect of having others present and overtly exhibiting their reactions may influence viewers who did not have any reactions themselves.

259

Advertising Control for Television (ACT), a lab procedure of The MSW Group, uses about 400 respondents representing four cities. It measures initial brand preference by asking participants which brands they most recently purchased. Respondents are then divided into groups of 25 to view a 30-minute program with seven commercials inserted in the middle. Four are test commercials; the other three are control commercials with established viewing norms. After viewing the program, respondents are given a recall test of the commercials. After the recall test, a second 30-minute program is shown, with each test commercial shown again. The second measure of brand preference is taken at this time, with persuasion measured by the percentage of viewers who switched preferences from their most recently purchased brand to one shown in the test commercials.

FIGURE 9–9

The Ad*Vantage/ACT
theatre methodology

Proponents argue that theatre tests offer distinct advantages. In addition to control, the established norms (averages of commercials' performances) indicate how one's commercial will fare against others in the same product class tested previously. Further, advocates say the brand preference measure is supported by actual sales results.

On-Air Tests Firms also insert commercials into actual TV programs in certain test markets, referred to as an **on-air test**. This technique offers all the advantages and disadvantages of field methodologies; however, one concern is associated with the resulting **day-after recall scores**. Lyman Ostlund notes that measurement errors may result from the natural environment—the position of the ad in the series of commercials shown, the adjacent program content, and/or the number of commercials shown.[8] While the testing services believe their methods overcome many of these criticisms, each still uses recall as one of the primary measures of effectiveness. Since recall tests best reflect the degree of attention and interest in an ad, claims that the tests predict the ad's impact on sales may be going too far. In 28 studies reviewed by Jack Haskins, only two demonstrated that factual recall could be related to sales.[9] Joel Dubow's research indicates that recall is a necessary but not sufficient measure, while research by Jones and Blair was even more demonstrative, noting that "it is unwise to look to recall for an accurate assessment of a commercial's sales effect."[10]

On the plus side, most of the testing services have offered evidence of both validity and reliability for on-air pretesting of commercials. Some firms claim their pretest and posttest results yield the same recall scores 9 out of 10 times—a strong indication of reliability and a good predictor of the effect the ad is likely to have when shown to the population as a whole.

Physiological Measures A less common method of pretesting finished commercials involves a laboratory setting in which physiological responses are measured. These measures indicate the receiver's *involuntary* response to the ad, theoretically eliminating biases associated with the voluntary measures reviewed to this point. (Involuntary responses are those over which the individual has no control, such as heartbeat and reflexes.) Physiological measures used to test both print and broadcast ads include pupil dilation, galvanic skin response, eye tracking, and brain waves.

Pupil dilation. Research in **pupillometrics** is designed to measure dilation and constriction of the pupils of the eyes in response to stimuli. Dilation is associated with action; constriction involves the body's conservation of energy. Pupil dilation suggests a stronger interest in (or preference for) an ad or implies arousal or attention-getting capabilities. Other attempts to determine the affective (liking or disliking) responses created by ads have met with less success. Because of high costs and some methodological problems, the use of pupillometrics has waned over the past decade. But it can be useful in evaluating certain aspects of advertising.

Galvanic skin response. Also known as **electrodermal response**, GSR measures the skin's resistance or conductance to a small amount of current passed between two electrodes. Response to a stimulus activates sweat glands, which in turn increases the conductance of the electrical current. Thus, GSR/EDR activity might reflect a reaction to advertising. In their review of the research in this area, Paul Watson and Robert Gatchel concluded that GSR/EDR (1) is sensitive to affective stimuli, (2) may present a picture of attention, (3) may be useful to measure long-term advertising recall, and (4) is useful in measuring ad effectiveness.[11] In interviews with practitioners and reviews of case studies, Priscilla LaBarbera and Joel Tucciarone also concluded that GSR is an effective measure and is useful, yet underused, for measuring affect, or liking, for ads.[12]

Eye tracking. A methodology that is more commonly employed is **eye tracking** (Figure 9-10), in which viewers are asked to view an ad while a sensor aims a beam of infrared light at the eye. The beam follows the movement of the eye and shows the exact spot on which the viewer is focusing. The continuous reading of responses demonstrates which elements of the ad are attracting attention, how long the viewer is focusing on them, and the sequence in which they are being viewed.

Eye tracking can identify strengths and weaknesses in an ad. For example, attractive models or background action may distract the viewer's attention away from the brand or product being advertised. The advertiser can remedy this distraction before fielding the ad. In other instances, colours or illustrations may attract attention and create viewer interest in the ad.

Brain waves. **Electroencephalographic (EEG) measures** can be taken from the skull to determine electrical frequencies in the brain. While EEG research has engaged the attention of academic researchers, it has been much less successful in attracting the interest of practitioners, though recently the technology has gained in attractiveness, as shown in IMC Perspective 19-2. The electrical impulses are used in three areas of research, alpha waves, hemispheric lateralization, and indirect methods.

- **Alpha activity** refers to the degree of brain activation. People are in an alpha state when they are inactive, resting, or sleeping. The theory is that a person in an alpha state is less likely to be processing information (recall correlates negatively with alpha levels) and that attention and processing require moving from this state. By measuring a subject's alpha level while viewing a commercial, researchers can assess the degree to which attention and processing are likely to occur.

- **Hemispheric lateralization** distinguishes between alpha activity in the left and right sides of the brain. It has been hypothesized that the right side of the brain processes visual stimuli and the left processes verbal stimuli. The right hemisphere is thought to respond more to emotional stimuli, while the left responds to logic. The right determines recognition, while the left is responsible for recall.[13] If these hypotheses are correct, advertisers could design ads to increase learning and memory by creating stimuli to appeal to each hemisphere. However, some researchers believe the brain does not function laterally, and an ad cannot be designed to appeal to one side or the other.

- **Indirect methods** use technologies originally designed for the medical field, such as positron emission tomography (PET) and functional magnetic resonance imaging (fMRI). Neuroscientists have teamed up with marketers to examine physiological reactions to ads and brands through brain scan imaging. PET tracks changes in metabolism while fMRI tracks blood flow, and both provide an indirect measure of brain activity. By monitoring the brain activity, scientists are learning how consumers make up their minds by measuring chemical activity and/or changes in the magnetic fields of the brain as well as how they react to commercials.

Objective:	Tracks viewers' eye movements to determine what viewers read or view in print ads and where their attention is focused in TV commercials or billboards.
Method:	Fibre optics, digital data processing, and advanced electronics are used to follow eye movements of viewers and/or readers as they process an ad.
Output:	Relationship among what readers see, recall, and comprehend. Scan paths on print ads, billboards, commercials, and print materials. (Can also be used to evaluate package designs.)

FIGURE 9–10

Eye movement research

FIGURE 9–11

The Starch Ad
Readership Report

Objective:	Determining recognition of print ads and comparing them to other ads of the same variety or in the same magazine.
Method:	Samples are drawn from 20 to 30 urban areas reflecting the geographic circulation of the magazine. Personal interviewers screen readers for qualifications and determine exposure and readership. Samples include a minimum of 200 males and females, as well as specific audiences where required. Participants are asked to go through the magazines, looking at the ads, and provide specific responses.
Output:	Starch Ad Readership Reports generate three recognition scores: • Noted score—the percentage of readers who remember seeing the ad. • Seen-associated score—the percentage of readers who recall seeing or reading any part of the ad identifying the product or brand. • Read-most score—the percentage of readers who report reading at least half of the copy portion of the ad.

similar ads elsewhere, expecting that such an ad would appear in the medium, or wanting to please the questioner. Interest in the product category also increases reporting of ad readership. Whether this false claiming is deliberate or not, it leads to an overreporting of effectiveness. On the flip side, factors such as interview fatigue may lead to an underreporting bias—that is, respondents not reporting an ad they did see.

Interviewer sensitivities. Any time research involves interviewers, there is a potential for bias. Respondents may want to impress the interviewer or fear looking unknowledgeable if they continually claim not to recognize an ad. There may also be variances associated with interviewer instructions, recordings, and so on, regardless of the amount of training and sophistication involved.

Reliability of recognition scores. Starch admits that the reliability and validity of its readership scores increase with the number of insertions tested, which essentially means that to test just one ad on a single exposure may not produce valid or reliable results.

In sum, despite critics, the Starch readership studies continue to dominate the posttesting of print ads. The value provided by norms and the fact that multiple exposures can improve reliability and validity may underlie the decisions to employ this methodology.

Recall Tests   There are several tests to measure recall of print ads. Perhaps the best known of these are the Ipsos-ASI Next*Print test and the Gallup & Robinson Magazine Impact Research Service (MIRS) (described in Figure 9-12). These **recall tests** are similar to those discussed in the section on pretesting broadcast ads in that they attempt to measure recall of specific ads.

In addition to having the same interviewer problems as recognition tests, recall tests have other disadvantages. The reader's degree of involvement with the product and/or the distinctiveness of the appeals and visuals may lead to higher-than-accurate recall scores, although in general the method may lead to lower levels of recall than actually exist (an error the advertiser would be happy with). Critics contend the test is not strong enough to reflect recall accurately, so many ads may score as less effective than they really are, and advertisers may abandon or modify them needlessly.

On the plus side, it is thought that recall tests can assess the ad's impact on memory. Proponents of recall tests say the major concern is not the results themselves but how they are interpreted. In one very interesting study of the effects of brand name suggestiveness on recall, Kevin Keller, Susan Heckler, and Michael Houston found that suggestive brand names (those that convey relevant attribute or benefit information about the product) facilitate the initial recall of the brand's benefits but

Objective:	Tracking recall of advertising (and client's ads) appearing in magazines to assess performance and effectiveness.
Method:	Test magazines are placed in participants' homes and respondents are asked to read the magazine that day. A telephone interview is conducted the second day to assess recall of ads, recall of copy points, and consumers' impressions of the ads. Sample size is 150 people.
Output:	Three measurement scores are provided: • Proven name registration—the percentage of respondents who can accurately recall the ad. • Idea communication—the number of sales points the respondents can recall. • Favourable buying attitude—the extent of favourable purchase reaction to the brand or corporation.

FIGURE 9-12

Gallup & Robinson
Magazine Impact
Research Service

inhibit recall of subsequently advertised claims. These results would seem to indicate that a suggestive brand name could facilitate initial positioning of the brand but make it more difficult to introduce new attributes at a later time.[14]

A very extensive longitudinal study was conducted by the Netherlands Institute of Public Opinion (NIPO) to assess the relationship between recall and recognition. The results indicated that the average correlation between recall and recognition in both newspapers and magazines was very high ($r = .96$ and $.95$, respectively). The study concluded that recall actually stems from recognition, in that 99 percent of 3,632 cases of recall also had recorded recognition. In addition, likable and interesting ads doubled the recall scores and increased the recall share of recognition. Creative advertising was much more effective for creating perceptions and recall than was the size of the ad.[15]

Posttests of Broadcast Commercials A variety of methods exist for posttesting broadcast commercials. The most common provide a combination of day-after recall tests, persuasion measures, and diagnostics. Test marketing and tracking studies, including single-source methods, are also employed.

Day-After Recall Tests The most popular method of posttesting employed in the broadcasting industry for decades was the *Burke Day-After Recall Test*. While a number of companies offered day-after recall methodologies, the "Burke test" for all intents and purposes became the generic name attached to these tests. While popular, day-after recall tests also had problems, including limited samples, high costs, and security issues (ads shown in test markets could be seen by competitors). In addition, the following disadvantages with recall tests were also suggested:

- DAR tests may favour unemotional appeals because respondents are asked to verbalize the message. Thinking messages may be easier to recall than emotional communications, so recall scores for emotional ads may be lower.[16] Other studies concluded that emotional ads may be processed differently from thinking ones and some ad agencies (e.g., Leo Burnett, BBDO) developed their own methods of determining emotional response to ads.[17]
- Program content may influence recall as the scores may vary depending upon the type of program or the particular episode. The result is potential inaccuracy in the recall score and in the norms used to establish comparisons.[18]
- A prerecruited sample may pay increased attention to the program and the ads contained therein because the respondents know they will be tested the next day. This effect would lead to a higher level of recall than really exists.

The major advantage of day-after recall tests is that they are field tests. The natural setting is supposed to provide a more realistic response profile. These tests are also popular because they provide norms that give advertisers a standard for comparing how well their ads are performing. In addition to recall, a number of different measures of the commercial's effectiveness are now offered, including persuasive measures and diagnostics. (The Burke test itself no longer exists.)

Comprehensive Measures As noted earlier in our discussion of pretesting broadcast commercials, a measure of a commercial's persuasive effectiveness is gathered by asking consumers to choose a brand that they would want to win in a drawing and then—after exposure to the ad—asking the question again. In theatre settings, this is accomplished by announcing a series of prize drawings, with viewers indicating which of the brands they would choose if they won. In field settings, it is accomplished by taking a brand preference measure when the video is delivered and then again the next day. Some of the services offer additional persuasion measures, including purchase-intent and frequency-of-purchase criteria.

Copy testing firms also provide diagnostic measures. These measures are designed to garner viewers' evaluations of the ads, as well as how clearly the creative idea is understood and how well the proposition is communicated. Rational and emotional reactions to the ads are also examined. While each of the measures just described provides specific input into the effectiveness of a commercial, many advertisers are interested in more than just one specific input. Thus, some companies provide comprehensive approaches in which each of the three measures just described (i.e., recall, persuasion, diagnostics) can be obtained through one testing program. Figure 9-13 describes one such comprehensive program, Ipsos-ASI's Next*TV test (Exhibit 9-2).

Test Marketing Many companies conduct tests designed to measure their advertising effects in specific test markets before releasing them nationally. The markets chosen are representative of the target market. For example, a company may test its ads in London, Ontario, Peterborough, Ontario, or Winnipeg, Manitoba, if the demographic and socioeconomic profiles of these cities match the product's market. A variety of factors may be tested, including reactions to the ads (for example, alternative copy points), the effects of various budget sizes, or special offers. The ads run in finished form in the media where they might normally appear, and effectiveness is measured after the ads run.

The advantage of test marketing of ads is realism. Regular viewing environments are used and the testing effects are minimized. A high degree of control can be attained if the test is designed successfully. For example, an extensive test market study was designed and conducted by Seagram and Time Inc. over three years to measure the effects of advertising frequency on consumers' buying habits. This

---

FIGURE 9-13

Ipsos-ASI's Next*TV

Objective:	To assist advertisers in copy testing of their commercials through multiple measures to determine (1) the potential of the commercial for impacting sales, (2) how the ad contributes to brand equity, (3) how well it is in line with existing advertising strategies and objectives, and (4) how to optimize effectiveness.
Method:	Consumers are recruited to evaluate a TV program, with ads embedded into the program as they would be on local prime-time television. Consumers view the program on a videotape in their homes to simulate actual field conditions. (The option to use local cable television programs with commercial inserts is also provided.)
Output:	Related recall (day-after recall) scores; persuasion scores, including brand preference shifts, purchase intent and frequency, brand equity differentiation, and relevance and communication; and reaction diagnostics to determine what viewers take away from the ad and how creative elements contribute to or distract from advertising effectiveness.

study demonstrated just how much could be learned from research conducted in a field setting but with some experimental controls. It also showed that proper research can provide strong insights into the impact of ad campaigns. (Many advertising researchers consider this study one of the most conclusive ever conducted in the attempt to demonstrate the effects of advertising on sales.)

The Seagram study also reveals some of the disadvantages associated with test market measures, not the least of which are cost and time. Few firms have the luxury to spend three years and hundreds of thousands of dollars on such a test. In addition, there is always the fear that competitors may discover and intervene in the research process. Test marketing can provide substantial insight into the effectiveness of advertising if care is taken to minimize the negative aspects of such tests.

Single-Source Tracking Studies More sophisticated approaches are **single-source tracking methods** that track the behaviours of consumers from the television set to the supermarket checkout counter. Participants in a designated area who have cable TV and agree to participate in the studies are given a card that identifies their household and gives the research company their demographics. The households are split into matched groups; one group receives an ad while the other does not, or alternate ads are sent to each. Their purchases are recorded from the bar codes of the products bought. Commercial exposures are then correlated with purchase behaviours. The single-source method can be used effectively to post-test ads, allowing for a variety of dependent measures and tracking the effects of increased ad budgets and different versions of ad copy—and even ad effects on sales.[19] After using scanner data to review the advertising/sales relationship for 78 brands, John Jones concluded that single-source data are beginning to fulfill their promise now that more measurements are available.[20]

A 10-year study conducted by Information Resources' BehaviorScan service demonstrated long-term effects of advertising on sales. The study examined copy, media schedules, ad budgets, and the impact of trade promotions on sales in 10 markets throughout the United States and concluded that advertising can produce sales growth as long as two years after a campaign ends.[21] (The study also concluded that results of copy recall and persuasion tests were unlikely to predict sales reliably.) A number of single-source methods have been used, among them BehaviorScan (Information Resources) and MarketSource. The ACNielsen company's Scantrack is another commonly employed single-source tracking system.

While single-source testing is a valuable tool, it still has some problems. One researcher says, "Scanner data focus on short-term sales effects, and as a result capture only 10 to 30 percent of what advertising does."[22] Others complain that the data are too complicated to deal with, as an overabundance of information is available. Still another disadvantage is the high cost of collecting single-source data. While the complexity of single-source data resulted in a slow adoption rate, this method of tracking advertising effectiveness became widely adopted in the 1990s.

Tracking Print/Broadcast Ads One of the more useful and adaptable forms of post-testing involves tracking the effects of the ad campaign by taking measurements at regular intervals. **Tracking studies** have been used to measure the effects of advertising on awareness, recall, interest, and attitudes toward the ad and/or brand as well as purchase intentions. (Ad tracking may be applied to both print and broadcast ads but is much more common with the latter.) Personal interviews, phone surveys, mall intercepts, and even mail surveys have been used. Sample sizes typically range

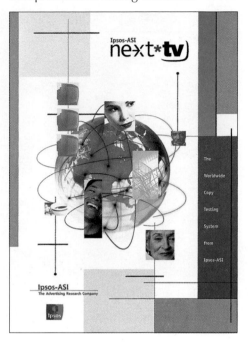

Exhibit 9-2 Ipsos-ASI offers a comprehensive testing measure.

267

Exhibit 9-3 Tracking studies provide useful measures.

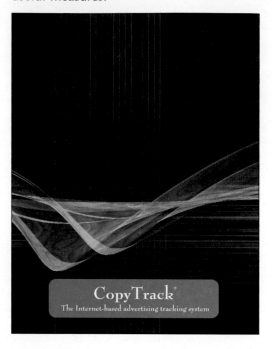

CopyTrack®
The Internet-based advertising tracking system

from 250 to 500 cases per period (usually quarterly or semi-annually). Tracking studies yield perhaps the most valuable information available to the marketing manager for assessing current programs and planning for the future. (See Exhibit 9-3.)

The major advantage of tracking studies is that they can be tailored to each specific campaign and/or situation. A standard set of questions can track effects of the campaign over time. The effects of various media can also be determined, although with much less effectiveness. Tracking studies have also been used to measure the differential impact of different budget sizes, the effects of flighting, brand or corporate image, and recall of specific copy points. Finally, when designed properly, as shown in Figure 9-14, tracking studies offer a high degree of reliability and validity.[23]

Some of the problems of recall and recognition measures are inherent in tracking studies, since many other factors may affect both brand and advertising recall. Despite these limitations, however, tracking studies are a very effective way to assess the effects of advertising campaigns.

In summary, you can see that each of the testing methods considered in this chapter has its strengths and its limitations. You may wonder: Can we actually test advertising effectiveness? What can be done to ensure a valid, reliable test? The next section of this chapter suggests some answers.

FIGURE 9–14

Factors that make or break tracking studies

1. Properly defined objectives
2. Alignment with sales objectives
3. Properly designed measures (e.g., adequate sample size, maximum control over interviewing process, adequate time between tracking periods)
4. Consistency through replication of the sampling plan
5. Random samples
6. Continuous interviewing (that is, not seasonal)
7. Evaluate measures related to behaviour (attitudes meet this criterion; recall of ads does not)
8. Critical evaluative questions asked early to eliminate bias
9. Measurement of competitors' performance
10. Skepticism about questions that ask where the advertising was seen or heard
11. Building of news value into the study
12. "Moving averages" used to spot long-term trends and avoid seasonality
13. Data reported in terms of relationships rather than as isolated facts
14. Integration of key marketplace events with tracking results (e.g., advertising expenditures, promotional activities associated with price changes, new brand introductions)

IMC PLANNING: PROGRAM FOR MEASURING EFFECTIVENESS

In this section, we offer some prescriptions for managers planning for evaluative research. In a significant industry move, 21 of the largest U.S. ad agencies endorsed a set of principles aimed at "improving the research used in preparing and testing ads, providing a better creative product for clients, and controlling the cost of TV commercials."[24] (We include it here due to the U.S. connection of many Canadian agencies.) This set of nine principles, called **PACT (Positioning Advertising Copy Testing)**, defines *copy testing* as research "which is undertaken when a decision is to be made about whether advertising should run in the marketplace. Whether this stage utilizes a single test or a combination of tests, its purpose is to aid in the judgment of specific advertising executions."[25] The nine principles of good copy testing are shown in Figure 9-15. Adherence to these principles may not make for perfect testing, but it goes a long way toward improving the state of the art and providing guidelines for effectiveness research.

CRITERIA FOR EFFECTIVE RESEARCH

When testing methods are compared to the criteria established by PACT, it is clear that some of the principles important to good copy testing can be accomplished readily. Principle 1 (providing measurements relative to the objectives sought) and principle 2 (determining a priori how the results will be used) are consistent with DAGMAR (i.e., Chapter 5) and are basic advertising management prescriptions along with principle 6 (providing equivalent test ads). Principles 3, 5, and 8 are largely in the control of the researcher. Principle 3 (providing multiple measurements) may require little more than budgeting to make sure more than one test is conducted. Likewise, principle 5 (exposing the test ad more than once) can be accomplished with a proper research design. Finally, principle 8 (sample definition) requires sound research methodology; any test should use the target audience to assess an ad's effectiveness. The most difficult factors to control are principles 4, 7, and 9.

The best starting point is principle 4, which states the research should be guided by a model of human response to communications that encompasses reception, comprehension, and behavioural response. It is the best starting point, in our opinion, because it is the principle least addressed by practising researchers. If you recall, Chapter 4 proposed a number of models that could fulfill this principle's requirements. Yet even though these models have existed for quite some time, few if any common research methods attempt to integrate them into their methodologies. Most current methods do little more than provide recall scores, despite the fact many researchers have shown that recall is a poor measure of effectiveness. Models that do claim to measure such factors as attitude change or brand preference change are often fraught with problems that severely limit their reliability. An effective measure must include some relationship to the communications process.

It might seem at first glance that principle 7 (providing a nonbiasing exposure) would be easy to accomplish. But lab measures, while offering control, are artificial and vulnerable to testing effects. And field measures, while more realistic, often

1. Provide measurements that are relevant to the objectives of the advertising.
2. Require agreement about how the results will be used in advance of each specific test.
3. Provide multiple measures (single measures are not adequate to assess ad performance).
4. Be based on a model of human response to communications—the reception of a stimulus, the comprehension of the stimulus, and the response to the stimulus.
5. Allow for whether the advertising stimulus should be exposed more than once.
6. Require that the more finished a piece of copy is, the more soundly it can be evaluated and require, as a minimum, that alternative executions be tested in the same degree of finish.
7. Provide controls to avoid the biasing effects of the exposure context.
8. Take into account basic considerations of sample definition.
9. Demonstrate reliability and validity.

FIGURE   9–15

Positioning Advertising Copy Testing (PACT)

lose control. The Seagram and Time study may have the best of both worlds, but it is too large a task for most firms to undertake. Some of the improvements associated with the single-source systems help to solve this problem. In addition, properly designed ad tracking studies provide truer measures of the impact of the communication. As technology develops and more attention is paid to this principle, we expect to see improvements in methodologies soon.

Last but not least is principle 9, the concern for reliability and validity. Most of the measures discussed are lacking in at least one of these criteria, yet these are two of the most critical distinctions between good and bad research. If a study is properly designed, and by that we mean it addresses principles 1 through 8, it should be both reliable and valid.

GUIDELINES FOR EFFECTIVE TESTING

Good tests of advertising effectiveness must address the nine principles established by PACT. One of the easiest ways to accomplish this is by following the decision sequence model in formulating promotional plans.

- *Use a consumer response model.* Early in this text we reviewed hierarchy of effects models and cognitive response models, which provide an understanding of the effects of communications and lend themselves to achieving communications goals. We also presented Rossiter and Percy's model for stating communication objectives which could also be a basis for measurement.
- *Establish communications objectives.* It is nearly impossible to show the direct impact of advertising on sales. The marketing objectives established for the promotional program are not good measures of communication effectiveness. On the other hand, attainment of communications objectives can be measured and leads to the accomplishment of marketing objectives.
- *Use both pretests and posttests.* From a cost standpoint—both actual cost outlays and opportunity costs—pretesting makes sense. It may mean the difference between success or failure of the campaign or the product. But it should work in conjunction with posttests, which avoid the limitations of pretests, use much larger samples, and take place in more natural settings. Posttesting may be required to determine the true effectiveness of the ad or campaign.

- *Use multiple measures.* Many attempts to measure the effectiveness of advertising focus on one major dependent variable—perhaps sales, recall, or recognition. As noted earlier in this chapter, advertising may have a variety of effects on the consumer, some of which can be measured through traditional methods, others that require updated thinking (recall the discussion on physiological responses). For a true assessment of advertising effectiveness, a number of measures may be required.
- *Understand and implement proper research.* It is critical to understand research methodology. What constitutes a good design? Is it valid and reliable? Does it measure what we need it to? There is no shortcut to this criterion, and there is no way to avoid it if you truly want to measure the effects of advertising.

A major study sponsored by the Advertising Research Foundation (ARF), involving interviews with 12,000 to 15,000 people, addressed some of these issues.[26] While we do not have the space to analyze this study here, note that the research was designed to evaluate measures of copy tests, compare copy testing procedures, and examine some of the PACT principles. Information on this study has been published in a number of academic and trade journals and by the ARF.

CHAPTER OBJECTIVES AND SUMMARY

1 To understand reasons for measuring promotional program effectiveness.

This chapter introduced issues and decisions concerning the measurement of advertising and promotion effectiveness. All marketing managers want to know how well their promotional programs are working. This information is critical for planning the next period, since program adjustments and/or maintenance are based on evaluation of current strategies.

While the need for understanding how programs are working appears critical, this chapter summarized the debate regarding whether measurement is in fact needed. We conclude that research measuring the effectiveness of advertising is important to the promotional program and should be an integral part of the planning process.

2 To know the various measures used in assessing promotional program effectiveness.

We summarized many types of decisions for advertising research. Managers must consider what parts of the promotional message need to be tested. We identified both creative strategy and creative tactic decisions as being important for testing. We also suggested that most other IMC tools had a key message that required effectiveness testing and that these advertising research methods were applied accordingly. Moreover,

research could occur prior to a campaign (i.e., pretesting) or after the campaign (i.e., posttesting), which represents another key decision. Whether a lab or field test is required also should be determined. Lab tests offer greater control with the cost of a lack of realistic setting while features of field tests are reversed. While there are many choices for research, a comprehensive, yet expensive, evaluation program would test all message variables, before and after a campaign, with both lab and field methods.

3 To evaluate alternative methods for measuring promotional program effectiveness.

The chapter described many research methods that cover the stages of developing a promotional program. Many of the tests originated with one firm and were later adapted by other firms. Many companies have developed their own testing systems in conjunction with their advertising or communication agency.

Concept tests, focus groups, and mall intercepts are used to test initial ideas for creative strategies and promotional messages. Comprehension and reaction tests along with consumer juries appeared useful to testing rough or preliminary examples of print ads and television storyboards.

Finished ads are also tested prior to launching the campaign. Investment in these tests reassures managers so that costly media buys can be avoided. We reviewed portfolio tests,

readability tests, and dummy advertising vehicles for evaluating completed print ads. Finished broadcast ads can be examined with theatre tests, on-air tests, and physiological measures.

Evaluations after the ads have been launched, known as posttests, offer greater confirmation of the promotion effectiveness. Print ad posttests include inquiry tests, recognition tests, and recall tests. Broadcast posttests include day-after recall tests, comprehensive measures, test marketing, single-source tracking studies, and tracking studies. Single-source research data offer strong potential for improving the effectiveness of ad measures since commercial exposures and reactions may be correlated to actual purchase behaviours.

4 To understand the requirements of proper effectiveness research.

Finally, we reviewed the criteria (defined by PACT) for sound research and suggested some ways to accomplish effective studies. It is important to recognize that different measures of effectiveness may lead to different results. Depending on the criteria used, one measure may show that an ad or promotion is effective while another states that it is not. This is why clearly defined objectives, evaluations occurring both before and after the campaigns are implemented, and the use of multiple measures are critical to determining the true effects of an IMC program.

KEY TERMS

alpha activity, *261*

comprehension and
   reaction tests, *256*

concept testing, *253*

consumer juries, *256*

day-after recall scores, *260*

electrodermal response, *260*

electroencephalographic
   (EEG) measures, *261*

eye tracking, *261*

field tests, *253*

Flesch formula, *258*

halo effect, *257*

hemispheric
   lateralization, *261*

indirect methods, *261*

inquiry tests, *263*

laboratory tests, *252*

on-air test, *260*

PACT (Positioning
   Advertising Copy
   Testing), *269*

portfolio tests, *257*

posttests, *251*

pretests, *251*

pupillometrics, *260*

recall tests, *264*

recognition method, *263*

rough tests, *254*

single-source tracking
   methods, *267*

split-run tests, *263*

testing bias, *252*

theatre testing, *258*

tracking studies, *267*

DISCUSSION QUESTIONS

1. Discuss some of the reasons why some companies decide not to measure the effectiveness of their promotional programs. Explain why this may or may not be a good strategy.

2. Discuss the differences between pretesting and posttesting. Give examples of each.

3. What is the difference between a lab test and a field test? When should each be employed?

4. Give examples of the various types of rough testing methodologies. Describe why a company might wish to test at this phase of the process. When might it wish to test only completed ads?

5. The bottom line for advertisers is to invoke some behaviour—for example, sales. Explain why it may be difficult to use sales to measure advertising effectiveness.

6. Why might a firm use theatre testing, on-air tests, and physiological measures to pretest its finished broadcast ads?

7. What limitations exist if one uses inquiry tests, recall tests, and recognition tests when performing market testing of ads?

8. Why are the PACT criteria important for testing effectiveness?

10 MEDIA PLANNING AND BUDGETING FOR IMC

■ CHAPTER OBJECTIVES

1 To know how a media plan is developed.

2 To know the process of deciding on and implementing media strategies and tactics.

3 To understand the theoretical and managerial approaches for media budget setting.

Mazda Innovates with Multiple Media

To launch the 2010 Mazda3, the brand organized an alternative reality game (ARG) with the assistance of its agency, Doner, the largest independent agency in the world. Called "33 Keys," the game featured "Time travel, secret police, underground rebellions and an evil empire hell-bent on enslaving mankind to a lifetime of conformity." Players engaged in real-life challenges much like the ones they watched on television reality shows, with the goal of finding the 33 keys hidden in the province of Quebec—one of which opened the custom-designed Essence. With 43 percent of sales occurring in Quebec, this market looked ideal for developing a unique opportunity to interact with customers during the four-week activity. According to the account director at Doner, "The consumer that buys the Mazda3 is into gaming, they're into high technology, they're into entertainment and they really like to be entertained with all types of advertising."

Players kept track of clues and challenges using the website (reperio.ca) and social media. TV and out-of-home media and event stunts provided storyline experiences and clues, and directed players to online media. Astral Media was the media partner, chosen for the fit among its media vehicles, the ARG, and Mazda customers. Popular Quebec-based media personalities including Marie-Claude Perron of MusiquePlus and Dominic Arpin of Energie actively participated in the storyline. In fact, Perron started the ARG by complaining on-air about graffiti on the billboard for her new (but fictitious) fashion show. Some watching her show picked up on the idea and discovered a countdown clock at the website, or found a mysterious blogger talking about events from the year 2033. According to Mazda's marketing director, "ARG offers a unique opportunity to engage consumers in something that's fun and brand consistent."

Shortly thereafter, a message from Xira initiated the game on all eight Astral TV stations with a roadblock scheduled at exactly 9:58 p.m. She gave a VIN that players entered online to receive clues in order to find the first key. The roadblock carried on every night during the first week. "There are so many different ways to communicate with a customer in a four or five year purchase cycle for a vehicle, that there's no one thing that influences that decision. So we have to be in different places and speak to customers at different times," commented the marketing director. Clues coming in from multiple sources kept the idea alive even within the ARG.

Sources: Carey Toane, "Audiences: Everybody's Getting in on the Game," *Strategy*, September 2009, p. 43; Kristin Laird, "Mazda Plays with 33 Keys," *Marketing Magazine*, April 22, 2009; "Zoom-Zoom Evolved: Mazda Takes Consumers on Futuristic Thrill Ride" newswire.ca, April 21, 2009.

Question:

1. What are the key advantages of Mazda's media plan?

As the opening vignette suggests, a marketer has many media opportunities available that require in-depth knowledge of all the alternatives. Media planners must now consider new options as well as recognize the changes that are occurring in traditional sources. Planning when, where, and how the message will be delivered is a complex and involved process resulting in a media plan. The purpose of the media plan is to identify and justify the decisions that will deliver the message to the target audience cost efficiently and will communicate the product, brand, and/ or service message effectively.

This chapter illustrates the media planning process, discusses the development of decisions for media strategy and tactics, and presents issues and decisions related to setting and allocating an IMC budget. We include budget setting for IMC in this chapter because of this inherent trade-off between media decisions and financial resources. We do not exclusively discuss budget issues for other IMC tools for two reasons. First, the remaining IMC tools are often dependent on media expenditures. For example, advertisers use media to direct visitors to their websites or other digital media alternatives, and public relations campaigns use media to encourage visits to events or participate in brand activities. Second, the planning process for all marketing communication tools follows or is consistent with established planning processes of advertising. Thus, the budgeting concepts with reference to advertising described here are directly used for or transferred to other IMC tools.

MEDIA PLANNING

In this section we provide a general overview of media planning to briefly highlight the context in which messages are delivered, describe the content of a media plan to understand how its content is consistent with other elements of IMC planning, and indicate the unique challenges with media planning not found in other areas of IMC planning.

OVERVIEW

Media planning is the series of decisions involved in delivering the promotional message to prospective purchasers and/or users of the product or brand. Media planning is a process whereby the decisions may be altered or abandoned as the plan develops. One primary decision is the type of media selected. Options include mass media such as television, newspapers, radio, and magazines, as well as out-of-the-home media such as outdoor advertising and transit advertising (Figure 10-1). Each medium has its own particular strengths and limitations that must be considered in light of the communication problem or opportunity with which the marketer is faced. This makes the media selection and all other media decisions very difficult. For example, the media planning process becomes even more complicated when the manager has to choose among alternatives within the same medium, like different television stations or shows and magazine titles.

A number of decisions must be made throughout the media planning process. The promotional planning model in Chapter 1 identified decisions such as selecting target audiences, establishing objectives, and formulating strategies for attaining them. The development of the media plan and strategies follows a similar path, except that the focus is to determine the best way to deliver the message. Thus, the media plan is generally comprised of a short section containing **media objectives**, an explanation of the **media strategy** decisions, and fine-tuning details that are known as media execution or **media tactics**. The activities involved in developing the media plan and the purposes of each are presented in Figure 10-2. Although this simplified template illustrates broadcast and print media, the general process is similar for all media and IMC tools.

FIGURE   10–1   Canadian market data: Net advertising revenues

Medium		2002	2003	2004	2005	2006	2007	2008
Television	Total	2,593	2,827	2,964	3,014	3,241	3,299	3,391
	National Spot	1,201	1,312	1,310	1,302	1,309	1,338	1,303
	Local Spot	386	389	383	385	393	407	400
	Network	480	503	544	539	633	581	641
	Specialty	509	607	708	769	882	948	1,025
	Infomercial	18	17	18	19	24	24	22
	Change	+1.6%	+9.0%	+4.8%	+1.7%	+7.5%	+1.8%	+2.8%
Daily Newspaper	Total	2,510	2,529	2,611	2,659	2,635	2,572	2,503
	National	576	580	599	610	605	590	575
	Local	1,108	1,116	1,152	1,174	1,163	1,135	1,105
	Classified	826	832	859	875	867	846	824
	Change	+0.4%	+0.7%	+3.2%	+1.9%	−0.9%	−2.4%	−2.7%
Radio	Total	1,080	1,171	1,209	1,313	1,388	1,467	1,547
	National	235	271	271	323	351	379	406
	Local	845	900	938	991	1,037	1,088	1,141
	Change	+3.0%	+8.4%	+3.3%	+8.6%	+5.7%	+5.7%	+5.5%
Internet	Total	176	237	364	562	900	1,241	1,602
	Search	—	—	—	—	343	478	602
	Display	—	—	—	—	314	432	490
	Classifieds/Directories	—	—	—	—	223	305	480
	Email	—	—	—	—	20	17	18
	Video	—	—	—	—	na	9	12
	Change	+81.4%	+34.7%	+53.6%	+54.4%	+60.1%	+37.9%	+29.1%
General Magazines	Total	558	610	647	665	682	718	692
	Change	+3.1%	+9.3%	+6.1%	+2.8%	+2.6%	+5.3%	−3.7%
Out-of-Home	Total	273	284	303	344	370	422	463
	Change	−2.8%	+4.2%	+6.4%	+13.6%	+7.7%	+14.0%	+9.7%
Catalogue/Direct Mail	Total	1,285	1,383	1,490	1,532	1,608	1,639	1,662
	Change	+1.7%	+7.6%	+7.7%	+2.8%	+5.0%	+1.9%	+1.4%
Yellow Pages	Total	1,060	1,121	1,168	1,208	1,256	1,281	1,299
	Change	+1.3%	+5.8%	+4.2%	+3.4%	+4.0%	+1.9%	+1.4%
Miscellaneous	Total	1,192	1,261	1,314	1,359	1,413	1,441	1,461
	Change	+1.3%	+5.8%	+4.2%	+3.4%	+4.0%	+1.9%	+1.4%
Total Advertising	Total	10,728	11,424	12,070	12,656	13,494	14,079	14,620
	National	5,719	6,238	6,705	7,122	7,838	8,352	8,859
	Local	5,008	5,186	5,365	5,534	5,656	5,727	5,761
	Change	+2.1%	+6.5%	+5.7%	+4.9%	+6.6%	+4.3%	+3.8%
Total Television		2,593	2,827	2,964	3,014	3,241	3,299	3,391
Total Advertising		10,728	11,424	12,070	12,656	13,494	14,079	14,620
TV Share of Total Advertising (%)		24.2%	24.7%	24.6%	23.8%	24.0%	23.4%	23.2%
Population (Millions)		31.4	31.7	32.0	32.3	32.6	32.9	33.3
Per Capita Television Advertising		83	89	93	93	99	100	102
Per Capita Total Advertising		342	361	377	392	413	428	439

"Sources: Television: CRTC; Daily Newspaper: CNA for Total, estimates for breakdown; Radio: CRTC; General Magazine: Magazines Canada; Outdoor: estimate of net revenue based on NMR; Direct Mail: Canada Post; Internet: IAB; Yellow Pages: estimates based on last report by TeleDirect (1999); Miscellaneous: includes estimates for Community Newspaper, Trade & Other Print; Population: Statistics Canada Mid-Year Population by Year.

Note: Some figures may differ from previous charts due to updating. From 1991 forward, the source for all broadcast figures has been changed from Statistics Canada to CRTC. TVB has used internal estimates to correctly reflect the breakdown of Network and Spot revenue.

Figures in red represent Industry estimates. Broadcast revenue is based on the broadcast calendar ie. in each year indicated, the figures represent the revenue from Sep.01 of the previous year to Aug.31 of the indicated year. All other figures are based on revenue for the indicated calendar year."

Source: Media Digest 09/10, Canadian Market Data, "Net Advertising Volume by Media," p. 13.

277

FIGURE 10–2   Activities involved in developing the media plan

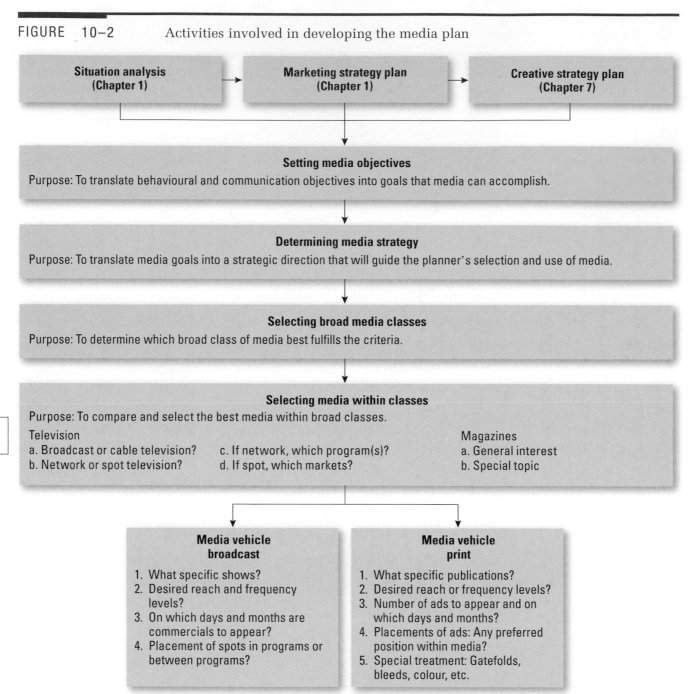

Media planning certainly occurs for advertising, but it is also necessary as part of the decision for other IMC tools as suggested above. Sales promotions often require media expenditure to communicate the offers available or for distribution. Public relations activities use media to communicate corporate activities with respect to sponsorship or community events. A number of media are available for direct marketing, and many aspects of media planning are applicable. In general, the guiding principles for media strategy and media tactics are applicable for the use of media to implement other IMC activities beyond advertising.

Finally, media planning experiences the challenge of developing a plan with limited financial resources as plans have a prescribed budget that the media planner must respect. All decisions within media planning for advertising face trade-offs to maximize or optimize communication and behavioural objectives. Extending this beyond advertising and the promotional planner is faced with the task of allocating expenditures across all IMC tools to achieve broader target audience objectives. In fact, the pressure of marketing managers to spend wisely in the promotional domain is more critical with recent pressures holding the marketing task more financially accountable as firms now calculate their return on marketing investment (ROIM).[1]

MEDIA PLAN

The media plan documents the decisions for finding the best way to get the advertiser's message to the market. In a basic sense, the goal of the media plan is to find the combination of media that enables the marketer to communicate the message in the most effective manner to the largest number of the target audience at the lowest cost. In this section, we review the media plan content regarding media objectives, media strategy, and media tactics.

Media Objectives   Just as the situation analysis leads to establishment of marketing and communication objectives, it should also lead to specific media objectives. The media objectives are not ends in themselves. Rather, they are derived from and are designed to lead to the attainment of communication and behavioural objectives, and contribute to achieving marketing objectives. Media objectives are the goals for the media program and should be limited to those that can be accomplished through media strategies. We now present examples of media objectives that are derived from three communication and two behavioural objectives.

Category Need

- Select media to sufficiently demonstrate how the target audience requires the product category.
- Provide sufficient number of exposures to ensure 80 percent of target audience understands the need for the product category.

Brand Awareness

- Select media to provide coverage of 80 percent of the target audience over a six-month period.
- Provide sufficient number of exposures to ensure 60 percent target audience brand recognition.
- Concentrate advertising during the target audience's peak purchasing time.

Brand Attitude

- Select media to ensure that 40 percent of the target audience have favourable beliefs regarding the brand's benefits and have positive emotions associated with the brand.
- Schedule creative executions over six months to heighten emotions associated with the brand and minimize message fatigue.

Brand Trial

- Select media to allow immediate purchase of brand.
- Schedule sufficient number of opportunities for target audience brand engagement.

Brand Repeat Purchase

- Select media to remind target audience of brand purchase.
- Provide sufficient advertising throughout the year to minimize target audience switching.

The content and exact number of media objectives is at the promotional planner's discretion. These examples merely illustrate the degree to which the link between objectives is not an easy step. The media objectives give direction for the media strategy and tactics decisions. Upon implementation, marketers need to know whether or not they were successful. Measures of effectiveness must consider two factors: (1) How well did these strategies achieve the media objectives? (2) How well did this media plan contribute to attaining the overall marketing and communications objectives? If the strategies were successful, they should be used in future plans. If not, their flaws should be analyzed.

Media Strategy   As Figure 10-2 indicates, the primary media strategy decision concerns the use of media, moving from a broad perspective to a more specific one. The **medium** is the general category of available delivery systems, which includes broadcast media (like TV and radio), print media (like newspapers and magazines), direct marketing, out-of-home advertising, and other support media. After or during this evaluation, the media planner will consider the relative strengths and limitations of broad **media class** options. IMC Perspective 10-1 shows how the advertising industry recognizes good media selection.

In making the media strategy decisions, a media planner will consider the strategic implications of three concepts. **Reach** is a measure of the number of different audience members exposed at least once to a media vehicle in a given period of time. **Coverage** refers to the potential audience that might receive the message through a vehicle. Coverage relates to potential audience; reach refers to the actual audience delivered. (The importance of this distinction will become clearer later in this chapter.) Finally, **frequency** refers to the number of times the receiver is exposed to the media vehicle in a specified period.

Media Tactics   After the general strategic direction of the media plan has been established, the media planner looks to more specific media decisions like the media vehicle. The **media vehicle** is the specific carrier within a media class. For example, *Maclean's* is a print vehicle; *Hockey Night in Canada* is a television vehicle. As described in later chapters, each vehicle has its own characteristics as well as its own relative strengths and limitations. Specific decisions must be made as to the value of each in delivering the message.

While making the media vehicle decision, the media planner evaluates the options carefully to maximize coverage, reach, and frequency, and minimize costs. For example, according to Figure 10-2, once print has been established the media planner has to decide which specific magazine(s) to select. In addition, certain placement factors need to be carefully evaluated. The tactical decisions include relative cost estimates that may lead to refinements in the allocation of the media dollars. Finally, the complete plan is summarized in a blocking chart. The chart may indicate gaps in media coverage or some other concern that would lead the media planner to perform additional evaluation prior to completing the media plan.

MEDIA PLANNING CHALLENGES

Since media planning is a series of decisions, a number of challenges contribute to the difficulty of establishing the plan and reduce its effectiveness. These problems include insufficient information, inconsistent terminologies, need for flexibility, role of media planner, and difficulty measuring effectiveness.

Insufficient Information   While a great deal of information exists about markets and the media, media planners often require more than is available. Some data are just not measured, either because they cannot be or because measuring them would be too expensive. The timing of measurements is also a problem; some

Strategy's B!G Awards recognizes advertisers with budgets over $20 million that represent at least $2 million for the agency. A recent year saw Hellmann's mayonnaise and Ogilvy receive bronze; Nissan and Capital C pick up silver for the Cube launch; and gold go to Lay's potato chips and its agency Juniper Park for the "Happiness Is Simple" campaign. We highlight the gold and bronze winners here; check out IMC Perspective 6-2 to read about the silver winner.

A Canadian agency based in Toronto rejuvenated the image of Lay's potato chips south of the border. With a focus on the ingredients of potatoes, all-natural cooking oil, and a dash of salt, the campaign reminded U.S. consumers that Lay's sourced the potatoes from local farms. In fact, about 80 farms in 27 states grow the spuds for the iconic American brand. To communicate these key facts, customized point-of-sale messages emphasized the state connection. For example, in Tennessee the message highlighted that the potatoes grew in that state.

Overall, Juniper Park produced 38 different versions of the message in more than 300 items, ranging from free-standing displays to cart-talkers to shelf blades for the Lay's sales force to set up or distribute in retail settings. To support the in-store signage, a TV commercial showed citizens arriving at a local farm and then waiting for the potatoes to explode out of the ground. After spuds burst forth like fireworks, everyone caught the falling chips from the sky with their bowls. The result proved tasty, as Lay's received the greatest acceptance in in-store signage from retailers ever, obtained extensive media exposure through journalists, and obtained a significant lift in sales.

Hellmann's Real Mayonnaise challenged its agency, Ogilvy, to encourage consumers to consider eating a greater proportion of their diet from real food. Since the product contains all-natural ingredients—vinegar, eggs, and canola oil—and features the word "real" as part of its name, the task fit the brand perfectly. But given the perception that mayonnaise is unhealthy, and price concerns with inflation of ingredients, the agency looked for a completely different approach. Hitting on the fact that a large percentage of Canadian food is not locally sourced, a three-minute ad entitled "Family Dinner" resonated emotionally with audiences who watched it at the website (eatrealeatlocal.ca) via YouTube. The website also provided links for locally grown food and offered information for buying Canadian food. Prominent among these tools were social media applications to encourage greater involvement through consumer pledges that facilitated donations to the Canadian food chain.

Other media jumped into the opportunity: CanWest produced editorial content on the subject, and Transcontinental committed itself extensively. For example, *Canadian Living* featured a wrap and editorial content, TV and online ads directed website visits, and sponsorship messages contributed to the overall exposure. Results appeared substantial, with the ad obtaining 50,000 hits in the first 10 days, with 105,000 pledges and 100,000 ad views in two months.

Sources: Carey Toane, "B!G Awards 2009," *Strategy,* November 2009, p. 17; Carey Toane, "Juniper Park Plants Lay's in Familiar Ground," *Strategy,* November 2009, p. 18; Carey Toane, "Nissan and Capital G Go Media Free," *Strategy,* November 2009, p. 19; Carey Toane, "Hellmann's and Ogilvy Get Real," *Strategy,* November 2009, p. 20.

Question

1. How are the winners considered innovative?

audience measures are taken only at specific times of the year. This information is then generalized to succeeding months, so future planning decisions must be made on past data that may not reflect current behaviours. Think about planning for TV advertising for the fall season. There are no data on the audiences of new shows, and audience information taken on existing programs may not indicate how these programs will do in the fall as most shows eventually lose their audience. The lack of information is even more of a problem for small advertisers, who may not be able to afford to purchase the information they require and rely on limited or out-of-date data.

Compared to media planners in the United States, Canadian media planners face additional pressures of insufficient information. The size of the American population permits extensive economies of scale, so it is not unexpected that larger U.S.-based media-buying organizations would have valuable resources. Combined with similar media consumption (e.g., popular television shows) between Americans and English-speaking Canadians, there is a movement to coordinate media purchasing across North America. The end result may be improved efficiency and effectiveness of the media purchase with the sharing of information.[2]

Inconsistent Terminologies   Problems arise because the cost bases used by different media often vary and the standards of measurement used to establish these costs are not always consistent. For example, print media may present cost efficiency data in terms of the cost to reach a thousand people (cost per thousand, or CPM), while broadcast and outdoor media use the cost per ratings point (CPRP). Audience information that is used as a basis for these costs has also been collected by different methods. Finally, terms that actually mean something different (such as *reach* and *coverage*) may be used synonymously, adding to the confusion.

Need for Flexibility   Most media plans are written annually so that all participants are well informed and results can be measured against objectives. However, advertisers find it necessary to alter their objectives and strategies due to the marketing environment. Thus, media planners juggle between requiring a document for action during the year with the need for flexibility. Here are a few examples of how the environment can be altered necessitating a change in the media plan.

- *Market opportunities.* Sometimes a market opportunity arises that the advertiser wishes to take advantage of. For example, a special television show may prompt an advertiser to shift its expenditures from another medium.
- *Market threats.* External factors may pose a threat to the firm, and a change in media strategy is dictated. For example, a competitor may alter its media strategy to gain an edge. Failure to respond to this challenge could create problems for the firm.
- *Availability of media.* Sometimes a desired medium (or vehicle) is not available to the marketer. Perhaps the medium does not reach a particular target audience or has no time or space available. There are still some geographic areas that certain media do not reach. Alternative vehicles or media must then be considered.
- *Changes in media vehicles.* A change in a particular media vehicle may require a change in the media strategy. A drop in ratings or a change in editorial format may lead the advertiser to use different programs or print alternatives.

Role of Media Planners   Media planners often face a number of expectations from other organizational players. Procurement specialists often put extensive pressure on the media decisions in an effort to save money. Clients request media plans prior to contracting services. Decision makers of all the main IMC tools often look to media planners as the implementer instead of being a key decision-making participant. There also is never-ending debate as to whether media planning buying should be part of an advertising agency or an independent agency.[3]

Difficulty Measuring Effectiveness   Because it is so hard to measure the effectiveness of advertising and promotions in general, it is also difficult to determine the relative effectiveness of various media or media vehicles. While progress is being made in this regard (particularly in the area of direct-response advertising), the media planner must usually guess at the impact of these alternatives.

While these problems complicate the media planning process, they do not render it an entirely subjective exercise. Media planners try to ensure that all media decisions are quantitatively determined, but sometimes managers rely on their experience and judgment when faced with these concerns. The next section of this chapter explores in more detail how media strategies are developed and ways to increase their effectiveness.

MEDIA STRATEGY DECISIONS

Having determined what is to be accomplished, media planners consider how to achieve the media objectives. They develop and implement media strategies that consist of five main topics for decision:

- media mix
- target audience coverage
- geographic coverage
- scheduling
- reach vs. frequency

THE MEDIA MIX

A wide variety of media are available to advertisers. While it is possible that only one might be employed, it is much more likely that a number of alternatives will be used. The behavioural and communication objectives, the characteristics of the product or service, the size of the budget, the target audience, and individual preferences are primary factors that determine the combination of media used. While an evaluation of each media occurs within the perspective of the communication situation a media planner faces, each medium has certain degrees of use with Canadians, as shown in Figure 10-3.

The context of the medium in which the ad is placed may also affect viewers' perceptions, and the creative strategy may require certain media. Therefore, within the media mix a single medium becomes the primary medium where a majority of the budget is spent or the primary effects occur. Because TV provides both sight and sound, it may be more effective in generating emotions than other media. The campaign to attract tourists to Newfoundland and Labrador used TV extensively to convey the experience of actually being in the province while viewing the ad. According to the agency, "Most tourism advertising around the world is an inventory of products, whereas our deep feeling is that the advertising should express and evoke the feeling of the place."[4] Magazines may create different perceptions from newspapers, so we regularly see some products in one form of print versus another.

It is possible to increase the success of a product significantly through a strong creative campaign. In some situations, the media strategy to be pursued may be the driving force behind the creative strategy, as the media and creative departments work closely together to achieve the greatest impact with the audience of the specific media. For example, in the case of the "Must drink more milk" campaign, six original ads ran on TV but eight cruder and cooler ads with animation ran on YouTube.[5]

Time Spent Weekly Per Capita Hours	Total Canada	Quebec (French)
Television	24.3	24.5
Radio	18.5	19.0
Internet	16.7	12.6
Daily Newspaper	2.7	2.9
Local Newspaper	0.4	0.4
Source: BBM Analytics RTS Fall 2009		

FIGURE 10-3

Where is the time spent? Adults 18+

By employing a media mix advertisers can add more versatility to their media strategies, since each medium contributes its own distinct advantages. By combining media, marketers can increase coverage, reach, and frequency levels while improving the likelihood of achieving overall communications and marketing goals. Chapters 11, 12, and 13 summarize the characteristics of each medium that make it better or worse for attaining specific communication objectives. We have organized these as media and media-usage characteristics.

Media Characteristics

- target audience selectivity
- target audience coverage
- geographic coverage
- scheduling flexibility
- reach
- frequency
- cost efficiency
- absolute cost for placement and production

Media-Usage Characteristics

- control for selective exposure
- attention
- creativity for cognitive responses
- creativity for emotional responses
- amount of processing time
- involvement
- clutter
- media image

Figure 10-4 provides a summary of the strengths and limitations of the media reviewed in the next three chapters. We continue with these characteristics for direct marketing and Internet marketing in their respective chapters. With so many competing variables, it becomes clear why media planners spend considerable efforts getting the media mix decision right. Finally, keep in mind that these are general characteristics that give guidance to the media mix decision. Citing these to make a media mix decision is not sufficient. Each strength and limitation needs to be related to the communication situation a specific brand faces and how the media characteristics will help the brand reach its relevant objectives.

284

FIGURE 10-4

Strengths and limitations of media characteristics

	Strengths	Limitations
Television	Target audience coverage	Selective exposure
	Geographic coverage	Target audience selectivity
	Creativity for emotional responses	Absolute cost
	Creativity for cognitive responses	Amount of processing time
	Reach	Involvement
	Frequency	Clutter
	Scheduling flexibility	Media image
	Cost efficiency	
	Attention	
	Media image	
Radio	Cost efficiency	Amount of processing time
	Absolute cost	Selective exposure
	Target audience selectivity	Attention
	Geographic coverage	Clutter
	Scheduling flexibility	Creativity for emotional responses without visual
	Creativity for cognitive responses	Involvement
	Reach	Target audience coverage
	Frequency	
	Media image	

	Strengths	**Limitations**
Magazines	Target audience selectivity	Target audience coverage
	Geographic coverage	Reach
	Selective exposure	Frequency
	Attention	Scheduling flexibility
	Involvement	Cost efficiency
	Amount of processing time	Absolute cost
	Creativity for cognitive responses	Clutter
	Creativity for emotional responses	
	Media image	
Newspapers	Scheduling flexibility	Target audience selectivity
	Reach	Clutter
	Frequency	Selective exposure
	Geographic coverage	Attention
	Cost efficiency	Creativity for emotional responses
	Absolute cost	
	Target audience coverage	
	Media image	
	Involvement	
	Processing time	
	Creativity for cognitive responses	
Outdoor	Frequency	Amount of processing time
	Attention	Media image
	Geographic coverage	Target audience selectivity
	Reach	Target audience coverage
	Cost efficiency	Absolute cost
	Selective exposure	Clutter
	Creativity for emotional responses	Low involvement
	Scheduling flexibility	Creativity for cognitive responses
Transit	Geographic coverage	Target audience coverage
	Reach	Target audience selectivity
	Frequency	Creativity for cognitive responses
	Amount of processing time	Creativity for emotional responses
	Selective exposure	Involvement
	Scheduling flexibility	Media image
	Cost efficiency	Clutter
	Absolute cost	Attention

FIGURE 10–4

(continued)

285

TARGET AUDIENCE COVERAGE

The media planner determines which target audiences should receive the most media emphasis. Developing media strategies involves matching the most appropriate media to this audience by asking, "Through which media and media vehicles can I best get my message to prospective buyers?" The issue here is to get coverage of the audience, as shown in Figure 10-5. The optimal goal is full audience coverage, shown in the second pie chart. Business marketing organizations often get

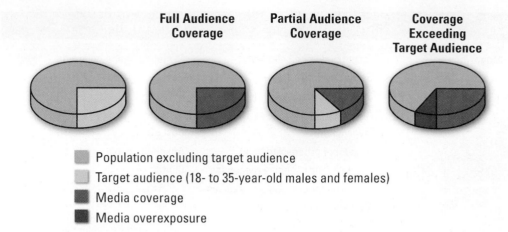

FIGURE 10–5

Marketing coverage
possibilities

Full Audience Coverage

Partial Audience Coverage

Coverage Exceeding Target Audience

 Population excluding target audience

 Target audience (18- to 35-year-old males and females)

 Media coverage

 Media overexposure

close to full audience coverage due to the small numbers of customers and potential customers. A B.C.-based firm, 4Refuel, advertised in trade and industry association publications to attract new customers and obtained considerable leverage for its $100,000. A newsletter offered for publication in the magazines acted as additional publicity and garnered the equivalent of $500,000 in exposure.[6]

More realistically, conditions shown in the third and fourth charts are likely to occur in most marketing situations. In the third chart, the coverage of the media does not allow for coverage of the entire audience, leaving some without exposure to the message. In the fourth chart, the marketer is faced with a problem of overexposure (also called **waste coverage**), in which the media coverage exceeds the targeted audience. If media coverage reaches people who are not sought as buyers and are not potential users, then it is wasted. This term is used for coverage that reaches people who are not potential buyers and/or users. Consumers may not be part of the intended target audience but may still be considered as potential—for example, those who buy the product as a gift for someone else.

The goal of the media planner is to extend media coverage to as many of the members of the target audience as possible while minimizing the amount of waste coverage. The situation usually involves trade-offs. Sometimes one has to live with less coverage than desired; other times, the most effective media expose people not sought. In this instance, waste coverage is justified because the media employed are likely to be the most effective means of delivery available and the cost of the waste coverage is exceeded by the value gained from their use.

A variety of factors can assist media planners in making the target audience coverage decision. Some will require primary research, whereas others will be available from published (secondary) sources. This research can show the number of consumers for a particular product category across many demographic variables. We review audience information in Chapters 11, 12, and 13, as each medium has its own method.

When examining these data, media planners are often more concerned with the percentage figures and index numbers than with the raw numbers. This is largely due to the fact that the numbers provided may not be specific enough for their needs, or they question the numbers provided because of the methods by which they were collected. Another key reason is that index numbers and percentages provide a comparative view of the market.

Overall, the **index number** is considered a good indicator of the potential of the market. This number is derived from the formula

$$\text{Index} = \frac{\text{Percentage of users in a demographic segment}}{\text{Percentage of population in the same segment}} \times 100$$

An index number over 100 means use of the product is proportionately greater in that segment than in one that is average (100) or less than 100. Depending on their overall strategy, marketers may wish to use this information to determine which groups are now using the product and target them or to identify a group that is currently using the product less and attempt to develop that segment. While the index is helpful, it should not be used alone. Percentages and product usage figures are also needed to get an accurate picture of the market. Just because the index for a particular segment of the population is very high, that doesn't always mean it is the only attractive segment to target. The high index may be a result of a low denominator (a very small proportion of the population in this segment).

Understanding coverage in a multimedia environment is proving difficult for media planners. Recent research suggests that younger consumers frequently engage in the consumption of more than one medium at a time. It suggests that up to 34 percent of young people aged 12–17 use the Internet while watching television.[7] This is a significant trend since coverage historically implied a reasonably close association with exposure and processing of the advertising message. Clearly, the communication is limited even further if other media are competing for the young people's attention.

GEOGRAPHIC COVERAGE

The question of where to promote relates to geographic considerations. The question is, where will the ad dollars be more wisely spent? Should we allocate additional promotional monies to those markets where the brand is already the leader to maintain market share, or does more potential exist in those markets where the firm is not doing as well and there is more room to grow? Perhaps the best answer is that the firm should spend advertising and promotion dollars where they will be the most effective—that is, in those markets where they will achieve the desired objectives. Two useful calculations that marketers examine to make this decision are the Brand Development Index and the Category Development Index.

The **Brand Development Index (BDI)** helps marketers factor the rate of product usage by geographic area into the decision process.

$$BDI = \frac{\text{Percentage of brand to total Canadian sales in the market}}{\text{Percentage of total Canadian population in the market}} \times 100$$

The BDI compares the percentage of the brand's total sales in a given market area with the percentage of the total population in the market to determine the sales potential for that brand in that market area. An example of this calculation is shown in Figure 10-6. The higher the index number, the more market potential exists. In this case, the index number indicates this market has high potential for brand development.

The **Category Development Index (CDI)** is computed in the same manner as the BDI, except it uses information regarding the product category (as opposed to the brand) in the numerator:

$$CDI = \frac{\text{Percentage of product category total sales in market}}{\text{Percentage of total Canadian population in market}} \times 100$$

$$BDI = \frac{\text{Percentage of product category sales in Ontario}}{\text{Percentage of total Canadian population in Ontario}} \times 100$$
$$= \frac{50\%}{34\%} \times 100$$
$$= 128$$

FIGURE 10-6

Calculating BDI

FIGURE 10–7

Using CDI and BDI to determine market potential

$$CDI = \frac{\text{Percentage of product category sales in Alberta}}{\text{Percentage of total Canadian population in Alberta}} \times 100$$

$$= \frac{8\%}{11\%} \times 100$$

$$= 80$$

$$BDI = \frac{\text{Percentage of total brand sales in Alberta}}{\text{Percentage of total Canadian population in Alberta}} \times 100$$

$$= \frac{15\%}{11\%} \times 100$$

$$= 136$$

The CDI provides information on the potential for development of the total product category rather than specific brands. When this information is combined with the BDI, a much more insightful promotional strategy may be developed. One might first look at how well the product category does in a specific market area. In Alberta, for example, the category potential is low (see Figure 10-7). The marketer analyzes the BDI to find how the brand is doing relative to other brands in this area. This information can then be used in determining how well a particular product category and a particular brand are performing and figuring what media weight (or quantity of advertising) would be required to gain additional market share, as shown in Figure 10-8.

In addition to the BDI and CDI considerations, some geographic decisions are based on the availability of the product. For example, Primus launched the first national Web telephone service in North America using voice over Internet protocol (VOIP) technology. The Talk Broadband offering promises long-distance savings of 15 percent and attempts to pre-empt cable companies in the long-distance phone market and sway current telephone users. While national in scope for the long term, the radio, print, and transit ads are shown in Toronto, Montreal, Vancouver, Halifax, Calgary, Ottawa, and Edmonton, cities where the product is initially sold.[8]

FIGURE 10–8

Using BDI and CDI indexes

	High BDI	**Low BDI**
High CDI	High market share Good market potential	Low market share Good market potential
Low CDI	High market share Monitor for sales decline	Low market share Poor market potential

High BDI and high CDI	This market usually represents good sales potential for both the product category and the brand.
High BDI and low CDI	The category is not selling well, but the brand is; probably a good market to advertise in but should be monitored for declining sales.
Low BDI and high CDI	Both the product category and the brand are doing poorly; not likely to be a good place for advertising.
Low BDI and low CDI	The product category shows high potential but the brand is not doing well; the reasons should be determined.

SCHEDULING

Obviously, companies would like to keep their advertising in front of consumers at all times as a constant reminder of the product and/or brand name. In reality, this is not possible or necessary for a variety of reasons. The primary objective of scheduling is to time promotional efforts to coincide with the highest potential buying times. For some products these times are not easy to identify; for others they are very obvious. Three scheduling methods available to the media planner—continuity, flighting, and pulsing—are shown in Figure 10-9.

Continuity refers to a continuous pattern of advertising, which may mean every day, every week, or every month. The key is that a regular (continuous) pattern is developed without gaps or nonadvertising periods. Such strategies might be used for advertising for food products, laundry detergents, or other products consumed on an ongoing basis without regard for seasonality.

A second method, **flighting**, employs a less regular schedule, with intermittent periods of advertising and nonadvertising. At some time periods there are heavier promotional expenditures, and at others there may be no advertising. Many banks, for example, spend no money on advertising in the summer but maintain advertising throughout the rest of the year. Snow skis are advertised heavily between October and April; less in May, August, and September; and not at all in June and July.

Pulsing is actually a combination of the first two methods. In a pulsing strategy, continuity is maintained, but at certain times promotional efforts are stepped up. In the automobile industry, advertising continues throughout the year but may increase in April (tax refund time), September (when new models are brought out), and the end of the model year.

There are certain advantages and disadvantages to each scheduling method, as shown in Figure 10-10. One comprehensive study indicates that continuity is more effective than flighting. On the basis of the idea that it is important to get exposure to the message as close as possible to when the consumer is going to make the purchase, the study concludes that advertisers should continue weekly schedules as long as possible.[9] The key here may be the "as long as possible" qualification. Given a significant budget, continuity may be more of an option than it is for those with more limited budgets.

An interesting twist on scheduling is with Campbell's soup, where ads are run when the temperature drops below −5 degrees. A 10-second ad appearing on the Weather Network demonstrates the falling temperature of a thermometer turning into a Campbell's soup can. The voice-over concludes with, "When it's cold outside . . . warm up with Campbell's," while the visual shows a bowl of soup and the Campbell's slogan "M'm! M'm! Good!" The campaign also features a Web banner in ads in daily e-mails sent by the Weather Network and in newspaper ads adjacent to the weather information in some Toronto newspapers.[10]

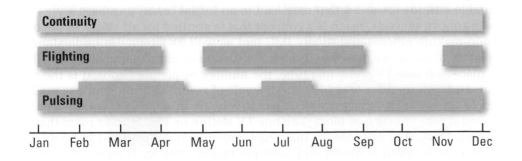

FIGURE 10−9

Three methods of promotional scheduling

Given the complexity and uncertainty for reach and frequency, it is not too surprising to see that these decisions are not always made on hard data. Says Joseph Ostrow, executive vice president/director of communications services with Young & Rubicam, "Establishing frequency goals for an advertising campaign is a mix of art and science but with a definite bias toward art."[12] Figure 10-12 summarizes the effects that can be expected at different levels of exposure on the basis of research in this area. In addition to these results, Joseph Ostrow has shown that while the number of repetitions increases awareness rapidly, it has much less impact on attitudinal and behavioural responses.[13]

Using Gross Ratings Points The media buyer typically uses a numerical indicator to know how many potential audience members may be exposed to a series of commercials. A summary measure that combines the program rating and the average number of times the home is reached during this period (frequency of exposure) is a commonly used reference point known as **gross ratings points (GRP)**:

$$GRP = Reach \times Frequency$$

GRPs are based on the total audience the media schedule may reach; they use a duplicated reach estimate. GRPs can be calculated for the total population aged 2+, Adults 18+, Adults 18–34, Adults 18–49, or several other measured demographic groups.

The advertiser must ask: How many GRPs are needed to attain a certain reach? How do these GRPs translate into effective reach? For example, how many GRPs must one purchase to attain an unduplicated reach of 50 percent, and what frequency of exposure will this schedule deliver? The following example shows how this process works. A purchase of 100 GRPs could mean 100 percent of the market is exposed once or 50 percent of the market is exposed twice or 25 percent of the market is exposed four times, and so on. This information must be more specific for the marketer to use it effectively. To know how many GRPs are necessary, the manager needs to know how many members of the intended audience the schedule actually reaches. The chart in Figure 10-13 helps make this determination.

In Figure 10-13, a purchase of 100 GRPs on one network would yield an estimated reach of 32 percent of the total households in the target audience. This figure would climb to 37.2 percent if two networks were used and 44.5 percent with three. Working backward through the formula for GRPs, the estimate of frequency of exposure—3.125, 2.688, and 2.247, respectively—demonstrates the trade-off between reach and frequency.

FIGURE 10–12

The effects of frequency

1. One exposure of an ad to a target group within a purchase cycle has little or no effect in most circumstances.

2. Since one exposure is usually ineffective, the central goal of productive media planning should be to enhance frequency rather than reach.

3. The evidence suggests strongly that an exposure frequency of two within a purchase cycle is an effective level.

4. Beyond three exposures within a brand purchase cycle or over a period of four or even eight weeks, increasing frequency continues to build advertising effectiveness at a decreasing rate but with no evidence of decline.

5. Although there are general principles with respect to frequency of exposure and its relationship to advertising effectiveness, differential effects by brand are equally important.

6. Nothing we have seen suggests that frequency response principles or generalizations vary by medium.

7. The data strongly suggest that wearout is not a function of too much frequency; it is more of a creative or copy problem.

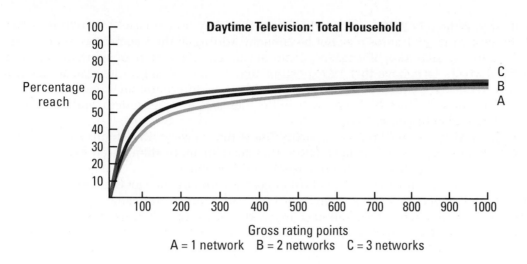

Daytime Television: Total Household

FIGURE   10–13

Estimates of reach
for network GRPs

Gross rating points
A = 1 network   B = 2 networks   C = 3 networks

Determining Effective Reach and Frequency   Since marketers have budget constraints, they must decide whether to increase reach at the expense of frequency or increase the frequency of exposure but to a smaller audience. A number of factors influence this decision. For example, a new product or brand introduction will attempt to maximize reach, particularly unduplicated reach, to create awareness in as many people as possible as quickly as possible. At the same time, for a high-involvement product or one whose benefits are not obvious, a certain level of frequency is needed to achieve effective reach.

Effective reach represents the percentage of a vehicle's audience reached at each effective frequency increment. This concept is based on the assumption that one exposure to an ad may not be enough to convey the desired message. As we saw earlier, no one knows the exact number of exposures necessary for an ad to make an impact, although advertisers have settled on three as the minimum. Effective reach (exposure) is shown in the shaded area in Figure 10-14 in the range of 3 to 10 exposures. Fewer than 3 exposures is considered insufficient reach, while more than 10 is considered overexposure and thus ineffective reach. This exposure level is no guarantee of effective communication; different messages may require more or fewer exposures. For example, Jack Myers, president of Myers Reports, argues that the three-exposure theory was valid in the 1970s when consumers were exposed

293

FIGURE   10–14   Graph of effective reach

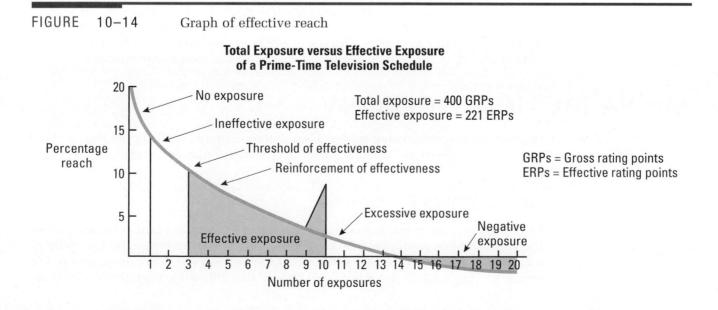

**Total Exposure versus Effective Exposure
of a Prime-Time Television Schedule**

Total exposure = 400 GRPs
Effective exposure = 221 ERPs

GRPs = Gross rating points
ERPs = Effective rating points

to approximately 1,000 ads per day. Now that they are exposed to 3,000 to 5,000 per day, three exposures may not be enough. Adding in the fragmentation of television, the proliferation of magazines, and the advent of a variety of alternative media leads Myers to believe that 12 exposures may be the minimum level of frequency required. Also, Jim Surmanek, vice president of International Communications Group, contends that the complexity of the message, message length, and recency of exposure also impact this figure.[14]

Since they do not know how many times the viewer will actually be exposed, advertisers typically purchase GRPs that lead to more than three exposures to increase the likelihood of effective reach and frequency.

Determining effective reach is further complicated by the fact that when calculating GRPs advertisers use a figure that they call **average frequency**, or the average number of times the target audience reached by a media schedule is exposed to the vehicle over a specified period. The problem with this figure is revealed in the following scenario.

Consider a media buy in which:

50 percent of audience is reached 1 time.
30 percent of audience is reached 5 times.
20 percent of audience is reached 10 times.
Average frequency = 4

In this media buy, the average frequency is 4, which is slightly more than the number established as effective. Yet a full 50 percent of the audience receives only one exposure. Thus, the average frequency number can be misleading, and using it to calculate GRPs might result in underexposing the audience.

Although GRPs have their problems, they can provide useful information to the marketer. A certain level of GRPs is necessary to achieve awareness, and increases in GRPs are likely to lead to more exposures and/or more repetitions—both of which are necessary to have an effect on higher-order objectives. Perhaps the best advice for purchasing GRPs is offered by Ostrow, who recommends the following strategies:[15]

- Instead of using average frequency, the marketer should decide what minimum frequency goal is needed to reach the advertising objectives effectively and then maximize reach at that frequency level.
- To determine effective frequency, one must consider marketing factors, message factors, and media factors. (See Figure 10-15.)

While the idea of minimum effective frequency has been used extensively in the advertising industry, there are some concerns with its use in more recent years.[16] In contrast, with the growth of more media outlets and enhanced syndicated data, minimum effective frequency within and across various combinations of media provide opportunity for more efficient and effective us of media expenditures.[17]

MEDIA TACTICS DECISIONS

Once the initial media strategy has been determined, the marketer addresses three media tactics decisions: media vehicle, relative cost estimates, and blocking chart.

MEDIA VEHICLE

Once the medium or media has been determined, the media planner must consider the most suitable media vehicle. Certain media vehicles enhance the creativity of a message because they create a mood that carries over to the communication. For example, think about the moods created by the following magazines: *Gourmet,*

Marketing Factors

- *Brand history.* New brands generally require higher frequency levels.
- *Brand share.* The higher the brand share, the lower the frequency level required.
- *Brand loyalty.* The higher the loyalty, the lower the frequency level required.
- *Purchase cycles.* Shorter purchasing cycles require higher frequency levels to maintain top-of-mind awareness.
- *Usage cycle.* Products consumed frequently usually require a higher level of frequency.
- *Share of voice.* Higher frequency levels are required with many competitors.
- *Target audience.* The ability of the target group to learn and to retain messages has a direct effect on frequency.

Message or Creative Factors

- *Message complexity.* The simpler the message, the less frequency required.
- *Message uniqueness.* The more unique the message, the lower the frequency level required.
- *New versus continuing campaigns.* New campaigns require higher levels of frequency.
- *Image versus product sell.* Image ads require higher levels of frequency than specific product sell ads.
- *Message variation.* A single message requires less frequency; a variety of messages requires more.
- *Wearout.* Higher frequency may lead to wearout.
- *Advertising units.* Larger units of advertising require less frequency than smaller ones.

Media Factors

- *Clutter.* The more advertising that appears in the media used, the more frequency is needed to break through the clutter.
- *Editorial environment.* The more consistent the ad is with the editorial environment, the less frequency is needed.
- *Attentiveness.* Media vehicles with higher attention levels require less frequency.
- *Scheduling.* Continuous scheduling requires less frequency than does flighting or pulsing.
- *Number of media used.* The fewer media used, the lower the level of frequency required.
- *Repeat exposures.* Media that allow for more repeat exposures require less frequency.

FIGURE 10–15

Factors important in determining frequency levels

Skiing, Travel, and *House Beautiful.* Each of these special-interest vehicles puts the reader in a particular mood. The promotion of fine wines, ski boots, luggage, and home products is enhanced by this mood. What different images might be created for a product advertised in the following media?

The *National Post* versus the *Toronto Star*
Architectural Digest versus *Reader's Digest*
A highly rated prime-time TV show versus an old rerun

The message may require a specific medium and a certain media vehicle to achieve its objectives. Likewise, certain media and vehicles have images that may carry over to the perceptions of messages placed within them. The explanation of these considerations is the **vehicle option source effect**, "the differential impact that the advertising exposure will have on the same audience member if the exposure occurs in one media option rather than another."[18] People perceive ads differently depending on their context.[19]

Sometimes advertisers find themselves objecting to the type of show or its content and decide not to advertise with a specific media vehicle. Microsoft initially planned to sponsor a special episode of *Family Guy* to promote Windows 7. The creators planned computer and Microsoft jokes; however, the "subversive and unique" humour regularly witnessed on the show proved too much for the executives (who, incidentally, watch the show themselves on a regular basis). In the end, Microsoft announced that the content "was not a fit with the Windows brand."[20]

An extension of this idea is the development of media engagement, where the media experiences of specific vehicles are identified along the global dimensions: inspiration, trustworthy, life enhancing, social involvement, and personal timeout. The purpose of this more detailed investigation of the media experience is to find a more specific link between the media vehicle and communication and behavioural effects.[21]

Related to the idea of directing messages to customers or non-customers, one author recommends finding a fit between the brand users and the media vehicle selected. Through the use of survey and syndicated data, the researcher concluded that demographic matching of target audience and media vehicle is less effective versus a similarity of brand and media vehicle users in terms of values. The author suggests that finding media vehicles that brand users are experiencing is possible for most major media.[22]

Once the media vehicle consideration is resolved, the media planner considers some other fine-tuning. The location within a particular medium (front page versus back page) and size of ad or length of commercial also merit examination. For example, research has demonstrated that readers pay more attention to larger ads.[23]

RELATIVE COST ESTIMATES

The value of any strategy can be determined by how well it delivers the message effectively to the audience with the lowest cost and the least waste. The media planner strives for optimal delivery by balancing costs associated with each of the media strategy decisions. Media planning is inherently a series of trade-offs between reach and frequency or geographic coverage and scheduling, among others. As these trade-offs are investigated and finalized, the media planner estimates and compares costs. Advertising and promotional costs can be categorized in two ways in terms of absolute cost and relative cost.

The **absolute cost** of the medium or vehicle is the actual total cost required to place the message. For example, a full-page four-colour ad in *Chatelaine* magazine costs about $42,000. **Relative cost** refers to the relationship between the price paid for advertising time or space and the size of the audience delivered. Relative costs are important because the manager must try to optimize audience delivery within budget constraints. Since a number of alternatives are available for delivering the message, the advertiser must evaluate the relative costs associated with these choices. For example, the media planner could compare the relative cost of reaching a member of the target audience in one magazine versus another. This decision can be influenced by the absolute cost of one magazine having a cheaper back page price versus another magazine. As the number of media alternatives rises, the number of comparisons grows considerably, potentially making this a tedious and difficult process. Media planners typically use two calculations, CPM and CPRP, to compare both media mix options or media vehicle options.

1. **Cost per thousand (CPM).** Magazines, and some other media, provide cost breakdowns on the basis of cost per thousand people reached. The formula for this computation is

$$CPM = \frac{\text{Cost of ad space (absolute cost)}}{\text{Circulation}} \times 1,000$$

	Canadian Living	Chatelaine
Per-page cost	$35,500	$46,505
Circulation	519,045	586,136
Calculation of CPM	$\dfrac{\$35,500 \times 1,000}{519,045}$	$\dfrac{\$46,505 \times 1,000}{586,136}$
CPM	$68.39	$79.34

FIGURE 10–16

Cost per thousand computations: *Canadian Living* versus *Chatelaine*

Figure 10-16 provides an example of this computation for two vehicles in the same medium—*Canadian Living* and *Chatelaine*—and shows that (all other things being equal) *Canadian Living* is a more cost-efficient buy. (We will come back to "all other things being equal" in a moment.)

Like magazines, newspapers now use the cost-per-thousand formula to determine relative costs. As shown in Figure 10-17, the *National Post* costs significantly more to advertise in than does *The Globe and Mail* (again, all other things being equal).

2. **Cost per ratings point (CPRP).** The broadcast media provide a different comparative cost figure, referred to as cost per ratings point or *cost per point (CPP)*, based on the following formula:

$$\text{CPRP} = \frac{\text{Cost of commercial time}}{\text{Program rating}}$$

An example of this calculation for a spot ad in a local TV market is shown in Figure 10-18. It indicates that *Survivor* would be more cost-effective than *CSI*.

	Globe and Mail	National Post
Cost per page	$64,800	$53,070
Circulation	335,013	240,030
Calculation	$\text{CPM} = \dfrac{\text{Page cost} \times 1,000}{\text{Circulation}}$	
	$= \dfrac{\$64,800 \times 1,000}{335,013}$	$\dfrac{\$53,070 \times 1,000}{240,030}$
	= $193.43	$221.10

FIGURE 10–17

Comparative costs in newspaper advertising

	CSI	Survivor
Cost per spot ad	$9,000	$8,000
Rating	20	19
Reach (households)	195,140	185,383
Calculation	$9,000/20	$8,000/19
CPRP (CPP)	$450	$421

FIGURE 10–18

Comparison of cost per ratings point: *CSI* versus *Survivor* in a local TV market

THEORETICAL APPROACHES IN BUDGET SETTING

Most of the approaches used to establish advertising budgets are based on marginal analysis or sales response models. These approaches are viewed as theoretical since academics have long debated the overall effects of advertising on sales, a topic that continually perplexes managers as well.

Marginal Analysis   Figure 10-21 graphically represents the concept of **marginal analysis**. As advertising/promotional expenditures increase, sales and gross margins also increase to a point, but then they level off. Profits are shown to be a result of the gross margin minus advertising expenditures. Using this theory to establish its budget, a firm would continue to spend advertising/promotional dollars as long as the marginal revenues created by these expenditures exceeded the incremental advertising/promotional costs. As shown on the graph, the optimal expenditure level is the point where marginal costs equal the marginal revenues they generate (point A). If the sum of the advertising/promotional expenditures exceeded the revenues they generated, one would conclude the appropriations were too high and scale down the budget. If revenues were higher, a higher budget might be in order.

Marginal analysis seems logical; however, it has weaknesses in two assumptions: that (1) sales are a direct result of advertising and promotional expenditures and this effect can be measured and (2) advertising and promotion are solely responsible for sales. Let us examine each of these assumptions in more detail.

1. *Assumption that sales are a direct measure of advertising and promotions efforts.* Previously, we discussed the fact that the advertiser needs to set communications objectives that contribute to accomplishing overall marketing objectives but at the same time are separate. One reason for this strategy is that it is often difficult, if not impossible, to demonstrate the effects of advertising and promotions on sales. In studies using sales as a direct measure, it has been almost impossible to establish the contribution of advertising and promotion.[26] Thus, to try to show that the size of the budget will directly affect sales of the product is misleading. A more logical approach would be to examine the impact of specific budgets for each communication tool on the attainment of specific communications objectives for each tool.

2. *Assumption that sales are determined solely by advertising and promotion.* This assumption ignores the remaining elements of the marketing mix—price, product, and distribution—which do contribute to a company's success. Environmental factors may also affect the promotional program, leading the marketing manager to assume the advertising was or was not effective when some other factor may have helped or hindered the accomplishment of the desired objectives.

FIGURE   10–21

Marginal analysis

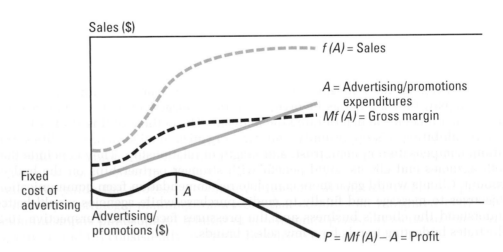

Sales Response Models   The sales curve in Figure 10-21 shows sales levelling off even though advertising and promotions efforts continue to increase. The relationship between advertising and sales has been the topic of much research and discussion designed to determine the shape of the response curve.

Almost all advertisers subscribe to one of two models of the advertising/sales response function: the concave-downward function or the S-shaped response curve.

- *The concave-downward function.* After reviewing more than 100 studies of the effects of advertising on sales, researchers concluded that the effects of advertising budgets follow the microeconomic law of diminishing returns.[27] That is, as the amount of advertising increases, its incremental value decreases. The logic is that those with the greatest potential to buy will likely act on the first (or earliest) exposures, while those less likely to buy are not likely to change as a result of the advertising. For those who may be potential buyers, each additional ad will supply little or no new information that will affect their decision. Thus, according to the **concave downward function model**, the effects of advertising quickly begin to diminish, as shown in Figure 10-22A. Budgeting under this model suggests that fewer advertising dollars may be needed to create the optimal influence on sales.
- *The S-shaped response curve.* Many advertising managers assume the **S-shaped response curve** (Figure 10-22B), which projects an S-shaped response function to the budget outlay (again measured in sales). Initial outlays of the advertising budget have little impact (as indicated by the essentially flat sales curve in range A). After a certain budget level has been reached (the beginning of range B), advertising and promotional efforts begin to have an effect, as additional increments of expenditures result in increased sales. This incremental gain continues only to a point, however, because at the beginning of range C additional expenditures begin to return little or nothing in the way of sales. This model suggests a small advertising budget is likely to have no impact beyond the sales that may have been generated through other means (for example, word of mouth). At the other extreme, more does not necessarily mean better: Additional dollars spent beyond range B have no additional impact on sales and for the most part can be considered wasted. As with marginal analysis, one would attempt to operate at that point on the curve in area B where the maximum return for the money is attained.

FIGURE   10–22   Advertising sales/response functions

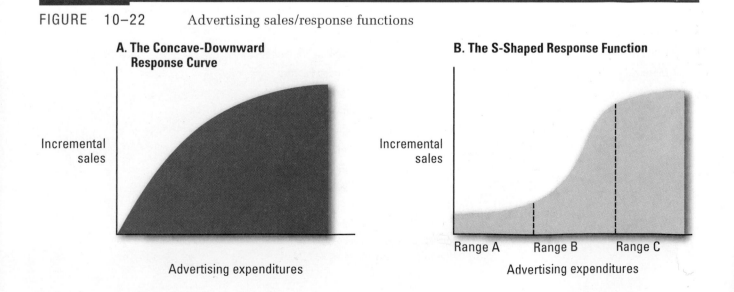

A. The Concave-Downward Response Curve

Incremental sales

Advertising expenditures

B. The S-Shaped Response Function

Incremental sales

Range A   Range B   Range C

Advertising expenditures

Even though marginal analysis and the sales response curves may not apply directly, they give managers insight into a theoretical basis of how the budgeting process should work. Some empirical evidence indicates the models may have validity. One study, based on industry experience, has provided support for the S-shaped response curve; the results indicate that a minimum amount of advertising dollars must be spent before there is a noticeable effect on sales.[28]

A weakness in attempting to use sales as a direct measure of response to advertising is that various situational factors may have an effect. In one comprehensive study, 20 variables were shown to affect the advertising/sales ratio. Figure 10-23 lists these factors and their relationships.[29] For a product characterized by emotional buying motives, hidden product qualities, and/or a strong basis for differentiation, advertising would have a noticeable impact on sales. Products characterized as large-dollar purchases and those in the maturity or decline stages of the product would be less likely to benefit. The study showed that other factors involving the market, customer, costs, and strategies employed have different effects.

The results of this study are interesting but limited, since they relate primarily to the percentage of sales dollars allocated to advertising and the factors influencing these ratios. As we will see later in this chapter, the percentage-of-sales method of budgeting has inherent weaknesses in that the advertising and sales effects may be reversed. So we cannot be sure whether the situation actually led to the advertising/sales relationship or vice versa. Thus, while these factors should be considered in the budget appropriation decision, they should not be the sole determinants of where and when to increase or decrease expenditures.

304

FIGURE 10-23   Factors influencing advertising budgets

Factor	Relationship of Advertising/Sales	Factor	Relationship of Advertising/Sales
Customer Factors		**Product Factors**	
Industrial products users	—	Basis for differentiation	+
Concentration of users	+	Hidden product qualities	+
Market Factors		Emotional buying motives	+
Stage of product life cycle		Durability	—
Introductory	+	Large dollar purchase	—
Growth	+	Purchase frequency	Curvilinear
Maturity	—	**Strategy Factors**	
Decline	—	Regional markets	—
Inelastic demand	+	Early stage of brand life cycle	+
Market share	—	High margins in channels	—
Competition		Long channels of distribution	+
Active	+	High prices	+
Concentrated	+	High quality	+
Pioneer in market	—	**Cost Factors**	
		High profit margins	+

Note: + relationship indicates a positive effect of advertising on sales; — relationship indicates little or no effect of advertising on sales.

MANAGERIAL APPROACHES IN BUDGET SETTING

This section reviews methods developed through practice and experience for setting budgets and the relative advantages and disadvantages of each. It is important to review many approaches since firms may employ more than one method and budgeting methods also vary according to the size and sophistication of the firm. One approach may be referred to as **top-down budgeting** because an amount is established at an executive level and then the monies are passed down to the various departments (as shown in Figure 10-24). Top-down methods include the affordable method, arbitrary allocation, percentage of sales, competitive parity, and return on investment (ROI). The major flaw associated with the top-down methods is that these judgmental approaches lead to predetermined budget appropriations often not linked to objectives and the strategies designed to accomplish them. A more effective budgeting strategy would be to consider the firm's communication objectives and budget what is deemed necessary to attain these goals. The idea is to budget so these promotional mix strategies can be implemented to achieve the stated objectives. This is known as bottom-up budgeting and we review two approaches: the objective and task method and payout planning.

The Affordable Method In the **affordable method**, the firm determines the amount to be spent in various areas such as production and operations. Then it allocates what's left to advertising and promotion, considering this to be the amount it can afford. The task to be performed by the advertising/promotions function is not considered, and the likelihood of under- or overspending is high, as no guidelines for measuring the effects of various budgets are established.

This approach is common among small firms where cash flow concerns are prominent. Unfortunately, it is also used in large firms, particularly those that are not marketing-driven and do not understand the role of advertising and promotion. For example, some high-tech firms focus on new product development and engineering and assume that the product, if good enough, will sell itself. In these companies, little money may be left for performing the advertising and promotions tasks.

The logic for this approach stems from "We can't be hurt with this method" thinking. That is, if we know what we can afford and we do not exceed it, we will

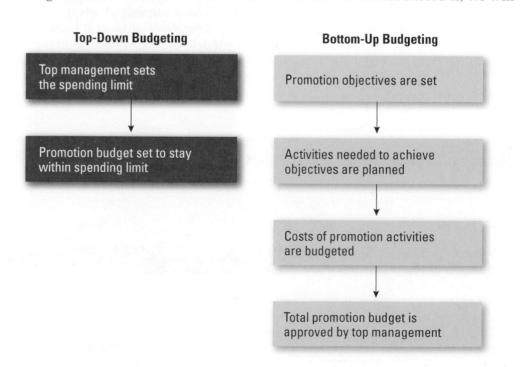

Top-Down Budgeting

Top management sets the spending limit

↓

Promotion budget set to stay within spending limit

Bottom-Up Budgeting

Promotion objectives are set

↓

Activities needed to achieve objectives are planned

↓

Costs of promotion activities are budgeted

↓

Total promotion budget is approved by top management

FIGURE 10–24

Top-down versus bottom-up approaches to budget setting

not get into financial problems. While this may be true in a strictly accounting sense, it does not reflect sound managerial decision making from a marketing perspective. Often this method does not allocate enough money to get the product off the ground and into the market. In terms of the S-shaped sales response model, the firm is operating in range A. Or the firm may be spending more than necessary, operating in range C. When the market gets tough and sales and/or profits begin to fall, this method is likely to lead to budget cuts at a time when the budget should be increased.

Arbitrary Allocation Perhaps an even weaker method than the affordable method for establishing a budget is **arbitrary allocation**, in which virtually no theoretical basis is considered and the budgetary amount is often set by fiat. That is, the budget is determined by management solely on the basis of what is felt to be necessary. In a discussion of how managers set advertising budgets, Melvin Salveson reported that these decisions may reflect "as much upon the managers' psychological profile as they do economic criteria."[30] While Salveson was referring to larger corporations, the approach is no less common in small firms and nonprofit organizations.

The arbitrary allocation approach has no obvious advantages. No systematic thinking has occurred, no objectives have been budgeted for, and the concept and purpose of advertising and promotion have been largely ignored. Other than the fact that the manager believes some monies must be spent on advertising and promotion and then picks a number, there is no good explanation why this approach continues to be used. Yet budgets continue to be set this way, and our purpose in discussing this method is to point out only that it is used—not recommended.

Percentage of Sales Perhaps the most commonly used method for budget setting (particularly in large firms) is the **percentage-of-sales method**, in which the advertising and promotions budget is based on sales of the product. Management determines the amount by either (1) taking a percentage of the sales dollars or (2) assigning a fixed amount of the unit product cost to promotion and multiplying this amount by the number of units sold. These two methods are shown in Figure 10-25.

Proponents of the percentage-of-sales method cite a number of advantages. It is financially safe and keeps ad spending within reasonable limits, as it bases spending on the past year's sales or what the firm expects to sell in the upcoming year. Thus, there will be sufficient monies to cover this budget, with increases in sales leading to budget increases and sales decreases resulting in advertising decreases. The percentage-of-sales method is simple, straightforward, and easy to implement.

FIGURE 10–25

Alternative methods for computing percentage of sales for Eve Cologne

Method 1: Straight Percentage of Sales		
2000	Total dollar sales	$1,000,000
	Straight % of sales at 10%	$100,000
2001	Advertising budget	$100,000

Method 2: Percentage of Unit Cost		
2000	Cost per bottle to manufacturer	$4.00
	Unit cost allocated to advertising	$1.00
2001	Forecast sales, 100,000 units	
2001	Advertising budget (100,000 × $1)	$100,000

Regardless of which basis—past or future sales—is employed, the calculations used to arrive at a budget are not difficult. Finally, this budgeting approach is generally stable. While the budget may vary with increases and decreases in sales, as long as these changes are not drastic the manager will have a reasonable idea of the parameters of the budget.

At the same time, the percentage-of-sales method has some serious disadvantages, including the basic premise on which the budget is established: sales. Letting the level of sales determine the amount of advertising and promotions dollars to be spent reverses the cause-and-effect relationship between advertising and sales. It treats advertising as an expense associated with making a sale rather than an investment.

Another problem with this approach was actually cited as an advantage earlier: stability. Proponents say that if all firms use a similar percentage, that will bring stability to the marketplace. But what happens if someone varies from this standard percentage? The problem is that this method does not allow for changes in strategy either internally or from competitors. An aggressive firm may wish to allocate more monies to the advertising and promotions budget, a strategy that is not possible with a percentage-of-sales method unless the manager is willing to deviate from industry standards.

The percentage-of-sales method of budgeting may result in severe misappropriation of funds. If advertising and promotion have a role to perform in marketing a product, then allocating more monies to advertising will, as shown in the S-shaped curve, generate incremental sales (to a point). If products with low sales have smaller promotion budgets, this will hinder sales progress. At the other extreme, very successful products may have excess budgets, some of which may be better appropriated elsewhere.

The percentage-of-sales method is also difficult to employ for new product introductions. If no sales histories are available, there is no basis for establishing the budget. Projections of future sales may be difficult, particularly if the product is highly innovative and/or has fluctuating sales patterns.

Finally, if the budget is contingent on sales, decreases in sales will lead to decreases in budgets when they most need to be increased. Continuing to cut the advertising and promotion budgets may just add impetus to the downward sales trend (Figure 10-26). On the other hand, some of the more successful companies have allocated additional funds during hard times or downturns in the cycle of sales. Companies that maintain or increase their ad expenditures during recessions achieve increased visibility and higher growth in both sales and market share (compared to those that reduce advertising outlays). For example, Sunkist can attribute at least some of its success in maintaining its strong image to the fact that it has maintained consistent levels of advertising expenditures over 80 years, despite recessions.[31]

A variation on the percentage-of-sales method uses a percentage of projected future sales as a base. This method also uses either a straight percentage of projected sales or a unit cost projection. One advantage of using future sales as a base is that the budget is not based on last year's sales. As the market changes, management must factor the effect of these changes on sales into next year's forecast rather than relying on past data. The resulting budget is more likely to reflect current conditions and be more appropriate. While this appears to be a remedy for some of the problems discussed here, the reality is that problems with forecasting, cyclical growth, and uncontrollable factors limit its effectiveness.

307

FIGURE   10–26

Investments pay off in later years

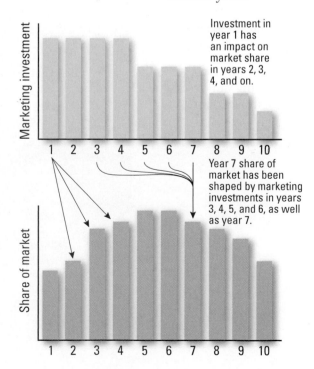

Investment in year 1 has an impact on market share in years 2, 3, 4, and on.

Year 7 share of market has been shaped by marketing investments in years 3, 4, 5, and 6, as well as year 7.

Competitive Parity   In many industries or product categories, we observe firms with similar advertising expenditures resulting from a competitive analysis. Competitors' advertising expenditures are available from market research firms, trade associations, and other advertising industry periodicals. Larger corporations often subscribe to services that track media and other communication expenditures. For example, videotape services provide competitors with information, and Nielsen's new technology (discussed in Chapter 11) allows full reporting of all commercials. Smaller companies often use a **clipping service**, which clips competitors' ads from local print media, allowing the company to work backward to determine the cumulative costs of the ads placed.

In the **competitive parity method**, managers establish budget amounts by matching the competition's percentage-of-sales expenditures. The argument is that setting budgets in this fashion takes advantage of the collective wisdom of the industry. It also takes the competition into consideration, which leads to stability in the marketplace by minimizing marketing warfare. If companies know that competitors are unlikely to match their increases in promotional spending, they are less likely to take an aggressive posture to attempt to gain market share. This minimizes unusual or unrealistic ad expenditures.

The competitive parity method has a number of disadvantages, however. For one, it ignores the fact that advertising and promotions are designed to accomplish specific objectives by addressing certain problems and opportunities. Second, it assumes that because firms have similar expenditures, their programs will be equally effective. This assumption ignores the contributions of creative executions and/or media allocations, as well as the success or failure of various promotions. Further, it ignores possible advantages of the firm itself; some companies simply make better products than others. A study by Yoo and Mandhachitara indicates that a competitive parity strategy must consider the fact that a competitor's advertising can actually benefit one's own firm, and that one competitor's gain is not always the other's loss. As shown in Figure 10-27 there are four different situations to determine how the competitive budgets may impact sales—only one of which involves the zero-sum scenario.[32]

Also, there is no guarantee that competitors will continue to pursue their existing strategies. Since competitive parity figures are determined by examination of

FIGURE   10–27

Competitors'
advertising outlays
do not always hurt

competitors' previous years' promotional expenditures (short of corporate espionage), changes in market emphasis and/or spending may not be recognized until the competition has already established an advantage. Further, there is no guarantee that a competitor will not increase or decrease its own expenditures, regardless of what other companies do. Finally, competitive parity may not avoid promotional wars.

In summary, few firms employ the competitive parity method as a sole means of establishing the promotional budget. This method is typically used in conjunction with the percentage-of-sales or other methods. It is never wise to ignore the competition; managers must always be aware of what competitors are doing. But they should not just emulate them in setting goals and developing strategies.

Return on Investment (ROI) In the percentage-of-sales method, sales dictate the level of advertising appropriations. But advertising causes sales. In the marginal analysis and S-shaped curve approaches, incremental investments in advertising and promotions lead to increases in sales. The key word here is *investment.* In the **ROI budgeting method**, advertising and promotions are considered investments, like plant and equipment. Thus, the budgetary appropriation (investment) leads to certain returns. Like other aspects of the firm's efforts, advertising and promotion are expected to earn a certain return.

While the ROI method looks good on paper, the reality is that it is rarely possible to assess the returns provided by the promotional effort—at least as long as sales continue to be the basis for evaluation. Thus, while managers are certain to ask how much return they are getting for such expenditures, the question remains unanswered, and ROI remains a virtually unused method of budgeting.

Objective and Task Method It is important that objective setting and budgeting go hand in hand rather than sequentially. It is difficult to establish a budget without specific objectives in mind, and setting objectives without regard to how much money is available makes no sense. For example, a company may wish to create awareness among X percent of its target market. A minimal budget amount will be required to accomplish this goal, and the firm must be willing to spend this amount.

The **objective and task method** of budget setting consists of three steps: (1) defining the communications objectives to be accomplished, (2) determining the specific strategies and tasks needed to attain them, and (3) estimating the costs associated with performance of these strategies and tasks. The total budget is based on the accumulation of these costs.

Implementing the objective and task approach is somewhat more involved. The manager must monitor this process throughout and change strategies depending on how well objectives are attained. As shown in Figure 10-28, this process involves several steps:

1. *Isolate objectives.* When the promotional planning model is presented, a company will have two sets of objectives to accomplish—the marketing objectives for the product and the communications objectives. After the former are established, the task involves determining what specific communications objectives will be designed to accomplish these goals. Communications objectives must be specific, attainable, and measurable, as well as time limited.
2. *Determine tasks required.* A number of elements are involved in the strategic plan designed to attain the objectives established. (These strategies constitute the remaining chapters in this text.) These tasks may include advertising in various media, sales promotions, and/or other elements of the promotional mix, each with its own role to perform.
3. *Estimate required expenditures.* Buildup analysis requires determining the estimated costs associated with the tasks developed in the previous step. For example, it involves costs for developing awareness through advertising, trial through sampling, and so forth.

FIGURE 10–28

The objective and
task method

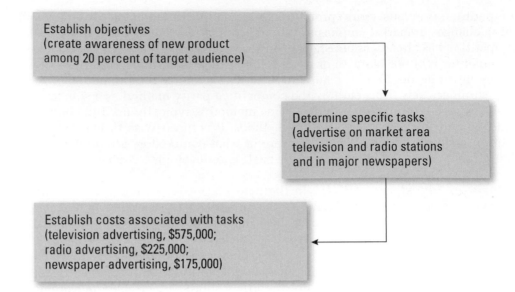

Establish objectives
(create awareness of new product
among 20 percent of target audience)

Determine specific tasks
(advertise on market area
television and radio stations
and in major newspapers)

Establish costs associated with tasks
(television advertising, $575,000;
radio advertising, $225,000;
newspaper advertising, $175,000)

4. *Monitor.* As we saw in Chapter 9 on measuring effectiveness, there are ways to determine how well one is attaining established objectives. Performance should be monitored and evaluated in light of the budget appropriated.
5. *Reevaluate objectives.* Once specific objectives have been attained, monies may be better spent on new goals. Thus, if one has achieved the level of consumer awareness sought, the budget should be altered to stress a higher-order objective such as evaluation or trial.

The major advantage of the objective and task method is that the budget is driven by the objectives to be attained. The managers closest to the marketing effort will have specific strategies and input into the budget-setting process.

The major disadvantage of this method is the difficulty of determining which tasks will be required and the costs associated with each. For example, specifically what tasks are needed to attain awareness among 50 percent of the target audience? How much will it cost to perform these tasks? While these decisions are easier to determine for certain objectives—for example, estimating the costs of sampling required to stimulate trial in a defined market area—it is not always possible to know exactly what is required and/or how much it will cost to complete the job. This process is easier if there is past experience to use as a guide, with either the existing product or a similar one in the same product category.

However, the process is especially difficult for new product introductions. As a result, budget setting using this method is not as easy to perform or as stable as some of the methods discussed earlier. Given this disadvantage, many marketing managers have stayed with those top-down approaches for setting the total expenditure amount. The objective and task method offers advantages over methods discussed earlier but is more difficult to implement when there is no track record for the product. The following section addresses the problem of budgeting for new product introductions.

Payout Planning The first months of a new product's introduction typically require heavier-than-normal advertising and promotion appropriations to stimulate higher levels of awareness and subsequent trial. After studying more than 40 years of Nielsen figures, James O. Peckham estimated that the average share of advertising to sales ratio necessary to launch a new product successfully is approximately 1.5:2.0.[33] This means that a new entry should be spending at approximately twice the desired market share, as shown in the two examples in Figure 10-29. For

New Brands of Food Products

Brand	Average share of advertising	Attained share of sales	Ratio of share of advertising to share of sales
101	34%	12.6%	2.7
102	16	10.0	1.6
103	8	7.6	1.1
104	4	2.6	1.5
105	3	2.1	1.4

FIGURE 10–29

Share of advertising/ sales relationship (two-year summary)

example, brand 101 gained a 12.6 percent market share by spending 34 percent of the total advertising dollars in this food product category.

To determine how much to spend, marketers often develop a **payout plan** that determines the investment value of the advertising and promotion appropriation. The basic idea is to project the revenues the product will generate, as well as the costs it will incur, over two to three years. Based on an expected rate of return, the payout plan will assist in determining how much advertising and promotions expenditure will be necessary when the return might be expected. A three-year payout plan is shown in Figure 10-30. The product would lose money in year 1, almost break even in year 2, and finally begin to show substantial profits by the end of year 3.

The advertising and promotion figures are highest in year 1 and decline in years 2 and 3. This appropriation is consistent with Peckham's findings and reflects the additional outlays needed to make as rapid an impact as possible. For example, that shelf space is limited, and store owners are not likely to wait around for a product to become successful. The budget also reflects the firm's guidelines for new product expenditures, since companies generally have established deadlines by which the product must begin to show a profit. Finally, building market share may be more difficult than maintaining it—thus the substantial dropoff in expenditures in later years. While the payout plan is not always perfect, it does guide the manager in establishing the budget. When used in conjunction with the objective and task method, it provides a much more logical approach to budget setting than the top-down approaches previously discussed.

IMC PLANNING: BUDGET ALLOCATION

Once the overall budget has been determined, the next step is to allocate it. The allocation decision involves determining the relative expenditures across IMC tools and markets while accounting for market-share goals, client/agency policies, and organizational characteristics.

	Year 1	Year 2	Year 3
Product sales	15.0	35.50	60.75
Profit contribution (@ $0.50/case)	7.5	17.75	30.38
Advertising/promotions	15.0	10.50	8.50
Profit (loss)	(7.5)	7.25	21.88
Cumulative profit (loss)	(7.5)	(0.25)	21.63

FIGURE 10–30

Example of three-year payout plan ($ millions)

311

IMC TOOLS

The promotional budget is allocated to broadcast, print, and out-of-home media as suggested in the media plan, and among other IMC tools such as sales promotion, public relations, Internet, and direct marketing. As noted in Chapter 1, firms are increasingly evaluating and employing all IMC tools to achieve their communication and behavioural objectives. The degree to which a firm engages in more tools to achieve its objectives influences the relative emphasis. Figure 10-31 summarizes examples of traditional media plans and others with evolving IMC tools.[34]

These examples are reflected in macro statistics cited earlier. As shown in Figure 10-1, total Canadian expenditures for media advertising, Internet, and catalogue/direct mail total $14.6 billion. Some of these IMC tools continue their strength over time. For example, television advertising consistently commands approximately one-quarter of all media expenditures at about $3.4 billion. However, the ratio among different types of television advertising has evolved, with less emphasis on spot advertising and greater emphasis for specialty channel advertising. Radio continues with consistent year after year growth of 5% and a strong local presence while receiving $1.6 billion in advertising revenue.

Representing print media, newspaper, consumer magazines, and specialty print typically constitute one-third of all media expenditures at almost $5 billion. In contrast, Internet grew from $200 million in 2002 to $1.6 billion in 2008 and 11 percent of all media expenditures, and appears as a key part of most IMC plans.

In comparison, other promotional tools constitute extensive expenditures. Public relations activities like sponsorship approach $1 billion, while promotional products approximate $2 billion in Canada. And while an accurate accounting for all sales promotion expenditures is difficult to achieve, estimating sales promotion expenditures at 2 percent of all Canadian retail sales culminates in a total of $7 billion.

As these macro statistics indicate, firms have a variety of tools and approaches for delivering messages to their target audiences, and careful consideration of the allocation across the tools each year is a central task for IMC planning. The budget allocation across media has been the focus of some research to find the right combination of media, and providing the optimal expenditure levels is a critical decision that has long lasting communication and financial implications. A study of the SUV market found that the effects of media mix for the Ford Explorer outperformed the effects of the media mix for the Jeep Grand Cherokee. The authors conclude that balance between image-oriented media versus more tactical media had stronger

FIGURE   10–31   Summary of examples of target and media choices

Brand	Target	Media
Toronto Star $500,000	Potential classified ad purchasers, ages 40–59, married, suburbs	Magazine, newspaper, radio, TV in elevators; high-traffic display, GO transit buses and shelters
Sprite $170,000	New consumers, urban youth, males, ages 16–18	Virtual community Habbo Hotel, transit shelter; donated basketball backboard and net to community centres; court chalk art; Sprite's animated spokesperson, Miles Thirst, hosts own MusiquePlus VJ show
Thermasilk $200,000	New consumers (repositioning); girls, ages 15–20	Virtual community Habbo Hotel, banner ads, microsite, contest, TV advertising
Home Depot	Women ages 30–49, professional, house proud	Domestic Divas via *Chatelaine* Internet site, contests, *Chatelaine* magazine, e-newsletter
BMW 525i	Men who like to drive; high income, urban; manager travelling in three major cities	*Air Canada* magazine and in-flight television; radio; outdoor (billboard, garages, elevator, gas pump); banner ads

effects for this set of data.[35] Another study concludes that some media have longer carryover effects versus other media which should also guide the media allocation decision for advertising.[36] The next research step is to assess the relative effects across different combinations of IMC tools.

MARKET SHARE GOALS

While the budget should be allocated according the specific promotional tools needed to accomplish the objectives, the size of the market affects the amount of money invested in promotion. In smaller markets, it is often easier and less expensive to reach the target audience. Too much of an expenditure in these markets will lead to saturation and a lack of effective spending. In larger markets, the target audience may be more dispersed and thus more expensive to reach.

For a variety of reasons, some markets hold more potential than others. When particular markets hold higher potential, the marketing manager may decide to allocate additional monies to them. Keep in mind that just because a market does not have high sales does not mean it should be ignored. The key is potential—and a market with low sales but high potential may be a candidate for additional appropriations.

Two studies in the *Harvard Business Review* discussed advertising spending with the goal of maintaining and increasing market share.[37] John Jones compared the brand's share of market with its share of advertising voice (the total value of the main media exposure in the product category). Jones classified the brands as "profit taking brands, or underspenders" and "investment brands, those whose share of voice is clearly above their share of market." His study indicated that for those brands with small market shares, profit takers are in the minority; however, as the brands increase their market share, nearly three out of five have a proportionately smaller share of voice.

Jones noted that three factors can be cited to explain this change. First, new brands generally receive higher-than-average advertising support. Second, older, more mature brands are often "milked"—that is, when they reach the maturity stage, advertising support is reduced. Third, there's an advertising economy of scale whereby advertising works harder for well-established brands, so a lower expenditure is required. Jones concluded that for larger brands, it may be possible to reduce advertising expenditures and still maintain market share. Smaller brands, on the other hand, have to continue to maintain a large share of voice.

James Schroer addressed the advertising budget in a situation where the marketer wishes to increase market share. His analysis suggests that marketers should focus on markets where competition is weak and/or underspending instead of advertising nationally. Figure 10-32 shows Schroer's suggestions for spending priorities in various markets.

One factor influencing these suggestions is **economies of scale** in advertising. It is argued that larger advertisers can maintain advertising shares that are smaller than their market shares because they get better advertising rates, have declining

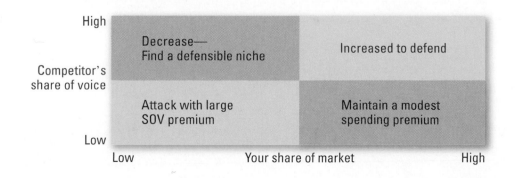

FIGURE 10–32

The share of voice (SOV) effect and ad spending: priorities in individual markets average costs of production, and accrue the advantages of advertising several products jointly. In addition, they are likely to enjoy more favourable time and space positions, cooperation of intermediaries, and favourable publicity.

Some studies have presented evidence that firms and/or brands maintaining a large share of the market have an advantage over smaller competitors and thus can spend less money on advertising and realize a better return.[38] Reviewing the studies in support of this position and then conducting research over a variety of small-package products, Kent Lancaster found that this situation did not hold true and that in fact larger brand share products might actually be at a disadvantage.[39] His results indicated that leading brands spend an average of 2.5 percentage points more than their brand share on advertising. The results of this and other studies suggest there really are no economies of scale to be accrued from the size of the firm or the market share of the brand.[40]

CLIENT/AGENCY POLICIES

Another factor that may influence budget allocation is the individual policy of the company or the advertising agency. The agency may discourage the allocation of monies to sales promotion, preferring to spend them on the advertising area. The agency may take the position that these monies are harder to track in terms of effectiveness and may be used improperly if not under its control. (In many cases commissions are not made on this area, and this fact may contribute to the agency's reluctance.)[41]

The orientation of the agency or the firm may also directly influence where monies are spent. Many ad agencies are managed by officers who have ascended through the creative ranks and are inclined to emphasize the creative budget. Others may have preferences for specific media. For example, some agencies position themselves as experts in cable TV programming and often spend more client money in this medium. Others tend to spend more monies on the Internet. Both the agency and the client may favour certain aspects of the promotional program, perhaps on the basis of past successes, that will substantially influence where dollars are spent.

ORGANIZATIONAL CHARACTERISTICS

In a review of the literature on how allocation decisions are made between advertising and sales promotion, George Low and Jakki Mohr concluded that organizational factors play an important role in determining how communications dollars are spent.[42] The authors note that the following factors influence the allocation decision. These factors vary from one organization to another, and each influences the relative amounts assigned to advertising and promotion:

- The organization's structure—centralized versus decentralized, formalization, and complexity.
- Power and politics in the organizational hierarchy.
- The use of expert opinions (e.g., consultants).
- Characteristics of the decision maker (preferences and experience).
- Approval and negotiation channels.
- Pressure on senior managers to arrive at the optimal budget.

One example of how these factors might influence allocations relates to the level of interaction between marketing and other functional departments, such as accounting and operations. The authors note that the relative importance of advertising versus sales promotion might vary from department to department. Accountants, being dollars-and-cents minded, would argue for the sales impact of promotions, while operations would argue against sales promotions because the sudden surges in demand that might result would throw off production schedules. The marketing department might be influenced by the thinking of either of these groups in making its decision.

CHAPTER OBJECTIVES AND SUMMARY

1 To know how a media plan is developed.

Media planning involves delivering the marketing communications message through different channels such as television, radio, print, and out-of-home, among others. Media planning is required for advertising to deliver the creative strategy but also for any other IMC tool. For example, a sales promotion offer might be communicated over the radio, a charity event that a brand sponsors could be found in a local city newspaper, or a transit ad possibly directs commuters to a firm's website.

A media is generally the end result of the media planning process, and it contains sections for objectives, strategy decisions, and tactical decisions. The media plan's objectives must be designed to support the overall marketing objectives and help achieve the behavioural and communications objectives determined for each target audience.

The basic task involved in the development of media strategy is to determine the best matching of media to the target audience, given the constraints of the budget. The media planner attempts to balance reach and frequency and to deliver the message to the intended audience with a minimum of waste coverage. Media strategy development has been called more of an art than a science, because while many quantitative data are available the planner also relies on creativity and non-quantifiable factors.

2 To know the process of deciding on and implementing media strategies and tactics.

This chapter discussed five media strategy decisions, including developing a proper media mix, determining target audience coverage, geographic coverage, scheduling, and balancing reach and frequency. A summary chart of strengths and limitations of media alternatives was provided. The list provides a starting point for planners who select the right combination of media based on the communication problem or opportunity.

The chapter also looked at key tactical decisions that fine-tune the media strategy. The media vehicle plays a key part in the media plan as the media planner makes a careful match among the viewers, listeners, and readers of the media and the profile of the target audience. Relative cost estimates guide the media planner's final decisions for vehicle selection by finding the most cost-efficient placement. Fine-tuning scheduling details are finalized with the realization of a blocking chart that summarizes all media decisions and costs across relevant time periods and geographic locations.

3 To understand the theoretical and managerial approaches for media budget setting.

This chapter summarized theoretical and managerial approaches for budget setting. Theoretical methods feature economic models (i.e., marginal analysis, sales response) that attempt to demonstrate the effects of advertising on sales, often without accounting for the effects of other marketing mix variables. Top-down managerial approaches include affordable, arbitrary allocation, percentage of sales, competitive parity, and return on investment. The methods are often viewed as lacking in any theoretical basis while ignoring the role of advertising and promotion in the marketing mix.

Bottom-up managerial approaches include the objective and task method and payout planning. In particular, the former connects the cost of advertising and promotion to the communication and behavioural objectives expected for the communication program as opposed to broader marketing objectives expected for the marketing program. While the objective and task method offers an improvement over the top-down approaches, firms continue to use a combination of approaches to make the budget decision.

KEY TERMS

absolute cost, *296*

affordable method, *305*

arbitrary allocation, *306*

average frequency, *294*

blocking chart, *299*

Brand Development Index (BDI), *287*

Category Development Index (CDI), *287*

clipping service, *308*

competitive parity method, *308*

concave downward function model, *303*

continuity, *289*

cost per ratings point (CPRP), *297*

cost per thousand (CPM), *296*

coverage, *280*

duplicated reach, *290*

economies of scale, *313*

effective reach, *293*

flighting, *289*

frequency, *280*

gross ratings points (GRP), *292*

index number, *286*

marginal analysis, *302*

media class, *280*

media objectives, *276*

media planning, *276*

media strategy, *276*

media tactics, *276*

media vehicle, *280*

medium, *280*

objective and task method, *309*

pass-along rate, *298*

payout plan, *311*

percentage-of-sales method, *306*

pulsing, *289*

reach, *280*

readers per copy, *298*

relative cost, *296*

ROI budgeting method, *309*

S-shaped response curve, *303*

target CPM (TCPM), *298*

top-down budgeting, *305*

unduplicated reach, *291*

vehicle option source effect, *295*

waste coverage, *286*

DISCUSSION QUESTIONS

1. Describe what is meant by waste coverage. The decision must often be made between waste coverage and undercoverage. Give examples when the marketer might have to choose between the two, and when it may be acceptable to live with waste coverage.

2. Media planning involves a trade-off between reach and frequency. Explain what this means. Under what circumstances would a planner emphasize reach? Frequency?

3. What is meant by readers per copy? How is this different from CPM? Explain the advantages and disadvantages associated with the use of both.

4. One long-time advertising agency executive noted that buying media is both an art and a science, with a leaning toward art. Explain what this means and provide examples.

5. Discuss some of the factors that are important in determining frequency levels. Give examples of each factor.

6. Describe the three methods of promotional scheduling. Give examples of products that might use each method.

7. Discuss some of the reasons managers continue to set budgets using "top-down" budgeting methods.

8. Explain the difference between investing in advertising and spending. Cite examples of companies that have successfully invested.

9. Figure 10-27 shows that advertising spending and effects may differ in different competitive environments. Explain each of the four scenarios presented and give examples of brands in each of the cells.

10. Explain the difference between the two sales response models. Provide examples of types of products that might follow each of these response curves.

BROADCAST MEDIA

■ CHAPTER OBJECTIVES

1 To consider the strengths and limitations of television as an advertising medium.

2 To understand how to purchase different types of television advertising, alternative time periods, and specialty television advertising.

3 To explain how television audiences are measured.

4 To summarize the strengths and limitations of radio as an advertising medium.

5 To identify how to purchase different radio formats and time periods.

6 To review how radio audiences are measured.

CORUS LINE OF CHANNELS FOR WOMEN

After establishing itself with a strong lineup of TV channels for children with YTV, Treehouse, and Discovery Kids, Corus Television expanded to cover the market for women equally well with channels like Cosmopolitan TV, VIVA, W Network, and W Movies. The flagship, W Network, attracts 10 million viewers per month and offers a wide variety of entertainment for women of all ages. Cosmopolitan TV "promises fun, flirty and irreverent entertainment" for women aged 18–34. VIVA reaches women aged 35–64 "with an enthusiasm for growth, learning and a passion for newfound interests." W Movies is expected to reach women aged 25–54. The channels are supported by websites (corusgetswomen.com) with content that is consistent with the channels.

The flanking strategy of having two niche channels to support the mainstream one is consistent with media vehicle options found with magazines. For example, Transcontinental has *Elle Canada* for women in their 20s, *Canadian Living* and *Homemakers* for women in their 30s and 40s, and *More* and *Good Times* for women older than 40. According to one industry expert the strategy is very sound in offering advertisers a wide variety of choices to reach particular groups of women, but the programming on each station needs to be different to attract distinctly unique audiences for the benefit of both viewers and advertisers. However, another expert felt that the flanking strategy works well for magazines but is significantly more difficult for TV.

Despite the uncertainty around whether the niche specialty TV offerings will be successful, Corus showed its capabilities with a recent package it produced for Dare Simple Pleasures cookies. For its Friday night movies on W and VIVA, the brand received multiple five-second billboards, 30-second ads, and 10-second closed-captioning spots. Corus also developed ads to attract viewers for the movies and used a similar "reinvention and transformation" theme consistent with Dare's message. The ads use an image of the cookie along with images from the movie and start with the following copy:

> This is a Simple Pleasures cookie—it has no cholesterol. That's good for your heart. What else is good for your heart? Finding true love, like in *Sense and Sensibility*. What else is sensible? Simple Pleasures cookies and Gwyneth Paltrow, who plays a first-class flight attendant. First Class has lots of leg room and Sandra Bullock has great legs in *Miss Congeniality*. How'd they get so strong? Calcium, like in Simple Pleasure cookies.

Advertisers are satisfied with customized opportunities such as this—and it appears that viewers are equally impressed with the uniqueness of specialty channels, as audience numbers continued to grow while conventional TV channels have felt some withdrawal recently.

Sources: Chris Powell, "Tuning In to Women," *Marketing Magazine*, February 23, 2009; Kristin Laird, "Corus Begins Simple Pleasures Campaign for Dare," *Marketing Magazine,* July 20, 2009; Matt Semansky, "Specialty TV Audience Continues to Grow," *Marketing Magazine,* May 27, 2009.

QUESTION:

1. Does this example imply that television has stronger target audience selectivity?

TV has virtually saturated households throughout Canada and most other countries and has become a mainstay in the lives of most people. The average Canadian household watches almost six hours of TV a day, and the average person (age 2+) watches about 3.5 hours of TV per day.[1] The large numbers of people who watch television are important to the TV networks and stations because they can sell time on these programs to marketers who want to reach that audience with their advertising messages. Moreover, the qualities that make TV a great medium for news and entertainment also encourage creative ads that can have a strong impact on current and potential customers.

Radio is also an integral part of our lives. For many people, radio is a constant companion in their cars, at home, even at work for information and entertainment. The average Canadian listens to the radio about two hours each day.[2] Like TV viewers, radio listeners are an important audience for marketers. In this chapter, we examine TV and radio media, including the general characteristics of each as well as their specific strengths and limitations. We examine how advertisers use TV and radio as part of their advertising and media strategies, how they buy TV and radio time, and how audiences are measured and evaluated for each medium.

TELEVISION

It has often been said that television is the ideal advertising medium. Its ability to combine visual images, sound, motion, and colour presents the advertiser with the opportunity to develop the most creative and imaginative appeals of any medium. However, TV does have certain characteristics that limit or even prevent its use by many advertisers.

STRENGTHS OF TELEVISION

TV has numerous strengths compared to other media, including creativity, target audience coverage, cost efficiency, attention, scheduling flexibility, geographic coverage, reach, frequency, and media image.

Creativity for Cognitive and Emotional Responses Perhaps the greatest advantage of TV is the opportunity it provides for presenting the advertising message. The interaction of sight, sound, and motion offers tremendous creative flexibility and makes possible dramatic, lifelike representations of products and services. TV commercials can be used to convey a mood or image for a brand as well as to develop emotional or entertaining appeals that help make a dull product appear interesting. The overall impact of TV's characteristics provides unlimited options for generating optimal cognitive and emotional responses to highly imaginative ads. For example the ads for Newfoundland and Labrador tourism showing fjords in Gros Morne National Park, the province's unique heritage architecture, and the L'Anse aux Meadows national historical site all come alive with beautiful cinematography and the directional skills of Alar Kivilo.[3]

Television is an excellent medium for demonstrating a product. Print ads are effective for showing a product such as a high definition television and communicating information regarding its features. However, a TV commercial like the acclaimed "Power Unleashed" spot for the Hitachi UltraVision plasma set shown in Exhibit 11-1 is very effective in portraying its rich colour, vivid detail, and lifelike picture.

Target Audience Coverage Television advertising makes it possible to reach large audiences. Nearly everyone, regardless of age, sex, income, or educational level, watches at least some TV. During prime time (6:00 p.m. to 11:00 p.m.) the

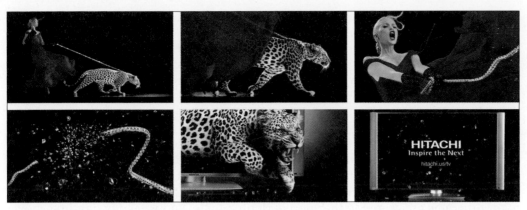

average Canadian watches almost two hours of TV each evening (see Figure 11-1). Most people watch on a regular basis; 99 percent of all Canadian households own a TV, and 65 percent have more than one. Marketers selling products and services that appeal to broad target audiences find that TV lets them reach mass markets.

Cost Efficiency   Compared to many other media, the cost to reach individuals by television is reasonably affordable. For example, one estimate is that the average cost per thousand (CPM) to reach English-speaking women 18 to 49 is about $18.[4] Because of its ability to reach large audiences in a cost-efficient manner, TV is a popular medium among companies selling mass-consumption products. Companies with widespread distribution and availability of their products and services use TV to reach the mass market and deliver their advertising messages at a very low cost per thousand. Television has become indispensable to large consumer packaged-goods companies, carmakers, and major retailers.

Attention   Television is basically intrusive in that commercials impose themselves on viewers as they watch their favourite programs. Unless we make a special effort to avoid commercials, most of us are exposed to thousands of them each year. This seemingly continuous exposure implies that viewers devote some attention

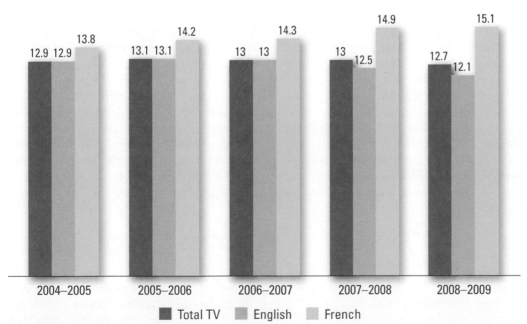

FIGURE   11–1

Weekly per-capita
hours: Total Canada

Source: BBM Canada—Broadcast Years

(i.e., selective attention) to many advertising messages. As discussed in Chapter 4, the low-involvement nature of consumer learning and response processes may mean TV ads have an effect on consumers simply through heavy repetition and exposure to catchy slogans and jingles. Research suggests that consumers watching their favourite programs pay greater attention to the program and subsequently to the embedded television commercial.[5]

Scheduling Flexibility Television has often been criticized for being a non-selective medium, since it is difficult to reach a precisely defined target audience through the use of TV advertising. But some selectivity is possible due to variations in the composition of audiences as a result of broadcast time and program content. For example, Saturday morning TV caters to children; Saturday and Sunday afternoon programs are geared to the sports-oriented male; and weekday daytime shows appeal heavily to homemakers. With the growth of specialty channels, advertisers refine their coverage further by appealing to groups with specific interests such as sports, news, history, the arts, or music.

Geographic Coverage Advertisers can also adjust their media strategies to take advantage of different geographic markets through spot ads in specific market areas. Ads can be scheduled to run repeatedly in more favourable markets. Alternatively, advertisers can obtain national coverage or regional coverage depending upon their marketing objectives.

Reach Television viewing is a closely monitored activity such that the size of the audience for a television program is known fairly quickly. Placement of TV ads on certain combinations of shows allows an advertiser to reach as many in its target audience as it feels necessary. Availability of airtime and amount of budget are the main constraints on allowing an advertiser to reach as large an audience as possible.

Frequency Scheduling television permits frequency in concentrated blocks throughout a program, evening, week, month, or season. Heightened frequency may be necessary for a new product launch or an effort to obtain switching, while lower levels of frequency may be feasible for advertisers desiring more continuous exposure.

Media Image Given the prominence television has with its mass-market characteristic, TV advertising often carries a high degree of acceptability. Television is usually viewed favourably due to the higher costs of placement and production, which demonstrates a level of acceptance or establishment for those who advertise with this medium. The evolution of advertisers putting their ads on video hosting sites is testament for media image. A 60-second ad for the redesigned Subaru Forester featured a collection of sumo wrestlers washing their filthy vehicle. With Forester virtually in every second of the ad, the message "Japanese SUVs just got a little sexier" is humorously communicated with the imagery of the wrestlers engaged in a variety of manoeuvres. So humorous, in fact, that it racked up 700,0000 views online that helped spur a 5 percent increase in the Japanese SUV market.[6]

LIMITATIONS OF TELEVISION

Although television is unsurpassed from a creative perspective, the medium has several limitations that preclude its use by many advertisers. These problems include absolute cost, target audience selectivity, processing time, clutter, selective exposure, involvement, and media image.

Absolute Cost Despite the efficiency of TV in reaching large audiences, it is an expensive medium in which to advertise. The high cost of TV stems not only from the expense of buying airtime but also from the costs of producing a quality commercial. Production costs for a national brand 30-second spot average nearly $300,000 and can reach over $1 million for more elaborate commercials.[7] More advertisers are using media-driven creative strategies that require production of a variety of commercials, which drive up their costs. Even local ads can be expensive to produce and often are not of high quality. The high costs of producing and airing commercials often price small- and medium-size advertisers out of the market.

Target Audience Selectivity Some selectivity is available in television through scheduling, but advertisers who are seeking a very specific, often small, target audience find the coverage of TV often extends beyond their market. Geographic selectivity can be a problem for local advertisers such as retailers, since a station bases its rates on the total market area it reaches. For example, stations in Ottawa reach viewers in western Quebec and eastern Ontario. The small company whose market is limited to the immediate Ottawa area may find TV an inefficient media buy, since the stations cover a larger geographic area than the merchant's trade area.

Audience selectivity is improving as advertisers target certain groups of consumers through the type of program or day and/or time when they choose to advertise. However, TV still does not offer as much audience selectivity as radio, magazines, newspapers, or direct mail for reaching precise segments of the market.

Processing Time TV commercials usually last only 30 or 15 seconds and leave nothing tangible for the viewer to examine or consider. Commercials have become shorter as the demand for a limited amount of broadcast time has intensified and advertisers try to get more impressions from their media budgets. Commercials lasting 15 seconds have grown from 21 percent in 1991 to 29 percent in 2009, while 30-second commercials moved from 67 percent to 53 percent.[8]

An important factor in the decline in commercial length has been the rising media costs. Many advertisers see shorter commercials as the only way to keep their media costs in line. A 15-second spot typically sells for about two-thirds the price of a 30-second spot. By using 15-second commercials, advertisers can run additional spots to reinforce the message or reach a larger audience. Some advertisers believe shorter commercials can deliver a message just as effectively as longer spots for much less money.

Clutter The problems of short messages are compounded by the fact that the advertiser's message is only one of many spots and other nonprogramming material seen during a commercial break, so it may have trouble being noticed. One of advertisers' greatest concerns with TV advertising is the potential decline in effectiveness because of such *clutter*.

Imagine counting the number of commercials, promotions for the news or upcoming programs, or public service announcements that appear during a station break and the concern for clutter becomes obvious. In the United States, one study sponsored by the advertising industry found a record level of clutter during prime-time television broadcasts on the major networks. The study analyzed one week of broadcasts during May and November of 1999 and found that the four major networks averaged 16 minutes and 43 seconds of nonprogramming content.[9] With all of these messages competing for target audiences' attention, it is easy to understand why the viewer comes away confused or even annoyed and unable to remember or properly identify the product or service advertised.

One cause of clutter is the use of shorter commercials and **split-30s**, 30-second spots in which the advertiser promotes two different products with separate messages. The Canadian Radio-television and Telecommunications Commission (CRTC), which regulates television, permits only 12 minutes of commercials per hour. However, when simulcast Canadian commercials are run, there is extra time since U.S. TV stations often show more than 12 minutes of commercials. To fill this time, Canadian stations run ads for other shows, public service announcements, or news/entertainment vignettes. Thus, Canadian viewers experience a different kind of clutter than their American counterparts.

Selective Exposure   When advertisers buy time on a TV program, they are not purchasing guaranteed exposure but rather the opportunity to communicate a message to large numbers of consumers. But there is increasing evidence that the size of the viewing audience shrinks by a third during a commercial break for a variety of reasons.[10] Thus, viewers engage in selective exposure to television commercials resulting from zapping and zipping.

Zapping refers to changing channels to avoid commercials. An observational study found as much as a third of program audiences may be lost to electronic zapping when commercials appear.[11] Zapping has been fuelled by the emergence of 24-hour continuous-format programming on cable channels as viewers can switch over for news headlines, sports scores, or a music video and then return to the program. Zapping occurs because commercials are viewed as unbelievable, a poor use of time, and annoying—and TV ads suffer from greater ad avoidance than other media like radio, magazines, and newspapers.[12] Research shows that young adults zap more than older adults, and men are more likely to zap than are women.[13]

A study on zapping found that during commercial breaks 29 percent of the audience stopped watching television or switched away to another channel.[14] This loss of viewers was partially compensated for by an average increase of 7 percent of new viewers who zapped in from another channel. The study also found that people stop viewing TV during a commercial break because they have a reason to stop watching television altogether or they want to find out what is being shown on other channels. The number of people zapping in and out during breaks was not caused by the type of products being advertised or by specific characteristics of the commercials. Research has also shown that zappers recalled fewer of the brands advertised than non-zappers and that most of the brands that were recalled by zappers were placed near the end of the commercial break, which is when viewers would be likely to return to a program.[15]

A representative sample of Canadians on what they do to limit their exposure to television, radio, and online advertising shows a number of alternatives. Figure 11-2 illustrates the frequencies of those efforts that most pertain to television. Canadians engage in considerable zapping—61 percent, or about double the amount of zapping cited in previous studies. Actual amount of zapping versus perceived amount of zapping may account for this difference. This would suggest that people's attitude toward an ad and their actual behaviour toward it are dramatically at odds. Alternatively, the different statistics may indicate a trend to increased zapping or more technological usage on the part of Canadians to avoid ads.[16]

A challenge facing television networks and advertisers is how to discourage viewers from zapping. The networks use certain tactics to hold viewers' attention, such as previews of the next week's show or short closing scenes at the end of a program. Some programs start with action sequences before the opening credits and commercials. Some advertisers believe that producing different executions of a campaign theme is one way to maintain viewers' attention. Others think the ultimate way to zap-proof commercials is to produce creative advertising messages that will attract and hold viewers' attention.

Zipping occurs when customers fast-forward through commercials as they play back a previously recorded program. A study of VCR use found that most viewers fully or partially zipped commercials when watching a prerecorded program.[17] PVR technology entered Canada in 2001, about five years after the launch of the TiVo and Relay brands in the United States. By 2010, household penetration reached 16 percent in Canada and 27 percent in the U.S.[18] A study by Forrester Research in

FIGURE 11–2 How Canadians avoid television advertising

		Age				
	Total (n=1285)	15–19 (n=120)*	20–29 (n=204)*	30–39 (n=246)*	40–49 (n=270)*	50+ (n=445)
Change TV channels	61	83	79	66	64	43
Use mute button	18	7	7	14	14	29
Leave room/walk away	14	8	9	13	17	18
Do something else	12	7	7	11	13	15
Turn it off	7	10	8	6	6	7
Fast forward through ads	6	1	4	5	8	9
Get food/drink	6	3	2	5	7	10
Do household task	4	2	3	3	4	5
Ignore it	4	2	4	2	3	6
Read something	3	1	1	1	2	7
Watch TV channels that don't have ads	2	–	3	2	2	2
Turn down volume	2	1	–	2	2	3
Other/don't know	4	4	4	5	3	3

*n = the number of respondents.

Note: Total does not equal 100 percent because more than one response was accepted.

Source: The Strategic Counsel, Toronto.

the U.S. suggests that users watch 60 percent of their viewing from recorded programming and skip about 90 percent of the ads. However, another study released by *Mediaweek* found that most consumers could recognize the brands advertised as they zipped through the commercials.[19] A Bureau of Broadcast Measurement of Canada study finds that three-quarters of Canadians using PVR are aware of the brands advertised when zipping past commercials and that half stop zipping and view the ads.[20] While there is potential for missed television commercials due to zipping, one author suggests that the data showing how and when viewers avoid commercials will provide valued information to make advertising more relevant, engaging, and efficient.[21]

Involvement   The cumulative effect of the varied television characteristics generally implies that it is a low-involvement medium. While its invasiveness can expose the message to us readily and perhaps hold our attention with significant creative strategies and tactics, the relatively short processing time and clutter make for less effective media for an advertiser to significantly persuade a target audience. While this assertion of television appears historically accurate, some alternative ideas are emerging. For example, some shows attract a devout cohort of viewers that are so engaged or connected with the program their attention to advertising is heightened.[22]

Media Image   To many critics of advertising, TV commercials personify everything that is wrong with the industry. Critics often single out TV commercials because of their pervasiveness and the intrusive nature of the medium. Consumers are seen as defenceless against the barrage of TV ads, since they cannot control the transmission of the message and what appears on their screens. Viewers dislike TV advertising when they believe it is offensive, uninformative, or shown too frequently, or when they do not like its content.[23] Studies have shown that of the various forms of advertising, distrust is generally the highest for TV commercials.[24] Also, concern has been raised about the effects of TV advertising on specific groups, such as children or the elderly.[25]

BUYING TELEVISION ADVERTISING TIME

A number of options are available to advertisers that choose to use TV as part of their media mix. They can purchase ads on shows that are shown across the national or regional network versus a local spot announcement in a few cities. They can sponsor an entire program. They can purchase time in a variety of program formats that appeal to various types and sizes of audiences. With the growth of new television services, advertisers decide the degree to which they want to advertise on specialty channels. We explore these four decisions in this section.

The purchase of TV advertising time is a highly specialized phase of the advertising business, particularly for large companies spending huge sums of money. Large advertisers that do a lot of TV advertising generally use agency media specialists or specialized media buying services to arrange the media schedule and purchase TV time. We conclude this section with a discussion on measuring TV audiences because it is a critical input for TV decisions.

TYPES OF TELEVISION ADVERTISING

A basic decision for all advertisers is allocating their TV media budget to network versus local or spot announcements. Most national advertisers use network schedules to provide national coverage and supplement this with regional or local spot purchases to reach markets where additional coverage is desired.

Network Advertising   A common way advertisers disseminate their messages is by purchasing airtime from a **television network**. A network assembles a series of affiliated local TV stations, or **affiliates**, to which it supplies programming and services. These affiliates, most of which are independently owned, contractually agree to preempt time during specified hours for programming provided by the networks and to carry the national advertising within the program. The networks share the advertising revenue they receive during these time periods with the affiliates. The affiliates are also free to sell commercial time in non-network periods and during station breaks in the pre-empted periods to both national and local advertisers. Figure 11-3 summarizes the Canadian and U.S. networks and independent stations, along with the amount of consumption for each.

Canada's television industry features four national networks. The Canadian Broadcasting Corporation (CBC) is a Crown corporation of the federal government of Canada and its network reaches virtually all English-language homes. Radio-Canada is the CBC cousin for the French-language network reaching viewers in Quebec and other Canadian provinces and territories. The Canadian Television Network (CTV) operates as a national English-language service in most Canadian provinces. Finally, TVA, a private French-language network, broadcasts to most Quebec households and a significant number of French-speaking viewers throughout Canada. Many regional networks also dot the Canadian landscape, as seen in the following list.

Access	CityTV	SHOPTV Canada
A Channel	CTV	TELE-QUEBEC
CP24	Canwest	Television Quatre Saisons
CBC	SUN TV	

The networks generally have affiliate stations throughout the country or region. As the list implies, some of the national networks operate regionally as well. When

Station Group	Fall			
	2005	**2006**	**2007**	**2008**
CBC O&O	4.6	4.8	4.5	4.6
CBC Affiliates	0.7	0.5	0.6	0.7
CBC Total	**5.5**	**5.5**	**5.1**	**5.3**
CTV	13.4	13.7	12.7	11.8
Independent English	8.3	8.8	8.3	8.2
Global	7.4	7.6	7.2	6.2
Radio Canada O&O	3.4	2.9	3.1	3.3
Radio Canada Affiliates	0.7	0.7	0.6	0.6
Radio Canada Total	**4.2**	**3.6**	**3.7**	**3.9**
TVA	7.9	7.1	8.1	8.2
Tele-Quebec	0.7	0.7	0.6	0.7
Quatre Saisons	2.9	3.3	2.7	1.2
Total CDN Conventional	**50.6**	**50.3**	**48.4**	**45.5**
US: ABC Affiliates	1.7	2.0	1.5	1.5
NBC Affiliates	2.0	1.7	1.2	1.3
CBS Affiliates	2.1	2.3	2.2	2.5
FOX Affiliates	1.5	1.4	1.7	1.6
PBS	0.9	1.0	0.9	1.0
Independent/UPN/WB	2.4	2.0	1.9	1.7
Total US Conventional	**9.3**	**10.4**	**9.4**	**9.6**
Cable/Prov.	1.8	1.9	0.4	0.4
International	0.2	0.3	0.4	0.4
VCR	4.7	4.6	4.3	3.9
PVR	0.3	0.6	1.1	1.8
Demand	n/a	n/a	0.3	0.4
CDN Specialty/Pay	25.8	25.4	28.0	30.8
US Specialty/Pay	4.7	5.3	5.4	6.1
Others	1.2	1.2	0.8	0.8
Total Hours (Millions)	**678.7**	**659.4**	**657.8**	**668.5**

Source: BBM Fall 2008 Sweep Surveys (Mon-Sun 6A-2A)

FIGURE 11–3

Share of hours tuned by station group

an advertiser purchases airtime from one of the national or regional networks, the commercial is transmitted through the affiliate station network. Network advertising truly represents a mass medium, since the advertiser can broadcast its message simultaneously through many networks (Figure 11-4). Another advantage of this advertising is a simplified purchase process as the advertiser works with only one party or media representative to air a commercial.

The larger networks (e.g., CTV) offer the most popular programs and generally control prime-time programming. Advertisers interested in reaching larger audiences generally buy network time during the prime viewing hours of 8 p.m. and 11 p.m. Availability of time can be a problem as many advertisers turn to network advertising to reach mass markets. Traditionally, most prime-time commercial spots, particularly on the popular shows, are sold during the buying period in May/June/July that occurs before the TV season begins. Advertisers hoping to use prime-time network advertising must plan their media schedules and often purchase TV

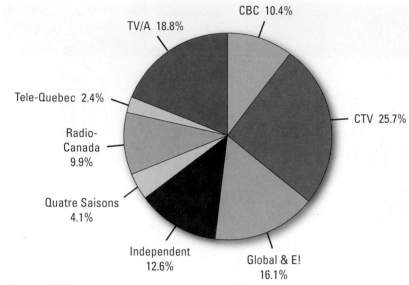

FIGURE 11–4

National television
audience share across
available Canadian
conventional
channels

Source: Media Digest 09/10

time as much as a year in advance. Demands from large clients who are heavy TV advertisers force the biggest agencies to participate in the up-front market. However, TV time is also purchased during the **scatter market** that runs through the TV season. Some key incentives for buying up front, such as cancellation options and lower prices, are available in the quarterly scatter market. Network TV can also be purchased on a regional basis, so an advertiser's message can be aired in certain sections of the country with one media purchase.

Spot Advertising   **Spot advertising** refers to commercials shown on local TV stations, with time negotiated and purchased directly from the individual stations or their national station representatives. **Station reps** act as sales agents for a number of local stations in dealing with national advertisers.

Spot advertising offers the national advertiser flexibility in adjusting to local market conditions. The advertiser can concentrate commercials in areas where market potential is greatest or where additional support is needed. This appeals to advertisers with uneven distribution or limited advertising budgets, as well as those interested in test marketing or introducing a product in limited market areas. National advertisers sometimes use spot television advertising through local retailers or dealers as part of their cooperative advertising programs and to provide local dealer support. This attractive option is most prevalent in Canada, with about 60 percent of all TV ads.

Sponsorship Advertising   Under a **sponsorship** arrangement, an advertiser assumes responsibility for the production and usually the content of the program as well as the advertising that appears within it. In the early days of TV, most programs were produced and sponsored by corporations and were identified by their name. Today most shows are produced by either the networks or independent production companies that sell them to a network; however, sponsorship is a good option in some situations.

A company might choose to sponsor a program for several reasons. Sponsorship allows the firm to capitalize on the prestige of a high-quality program, enhancing the image of the company and its products. Another reason is that the sponsor has control over the number, placement, and content of its commercials. Commercials can be of any length as long as the total amount of commercial time does not exceed network or station regulations. Advertisers introducing a new product line often sponsor a program and run commercials that are several minutes long to introduce and explain the product. For example, Becel sponsored (in part) the 2010 Academy Awards on CTV and showed a mini-film (i.e., a two-minute commercial) that depicted the brand's support for the Heart & Stroke Foundation's campaign for women's heart health. While these factors make sponsorship attractive to some companies, the high costs of sole sponsorship limit this option to large firms.

Scotiabank provides another example of innovative sponsorship. Historically, Scotiabank was successful with its sponsorship of CTV's "Business Report," shown during its *Canada AM* morning show. Looking for a consistent message across many of CTV's banners, Scotiabank hit on the solution of using the Report on Business Television's financial news show *Dollars & Sense,* as shown in Figure 11-5.[26]

TIME PERIODS AND PROGRAMS

Another decision in buying TV time is selecting the right program and time period for the advertiser's commercial messages. The cost of TV advertising time varies depending on the particular program and the time of day, since audience size varies as a function of these two factors. As for the particular program, *Hockey Night in Canada* is a popular selection due the audience size and composition. For these reasons, Red Baron beer produced by Brick Brewing Co. selected this program to launch its first-ever TV ad after extensive use of radio and out-of-home for many years.[27]

TV time periods are divided into **dayparts**, which are specific segments of a broadcast day. The time segments that make up the programming day vary from station to station. The various daypart segments attract different audiences in both size and nature, so advertising rates vary accordingly. Figure 11-6 shows how the viewership distribution varies across different dayparts. Prime time draws about 45 percent of per capita television consumption. Since firms that advertise during prime time must pay premium rates, this daypart is dominated by the large national advertisers.

329

Participants: Report on Business Television, CTV Newsnet, Canada AM, CTV News, CTV.ca, ROBTV.com and other relevant Bell Globemedia websites.

Run: For 10 weeks starting Oct. 6, 2003 and for 20 weeks starting Jan. 5, 2004.

Production: 150 original two-minute *Dollars & Sense* segments airing on Report on Business Television; 30 original 30-second *Dollars & Sense* interstitial vignettes airing on CTV Newsnet and *Canada AM.*

Online: Digitized content so interstitials and long-version *Dollars & Sense* segments are available online supporting the advertising.

Component breakdown:

Report on Business Television runs two-minute editorial segments titled *Dollars & Sense*; airing four times per day, with unique content, Monday to Friday. Editorial segments are sponsored by Scotiabank and packaged with a 10-second opening and closing billboard and a 30-second adjacent Scotiabank commercial. Scotiabank-branded stock ticker appears on screen during the editorial content.

CTV Newsnet runs 30-second *Dollars & Sense* interstitial vignettes (similar content to longer version but more compact and focused in-content delivery), airing two times per day, Monday to Friday; 30-second commercial adjacency following interstitial; 10-second customized closed captioning campaign promoting "*Dollars & Sense* brought to you by Scotiabank," Monday to Saturday.

Canada AM runs 30-second *Dollars & Sense* interstitial in fixed position on Wednesdays and Fridays with 30-second commercial adjacency.

CTV News runs 10-second customized closed-captioning campaign promoting "*Dollars & Sense* brought to you by Scotiabank," Monday to Friday.

FIGURE 11–5

The *Dollars & Sense* breakout

FIGURE   11–6   Percentage distribution of weekly per capita hours by daypart: Total Canada

Audiences Dayparts	Ind. 2+ % T min	A18+ % T min	F18+ % T min	M18+ % T min	T12–17 % T min	C2–11 % T min
M–F 6a–4:30p	22.8	22.3	24.4	20.0	20.3	29.7
M–F 4:30p–7p	7.1	6.9	7.2	6.5	8.7	9.4
M–Su 7p–11p	41.0	41.9	41.4	42.5	41.8	30.3
M–Su 11p–2a	11.6	12.3	11.5	13.3	9.0	4.1
Sa 6a–7p	8.1	7.6	7.2	8.0	9.7	13.3
Su 6a–7p	9.4	9.0	8.3	9.8	10.6	13.3

Source: BBM Fall 2001 & 2005; BBM-NMR-PPM Fall 2008.

The various dayparts are important to advertisers since they attract different demographic groups. For example, daytime TV generally attracts women; early morning attracts women and children. The late-fringe (late-night) daypart period has become popular among advertisers trying to reach young adults. Audience size and demographic composition also vary depending on the type of program.

SPECIALTY TELEVISION ADVERTISING

Canada has an extensive variety of specialty networks and digital specialty networks that advertisers run commercials on to reach specific target audiences. These specialty networks require either cable or satellite technology on the part of consumers to access this entertainment. We will briefly review these two technologies and then discuss the advertising on these specialty channels.

Cable and Satellite Technology   Perhaps the most significant development in the broadcast media has been the expansion of **cable television**. Cable, or CATV (community antenna television), which delivers TV signals through fibre or coaxial wire rather than the airways, was developed to provide reception to remote areas that could not receive broadcast signals. Canadians readily accepted cable in the 1970s since it was also the easiest (or only) method of receiving the feed of American channels. Today, cable penetration stands at about 62 percent, down from 76 percent in 1995.[28]

Direct broadcast satellite (DBS) services emerged in the 1990s. TV and radio programs are sent digitally from a satellite to homes equipped with a small dish. DBS companies have been aggressively marketing their service, superior picture quality, and greater channel choice as subscribers receive as many as 200 channels that include news, music, and sports in crisp, digital video and CD-quality sound. However, the pendulum can swing back the other way as more cable operators offer digital cable that allows them to match the number of channels received on satellites. Total satellite and digital cable penetration reached 67 percent in 2009. Combined, basic cable, digital cable, and satellite penetration in Canada stands at 90 percent.[29]

Cable and satellite subscribers pay a monthly fee and receive many channels, including the local Canadian and American network affiliates and independent stations, various specialty networks, American superstations, and local cable system channels. Both operators also offer programming that is not supported by commercial sponsorship and is available only to households willing to pay a fee beyond the

330

monthly subscription charge (e.g., The Movie Channel). Cable and satellite broaden the program options available to the viewer as well as the advertiser by offering specialty channels, including all-news, pop music, country music, sports, weather, educational, and cultural channels as well as children's programming.

Another feature offered by these television service providers is time shifting, which allows viewers to watch network feeds from other time zones. If viewers in Toronto miss their favourite show at 8 p.m., for example, they can watch the Vancouver feed three hours later. The problem is that those viewers are also seeing ads intended for Vancouver residents. So, while a national company may run a price promotion intended only for Western Canada, someone in the East may see the ad while watching a time-shifted signal and become annoyed when the promotion doesn't seem to exist. Even though Canada is the only country that allows time shifting, broadcasters recognize this is how cable and satellite companies have, in part, sold digital TV services. As a solution, CanWest has proposed to the CRTC that providers adopt "simultaneous substitution"—a solution modelled on how Canadian networks simulcast American programs.[30]

Specialty Networks   The proliferation of channels in both technologies has influenced the nature of television as an advertising medium. Expanded viewing options have led to considerable audience fragmentation. Much of the audience growth of specialty networks has come at the expense of national and regional networks. Specialty networks now have about 37 percent of the viewing audience. Many specialty networks have become very popular among consumers, leading advertisers to re-evaluate their media plans and the prices they are willing to pay for network and spot commercials on network affiliate stations. Advertising on specialty networks reached $1,025 million in 2008, up from $708 million in 2004. In comparison, all other television ad revenue increased from $2.256 billion in 2004 to $2.366 billion in 2008. The dominance of specialty TV is one reason why conventional networks are moving in this direction, as described in IMC Perspective 11-1.

This change in advertising revenue indicates that advertisers are using specialty networks to reach specific target audiences. Advertisers are also interested in specialty networks because of their low cost and flexibility. Advertising rates on cable programs are much lower than those for the shows on the major networks. This makes TV a much more viable media option for smaller advertisers with limited budgets and those interested in targeting their commercials to a well-defined target audience. Also, specialty network advertisers generally do not have to make the large up-front commitments the networks require, which may be as much as a year in advance.

In addition to costing less, specialty networks give advertisers much greater flexibility in the type of commercials that can be used. While most network commercials are 30- or 15-second spots, commercials on specialty networks can be longer (e.g., **infomercials** ranging from 3 to 30 minutes in length). Direct-response advertisers often use these longer ads to describe their products or services and encourage consumers to call in their orders during the commercial. The use of infomercials by direct-response advertisers is discussed in Chapter 16. Finally, specialty network advertising can be purchased on a national or a regional basis. Many large marketers advertise on specialty networks to reach large numbers of viewers across the country with a single media buy. Regional advertising on specialty networks is available but limited.

While specialty networks have become increasingly popular among national, regional, and local advertisers, they still have limitations. One concern is that specialty networks are overshadowed by the networks. The average person will watch more hours per week of a CBC or CTV affiliate than a single specialty network, although this is changing. Figure 11-7 shows a summary of the more highly viewed specialty channels. For example, the average Canadian watches TSN an average of 3.6 hours per week. Although specialty networks' share of the TV viewing audience has increased

Network Channel Changes

The Bureau of Broadcast Measurement of Canada reported that TV viewing is 55 percent and 37 percent for conventional channels and specialty channels, respectively. Regarding the rise of specialty channels, one media buyer commented, "Absolutely it's more cost-effective and cost-efficient. It's one of the reasons more advertisers have been migrating and spending a larger portion of their dollars with specialty versus conventional stations." In fact, specialty channels change their format quickly to adjust to market conditions. For example, Corus renamed its Scream channel to Dusk and moved the genre to suspense rather than horror to woo both women and advertisers. The impetus for the move gained momentum when it added the show *Supernatural* to its lineup and saw a 100 percent increase in the women 18–49 audience.

For this reason, networks are buying specialty channels and in some cases revamping the lineup. For example, Canwest replaced Fine Living Canada with the DIY Network. Since many HGTV shows had a DIY angle, the potential to develop this channel with an already established base of 2 million subscribers appeared solid. And given its past success of increased audience sizes for Showcase Diva and History, Canwest executives confidently predicted future success with DIY.

While networks look to specialty channels for increased revenue, they also looked online but the profitability of these ventures has not fully materialized. CTV's offerings developed well but the results are a paradox, as suggested by one executive: "The problem is that it's a very low-margin business. Unlike television, the more viewers watch video online, the more broadband and bandwidth has to be purchased, so there's a cost of retaining and having viewers on your site." So to balance the scale and get more profits, the specialty channels are a significant cash cow.

And the networks are not stopping there. One media expert offered five ways in which TV could evolve in the future according to the ambitions of major Canadian networks. One is that, except for the CBC, Canadian networks do not produce content like networks do in the U.S., and receive only advertising revenue. Increasingly, Canadian networks seek additional compensation for giving programs an initial point of distribution. Two, networks are increasingly putting pressure on the CRTC to stop the delivery of free TV and allow them to charge cable and satellite carriers a fee. Three, costs and smaller audiences have led to CTV and Global planning to abandon some smaller local stations. A continuation of this trend will erode local programming even further. Four, networks will likely continue buying more specialty channels since they offer a steady stream of revenue via the fees consumers pay. Five, networks may align themselves with particular U.S. networks for programming.

Sources: Melita Kuburas, "The Fall TV Fixer-Upper," *Strategy*, July 2009, p. 22; Grant Robinson, "Television's New Age," *The Globe and Mail*, April 27, 2009.

Question:

1. Explain why specialty channels are an attractive media vehicle for advertisers.

---

significantly, the viewers are spread out among the large number of channels available. Collectively, the specialty channels contribute to greater audience fragmentation as the number of viewers who watch any one cable channel is generally quite low. Figure 11-8 shows a breakout of television viewership across all formats.

The emergence a few years ago of dozens of digital specialty channels raises the question as to how well they are performing in attracting audiences in sufficient numbers for advertisers to consider them as a viable television vehicle. While their share of 1 or 2 percent of the television market may be considered disappointing, another perspective suggests that a more realistic benchmark should be used. Since access to a specific digital specialty channel requires a subscription similar to that of magazines, a more important comparison is to look at the leaders for each medium. In fact, about three-quarters of the digital specialty channels have more than half a million subscribers, something only three subscription magazines can claim.[31]

Recent research suggests that over the past few years 45 percent of all viewers watch more programs on specialty channels, with 41 percent indicating their perception that these channels have more interesting/entertaining programming versus

Specialty	Fall 2008			Fall 2007		
	Hours (000)	Reach (000)	Avg Hrs	Hours (000)	Reach (000)	Avg Hrs
ARTV (ARTV)	1,336	612	2.2	903	519	1.7
Report on Business Telev. Business News Network (BNN)	1,989	561	3.5	1,417	383	3.7
Bravo! (BRAVO)	3,529	1,672	2.1	3,902	1,788	2.2
Canal D (CANALD)	2,286	993	2.3	1,912	929	1.5
Canal Vie (VIE)	3,336	1,269	2.6	2,608	1,119	2.3
CBC Newsworld (CBC SP)	6,149	2,552	2.4	5,263	2,109	2.5
Comedy Network, the (COMEDY)	3,063	2,138	1.4	2,945	2,175	1.4
Country Music Television (CMT)	2,658	1,377	1.9	2,945	1,470	2.0
CP24 (CP 24)	3,463	1,183	2.9	3,004	962	3.1
CTV NewsNet (CTVNNT)	2,789	1,229	2.3	2,588	1,204	2.2
DejaView (DEJAVU)	1,056	416	2.5	1,024	420	2.4
Discovery Channel (DISCVY)	6,136	3,438	1.8	5,266	3,202	1.7
Fairchild Television (FAIR TV)	1,825	150	12.2	1,462	173	8.5
Family Channel, the (FAMILY)	10,407	2,878	3.6	9,596	2,693	3.6
Food Network Canada (FOOD)	3,760	1,871	2.0	3,690	1,719	2.1
HGTV Canada (HGTV)	5,491	2,639	2.1	5,223	2,405	2.2
Historia (HISTFR)	1,527	718	2.1	1,085	529	2.1
History Television (HISTTV)	7,182	2,803	2.6	4,504	2,153	2.1
MuchMoreMusic (MMM)	1,279	929	1.4	964	796	1.2
MuchMusic (MMUSIC)	1,632	1,070	1.5	2,115	1,208	1.8
Mystery (MYS E)	1,371	492	2.8	1,282	452	2.8
RDI (RDI)	5,261	1,311	4.0	4,046	1,106	3.7
RDS - Le Reseau des Sports (RDS)	9,981	2,370	4.2	8,321	2,003	4.2
Rogers SportsNet (ROGRSP)	11,635	3,985	2.9	10,018	3,423	2.9
Score Television Network, the (SCORE)	1,720	896	1.9	1,996	973	2.1
Series+ (SERIES)	3,484	856	4.1	4,504	851	5.3
Showcase (SHWCSE)	2,500	1,603	1.6	2,329	1,398	1.7
Showcase Action (ACTION)	1,010	506	2.0	894	417	2.1
Showcase Diva (DIVA)	1,342	593	2.3	611	341	1.8
Space (SPACE)	3,106	1,278	2.4	3,094	1,240	2.5
Telelatino (LATINO)	1,227	410	3.0	1,251	469	2.7
Teletoon English (TOON E)	3,396	1,596	2.1	3,546	1,771	2.0
Teletoon French (TOON F)	2,079	790	2.6	1,987	724	2.8
Treehouse (TREE)	7,366	1,814	4.1	8,985	1,987	4.5
TSN (TSN)	18,190	5,082	3.6	12,450	4,160	3.0
TV5 (TV5)	1,527	540	2.8	1,639	532	3.1
TVTropolis (TV TROP)	2,613	1,822	1.4	2,961	2,084	1.4
Vision TV (VISION)	3,083	1,321	2.3	1,682	1,012	1.7
VRAK TV (VRAKTV)	2,358	792	3.0	2,525	859	2.9
W Network (WNET+)	4,861	2,367	2.1	4,282	2,285	1.9
Weather Network, the (WEATHR)	2,743	1,959	1.4	2,429	1,719	1.4
YTV	6,892	2,653	2.6	6,144	2,457	2.5
Ztele	1,334	654	2.0	1,228	607	2.0S

Source: Nielsen Media Research, People Meter Data; BBM Canada—Weekly Hours Tuned & Weekly Reach by Network

FIGURE 11-7

Average hours watched/week for selected specialty channels

333

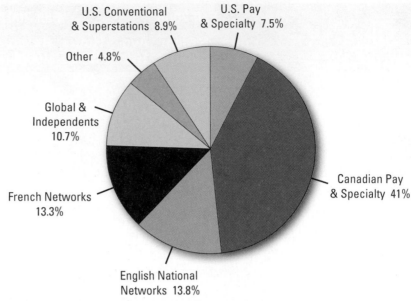

FIGURE 11–8

Viewing habits of
Canadians 2+ by
station groups

Source: BBM Fall 2008 Sweep Surveys (Mon-Sun 6A-2A)

conventional channels. Furthermore, 37 percent devote more than half of their
viewing time to specialty channels, and a similar number will consider a specialty
channel first when they do not have a planned program to watch. With cost per rating point being about 50 percent lower and a greater ability to target an audience, it
is not surprising to see that advertising revenues for specialty channels are growing
significantly faster compared to conventional channels.[32]

MEASURING THE TELEVISION AUDIENCE

One of the most important considerations in TV advertising is the size and composition of the viewing audience. Audience measurement is critical to advertisers as
well as to the networks and stations. Advertisers want to know the size and characteristics of the audience they are reaching when they purchase time on a particular
program. And since the rates they pay are a function of audience size, advertisers
want to be sure audience measurements are accurate. Audience size and composition are also important to the network or station, since they determine the amount
it can charge for commercial time. Shows are cancelled once they fail to attract
enough viewers to make their commercial time attractive to potential advertisers. In
this section, we examine how audiences are measured and how advertisers use this
information in planning their media schedules.

Audience Measurement   Television audiences are measured and communicated
by the Bureau of Broadcast Measurement of Canada (BBM). BBM is a not-for-profit
broadcast research company based on cooperation among the Canadian Association
of Broadcasters, the Association of Canadian Advertisers, and Canadian advertising
agencies. BBM Canada collects TV audience measurement data with two methods:
portable people meter (PPM) for national and some local markets, and diary for
remaining local markets. This current data collection arrangement has undergone
tremendous change over the past few years.

Historically, BBM measured local market audiences with the diary method and
Nielsen Media Research measured national audiences technologically. A meter
attached to the household TV recorded when individuals watched. Over time,
Nielsen expanded to a few local cities and BBM followed by introducing the same
meter technology for national and some local markets. During this development,

BBM introduced PPM technology to measure French-speaking audiences in Quebec. For a period of a few years, duplication of audience measurement in Canada existed between the two organizations until the current situation emerged.

Currently, BBM's portable people meter collects data nationally and in the four largest local markets: Montreal (French), Toronto-Hamilton, Calgary, and Vancouver-Victoria. People in the panel wear a device that automatically records a silent audio signal emitted from programming. In fact, the PPM is capable of receiving the signal from other media such as radio, cinema, or any medium that emits a sound. The device records information regarding station, program, and time. Each evening, the device is placed in a docket and the data are transferred to BBM. The new method offers numerous measurement benefits over the previous technology; we highlight four major ones here:

- unobtrusive, as the person does not interact with the device while measurement occurs
- individual level measurement instead of a household or television basis
- measures exposure to multiple media for each individual
- measures exposure of recorded programming from any technology (e.g., PVR)

BBM Canada also uses the diary research method for collecting television audience information in 40 local markets. A booklet for each television owned in the household is sent to a representative sample of households. BBM gathers viewership information from this sample and then projects this information to the total viewing area. The diary method works as follows. Each person aged two years or older records his or her viewing for one week in the booklet. The recordings are based on 15-minute increments from 6:00 a.m. until 2:00 a.m. Viewers write down station call letters, channel numbers, programs, and who is watching. The booklet also contains a number of basic demographic questions to be completed by each individual. As expected, the diary method is a substantially weaker measurement system than the original (and new) meter technology; however, the cost efficiencies and ease of use of the PPM will likely lead to expansion to local markets in future.

To help its customers understand the data, BBM Canada provides an extensive array of products. Market reports are a summary of the audience sizes across all markets by time block, program listings, and time period. Their reach book summarizes the demographic information across each province, data area, and station. BBM Canada also offers guidelines on population estimates and booklets that assist its members in understanding the geographic boundaries studied and the research methodology. BBM Canada's television data book breaks down viewing habits across different markets with user-friendly graphs and charts. The EM Stats Card provides detailed information for each extended market in terms of cable, satellite, PVR, and VCR penetration in addition to other similar macro-level data. Finally, two different documents tabulate the audiences for the different television shows. As a complement, BBM Canada also offers four different software packages that allow its members to analyze the data in a variety of ways.

Audience Measures   The data collected allow for the calculation of two critical audience measures, program rating and share of audience. A **program rating** is the percentage of people in a geographic area tuned in to a specific program during a specific time period. The program rating is calculated by dividing the number of people tuned to a particular show by the total number of people in the geographic area. A **ratings point** represents 1 percent of all the people in a particular area tuned to a specific television program. As suggested above, a program rating is calculated nationally and for each local market.

The program rating is the key number to the stations, since the amount of money they can charge for commercial time is based on it. Ratings points are very important to the networks as well as to individual stations. A 1 percent change in a program's ratings over the course of a viewing season can gain or lose substantial dollars in advertising revenue. Advertisers also follow ratings closely, since they are the key measure for audience size and commercial rates.

Another important audience measurement figure is the **share of audience**, which is the percentage of people using TV in a specified time period that are tuned to a specific program. Audience share is always higher than the program rating unless all people are watching television (in which case they would be equal). Share figures are important since they reveal how well a program does with the available viewing audience. For example, late at night the size of the viewing audience drops substantially, so the best way to assess the popularity of a late-night program is to examine the share of the available audience it attracts relative to competing programs. Again, share of audience is calculated nationally and for each local market.

Since the data are recorded on a minute-by-minute basis for the PPM and 15-minute increments for the diary method, the program ratings and share of audience can be examined over different time intervals. In fact, some believe that the ability of new technology to measure audiences with short time intervals on a minute basis will provide unexpected research results regarding TV viewing behaviour in the future.[33] Also, since the demographic and other consumer data are recorded, these measures can be investigated in great detail for many target audience profile variables. The sheer complexity and extensiveness of the data makes advanced software and analysis paramount.

Audience Measurement Reporting   The collected television data are analyzed with software applications from different suppliers. BBM Analytics is a subsidiary of BBM and offers numerous solutions for examining the program ratings and share of audience data extensively by time, by different audience characteristics. While Nielsen no longer collects TV audience data in Canada, it remains a major player as a third-party processor with its sophisticated software. For example, it is capable of determining the audience size by person and by household with various distribution skews, many reach levels over time (i.e., daily, weekly, monthly), and other usage statistics in terms of amount of TV consumed. Numerous other third-party processors exist as it is a competitive market for turning data into valuable media planning information.

Media buying agencies and advertising agencies subscribe to these data and analytic services and use the information for developing media plans for their clients. Advertisers can access some of this aggregate information through the Television Bureau. The TVB is an industry association for television networks, television stations, and firms that sell television advertising time. It offers resources to those in the television industry to demonstrate the value and importance of television as a medium versus competing media (e.g., magazines). It publishes basic facts garnered from the aforementioned sources and conducts primary research through independent market research firms. Based on this research, television consistently outperforms the other media on a number of variables. Television reaches 88 percent of the country on a daily basis and 95 percent on a weekly basis, and it is perceived as being the most authoritative (47 percent) and most influential (62 percent) compared to radio, the Internet, daily newspapers, and magazines.[34]

RADIO

In contrast to television, radio has evolved into a primarily local advertising medium characterized by highly specialized programming appealing to very narrow segments of the population. The importance of radio is best demonstrated by the numbers. Radio reaches 91 percent of all Canadians over the age of 12 each week and has grown into a ubiquitous background to many activities (Figure 11-9). The average Canadian listens to radio about two hours per day. The pervasiveness of this medium continues as radio advertising revenue grew from $1.05 billion in 2001 to

National Brands Give Radio a Spin

A primary strength of radio is its cost efficiency and low absolute cost, which is very appealing for local and/or small businesses. Most radio stations offer creative and recording services for these brands to develop a message or an entire campaign. For example, the Looking Glass Foundation of B.C. increased its funding through donations by successfully using radio so that it could develop a property to better serve those with eating disorders. But the continued growth of radio advertising revenue, now at $1.3 billion, suggests that its strength as a media choice for national or regional brands must be a factor—as evidenced by some recent examples.

Boston Pizza used radio in Quebec for a 13-week campaign to promote its "Mangiare, Mangiare" theme for special meals at $9.95. A popular star, Marc Hervieux, sings opera in Italian for a while until he humorously ends the solo due to his lack of rhyming skills. The 10-second spot's use of Italian intended to break through the clutter and remind consumers that Boston Pizza offered authentic Italian food. The chain also used 30-second sponsorships for news, weather, and traffic in French on two Astral Media stations.

James Ready Beer successfully transferred its creative concept from outdoor to radio. Long known for its relatively inexpensive price, "Help Us Keep This Beer a Buck," the brewery used only half a billboard, saying that it was saving money so the price of the beer would stay reasonable. The ad invited consumers though various channels (newspaper ads, e-mail, in-case newsletters) to create the rest of the ad, which culminated in over 100 unique "co-op" messages. In fact, the brewer and media company placed the ads in the same vicinity of their residence. For radio, the concept emerged as "Share Our Radio Space," where fans could complete the ending of the radio spots. The ads could be anything from marriage proposals to band gigs, or whatever an individual wanted to market. The ads began on various rock stations in seven Ontario cities.

Lay's potato chips used a radio call-in show as the style for its national ad campaign. Farmer Joe Oulton, the same person featured in three TV spots, received calls from people asking for directions. Instead of actually helping them, Joe directed the questioner to the local farm where Lay's grew its potatoes. The 20 ads featured local scenarios—like a lost Calgarian on the Edmonton Trail—to add a bit of folksy humour to the message of authentic home-grown potatoes in every bite.

Sources: Brian Dunn, "Boston Pizza Promotes Specials with Radio Spots," *Marketing Magazine*, April 13, 2009; Carey Toane, "James Ready Shares the Radio Waves," *Strategy*, June 2009, p. 8; Carey Toane, "Outdoor," *Strategy*, June 2009, p. 45; Emily Wexler, "Radio," *Strategy*, June 2009, p. 46.

Question:

1. How does radio help these brands achieve their communication objectives?

$1.55 billion in 2008. In this section, we review radio's strengths for advertisers to communicate messages to their current and potential customers and summarize the inherent limitations that affect its role in the advertiser's media strategy. We also show how buying radio time is mostly similar to that of television. IMC Perspective 11-3 highlights radio's recent attractiveness.

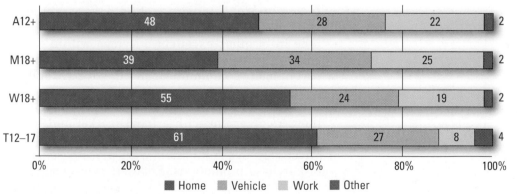

FIGURE 11-9

Percentage of listening by location and demographic

Source: BBM Survey 1, 2006, National, Mo-Su, 5a-1a, AQH Audience.

STRENGTHS OF RADIO

Radio has many strengths compared to other media, including cost efficiency and absolute cost, reach and frequency, target audience selectivity, geographic coverage, scheduling flexibility, creativity for cognitive responses, and image.

Cost Efficiency and Absolute Cost   One of the main strengths of radio as an advertising medium is its low cost. Radio commercials are very inexpensive to produce. They require only a script of the commercial to be read by the radio announcer or a copy of a prerecorded message that can be broadcast by the station. The cost for radio time is also low. The low relative costs of radio make it one of the most efficient of all advertising media, and the low absolute cost means the budget needed for an effective radio campaign is often lower than that for other media.

Reach and Frequency   The low cost of radio means advertisers can build more reach and frequency into their media schedule within a certain budget. They can use different stations to broaden the reach of their messages and multiple spots to ensure adequate frequency. Radio commercials can be produced more quickly than TV spots, and the companies can afford to run them more often.[35] Many national advertisers also recognize the cost efficiency of radio and use it as part of their media strategy. Figures 11-10 and 11-11 indicate the degree of reach.

Target Audience Selectivity   Another major advantage of radio is the high degree of audience selectivity available through the various program formats and geographic coverage of the numerous stations. Radio lets companies focus their advertising on specialized audiences such as certain demographic and lifestyle groups. Most areas have radio stations with formats such as adult contemporary, easy listening, classical music, country, news/talk shows, jazz, and all news, to name a few. BBM tracks radio listeners across 20 different radio formats. Elusive consumers like teenagers, students, and working adults can be reached more easily through radio than most other media. Furthermore, light television viewers spend considerably more time with radio than with TV and are generally an upscale market in terms of income and education level. Light readers of magazines and newspapers also spend more time listening to radio.

Geographic Coverage   Radio is essentially a local media. In this respect, since all listeners can tune in, it offers excellent coverage within its geographic scope. Radio stations become an integral part of many communities, and the deejays and program hosts may become popular figures. Advertisers often use radio stations and personalities to enhance their involvement with a local market and to gain influence with local retailers. Radio also works very effectively in conjunction with place-based/point-of-purchase promotions. Retailers often use on-site radio broadcasts combined with special sales or promotions to attract consumers to their stores and get

338

FIGURE   11–10

Percentage weekly reach and hours tuned by major demographic

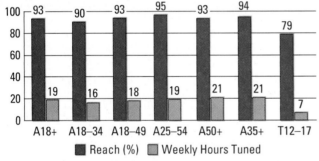

Source: BBM Survey 1 2006, National, Mo-Su, 5a-1a; BBM Survey 1 2008, National, Mo-Su, 5a-1a

FIGURE   11–11

Percentage weekly reach by major demographic, by location

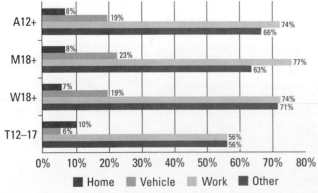

Source: FFM Survey 1 2006, Mo-Su, 5a-1a; BBM Survey 1 2008, Mo-Su, 5a-1a.

them to make a purchase. Live radio broadcasts are also used in conjunction with event marketing.

Scheduling Flexibility   Radio is probably the most flexible of all the advertising media because it has a very short closing period, which means advertisers can change their message almost up to the time it goes on the air. Radio commercials can usually be produced and scheduled on very short notice. Radio advertisers can easily adjust their messages to local market conditions and marketing situations.

Creativity for Cognitive Responses   The verbal nature of radio ads makes them ideal for long copy to select target audiences who may appreciate greater detailed information for some products. Alternatively, radio ads can also provide more concise brand information in a timely manner. Moreover, both of these factors are highly relevant for those listening in their car, which is a significant percentage of radio listenership. In either case, the informative nature of radio advertising makes it an opportunistic medium to connect with a target audience on a more rational level.

Media Image   Radio advertising in general has a good media image. Consumers rely on radio for news, weather, and traffic information, not to mention the obvious program content. Thus, radio is well appreciated and this spills over to the ads, as 77 percent of Canadians feel that radio advertising is acceptable.

LIMITATIONS OF RADIO

Several factors limit the effectiveness of radio as an advertising medium, among them creativity for emotional responses, amount of processing time, target audience coverage, listener attention, selective exposure, clutter, and involvement. The media planner must consider them in determining the role the medium will play in the advertising program.

Creativity for Emotional Responses   A major drawback of radio as an advertising medium is the absence of a visual image. The radio advertiser cannot show the product, demonstrate it, or use any type of visual appeal or information. While the creative options of radio are limited, many advertisers take advantage of the absence of a visual element to let consumers create their own picture of what is happening in a radio message. Some ads encourage listeners to use their imagination when processing a commercial message.

Radio may also reinforce television messages through a technique called **image transfer**, where the images of a TV commercial are implanted into a radio spot.[36] First the marketer establishes the video image of a TV commercial. Then it uses a similar, or even the same, audio portion (spoken words and/or jingle) as the basis for the radio counterpart. The idea is that when consumers hear the radio message, they will make the connection to the TV commercial, reinforcing its video images. Image transfer offers advertisers a way to make radio and TV ads work together. This promotional piece put out by the Radio Advertising Bureau of the U.S. shows how the image transfer process works (Exhibit 11-2).

Amount of Processing Time   A radio commercial is, like a TV ad, a short-lived and fleeting message that is externally paced and does not allow the receiver to control the rate at which it is processed.

Exhibit 11-2   The Radio Advertising Bureau promotes the concept of imagery transfer.

FIGURE 11–12

Share of radio hours tuned by major station—
English 18+

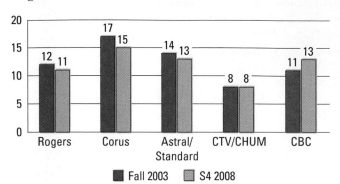

Source: BBM, Mo-Su, 5a-1a; as reported in CMDC Ownership and Market
Share Report.

FIGURE 11–13

Share of radio hours tuned by major station—
French 18+

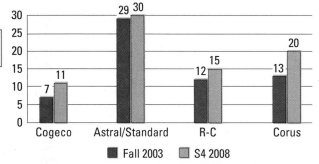

Source: BBM, Mo-Su, 5a-1a; as reported in CMDC Ownership and Market
Share Report.

Target Audience Coverage Another problem with radio is the high level of audience fragmentation due to the large number of stations. The percentage of the market tuned to any particular station is usually very small. The top-rated radio station in many major metropolitan areas with a number of AM and FM stations may attract less than 10 percent of the total listening audience. Advertisers that want a broad reach in their radio advertising media schedule have to buy time on a number of stations to cover even a local market. With recent media mergers in Canada, syndicated radio stations now provide advertisers with greater coverage, thus minimizing this limitation to a lesser degree. Figure 11-12 and Figure 11-13 highlight the major players for English and French listeners.

Listener Attention Another problem that plagues radio is that it is difficult to retain listener attention to commercials. Radio programming, particularly music, is often the background to some other activity and may not receive the listener's full attention. Thus they may miss all or some of the commercials. This is slightly less of a concern because radio is with consumers throughout the day while doing many activities (Figure 11-14).

Selective Exposure One environment where radio has a more captive audience is in cars. But getting listeners to expose themselves to commercials can still be difficult. Most people preprogram their car radio and change stations during commercial breaks. A study by Avery Abernethy found large differences between exposure to radio programs versus advertising for listeners in cars. They were exposed to only half of the advertising broadcast and changed stations frequently to avoid commercials.[37] While radio, like television, does suffer from a degree of selective exposure, research suggests ad avoidance is about 30 percent for radio and 40 percent for television.[38]

FIGURE 11–14

Activities while listening to radio—18+, some/most of the time

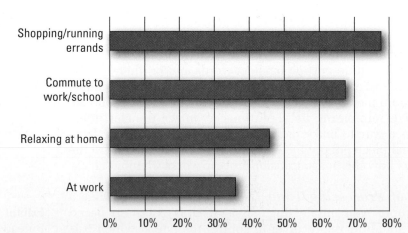

Source: Radio Marketing Bureau, Foundation Research Study 2009. adults 18+.

Chapter 11 Broadcast Media

Clutter Clutter is just as much a problem with radio as with other advertising media. Radio stations can play as many minutes of advertising as they like. Most radio stations carry an average of nearly 10 minutes of commercials every hour. During the popular morning and evening rush hours, the amount of commercial time may exceed 12 minutes. Advertisers must create commercials that break through the clutter or use heavy repetition to make sure their messages reach consumers.

Involvement Similar to television, radio is generally considered a low-involvement medium since it is faced with the same characteristics of short processing time and clutter. In fact, it may be seen as being less involving since it has the additional limitation of no visual.

BUYING RADIO TIME

The purchase of radio time is similar to that of television; advertisers can make either network or spot buys. Since these options were reviewed in the section on buying TV time, we discuss them here only briefly.

Network Radio Advertising time on radio can be purchased on a network basis. This is a relatively new option for advertisers, who can now run ads on the CHUM radio network, the Team Sports Radio Network, and a few others. Using networks minimizes the amount of negotiation and administrative work needed to get national or regional coverage, and the costs are lower than those for individual stations. However, the number of affiliated stations on the network roster and the types of audiences they reach may vary, so the use of network radio reduces advertisers' flexibility in selecting stations.

Spot Radio National advertisers can also use spot radio to purchase airtime on individual stations in various markets. The purchase of spot radio provides greater flexibility in selecting markets, individual stations, and airtime and adjusting the message for local market conditions. By far the heaviest users of radio are local advertisers; the majority of radio advertising time is purchased from individual stations by local companies. Auto dealers, retailers, restaurants, and financial institutions are among the heaviest users of local radio advertising.

TIME CLASSIFICATIONS

As with television, the broadcast day for radio is divided into various time periods or dayparts, as shown in Figure 11-15. The size of the radio listening audience varies widely across the dayparts, and advertising rates follow accordingly. The largest radio audiences (and thus the highest rates) occur during the early morning and

Time Block		Women 18+	Men 18+	Teens	Total
Breakfast	Mo–Fr 6–10a	48	48	4	100
Midday	Mo–Fr 10a–4p	51	48	1	100
Drive	Mo–Fr 4–7p	46	49	5	100
Evening	Mo–Fr 7p–12a	44	42	9	100
Source: BBM Survey 1 2006, National, AQH Audience					

FIGURE 11–15

Audience composition by daypart (%)

late afternoon drive times. Radio rates also vary according to the number of spots or type of audience plan purchased, the supply and demand of time available in the local market, and the ratings of the individual station. Rate information is available directly from the stations and is summarized in CARD. Some stations issue grid rate cards. However, many stations do not adhere strictly to rate cards. Their rates are negotiable and depend on factors such as availability, time period, and number of spots purchased.

MEASURING THE RADIO AUDIENCE

As noted earlier, BBM Canada also provides information on radio listenership using the PPM and a diary method similar to television. Surveys are done twice per year in over 130 radio markets. BBM Canada publishes many reports associated with these surveys. Market reports summarize each radio station's audience by occupation, language, and other important characteristics. Other similar reports with greater aggregation across regions are also published. As for television, BBM Canada provides its members with many supporting documents to understand how to use radio as a communication tool. It also offers many software applications so that advertisers can purchase radio media effectively and efficiently. The three basic elements in the BBM Canada reports are:

- Person estimates—the estimated number of people listening.
- Rating—the percentage of listeners in the survey area population.
- Share—the percentage of the total estimated listening audience.

These three estimates are further defined by using quarter-hour and cume figures. The **average quarter-hour (AQH) figure** expresses the average number of people estimated to have listened to a station for a minimum of five minutes during any quarter-hour in a time period. This figure helps to determine the audience and cost of a spot schedule within a particular time period.

Cume stands for cumulative audience, the estimated total number of different people who listened to a station for at least five minutes in a quarter-hour period within a reported daypart. Cume estimates the reach potential of a radio station.

The **average quarter-hour rating (AQH RTG)** expresses the estimated number of listeners as a percentage of the survey area population. The **average quarter-hour share (AQH SHR)** is the percentage of the total listening audience tuned to each station. It shows the share of listeners each station captures out of the total listening audience in the survey area.

Audience research data on radio are often limited, particularly compared with TV, magazines, or newspapers. The BBM audience research measurement mostly focuses on demographics and a handful of lifestyle factors. Most users of radio are local companies that cannot support research on radio listenership in their markets. Thus, media planners do not have as much audience information available to guide them in their purchase of radio time as they do with other media.

The Radio Marketing Bureau (RMB) is an organization that plays a similar role for radio as the Television Bureau of Canada, discussed earlier in this chapter, does for TV. It acts as a resource for radio stations and those involved with selling airtime for radios. Its mission is to educate advertisers on the effective use of the radio medium and to assist advertisers in meeting their communication objectives. The Radio Marketing Bureau offers professional services to advertisers if needed. It also offers a training and certificate program for those working in the radio industry. Finally, this organization does some research to help support radio as a viable communication medium.

IMC PLANNING: STRATEGIC USE OF BROADCAST MEDIA

We continue with our IMC planning sections by relating the use of TV and radio with respect to achieving communication and behavioural objectives in general and in terms of the different stages of the consumer decision-making process for the target audience. This builds on our discussions in earlier chapters and highlights the importance of planning creative and media together.

TELEVISION

The creative opportunities and many types of television allow it to play a variety of roles in the decision-making process for the target audience. We link the different types of ads with communication objectives and decision-making processes because the integration of television with other media or tools is predicated upon which types of TV ads will be run. For example, the suggestion to combine TV with Internet advertising, an event sponsorship, or perhaps out-of-home media is contingent on how the two media are planned to influence the target audience. As promotional planners decide upon TV as part of their IMC plan, it is critical to consider its communication objectives in relation to the objectives the other tools will contribute.

Promotional managers can plan for ads to influence their target audience at the pre-purchase and need recognition stages. These kinds of ads could focus on one key benefit or consumption experience, and identify the brand sufficiently to contribute to awareness. For example, some car ads fit this role quite nicely, like the commercials positioning the Toyota Corolla as a reliable vehicle. The plan included other media to encourage further progress through the decision-making process. In this case, the Corolla utilized newspaper advertising for additional explanation and support of the reliability (e.g., information search), and transit station posters as a reminder for a test drive (e.g., purchase decision). For Corolla, the media selection, including television, planned a particular role for each selection to encourage all aspects of the decision-making process, each with particular attitudinal communication objectives.

Alternatively, marketers could provide a television message with information to influence their target audience while evaluating alternative brands. The WestJet ads communicated the enhanced service level compared to its previous discount offering to encourage Air Canada consumers to switch; this message would be critical at the alternative evaluation stage. The many executions showed the variety of customer experiences enhanced by the commitment level of the staff to serve its customers in an exemplary manner.

Finally, planners often schedule ads that have more immediate purchase intention or purchase facilitation objectives for the target to take action. An additional type of car ad communicates a promotional event or encourages a dealer visit for a test drive. Virtually all car brands resort to TV ads like this, yet the intensity of the "call to action" and the frequency varies considerably. When these ads are run, car brands typically are not running other types of TV ads but might have instructions to consult the newspaper for additional information. Another example in the social marketing realm is the United Way of Toronto's TV ads that showed a "helping hand" in two different scenarios with a verbal message requesting donations and the Internet address shown visually.

343

RADIO

While all media are inherently in competition for advertising revenue spent by media planners, radio finds itself with a very significant niche of flexibility that allows it to be in the plans for national brands like Bell and local advertisers like the pizzeria just around the corner. Moreover, the characteristics of the medium allow planners to integrate radio with virtually any other media or IMC tool.

Whether we are considering a national advertiser like Bell or a local business, oftentimes the purchase decision stage is the one where maximum influence occurs. For example, many radio messages have a time frame for encouraging purchase through participation with a price promotion. Retailers use radio extensively for various sales, for instance. Alternatively, other radio messages might remind the target audience of entertainment and leisure activities occurring in the city or province within a time frame requiring more immediate action. In these situations, the key communication objectives attained are brand purchase intention or brand purchase facilitation. As we can see from these points, the scheduling flexibility of radio permits attainment of particular communication objectives or messaging consumers exactly when they are planning to make a purchase decision.

The lower costs associated with radio can contribute to building brand equity or an identifiable positioning through the affordability of repetition. A recent example of this is the prevalent use of radio by Sleep Country Canada, with owner Christine McGee as the spokesperson. The radio ads give the central positioning as a leading mattress retailer much added frequency beyond its television commercials, thus indicating a natural way to build brands by integrating a consistent message across two broadcast media (see Figure 11-16 and Figure 11-17).

Radio's flexibility and cost implications allow it to support other IMC tools. It can suggest that the target audience visit a brand's Internet site or look for a direct mail piece sent to their home—again, both are action-oriented with a time frame—or with some kind of intention on the part of the receiver of the message. One study found a high percentage of listeners check the Internet, perform a search, type in a web address, or visit the radio station's website after hearing about something on the radio.[39]

As noted above with price promotions, many other sales promotions can be communicated through radio, particularly those affiliated with sponsorships. Radio can be a key integrating medium to generate awareness of the other IMC tools for further communication in the target audience's decision making.

FIGURE   11–16   Radio's influence on Internet

Agree/Strongly Agree to Statement	Adults 18+	Working adults	Adults w/kids	A18–34	A25–54	HHI $100K+
I check the Internet after hearing about something on radio	41%	42%	47%	46%	44%	43%
Radio ads prompted search the Internet	45%	45%	54%	45%	48%	50%
I have typed website address in my browser just after heard on radio	35%	35%	43%	35%	38%	35%

Source: Radio Marketing Bureau, Foundation Research Study 2009. adults 18+.

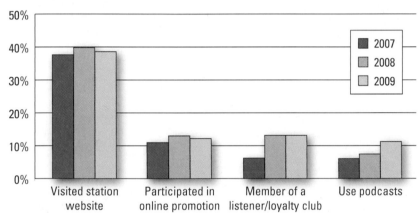

Source: Radio Marketing Bureau, Foundation Research Study 2009. adults 18+.

FIGURE   11–17

Local radio stations online

CHAPTER OBJECTIVES AND SUMMARY

1 To consider the strengths and limitations of television as an advertising medium.

Television is a pervasive medium in most consumers' daily lives and offers advertisers the opportunity to reach vast audiences with very frequent messages. Over the past 60 years, national advertisers, and many local ones, employed TV as their leading medium. No other medium offers its creative capabilities; the combination of sight, sound, and movement give the advertiser a vast number of options for presenting a commercial message. As a primary medium for these advertisers, the creative opportunities of television contribute to the brand's awareness and help in establishing or maintaining a brand's position. Television also offers advertisers mass coverage at a low relative cost. Variations in programming and audience composition are helping TV offer scheduling opportunities and some audience selectivity to advertisers.

While television is often viewed as the ultimate advertising medium, it has several limitations, including the high absolute cost of producing and airing commercials, low target audience selectivity, short processing time, extensive clutter, high selective exposure, and distrustful image. Despite these concerns, consumers generally appreciate brands more if they are advertised on television because the expenditure signals a stronger and more reputable brand.

2 To understand how to purchase different types of television advertising, alternative time periods, and specialty television advertising.

Television advertising is time dependent rather than space-oriented like print advertising. Advertisers select the time, day, week, and month in which they want their ads to be seen. Television is a system of affiliated stations belonging to a network, as well as individual stations, which broadcast programs and commercial messages. Advertising can be done on national or regional network programs or purchased in spots from local stations. The growth of specialized stations in recent years offers advertisers niche audiences and stronger selectivity than in the past.

3 To explain how television audiences are measured.

Information regarding the size and composition of national and local TV audiences is provided by BBM Canada. The amount of money a network or station can charge for commercial time on its programs is based on its audience measurement figures. This information is also important to media planners, as it is used to determine the combination of shows needed to attain specific levels of reach and frequency with the advertiser's target audience.

4 To summarize the strengths and limitations of radio as an advertising medium.

The role of radio as an entertainment and advertising medium has evolved into a primarily local one that offers highly specialized programming appealing to narrow segments of the market. Radio offers strengths in terms of cost efficiency and absolute cost, reach and frequency, target audience selectivity, geographic coverage, scheduling flexibility, creativity for cognitive responses, and media image.

The major drawback of radio is its weak creativity owing to the absence of a visual image. The short and fleeting nature of the radio commercial, the highly fragmented nature of the radio audience, low involvement, and clutter are also problems.

5 To identify how to purchase different radio formats and time periods.

As with TV, the rate structure for radio advertising time varies with the size of the audience delivered. It differs from television in that purchases are not tied to individual shows or programs. Instead, packages are offered over a period of days, weeks, or months.

6 To review how radio audiences are measured.

The primary source of listener information is BBM. The new PPM technology for television works with radio as well, although the diary method remains for smaller radio markets.

KEY TERMS

affiliates, *326*

average quarter-hour (AQH)
figure, *342*

average quarter-hour rating
(AQH RTG), *342*

average quarter-hour share
(AQH SHR), *342*

cable television, *330*

cume, *342*

dayparts, *329*

direct broadcast satellite
(DBS) services, *330*

image transfer, *339*

infomercials, *331*

program rating, *335*

ratings point, *335*

scatter market, *328*

share of audience, *336*

split-30s, *323*

sponsorship, *328*

spot advertising, *328*

station reps, *328*

television network, *326*

zapping, *324*

zipping, *324*

DISCUSSION QUESTIONS

1. Discuss the strengths of television as an advertising medium and the importance of these factors to major national advertisers and to smaller local companies.

2. Television is often described as a mass medium that offers little selectivity to advertisers. Do you agree with this statement? What are some of the ways selectivity can be achieved through TV advertising?

3. Choose a particular television daypart other than prime time and analyze the products and services advertised during this period. Why do you think these companies have chosen to advertise during this daypart?

4. Explain what is meant by zapping and zipping and how they affect television viewing behaviour. Discuss some of the ways that advertisers can deal with these problems.

5. Discuss the strengths and limitations of advertising on specialty channels. Discuss how both large national advertisers and small local companies might use cable TV effectively in their media plans.

6. Discuss the methods used to measure network and local TV viewing audiences. Do you think the measurement methods used for each are producing reliable and valid estimates of the viewing audiences? How might they be improved?

7. Discuss how personal video recorders will influence consumers' television viewing and how advertisers will likely respond to the changes.

8. What are the strengths and limitations of advertising on radio? What types of advertisers are most likely to use radio?

9. What is meant by image transfer in radio advertising? Find an example of a radio campaign that is using this concept and evaluate it.

PRINT MEDIA

■ CHAPTER OBJECTIVES

1 To identify the different types of magazines offered as an advertising medium.

2 To analyze the strengths and limitations of magazines as an advertising medium.

3 To describe how space is purchased in magazines, how readership is measured, and how rates are determined.

4 To identify the types of newspapers offered as an advertising medium and the format of newspaper ads.

5 To explain how advertising space is purchased in newspapers, how readership is measured, and how rates are determined.

6 To summarize the strengths and limitations of newspapers as an advertising medium.

Newspapers Continue to Thrive

Popular opinion suggests that newspapers are on their deathbed and this print option is no longer a viable advertising medium; however, nothing could be further from the truth. According to the chairman of Mediabrands Canada, "I believe newspapers will be around in their print form for many, many years to come." So why is this industry leader so confident?

Most Canadian newspapers remain quite profitable as readers continue to seek out information and have kept readership levels relatively steady. And readers seek this information from a credible and trusted source, like a newspaper, in the face of less credible sources found on the Internet. So, while many newspapers have found a growing niche of some readers getting news through their online version, a core group of print readers remain. "If you aggregate the print format plus the web, you could argue that newspapers are actually reaching more people than ever before" suggests one consultant.

Another factor is that newspaper advertising is effective for certain types of products that regularly buy space. Suni Boot, CEO of ZenithOptimedia, is quite clear about this, "Newspapers draw attention. There's an immediacy to it. There's a credibility to it. It's still a very, very good retail medium." In fact, most agree that newspapers get a brand's message to the right audience at the right place at the right time. Howard Chang of Top Drawer Creative echoes this, suggesting that newspaper advertising is contributing to the growth in sales for its client Golf Town. Penny Stevens of Media Experts also commented, "We're very lucky with a bunch of our clients that allow us to see sales on a day in-day basis so we get a very strong sense of what is working and what is not working."

Canadian newspapers have done much better than U.S. ones as they face a more friendly media environment. The U.S. has double the number of radio stations per capita, which siphon local advertising revenue away from newspapers. And Canadian newspapers have integrated their print and online versions more effectively to shore up readership. Canadian newspapers base advertising rates on readership instead of circulation, so multiple readers in a household contribute to solid streams.

One publisher remarked that, "You're seeing an extraordinary fracturing of audiences in television and radio and you're also seeing a very rapid aging of television audience so that we may actually get to the situation again where newspapers, by a huge margin, are the only medium that's really talking very broadly to the population. We may be the only mass media that's left."

Sources: "Evolving, Yes. Dying, Not At All," *Ottawa Citizen*, April 25, 2009, p. A14; David Akin, "Second in a Series," *Ottawa Citizen*, April 26, 2009, p. A7; David Akin, "A Tale of Two Countries," *Ottawa Citizen*, April 27, 2009, p. A4.

QUESTION:

1. Do you agree with the positive claims of newspapers as an advertising vehicle?

Thousands of magazines are published in Canada and throughout the world. They appeal to nearly every specific consumer interest and lifestyle, as well as to thousands of businesses and occupations. By becoming a highly specialized medium that reaches specific target audiences, the magazine industry has prospered. Newspapers are still the primary advertising medium in terms of both ad revenue and number of advertisers. Newspapers are particularly important as a local advertising medium for many retail businesses and are often used by large national advertisers as well.

The role of print media differs from that of broadcast media because detailed information can be presented that readers may process at their own pace. Print media are not intrusive like radio and TV, and generally require some effort on the part of the reader for the advertising message to have an impact. For this reason, magazines and newspapers are often referred to as *high-involvement media*.[1] This chapter focuses on these two major forms of print media. It examines their unique strengths and limitations, along with factors that are important in determining when and how to use magazines and newspapers in the media plan.

EVALUATION OF MAGAZINES

Magazines serve the educational, informational, and entertainment needs of a wide range of readers in both the consumer and business markets. Magazines are the most specialized of all advertising media. While some magazines are general mass-appeal publications, most are targeted to a very specific audience. There is a magazine designed to appeal to nearly every type of consumer in terms of demographics, lifestyle, activities, interests, or fascination. Numerous magazines are targeted toward specific businesses and industries as well as toward individuals engaged in various professions. The wide variety makes magazines an appealing medium to many advertisers.

CLASSIFICATIONS OF MAGAZINES

To gain some perspective on the various types of magazines available and the advertisers that use them, consider the way magazines are generally classified. Canadian Advertising Rates and Data (CARD), the primary reference source on periodicals for media planners, divides magazines into four broad categories based on the audience to which they are directed: consumer, ethnic, farm, and business publications. Each category is then further classified according to the magazine's editorial content and audience appeal. We also examine the opportunity of foreign publications.

Consumer Magazines   Consumer magazines are bought by the general public for information and/or entertainment. CARD divides over 800 domestic consumer magazines into 48 classifications, among them general interest, women's, city/ regional, entertainment, and sports, as seen in Figure 12-1. Figure 12-2 tabulates the circulation figures to show that the majority of all magazines have circulations below 50,000 and only 26 publications (3 percent) have circulations above 500,000. Figures 12-3 and 12-4 show the top Canadian magazines in terms of circulation for both official languages. Magazines can also be classified by frequency—weekly, monthly, and bimonthly are the most common—and by distribution—subscription, store distribution, or controlled (free).

Consumer magazine advertising reached $692 million in 2008, up from $541 million in 2001. Annual circulation hit 770 million copies in 2008. Consumer magazines are best suited to marketers interested in reaching general consumers of products

Rank	Editorial Category	2008 Circulation (average circulation, 000's)
1	General Interest	7,863
2	Women's	6,072
3	City	5,471
4	TV and Radio	5,141
5	Health	4,512
6	Homes/Gardening	4,248
7	Entertainment	4,420
8	Mature	4,131
9	Sports/Recreation	3,624
10	Food and Beverage	3,496

Source: CARD

FIGURE 12–1

Top editorial

Circulation Size	# of Titles	% of Total Titles
1 million+	7	0.8
500,000 to 999,999	19	2.2
250,000 to 499,999	28	3.3
100,000 to 249,999	129	15.1
50,000 to 99,999	159	18.6
20,000 to 49,999	275	32.0
1 to 19,999	240	28.0

Source: Titles Reporting Circulation in CARD

FIGURE 12–2

Circulation distribution

Publication	Magazine Class	Circulation (000's)	Readership (PMB 2008 All 12+ 000's)
CAA Magazine (excluding Manitoba)	General Interest	1,484	2,305
Canadian Living	Women's	516	3,959
Chatelaine	Women's	601	3,768
Famous	Entertainment	623	1,222
Food & Drink	Food & Beverage	526	2,304
Movie Entertainment	Entertainment	521	1,888
Readers Digest	General Interest	955	6,564
Starweek	TV & Radio	616	992
Tribute	Entertainment	500	1,539
Westworld	General Interest	1,155	1,255
What's Cooking	Food & Beverage	1,409	3,705

Source: Media Digest 09/10, p. 51

FIGURE 12–3

Top English-language magazines by circulation and readership

FIGURE 12–4

Top French-language magazines by circulation and readership

Publication	Magazine Class	Circulation (000's)	Readership (PMB 2008 All 12+ 000's)
Châtelaine	Women's	206	895
Coup de Pouce	Women's	230	1,254
Primeurs	TV & Radio	386	380
Qu'est-ce qui mijote	Food & Beverage	610	1,392
Selection du Readers Digest	General Interest	255	1,064
Touring (French & English)	General Interest	681	1,171

Source: Media Digest 09/10, p. 53

and services as well as to companies trying to reach a specific target audience. For example, the Intel ad in Exhibit 12-1 could be found in general magazines since so many people own laptop computers, while the Under Armor ad in Exhibit 12-2 might fit better in a specialty sports magazine. Figure 12-5 shows the most prevalent advertising product categories.

While large national advertisers tend to dominate consumer magazine advertising in terms of expenditures, consumer magazines are also important to smaller companies selling products that appeal to specialized markets. Special-interest magazines assemble consumers with similar lifestyles or interests and offer marketers an efficient way to reach these people with little wasted coverage or circulation. For example, a manufacturer of ski equipment such as Nordica, Rossignol, or Salomon might find *Ski Canada* magazine the best vehicle for advertising to serious skiers. Not only are these specialty magazines of value to firms interested in reaching a specific market segment, but their editorial content often creates a very favourable advertising environment for relevant products and services (see Exhibit 12-3).

The growth of free, customized magazines from retailers with controlled distribution is an emerging trend. Foremost are *Food & Drink* and *Chill* distributed in the liquor and beer stores in Ontario. HBC's *Belle* targets upscale females ages 35 to 55 with household income greater than $100,000—representing HBC's best customers. Past purchasing behaviour through credit cards and rewards cards identified this attractive segment as being interested in fashion, beauty, and home decor. *Belle* offers editorial content to fit the target's lifestyle while showing selective products and brands. Harry Rosen's *Harry* magazine is distributed to the chain's top 100,000 customers and has a newsstand presence of about 10,000. It features 50 pages of paid advertising from selective advertisers like Mercedes, Lexus, Armani, and Hugo Boss (Exhibit 12-4)

Ethnic Publications CARD currently lists 207 magazines directed to persons with various backgrounds based on ethnicity. The majority of these are written in English, with French, Arabic, Chinese, Portuguese, and Punjabi languages showing

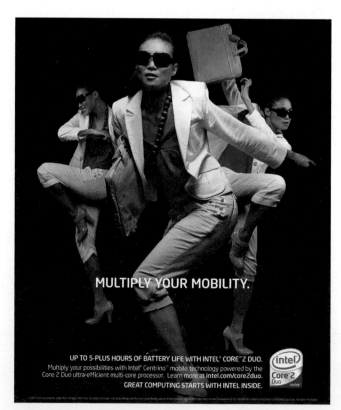

Exhibit 12-1 Intel's ad appeals well in general consumer magazines.

the most other language titles. Some of these publications have low circulation figures or do not have an authenticated circulation. Thus, the cost of advertising in these publications is currently very low.

Farm Publications   The third major CARD category consists of all the magazines directed to farmers and their families. About 95 publications are tailored to nearly every possible type of farming or agricultural interest (e.g., *Ontario Milk Producer, Ontario Produce Farmer*). A number of farm publications are directed at farmers in specific provinces or regions, such as *Alberta Beef*. Farm publications are not classified with business publications because historically farms were not perceived as businesses.

Business Publications   Business publications are those magazines or trade journals published for specific businesses, industries, or occupations. CARD lists about 780 business magazines and trade journals, and breaks them into 80 categories. The major categories include:

Advertiser Category	Rank* 2008	2007
Toiletries & Toilet Goods	1	1
Food & Food Products	2	2
Business & Consumer Services	3	3
Retail Stores	4	4
Drugs & Remedies	5	5
Travel, Hotels, & Resorts	6	7
Apparel, Footwear, & Accessories	7	9
Automotive	8	6
Entertainment & Amusement	9	8
Household Equipment & Supplies	10	12

*Advertising dollars
Source: LNA 2006

FIGURE 12–5

The most prevalent advertising product categories

353

FIGURE 12–7

U.S. spill trends

Year	Total Spill Circ (000's)	Index	Avg Circ/Title	Index
1983	10,705	100	26,303	100
1989	9,969	93	21,031	80
1998	9,155	86	16,203	62
2000	8,518	80	15,716	60
2002	8,160	76	15,396	59
2004	7,899	74	14,055	53
2006	7,666	72	13,664	52
2008	7,322	68	13,435	51

Source: ABC

where the receiver's identity is known (e.g., addressed direct mail). Most magazines are published for readers with very specific reading requirements. The magazines reach all types of consumers and businesses and allow advertisers to target their advertising to groups that are consistent with their segmentation strategies along the lines of demographics, socioeconomics, and lifestyle (e.g., activities and interests). For example, *PhotoLife* is targeted toward camera buffs, *Exclaim!* reaches those with an avid interest in music, and *What!* claims to be "the voice and choice of Canadian youth."

One Canadian success story is the lifestyle magazine *Vice,* which has an international circulation of 350,000 and has versions in the U.S., the U.K., and Japan, with plans for versions in Scandinavia, Germany, Holland, and France. Designed for the hip, urban, young consumer, *Vice* has steadily built an "edgy" reputation—making some advertisers critical of the magazine's content and wary of advertising in it. Another lifestyle magazine is *Nuvo,* a refined publication (non-paid circulation) catering to the very affluent who appreciate a refined lifestyle of luxury.[4]

Another successful interest magazine is *Hello!,* which features photos of and articles about celebrities. In the first two years of its Canadian edition circulation reached almost 100,000, putting it in the top 20 percent. The uniquely Canadian edition found a niche where its focus on celebrities did not follow old ways of

FIGURE 12–8

Canada continues to outpace the U.S. in magazine page growth

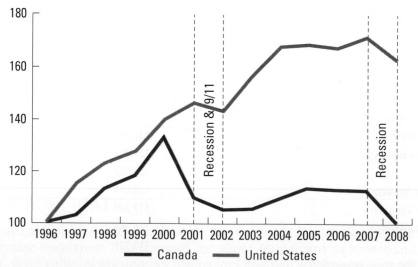

Source: PIB; Leading National Advertisers, 1996–2008

telling the stories but found a distinctive voice. Its latest challenge has concerned the reluctance of advertisers to run ads in consecutive weeks due to their familiarity with mostly monthly magazine ad purchases.[5]

In addition to providing selectivity based on interests, magazines can provide advertisers with high demographic selectivity. *Demographic selectivity,* or the ability to reach specific demographic groups, is available in two ways. First, most magazines are, as a result of editorial content, aimed at fairly well-defined demographic segments. *Canadian Living* and *Chatelaine* (Exhibit 12-6) are read predominantly by women; *The Hockey News* is read mostly by men. Older consumers can be reached through publications like *FiftyPlus.*

Selectivity can be applied effectively by tailoring the message by language. As you might expect, Canada has magazines written in both English and French. In fact, the latter has seen tremendous change recently with the relaunching of several titles prompting significant readership and ad revenue growth.[6] International ad campaigns like Heineken's translated for use in French publications (Exhibit 12-7).

Two technological developments allow advertisers to deliver personalized messages to tightly targeted audiences: selective binding and ink-jet imaging. **Selective binding** is a computerized production process that allows the creation of hundreds of copies of a magazine in one continuous sequence. Selective binding enables magazines to target and address specific groups within a magazine's circulation base. They can then send different editorial or advertising messages to various groups of subscribers within the same issue of a publication. **Ink-jet imaging** reproduces

Exhibit 12-6 *Chatelaine* allows for demographic selectivity.

Exhibit 12-7 Translated versions of Heineken's international campaign appeared in Canadian and worldwide publications.

Exhibit 12-8 City magazines such as *Toronto Life* offer advertisers high geographic selectivity.

Toronto Life, August 2010. Printed with permission.

a message by projecting ink onto paper rather than using mechanical plates. This process makes it possible to personalize an advertising message. These innovations permit advertisers to target their messages more finely and let magazines compete more effectively with direct mail and other direct-marketing vehicles.

Geographic Coverage One way to achieve specific geographic coverage is by using a magazine that is targeted toward a particular area. One of the more successful media developments of recent years has been the growth of city magazines in some Canadian cities. *Toronto Life, Vancouver Magazine,* and *Montréal Scope,* to name a few, provide residents of these areas with articles concerning lifestyle, events, and the like in these cities and their surrounding metropolitan areas (Exhibit 12-8).

Another way to achieve selective geographic coverage in magazines is through purchasing ad space in specific geographic editions of national or regional magazines. A number of publications (e.g., *Maclean's, Chatelaine*) divide their circulation into groupings based on regions or major metropolitan areas and offer advertisers the option of concentrating their ads in these editions.

CARD lists the consumer magazines offering geographic editions. Regional advertisers can purchase space in editions that reach only areas where they have distribution, yet still enjoy the prestige of advertising in a major national magazine. National advertisers can use the geographic editions to focus their advertising on areas with the greatest potential or those needing more promotional support. They can also use regional editions to test-market products or alternative promotional campaigns in various regions of the country.

Ads in regional editions can also list the names of retailers or distributors in various markets, thus encouraging greater local support from the trade. The trend toward regional marketing is increasing the importance of having regional media available to marketers. The availability of regional and demographic editions can also reduce the cost per thousand for reaching desired audiences.

Creativity for Cognitive and Emotional Responses One of the most valued attributes of magazine advertising is the reproduction quality of the ads. Magazines are generally printed on high-quality paper stock and use printing processes that provide excellent reproduction in black and white or colour. Since magazines are a visual medium where illustrations are often a dominant part of an ad, this is a very important property. The reproduction quality of most magazines is far superior to that offered by the other major print medium of newspapers, particularly when colour is needed. The use of colour has become a virtual necessity in most product categories. The creative Hyundai ad encourages both types of responses, along with an invitation to visit a website (Exhibit 12-9).

In addition to their excellent reproduction capabilities, magazines also offer advertisers options in terms of the type, size, and placement of the advertising material. Some magazines offer (often at extra charge) a variety of special opportunities to enhance the creative appeal of the ad such as gatefolds, bleed pages, inserts, and creative space buys.

Exhibit 12-9
Hyundai's ad evokes
all sorts of responses.

Gatefolds enable an advertiser to make a striking presentation by using a third page that folds out and gives the ad an extra-large spread. Gatefolds are often found at the inside cover of large consumer magazines, or on some inside pages. Advertisers use gatefolds to make a very strong impression, especially on special occasions such as the introduction of a new product or brand. For example, automobile advertisers often use gatefolds to introduce new versions of their cars each model year. **Bleed pages** are those where the advertisement extends all the way to the end of the page, with no margin of white space around the ad. Bleeds give the ad an impression of being larger and make a more dramatic impact (Exhibit 12-10).

Various **inserts** are used in many magazines designed for promotion such as recipe booklets, coupons, and even product samples. Cosmetics companies use scented inserts to introduce new fragrances, and others use them to promote products for which scent is important (e.g., deodorants, laundry detergents). Current technologies are being refined and made more cost-effective to enhance the reading of advertising messages. Newer options include anaglyphic images (three-dimensional materials that are viewed with coloured glasses); lenticular (colour) images printed on finely corrugated plastic that seem to move when tilted; and pressure- or heat-sensitive inks that change colour on contact. **Creative space buys** are another option in magazines, where advertisers purchase space units in certain combinations to increase the impact of their media budget. IMC Perspective 12-1 describes some new creative approaches for magazines.

Reader Involvement and Amount of Processing Time   A distinctive strength offered by magazines is their long life span. TV and radio are characterized by fleeting messages that have a very short life span; newspapers are generally discarded soon after being read. Magazines, however, are generally read over

Exhibit 12-10   Absolut continues to use bleed pages for its new campaign.

359

Magazines Get Creative and Digital

Magazines always look for ways to innovate despite their longevity of publishing for decades. There are always new cohorts of consumers to attract; for example, eventually new people gravitate to a sport (e.g., mountain biking) or recreational activity (e.g., cottage life) and decide they would like to read something about it. Or magazines may attempt to attract lapsed readers with creative ideas.

Time recently experimented with a customized magazine in an attempt to mimic in printed form the personalized news feeds found online. Entitled "mine," subscribers selected content from five of eight magazines in the sports, lifestyle, finance, and general news genres. Lexus prompted the idea as a new advertising approach and acted as the sole advertiser by purchasing 4 of the 36 pages. According to the Lexus VP, "Our message of 'driver inspired' and 'customization' will come through a lot stronger." Supporting this sentiment, a *Time* executive surmised that the initiative provided the right balance between reader choice, advertising, and the company's editorial control.

Esquire moved in the direction of technology with its innovation. When people held up a 3D bar code on the cover to a webcam they received digital enhancements. *GQ* magazine recently offered an iPhone app for consumers to access an identical version of their issue. The ads included a tag so that users could go to the brand's website. *Fortune* magazine allowed Flyp Media to experiment by recasting its stories in a new digital format with video, music, and hyperlinks—a completely new experience. Another digital approach is a joint venture where

different publishers offer an online storefront for loading digital versions for various viewer pleasures (e.g., laptop, smartphone, e-reader). But as these options are considered, the essence and uniqueness of a magazine—colour photography and design—becomes endangered.

Consumers who are polled are reluctant to pay for online subscriptions after receiving similar content for free at various sites. Rogers Media offers its magazines for free online, but others who do charge make very little in comparison to what is earned with the paper version. Essentially publishers are beyond "Can we go digital?" and are looking at it as "Can we make money with digital?"

However, Canadian fashion magazines—*Flare, Fashion,* and *Elle Canada*—continue to stay the course with their authentic versions that have an international look while retaining their Canadian focus on homegrown designers, models, and musical artists. Enhanced promotional efforts to encourage single-issue purchases and subscriptions help to keep paper readership alive.

Sources: Amy Verner, "Canadian Fashion Mags See Black," *The Globe and Mail,* August 8, 2009, p. L1; Susan Krashinsky, "The Future of Magazines," *The Globe and Mail,* December 18, 2009, p. B1; "Toyota, *Time* Create Personalized Magazine," *The Globe and Mail,* March 18, 2009, p. B8; "Flyp Turning Magazines Upside-down," *Marketing Magazine,* May 26, 2009.

Question:

1. How is the experience of reading a print magazine similar to or different from a digital version of the same title?

---

several days and are often kept for reference. They are retained in the home longer than any other medium and are generally referred to on several occasions. A summary of research regarding magazine audience usage cites a number of positive findings.[7] Readers devote about 40 minutes to reading a magazine with a high degree of interest. Readers focus on the magazine and engage in less multi-tasking. Finally, nearly 75 percent of consumers retain magazines for future reference. One benefit of the longer life of magazines is that reading occurs at a less hurried pace and there is more opportunity to examine ads in considerable detail. This means ads can use longer and more detailed copy, which can be very important for high-involvement and complex products or services. The permanence of magazines also means readers can be exposed to ads on multiple occasions and can pass magazines along to other readers.

Media Image Another positive feature of magazine advertising is the prestige the product or service may gain from advertising in publications with a favourable image. Companies whose products rely heavily on perceived quality, reputation, and/or image often buy space in prestigious publications with high-quality editorial content whose consumers have a high level of interest in the advertising pages. For example, *Flare* covers young women's fashions in a very favourable environment, and a clothing manufacturer may advertise its products in these magazines to enhance the prestige of its lines. *Canadian Geographic* provides an impressive editorial environment that includes high-quality photography. The magazine's upscale readers are likely to have a favourable image of the publication that may transfer to the products advertised on its pages. Media planners rely on their experiences to assess a magazine's prestige and reader opinion surveys in order to select the best magazine title.

Selective Exposure and Attention   With the exception of newspapers, consumers are more receptive to advertising in magazines than in any other medium. Magazines are generally purchased because the information they contain interests the reader, and ads provide additional information that may be of value in making a purchase decision. Some magazines, such as bridal or fashion publications, are purchased as much for their advertising as for their editorial content.

In addition to their relevance, magazine ads are likely to be received favourably by consumers because, unlike broadcast ads, they are nonintrusive and can easily be ignored. The majority of magazine readers welcome ads; only a small percentage have negative attitudes toward magazine advertising. Consumers generally enjoy magazines over other media along many measures such as advertising receptivity, inspirational, trustworthy, life-enhancing, social interaction, and personal timeout. Furthermore, readers believe advertising contributes to the enjoyment of reading a magazine more strongly than other media and they have stronger attitudes to magazine ads versus ads in other media.[8]

Advertisers take advantage of this strength with clever creative tactics. For example, Audi and *Maclean's* teamed up to put an ad on the magazine cover that looked entirely normal except for a discreetly placed "open here" message. Readers lifted a small flap to reveal the car ad—which proclaimed the AQ was foxy compared to a generic "boxy" competitor.[9] *Vice* magazine managed to put a BMW ad on its cover that could be seen only in the dark. The publisher distributed copies to nightclubs, where the ad would become visible.[10]

LIMITATIONS OF MAGAZINES

Although the strengths offered by magazines are considerable, they have certain drawbacks too. These include the costs of advertising, their limited reach and frequency, the long lead time required in placing an ad, weak target audience coverage, and the problem of clutter.

Absolute Cost and Cost Efficiency   The cost of advertising in magazines varies according to size of audience reached and selectivity. Advertising in large mass-circulation magazines like *Maclean's* can be very expensive. For example, a full-page, four-colour ad in *Maclean's* magazine's national edition (circulation 362,000) cost $37,000. Popular positions such as the back cover cost even more.

Like any medium, magazines must be considered not only from an absolute cost perspective but also in terms of relative costs. Most magazines emphasize their efficiency in reaching specific target audiences at a low cost per thousand. Media planners generally focus on the relative costs of a publication in reaching their target audience. However, they may recommend a magazine with a high cost per thousand because of its ability to reach a small, specialized market segment. Of course, advertisers with limited budgets will be interested in the absolute costs of space in a magazine and the costs of producing quality ads for these publications.

Reach and Frequency   Magazines are generally not as effective as other media in offering reach and frequency. While adults in Canada read one or more consumer magazines each month, the percentage of adults reading any individual publication tends to be much smaller, so magazines have a thin penetration of households. For example, *Maclean's* has a high circulation, but it represents only 3 percent of the 12.8 million households in Canada.

Thus, advertisers seeking broad reach must make media buys in a number of magazines, which means more negotiations and transactions. For a broad reach strategy, magazines are used in conjunction with other media. Since most magazines are monthly or at best weekly publications, the opportunity for building frequency through the use of the same publication is limited. Using multiple ads in the same issue of a publication is an inefficient way to build frequency. Most advertisers try to achieve frequency by adding other magazines with similar audiences to the media schedule.

Scheduling Flexibility   Another drawback of magazines is the long lead time needed to place an ad thus reducing scheduling flexibility. Most major publications have a 30- to 90-day lead time, which means space must be purchased and the ad must be prepared well in advance of the actual publication date. No changes in the art or copy of the ad can be made after the closing date. This long lead time means magazine ads cannot be as timely as other media, such as radio or newspapers, in responding to current events or changing market conditions.

Target Audience Coverage   The flipside of the strength of target audience selectivity is the limitation of magazines in providing extensive target audience coverage. Even though a magazine may draw an audience with a particular interest, for example, hockey with *The Hockey News,* the number of people reading the publication versus the number of people who actually play hockey is substantially disproportionate.

Clutter   While the problem of advertising clutter is generally discussed in reference to the broadcast media, it is not as serious an issue for print media since consumers tend to be more receptive and tolerant of print advertising. They can also control their exposure to a magazine ad simply by turning the page. The clutter problem for magazines is something of a paradox: The more successful a magazine becomes, the more advertising pages it attracts, and this leads to greater clutter. In fact, magazines generally gauge their success in terms of the number of advertising pages they sell.

Magazine publishers do attempt to control the clutter problem by maintaining a reasonable balance of editorial pages to advertising. However, many magazines contain ads on more than half of their pages. This clutter makes it difficult for an advertiser to gain readers' attention and draw them into the ad. Thus, many print ads use strong visual images, catchy headlines, or some of the creative techniques discussed earlier to grab the interest of magazine readers. Some advertisers create their own custom magazines to sidestep the advertising clutter problem as well as to have control over editorial content. A number of companies have also been publishing their own magazines to build relationships with their customers.

Fashion retailer Holt Renfrew custom-published its own shopping magazine, *Holt's,* to reach a sophisticated clientele who shop all around the world. This contributed to Holt Renfrew's established connections with the high-profile publication *Lucky,* where the fashion retailer consistently linked its brand with the world-renowned fashion and beauty brands through product placement and cooperative media opportunities. In the future, Holt Renfrew looks to establish more permanent advertising placements in Canada's newest fashion magazines—*Loulou, Fashion Shops,* and *Shopping Clin d'oeil*—and achieve an optimal balance between custom-published and regular magazines.[11]

BUYING MAGAZINE ADVERTISING SPACE

The strengths and limitations of magazines are part of the decision to use this medium. Another key factor is a complete understanding of the readers of magazines to assess whether there is a fit between them and the target audience of the promotion plan. In this section, we review a few issues related to this part of the decision: circulation and readership, audience measurement, and magazine advertising rates.

MAGAZINE CIRCULATION AND READERSHIP

Two of the most important considerations in deciding whether to use a magazine in the advertising media plan are the size and characteristics of the audience it reaches. Media buyers evaluate magazines on the basis of their ability to deliver the advertiser's message to as many people as possible in the target audience. To do this, they must consider the circulation of the publication as well as its total readership, and match these figures against the audience they are attempting to reach.

Circulation   Circulation figures represent the number of individuals who receive a publication through either subscription or store purchase, or through controlled distribution (free). Given that circulation figures are the basis for a magazine's advertising rates and one of the primary considerations in selecting a publication for placement, the credibility of circulation figures is important. Most major publications are audited by the Audit Bureau of Circulations (ABC), which was organized in 1914 and is sponsored by advertisers, agencies, and publishers. The Canadian division of this U.S.-based organization is known as the Canadian Circulations Audit Board. ABC collects and evaluates information regarding the subscriptions and sales of magazines and newspapers to verify their circulation figures. Only publications with 70 percent or more paid circulation (which means the purchaser paid at least half the magazine's established base price) are eligible for verification audits by ABC. Certain business publications are audited by the Business Publications Audit (BPA) of Circulation. Many of these are published on a **controlled-circulation basis**, meaning copies are sent (usually free) to individuals who the publisher believes can influence the company's purchases.

ABC provides media planners with reliable figures regarding the size and distribution of a magazine's circulation, which helps them evaluate its worth as a media vehicle. The ABC statement also provides detailed circulation information that gives a media planner an indication of the quality of the target audience. For example, it shows how the subscription was sold, the percentage of circulation sold at less than full value, the percentage of circulation sold with some kind of incentive, and the percentage of subscriptions given away. Many advertisers believe that subscribers who pay for a magazine are more likely to read it than are those who get it at a discount or for free. Media buyers are generally skeptical about publications whose circulation figures are not audited and will not advertise in unaudited publications. Circulation data, along with the auditing source, are available from CARD or from the publication itself.

Readership   Advertisers are often interested in the number of people a publication reaches as a result of secondary, or pass-along, readership. **Pass-along readership** can occur when the primary subscriber or purchaser gives a magazine to another person or when the publication is read in doctors' waiting rooms or beauty salons, on airplanes, and so forth.

Advertisers generally attach greater value to the primary in-home reader than the pass-along reader or out-of-home reader, as the former generally spends more time with the publication, picks it up more often, and receives greater satisfaction from it. Thus, this reader is more likely to be attentive and responsive to ads. However, the value of pass-along readers should not be discounted. They can greatly expand a magazine's readership.

The **total audience**, or **readership**, of a magazine is calculated by multiplying the readers per copy (the total number of primary and pass-along readers) by the circulation of an average issue. For example, *Flare* has a circulation of 160,000 and 11 readers per copy for a total audience of 1.5 million. However, rate structures are generally based on the more verifiable primary circulation figures, and many media planners devalue pass-along readers by as much as 50 percent. Total readership estimates are reported by the Print Measurement Bureau (PMB), to which we now turn our attention.

MAGAZINE AUDIENCE MEASUREMENT—PMB

Print Measurement Bureau (PMB) is a non-profit Canadian industry association of nearly 500 members drawn from advertisers, print magazine publishers, and advertising agencies. Its primary mandate is to collect readership information for print magazines, which allows all three constituents to make more effective advertising decisions. Its foremost research is known simply as the **PMB study**.

The first national PMB study was conducted in 1973 and originally concerned print magazines only. It has grown since then and is now Canada's primary syndicated source for print and non-print media exposure, as well as responses to survey questions. The current study has resulted in a two-year database of 30,000 respondents, over 2,500 products, and over 3,500 brands.

The research method is an in-home interview conducted throughout the year. Respondents are screened by asking whether they have read any of the listed publications within the past 12 months; they are subsequently qualified if they have read the publications recently enough, depending upon the frequency of publication (e.g., weekly, monthly). A number of reading-related questions are asked, including frequency of reading, number of reading occasions, time spent reading, source of copy, where read, and interest.

Respondents are then asked many demographic, lifestyle, media consumption, product usage, retail shopping, and psychographic questions. The demographic questions are quite exhaustive and total over 20 in number. The lifestyle questions include life events, leisure activities, education, sporting activities, and attendance of sporting events. Media consumption questions are very extensive and include TV viewing, radio listening, community and daily newspaper reading, transit usage, distance travelled, shopping mall trips, and Yellow Pages usage. Product usage data are recorded for 17 broad product categories (e.g., personal care, groceries, financial, business, and so on). Questions pertaining to shopping at approximately 30 different retail environments are also asked. And finally, many questions are asked to determine psychographic clusters for nine broad product categories and one general societal category.

The data available for analysis is a virtual gold mine of information for media planners. They can relate many of the variables together to accurately reach a specific target audience in terms of their behaviour (i.e., the primary target variable), demographics, lifestyle, and psychographics. The database works with specialized software to allow media planners to make their effective decisions efficiently.

One final useful feature of the PMB study is "return to sample." Individual firms can confidentially re-contact respondents to ask them proprietary questions with respect to specific brand attitudes, purchase intentions, or purchase influences. An advertiser would then have the broad data tied in with some specific measures of its own brand.

MAGAZINE ADVERTISING RATES

Magazine rates are primarily a function of circulation: the greater the circulation, the higher the cost of the ad. Other variables include the size of the ad, its position in the publication, the particular editions (geographic, demographic) chosen, any special mechanical or production requirements, the number and frequency of insertions, and whether the circulation is controlled (free) or paid.

Advertising space is generally sold on the basis of space units, such as full-page, half-page, quarter-page, or double-page spread (two facing pages); a greater cost is incurred for ads requiring more space. Advertisers use larger ads since they result in stronger advertising recall. Research suggest that full-page ads account for 20 percent stronger recall than half-page ads, and that a double-page spread can be 15 percent stronger than a single page.[12]

Ads can be produced or run using black and white, black and white plus one colour, or four colours. The more colour used in the ad, the greater the expense because of the increased printing costs. Colour ads are so prominent in magazines that many do not even quote a non-colour cost in their CARD listing. Advertising recall scores are stronger for colour versus non-colour by up to 25 percent.[13] Ads placed inside the front cover, inside the back cover, and outside the back cover will also be more costly and yield stronger recall (10 to 20 percent) than a regular inside page. Ads requiring special mechanical production or specific location will also cost extra. The magazine's capabilities are identified on the CARD listing.

Rates for magazine ad space can also vary according to the number of times an ad runs and the amount of money spent during a specific period. The more often an advertiser contracts to run an ad, the lower the space charges. Volume discounts are based on the total space purchased within a contract year, measured in dollars or number of insertions.

EVALUATION OF NEWSPAPERS

Newspapers, the second major form of print media, are one of the largest of all advertising media in terms of total dollar volume. In 2008 more than $2.5 billion was spent on daily newspaper advertising, or about 18 percent of the total advertising expenditures in Canada. Newspapers are an especially important advertising medium to local advertisers, particularly retailers. However, newspapers are also valuable to national advertisers. Newspapers vary in terms of their format, the type of advertising, and their strengths and limitations as an advertising medium.

TYPES OF NEWSPAPERS

The traditional role of newspapers has been to deliver prompt, detailed coverage of news as well as to supply other information and features that appeal to readers as shown in Figure 12-9. The vast majority of newspapers are daily publications serving a local community. However, weekly, national, and special-audience newspapers have special characteristics that can be valuable to advertisers.

Daily Newspapers Daily newspapers, which are published each weekday, are found in cities and larger towns across the country. Some areas have more than one daily paper and are known as competitive markets, while the vast majority of smaller Canadian cities and towns have one publication. Daily newspapers are read by about 50 percent of adults each weekday and nearly 75 percent each week. They provide detailed coverage of news, events, and issues concerning the local area as well as business, sports, and other relevant information and entertainment. In 2008,

FIGURE 12–9

Secondary topics, read after news

Men 18+		Women 18+	
Sports	54%	Arts/Entertainment	52%
Business/Finance	41%	Health	48%
Editorial/Opinion	36%	Food	45%
Arts/Entertainment	32%	Fashion/Lifestyle	42%
Automotive	29%	Editorial/Opinion	38%
Source: 2009 NADbank			

there were 124 daily newspapers in Canada; of these, 111 were English-language papers and 13 were French-language papers, with a total circulation of 6 million. Most daily newspapers charge a price (or subscription fee); however, free dailies emerged on the market a decade ago and now represent substantial circulation and advertising revenue. Each of Canada's largest six cities has at least one free daily under the *Metro* or *24 hours* banner.

Community Newspapers Most community newspapers publish weekly and originate in small towns where the volume of news and advertising cannot support a daily newspaper. Canada had 1,100 community newspapers in 2009 with a total circulation of 17 million. Community newspapers also dot the suburbs of many larger Canadian cities. These papers focus primarily on news, sports, and events relevant to the local area and usually ignore content covered by the city-based daily newspaper. Community newspapers appeal primarily to local advertisers because of their geographic focus and lower absolute cost. Most national advertisers avoid community newspapers because of their duplicate circulation with daily papers in the large metropolitan areas.

While smaller daily and community newspapers have historically been a fragmented market and difficult for national or regional advertisers to use as an effective newspaper vehicle, their emerging force in Ontario promises to create an interesting opportunity. Recently, Osprey Media Group purchased many daily newspapers in small towns and cities (e.g., Kingston, Sarnia, Sudbury, etc.) with a total circulation of 622,000. When combined with weekly newspapers, the new media giant can reach nearly 1 million people in 45 markets. In total, Osprey owns 22 dailies and 24 weeklies. In comparison, two other similar companies own 60-plus newspapers, thus indicating the beginning of some concentration in the media option. The implication for advertisers is significant. In addition to providing advertisers with the ability to reach many local markets easily, these newspapers allow advertisers to reach a very attractive market since disposable income tends to be higher in those towns and cities with lower property/mortgage costs.[14]

National Newspapers Newspapers in Canada with national circulation include the *National Post* and *The Globe and Mail*. Both are daily publications and have editorial content with a national appeal. The *National Post* has a weekday circulation of about 192,000 and a Saturday circulation of almost 208,000. *The Globe and Mail* has a weekday circulation of about 335,000 and a Saturday circulation of approximately 391,000. National newspapers appeal primarily to large national advertisers and to regional advertisers that use specific geographic editions of these publications.

Internet Newspapers Major Canadian daily newspapers, the two national newspapers, and some community newspapers offer an Internet version of their publications. Regular newspapers charge for subscription or individual papers at newsstands and rely on advertising revenue to support the distribution of editorial content. Internet versions are similar in this respect; the publishing firms have experimented with different combinations of fees and banner ads. Recently, Can-West allowed newspaper subscribers free access to the complete digital version of the newspaper. Online readership has grown from 10 percent in 2001 to almost 20 percent, but it is substantially lower than the 80 percent for the original version. Consumers are currently in the process of evolving their newspaper consumption habits as shown in Figure 12-10. For example, portals offer news and features similar to online newspapers, so the competition for an audience may be different in a new media environment.[15]

Special-Audience Newspapers   A variety of papers offer specialized editorial content and are published for particular groups, including labour unions, professional organizations, industries, and hobbyists. Many people working in advertising and marketing read *Marketing Magazine.* Specialized newspapers are also published in areas with large foreign-language-speaking ethnic groups, among them Chinese. Newspapers targeted at various religious and educational groups compose another large class of special-interest papers. A recent trend has been the establishment of local business newspapers. In western Canada, *Business Edge* reaches 47,000 readers in Alberta and 30,000 in B.C. It receives advertising from regional and small firms, and also from large firms like Telus and Rogers Wireless.[16]

Newspaper Supplements   Although not a category of newspapers per se, some papers include magazine-type supplements. For example, *The Globe and Mail* publishes a glossy *Report On Business* magazine at the end of each month.

TYPES OF NEWSPAPER ADVERTISING

The ads appearing in newspapers can also be divided into different categories. The major types of newspaper advertising are display and classified. Other special types of ads and preprinted inserts also appear in newspapers.

Display Advertising   **Display advertising** is found throughout the newspaper and generally uses illustrations, headlines, white space, and other visual devices in

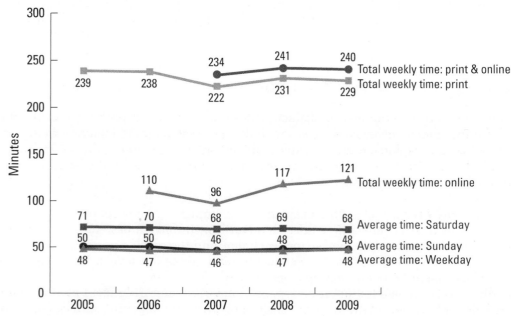

FIGURE   12–10

Time spent reading, weekday and weekend, in minutes 2005-2009, 19 trended markets

Source: 2009 NADbank

addition to the copy text. The two types of display advertising in newspapers are local and national (general).

Local advertising refers to ads placed by local organizations, businesses, and individuals who want to communicate with consumers in the market area served by the newspaper. Supermarkets and department stores are among the leading local display advertisers, along with numerous other retailers and service operations such as banks and travel agents.

National or general advertising refers to newspaper display advertising done by marketers of branded products or services that are sold on a national or regional level. These ads are designed to create and maintain demand and to complement the efforts of local retailers that stock and promote the advertiser's products. Major retail chains, automakers, and airlines are heavy users of newspaper advertising.

Classified Advertising **Classified advertising** provides newspapers with revenue; however, online classifieds have eaten into this market considerably. These ads are arranged under subheads according to the product, service, or offering being advertised. Employment, real estate, and automotive are the three major categories of classified advertising. While most classified ads are just text set in small type, some newspapers also accept classified display advertising. These ads are run in the classified section of the paper but use illustrations, larger type sizes, white space, borders, and even colour to stand out.

Special Ads Special advertisements in newspapers include a variety of government and financial reports and notices and public notices of changes in business and personal relationships. Other types of advertising in newspapers include political or special-interest ads promoting a particular candidate, issue, or cause.

Inserts **Preprinted inserts** do not appear in the paper itself; they are printed by the advertiser and sent to the newspaper to be inserted before delivery. Many retailers use inserts such as circulars, catalogues, or brochures in specific circulation zones to reach shoppers in their particular trade areas. Car companies often include poster-like inserts that people may choose to keep. A recent trend is for inserts to become more creative. Belairdirect insurance used inserts that looked like file folders similar to what consumers would use while researching this purchase. For the holiday season a Molson's insert looked like a beer fridge; upon opening, consumers could see cases on flaps that could be opened that had promotional information underneath, like PIN codes for an online contest to win a beer fridge or links to Facebook fan pages.[17]

STRENGTHS OF NEWSPAPERS

Newspapers have a number of characteristics that make them popular among both local and national advertisers. These include their reach and frequency, scheduling flexibility, geographic coverage, reader involvement and amount of processing time, media image, creativity for cognitive responses, absolute cost and cost efficiency, and target audience coverage.

Reach and Frequency One of the primary strengths of newspapers is the high degree of market coverage they offer an advertiser. In most areas, 40 to 50 percent of households read a daily newspaper each day, and the reach figure hits the higher end among households with higher incomes and education levels. Most areas are served by one or two daily newspapers.

The extensive penetration of newspapers makes them a truly mass medium and provides advertisers with an excellent opportunity for reaching all segments of the population. Also, since many newspapers are published and read daily, the advertiser can build a high level of frequency into the media schedule.

Scheduling Flexibility   Another strength of newspapers is the flexibility they offer advertisers in terms of requirements for producing and running the ads. Newspaper ads can be written, laid out, and prepared in a matter of hours. For most dailies, the closing time by which the ad must be received is usually only 48 hours before publication (although closing dates for supplements and for special ads, such as those using colour, are longer). The short production time and closing dates make newspapers an excellent medium for responding to current events or presenting timely information to consumers. For example, the Archdiocese of Montreal ran an ad a few days after the terrorist attacks of September 11, 2001 that showed the repeated text of the Lord's Prayer in the shape of the twin towers. The meanings of this message are numerous for many people; however, the most significant point is that the message would not have been as effective if it had been placed in a magazine a month later.[18]

Geographic Coverage   Newspapers generally offer advertisers targeted geographic or territorial coverage. Advertisers can vary their coverage by choosing a paper—or combination of papers—that reaches the areas with the greatest sales potential. National advertisers take advantage of the geographic coverage of newspapers to concentrate their advertising in specific areas they can't reach with other media or to take advantage of strong sales potential in a particular area. For example, more expensive automobile manufacturers advertise in Toronto newspapers that reach the greater Toronto area and beyond with their wide distribution.

A number of companies use newspapers in their regional marketing strategies. Newspaper advertising lets them feature products on a market-by-market basis, respond and adapt campaigns to local market conditions, and tie in to more retailer promotions, fostering more support from the trade.

Local advertisers like retailers are interested in geographic coverage within a specific market or trade area. Their media goal is to concentrate their advertising in the areas where most of their customers are. Many newspapers now offer advertisers various geographic areas or zones for this purpose.

Reader Involvement and Amount of Processing Time   Another important feature of newspapers is consumers' level of acceptance and involvement with papers and the ads they contain. The typical newspaper reader spends considerable time each day reading. Most consumers rely heavily on newspapers not only for news, information, and entertainment but also for assistance with consumption decisions.

Many consumers actually purchase a newspaper *because* of the advertising it contains. Consumers use retail ads to determine product prices and availability and to see who is having a sale. One aspect of newspapers that is helpful to advertisers is readers' knowledge about particular sections of the paper. Most of us know that ads for automotive products and sporting goods are generally found in the sports section, while ads for financial services are found in the business section. The weekly food section in many newspapers is popular for recipe and menu ideas as well as for the grocery store ads and coupons offered by many stores and companies.

Media Image   The value of newspaper advertising as a source of information has been shown in several studies. One study found that consumers look forward to ads in newspapers more than in other media. In another study, 80 percent of consumers said newspaper ads were most helpful to them in doing their weekly shopping. Newspaper advertising has also been rated the most believable form of advertising in numerous studies. IMC Perspective 12-2 reflects on the positive image of newspaper advertising.

The essence of the newspaper is a recording of history. Stacked in numerous locations in Ottawa are copies of newspapers from all across the country dating back two centuries, preserved by Library and Archives Canada. For some reason, the staying power of the medium and the social implications of knowing what is happening make the newspaper popular still today.

Most other media are dependent upon newspapers because of their extensive research capabilities and larger journalistic staff. Moreover, the population intuitively understands the journalistic credence of the medium as a result of this wealth of knowledge and expertise. The chief conservator of the Archives reflects upon newspapers as an intellectual journey with subtle experiences of all the elements: headline, photos, articles compiled, and variety of stories—it surpasses all other media. "The kind of investigative, background material along with agenda-setting, enterprise reporting and analysis and interpretation providing contest to today's news is, I think a role that absolutely must continue."

And with that role comes respect from bloggers who appreciate the professionalism, fairness, and balanced reporting so understood by all who read a newspaper. In fact, the historic importance of the newspaper for chronicling the events of time and involving itself in the community is well-respected by citizens. So it appears this integral source has staying power that will allow newspapers to be a strong content provider for an advertiser to surround itself with.

This role is exemplified by the *Ottawa Citizen,* the longest-running business in our nation's capital. The newspaper has contributed back to the community in the form of $18 million in free or low-cost advertising space for non-profit organizations for program or event support. Like other good businesses, the *Citizen* contributed $500,000 for literacy and the United Way. For newspapers, journalistic integrity and philanthropy are intrinsically related. It is this fitting in with and support of the community that helps newspapers retain their strong media image and the confidence of readers that the advertising will be informative and useful for purchasing.

This reputation of newspapers as a trusted entity for information allows them to thrive online. The combined print and online readership of news from journalistic organizations is stronger than the peak of newspaper-only readership. The managing editor of the *Vancouver Sun,* Kirk LaPointe, concludes, "Online isn't replacing the paper as much as it's complementing it. The advantage for the local newspaper/site is the local condition and hyper-local content, in particular the thorough investigation and rigorous scrutiny that an individual blogger could not afford. It has built equity and a trusted relationship, and the new ways of creating and sharing content simply enhances that covenant. The growth in traffic is a positive sign that people return to a source they have trusted."

Sources: David Akin, "A Tale of Two Countries," *Ottawa Citizen,* April 27, 2009, p. A4; Randy Boswell, "It's Not Just the Headline," *Ottawa Citizen,* April 28, 2009, p. A7; Doug Fisher, "A Legacy of Ink-Stained Citizenship," *Ottawa Citizen,* April 29, p. A5; Kirk LaPointe, "Internet Not a Threat," *Ottawa Citizen,* April 30, 2009, p. A11.

Question:

1. Why are newspapers a stronger or weaker alternative as an advertising medium compared to online blogs?

Creativity for Cognitive Responses Newspapers offer the opportunity for extremely long copy, perhaps a thousand words extolling the attributes and benefits of a product. The option of considerable explanation of a product could be quite important for marketers looking to persuade consumers who are at the information search stage of the decision-making process. Furthermore, newspapers offer numerous creative options as ads can be run in various sizes, shapes, and formats to persuade the reader. Magazine innovations described earlier are adapted to newspapers as well. *Metro* agreed to print all 540,000 copies of an entire edition on special green paper for Dove's Cool Moisture product line. The special media buy included a front-page ad, a double-page spread inside, and a product sample attached to the front.[19]

Absolute Cost and Cost Efficiency Newspapers assist small companies through free copywriting and art services. Small advertisers without an agency or advertising department often rely on the newspaper to help them write and produce their ads. Production costs of ads are reasonable since many are comprised of simple copy with a standard image or photo-stock visual. The creative flexibility of newspapers in terms of size and format of the ad makes it difficult to exactly conclude the cost implications of this media. Small and local businesses can run a small ad with a reasonable CPM (cost per thousand) compared to magazines.

Target Audience Coverage   Coverage of a specific target audience is argued to be a limitation for the newspaper in comparison to its print cousin, the magazine. However, placement of ads in certain newspaper sections that recur every day (e.g., sports, business, entertainment) or once a week (e.g., food, cars, finance) can be advantageous for some marketers.

LIMITATIONS OF NEWSPAPERS

While newspapers have many strengths, like all media they also have limitations that media planners must consider. The limitations of newspapers include their creativity for emotional responses, selective exposure and attention, target audience selectivity, and clutter.

Creativity for Emotional Responses   One of the greatest limitations of newspapers as an advertising medium is their poor reproduction quality. The coarse paper stock used for newspapers and the absence of extensive colour limits the quality of most newspaper ads. Newspapers have improved their reproduction quality in recent years, and colour reproduction has become more available. Also, advertisers desiring high-quality colour in newspaper ads can turn to such alternatives as freestanding inserts or supplements. However, these are more costly and may not be desirable to many advertisers. As a general rule, if the visual appearance of the product is important, the advertiser will not rely on newspaper ads. Ads for food products and fashions generally use magazines to capitalize on their superior reproduction quality and colour.

Selective Exposure and Attention   Unlike magazines, which may be retained around the house for several weeks, a daily newspaper is generally kept less than a day. So an ad is unlikely to have any impact beyond the day of publication, and repeat exposure is very unlikely. Compounding this problem are the short amount of time many consumers spend with the newspaper and the possibility they may not even open certain sections of the paper. Media planners can offset these problems somewhat by using high frequency in the newspaper schedule and advertising in a section where consumers who are in the market for a particular product or service are likely to look.

Target Audience Selectivity   While newspapers can offer advertisers geographic selectivity, they are not a selective medium in terms of demographics or lifestyle characteristics. Most newspapers reach broad and very diverse groups of consumers, which makes it difficult for marketers to focus on narrowly defined market segments. For example, manufacturers of fishing rods and reels will find newspapers very inefficient because of the wasted circulation that results from reaching all the newspaper readers who don't fish. Thus, they are more likely to use special-interest magazines. Any newspaper ads for their products will be done through cooperative plans whereby retailers share the costs or spread them over a number of sporting goods featured in the ad.

Clutter   Newspapers, like most other advertising media, suffer from clutter. Because a substantial amount of the average daily newspaper in Canada is devoted to advertising, the advertiser's message must compete with numerous other ads for

371

consumers' attention and interest. Moreover, the creative options in newspapers are limited by the fact that most ads are black and white. Thus, it can be difficult for a newspaper advertiser to break through the clutter without using costly measures such as large space buys or colour. Some advertisers use creative techniques like island ads—ads surrounded by editorial material. Island ads are found in the middle of the stock market quotes on the financial pages of many newspapers.

BUYING NEWSPAPER ADVERTISING SPACE

As in the case of magazines, advertisers look for a strong fit between the target audience of their brand and the newspaper's audience. In this section, we review a few issues related to this part of the decision: circulation and readership, audience measurement, and newspaper advertising rates.

NEWSPAPER CIRCULATION AND READERSHIP

The media planner must understand the size and reading usage characteristics of the audience reached by a newspaper when considering its value in the media plan. Like any other media, advertisers are concerned with the size of the audience reached through a particular vehicle. Thus, the circulation, or number of readers, is an important statistic evaluated. And while the size is important, advertisers are also interested in the amount of reading occurring and similar usage statistics prior to making their decision regarding newspapers.

Circulation The basic source of information concerning the audience size of newspapers comes from circulation figures available through CARD, discussed earlier in this chapter. The Audit Bureau of Circulation (ABC) verifies circulation figures for many newspapers, as illustrated in the magazine media section. Advertisers using a number of papers in their media plan generally find CARD to be the most convenient source. The Canadian Community Newspapers Association (CCNA) verifies the circulation if an advertiser decides to use this vehicle.

The CCNA is a network of seven regional newspaper associations: Atlantic Community Newspapers Association, the Quebec Community Newspapers Association, the Ontario Community Newspapers Association, the Manitoba Community Newspapers Association, the Saskatchewan Weekly Newspapers Association, the Alberta Weekly Newspapers Association, and the British Columbia & Yukon Community Newspapers Association. Membership of an individual community newspaper in a regional association includes membership in the national association. CCNA currently represents more than 700 English-language community newspapers with a total first-edition circulation of more than 9 million copies per week.

The CCNA gives an individual community newspaper a national voice in working with the public, business, and government, and its mission is to ensure a strong community newspaper industry. For advertisers, the CCNA plays a strong role in coordinating the placement of ads throughout the network. Its services include a "one-order, one-bill" system, ROP ads and pre-printed inserts, digital transmission of ads, Geographic Information System (GIS), and national or regional classified advertising. Currently, CCNA does not have audience information like NADbank; however, in June 2002, CCNA announced the implementation of a readership study. Despite this limitation, CCNA claims that community newspapers offer key benefits: precise coverage of specific markets with no wasted circulation, strong household penetration, state-of-the-art newspaper reproduction, and audited circulation figures.

CCNA has a self-administered audit program for all its members. The program includes a manual with detailed instructions and necessary forms. The member

372

newspaper collects its own circulation data according to the VC rules and regulations. These data are reported to the CCNA and the CCNA circulation auditor or a public (chartered) accountant audits the data thoroughly and a circulation report is published.

Newspaper circulation figures are generally broken down into three categories: the city zone, the retail trading zone, and all other areas. The **city zone** is a market area composed of the city where the paper is published and contiguous areas similar in character to the city. The **retail trading zone** is the market outside the city zone whose residents regularly trade with merchants within the city zone. The "all other" category covers all circulation not included in the city or retail trade zone.

Sometimes circulation figures are provided only for the primary market, which is the city and retail trade zones combined, and the other area. Both local and national advertisers consider the circulation patterns across the various categories in evaluating and selecting newspapers.

Readership   Circulation figures provide the media planner with the basic data for assessing the value of newspapers and their ability to cover various market areas. However, the media planner also wants to match the characteristics of a newspaper's readers with those of the advertiser's target audience. Data on newspaper audience size and characteristics are available from NADbank. Figures 12-11 to 12-14 give an overview of the Canadian newspaper reader.

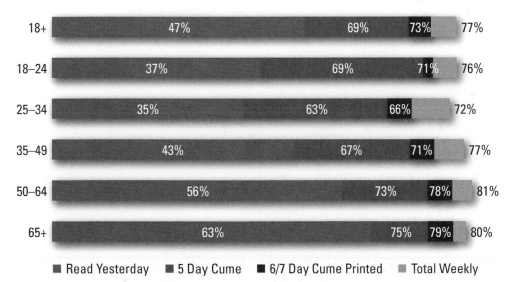

FIGURE   12–11

Daily newspaper readership by age, all markets, adults 18+

373

Source: 2009 NADbank Study

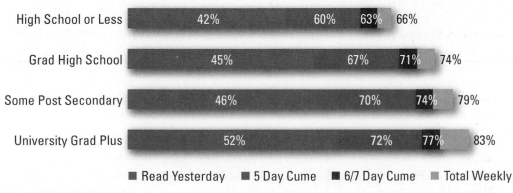

FIGURE   12–12

Daily newspaper readership by education, all markets, adults 18+

Source: 2009 NADbank Study

FIGURE 12–13

Daily newspaper readership by income, all markets, adults 18+

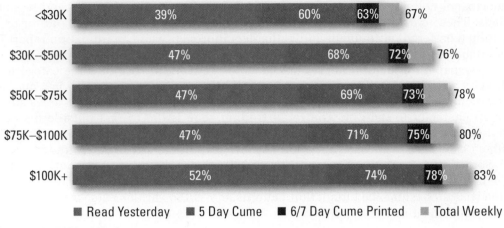

Source: 2009 NADbank Study

FIGURE 12–14

Daily newspaper readership by occupation, all markets, adults 18+

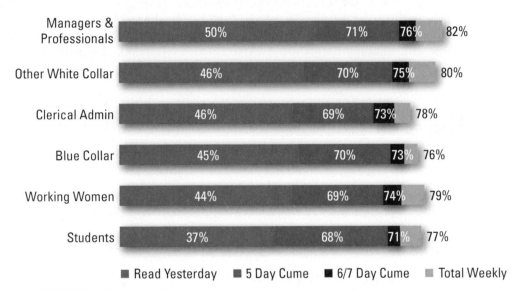

Source: 2009 NADbank Study

DAILY NEWSPAPER AUDIENCE MEASUREMENT

For newspapers, we summarize two important organizations that are involved with audience measurement: NADbank and Combase. The former concerns itself with city newspapers, while the latter's focus is community newspapers.

NADbank   Newspaper Audience Databank Inc. (NADbank) is an organization comprised of newspaper, advertising agency, and advertiser members. Its primary mandate is to publish audience research information for Canadian daily newspapers. The purpose of this research is to provide its members with valid readership information to facilitate the buying and selling of newspaper advertising space.

NADbank uses a phone interview of respondents that takes approximately 15 minutes. The interview asks questions pertaining to readership of local and non-local newspapers, time spent reading, frequency of reading, method of receipt of newspapers into the home or outside the home, readership of TV magazine publications, radio listening, TV viewing and magazine readership, Internet readership of online newspapers, demographics, and media reliance. Product usage data are collected by a self-completion questionnaire that is sent to respondents after the telephone interview. These questions focus on 29 product categories and 20 retail shopping categories.

The study is conducted in 53 Canadian urban markets covering 83 Canadian paid daily newspapers. Twenty-two markets annually are measured for both the readership and product data, while 31 markets are measured for readership data every three years. The measurement period for NADbank is comprised of two waves. The Winter/Spring wave covers the period from January to June. The Fall wave measures the period from September to December.

The readership study indicated that adults read the newspaper an average of 48 minutes per weekday and an average of 88 minutes on the weekend. The reach of newspapers is quite pervasive even though there are many media choices and reading is more time-consuming and involving than other media. For example, 48 percent of adults 18 and older across all markets read a newspaper yesterday, 48 percent read a newspaper last weekend, and 73 percent have read a newspaper in the past week.

As we have seen in the audience measurement for other media, the NADbank data are available to use with specialized software from two authorized suppliers (IMS and Harris/Telmar). It provides consultation services to assist its members who use the information. Proprietary questions may also be added to the survey if an advertiser or marketer wants to link brand-specific data with the media and product usage data.

ComBase ComBase administers the audience measurement for CCNA. ComBase is also the name of the study. ComBase is an organization with a composition and mandate similar to that of NADbank. The independent board features newspapers, advertisers, and advertising agencies. Its mandate is to publish audience research information of the community newspapers throughout Canada to allow them to sell their advertising space more effectively. The most recent study occurred in 2009.

The "Recent Reading" methodology used by ComBase is as thorough as the NADbank and PMB studies. In fact, an independent organization, the Canadian Advertising Research Foundation (CARF), appraised and endorsed the methodology. Of note, the survey determines all the publications read with an intensive investigation over a three-month time period. The survey also features excellent sample sizes and response rates and conducts the survey appropriately over time to ensure authenticity.

ComBase conducts 10-minute telephone interviews in English with adults selected at random. The interviewer asks questions pertaining to readership of community newspapers, local and non-resident; readership of daily newspapers, including nationals; readership of other print press including shoppers, agricultural press, and alternative publications; number of papers read; frequency of reading; newspaper preferred if more than one is read; rating of newspapers read; radio listening and TV viewing; and demographic information about the respondent and household.

Results of the data can be compiled along a number of dimensions: Census Metropolitan Area (CMA) with population of 100,000 or more in an urbanized core; Census Agglomeration (CA) with population of 10,000 or more in an urbanized core; suburbs; newspaper distribution areas; Census Subdivisions (CSD) like towns and villages; economic regions with areas of common economic interests as defined by Statistics Canada; and provinces. Data can be accessed and used with existing media software, similar to the situation with NADbank. The following results demonstrate the significance of community newspapers:

- 70 percent read last weekday's issue of their community newspaper
- 48 percent read yesterday's weekday daily
- 25 percent of readers are exclusive
- 40 percent of Canadians are light TV viewers
- 26 percent of Canadians did not listen to radio yesterday.

NEWSPAPER ADVERTISING RATES

Advertisers are faced with a number of options and pricing structures when purchasing newspaper space. The cost of advertising space depends on the circulation, and whether the circulation is controlled (free) or paid. It also depends on factors such as premium charges for colour in a special section, as well as discounts available. National rates can be about 15 percent higher than local rates, to account for agency commission. Figures 12-15 and 12-16 provide a summary of newspaper advertising rates.

Newspaper space is sold by the **agate line** and **column width**. A line (or agate line) is a unit measuring one column wide and 1/14-inch deep. One problem with this unit is that newspapers use columns of varying width, from 6 columns per page to 10 columns per page, which affects the size, shape, and costs of an ad. (Note that these columns are not the actual columns viewed while reading the newspaper.) This results in a complicated production and buying process for national advertisers that purchase space in a number of newspapers.

Advertisers need to know the number of lines and number of columns on a newspaper page in order to calculate the cost of an ad. For example, the following calculation is for the weekday cost of a full-page ad in the national edition of the *National Post*. The paper has 301 lines and 10 columns per page, and the open cost per line is $17.69.

$$10 \text{ columns} \times 301 \text{ lines} \times \$17.69/\text{line per column} = \$53,247$$

This calculation could be done differently with the same result when the entire length of the paper is known (301 lines/14 agate lines per column inch).

$$10 \text{ columns} \times 21.5 \text{ inches} \times 14 \text{ agate lines per column inch} \times \$17.69 = \$52,247$$

FIGURE 12–15

Daily newspaper circulation and cost by region

	Atlantic	Quebec	Ontario	Prairies	BC & Yukon	Total
Number of Markets	13	6	35	14	26	94
Number of Dailies	14	13	44	21	32	124
Circulation	359,940	1,234,303	2,682,485	921,080	825,363	6,023,171
BW Line Rate ($)	24	64	210	64	83	445
Full Page BW ($)	68,142	123,970	487,821	157,027	128,876	965,836
Full Page Colour ($)	82,182	153,054	562,289	193,359	153,155	1,144,039

Source: CARD Spring/Summer 2009, Media Digest 09/10, p. 38

FIGURE 12–16

Daily newspaper circulation and cost by population groups

	1MM+	500M–1MM	100M–500M	50M–100M	Under 50M	Total
Number of Markets	6	3	26	24	35	94
Number of Dailies	29	5	30	25	35	124
Circulation	4,093,744	447,254	932,057	329,567	220,549	6,023,171
Full Page BW ($)	520,502	63,567	211,187	86,285	84,295	965,836
Full Page Colour ($)	609,347	86,712	245,451	100,436	102,093	1,144,039

Source: CARD Spring/Summer 2009, Media Digest 09/10, p. 38

This principle can be used to calculate the cost of ads of various sizes. For example, for an ad that is 5 columns wide and 6 inches deep, the calculation would then be the following:

$$5 \text{ columns} \times 6 \text{ inches} \times 14 \text{ agate lines per column inch}$$
$$\times \$17.69 \text{ per column inch} = \$7{,}430$$

Newspaper rates for local advertisers continue to be based on the column inch, which is 1 inch deep by 1 column wide. Advertising rates for local advertisers are quoted per column inch, and media planners calculate total space costs by multiplying the ad's number of column inches by the cost per inch.

Most newspapers have an **open-rate structure**, which means various discounts are available. These discounts are generally based on frequency or bulk purchases of space and depend on the number of column inches purchased in a year. The above calculations used the most expensive cost based on a one-time ad. The maximum discount puts the cost per line at $11.82, about one-third less expensive. A full-page ad would drop from $53,247 to $35,578, a savings of $17,669.

Newspaper space rates also vary with an advertiser's special requests, such as preferred position or colour. The basic rates quoted by a newspaper are **run of paper (ROP)**, which means the paper can place the ad on any page or in any position it desires. While most newspapers try to place an ad in a requested position, the advertiser can ensure a specific section and/or position on a page by paying a higher **preferred position rate**. Colour advertising is also available in many newspapers on an ROP basis or through preprinted inserts or supplements.

Recently, advertising rates have come under fire from media buyers with an equally contentious response from the media vendors. Historically, media buyers paid what newspapers set as their price without much criticism. However, newspaper rates have been questioned from larger advertising agencies and media buying organizations that have emerged with amalgamations in the industry. While media buyers usually investigate and evaluate the audience size and price for television advertising rates, this behaviour was not generally expected with newspapers. In particular, the *National Post* and *The Globe and Mail* reacted strongly to those buyers who have put increased pressure on lower rates as they represent very large advertisers who purchase millions of agate lines per year. To contribute to the discussion, *The Globe and Mail* worked with an independent data analysis firm that tracked the sales impact of newspaper ad placement.[20]

IMC PLANNING: STRATEGIC USE OF PRINT MEDIA

In the previous chapter, we ended with a discussion of the use of broadcast media to achieve strategic IMC objectives. In this IMC planning section, we investigate the use of magazines and newspapers to achieve communication and behavioural objectives at different stages of the target audience's decision-making process.

MAGAZINES

The selectivity and creativity options for magazines allow promotional planners a multitude of opportunities for establishing and maintaining very unique brand positions across all potential target audiences. For example, if research indicates a high proportion of non-users in certain lifestyle publications, the promotional planner can develop print ads with extensive copy to build category need as well as sufficient brand coverage for awareness while communicating the most appropriate brand benefit message for persuasion. Alternatively, research in other publications might indicate strong brand development and a high degree of current customers, thus allowing the promotional planner the opportunity to use messages that maintain the strong brand equity. This might suggest a more emotional message with enticing visuals for low-involvement processing.

While the decision to offer more customized messages to each audience is met with some amount of risk, it is mitigated by the consistency in the creative theme and creative tactics such as the design elements (e.g., layout). This possible scenario for promotional planners suggests that ads directed toward non-users could be developed to influence the pre-purchase and need recognition stages, whereas the ads for the customer could attempt to influence the purchase decision stage, as the brand would be encouraging a repeat purchase objective.

Extending this argument geographically is another strategic opportunity for promotional planners. For example, if the brand has a low brand development index in one part of the country, more persuasive switching messages directed to consumers at the purchase decision stage might be considered through regional or city editions. Alternatively, other regional editions could be examined if the brand has a high brand development index and the promotional planner concentrates on brand maintenance messages that focus, for example, on post-purchase satisfaction.

As the use of these key strengths of magazines implies, promotional planners can use magazines to attain virtually any of the communication objectives with any type of target audience and create the unique brand positions desired. Granted, certain costs are associated with this strategic use of magazines; the promotional planner can schedule the placements over time so as not to break the budget.

These strengths of magazines allow print to work with other media and IMC tools. Visuals can be the same as those from TV commercials to enhance message frequency. Headlines could be consistently used across out-of-home media and print ads. Sales promotions can be added to the message, like coupons or Internet site links to register for samples. Brand-building charity sponsorship or events can be communicated if they especially resonate with the readership audience. In short, magazines offer a degree of potential integration in the IMC plan.

NEWSPAPERS

The strategic use of this medium is similar to radio in that national and local advertisers design messages with related objectives. National advertisers employ newspapers for brand-building messages they wish to disseminate across the country or in select regions. These ads take a few general forms. One kind of ad builds awareness and benefit beliefs at the pre-purchase and need recognition stages due to the broad reach of newspapers. With the majority of Canadian households reading newspapers on a regular basis, brands naturally reach their target audience and those who may not be in the market for such products. Other types of ads contribute at the information search stage for the target audience. The involved nature of the messages that can be creatively communicated in a more rational manner to fit the editorial context permits promotional planners to persuade their audience via high-involvement, informational brand attitude. One limitation with the opportunity is that the number of consumers actually in the market at this stage is fewer, thus making the purchase less cost-efficient. Finally, national advertisers utilize newspapers for executing information regarding sales promotions. For example, automobile manufacturers and large retailers are some of the largest advertisers who communicate their price and other promotions in newspapers to influence consumers at the purchase decision stage.

As noted in the cost implications discussion, newspapers offer local advertisers and small businesses (e.g., retailers, services) a tremendous opportunity for reaching an entire city for a reasonable cost. These advertisers can design ads to meet any communication objectives. A perusal of the local newspaper will identify ads that are clearly trying to build awareness and communicate certain brand benefits. However, the daily/weekly time frame of newspapers reveals that many ads have stronger purchase intention objectives.

Like magazines, newspapers offer good potential for integrating with other media and IMC tools. Oftentimes, television and radio commercials suggest that consumers "see newspaper for details." In this case, the initial ads are influencing the target audience at the need recognition stage and the newspaper is influencing the information search stage. Many public relations activities like sponsorship of charity events in the local community are conveyed in newspapers since they act as a planning resource for things to do in one's city.

CHAPTER OBJECTIVES AND SUMMARY

1 To identify the different types of magazines offered as an advertising medium.

Magazines are a very selective medium and are very valuable for reaching specific types of customers and market segments. The four broad categories of magazines are consumer, ethnic, farm, and business publications. Each of these categories can be further classified according to the publication's editorial content and audience appeal.

2 To analyze the strengths and limitations of magazines as an advertising medium.

The strengths of magazines include their target audience selectivity, geographic coverage, creativity, reader involvement and amount of processing time, media image, and selective exposure and attention levels. Limitations of magazines include their high cost, limited reach and frequency, long lead time, weak target audience coverage, and the advertising clutter in most publications.

3 To describe how space is purchased in magazines, how readership is measured, and how rates are determined.

Advertising space rates in magazines vary according to a number of factors, among them the size of the ad, position in the publication, particular editions purchased, use of colour, and number and frequency of insertions. Rates for magazines are compared on the basis of cost per thousand, although other factors such as the editorial content of the publication and its ability to reach specific target audiences must also be considered. Readership is verified with an audit function so advertisers are confident that the number claimed by the individual titles is accurate. Extensive information about magazine readers is available to those who subscribe to the PMB data. The PMB is one of the most sophisticated and extensive readership studies in the world.

4 To identify the types of newspapers offered as an advertising medium and the format of newspaper ads.

A variety of newspapers are available for advertisers including, daily, community, national, Internet, and special audience. Newspapers offer great flexibility regarding the type of ad including display, classified, and inserts.

5 To explain how advertising space is purchased in newspapers, how readership is measured, and how rates are determined.

Newspaper ads are sold as a full page or any partial page the advertiser desires. The line and column characteristics of newspapers allow nearly unlimited sizes, although most ads follow conventional sizes of half-page, quarter-page, and so on, with smaller advertisers selecting smaller spaces. Advertising rates are determined by the size of the ad and the circulation. Extensive research is conducted to ensure that the number of readers is accurate. Additional research of newspaper readers provides a detailed profile of their characteristics.

6 To summarize the strengths and limitations of newspapers as an advertising medium.

Newspapers represent a strong advertising medium in terms of total advertising revenue, despite negative growth during the past three years. Newspapers are a very important medium to local advertisers, especially retailers. Newspapers are a broad-based medium and reach a large percentage of households in a particular area. Newspapers' other advantages include scheduling flexibility, geographic coverage, reader involvement and amount of processing time, media image, creativity for cognitive responses, and absolute cost and cost efficiency. Drawbacks of newspapers include their creativity for emotional responses, selective exposure and attention, target audience selectivity, and clutter. The use of special inserts and supplements allows advertisers to overcome some of these limitations to a degree. However, newspapers face increasing competition from Internet media as the World Wide Web continues to grow as an information resource for consumers.

KEY TERMS

agate line, *376*
bleed pages, *359*
city zone, *373*
classified advertising, *368*
column width, *376*

controlled-circulation basis, *363*
creative space buys, *359*
display advertising, *367*
gatefolds, *359*
ink-jet imaging, *357*

inserts, *359*
open-rate structure, *377*
pass-along readership, *363*
PMB study, *364*
preferred position rate, *377*
preprinted inserts, *368*

retail trading zone, *373*
run of paper (ROP), *377*
selective binding, *357*
selectivity, *355*
total audience/ readership, *364*

DISCUSSION QUESTIONS

1. Discuss the strengths and limitations of magazines as an advertising medium. How do magazines differ from television and radio as advertising media?

2. Describe what is meant by selectivity with regard to the purchase of advertising media and discuss some of the ways magazines provide selectivity to advertisers.

3. Explain why advertisers of products such as cosmetics or women's clothing would choose to advertise in magazines such as *Flare*, *Elle Canada*, or *Chatelaine*.

4. Discuss how circulation figures are used in evaluating magazines and newspapers as part of a media plan and setting advertising rates.

5. If you were purchasing magazine ad space for a manufacturer of snowboarding equipment, what factors would you consider? Would your selection of magazines be limited to snowboarding publications? Why or why not?

6. The number of magazines has increased substantially in the past five years. What could have caused this recent trend?

7. Discuss the strengths and limitations of newspapers as an advertising medium. How might the decision to use newspapers in a media plan differ for national versus local advertisers?

8. What factors could explain the lower readership of newspapers compared to a few years ago?

OUT-OF-HOME AND SUPPORT MEDIA

■ CHAPTER OBJECTIVES

1   To describe out-of-home and support media available to the marketer in developing an IMC program.

2   To know how audiences for out-of-home and support media are measured.

3   To develop an understanding of the strengths and limitations of out-of-home and support media.

CADBURY'S OUTDOOR ADVENTURES

Lesya Lysyj, VP Marketing for Cadbury North America, oversees a team of 50 who have worked to drive the company's chocolate, candy, cough drop, and gum brands to new heights. The team—20 of whom are based in Toronto—have come up with fun and innovative marketing communication activities in which out-of-home and other support media have played a key role. Some of its best work has occurred with Creme Egg, Dairy Milk, Caramilk, Cadbury Chocolate, and Dentyne.

With its high-profile location and outdoor media options, Toronto's Dundas Square was ideal to feature a Cadbury brand. A billboard for the Creme Egg relied on precipitation to completely reveal a gooey adventure for all to see in person or online. A pendulum-like device with a giant egg at one end and a box that collected snow and rain at the other eventually tilted so that the egg made contact with a fan. The ensuing contact broke the egg and released the faux cream filling upon the billboard. According to one Cadbury executive, "Canadians just love to talk the weather and express great interest in the weather conditions, particularly in Toronto. The building of the billboard was a great opportunity to celebrate the fun, gooey, messy playfulness of the Creme Egg just in time for Easter."

In the past, a 3D billboard topped by a mechanized figure ate a piece of Dairy Milk bar in Dundas Square, and Cadbury later used the same location to support its "Eyebrows" campaign, which originated in the UK and moved to Canada after great success. In various media locations, messages using people's eyebrows could be decoded to win prizes or carry on in the game.

A rejuvenated campaign for the Caramilk "Secret" featured 50 interactive audioboards in the Toronto subway system among other media like TV, print, and online. A series of interpretive reveals of the secret kept the mystery and discovery experience exciting for consumers. Cadbury promoted consumption with a Chocolate Couture Fashion Show where fashion designers and chocolate artists teamed up to create an outfit made of chocolate.

For its chewing gum brands, Cadbury also contracted out-of-home media. A revised Dentyne campaign encouraged "face-time" with friends, for which one would naturally want Dentyne-like fresh breath. Some ads pictured images of a man and a woman kissing with Internet-inspired messages such as "friend request accepted," "the original instant message," and "the original voicemail." Another showed a group of friends on or beside a couch with the message "chatroom full."

Sources: Katie Bailey, "Cadbury's Dairy Milk Decodes Brow Language," *Strategy*, November 2009, p. 50; Jonathan Paul, "Cadbury Spills the Caramilk Secret," *Strategy*, July 2009, p. 6; Emily Wexler, "Getting Cadbury More Face Time," *Strategy*, March 20, p. 20; Chris Powell, "Dundas Square to Get Creamed by Cadbury," *Marketing Magazine*, February 25, 2009.

QUESTION:

1. Why do chocolate bar brands use outdoor advertising?

Every time we step out of the house, we encounter media directing an advertising message to us. Often we see ads while travelling. Many places we go to for leisure have advertising. **Out-of-home media** is quite pervasive as it delivers advertising messages that we experience while moving throughout our town or city while accomplishing our day-to-day activities. Some are new to the marketplace, and others have been around a while. In this chapter, we review three broad categories of out-of-home media: outdoor, transit, and place-based (Figure 13-1) that generated $463 million in advertising revenue in 2008. The term out-of-home media is adopted because it encompasses media that are located in public spaces.

We also encounter messages from other media, known as **support media**. These media are used to reach those in the target audience that primary media may not, or to reinforce the message contained in primary media. We conclude this chapter by summarizing two broad types: promotional products and product placement. The term "promotional media" might be more appropriate; however, the notion of support media has existed for some time and remains relatively accurate. Its function as a public dissemination of a brand's messages is similar to that of out-of-home media, allowing this chapter to have a consistent theme. Finally, for each out-of-home and support medium, we offer a summary of strengths and limitations; these are generalizations, however, and advertisers can certainly find some exceptions as these media continue to flourish and innovate.

OUTDOOR MEDIA

Outdoor media are pervasive, and it appears that we are surrounded. However, the amount spent on this medium is a portion of the $463 million spent on out-of-home media. In contrast, advertising on the Internet is over three times larger than out-of-home. Despite this paradox of both large and small scale, the growth of outdoor media options and its contribution to sales may be a key factor in its continued interest to advertisers. In a study reported by BBDO advertising, 35 percent of consumers surveyed said they had called a phone number they saw on an out-of-home ad.[1] Another study showed that outdoor advertising can have a significant effect on sales, particularly when combined with a promotion.[2] We now describe outdoor media options available, the audience measurement, and their strengths and limitations as an advertising medium.

OUTDOOR MEDIA OPTIONS

A variety of outdoor media options and the companies that sell them can be seen in Figure 13-2. Most outdoor operators can present examples of past outdoor campaigns

FIGURE 13–1

Out-of-home media

Outdoor	Transit	Place-Based
Horizontal/vertical poster	Interior horiz./vert. poster	Bar, restaurant, hotel
Backlit poster	Exterior bus poster	Mall, cinema
Superboard, spectacular	Super-bus, bus mural	Airport poster/video display
Video/electronic display	Station video display	Arena, stadium
Street level/transit shelter poster	Station poster	Golf, ski, fitness centre
Wall banner, mural	Station domination	Office building
Mobile signage	Taxi	University, college
Aerial, bench, receptacle, parking lot, bike rack	In-flight video/magazine	Washroom, elevator

FIGURE   13–2   Outdoor media operators

Operator	Poster	Super-board	Backlit Poster	Street Furniture	Mural Advertising	Outdoor Digital	Media Inventory	Total Media Percentage Share
Pattison	10,304	379	146	6,715	10	6	17,500	41%
CBS	6,579	271	182	9,147	11	—	16,190	38%
Astral Media Outdoor	1,976	123	12	5,292	13	21	7,437	18%
All Others	445	46	8	605	4	36	1,144	3%
Industry Total	19,304	819	348	21,759	38	63	42,331	100%

Source: COMB; CARD, April 2006/Vendor Rate Cards

producing awareness and other communication effects. The examples can be for a product category or for individual campaigns. The operators can also provide maps to illustrate the locations and other relevant data (e.g., demographics).

Posters describe the typical billboard, which can be horizontal (e.g., 3m by 6m) or vertical (e.g., 4m by 5m). These displays are front lit for visibility at night and are located in areas with high vehicle traffic. They may be purchased on an individual basis or for a certain level of GRPs in cities such as Toronto or in smaller markets such as Timmins, Ontario. As the name implies, **backlit posters** are posters of generally the same size that have a light behind them so that they are more clearly illuminated. These units are located at major intersections or high-traffic-volume areas in or near major cities in Canada.

Larger billboards, known as **bulletins**, **superboards**, or **spectaculars**, are larger displays (two to three times larger) that have a variety of sizes depending upon the media company. These displays are sold on a per location basis due to their size and the low number of options available in major Canadian markets. Research on billboards is lacking in comparison to other media, but one recent study on why billboards are used found that managers rated visibility and media efficiency as more influential than local presence and tangible results (e.g., sales). The most critical factors for billboard success included name identification, location, readability, and clarity. A secondary set of factors suggested IMC and visuals, while the third group indicated creative and information. This implies that allowing the target audience to clearly read the brand identification at the right place is paramount over the most creative or informative ad.[3]

Smaller backlit displays, known as **street-level posters** and measuring about 2m by 1m, are available across the country and are also posted in transit shelters (some in the industry refer to this as "street furniture"). A recent study conducted in Europe makes a number of conclusions regarding their usefulness.[4]

- Clear branding and inclusion of new-product information enhances product recognition.
- Large amounts of text and pictures of people delay product recognition.
- Lengthy, large headlines, information cues, and humour delay brand recognition.
- Short headlines, longer body text, and a product shot enhance the creative appeal.
- Specifying a brand name in the headline or providing price information reduces appeal.

A number of innovative outdoor tools have emerged in Canada. Some firms are setting up large video-display units that have full animation and colour. For example, Dundas Square, near the Eaton Centre in downtown Toronto, features

385

Exhibit 13-1 Outdoor media goes beyond two dimensions.

Exhibit 13-2 Murals are part of the outdoor landscape.

a 12-metre-wide by 9-metre-high full-colour video screen in addition to eight display faces and Canada's largest neon sign, at 18 metres in diameter. Many of Canada's largest advertisers secure space in this very prominent location, which receives extensive pedestrian and vehicular traffic (see Exhibit 13-1).[5] Electronic message signs offer short ads (e.g., 10 seconds) on a 2- or 3-minute rotation. As expected, both of these displays are located in high-traffic locations in a few large urban markets, with various sizes and packages available depending on the media firm. The growth of outdoor video displays is such that the firms offer network services, thereby reaching many viewers across the country. Murals and wall banners are sold in a few major markets in Canada (e.g., Toronto, Vancouver) with varying sizes (Exhibit 13-2).

A number of firms offer **mobile signage** by placing displays on trucks or vehicles. These are sold by the number of vehicles and the number of months. And mobile messages with advertising-wrapped cars are driving into Canada, after growing substantially in the U.S. in the past decade. CityFlitz offers a fleet of 35 Minis with a cost of $4,500 per month for the advertiser. With a claimed exposure of at least 50,000 people, the CPM clicks in at a mere $3, far cheaper than static billboards located in the same place for one month. In addition, the cars are WiFi equipped, offering additional opportunity for inventive marketers. The logistics of driving are covered by members who join the company and rent the car for only $1 per day.[6] Finally, we find outdoor media in some unusual outdoor locations. Signage is placed on benches, parking lots, bicycle racks, garbage receptacles, and in the air through aerial advertising on airplanes or hot-air balloons. It seems that no matter where we turn outside, there will be some form of advertising message directed toward us.

Historically, advertisers considered outdoor advertising as a support medium to broadcast or print. However, current usage indicates outdoor ads can be used successfully as a primary medium, as shown by Clover Leaf's recent strategic emphasis. Hoping to expand the overall tuna category to both men and women with its flavoured varieties (e.g., sun-dried tomato and basil), the only nationally distributed tuna producer showed interesting and innovative ways of thinking about tuna (e.g., salad or wraps) with its more exotic taste sensations. Outdoor (e.g., posters, transit shelters, street columns) became the focal point to communicate the images and messages that easily transferred to other out-of-home media (e.g., in-store, health club posters) and sales promotions (e.g., coupons, samples).[7] IMC Perspective 13-1 identifies examples where out-of-home ads are very creative and play a key role in the IMC plan.

The aforementioned outdoor options are typically purchased for four weeks and provide anywhere from 25 GRPs to 150 GRPs per day, depending upon the number of displays or showings chosen within a local market. Recall from Chapter 10 that one GRP represents 1 percent of the market exposed to the ad once. Thus, buying 50 GRPs possibly implies that the marketer reaches 50 percent of the market once per day.

FIGURE 13–3   Outdoor media schedule

Market	12+ Pop'n	Operator	Product	Panel Numbers	GRPs/ wk	Target 12+ Impr/ wk	4 wks
Montreal CMA	3,293.3	Astral	Horizontal	23	178	23,442	66.1/10.8
		Pattison	Horizontal	26	176	23,152	63.2/11.1
		CBS	Horizontal	26	182	23,969	67.9/10.7
		Astral	Column	51	175	23,095	58.4/12.0
		Pattison	Street Furniture	53	176	23,231	58.1/12.1
		CBS	Street Furniture	62	175	23,087	68.4/10.2
			Mix		1,062	13,976	90+
Toronto CMA	4,783.6	Astral	Horizontal	42	177	33,930	60.1/11.8
		Pattison	Horizontal	60	178	34,021	66.4/10.7
		CBS	Horizontal	49	177	33,847	68.6/10.3
		Astral	Street Furniture	73	176	33,627	66.7/10.5
		Pattison	Street Furniture	108	177	33,778	43.3/16.3
		CBS	Street Furniture	63	176	33,681	62.7/11.2
			Mix		1,061	202,884	90+
Vancouver CMA	2,002.8	Pattison	Horizontal	23	173	14,214	68.8/10.3
		CBS	Horizontal	19	178	14,630	58.5/12.5
		Pattison	Street Furniture	40	174	14,301	64.3/11.1
		CBS	Street Furniture	30	172	14,163	68.9/10.3
			Mix		697	57,308	90+

Source: COMBNavigator; Media Digest 09/10 p. 59

Figure 13-3 illustrates hypothetical schedules in Canada's three leading markets with various outdoor media based on 25 GRPs/day (175 GRPs/week). It is impossible to get exactly 175 GRPs due to buying a specific number of displays that have different exposure levels. Each medium selected provides different resulting reach and frequency estimates, although most are in the same range. The first line shows a reach of 66 percent with a frequency of 10.8 over the four-week time period, which is consistent with the 178 GRPs for each of the four weeks (i.e., 4 weeks × 178 GRPs/week = 66 × 10.8). The cost for such a plan is currently unavailable as most of these media companies report "call for rates" in CARD.

AUDIENCE MEASUREMENT

COMB   Audience measurement to determine the amount of reach and frequency is done by the Canadian Out-of-Home Measurement Bureau (COMB), an independent organization comprised of members from advertisers, advertising agencies, and media firms known as outdoor operators. COMB maintains a national database of all products for outdoor operators in order to calculate daily or weekly audience averages for each medium in all markets. COMB acts as an auditor to ensure an authentic media purchase and produces specific reports as documentation. COMB

Out-of-Home Creativity

While TV is often seen as the prime media for creative, advertising is also very creative with out-of-home media seen across the country for a variety of products and invented from many different agencies. The Vancouver team of the Taxi agency created a pint-sized outdoor campaign that fit its client, West Valley Market. The local independent store wanted to distance itself from the ads for big-box stores, so the miniature campaign proved to be a perfect contrast. About 500 small pots planted with vegetables found their way to doorsteps and public places for consumers to take and had the message "A small taste of the farm—West Valley Market." Later, mini models of things like farms and gardens dotted the area and had messages like "A small taste of Japan," or "A small taste of Italy."

The Vancouver team of the Rethink agency demonstrated Parissa Wax Strips on the beach with help from a man with a hairy back. The brand name—groomed using wax into the man's hair—attracted the attention of sunbathers, who clearly perceived the need for the product! "We thought this was a fun way to draw attention to our product at a place where smooth, silky skin is an absolute must—the beach," commented Parissa's VP. Rethink estimated the resulting publicity garnered $250,000 in exposure. Rethink also promoted a personal trainer's services by having a person ride a stationary bike beside morning commuters with the message "Escape your boring gym."

The out-of-home ads developed by Nolin BBDO for the Quebec Federation of Milk Producers comforted Quebecers with cheery messages changed weekly that of course reminded consumers to drink milk. Montreal and Quebec businesses could win visits featuring heart-warming messages along with milk and cookies to keep them happy and chase away the winter blues. Additional comforting messages occurred in the subway system.

The Toronto group of Venture Communications turned the stairway of Toronto's Union Station from street level to track level with a virtual trek down a ski hill with wall-to-wall images of the Alberta Rockies. "We felt our ski messaging would have a large impact on the quarter-million commuters who frequent the station on a daily basis," commented a director of Travel Alberta. Other media complemented the initial eye-opener and included store kiosks, direct mail, and a website (skicanadianrockies.com) where visitors could experience video clips of the hills and plan a vacation.

The Media Merchants of Vancouver projected video images onto building walls in Montreal, Toronto, Calgary, and Vancouver using a hand-held projector with ads for a Burger King promotion connected to the movie *Transformers: Revenge of the Fallen.* Operators handed out coupons and carried the speakers in backpacks. The technology allowed advertising at night in places where outdoor ads do not exist and vehicle ads cannot reach.

Sources: Tim Shepherd, "West Valley Market's Lilliputian Strategy," *Strategy,* September 2009, p. 10; Hollie Shaw, "With the West Coast in the Grip of Hot Weather, Things Can Get a Little Hairy," *National Post,* July 31, p. FP10; Hollie Shaw, "Rethinking Vancouver's Streets," *National Post,* August 14, 2009, p. FP10; Theresa Wood, "Milk Coats Quebec with Cheer," *Strategy,* March 2009, p. 6; Emily Wexler, "Travel Alberta's Subway Slopes," *Strategy,* January 2009, p. 8; Jonathan Paul, "Parissa Brings Sexy Back-Vertising," *Strategy,* September 2009, p. 10; Jonathan Paul, "Media Merchants Ninja," *Strategy,* July 2009, p. 7.

Question:

1. Which of these ideas appears most creative?

---

conducts 6,000 randomly selected field audits per year, calculates performance statistics for all operators, and disseminates these findings to all members.

COMB's methodology to determine the reach and frequency is comprehensive. COMB obtains traffic circulation numbers from municipalities, and then analyzes these data with respect to three key questions:

- What is the average number of people in the vehicle?
- What is the vehicle's origin within the CMA?
- Is the sign illuminated? If so, for how long?

This analysis is known as the total number of circulations. These circulations are applied to each poster along a certain part of the road called a link. The numbers are adjusted to account for time-of-day variations throughout the week to arrive at an adjusted circulation, which is then divided by the target population so that the reach is expressed as 1 percent of the population.

This involved measurement process has resulted in a system that COMB claims as being the most accurate and reliable method in the world. In contrast, some media buyers are concerned that the measurement tracks opportunity for exposure and not actual exposure to the ads. While this discrepancy is an inherent problem with all media, it appears to be particularly strong with outdoor media. Furthermore, it is not clear how many people are in each vehicle that may be exposed to the ads. Despite this success and constructive criticism, COMB strives to find the best system possible to ensure a larger piece of the advertising industry beyond its usual 4-percent share compared to broadcast or print.

Recently, COMB tested the use of a global positioning system (GPS) to track driving behaviour more accurately in selected Canadian cities. The device was installed in cars to track driving patterns and to track which outdoor ads drivers had driven past. Pre- and posttest interviews obtained demographic and other information that was linked to other data sources to estimate reach and frequency. Preliminary results indicated that people were exposed to many ads but with less frequency to each ad, thus suggesting the usefulness of maximizing reach over frequency with outdoor ads.

OMAC The Out-of-Home Marketing Association of Canada (OMAC), formed in 2005, is a membership among five founding media companies—Astral Media Outdoor, NEWAD, Pattison Outdoor, CBS Outdoor, and Zoom Media—and four others that have joined more recently—Lamar Transit, Metromedia Plus, OBN, and Titan 360. Combined, the nine firms own 90 percent of the out-of-home media opportunities. OMAC's mission is to develop the market for this medium, implement new industry initiatives, establish guidelines, and act on behalf of the industry on any issues. Like other organizations that represent a particular medium, OMAC commissions research to demonstrate its effectiveness that acts as key information for decision makers.

OMAC undertook two "Day in the Life" (DIL) studies. The first, DIL I, investigated time spent inside/outside home, out-of-home exposure, commuting habits, and related shopping behaviour. Based on telephone interviews with 2,500 Canadians age 12+ in major markets, the study found that the average person spends 55 percent of the day (while awake) out of the home and one-third in the home. On a typical weekday, urban Canadians spend as much time exposed to out-of-home media (3.8 hours) as to television and the Internet (Figure 13-4). The typical urban Canadian drives nearly 130 kilometres a week, with commuting to and from work accounting for half this distance and taking 65 minutes. Many urban workers (73 percent) use a vehicle to get to work, with the incidence of travelling by vehicle increasing significantly among suburbanites.

Figure 13-5 shows when people do their shopping; more than 50 percent shop on their way to work or home. From a measurement standpoint, advertisers can be confident that out-of-home media reach a substantial portion of the population while they are planning to or actually shopping. In fact, 87 percent either shop closer to work, closer to home, or somewhere equally close to both places. Out-of-home advertising also wields considerable influence on purchase decisions. The study found that in the past three months, 30 percent of people visited a specific website after seeing it promoted on out-of-home advertising; 25 percent learned about a store/product/sale that motivated them to visit a specific store; and 17 percent were prompted to purchase or seek information about a new product.

The second Day in the Life study, DIL II, investigated the relevance and impact of out-of-home media versus other media. Figure 13-6 suggests that consumers do not believe there is too much out-of-home advertising compared to other media.[8]

389

FIGURE 13–4

Time exposed to various media

	Average Time Exposed per Day (Hours)		
	Week Day	**Saturday**	**Sunday**
Out-of-Home Stimulus	3.8	4.7	4.7
Radio	2.2	1.3	1.1
Internet	3.6	2.6	2.4
Newspapers	0.5	0.6	0.4
Magazines	0.4	0.3	0.2
Television	3.8	3.1	3.1

Source: Out-of-Home Marketing Association of Canada, A Day in the Life I

FIGURE 13–5

Time of day when workers shop

Source: Out-of-Home Marketing Association of Canada, A Day in the Life I

FIGURE 13–6

Perceptions of amount of advertising by medium

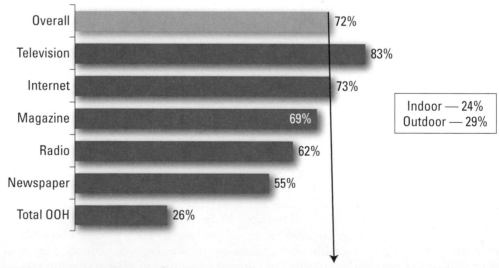

Source: Out-of-Home Marketing Association of Canada, A Day in the Life II

Another source of measurement is innovative technology that tracks a driver's eye movement to assess which ads are actually seen while driving. Taking into account the size of the ad and the distance from the road, this new method is well established in the United Kingdom and is demonstrating more accurate numbers and some believe it has led to a growth of advertising revenue that now stands at 8 percent.[9]

390

Member companies of OMAC (Pattison, Astral, CBS) commissioned the Outdoor Advertising Consumer Exposure Study (OACES) to investigate the usefulness of this research for Canada. The study used 27 randomly selected drivers and passengers from Ottawa and Montreal, who were asked to drive a predetermined route that passed by a variety of outdoor advertising products and consisted of a variety of different driving conditions. The route was driven at different times of day, respondents' eye movements were tracked using a headband eye camera, and the entire visual interaction was also video recorded. An outdoor ad was considered "seen" if a driver or passenger fixated on it for at least 200 milliseconds. The study found that 55 percent of the ads selected for analysis were seen by the 27 drivers and passengers tested. Passengers, unsurprisingly, were more likely to see them (some 73 percent, versus 52 percent of drivers who saw them). Those people who looked at advertising looked at an ad an average of 2.04 times on a single drive-by. Out-of-home ads with three rotating faces were looked at more often, 2.46 times, compared with 1.9 times for a standard poster. In total, 535 outdoor exposures were eye-tracked during the study. Neither drivers nor passengers knew the study was related to advertising with most of them thinking it was something to do with the transport ministry.[10]

STRENGTHS OF OUTDOOR MEDIA

Reach   With proper placement, a broad base of exposure is possible in a given market, with both day and night presence. A 100 GRP **showing** (the percentage of duplicated audience exposed to an outdoor poster daily) could yield exposure to an equivalent of 100 percent of the marketplace daily! This level of coverage is likely to yield high levels of reach.

Frequency   Because purchase cycles for outdoor media are typically for 4-week periods, consumers are usually exposed a number of times, resulting in high levels of frequency.

Geographic Coverage   Outdoor media can be placed along highways, near stores, or on mobile billboards, almost anywhere that the law permits. Local, regional, or even national markets may be covered.

Creativity for Emotional Responses   As shown in Exhibits 13-1 and 13-2, outdoor ads can be very creative. Large print, colours, and other elements attract attention and tend to generate short emotional responses that connect the target audience to the brand.

Cost Efficiency   Outdoor ads usually have a very competitive CPM when compared to other media. The average CPM of outdoor ads is less than that of radio, TV, magazines, and newspapers.

Scheduling Flexibility   Modern technologies have reduced production times for outdoor advertising to allow for rapid turnaround time. Placement can be done on a monthly basis assuming availability exists.

Selective Exposure   On the one hand, outdoor ads are difficult for consumers to avoid since they are so pervasive. Moreover, a consumer has little control like television or radio to change the channel or station. On the other hand, consumers can deliberately ignore outdoor ads; however, the high profile of the ads makes this a difficult task at times.

Attention   The sheer size, strategic placement, and the creative elements of colour make outdoor advertising an attractive medium to draw the attention of the target audience.

LIMITATIONS OF OUTDOOR MEDIA

Target Audience Coverage With the broad base reach of outdoor advertising, it is difficult to ensure that the specific target audience coverage is sufficient. While it is possible to reach an audience with select location placement, in many cases the purchase of outdoor ads results in a high degree of waste coverage. It is not likely that everyone driving past a billboard is part of the target audience.

Amount of Processing Time Because of the speed with which most people pass by outdoor ads, exposure time is short, so messages are limited to a few words and/or an illustration.

Creativity for Cognitive Responses Lengthy appeals are not physically possible in many instances, and if they were, they have less likelihood of complete comprehension. Thus, it is expected that outdoor ads suffer from their inability to fully persuade consumers with an involved message.

Absolute Cost A basic level of 25 GRPs per day over four weeks in 10 or even three major cities can be quite prohibitive for many advertisers. For smaller businesses, selecting a few strategic locations in a local market could overcome this limitation.

Media Image Outdoor advertising has suffered some image problems as well as some disregard among consumers. This may be in part due to fatigue of the high frequency of exposures that may lead to wearout—people are likely to get tired of seeing the same ad every day.

Target Audience Selectivity Reaching a specific target audience is challenging due to the broad exposure of outdoor media in general. However, strategic use can overcome this limitation, for example by using reminder ads for a type of product near the retail outlets.

Clutter By its very nature, outdoor ads have competing messages. At any streetscape or location where outdoor ads are featured, it is very likely that other messages will be also vying for consumer attention, as seen in Exhibit 13-3.

Exhibit 13-3
Competing messages present a challenge with outdoor media.

Low Involvement The overall effect of the short repeated message is that out-door ads tend to be considered a low-involvement media.

TRANSIT MEDIA

Another form of out-of-home advertising is **transit advertising**. While similar to outdoor in the sense that it uses posters, digital, and video messages, transit is targeted at the millions of people who are exposed to commercial transportation facilities, including buses, subways, light-rail trains, and airplanes. We now describe transit media options available, and their strengths and limitations as an advertising medium.

TRANSIT MEDIA OPTIONS

Some of the most common transit ads viewed are the **interior transit cards** placed above the seating. Ads are positioned in backlit units above windows and along both sides of the bus, streetcar, subway, or light-rail transit cars. **Interior door cards** are available in major markets where there is subway-like transit. These cards are placed on both sides of the doors and are about 50 percent larger than the aforementioned cards. **Exterior posters** may appear on the sides, backs, and/or roofs of buses, taxis, trains, and subway and street cars (see Exhibit 13-4). Various sizes are available depending on the media company and the transit vehicles, however the two most common are "seventies" (.5 m × 1.8 m) and "king" (.75 m × 3.5 m) that are seen on buses and so on. The former gets its name from the length actually sold with a width of 70 inches.

Discovery Channel has always used out-of-home media to establish itself as a legitimate television alternative and to advertise its specific series, specials, or theme weeks. For example, during Shark Week, they turned transit shelters into giant shark tanks. Following this, a summer transit shelter campaign in downtown Toronto attempted to establish an audience for *Nefertiti Resurrected* and to increase awareness and viewership of Discovery Channel in general. The ads featured an air of glamour and mystery to attract new viewers. In addition, Nefertiti models passed

Exhibit 13-4
Electronic outside posters often appear on taxicabs.

Exhibit 13-5 Station posters can be used to attract attention.

by the transit ads during a two-week period and allowed people to ask questions and take photographs. Discovery Channel believes these transit ads and street-level events played an important supporting role with the on-air ads in setting a record audience 10 percent higher than previously achieved.[11]

Station posters are of varying sizes and forms that attempt to attract the attention of those waiting for a subway-like ride. The most common size is 1m by 2m. As Exhibit 13-5 shows, station posters can be very attractive to attract attention. Similar-sized posters are found at bus or streetcar **transit shelters** and often provide the advertiser with expanded coverage where other outdoor boards may be restricted. Many of these are sold by outdoor media companies as they are identical to street-level posters, but some are listed in transit. Larger station posters are available as well; Metromedia offers super vertical subway posters and platform posters, for example.

Recent innovations in transit media include the super-bus, where an advertiser "owns" the bus and places a vinyl ad on its entire surface. This is often done for a longer-term contract of a half- or full year because of the application on the bus. On a less grand scale in a few select markets, smaller bus murals can be applied to the side or tail for a shorter period of time. Similar wraps are also possible for subway cars. Recently, the Toronto and Montreal subway systems have featured station domination, where a single advertiser can be the sole sponsor of all points of communication within that station. This could include wrapping a number of different parts of the infrastructure and erecting sizable murals and posters. **Subway online** is located in the 10 busiest subway stations in Toronto. It features digital news centres with video capabilities that deliver news, sports, and weather highlights with 20-second ads.

Transit media are sold in select markets on a four-week basis with a certain desired level of GRPs. The range of GRPs is quite varied, going from a low of 5 GRPs to a high of 100 GRPs. Other purchases of transit media are based on the number of showings. For example, if an operator has the rights to 400 buses or subway cars, then an advertiser could typically buy displays in varying numbers (i.e., 25 percent, 50 percent, 75 percent, 100 percent) over a four-week time period. Figure 13-7 illustrates a schedule as seen with outdoor to show that the selection decision is quite similar. Unlike outdoor advertising, there is no industry association to document circulation or authenticate reach and frequency levels despite their use in pricing of the media purchase. However, some information is gained from the research conducted by BBM so that rough estimates of exposure are possible. OMAC's DIL research also touches on transit to a degree, as seen in Figure 13-8 where most people find transit advertising acceptable.

Transit media viewed while travelling *between* cities and towns presents similar transit and terminal (i.e., airport, train, bus) options. Free magazines are published by travel operators (see Exhibit 13-6). In-flight videos are common on international and some domestic flights. For example, Air Canada sells different packages depending on the type of show (e.g., news, movie). Some of these commercial messages are as long as three minutes. In-flight radio is a pleasant way to pass the time while flying, and offers another opportunity for advertisers to deliver an audio message beyond standard radio. Ads can be placed on various collateral material such as boarding passes, ticket jackets, and meal trays.

FIGURE   13–7   Four-week transit reach and frequency schedule

							All Persons 12+		
Operator	**Territory**	**12+ Pop'n (000)**	**Transit System**	**Product**	**Posters**	**GRPs/ wk**	**Impr/ wk**	**4Wks**
Metro Media Plus	Montreal CMA	3,250	bus	King	281	350	11,375	76/18.5
			bus	Seventy	351	350	11,375	70/19.9
			bus	Standard Interior	2,791	350	11,375	34/41.4
			Metro	Mix		1,400	45,501	99/56.6
CBS	Toronto CMA	4,704.8	bus/streetcar	King	407	350	16,467	78/18.0
			bus/streetcar	Seventy	508	350	16,467	73/19.3
			bus/streetcar	Standard Interior	3,325	350	16,467	38/36.9
			subway/LRT	Standard Interior	2,692	350	16,467	34/40.7
				Mix		1,400	65,868	99/56.6
Lemar	Vancouver CMA	2,006.8	bus	King	174	350	7,024	77/18.2
			bus	Seventy	217	350	7,024	71/19.6
			bus	Standard Interior	1,603	350	7,024	26/53.8
			SkyTrain	Standard Interior	1,728	350	7,024	26/53.8
				Mix		1,400	28,095	99/56.6

Source: Media Digest 09/10, p. 69

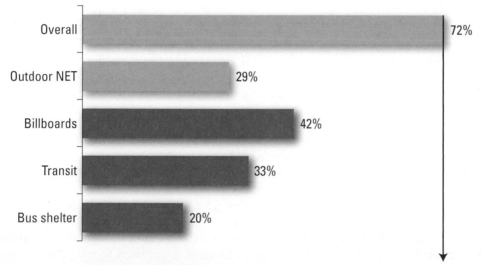

Source: Out-of-Home Marketing Association of Canada

FIGURE   13–8

Perceived amount of advertising by outdoor medium

STRENGTHS OF TRANSIT MEDIA

Amount of Processing Time   Long length of exposure to an ad is a major strength of indoor forms. The audience is essentially a captive one, with nowhere else to go and nothing much to do. As a result, riders are likely to read the ads—more than once.

Reach   Transit advertising benefits from the absolute number of people exposed. Millions of people ride mass transit every week, providing a substantial number of potential viewers that can be reached.

Exhibit 13-6 In-flight magazines are available on most carriers.

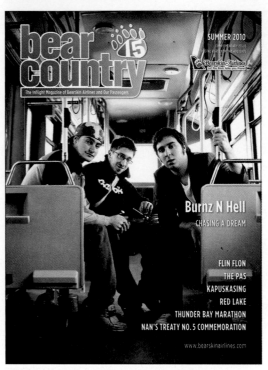

Frequency   Because our daily routines are standard, those who ride buses, subways, and the like are exposed to the ads repeatedly. If you rode the same subway to work and back every day, in one month you would have the opportunity to see the ad 20 to 40 times. The locations of station and shelter signs also afford high frequency of exposure.

Geographic Coverage   For local advertisers in particular, transit advertising provides an opportunity to reach a very select segment of the population. A purchase of a location in a certain neighbourhood will lead to exposure to people of specific ethnic backgrounds, demographic characteristics, and so on.

Absolute Cost and Cost Efficiency   Transit advertising tends to be one of the least expensive media in terms of both absolute and relative costs. An ad on the side of a bus can be purchased for a very reasonable CPM.

Selective Exposure   Similar to outdoor advertising, transit ads are quite pervasive for those using the service and consumers have little control over the use of the media.

Scheduling Flexibility   The capacity available for transit ads makes it fairly good for placement. Ads can be produced quickly and inserted internally or externally.

LIMITATIONS OF TRANSIT MEDIA

Media Image   To many advertisers, transit advertising does not carry the image they would like to represent for their products or services. Some advertisers may think having their name on the side of a bus or in a bus does not reflect well on the firm.

Target Audience Selectivity   While a strength of transit advertising is the ability to provide exposure to a large number of people, this audience may have certain lifestyles and/or behavioural characteristics that are not true of the target audience as a whole. For example, in rural or suburban areas mass transit is limited or non-existent, so the medium is not very effective for reaching these people.

Target Audience Coverage   While geographic selectivity may be an advantage, not everyone who rides a transportation vehicle or is exposed to transit advertising is a potential customer. For products that do not have specific geographic segments, this form of advertising incurs a good deal of waste coverage. Another problem is that the same bus may not run the same route every day. To save wear and tear on the vehicles, some transit companies alternate city routes (with much stop and go) with longer suburban routes. Thus, a bus may go downtown one day and reach the desired target group but spend the next day in the suburbs, where there may be little market potential.

Creativity for Emotional and Cognitive Responses   It may be very difficult to place colourful and attractive ads on cards, thus limiting their emotional content. And while much copy can be provided on inside cards, the short copy on the outside of a bus provides less rational persuasion.

Clutter Inside ads suffer from clutter of competing ads and outside ads feel the pressure of other street-level ads. Furthermore, the environment is cluttered in another sense as sitting or standing on a crowded subway may not be conducive to reading advertising, let alone experiencing the mood the advertiser would like to create.

Attention The smaller size and location of interior transit ads make it difficult to use the creative elements to attract attention. The movement of transit vehicles makes it difficult to perceive the message.

Involvement Like outdoor advertising, with shorter copy and seemingly fleeting messages of short copy, transit ads are generally considered to be low-involvement media.

PLACE-BASED MEDIA

The variety of out-of-home media continues to increase, and the idea of bringing an advertising medium to consumers wherever they may be underlies the strategy behind place-based media. In this section we summarize a few of the more prevalent options that include both print and video messages and highlight their strengths and limitations.

PLACE-BASED MEDIA OPTIONS

As Figure 13-1 indicated at the start of this chapter, there are a number of locations in which advertising messages reach consumers. Many of these are options occur where consumers engage in leisure or recreational activities, while some are where consumers work or study. Many of these media occur indoors, which is a term that some media companies currently use. Figure 13-9 summarizes the options and the media operators who run most indoor advertising in Canada.

In all of these locations there are poster or print messages, and in many there are video or digital applications. There is also growth in some of these locations that allows consumers to interact with their hand-held mobile device. Given the interaction with websites and text messages after viewing ads (Figure 13-10 and Figure 13-11), it appears this "on-the-spot" follow-up to messages will be a new evolution in advertising and consumer response behaviour.

FIGURE 13–9 Place-based media operators

Operator	Classic & Miniboard	Extra Lit & Backlitboard	Mega Lit & Bigboard	Digital Screen & eBoard	Mall Poster	Media Inventory	Total Media Share
Zoom Media	17,568	346	240	810		18,964	49%
NEWAD	17,268	260	217	403		18,148	47%
Pattison					1,623	1,623	4%
Industry Total	34,836	606	457	1,213	1,623	38,735	
Source: Canadian Out-of-Home Measurement Bureau							

FIGURE   13–10

Percentage visiting a website within past three months after seeing indoor/outdoor ad

	DITL 1	DITL 2
Toronto	29.5	36.9
Montreal	27.8	37.7
Vancouver	27.6	38.3
Females	29.5	38.5
Males	29.0	35.7

Source: Out-of-Home Marketing Association of Canada

FIGURE   13–11

Percentage sending a text message within past three months after seeing indoor/outdoor ad

	DITL 1	DITL 2
Toronto	4.8	4.7
Montreal	3.2	6.0
Vancouver	3.2	6.9
Females	2.7	4.3
Males	4.4	6.5

Source: Out-of-Home Marketing Association of Canada

An original example of place-based media is the mall poster. It is often backlit, like the transit shelter or transit-station poster, and is located throughout a shopping mall. The key feature of the mall poster is that it is in the shopping environment and therefore one step closer to the actual purchase. These posters are sold in most markets across the country similarly to outdoor posters with individual spot buys and varying levels of GRPs. Firms also sell various sizes of mall banners for branding purposes. Video or digital displays are growing in various retail locations as well.

An example of video messages occurring out of home at a specific location is cinema or movie theatre ads. Today, it is estimated that about $25 million to $30 million in advertising is spent in theatres on commercials, slides, posters, and sales promotions, with about $15 million of that for the commercials. Since the commercials last 60 to 90 seconds, advertisers have a unique opportunity to communicate for a longer period of time than with a typical TV ad. In fact, 95 percent of the theatre ads are also shown on television, albeit in a shortened format. Cinema ads lead other public video media as it now reports audience measurement information. One study estimated that total recall (aided plus unaided) reached 74 percent compared to 37 percent for radio and 32 percent for television.[12]

Research on consumer attitudes toward cinema ads in general found a number of sources of negativity in terms of restriction (e.g., less communication, captive, delayed gratification, minimizing escapism) and equity (unfair, time-waster, payment); however, many people enjoy the experience of specific ads (entertaining, liking the ad, involved, ad congruent with movie) as long as it is not shown too many times. It appears this, like other media, has a tension of both positive and negative reactions.[13]

Despite this mixed view, advertisers sometimes develop ads specifically for cinemas; Toyota took advantage of that idea with a scene set in a car at a drive-in movie theatre. The movie showed a montage of Toyota vehicles over the past 20 years to reinforce the message that 80 percent of all Toyotas sold in the past 20 years are still on the road. A creative director for the agency commented, "Toyota likes cinema. We get good recall results from it. Those ads create good drama for the brand."[14]

Airport terminals are another place where extensive signage occurs; an airport is very similar to a mall, with shopping concourses and restaurant areas. Displays are available ranging from smaller backlit posters in the terminal to superboards near the terminal and various other types of displays depending upon the media company and terminal. An exploratory study of airport terminal advertising reports the following conclusions.[15] One, ads are more likely to be processed when in the main concourse or near retail outlets. Two, the situational variable of the person's activity influences their degree of processing. Three, repetition of a simple message is necessary, but with less frequency. Four, various elements of the ad influence recall and recognition differently, thus necessitating decisions on design and communication objective. Five, frequent flyers' responses are strong up to a point then taper off after receiving a repetitious message.

Lexus innovated with a touch screen attached to the window of its new luxury crossover vehicle. The screen allowed consumers to interact with the vehicle's advanced features. A high-contrast rear-projection film adhesive located inside allowed the touch screen to be seen from the outside. Lexus used the message "Reinventing the vehicle that invented it all" and placed the RX in Toronto's major airport for 13 weeks to obtain 64,000 interactions and 1.3 million envious glances.[16]

Like malls, a number of place-based media are outdoor media brought into a particular environment. Backlit posters, superboards, electronic message signs, and video displays are used in many locations for leisure such as movie theatres, hotels, restaurants and bars, sports stadiums or arenas, athletic venues such as golf, ski, or fitness centres, or wherever a sufficient number of people congregate. The OMAC DIL research estimates that the average Canadian spends on leisure 1.3 and 2.2 hours per weekday and weekend day, respectively. For example, 55 percent visited a restaurant or bar four times per month for an average of two hours, and 24 percent visited a health club eight times per month for an average of 1.4 hours. Advertising in office buildings or convention centres or similar venues also reaches those who are at work, where a considerable amount of time is spent. The method of selling the time or space is similar to that described above.

Continuing this idea of bringing a message to a target audience based on where they are illustrates two emerging place-based media outlets. Firms attempt to reach younger consumers on the campuses of many universities and colleges with various sizes of indoor posters that are standard and non-standard. Research confirms the average student's experience as each campus visit averages five hours—plenty of exposure time for messages in various university/college buildings. Furthermore, with closed-circuit television, firms attempt to reach travellers in hotels, or patients in medical waiting rooms. And to reach virtually anyone and everyone, it is possible to place print and video ads inside elevators or washrooms, and print ads on floors or escalator handrails. Despite the prevalence of all these place-based media, Canadians do not believe it is too much (Figure 13-12).

STRENGTHS OF PLACE-BASED MEDIA

Target Audience Selectivity The main purpose of place-based media is to reach a specific target audience or to reach the target audience while closer to the purchase decision in terms of time and space. For example, ads in fitness clubs could contain messages for athletic gear, mall posters could have ads for food outlets that are located in the mall food court, and movies could attract a certain crowd who fit with particular brands more than others.

Absolute Cost and Cost Efficiency The absolute cost and CPM are generally reasonable compared to other media options.

Creativity for Cognitive and Emotional Responses Because the target and place are intertwined, the message may generate more in-depth cognitive responses or stronger emotional responses. For example, creative lifestyle messages can be

FIGURE 13–12

Perceived amount of
advertising by indoor
medium: Percentage
having "too much"
advertising

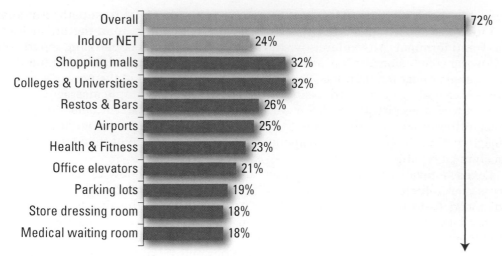

Source: Out-of-Home Marketing Association of Canada

prominent in poster ads located in clubs or bars. Large-scale spectaculars have been used to create fantastic visual effects to generate positive feelings. The special mood created in the movie theatre compared to at-home consumption makes the experience richer, and advertisers use theatre ads as an emotional spike that can transfer to the product more readily, especially if the theatre is located next to a mall or store where the product may be sold.

Control for Selective Exposure   Since many of these media options have captive or nearly captive audiences, the opportunity for consumers to avoid the ads or direct their attention elsewhere is minimal compared to other media. For example, once sitting in a movie theatre, it is very difficult for the average person to not watch the ad.

Attention and Involvement   With the above strengths of many place-based media options, the collective conclusion suggests that the target audience may be more involved with the advertising message than some other similar media in different contexts. The growth of video and digital messages in many locations offers greater opportunity to gain attention, and with a degree of target audience selectivity the creative can be customized with appropriate headlines for print messages.

LIMITATIONS OF PLACE-BASED MEDIA

Media Image   Often, place-based media are exposed to consumers when they do not expect a selling message to occur, which may cause some amount of resentment. Consumers appear to be generally accustomed to ads in malls since they are so similar to the store signage. Cinema ads, in contrast, experienced negative reaction when first introduced.[17] However, more recently we find mixed research results; one study reports a high percentage of viewers claim to not mind this form of advertising.[18] Other research suggests a negative image remains concerning how the ad infringes upon patrons' time prior to the movie, removes control for avoidance, delays movie enjoyment, minimizes the escapism feeling of being in the theatre, makes too much money for the theatre, steals personal time, and represents an unwarranted cost.[19] We have provided additional details for cinema ads as research exists compared to other media and to suggest that some points may be relevant for other place-based media.

Clutter   The clutter that consumers feel while watching television may be similar as the video displays generally play a block of commercials, although this can be lessened in some options like cinema ads where one or two video ads could play. Similarly, some locations have multiple posters of varying sizes, thus giving a similar clutter experience as reading the newspaper or magazine.

Reach and Frequency   Place-based media plays more of a supporting role to other media since it is very difficult to ensure high levels of either reach or frequency. Some exceptions can be considered, but in general media planners will look for other media to maximize these two factors.

Target Audience and Geographic Coverage   The logistical availability of these types of media makes full target audience coverage difficult or quite challenging to implement, or nearly impossible to get complete geographic coverage.

Amount of Processing Time   For the most part, place-based media suffer from very short messages to target audiences that are more likely preoccupied with some other task. Some evidence of strong recall suggests that the processing may be stronger for more creative executions, where additional processing occurs.

Scheduling Flexibility   While not a complete or comprehensive limitation, the logistics of changing place-based media makes the scheduling, which is done on a monthly basis, put certain restrictions on an advertiser for a timely message. Placement for cinema ads generally requires eight weeks, and category exclusivity in certain distribution outlets further limits the availability and scheduling ease with this media option.

401

PROMOTIONAL PRODUCTS

The Promotional Products Association International (PPAI), a trade association, defines **promotional products marketing** as "the advertising or promotional medium or method that uses promotional products, such as ad specialties, premiums, business gifts, awards, prizes, or commemoratives." Promotional product marketing is a recent name for what used to be called specialty advertising. Specialty advertising has now been provided with a new definition:

> A medium of advertising, sales promotion, and motivational communication employing imprinted, useful, or decorative products called advertising specialties, a subset of promotional products. Unlike premiums, with which they are sometimes confused (called advertising specialties), these articles are always distributed free—recipients don't have to earn the specialty by making a purchase or contribution.[20]

Specialty advertising is often considered both an advertising and a sales promotion medium. In our discussion, we treat it as an advertising medium in the IMC program, as it often communicates or represents the brand and its positioning.

The promotional product industry in Canada is substantial; the Canadian trade association is known as the Promotional Product Professionals of Canada (PPPC) (see www.promocan.com). One of its main tasks is to compile research information for its members, which we highlight briefly. Distributor revenue topped $3.9 billion in 2008, up from $1.2 billion in 1998 (Figure 13-13). The 2008 figure is two times greater than all Internet advertising in 2008. Figure 13-14 shows the percentage of sales by product category. Wearables/apparel accounted for the bulk at 30 percent, while the next highest, writing instruments, clipped in at 9 percent. Figure 13-15 shows the percentage of sales by program type. Business gifts, brand awareness, public relations, and trade shows account for nearly half of all revenue.[21]

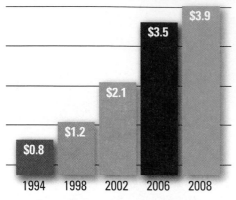

FIGURE 13–13

Promotional products revenue

Growth of promotional products

Source: Promotional Product Professionals of Canada, 2009 Sales Volume Study Highlights

Some trends are supporting the growth of promotional products. Thanks to the Internet, it is now logistically easier to distribute the products than in the past. Since clothing is the largest product category, its growth stemmed from a steady change toward more casual dressing at work and from many name brands such as Nike getting into the market. Other big brands like Apple make their product lines available, thus spurring on the overall demand for promotional products. Promotional product organizations have become more sophisticated in their selling as they try to build a brand with promotional planners. For example, both parties carefully consider whether the promotional product needs to be directly tied to the type of product, and the degree to which the promotional product needs to last a long time or for a shorter time period.[22]

As suggested above, thousands of advertising specialty items exist—ballpoint pens, coffee mugs, key rings, calendars, T-shirts, and matchbooks. Unconventional specialties such as plant holders, wall plaques, and gloves with the advertiser's name printed on them are also used to promote a company or its product; so are glassware, trophies, awards, and vinyl products. Specialty items are used for many promotional purposes. It can generate or improve awareness when introducing new products or reinforcing the name of an existing company or products. The variety of promotional products makes it a virtual certainty that a manager will be able to strengthen attitudes with an item that represents the brand appropriately. Oftentimes promotional products

402

FIGURE 13–14   Distribution product category breakdown

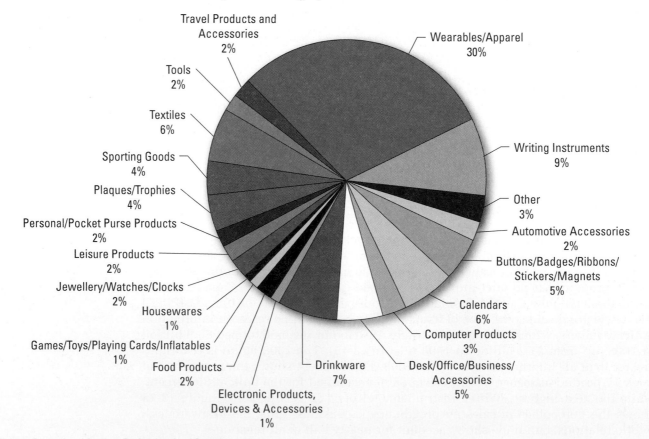

Source: Promotional Product Professionals of Canada

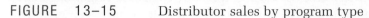

FIGURE   13–15   Distributor sales by program type

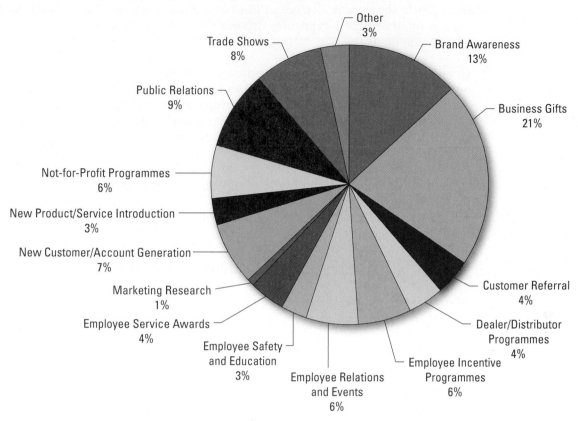

Source: Promotional Product Professionals of Canada

403

are used to thank customers for patronage and encourage repeat purchasing. Promotional products support other IMC tools like sales promotion or public relations, so they contribute substantially to the overall promotional mix. In summary, many companies use promotional products as a way to fully communicate with their customers, suppliers, employees, and the general public.

STRENGTHS OF PROMOTIONAL PRODUCTS

Target Audience Selectivity and Coverage   Because specialty advertising items are generally distributed directly to target customers, the medium offers a high degree of selectivity. The communication is distributed to the desired recipient, reducing waste coverage.

Creativity for Cognitive Responses   As the variety of specialty items in Figure 13-14 demonstrates, this medium offers a high degree of flexibility. A message as simple as a logo or as long as is necessary can be distributed through a number of means. Both small and large companies can employ this medium, limited only by their own creativity.

Frequency   Most forms of specialty advertising are designed for retention. Key chains, calendars, and pens remain with the potential customer for a long time, providing repeat exposures to the advertising message at no additional cost. One set of statistics suggests 50 percent of all promotional products are kept for a year or longer.

Absolute Cost and Cost Efficiency   Some specialty items are rather expensive (for example, leather goods), but most are affordable to almost any size organization. While they are costly on a CPM basis when compared with other media, the high number of repeat exposures drives down the relative cost per exposure of this advertising medium.

Creativity for Emotional Responses   Promotional products are perhaps the only medium that generates goodwill in the receiver. Because people like to receive gifts and many of the products are functional (key chains, calendars, etc.), consumers are grateful to receive them. In a recent study of users of promotional products, goodwill was cited as the number 1 reason for use.

Attention, Involvement, Amount of Processing Time   These would all be considered strengths of promotional products assuming the recipient appreciates the actual item, whether it is clothing or some kind of office product. Certainly the selection of the item in question will heavily influence consumer reaction.

LIMITATIONS OF PROMOTIONAL PRODUCTS

Media Image   While most forms of specialty advertising are received as friendly reminders of the store or company name, the firm must be careful choosing the specialty item. The company image may be cheapened by a chintzy or poorly designed advertising form.

Clutter   With so many organizations now using this advertising medium, the marketplace may become saturated. While one can always use another ballpoint pen or book of matches the value to the receiver declines if replacement is too easy, and the likelihood that you will retain the item or even notice the message is reduced. The more unusual the specialty, the more value it is likely to have to the receiver.

Scheduling Flexibility   The lead time required to put together a promotional products message is significantly longer than that for most other media.

Reach   An advertiser hoping to expand the market through wider reach would likely find promotional products a weaker choice. As a support media, it thrives on assisting existing media that have reach as their strength.

Geographic Coverage   While promotional products can be distributed essentially anywhere, the cost implications would severely curtail this as a feasible feature for most advertisers.

Selective Exposure   Recipients of promotional products are in complete control as to whether they choose to display or show the item. It is entirely possible that a tremendous investment could receive very minimal exposure to the intended target audience.

PROMOTIONAL PRODUCTS RESEARCH

Owing to the nature of the industry, specialty advertising has no established ongoing audience measurement system. Research has been conducted in an attempt to determine the impact of this medium, however, including the following reports.

A study by Schreiber and Associates indicated 39 percent of people receiving advertising specialties could recall the name of the company as long as six months later, and a study conducted by AC Nielsen found that 31 percent of respondents were still using at least one specialty item they had received a year or more earlier.[23]

A study by Gould/Pace University found the inclusion of a specialty item in a direct-mail piece generated a greater response rate and 321 percent greater dollar purchases per sale than mail pieces without such items.[24] Studies at Baylor University showed that including an ad specialty item in a thank-you letter can improve customers' attitudes toward a company's sales reps by as much as 34 percent and toward the company itself by as much as 52 percent.[25] Finally, Richard Manville Research reported the average household had almost four calendars; if they had not been given such items free, two-thirds of the respondents said they would purchase one, an indication of the desirability of this particular specialty item.[26]

More recent research conducted by PPAI (www. ppai.org) shows the pronounced communication effect of promotional products when combined with media. The results of one experiment shown in Figure 13-16 illustrate the stronger impressions that occur when a promotional product is combined with TV and print ads for a local pizzeria. Another survey of more than 550 business travellers at a U.S. airport found that 71 percent had received a promotional product within the past 12 months; 34 percent actually had the item with them at the time of the survey; and 76 percent recalled the brand name. A field experiment at a trade show indicated that visits to a firm's booth increased significantly when a modest promotional product (i.e., magnet) and a promise to receive a more valuable item (i.e., T-shirt) were mailed to registrants prior to the show compared with a simple invitation.

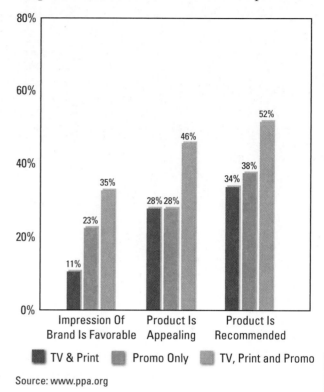

FIGURE 13-16

Respondents' evaluation of a brand or product

Source: www.ppa.org

PRODUCT PLACEMENT

An increasingly common way to promote a brand is **product placement**, where the actual product or an ad for it is part of a movie, TV show, or video game. Like specialty advertising, product placement is sometimes considered a promotion rather than an advertising form. This distinction is not a critical one, and we have decided to treat product placement as a form of advertising. We review a few key product placement decisions and their corresponding strengths and limitations.

PRODUCT PLACEMENT DECISIONS

With up to $4 billion in North American revenue and up to 50 percent of all movies and television shows using product placement, advertising through this promotional medium is certainly big business (Figure 13-17). For example, we have recently seen GM vehicles featured in a popular movie (see Exhibit 13-7). While movie and TV product placement accounts for the majority of the revenue, in the gaming world, North American advertising revenue is expected to reach close to $1 billion by 2008. It should be noted that it is difficult to assess the accuracy of these figures.

FIGURE 13–17

Expenditures on
product placement
continue
to increase

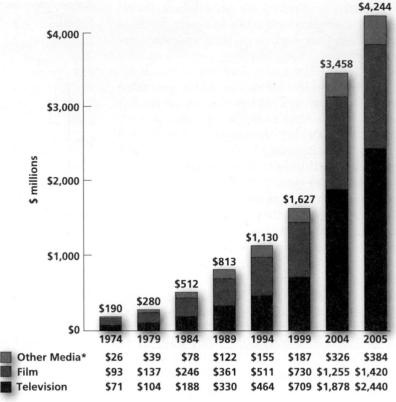

	1974	1979	1984	1989	1994	1999	2004	2005
Other Media*	$26	$39	$78	$122	$155	$187	$326	$384
Film	$93	$137	$246	$361	$511	$730	$1,255	$1,420
Television	$71	$104	$188	$330	$464	$709	$1,878	$2,440

*Magazines, newspapers, videogames, Internet, recorded music, books, radio

Source: Adapted from *PQ Media*, February 2006

Most product placements are free or provided in exchange for trade. Product placement agencies contend that as much as 70 to 95 percent of their placements are for trade.[27] An in-depth study of the product placement industry also supports this contention.[28]

Much of the logic behind product placement is that since the placement is embedded in the script or program setting it cannot be avoided, thereby increasing exposure. Given the lack of intrusiveness of the placement, consumers may not have the same negative reactions to it as they may to a commercial. Assuming a marketer

Exhibit 13-7
GM cars and trucks
were prominently
placed in the movie
Transformers.

selected the right movie or TV vehicle, product placement contributes to higher awareness by its sheer volume of exposure. More successful product placement contributes to its brand position and requires a number of decisions.[29] Similarly for video games, research supports about 30 percent unaided brand recall; 70 percent believe that ads in games make the experience feel realistic.[30]

A primary issue to resolve concerns the source as represented by the plot, scenes, or characters of the movie or TV show. The creative use of the product profoundly impacts the experience ranging from a central role in the scene to a mere showing of the product to having a central character use or talk about the product.[31] Recent examples of product placement occurring in Canada or as a result of movie or television production being filmed in Canada are quite numerous.[32]

Related to the above two issues is the amount of time the product is featured and how many different vehicles a marketer wants to be exposed in. While a marketer and its agent obviously try to negotiate the most favourable situation on all these issues, they are also dependent upon the director's final artistic decision.[33] For example, product placement moved to animated shows with the placement of the Reach 400 Max toothbrush on the TV sitcom *Bob and Margaret* in the form of a five- to 10-second virtual placement that was blended into the show's program about a dentist. Reach managers felt the placement balanced the requirements of not too blatant, but noticed. Placement support included a tune-in spot for the show that featured the toothbrush along with the Reach commercial in the promotion schedule, and closed captioning sponsorship of the show. The Reach toothbrush's placement offered more control than usual since the program already existed with an established time slot, and the virtual placement material (i.e., logo, product visual) provided by Reach fit appropriately into established scenes.[34] IMC Perspective 13-2 explores product placement trends in Canada.

Finally, as a support medium, product placement needs to work with other marketing communication tools to achieve its maximum contribution. Much of the product placement in Quebec reality television shows is linked with sponsorship arrangements. For example, GM Canada sponsors *Le Grand blond avec un show surnois*, a late-night talk show, and *Testostérone*, a men's show, in addition to having product placement as an important element. Similarly, *Ma Maison Rona* is a sponsored reality television show based on renovating someone else's home that naturally included trips to Rona for material.[35] Rona goes one step further as this product placement occurs during its mass media campaign.[36]

As these examples illustrate, product placement has taken an overt step, which is referred to as content sponsorship. This occurs when an advertiser sponsors a specific program and receives product placement, integration, and other promotional considerations in return. In reality this is somewhat of a return to the early days of television, when shows were sponsored by advertisers. Another approach is the use of "advertainment," which is the creation of video and/or music content by an advertiser in an attempt to entertain viewers while advertising their products. These ideas have also transferred to video games (Exhibit 13-8).

Another overt step is the use of virtual ads, a form of camera trickery where products are digitally embedded upon a show. Global digitally inserted consumer products into several U.S. programs. Editors spend hours blending a two-dimensional image of a product into a show, shot by shot. Virtual products are often added to the background or foreground of a scene. But transition shots—usually outdoor city images—provide a blank canvas on which to plaster ads. Virtual ads can be cheaper than traditional advertising and standard product placement at $10,000 an episode; a 30-second spot on the same broadcast is $36,000. While virtual ads are an inconsequential sliver of Canada's $3-billion TV advertising market, they are on the minds of executives at every major network in large part because they provide an unregulated revenue source. The CRTC monitors virtual ads, but has no plans to force networks to include them in the 12 minutes of ad time permitted during each 60-minute slot.[37]

At one time Cheese Whiz concluded its ads with the slogan "You know you want it"—but recently, it found itself starring in the hit TV show *Corner Gas*. Comedian Brent Butt built a comedy gag around the brand and it appeared a dozen times for a total of three minutes. With a knack of writing brands into the script, *Corner Gas* became the leader in product placement in Canada while it aired for six years.

Historically, TV got its start with complete sponsorship of shows from consumer products where the pauses between live scenes spliced in their messages. Soap companies originally sponsored soap operas, hence the name, and game shows always displayed brand name prizes. Nowadays, the placement moves from fairly obvious promotional messages found on reality shows to much more subtle visuals as the product is seen and noticed but becomes part of the natural storyline.

Since Canadians watch a substantial amount of American programming, much of this history is a U.S. trend. Product placement on Canadian television is not of the same magnitude. One CanWest executive noted, "If you're a U.S. network getting a $200,000 fee for placement, that kind of money is worth the trouble. But as a Canadian broadcaster charging one-tenth of that, $20,000 just isn't worth it. Despite this concern the product placement has grown recently in Canada. CBC integrated brands into a number of shows such as *Being Erica, Little Mosque on the Prairie,* and *Heartland,* and its revenue for non-sports product integration increased by 1,000 percent during the past two years. Two other major networks also expanded in this direction but implementation concerns make this a risky adventure.

Producers of one hit show find the product placement proposal far too blatant and uninspired and avoid the concept altogether. Although open to the idea, a commercial-like premise of the placement cannot be a natural fit with the characters. Another concern is the time delay where the show's production may not coincide with the advertising schedule and message evolution. Some are also concerned with the ability to accurately measure the effects in comparison to established procedures in advertising.

Given these limitations, one new idea, which returns to the historical sponsorship approach, is to insert ads for brands that naturally fit in a storyline. For example, if the story has a restaurant scene, then an ad for a restaurant could play immediately thereafter. One network that tested the idea found improved measures of overall effectiveness and brand resonance.

Sources: Jennifer Wells, "The Right Breaks at the Right Time," *The Globe and Mail,* May 29, 2009, p. B5; Simon Houpt, "Why Timbits Aren't Likely to Drive the Plot of *The Border*," *The Globe and Mail,* August 21, 2009, p. B 4.

Question

1. In what way do you think product placement is effective?

While product placement appears promising, research indicates that its greatest strength lies in maintaining existing loyalty of current customers who see the product they favour actually consumed in a realistic situation by a character they can relate to or identify with. Furthermore, consumers indicate that real products are expected and preferred compared to some kind of generic unrecognizable brand.[38]

STRENGTHS OF PRODUCT PLACEMENT

Reach   A large number of people see movies each year. The average film is estimated to have a life span of 3½ years, and most of these moviegoers are very attentive audience members. When this is combined with the increasing home video rental market and network and specialty channels, the potential exposure for a product placed in a movie is enormous.

Frequency   Depending on how the product is used in the movie (or program), there may be ample opportunity for repeated exposures (or many, to those who like to watch a program or movie more than once).

Exhibit 13-8
Guitar Hero is a hit with consumers as well as advertisers.

Creativity for Emotional Responses   We previously discussed the advantage of source identification that occurs with a creative message. When consumers see their favourite movie star wearing Oakleys, drinking Gatorade, or driving a Mercedes, this association may lead to a favourable product image. Most of those involved in product placement believe that association with the proper source is critical for success.

Cost Efficiency   While the cost of placing a product may range from free samples to a million dollars, these are extremes. The CPM for this form of advertising can be very low, owing to the high volume of exposures it generates.

Geographic Coverage   The potential for geographic coverage is substantial as a top movie or television show could have national or international coverage. We emphasize the importance of this qualifying aspect, as entertainment viewers can be fickle.

Selective Exposure   It is very difficult for a theatre audience member to physically avoid the product placement through some form of zipping or zapping!

Clutter   With category exclusivity rights within a vehicle and the fact that any show or movie has only a few product placements, the potential for clutter is very low. However, the plot, scenes, and dialogue act as a form of clutter that can be overcome with creative use of product placement.

Involvement   A product placement done properly has direct relevance for the character or situation and is almost a transformational experience for the audience member who is paying full attention to the entertainment.

LIMITATIONS OF PRODUCT PLACEMENT

Absolute Cost   While the CPM may be very low for product placement in movies, the absolute cost of placing the product may be very high, pricing some advertisers out of the market.

409

Amount of Processing Time and Attention While the way some products are exposed to the audience has an impact, there is no guarantee viewers will notice the product. Some product placements are more conspicuous than others. When the product is not featured prominently, the advertiser runs the risk of not being seen (although, of course, the same risk is present in all forms of media advertising). Furthermore, some product placements last only for a few seconds.

Creativity for Cognitive Responses The appeal that can be made in this media form is limited. There is no potential for discussing product benefits or providing detailed information. Rather, appeals are limited to source association, use, and enjoyment. The endorsement of the product is indirect, and the flexibility for product demonstration is subject to its use in the film.

Scheduling Flexibility In many movies, the advertiser has no say over when and how often the product will be shown. Fabergé developed an entire Christmas campaign around its Brut cologne and its movie placement, only to find the movie was delayed until February.

Media Image Many TV viewers and moviegoers are incensed at the idea of placing ads in programs or movies. These viewers want to maintain the barrier between program content and commercials. If the placement is too intrusive, they may develop negative attitudes toward the brand.

Target Audience Selectivity By its very nature of being cast in a movie, the potential for exposure beyond a brand's target audience is enormous. Although a certain amount of selectivity is viable through the type of movie or show, there is likely considerable wasted coverage.

Target Audience Coverage Movie attendance is historically strong; however, in many cases it will be difficult to reach a substantial portion of one's audience with a single movie. Similarly, even a hit television show may reach only a portion of a brand's target audience.

AUDIENCE MEASUREMENT FOR PRODUCT PLACEMENT

To date, no audience measurement is available except from the providers. Potential advertisers often have to make decisions based on their own creative insights (see Exhibit 13-9) or rely on the credibility of the source. However, at least two studies have demonstrated the potential effectiveness of product placements. Research provided by Pola Gupta and Kenneth Lord showed that prominently displayed placements led to strong recall.[39] A study by Pola Gupta and Stephen Gould indicated that viewers are accepting of promotional products and in general evaluate them positively, though some products (alcohol, guns, cigarettes) are perceived as less acceptable.[40]

IMC PLANNING: STRATEGIC USE OF OUT-OF-HOME AND SUPPORT MEDIA

Previously, the strategic use of out-of-home and support media might have been considered an oxymoron, as both types appeared in promotional planners' budgets after money had been allocated to other more "valuable" media. An IMC perspective toward media selection provides a new look at how these types of opportunities can

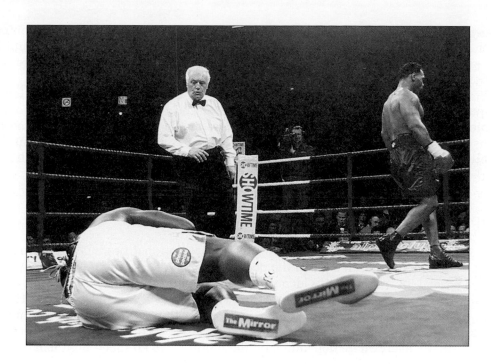

Exhibit 13-9
Ads often appear in
the strangest places.

achieve communication and behavioural objectives, primarily at the pre-purchase and purchase decision stages.

OUT-OF-HOME MEDIA

For the most part, outdoor, transit, and place-based media tend to have two primary objectives. The first is awareness, as these media share common strengths of cost efficiency with extensive reach and frequency levels in the geographic areas in which the media are located or placed. The ability to use clever images and head-lines or very short-copy messages permits these messages to have some emotional relevance to help ensure brand recognition or recall. Moreover, these two design elements can be consistent with creative messages from other media to ensure addi-tional message frequency with the intention to build awareness more strongly.

In general, these media are limited in their ability to build category need or influ-ence brand attitudes beyond maintaining the current attitude of the target audience. Many brands will use these media as an inexpensive, yet cost-effective way of com-municating simple brand preference messages directed toward current customers or messages to reinforce the general market position of the brand to all potential con-sumers. Given the limited nature of these media to influence attitudes extensively with short messages, they typically are good for building communication effects at the pre- and post-purchase stages.

Most place-based media typically offer the opportunity for promotional plan-ners to achieve a second objective: brand purchase intention. Since the messages for place-based media are context-dependent in terms of location or time, they can provide the right situational motive to spur on a store visit or more immediate sale. Some particular place-based media, like movie theatres, are vehicles for additional exposure of the more traditional broadcast and print media ads and thus permit strong brand positioning strategy opportunities. As noted in the chapter, movie theatres can show longer and more specialized ads that brands may be reluctant to show in a broadcast environment.

Given the broad reach and public nature of these media, oftentimes they are more general and have a less clear behavioural objective. However, given that many messages are reinforcing existing attitudes, it appears a substantial number of these ads attempt to influence repeat purchasing. Recent application of out-of-home messages including connections to mobile hand-held devices suggests greater opportunity for brand switching for trial purchases.

From an integration perspective, out-of-home or transit media provide additional frequency of a creative message that has been placed in broadcast or print media. Typically, we do not see advertisers using these media for executing sales promotions except in some poster locations. This medium is also used to some extent for public relations activities, and we infrequently observe any connection to direct marketing or Internet applications.

SUPPORT MEDIA

The size and growth of support media such as promotional products and product placement is almost hidden given the degree to which it fits into our everyday life or our normal TV, movie, and video game consumption habits. In this regard, they are similar to out-of-home media that are a part of our everyday experiences. However, for these two support media, the exposure is both more widespread and more narrow. Promotional products are more widespread as we are selectively observing them virtually everywhere depending on the product. Given that a high percentage is wearable, we witness brand names on shirts, hats, and so on almost constantly. Product placement is clearly narrower, as it is limited within the time frame and scope of the vehicle it is delivered in. These characteristics suggest that both are excellent for building awareness, much like out-of-home media, and could be especially useful for all stages of the target audience's decision-making process.

Promotional products and product placement offer brand-building capabilities much like some specialized place-based media such as movie theatres. The vehicle in which the brand is associated provides an additional source effect that puts significant context around the brand experience. For example, observing a particular brand in a movie approximates an endorsement from both the character and the actor. This is consistent with viewing a television commercial with the same actor, but even more so as the emotion and involvement with the movie compounds the positive effect. Given this more profound viewing experience, it is no wonder advertisers are willing to pay substantial parts of their budget to have the brand featured in a few seconds of a popular movie.

The independence of these kinds of media suggests more limited opportunity for integration. However, some opportunities are pursued. Public relations activities are often used to connect the brand and its product placement in a movie or television show. For example, for some blockbuster placements, like showing a new car model in a movie, news media will report the appearance in both traditional versions and on the Internet. Recently, news media have reported upon the placement of brands in various video games. Naturally, the Internet offers a wide variety of information content, and a brand can highlight its placement on its own site.

CHAPTER OBJECTIVES AND SUMMARY

1 To describe out-of-home and support media available to the marketer in developing an IMC program.

This chapter introduced the vast number of out-of-home and support media available to marketers. Out-of-home media include outdoor, transit, and place-based. Support media include promotional products and product placement. While these constitute many examples and options for a marketer, it seems the choices are quite endless at times.

2 To know how audiences for out-of-home and support media are measured.

Outdoor advertising audience measurement is very strong in Canada. The industry association, COMB, has established a strong research methodology for ensuring accurate estimates of exposure levels. This research has expanded to some place-based media such as those found in restaurants and hotels as well as health and fitness outlets. Documentation for transit audiences is less thorough, although some degree of assessment is possible. Research of audience size for the support media of promotional products and product placement is mixed. Clearly, product placements in movies and TV shows rely on movie ticket sales (and later video purchase and rentals) and audience size estimates for television viewing.

3 To develop an understanding of the strengths and limitations of out-of-home and support media.

Collectively, these media offer a variety of strengths although they are not consistent across the five topics examined; however, a handful are true almost across the board. For the most part, the public nature of these media leads to high numbers of people reached, which in turn suggests relatively positive cost efficiency allowing advertisers to extend their frequency levels. Secondly, each medium allows for some degree of creativity for either emotional or cognitive responses. In addition, many of the media discussed here have effectively demonstrated their power to obtain positive communication and business effects. But each medium also has limitations. Perhaps the major weakness with most is the lack of audience measurement and verification. While there is improvement in this area, the advertiser is forced to make decisions without hard data or based on information provided by the media.

KEY TERMS

backlit posters, *385*
bulletins, *385*
exterior posters, *393*
interior door cards, *393*
interior transit cards, *393*
mobile signage, *386*

out-of-home media, *384*
posters, *385*
product placement, *405*
promotional products marketing, *401*

showing, *391*
spectaculars, *385*
station posters, *394*
street-level posters, *385*
subway online, *394*

superboards, *385*
support media, *384*
transit advertising, *393*
transit shelters, *394*

DISCUSSION QUESTIONS

1. What are promotional products? List some of the advantages and disadvantages of this medium. Provide examples where the use of this medium would be appropriate.

2. Discuss some of the merits of in-flight advertising. What types of products might most effectively use this medium?

3. Explain how out-of-home and support media might be used as part of an IMC program. Take any three of the media discussed in the chapter and explain how they might be used in an IMC program for automobiles, cellular telephones, and Internet services.

4. A prevalent strategy among advertisers is to get themselves into television shows and movies. Discuss the possible advantages and disadvantages that might result from such exposures.

5. Explain how outdoor ads can be creative and foster emotional responses. Why would brands use outdoor ads for this purpose?

6. Discuss advantages and disadvantages associated with advertising in movie theatres. For what types of products and/ or services might these media be most effective?

7. What are place-based media? Explain what type of advertisers would most benefit from their use.

8. Many forms of transit advertising exist. What products might be successfully advertised in each type?

SALES PROMOTION

■ CHAPTER OBJECTIVES

1 To understand the role of sales promotion in a company's integrated marketing communications program and to examine why it is increasingly important.

2 To identify the objectives, strategy, and tactical components of a sales promotion plan.

3 To examine the consumer and trade sales promotion strategy options and the factors to consider in using them.

4 To understand key IMC issues related to sales-promotion decisions.

CREATIVE CONSUMER DIGITAL SALES PROMOTION

Consumer-generated content has gained momentum as consumers have become a key part of contests for a number of different brands, including Honda, Absolut, Scotiabank/Cineplex, and LG. Each activity featured uses digital connections and other media as ways to gain entry.

Part of Honda's marketing communication for its compact car is the Civic Nation, an approach to building strong feeling through driving the vehicle and a way for individual consumers to customize their experience with a mass-marketed product. The "United We Drive" theme took a new direction with a contest where musical souls could create an "Anthem for a Nation" using samples of music from hip-hop artist Saukrates. Multimedia directed those interested to a website (civicnation.ca) where they developed a 30-second electronica, hip-hop, or electropop track. After voting, the winning selections played as the intro for a radio show. The second and third phases of the campaign culminated in a full Civic Nation anthem.

Using Facebook, Absolut invited Vancouver's artists, writers, visual artists, musicians, curators, filmmakers, and gallery owners to create artwork, series, or educational programs that reflected the brand's values of "engaging," "visionary," "bold," and "perfection." The best effort received an award of $120,000. The popular vodka maker obtained only 30 entries, with about half worthy of serious evaluation. Given the historical close connection of Absolut and artists the low number appears startling, yet executives were satisfied because the task demanded excellence in order to find a long-lasting artistic partner to portray the brand. In fact, for complete success the artistic work had to demonstrate a partnership with the brand and its values.

A joint marketing effort between Scotiabank and Cineplex is the Scene card, where users collect points for using the bank's product and redeem them for movie tickets. In a recent contest, interested Scene card members produced 15-second ads to promote the loyalty program. From the 128 submissions, judges selected the winner from five finalists; all five were played on Cineplex screens. Surprisingly, people from 83 countries viewed the entries online, and the winner obtained 65,000 votes.

The Canadian division of LG conceived the inaugural LG "Life's Good" Film Festival, where aspiring filmmakers from all over the world could submit a high-definition film up to five minutes in length that expressed an uplifting message consistent with the brand's slogan. LG partnered with Google, YouTube, and Film.com and a dedicated website (LGfilmfest.com) to announce the contest and allow viewership. Categories included animation, sports, narrative, and fashion and music, with three category winners receiving $10,000 and a fourth overall winner receiving $100,000.

Sources: Garine Tcholakina, "Honda Drives Civic Nation Mix-Off," *Strategy,* November 2009, p. 40; Jonathan Paul, "Wannabe Filmmakers Get Scene," *Strategy,* February 2009, p. 7; Jonathan Paul, "Life's Good, But LG Thinks It's Better in HD," *Strategy,* September 2009, p. 8; Denise Ryan, "Can You Brand the West Coast?" *National Post,* November 16, 2009, p. B16.

QUESTION:

1. How do these contests help build the brands?

directed to the ultimate consumer. The goal of a pull strategy is to create demand among consumers and encourage them to request the product from the reseller who in turn will order the product. Thus, stimulating demand at the end-user level pulls the product through the channels of distribution.

Whether to emphasize a push or a pull strategy depends on a number of factors, including the company's relations with the trade, its promotional budget, and demand for the firm's products. Companies that have favourable channel relationships may prefer to use a push strategy and work closely with channel members to encourage them to stock and promote their products. A firm with a limited promotional budget may not have the funds for sales promotion that a pull strategy requires and may find it more cost-effective to build distribution and demand by working closely with resellers. When the demand outlook for a product is favourable because it has unique benefits, is superior to competing brands, or is very popular among consumers, a pull strategy may be appropriate. Companies often use a combination of push and pull strategies, with the emphasis changing as the product moves through its life cycle.

GROWTH OF SALES PROMOTION

Sales promotion has been part of marketing for years, however its role and importance in an IMC program has evolved. Historically, advertising received the major budget allocation for most consumer-products companies' plans. In the 1980s and 1990s, the proportion of the marketing budget allocated to sales promotion rose sharply, mostly due to increased trade promotion but also due to more attractive and creative consumer promotions. Current estimates suggest marketers spend between 60 and 75 percent of their promotional budgets on sales promotion, with the remainder allocated to media advertising.[4] Many factors have led to the shift in marketing dollars to sales promotion. Among them are the strategic importance of sales promotion, reaching a specific target audience, increased promotional sensitivity, declining brand loyalty, brand proliferation, short-term focus, increased accountability, growing power of retailers, and competition.

Strategic Importance of Sales Promotion Increased sophistication and a more strategic importance elevated sales promotion's role in the IMC program of many companies.[5] In the past, sales promotion specialists participated in planning after key strategic branding decisions were made to develop a promotional program that could create a short-term increase in sales. However, companies now include promotional specialists as part of their strategic brand-building team, and promotional agencies offer integrated marketing services and expertise to enhance brand equity (see Exhibit 14-1). Critics contend that if the trend toward spending more on sales promotion at the expense of media advertising continues, brands may lose the equity that advertising helped create. However, not all sales promotion activities detract from the value of a brand, as the next example illustrates.

With the mystique of the Stanley Cup, the NHL, and CBC's *Hockey Night in Canada,* corporate partners Pepsi, Lay's,

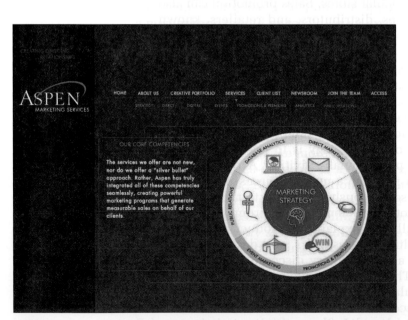

Exhibit 14-1 Aspen Marketing Services touts its IMC capabilities.

420

and Gatorade invited fans to submit a video or photo showing their ritual for watching NHL playoff hockey and what the Cup means to them (Exhibit 14-2). The winner of the inaugural promotion received a $25,000 grand prize package comprising a hockey shrine built in their home designed by *Hockey Night in Canada,* a Samsung HDTV home theatre system, *HNIC* leather chairs and memorabilia, an Xbox 360 game system, and a supply of Pepsi, Lay's, and Gatorade products. This ultimate playoff party was captured for broadcast during a playoff game on *HNIC,* punctuated by six-time Stanley Cup champion Mark Messier delivering the Holy Grail itself as the guest of honour. The campaign was supported by *HNIC* broadcasts, a dedicated website, retail point-of-purchase creative, and special-edition Pepsi, Lay's, and Gatorade packaging. The public viewed the three finalists online a total of 40,000 times and voted for the ultimate winner, which was announced during game 2 of the Stanley Cup final featuring the Anaheim Ducks and Ottawa Senators. During the promotion, the website attracted more than 100,000 visitors, 70 percent of them unique, and produced more than 700,000 page views.[6]

Exhibit 14-2 The Stanley Cup became the focal point of the promotion.

421

Reaching a Specific Target Audience Marketing efforts focus on specific market segments, and firms use sales promotions to reach geographic, demographic, psychographic, and ethnic audiences. Sales promotion programs can also be targeted to specific user-status groups such as customers or non-customers, as well as non-category users or light versus heavy users. Sales promotion tools have become one of the primary vehicles for geographic-based programs tied into local flavour, themes, or events. For example, in an effort to increase traffic during lunch and dinner, a major western Canadian franchisee of 25 Denny's Restaurants used advertising (e.g., radio, newspaper), sales promotion (e.g., featured menu prices, guarantees), and public relations (e.g., sponsorship of junior hockey) to increase sales by 15 percent.[7]

Increased Promotional Sensitivity Marketers are making greater use of sales promotion in their marketing programs because consumers respond favourably to the incentives it provides. A major research project completed by Promotion Decisions Inc. in 1999 tracked the purchase behaviour of more than 33,000 consumers and their response to both consumer and trade promotions. The results showed that 42 percent of the total unit volume of the 12 packaged-goods products analyzed were purchased with some type of incentive, while 58 percent were purchased at full price. Coupons were particularly popular among consumers, as 24 percent of the sales volume involved the use of a coupon.[8]

Declining Brand Loyalty Another major reason for the increase in sales promotion is that consumers have become less loyal to one brand. Some consumers are always willing to buy their preferred brand at full price without any type of promotional offer. However, many consumers are loyal coupon users and/or are conditioned to look for deals when they shop. They may switch back and forth among a set of brands they view as essentially equal. These brands are all perceived as being satisfactory and interchangeable, and favourable brand switchers (discussed in Chapter 3) purchase whatever brand is on special or for which they have a coupon.

Brand Proliferation Many mature product categories are saturated with new brands that may lack significant advantages that can be communicated in an

Exhibit 14-3 A premium offer is used to provide extra incentive to purchase Kellogg's Corn Flakes.

advertising campaign. Thus, companies increasingly depend on sales promotion to encourage consumers and trade members to try or adopt these brands. Marketers rely on samples, coupons, rebates, premiums, and other innovative promotional tools to achieve consumer trial of their new brands and encourage repeat purchase (Exhibit 14-3). Marketers face competitive pressure to obtain shelf space for new products in stores as retailers favour new brands with strong sales promotion support that will bring in more customers and boost their sales and profits. Retailers often require special discounts or allowances from manufacturers just to handle and list a new product that requires additional investment in a brand's sales promotion budget.

Short-Term Focus Increased sales promotion is motivated by marketing plans and reward systems geared to short-term performance measures of quarterly and yearly market share and sales volume. Some think the packaged-goods brand management system has contributed to marketers' increased dependence on sales promotion at the expense of brand building activities. Marketing or brand managers use promotions to help them move products into the retailers' stores at the request of the sales people, who also face short-term quotas or goals. Many managers view consumer and trade promotions as the most dependable way to generate short-term sales, particularly when they are price-related. The reliance on sales promotion is particularly high in mature and slow-growth markets, where it is difficult to stimulate consumer demand through advertising. This has led to concern that managers have become too dependent on the quick sales fix that can result from a promotion and that the brand franchise may be eroded by too many deals.

Increased Accountability An increased emphasis on the return on investment of marketing expenditures from senior management puts pressure on marketing or brand managers and the salesforce to produce short-term results. Sales promotion is more economically accountable than advertising. In companies struggling to meet their sales and financial goals, top management is demanding measurable, accountable ways to relate promotional expenditures to sales and profitability. Managers who are being held accountable to produce results often use price discounts or coupons, since they produce a quick and easily measured jump in sales. It takes longer for an ad campaign to show some impact, and the effects are more difficult to measure. Marketers also feel pressure from the trade as retailers demand sales performance from their brands. Real-time data available from computerized checkout scanners makes it possible for retailers to monitor promotions and track the results they generate on a daily basis.

Growing Power of Retailers One reason for the increase in sales promotion is the power shift in the marketplace from manufacturers to retailers. Historically, consumer products manufacturers created consumer demand for their brands by using heavy advertising and some consumer promotions, and exerted pressure on retailers to carry the products. Retailers did very little research and sales analysis; they relied on manufacturers for information regarding the sales performance of individual brands. With the advent of optical checkout scanners and sophisticated in-store computer systems, retailers gained access to data concerning how quickly products turn over, which sales promotions are working, and which products make money.[9] Retailers use this information to analyze sales of manufacturers' products and then demand discounts and other promotional support from manufacturers of lagging brands. Companies that fail to comply with retailers' demands for more trade support often have their shelf space reduced or even their product dropped.

Competition   Another factor for increased sales promotion is manufacturers' reliance on trade and consumer promotions to gain or maintain competitive advantage. For mature and stagnant markets, brands prefer sales promotion over advertising. Exciting, breakthrough creative ideas are difficult to achieve on a regular basis, so there can be an overreliance on sales promotion. Many companies are tailoring their trade promotions to key retail accounts and developing strategic alliances with retailers that include both trade and consumer promotional programs to achieve differentiation. A major development in recent years is **account-specific marketing**, whereby a manufacturer collaborates with an individual retailer to create a customized promotion that accomplishes mutual objectives—like the one between Sunsilk and Walmart (see Exhibit 14-4). However, retailers may use a promotional deal with one company as leverage to seek an equal or better deal with its competitors as consumer and trade promotions are easily matched by competitors.

Exhibit 14-4   Sunsilk developed an account-specific promotion for Walmart.

SALES PROMOTION PLAN

In this section, we examine the various parts of a sales promotion plan. First, we consider some objectives marketers have for sales promotion programs. Next, we illustrate why the various sales promotion decisions are strategic options. Finally, we discuss the key tactics that are critical for all sales promotions. We focus on the consumer market to illustrate these ideas. Application to the trade market is readily done once the concept is understood.

OBJECTIVES OF CONSUMER SALES PROMOTION

As with any promotional mix element, marketers plan consumer promotions by conducting a situation analysis and determining sales promotion's specific role in the IMC program. They must decide what the promotion is designed to accomplish and to whom it should be targeted. Setting clearly defined objectives and measurable goals for their sales promotion programs is consistent with the planning process explained in previous chapters. While the basic goal is to induce brand purchase, the marketer may have different objectives for new versus established brands or new versus current customers. We use the ideas developed in Chapter 5 to highlight how sales promotions can help achieve behavioural and communication objectives. In particular, the latter considers the long-term cumulative effect on the brand's image and position.

Trial Purchase   One of the most important uses of sales promotion techniques is to encourage consumers to try a new product or service. While thousands of new products are introduced to the market every year, many fail within the first year due to a lack of the promotional support needed to encourage initial brand trial by enough consumers. Many new brands are merely new versions of an existing product without unique benefits, so advertising alone cannot induce trial. Sales promotion tools have become an important part of new brand introduction strategies; the level of initial trial can be increased through techniques such as sampling, couponing, and refund offers.

423

A trial purchase objective is also relevant for an established brand that uses a sales promotion to attract nonusers of the product category. Attracting nonusers of the product category can be very difficult, as consumers may not see a need for the product. Sales promotions can appeal to nonusers by providing them with an extra incentive to try the product, but a more common strategy for increasing sales of an established brand is to attract consumers who use a competing brand. This can be done by giving them an incentive to switch, such as a sample, coupon, premium offer, bonus pack, or price deal.

Repeat Purchase   The success of a new brand depends not only on getting initial trial but also on inducing a reasonable percentage of people who try the brand to repurchase it and establish ongoing purchase patterns. Promotional incentives such as coupons or refund offers are often included with a sample to encourage repeat purchase after trial. For example, when Peek Freans introduced its Lifestyle Selections brand of cookie, it distributed free samples along with a 50-cent coupon and a contest offer with the winner receiving a trip to Las Vegas. The samples allowed consumers to try the new cookie, while the coupon provided an incentive to purchase it.

A company can use sales promotion techniques in several ways to retain its current customer base through continued repeat purchases. One way is to load them with the product, taking them out of the market for a certain time. Special price promotions, coupons, or bonus packs can encourage consumers to stock up on the brand. This not only keeps them using the company's brand but also reduces the likelihood they will switch brands in response to a competitor's promotion.

Increasing Consumption   Many marketing managers are responsible for established brands competing in mature markets, against established competitors, where consumer purchase patterns are often well set. Awareness of an established brand is generally high as a result of cumulative advertising effects, and many consumers have probably tried the brand. These factors can create a challenging situation for the brand manager. Sales promotion can generate some new interest in an established brand to help increase sales or defend market share against competitors.

Marketers attempt to increase sales for an established brand in several ways, and sales promotion can play an important role in each. One way to increase product consumption is by identifying new uses for the brand. Sales promotion tools like recipe books or calendars that show various ways of using the product often can accomplish this. One of the best examples of a brand that has found new uses is Arm & Hammer baking soda. Exhibit 14-5 shows a clever freestanding insert (FSI) coupon that promotes the brand's new fridge–freezer pack, which absorbs more odours in refrigerators and freezers.

Build Brand Equity   A final objective for consumer promotions is to enhance or support the brand's IMC effort. Although maintaining or building brand equity and image has traditionally been viewed as being accomplished by media advertising, it has also become an important objective for sales promotions. Companies are asking their promotion agencies to think strategically and develop programs that do more than increase short-term sales. They want promotions that require consumer involvement with their brands. Sales promotion techniques such as contests or sweepstakes and premium offers are often used to draw attention to an ad, increase involvement with the message and product/service, and help build relationships with consumers.

Marketers often turn to sales promotion in the fall to reach students of all ages who are going back to school. For example, DaimlerChrysler displayed its new PT Cruiser and Neon RT to university students at nine campuses across Canada during a September orientation week as part of its "Coolest car on campus" campaign. A contest allowed students to paint a PT Cruiser

Exhibit 14-5   Arm & Hammer used this FSI to promote a specific use for the product.

with water-based paint, with the winning university receiving the car for a campus drive-safe program. In addition, students dressed up in costumes in front of the car, and photos were sent to their parents as part of the "I'll be graduating before you know it" campaign.[10]

CONSUMER SALES PROMOTION STRATEGY DECISIONS

Strategic decisions for sales promotions fall into three broad categories: sales promotion strategy options, application across product lines, and application across geographic markets.

Sales Promotion Strategy Options   Our view of sales promotions is that the options identified in Figure 14-1 are important strategic choices for a marketer. Essentially, the key strategic decision for a marketer concerns the most appropriate sales promotion option that will best achieve the behavioural objective for the target audience. Two characteristics of sales promotions help guide the strategic direction of the sales promotion plan: the degree to which the sales promotion is "franchise building," and whether the incentive of the sales promotion is immediate or delayed.

Franchise-Building Characteristic   Sales promotion activities that communicate distinctive brand attributes and contribute to the development and reinforcement of brand identity are **consumer franchise-building (CFB) promotions**.[11] Consumer sales promotion efforts cannot make consumers loyal to a brand that is of little value or does not provide them with a specific benefit. But they can make consumers aware of a brand and, by communicating its specific features and benefits, contribute to the development of a favourable brand attitude. Consumer franchise-building promotions are designed to build long-term brand preference and help the company achieve the ultimate goal of full-price purchases that do not depend on a promotional offer. Many specialists in the promotional area stress the need for marketers to use sales promotion tools to build a franchise and create long-term continuity in their promotional programs. Well-planned CFB activities can convert consumers to loyal customers.

For years, franchise or image building was viewed as the exclusive realm of advertising, and sales promotion was used only to generate short-term sales increases. But now marketers are recognizing the image-building potential of sales promotion and realizing its CFB value. A survey of senior marketing executives found that 88 percent believe consumer promotions can help build a brand's equity, and 58 percent think trade promotions can contribute.[12] The Peek Freans contest (mentioned above) contributed to building the brand as it reinforced the image of the cookie as being better for the consumer (e.g., healthier). Since the cookie was good, the winner had to go to "Sin City in order to be bad."

Nonfranchise-Building Characteristic   **Nonfranchise-building (non-FB) promotions** are designed to accelerate the purchase decision process and generate an immediate increase in sales. These activities do not communicate information about a brand's unique features or the benefits of using it, so they do not contribute to the building of brand equity and image. Price-off deals, bonus packs, and rebates or refunds are examples of non-FB sales promotion techniques. Short-term non-FB promotions have their place in a firm's promotional mix, particularly when competitive developments call for them since they can switch customers from other brands. But their limitations must be recognized when a long-term marketing strategy for a brand is developed.

Trade promotions are mostly viewed as being nonfranchise-building. First, many of the promotional discounts and allowances given to the trade are never passed on to consumers. Second, trade promotions that are forwarded through the channels reach consumers in the form of lower prices or special deals and lead them to buy on the basis of price rather than brand benefits. Like consumer sales promotions, a franchise-building characteristic can be built into the trade promotion program with activities that do not have a price focus.

Incentive Characteristic   Sales promotions provide consumers with an extra incentive or reward for engaging in a certain form of behaviour, such as purchasing a brand. For some sales promotion tools the incentive that the consumer receives is immediate, while for others the reward is delayed and not realized immediately. Using their situation analysis, marketers decide the relative balance between immediate or delayed incentives. The decision is based on the target audience(s) and the intended behavioural objective(s). The chart in Figure 14-2 outlines which sales promotion tools can be used to accomplish various behavioural objectives and identifies whether the extra incentive or reward is immediate or delayed.[13]

Some of the sales promotion techniques are listed in Figure 14-2 more than once because they can be used to accomplish more than one objective with both immediate and delayed incentives. For example, loyalty programs can be used to retain customers by providing both immediate and delayed rewards. Shoppers who belong to loyalty programs sponsored by supermarkets, and who receive discounts every time they make a purchase, are receiving immediate rewards that are designed to retain them as customers. Some loyalty promotions, such as frequency programs used by airlines and hotels, offer delayed rewards by requiring that users accumulate points to reach a certain level before the points can be redeemed. Loyalty programs can also be used by marketers to help build brand equity. For example, when an airline or hotel sends its frequent users upgrade certificates, the practice helps build relationships with these customers and thus contributes to brand equity.

One explanation for how sales promotion incentives work lies in the theory of **operant conditioning**. Individuals act on an aspect of the environment that reinforces behaviour. In a promotion context, if a consumer buys a product with a sales promotion and experiences a positive outcome, the likelihood that the consumer will use this product again increases. If the outcome is not favourable, the likelihood of buying the product again decreases. Two aspects of reinforcement relevant to sales promotion strategies are schedules of reinforcement and shaping.

FIGURE   14–2   Consumer sales promotion tools for various objectives

Communication and Behavioural Objectives

Consumer Reward Incentive	Trial purchase	Repeat purchase/ customer loading	Support IMC program/ build brand equity
Immediate	• Sampling • Instant coupons • In-store coupons • In-store rebates	• Price-off deals • Bonus packs • In- and on-package free premiums • Loyalty programs	• Events • In- and on-package free premiums
Delayed	• Media- and mail-delivered coupons • Mail-in refunds and rebates • Free mail-in premiums • Scanner- and Internet-delivered coupons	• In- and on-package coupons • Mail-in refunds and rebates • Loyalty programs	• Self-liquidating premiums • Free mail-in premiums • Contests and sweepstakes • Loyalty programs

426

Different **schedules of reinforcement** result in varying patterns of learning and behaviour. Learning occurs most rapidly under a *continuous reinforcement schedule,* in which every response is rewarded—but the behaviour is likely to cease when the reinforcement stops. This implies promotional offers like loyalty programs should carry on indefinitely so that customers would not switch. Learning occurs more slowly but lasts longer when a *partial or intermittent reinforcement schedule* is used and only some of the individual's responses are rewarded. This implies that an IMC program should have a sales promotion with partial reinforcement schedule. The firm does not want to offer the incentive every time (continuous reinforcement), because consumers might become dependent on it and stop buying the brand when the incentive is withdrawn. A study that examined the effect of reinforcement on bus ridership found that discount coupons given as rewards for riding the bus were as effective when given on a partial schedule as when given on a continuous schedule.[14] The cost of giving the discount coupons under the partial schedule, however, was considerably less.

Reinforcement schedules can also be used to influence consumer behaviour through a process known as **shaping**, the reinforcement of successive acts that lead to a desired behaviour pattern or response.[15] In a promotional context, shaping procedures are used as part of the introductory program for new products. Figure 14-3 provides an example of how samples and discount coupons can be used to introduce a new product and take a consumer from trial to repeat purchase. Marketers must be careful in their use of shaping procedures: If they drop the incentives too soon, the consumer may not establish the desired behaviour; but if they overuse them, the consumer's purchase may become contingent on the incentive rather than the product or service.

Application across Product Lines   Another part of the strategic sales promotion decision is the degree to which each sales promotion tool is applied to the range of sizes, varieties, models, or products. Overall, there are three important product decisions for sales promotions. The first concerns whether the sales promotion should be run on the entire line or on individual items. If the latter option is selected (i.e., selective application), the second decision concerns which specific items. The marketer could run a promotion on either the more or less popular items. Similarly, the marketer could focus on higher or lower price points. Sometimes, a sales promotion is offered on a unique product format or size instead of the regular product. For example, Kellogg's bundled three brands of cereal with plastic in one sales promotion in which each size was not the standard size typically distributed. Thus, the third strategic issue concerns whether the sales promotion is run on the "regular" stock or some other special version.

Application across Geographic Markets   Sales promotions can be run nationally or in select markets. Local or regional market conditions, with respect to consumer demand and competitive intensity, tend to dictate the degree of tailoring sales promotions for each geographic market. Intuitively, it appears that many marketers would be faced with situations where offering unique sales promotions for each geographic market would achieve optimal communication and behavioural effects; however, there are three factors that marketers need to consider. First, a regional focus requires additional managerial commitment in planning and implementation. Second, achieving objectives

FIGURE   14–3

Applications of shaping procedures for sales promotion

Behaviour Change	Type of Sales Promotion
Induce product trial	Free samples distributed; large discount coupon
Induce purchase with little financial obligation	Discount coupon prompts purchase with little cost; coupon good for small discount on next purchase enclosed
Induce purchase with moderate financial obligation	Small discount coupon prompts purchase with moderate cost
Induce purchase with full financial obligation	Purchase occurs without coupon assistance

more specifically may result in greater expense, thus necessitating a cost–benefit analysis. Finally, national accounts may not be too receptive, with different types of sales promotions in one province versus another.

CONSUMER SALES PROMOTION TACTICS DECISIONS

A coupon can be received with a value anywhere from 50¢ to $2.00 for many consumer products, early in the year or later in the year, often or not so often, or from any number of outlets (e.g., direct mail, magazine). As this implies, for each sales promotion option the marketer faces a number of key tactical decisions: value of the incentive, timing, and distribution. We briefly describe each of these in order to put together a comprehensive sales promotion plan.

Value of Incentive   Whether the marketer is offering some sort of price discount or a consumer franchise-building sales promotion such as a premium, eventually the marketer has to decide the value of the sales promotion. For example, should the coupon be the equivalent of a 10- or a 20-percent discount? This decision is contingent upon the threshold at which consumers will respond to a sales promotion and the number of potential consumer responses; each will contribute to the total cost of the sales promotion. Similarly, if a beer company is offering a premium, a strategic decision has to be made as to the relative value of the premium: for example, a T-shirt worth $10 to $15 or perhaps a "cozy" worth a couple of dollars.

A non-economic interpretation of value is also possible. Hostess Frito-Lay has used various in-pack collectibles (e.g., stickers) of well-known entertainment or pop-culture icons (e.g., *The Simpsons, Star Wars*) that attract young, impulse-purchase consumers. The focus of these sales promotions transfers well to point-of-sale displays to attract consumers' attention and to meet retailers' need for innovative merchandising to move product off the shelves. For example, Hostess Frito-Lay has used Marvel comic-book characters on packaging and convenience-store point-of-sale displays, and offered limited-edition comic books as part of a trivia challenge in association with Teletoon.[16]

Timing   The time element of the sales promotion is important in a few directions that are mutually dependent. A marketer has to decide during which months, weeks, or days the sales promotion will be offered. Seasonal or some other consumption pattern discovered through market research or the situation analysis may guide this choice. Secondly, sales promotions can be offered for one day, one week, a few weeks, or even a few months. Target audience and behavioural objectives typically guide this duration decision. Finally, the frequency of the sales promotion is a final timing consideration. If coupons have been decided, the marketer needs to decide whether one will be offered every six months or perhaps two every six months.

Distribution   For most sales promotions, there is a logistical consideration as to how the promotion will get to the consumer or how the consumer will get to the sales promotion. There are many choices for sales promotions, such as coupons (e.g., direct mail, in-ad), while for others, such as premiums, the choices may be limited. We discuss some of the distribution options for each sales promotion in the next section, where we describe each sales promotion and its strengths and limitations.

CONSUMER SALES PROMOTION STRATEGY OPTIONS

A number of consumer sales promotions that managers may select from to develop a strategic sales promotion plan were identified in Figure 14-1. Each of these options can assist the promotional planner in achieving the objectives just discussed. We now review each of these options by describing their characteristics, distribution methods, and strengths and limitations.

SAMPLING

Sampling involves a variety of procedures whereby consumers are given some quantity of a product for no charge to induce trial. Sampling is generally considered the most effective way to generate trial, although it is also the most expensive. As a sales promotion technique, sampling is often used to introduce a new product or brand to the market; however, sampling is used for established products as well. Some companies do not use sampling for established products, reasoning that samples may not induce satisfied users of a competing brand to switch and may just go to the firm's current customers, who would buy the product anyway. This may not be true when significant changes (new and improved) are made in a brand.

Sampling can have strong consumer franchise building strength if supported within the IMC program. McDonald's initiated its free coffee offer with extensive advertising in many media: TV, billboard, and out-of-home spectaculars. The ads conveyed that it was a premium roast coffee made with 100 percent Arabica beans, hand-picked and fire-roasted for a full-bodied flavour—a clear reason to enjoy the sample even more and increase the likelihood of actual purchase with a change in consumer attitude.[17]

Packaged goods (e.g., food, health care) producers are heavy users of sampling since their products meet the three criteria for an effective sampling program:

- The products are of relatively low unit value, so samples do not cost too much.
- The products are divisible, which means they can be broken into small sample sizes that are adequate for demonstrating the brand's features and benefits to the user.
- The purchase cycle is relatively short, so the consumer will consider an immediate purchase or will not forget about the brand before the next purchase occasion.

One of the cleverest samples that seems to satisfy these criteria occurred within four subway ads in Toronto. Commuters plugged their headphones into an audio jack to hear book excerpts, much like sampling music online or in a store. The recording ended with "HarperCollins: We tell the world's greatest stories."[18]

Strengths of Sampling   Samples are an excellent way to induce a prospective buyer to try a product or service. A major study conducted by the Promotion Marketing Association in 2002 found that the vast majority of consumers receiving a sample either use it right away or save it to use later.[19] Sampling generates much higher trial rates than advertising or other sales promotion techniques.

Getting people to try a product leads to a second benefit of sampling: consumers experience the brand directly, gaining a greater appreciation for its benefits. This can be particularly important when a product's features and benefits are difficult to describe through advertising. Many foods, beverages, and cosmetics have subtle features that are most appreciated when experienced directly. Nearly 70 percent of the respondents in the PMA survey indicated that they have purchased a product they did not normally use after trying a free sample. The study also found that samples are even more likely to lead to purchase when they are accompanied with a coupon.

Limitations of Sampling   While samples are an effective way to induce trial, the brand must have some unique or superior benefits for a sampling program to be worthwhile. Otherwise, the sampled consumers revert back to other brands and do not become repeat purchasers. The costs of a sampling program can be recovered only if the program gets a number of consumers to become regular users of the brand at full retail price.

Another possible limitation to sampling is that the benefits of some products are difficult to gauge immediately, and the learning period required to appreciate the brand may require supplying the consumer with larger amounts of the brand than are affordable. An example would be an expensive skin cream that is promoted as preventing or reducing wrinkles but has to be used for an extended period before any effects are seen.

Sampling Methods   One decision the promotional manager must make is how to distribute the sample. The sampling method chosen is important not only in terms of costs but also because it influences the type of consumer who receives the sample. The best sampling method gets the product to the best prospects for trial and subsequent repurchase. We now review the distribution options available.

Door-to-door sampling, in which the product is delivered directly to the prospect's residence, is used when it is important to control where the sample is delivered. This distribution method is very expensive because of labour costs, but it can be cost-effective if the marketer has information that helps define the target audience and/or if the prospects are located in a well-defined geographic area.

Sampling through media, in which goods are delivered through print media like newspaper and magazines as they are delivered to residences. Newspapers use bags with advertising on the outside and the sample is tucked inside with the reading material, or an extension is put on the bag allowing greater visibility of the promotional offer. Magazines have similar capabilities but for smaller products.

Sampling through the mail is common for small, lightweight, nonperishable products. A major advantage of this method is that the marketer has control over where and when the product will be distributed and can target the sample to specific market areas. Many marketers use information from geodemographic target marketing programs to better direct their sample mailings. Sampling requests obtained from various sources (e.g., phone, Internet, mail) are usually mailed to consumers. The main drawbacks to mail sampling are postal restrictions and costs.

In-store sampling occurs when the marketer hires temporary demonstrators who set up a table or booth, prepare small samples of the product, and pass them out to shoppers. This approach can be very effective for food products, since consumers get to taste the item and the demonstrator can give them more information about the product while it is being sampled. Demonstrators may also give consumers a cents-off coupon for the sampled item to encourage immediate trial purchase. This sampling method can be very effective with direct product experience but it requires greater investment, extensive planning, and retailer cooperation.

On-package sampling, where a sample of a product is attached to another item, is another common sampling method (see Exhibit 14-6). This procedure can be very cost-effective, particularly for multiproduct firms that attach a sample of a new product to an existing brand's package. A drawback is that since the sample is distributed only to consumers who purchase the item to which it is attached, the sample will not reach nonusers of the carrier brand. Marketers can expand this sampling method by attaching the sample to multiple carrier brands and including samples with products not made by their company.

Event sampling is a popular way of distributing samples. Many marketers use sampling programs that are part of integrated marketing programs that feature events, media tie-ins, and other activities that provide consumers with a total sense of a brand rather than just a few tastes of a food or beverage or a trial size of a packaged-goods product. Event sampling can take place at venues such as concerts, sporting events, and cultural festivals.

Location sampling allows many companies to use specialized sample distribution services that help the company identify consumers who are nonusers

Exhibit 14-6 Armor All uses on-package samples for related products.

of a product or users of a competing brand and develop appropriate procedures for distributing a sample to them. Many university and college students receive sample packs at the beginning of the semester that contain trial sizes of such products as mouthwash, toothpaste, headache remedies, and deodorant.

The Internet is yet another way companies are making it possible for consumers to sample their products. Software, information, or entertainment products can be easily delivered electronically in the digital age.

Promotional planners are not limited to one method. In fact, **multiple methods** for sample requests and delivery can occur. For example, with the decline of the wet cat food in a can category, Effem looked to samples to launch its Whiskas Flavour Lock pouch and its Temptations treat cat food in two new product formats—wet cat food in a convenient pouch and tasty treats as a cat snack. Using a database, Effem delivered samples to a total of 250,000 households in less than four months. Print ads, online ads, and retail point-of-sale supported the direct contact. Consumers also responded with an online request and received one of three samples through the mail. Consumers requested about 20 percent of the samples online, making this Canadian site the second most visited international site owned by Effem's parent, Mars Corporation. Whiskas' market share in the wet pouch category increased by 1.5 percent and volume by weight rose 20 percent, with Whiskas the only brand growing in the declining wet cat food category. Temptations increased its share by 7 percent and maintained its lead in the treat category.[20]

COUPONS

The oldest, most widely used, and most effective sales promotion is the cents-off coupon. These characteristics are a function of options with its tactical considerations: the variability in discount offered (e.g., $.50, $1.00), time flexibility in terms of offer and expiration (e.g., limited, unlimited), and how it is distributed (e.g., media, direct, package, retailer), allowing it to fit in many of the cells of Figure 14-2. Research indicates that the average Canadian household receives about 200 coupons per year and uses about eight coupons, a 4 percent redemption rate.[21]

Currently, extensive research on coupons in Canada is not available; however, we present a couple of items from the U.S. in Figure 14-4. The average U.S. household received considerably more coupons—as much as 10 times more—yet the redemption is only about one percent. The face value and length of time data in Figure 14-4 are reasonably consistent with historical Canadian data.

Strengths of Coupons Coupons have a number of strengths that make them popular sales promotion tools for both new and established products. First, coupons make it possible to offer a price reduction only to those consumers who are price-sensitive. Such consumers generally purchase because of coupons, while those who

431

	2009
Quantity distributed	311 billion
Quantity redeemed	3.2 billion
Average face value coupons *distributed*	$1.37
Average face value coupons *redeemed*	$1.09
Average valid period	150 days
Consumer savings	$3.5 billion
Source: NCH 2010 Coupon Facts Report	

FIGURE 14–4

U.S. coupon facts

are not as concerned about price buy the brand at full value. Coupons also make it possible to reduce the retail price of a product without relying on retailers for cooperation, which can often be a problem. Coupons are generally regarded as second only to sampling as a promotional technique for generating trial. Since a coupon lowers the price of a product, it reduces the consumer's perceived risk associated with trial of a new brand. Coupons can encourage repurchase after initial trial. Many new products include a cents-off coupon inside the package to encourage repeat purchase. Coupons can also be useful promotional devices for established products. They can encourage nonusers to try a brand, encourage repeat purchase among current users, and get users to try a new, improved version of a brand. Coupons may also help coax users of a product to trade up to more expensive brands.

Limitations of Coupons   There are a number of problems with coupons. First, there is potential that coupons will not achieve their intended objective. Coupons intended to attract new users to an established brand can be and are redeemed by consumers who already use the brand. Rather than attracting new users, coupons can end up reducing the company's profit margins among consumers who would probably purchase the product anyway. Due to the incentive, conditions, and expiry date, coupons remain less effective than sampling for inducing initial product trial in a short period.

Second, it can be difficult to estimate how many consumers will use a coupon and when. Response to a coupon is rarely immediate; it typically takes anywhere from two to six months to redeem one. A study of coupon redemption patterns by Inman and McAlister found that many coupons are redeemed just before the expiration date rather than in the period following the initial coupon drop.[22] Many marketers are attempting to expedite redemption by shortening the time period before expiration. The average length of time from issue date to expiration date for coupons in 2005 was 183 days. The uncertainty in knowing the redemption rate and timing makes for more difficult financial planning for coupons.

A third problem with coupons involves low redemption rates and high costs. Couponing program expenses include the face value of the coupon redeemed plus costs for production, distribution, and handling of the coupons. Figure 14-5 shows the calculations used to determine the costs of a couponing program using an FSI (freestanding insert) in the newspaper and a coupon with an average face value of

432

FIGURE   14–5

Calculating couponing costs

Cost per Coupon Redeemed: An Illustration	
1. Distribution cost 5,000,000 circulation × $15/M	$75,000
2. Redemptions at 2%	100,000
3. Redemption cost 100,000 redemptions × $.75 face value	$75,000
4. Retailer handling cost and processor fees 100,000 redemptions × $10	$10,000
5. Total program cost Items 1 + 3 + 4	$160,000
6. Cost per coupon redeemed Cost divided by redemption	$1.60
7. Actual product sold on redemption (misredemption estimated at 20%) 100,000 × 80%	80,000
8. Cost per product moved Program cost divided by amount of product sold	$2.00

75 cents. The marketer should track costs closely to ensure the promotion is economically feasible.

Recent research on coupon face value indicates that testing for the most appropriate level is important for determining the most efficient (i.e., cost per coupon redeemed) coupon program. Since a coupon program combines redemption, printing, distribution, and handling costs, the face value and corresponding redemption rate can influence the overall efficiency of the program. The research tested a number of direct mail and FSI offers from various firms selling major grocery brands with different face values and consistent communication elements across all offers. The results indicate that moving from $.50 to $1.00 off nearly doubles the redemption rate (e.g., 2 percent to 4 percent), while moving from $1.00 to $1.50 off improves the redemption rate at a slower rate (e.g., 4 percent to 5 percent). Overall, this curvilinear relationship between face value and redemption rate made the $1.00 offer 20 percent and 12 percent more cost-efficient versus the $.50 and $1.50 offers, respectively. Conclusions from the research suggest the choice of face value should not make the program go over budget, the face value and redemption rate connection will vary by brand, lower face values may not be the most cost-efficient program, higher face values are good for brand trial, and lower face values are good for brand retrial.[23]

A final problem with coupon promotions is misredemption, or the cashing of a coupon without purchase of the brand. Coupon misredemption or fraud occurs in a number of ways, including:

- Redemption of coupons by consumers for a product or size not specified on the coupon.
- Redemption of coupons by salesclerks in exchange for cash.
- Gathering and redeeming coupons by store managers/owners without actually selling the product.
- Printing of counterfeit coupons that are redeemed by unethical merchants.

Coupon Distribution Coupons can be disseminated to consumers in a number of ways, including newspaper freestanding inserts, direct mail, newspapers (either in individual ads or as a group of coupons in a cooperative format), magazines, packages, and the Internet. Figure 14-6 summarizes the U.S. coupon redemption rates for each media type.

Distribution through newspaper *freestanding inserts* (FSIs) is by far the most popular method for delivering coupons to consumers for a number of reasons, including their high-quality four-colour graphics, competitive distribution costs, national same-day circulation, market selectivity, and the category exclusivity given by FSI company. Because of their consumer popularity and predictable distribution, coupons distributed in FSIs are also a strong selling point with the retail trade. On the other hand, FSIs suffer from a low redemption rate and their widespread distribution may lead to a clutter problem.

Direct mail coupons are often sent by local retailers or through co-op mailings where a packet of coupons for different products is sent to a household. Direct-mail couponing has several advantages. First, the mailing can be sent to a broad audience or targeted to specific geographic or demographic segments. Second, firms that mail their own coupons through addressed mail can be quite selective about recipients. Third, direct-mail coupons can also be

FIGURE 14–6 U.S. coupon redemption rates, 2009

Free Standing Insert	0.8%
Newspaper	0.7%
Magazine	0.9%
Direct Mail	2.7%
Regular In-Pack	4.3%
Regular On-Pack	6.5%
In-Pack Cross-Ruff	3.0%
On-Pack Cross-Ruff	3.8%
Instant On-Pack	20.8%
Instant On-Pack Cross-Ruff	8.5%
On-Shelf Distributed	7.9%
Handout Electronically Dispensed	7.9%
All Other Handouts In-Store	3.1%
All Other Handouts Away from Store	2.5%
Internet	15.9%

Source: NCH Marketing Services, Inc.

combined with a sample, which makes it a very effective way to gain the attention of consumers. Finally, the above strengths generally give this method a redemption rate higher than FSI. The major disadvantage of direct-mail coupon delivery is the expense relative to other distribution methods. The cost per thousand for distributing coupons through co-op mailings ranges from $10 to $15, and more targeted promotions can cost $20 to $25 or even more. Also, the higher redemption rate of mail-delivered coupons may result from the fact that many recipients are already users of the brand who take advantage of the coupons sent directly to them.

The use of *newspapers* and *magazines* as couponing vehicles offers a print media alternative. The advantages of newspapers as a couponing vehicle include market selectivity, shorter lead times with timing to the day, cooperative advertising opportunities that can lead to cost efficiencies, and promotional tie-ins with retailers. Other advantages of newspaper-delivered coupons are the broad exposure and consumer receptivity. Many consumers actively search the newspaper for coupons, especially on "food day" (when grocery stores advertise their specials). This enhances the likelihood of the consumer at least noticing the coupon. Distribution of coupons through magazines can take advantage of the selectivity of the publication to reach specific target audiences, along with enhanced production capabilities and extended copy life in the home. One feature of these print options is that the distribution cost is not a factor if the advertiser was planning to run a print ad in the first place.

Placing coupons either *inside* or on the *outside* of the package has virtually no distribution costs and a much higher redemption rate than other couponing methods. An in/on pack coupon that is redeemable for the next purchase of the same brand is known as a **bounce-back coupon**. Bounce-back coupons are often used with product samples to encourage the consumer to purchase the product after sampling. They may be included in or on the package during the early phases of a brand's life cycle to encourage repeat purchase, or they may be a defensive manoeuvre for a mature brand that is facing competitive pressure and wants to retain its current users. The main limitation of bounce-back coupons is that they go only to purchasers of the brand and thus do not attract nonusers. A bounce-back coupon placed on the package for a Kellogg's cereal bar is shown in Exhibit 14-7.

Another type of in/on pack coupon is the **cross-ruff coupon**, which is redeemable on the purchase of a different product, usually one made by the same company but occasionally through a tie-in with another manufacturer. Cross-ruff coupons can be effective in encouraging consumers to try other products or brands. Companies with wide product lines, such as cereal manufacturers, often use these coupons. Yet another type of package coupon is the **instant coupon**, which is attached to the outside of the package so that the consumer can rip it off and redeem it immediately at the time of purchase. They can be selectively placed in terms of promotion timing and market region. Some companies prefer instant coupons to price-off deals because the latter require more cooperation from retailers and can be more expensive, since every package must be reduced in price.

Another distribution method that has experienced strong growth is **in-store couponing**, which includes all co-op couponing programs distributed in a retail store environment. Coupons are distributed to consumers in stores in several ways, including tear-off pads, handouts in the store (sometimes as part of a sampling demonstration), on-shelf dispensers, and electronic dispensers. These in-store coupons have several advantages: They can reach consumers when they are ready to make a purchase, increase brand awareness on the shelf, generate impulse buying, and

Exhibit 14-7 Kellogg Company uses an on-package coupon to encourage repurchase.

encourage product trial. They also provide category exclusivity. In-store couponing removes the need for consumers to clip coupons from FSIs or print ads and then remember to bring them to the store.

While many marketers are using the Internet for online promotions, online coupons account for a small percentage (i.e., one percent) of all coupons distributed, although many find it appealing to be able to download to a loyalty card and simply swipe at the point of sale.[24] A major problem that has kept marketers away from "e-couponing" is the risk of fraud, as it is too easy for consumers or unscrupulous retailers to mass-duplicate online coupons by printing out several, or by photocopying the black-and-white prints. There are ways to deal with this problem, such as coding coupons and verifying them in-store when they are redeemed. However, this is time-consuming and not very popular with retailers. Two alternatives are now on the scene in Canada. Two websites, Coupons.com and Save.ca, allow consumers to print or receive coupons in the mail, respectively. Currently, the fraud problem is not a significant concern in Canada.[25] The famous blue Valpak, distributed to households through the mail system, is now available online (Exhibit 14-8). IMC Perspective 14-1 summarizes how coupons have gone digital.

Exhibit 14-8 Valpak's coupons are now available online.

PREMIUMS

Premiums are a sales promotion device used by many marketers. A **premium** is an offer for an item of merchandise or service either free or at a low price that is an extra incentive for purchasers. Many marketers are eliminating toys and gimmicks in favour of value-added premiums that reflect the quality of the product and are consistent with its image and positioning in the market.

Strengths of Premiums Premiums are usually small gifts or merchandise included in a product package or sent to consumers who mail in a request along with a proof of purchase. In/on-package free premiums include toys, balls, trading cards, or other items included in cereal packages, as well as samples of one product included with another. McDonald's is a leader in the restaurant market for giving free premiums with its Happy Meal for children (Exhibit 14-9). Package-carried premiums have high impulse value and can provide an extra incentive to buy the product.

Premiums also are useful in building brand image and co-branding. For example, a successful Canadian in-package premium was the General Mills giveaway of six CD-ROM computer games including Monopoly Junior and Clue. Modelled after a similar premium offer in the U.S., the Canadian division worked with only one games supplier, Hasbro, versus a couple of partners used south of the border. Hasbro was selected because both it and

Exhibit 14-9 McDonald's Happy Meal uses toys to help attract children.

IMC PERSPECTIVE 14-1
Coupons Go Digital

An old favourite, the coupon, is getting a new lease on life with the advent of technology. In Canada, a new website (Couponclick.ca)-distributes coupons that can be instantly downloaded and printed. Each voucher contains a code tracked to the individual consumer for measurement effectiveness and security purposes. While online coupon distribution got off to a slow start relative to other aspects of marketing, like simple (banner) ads, growth finally arrived as the number grew from 1.6 million in December 2007 to 2.6 million in 2009 according to comScore.

Research supports potential demand for a new online distribution entry; Ipsos Reid reports that about half the population would be "extremely likely" or "very likely" to download coupons. Projecting into the future, the president of the new venture suggested, "The technology provides marketers with a direct link to customers, and the ability to gather rich, aggregated information on coupon users that enhances customer relationship management efforts and enables the creation of customized promotions."

Another step in the digitization of coupons is the capability of using them with mobile devices. The process begins with a website (Samplesaint.com) to transmit the offer to an Internet-enabled phone. Upon purchase, a cashier scans the bar code on the phone's screen, thereby redeeming the coupon and deleting it from the phone. Another application allows manual entry of the coupon code; however, retailers find the process cumbersome as mistakes get made, and costly as the process requires more time leading to higher labour costs. So there is hope to implement online coupons with a streamlined process.

Critics identify numerous concerns with the new method, including incompatible devices, software problems, the risk of dropping expensive phones during the exchange, and inaccurate reading of data by retail scanners. However, the new service claims it has all the difficulties addressed, and has control over people being able to re-use the coupon or e-mail it to others. A significant advantage of digital distribution is a higher redemption rate (mid-teens), since consumers are seeking out a desired brand rather than sorting through newspaper inserts.

How consumers find the coupon websites is also digitally influenced. Blogs put together by shoppers recommend various websites offering coupons and criticize and praise different retailers and their coupon offerings. For example, popular blogger Consumerqueen.com complained about Old Navy's lack of intensity, and the clothing retailer immediately responded by increasing its frequency. Many blogs feature the opinions of expert household shoppers—namely, moms—and are turning into a significant marketing force with Nielsen tracking their traffic. Nielsen ranks mother-oriented blogs by how much chatter they garner, their number of followers on Twitter, and how many times consumers link to them from other blogs. According to a partner at an international marketing consulting firm, "Moms are turning to their new set of online friends and families to make all kinds of purchasing decisions. Women are trusting women bloggers."

Sources: Kristin Laird, "Promopost Launching New Click-and-Save-Service," *Marketing Magazine,* June 4, 2009; Andrew Lavallee, "Unilever Begins 'Holy Grail' Test of Mobile Coupons," *The Globe and Mail,* May 29, 2009, p. B7; Anne D'Innocenzio, "Come On, Cough Up the Coupons," *The Globe and Mail,* June 4, 2009, p. L6.

Question:

1. What are the advantages of digital coupons over media-distributed coupons?

General Mills represent quality and heritage. The premium was so popular that store employees witnessed consumers searching through cases to find the game they wanted, as well as some consumers leaving the store with only the CD-ROM after purchasing the cereal. For competitive reasons, executives at General Mills were not willing to reveal results, but did admit that the consumer reaction was beyond belief given the empty shelves.[26]

A third benefit of premiums is their ability to work with rest of the IMC program effectively to build the brand image. For example, Labatt had a winner with the Labatt Blue NHL Crazy Coldie Program during the Stanley Cup playoffs. Each case of Double Blue (i.e., 12 Blue and 12 Blue Light) had a "coldie" (i.e., holder to keep beer cold) in the shape of the jersey of one of the 30 teams. While the in-pack premium is relatively inexpensive, it resonated with the 19–34 male market that pushed sales to a 300-percent market share growth during the promotional program. Success can be partly attributed to the promotion's ads, where three humorous spots showed consumers trying to wear the "coldie jersey" despite its obvious small size and a host of other promotional support activities such as a contest and special events.[27]

Fourth, premiums can also encourage trade support and gain in-store displays for the brand and the premium offer. General Mills Canada was at it again with a successful premium during the Christmas season. Customers received a beanbag version of the Pillsbury Doughboy for $2.99 with the purchase of two refrigerated-dough products. This marked the first time the brand icon had ever been directly merchandised! Pillsbury had the perfect opportunity because the Doughboy is the second-most recognized icon in North America, after Coca-Cola's Polar Bears. Even more impressive was the retailer participation and consumer acceptance. All retailers in Canada ran with the deal, and more than 200,000 Doughboys found a new home. And just to make sure that consumers liked the idea even more, the Doughboy came in three models: one holding a candy cane, another, a stocking, and the third, gifts.[28]

Limitations of Premiums   There are some limitations associated with the use of premiums. First, there is the cost factor, which results from the premium itself as well as from extra packaging that may be needed. Finding desirable premiums at reasonable costs can be difficult, particularly for adult markets, and using a poor premium that costs less may do more harm than good. A solution to this is to offer **self-liquidating premiums** requiring the consumer to pay some or all of the cost of the premium (as described above). The marketer usually purchases items used as self-liquidating premiums in large quantities and offers them to consumers at lower-than-retail prices. The goal is not to make a profit on the premium item but rather just to cover costs and offer a value to the consumer. A second limitation is that some offers require the consumer to send in more than one proof of purchase to receive the premium. This requires effort from the consumer and money for the mailing and does not offer an immediate reinforcement or reward. A third limitation is that the marketer faces the risk of poor acceptance and is left with a supply of items with a logo or some other brand identification that makes them hard to dispose of. Thus, it is important to test consumers' reaction to a premium incentive and determine whether they perceive the offer as valuable. Another option is to use premiums with no brand identification, but that detracts from their consumer franchise-building value.

CONTESTS AND SWEEPSTAKES

Contests and sweepstakes are an increasingly popular consumer sales promotion since they seem to have an appeal and glamour that other promotions like coupons lack. A **contest** is a promotion where consumers compete for prizes or money on the basis of skills or ability. The company determines winners by judging the entries or ascertaining which entry comes closest to some predetermined criteria. Contests usually provide a purchase incentive by requiring a proof of purchase or an entry form that is available from a dealer or advertisement. Some contests require consumers to read an ad or package or visit a store display to gather information. Marketers must be careful not to make their contests too difficult to enter, as doing so might discourage participation among key prospects in the target audience.

A **sweepstakes** is a promotion where winners are determined purely by chance; it cannot require a proof of purchase as a condition for entry. Entrants need only submit their names for the prize drawing. While there is often an official entry form, handwritten entries must also be permitted. One form of sweepstakes is a **game**, which also has a chance element or odds of winning. Scratch-off cards with instant winners are a popular promotional tool. Some games occur over a longer period and require more involvement by consumers. Promotions where consumers must collect

Exhibit 14-10   Advertisements are often used to deliver messages about promotions such as a sweepstakes.

game pieces are popular among retailers and fast-food chains as a way to build store traffic and repeat purchases. For example, McDonald's has used promotions based on the game Monopoly several times in recent years.

Because they are easier to enter, sweepstakes attract more entries than do contests. They are also easier and less expensive to administer, since every entry does not have to be checked or judged. Choosing the winning entry in a sweepstakes requires only the random selection of a winner from the pool of entries or generation of a number to match those held by sweepstakes entrants. Experts note that the costs of mounting a sweepstakes are also very predictable. Companies can buy insurance to indemnify them and protect against the expense of awarding a big prize. In general, sweepstakes present marketers with a fixed cost, which is a major advantage when budgeting for a promotion. Exhibit 14-10 shows an ad for a sweepstakes where the prize and brand are closely aligned to build brand equity, another key feature of these promotions.

Strengths of Contests and Sweepstakes   A recent study suggests that sales can be enhanced by trial and repeat purchases through a sweepstakes advertised via in-store ad-pads. A 12-week experiment of 20 mass-merchandiser outlets— 10 test and 10 control stores—revealed that a major household product increased its sales by 70 percent in the test stores during the four-week test period compared to the previous four-week period that featured no advertising or promotion. Furthermore, during the posttest four-week period that had no ad-pad, sales hit a 30-percent increase.[29] Clearly, non-customers either recalled the sales promotion and ad message, or new or existing customers returned for a repeat purchase. In either case, the improved communication and behavioural effects of the promotion make it useful for both manufacturers and retailers.

Contests and sweepstakes can involve consumers with a brand by making the promotion product relevant or by connecting the prizes to the lifestyle, needs, or interests of the target audience. Procter & Gamble teamed up with MuchMusic for two contests to promote its Cover Girl brand of makeup. In January 2001, seven lucky winners received a live, on-air makeover with celebrity hair and makeup artists. Another contest, "Prom Night 2001," featured one winner and nine friends receiving a makeover and a limousine ride to their prom, among other prizes.[30]

Contests can be designed to be consistent with the brand positioning strategy used in advertising. Axe deodorant body spray used an unusual skill or ability in its recent contest in Quebec. It sent camera teams to popular clubs and asked men to recite their best "pick-up" lines. Winners received dinner and a shopping spree and their victorious efforts were shown on MusiquePlus. While this is certainly provocative, it is quite fitting with the sexual allurement communicated in Axe's recent television commercials.[31]

Limitations of Contests and Sweepstakes   Many sweepstakes and/or contest promotions do little to contribute to consumer franchise building for a product or service and may even detract from it. The sweepstakes or contest often becomes the dominant focus rather than the brand, and little is accomplished other than giving away substantial amounts of money and/or prizes. Many promotional experts question the effectiveness of contests and sweepstakes. Some companies have cut back or even stopped using them because of concern over their effectiveness and fears that consumers might become dependent on them.[32]

Despite this challenge it is possible to overcome this limitation. O.K. Tire connected to the local community where its dealers are located with a positive consumer-franchise building contest to launch its re-branding strategy. O.K. Tire offered 40 prizes totalling $50,000 to local community groups that were identified on ballots entered at one of the 230 dealerships. Results included current customers filling out many ballots while visiting a dealership for service, new customers acting upon the television and radio ads to try O.K. Tire, increased word-of-mouth communication in many locales, and enhanced personal communication with an emphasis on the dealer as a trusted neighbourhood business.[33]

Numerous legal considerations affect the design and administration of contests and sweepstakes.[34] But companies must still be careful in designing a contest or sweepstakes and awarding prizes. Most firms use consultants that specialize in the design and administration of contests and sweepstakes to avoid any legal problems, but they may still run into problems with promotions.

A final problem with contests and sweepstakes is participation by professionals or hobbyists who submit many entries but have no intention of purchasing the product or service. Because it is illegal to require a purchase as a qualification for a sweepstakes entry, people can enter as many times as they wish. Professional players sometimes enter one sweepstakes several times, depending on the nature of the prizes and the number of entries the promotion attracts. There are even newsletters that inform them of all the contests and sweepstakes being held, the entry dates, estimated probabilities of winning for various numbers of entries, how to enter, and solutions to any puzzles or other information that might be needed. The presence of these professional entrants not only defeats the purpose of the promotion but also may discourage entries from consumers who think their chances of winning are limited.

REFUNDS AND REBATES

Refunds (also known as rebates) are offers by the manufacturer to return a portion of the product purchase price, usually after the consumer supplies some proof of purchase. Consumers are generally very responsive to rebate offers, particularly as the size of the savings increases. Rebates are used by makers of all types of products, ranging from packaged goods to major appliances, cars, and computer software (Exhibit 14-11).

Packaged-goods marketers often use refund offers to induce trial of a new product or encourage users of another brand to switch. Consumers may perceive the savings offered through a cash refund as an immediate value that lowers the cost of the item, even though those savings are realized only if the consumer redeems the refund or rebate offer. Redemption rates for refund offers typically range from 1 to 3 percent for print and point-of-purchase offers and 5 percent for in/on-package offers.

Refund offers can also encourage repeat purchase. Many offers require consumers to send in multiple proofs of purchase. The size of the refund offer may even increase as the number of purchases gets larger. Some packaged-goods companies are switching away from cash refund offers to coupons or cash/coupon combinations. Using coupons in the refund offer enhances the likelihood of repeat purchase of the brand.

Strengths and Limitations of Refunds and Rebates
Rebates can help create new users and encourage brand switching or repeat purchase behaviour, or they can be a way to offer a temporary price reduction. The rebate may be perceived as an immediate savings even though many consumers do not follow through on the offer. This perception can influence

Exhibit 14-11 Pennzoil uses a refund offer that is tied to a future purchase.

purchase even if the consumer fails to realize the savings, so the marketer can reduce price for much less than if it used a direct price-off deal.

Some limitations are associated with refunds and rebates. Many consumers are not motivated by a refund offer because of the delay and the effort required to obtain the savings. They do not want to be bothered saving cash register receipts and proofs of purchase, filling out forms, and mailing in the offer.[35] A study of consumer perceptions found a negative relationship between the use of rebates and the perceived difficulties associated with the redemption process.[36] The study also found that consumers perceive manufacturers as offering rebates to sell products that are not faring well. Nonusers of rebates were particularly likely to perceive the redemption process as too complicated and to suspect manufacturers' motives. This implies that companies using rebates must simplify the redemption process and use other promotional elements such as advertising to retain consumer confidence in the brand.

When small refunds are being offered, marketers may find other promotional incentives such as coupons or bonus packs more effective. They must be careful not to overuse rebate offers and confuse consumers about the real price and value of a product or service. Also, consumers can become dependent on rebates and delay their purchases, or purchase only brands for which a rebate is available. Many retailers have become disenchanted with rebates and the burden and expense of administering them.[37]

BONUS PACKS

Bonus packs offer the consumer an extra amount of a product at the regular price by providing larger containers or extra units (Exhibit 14-12). Bonus packs result in a lower cost per unit for the consumer and provide extra value as well as more product for the money. There are several advantages to bonus pack promotions. First, they give marketers a direct way to provide extra value without having to get involved with complicated coupons or refund offers. The additional value of a bonus pack is generally obvious to the consumer and can have a strong impact on the purchase decision at the time of purchase.

Bonus packs can also be an effective defensive manoeuvre against a competitor's promotion or introduction of a new brand. By loading current users with large amounts of its product, a marketer can often remove these consumers from the market and make them less susceptible to a competitor's promotional efforts. Bonus packs may result in larger purchase orders and favourable display space in the store if relationships with retailers are good. They do, however, usually require additional shelf space without providing any extra profit margins for the retailer, so the marketer can encounter problems with bonus packs if trade relationships are not good. Another problem is that bonus packs may appeal primarily to current users who probably would have purchased the brand anyway, or to promotion-sensitive consumers who may not become loyal to the brand.

PRICE-OFF DEALS

Another consumer sales promotion tool is the direct **price-off deal**, which reduces the price of the brand. Price-off reductions are typically offered right on the package through specially marked price packs, as shown in Exhibit 14-13. Typically, price-offs range from 10 to 25 percent off the regular price, with the reduction coming out of the manufacturer's profit margin, not the retailer's. Keeping the retailer's margin during a price-off promotion maintains its support and cooperation.

Marketers use price-off promotions for several reasons. First, since price-offs are controlled by the manufacturer, it can make sure the promotional discount reaches the consumer rather than being kept by the trade. Like bonus packs, price-off deals usually present a readily apparent value to shoppers, especially when they have

Exhibit 14-12 Bonus packs provide more value for consumers.

a reference price point for the brand and thus recognize the value of the discount.[38] So price-offs can be a strong influence at the point of purchase when price comparisons are being made. Price-off promotions can also encourage consumers to purchase larger quantities, preempting competitors' promotions and leading to greater trade support.

Price-off promotions may not be favourably received by retailers, since they can create pricing and inventory problems. Most retailers will not accept packages with a specific price shown, so the familiar X amount off the regular price must be used. Also, like bonus packs, price-off deals appeal primarily to regular users instead of attracting nonusers. Finally, the federal government has regulations regarding the conditions that price-off labels must meet and the frequency and timing of their use.

Services also offer discounts, as seen with Milestone's "Wednesday Date Night" promotion. Each Wednesday the casual dining chain offered patrons dinner for two for $50 when ordering off a special menu. Radio communicated the promotion and the dating theme prevailed in the execution. Management saw the promotion as a way of distinguishing the brand from competitors like The Keg and Moxies.[39]

Electronic products are often discounted, and one market where fierce discounting has occurred is e-books. The whole book market is in a degree of turmoil, with two formats—print and electronic versions—and royalty arrangements based on the initial print form, thus influencing the cost structure. Consequently, publishers recently discounted e-books to $10 when selling hardcover equivalents for $30.[40]

Exhibit 14-13 Examples of price-off packages.

FREQUENCY PROGRAMS

One of the fastest growing areas of sales promotion is the use of **frequency programs** (also referred to as *continuity* or *loyalty programs*). Frequency programs have become commonplace in a number of product and service categories, particularly travel and hospitality, as well as among retailers. Virtually every airline, car rental company, and hotel chain has some type of frequency program. Loyalty programs are also used by a variety of retailers, including grocery stores, department stores, home centres, bookstores, and even local bagel shops.

There are a number of reasons why frequency programs have become so popular. Marketers view these programs as a way of encouraging consumers to use their products or services on a continual basis and as a way of developing strong customer loyalty. Many companies are also realizing the importance of customer retention and understand that the key to retaining and growing market share is building relationships with loyal customers. Frequency programs also provide marketers with the opportunity to develop databases containing valuable information on their customers that can be used to better understand their needs, interests, and characteristics as well as to identify and track a company's most valuable customers. These databases can also be used to target specific programs and offers to customers to increase the amount they purchase and/or to build stronger relationships with them. For example, the WD-40 Fan Club is a loyalty program for the brand that provides members with product information, usage tips, newsletters, downloads of games, and other benefits (Exhibit 14-14). The fan club has nearly 70,000 members who educate each other about creative ways to use the solvent and serve as advocates for the brand.[41]

Exhibit 14-14 The WD-40 Fan Club is a popular customer loyalty program.

441

As frequency programs become more common, marketers will be challenged to find ways to use them as a means of differentiating their product, service, business, or retail store. It has been argued that many of the loyalty programs developed by marketers are really short-term promotions that overreward regular users and do little to develop long-term loyalty.[42] A recent study by a loyalty marketing firm found that 66 percent of consumers say that discounts are the main reason they participate in loyalty programs. This study also found that many consumers drop out of loyalty programs because of the length of time it takes to accumulate reward points.[43] Marketers must find ways to make their loyalty programs more than just discount or frequent-buyer programs. This will require the careful management of databases to identify and track valuable customers and their purchase history and the strategic use of targeted loyalty promotions.

Many retailers use various points systems in Canada with names like HBC and PC, while others are attempting to innovate. The Gap tested a new loyalty program in Vancouver with the idea of launching it globally if successful. Called Sprize, it allows consumers to buy an item at full price and receive an automatic credit on future purchases if it goes on sale within 45 days. Communication of the program used the theme "Shopping turned on its head." Stores literally turned all sorts of signage upside down, and radio also supported the announcement. Other retailers who began or augmented their loyalty programs recently include Sobeys and Canadian Tire. Club Sobeys passed the one million member mark in the first six weeks of its points program, which allows redemption for in-store savings, food rewards, and Aeroplan miles. Canadian Tire "money" is obtained by consumers for cash purchases that can be used for future purchases; about $100 million is distributed annually. Speculation abounds that the program may be discontinued; however, recently the chain offered a $1 coin instead of its normal paper currency for a two-day December promotion to invigorate the offer and drive traffic for holiday purchases.[44]

EVENT MARKETING

Event marketing has become very popular in recent years. It is important to make a distinction between *event marketing* and *event sponsorships,* as the two terms are often used interchangeably yet they refer to different activities. **Event marketing** is a type of promotion where a company or brand is linked to an event or where a themed activity is developed for the purpose of creating experiences for consumers and promoting a product or service. Pepsi associated its Mountain Dew brand with various action sports (Exhibit 14-15), while an energy drink company established

Exhibit 14-15
Pepsi established the AST Dew Tour.

Marketing events in various locations that included live brand representatives were carried on in full force recently for Perrier, Adidas, Coppertone, and Fido.

Perrier fans who signed up online (Societeperrier.ca) received a special PIN code that allowed them to attend "soirees" at upscale nightclubs. These exclusive parties occurred in branded VIP areas and offered a free Perrier cocktail, a taxi voucher, and complimentary Perrier all evening. Each club displayed bar mats, coasters, stirsticks, candles, and tent cards describing the three cocktails. Brand reps gave out business cards to invite registrations, and other communication occurred with wild postings via e-mail, Facebook, and Twitter.

A Montreal agency, Sid Lee, developed the first global campaign for Adidas Originals products, a line-up that celebrates the authentic fashion of the three stripes. The theme "Celebrate Originality" expressed the wide-ranging cultural presence of the brand and youth culture. A house party with various international stars and regular young people played a key part as clips played on various Canadian music stations. For example, a three-minute segment appeared on *Much on Demand,* a two-minute ad sponsored the show, and VJs wearing Adidas clothing announced a contest for gear to allow winners to host their own house party.

A Coppertone executive said NEWAD received the nod as the agency for its latest event because of its "outstanding creativity, passion and strong strategic planning skills." A NEWAD manager gushed, "So it's great because they are listening to our recommendations and the client

moved forward with our plan." Enter the Coppertone Sun Protection Patrol, a street team that distributes samples and educational materials in Canada's three largest cities. To get around, the team travelled in a branded truck that acted as a mobile education centre to visit key events. The team took instant pictures of visitors to assess their skin for sun damage, and nurses provided guidance and recommended Coppertone skin care options.

Fido sponsored a series of underground artsy events/parties called Fido Sessions that centred on art, culture, design, and fashion in areas where young, hip people live, work, and play. The location and the events remained a mystery until two giant dolls eventually joined after eight days of getting closer together. The four-storey, white, featureless dolls had no identity except for a text shortcode where people could learn about the events. A team of people dressed as mini dolls deployed the message as well through wild postings, chalk art, night projections, tree hangers, and flying cloud logos. The lack of branding fit with the underground nature of the events—although participants could order drinks with Fido phones.

Sources: Kristin Laird, "Perrier Goes Clubbing in Toronto," *Marketing Magazine,* November 27, 2009; Kristin Laird, "NEWAD hired to take Coppertone to the Streets," *Marketing Magazine,* May 29, 2009; Jonathan Paul, "Adidas's Hipster House Party: 60 Is the New 20-Something," *Strategy,* April 2009; p. 28; Jonathan Paul, "Promotion," *Strategy,* June 2009, p. 443.

Question:

1. How do these party events help build the brand?

Red Bull Crashed Ice where the finals are televised on TSN. Event marketing allows marketers to develop integrated marketing programs including promotional tools that create experiences for consumers in an effort to associate their brands with certain lifestyles and activities. Marketers use events to distribute samples as well as information about their products and services, or to let consumers actually experience the product. IMC Perspective 14-2 describes a few recent events.

An **event sponsorship** is an integrated marketing communications activity where a company develops actual sponsorship relations with a particular event (e.g., concert, art exhibition, cultural activity, social change, sports) and provides financial support in return for the right to display a brand name, logo, or advertising message and be identified as a supporter of the event. Part of the confusion between these two promotions arises from the fact that event marketing often takes place as part of a company's event sponsorship. We describe examples of the former concept here and address the latter in the next chapter as it relates more closely to public relations activities.

Two notable events to distribute samples in situations that reinforced their brand positioning strategy achieved great success. Aveeno, a marketer of skin care products, launched its 2004 Snowfest tour with product sampling, a contest, and an "Après Ski" party at 16 ski hills across Canada. Activities such as these can enhance the post-event advertising or can benefit from pre-event advertising. For instance, Aveeno used print and online ads to round out its IMC campaign.[45] An event run by Coffee-Mate was almost an anti-event with a "tease, taste and reveal" approach. It distributed 800,000 free cups of coffee with Coffee-Mate liquid at high-traffic locations (e.g., offices, commuter hubs, arenas) in six Canadian cities. To overcome the Coffee-Mate equals powder association, it did not disclose the brand until after the consumer had tasted the product.[46]

Volvo Cars of Canada doubled its investment on event marketing recently; the bulk of the dollars were spent on established events like the Volvo Golf Challenge and Volvo Ski Series, but Volvo also included a new event, Local 416. Initiated in Toronto, the event involved artists creating work inspired by the automaker's new C30—a three-door coupe aimed at urban professionals ages 25–35 with no children. Local 416 featured the work of one artist, a DJ, and a fashion designer in a downtown art gallery over four weeks. Volvo positioned the event as a "physical extension" of Volvo's global positioning of the car as "a product of free will." Volvo acted as host so as to not compromise the arts and the artists. The event occurred while Volvo launched four new vehicles, which has allowed the company to expand its marketing budget beyond mainstream media outlets.[47]

TRADE SALES PROMOTION

Trade sales promotions that managers may select from to develop a strategic sales promotion plan were identified in Figure 14-1. Each of these options can assist the promotional planner in achieving the objectives with various resellers. The objectives are similar to those of consumer sales promotions since the promotion acts as a behavioural incentive. We now review objectives and strategic options for trade sales promotions.

OBJECTIVES OF TRADE SALES PROMOTION

Like consumer promotions, sales promotion programs targeted to the trade should be based on well-defined objectives and measurable goals and a consideration of what the marketer wants to accomplish. Typical objectives for promotions targeted to marketing intermediaries such as wholesalers and retailers include obtaining distribution for new products, maintaining trade support for established brands, building retail inventories, and encouraging retailers to display established brands.

Obtain Distribution for New Products Trade promotions are often used to encourage retailers to give shelf space to new products. Essentially, this translates into a trial purchase objective like we saw with consumer promotions. Manufacturers recognize that only a limited amount of shelf space is available in supermarkets, drugstores, and other major retail outlets. Thus, they provide retailers with financial incentives to stock new products. While trade discounts or other special price deals are used to encourage retailers and wholesalers to stock a new brand, marketers may use other types of promotions to get them to push the brand. Merchandising allowances can get retailers to display a new product in high-traffic areas of stores, while incentive programs or contests can encourage wholesale or retail store personnel to push a new brand.

Maintain Trade Support for Established Brands Trade promotions are often designed to maintain distribution and trade support for established brands. Clearly, this objective is akin to a repeat purchase objective that we saw with consumer sales promotion. Brands that are in the mature phase of their product life cycle are vulnerable to losing wholesale and/or retail distribution, particularly if they are not differentiated or face competition from new products. Trade deals induce wholesalers and retailers to continue to carry weaker products because the discounts increase their profit margins. Brands with a smaller market share often rely heavily on trade promotions, since they lack the funds required to differentiate themselves from competitors through media advertising. Even if a brand has a strong market position, trade promotions may be used as part of an overall marketing strategy.

Build Retail Inventories   Manufacturers often use trade promotions to build the inventory levels of retailers or other channel members, another form of repeat purchasing. There are several reasons why manufacturers want to load retailers with their products. First, wholesalers and retailers are more likely to push a product when they have high inventory levels rather than storing it in their warehouses or back rooms. Building channel members' inventories also ensures they will not run out of stock and thus miss sales opportunities.

Some manufacturers of seasonal products offer large promotional discounts so that retailers will stock up on their products before the peak selling season begins. This enables the manufacturer to smooth out seasonal fluctuations in its production schedule and pass on some of the inventory carrying costs to retailers or wholesalers. When retailers stock up on a product before the peak selling season, they often run special promotions and offer discounts to consumers to reduce excess inventories.

Encourage Retailers to Display Established Brands   Another objective of trade-oriented promotions is to encourage retailers to display and promote an established brand. This could be analogous to increased consumption as seen with consumer sales promotion objectives, since the retailer demonstrates increased commitment. Marketers recognize that many purchase decisions are made in the store and promotional displays are an excellent way of generating sales. An important goal is to obtain retail store displays of a product away from its regular shelf location. A typical supermarket has approximately 50 display areas at the ends of aisles, near checkout counters, and elsewhere. Marketers want to have their products displayed in these areas to increase the probability shoppers will come into contact with them. Even a single display can increase a brand's sales significantly during a promotion. Manufacturers often use multifaceted promotional programs to encourage retailers to promote their products at the retail level. For example, a manufacturer will combine its advertising and consumer sales promotions and offer them at the same time as the trade promotion.

TRADE SALES PROMOTION STRATEGY OPTIONS

Manufacturers use a variety of trade promotion tools as inducements for wholesalers and retailers. Next we examine some of the most often used types of trade promotions and some factors marketers must consider in using them. These promotions include trade allowances, point-of-purchase displays, cooperative advertising, contests and incentives, events, sales training programs, and trade shows.

Trade Allowances   Probably the most common trade promotion is some form of **trade allowance**, a discount or deal offered to retailers or wholesalers to encourage them to promote, display, or stock the manufacturer's products. Types of allowances offered to retailers include buying allowances, promotional or display allowances, and slotting allowances.

445

Buying Allowances   A buying allowance is a deal or discount offered to resellers in the form of a price reduction on merchandise ordered during a fixed period. These discounts are often in the form of an **off-invoice allowance**, which means a certain per-case amount or percentage is deducted from the invoice. A buying allowance can also take the form of *free goods*; the reseller gets extra cases with the purchase of specific amounts (for example, 1 free case with every 10 cases purchased).

Promotional (Display) Allowances   Manufacturers often give retailers allowances or discounts for performing certain promotional or merchandising activities in support of their brands. These merchandising allowances can be given for providing special displays away from the product's regular shelf position, running in-store promotional programs, or including the product in an ad. The manufacturer generally has guidelines or a contract specifying the activity to be performed to qualify for the promotional allowance. The allowance is usually a fixed amount per case or a percentage deduction from the list price for merchandise ordered during the promotional period.

Slotting Allowances   Retailers often demand a special allowance for agreeing to accept a new product. *Slotting allowances,* also called *stocking allowances, introductory allowances,* or *street money*, are fees retailers charge for providing a slot or position to accommodate the new product. Retailers justify these fees by pointing out the costs associated with taking on so many new products each year, such as redesigning store shelves, entering the product into their computers, finding warehouse space, and briefing store employees on the new product.[48] They also note they are assuming some risk, since so many new product introductions fail.

Slotting fees can range from a few hundred dollars per store to $50,000 or more for an entire retail chain. Manufacturers that want to get their products on the shelves nationally can face substantial slotting fees. Many marketers believe slotting allowances are not appropriate and say some 70 percent of these fees go directly to retailers' bottom lines. Retailers can continue charging slotting fees because of their power and the limited availability of shelf space in supermarkets relative to the large numbers of products introduced each year. Large manufacturers with popular brands are less likely to pay slotting fees than smaller companies that lack leverage in negotiating with retailers.

A recent study by Paul Bloom, Gregory Gundlach, and Joseph Cannon examined the views of manufacturers, wholesalers, and grocery retailers regarding the use of slotting fees. Their findings suggest that slotting fees shift the risk of new product introductions from retailers to manufacturers and help apportion the supply and demand of new products. They also found that slotting fees lead to higher retail prices, are applied in a discriminatory fashion, and place small marketers at a disadvantage.[49]

Strengths of Trade Allowances   Buying allowances are used for several reasons. They are easy to implement and are well accepted, and sometimes expected, by the trade. They are also an effective way to encourage resellers to buy the manufacturer's product, since they will want to take advantage of the discounts being offered during the allowance period. Manufacturers offer trade discounts expecting wholesalers and retailers to pass the price reduction through to consumers, resulting in greater purchases.

Promotional allowances provide brands that sell in retail stores the opportunity to have specialized displays to feature their product. Promotional allowances also permit a brand to obtain a favourable end-of aisle location or some other prominent place where high traffic occurs, thus ensuring greater exposure. Brands would like to reproduce the imagery from their commercials or any other advertising vehicle where brand recognition at the point of sale is required. Extensive and elaborate displays would also reinforce the positioning strategy of the brand and contribute to its overall brand development. Thus, retailers prefer to merchandise a brand that has a consistent and well thought out strategy so that they will not be stuck with inventory unsold due to a lack of in-store communication.

Limitations of Trade Allowances   Marketers give retailers these trade allowances so that the savings will be passed through to consumers in the form of lower prices, but companies such as Procter & Gamble claim that only 30 percent of trade promotion discounts actually reach consumers because 35 percent is lost in inefficiencies and another 35 percent is pocketed by retailers and wholesalers. Moreover, many marketers believe that the trade is taking advantage of their promotional deals and misusing promotional funds.

For example, retailers and wholesalers engage in a practice known as **forward buying**, where they stock up on a product at the lower deal or off-invoice price and resell it to consumers after the marketer's promotional period ends. Another common practice is **diverting**, where a retailer or wholesaler takes advantage of the promotional deal and then sells some of the product purchased at the low price to a store outside its area or to an intermediary that resells it to other stores.

In addition to not passing discounts on to consumers, forward buying and diverting create other problems for manufacturers. They lead to huge swings in demand that cause production scheduling problems and leave manufacturers and retailers always building toward or drawing down from a promotional surge. Marketers also worry that the system leads to frequent price specials, so consumers learn to make purchases on the basis of what's on sale rather than developing any loyalty to their brands.

The problems created by forward buying and diverting led Procter & Gamble, one of the country's most powerful consumer products marketers, to adopt **everyday low pricing (EDLP)**, which lowers the list price of over 60 percent of its product line by 10 to 25 percent while cutting promotional allowances to the trade. The price cuts leave the overall cost of the product to retailers about the same as it would have been with the various trade allowance discounts. Although some retailers reacted negatively to this strategy, P&G claimed success and continued with the plan internationally.[50]

Point-of-Purchase Displays   Point-of-purchase displays are an important promotional tool because they can help advertisers obtain more effective in-store merchandising of products. In one sense, a display acts as a "medium" since it is an important method of transmitting an advertising-like message when consumers are making a purchase decision. In fact, the Point of Purchase Advertising Institute (POPAI) estimates that approximately two-thirds of consumers' purchase decisions are made in the store; some impulse categories demonstrate an 80-percent rate.[51] We put medium in quotes because often many types of displays do not appear to be typical media; in fact, however, a display shares similar characteristics with place-based media (discussed in Chapter 13). A display is also viewed as a sales promotion since many of the messages include a sales promotion and most require the participation of retailers that necessitates a payment that is often recorded as a trade promotion expense in the budget. Figure 14-7 identifies many types of point-of-purchase displays; Exhibit 14-16 shows a point-of-purchase display for Wilson baseball gloves.

Exhibit 14-16   This award-winning point-of-purchase display plays an important role in the merchandising of Wilson.

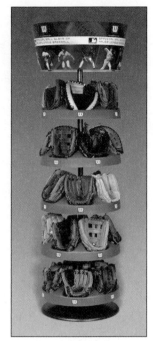

447

On-premise sign	Pre-assembled display	Display card	TV display
Window display	Display shipper	Shelf sign	LED board
Modular display rack	Wall display	Stand-up rack	End-of-aisle display

FIGURE   14–7

Types of point-of-purchase displays

Strengths of Point-of Purchase Displays It's easy to see why advertisers use point-of-purchase displays extensively. The main purpose is to reach the target audience while they are making the brand choice, so naturally a message or promotion attempting to influence a decider appears imperative. Indeed, key or deterministic benefits can be communicated just prior to purchase as these benefits may become salient only during the final choice decision. Recent innovations in point-of-purchase options—such as video screens at cash registers—attempt to bring the emotion of television commercials to the store environment so that consumers feel the same way just prior to purchasing the product. Since consumers are in the process of shopping, point-of-sale media have a tremendous opportunity for attracting the attention of the target audience. In general, consumers are seeking additional information or sensory experience as they consider the product selection. Coverage objectives also can be achieved by distributing point-of-purchase displays across the country through retail chains. For example, a brand could have displays in virtually all grocery stores at the same time with placement agreed among personnel at a few head offices. A key strength of point-of-sale display is that it is communicating to virtually all people who are considering purchasing in a particular category except those going direct through the Internet or catalogues. It may be difficult to suggest that point-of-purchase displays are universally involving. However, it appears reasonable to suggest that if the target audience has not avoided a certain part of the store and also paid attention to a display, then the potential is strong that the relevant messages will resonate such that a sufficient amount of consideration will be given. And finally, the absolute cost and CPM are generally reasonable compared to other media options.

Limitations of Point-of Purchase Displays Despite these strengths, point-of-purchase displays have limitations. One source of discontent for a consumer is that the shopping experience may be hindered by many promotional messages. Consumers have complete control over where they want to look in a store, how much time they prefer to stay in one area, and whether they want to look at any form of in-store communication. If an advertiser desires to be there, so does the competition. The clutter consumers feel while watching television or reading a magazine may be felt in the purchase environment. Processing of point-of-sale media requires a consumer's presence in the retail environment. So, except for circumstances where a consumer is entering an establishment repeatedly, the likelihood of an advertiser achieving sufficient frequency through this medium is quite limited. Finally, a marketer is reliant on the retailer, who may not install or set up the display correctly and also requires payment.

Cooperative Advertising

A trade promotion that has consumer effects like point-of-purchase display is **cooperative advertising**, where the cost of advertising is shared by more than one party. There are three types of cooperative advertising. Although the latter two are not exactly trade promotion, they involve the trade at times and are consistent with cooperative advertising.

The most common form of cooperative advertising is **vertical cooperative advertising**, in which a manufacturer pays for a portion of the advertising a retailer runs to promote the manufacturer's product and its availability in the retailer's place of business. Manufacturers generally share the cost of advertising run by the retailer on a percentage basis (usually 50/50) up to a certain limit.

The amount of cooperative advertising the manufacturer pays for is usually based on a percentage of dollar purchases. If a retailer purchases $100,000 of product from a manufacturer, it may receive 3 percent, or $3,000, in cooperative advertising money. Large retail chains often combine their co-op budgets across all of their stores, which gives them a larger sum to work with and more media options.

Cooperative advertising can take on several forms. Retailers may advertise a manufacturer's product in, say, a newspaper ad featuring a number of different products, and the individual manufacturers reimburse the retailer for their portion of the ad. Or the ad may be prepared by the manufacturer and placed in the local media by the retailer. Exhibit 14-17 shows a cooperative ad format that retailers can use by simply inserting their store name and location.

Cooperative advertising expenditure growth occurred recently as companies moved money out of national advertising to this trade avenue because they believe it achieves strong communication effects in local markets. There is also a trend toward more cooperative advertising programs initiated by retailers, which approach manufacturers with catalogues, promotional events they are planning, or advertising programs they have developed in conjunction with local media and ask them to pay a percentage of the cost. Manufacturers often go along with these requests, particularly when the retailer is large and powerful.[52]

Horizontal cooperative advertising is advertising sponsored in common by a group of retailers or other organizations providing products or services to the market. For example, automobile dealers who are located near one another often allocate some of their ad budgets to a cooperative advertising fund. **Ingredient-sponsored cooperative advertising** is supported by raw materials manufacturers; its objective is to help establish end products that include the company's materials and/or ingredients. Perhaps the best-known, and most successful, example of this type of cooperative advertising is the "Intel Inside" program, sponsored by Intel Corporation (Exhibit 14-18).

Contests and Incentives Manufacturers may develop contests or special incentive programs to stimulate greater selling effort and support from reseller management or sales personnel. Contests or incentive programs can be directed toward managers who work for a wholesaler or distributor as well as toward store or department managers at the retail level. Manufacturers often sponsor contests for resellers and use prizes such as trips or valuable merchandise as rewards for meeting sales quotas or other goals.

Contests or special incentives are often targeted at the sales personnel of the wholesalers, distributors/dealers, or retailers. These salespeople are an important link in the distribution chain because they are likely to be very familiar with the market, more frequently in touch with the customer (whether it be another reseller or the ultimate consumer), and more numerous than the manufacturer's own sales organization. Manufacturers often devise incentives or contests for these sales personnel. These programs may involve cash payments made directly to the retailer's or wholesaler's sales staff to encourage them to promote and sell a manufacturer's product. These payments are known as **push money** (pm) or *spiffs*. For example, an appliance manufacturer may pay a $25 spiff to retail sales personnel for selling a certain model or size. In sales contests, salespeople can win trips or valuable merchandise for meeting certain goals established by the manufacturer. As shown in Figure 14-8, these incentives may be tied to product sales, new account placements, or merchandising efforts.

Exhibit 14-17 This Bridgestone Golf ad is an example of vertical cooperative advertising.

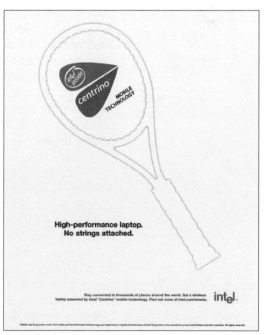

Exhibit 14-18 The "Intel Inside" cooperative advertising program has been extremely successful.

FIGURE 14-8

Three forms of
promotion targeted to
reseller salespeople

- **Product or Program Sales**
  Awards are tied to the selling of a product, for example:
    Selling a specified number of cases
    Selling a specified number of units
    Selling a specified number of promotional programs

- **New Account Placements**
  Awards are tied to:
    The number of new accounts opened
    The number of new accounts ordering a minimum number of cases or units
    Promotional programs placed in new accounts

- **Merchandising Efforts**
  Awards are tied to:
    Establishing promotional programs (such as theme programs)
    Placing display racks, counter displays, and the like

450

While contests and incentive programs can generate reseller support, they can also be a source of conflict between retail sales personnel and management. Some retailers want to maintain control over the selling activities of their sales staff. They don't want their salespeople devoting an undue amount of effort to trying to win a contest or receive incentives offered by the manufacturer. Nor do they want their people becoming too aggressive in pushing products that serve their own interests instead of the product or model that is best for the customer.

Events   Often, event marketing or event sponsorship programs directed to consumers are also linked to the trade as a way to foster good relationships among channel members and to enhance merchandising activities. For example, a tour of famous figure skaters—Kurt Browning, Elvis Stojko, Brian Orser, Isabelle Brasseur, Lloyd Eisler, Josée Chouinard, and Shae-Lynn Bourne—performed in many small Canadian cities with sponsorship from Procter & Gamble's Nice'n Easy brand of hair colour for women. People in many of these towns did not normally have the opportunity to see such shows, and P&G felt a need to more directly connect with markets that had strong consumer acceptance for this product. As part of the sponsorship, P&G ran various promotions with its retail distributors and customized the programs to meet their respective needs in addition to the usual contests and incentives. Zellers, Loblaws, and Shoppers Drug Mart hosted in-store autograph sessions. Walmart organized tickets for the Children's Miracle Network and skating seminars for local clubs.[53]

Sales Training Programs   Another form of manufacturer-sponsored promotional assistance is sales training programs for reseller personnel. Many products sold at the retail level require knowledgeable salespeople who provide consumers with information about the features and benefits of various brands and models (e.g., cosmetics, appliances, computers). Manufacturers provide sales training assistance to retail salespeople through training sessions so that retail personnel can increase their knowledge of a product or a product line. These training sessions present information and ideas on how to sell the manufacturer's product and may also include motivational components.

Manufacturers also provide sales training assistance to retail employees through their own salesforce. Sales reps educate retail personnel about their product line and provide selling tips and other relevant information. The reps can provide ongoing sales training as they come into contact with retail sales staff on a regular basis and can update them on changes in the product line. Sales reps often provide resellers sales manuals, product brochures, reference manuals, and other material. Many companies provide videos for retail sales personnel that include product information, product-use demonstrations, and ideas on how to sell their product. These selling aids can often be used to provide information to customers as well.

Trade Shows Another important promotional activity targeted to resellers is the **trade show**, a forum where manufacturers can display their products to current as well as prospective buyers. According to the Trade Show Bureau, nearly 100 million people attend the 5,000 trade shows each year in the United States and Canada, and the number of exhibiting companies exceeds 1.3 million. In many industries, trade shows are a major opportunity to display one's product lines and interact with customers. They are often attended by important management personnel from large retail chains as well as by distributors and other reseller representatives.

A number of promotional functions can be performed at trade shows, including demonstrating products, identifying new prospects, gathering customer and competitive information, and even writing orders for a product. Trade shows are particularly valuable for introducing new products, because resellers are often looking for new merchandise to stock. Shows can also be a source of valuable leads to follow up on through sales calls or direct marketing. The social aspect of trade shows is also important. Many companies use them to entertain key customers and to develop and maintain relationships with the trade. A recent academic study demonstrated that trade shows generate product awareness and interest and can have a measurable economic return.[54]

IMC PLANNING: STRATEGIC USE OF SALES PROMOTION

451

Rather than separate activities competing for a firm's promotional budget, advertising and sales promotion should be viewed as complementary tools. When properly planned and executed to work together, advertising and sales promotion can have a more complete and persuasive communication effect that is much greater than that of either promotional mix element alone. Proper coordination of advertising and sales promotion is essential for the firm to take advantage of the opportunities offered by each tool and get the most out of its promotional budget. Successful integration of advertising and sales promotion requires decisions concerning not only the allocation of the budget to each area but also the coordination of the ad and sales promotion themes, the timing of the various promotional activities, the brand equity implications of sales promotion, and the measuring of sales promotion effectiveness.

BUDGET ALLOCATION

While many companies are spending more money on sales promotion than on media advertising, it is difficult to say just what percentage of a firm's overall promotional budget should be allocated to advertising versus consumer and trade promotions. This allocation depends on a number of factors, including the specific promotional objectives of the campaign, the market and competitive situation, and the brand's stage in its life cycle.

Consider, for example, how allocation of the promotional budget may vary according to a brand's stage in the product life cycle. In the introductory stage, a large amount of the budget may be allocated to sales promotion techniques such as sampling and couponing to induce trial. In the growth stage, however, promotional dollars may be used primarily for advertising to stress brand differences and keep the brand name in consumers' minds.

When a brand moves to the maturity stage, advertising is primarily a reminder to keep consumers aware of the brand. Consumer sales promotions such as coupons, price-offs, premiums, and bonus packs may be needed periodically to maintain consumer loyalty, attract new users, and protect against competition. Trade promotions are needed to maintain shelf space and accommodate retailers' demands for better margins as well as encourage them to promote the brand. A study on the synergistic effects of advertising and promotion examined a brand in the mature phase of its life cycle and found that 80 percent of its sales at this stage were due to sales promotions. When a brand enters the decline stage of the product life cycle, most of the promotional support will probably be removed and expenditures on sales promotion are unlikely.

CREATIVE THEMES

To integrate the advertising and sales promotion programs successfully, the theme of consumer promotions should be tied in with the advertising and positioning theme wherever possible. Sales promotion tools should attempt to communicate a brand's unique attributes or benefits and to reinforce the sales message or campaign theme. In this way, the sales promotion effort contributes to the consumer franchise-building effort for the brand.

At the same time, media advertising and other IMC tools should be used to draw attention to a sales promotion program such as a contest, sweepstakes, or event or to a special promotion offer such as a price reduction or rebate program. An excellent example of this is the award-winning "Win 500 Flights" sweepstakes that was developed by MasterCard and its promotional agency, Armstrong Partnership. The sweepstakes was developed under the umbrella of MasterCard's "Priceless" campaign theme and thus was designed to deliver on the brand promise that MasterCard understands what matters most to consumers—in this case travelling for any reason at all. The primary objective of the integrated marketing campaign was to drive MasterCard use during the key summer travel season. Consumers using their MasterCard from July 1 to August 31 were automatically entered in the sweepstakes for a chance to win 500 airline tickets to anywhere that could be shared with family and friends. Media advertising including television, print, out-of-home, and online banner ads were used to promote the sweepstakes, along with an extensive public relations campaign. Exhibit 14-19 shows one of the print ads used to promote the "Win 500 Flights" sweepstakes.

Exhibit 14-19 MasterCard used media advertising to promote its sweepstakes.

MEDIA SUPPORT

Media support for a sales promotion program is critical and should be coordinated with the media program for the ad campaign. Media advertising is often needed to deliver such sales promotion materials as coupons, sweepstakes, contest entry forms, premium offers, and even samples. It is also needed to inform consumers of a promotional offer as well as to create awareness, interest, and favourable attitudes toward the brand.

By using advertising in conjunction with a sales promotion program, marketers can make consumers aware of the brand and its benefits and increase their responsiveness to the promotion. Consumers are more likely to redeem a coupon or respond to a price-off deal for a brand they are familiar with than one they know nothing about. Moreover, product trial created through sales promotion techniques such as sampling or high-value couponing is more likely to result in long-term use of the brand when accompanied by advertising.[55]

Using a promotion without prior or concurrent advertising can limit its effectiveness and risk damaging the brand's image. If consumers perceive the brand as being promotion dependent or of lesser quality, they are not likely to develop favourable attitudes and long-term loyalty. Conversely, the effectiveness of an ad can be enhanced by a coupon, a premium offer, or an opportunity to enter a sweepstakes or contest.

To coordinate their advertising and sales promotion programs more effectively, many companies are getting their sales promotion agencies more involved in the advertising and promotional planning process. Rather than hiring agencies to develop individual, nonfranchise-building types of promotions with short-term goals and tactics, many firms are having their sales promotion and advertising agencies work together to develop integrated promotional strategies and programs. Figure 14-9 shows how the role of sales promotion agencies is changing.

BRAND EQUITY

The increasing use of sales promotion in marketing programs is a fundamental change in strategic decisions about how companies market their products and services. The value of this increased emphasis on sales promotion has been questioned by several writers, particularly with regard to the lack of adequate planning and management of sales promotion programs.[56] These concerns lead some to believe that sales promotion can be overused by too much frequency, too valuable an economic offering, or offering too many promotions.

Overuse of sales promotion can be detrimental to a brand in several ways. A brand that is constantly promoted may lose perceived value. Consumers often end up purchasing a brand because it is on sale, they get a premium, or they have a coupon, rather than basing their decision on a favourable attitude they have developed. When the extra promotional incentive is not available, they switch to another brand. A recent study by Priya Raghubir and Kim Corfman examined whether price promotions affect pretrial evaluations of a brand.[57] They found that offering a price promotion is more likely to lower a brand's evaluation when the brand has not been promoted previously compared to when it has been frequently promoted; that price promotions are used as a source of information about a brand to a greater extent when the evaluator is not an expert but does have some product or industry

Traditional	New and Improved
1. Primarily used to develop short-term tactics or concepts.	1. Used to develop long- and short-term promotional strategies as well as tactics.
2. Hired/compensated on a project-by-project basis.	2. Contracted on annual retainer, following formal agency reviews.
3. Many promotion agencies used a mix—each one hired for best task and/or specialty.	3. One or two exclusive promotion agencies for each division or brand group.
4. One or two contact people from agency.	4. Full team or core group on the account.
5. Promotion agency never equal to ad agency—doesn't work up front in annual planning process.	5. Promotion agency works on equal basis with ad agency—sits at planning table up front.
6. Not directly accountable for results.	6. Very much accountable—goes through a rigorous evaluation process.

FIGURE 14-9

The shifting role of the promotion agency

knowledge; and that promotions are more likely to result in negative evaluations when they are uncommon in the industry. The findings from this study suggest that marketers must be careful in the use of price promotions as they may inhibit trial of a brand in certain situations.

Alan Sawyer and Peter Dickson have used the concept of *attribution theory* to examine how sales promotion may affect consumer attitude formation.[58] According to this theory, people acquire attitudes by observing their own behaviour and considering why they acted in a certain manner. Consumers who consistently purchase a brand because of a coupon or price-off deal may attribute their behaviour to the external promotional incentive rather than to a favourable attitude toward the brand. By contrast, when no external incentive is available, consumers are more likely to attribute their purchase behaviour to favourable underlying feelings about the brand.

Another potential problem with consumer-oriented promotions is that a **sales promotion trap** or spiral can result when several competitors use promotions extensively.[59] Often a firm begins using sales promotions to differentiate its product or service from the competition. If the promotion is successful and leads to a differential advantage (or even appears to do so), competitors may quickly copy it. When all the competitors are using sales promotions, this not only lowers profit margins for each firm but also makes it difficult for any one firm to hop off the promotional bandwagon.[60] This dilemma is shown in Figure 14-10. A number of industries have fallen into this promotional trap. In the cosmetics industry, gift-with-purchase and purchase-with-purchase promotional offers were developed as a tactic for getting buyers to sample new products. But they have become a common, and costly, way of doing business.[61]

Marketers must consider both the short-term impact of a promotion and its long-term effect on the brand. The ease with which competitors can develop a retaliatory promotion and the likelihood of their doing so should also be considered. Marketers must be careful not to damage the brand franchise with sales promotions or to get the firm involved in a promotional war that erodes the brand's profit margins and threatens its long-term existence. Marketers are often tempted to resort to sales promotions to deal with declining sales and other problems when they should examine such other aspects of the marketing program as channel relations, price, packaging, product quality, or advertising.

454

FIGURE 14–10

The sales promotion trap

| | **Our Firm** | |
All Other Firms	**Cut back promotions**	**Maintain promotions**
Cut back promotions	Higher profits for all	Market share goes to our firm
Maintain promotions	Market share goes to all other firms	Market share stays constant; profits stay low

FIGURE 14–11 Conceptual framework analysis

Sales Promotions		Communication Factors			
		Attention/ Impression	Communication/ Understanding	Persuasion	Purchase
	FSI coupons	✓✓	✓✓✓	✓✓	✓✓
	On-shelf coupons	✓✓✓	✓✓✓	✓✓✓	✓✓✓
	On-pack promotions	✓	✓	✓✓	✓
	Bonus packs	✓✓✓	✓✓	✓✓	✓✓
	EDLP	✓	✓✓	✓✓	✓

Promotional tendency to fulfill factor: ✓✓✓ = Strong; ✓✓ = Moderate; ✓ = Weak

MEASURING SALES PROMOTION EFFECTIVENESS

Elizabeth Gardener and Minakshi Trivedi offer a communications framework to allow managers to evaluate sales promotion strategies over a given set of specific criteria. Borrowing from advertising applications, and using four communications goals—attention, comprehension (understanding), persuasion, and purchase—the researchers show the impact of four promotional tools and everyday low pricing (EDLP) on each goal (Figure 14-11). In addition, the impact of everyday low pricing, Procter & Gamble's strategy for discontinuing the use of sales promotions, is also discussed in the article.[62]

The implication of this study is that sales promotions can be evaluated with a framework similar to the one we summarized in Chapter 4. Much of the advertising research methods and measures discussed in Chapter 8 can be used in the context of sales promotions. For example, pre- or post-surveys can be used to assess brand awareness or brand attitude (i.e., attribute or benefit beliefs) associated with the sales promotion. Furthermore, assessment of attention, cognitive, and emotional responses of the promotional offer can also be measured with the appropriate method. From a behavioural standpoint, measurement of switching and loyalty is assessed with scanner data. Other aspects of behaviour can be measured by counting the number of inquiries, coupon redemptions, and contest entries.

CHAPTER OBJECTIVES AND SUMMARY

1   To understand the role of sales promotion in a company's integrated marketing communications program and to examine why it is increasingly important.

Sales promotion is an inducement or incentive and an acceleration tool that is offered as value to any person or organization within the overall marketing system, such as consumers and any trade members like wholesalers and retailers. Marketers have been allocating more of their promotional dollars to sales promotion to influence purchasing behaviour. Some reasons for this shift include the strategic importance of sales promotions, reaching a specific target audience, increased promotional sensitivity, declining brand loyalty, brand proliferation, short-term focus of managers and increased accountability of promotional managers, and growing power of retailers and the competition.

2   To identify the objectives, strategy, and tactical components of a sales promotion plan.

The objectives of sales promotion are often stated in terms of brand behaviour such as trial, re-trial, and repeat purchases, or product category trial or re-trial. Sales promotions can be characterized as either franchise building or nonfranchise building. The former contribute to the long-term development and reinforcement of brand identity and image; the latter are designed to accelerate the purchase process and generate immediate increases in sales. Sales promotion can also be looked at in terms of their incentive characteristic that can be immediate or delayed. Tactical considerations for sales promotion include the amount of the incentive, the timing of the promotion in terms of schedule and duration, and the distribution of the sales promotion.

3   To examine the consumer and trade sales promotion strategy options and the factors to consider in using them.

Sales promotion techniques can be classified as either trade or consumer. A number of consumer sales promotion techniques were examined in this chapter, including sampling, couponing, premiums, contests and sweepstakes, refunds and rebates, bonus packs, price-off deals, frequency programs, and event marketing. The characteristics of these promotional tools were examined, along with their strengths and limitations. We also identified trade promotions including trade allowances, point-of-purchase displays, cooperative advertising, contests and incentives, events, sales training programs, and trade shows.

4   To understand key IMC issues related to sales-promotion decisions.

Advertising and sales promotion should not be viewed as separate activities but rather as complementary tools. When planned and executed properly, advertising and sales promotion can produce a synergistic effect that is greater than the response generated from either promotional mix element alone. To accomplish this, marketers must coordinate budgets, advertising and promotional themes, media scheduling and timing, and target audiences. Extensive sales promotion can result in diminished brand equity when marketers become too dependent on the use of sales promotion techniques and sacrifice long-term brand position and image for short-term sales increases. Many industries experience sales promotion traps when a number of competitors use promotions extensively and it becomes difficult for any single firm to cut back on promotion without risking a loss in sales. Overuse of sales promotion tools can lower profit margins and threaten the image and even the viability of a brand.

KEY TERMS

account-specific
    marketing, **423**
bonus packs, **440**
bounce-back coupon, **434**
consumer franchise-
    building (CFB)
    promotions, **425**
consumer sales
    promotion, **419**
contest, **437**
cooperative advertising, **448**
cross-ruff coupon, **434**
diverting, **447**
event marketing, **442**

event sponsorship, **443**
everyday low pricing
    (EDLP), **447**
forward buying, **447**
frequency programs, **441**
game, **437**
horizontal cooperative
    advertising, **449**
ingredient-sponsored
    cooperative
    advertising, **449**
instant coupon, **434**
in-store couponing, **434**
multiple methods **431**

nonfranchise-
    building (non-FB)
    promotions, **425**
off-invoice allowance, **446**
operant conditioning, **426**
premium, **435**
price-off deal, **440**
promotional pull
    strategy, **419**
promotional push
    strategy, **419**
push money, **449**
refund, **439**
sales promotion, **418**

sales promotion trap, **454**
sampling, **429**
schedules of
    reinforcement, **427**
self-liquidating
    premiums, **437**
shaping, **427**
sweepstakes, **437**
trade advertising, **419**
trade allowance, **445**
trade sales promotion, **419**
trade show, **451**
vertical cooperative
    advertising, **448**

DISCUSSION QUESTIONS

1. What are the differences between consumer and trade sales promotion? Discuss the role of each in a marketer's IMC program.

2. Discuss how sales promotion can be used as an acceleration tool to speed up the sales process and maximize sales volume.

3. Discuss the factors that have led to companies shifting more of their marketing budgets to sales promotion. Discuss the pros and cons of this reallocation of marketers' advertising and promotion budgets.

4. What are the differences between consumer franchise-building and nonfranchise-building promotions? Find

an example of a promotional offer you believe contributes to the equity of a brand and explain why.

5. Discuss how sales promotion progress can be integrated with a company's online strategy and how the Internet can be used as part of a company's sales promotion efforts.

6. What is meant by a sales promotion trap? Find an example of an industry where a promotional war is currently taking place. What are the options for a marketer involved in such a situation?

7. Canadian Tire and Pillsbury each used an aspect of their brand for a sales promotion for

the first time ever. Does this damage the brand at all in light of some concerns about sales promotion raised in this chapter? What other brand has a long-standing icon that could be used for a sales promotion?

8. Explain why it is important for sales promotion to contribute to brand equity. In what circumstances will brand equity enhancement not be a priority?

9. The number of coupons directed to consumers grew significantly in recent years. Discuss why this occurred based on issues of distribution, redemption, profitability, type of coupon, and expiration date.

PUBLIC RELATIONS

■ CHAPTER OBJECTIVES

1 To recognize the role of public relations in the promotional mix.

2 To know how to compile a public relations plan.

3 To understand how public relations is generated through media publicity.

4 To understand the strengths and limitations of media publicity.

5 To understand how public relations is managed through corporate advertising.

AWARD-WINNING SOCIALLY RESPONSIBLE MARKETING

The vast majority of Canadians believe it is important for companies to implement programs that improve society, social causes, or the environment, so it seems natural to see *Strategy* award recognition to the best corporate social responsibility efforts in various categories.

Cisco created a social networking site (onemillion actsofgreen.com) focused on environmental sustainability. The site fit the technology company's global "Human Network" campaign and allowed Canadians to post their "green" ideas such as riding a bike to work. Cisco partnered with the CBC for outreach to encourage participation by having the program featured on *Hockey Night in Canada* and *The Hour*. The sport vehicle continued with on-air mentions from NHL and NBA players. Extensive direct communication occurred with online video, newsletters, and e-mail. Many organizations jumped onboard by encouraging employee involvement. At the time of the award, the site had hit 1.3 million acts from 33,000 registered users, with 186,000 unique visitors having spent an average of 17 minutes. Positive publicity through numerous articles in media and comedians spoofing the initiative proved such remarkable acceptance that this Canadian idea went global.

Rona invented the Fab Shop program as part of its sponsorship of the 2010 Olympics and stayed true to its positioning of "Building Canada." All Olympics include an on-site carpentry workshop where various items are produced, and Rona ensured that at-risk youth received an employment opportunity at the workshop in Vancouver. Rona worked with multiple parties to implement an idea where employees eventually became certified carpenters. The home building retailer highlighted one successful participant in a TV spot to truly show that Rona owned the line "Building Canada's Games."

At the time of the award two groups of trainees had completed the program, with a third still to finish. Awareness of Rona ads improved—recall by 4 percent and recognition by 10 percent—and other communication measures showed improvement as well.

Mountain Equipment Co-op (MEC) and Canadian Parks and Wilderness Society joined together to increase the percentage of Canadian wilderness under government control. Compared to Alaska at 40 percent and Australia's Great Barrier Reef at 33 percent, only 10 percent of our land is protected. MEC developed a social networking site (thebigwild.org) to gather supporters and allow them to communicate. Though the external communication appeared somewhat limited, the site attracted 60,000 visitors in the first six months; 20 percent of visitors registered, and 50 percent of registrants set up active profiles. Usage of various social media tools on the site suggested tremendous success.

Sources: Carey Toane, "Introduction," *Strategy*, May 2009, p. 29; Carey Toane, "Overall Winner: Cisco's One Million Acts of Green," *Strategy*, May 2009, p. 30; Carey Toane, "Top Community Program: Rona's Olympic Fab Shop," *Strategy*, May 2009, p. 32; Carey Toane, "Top Eco Program: Mountain Equipment Co-op's Big Wild," *Strategy*, May 2009, p. 36.

QUESTION:

1. What is the key redeeming characteristic of each of these award winners?

Public relations, publicity, and corporate advertising all have promotional program elements that may be of great benefit to marketers. They are integral parts of the overall promotional effort that must be managed and coordinated with the other elements of the promotional mix. However, these three tools do not always have the specific objectives of product and service promotion, and often involve other methods of reaching their target audiences. Typically, these activities are designed more to change attitudes toward an organization or issue than to promote specific products or affect behaviours directly. Some aspects of these tools assist the marketing of products periodically for firms with a new view of the role of these tools. This chapter explores the domain of public relations, its related topic of publicity generated by news media, corporate advertising, the strengths and limitations of each, and the process by which they are planned and implemented.

PUBLIC RELATIONS

What is public relations? How does it differ from other elements of marketing communication discussed thus far? Perhaps a good starting point is to define what the term *public relations* has traditionally meant, to introduce its new role, and to compare it to publicity.

THE TRADITIONAL DEFINITION OF PR

A variety of books define **public relations**, but perhaps the most comprehensive definition is that offered by the *Public Relations News* (the weekly newsletter of the industry):

> the management function which evaluates public attitudes, identifies the policies and procedures of an organization with the public interest, and executes a program of action (and communication) to earn public understanding and acceptance.[1]

Public relations is indeed a management function. The term *management* should be used in its broadest sense; it is not limited to business managements but extends to other types of organizations, including nonprofit institutions. In this definition, public relations requires a series of stages, including:

- The determination and evaluation of public attitudes.
- The identification of policies and procedures of an organization with a public interest.
- The development and execution of a communications program designed to bring about public understanding and acceptance.

This definition reveals that public relations involves much more than activities designed to sell a product or service. The PR program may involve some of the promotional program elements previously discussed but use them in a different way. For example, press releases may be mailed to announce new products or changes in the organization, special events may be organized to create goodwill in the community, and advertising may be used to state the firm's position on an issue.

THE NEW ROLE OF PR

An increasing number of marketing-oriented companies have established new responsibilities for public relations. PR takes on a broader (and more marketing-oriented) perspective, designed to promote the organization as well as its products and/or services.

The way that companies and organizations use public relations might best be viewed as a continuum. On one end of the continuum is the use of PR from a traditional perspective. In this perspective public relations is viewed as a nonmarketing function whose primary responsibility is to maintain mutually beneficial relationships between the organization and its publics. In this case, customers or potential customers are only part of numerous publics—employees, investors, neighbours, special-interest groups, and so on. Marketing and public relations are separate departments; if external agencies are being used, they are separate agencies.

At the other end of the continuum, public relations is considered primarily a marketing communications function. All noncustomer relationships are perceived as necessary only in a marketing context.[2] In these organizations, public relations reports to marketing. Thus, for many companies the PR function is moving more and more toward a "new role," which is much closer to a marketing function than a traditional one. The new role of public relations envisions both strong marketing and strong PR departments. Rather than each department operating independently, the two work closely together, blending their talents to provide the best overall image of the firm and its product or service offerings. Toyota Canada took this one step further by recently merging its advertising and public relations departments.[3]

Writing in *Advertising Age,* William N. Curry notes that organizations must use caution in establishing this relationship because PR and marketing are not the same thing, and when one becomes dominant, the balance required to operate at maximum efficiency is lost.[4] He says losing sight of the objectives and functions of public relations in an attempt to achieve marketing goals may be detrimental in the long run. Others take an even stronger view that if public relations and marketing distinctions continue to blur, the independence of the PR function will be lost and it will become much less effective.[5] In fact, as noted by Cutlip, Center, and Broom, marketing and public relations are complementary functions, "with each making unique but complementary contributions to building and maintaining the many relationships essential for organizational survival and growth. To ignore one is to risk failure in the other."[6] This position is consistent with our perception that public relations is an important part of the IMC process, contributing in its own way but also in a way consistent with marketing goals.

PUBLICITY

Publicity refers to the generation of news about a person, product, service, or organization that appears in broadcast or print media, and now on the Internet. In some instances, it appears that publicity and public relations occur at the same time or in close proximity. For example, Maple Leaf Foods faced the absolute worst experience in its long history when consumers perished or became severely ill from eating its contaminated meat products. In response, CEO Michael McCain took a strong leadership role in reassuring Canadians. In doing so, Maple Leaf Foods used extensive public relations activities at varying stages of the identification and solution of the problem to address the situation such that consumers were exposed to both publicity (i.e., information coming from the media) and public relations (i.e., information coming from Maple Leaf Foods itself). Mr. McCain met with journalists on a regular basis at press conferences and acted as the main spokesperson in corporate advertising messages that communicated the actions the company had undertaken to prevent further problems. Maple Leaf's television messages reached many Canadians and became a key part of the Maple Leaf Foods channel on YouTube (see Exhibit 15-1).

In other instances, it seems that publicity is the end result or effect of the public relations effort. Because marketers like

Exhibit 15-1 Maple Leaf Food responds to a crisis.

Exhibit 15-2 A lack of branded flowers provided an advertising opportunity for FLO.

to have as much control as possible over the time and place where information is released, they often provide the news media with pre-packaged material. One way to do this is with the **video news release (VNR)**, a publicity piece produced by publicists so that stations can air it as a news story. Print media publications also receive material from brands with the intention of getting an editorial story written. A branded flower company, FLO, successfully used this idea by having gardening stories written in women's magazines that prominently featured the brand name and its imagery. The campaign included out-of-home, print, and radio media along with vibrant point-of-sale display carts, banners, and labels. Additional support occurred with signature information on delivery trucks along with the website address (flocanada.ca). By all accounts, the plan firmly planted FLO as a quality brand in the undifferentiated flower market (Exhibit 15-2).

Given the above scenarios, there are at least three complications for understanding public relations and publicity. First is the fact that publicity typically lasts for a short period of time. The communication effect of an article in the newspaper about a new product may last for a few weeks. Alternatively, public relations is a concerted program, with many exposures extending over a period of time that have a lasting communication effect. A second complication is that public relations is designed to provide positive information about a firm and is usually controlled by the firm or its agent. Publicity, on the other hand, is not always positive and is not always under the control of, or paid for by, the organization. One factor that distinguishes publicity from the other IMC program elements is its sheer power as a form of communication, which gives rise to the final complication. Some of the more powerful incidents of publicity are unplanned by the corporation, and the focus is on the successful and unsuccessful reactions of the organization to positive or negative events. IMC Perspective 15-1 identifies negative publicity some brands recently received and their public relations activities afterward.

PUBLIC RELATIONS PLAN

Public relations is an ongoing process requiring formalized policies and procedures for dealing with problems and opportunities. A public relations plan is required, as in the case for an advertising plan or a sales promotion plan. Moreover, the public relations plan needs to be integrated into the overall marketing communications program. A public relations plan can be structured like the other IMC tools we have discussed thus far. It starts with a situation analysis and includes decisions with respect to target audiences, behavioural objectives, communication objectives, strategy, and tactics. Once the plan is written, marketers should ask themselves some of the questions in Figure 15-1 to determine whether their public relations plan is complete. Given the broad nature of public relations, there are many options for each part of the plan that we now discuss.

Car Companies Repair Damage

With news reports of bankruptcy for GM and of recalls for Toyota, the negative publicity could not get much worse. How did these two automakers fare in their response to implement appropriate public relations and foster more positive publicity through the media? For the Canadian divisions of these two global giants the perception of the international difficulties appeared significant, since GM Canada did not declare bankruptcy and many Toyota models sold in Canada did not falter.

As GM in the U.S. moved toward the "Rebirth of the American Car" in its ads to restore its corporate reputation, the Canadian version of the ad made no reference to the bankruptcy and did not have American imagery (i.e., the U.S. flag). Instead, a message of reinvention that highlighted the strong brands and models emphasized a more positive and future-oriented direction. According to the advertising director for GM Canada, "The early feedback on the campaign is extremely positive. We are thinking it is coming across in the right tone and manner—acknowledging the situation we are in and moving forward in a positive direction."

Because of the recall Toyota halted sales of the affected models, and its North American advertising response to the negative publicity focused on its reputation for quality. The managing director for Toyota Canada released a four-minute online video that clarified the situation here. Since the problem of the gas pedal sticking affected only one Canadian model, the extensiveness of the problem was not as severe. However, Toyota Canada did offer a "voluntary safety improvement campaign," where it replaced the parts on models recalled only in the U.S. even though the parts on the Canadian versions were manufactured with different materials and would not cause problems. Toyota Canada executives also appeared on television news shows. Extensive communication occurred on the company's website, and Toyota directly contacted all owners to explain the solution and how it planned to resolve the problem.

The managing director confirmed, "I believe the whole process we're engaged in now is extremely important in terms of continuing to maintain customer confidence and support for our brand. Going forward, I hope people will understand that there has been an incredibly fast response to this issue because the company turned all of its resources to try to deal with the issue of the sticking acceleration pedal." And GM responded equally fast to Toyota's difficulty by extending its loyalty discount of $1,000 to Toyota owners who terminate their lease.

Shortly thereafter, Toyota Canada faced additional negative publicity as a recall and criminal investigation in the U.S. regarding faulty floor mats spilled over. Toyota Canada models featured different mats, so the problem of drivers losing control of the vehicle did not occur. Given the "global media environment," Toyota Canada continued to take extra precautions with voluntary measures to reassure customers that they owned safe vehicles.

Sources: Hollie Shaw, "GM Reinvented," *National Post,* June 26, 2009, p. FP10; Rupal Parekh and Michael Bush, "GM Lures Toyota Owners Hit by Recall," *Marketing Magazine,* January 28, 2010; "Toyota Launches Ad Blitz to Reassure Customers," *Marketing Magazine,* February 1, 2010; "*Marketing*'s Q&A: Toyota Boss Talks Brand Re-Building After Massive Recall," *Marketing Magazine,* February 2, 2010; "Toyota Canada Launches Campaign to Distance Itself from U.S. Problems," *Marketing Magazine,* February 23, 2010.

Questions

1. What is your assessment of how Toyota Canada handled the recall situation?

SITUATION ANALYSIS

Some elements of the situation analysis from the marketing plan or IMC plan are reviewed. An additional key piece of information is a current assessment of people's attitudes toward the firm, its product or service, or specific issues beyond those directed at a product or service. Why are firms so concerned with the public's attitudes? One reason is that these attitudes may affect sales of the firm's products. Second, no one wants to be perceived as a bad citizen. Corporations exist in communities where their employees work and live. Negative attitudes carry over to employee morale and may result in a less-than-optimal working environment internally and in the community.

FIGURE 15–1

Ten questions for evaluating public relations plans

1. Does the plan reflect a thorough understanding of the company's business situation?
2. Has the PR program made good use of research and background sources?
3. Does the plan include full analysis of recent editorial coverage?
4. Do the PR people fully understand the product's strengths and weaknesses?
5. Does the PR program describe several cogent, relevant conclusions from the research?
6. Are the program objectives specific and measurable?
7. Does the program clearly describe what the PR activity will be and how it will benefit the company?
8. Does the program describe how its results will be measured?
9. Do the research, objectives, activities, and evaluations tie together?
10. Has the PR department communicated with marketing throughout the development of the program?

Due to their concerns about public perceptions, many privately held corporations, publicly held companies, utilities, and the media survey public attitudes. The reasons for conducting this research are many:

- *It provides input into the planning process.* Once the firm has determined public attitudes, these become the starting point in the development of programs designed to maintain favourable positions or change unfavourable ones.
- *It serves as an early warning system.* Once a problem exists, it may require substantial time and money to correct. By conducting research, the firm may be able to identify potential problems and handle them effectively before they become serious issues.
- *It secures support internally.* If research shows that a problem or potential problem exists, it will be much easier for the public relations arm to gain the support it needs to address this problem.
- *It increases the effectiveness of the communication.* The better the firm understands a problem, the better it can design communications to deal with it.[7]

DETERMINE RELEVANT TARGET AUDIENCES

The target audiences for public relations efforts vary, and as we saw earlier each will have unique behavioural and communication objectives. These audiences may be internal or external to the firm. **Internal audiences** are connected to the organization in some way and include the employees of the firm, shareholders and investors, members of the local community, suppliers, and current customers. **External audiences** are those people who are not closely connected with the organization (e.g., the public at large). It may be necessary to communicate with both groups on an ongoing basis for a variety of reasons and it is likely that those who are not in the target audience will in fact receive the message, like we observe with product advertising.

Employees of the Firm Maintaining morale and showcasing the results of employees' efforts are often prime objectives of the public relations program. Organizational newsletters, notices on bulletin boards, paycheque envelope stuffers, direct mail, and annual reports are some of the methods used to communicate with these groups. Personal methods of communicating may be as formal as an established grievance committee or as informal as an office Christmas party. Other social events, such as corporate sports teams or picnics, are also used to create goodwill.

Shareholders and Investors   An annual report like the one in Exhibit 15-3 provides shareholders and investors with financial information regarding the firm. While this is one purpose, annual reports are also a communications channel for informing this audience about why the firm is or is not doing well, future plans, and other information that goes beyond numbers.

For example, McDonald's has successfully used annual reports to fend off potential PR problems. One year the report described McDonald's recycling efforts to alleviate consumers' concerns about waste; another report included a 12-page spread on food and nutrition. Other companies use similar strategies, employing shareholders' meetings, video presentations, and other forms of direct mail. Companies have used these approaches to generate additional investments, to bring more of their stocks "back home" (i.e., become more locally controlled and managed), and to produce funding to solve specific problems, as well as to promote goodwill.

Community Members   People who live and work in the community where a firm is located or doing business are often the target of public relations efforts. Such efforts may involve ads informing the community of activities that the organization is engaged in—for example, reducing air pollution, or cleaning up water supplies. Demonstrating to people that the organization is a good citizen with their welfare in mind may also be a reason for communicating to these groups. Exhibit 15-4 features an ad to draw community members' attention to an energy company's concern for the environment.

Exhibit 15-3   Annual reports serve a variety of purposes

465

Suppliers and Customers   An organization wishes to maintain *goodwill* with its suppliers as well as its consuming public. If consumers think a company is not socially conscious, they may take their loyalties elsewhere. Suppliers may be inclined to do the same. Indirect indications of the success of PR efforts may include more customer loyalty, less antagonism, or greater cooperation between the firm and its suppliers or consumers. Historically, most people viewed public relations as a communications strategy to maintain customers. Cisco, Novell, and Sony recently used public relations effectively to attract new Canadian customers in their distribution channels. Each firm experienced substantial sales increases with specific tools to reach particular audiences that had not perceived the benefits offered.[8] Exhibit 15-5 shows how one firm reaches out to its customers and offers professional seminars.

The Media   Perhaps one of the most critical external publics is the media, which determine what you will read in your newspapers or see on TV, and how this news will be presented. Because of the media's power, they should be informed of the firm's actions. Companies issue press releases and communicate through conferences, interviews, and

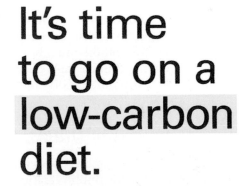

Exhibit 15-4   BP demonstrates concern for the public.

Exhibit 15-5 Syngenta provides information to customers.

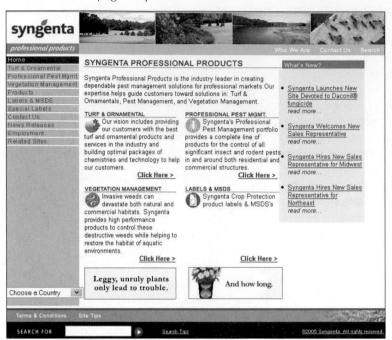

special events. The media are generally receptive to such information so long as it is handled professionally; reporters are always interested in good stories.

Educators A number of organizations provide educators with information regarding their activities. The Canadian Marketing Association and the Promotional Products Association of Canada, among others, keep educators informed in an attempt to generate goodwill as well as exposure for their causes. These groups and major corporations provide information regarding innovations, state-of-the-art research, and other items of interest.

Civic and Business Organizations Local nonprofit civic organizations also serve as gatekeepers of information. Companies' financial contributions to these groups, speeches at organization functions, and sponsorships are all designed to create goodwill. Corporate executives' service on the boards of nonprofit organizations also generates positive public relations.

Governments Public relations often attempts to influence government bodies directly at both local and national levels. Successful lobbying may mean immediate success for a product, while regulations detrimental to the firm may cost it millions.

Financial Groups In addition to current shareholders, potential shareholders and investors may be relevant target markets. Financial advisers, lending institutions, and others must be kept abreast of new developments as well as financial information, since they offer the potential for new sources of funding. Press releases and corporate reports play an important role in providing information to these publics.

BEHAVIOURAL OBJECTIVES

The framework for behavioural objectives discussed in Chapter 5 is readily applicable for public relations. Recall that behavioural objectives are trial purchase, repeat purchase, purchase-related action, or consumption. No matter what target audiences are selected in the prior step, an astute marketer will know that it is important to understand the type of behaviour desired as a result of the communication. The idea of a "purchase" seems incongruous for some public relations situations, so the marketer may have to view this as the target audience "buying into the idea" or some other specific behaviour in order to carefully define the objectives.

COMMUNICATION OBJECTIVES

The communication objectives of Chapter 5 can similarly be used for public relations. Communication objectives include category need, brand awareness, brand attitude, purchase intention, and purchase facilitation. Each of these can be the focus of the public relations plan, although slight modifications are needed. For example, the "brand" may in fact be the corporation itself or a new product that is talked about in a press release. In addition, the notion of a "category" has to be adjusted. Some target audiences want to be affiliated with "good corporate citizens" that are responsible to the community, the environment, or some other issue. Often, then, the "category" will be related to the particular topic or focus of the public relations message.

Awareness is critical for a brand and is important for the organization. Many organizations engage in various social causes because the exposure of their name will enhance the general public's recall and recognition at a later point in time.

We started off by highlighting the importance of existing attitudes of the target audiences. Clearly, then, the public relations plan should have a specific section that outlines the attitude change or modification desired. It should also illustrate the key motives addressed and what attributes or benefits of the firm or product the message should focus on.

STRATEGY

The strategy decisions for public relations are twofold, as we saw with advertising: message and media. The primary message decisions concern the degree to which the message will have a marketing or corporation focus, and the creative associated with the message. We will briefly describe some issues related to this decision in this section. Like advertising, there are a number of options to disseminate the message—news media, advertising media, and events. We will discuss these in more detail in the next major section.

Focus of the Message Thomas L. Harris has referred to public relations activities designed to support marketing objectives as **marketing public relations (MPR)** functions.[9] Marketing objectives that may be aided by public relations activities include raising awareness, informing and educating, gaining understanding, building trust, giving consumers a reason to buy, and generating consumer acceptance. These points are consistent with the behavioural and communications objective of our framework. Marketing public relations can be used effectively in the following ways:

- Building marketplace excitement before media advertising breaks.
- Creating news about a new advertising or promotional campaign.
- Introducing a product with little or no advertising.
- Influencing the influentials—that is, providing information to opinion leaders.
- Defending products at risk with a message of reassurance.
- Constructively promoting a product.

IKEA Canada's innovative activities successfully increase media exposure and exemplify marketing public relations. In fact, a key source of many zany ideas originated from its consumer surveys—shopping at IKEA was seen as a bit stressful for some couples so it hosted relationship seminars on Valentine's Day. IKEA's Relax event noted the fact that many Canadians found relaxing to be more naughty than sex. This prompted IKEA to issue instructions for making a restful home along with an "IKEA Adrenaline Index" on the website featuring humorous questions to assess people's stress levels. Store openings and catalogue launches both receive ambitious events to ensure the media cover the story. IKEA sees the value of these activities and invests heavily, with a 50 percent budget increase and each event receiving a $500,000 allotment.[10]

The historical role of public relations is one of communicating a favourable image of the corporation as a whole. The domain of this image, or reputation management, concerns every facet of how the organization interacts with its many social, economic, political, and charitable constituents, in addition to the general public locally, nationally, and internationally.

Given the two broad directions of the actual message, marketing versus corporate, an organization has to decide the relative degree of the message's impact over the course of a year or even longer, as public relations tends to have a lasting communication effect. Too much of a focus in either direction and the organization loses the opportunity to communicate fully.

Creative of the Message　We will discuss the many tools for public relations shortly; however, in deciding what message to communicate, the marketer is faced with the decision as to whether the creative strategy of advertising or other IMC tools should be adopted for public relations. On the one hand, there is the argument that all communications should have a common look and feel to them. To counter this, one could argue that unique target audiences with a specific message should have an appropriate associated creative.

Honda developed the "Blue Skies for Our Children" theme and directed messaging to children with TV, print, online banner, and POS ads, elevator wraps, and digital brochures as part of an Earth Day launch of Honda's longstanding commitment to the environment. Its website (hondabluesky.ca) contained three sections, Yesterday, Today, and Tomorrow, with the latter showing interviews of children to symbolically show what Honda plans to do beyond its current Insight vehicle.[11]

Delivery of the Message　In the course of defining public relations and publicity, and explaining the content of a public relations plan, we have generally described two mechanisms for the delivery of the message. Various news media outlets are available and the media have the choice of publishing or not publishing the materials that organizations submit for their consideration. Alternatively, organizations can turn to other options where they control the dissemination of the message through different types of corporate advertising opportunities in which the organization is responsible for the costs, much like regular product advertising we have covered thus far.

TACTICS

The choice of news media or corporate advertising dictates the types of tactics employed. When using news media, a marketer would need to know how to make a media presentation, whom to contact, how to issue a press release, and what to know about each medium addressed, including TV, radio, newspapers, magazines, and direct-response advertising. In addition, decisions have to be made regarding alternative media such as news conferences, seminars, events, and personal letters, along with insights on how to deal with government and other legislative bodies. Because this information is too extensive to include as a single chapter in this text, we suggest you peruse one of the many books available on this subject for additional insights. For corporate advertising, many considerations have been addressed in the advertising message chapters (Chapters 7 and 8) and the media chapters (Chapters 10 to 13).

PUBLIC RELATIONS EFFECTIVENESS

As with the other promotional program elements, it is important to evaluate the effectiveness of the public relations efforts. In addition to determining the contribution of this program element to attaining communications objectives, the evaluation tells management:

- How to assess what has been achieved through public relations activities;
- How to measure public relations achievements quantitatively;
- How to judge the quality of public relations achievements and activities.

As shown in Figure 15-2, a number of exposure measures may be used to assess the effects of PR programs through news media. Raymond Simon suggests additional managerial approaches and research methods for accomplishing this evaluation process, including the following[12]:

- *Management by objectives.* Executives and their managers act together to identify communication objectives to be attained and the responsibilities of the managers. These objectives are then used as a standard to measure accomplishments.
- *Matching objectives and results.* Specific communications objectives should be related to actions, activities, or media coverage.
- *Personal observation and reaction.* Personal observation and evaluation by one's superiors should occur at all levels of the organization.
- *Public opinion and surveys.* Research in the form of public opinion surveys may be used to gather data to evaluate program goal attainment.
- *Internal and external audits.* Internal audits involve evaluations by superiors or peers within the firm to determine the performance of the employee (or his or her programs). External audits are conducted by consultants or other parties outside the organization.

Others suggest comprehensive approaches like we have seen with advertising. Walter Lindenmann says three levels of measures are involved: (1) the basic, which measures the actual PR activities undertaken; (2) the intermediate, which measures audience reception and understanding of the message; and (3) the advanced, which measures the perceptual and behavioural changes that result.[13] We remind you that this approach is entirely consistent with the exposure, processing, and communications effects model described in Chapter 4. An application of these concepts is conveyed in Figure 15-3, which is a model developed by Ketchum Public Relations for tracking the effects of public relations. Some organizations may use a combination of measures, depending on their specific needs. For example, Hewlett-Packard uses impression counts, awareness and preference studies, in-house assessments, press clippings counts, and tracking studies.[14]

MEDIA PUBLICITY

In this section, we discuss how organizations can achieve public relations communication objectives through publicity generated through the media. We refer to this as *media publicity*; that is, publicity that the firm attempts to control by influencing the media to report an organization's story to the public. In this section we review different ways to reach the media and consider the strengths and limitations of this option. When considering the significance of this assessment, keep in mind that

---

A system for measuring the effectiveness of the public relations program has been developed by Lotus HAL. The criteria used in the evaluation process follow:

- Total number of impressions over time
- Total number of impressions on the target audience
- Total number of impressions on specific target audiences
- Percentage of positive articles over time
- Percentage of negative articles over time
- Ratio of positive to negative articles
- Percentage of positive/negative articles by subject
- Percentage of positive/negative articles by publication or reporter
- Percentage of positive/negative articles by target audience

FIGURE 15–2

Criteria for measuring the effectiveness of PR

FIGURE 15–3   The Ketchum Effectiveness Yardstick (KEY); a strategic approach to the measurement of public relations results

At Ketchum, we believe strongly that it is possible to measure public relations effectiveness. We also believe strongly that measuring public relations results can be done in a timely and cost-efficient manner.

Our strategic approach to public relations measurement involves a two-step process:

1. Setting in advance very specific and clearly defined public relations goals and objectives, and,

2. Pinpointing those levels of measurement that are crucial to the organization in determining to what extent those specific public relations goals and objectives have been met.

In the model, there are three levels for measuring PR effectiveness:

- Level #1—the Basic level for measuring public relations OUTPUTS. This measures the amount of exposure an organization receives in the media, the total number of placements, the total number of impressions, and/or the likelihood of having reached specific target audience groups. Research tools often used when conducting Level #1 measurement include content analysis or publicity tracking studies, secondary analysis, segmentation analysis, and basic public opinion polls.

- Level #2—the Intermediate level for measuring public relations OUTGROWTHS. Outgrowths measure whether or not target audience groups actually received the messages directed at them, paid attention to them, understood the messages, and retained those messages in any shape or form. Research tools often used when conducting Level #2 measurement include focus groups; in-depth interviews; telephone, mail, face-to-face, or mall intercept surveys; testing techniques; and recall studies.

- Level #3—the Advanced level for measuring public relations OUTCOMES. This measures opinion, attitude, and/or behaviour change to determine if there has been a shift in views and/or how people act when it comes to an organization, its products, or its services. Research tools often used when conducting Level #3 measurement include before-and-after studies, experimental and quasi-experimental research, ethnographic studies, communications audits, and multivariate analyses of data.

- The different levels of measuring public relations impact can be plotted on a yardstick in a hierarchial fashion. Here is a graphic displaying the KETCHUM EFFECTIVENESS YARDSTICK (KEY), which summarizes from left to right these levels of public relations measurement:

Level #1	Level #2	Level #3
Basic—Measuring	Intermediate—Measuring	Advanced—Measuring
OUTPUTS	OUTGROWTHS	OUTCOMES
Media placements	Receptivity	Opinion change
Impressions	Awareness	Attitude change
Targeted	Comprehension	Behaviour change
Audiences	Retention	

More detailed information about Ketchum's strategic approach to measuring public relations effectiveness may be obtained by contacting Graham Hueber, Vice President and Director of Research at Ketchum.

consumers receive the message through all the media discussed thus far, so the effects can be somewhat varied.

MEDIA OPTIONS

A number of media options are available for communicating with various target audiences, including press releases, press conferences, exclusives, interviews, and community involvement.

Press Releases   One of the most important publics is the press. To be used by the press, information must be factual, true, and of interest to the medium as well as to its audience. The source of the **press release** can do certain things to improve the likelihood that the "news" will be disseminated, such as ensuring that it reaches the right target audience, making it interesting, and making it easy to pass along.

The information in a press release won't be used unless it is of interest to the readers of the medium it is sent to. For example, financial institutions may issue press releases to business trade media and to the editor of the business section of a general-interest newspaper. Information on the release of a new rock album is of more interest to radio disc jockeys than to TV newscasters; sports news also has its interested audiences.

Press Conferences   We are all familiar with **press conferences** held by political figures. While used less often by organizations and corporations, this form of delivery can be very effective as scenes of corporate spokespeople will be viewed on television. The topic must be of major interest to a specific group before it is likely to gain coverage. Companies often call press conferences when they have significant news to announce, such as the introduction of a new product or advertising campaign. On a local level, community events, local developments, and the like may receive coverage. Sports teams use this tool to attract fan attention and interest when a new star is signed. The development of technology has allowed the delivery of press conferences to occur remotely where reporters receive the presentation and participate in the follow-up question and answer session.

A medium-sized Canadian company, Atelier America, used media relations to announce its innovative method of reproducing oil on canvas masterpieces. All major U.S. media organizations covered the press conference in New York City. The story circulated through all major U.S. cities and Europe and peaked with coverage on ABC's *World News Tonight* with Peter Jennings. Almost immediately, telephone orders emerged that could be tracked accurately with the media coverage. Previously weak Internet orders reversed overwhelmingly.[15]

Exclusives   Although most public relations efforts seek a variety of channels for distribution, an alternative strategy is to offer one particular medium exclusive rights to the story if that medium reaches a substantial number of people in the target audience. Offering an **exclusive** may enhance the likelihood of acceptance, and sometimes the media actually use these exclusives to promote themselves.

Interviews   Interviews occur on a variety of news or information shows. Usually, someone will raise specific questions and a spokesperson provided by the firm will answer them. Oftentimes, the president or owner will give interviews when there is important news about the firm.

Community Involvement   Many corporations enhance their public images through involvement in the local community that often is covered by the media. This involvement may take many forms, including membership in local organizations and contributions to or participation in community events. For example, Rogers employees work throughout many neighbourhoods on Halloween night to promote community safety. It also includes organizations participating in emergencies.

STRENGTHS OF MEDIA PUBLICITY

Credibility   Public relations communication through media publicity is not perceived in the same light as advertising. Consumers understand that most advertising is directly paid for by the sponsoring organization. Obviously some exceptions occur, such as public service announcements heard on the radio, for example. The

Exhibit 15-6 Edward Jones promotes its JD Power Award.

fact that the media are not being compensated for providing the information may lead receivers to consider the news more truthful and credible. For example, an article in newspapers or magazines discussing the virtues of ibuprofen may be perceived as much more credible than an ad for a particular brand of ibuprofen. And while some firms present the media with news releases or press kits and incur some cost, consumers generally perceive the media source to be reasonably trustworthy with its reporting expertise.

Endorsement Information from media publicity may be perceived as an endorsement by the media vehicle in which it appeared. Automotive awards presented in magazines such as *Motor Trend* carry clout with potential car buyers, and car companies often advertise their achievements. A number of auto manufacturers advertised their high customer satisfaction ratings reported by J. D. Power & Associates, an independent research firm specializing in satisfaction research. Exhibit 15-6 shows that it extends to other industries. Taken together, the credibility and endorsement effects constitute a significantly positive media image.

Cost In both absolute and relative terms, the cost of media publicity is very low, especially when the possible effects are considered. While a firm can employ public relations agencies and spend millions of dollars, for smaller companies this form of communication may be the most affordable alternative available. Many public relations programs require little more than the time and expenses associated with putting the program together and getting it distributed, yet they still accomplish their objectives.

Avoidance of Clutter Because they are typically perceived as news items, media publicity messages are not subject to the clutter of ads. A story regarding a new product introduction or breakthrough is treated as a news item and is likely to receive attention.

Reach Specific Audiences Because some products appeal only to small market segments, it is not feasible to engage in advertising and/or promotions to reach them. If the firm does not have the financial capabilities to engage in promotional expenditures, the best way to communicate to these groups is through media publicity.

Image Building Effective public relations helps to develop a positive image for the organization. The examples discussed thus far have indicated strong image-building capabilities with proactive public relations. News about a product may in itself serve as the subject of an ad. Exhibit 15-7 demonstrates how General Mills used favourable publicity from a variety of sources to promote the importance of whole grains in a healthy diet and promote the use of whole grains in its cereal.

Frequency Potential Still another reason for publicity's power is the frequency of exposure it generates. For example, a successful public relations activity could generate exposure in multiple media (i.e., broadcast, print, Internet).

LIMITATIONS OF MEDIA PUBLICITY

Weaker Brand or Corporate Identification Effect Perhaps the major disadvantage of media publicity is the potential for not completing the communications process. While these messages can break through the clutter of commercials, the receiver may not make the connection to the source. Many firms' PR efforts are never associated with their sponsors in the public mind.

Inconsistent Message Media publicity may also misfire through mismanagement and a lack of coordination with the marketing department. When marketing and PR departments operate independently, there is a danger of inconsistent communications or redundancies in efforts.

Timing Timing of media publicity is not always completely under the control of the marketer. Unless the press thinks the information has very high news value, the timing of the press release is entirely up to the media—if it gets released at all. Thus, the information may be released earlier than desired or too late to make an impact.

Accuracy The information contained in a press release sometimes gets lost in translation—that is, it is not always reported the way the provider wishes it to be. As a result, inaccurate information, omissions, or other errors may result.

Exhibit 15-7 General Mills capitalizes on positive publicity.

CORPORATE ADVERTISING

For purposes of this text we use the term **corporate advertising** for marketing communication implemented for the direct benefit of the corporation rather than its products or services. This method of delivery is selected over media publicity since the firm exerts complete control over the communication process rather than relying on the media acceptance for publicity to occur. Marketers seek attainment of corporate advertising's objectives by implementing image advertising, cause-related advertising, and sponsorship. More recently, the latter two have moved to the product level in communications strategy so the distinction has blurred. We cover these three topics in this section, but first we look at the purpose of corporate advertising, namely the management of corporate reputation.

CORPORATE REPUTATION

Earlier in this text we suggested that the communications framework described for advertising can be applied to other communication tools, and previously in this chapter we highlighted that it can be used for various public relations tools. This thought is echoed with a summary of the planning process used by executives of a leading public relations firm, Fleishman-Hillard Canada, in its efforts to assist clients with reputation management[16]:

- Gain a detailed, forward-looking understanding of corporate business objectives, competitive positioning, and the desired corporate reputation or corporate brand. This is best accomplished through interviews with senior corporate and business unit executives.
- Define the key audience, and derive audience-specific behavioural and attitudinal objectives and audience-specific corporate positioning attributes.
- Assess current perceptions of the company held by each key stakeholder group or audience on each of the key reputational attributes.
- Implement reputation-management programs throughout the corporation.
- Establish an ongoing plan to measure and monitor corporate reputation, and use reputation measurement to refine communications programs.

We highlight the issue of corporate reputation, a term that is used in public relations to convey the idea of corporate image, since a key outcome of corporate advertising is to influence overall perceptions of the organization. Clearly, the notion of corporate reputation is attitudinal, thus indicating that the general framework suggested in this text can be applied to all IMC tools. Furthermore, all methods described in Chapter 9 (e.g., focus groups, interviews, surveys) are readily applied for measuring corporate advertising effectiveness. Various news organizations publish polls that ask Canadians their opinion about corporations. Figure 15-4 summarizes the findings from the 2009 corporate reputation survey by *Marketing Magazine*/Leger, where 1,500 respondents rated the quality of products offered by the companies.[17]

Google's first entry into this annual poll saw the digital brand land in the number one spot. While Google did not engage in any corporate advertising per se, executives acknowledged that it received extensive positive media coverage while launching many new products over the past year. Tim Hortons clinched the top 5 once again; executives for Canada's famous coffee retailer believe organizational commitment to the Tim Hortons Children's Foundation, strong value proposition, and a great promotion in "Roll-Up-The-Rim" keep the brand at the forefront.[18]

A few years ago, Maple Leaf Foods stood in 15th place with a score of 72.[19] However, it placed 21st with a score of 66 just prior to the listeria crisis, and fell to a rating of 8 thereafter. After its public relations communications, which included an apology

FIGURE 15–4

The Top 10 companies in the 2009 *Marketing/* Leger Corporate Reputation Survey

2009 Rank	Company	Score*	% Good Opinion	% Bad Opinion	2008 Rank
1	Google	91	92.6	1.7	—
2	Sony	83	87.3	4.3	3
3	Tim Hortons	83	89.9	7.4	2
4	President's Choice	83	87.5	5.0	—
5	Shoppers Drug Mart	81	85.8	4.5	6
6	Staples Business Depot	79	84.8	5.5	1
7	Panasonic	79	82.4	3.1	5
8	Kraft	78	86.0	7.8	8
9	Toyota	77	80.2	2.9	10
10	Canadian Tire	77	86.1	9.1	4

*Final score is rounded up to the nearest whole number

Source: *Marketing Magazine*, May 18, 2009. Available online at http://www.marketingmag.ca/english/news/ marketer/article.jsp?content=20090522_102539_2388.

and a commitment to improvement, its reputation recovered to 33 in the ranking. Experts believe continued good faith shown by the company and advertising that demonstrates employee expertise in food production will allow one of Canada's own brands to fully recover.[20]

IMAGE ADVERTISING

One form of corporate advertising is devoted to promoting the organization's overall image. **Image advertising** may accomplish a number of objectives, including creating goodwill both internally and externally, creating a position for the company, specifying a firm's perspective on an issue, and generating resources, both human and financial.

Positioning   Firms, like products, need to establish a position in the marketplace, and corporate image advertising activities are one way to accomplish this objective. A well-positioned product is much more likely to achieve success than is one with a vague or no image. The same holds true of the firm. Companies with strong positive corporate images have an advantage over competitors that may be enhanced when they promote any aspect of their organization or products. As shown in Exhibit 15-8, ads are often designed to create an image of the firm in the public mind. The exhibit shows how Tyco is attempting to create an image of itself as a market leader and health care expert, not a toy company.

Coca-Cola used sponsorship of the 2010 Olympics to advertise its new position of being more environmentally responsible. Coke believed it needed to improve the brand's image and connected the new initiative with its long association with the Olympics as a sponsor since 1928. The first step featured the message of a new, more eco-friendly container, made in part from sugar cane and molasses. Other activities communicated include Coke's commitment to use less water during production and a drive toward ensuring greater recycling. For example, Coke established branded recycling depots (i.e., bins, signage), donated clothing made from recycled bottles, and had employees wear similar clothing.[21]

HBC also took its Olympic connection as an opportunity to energize its image with an emotional and nostalgic message by invoking the role of the company in Canada's history during a 60-second ad. With lots of imagery of people conquering or enjoying the Canadian outdoors during the winter, executives hoped viewers believed the company's history and Canada's history are forged together.[22]

Television Sponsorship   A firm often runs corporate image advertising on TV programs or specials. By associating itself with high-quality or educational programming, the firm hopes for a carryover effect that benefits its own image. IBM acted as the sponsor (i.e., sole advertiser) for a number of newscasts on CBC and Canwest that addressed seven major themes, such as "The Smart City" and "Building Sustainable Value." As part of IBM's "Smarter Planet" brand positioning, the effort encouraged the media partners to investigate the themes within their existing news programs. For instance, the CBC investigated the topics on *The Nature of Things* and *Mansbridge One on One,* while Canwest linked in its *Global News* and *Financial Post* properties.[23]

Recruitment   The promotional piece presented in Exhibit 15-9 is a good example of corporate image advertising designed to attract new employees. If you are a graduating senior considering a career in the new Internet economy, this ad, promoting a corporate image for the company, will interest you.

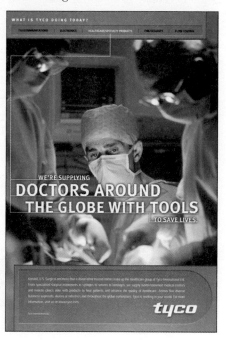

Exhibit 15-8   Tyco uses image advertising to avoid confusion.

Exhibit 15-9 Corporate image advertising designed to attract employees.

A passion for the business of **accounting**.

There is a select group of individuals in this world who have a passion for accounting. Yes, accounting. And that group happens to be the accountants at Grant Thornton. Our passion for what we do for our clients, our expertise and partner involvement, have been the hallmark of Grant Thornton LLP in the U.S. for 80 years. And you get the benefit of Grant Thornton International member firms in 112 countries. Give our CEO, Ed Nusbaum a call at 312.602.8005 or contact our partners at **www.GrantThornton.com**. Leave your business card information and we'll send you a free copy of the latest Grant Thornton Business Leaders Survey. It'll give you an enlightening look at emerging issues that could affect your company's growth and profits in uncertain times. Call us today. Find out how it feels to work with people who love what they do.

Grant Thornton
A passion for the business of accounting

The employment section of most major metropolitan newspapers is an excellent place to see this form of corporate image advertising at work. Notice the ads in these papers and consider the images the firms are presenting.

Financial Support Some corporate advertising is designed to generate investments in the corporation. By creating a more favourable image, the firm makes itself attractive to potential stock purchasers and investors. More investments mean more working capital, more monies for research and development, and so on. In this instance, corporate image advertising is almost attempting to make a sale; the product is the firm.

Advocacy Firms often take positions on certain social, business, or environmental issues that influence their image and the public's perception. Such **advocacy advertising** is concerned with propagating ideas and elucidating controversial social issues of public importance in a manner that supports the interests of the sponsor.[24]

While still portraying an image for the company or organization, advocacy advertising does so indirectly, by adopting a position on a particular issue rather than promoting the organization itself. The ads may be sponsored by a firm or by a trade association and are designed to tell readers how the firm operates or management's position on a particular issue.

The reason for the advertising can be due to the firm's negative publicity or the firm's inability to place an important message through public relations channels, or because the firm just wants to get certain ideas accepted or have society understand its concerns.

TO SOME, IT'S PRECIOUS METAL.

HABITAT FOR HUMANITY BELIEVES THAT EVERY FAMILY DESERVES A SAFE,

Habitat for Humanity

DECENT HOME. AT WHIRLPOOL, WE SHARE THAT BELIEF. WE DONATE A REFRIGERATOR AND RANGE TO EVERY HABITAT HOME. AND EVERY YEAR, THOUSANDS OF WHIRLPOOL EMPLOYEES VOLUNTEER THEIR OWN TIME TO HABITAT. TOGETHER WE CAN ELIMINATE POVERTY HOUSING, ONE FAMILY AT A TIME. JOIN US TODAY.

Whirlpool

WHIRLPOOL.COM

Exhibit 15-10 Whirlpool supports the effort for affordable housing.

CAUSE-RELATED ADVERTISING

An increasingly popular method of image building is **cause-related marketing**, in which companies link with charities or nonprofit organizations as contributing sponsors. The company benefits from favourable publicity, while the charity receives much-needed funds. Companies also take the opportunity to advertise their involvement (Exhibit 15-10). Spending on cause-related marketing has increased considerably in the past decade. Proponents of cause marketing say that association with a cause may differentiate one brand or store from another, increase consumer acceptance of price increases, generate favourable publicity, and even win over skeptical officials who may have an impact on the company.[25] IMC Perspective 15-2 describes Becel's longstanding association with the Heart & Stroke Foundation.

Cause marketing relationships can take a variety of forms. Making outright donations to a nonprofit cause, having companies volunteer for the cause, donating materials or supplies, running public service announcements, or even providing event refreshments are some ways companies get involved. However, like most marketing communication activities, brands look for unique opportunities to facilitate the communication process effectively and efficiently. For example, KitchenAid found a unique way to get involved with the Canadian Breast Cancer

Heart Matters with Becel

Unilever developed Becel in the 1950s after scientific research established the link between heart disease and saturated fats. With a brand mission to improve the heart health of its consumers, marketing communication emphasized this characteristic, especially in Canada. Although the style of the advertising has evolved since its debut in our country more than 30 years ago, Canadians readily accepted the heart-healthy message; Becel owns half of the margarine market. And the success of Canadian marketing of Becel allowed some of its messages and creative elements to be communicated internationally.

As part of its marketing communication, Becel has supported the Heart & Stroke Foundation for decades with a variety of activities. It started with partnership to produce a cookbook in 1988, which sold 500,000 copies. Another milestone that began in 1997 is the Becel Heart & Stroke Ride for Heart, a bikeathon where people ride on major highways to raise money for the Foundation. In 2010, 13,000 participated in the Toronto event and raised $3.2 million. Becel spent about 5 percent of its marketing budget publicizing the event.

More recently, Becel became the founding sponsor for the Foundation's Heart Truth campaign designed to inform the public that heart disease is the leading cause of death among women. The key message focused on how supporters could help save the life of a woman they loved (e.g., mother, sister, friend). Extensive TV ads and sponsorship of women's shows heightened awareness during February's health month. Print and PR communicated the Foundation's Red Dress Fashion Show featuring Canadian celebrities and benefit concerts. All communication drove women to the website (loveyourheart.ca) for resources and media content. After three months, awareness of heart disease increased from 13 percent to 23 percent, and Becel's sales grew by 9 percent.

Becel added a new element for 2010, a two-minute film entitled *The Heart* that premiered during the Academy Awards on March 7. The message of the film took a new direction by artistically encouraging women to think of themselves and their heart health. A montage of images of a woman's life as she cared for her family ensued as heartfelt music kept pace. Pre-broadcast publicity occurred with *eTalk Daily* host Tanya Kim and stories placed in print and broadcast media. Post-broadcast messaging with *eTalk* continued along with placement of the film in Cineplex movie theatres and online placements on YouTube, VideoEgg, CTV pre-roll, and Facebook. Becel filmed a separate execution for Quebec that aired during the French-language Cinematic awards show *Les Jutra*.

Sources: Katie Bailey, "Becel to Debut *The Heart* at Oscars," *Strategy*, February 25, 2010; Emily Wexler, "Becel's Margaret McKellar: Marketing *With Heart*," *Strategy*, June 2009, p. 18; Carey Toane, "Top Health Awareness Program: Becel's Heart Truth," *Strategy*, May 2009, p. 37; Natalia Williams, "All Heart—Becel," *Strategy*, August 1, 2006.

Question:

1. What would be the next step in Becel's support for the Heart & Stroke Foundation?

Foundation. Its consumers hosted at-home parties and their guests donated money instead of bringing the host a gift (e.g., bottle of wine, flowers). Hosts could browse "cookforthecure.ca" for recipes, and so on, and submit the funds that were raised.[26]

Virgin Mobile's Re*Generation program raised money for clothing for at-risk and homeless youth and donated the money to non-profit organizations like the Broadway Youth Resource Centre in Vancouver. One fundraising activity saw Lady Gaga perform at a Toronto nightclub, while another featured contributions for every Samsung Re*Generation phone sold.[27] For more than 10 years, Honda supported the non-profit organization ABC Canada Literacy Foundation by encouraging its dealers to get involved in activities on Family Literacy Day (January 27).[28] And Food Banks Canada received a total of $2.5 million from Kraft over the past few years in a matching donations program. Kraft recently extended the idea with a recipe program that included a partnership with American Greetings. For every recipe e-card forwarded to a friend Kraft donated $2, up to a maximum of $50,000.[29] All three of these activities are examples of a brand finding a creative way of supporting a non-profit organization responsible for helping others and receiving some marketing communication benefit in return.

Companies also become involved in causes that reinforce their brand or corporate mandate by establishing a worthy cause themselves rather than working with an existing organization as described above. For example, Indigo established the Love of Reading Foundation and donated $7.5 million to 70 schools in support of library renovations and book purchases. Recently, it teamed up with a publisher of children's books, where a portion of sales contributed to the fund. A 60-second public service announcement and other media advertised the initiative, which also helped the publisher expand its franchise to a new merchandising product line based on a book character.[30] An international chocolate brand established the Cadbury's Cocoa Partnership, a 10-year, $80 million program to help cocoa farmers in developing countries where its beans are purchased. The Canadian division launched a Bicycle Factory program to send 5,000 bicycles to Ghana, allowing the recipients to travel. Cadbury featured a host of advertising and promotional activities designed to get Canadian consumers involved. For example, a website allowed consumers to enter the code on its package to "buy" one part for a bike. Each bike requires 100 parts, so after 500,000 chocolate bars the collaboration achieved its mandate.[31]

This approach of creating a cause organization through the brand is a new trend in cause-related advertising, and Canadian Tire's effort combined both established and new approaches. To assist children without financial resources to participate in sports, Canadian Tire donated money to local chapters of groups like Big Brothers and Big Sisters and funded its own Jumpstart charitable program where it earmarked a portion of sales to the program and then donated the money. Advertising for the program consisted of TV spots, onsite radio remotes, and various digital tools.[32]

While companies receive public relations benefits from their association with causes, with 80 percent of consumers saying they have a more positive impression of companies that support a cause, they sometimes receive financial rewards as well.[33] An Ipsos Reid poll illustrated the current benefits that Canadians regard as socially responsible activities:

- 76 percent of Canadians think Canadian companies are doing a good job in terms of doing business in a socially responsible way (14 percent say companies are doing a "very good" job, while 62 percent say companies are doing a "somewhat good" job).
- 23 percent give Canadian companies poor marks (16 percent say companies are doing a "somewhat poor" job and 6 percent say they are doing a "very poor" job).
- 55 percent say they have consciously decided to buy a product or service from one company over another because they felt the company was a good corporate citizen, while 52 percent have consciously refused to buy a product or a service from a company not conducting business in a socially responsible way.
- While Canadians want to see companies operate in a socially responsible manner, they do question the motives of companies that undertake socially responsible activities (68 percent think companies are motivated by their bottom line, while 29 percent say companies care about being socially responsible).
- However, Canadians like good news (68 percent say that a corporate social responsibility news story about a company being singled out for a very positive action is more likely to grab their attention than a story about a company being highlighted for a very negative action).
- Women are more likely than men to want to read about a company's positive action (71 percent versus 64 percent).[34]

At the same time, not all cause marketing is a guarantee of success. Cause marketing requires more than just associating with a social issue, and it takes time and effort. Companies can get into trouble by misleading consumers about their relationships. It is also possible to waste money by hooking up with a cause that offers little connection or relation to their brand. Firms need to avoid picking the wrong cause—finding that their customers and potential customers either have little interest in or don't like the cause. Finally, the results of cause-marketing efforts can sometimes be hard to quantify.

SPONSORSHIP

Corporate sponsorship of different events plays a major role in the public relations plans of many organizations. While some companies sponsor specific events with primarily traditional public relations objectives in mind, a separate and more marketing-oriented use of sponsorships is also on the increase. And some event sponsorship occurs for product-level brands compared to corporate brands. In either case, the decisions involved are comparable—we turn to some of these in this section, beginning with a brief overview.

Overview   Activities where a fee is paid in exchange for various marketing communication benefits for an organization are known as **event sponsorship**. This type of public relations can take on a variety of forms, as shown in Figure 15-5. An organization agrees to sponsor an event since it provides exposure to a selective audience, and potentially a larger audience with television coverage or photos or video posted on the Internet. A further benefit includes the ability to have the organization associated with the event, thus providing additional development of the corporate or product brand. In the course of developing this section we will highlight others.

In response to the growth of sponsorship, industry members recently established the Sponsorship Marketing Council of Canada to demonstrate sponsorship as a valuable communication tool by establishing practices and measurement tools to validate the investment.[35] Other activities include establishing an awards program recognizing the best sponsorship in four categories: arts and entertainment, sports, causes, and special interest. Kraft Hockeyville recently won gold in the sports category, gold for continued success, and Best of Show for 2009 (following up its 2007 Best of Show recognition). The program launched in 2006 as a grassroots competition to find the place where hockey lives in Canada, bringing together Kraft Canada, the CBC, the NHL, and the NHL Players' Association. To enter, people submitted a 500-word essay plus photos to support their community. Kraft Hockeyville 2009 attracted 7,183 entries and 481 community profiles. The final ballot beat all previous records, with 9.3 million votes cast. As title sponsor, Kraft attempted to increase brand loyalty, showcase community responsibility, and create retail excitement that drives sales. A number of key metrics support achievement. Consumers completely

	1998	2002	2006	2009
Sports	$4,556	$6,430	$8,935	$11,280
Entertainment tours/attractions	680	865	1,377	1,640
Festivals, fairs, events	612	834	609	756
Causes	544	828	1,303	1,510
Arts	408	610	743	820
Associations/membership organizations			404	496
Total	$6,800	$9,567	$13,371	$16,510

Source: Adapted from *Promo*, June 1, 2002; *Promo Xtra*, January 24, 2007; *Promo*, January 28, 2010.

FIGURE   15–5

Annual sponsorship spending in North America by property ($ millions)

accepted the retail-level initiatives; consumption grew by 4.4 percent for 2009. Each year, Kraft Hockeyville became the number one CBC show website. PR coverage attained 330 million media impressions—close to triple the previous record.[36]

A high-profile Canadian festival where many international stars make an appearance is the Toronto Film Festival, which has celebrated its 34th anniversary. Like many star-studded affairs, a pre-eminent occasion is the walk down the red carpet taken by the noted celebrities—the perfect location for sponsorship. And so thought the executives at Holt Renfrew; the upscale retailer had its logo imprinted at close intervals along the path toward the gala theatre entrance. Holt Renfrew began its sponsorship of the red carpet in 2004, and its executives appear pleased with the relationship: "In many red carpet pictures you can see the Holt Renfrew logo," and "It's a nice fit, the worlds of fashion and film coming together." The fashion leader spends its marketing dollars on traditional and digital media, catalogues, fashion shows, glitzy parties, and eye-catching store windows, yet the film sponsorship has represented only one percent of its marketing budget and produces the strongest impact.[37]

As expected, a number of specific decisions are associated with event sponsorship including the types of sponsorship, target audience fit, target audience exposure, and brand positioning. We explore these important sponsorship decisions in the context of sports sponsorship for illustrative purposes because it represents the dominant expenditure—more than $16 billion in North America in 2009. Each idea can be readily adapted to other events, for example entertainment or arts festivals. Sports sponsorship can be successful with clear objectives, a good positioning strategy, adequate budget, the appropriate sporting vehicle, and key tactical implementation, characteristics we have seen in other types of promotional plans.[38]

Types of Sponsorship Sport sponsorship involves endorsement deals or sponsoring a team, league, event, athlete, or organization, along with stadium naming or broadcast rights. The goal is to associate a brand with its target audience's entertainment consumption or lifestyle, thus enriching the overall brand experience. One thought on the topic suggested three levels of sponsorship.[39] *Proprietary* has little or no external sanctioning or partnerships; Nike's RunTO featured a running event throughout the entire city of Toronto. *Affiliated advertising* utilizes the assets of a sponsorship or association. For example, the Esso Legends of Hockey brings together the Hockey Hall of Fame, NHL, NHL Players' Association, and NHL Alumni. *Programming* lives within a larger event or sponsorship, for example Powerade's "Thirst for Soccer" that visits youth soccer tournaments across Canada.

Working with an athletic sponsorship is similar to sponsorship with a team, but with a few unique issues. Foremost is ensuring a fit between the athlete and the company or brand. Exposure arrangements regarding an athlete's identity (i.e., name, image, and likeness), amount and type of service, and corporate logo placement need to be established. Rounding out the arrangement is the strategic communication use of an athlete in advertising, public relations, or sales promotion and conditions for the sponsor to protect its investment (e.g., an ethics clause).[40]

Brand Positioning Many companies are attracted to event sponsorships because effective IMC programs can be built around them and promotional tie-ins can be made to local, regional, national, and even international markets. Companies are finding event sponsorships an excellent platform from which to build equity and gain affinity with target audiences as well as a good public relations tool for the corporation in general.

While the overall market position of the brand may be well established throughout the marketing plan, sport sponsorship permits a brand positioning strategy to a unique and well-defined target audience that the brand has specific communication and behavioural objectives. For example, a sports sponsorship could enable a brand to establish awareness and new brand associations as it reaches new customers to develop trial purchases.

However, brands should be prepared to spend accordingly to achieve their objectives, as the initial sponsorship investment requires additional advertising or sales promotion expenditures. As the foundation is critical, brands should ensure that the rights and benefits of the sports sponsorship allow the brand to achieve its objectives and positioning. For example, sponsorship in hockey can have limits without the clearance from various stakeholders (e.g., NHL, NHL Players' Association, and Hockey Canada). Finally, picking the right sponsorship that has the right profile at the right time and a partner that is receptive to making the deal work is paramount for successful implementation.

Target Audience Fit   Most companies focus their marketing efforts on specific market segments and are always looking for ways to reach these target audiences. Many marketers are finding that event sponsorships are very effective ways to reach specific target audiences based on geographic, demographic, psychographic, and ethnic characteristics. For example, golf tournaments are a popular event for sponsorship by marketers of luxury automobiles and other upscale products and services. The golf audience is affluent and highly educated, and marketers believe that golfers care passionately about the game, leading them to form emotional attachments to brands they associate with the sport. Alternatively, brands will look to many similar venues to reach a consistent target audience that fits. For example, BMO Financial supports Figure Skating Canada, Equestrian at Spruce Meadows in Calgary, and the Canadian Opera Company.[41] The Telus World Ski and Snowboard Festival allows the national telecommunications firm to reach its youth market with its sponsorship investment.[42]

Target Audience Exposure   Many marketers are attracted to event sponsorship because it gets their company and/or product names in front of consumers. By choosing the right events for sponsorship, companies can get visibility among their target market. Canadian amateur athletes and semi-pro sports organizations have been working with marketers to develop sponsorships that benefit both parties. Alpine Canada Alpin (ACA), the governing body for Canadian alpine ski racing, generated $1.9 million in sponsorship deals representing 25 percent of its annual budget compared to 16 percent from the public sector for the 2000–01 season. It signed deals with Wrigley Canada, General Motors, and Fido cellphones. The key success factor in landing these deals is the fact that World Cup ski races had TV audiences of more than 30 million.[43]

Brand Activities   Most sponsored properties include guidelines on what level of marketing the brand's support permits in terms of the number and size of signs, for example. Some sponsored properties allow extensive brand activation to occur, while others place significant limitations on the type of brand activities permitted during the exposure. For example, Levi Strauss & Co. was a secondary sponsor of Crankworx, a mountain bike festival in Whistler, B.C. To gather momentum, Levi's staged mock photo shoots where staff acted as "model scouts" and approached festival attendees in the brand's 17–24 target to pose for mock ads. The posters were put up on-site, and event attendees were encouraged to vote for their favourite "model" via text messages or ballots (two winners later appeared in a real Levi's ad published in *Exclaim!* magazine). Levi's did the same thing at a Virgin Festival in Toronto with a "Best Impressions" competition. Music festival goers voted for their favourite Levi's "model," and the winner appeared in the November issue of *Exclaim!* In contrast, events like the Calgary Stampede and the Rogers Cup tennis tournament place companies in strict sponsorship categories based on their investment level and take steps to ensure that each sponsor receives a level of exposure consistent with their investment. For example, sampling is closely controlled because this method often attracts greater attention.[44]

Measuring Sponsorship Effectiveness   As we have seen with other communication tools, sponsorship planning follows a general framework of performing a situation analysis with relevant consumer and competitive research, establishing objectives (i.e., marketing, communication, behavioural), developing strategy and tactics, and outlining the criteria and measures of effectiveness to assess whether objectives have been met. A major issue that faces the event sponsorship industry is incomplete research. As marketers become interested in targeted audiences, they will want more evidence that event sponsorship is effective and a good return on their investment.

Despite this concern, the growth in sponsorship investments has led to a corresponding emergence of measuring the effectiveness of sponsorships. Essentially, measures of sponsorship effectiveness can be categorized as exposure-based methods or tracking measures[45]:

- *Exposure methods.* Exposure methods can be classified as those that monitor the quantity and nature of the media coverage obtained for the sponsored event and those that estimate direct and indirect audiences. These measures have been commonly employed by corporations, but heavily criticized by scholars. Pham argues that media coverage is not the objective of sponsorships and should not be considered a measure of effectiveness. He argues that the measures provide no indication of perceptions, attitude change, or behavioural change and should therefore not be considered as measures of effectiveness.[46]
- *Tracking measures.* These measures are designed to evaluate the awareness, familiarity, and preferences engendered by sponsorship based on surveys. A number of empirical studies have measured recall of sponsors' ads, awareness of and attitudes toward the sponsors and their products, and image effect including brand and corporate images. Moreover, the tracking measures could be done for current customers, potential customers, and the general public before, during, and after the event to get a complete picture of the sponsorship.[47]

While each of these measures has its advantages and disadvantages, we suggest using several in assessing the impact of sponsorships. In fact, the selection of appropriate measures is so critical that some recommend they may have to be customized for each sponsorship activity.[48] One innovative and comprehensive measurement system is SponsorScope, developed by Fusion Alliance Marketing, a division of Cossette Communication Group. Their tool examines items like the media used, media and sponsor visibility, and usage of sales promotion tools, along with items like the number of event sponsors, the event's reputation, category exclusivity, leveraging potential for employees, and the event's communication plan.[49]

IMC PLANNING: STRATEGIC USE OF PR

As discussed in this chapter, public relations activities often communicate infrequently to a broader population and attempt to persuade the target audience on more global or abstract attributes of the company and its brand. With this in mind, public relations generally does not influence the decision-making process because the activities are not sequenced to match the purchase and consumption behaviour of consumers, as they are in advertising or sales promotion. For that matter, it is unlikely that a single public relations activity would coincide exactly with decision making for any other stakeholder that might be a target audience for the organization.

For example, the CIBC is the title sponsor for Run for the Cure, an annual event to raise funds for the Canadian Breast Cancer Foundation. The late-September event features considerable lead-up media exposure funded by CIBC and other sponsors; however, this timing does not necessarily fit for all customers and non-customers of CIBC since financial products and services are purchased year-round. Presumably, CIBC expects this sponsorship activity to have a broad, long-term benefit associated with the corporate brand that consumers and all other internal and external stakeholders would retain during the year and until the event returns.

Advertising and PR often reinforce one another. The launch of a new advertising campaign is helped with additional exposure through news media in the form of announcements in the newspaper, clips shown on television, or information and complete ads posted on the Internet. Sometimes, brands take advantage of favourable publicity and make note of this in their advertising or make it a central theme in a particular message. Alternatively, if the corporation involved itself with sponsorship of arts, a cause, or sports, the advertising can make reference of this for regular brand messages beyond advertising messages dedicated to communicating information about the sponsorship. For these reasons, it is no wonder we have seen extensive proliferation of various public relations expenditures in recent years.

PR and sales promotion often work hand-in-hand, and Tabi International provides a good example of this. Each season Tabi, like most fashion retailers or clothes designers, provides press releases to fashion, lifestyle, and marketing/business media with the intention of obtaining exposure through news articles in magazines, newspapers, or the Internet. To spark the presentation, the upscale retailer established the Tabi Face of 40+ contest as the central theme to launch its autumn fashions. The contest encouraged women over 40 to enter and be selected to model in a photo shoot published in the 40th anniversary edition of *Homemakers* magazine, along with *Canadian Living* magazine.[50]

Internet sites for corporations are a primary vehicle for communicating basic facts, especially the corporation's social and community interests, and for disseminating some common public relations tools. For example, firms regularly put copies of their press releases on their sites and also include video clips of various corporate activities like speeches or annual shareholder meetings. The ability of virtually anyone to obtain basic company information through the Internet makes it a desirable tool for firms to project their best image with timely content to ensure strong reputation management. However, the darker side of the Internet appears in the form of unwarranted negative publicity for many brands. Even the average person may try to sabotage organizations that have appropriate corporate missions, sell legitimate products, and follow the laws of the land.

483

CHAPTER OBJECTIVES AND SUMMARY

1 To recognize the role of public relations in the promotional mix.

This chapter examined the role of public relations. Public relations is typically accomplished through publicity generated through news media and corporate advertising. We noted that these areas are all significant to the marketing communication effort and are usually considered differently from the other promotional elements. The reasons for this special treatment stem from the facts that (1) they are typically not designed to promote a specific product or service, and (2) in many instances it is harder for the consumer to make the connection between the communication and its intent.

In many firms, PR is a separate department operating independently of marketing; in others, it is considered a support system. Many large firms have an external public relations agency, just as they have an outside ad agency. Thus, public relations is useful with its traditional responsibilities; however, increasingly more marketing-oriented firms use this tool at the brand or product level for enhanced communication efforts.

2 To know how to compile a public relations plan.

Like all aspects of IMC, a public relations plan begins with a situation analysis, in particular an evaluation of public attitudes to the firm through a survey methodology in order to gauge an accurate reading. Influencing the right audience is another critical element as the organization must decide to communicate with groups such as employees, investors, community, suppliers, customers, media, educators, and any other relevant societal stakeholder. Objectives need to be set, consistent with the behaviour and communication ideas suggested earlier in this book.

An appeal of sorts is also established for public relations much like we saw in advertising examples; a clear message with a focus that often has creative elements. The delivery of the message can occur through some of the established media channels discussed already, and through the media to generate publicity. Finally, tactical considerations and effective measures need to be established for full implementation.

3 To understand how public relations is generated through media publicity.

News about a person, product, service, or organization that appears in broadcast or print media or on the Internet is known as publicity. It can occur through a story a journalist decides to write. In this case, publicity can be positive or negative and the firm is in more of a reactionary mode; preparedness for this scenario is certainly possible and recommended. Alternatively, a firm can seek media coverage for important news by communicating with the media through many tools with the planned intention of receiving positive stories. Firms use press releases, press conferences, exclusives, interviews, and community involvement, and may use other creative means to persuade journalists to cover them.

4 To understand the strengths and limitations of media publicity.

Messages about a company that consumers receive through the media have many strengths, including credibility, endorsement, low cost, less clutter, ability to reach specific audiences, image building, and frequency potential. Limitations include whether the brand is actually stronger, and a lack of control leading to an inconsistent message, poor timing, and possible inaccuracy.

5 To understand how public relations is managed through corporate advertising.

Corporate advertising involves the reputation management of the firm through advertising and promotional activities designed to put the firm in the most favourable public position. Corporate advertising is a general term to cover all marketing communication that usually includes image advertising, cause-related advertising, and sponsorship. Corporate advertising can be controversial because sometimes the source of the message is top management, who may have their own intentions and motivations. This element of communication definitely has its place in the promotional mix but should follow the planning suggestions outlined in this chapter in order to be effective.

KEY TERMS

advocacy advertising, *476*

cause-related marketing, *476*

corporate advertising, *473*

event sponsorships, *479*

exclusive, *471*

external audiences, *464*

image advertising, *475*

internal audiences, *464*

marketing public relations (MRP), *467*

press conference, *471*

press release, *471*

public relations, *460*

publicity, *461*

video news release (VNR), *462*

DISCUSSION QUESTIONS

1. Some marketers and PR people believe public relations should replace advertising as the primary tool for introducing new products. Explain why this would or would not be a good plan.

2. Explain why traditional public relations practitioners might be unhappy with the organization's use of MPRs. Take a position as to whether this criticism is justified.

3. List and describe the advantages and disadvantages of the use of public relations in an IMC program. Provide an example of an appropriate use of public relations in this mix.

4. What is a video news release (VNR)? Provide an example of a situation in which a company might employ the use of a VNR. Discuss some of the ethical implications (if any) in using this tool.

5. Many companies are now taking the position that their charitable contributions should lead to something in return—for example, sales or increased visibility. Discuss the pros and cons of this position.

6. Many companies are now trying to generate as much free publicity as they can. Cite some examples of this, and discuss the advantages and disadvantages associated with this strategy.

7. Describe some criteria used by firms to measure public relations effectiveness.

DIRECT MARKETING

■ CHAPTER OBJECTIVES

1 To recognize the purpose of direct marketing as a communications tool.

2 To appreciate the importance of a database for direct marketing.

3 To understand the decisions of a direct marketing plan.

4 To demonstrate the use of direct-response media.

5 To determine the strengths and limitations of direct marketing.

CREATIVE DIRECT MAIL GETS RESULTS

Stunning commercials (also shown online before or after the TV placement), fabulous print layouts, extraordinary outdoor spectaculars, and innovative digital applications continue to abound in today's advertising world, but what about direct mail? Creative executions for direct mail still produce winners for business marketing communication tasks, as evidenced in the following examples.

Grey Advertising won a Gold Lion at the 2010 Cannes Awards with its innovative execution for its client, GGRP, a premier sound design house located in Vancouver. GGRP needed a message to rejuvenate its image for creativity in sound to existing and new North American clients who truly appreciated the audio art the company could produce. The idea picked up on the love audiophiles have for vinyl, an expressive medium for sound that has resurged in popularity. The direct mail piece featured a cardboard record player that also acted as the envelope along with a vinyl 45. Users spun the record with a pencil and the cardboard naturally amplified the vibrations going through the needle. A response rate of almost 100 percent resulted, as all recipients either talked about it or wanted more copies. It also became an Internet hit, with hundreds of blog reports, extensive YouTube hits on the video showing how to set up the record player, and 70,000 hits to the GGRP website.

Target Marketing and Communications won Best in Show honours and Direct Mail Gold with its execution for its client the Canadian Sea Turtle Network (CSTN) at the ICE Awards. The agency arranged to have an issue of *National Geographic* dedicated to CSTN's efforts to save the leatherback turtles, which included a handwritten note from the executive director of the CSTN and was wrapped in an actual fish net. The recipients, journalists, and bloggers with environmental and conservation background, who had the most potential to be key influencers, had to physically cut the net to read the magazine and card. Commenting on the creative, Target's president said, "We wanted to differentiate it from everything else that landed in their 'in' tray. It's differentiated in every way, not only their shape, size and weight, but they actually have to free the magazine, which is relevant with what CSTN is working to do."

Bos created an imaginative secret society for wheat and barley farmers to market Syngenta's new herbicide, and *Strategy* recognized this effort in one of its awards. The new premium product sold in limited quantities proved to be the inspiration as 1,500 top tier growers received the kit. Inside, the luxe paper, gold ink, embossing, and wax seal invited them into the "No Compromise Club" to guarantee a supply of the new weed killer. The package included a leather wallet and a code allowing online registration for a gift, such as a leather-bound poker set. A 53 percent response rate suggested tremendous success for the agency.

Sources: Emily Wexler, "Cannes Lions: Grey Canada Wins Direct Gold," *Strategy*, June 21, 2010; www.canneslions.com; Jeromy Lloyd, "Target Nets Top ICE Award for Turtle Campaign," *Marketing Magazine*, October 29, 2009; Kristin Laird, "Not Interested in Snail Mail? How about Some Turtle Mail?" *Marketing Magazine*, July 22, 2009; Emily Wexler, "Direct Mail," *Strategy*, June 2009, p. 41.

QUESTION:

1. What are the common elements across all three examples?

In this chapter, we discuss direct marketing and its role as a communications tool. Direct marketing includes programs that use direct-response media such as direct mail, catalogues, telemarketing, and infomercials. In essence, it uses each of the media we have discussed thus far, but with a more immediate behavioural objective in addition to communication objectives. The significance of direct response media is seen with direct mail and catalogues accounting for nearly $1.7 billion in advertising revenue for 2008. We begin with an overview of direct marketing and the use of databases; a critical implementation resource. We then identify key decisions for direct-marketing programs and the use of direct-response media. The chapter concludes with a summary of the strengths and limitations of this marketing tool.

DIRECT MARKETING

While most companies continue to rely primarily on the other promotional mix elements to move their products and services through intermediaries, an increasing number are going directly to the consumer. These companies believe that the traditional promotional mix tools, such as advertising and sales promotion, are effective in creating brand image, conveying information, and/or creating awareness. However, going direct with these same tools can generate an immediate behavioural response that makes direct marketing a valuable tool in the integrated communications program. For this section we briefly define the purpose of direct marketing and illustrate the importance of databases for implementation.

DEFINING DIRECT MARKETING

As noted in Chapter 1, **direct marketing** is a system of marketing by which organizations communicate directly with target customers to generate a response or transaction. This response may take the form of a phone inquiry, a retail visit, or a purchase. In his *Dictionary of Marketing Terms,* Peter Bennett defines direct marketing as:

> The total of activities by which the seller, in effecting the exchange of goods and services with the buyer, directs efforts to a target audience using one or more media (direct selling, direct mail, telemarketing, direct-action advertising, catalogue selling, cable TV selling, etc.) for the purpose of soliciting a response by phone, mail, or personal visit from a prospect or customer.[1]

Clearly, at this time we would add a visit to a brand's website or other new Internet media applications. Direct marketing involves marketing research, segmentation, strategic and tactical decisions, and evaluation as shown in our planning model in Chapter 1. For the execution, direct marketing uses a set of **direct-response media**, including direct mail, telemarketing, interactive TV, print, the Internet, and other media to reach both customers and prospective customers. The use of direct-response media differs depending on whether the identity of the target audience is known. For example, direct mail can be addressed, where the person's name and address is on the communication sent to the home (or business) location. In contrast, unaddressed mail reaches homes and is delivered in bulk to selective geographic areas decided by the promotional planner. Exhibit 16-1 shows how direct mail is used to encourage travel.

In either case, an important element of direct marketing and the selection of the most appropriate direct-response media is the development and use of a database. We briefly examine the content and use of a database for the purpose of marketing communication as it has implications for all direct-response media described in this chapter and for digital media discussed in the next chapter.

DEVELOPING A DATABASE

As we have discussed throughout this text, market segmentation and targeting are critical components of any promotional program. Direct-marketing programs employ these principles even more than others, since the success of a direct-marketing program is in large part tied to the ability to reach a very specific target audience. To segment and target their audiences, direct marketers use a **database**, a listing of customers and/or potential customers. This database is a tool for **database marketing**—the use of specific information about individual customers and/or prospects to implement more effective and efficient marketing communication.[2] In this section we look at using database information, the sources of database information, and how to determine the effectiveness of the database.

Using Database Information Figure 16-1 demonstrates how database marketing works. The creation and development of the database is the first and obviously a necessary step for this program. The database contains names, addresses, and postal codes; more sophisticated databases include information on demographics and psychographics, purchase transactions and payments, personal facts, neighbourhood data, and even credit histories (see Figure 16-2). Canada's privacy legislation places limitations on what marketers can

Exhibit 16-1 Saskatchewan encourages visits through direct mail.

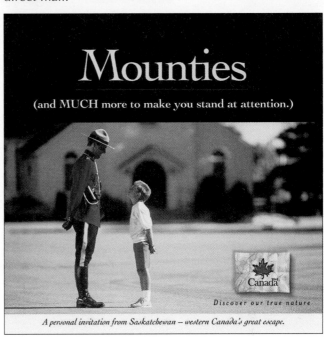

A personal invitation from Saskatchewan – western Canada's great escape.

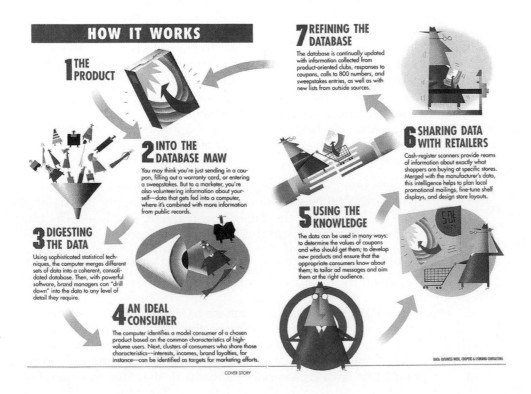

HOW IT WORKS

1 THE PRODUCT

2 INTO THE DATABASE MAW
You may think you're just sending in a coupon, filling out a warranty card, or entering a sweepstakes. But to a marketer, you're also volunteering information about yourself—data that gets fed into a computer, where it's combined with more information from public records.

3 DIGESTING THE DATA
Using sophisticated statistical techniques, the computer merges different sets of data into a coherent, consolidated database. Then, with powerful software, brand managers can "drill down" into the data to any level of detail they require.

4 AN IDEAL CONSUMER
The computer identifies a model consumer of a chosen product based on the common characteristics of high-volume users. Next, clusters of consumers who share those characteristics—interests, incomes, brand loyalties, for instance—can be identified as targets for marketing efforts.

5 USING THE KNOWLEDGE
The data can be used in many ways: to determine the values of coupons and who should get them; to develop new products and ensure that the appropriate consumers know about them; to tailor ad messages and aim them at the right audience.

6 SHARING DATA WITH RETAILERS
Cash-register scanners provide reams of information about exactly what shoppers are buying at specific stores. Merged with the manufacturer's data, this intelligence helps to plan local promotional mailings, fine-tune shelf displays, and design store layouts.

7 REFINING THE DATABASE
The database is continually updated with information collected from product-oriented clubs, responses to coupons, calls to 800 numbers, and sweepstakes entries, as well as with new lists from outside sources.

DATA: BUSINESS WEEK, COOPERS & LYBRAND CONSULTING

COVER STORY

FIGURE 16–1

How database marketing works

489

FIGURE 16–2

Contents for a comprehensive database

Consumer Database	Business-to-Business Database
Name	Name of company/contact/decision maker(s)
Address/postal code	Title of contact
Telephone number	Telephone number
Length of residence	Source of order/inquiry or referral
Age	Credit history
Gender	Industrial classification
Marital status	Size of business
Family data (number of children, etc.)	Revenues
Education	Number of employees
Income	Time in business
Occupation	Headquarters location
Transaction history	Multiple locations
Promotion history	Purchase history
Inquiring history	Promotion history
Unique identifier	Inquiry history
	Unique identifier

do with information stored in their databases. We refer you to www.privcom.gc.ca for a complete guide.

The database permits extensive and advanced statistical analysis to identify specific audiences for which a customized and/or personalized advertising or promotional offer can be delivered through a direct-response medium. For example, Knorr delivered direct mail pieces, also containing a coupon, to households according to demographic and purchase behaviour potential along 10 different characteristics. Those most likely to respond included past Knorr consumers interested in the frozen food category who had sufficient disposable income to afford a premium product. The various combinations of the 10 characteristics provided many opportunities to reach various target audiences ranging from very low to extremely high levels of audience attractiveness. The results indicated a 10 percent response rate, substantially higher than the projected 3 percent. One of the more attractive target audiences attained a response rate of 50 percent.

As this example shows, the database serves as the foundation from which the direct-marketing programs evolve. Databases are used to achieve the above trial purchase objective and other functions[3]:

- *Improving the selection of market segments.* Some consumers are more likely to be potential purchasers than others, as the Knorr example illustrates. By analyzing the characteristics of the database, a marketer like Knorr can target a potential audience that has a stronger likelihood of responding to the offer (e.g., use coupon, trial purchase). Other marketers, like catalogue companies such as Lands' End, Sears, and the Gap, have researched their customer lists and become efficient by targeting only those who are most likely to purchase their products.
- *Stimulate repeat purchases.* Once a purchase has been made, the customer's name and other information are entered into the database. These people are proven users who offer high potential for repurchase. Magazines, for example, routinely send out renewal letters and/or call subscribers before the expiration date. Companies like lawn care services and car dealers, for example, build a base of customers and contact them when they are "due" to repurchase.

Exhibit 16-2
Costco mails promotional offers to its members.

Costco mails promotions to members regularly to encourage return visits (Exhibit 16-2).

- *Cross-sell.* Customers who demonstrate a specific interest also constitute strong potential for other products of the same nature. For example, the National Geographic Society has successfully sold globes, maps, videos, travel magazines, and an assortment of other products to subscribers who obviously have an interest in geography and/or travel. Likewise, Victoria's Secret has expanded its clothing lines primarily through sales to existing customers.

- *Customer relationship management.* Customer relationship management (CRM) requires that the marketer develop and maintain a significant amount of information about its clients. The aim of CRM is to establish and maintain a relationship with one's customers through personalized communication and customized product/service offerings. CRM relies on software technology and an extensive database specifically designed to implement the management of customer relationships. For example, Exhibit 16-3 shows various brands that have a continuity program, a key part of CRM since it provides an incentive for repeat purchase. Timely communication and appropriate promotional offers that fit with the customer's past purchase behaviour is the hallmark of CRM, of which a database and direct-response media are imperative.

Numerous companies have established comprehensive databases on existing and potential customers both in North America and internationally. Database marketing has become so ubiquitous that many people are concerned about invasion of privacy. Direct marketers are concerned as well. The Canadian Marketing Association (CMA) and the Canadian Advertising Foundation (CAF) have asked members to adhere to ethical rules of conduct in their marketing efforts. They point out that if the industry does not police itself, the government will do it.

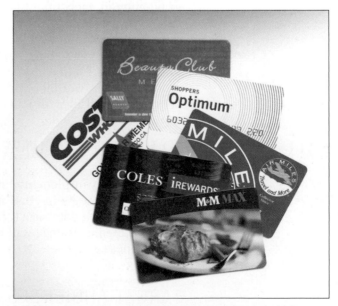

Exhibit 16-3 The databases for these brands help facilitate CRM.

491

Sources of Database Information   There are many sources of information for direct-marketing databases:

- *Statistics Canada.* Census data provide information on almost every household in Canada. Data include household size, demographics, income, and other information.
- *Canada Post.* Postal codes provide information on both household and business locations.
- *List services.* Many providers of lists are available. The accuracy and timeliness of the lists vary.
- *Info Canada.* Provincial Business Directory provides information regarding business lists. Direct Mail List Rates and Data contains thousands of list selections, published by province.
- *Marketing research houses.* Large research houses conduct annual studies of customers who buy at home via mail or telephone. They compile information on total orders placed, types of products purchased, demographics, and purchase satisfaction, among others.
- *Loyalty programs.* Continuity programs designed to enhance loyalty are a new source of consumers with precise purchase patterns.
- *Others.* The Canadian Marketing Association, Dunn and Bradstreet, Fortune 500, *The Book of Lists,* and other published periodicals of this nature all contain listed information that can be used for these purposes.

Consumer-goods manufacturers, banks, credit bureaus, retailers, charitable organizations, and other business operations also sell lists and other selected information. Companies can build their own databases through completed warranty cards, surveys, and so on.

Determining the Effectiveness of the Database   While many companies maintain a database, many do not use them effectively. Collecting names and information is not enough; the list must be kept current, purged of old and/or inactive customers, and updated frequently. The more information about customers that can be contained in the database, the more effective it will be. An **RFM scoring method** is often used for this purpose. RFM stands for the recency, frequency, and monetary transactions between the company and the customer. More specifically, data need to be entered each time there is a transaction so that the company can track how recently purchases have been made, how often they are made, and what amounts of money are being spent. In addition, tracking which products and/or services are used increases the ability for databases to conduct the activities previously mentioned in this section. By analyzing the database on a regular basis, the company or organization can identify trends and buying patterns that will help it establish a better relationship with its customers by more effectively meeting their needs.

DIRECT-MARKETING PLAN

To successfully implement direct-marketing programs, companies must make a number of decisions. As in other marketing programs, they must determine (1) whom to target by using a database; (2) what the program's objectives will be; (3) what direct-response media strategy will be employed; and (4) how to measure direct-marketing effectiveness.

TARGET AUDIENCES FOR DIRECT MARKETING

As the database description suggested, direct marketing is especially useful to target specific current customers. Well-managed firms have extensive records of their customers in terms of their purchases and other relevant characteristics, allowing for much more meaningful communication as it can be personalized and customized. Alternatively, the database section identified other sources to compile a database of non-customers. Businesses are often expanding geographically or along some other dimension (e.g., demographic, socioeconomic) where an accurate database and direct marketing could generate trial among prospects. As the earlier Knorr example showed, many other segmentation variables are used to more accurately profile the target audience for the marketing communication.

Thus far we have discussed direct marketing and the use of databases with the idea that the identity of the receiver is known. While this is true in many applications, direct marketing is also used with broader media (i.e., television) and with media that allow for delivery without identity (i.e., unaddressed direct mail). In these situations, databases are (or should be) used to identify the most relevant profile variables to ensure the highest response rate possible. For example, if a firm decides to use unaddressed direct mail, it can use census data and postal codes to select more attractive regions within a town or city. For example, Nubody's Fitness targeted its unaddressed monthly mail drop of 190,000 pieces with key demographic variables, leading to stronger retail visits and phone enquiries.[4]

Sometimes, a direct mail piece has an address—easily determined and compiled with computer databases—but no name, or "to resident." For example, Rogers can mail promotional pieces such as the one in Exhibit 16-4 to exact addresses where its database indicates no current customer, especially if it served the residence via a prior owner or tenant.

A third idea for targeting occurs through profiling current customers and using the information to select prospective customers from an alternative database. Working with Canada Post, the Canadian Cancer Society followed this approach with an experiment. They identified four different groups: (1) profiled postal code and receive mail, (2) profiled postal code and receive no mail, (3) non-profiled postal code and receive mail, and (4) non-profiled postal code and receive no mail. The results found a 13.5 percent higher response rate for profiled segments, with net revenue being 19.2 percent higher.[5]

DIRECT-MARKETING OBJECTIVES

The direct marketer seeks an immediate behavioural response. As such, the behavioural objectives identified in Chapter 5 become much more salient in direct marketing. Direct marketers can attempt to achieve brand trial, re-trial, switching, or category trial objectives. A databases of consumers' past purchase history information helps identify those who have not previously purchased the brand. For databases containing current customer purchase history, the direct marketer can attempt to influence the rate, amount, or timing of purchases. Oftentimes, direct marketing attempts to bring consumers along in their decision-making process. Thus, purchase-related behaviour can be an objective through retail visits that manifest in many ways such as test driving cars or trying on shoes and clothes, requests for service such as obtaining free estimates, or experiencing other marketing communication. Repeat consumption is also an objective with current customers. For example, financial-service firms

Exhibit 16-4 Rogers uses direct mail to entice switching.

can use direct marketing to encourage additional visits by its customers for yearly financial planning advice.

A behavioural response is not the only objective for direct marketing. All communication objectives and how the message and offers influence attitudes is still very relevant for direct marketing. As we noted in Chapter 5, brand objectives (i.e., awareness, attitude) are considerations for all pieces of marketing communication. In fact, direct marketers are very innovative, with clever creative approaches to attract attention and encourage processing the message so that a communication effect occurs even if the receiver declines the call to action. A typical objective of perhaps a 2 to 3 percent response rate suggests that communication objectives are as valuable here as in other marketing communication tools, since more than 90 percent are viewing the direct marketing in the same light.

DIRECT-RESPONSE MEDIA

Direct-response media include many media, of which we discuss direct mail, catalogue, broadcast, print, and telemarketing. To help achieve the previously identified objectives, these media generally follow a couple of approaches. In the **one-step approach**, the medium is used directly to obtain an order. For example, TV commercials for products such as workout equipment or magazine subscriptions urge viewers to phone a toll-free number to place an order immediately. The **two-step approach** involves the use of more than one medium. The first effort is designed to screen, or qualify, potential buyers. The second effort generates the response. For example, business marketing companies use telemarketing to screen on the basis of interest, then follow up to interested parties with more information designed to achieve an order or use personal selling to close the sale. IMC Perspective 16-1 describes an innovative application of this method.

Direct Mail   Direct mail is a significant medium; 18 billion pieces generated as much advertising revenue as the Internet during 2008 in Canada. Canada Post has a strong interest in developing the market for direct mail and provides extensive research and service to facilitate this goal, especially for small businesses concerned with reaching their customers and prospects with a low cost option.

Canada Post research statistics show that 66 percent of Canadians read addressed direct mail right away when it arrives. Another 27 percent of Canadians keep it to review later at a time more convenient to them. Attitudinally, 72 percent of Canadians look forward to seeing what is in their mailbox, and 63 percent claim receiving mail is a real pleasure. Consumers are quite favourable to reading mail if they are a customer of the sender, it is a promotional offer, or they have seen previous ads. Currently, Canadians prefer mail over e-mail by a four to one ratio from businesses marketing their products.[6]

Many advertisers shied away from direct mail in the past, fearful of the image it might create or harbouring the belief that direct mail was useful only for low-cost products. But this is no longer the case. For example, Porsche Cars North America Inc. uses direct mail to target high-income, upscale consumers who are most likely to purchase its expensive sports cars (Exhibit 16-5). In one example, Porsche developed a direct mail piece that was sent to a precisely defined target: physicians in specialties with the highest income levels. This list was screened to match the demographics of Porsche buyers and narrowed further to specific geographic areas. The direct mail piece was an X-ray of a Porsche 911 Carrera 4

Exhibit 16-5   Porsche targets direct mail to upscale audiences.

Dove and the Shoppers Drug Mart Double Loyalty Club

With just over 10 million members, Shoppers Drug Mart isn't the only one happy about the success of its Shoppers Optimum loyalty program. Marketers often see sales of their brands spike when they invest in a Shoppers Optimum promotion since participating consumers receive bonus points toward in-store discounts. Now, Unilever—one of the drugstore chain's largest vendors—has upped the ante, running a loyalty initiative specifically for Dove that exists within the Shoppers Optimum program. Called Dove Optimum Rewards, membership gives consumers the opportunity to earn double the points when they buy two or more different Dove products. "We've created a club within a club," says Gabriel Verkade, retail activation manager of national accounts at Toronto-based Unilever.

Dove Optimum Rewards is the first vendor program of its kind for Shoppers Drug Mart. As the loyalty segment matures, experts suggest this is just the start of what they're calling "loyalty program guardians," where marketers ranging from retailers to hotels create new and innovative partnerships with vendors. Before Shoppers Drug Mart partnered with Dove, rival packaged goods companies had approached the retailer about creating a vendor subprogram within Shoppers Optimum. Ultimately, Shoppers Drug Mart chose Dove because the brand ties nicely into the retailer's identity, focusing on health, beauty, and convenience, and had many SKUs to drive sales.

The four-week introductory campaign for Dove Optimum Rewards included a permission-based e-mail to one million Shoppers Optimum members, as well as to the permission-based e-mail lists of *Chatelaine* and mochasofa.ca; a national two-page flyer delivered to 4.4 million homes; an ad in *Glow* magazine; and signage, posters, and header cards in more than 974 Shoppers Drug Mart and Quebec-based Pharmaprix[MD] stores. The advertising included a coupon which, when scanned at the checkout, signed up Shoppers Optimum members to the Dove program. Shoppers Optimum members can also register online at www.shoppersdrugmart.ca/dove. Once registered, Shoppers Optimum card holders are automatically tagged as Dove Optimum Rewards members—in other words, no need for customers to carry yet another loyalty card.

Unilever aims to do more than just encourage trial among customers who typically purchase only a single Dove product. Unilever ultimately wants to develop a relationship with these customers through the new Dove Optimum database. Verkade says strict privacy regulations mean Shoppers Drug Mart doesn't give vendors access to its Shoppers Optimum database—which includes everything from the typical amount of a member's shopping basket to their demographic profile. But, the Shoppers Drug Mart/Unilever partnership does give Unilever access to information about the Dove Optimum Rewards members and the ability to work with Shoppers to better target them.

For Dove, the challenge is keeping the Dove Optimum Rewards program top of mind so that consumers realize that it is, in fact, a club within a club. "Once they are enrolled, our challenge is reminding them that they have joined an additional program and of the value they are receiving from it," says Verkade. That might mean a combination of direct mail, flyers, and e-mail or promotions on existing or new products, but also more value-added, enriched content, such as a booklet about beauty tips or information on managing sensitive skin.

Source: Chris Daniels, "The Layered Look," *Marketing Magazine*, March 26, 2007.

Questions

1. Explain how Dove's relationship to the Shoppers Optimum program works.
2. What concerns would you have about this joint promotion?

Exhibit 16-6 Maserati used direct mail to introduce its new automobiles.

Be one of the first to test drive the new Maserati GranTurismo and Quattroporte Sport GT S...

...and also receive another reward

written in the language of the medical audience. This creative campaign generated one of the highest response rates of any mailing by Porsche.[7] The material shown in Exhibit 16-6 is just one piece that was sent by Maserati to market its new Gran Turismo and Quattroporte Sport GT S automobiles.

Direct mail works well as the first step in the two-step approach for message delivery. Tourism Yukon's direct mail initiate obtained a 20 percent response rate for website visits versus 5 percent for its online ads presenting the same message. Bear Mountain Resort delivered brochures to two selective markets that encouraged online registration to view their new condominiums and garnered a 37 percent response versus a 14 percent response for past newspaper ads.[8]

Keys to the success of direct mail are the **mailing list**, which constitutes the database from which names are generated, and the ability to segment markets. Lists have become more current and more selective, eliminating waste coverage. Segmentation on the basis of geography (usually through postal codes), demographics, and lifestyles has led to increased effectiveness. The most commonly used lists are of individuals who have already purchased direct mail products.

The importance of the list itself has led to a standalone business as many companies profit from selling the names of purchasers of their products and/or services to list firms. There are also a growing number of list-management companies springing up on the Internet. Canadian mailing lists sorted by association or type of vocation are available, and Canadian companies such as www.interactdirect.com, based in London, Ontario, are becoming more common.

Catalogues   Some companies rely solely on catalogue sales. For example, Yves Rocher is a firm that markets botanical beauty care products for women. It expanded into Canada with its small catalogues and sells directly to consumers. Lee Valley Tools of Ottawa began as a mail order catalogue company 30 years ago, but has branched out to retail stores across the country and online sales.

Companies also use catalogues in conjunction with their more traditional sales and promotional strategies. For example, companies such as Canadian Tire and Sears sell directly through catalogues but also use them to inform consumers of product offerings available in the stores.

IKEA prints 6 million catalogues per year and its executives view the catalogue as the company's "main marketing tool" since it naturally encourages consumers to visit the retail outlets or the Internet site. But, more importantly, the catalogue is a strong brand-building tool to demonstrate how IKEA's products can improve the homes of millions of consumers.[9]

Home Depot started out as the headquarters for contractors and handy home renovators, but in Canada it started a decorating catalogue, "The Home Depot Dreambook," to inspire women looking to improve their homes. Thus, catalogues can be used as a direct-marketing tool to attract a new target audience while not alienating the original loyal customer.[10]

In addition to the traditional hard copies, catalogues are now available on the Internet for both consumers and business-to-business customers. In some instances in the consumer market the catalogue merchandise is available in retail stores as well. In others, the catalogue and retail divisions are treated as separate entities. For example, purchases made through the Eddie Bauer catalogue can be exchanged or returned to the retail stores. At the Gap, the catalogue is used to supplement the inventory in stock, and phone orders for different sizes and so on can be made from the store and shipped for free.

Broadcast Media Two broadcast media are available to direct marketers: television and radio. While radio was used quite extensively in the 1950s, its use and effectiveness have dwindled substantially in recent years. Thus, the majority of direct-marketing broadcast advertising now occurs on TV. Direct-response TV encompasses direct-response TV spots, infomercials, and home shopping shows (teleshopping).

TV Spots Referred to in the direct-marketing industry as *short-term programs,* these spots include direct-response commercials for products such as magazines and household goods. In **direct-response advertising**, the product or service is offered and a sales response is solicited through either the one- or two-step approach. Toll-free phone numbers are included so that the receiver can immediately call to order. Many companies run direct-response television commercials to encourage website visits. For example, in its effort to move from a soup company to a food company, the Campbell Company of Canada ran nine ads with a celebrity chef demonstrating different cooking methods that directed consumers to a website, www.power2cook.ca, and followed up with extensive direct mail pieces to 2 million Canadians.[11]

Infomercials The lower cost of commercials on cable and satellite channels has led advertisers to a new form of advertising. An **infomercial** is a long commercial that ranges from 3 to 60 minutes. Many infomercials are produced by the advertisers and are designed to be viewed as regular TV shows. Consumers dial a 1-800 or 1-900 number to place an order. Relatively speaking, infomercials in Canada are less significant in terms of expenditures, with only $22 million in revenue for 2008, a decline of $2 million. The video capabilities of the Internet may diminish this further over the next few years. Despite this, infomercials are popular with small firms and have been adopted by mainstream marketers, like Apple and Microsoft, and niche marketers like Bentley (Exhibit 16-7). One study compared the communication effects of a one-minute ad, 15-minute infomercial, 30-minute infomercial, and direct experience (i.e., interacting with the product). The authors concluded that infomercials provided results more closely related to direct experience than a one-minute ad, presumably because both messages allow for extensive cognitive and emotional process during a longer duration.[12]

As to their effectiveness, studies indicate that infomercials get watched and sell products. One study profiling infomercial viewers and buyers demonstrated that this advertising medium is indeed effective with a broad demographic base, not significantly different from the infomercial non-shopper in age, education, income, or gender. There are also a number of differences between infomercial shoppers and non-shoppers.[13]

Teleshopping The development of toll-free telephone numbers, combined with the widespread use of credit cards, has led to a dramatic increase in the number of people who shop via their TV sets. Jewellery, kitchenware, fitness products, electronics, and a variety of items are now promoted (and sold) this way. The Shopping Channel (TSC) is Canada's broadcast retailer available on all delivery formats

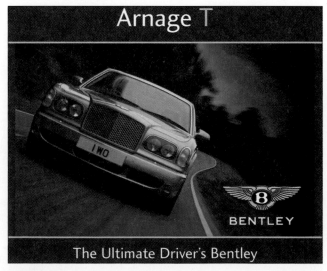

Exhibit 16-7 Bentley uses an infomercial to attract buyers.

Exhibit 16-8 A direct-response print ad.

Hand painted on glass...complete with wrought-iron stand.

(cable, satellite) across the country. And, of course, the lines of communication get blurred even more as TSC is available in catalogue form and on the Internet.

Print Media Magazines and newspapers are difficult media to use for direct marketing. Because these ads have to compete with the clutter of other ads and because the space is relatively expensive, response rates and profits may be lower than in other media. Exhibit 16-8 shows a direct ad that appeared in a magazine. Direct-to-consumer magazines hit Canada when the Hudson's Bay Company launched Canada's first publication, *Lifestyle,* to the 500,000 members within its HBC Rewards database. HBC planned to measure the consumer response to specific promotions, and advertisers within the magazine could also join in so that they too could track their results.[14]

Telemarketing Communication resulting in sales via the telephone is known as **telemarketing**. There are two types of telemarketing. Outbound telemarketing refers to calls made by a company or its sponsor to a potential buyer or client, soliciting the sale of products, services, donations, votes, or any other "value" issue. Inbound telemarketing occurs when a company has advertised its 1-800 number or its website address, for example, asking the customer to call the number, visit the store, or log on to the website. Both for-profit and charitable organizations have employed this medium effectively in one- and two-step approaches.

As telemarketing continues to expand in scope, a new dimension referred to as **audiotex** or **telemedia** has evolved. Tom Eisenhart defines telemedia as the "use of telephone and voice information services (900, 800, and 976 numbers) to market, advertise, promote, entertain, and inform."[15] Many telemedia programs are interactive. Figure 16-3 shows more specifically how 800/900 numbers are used as marketing tools.[16]

FIGURE 16–3 The use of 800, 900, and 976 numbers in marketing

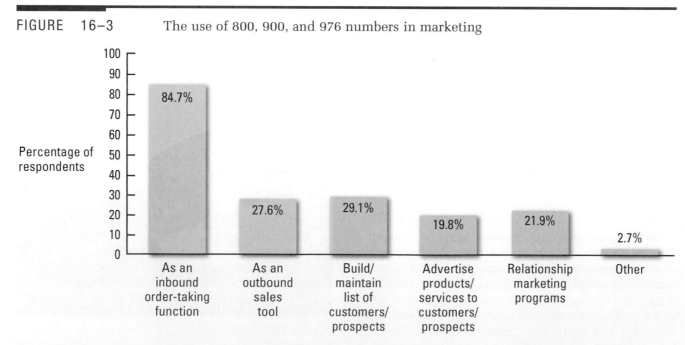

Note: *Direct* forecast survey was conducted by Jacobson Consulting Applications. The firms mailed a four-page questionnaire to direct-marketing executives, on an *n*th name basis from *Direct*'s circulation list. There were 565 responses.

Problems associated with telemarketing include its potential for fraud and deception and its potential for annoyance. However, data on call centres in Canada show that most call centres are well managed. The majority communicate clearly if the interaction is recorded, follow the laws governing telemarketing, and work with their employees to ensure appropriate interactions.[17] Those in the telemarketing and telemedia industry have responded to public criticisms. As more and more large companies use telemedia, its tarnished image will likely brighten up.

DIRECT-MARKETING EFFECTIVENESS

For direct-marketing programs that do not have an objective of generating an immediate behavioural response, traditional measures of advertising effectiveness can be applied. In those situations requiring a direct response, measuring the effectiveness should include some specific behavioural measure in addition to the communication measures. Using the cost per order (CPO), advertisers can evaluate the relative effectiveness of an ad in only a few minutes based on the number of calls generated. By running the same ad on different stations, a direct marketer can determine the relative effectiveness of the medium itself. For example, if the advertiser targets a $5 return per order and a broadcast commercial (production and print) costs $2,500, the ad is considered effective if it generates 500 orders. Similar measures have been developed for print and direct mail ads.

Tracking the behavioural effects is exactly what Sprint Canada emphasized during the launch of its "Red Is Smarter" campaign. Each creative execution contained a unique toll-free number in a controlled region so that it could gauge the impact of different persuasive messages when the call centre received the inbound consumer response. Sprint Canada used the same idea for different promotional offers.[18]

499

EVALUATION OF DIRECT MARKETING

We presented many strengths and limitations of direct marketing thus far, but summarize these factors in a concluding section as we have done in previous chapters. Given that direct marketing employs different media, each with its own characteristics, these conclusions are generalizations in which some variation can be expected.

STRENGTHS OF DIRECT MARKETING

Target Audience Selectivity   Marketers can purchase lists of recent product purchasers, car buyers, bank card holders, and so on. These lists may allow segmentation on the basis of geographic area, occupation, demographics, and job title, to mention a few. Combining this information with the geocoding capabilities of PRIZM or VALS (discussed in Chapter 3), marketers can develop effective segmentation strategies.

Target Audience Coverage   Direct marketing lets the advertiser reach a high percentage of the selective target audience and reduces or eliminates waste coverage. Since the database allows precise target audience profiles, the direct-response media selected can achieve a strong level of hits. For example, while not everyone drives on highways where there are billboards or pays attention to TV commercials, virtually everyone receives mail. A good list allows for minimal waste, as only those consumers with the highest potential are targeted. For example, a political candidate can direct a message at a very select group of people (those living in a certain postal code, or members of McGill University Alumni, or the Royal Vancouver Yacht Club, say); in the same vein, a music club can target recent purchasers of MP3 players, or a medical software supplier can target all M.D.s in the medical association directories.

Frequency Depending on the medium used, it may be possible to build frequency levels. The program vehicles used for direct-response TV advertising are usually the most inexpensive available, so the marketer can afford to purchase repeat times. Frequency may not be so easily accomplished through the mail, since consumers may be annoyed to receive the same mail repeatedly.

Creativity for Cognitive and Emotional Responses Direct marketing can take on a variety of creative forms. For example, the Discovery Network sent 17-inch TV sets to media buyers through the mail. The only message accompanying the TV sets was one on the cord that said "Plug me in" and another on a videotape that read "Play me." Upon doing so, the recipient was greeted with a 7-minute promotional video. Direct mail pieces also allow for detailed copy that provides a great deal of information. The targeted mailing of CDs or DVDs containing product information has increased dramatically, as companies have found this a very effective way to provide potential buyers with product information.

Scheduling Flexibility While many media require long-range planning and have long closing dates, direct-response advertising can be much more timely. Direct mail, for example, can be put together very quickly and distributed to the target population. TV programs typically used for direct-response advertising are older, less sought programs that are likely to appear on the station's list of available spots. Another common strategy is to purchase available time at the last possible moment to get the best price.

Personalization No other advertising medium can personalize the message as well as direct media. Parents with children at different age levels can be approached, with their child's name included in the appeal. Car owners are mailed letters congratulating them on their new purchase and offering accessories. Computer purchasers are sent software solicitations. Graduating college and university students receive very personalized information that recognizes their specific needs and offers solutions (such as credit cards). With the ability of direct marketing to personalize and customize its messages through a relevant direct-response media, we suggest that a considerable amount is fairly strong for attention and involvement of the message.

Costs While the CPM for direct mail may be very high on an absolute and a relative basis, its ability to specifically target the audience and eliminate waste coverage reduces the actual CPM. The ads used on TV are often among the lowest-priced available, and a video can be delivered for less than $1 (including postage). A second factor contributing to the cost-effectiveness of direct-response advertising is the cost per customer purchasing. Because of the low cost of media, each sale generated is very inexpensive.

LIMITATIONS OF DIRECT MARKETING

Media Image Many people believe unsolicited mail promotes junk products, and others dislike being solicited. Likewise, direct-response ads on TV are often low-budget ads for lower-priced products, which contributes to the image that something less than the best products are marketed in this way. Some of this image is being overcome by the home shopping channels, which promote some very expensive products. Telemarketing is found to be irritating to many consumers.

500

Target Audience Coverage   One of the advantages cited for direct mail was targeting potential customers specifically. But the effectiveness of these methods depends on the accuracy of the lists used. People move, change occupations, and so on, and if the lists are not kept current, selectivity will decrease. Computerization has greatly improved the currency of lists and reduced the incidence of bad names; however, the ability to generate lists is becoming a problem.[19]

Control for Selective Exposure   While target audience selectivity attempts to address this factor, consumers exert tremendous control with respect to direct marketing. It is easy to simply toss a direct mail piece in one's paper recycling bin. As seen in the discussion for television, consumers can readily zip or zap a direct message, and consumers usually have to actively seek and select an infomercial.

Reach   The selectivity of direct marketing and the cost associated with it suggest that achieving high levels of reach are neither feasible nor even a realistic characteristic of the purpose of this marketing approach.

IMC PLANNING: STRATEGIC USE OF DIRECT MARKETING

Direct marketing is now an important component in the integrated marketing programs of many organizations. In some cases it is used as a tool for an immediate response and in other cases it plays a key role in building the brand by moving through the target audience's decision-making process. In addition, direct-marketing activities support and are supported by other elements of the promotional mix.

501

DECISION-MAKING PROCESS

As described in this chapter, direct marketing tools are typically employed to persuade immediate consumer action. At this point, it is critical that the promotional manager plan for a specific action in order to select the most appropriate direct-response media. In Chapter 5 we reviewed different types of behavioural objectives for promotional communication, which we will use to develop some IMC planning prescriptions. Trial and repeat purchasing objectives suggest that much of direct marketing involves influence at the purchase decision stage.

Trial objectives require a broader-based direct-response medium, much like what is seen in advertising media decisions. Typically, wide-ranging direct mail pieces targeted by census track and income dispersions allow firms to reach as many potential consumers as possible. In this situation, the database used relies on more public sources, and a manager may use unaddressed drop-offs. Alternatively, for more targeted messages, brands may rely upon the list services and provide addressed mailings. Alternatively, with a database of existing customers, cross-selling of other products is now a trial purchase for the promotional planner's brand in a new product category. This trial purchase may be relatively new and be viewed as a purchase within the product category, thus requiring a direct-response medium providing considerable information.

We mentioned that existing customer databases are used for repeat purchases. Repeat purchasing objectives involve the timing, amount, and rate of consumer purchases. These different options suggest other criteria for evaluating the different direct-media options. For example, repeat purchasing objectives for specific timing might suggest telemarketing if the managers have current databases and permission to call upon its current customers. A favourite direct-response medium for many firms is bill inserts delivered monthly to enhance frequency and thus improve the amount and rate of purchase. Thus, the opportunity of promotional planners to match the specific objectives with the right direct-response medium requires full consideration.

Purchase-related behaviour objectives frequently involve influencing consumers at earlier stages in their decision making. For example, direct mail pieces may be delivered to encourage need recognition and prompt the target audience to make a sales enquiry at the retail location or over the telephone, or to visit the Internet site for further understanding of the brand during the information search stage. Alternatively, telephone calls can be made as follow up after the sales enquiry to ensure that the brand is seriously considered at the alternative evaluation stage.

DIRECT MARKETING AND IMC TOOLS

Obviously, direct marketing is in itself a form of advertising. Whether through mail, print, or TV, the direct-response offer is an ad. It usually contains a contact number, a form that requests mailing information, or a link to an Internet site. Sometimes the ad supports the direct-selling effort. For example, Victoria's Secret runs image ads to support its store and catalogue sales. Direct-response ads or infomercials are also referred to in retail outlet displays.

Public relations activities often employ direct-response techniques. Private companies may use telemarketing activities to solicit funds for charities or co-sponsor charities that use these and other direct-response techniques to solicit funds. Likewise, corporations and/or organizations engaging in public relations activities may include contact numbers or Internet addresses in their ads or promotional materials.

Telemarketing and direct selling are two methods of personal selling. Non-profit organizations such as charities often use telemarketing to solicit funds. For-profit companies are also using telemarketing with much greater frequency to screen and qualify prospects (which reduces selling costs) and to generate leads. Direct mail pieces are often used to invite prospective customers to visit auto showrooms to test-drive new cars; the salesperson then assumes responsibility for the selling effort.

Direct mail is often used to notify consumers of sales promotions like sales events or contests. Ski shops regularly mail announcements of special end-of-season sales. Whistler Ski Resort and Intrawest constantly mail out promotions to their customer database announcing promotional and seasonal vacation packages, room rates, and lift ticket specials. Consumer packaged goods firm Garnier used both addressed (5 percent redemption) and unaddressed mail (1.5 percent redemption) with extensive profiling to deliver a sample and coupon offer for its Long and Strong brand.[20] The Bay, Sears, and other retail outlets call their existing customers to notify them of special sales promotions. In turn, the sales promotion event may support the direct-marketing effort since databases are often built from the names and addresses acquired from a promotion, permitting other direct marketing follow-up.

CHAPTER OBJECTIVES AND SUMMARY

1 To recognize the purpose of direct marketing as a communications tool.

This chapter introduced the field of direct marketing, which involves a variety of methods and media. The versatility of direct marketing offers many different types of companies and organizations a promotional and selling tool that seeks to obtain a more immediate behavioural response from the target audience.

2 To appreciate the importance of a database for direct marketing.

The success of a direct marketing program is predicated on a database. The database contains extensive information for each customer or prospect in terms of demographic variables. More thorough databases will have additional variables on purchase history, socioeconomic characteristics, media exposure, and any other relevant segmentation variable the marketer believes necessary. The intrusive nature of the direct marketing and the use of databases make some marketers hesitant to use direct-marketing tools. However, self-policing of the industry and involvement by large, sophisticated companies have led to significant improvements allowing direct marketing to continue growing.

3 To understand the decisions of a direct marketing plan.

Direct marketing involves careful target audience profiling through the use of the database. Direct marketers can target lapsed customers in an attempt to generate re-trial. Alternatively, they can target current customers and try to encourage repeat purchasing of the brand, but with additional products (i.e., cross-selling). Databases garnered from other means can be compiled to develop stronger trial among non-category users or non-brand users. Thus, a critical part of the direct marketing plan is profiling the target audience and selecting the corresponding objective, since this guides the promotional offer and the selection of the most appropriate direct-response media.

4 To demonstrate the use of direct-response media.

Direct marketing is executed with a variety of direct-response media including direct mail, catalogues, broadcast, print, telemarketing, and new digital applications. We summarized the initial ones in this chapter and examine the latter in the next chapter. These media are used in a specific manner to encourage consumers to take some kind of action in terms of a purchase or getting involved with another medium or another IMC tool such as sales promotion.

5 To determine the strengths and limitations of direct marketing.

Advantages of direct marketing include target audience selectivity, target audience coverage, frequency, creativity for cognitive and emotional responses, scheduling flexibility, personalization leading to stronger attention and involvement, and costs. At the same time, a number of disadvantages are associated with the use of direct marketing including media image, target audience coverage, control for selective exposure, and reach.

KEY TERMS

audiotex, **498**

database, **489**

database marketing, **489**

direct marketing, **488**

direct-response advertising, **497**

direct-response media, **488**

infomercial, **497**

mailing list, **496**

one-step approach, **494**

RFM scoring method, **492**

telemarketing, **498**

telemedia, **498**

two-step approach, **494**

DISCUSSION QUESTIONS

1. Explain how companies use database marketing. Name some of the companies that may have information in their database. Explain how this information is used to reach a target audience.

2. What is the difference between the one- and two-step approaches to direct marketing? Give examples of companies that pursue both methods.

3. As the Internet continues to grow in popularity, some marketers predict that the print catalogue will cease to exist, replaced by Internet catalogues. Others disagree. Explain some of the reasons why this situation may or may not occur.

4. Describe the various forms of direct-response advertising. Discuss some of the reasons for the success of direct-response advertising.

5. Many marketers thought that the Internet would hurt the direct mail catalogue industry. In fact, this has not been the case. Explain some of the similar characteristics of catalogue shopping and shopping on the Internet. Then explain why you think the mail catalogue business has not been hurt.

6. Explain why companies like KitchenAid, Soloflex, and others have been successful in adopting direct-marketing techniques. Describe the conditions that contribute to the successful implementation of direct-marketing programs.

7. Identify some of the factors that have contributed to the growth of direct marketing. Do you see these factors as being relevant today? Discuss why or why not, and the impact they will have on direct marketing in the future.

8. One of the disadvantages associated with direct-marketing media is the high cost per exposure. Some marketers feel that this cost is not really as much of a disadvantage as is claimed. Argue for or against this position.

9. Give an example of how companies might use direct marketing as part of an IMC program. Provide examples of both consumer and business marketers.

10. Direct marketing has been beset by a number of problems that have tarnished its image. Discuss some of these and what might be done to improve direct marketing's image.

The chapter opener illustrates a company that effectively integrates the Internet into its marketing communication program by viewing the Internet as a medium to reach its target audience. In this chapter we will discuss Internet media from a communication perspective. Internet media is a valuable component of the integrated marketing communications program and, like other components, is most effective when used in conjunction with other elements.

We begin this chapter by briefly exploring how promotional planners can view the Internet as a communication medium. Next, we investigate the many ways the Internet can be used within a promotional program. We conclude by summarizing the methods for measuring Internet communication effectiveness and presenting the key strengths and limitations of Internet media.

INTERNET COMMUNICATION

While the **Internet** and the **World Wide Web (WWW)** are ways for marketers and consumers to conduct transactions for goods and services, our focus for this chapter is to consider these digital tools as media for communication and facilitation of all aspects of the promotional program. In the academic literature, there are a number of marketing domains investigated beyond advertising.[1] Our particular interest is Internet advertising research that examines the effectiveness of Internet advertising, interactivity, how advertising works, attitude to the Internet ad (including websites), and finally comparisons to other media.[2] As this suggests, the Internet has consumers—both current customers and potential customers—and marketers connecting or seeking to connect with these consumers through advertising and other tools. Furthermore, advertisers would like to know as much as possible about Internet users as one means of knowing whether investments are worthwhile. In this section, we briefly review some basic facts about Canadian Internet users and explore the basic marketing communication function of Internet media.

INTERNET USERS

A profile of Canadian Internet users is summarized in Figure 17-1. Approximately 80 percent of all Canadians used the Internet at any location during the past 12 months, up from 68 percent in 2005. The usage rate between men and women is fairly equal for all three time periods. Internet usage declines with age; most young Canadians ages 18–34 use the Internet, while those over 55 use the Internet below the 80 percent level. One-person households are least likely to use the Internet.

Internet use is greatly influenced by socioeconomic status. Individuals with higher incomes and higher levels of education are much more likely to use the Internet, although it is not perfectly correlated since the usage rate for the lowest income quartile is higher than the second lowest income quartile. There is greater disparity in the usage rate for education, ranging from 51 percent to 95 percent, than for income, ranging from 70 percent to 92 percent.[3] Figure 17-2 illustrates that Canadians spend about 18 hours a week actively using the Internet, or about 1.5 hours per day. What are we doing there for so long?

Figure 17-3 summarizes the types of usage during the past 12 months, such as searching or viewing various kinds of news and information, enjoying a variety of entertainment, banking, communicating, and contributing content. Clearly, the extensive activities Canadians engage in on the Internet allow advertisers many opportunities to reach specific customer groups, lifestyles, or virtually any marketing segmentation variable. In fact, some opportunities may be *very* good—the Internet appears to have spurred greater consumption of news when adding up the total exposure from traditional and digital media.[4] Further to this is the development of user-generated content such as product reviews, forum or journal posts,

	Any location[a]			
	2005	**2007**	**2009**	
	% of individuals[b]			
All Internet users	67.9	73.2	80.3	
Household type				
Single family households with unmarried children under age 18	80.9	86.4	91.1	
Single family households without unmarried children under age 18	62.5	67.5	76.4	
One-person households	48.7	53.0	63.1	
Multi-family households	78.8	80.6	86.4	
Sex				
Males	68.0	74.1	81.0	
Females	67.8	72.3	79.7	
Age				
34 years and under	88.9	93.1	96.5	
35 to 54 years	75.0	79.8	87.8	
55 to 64 years	53.8	60.8	71.1	
65 years and over	23.8	28.8	40.7	
Level of education				
Less than high school	31.2	43.2	50.7	
High school or college	72.0	76.8	83.4	
University degree	89.4	92.5	94.7	
Personal income quartile[c]				
Lowest quartile	58.7	68.8	76.2	
Second quartile	56.9	60.7	69.9	
Third quartile	71.3	75.5	83.1	
Highest quartile	83.2	87.9	92.1	

FIGURE 17–1

Characteristics of individuals using the Internet

Notes:

a. Internet access from any location includes use from home, school, work, public library or other, and counts an individual only once, regardless of use from multiple locations.

b. Percent who have used the Internet for personal, non-business reasons in the past 12 months. The target population for the Canadian Internet Use Survey (CIUS) has changed from individuals 18 years of age and older in 2005 to 16 years of age and older in 2007.

c. Canadian Internet Use Survey (CIUS) divides income into quartiles of four equal groups based on the respondent's personal income, each representing 25% of the income spectrum from highest to lowest.

Source: Statscan, "Characteristics of Individuals Using the Internet." CANSIM. Last modified May 10, 2010.

509

	2009	**2008**	**2007**
Actively using the Internet	18.1	14.9	15.0
Watching TV	16.9	15.8	15.1
Listening to the radio	8.9	10.0	9.1
Reading newspapers	2.9	3.3	3.0
Reading magazines	1.4	1.6	1.5

FIGURE 17–2

Time spent on various media in past week

Source: Ipsos Canadian Inter@ctive Reid Report: http://www.ipsos-na.com/news-polls/pressrelease.aspx?id=4720.

FIGURE 17-3

Internet use by individuals by type of activity, Internet users at home*

	2005	2007	2009
	% of individuals		
E-mail	91.3	92.0	93.0
Participating in chat groups or using a messenger	37.9	—	—
Use an instant messenger	—	49.9	44.8
Searching for information on Canadian municipal, provincial, or federal government	52.0	51.4	56.5
Communicating with Canadian municipal, provincial, or federal government	22.6	25.5	26.9
Searching for medical or health-related information	57.9	58.6	69.9
Education, training or school work	42.9	49.5	50.3
Travel information or making travel arrangements	63.1	66.1	66.2
Paying bills	55.0	—	—
Electronic banking	57.8	—	—
Search for employment	—	32.3	34.9
Electronic banking or paying bills	—	62.5	66.7
Researching investments	26.2	25.5	27.1
Playing games	38.7	38.7	42.1
Obtaining or saving music	36.6	44.5	46.5
Obtaining or saving software	31.8	32.5	35.0
Viewing the news or sports	61.7	63.7	67.7
Obtaining weather reports or road conditions	66.6	69.8	74.6
Listening to the radio over the Internet	26.1	28.1	31.8
Downloading or watching television	8.5	15.7	24.7
Downloading or watching a movie	8.3	12.5	19.8
Researching community events	42.3	44.3	50.0
General browsing (surfing)	84.0	76.0	77.7
Research other matters (family history, parenting)	—	69.5	72.7
Contribute content (blogs, photos, discussion groups)	—	20.3	26.7
Make telephone calls	—	8.7	13.8
Sell goods or services (through auction sites)	—	8.9	13.4
Other Internet activity	10.9	1.5	7.8

*Internet users at home are individuals who answered that they used the Internet from home in the past twelve months.

Source: Statscan, "Characteristics of Individuals Using the Internet." CANSIM. Last modified May 10, 2010.

blogs, websites, wikis, audio files, video files, podcasts—all contribute to an enormous amount of word-of-mouth communication. A recent study documented how much certain types of psychographic groups relied on these sources of information when making purchase decisions.[5]

Figure 17-4 summarizes the goods and services purchased or "shopped for" on the Internet during the past 12 months. Topping the list for actual goods and services purchased online are travel and books, magazines, and newspapers. About 40 percent of all Canadians say they shop for electronics, housewares, travel, and clothing on the Internet, and many other product categories demonstrate reasonably high numbers suggesting that the Internet has become a primary external source of information in consumers' decision making.

Window shoppers* browsing for	2005	2007
Computer software	18.6	18.5
Computer hardware	19.8	20.5
Music	21.5	23.7
Books, magazines and online newspapers	28.3	30.6
Videocassettes and digital videodiscs (DVD)	17.7	18.8
Other entertainment products	22.5	26.4
Food, condiments and beverages	7.5	8.2
Prescription drugs	2.4	2.7
Other health products, beauty and vitamins	11.0	12.8
Clothing, jewellery and accessories	36.9	40.6
Housewares	39.0	42.8
Consumer electronics	42.4	43.7
Automotive products	25.8	28.0
Travel arrangements	36.7	41.5
Flowers—gifts	11.9	13.4
Sports equipment	15.7	16.6
Toys and games	18.3	21.2
Real estate	16.2	18.7

*Window shoppers: Refers to Internet users who reported, during the preceding twelve months, having used the Internet to browse for goods or services without placing an order directly over the Internet for that product.

Source: Statscan, "Characteristics of Individuals Using the Internet." CANSIM. Last modified November 18, 2008.

FIGURE 17-4

Internet shopping by type of product and service

WEBSITE COMMUNICATION

When organizations first began using the Internet for marketing communication, they put up websites primarily for information purposes. Thus, one role of the **website** is to act as the place where information is made available by the site owner to Internet users. To attract visitors to the site—and to have them return—requires a combination of creativity, effective marketing, frequent updates, and the use of other media to direct consumers. Over time an additional role of the website emerged as sites became much more creative, with technological advances allowing fancier graphics, audio, and animation. This new role created unique brand messages unlike consumers had previously experienced.

We investigate website communication since the purpose of many digital marketing communication tools is to direct users to the website (or to an application that shares many of the characteristics of a website). Also, a website is a marketing communications medium, allowing companies to create awareness and influence attitudes by providing information and inviting consumers to interact with the new medium. Let's first look at these communication objectives that companies want to achieve.

WEBSITE COMMUNICATION OBJECTIVES

From a purely communications standpoint, websites typically attempt to achieve four broad communication objectives: develop awareness, disseminate information, build a brand image, and facilitate interaction. These latter three are attitudinal in nature and are consistent with the ideas presented in earlier chapters.

Exhibit 17-1 Snapple offers a number of reasons to visit its website.

Develop Awareness Communicating on a website can be useful in enhancing or creating awareness of an organization as well as its specific product and service offerings. Websites for well-established products offer additional interactive exposure of the brand in terms of its key messages and typical signature (e.g., logo, slogan, colours). Exhibit 17-1 shows how Snapple creates a fun experience for consumers to enjoy the brand and keep awareness strong. For small companies with limited budgets, a website is an opportunity to create awareness well beyond what might be achieved through traditional media. However, the Internet may not be the optimal medium for awareness in these situations due to its limited reach without other communication to direct consumers to the website.

Disseminate Information One of the primary objectives for using a website is to provide in-depth information about a company's products and services. In business-to-business markets, having a website has become a necessity, as more and more buyers expect that a company will have a site providing them with detailed information about its offerings (Exhibit 17-2). In the public sector, all levels of government use the Internet to provide citizens with a wide range of information on its services and policies. For example, we have cited Internet usage statistics in this chapter from research conducted by Statistics Canada. For many consumer companies, their websites serve as a means of communicating more information about their products and services.

Build a Brand Image Many websites are designed to reflect the image a company wants to portray. For example, the consumer sites at molsoncanadian.ca and labattblue.ca are excellent examples of image building. Interestingly, one of the difficulties traditional marketers have experienced is that of creating a brand image

Exhibit 17-2 Caterpillar's website is designed to provide easy access to information.

on the Internet. While some companies have been successful, others have not fared as well and realize that branding and image-creating strategies must be specifically adapted to this medium. According to David Aaker, the Internet—as part of an integrated marketing communications program—can be a useful tool for branding.[6] Many websites provide a transformational experience with video, animation, and other new tools to make the brand experience truly unique and interactive, beyond what consumers experience with other media.

We believe that the Internet—as part of an integrated marketing communications program—can be used for branding purposes, as well as for other objectives. This belief is reiterated in a recent article from an MSN Canada executive who believes the quality of the recent creative work on the Internet has vastly surpassed creative efforts from previous years. Combined with the average 30 hours per month on the Internet and advertising expenditures growing at a 40 percent annual rate, astute promotional planners will very soon master online brand building.[7] A study by the marketing research firm Millward Brown published in the *Journal of Advertising Research* concludes that Internet media are capable of building a brand like other established advertising media, although certain caveats seen elsewhere remain. For example, ensuring that the right message is communicated within the appropriate media vehicle is critical, a key conclusion that we have seen with more established media.[8] IMC Perspective 17-1 documents activities of a new brand entering the Canadian wireless market that used Internet media extensively.

Exhibit 17-3   Vocalpoint is a website where mothers exchange ideas about goods and services.

Facilitate Interaction   Some companies set up websites that have a variety of names, but in essence their purpose is to interact with consumers, or some other target, on regular basis, especially if there is a membership component so that the company can obtain (with permission) personal information and follow up using other forms of communication such as e-mail. For example, Procter & Gamble established a website (www.vocalpoint.com) where moms can share information (Exhibit 17-3). Vocalpoint is an online community whose mission is to help companies do a better job developing products and services that moms care about and want to talk about. The site offers moms access to information, products, and samples as well as the ability to influence products and programs and help shape marketing programs. The Vocalpoint moms are able to share their opinions and feedback on new ideas and products, and spread the word to friends if they think the idea or product is worth talking about. Membership in the community and the sharing of opinions is entirely voluntary, although on occasion Vocalpoint moms are asked to participate in research and are compensated in the same way as participants in a focus group or any other paid consumer research program.[9]

WEBSITE STRATEGY

Making a site work and having one work successfully are not the same thing; whether a site is effective is determined by what management hopes to achieve through the site. As already noted, some sites are offered for informational purposes only (this

Wind Mobile entered the wireless phone market in select cities with extensive use of digital media that started even before consumers could purchase the service and handsets. The brand planned to spend 30 percent of its $30 million to $40 million first-year budget online, so it's not too surprising to see that digital took the lead initially. The brand is well established with 22 million subscribers in Italy and Greece. The parent company, Globalive, won the rights to be one of three new entrants in the Canadian market in late 2008. The brand began its marketing communication with a website (windmobile.ca) by the summer of 2009 that featured a blog and a community forum section with the purpose of interacting with dissatisfied customers of other wireless brands.

In November, Wind launched a series of Web videos and online ads to go with their print ads despite the service not yet being operational. A review of the application to enter the market by the government delayed the service. The ads showed real consumers as they encountered fees being applied to everyday situations where it would be preposterous to do so, such as having to pay to lock one's bike to a bike rack for three years. Featuring a hidden-camera execution style, the ads highlighted the unique offerings of the new brand (i.e., no contracts, no hidden fees, no extra roaming fees). Wind hoped to illustrate the current state of Canada's wireless industry and to demonstrate the need for increased choice for consumers. An additional website (wirelesssoapbox.com) also continued the dialogue with consumers. With the review completed in December, Wind faced the existing direct competition and anticipated the launch of three other new brands in the new year.

By December, the message moved to "The Power of Conversation," with an emphasis on how the phone can facilitate conversation and the conversations Wind had with consumers from its websites. A new ad paid tribute to its new customers with triumph-themed music and heroic images of people on chariots, horses, or pedestals while dressed in classical outfits. An announcement launch event included a six-metre statue, similar to the ad images, to demonstrate the brand's commitment to consumers. The company's chief customer officer announced, "We wanted to do a monument to customers, to our community online."

Analysts predicted that Wind Mobile reached 30,000 customers in Toronto, Calgary, and Edmonton by March 2010. While executives did not dispute the number, they remained confident that the brand would prevail, as demonstrated by the chairman: "It is premature to draw any conclusions about how things are going with Wind. Wind is still on target to be in five major Canadian cities by September and have 1.5 million subscribers within three years."

Sources: Kristin Laird, "Wind Blowing into Canadian Wireless Market," *Marketing Magazine,* August 13, 2009; Kristin Laird, "Globalive Waits for Approval but Begins Advertising," *Marketing Magazine,* November 30, 2009; Jonathan Paul, "Brilliant! Wind Mobile Blows Its Horn with Viral Vids," *Strategy,* November 2009, p. 70; "New Wireless Brand Could Be in Market Next Week," *Marketing Magazine,* December 11, 2009; Simon Houpt, "Wind Finally Gets Its Moment in the Sun," *The Globe and Mail,* December 18, 2009 p. B7.

Question:

1. Does it appear that Wind is relying too much on digital?

tends to be more common in the business-to-business market than in the consumer market), while others approach the market with more transformational purposes as they become a valuable resource for important life experiences.

Dove's website (Dove.ca) is an example of this newer trend, with multiple capabilities and an extensive array of text, video, graphics, and photos (Exhibit 17-4). Its main menu offers six selections: Products, Connections, Expertise, Features, Offers, and Campaign for Real Beauty. The website helps develop a long-term relationship with women and girls, contributes to the brand image for Dove, and supports sales. Its Products section is a clear approach for providing basic factual information for each type of product (e.g., bar/body wash). The Connections section allows for interaction with blogs and discussion forums along with writing from various Dove personnel. Expertise is offered in one menu item so that consumers can be more knowledgeable about self-care and the products. The Features menu provides video and various interactive experiences for different ages. As the title implies, the Offers section highlights the latest promotions. And, finally, the overall theme of Dove's marketing, Campaign for Real Beauty, has its own section where consumers can learn about the esteem fund. Furthermore, this menu item offers information for specific individuals (e.g., girls, mothers, educators). Surrounding the content displayed for each menu item are various "banner ad–like" boxes for multiple products. As this state-of-the-art example from Dove demonstrates, a website can be an effective marketing tool to achieve any or all communication objectives, and in fact achieve different types of behavioural objectives identified in Chapter 5 for multiple audiences at varying stages of the decision-making process as identified in Chapter 3.

Exhibit 17-4 Dove's website has many transformational features.

A consumer interacting with a website raises the question as to what is meant by interactivity. Interactivity is the extent to which an actor involved in a communication episode perceives the communication to be reciprocal, responsive, speedy, and characterized by the use of nonverbal information.[10]

Applying this idea, a website demonstrates reciprocity if it offers multiple opportunities for the consumer to act upon, such as links, buttons, or connections to other utilities like social media. It also shows responsiveness if every action produces a relevant and appropriate outcome. Extensive use of pictures, sounds, and animation implies nonverbal information. Finally, quick response suggests the website is strong on the speedy characteristic. Notably absent from this definition is the notion of control, since it is a media usage characteristic of both interactive media and non-interactive media as described in Chapter 10. Empirical findings supported this definition of interactivity, which was also found to be a strong predictor of attitude to the website and media involvement.[11] Furthermore, preliminary research indicates that more interactive websites generate deeper information processing and message believability, leading to stronger attitudes to the brand and website.[12]

This attitudinal communication effect is another source of recent findings where researchers investigate what design factors lead to a consumer's positive attitude to the website.[13] Additionally, research investigates the impact of attitude to the website to brand attitude or company attitude.[14] This effect has been investigated for both high/low involvement and informational/transformational brand attitudes, previously discussed in Chapter 8.[15] Finally, research also looks at the attitudinal effects on purchase intentions.[16] Figure 17-5 summarizes these ideas, which are similar to the models described in Chapter 4. Many of the advertising principles established in other media are being investigated with Internet media, and it remains to be seen whether it will be completely similar or with some variation. In the end, however, the notion of Internet advertising is now common terminology.

515

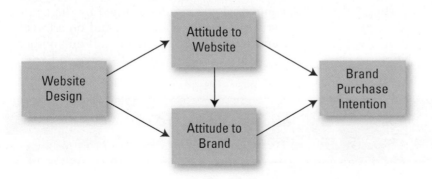

FIGURE 17–5

Model of website advertising effects

To illustrate some of these ideas we turn to the microsite for Bull's-Eye barbecue sauce. Its creative video clips end with a merit theme as the viewer obtains a "badge of brotherhood," and its tips for grilling celebrate the barbecuing experience for men aged 25–45 who are very protective of the tools of their trade—in this case, cooking meat in the great outdoors of one's patio. Guys can send videos of their bolder endeavours to a social media site, where they can enter for chances in a contest for a trip to Las Vegas.[17] Presumably, the key design elements of the microsite lead to these consumers having a stronger attitude to both Bull's-Eye and the site, leading to increased intentions and actual trial.

INTERNET MEDIA OPTIONS

The remarkable power of the Internet is the opportunity for promotional planners to view it as a multiple IMC tool. A primary decision for managers is to strategically use the features of the Internet to achieve communication and behavioural objectives. Various brands treat it as a media channel for advertising; a sales promotion through games and online experiences; a form of sophisticated public relations; and finally a direct-response communication mechanism. This perspective is different than using the Internet with advertising or using the Internet with sales promotion, which we examine toward the end of the chapter. We now investigate each of these options, but begin with the idea of how promotional planners target specific audiences with Internet media.

METHODS OF REACHING TARGET AUDIENCES

Communicating to specific target audiences with Internet media is done by various methods resulting from the nature of the technology and consumer adaptation to the media within their everyday lives. The Advertising Research Foundation suggests reaching target audiences through behaviour, context, geography, site loyalty, and time of day. We now briefly define each of these approaches to illustrate that in terms of communication the Internet shares some characteristics with other media.[18]

Behavioural Targeting   Another Internet advertising concept that has only recently gained acceptance is **behavioural targeting**. Behavioural targeting is based on advertisers targeting consumers according to their website-surfing behaviours. By compiling clickstream data and Internet protocol (IP) information, segments of potential buyers can be identified and ads directed specifically to them. For example, by tracking an individual's visits to a number of automobile websites, an ad for cars or a dealership could be served to that individual. A frequent visitor to employment classifieds might be a promising target for an employment service firm, and so on.

Contextual Targeting   Advertisers who target their ads based on the content of the Internet page are using **contextual targeting**. Whereas behavioural targeting tracks surfing behaviours, contextual ads are determined by the content on the Web page. For example, an advertiser may place an airline ad on a travel site, or a golf club ad on a golf site, or even in or near a story about golf on another site. The Canadian Nurses Association placed its 3-image Flash ad shown in Exhibit 17-5 on

Exhibit 17-5
Employment ads are placed on job search and other work-related websites.

The national job board of the Canadian Nurses Association

job search sites like Workopolis and Monster. In September 2005, Yahoo announced that it would provide a service to automatically place advertisers' messages near relevant content sites, including blogs—a service also offered by Google, though Google has had difficulty implementing the service.[19]

Geographic Targeting   Increasingly, advertisers are adjusting their Internet communication messages depending upon where the user is located. This information can be determined with the user's voluntary declaration of residence (e.g., country, city, etc.) and to some degree with technological features. For example, different versions of travel websites (e.g., Travel Alberta) can emerge depending upon where the information seeker is living. Research suggests stronger consumer response with more tailored messages based on geography.

Site-Loyalty Targeting   Websites fit into a variety of categories, much like television specialty channels, and recent research indicates that consumers have an affinity for or are very loyal to particular sites for their information or entertainment needs. More loyal users tend to spend more time at a favourite site and have much more positive attitudes toward the site's relevance, content, and features. More importantly, users have more positive attitudes of the advertising for the sites they are more loyal toward and exhibit stronger awareness for advertised brands.

Time of Day Targeting   Consumer variation in media usage akin to television and radio is found with Internet media. Television viewers are not consistently the same across the whole day, from early morning viewers to those watching daytime television versus the prime-time audience. Similarly, radio's audience size and composition varies considerably, especially during driving to and from work. Internet media are following a similar pattern, with groups of working people accessing Internet media during the day for business purposes, primarily in the morning. It declines during the afternoon and dinner time and then peaks once again during the evening for leisure purposes. Recent Canadian data suggest that the biggest growth in Internet media use is daytime access of news and information sites, at 21 percent versus overall Internet media use growth of 13 percent.[20]

ADVERTISING

Today, companies and organizations promoting their products and services must consider the Internet like they would any other media. The Interactive Advertising Bureau (IAB) of Canada estimated that online advertising revenue reached $1.8 billion in 2009 (Figure 17-6). This is still lower than the $3.1 billion spent on television and is almost on par with daily newspapers at $2.0 billion. Internet advertising

FIGURE   17–6   Canadian online advertising revenue, ten-year growth trend

	2000	2001	2002	2003	2004	2005	2006	2007	2008	2009
Total Cda Millions ($)	98	86	176	237	364	562	900	1,241	1,602	1,822
% growth/yr	96	–12	105	35	54	54	60	38	29	14
French Cda Millions ($)	—	—	—	—	65.5	124	189	260	317	352
% growth/yr	—	—	—	—	—	89	52	38	22	11

Note: Online Advertising Revenues for French Canada were not able to be determined accurately until 2004.

Source: Interactive Advertising Bureau of Canada

FIGURE   17–7

Distribution of online
revenue by major
product category

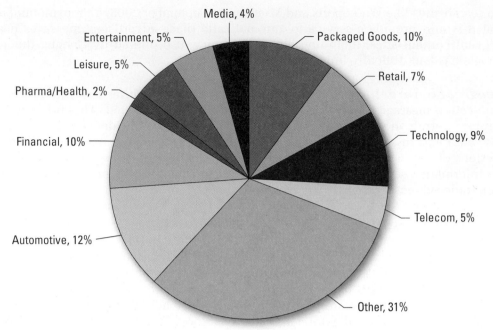

Source: Interactive Advertising Bureau of Canada

revenue accounted for 13 percent of the total advertising revenue in Canada, yet reached more than 20 percent for five European countries and 14 percent for the United States.[21] Some are perplexed that Internet advertising revenue is not a higher percentage of the total given that Canada has one of the world's highest broadband penetration rates.[22] The types of products advertised on the Internet in 2009 are shown in Figure 17-7. Coastal Contacts, located in Vancouver, is a successful online advertiser and is one of the world's largest online retailers of prescription eyewear.[23] The types of online advertising used by companies are shown in Figure 17-8. We now discuss these various options.

Banners   A common form of advertising on the Internet is with **banner ads**. Banner ads take their name and format from ads found in other media (e.g., newspapers). While initially most often taking the form of a vertical rectangle across the top of an Internet page, now square and vertical rectangles of varying standard sizes

FIGURE   17–8   Canadian online advertising revenue, by advertising vehicle, five-year trend

Advertising Vehicle	2005 $ (millions)	2006 $ (millions)	% change	2007 $ (millions)	% change	2008 $ (millions)	% change	2009 $ (millions)	% change
Search	197	343	74	478	39	622	30	741	19
Display	230	314	37	432	38	490	13	578	18
Classifieds/Directories	124	223	80	305	37	460	51	467	2
Video	—	—	NA	9	NA	12	33	20	67
Email	11	20	82	17	−15	18	6	13	−28
VideoGaming	—	—	NA	—	NA	—	NA	3	NA
Total	551	880	60%	1,241	41%	1,602	29%	1,822	14%

Source: Interactive Advertising Bureau of Canada

are available with placement in various page locations (Exhibit 17-6). Although there continues to be innovation with new digital applications, the majority of banner ads initially look like a print ad found in newspapers or magazines and are referred to as display ads, the same name used in the original media. Banner advertising revenue hit $490 million in 2008, up from $216 million in 2006, and clearly rivals magazines at $692 million. Banner ads are found in all sorts of vehicles on the Internet, and this revenue total includes ads also found in social media outlets like Facebook. Naturally, banner ads have a link embedded allowing users to move to any other digital location, usually a brand or company website, and more recent developments allow for different interactive features. While the click-through is about 0.1 percent these days, one industry study employing eye-tracking methodology provides strong evidence that banner ads may be very effective in creating recall and brand building. The study also revealed a strong dislike for flashing banner ads, indicating that viewers almost immediately dismiss them.[24] In addition, a Ponemon Institute study conducted in 2004 showed that 66 percent of respondents said they would find relevant banner ads less annoying, while 52 percent indicated they would even be likely to respond to a relevant banner ad.[25]

Since banner ads are the original marketing communication found on the Internet and account for extensive advertising revenue, it is not surprising to see a number of academics investigating their usefulness. Much of this research builds on existing studies done for other media with an interest in predicting awareness (i.e., recall and recognition), attitude to the brand, attitude to the ad, attitude to the advertising format, purchase intention, and click-through rates—all communication and behavioural effects discussed earlier. A number of familiar topics recently have been investigated. One study looked at the effects of forced exposure; that is, whether the user had control to avoid the ad.[26] Other research has shown the importance of congruence between the website (i.e., media vehicle) or the search engine keywords imputed and the brand advertised.[27] Another inquiry looked at whether the audience was familiar or unfamiliar with the advertised brand, a key factor in advertising planning that has been covered extensively in this book.[28] Other research has begun to investigate the effects of message content design elements and format of the ads on both communication and behavioural effects.[29] Furthermore, media scheduling and duration of exposure of the banner ads replicate findings of advertising from other media. For example, longer exposure and repetition are generally important in achieving desired effects.[30] And while existing research begins to uncover how banner ads work, a new innovation comes along where banner ads will instantly turn into an interactive microsite without redirection that allows the downloading of promotional items (e.g., a coupon). Later, the new ads will include provisions for feedback (e.g., sign-up) and transactions.[31]

Pop-Ups/Pop-Unders While Internet users are browsing, a window—or maybe even a creature of some sort—might appear on their screen with a message. These advertisements are known as **pop-ups**, and appear when users access certain sites. Pop-ups are usually larger than banner ads but smaller than a full screen. **Pop-unders** are ads that appear underneath the Web page and become visible only when the user leaves the site. While there exists some disagreement on their usefulness for advertising, consumer complaints have led Google and others to no longer accept these advertising forms. A study conducted by TNS revealed that 93 percent of respondents found pop-up ads annoying or very annoying.[32] In contrast, one academic study concludes that these ads may be more welcomed when users are in a more entertainment-minded mood, the ads are relevant, or the ads provide value in some manner.[33] The frequency and effectiveness of these ads have been greatly reduced given the opportunity for Internet users to use an application that blocks the ads before they appear on the screen. Some marketers believe that pop-ups and pop-unders are in the decline stage of their life cycle.

Exhibit 17-6 Banner ad formats.

Interstitials **Interstitials** are ads that emerge on the screen while a site's content downloads. Although some advertisers believe that interstitials are irritating and more of a nuisance than a benefit, a study conducted by Grey Advertising found that only 15 percent of those surveyed felt that the ads were irritating (versus 9 percent for banner ads) and that 47 percent liked the ads (versus 38 percent for banners). Perhaps more importantly, while ad recall of banner ads was approximately 51 percent, recall of interstitials was much higher, at 76 percent. A new form of interstitial is in-person ads, where a person begins speaking to the user, so the effect is similar to experiencing a presentation from a sales person.

Sponsorship Another common form of advertising is **sponsorship**, of which there are two types. Regular sponsorship occurs when a company pays to sponsor a section of a site. A more involved agreement is the **content sponsorship**, in which the sponsor not only provides dollars in return for name association but also participates in providing the content itself. In some cases, the site is responsible for providing content and having it approved by the sponsor; in other instances, the sponsor may contribute all or part of the content.

For example, a Nature Valley/Sympatico microsite emerged when users selected certain subject sections from the Sympatico portal. The repackaged look of the website provided links to various outdoor activities like hiking, golfing, and skiing. These links informed users about these recreational activities, provided recommendations on how to enjoy their experiences, and gave suggestions on what to eat (i.e., Nature Valley Chewy Trail Mix). The microsite featured an advergame that was tied to receiving a free sample delivered to the user's home. Executives believed in promotions targeted to adults aged 25–49 who enjoyed an active lifestyle but were not health-obsessed. Post-promotion results appeared impressive. The Nature Valley brand received an 18-percent increase in message association scores, a 35-percent increase in unaided brand awareness, and 20,000 unique visitors played the advergame.[34]

Push Technologies **Push technologies**, or **webcasting** technologies, allow companies to "push" a message to consumers rather than waiting for them to find it. Push technologies dispatch Internet pages and news updates and may have sound and video geared to specific audiences and even individuals. For example, a manager whose job responsibilities involve corporate finance might log on to his or her computer and find that new stories are automatically there on the economy, stock updates, or a summary of a speech. Companies provide screen savers that automatically "hook" the viewer to their sites for sports, news, weather reports, and/or other information that the viewer has specified. Users can use **personalization**—that is, they can personalize their sites to request the kinds of specific information they are most interested in viewing. For example, sports fans can have updates sent to them through sites providing sports information. The service is paid for by advertisers who flash their messages on the screen and therefore it is similar to a sponsorship.

Links While considered by some to not be a type of advertising, **links** serve many of the same purposes as are served by the types discussed above. A visitor to one site may click on a link that provides additional information and/or related materials at another site. Thus someone on TSN.ca may link to Nike.com and find information on sports-related products. Google's application of Adsense and Adwords is an example of this form of advertising that has grown significantly the past few years.

Paid Search A substantial form of advertising on the Internet is that of **paid search**, or search engine advertising in which advertisers pay only when a consumer clicks on their ad or link from a search engine page. Search advertising revenue reached $602 million in Canada for 2008. In an effort to more specifically target customers that may be interested in their offerings, advertisers buy ads on search engine sites such as Google, Yahoo, or MSN so that when the visitor to the site keys in a specific search word or phrase, an advertisement targeted to that category appears. For example, typing in the word *automobile* could lead to a Ford ad (or commercial). Advertisers bid for the placement; those who pay the most get the best locations. More sophisticated search engines look at meta-tags (keywords that describe the document or site) as well as the content, link structure, and link popularity. Search results are provided in the form of organic (nonpaid listings) and sponsored links, as seen in Exhibit 17-7. Proponents of sponsored search contend that it allows companies to specifically target those interested in their products and/or services, and add that even small companies can compete equitably since they pay only when a user clicks on their ad. Opponents accuse paid search of wasted money because advertisers pay top dollar for the place-

Exhibit 17-7   Results of a Google search for flowers.

ments upon which consumers click, even though they likely would have gone there anyway. However, one example by Yahoo finds a 60 percent higher click-through rate beyond display ads arising from a search versus display ads placed without connection to past search engine use.[35]

Jeff Quipp, CEO of Toronto-based Search Engine People, makes the following recommendations for paid search success. One, the titles for the pages should labelled and unique, and the text should not be embedded in visuals. Two, content should be unique and valuable so that designers of other sites will see value and include a link on their site. Three, to increase a ranking on search, pay the extra money for the search terms and do what is necessary in messaging to ensure strong click-through rates. Four, optimize customization through past search history.[36]

Online Commercials   The increased penetration of broadband into households has increased the use of streaming video advertising messages. The equivalent of traditional television commercials, online commercials are appearing on the Net. Some companies have created their own Web commercials, while others run the same spots they show on TV. A number of companies have been successful in blending the two media, showing the commercial on TV and then directing interested viewers to the Web if they wish to see it again or to view longer versions. The growth of consumers watching TV shows online has led to $55 million in advertising revenue that is currently accounted for within the TV figures.[37]

Radio-Canada, responsible for CBC programming in French, undertook an experiment with several industry personnel and placed its TV ads on the broadcaster's Internet site for a period of one month. TV spots directed viewers to this option. With an eye to seeing whether consumers would be interested in the concept and to determine the most appropriate measurement and compensation system, the trial appeared successful. About 41,000 unique visitors watched an average of four commercials each, and 90 percent of the feedback e-mails contained positive comments. The future of this idea as a permanent option appears possible as those involved continue to investigate issues of viability, costs to marketers, fees to rights-holders, time, and bandwidth.[38]

Video on Demand   Video clips of various entertainment activities (which include ads or are sponsored) are also available through the Internet. CTV's Broadband Network ushered in a new route for advertisers to reach their audiences via Internet media. Viewers watch free shows along with embedded commercials, similar to

Video on the Internet has made great strides recently as trade publications like *Strategy* recognized creativity with awards and overnight sensations emerged; however, spoofs and financial concerns raise concerns for this new media opportunity.

Strategy presented two cyber-awards for innovative video messages. The agency Taxi invited break dancers to a faux dance audition, and upon completion the dancers did their moves while solving a jigsaw puzzle, playing Jenga, or twisting a Rubik's cube, all while being filmed. The resulting ad circulated on various video sites with the purpose of promoting the "Go! Go! Break Steady" video game for Xbox Live, a puzzle-based game developed by Little Boy Games of Vancouver.

Dove's interactive romantic comedy video located at its own website (wakinguphannah.ca) to promote its new Go Fresh product line of soap, shampoo, lotion, deodorant, and body mist targeted to women in their twenties featured a storyline where users decided the ending by clicking different videos at the completion of each scene. With a total of 19 clips and seven possible endings, women experienced the highs and lows of Hannah's day (e.g., blind date, boss, etc.) while witnessing her e-mail, voicemail, text messages, and photos. A total of 270,000 visits occurred during the first six months, with an average length of over three minutes, to help Dove exceed its sales target by 48 percent.

Multiple video genres abound on YouTube; one type features people displaying their talents with the hopes of being discovered. In fact, TV stations and other content providers eagerly watch to find the next big hit or to test ideas for shows online. The video becomes almost a commercial, with a demonstration-like execution style or perhaps even a sample. In either case, a venture like Nadia G's *Bitchin' Kitchen* got discovered by the Food Network so that the online sketch comedy video could find a new home on TV.

However, executives at Microsoft must be wondering about Internet video messages after numerous spoofs of its ad for Windows 7 digitally appeared seemingly everywhere. The ad encouraged consumers to host a party where everyone would explore the features of the new operating system. According to one Microsoft manager, "It's giving people the opportunity to experience the product. The TV and online advertising will create awareness, but people have got to get their hands on it." So the house party seemed the perfect solution, and despite some mockery 50,000 signed up to be a host!

And what of Google's YouTube—how can it possibly host all this video? Twenty hours uploaded per minute works out to almost 30,000 hours per day, which translates to over 10 million hours per year. One estimate pegged the loss at about a half-billion dollars a year, so the question arises as to how sustainable online video messages will be in the future since this social medium sells ads on fewer than 10 percent of its videos.

Sources: Hollie Shaw, "Delivering the Story," *National Post,* October 23, p. FP12; Anonymous, "YouTubeLand," *National Post,* August, 22, 2009, p. FP1; Carey Toane, "Cyber," *Strategy,* June 2009, p. 49; Farhad Manjoo, "Everybody's Surfing: No One's Paying," *National Post,* April 20, p. A10.

Question:

1. How similar or different is watching a video message online to watching one on TV or elsewhere?

---

the existing television model. Initial programming had five or six minutes of commercials per 22-minute show, running before, after, and during the show. As an alternative, CHUM offered its shows on specific Internet sites for each program, such as MuchMusic, rather than a central "network" location.[39] The future of advertising through streamed television shows is a new, promising opportunity for promotional planners, even though the innovation is in the early stages of development for the sender and the receiver. Internet Protocol Television, IPTV, gained ground in 2006 and 2007, and service providers expected about one million Canadian subscribers by the end of 2008.[40] The growth of video messages on the Internet is summarized in IMC Perspective 17-2.

Podcasting **Podcasting** is a medium that uses the Internet to distribute audio and video files for downloading to various portable handheld devices for learning or entertainment purposes. The enhanced control of this medium allows users to time-shift and place-shift their media consumption. Like other media alternatives, advertising opportunities are present. For example, Volvo sponsored a podcast for $60,000 that was downloaded 150,000 times, while other initial sponsorships garnered $25 per thousand. In addition, metrics for understanding the audience size (Exhibit 17-8) emerged similar to other media (e.g., podtrac.com). After this initial development, a recent study investigated how podcasting worked. The findings indicate an average of 2.4 ads per podcast with an average length of 16 seconds, consistent with a length seen on television and ads shown prior to video clips on news or portal sites. The majority of the ads (i.e., 75 percent) preceded or ended the podcast with a sponsorship message, much like the early days of television in the 1950s. In most cases, the content provider acknowledged sponsorship message with familiar phrases like, "brought to you by" (19 percent), "support" (18 percent), "break" (16 percent), "sponsors" (13 percent), and "thanks" (6 percent). The specificity of the podcast content allowed for very targeted ads (60 percent), such as automobile brands sponsoring a car-care podcast; thus, we see a very strong media vehicle source effect much like magazines.[41] It appears a familiar advertising model with a sponsorship approach will continue to grow; however, the content of a podcast is also a message with possible commercial intent. For example, in order to increase demand for fine wine consumption, a podcast describing the nuances of grapes, vintages, tasting, and so on could act as a means of switching consumers who currently purchase less premium brands.

Exhibit 17-8 Audiences for podcasts represent a new advertising opportunity.

RSS **Really Simple Syndication (RSS)** is a specification that uses XML to organize and format Web-based content in a standard way. Content owners create an RSS feed, which usually consists of titles and brief descriptions of about 10 articles elsewhere on the site. The difference between Web content and an RSS feed is that the latter can send out notifications whenever new material is available.[42] Because the alerts can be customized to the viewers' preferences, advertisers have found it useful for disseminating information to those who may be most interested.

Blogs A **blog** (or weblog) is a Web-based publication consisting primarily of periodic articles, normally presented in reverse chronological order. As noted, blogs may reflect the writings of an individual, a community, a political organization, or a corporation, and they offer advertisers a new way to reach their target audiences. Some marketers are excited about the potential of blogs to reach large audiences at a small cost. Companies have experimented with corporate blogs to put forth a friendly public relations face to the general public and allow some interactions.

Personal bloggers often find themselves as key influencers for consumers while describing their product experiences. For some consumers, a blogger has a strong source credibility effect. In this respect, bloggers are acting similarly to journalists who feature product stories in newspapers or magazines. Marketers are also starting to recognize that mothers who blog are particularly successful in this role as mothers seem to trust other mothers considerably. For example, McDonald's recruited five mothers for behind-the-scenes tours. As they wrote about their experiences, the testimonials resonated like the most perfect commercial: "McDonald's hamburgers are made from 100% Canadian beef. No fillers, no additives. No preservatives. Beef. That's it. I promise. And I can make this promise to you because I was there to see it."[43]

523

Advertisers also sponsor personal blogs, or an individual blog that is part of a collection of blogs such as the yummymummyclub.ca. Erica Ehm, a famous media host, documented a trip to Alberta on her blog, which included photos taken with a Sony camera. One page of the blog ended with the brand prominently displayed with a sponsorship notice that provided full disclosure of the relationship between the blogger and the brand. Some are critical of this process and suggest that it circumvents the "idea" of a blog, while others are concerned that bloggers do not communicate the advertiser's exact financial contribution. In defence, bloggers cite industries (e.g., fashion, travel) where free goods are routinely passed along for endorsement. Currently, Advertising Standards Canada, the self-regulatory body for marketers, has no plans for potential disguised advertising techniques in blogs.[44]

Social Media   Without question, social media has exploded in popularity during the past few years, with social networking or social utility sites as prominent Web destinations. Figure 17-9 shows data from a panel study conducted by Zinc Research and Dufferin Research that demonstrates Facebook's dominance in the Canadian market. Social networking in general, and Facebook in particular, is predominantly a younger person's activity, and the data in Figure 17-10 highlight this across four age groups. Figure 17-11 summarizes some of the reasons why characteristics of social networking are important for its users.

In many ways, from an advertising standpoint Facebook and other social media offer themselves as media vehicles much like a specific magazine or television show might. There is a placement of a print or video message within a content environment (or via a link). These messages are similar to the ads described above, such as a banner ad with a link to a brand's website or video messages created by the brand or by users (Exhibit 17-9).

The targeting abilities of these tools make them a very attractive opportunity for advertisers, allowing for complete choice and substantial precision among all the methods described earlier in the targeting section. Facebook, for example, provides some guidelines on how the targeting and costing operates in this new media environment, and for the most part the steps are similar to what we have seen for other media but with simpler, "point and click" options as opposed to other more involved logistical arrangements.

524

FIGURE   17–9

Awareness of social networking websites, September 2009

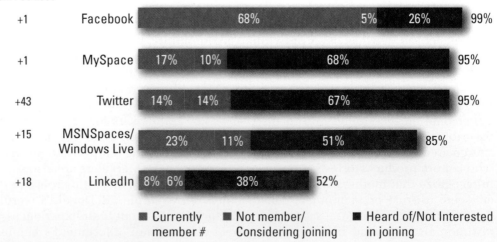

Source: Zinc Research, Dufferin Research

Proxied Penetration Rates* (%)
Total Canada; 9.41 million; 18+ –8.04 million

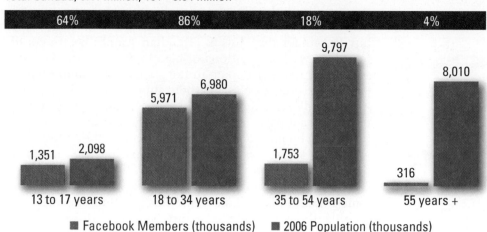

| 64% | 86% | 18% | 4% |

9,797

8,010

6,980

5,971

1,351   2,098

1,753

316

13 to 17 years   18 to 34 years   35 to 54 years   55 years +

■ Facebook Members (thousands)   ■ 2006 Population (thousands)

Source: Zinc Research, Dufferin Research

FIGURE   17–10

Facebook members
by age, April 2008

In another sense these media are completely unique, with the development of "fan" pages that allow an instant connection to exciting brand content, making the whole page a commercial experience in which the user may not even perceive (or may not be concerned about) the advertising due to their pervasive brand loyalty. Fan pages can offer virtually any marketing communication tool depending on the brand's objective. For example, during the summer of 2010 the Molson Canadian

525

"How important are the following aspects of social networking sites to you. . .?"

■ Very important   ■ Somewhat important

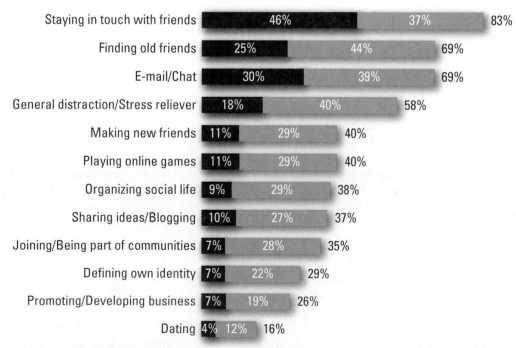

	Very important	Somewhat important	Total
Staying in touch with friends	46%	37%	83%
Finding old friends	25%	44%	69%
E-mail/Chat	30%	39%	69%
General distraction/Stress reliever	18%	40%	58%
Making new friends	11%	29%	40%
Playing online games	11%	29%	40%
Organizing social life	9%	29%	38%
Sharing ideas/Blogging	10%	27%	37%
Joining/Being part of communities	7%	28%	35%
Defining own identity	7%	22%	29%
Promoting/Developing business	7%	19%	26%
Dating	4%	12%	16%

Source: Zinc Research, Dufferin Research

FIGURE   17–11

Usage of social
networking sites,
September 2009

Exhibit 17-9 Facebook uses banner ads to generate revenue.

Facebook page featured about 430,000 fans who could watch 6 Molson videos and 32 videos posted by fans or other consumers. Similarly, Molson posted 6 photo albums, while fans posted about 1,300 photos. Concert information and links to buy tickets for the Molson Canadian Amphitheatre could be found, as well as locations of bars to attend. True fans could read about and participate in the "Seize the Summer" promotion by earning badges for their summer experiences, much like a child's summer camp experience, that could be recorded on a personal page. This final step required the permission of the user, who had to agree to let Molson do the following four activities: (1) access my basic information (i.e., name, profile picture, gender, networks, user ID, list of friends, and any other information I've shared with everyone); (2) send me an e-mail (i.e., Molson Canadian Seize the Summer may e-mail me directly at. . .); (3) post to my wall (i.e., Molson Canadian Seize the Summer may post status messages, notes, photos, and videos to my wall); (4) access my data any time (i.e., Molson Canadian Seize the Summer may access my data when I'm not using the application).

The implications of giving this kind of access to a company are interesting. The data could, over time, be compiled into a database and act as a resource for other marketing activities. For example, for a product like a beer brand a sophisticated marketer might want to figure out when a group of friends are planning to go to a particular bar, and then send out a promotional team to the same bar. Additional direct digital marketing activities may be developed such that a group of friends could be invited to an event.

Interactive Games A burgeoning vehicle is the placement of ads within interactive games, or the development of games that in fact act as an ad for the brand. The potential of this market will be interesting to watch over the next decade, but already firms are moving in this direction. Game developer EA recently purchased an interactive games company to pursue the path of playing games within a social networking site.[45] Fuel Industries of Ottawa worked deals to develop brand content in some of the games it develops for clients.[46] Dynamic ads in games allow links to other websites: Microsoft and Ubisoft of Montreal targeted game developers by placing ads in a game they frequent.[47] Nissan established its own game on a website (nissangooddecision.com) that provided an interactive feature to help consumers in their search for a new car.[48] Koodo used a series of videos on YouTube where consumers could chase a life-size gingerbread man through the streets—clearly from the imaginations of marketers![49]

SALES PROMOTION

Consumers experiencing Internet media through a variety of applications like websites, social utilities, blogs, podcasts, and video-on-demand allow promotional planners to offer innovative sales promotions, largely to encourage repeat purchasing or repeat consumption. Innovative advertisers create specialized groups on Facebook, a leading social utility application, to communicate and interact with loyal customers. In these environments, the members receive various treats. For example *Spider-Man* movie fans who joined the Facebook group obtained electronic icons of the webbed hero for their computer. Loyal customers are rewarded with other related electronic items provided to them through social utilities and websites—such as ringtones, desktop wallpapers, and emoticons, skins, winks, and pictures for instant message services.

Related to this are virtual environments where consumers can immerse themselves in alternative realities. Habbo Hotel offers online visitors the opportunity to interact with one another as though they are guests in a hotel (Exhibit 17-10). The Canadian Habbo Hotel was attracting 300,000 youth each month, so Sprite looked at the game to bring its hip animated spokesperson "Miles Thirst" to life. Instead of being merely associated with the environment, Sprite wanted to become an integral part of it—starting with the largest club within Habbo Hotel, which Sprite renovated and renamed "Club Thirst" so visitors could meet Miles Thirst. They created a penthouse and set it up as a place where Habbo visitors could get together with Miles twice a week over a six-month campaign. Another simulated experience at the Habbo Hotel is ordering virtual drinks from the bar. Normally, visitors are served a generic Habbo cola. In this campaign, visitors quenched their thirst with Sprite—a welcome addition that provided an exciting new "real-life" dimension to the overall Habbo experience. The results of the campaign were incredible. Brand likability, purchase intent, and consumption for Sprite improved dramatically. One control group study that compared teens who had not visited Habbo Hotel to those who had showed a 90-percent increase in Sprite product consumption among Habbo visitors.[50]

Exhibit 17-10 Consumers visited Miles Thirst at the Habbo Hotel.

In this sense, these services have become digital "gifts" or "premiums," as described in the sales promotion chapter. Although the non-virtual world usually considered tangible goods to be the premium, the digital age has spawned the concept of intangible gifts that become highly valued. Another example occurs where various types of points systems allow repeat customers to generate even further rewards—a virtual continuity program for avid Internet media users who are brand loyal. Also, many brands offer advergames, skill-challenging endeavours that keep customers amused while offering brand messages during play. Thus, Internet media allow previously intangible sales promotions to create value through intangible benefits for continued usage.

Finally, one of the most significant rewards for loyal customers has been the delivery of enhanced content in terms of information or entertainment. Loyal customers are rewarded with exclusive video for their participation. To give thanks, advertisers provide enhanced levels of information where this is deemed valuable. In this sense, the content is not the product witnessed as it is perceived as a bonus, something fitting the original definition of a sales promotion.

PUBLIC RELATIONS

The Internet is a useful medium for conducting public relations activities. Many sites devote a portion of their content to public relations, including the provision of information about the company, its philanthropic activities, and annual

Exhibit 17-11   Chrysler uses its website for public relations purposes.

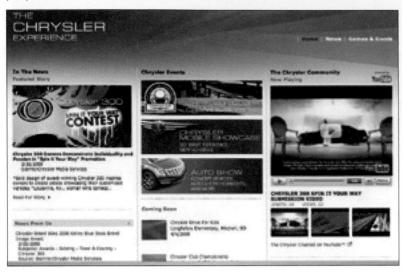

reports. Companies have used the Web to establish media, government, investor, and community relationships; deal with crises; and even perform corporate image, advocacy, and cause-related advertising. Companies have used their websites to address issues as well as to provide information about products and services, archive press releases, link to other articles and sites, and provide lists of activities and events. Other Internet tools, including e-mails and e-mail newsletters, have also been used effectively.

An excellent example of the use of public relations on the Internet is provided by Chrysler (Exhibit 17-11). The site provides up-to-date news stories and other forms of content, photo images, and cross-references to other sites or media as well as press kits and a calendar of upcoming events. It also provides information about Chrysler automobiles and the corporation itself and allows for customer feedback and registration for updates. In addition, DaimlerChrysler's homepage contains many of the articles written about the corporation, including awards won and philanthropic efforts achieved such as its concern for the environment and its $1.1 million support for Hurricane Katrina victims.

At the same time, many philanthropic and nonprofit organizations have found the Internet to be a useful way to generate funds. Several companies have developed sites to perform the functions that are required in traditional fundraising programs. For example, Ben & Jerry's uses its website to promote its products and image as well as showcasing the causes it supports and champions such as global warming, peace, and social and environmental issues (see Exhibit 17-12). Charitable organizations have also formed sites to handle public relations activities, provide information regarding the causes the charity supports, collect contributions, and so on. In an example of integrating the Internet with public relations and television, companies have found the Internet to be extremely useful for providing information in times of a crisis, and for gathering feedback about their products and services and about themselves.

Exhibit 17-12

Ben & Jerry's supports global causes through its website.

DIRECT MARKETING

Our discussion of direct marketing and the Internet will approach the topic from the perspective of e-mail and mobile.

E-Mail Direct mail on the Internet is essentially an electronic version of regular mail. Like regular mail it is highly targeted, relies heavily on lists, and attempts to reach consumers with specific needs through targeted messages. Consumers can opt to have specific types of e-mail sent to them and other types not sent. For example, collectors of Air Miles can subscribe to notices sent out for different promotional offers (Exhibit 17-13).

Alternatively, companies can use e-mail for different purposes. For example, Bell uses e-mail for different customer stages when communicating its Internet service. It sends e-mail to new consumers in order to obtain personal information and make the new user comfortable with the Internet. Later, when the data analysis of usage behaviour indicates a high probability of a customer leaving, Bell sends out a customized e-mail to encourage the customer to stay. The results have been impressive as the firm has noted a substantial drop in its percentage of customers leaving, also known in the industry as churn. Finally, subsequent data analysis identifies customers who may be using services that do not fully meet their needs, and Bell sends out an e-mail communicating a more appropriate service level. In some cases it has sent direct mail, but it received a substantially lower response rate.[51]

Catalogue companies keep in touch with customers via e-mail for purchase facilitation and information updates (Exhibit 17-14). Another usage is sending publications when consumers subscribe. A detailed and sophisticated database is developed from consumers agreeing to opt in since they provide segmentation-like information. Two successful sites (thrilllist.com, urbandaddy.com) send out publications to men that are consistent with the regular content not sent digitally. Each publication has a growing e-mail list and sends customized content that is quite distinct from one another with unique positioning approaches.[52]

Sometimes, users may also receive less targeted, unwanted e-mails referred to as **spam**. However, legitimate and enlightened marketers accept the practice of permission-based marketing as described above. Figure 17-12 summarizes the different types of advertising and promotion messages that Canadian consumers are most interested in receiving via e-mail.

Research investigated two of the behavioural responses: visiting the brand's website, and forwarding the e-mail to a friend. In a study for cosmetic and body care products sold in retail stores, more useful permission-based e-mail messages yielded fewer website visits, presumably because the information satisfied consumer requirements. However, more useful, more interesting, and more frequent e-mail messages resulted in more store visits, presumably to examine or buy the product. Consumers perceived useful e-mails as offering sales promotion information, or information about new products.[53]

Exhibit 17-13 E-mails sent from Air Miles inform members on how they can spend their reward miles.

Exhibit 17-14 Road Runner Sports has used the Internet to market to runners.

FIGURE 17–12

Registering to receive
e-mail/types of sites
registered

	2004	2010
Entertainment	48%	40%
E-Commerce/Retail	30%	28%
Travel	26%	28%
Health/Fitness	29%	27%
News/Information	36%	27%
Finance/Banking	20%	27%

Source: Ipsos-Reid, 2004 E-mail Marketing Study, 2010 Inter@ctiv Reid Report

Another study found pass-along rates for different types of e-mail: humour (88 percent), news (56 percent), health care and health information (32 percent), finance (24 percent), and sports (24 percent). Overall, 89 percent of the U.S. sample shared content with others via e-mail, with 63 percent sharing content at least once a week, and a whopping 75 percent forwarding content to as many as six others. However, 75 percent contend branded content makes no impact on whether they forward a message. Heather Clark, associate director of creative strategy at Henderson Bas in Toronto, who has worked on campaigns for ING Direct and Levi's, cautions there is potential for dismal failure as the chance of a commercial message being passed along using e-mail is extremely low. Apart from humour, one tactic that will help is incentives, such as an extra entry in a sweepstakes contest. A third factor is recognizing the consumer is in charge with an optional "send to a friend" feature and a chance for recipients to personalize the message before they forward it.[54]

In another sample of 1,259 forwarded e-mails from 34 participants, a study found extraordinary dispersion in the number forwarded during the one-month time frame. One person forwarded 177 messages and two others forwarded more than 100, while three people sent one each. Overall, participants forwarded about 40 percent of the e-mails received, which ranged from 0 percent to 100 percent. The implication of finding a "lead sender" for an e-mail forwarding campaign appears critical for success, much like a lead user in a diffusion of innovation. Additional qualitative research in the study finds that participants experienced substantial positive and negative emotional responses when receiving forwarded e-mail.[55]

It is important to note that the pass-along of e-mail is an outcome and not a strategy.[56] It is a manifestation of the cognitive and emotional responses of the receiver to the message. The similarity to a TV ad would be to recall the ad and tell someone about it, or to call out to a family member, "Hey Dad, come check out this ad on TV." Secondly, e-mail can experience extensive pass-along yet have minimal benefit for the brand since it entails a single exposure of a brand message for many of the receivers, who simply delete it after viewing.[57]

Mobile Advertising revenue for mobile totalled almost $12 million in 2008 and is summarized in Figure 17-13. Three main sources are short message service (SMS), mobile content, and display/sponsorship, although mobile search and mobile applications appear to be strong contenders for the future. Research to conduct these data carefully outlined what types of charges are not counted as advertising revenue given the unique delivery via mobile devices. Many marketing communication managers are excited with these new developments; however, it remains to be seen what level they will grow to, what media they may replace, and how fast they will grow. We now briefly describe these new options.

Short-Message Service Canadian cellphone carriers agreed to connect their networks so that text messages could be sent to any cellphone handset regardless of the carrier used. For example, Telus customers could send a message to a friend who

	2006 $ (thousands)	2007 $ (thousands)	percent change	2008 $ (thousands)	percent change
Mobile Messaging (SMS)	801	2,080	160	3,211	54
Mobile Content	104	219	111	5,113	2,235
Mobile Advertising (Display/Sponsorship)	81	140	73	3,329	2,278
Mobile Applications	8	121	1,413	238	97
Mobile Search	0	0	0	0	0
Other	100	103	3	0	−100
Total	1,094	2,663	143	11,891	347

Source: Interactive Advertising Bureau of Canada

FIGURE   17–13

Advertising revenue by mobile advertising vehicle

used Rogers, Bell Mobility, or Fido rather than only to another Telus user.[58] This technological evolution paved the way for marketers to develop innovative two-way communication. Rather than send text messages one way, like e-mail, marketers conceived the idea of creating short codes as part of a short-message service (SMS), so that consumers could immediately respond to relevant ads using their cellphone. For example, if "24BLUE" is seen on a billboard, the consumer could type this in and receive whatever promotional offer or information Labatt wanted to send as part of its overall promotional program. Overall, the SMS becomes a permission-based pull communication as only those interested in the promotional messages respond accordingly. Moreover, the marketer can reach any cellphone user with the technology standardization.[59]

Current research suggests that Canadians lag in text message usage, at 25 percent compared to 36 percent in the U.S. and 70 to 85 percent in various European countries. Although the domestic growth is impressive, moving from 3.7 million messages per day in 2005 to 8.7 million messages per day in 2006, only 12 percent are willing to receive relevant text messages from marketers. Despite the usefulness of SMS for marketing purposes remaining elusive, many brands planned and executed new communication and promotional offers. One expert estimated that main brands launched about 500 programs during the three years from 2005 to 2007.[60]

For example, Warner Music and 7-Eleven promoted to listeners of a local Winnipeg radio station to text in the message "Secret Events" for exclusive directions to locations where they could win a free CD or a free Slurpee. The success of this kind of communication is boosted by the fact that virtually all text messages are actually read by the cellphone customer.[61] Intrawest's promotional codes at point of sale generated a 50 percent redemption for a 25 percent discount on a hotel rental. Reactine provided information on pollen levels at locations and times when allergy sufferers needed the information. Molson Canadian Rocks Revealed allowed consumers to text the name of a mystery band based on clues provided. In turn, winners received virtual tickets scanned at the venue for admission. Various digital signage locations with unique words allowed Nissan to track which Versa messages received the most frequent contest entries.[62] Companies also found innovative ways to interact with their customers, going beyond promotional offers to attract switchers. For example, pharmaceutical company Janssen-Ortho, manufacturer of a contraceptive patch for women, sends weekly reminders to change the patch to women who have requested the alert.[63]

One limitation of SMS codes is the time delay of four to six weeks for registration with the Canadian Wireless Telecommunications Association (CWTA), which is responsible for ensuring that legitimate codes are launched to protect consumers from spam. Another limitation is that carriers are not fully consistent in working with all the different types of codes, as Telus no longer accepts one type.

Finally, marketers are still concerned about the proper metrics by which to measure success.[64]

As the above suggests, these promotional messages have content much like other forms of marketing communication with a particular source and message structure. A study investigated the effects of these variables in an experiment of short messages sent to gamers during a LAN party. The source was either a brand or a member of the party, while the message structure was either normal advertising language or shorthand text language, similar to what is sent in short text messages by users on a day-to-day basis.[65] Thus, while this new "medium" is an alternative for sending the message, the principles discussed thus far in terms of positioning and advertising messages remain relevant for understanding attitudinal responses and purchase intentions.

SMS codes eventually may be replaced with 2D (two-dimensional) barcodes, also known as QR (quick response). Consumers snap a picture of the code—from an out-of-home ad, for example—and their browser locates the programmed destination, likely a website or promotion offer. Labatt tested the idea with a tie-in to film festivals and received about 1,000 interested users for its Stella Artois beer. Consumers are required to load the software, but some phones are now coming pre-loaded. With consumers opting in at 20 percent, the software is picking up detailed exposure information on number of scans, who is scanning, and where.[66]

Mobile Content   This form includes things like multimedia messaging services, ringtones, graphics, video, and java games/applications. For a few years now, phones have permitted users to receive video content known as multimedia messaging services (MMS). For some it appears much like watching television, but with a few differences. The type of programming is currently limited to sports, entertainment, or news. Some experts believe that eventually the content on cellphones will be different from what is found on traditional TV, since the media consumption is more impulsive when users have free time while away from home.[67] For example, CHUM offered snippets of its show *Fashion Television* but added additional clips for cellphone users, which had greater potential for e-mailing to friends. Also, P&G sponsored a MuchMusic VJ search video sent to cellphones containing the advertiser's brand. Even with these content initiatives, some believe ads need to evolve to fit the small screen and the more personal link to the technology consumers have compared with television.[68]

Whatever programming implications arise, the development of this Internet media option is contingent upon the degree of advertising and the potential audience size. The method of advertising remains elusive as planners envision three payment options, as seen in TV: paid content where the user would pay a fee for each video received (i.e., a pay per view movie or hockey game); free content supported by advertising (i.e., a regular show or hockey game); or subscription content based on a monthly fee (i.e., a movie channel or centre-ice hockey package).[69]

New phones with advanced features called smartphones allow users to receive other content, and thus a new category of advertising has emerged in the past couple of years. For example, *The Score* was one of the first firms to offer an iPhone application for stats information. It charged advertisers premium Web pricing for ads placed within it due to its ability to obtain a 6 percent click-through rate (versus 1 percent for online ads). Other content includes games that are branded by advertisers, much like what consumers could access from a home PC or laptop. For example, Audi provided a racing game in support of its A4. With about 21 million phone users current estimates peg smartphone penetration at 25 percent, with many in the industry hoping consumers will continue to upgrade as their current plans conclude. Given the opportunity for greater reach, these advertising avenues may continue to have substantial annual growth.[70]

However, a recent study cautioned marketers, as it found that consumers' usage rate of the advanced features appeared quite low. The use of smartphones for social media fell well below usage for actual calling, texting, and using the smartphone as an alarm clock. Many users admitted ignorance on whether their smartphone had a GPS function, and many simply did not use it. Furthermore, consumers appeared confused regarding the difference between a mobile website and an application.[71] Another concern is the issue of figuring out the advertising payment method. How consumers are going to get content and who is going to pay for it are questions that marketers are still wrestling with.[72]

Display/Sponsorship   The online equivalent to display/sponsorship is naturally emerging on mobile devices, so material mentioned previously is relevant in this wireless environment. With consumers beginning to browse the Internet with their mobile device, how banner ads and other media will operate here remains to be seen.

Mobile Search   While searching with the mobile device occurs as in other computer environments, the GPS feature on new phones gives retailers and event marketers a greater opportunity to persuade consumers. The coordinates signalled from the device are tracked, allowing brand information to be placed higher in the search. This local search approach can be a better investment for smaller brands, such as single-shop retail outlets.[73]

Mobile Applications   Known as "apps" for short, these small programs can be downloaded to the phone for many purposes. They act as ads in many ways since they generally carry brand identification and some kind of brand experience. An entertainment app, like Carling's Fill & Drink, lets a user pretend to be drinking a beer as the glass slowly empties after the phone is tipped. In a way, the experience is like watching a mini commercial. Some apps, like Chanel's, allow consumers to keep up to date with a brand to know when fashion shows or other events occur. This kind of app seems to work like a mini website ad. Some other apps have ads embedded in them and the ads appear like other media, supporting content. The opportunity for apps appears good for advertising; though they have been around for 10 years, the number of apps is growing due to the increasing number and quality of phones and improved distribution for apps.[74]

MEASURING INTERNET EFFECTIVENESS

Measuring the effectiveness of the Internet is accomplished by a variety of methods, most of which can be done electronically. Audience information (demographics, psychographics, and so on) and exposure were the initial measures of effectiveness; however, fully measuring communication effects is an emerging trend.

AUDIENCE MEASURES

When the Internet marketing industry first developed its own audience size measures, concerns with the research methods led to a slower adoption rate by traditional media buyers. In an attempt to respond to criticism of the audience metrics used, as well as to standardize the measures used to gauge effectiveness, the Interactive Advertising Bureau (IAB)—the largest and most influential trade group—formed a task force consisting of global corporations involved in advertising and research. The final reports of the task force are available from iab.net and contain both American and international guidelines (see also iabcanada.com).

The basic problem facing Internet media concerns a standardized method for determining the size of the audience. The report identified the technical procedures for accurately reporting whether an ad impression has occurred. This answers the fundamental expectation of advertisers as to whether the receiver of the message actually experienced an opportunity to see the ad (i.e., degree of exposure to the message). Another aspect concerns the accepted procedures for auditing the data, much like we see in traditional print media. Another key part of the report included guidelines for presenting data in terms of time of day, week, and month, much like we see in broadcast media. Finally, industry representatives agreed upon substantial guidelines for disclosure of research methodology, again consistent with all major media described in previous chapters. In future, advertisers can look forward to more authentic data to assess the viability of committing increased resources for Internet communication.

EXPOSURE AND PROCESSING MEASURES

The electronic recording of Internet user behaviour allows advertisers to investigate a multitude of ways of understanding what has been looked at on a website and for how long, along with user characteristics.[75] Figure 17-14 summarizes measures to track whether pages are actually loaded and therefore have an opportunity to be seen; this would be equivalent to the data recorded by the portable people meter that tracks exposure to TV and other signals. Figure 17-15 shows other measures that can be used as a proxy for the degree of processing since they show how long the browser is loaded.

COMMUNICATION EFFECTS MEASURES

The movement for comprehensive communication effects measurement reveals that the Internet has its own set of criteria for measuring effectiveness and is also borrowing from traditional measures. Many companies that provide research information in traditional media now extend their reach into the Internet world. Academics publish articles related to measuring effectiveness on the Internet, such as consumers' attitudes toward a site or consumers' attitude to an ad (i.e., banner ads).[76] We now summarize a few emerging communication effects measures.

Cross-Media Optimization Studies One of the more extensive attempts to measure the effectiveness of integrating interactive and traditional media is through

534

FIGURE 17–14

Measures of exposure

Type of Measure	What Is Measured
Page impression	Number of users exposed to a Web page
Visits	Number of user sessions
Unique visitors	Number of unique users
Ad impression	Number of users exposed to an ad
Clicks	Number of user interactions with an ad
Click-through rate	Percentage of ads exposed that users click

FIGURE 17–15

Measures of processing

Type of Measure	What Is Measured
Average time per visit	Number of users exposed to a Web page
Average time per visitor	Number of user sessions

cross-media optimization studies. As noted by the IAB, the objective of these studies is the following:

> [To] help marketers and their agencies answer the question "What is the optimal mix of advertising vehicles across different media, in terms of frequency, reach and budget allocation for a given campaign to achieve its marketing goals?" . . . The [cross-media] studies simultaneously measure online and offline advertising in the same campaign to determine the optimal weight and mix of each medium.[77]

What makes these studies important is that they provide insight into (1) the relative contributions of each medium in the mix, (2) the combined contribution of multiple media, (3) optimal media budget allocations, and (4) actionable media mix strategies. Figure 17-16 details the results of the most recent findings.

Online Measuring   Firms are developing methods similar to those found in other media (i.e., PMB study) to measure demographics, psychographics, location of Web access, media usage, and buying habits. Clients can determine who saw their ads, determine reach, and ascertain whether the right target audience was reached. Advertisers can test the impact of their messages, receiving a report detailing impressions and clicks by time of day and day of the week.

Recall and Retention   A number of companies use traditional measures of recall and retention to test their Internet ads. The same measures have been used to pretest online commercials as well.

Surveys   Survey research, conducted both online and through traditional methods, is employed to determine everything from site usage to attitudes toward a site.

Tracking   Some companies now provide information on specific communication measures like brand awareness, message association, brand attitude, and purchase intention.

FIGURE   17–16   Results of cross-media studies

Company and Product	Objective	Methodology	Results
Ford F-150 pick up truck	To increase sales	Use English/Spanish TV, outdoor, print, direct mail, radio, Internet, experimental design, behavioural tracking	49% exposure to online ads; 6% sales increase directly attributable to online; website visitors twice as likely to buy as nonvisitors
ING Investment Management funds	Brand familiarity; purchase consideration	Use TV, magazines, online, survey design, continuous tracking	Use of three media together more effective than any one or two alone
Universal Studios movies	Release of *ET: The Extra Terrestrial* on DVD; to generate purchase interest among 25–49 market	Survey design, continuous tracking	Use of TV and rich media more effective than banner ad or TV alone
Unilever Dove Nutrium soap products	To increase awareness, image, purchase intent	Use TV, print, interactive, ratings information, media cost	Combining interactive led to increase in awareness, branding, purchase, purchase intent

Source: Interactive Advertising Bureau.

MEASURES OF BEHAVIOUR

Finally, Internet data are very adept at measuring the browsing behaviour of users through a variety of means as shown in Figure 17-17.

SOURCES OF MEASUREMENT DATA

An enormous number of sources provide information about the Internet. Below, we provide a partial list just to give some indication of the types of information available. Most of the companies listed are the largest and/or most cited sources, and the list is by no means intended to be exhaustive:

- *Arbitron.* Arbitron provides demographic, media usage, and lifestyle data on users of the Internet as well as other interactive media.
- *MRI* and *SMRB.* Both of these companies now provide information regarding viewership profiles for the Internet and other interactive media. Nielsen offers similar data.
- *Audit Bureau of Circulations.* This print agency is developing a product called WebFacts to certify Web counts.
- *Internet Advertising Bureau (IAB).* A trade organization of the Internet, IAB provides information on statistics, usage, and strategies regarding the Internet.
- *eMarketer.* This company publishes comparative data from various research sources and explains the different methods used to arrive at the projections. It also publishes its own projections.
- *Nielsen Net Ratings.* Nielsen provides audience information and analysis based on click-by-click Internet behaviour through a meter installed on users' computers at home and work.
- *Jupiter MediaMetrics.* This large merged firm provides statistics and website information, including data on users, projections, trends, and so on.

EVALUATION OF INTERNET MEDIA

As we have done for other media thus far in the text, we summarize the strengths and limitations of Internet media for delivering a message.

STRENGTHS OF INTERNET MEDIA

Target Audience Selectivity A major strength of the Internet is the ability to target very specific groups of individuals with a minimum of waste coverage. For those in the business-to-business market, the Internet resembles a combination trade magazine and trade show, as only those most interested in the products and/or services that a site has to offer will visit the site (others have little or no reason to do so). In the consumer market, sites are becoming more tailored to meet consumers' needs and wants through personalization and other targeting techniques. As a result

FIGURE 17–17

Measures of behaviour

Type of Measure	What Is Measured
Repeat visitor percentage	Number of repeat visitors as a percentage of total visitors
Frequency	Number of visits by unique visitors
Recency	Average interval between user visits

of precise targeting, messages can be designed to appeal to the specific needs and wants of the target audience. The interactive capabilities of the Net make it possible to carry on one-to-one marketing with increased success in both the business and the consumer markets.

Involvement and Processing Time   Because the Internet is interactive, it provides strong potential for increasing customer involvement and satisfaction and almost immediate feedback for buyers and sellers. A main objective of most websites is to provide significant brand content to allow consumers to enjoy a rich experience.

Control for Selective Exposure   Perhaps the greatest strength of the Internet is its availability as an information source. Internet users can find a plethora of information about almost any topic of their choosing merely by conducting a search using one of the search engines. Once they have visited a particular site, users can garner a wealth of information regarding product specifications, costs, purchase information, and so on. Links will direct them to even more information if it is desired. Moreover, this control is very quick compared to all other media.

Creativity   Creatively designed sites can enhance a company's image, lead to repeat visits, and positively position the company or organization. Technological advances have made the Internet as enjoyable to use as broadcast and print media for both cognitive and emotional responses.

Costs   For many smaller companies with limited budgets, the Internet enables them to gain exposure to potential customers that heretofore would have been impossible. For a fraction of the investment that would be required using traditional media, companies can gain national and even international exposure in a timely manner.

LIMITATIONS OF INTERNET MEDIA

Target Audience Coverage   In the past, one of the greatest limitations of the Internet was the lack of reliability of the research numbers generated. A quick review of forecasts, audience profiles, and other statistics offered by research providers will demonstrate a great deal of variance—leading to a serious lack of validity and reliability. The recent actions by IAB will reduce these concerns. And while the future looks promising, advertisers should continue to proceed with caution when using these data.

Clutter   As the number of ads proliferates, the likelihood of one ad's being noticed drops accordingly. The result is that some ads may not get noticed, and some consumers may become irritated by the clutter. Some studies already show that banner ads may be losing effectiveness for this very reason.

Reach   While the Internet numbers are growing in leaps and bounds, its reach is still far behind that of television. As a result, as discussed earlier, Internet companies have turned to traditional media to achieve reach and awareness goals.

Media Image   A poor media image is due to annoying characteristics, deception, and privacy. Numerous studies have reported on the irritating aspects of some Internet tactics, like e-mail spam and pop-ups and pop-unders, that deter visitors from repeat visits. Attempts by advertisers to target children with subtle advertising messages have proven to be a significant concern. In addition, data collection

537

without consumers' knowledge and permission, hacking, and credit card theft are a number of problems confronting the Internet. Like direct marketing, Internet marketers must be careful to respect users' privacy. Again, IAB has issued guidelines to improve this concern.

IMC PLANNING: STRATEGIC USE OF INTERNET MEDIA

The print, video, and audio characteristics of Internet media, along with various types of applications (e.g., websites, banner ads, streaming video, sponsorship, promotions, social utilities, etc.), positions it as being capable of communicating with customers and non-customers to achieve all communication and behavioural objectives, and to influence consumers at every stage of their decision-making process. The challenge for promotional planners is to select the correct application that fits the target audience and allows for the achievement of the most relevant objective along with the most appropriate message that supports the brand-positioning strategy. This is not an easy task, as there are multiple combinations of digital media opportunities for consideration. It makes their integration an interesting aspect of marketing communication, as seen in the following examples:

- Ben & Jerry's used e-mail, Facebook, Twitter, and finally a specialized website to run a contest for consumers to name a new flavour of ice cream.[78]
- Banff Lake Louise Tourism regularly used videos, blogs, Facebook, and Twitter, and quickly took them all to a new level when a squirrel from a photo taken at the lake began to appear in hundreds of other photos on the Internet. The "crasher" squirrel's popularity exploded so much, it was featured on billboards and other media.[79]
- Silk Canada created a microsite (sipsavoursmile.ca) to communicate the improved flavour of its soy beverages and allowed consumers to participate in a contest by uploading photos. Other activities included social networking, banner ads, in-store point-of-purchase, and mass media.[80]
- Pepsi sponsored an Internet radio station that broadcast live from a music event hosted by the Podcast Playground, ran a Twitter feed, and sent employees to post content on Twitter, YouTube, and a blog. The company also first communicated the new Pepsi online.[81]

One Canadian Google manager suggested that marketers will need to think about planning issues similar to those found in other media, like how to break through the clutter and how to deliver messages digitally across a wide spectrum of vehicles. At the same time, marketers would have to figure out a way to tap into the resources of the many online connections consumers have through their friends on social networking applications.[82] While this appears to be a solid recommendation, some brands seem to use every conceivable option for Internet media communication.

A second planning issue concerns how Internet media may or may not be better than other media for advertising purposes. Early research investigated whether Internet or TV produced better results and found that the former appeared stronger for high-involvement purchases only.[83] Other research compared the same ad delivered via print media to Internet media and found similar communication effects; however, ads with promotional messages (i.e., discounts) delivered better in print.[84]

A third planning issue pertains to how Internet media are integrated with other media for advertising purposes. One early study concluded that offline advertising increased awareness and subsequent website visits while online ads contributed to website visits. Neither affected the brand equity, as the actual visit to the website played more strongly in that regard.[85] Another study found that a combined

TV–Internet message performed better in terms of processing and stronger communication effects versus two TV messages or two Internet messages.[86] The conclusions of a print and Internet study recommended that print ads convey clear reasons to motivate readers to visit the website versus merely placing the website address in the ad.[87]

A fourth planning issue is how Internet media are increasingly part of a complete IMC program. For example, *Gillette Drafted: The Search for Canada's Next Sportscaster* hooked up in a promotional tie-in with *The Score* and used virtually all IMC tools including its own website (Drafted.ca), product placements with contestants on the sports show, *The Score*'s website, and mass media.[88] Other research uncovered the significant communication effect of direct-response media through mobile devices after viewers received advertising or promotional TV messages that prompted continued interaction.[89]

Internet media often work with other IMC tools. Promotional planners using print, broadcast, or out-of-home media would need to investigate the degree to which the advertising campaign in these media would be directly transferred to Internet advertising. This is commonly done and there are many examples. Alternatively, the Internet advertising could take a substantially different direction as some microsites, for example, have allowed brands to take a more experiential or informational track and have a substantially different role and message compared to what is more publicly available.

Internet advertising supports sales promotion activities designed to encourage trial and repeat purchases with banner ads or sponsored search links that direct consumers to contests or price promotional offers. Internet advertising is used successfully for public relations activities as links to corporate websites are found on relevant websites (e.g., financial information sites) and other mechanisms are available to direct consumers to corporate information to influence appropriate stakeholders. Finally, Internet advertising assists in direct-response marketing as it facilitates communication to the websites for conducting transactions.

Internet media as sales promotion is a new opportunity for marketers, with some brands having success. This can work very well with media advertising and sales promotions, as seen in some of the decorative options delivered to computer users. These fun activities are consistent with both the brand image and consumer experience, with sales promotions offering additional exposure and increasing meaningful brand experiences. For example, note the value of branded emoticons or icons or murals (e.g., SpiderMan, cited earlier) to continually remind consumers of past communication in other forms.

Internet media as public relations supports considerable advertising for many consumer packaged goods and food products. Broadcast and print ads for such products create images and persuade consumers with an appropriate brand-positioning strategy. However, some consumers desire more information on usage or would like to know the exact ingredients in more detail. The Internet site for Becel margarine offers a wonderful array of information for consumers desiring a more involved message about the brand and acts as a tremendous public relations resource by presenting a comprehensive and honest assessment of the brand.

Internet media for direct-response advertising works very well for Belairdirect. Many of the insurance company's print and radio ads suggest that consumers visit its Internet site to compare quotes from Belairdirect and up to five competitors. In this sense, Internet media function beyond mere communication like a regular informational website, especially considering that for a few years the focus of all the ads has been to encourage a direct response via the Internet medium.

The general idea suggested here is that the power of the Internet allows promotional planners to adapt their utilization of Internet media as multiple IMC tools that can work with what we might call media advertising—and perhaps with each of the other tools, with the right campaign and inventiveness.

CHAPTER OBJECTIVES AND SUMMARY

1 To provide an overview of Internet users.

Internet communication has become relatively common for a vast majority of the population, as seen in the statistics presented. While older segments of the population rely on these media less than younger groups do, the fact that the average hourly per capita consumption reached 18 hours per week suggests that Internet communication will be the significant media of the future. This appears especially true as consumers perform more activities online, including using company websites as a source of information for shopping.

2 To identify website communication in terms of objectives and strategy.

Website communication can be used for any or all of the communication objectives described in this book. They contribute to building brand awareness, disseminating information, building a brand image, and fostering interaction between consumers and the company. The unlimited creativity we have witnessed with websites is remarkable, and something that many might not have dreamed possible two decades ago. This creativity has given rise to consumers, practitioners, and academics referring to it as website advertising or Internet advertising. They apply existing models to understand how attitudes to the website and brand attitude are influenced by strategic and tactical design elements, much like what occurs with print and broadcast media.

3 To evaluate the different ways of advertising via the Internet.

Advertising on the Internet permits extensive targeting in terms of behaviour, context, geography, site loyalty, and time of day. Certainly other ideas are possible given the amount of data companies collect, but these are on the forefront. Targeting occurs through numerous routes such as banners, pop-ups/pop-unders, interstitials, sponsorships, push technologies, links, paid searches, online commercials, videos-on-demand, podcasts, RSS feeds, blogs, social media, and interactive games.

4 To explore other IMC tools delivered via the Internet such as sales promotion, public relations, and direct marketing.

The role of the Internet in an IMC program was discussed, with an explanation of how all the IMC program elements can be used with the Internet. As we saw in Chapter 14, the Internet is used to facilitate sales promotions. For example, it seems every contest for brands of large companies has an online entry component. However, the Internet has permitted the application of sales promotions through various samples and premiums that can be digitized. PR has moved to the Internet as well, with companies using many of the advertising routes for corporate purposes. It is in the area of direct marketing communication we see extensive development through e-mail and mobile (i.e., MMS, content, display, search) applications.

5 To highlight measures of Internet effectiveness.

Like other media we concentrated on different measures of effectiveness for each stage of the communication process. Measures are obtained for exposure, processing, and communication effects and behavioural responses. The majority of these are tracked digitally; however, communication effects require direct measurement or some proxy.

6 To review the strengths and limitations of Internet media.

We viewed the Internet as a means for communication to reach audiences much like other media, as a way to deliver a message and interact with current and potential customers. With this in mind, Internet media currently offer numerous strengths. Advertisers can direct tailored messages to very selective target audiences. And with technological advances, the creative messages can be richly experienced both cognitively and emotionally for considerable amounts of time as the users themselves decide what they would like to receive and not receive. Finally, this incredible messaging ability is possible at a reasonably low absolute and relative cost.

There are some limitations, however. It is unclear to marketers the degree to which the target audience can be covered and reached. Internet media can be viewed as tremendous clutter as users move among various websites. And, finally, severe problems regarding advertising delivery, illegal activities, and privacy concerns remain significant drawbacks.

7 To understand the role of Internet media in an IMC program.

The Internet has been the most rapidly adopted medium of our time. It holds great potential for both business-to-business and consumer marketers. However, contrary to popular belief, the

Internet is not a stand-alone medium. Its role in an integrated marketing communications program strengthens the overall program as well as the effectiveness of the Internet itself.

KEY TERMS

banner ads, *518*
behavioural targeting, *516*
blog, *523*
content sponsorship, *520*
contextual targeting, *516*
Internet, *508*

interstitials, *520*
links, *520*
paid search, *520*
personalization, *520*
podcasting, *522*

pop-ups/pop-unders, *519*
push technologies, *520*
Really Simple Syndication (RSS), *523*
spam, *529*

sponsorship, *520*
webcasting, *520*
website, *511*
World Wide Web (WWW), *508*

DISCUSSION QUESTIONS

1. While some believe that the Internet poses a threat to traditional media others disagree, arguing that it is just another tool for marketers. Explain some of the arguments on both sides. What is your conclusion?

2. The Internet is growing at an extremely rapid pace. At the same time, there are indications that this growth will slow. Discuss some factors that may lead to decreased growth of the use of Internet media.

3. Discuss the objectives marketers may be seeking in their use

of the Internet. Which is the Internet best suited for?

4. Explain the different forms that advertisers might use to advertise on the Internet. Discuss some of the advantages and disadvantages associated with each.

5. One of the most difficult objectives to achieve on the Internet is creating a strong brand. Discuss the factors that make brand-building both difficult and possible.

6. Discuss some of the ways that marketers attempt to measure the effectiveness of their programs on the Internet. How

do these measures relate to more traditional measures? Describe the advantages and disadvantages of traditional versus Internet measures.

7. Discuss some of the advantages of using the Internet. For which types of advertisers is the Internet best suited? Why?

8. Many marketers believe the Internet offers much more potential to business-to-business marketers than it does to consumer marketers. Detail some of the reasons why they feel this way and draw a conclusion as to the merits of this argument.

REGULATORY, ETHICAL, SOCIAL, AND ECONOMIC ISSUES FOR IMC

■ CHAPTER OBJECTIVES

1 To be familiar with the advertising regulation system in Canada.

2 To evaluate the ethical perspectives of advertising.

3 To understand the social effects of advertising.

4 To examine the economic role of advertising and its effects on consumer choice, competition, and product costs and prices.

TTC DENIES ADVERTISERS

"The idea is to let people know we're freshening up the radio experience and giving consumers a reason not to discard their radio in favour of other options. We're actually going to breathe new life into the medium; we're going to give them a reason not to get rid of their radio," extolled the director of branding and communication for Astral Media Radio when talking about the ads for Toronto's Virgin Radio 99.9. Three ads showed a radio resting at the edge of a bridge, sitting beside a bathtub, and standing at the edge of subway platform—all with the impression of the radio about to commit suicide—with the copy "Give Your Radio a Reason to Live."

Ads with a suicide theme have been rejected over the past decade. In 2001, a potato impaled itself on a fork after discovering an empty Imperial margarine container, which required Unilever to pull the ad. In 2007, a robot jumped off a bridge after dropping a screw while assembling a GM vehicle, which required GM to revise the ad. Virgin Radio was stopped in its tracks when the Toronto Transit Commission (TTC) denied the placement of the subway platform ad for bus shelters, even though the first two ads had appeared on bus shelters for the previous six weeks. Interestingly, ownership of the shelters and the placement of the ads is the domain of Astral Media, not the TTC; however, a contract stipulates that any TTC request for removal of ads must be honoured by Astral.

And suicide is not the only subject that may be taboo. "To blatantly advertise cheating in this manner where people of all ages, including children, are open to it, means people may be incredibly offended. People are generally outraged by that type of a lifestyle and to advertise it in such a public fashion, in my opinion, is wrong," announced the executive director of the Institute of Marriage and Family Canada as he reacted to the possible placement of ads on TTC streetcars from the Ashley Madison Agency, an online dating site that promotes adultery.

The planned campaign featured a streetcar's exterior wrapped with the slogan, "Life Is Short. Have an Affair." The phrase would also be placed in all other advertising slots. If successful, the campaign would be extended to 10 streetcars, for total revenue of $200,000 for the TTC. Responding to criticism of the campaign, the owner of Ashley Madison commented, "No one is going to have an affair because they read an ad on the side of a streetcar. They're going to have an affair because there are issues with their long-term relationships."

A day after the Ashley Madison controversy hit the news, the TTC's advertising review committee decided not to run the ads. According to one voter, "When it's a core fundamental value around cheating or lying, we're not going to let those kinds of ads go on. It's not about sexuality, it's about cheating. We would not have accepted an ad that said 'Life is short, cheat on your exams.' It's frankly a no-brainer." Despite not getting the ad placed, Ashley Madison declared victory with all the free media coverage it received.

Sources: Kenyon Wallace, "TTC Flirts with Online Adulterers," *National Post*, December 11, 2009, p. A1; Kenyon Wallace, "Pro-adultery Agency Loses TTC Ad Bid," *National Post*, December 12, 2009, p. A21; Chris Powell, "Astral Campaign Gives Radio Hope," *Marketing Magazine*, March 5, 2009; "Toronto Unhappy About Virgin Suicides," *Marketing Magazine*, April 17, 2009; Jeff Gray, "Suicide Ad Irks Transit Authority," *The Globe and Mail*, April 17, 2009, p. A3; www.torontoist.com.

QUESTION:

1. Do you agree with TTC's decisions?

> If I were to name the deadliest subversive force within capitalism, the single greatest source of its waning morality—I would without hesitation name advertising. How else should one identify a force that debases language, drains thought, and undoes dignity?[1]

As this quote suggests, not everyone shares the positive view regarding the role of marketing communication in today's society that our text illustrates thus far. Our perspective looks at advertising and other promotional tools as marketing activities used to convey information to consumers and influence their behaviour in an appropriate manner to facilitate a mutually satisfying exchange. Advertising and promotion are the most visible of all business activities and face scrutiny from scholars, economists, politicians, sociologists, government agencies, social critics, special-interest groups, and consumers, who criticize advertising for its excessiveness, the way it influences society, the methods it uses, its exploitation of consumers, and its effect on our economic system.

Advertising is a very powerful force, and this text would not be complete without a look at the criticisms regarding its ethical, social, and economic effects as well as some defences against these charges. Before we entertain this debate, we review the regulations affecting advertising in Canada. The various perspectives presented reflect judgments of people with different backgrounds, values, and interests. Some students may see nothing wrong with some ads while others may oppose ads on moral and ethical grounds (Exhibit 18-1). We attempt to present the arguments on both sides of these controversial issues and allow individuals to draw their own conclusions.

ADVERTISING REGULATION IN CANADA

Regulation of advertising in Canada occurs through both government regulation and self-regulation. In this section, we review both of these topics. With respect to government regulation, we focus on four prevalent domains. The Canadian Radio-television and Telecommunications Commission (CRTC) is responsible for laws and regulations concerning broadcasting and telecommunications, so its role in advertising is relevant. The *Competition Act* regulates misleading or deceptive ads. Health Canada has placed stringent laws for tobacco promotion. Finally, the

Exhibit 18-1
Some magazines refused to run this Benetton ad.

Quebec government has strong regulations with respect to advertising to children. In the other direction, the Advertising Standards Council (ASC) acts as the self-regulation body for the advertising industry. Responsibility for many of the federal laws regarding the content of advertising messages for specific product categories has been transferred to ASC by the request of the federal government.

CANADIAN RADIO-TELEVISION AND TELECOMMUNICATIONS COMMISSION (CRTC)

The mandate of the CRTC is to ensure that the *Broadcasting Act of 1991* and the *Telecommunications Act of 1993* are upheld throughout Canada. The broad objective of both acts is to make certain that all Canadians can receive broadcasting and telecommunications services. In attaining its mandate, the CRTC is required to delicately balance the needs of citizens, industries, and various interest groups with respect to programming and costs. For purposes of advertising, we will concentrate on the broadcasting side.

The CRTC regulates more than 5,900 media organizations (i.e., television, cable distribution, AM and FM radio, pay and specialty television, direct-to-home satellite systems, multipoint distribution systems, subscription television, and pay audio). The CRTC is responsible for granting the licences for these media and ensuring that they comply with the *Broadcasting Act*. Within the context of the *Broadcasting Act,* the CRTC focuses on a number of relevant issues (i.e., content, competition, technology). There are three areas for broadcasting ads where the CRTC is involved significantly:

- *Signal substitution.* In an effort to keep advertising revenue in Canada, the CRTC allows television broadcasters to substitute Canadian-sponsored ads on programming originating from the U.S. when shows are delivered at the same time on both Canadian and American networks. While this appears acceptable to most Canadians most of the time, football viewers often feel left out when some U.S. ads are not part of the domestic feed for the Super Bowl.
- *Advertising limits.* The CRTC ensures that TV stations and specialty services carry 12 minutes of advertising during the broadcast day, which lasts 18 hours beginning at 6:00 a.m. However, public service announcements or "ads" for Canadian TV shows are not counted in this total.
- *Infomercials.* An infomercial is a program lasting more than 12 minutes that combines the promotion of a product in an engaging, entertainment-like style. The CRTC approves all infomercials for any television station, network, or specialty service.

There are three areas where the CRTC is not involved significantly:

- *False or misleading ads.* The CRTC does not address complaints of these types of ads and refers complaints to the Competition Bureau of the federal government. The CRTC has left this for the ASC as well.
- *Alcohol and drugs.* There are regulations for advertising these products, but the CRTC has disbanded the screening process of the ads. This is now the responsibility of the ASC, and we will summarize this later in this section.
- *Internet.* The CRTC does not regulate the content on the Internet or require licences for those that "broadcast" on this medium. It currently is investigating whether video content delivered via the Internet falls under the jurisdiction of the broadcast code since it is technically not a broadcast like original TV and radio signals.[2]

As a regulator, the CRTC recently evaluated a highly topical application that would have changed the advertising industry. A marketing firm with the support of the Canadian Association of Advertisers wanted to insert Canadian ads during feeds

545

from U.S. specialty services (e.g., TBS, A&E). The Canadian Association of Broadcasters argued against this change suggesting that sufficient advertising capacity existed in Canada, and that increased capacity would reduce advertising revenue.[3] The CRTC denied the application.

COMPETITION ACT

The federal *Competition Act* prevents false or misleading advertising. Significantly revised in 1999, most of the act contains civil provisions to ensure compliance with the act rather than seeking punishment. In this situation, the goal is not so much to prove deliberate intent, but rather to remedy the situation with the most appropriate solution, such as cease and desist orders. Some criminal provisions still exist for the most serious offences, where false advertising occurred knowingly. Enforcement of the act falls under the jurisdiction of the Competition Bureau of Industry Canada. Some examples of what is not permissible are shown in Figure 18-1.[4] In 2009, the Act underwent revision with respect to deceptive marketing, items pertaining to pricing, and some other amendments. In particular, the fines for misleading representation in advertising increased substantially for non-criminal offences.[5] Industry people expect strong enforcement in the coming years, since Moores and the Brick have both received warnings for inappropriate communication for their sales promotions. Some questioned whether the changes were constitutional or whether the expanded situations of misrepresentation were clearly identified; nevertheless, the laws are currently in place.[6]

REGULATION OF TOBACCO ADVERTISING

Tobacco products are severely restricted by Health Canada regulations on their use of traditional advertising media. One avenue that tobacco companies turned to fairly quickly when the restrictions were enacted many years ago was to sponsor various arts, cultural, and sporting events; however, this option was discontinued in 2003. Print ads communicating these sponsorships were the only permitted advertising, so the new restriction appears to present even greater limits. Currently, tobacco firms also face significant packaging requirements such as presenting graphic images of the consequences of tobacco use, disallowing any reference to "light," and including a full list of ingredients. With such limited options to attract new users or retain existing consumers, the tobacco companies have been very creative with interesting media choices recently.

FIGURE 18-1 Advertising and marketing law in Canada

Guideline	Advertising Claim	Misleading Content
Cannot make false claims	Buy this vacuum and get a year's supply of vacuum bags absolutely free	There is a $12 administration fee for the vacuum bags
Even if claim is true, do not give false impression	Drive away in a Corvette for just $39,000	The visual display is a version with a sport package and costs $50,000
Avoid double meanings	Number one in the category	Best in sale, but not in quality
Disclaimers should not contradict headlines or body copy	Don't pay a cent until 2014	Fine-print says except for taxes and $750 freight

Source: Adapted from *Advertising and Marketing Law In Canada,* Brenda Pritchard and Susan Vogt, LexisNexis, Butterworths, 2006.

Underground marketing has emerged where communication of the brands occurs through exclusive distribution in select bars, pubs, and nightclubs. Through mechanisms such as these, the tobacco companies can get customers to register so that direct marketing techniques can take place, such as contest offers. And 1-800 numbers on tobacco packaging get customers to engage with the tobacco firms directly using creative angles. Point-of-sale communication has also been a competitive tactic that the companies aggressively pursue. Some companies have begun to use the Internet, but thus far mostly as a means of communicating sponsorship deals. Currently all of these IMC tools are legal, and we will find out whether the future looks bright for tobacco manufacturers, as they continue to innovate, or cloudy if the government steps in even further.[7]

REGULATIONS ON ADVERTISING TO CHILDREN

Although no federal laws specifically regulate advertising to children, the Broadcast Code for Advertising to Children acts as an important guide to ensure that children are not easily manipulated with exaggerated claims. In contrast, the province of Quebec provides strict regulations. According to the *Consumer Protection Act of Quebec,* it is illegal to direct commercial advertising messages to persons younger than 13 years of age. Provisions are in place to determine whether or not an ad is directed to children. Specifically, the provisions concern the product, the way the ad is presented, and the time and place the ad is shown. One exception to the law is a regularly published magazine that is for sale. These magazines, however, have 16 guidelines with respect to their advertising claims; the types of products; the portrayal of people's behaviour, motivation, or attitude reflected in the ad; and the source of the message (i.e., a person or character).

To apply the law, the Quebec government provides summary guidelines for advertisers to follow, and it also provides screening services for advertisers if they are uncertain whether an item contravenes the law. The purpose of the guidelines is to ensure that advertisers fully understand and correctly interpret the law. The guidelines pertain to precisely describing the types of advertising appeals that are not permitted, clearly defining what is meant by a children's TV program, and exactly stating the percentage of children in the audience that constitutes a children's TV program. The guidelines include the degree to which messages can be directed toward children depending upon whether the product is exclusively for children (i.e., candy), partially for children (i.e., cereal), or not for children. There are also specific guidelines for public service announcements directed to children, even though there is no commercial message. Ethical Perspective 18-1 identifies some new trends on this topic.

ADVERTISING STANDARDS COUNCIL (ASC)

The ASC is a not-for-profit, self-regulatory industry body with a mandate to create and maintain community confidence in advertising. The ASC represents advertisers, media organizations, and advertising industry suppliers and has more than 200 corporate members. Its Standards Division administers the industry's self-regulatory codes (i.e., *Canadian Code of Advertising Standards, Gender Portrayal Guidelines*), handles complaints about advertising, and administers any disputes that arise between advertisers. Its Advertising Clearance Division previews advertisements in five industry categories, as well as ads directed toward children, ensuring that advertisers will follow applicable legislation, regulatory codes, and industry standards. An example of one of its public service ads is shown in Exhibit 18-2.

New Directions for Advertising to Children

Even though Quebec's stringent guidelines regarding advertising to children should be a sufficient deterrent, some advertisers push the limit—as seen by a recent episode with Vachon, maker of the Jos Louis and Passion Flakie treats. Recently, Vachon created a cartoon character named Igor to represent its chocolate-filled, gorilla-shaped muffins. Vachon placed the imagery on CDs, DVDs, and other materials for daycare centres to use when entertaining the children.

In this situation Vachon tested the laws in three ways— the product, the message, and the time and place—and faced a $44,000 fine. It appears that the Quebec government is getting tougher with not-so-healthy products with the higher incidence of child obesity. However, there are indications that brands of healthier products, or a corporate initiative to encourage children to stay active, might not be as scrutinized. So while there are laws governing advertising to children in Quebec, the consistent application appears murky given the ethical implications.

One organization that has been at the forefront of this issue for decades is the CBC. It has always reserved the 7:00 a.m. to 11:00 a.m. slot for children's programming that is shown completely free. Advertising to children is legal in other parts of Canada; however, a movement toward what occurs in the province of Quebec appeared on the horizon with the development of the Canadian Children's Food & Beverage Advertising Initiative, which put limits on TV advertising for those products. However, other products are not covered—so what are parents to think about activities like one proposed by Future Shop?

The retailer approached the Toronto District School Board with an offer to fund a new computer lab for $50,000 if the Board painted the walls in the same red and grey colours of the brand's identity. Yet high school children are teenagers and beyond the ages for Quebec's laws and the Food & Beverage Initiative, thus complicating the issue in another direction and raising another question: At what age should advertising to children be controlled or regulated?

During this debate, the same issue emerged where it seemed that so-called "good" products would be acceptable advertisers, yet "bad" products like sugary or fatty food would not be fitting advertisers in schools. However, the backlash of invasive advertising suggests caution, as one expert commented: "Some people may actually feel they're being manipulated." For some the issue is not so much what kind of products, but more desire to minimize the amount of exposure to advertising children receive. Suggested one advocate, "When children are saturated with advertising, literally everywhere they are now, it's so much more important that we have spaces that are commercial-free where there aren't advertising pressures on children."

Sources: Jean-Francois Ouellet, "Vachon's Igor Crossed the Line in Quebec," *National Post,* March 10, 2009, FP13; Carly Weeks, "A Lesson in Breeding Brand Loyalty," *The Globe and Mail,* April 15, 2009, p. L1; Susan Krashinsky, "Cookie Monster Has Spoken, Advertisers Have Listened," *The Globe and Mail,* July 17, 2009, B4.

Question:

1. What limits or controls do you believe should be in place for children of varying ages?

Canadian Code of Advertising Standards   The Code, as it is known, describes what is not acceptable advertising. According to the ASC, "Advertising is defined as any message (the content of which is controlled directly or indirectly by the advertiser) expressed in any language and communicated in any medium to Canadians with the intent to influence their choice, opinion or behaviour." The Code pertains to the content of ads only. It does not limit the promotion of legal products or the demonstration of products for their intended purpose. The intention of the Code is to provide standards so that responsible and effective advertising results without minimizing the right of firms to advertise. It does not supersede any other laws or regulations.

The Code is used as the criteria to assess whether a complaint is legitimate or not, and the ASC is very clear in how it uses the Code to resolve complaints. "The context and content of the advertisement and the audience actually, or likely to be, or intended to be, reached by the advertisement, and the medium/media used to deliver the advertisement, are relevant factors in assessing its conformity with the Code."

The Code is supported by all member organizations as it sets the standard for advertising with respect to honesty, truth, accuracy, fairness, and propriety. Members are expected to follow the Code both in letter and in spirit and are expected to substantiate any advertised claims when requested. The Code contains 14 clauses:

1. Accuracy and Clarity
2. Disguised Advertising Techniques
3. Price Claims
4. Bait and Switch
5. Guarantees
6. Comparative Advertising
7. Testimonials
8. Professional or Scientific Claims
9. Imitation
10. Safety
11. Superstitions and Fears
12. Advertising to Children
13. Advertising to Minors
14. Unacceptable Depictions and Portrayals

In 2003, ASC updated clauses 6, 10, and 14 as part of its ongoing mandate to ensure that the Code reflects current practices and fairness. While on the surface the changes were just a few words for each clause, the meaning permitted a more reasonable and flexible interpretation. For the past decade, ASC has compiled "interpretation guidelines" so that members could understand how ASC will evaluate ads in terms of specific codes or advertising trends.[8] The first and fourth guidelines concern Clauses 10 or 14 and motor vehicle advertising. The second guideline provides extensive documentation on advertising to children pertaining to Clause 12. Environmental claims and how they are related to Clause 1, the Competition Bureau, and the Canadian Standards Association is the topic of the third guideline.

Exhibit 18-2 Ad by ASC communicating its purpose.

ASC helps protect Canadians from false messaging in advertising. Because among all the pretty words and pictures – truth matters.

ASC Advertising Standards Canada
adstandards.ca

As part of the second guideline, ASC acts as the administrator for the Canadian Children's Food and Beverage Advertising Initiative.[9] Canada's largest food and beverage marketers have committed to not engage in advertising directed primarily to children under 12 years of age, although some committed to advertise only "better-for-you" products to children. The initiative is in response to the growing obesity problem among children. In doing so, the marketers agreed to five core principles for advertising directed to children under 12 years of age:

- Devote at least 50 percent of television, radio, print, and Internet advertising to further the goal of promoting healthy dietary choices and/or healthy active living.
- Incorporate only products that represent healthy dietary choices in interactive games primarily directed to children under 12 years of age.
- Reduce the use of third-party licensed characters in advertising for products that do not meet the CAI's product criteria.
- Not pay for or actively seek to place food and beverage products in program/editorial content of any medium.
- Not advertise food or beverage products in elementary schools.

The first annual report, published in July 2009, concluded that all 16 founding members had fully complied by the end of 2008. By 2010, the number of committed organizations had grown to 19.

Gender Portrayal Guidelines   The guidelines, based on a previous CRTC task force, attempt to ensure that women and men are portrayed appropriately and equally in advertising. The ASC presents the guidelines as the direction of areas or topics from which complaints or issues have arisen over the past 30 years. There are six overall clauses, pertaining to authority, decision making, sexuality, violence, diversity, and language. For example, some might find the passionate theme of the Campari ad featuring Salma Hayek as conveying overt sexuality (Exhibit 18-3).

When interpreting the guidelines, the ASC has four suggestions that advertisers should consider. The overall impression of the ad should not violate the spirit of gender equality; there are clauses specifically addressed toward women, as men are at less risk of being negatively portrayed. History and art should not be used as an excuse for violating a clause. Finally, certain products and how they are advertised are amenable to more appropriate media.

Complaint Process   The Standards Division handles complaints in three streams. **Consumer complaints** are those from ordinary citizens who believe that an ad is unacceptable. The ASC receives these complaints directly as well as through government departments and agencies at all levels, the Better Business Bureau, the CRTC, and the Canadian Broadcast Standards Council. **Special interest group complaints** are those from a demonstrated organization that expresses a unified viewpoint. Complaints from other advertisers are known as **trade disputes**. While there is a distinct complaint process for consumers and special interest groups, the general procedures for each have a degree of similarity that we will touch upon. One difference, however, is that ASC first determines that the special interest group complaint is not a disguised trade dispute.

The initial complaint is authenticated to make sure that it is, in fact, a consumer or special interest group complaint and not a trade dispute. From there, the complaint is evaluated to determine whether it legitimately violates a Code provision or whether it is not a legitimate complaint. Reasons for a complaint not being legitimate include that the complaint did not identify a specific advertiser, that the ad was no longer current, and that the communication was not advertising. This initial assessment occurs at the national (i.e., Toronto) or regional (i.e., Alberta, Atlantic, British Columbia) Consumer Response Councils for English ads, and le Conseil des normes in Montreal for French ads. If the complaint is valid, the advertiser is contacted and has an opportunity to respond to the complaint before the Council makes a formal ruling. On the other hand, the advertiser can take an appropriate action to remedy the complaint as part of the response. In these cases, the advertiser would not be identified in the ASC complaints report. An advertiser who responds and does not remedy the situation can be identified in the report if the Council upholds the complaint.

The Council for Canadians filed a special interest group complaint against Nestlé for a claim that "most water bottles avoid landfill sites and are recycled" in a *Globe*

Exhibit 18-3
This TV ad was part of a global campaign that celebrated the passionate history of the brand.

and Mail ad. Its complaint cited a statement from Nestlé's annual report stating the contrary. And while this appeared to be a complaint with merit, ASC dismissed the case since the Council went public with its complaint thereby contravening the confidentiality requirement of the proceedings.[10] Sierra Club Canada filed a special interest complaint concerning a Canwest piece that stated, "in partnership with Shell Canada." The oil company put the advertorial series together as a public relations information source for the media, the government, and the general public. An editor with the media organization stated that the layout of the ad was not consistent with the editorial content and that "readers would realize the pages are advertisements for Shell." However, the executive director of Sierra Club concluded they appeared like neither advertising nor editorial.[11]

For trade disputes, there is a formal adjudication procedure where each party represents its point of view at a hearing if an initial first stage resolution is unsuccessful. An appeal of the decision is possible, but eventually there is a resolution if an advertiser is found in violation. As members of the ASC, they follow the recommendations of ASC similar to the consumer and special interest process. However, recently a situation emerged where for the first time ever an advertiser did not follow ASC's decision. Rogers disputed a Bell advertising claim and ASC upheld the complaint, suggesting Bell amend the ad or stop showing it. Bell did not participate in the hearing or comply with the decision since it was not a member and continued running the ad. In turn, and for the first time, ASC asked media companies to refrain from airing the ad.[12]

Complaints Report   The ASC has published a more comprehensive annual report since 1997. This format includes the identification of advertisers and the details of all complaints. Previously, the annual report provided global statistics. Figure 18-2 shows a capsule summary of the past few years. For each statistic, the first data point is the number of complaints, while the second is the number of ads those ads represent. The ratio of the number of complaints to the number of ads indicates that the number of complaints per ad is fewer than two. This underscores the fact that the content of the complaint is justification for investigating an ad. The percentage of complaints upheld has seen some modest movement, as expressed by the number of complaints received, pursued, and evaluated by the council.

In 2009, television, Internet, and out-of-home media generated 44 percent, 14 percent, and 9 percent of all complaints, respectively. In comparison, these same top three media accounted for 59 percent, 8 percent, and 7 percent, respectively. With increased online advertising expenditure, we now see a greater number of complaints. A pattern on the source of the complaint occurs each year, with clause 1 (accuracy and clarity) and clause 3 (price), clause 14 (unacceptable depictions and

	2009	2008	2007
Number of Complaints (ads)			
Received	1,228 (760)	1,445 (980)	1,119 (778)
Pursued	1,034 (624)	1,069 (669)	801 (554)
Evaluated by Council	133 (89)	241 (83)	194 (88)
Upheld by Council	80 (56)	193 (56)	126 (66)
Upheld Complaints (ads)			
Received	7% (7%)	13% (6%)	11% (8%)
Pursued	8% (9%)	18% (8%)	16% (12%)
Evaluated by Council	60% (63%)	80% (67%)	75% (75%)

FIGURE 18–2

Summary of complaints from the Advertising Standards Council's annual Complaints Report portrayals), and clause 10 (safety) consistently receiving the most complaints. We now briefly review ads that achieved notoriety over the past decade, summarized from past reports found at the ASC website.

Complaints for Debate   One of the most controversial rulings occurred in 2001. A Ford Motor Company TV ad showed a young female shoving a male store clerk into the hatchback of her car and driving away with him. This ad received nine complaints, and the Council upheld the complaints, citing clause 14 as the ad depicted an abduction, which is an unlawful activity. Ford appealed the decision; however, the Appeal Panel confirmed the original decision. Ford's post-appeal statement makes this example an interesting debate:

> Ford of Canada did not intend to offend any segment of the population in this particular advertisement; rather the aim of the ad was to show the attributes of the Focus. The identical advertisement shown in Quebec (both in English and in French) was determined not to contravene the *Code* by the Consumer Response Council and Appeal Panel in Quebec. Particulars of this complaint were provided to the press by a consumer complainant even though this process is intended to be confidential. Subsequent to the Appeal Decision, Margaret Wente, in a lengthy *Globe and Mail* article dated January 31, 2002, gave strong positive support for the ad. However, in light of the decision of the ASC Appeal Panel, Ford of Canada will withdraw the current English advertisement.[13]

In early 2004, a television ad for an alcohol beverage depicted two women engaging in a passionate kiss. The 113 complaints indicated that the scene was inappropriate for family viewing programming. Council upheld this complaint, stating, "the commercial displayed obvious indifference to conduct or attitudes that offended standard of public decency prevailing among a significant segment of the population." Council concluded that the ad in question did not contravene the code providing it was shown later than 9:30 in the evening.

A Kia Canada television commercial caused controversy during 2007 and received 77 complaints from individuals and those in the law-enforcement profession. The advertised vehicle contained two adults "making out," after which the woman returned to a police car wearing an officer's uniform. Council upheld the complaint citing clause 14(c) and concluded that the ad demeaned female officers in particular and all law-enforcement officials in general. Kia responded to the complaint with the following statement:

> As a responsible advertiser, Kia Canada Inc. [Kia] is aware of Advertising Standards Canada [ASC] guidelines, of which its media service agencies are members, and strives to adhere to the spirit of which they have been written. While not in agreement with the Council's final decision, Kia respects it and the process by which it was achieved. Kia believes it has responded to the subject of the complaints by making revisions to the commercial in question, and in adherence to the ASC's Advertising Standards Code.[14]

However, Kia's concern became more public when it ran an edited version of the ad that did not show the woman leaving the car. Instead, words on the screen announced a more suitable ending to the commercial for all audiences. The final scene featured a goat eating in a meadow for 10 seconds while light-hearted music played. We leave the interpretation of this revised ending for interested students to debate![15]

Also in 2007, the council determined certain Dairy Queen ads showed an unsafe act and reinforced bullying behaviour as the TV ad characters restrained others while eating Dairy Queen ice cream. The response from managers of the brand appears to suggest caution to advertisers with co-branding messages:

> Dairy Queen is all about creating smiles and stories for families and often uses irreverent, off-beat humour in its commercials. The Kit Kat commercial was meant to

accentuate this in a humorous way how families interact in a playful manner. Although we are not in agreement with the Council's decision, we are respectful of the process.[16]

An ad from Auto Trader, part of an overall campaign that compared buying a used car online to meeting another person with an online dating service, received only six complaints. However, the complaint, the council decision, and the advertiser statement cover new ground:

> In a television commercial, a man and a woman met in a coffee shop for the first time. After exchanging names, the woman asked the man if she could "take a quick peek". The man obliged by lowering his pants so the woman could look at his private parts from various angles. In the audio portion of the commercial the announcer said that "You can do that on Auto Trader—where you can research your car before you buy it."[17]

The complaint alleged that the ad depicted a demeaning portrayal of men and offended standards of public decency. However, the council agreed with the latter point but concluded that the ad denigrated both men and women. Auto Trader's rebuttal statement takes into account the media time frame and media vehicle, two critical points that ASC highlighted in previous rulings for more acceptable adult messages. And its inclusion as part of a television show makes this case another one for debate:

> Trader Corporation is not condoning the behaviour in the commercial "Research". We believe it is clear to anyone viewing that the actions in the commercial are exaggerated and, via the copyline "You can do that on AutoTrader.ca", clearly portrayed as behaviour that is not socially acceptable. Rather these actions are used in a humourous and entertaining manner to support the campaign message—It is easier to find your perfect "match" (car) with Auto Trader. Our belief that most people understand the humour is supported not only by positive reviews by the advertising press for its empowering message to female car buyers but also by quantifiable market research that indicates that the commercial performed significantly above industry norms on scores such as 'enjoyable' and 'appropriate and fits my lifestyle'. We have also tried to put it into adult-oriented television programs which match the content of the ads realizing that the commercial is somewhat risque for Canadian standards. It is also interesting to note that the commercial was recently selected for the U.S.-based show World's Funniest TV Commercials.[18]

We included some of these recent cases as they represent milestones in the relationship between ASC and it members. They show disagreement between ASC administrators (i.e., Ford), one of the most complaints ever (i.e., alcohol beverage), the most unexpected reaction from a member (i.e., Kia), a difficulty with co-branding (i.e., Dairy Queen), and a substantial rebuttal (i.e., Auto Trader). Exhibit 18-4 shows the most recent ad from ASC.

Clearance Process The ASC provides clearance services for ads for many product categories and ads directed toward children for all jurisdictions except Quebec.

- *Alcohol.* The ASC adheres to the CRTC *Code for Broadcast Advertising of Alcoholic Beverages.* The CRTC disbanded clearance services

Exhibit 18-4 An ASC ad humourously shows how truth in advertising is important.

553

Exhibit 18-6 This Airwalk ad was criticized for being suggestive and symbolizing sexual submission.

558

Advertising critics are particularly concerned about the use of sexual appeals to glorify the image of liquor and beer or to suggest they can enhance one's own attractiveness. Some women's groups criticized the Airwalk ad shown in Exhibit 18-6, arguing that it showed a submissive and sexually available woman. A critic argued that the ad contains a number of symbolic cues that are sexually suggestive and combine to reinforce an image of the woman's sexual submission to the man.[30] Thus, another common criticism of sexual appeals is that they can demean women (or men) by depicting them as sex objects.

Recently, Skyy Spirits has used provocative, sexually oriented ads to promote its popular namesake vodka brand. Some of its ads, which use stylized images placing the brand's distinctive blue bottle in suggestive situations, have been criticized by some groups (Exhibit 18-7). However, a company spokesperson has responded to the criticisms by noting, "Style is a maker of interpretation and like with all art we appreciate all points of view."[31]

Attitudes toward the use of sex in advertising is a polarizing issue as opinions regarding its use vary depending upon the individual's values and religious orientation, as well as across various demographic groups including age, education, and gender. A recent study found major differences between men and women in their attitudes toward sex in advertising.[32] As shown in Figure 18-4, while almost half of men said they liked sexual ads, only 8 percent of women felt the same way. Most men (63 percent) indicated that sexual ads have high stopping power and get their attention, but fewer women thought the same (28 percent). Also, most women (58 percent) said there is too much sex in advertising, versus only 29 percent of the men. Women were also much more likely than men to say that sexual ads promote a deterioration of moral and social values and that they are demeaning of the models used in them.

Shock Appeals With the increasing clutter in the advertising environment, advertisers continue to use sexual appeals that may offend some people but catch the attention of consumers and may even generate publicity for their companies. In recent years there has been an increase in what is often referred to as a shock appeal, in which marketers use nudity, sexual suggestiveness, or other startling images to get consumers' attention. A shock appeal is not new; Benetton (Exhibit 18-8) used this approach in ads for many years, yet it remains an interesting example and continues to intrigue students today. Many advertising experts argue that what underlies the use of shock appeals is the pressure on marketers and their agencies to do whatever it takes to get their ads noticed. However, critics argue that the more advertisers use the appeal, the more shocking the ads have to be to get attention. How far advertisers can go with this appeal will probably depend on the public's reaction.

Exhibit 18-7 Ads are often criticized for being sexually suggestive.

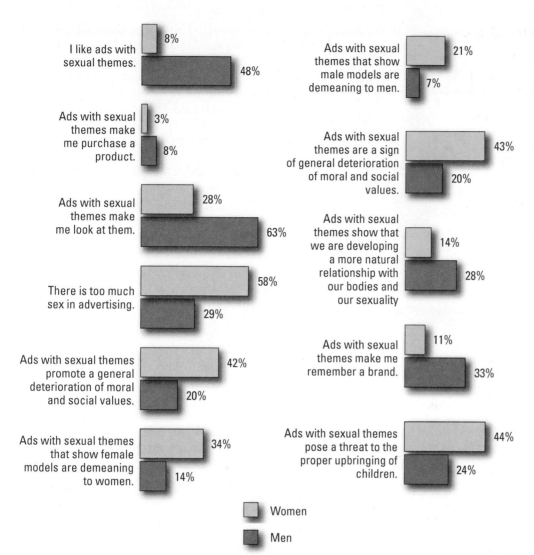

FIGURE 18–4

Attitudes toward sex in advertising, men vs. women

I like ads with sexual themes. — 8% / 48%

Ads with sexual themes make me purchase a product. — 3% / 8%

Ads with sexual themes make me look at them. — 28% / 63%

There is too much sex in advertising. — 58% / 29%

Ads with sexual themes promote a general deterioration of moral and social values. — 42% / 20%

Ads with sexual themes that show female models are demeaning to women. — 34% / 14%

Ads with sexual themes that show male models are demeaning to men. — 21% / 7%

Ads with sexual themes are a sign of general deterioration of moral and social values. — 43% / 20%

Ads with sexual themes show that we are developing a more natural relationship with our bodies and our sexuality — 14% / 28%

Ads with sexual themes make me remember a brand. — 11% / 33%

Ads with sexual themes pose a threat to the proper upbringing of children. — 44% / 24%

Women
Men

When advertisers have gone too far, they are likely to pressure the advertisers to change their ads and the media to stop accepting them. Exhibit 18-9 shows a more recent Benetton ad. While marketers and ad agencies often acknowledge that their ads push the limits with regard to taste, they also complain about a double standard that exists for advertising versus editorial television program content. They argue that even the most suggestive commercials are bland compared with the content of many television programs.

ADVERTISING AND CHILDREN

One of the most controversial topics advertisers must deal with is the issue of advertising to children. TV is a vehicle through which advertisers can reach children easily. Children between the ages of 2 and 11 watch an average of 15.5 hours of TV a week. Studies show that television is an important source of information for children about products.[33] Concern has also been expressed about marketers' use of other promotional vehicles and techniques such as radio ads, point-of-purchase displays, premiums in packages, and the use of commercial characters as the basis for TV shows.

Exhibit 18-8 Benetton's "Death Row" ads created a major controversy.

559

Exhibit 18-9 Benetton's advertising continues to focus on socially relevant issues.

Critics argue that children, particularly young ones, are especially vulnerable to advertising because they lack the experience and knowledge to understand and evaluate critically the purpose of persuasive advertising appeals. Research has shown that preschool children cannot differentiate between commercials and programs, do not perceive the selling intent of commercials, and cannot distinguish between reality and fantasy.[34] Research has also shown that children need more than a skeptical attitude toward advertising; they must understand how advertising works in order to use their cognitive defences against it effectively.[35] Because of children's limited ability to interpret the selling intent of a message or identify a commercial, critics charge that advertising to them is inherently unfair and deceptive and should be banned or severely restricted.

At the other extreme are those who argue that advertising is a part of life and children must learn to deal with it in the **consumer socialization process** of acquiring the skills needed to function in the marketplace.[36] They say existing restrictions are adequate for controlling children's advertising. A recent study by Tamara Mangleburg and Terry Bristol provided support for the socialization argument. They found that adolescents developed skeptical attitudes toward advertising that were learned through interactions with socialization agents such as parents, peers, and television. They also found that marketplace knowledge plays an important role in adolescents' skepticism toward advertising. Greater knowledge of the marketplace appears to give teens a basis by which to evaluate ads and makes them more likely to recognize the persuasion techniques used by advertisers.[37]

The *Children's Code* and the Food and Beverage Initiative discussed earlier recognize the above debate explicitly to find a balance between these two points of view. A study comparing the attitudes of business executives and consumers regarding children's advertising found that marketers of products targeted to children believe advertising to them provides useful information on new products and does not disrupt the parent–child relationship. However, the general public did not have such a favourable opinion. Older consumers and those from households with children had particularly negative attitudes toward children's advertising.[38] Clearly, companies communicating directly to children need to be sensitive to the naiveté of children as consumers to avoid potential conflict with those who believe children should be protected from advertising.

Finally, while we have been concerned with ads directed toward children, advertisers need to be careful not to unwittingly produce ads directed toward adults that make an impression upon children. For example, ASC published a bulletin, consistent with CRTC regulations, stating that marketers of alcoholic beverages could not use a spokesperson that is perceived as a role model for children. This arose from Molson's use of Don Cherry for its "Bubba" beer ads.[39]

SOCIAL EFFECTS OF ADVERTISING

Concern is often expressed over the impact of advertising on society, particularly on values and lifestyles. While a number of factors influence the cultural values, lifestyles, and behaviour of a society, the overwhelming amount of advertising and its prevalence in the mass media lead many critics to argue that advertising plays a major role in influencing and transmitting social values. While there is general agreement that advertising is an important social influence agent, opinions as to the value of its contribution are often negative. Advertising is criticized for encouraging materialism, manipulating consumers to buy things they do not really need, perpetuating stereotypes, and controlling the media.

ADVERTISING ENCOURAGES MATERIALISM

Critics claim advertising has an adverse effect on consumer values by encouraging **materialism**, a preoccupation with material things rather than intellectual or spiritual concerns. Critics contend that an ad like the one shown in Exhibit 18-10 can promote materialistic values. In summary, they contend that advertising:

- Seeks to create needs rather than merely showing how a product or service fulfills them.
- Surrounds consumers with images of the good life and suggests the acquisition of material possessions leads to contentment and happiness and adds to the joy of living.
- Suggests material possessions are symbols of status, success, and accomplishment and/or will lead to greater social acceptance, popularity, sex appeal, and so on.

This criticism of advertising assumes that materialism is undesirable and is sought at the expense of other goals, but some believe materialism is acceptable. For example, some consumers believe their hard work and individual effort and initiative allows for the accumulation of material possessions as evidence of success. Others argue that the acquisition of material possessions has positive economic impact by encouraging consumers to keep consuming after their basic needs are met. Many believe economic growth is essential and materialism is both a necessity and an inevitable part of this progress.

Economist John Kenneth Galbraith, often a vocal critic of advertising, describes the role advertising plays in industrialized economies by encouraging consumption:

> Advertising and its related arts thus help develop the kind of man the goals of the industrial system require—one that reliably spends his income and works reliably because he is always in need of more. In the absence of the massive and artful persuasion that accompanies the management of demand, increasing abundance might well have reduced the interest of people in acquiring more goods. Being not pressed by the need for these things, they would have spent less reliably to get more. The consequence—a lower and less reliable propensity to consume— would have been awkward for the industrial system.[40]

It has also been argued that an emphasis on material possessions does not rule out interest in intellectual, spiritual, or cultural values. Defenders of advertising say consumers can be more interested in higher-order goals when basic needs have been met. Raymond Bauer and Stephen Greyser point out that consumers may purchase material things in the pursuit of nonmaterial goals.[41] For example, a person may buy an expensive stereo system to enjoy music rather than simply to impress someone or acquire a material possession.

Even if we assume materialism is undesirable, there is still the question of whether advertising is responsible for creating and encouraging it. While many critics argue that advertising is a major contributing force to materialistic

Exhibit 18-10   Critics argue that advertising contributes to materialistic values.

Exhibit 18-11 The advertising industry argues that advertising reflects society.

values, others say advertising merely reflects the values of society rather than shaping them.[42] They argue that consumers' values are defined by the society in which they live and are the results of extensive, long-term socialization or acculturation.

The argument that advertising is responsible for creating a materialistic and hedonistic society is addressed by Stephen Fox in his book *The Mirror Makers: A History of American Advertising and Its Creators.* Fox concludes advertising has become a prime scapegoat for our times and merely reflects society. Regarding the effect of advertising on cultural values, he says:

> To blame advertising now for those most basic tendencies in American history is to miss the point. It is too obvious, too easy, a matter of killing the messenger instead of dealing with the bad news. The people who have created modern advertising are not hidden persuaders pushing our buttons in the service of some malevolent purpose. They are just producing an especially visible manifestation, good and bad, of the American way of life.[43]

The ad shown in Exhibit 18-11 was developed by the American Association of Advertising Agencies and suggests that advertising is a reflection of society's tastes and values, not vice versa. The ad was part of a campaign that addressed criticisms of advertising.

Advertising does contribute to our materialism by portraying products and services as symbols of status, success, and achievement and by encouraging consumption. As Richard Pollay says, "While it may be true that advertising reflects cultural values, it does so on a very selective basis, echoing and reinforcing certain attitudes, behaviours, and values far more frequently than others."[44]

ADVERTISING MAKES PEOPLE BUY THINGS THEY DON'T NEED

A common criticism of advertising is that it manipulates consumers into buying things they do not need. Many critics say advertising should just provide information useful in making purchase decisions and should not persuade. They view information advertising (which reports price, performance, and other objective criteria) as desirable but persuasive advertising (which plays on consumers' emotions, anxieties, and psychological needs and desires such as status, self-esteem, and attractiveness) as unacceptable. Persuasive advertising is criticized for fostering discontent among consumers and encouraging them to purchase products and services to solve deeper problems. Critics say advertising exploits consumers and persuades them to buy things they don't need.

Defenders of advertising offer a number of rebuttals to these criticisms. First, they point out that a substantial amount of advertising is essentially informational in nature.[45] Also, it is difficult to separate desirable informational advertising from undesirable persuasive advertising. Shelby Hunt, in examining the *information–persuasion dichotomy,* points out that even advertising that most observers would categorize as very informative is often very persuasive.[46] He says, "If advertising critics really believe that persuasive advertising should not be permitted, they are actually proposing that no advertising be allowed, since the purpose of all advertising is to persuade."[47]

Defenders of advertising also take issue with the argument that it should be limited to dealing with basic functional needs. In our society, most lower-level needs recognized in Maslow's hierarchy, such as the need for food, clothing, and shelter, are satisfied for most people. It is natural to move from basic needs to higher-order ones such as self-esteem and status or self-actualization. Consumers are free to choose the degree to which they attempt to satisfy their desires, and wise advertisers associate their products and services with the satisfaction of higher-order needs.

Proponents of advertising offer two other defences against the charge that advertising makes people buy things they do not really need. First, this criticism attributes too much power to advertising and assumes consumers have no ability to defend themselves against it. Second, it ignores the fact that consumers have the freedom to make their own choices when confronted with persuasive advertising. While they readily admit the persuasive intent of their business, advertisers are quick to note it is extremely difficult to make consumers purchase a product they do not want or for which they do not see a personal benefit. If advertising were as powerful as the critics claim, we would not see products with multimillion-dollar advertising budgets failing in the marketplace. The reality is that consumers do have a choice, and they are not being forced to buy. Consumers ignore ads for products and services they do not really need or that fail to interest them.

ADVERTISING AND STEREOTYPING

Advertising is often accused of creating and perpetuating stereotypes through its portrayal of women and ethnic minorities.

Women The portrayal of women in advertising is an issue that has received a great deal of attention through the years.[48] Advertising has received much criticism for stereotyping women and failing to recognize the changing role of women in our society. Critics have argued that advertising often depicts women as preoccupied with beauty, household duties, and motherhood, or shows them as decorative objects or sexually provocative figures. The various research studies conducted through the years show a consistent picture of gender stereotyping that has varied little over time. Portrayals of adult women in American television and print advertising have emphasized passivity, deference, lack of intelligence and credibility, and punishment for high levels of effort. In contrast, men have been portrayed as constructive, powerful, autonomous, and achieving.[49]

Research on gender stereotyping in advertising targeted to children has found a pattern of results similar to that reported for adults. A recent study found sex-role stereotyping in television advertising targeted at children in the United States as well as in Australia.[50] Boys are generally shown as being more knowledgeable, active, aggressive, and instrumental than girls. Nonverbal behaviours involving dominance and control are associated more with boys than girls. Advertising directed toward children has also been shown to feature more boys than girls, to position boys in more dominant, active roles, and to use male voiceovers more frequently than female ones.[51]

While stereotyping still exists, advertising's portrayal of women is improving in many areas as many advertisers now portray women realistically. Researchers Steven Kates and Glenda Shaw-Garlock argue that the transformed social positioning of women in North American society is perhaps the most important social development of this century.[52] They note that as women have crossed the boundary from the domestic sphere to the professional arena, expectations and representations of women have changed as well. For example, magazines incorporate and appeal to the sociocultural shifts in women's lives. Many advertisers are now depicting women in a diversity of roles that reflect their changing place in society. In many ads, the stereotypic character traits attributed to women have shifted from weak and dependent to strong and autonomous.[53] The ad for Network Solutions shown in Exhibit 18-12 is an example of how advertisers are changing the way they portray women in their ads.

Exhibit 18-12 Many advertisers now portray women in powerful roles.

This trend is seen in the 2009 annual report published by Advertising Standards Canada (ASC). It received a total of 541 complaints associated with clause 14 (unacceptable depictions and portrayals) in 2009. However, most of these concerned personal taste or preference and the council ultimately upheld 13 complaints for 5 ads. This represented a total of fewer than one percent of all complaints for this clause (5/541). Of these five, two represented unacceptable depictions of women and one represented an unacceptable depiction of men. As Figure 18-2 indicated, ASC upheld complaints for 56 ads in 2009, so these 5 ads accounted for only 9 percent of the total number of complaints (5/56). In contrast, ASC received 434 complaints for clause 1 (accuracy and clarity) and clause 3 (price claims) combined and upheld 63 complaints for 47 ads, which accounted for the clear majority at 84 percent (47/56).[54]

While the statistics are a positive indication, the issue of digitally altering photographic images is a concern. A recent illustration occurred with a Polo Ralph Lauren ad, where one astute viewer commented, "Dude, her head's bigger than her pelvis." Upon investigation, Polo apologized and claimed the mistake would not occur in future.[55] Ethical Perspective 18-2 shows Dove's criticism of digital manipulation in the beauty industry. So while the depiction and portrayal aspects reflect a positive trend, the use of such tactics still gives unrealistic images that a company like Dove is drawing attention toward.

It should be noted that portrayal and depiction problems occurring in advertising are not necessarily reflected in the statistics, as advertising gets amended or withdrawn prior to anyone making a complaint to ASC. And if the ad is no longer running, then ASC does not investigate. In the case of a Loblaws flyer featuring Joe Fresh ads for women's underwear and night clothes, the retailer immediately pulled its flyers once a few consumers complained directly and a media story questioned whether the images should be displayed in such a public manner. One vice president for the brand noted, "We stand by the flyer. We think the photography is beautiful, and we have definitely seen a positive reflection in our sales since the flyer went out. Ironically, the *Citizen* ran the picture and . . . claims it's disturbing . . . yet is showing it."[56]

Finally, the shoe is on the other foot, so to speak, as one advertising professional observed that some ads portray a stereotype of men as dumb, goofy, or inept. Deborah Adams, senior vice-president of Harbinger Communications, a consultancy firm that focuses on marketing to women, recounted a comment from a woman on their market research panel, "You know, if you want to make inroads with me, if you want to resonate with me, you really shouldn't be showing my husband as an idiot."[57] Which is precisely the reason why the ASC guidelines on depictions and portrayal include both women and men.

Visible Minorities Several U.S. academic studies in the late 1980s and early 1990s examined the incidence of visible minorities in advertising. A study conducted in 1987 found that 11 percent of the people appearing in commercials were African-Americans.[58] Another study conducted two years later found that

Dove Challenges the Stereotypical Norms of Beauty

The vast majority of ads for clothing, jewellery, cosmetics, and beauty care products use physically attractive models who are usually tall and slender and have flawless features. Consequently, most women believe that the media and advertising set an unrealistic standard of beauty that they cannot achieve. More than two-thirds of the women in a recent worldwide study expressed this viewpoint. Only 13 percent of the women indicated that they are very satisfied with their body weight and shape, only 2 percent of the women around the world considered themselves beautiful, and more than half of the women said their bodies disgust them. Inspired by these findings, Unilever's Dove, the global beauty brand, launched an IMC campaign to challenge the stereotypical view of beauty, celebrate diversity, and make women feel beautiful every day.

Dove's Campaign for Real Beauty has been praised as a catalyst for societal change and widening the definition and discussion of beauty. IT launched globally in September 2004 with a much-talked-about ad campaign featuring real women whose appearances are outside the stereotypical norms of beauty. The ads asked viewers to judge the women's looks (Oversized? Outstanding? or Wrinkled? Wonderful?) and invited them to cast their votes and join in a discussion of beauty issues on a special website (campaignforrealbeauty.ca). In June 2005, Dove kicked off the second phase with advertising featuring six "real women" with real bodies and real curves. These "real women" were not professional models, varied in shape and size, and came from all walks of life. The images of the real women showed the women posing proudly and confidently in their underwear. The photos were not altered or retouched as is often done when shooting images of models.

The second phase addressed the issue of body image and encouraged women to "Stand firm to celebrate their curves"—and supported the new line of Dove firming products with messages encouraging women to challenge beauty stereotypes. The campaign reached women through national and local television and magazine advertising as well as interactive billboards, transit station signage, and bus ads. The website allowed women to engage in ongoing dialogue about beauty by posting to discussion boards, to hear other women's perspectives on beauty, and to download research studies about beauty. The campaign also featured customized retail promotions and partnerships, local events to foster discussion about real beauty, and cause-related marketing with the Dove Self-Esteem Fund.

Dove has continued to find creative ways to keep the Campaign for Real Beauty fresh and relevant over time. In 2006, Dove's agency (Ogilvy & Mather–Toronto) created the "Evolution" video that used time-lapse photography to show the transformation of an average-looking woman into a glamorous billboard model using makeup artistry,

stylists, and Photoshop enhancements. The video ended with the message: "It's no wonder our perception of beauty is distorted." The video was first shown on Dove's website and was passed around online, and received millions of viewings after being posted on YouTube. The video won both the Cyber and Film Grand Prix at the 2007 Cannes Advertising Festival. In 2007 Dove followed up "Evolution" with another successful viral video called "Onslaught" that opens with a close-up of a sweet-faced, redheaded little girl and then is followed by a barrage of beauty industry images such as ultrathin and curvaceous women, lingerie models, scenes of plastic surgery, and women shrinking and expanding via fad diets—all leading up to the tagline, "Talk to your daughter before the beauty industry does."

Some critics note that there is somewhat of a contradiction in the message of the "real beauty" campaign because it still suggests women need Dove's products such as skin creams, moisturizers, firming lotions, and anti-aging creams to be beautiful. Critics also argue that the campaign is really just a creative way to sell more products, since it has led to double-digit sales increases for many Dove brands. However, many believe these ads send a simple message that many parents have tried to teach their daughters for years: Be happy with who you are.

Sources: Jack Neff, "Soft Soap," *Advertising Age*, September 24, 2007, pp. 1, 30; Laurel Wentz and Brooke Capps, "'Evolution' Win Marks Dawn of New Cannes," *Advertising Age*, June 25, 2007, pp. 1, 53; Rich Thomaselli, "Beauty's New, ER, Face," *Advertising Age*, August 15, 2005, pp. 1, 21; Theresa Howard, "Ad Campaigns Tell Women to Celebrate Who They Are," *USA TODAY*, July 8, 2005, p. 5B; "Real Women Bare Their Real Curves," press release, Edelman/Unilever, June 23, 2005.

Question

1. What is your personal reaction to the campaign?

Exhibit 18-13 IKEA broke new ground with this ad showing an interracial couple shopping for furniture.

African-Americans appeared in 26 percent of all ads on network TV that used live models but Hispanics appeared in only 6 percent of the commercials with live models. The researchers also found that TV ads in which blacks appeared were overwhelmingly integrated (Exhibit 18-13) and that blacks were likely to have played either minor or background roles in the majority of the ads.[59] A study conducted in 1995 found that 17 percent of prime-time network TV ads featured African-Americans as dominant characters and the majority of commercials featured them in minor roles.[60] A recent study by Corliss L. Green found that ads targeting African-Americans through racially targeted media, especially with race-based products, benefit from featuring African-American models with a dominant presence in the ad.[61]

A recent study of U.S. prime-time TV commercials found that Asian male and female models are overrepresented in terms of their proportion of the U.S. population (3.6 percent), appearing in 8.4 percent of the commercials. However, Asian models were more likely than members of other minority groups to appear in background roles, and Asian women were rarely depicted in major roles. The study also found that portrayals of Asian-Americans put more emphasis on the work ethic and less on other aspects of their lives.[62]

It may be difficult to generalize these findings to Canada; however, we should keep in mind that Canadians are exposed to these ads when watching U.S. television programs that do not simulcast Canadian commercials or when reading American magazines. So to a degree, Canadian consumers will experience and perceive some amount of imbalance through this exposure.

Visible minorities comprise about 18 percent of Canada's population, of which 23 percent are Chinese, 19 percent are South Asians, and 19 percent are black. Recent Canadian trends and commentary by practitioners suggest that the portrayal of visible minorities can be improved in Canadian advertising, even though there has been significant improvement over the past five years. For example, a recent study suggests that 45 percent of all Canadians feel that advertising is directed to whites, and 48 percent feel that visible minorities are underrepresented.[63] Walmart is an example of one leader that initiated multicultural ads. It began in 1997; with its agency's assistance, Walmart used Print Measurement Bureau and Census Canada data and identified a large and growing segment of the population that did not receive the existing advertising. Executives also truly believed that communicating to customers in a language of their choice was a sign of respect. In that first year, Walmart produced original TV creative for four ethnic groups: Italian, Portuguese, Cantonese, and South Asian, all but the latter in their own language. From then on, multicultural ads continued and the retailer remains one of a handful of companies producing original creative for ethnic TV.[64]

ADVERTISING AND THE MEDIA

The fact that advertising plays such an important role in financing the media has led to concern that advertisers may influence or even control the media. It is well documented that *economic censorship* occurs, whereby the media avoid certain topics or even present biased news coverage in acquiescence to advertiser demands.[65] In fact, Professors Lawrence Soley and Robert Craig say, "The assertion that advertisers attempt to influence what the public sees, hears, and reads in the mass media is perhaps the most damning of all criticisms of advertising, but this criticism isn't acknowledged in most advertising textbooks."[66] We will address this important issue in this book by considering arguments on both sides.

Arguments Supporting Advertiser Control   Some critics charge that the media's dependence on advertisers' support makes them susceptible to various forms of influence, including exerting control over the editorial content of magazines and newspapers; biasing editorial opinions to favour the position of an advertiser; limiting coverage of a controversial story that might reflect negatively on a company; and influencing the program content of television.

Newspapers and magazines receive nearly 70 percent of their revenue from advertising; commercial TV and radio derive virtually all their income from advertisers. Small, financially insecure newspapers, magazines, or broadcast stations are the most susceptible to pressure from advertisers, particularly companies that account for a large amount of the media outlet's advertising revenue. A local newspaper may be reluctant to print an unfavourable story about a car dealer or supermarket chain on whose advertising it depends. A survey of 147 daily newspapers found that more than 90 percent of editors have been pressured by advertisers and more than one-third of them said advertisers had succeeded in influencing news at their papers.[67]

Individual TV stations and even the major networks also can be influenced by advertisers. Programming decisions are made largely on the basis of what shows will attract the most viewers and thus be most desirable to advertisers. Critics say this often results in lower-quality television as educational, cultural, and informative programming is usually sacrificed for shows that get high ratings and appeal to the mass markets.

Arguments against Advertiser Control   The commercial media's dependence on advertising means advertisers can exert influence on their character, content, and coverage of certain issues. However, media executives offer several reasons why advertisers do not exert undue influence over the media.

First, they point out it is in the best interest of the media not to be influenced too much by advertisers. To retain public confidence, they must report the news fairly and accurately without showing bias or attempting to avoid controversial issues. Media executives point to the vast array of topics they cover and the investigative reporting they often do as evidence of their objectivity. They want to build a large audience for their publications or stations so that they can charge more for advertising space and time.

Media executives also note that an advertiser needs the media more than they need any individual advertiser, particularly when the medium has a large audience or does a good job of reaching a specific market segment. Many publications and stations have a very broad base of advertising support and can afford to lose an advertiser that attempts to exert too much influence. This is particularly true for the larger, more established, financially secure media. For example, a consumer products company would find it difficult to reach its target audience without network TV and could not afford to boycott a network if it disagreed with a station's editorial policy or program content. Even the local advertiser in a small community may be dependent on the local newspaper, since it may be the most cost-effective media option available.

The media in Canada are basically supported by advertising; this means we can enjoy them for free or for a fraction of what they would cost without advertising. The alternative to an advertiser-supported media system is support by users through higher subscription costs for the print media and a fee or pay-per-view system with TV. The ad in Exhibit 18-14, part of a campaign by the International Advertising

Exhibit 18-14 This ad points out how advertising lowers the cost of newspapers for consumers.

Exhibit 18-15   MADD encourages people to take action against drinking and driving.

568

Association, explains how advertising lowers the cost of print media for consumers. Another alternative is government-supported media like those in many other countries, but this runs counter to most people's desire for freedom of the press. Although not perfect, our system of advertising-supported media provides the best option for receiving information and entertainment.

ADVERTISING AND SOCIAL BENEFIT

This social effects discussion has focused on how advertising is used (or abused) for marketing products and services. It is important to note that advertising and other IMC tools play an important role in many activities that provide tremendous social benefit in a number of ways.

As discussed in Chapter 15, companies use advertising in their sponsorship or cause-related activities that encourage participation to help raise money for important causes. For example, communicating to the thousands who participated in CIBC's Run for the Cure and Becel's Ride for Heart efforts would not be possible without advertising—and, more importantly, would not occur without existing advertising industry and infrastructure.

Organizations dealing with social problems, such as alcohol-impaired driving, use advertising to influence attitudes and behaviour. Exhibit 18-15 identifies one organization that uses advertising and other marketing communication tools to achieve these objectives. Their messages try to persuade those at risk to not engage in the behaviour or take precautions. One study reviewing the effects of mass media campaigns found a 13 percent decline in alcohol-related crashes and concluded that the social benefit of the advertising clearly outweighed the cost of the advertising.[68] Furthermore, advertising attempts to influence social norms by giving friends and family the courage to intervene. A multimedia ad campaign from the provincial distributor of alcohol in Ontario supported this idea. Its research indicated that consumers often feel embarrassed or awkward when stopping someone from drinking and driving. An interactive website (deflatetheelephant.com) allowed users to practise, with the elephant shrinking as they achieved success.[69]

Non-profit organizations that raise funds for their worthy causes rely on advertising as well. The United Way campaigns are certainly successful, with thousands of volunteers; however, the whole campaign requires some assistance with advertising. To facilitate the delivery of various government services or implementation of policy, advertising is used extensively. Transit systems, generally a part of most city governments, rely on advertising to communicate routes, and so on. Provincial governments encourage visitors from other provinces to plan a vacation.

ECONOMIC EFFECTS OF ADVERTISING

Advertising plays an important role by making consumers aware of products and services and providing them with information for decision making. However, it is also a powerful force that can affect the functioning of our entire economic system. Advertising can encourage consumption and foster economic growth, facilitate entry into markets for a firm or a new product or brand; and lead to economies of scale in production, marketing, and distribution, thereby increasing the standard of living. In contrast, critics view advertising as a detrimental force that not only fails to perform its basic function of information provision adequately but also adds to the cost of products and services and discourages competition and market entry, leading to industrial concentration and higher prices for consumers.

To resolve this debate we turn to economists who generally take a macroeconomic perspective: they consider the economic impact of advertising on an entire industry or on the economy as a whole rather than its effect on an individual company or brand. Our examination of the economic impact of advertising focuses on these broader macro-level issues. We consider its effects on consumer choice, competition, and product costs and prices.

EFFECTS ON CONSUMER CHOICE

Some critics say advertising hampers consumer choice, as large advertisers use their power to limit our options to a few well-advertised brands. Economists argue that advertising is used to achieve (1) **differentiation**, whereby the products or services of large advertisers are perceived as unique or better than competitors', and (2) brand loyalty, which enables large national advertisers to gain control of the market, usually at the expense of smaller brands.

Larger companies often end up charging a higher price and achieve a more dominant position in the market than smaller firms that cannot compete against them and their large advertising budgets. When this occurs, advertising not only restricts the choice alternatives to a few well-known, heavily advertised brands but also becomes a substitute for competition based on price or product improvements.

Heavily advertised brands dominate the market in certain product categories, such as soft drinks, beer, and cereals.[70] But advertising generally does not create brand monopolies and reduce the opportunities for new products to be introduced to consumers. In most product categories, a number of different brands are on the store shelves and thousands of new products are introduced every year. The opportunity to advertise gives companies the incentive to develop new brands and improve their existing ones. When a successful new product such as a smartphone is introduced, competitors quickly follow and use advertising to inform consumers about their brand and attempt to convince them it is superior to the original. Companies like Head & Shoulders recognize that advertising has been an important part of their success (Exhibit 18-16).

EFFECTS ON COMPETITION

One of the most common criticisms economists have about advertising concerns its effects on competition. They argue that power in the hands of large firms with huge advertising budgets creates a **barrier to entry**, which makes it difficult for other firms to enter the market. This results in less competition

Exhibit 18-16 Head and Shoulders advertisements inform consumers of its uniqueness.

and higher prices. Economists note that smaller firms already in the market find it difficult to compete against the large advertising budgets of the industry leaders and are often driven out of business. For example, the Canadian beer industry is dominated by two national brewers, Molson and Labatt, which account for over 90 percent of the market. With their high advertising and promotion expenditures, these companies are spending much less per barrel than smaller firms, making it very difficult for the latter to compete.

Large advertisers clearly enjoy certain competitive advantages. First, there are **economies of scale** in advertising, particularly with respect to factors such as media costs. Firms such as Procter & Gamble, which spends millions of dollars per year on advertising and promotion, are able to make large media buys at a reduced rate and allocate them to their various products. Large advertisers usually sell more of a product or service, which means they may have lower production costs and can allocate more monies to advertising, so they can afford the costly but more efficient media like network television. Their large advertising outlays also give them more opportunity to differentiate their products and develop brand loyalty. To the extent that these factors occur, smaller competitors are at a disadvantage and new competitors are deterred from entering the market.

While advertising may have an anticompetitive effect on a market, there is no clear evidence that advertising alone reduces competition, creates barriers to entry, and thus increases market concentration. Lester Telser noted that high levels of advertising are not always found in industries where firms have a large market share. He found an inverse relationship between intensity of product class advertising and stability of market share for the leading brands.[71] These findings run contrary to many economists' belief that industries controlled by a few firms have high advertising expenditures, resulting in stable brand shares for market leaders.

Defenders of advertising say it is unrealistic to attribute a firm's market dominance and barriers to entry solely to advertising. There are a number of other factors, such as price, product quality, distribution effectiveness, production efficiencies, and competitive strategies. Industry leaders often tend to dominate markets because they have superior product quality and the best management and competitive strategies, not simply the biggest advertising budgets.[72] While market entry against large, established competitors is difficult, companies with a quality product at a reasonable price often find a way to break in. Moreover, they usually find that advertising actually facilitates their market entry by making it possible to communicate the benefits and features of their new product or brand to consumers.

EFFECTS ON PRODUCT COSTS AND PRICES

A major area of debate among economists, advertisers, consumer advocates, and policymakers concerns the effects of advertising on product costs and prices. Critics argue that advertising increases the prices consumers pay for products and services. First, they say the large sums of money spent advertising a brand constitute an expense that must be covered and the consumer ends up paying for it through higher prices. This is a common criticism from consumer advocates. Several studies show that firms with higher relative prices advertise their products more intensely than do those with lower relative prices.[73]

A second way advertising can result in higher prices is by increasing product differentiation and adding to the perceived value of the product in consumers' minds. Paul Farris and Mark Albion note that product differentiation occupies a central position in theories of advertising's economic effects.[74] The fundamental premise is that advertising increases the perceived differences between physically homogeneous products and enables advertised brands to command a premium price without an increase in quality.

Critics of advertising generally point to the differences in prices between national brands and private-label brands that are physically similar, such as cotton balls or tea bags, as evidence of the added value created by advertising. They see consumers' willingness to pay more for heavily advertised national brands rather than purchasing the lower-priced, nonadvertised brand as wasteful and irrational. However, consumers do not always buy for rational, functional reasons. The emotional, psychological, and social benefits derived from purchasing a national brand are important to many people. Moreover, say Albion and Farris,

> Unfortunately there seems to be no single way to measure product differentiation, let alone determine how much is excessive or attributable to the effects of advertising . . . Both price insensitivity and brand loyalty could be created by a number of factors such as higher product quality, better packaging, favorable use experience and market position. They are probably related to each other but need not be the result of advertising.[75]

Proponents of advertising offer several other counterarguments to the claim that advertising increases prices. They acknowledge that advertising costs are at least partly paid for by consumers. But advertising may help lower the overall cost of a product more than enough to offset them. For example, advertising may help firms achieve economies of scale in production and distribution by providing information to and stimulating demand among mass markets. These economies of scale help cut the cost of producing and marketing the product, which can lead to lower prices—if the advertiser chooses to pass the cost savings on to the consumer.

Advertising can also lower prices by making a market more competitive, which usually leads to greater price competition. A study by Lee Benham found that prices of eyeglasses were 25 to 30 percent higher in states that banned eyeglass advertising than in those that permitted it.[76] Robert Steiner analyzed the toy industry and concluded that advertising resulted in lower consumer prices. He argued that curtailment of TV advertising would drive up consumer prices for toys.[77] Finally, advertising is a means to market entry rather than a deterrent and helps stimulate product innovation, which makes markets more competitive and helps keep prices down.

Overall, it is difficult to reach any firm conclusions regarding the relationship between advertising and prices. After an extensive review of this area, Farris and Albion concluded, "The evidence connecting manufacturer advertising to prices is neither complete nor definitive . . . consequently, we cannot say whether advertising is a tool of market efficiency or market power without further research."[78]

Economist James Ferguson argues that advertising cannot increase the cost per unit of quality to consumers because if it did consumers would not continue to respond positively to advertising.[79] He believes advertising lowers the costs of information about brand qualities, leads to increases in brand quality, and lowers the average price per unit of quality.

SUMMARIZING ECONOMIC EFFECTS

Albion and Farris suggest that economists' perspectives can be divided into two principal schools of thought that make different assumptions regarding the influence of advertising on the economy.[80] Figure 18-5 summarizes the main points of the "advertising equals market power" and "advertising equals information" perspectives.

Advertising Equals Market Power The belief that advertising equals market power reflects traditional economic thinking and views advertising as a way to change consumers' tastes, lower their sensitivity to price, and build brand loyalty among buyers of advertised brands. This results in higher profits and market

FIGURE 18–5 Two schools of thought on advertising's role in the economy

Advertising = Market Power		Advertising = Information
Advertising affects consumer preferences and tastes, changes product attributes, and differentiates the product from competitive offerings.	Advertising	Advertising informs consumers about product attributes but does not change the way they value those attributes.
Consumers become brand loyal and less price sensitive and perceive fewer substitutes for advertised brands.	Consumer buying behaviour	Consumers become more price sensitive and buy best "value." Only the relationship between price and quality affects elasticity for a given product.
Potential entrants must overcome established brand loyalty and spend relatively more on advertising.	Barriers to entry	Advertising makes entry possible for new brands because it can communicate product attributes to consumers.
Firms are insulated from market competition and potential rivals; concentration increases, leaving firms with more discretionary power.	Industry structure and market power	Consumers can compare competitive offerings easily and competitive rivalry increases. Efficient firms remain, and as the inefficient leave, new entrants appear; the effect on concentration is ambiguous.
Firms can charge higher prices and are not as likely to compete on quality or price dimensions. Innovation may be reduced.	Market conduct	More informed consumers pressure firms to lower prices and improve quality; new entrants facilitate innovation.
High prices and excessive profits accrue to advertisers and give them even more incentive to advertise their products. Output is restricted compared with conditions of perfect competition.	Market performance	Industry prices decrease. The effect on profits due to increased competition and increased efficiency is ambiguous.

Exhibit 18-17 This ad promotes the value of advertising in building strong brands.

power for large advertisers, reduces competition in the market, and leads to higher prices and fewer choices for consumers. Proponents of this viewpoint generally have negative attitudes regarding the economic impact of advertising.

Advertising Equals Information The belief that advertising equals information takes a more positive view of advertising's economic effects. This model sees advertising as providing consumers with useful information, increasing their price sensitivity (which moves them toward lower-priced products), and increasing competition in the market. Advertising is viewed as a way to communicate with consumers and tell them about a product and its major features and attributes. More informed and knowledgeable consumers pressure companies to provide high-quality products at lower prices. Efficient firms remain in the market, whereas inefficient firms leave as new entrants appear. Proponents of this model believe the economic effects of advertising are favourable and think it contributes to more efficient and competitive markets. Exhibit 18-17 shows an ad from the International Advertising Association used to support this positive role of advertising.

To me it means that if we believe to any degree whatsoever in the economic system under which we live, in a high standard of living and in high employment, advertising is the most efficient known way of moving goods in practically every product class.

My proof is that millions of businessmen have chosen advertising over and over again in the operations of their business. Some of their decisions may have been wrong, but they must have thought they were right or they wouldn't go back to be stung twice by the same kind of bee.

It's a pretty safe bet that in the next 10 years many Americans will be using products and devices that no one in this room has even heard of. Judging purely by past performance, American advertising can be relied on to make them known and accepted overnight at the lowest possible prices.

Advertising, of course, makes possible our unparalleled variety of magazines, newspapers, business publications, and radio and television stations.

It must be said that without advertising we would have a far different nation, and one that would be much the poorer—not merely in material commodities, but in the life of the spirit.

Leo Burnett

These excerpts are from a speech given by Leo Burnett on the American Association of Advertising Agencies' 50th anniversary, April 20, 1967.

FIGURE   18–6

This message describes the positive economic effects of advertising

The debate over the economic effects of advertising will likely continue; however, the point of view expressed by Leo Burnett many years ago seems relevant today with the growth of mobile devices and other innovations (Figure 18-6). While many advertising and marketing experts agree that advertising and promotion play an important role in helping to expand consumer demand for new products, not everyone would agree that this is desirable.

CHAPTER OBJECTIVES AND SUMMARY

1 To be familiar with the advertising regulation system in Canada.

Various levels of government regulate different aspects of Canadian advertising; however, self-regulation of these laws is quite prominent in Canada. This self-regulation occurs through the Advertising Standards Council (ASC), a non-profit organization of advertising industry members. The ASC responds to all complaints with respect to advertising and publishes an annual report that summarizes the complaints it receives each year. The ASC is also responsible for clearing ads prior to their airing for a number of products. Some of the ASC's responsibilities have been given to it as the federal government has withdrawn services with the belief that industry is sufficiently responsible.

2 To evaluate the ethical perspectives of advertising.

Even though there appears to be sufficient control of advertising, it is a very powerful institution that has been the target of considerable criticism regarding its ethical, social, and economic impact. The criticism

of advertising concerns the specific techniques and methods used as well as its effect on societal values, tastes, lifestyles, and behaviour. Critics argue that advertising is deceptive and untruthful; that it is often offensive, irritating, or in poor taste; and that it exploits certain groups. Many people believe advertising should be informative only and advertisers should not use subjective claims, puffery, embellishment, or persuasive techniques.

Advertising often offends consumers by the type of appeal or manner of presentation used; sexually suggestive ads and nudity receive the most criticism. Advertisers say their ads are consistent with contemporary values and lifestyles and are appropriate for the target audiences they are attempting to reach. Advertising to children is an area of particular concern, since critics argue that children lack the experience, knowledge, and ability to process and evaluate persuasive advertising messages rationally.

3 To understand the social effects of advertising.

The pervasiveness of advertising and its prevalence in the mass

media have led critics to argue that it plays a major role in influencing and transmitting social values. Advertising has been charged with encouraging materialism, manipulating consumers to buy things they do not really want or need, and perpetuating stereotypes through its portrayal of certain groups such as women and visible minorities.

4 To examine the economic role of advertising and its effects on consumer choice, competition, and product costs and prices.

Advertising has also been scrutinized with regard to its economic effects. The basic economic role of advertising is to give consumers information that helps them make consumption decisions. Some people view advertising as a detrimental force that has a negative effect on competition, product costs, and consumer prices. Economists' perspectives regarding the effects of advertising follow two basic schools of thought: the advertising equals market power model and the advertising equals information model. Arguments consistent with each perspective were considered in analyzing the economic effects of advertising.

KEY TERMS

barrier to entry, **569**
consumer complaints, **550**
consumer socialization
process, **560**

differentiation, **569**
economies of scale, **570**
ethics, **555**

materialism, **561**
puffery, **555**

special interest group
complaints, **550**
trade disputes, **550**

DISCUSSION QUESTIONS

1. Explain why you agree or disagree with the rulings of the ASC presented in this chapter regarding the Ford Focus and Kia automobile ads.

2. Discuss the role of ethics in advertising and promotion. How do ethical considerations differ from legal considerations?

3. What is meant by shock advertising? Evaluate the arguments for and against the use of shock advertising by marketers.

4. Evaluate the arguments for and against advertising to children. Do you feel restrictions are needed for advertising and other forms of promotion targeted to children?

5. A common criticism of advertising is that it stereotypes women. Discuss the ways this might occur. Do you think the Airwalk ad shown in Exhibit 18-6 is suggestive and symbolizes sexual submission?

6. Discuss how attitudes toward the use of sex in advertising differ between men and women. Discuss the implications of these attitudinal differences for marketers who are developing ads for each gender.

7. With which position do you agree: "Advertising determines Canadian consumers' tastes and values and is responsible for creating a materialistic society," or "Advertising is a reflection of society and mirrors its tastes and values"?

8. Discuss how advertising can impact consumer choice, as well as its impact on product costs and the prices paid for products and services.

9. Discuss the two major perspectives of the economic impact of advertising: "advertising equals market power" versus "advertising equals information."

ENDNOTES

CHAPTER ONE

1. "AMA Board Approves New Marketing Definition," *Marketing News,* March 1, 1985, p. 1.
2. Richard P. Bagozzi, "Marketing as Exchange," *Journal of Marketing, 39,* October 1975, pp. 32–39.
3. Kristin Laird, "Art Is Joyful for BMW," *Marketing Magazine,* May 8, 2009.
4. J. Paul Peter and Jerry C. Olson, *Consumer Behavior* (Burr Ridge, IL.: Richard D. Irwin, 1987), p. 505.
5. Michael R. Solomon, "The Role of Products as Social Stimuli: A Symbolic Interactionism Perspective," *Journal of Consumer Research,* December 1983, pp. 319–29.
6. Matt Semansky, "Labatt Defends Kokanee's Mountain Territory," *Marketing Magazine,* September 17, 2009.
7. Michelle Warren, "Flight of the Stinger," *Marketing Magazine,* May 1, 2006; Michelle Warren, "The Trouble with Tag Lines," *Marketing Magazine,* March 6, 2006.
8. Kevin Lane Keller, "Conceptualizing, Measuring, and Managing Customer Based Brand Equity," *Journal of Marketing, 57,* January 1993, pp. 1–22.
9. Sreedhar Madhavaram, Vishag Badrinarayanan, and Robert E. McDonald, "Integrated Marketing Communication (IMC) and Brand Identity as Critical Components of Brand Equity Strategy," *Journal of Advertising, 34*(4), pp. 69–80.
10. Canada's Most Valuable Brands 2009, Brand Finance (http://www.level5.ca/pdf/Brand_Finance_Canada-Press%20Release-Most_Valuable_Brands_2009.pdf).
11. Peter and Olson, *Consumer Behavior,* p. 571.
12. Paul W. Farris and David J. Reibstein, "How Prices, Ad Expenditures, and Profits Are Linked," *Harvard Business Review,* November–December 1979, pp. 172–84.
13. Dhruv Grewal, Kent B. Monroe, & R. Krishnan, "The Effects of Price-Comparison Advertising on Buyers' Perceptions of Acquisition Value, Transaction Value, and Behavioral Intentions," *Journal of Marketing, 62,* April 1998, pp. 46–59; Daniel J. Howard & Roger A. Kerin, "Broadening the Scope of Reference Price Advertising Research: A Field Study of Consumer Shopping," *Journal of Marketing, 70,* October 2006, pp. 185-204.

14. Roger A. Kerin, Steven W. Hartley, Eric N. Berkowitz, and William Rudelius, *Marketing,* 8th ed. (Burr Ridge, IL: Irwin/McGraw-Hill, 2006).
15. Michael L. Ray, *Advertising and Communication Management* (Englewood Cliffs, NJ: Prentice Hall, 1982).
16. Ralph S. Alexander, ed., *Marketing Definitions* (Chicago: American Marketing Association, 1965), p. 9.
17. BBM.CA, Weekly Top 30 Programs.
18. "Analysis of the Economics of Canadian Television Programming." Study performed by Nodicity Group Ltd., March 2009.
19. Arjun Chaudhuri, "How Brand Reputation Affects the Advertising-Brand Equity Link," *Journal of Advertising Research,* May-June 2002, pp. 33–43.
20. Kristin Laird, "Broil King Heats Up Advertising for Summer," *Marketing Magazine,* May 5, 2009.
21. Jeromy Lloyd, "Amex Invests in Major Brand Campaign," *Marketing Magazine,* October 6, 2009.
22. H. Frazier Moore and Bertrand R. Canfield, *Public Relations: Principles, Cases, and Problems,* 7th ed. (Burr Ridge, IL: Irwin, 1977), p. 5.
23. Karin Scott, "Beyond Press Coverage," *Marketing Magazine,* June 16, 2003.
24. Kristin Laird, "Tim Hortons Is Turning Green," *Marketing Magazine,* June 1, 2009.
25. Michelle Warren, "Pub Visits Lead Guinness Holiday Push," *Marketing Magazine,* January 27, 2003.
26. Don E. Schultz, "Integrated Marketing Communications: Maybe Definition Is in the Point of View," *Marketing News,* January 18, 1993, p. 17.
27. Don Shultz and Philip Kitchen, "Integrated Marketing Communications in US Advertising Agencies: An Exploratory Study," *Journal of Advertising Research,* September-October 1997, pp. 7-18.
28. Joep P. Cornelissen and Andrew R. Lock, "Theoretical Concept or Management Fashion? Examining the Significance of IMC," *Journal of Advertising Research,* September–October 2000, pp. 7–15.
29. Philip J. Kitchen, Joanne Brignell, Tao Li, and Graham Spickett Jones, "The Emergence of IMC: A Theoretical Perspective," *Journal of Advertising Research,* March 2004, pp. 19–30.
30. Don E. Schultz, "IMC Receives More Appropriate Definition," *Marketing News,* September 15, 2004, pp. 8–9.

31. Dong Hwan Lee and Chan Wook Park, "Conceptualization and Measurement of Multidimensionality of Integrated Marketing Communications," *Journal of Advertising Research,* September 2007.
32. Mike Reid, Sandra Luxton, and Felix Mavondo, "The Relationship between Integrated Marketing Communication, Market Orientation, and Brand Orientation," *Journal of Advertising, 34*(4) pp. 11–23.
33. George Low, "Correlates of Integrated Marketing Communications," *Journal of Advertising Research,* January–February 2000, pp. 27–39.
34. Joep P. Cornelissen and Andrew R. Lock, "Theoretical Concept or Management Fashion? Examining the Significance of IMC," *Journal of Advertising Research,* September–October 2000, pp. 7–15.
35. Harlan E. Spotts, David R. Lambert, and Mary L. Joyce, "Marketing Déjà Vu: The Discovery of Integrated Marketing Communications," *Journal of Marketing Education, 20,* no. 3 (December 1998), pp. 210–18.
36. Lisa d'Innocenzo, "Inside P&G," *Strategy,* June 2006.
37. Tom Duncan and Sandra E. Moriarty, "A Communication-Based Model for Managing Relationships," *Journal of Marketing 62,* no. 2, (April 1998), pp. 1–13.
38. Philip J. Kitchen, Joanne Brignell, Tao Li, and Graham Spickett Jones, "The Emergence of IMC: A Theoretical Perspective," *Journal of Advertising Research,* March 2004, pp. 19–30.
39. Chris Powell, "Idol Worship," *Marketing Magazine,* November 10, 2003; and Danny Kucharsky, "Because You're Worth It," *Marketing Magazine,* February 9, 2004.
40. Leonard L. Berry, "Relationship Marketing of Services—Growing Interest, Emerging Perspectives," *Journal of the Academy of Marketing Science, 23,* no. 4, 1995, pp. 236–45; Jonathan R. Capulsky and Michael J. Wolfe, "Relationship Marketing: Positioning for the Future," *Journal of Business Strategy,* July–August 1991, pp. 16–26.
41. B. Joseph Pine II, Don Peppers, and Martha Rogers, "Do You Want to Keep Your Customers Forever?" *Harvard Business Review,* March–April 1995, pp. 103–14.
42. Lisa M. Keefe, "What Is the Meaning of 'Marketing'?" *Marketing News,* September 15, 2004, pp. 17–18.

43. Adrian Payne and Pennie Flow, "Strategic Framework for Customer Relationship Management," *Journal of Marketing, 69*(October) pp. 167-176.
44. Michelle Halpern, "In Your Face," *Marketing Magazine*, July 16, 2007; Rob Gerlsbeck, "Socially Awkward," *Marketing Magazine*, November 20, 2006.
45. Anthony J. Tortorici, "Maximizing Marketing Communications through Horizontal and Vertical Orchestration," *Public Relations Quarterly, 36*(1), 1991, pp. 20–22.
46. Mike Reid, "Performance Auditing of Integrated Marketing Communication (IMC) Actions and Outcome," *Journal of Advertising, 34*(4), pp. 41-54.
47. Paul-Mark Rendon, "Melitta Brews National Pormotions," *Marketing Magazine*, March 8, 2004.
48. Paul-Mark Rendon, "Where Above Meets Below," *Marketing Magazine*, May 8, 2006.

CHAPTER TWO

1. Jack Neff, "P&G Redefines the Brand Manager," *Advertising Age*, October 13, 1997, pp. 1, 18, 20.
2. Thomas J. Cosse and John E. Swan, "Strategic Marketing Planning by Product Managers—Room for Improvement?" *Journal of Marketing, 47* (Summer 1983), pp. 92–102.
3. Sharon Horsky, Steven C. Michael, and Alvin J. Silk, "The Internalization of Advertising Services: An Inter-Industry Analysis," Working Paper, Harvard Business School, 2008.
4. M. Louise Ripley, "What Kind of Companies Take Their Advertising In-House?" *Journal of Advertising Research*, October/November 1991, pp. 73–80.
5. Horsky, Michael, and Silk, "The Internalization of Advertising Services: An Inter-Industry Analysis."
6. Jeromy Lloyd, "A New Kind of MARCOM," *Marketing Magazine*, August 31, 2009.
7. "*Marketing*'s 2009 Agency Family Tree," *Marketing Magazine*, July 20, 2009 p 16-23.
8. Jon Steel, *Truth, Lies & Advertising: The Art of Account Planning* (New York: Wiley, 1998).
9. "Call in the Specialists," *Marketing Magazine*, June 4, 2001.
10. Jeffery Thibodeau, "Better Ways to Get Paid," *Marketing Magazine*, March 22, 2004.
11. www.aca-online.com.
12. Paul-Mark Rendon, "Pay as You Play," *Marketing Magazine*, June 21, 2004.
13. "The Benefits of PBR," *Marketing Magazine*, July 9, 2001; "Executive Summary," *Marketing Magazine*, July 9, 2001; "Finding the Right PBR Performance Measures," *Marketing Magazine*, July 16, 2001.

14. Rob Gerlsbeck, "Creative Compensation," *Marketing Magazine*, April 17, 2006.
15. Chris Daniels, "Part-Time Partners," *Marketing Magazine*, June 23, 2003.
16. Michelle Warren, "Project Work," *Marketing Magazine*, April 19, 2004; Michelle Warren, "The Year of Treading Water," *Marketing Magazine*, November 24, 2003.
17. Fred Beard, "Marketing Client Role Ambiguity as a Source of Dissatisfaction in Client–Ad Agency Relationships," *Journal of Advertising Research*, (September/October 1996), pp. 9–20; Paul Michell, Harold Cataquet, and Stephen Hague, "Establishing the Causes of Disaffection in Agency-Client Relations," *Journal of Advertising Research*, 32, 2, 1992, pp. 41–48; Peter Doyle, Marcel Corstiens, and Paul Michell, "Signals of Vulnerability in Agency-Client Relations," *Journal of Marketing*, 44 (Fall 1980), pp. 18–23; and Daniel B. Wackman, Charles Salmon, and Caryn C. Salmon, "Developing an Advertising Agency–Client Relationship," *Journal of Advertising Research 26*, no. 6 (December 1986/January 1987), pp. 21–29.
18. Mukund S Kulkarni, Premal P. Vora, and Terence A. Brown, "Firing Advertising Agencies," *Journal of Advertising, 32*(3), pp. 77-86.
19. Matt Semansky, "A Tighter Grip" *Marketing Magazine*, February 23, 2009.
20. Prema Nakra, "The Changing Role of Public Relations in Marketing Communications," *Public Relations Quarterly, 1* (1991) pp. 42–45.
21. "A Potent New Tool for Selling: Database Marketing," *Business Week*, September 5, 1994, pp. 56–62.
22. "Ad Firms Falter on One-Stop Shopping," *The Wall Street Journal*, December 1, 1988, p. 81; and "Do Your Ads Need a Superagency?" *Fortune*, April 27, 1987, p. 81.
23. Hy Haberman, "Walking the Talk on Integration," *Marketing Magazine*, February 9, 2004.
24. Philip J. Kitchen and Don E. Schultz, "A Multi-Country Comparison of the Drive for IMC," *Journal of Advertising Research*, January/February 1999, pp. 21–38; William N. Swain, "Perceptions of IMC after a Decade of Development: Who's at the Wheel and How Can We Measure Success," *Journal of Advertising Research* (March 2004) pp. 46–67.
25. David N. McArthur and Tom Griffin, "A Marketing Management View of Integrated Marketing Communications," *Journal of Advertising Research, 37*, no. 5, September/October 1997, pp. 19–26; Adrienne Ward Fawcett, "Integrated Marketing—Marketers Convinced: Its

Time Has Arrived," *Advertising Age*, November 6, 1993, pp. S1–2.
26. Michelle Warren, "What Marketers Want," *Marketing Magazine*, November 24, 2003.
27. Kevin Astle, "The Shaky State of Marketer–Agency Relations," *Marketing Magazine*, November 24, 2003.

CHAPTER THREE

1. Leon G. Schiffman and Leslie Lazar Kannuk, *Consumer Behavior*, 4th ed. (Englewood Cliffs, NJ: Prentice Hall, 1991), p. 192.
2. Eric N. Berkowitz, Roger A. Kerin, Steven W. Hartley, and William Rudelius, *Marketing*, 6th ed. (Burr Ridge, IL: Irwin/McGraw-Hill, 2000), p. 14.
3. A. H. Maslow, "'Higher' and 'Lower' Needs," *Journal of Psychology, 25* (1948), pp. 433–36.
4. For an excellent discussion of memory and consumer behaviour, see James R. Bettman, "Memory Factors in Consumer Choice: A Review," *Journal of Marketing, 43* (Spring 1979),pp. 37–53.
5. Danny Kucharsky, "World Wide Vacations," *Marketing Magazine*, June 12, 2006.
6. Chris Powell, "iPhone Helping Changing Canadian Wireless Attitudes," *Marketing Magazine*, April 9, 2009.
7. Gilbert Harrell, *Consumer Behavior* (San Diego: Harcourt Brace Jovanovich, 1986), p. 66.
8. Raymond A. Bauer and Stephen A. Greyser, *Advertising in America: The Consumer View* (Boston: Harvard Business School, 1968).
9. J. Paul Peter and Jerry C. Olson, *Consumer Behavior*, 2nd ed. (Burr Ridge, IL: Irwin/McGraw-Hill, 1990), p. 73.
10. Gordon W. Allport, "Attitudes," in *Handbook of Social Psychology*, ed. C. M. Murchison (Winchester, MA: Clark University Press, 1935), p. 810.
11. Robert B. Zajonc and Hazel Markus, "Affective and Cognitive Factors in Preferences," *Journal of Consumer Research, 9* (1982), pp. 123–31.
12. Alvin Achenbaum, "Advertising Doesn't Manipulate Consumers," *Journal of Advertising Research*, April 2, 1970, pp. 3–13.
13. William D. Wells, "Attitudes and Behavior: Lessons from the Needham Lifestyle Study," *Journal of Advertising Research*, February–March 1985, pp. 40–44; and Icek Ajzen and Martin Fishbein, "Attitude–Behavior Relations: A Theoretical Analysis and Review of Empirical Research," *Psychological Bulletin*, September 1977, pp. 888–918.
14. Joel B. Cohen, Paul W. Minniard, and Peter R. Dickson, "Information

Integration: An Information Processing Perspective," in *Advances in Consumer Research*, vol. 7, ed. Jerry C. Olson (Ann Arbor, MI: Association for Consumer Research, 1980), pp. 161–70.

15. Peter and Olson, *Consumer Behavior*, p. 182.

16. Peter L. Wright and Fredric Barbour, "The Relevance of Decision Process Models in Structuring Persuasive Messages," *Communications Research*, July 1975, pp. 246–59.

17. James F. Engel, "The Psychological Consequences of a Major Purchase Decision," in *Marketing in Transition*, ed. William S. Decker (Chicago: American Marketing Association, 1963), pp. 462–75.

18. Richard L. Oliver, *Satisfaction: A Behavioral Perspective on the Consumer* (New York: McGraw-Hill, 1997).

19. John A. Howard and Jagdish N. Sheth, *The Theory of Consumer Behavior* (New York: John Wiley & Sons, 1969).

20. Lyman E. Ostlund, *Role Theory and Group Dynamics in Consumer Behavior: Theoretical Sources*, ed. Scott Ward and Thomas S. Robertson (Englewood Cliffs, NJ: Prentice Hall, 1973), pp. 230–75.

21. James Stafford and Benton Cocanougher, "Reference Group Theory," in *Perspective in Consumer Behavior*, ed. H. H. Kassarjian and T. S. Robertson (Glenview, IL: Scott, Foresman, 1981), pp. 329–43.

22. Jagdish N. Sheth, "A Theory of Family Buying Decisions," in *Models of Buying Behavior*, ed. Jagdish N. Sheth (New York: Harper & Row, 1974), pp. 17–33.

23. Larry Percy, John R. Rossiter, and Richard Elliot, *Strategic Advertising Management* (Oxford University Press, 2001).

24. Eve Lazarus, "Tea's Time," *Marketing Magazine*, September 25, 2006.

25. Mary Maddever, "Media," *Strategy*, June 2009, p. 44.

26. Norma Ramage, "Educating the Young," *Marketing Magazine*, March 22, 2004.

27. Edward M. Tauber, "Research on Food Consumption Values Finds Four Market Segments: Good Taste Still Tops," *Marketing News*, May 15, 1981, p. 17; Rebecca C. Quarles, "Shopping Centers Use Fashion Lifestyle Research to Make Marketing Decisions," *Marketing News*, January 22, 1982, p. 18; and "Our Auto, Ourselves," *Consumer Reports*, June 1985, p. 375.

28. Michael R. Soloman, *Consumer Behavior: Buying, Having, and Being*, 8th Edition, Pearson Prentice Hall: 2009.

29. Norma Ramage, "Chinese Theme Added to Bell Effort," *Marketing Magazine*, February 2, 2004.

30. Celine Wong, "Can't Knock the Hustle," *Marketing Magazine*, May 3, 2004.

31. For an excellent discussion of social class and consumer behaviour, see Richard P. Coleman, "The Continuing Significance of Social Class to Marketing," *Journal of Consumer Research, 10*, no. 3, December 1983, pp. 265–80.

32. Chris Daniels, "Almost Rich, *Marketing Magazine*, April 26, 2004.

33. Russell Belk, "Situational Variables and Consumer Behavior," *Journal of Consumer Research*, December 1975, pp. 157–64.

34. Norma Ramage, "Marks Work Wearhouse Tries on New Women's Line," *Marketing Magazine*, September 2, 2009.

35. John Rossiter and Larry Percy, *Advertising Communications and Promotion Management* (New York: McGraw Hill, 1996).

36. Chris Powell, "TMN Puts Spotlight on Subscribers," *Marketing Magazine*, February 23, 2004.

37. Dave Scholz and Jean-Marc Leger, "The Fickle Beer Consumer," *Marketing Magazine*, May 10, 2004.

38. Thomas J. Reynolds and Carol B Phillips, "In Search of True Brand Equity Metrics: All Market Share Ain't Created Equal," *Journal of Advertising Research*, June 2005.

39. Scholz and Leger.

40. Melita Kuburas, "Initiative's Meaghan Stafford: Savvy Hyper-Targeter Hits Her Mark," *Strategy*, June 2009, p. 25.

41. Theresa Wood, "Design," *Strategy*, June 2009, p. 48.

42. Sarah Dobson, "Coffee Crisp Targets Caffeine Crowd," *Marketing Magazine*, February 10, 2003.

43. Eve Lazarus, "Vancouver's Driving Force," *Marketing Magazine*, August 28, 2006.

44. "Interactive IMC: The Relational-Transactional Continuum and the Synergistic Use of Customer Data," *Journal of Advertising Research*, June 2006, pp. 146-159.

45. Ace Alvarez, "How to Send Happiness," *Marketing Magazine*, August, 28, 2006.

46. Lisa D'Innocenzo, "Is Your Target a Man's Man? Then Reach Out to Women," *Strategy Magazine*, February 2006.

CHAPTER FOUR

1. Wilbur Schram, *The Process and Effects of Mass Communications* (Urbana: University of Illinois Press, 1955).

2. Ibid.

3. Joseph Ransdell, "Some Leading Ideas of Peirce's Semiotic," *Semiotica, 19* (1977), pp. 157–78.

4. For an excellent article on the application of semiotics to consumer behaviour and advertising, see David G. Mick, "Consumer Research and Semiotics: Exploring the Morphology of Signs, Symbols, and Significance," *Journal of Consumer Research, 13*, no. 2, September 1986, pp. 196–213; see also Edward F. McQuarrie and David Glen Mick, "Figures of Rhetoric in Advertising Language," *Journal of Consumer Research, 22*, March 1996, pp. 424–38.

5. Ian Herbert, "Spray It, Don't Say It," *US News & World Report*, May 30, 2005, p. 58; Kris Oser, "AXE's Latest Sex Ad Is a Digital Game," www. Adage.com, May 20, 2005, pp. 1–3; Christine Bittar, "Bringing Down the House: AXE Shakes Its Groove Thang," *Brandweek*, March 22, 2004, p. R4; Jack Neff, "Analyzing AXE Man," *Advertising Age*, June 21, 2004, pp. 4–5.

6. Barry L. Bayus, "Word of Mouth: The Indirect Effect of Marketing Efforts," *Journal of Advertising Research*, June/July 1985, pp. 31–39; Robert E. Smith and Christine A. Vogt, "The Effects of Integrating Advertising and Negative Word-of-Mouth Communications on Message Processing and Response," *Journal of Consumer Psychology, 4*, no. 2, 1995, pp. 133–51.

7. Larry Yu, "How Companies Turn Buzz Into Sales," *MIT Sloan Management Review*, Winter 2005, pp. 5–6.

8. John E. Hogan, Katherine N. Lemon, Barak Libai, "Quantifying the Ripple: Word-of-Mouth and Advertising Effectiveness," *Journal of Advertising Research*, pp. 271-280; Jeffrey Graham and William Havlena, "Finding the Missing Link: Advertising's Impact on Word of Mouth, Web Searches, and Site Visits," *Journal of Advertising Research*, December 2007, pp. 427–435.

9. Paul Brent, "From Broadcast to Broadband," *Marketing Magazine*, April 30, 2007.

10. Jonathan Paul, "Carrying the Torch for Coke," *Strategy*, February 2009, p. 19.

11. Emily Wexler, "Roundtable: Surviving the Social Revolution," *Strategy*, October 2009, p. 17.

12. E. K. Strong, *The Psychology of Selling* (New York: McGraw-Hill, 1925), p. 9.

13. Robert J. Lavidge and Gary A. Steiner, "A Model for Predictive Measurements of Advertising Effectiveness," *Journal of Marketing, 24*, October 1961, pp. 59–62.

14. Everett M. Rogers, *Diffusion of Innovations* (New York: Free Press, 1962), pp. 79–86.

15. William J. McGuire, "An Information Processing Model of Advertising Effectiveness," in *Behavioral and Management Science in Marketing*, ed. Harry J. Davis and Alvin J. Silk (New York: Ronald Press, 1978), pp. 156–80.

16. Anthony G. Greenwald and Clark Leavitt, "Audience Involvement in

Advertising: Four Levels," *Journal of Consumer Research, 11,* no. 1 (June 1984), pp. 581–92; and Judith L. Zaichkowsky, "Conceptualizing Involvement," *Journal of Advertising, 15,* no. 2 (1986), pp. 4–14.

17. Michael L. Ray, "Communication and the Hierarchy of Effects," in *New Models for Mass Communication Research,* ed. P. Clarke (Beverly Hills, CA: Sage, 1973), pp. 147–75.

18. Robert E. Smith, "Integrating Information from Advertising and Trial: Processes and Effects on Consumer Response to Product Information," *Journal of Marketing Research, 30.*

19. DeAnna S. Kempf and Russell N. Laczniak, "Advertising's Influence on Subsequent Product Trial Processing," *Journal of Advertising, 30,* no. 3, Fall 2001, pp. 27–38.

20. Herbert E. Krugman, "The Impact of Television Advertising: Learning without Involvement," *Public Opinion Quarterly, 29* (Fall 1965), pp. 349–56.

21. Scott A. Hawkins and Stephen J. Hoch, "Low-Involvement Learning: Memory without Evaluation," *Journal of Consumer Research, 19,* no. 2 (September 1992), pp. 212–25.

22. Jerry C. Olson, Daniel R. Toy, and Phillip A. Dover, "Mediating Effects of Cognitive Responses to Advertising on Cognitive Structure," in *Advances in Consumer Research, 5,* ed. H. Keith Hunt (Ann Arbor, MI: Association for Consumer Research, 1978), pp. 72–78.

23. Anthony A. Greenwald, "Cognitive Learning, Cognitive Response to Persuasion and Attitude Change," in *Psychological Foundations of Attitudes,* ed. A. G. Greenwald, T. C. Brock, and T. W. Ostrom (New York: Academic Press, 1968); Peter L. Wright, "The Cognitive Processes Mediating Acceptance of Advertising," *Journal of Marketing Research, 10* (February 1973), pp. 53–62; Brian Wansink, Michael L. Ray, and Rajeev Batra, "Increasing Cognitive Response Sensitivity," *Journal of Advertising, 23,* no. 2 (June 1994), pp. 65–76.

24. Peter Wright, "Message Evoked Thoughts, Persuasion Research Using Thought Verbalizations," *Journal of Consumer Research, 7,* no. 2 (September 1980), pp. 151–75.

25. Morris Holbrook and Rajeev Batra, "Assessing the Role of Emotions as Mediators of Consumer Responses to Advertising," *Journal of Consumer Research, 14*(3), December 1987, pp. 404-420.

26. Raffi Chowdhury, Douglas Olson, John Pracejuc, "Affective Responses to Images in Print Advertising," *Journal of Advertising, 37*(3), Fall 2008, pp. 7-18.

27. Scott B. Mackenzie, Richard J. Lutz, and George E. Belch, "The Role of Attitude toward the Ad as a Mediator of Advertising Effectiveness: A Test of

Competing Explanations," *Journal of Marketing Research, 23* (May 1986), pp. 130–43; and Rajeev Batra and Michael L. Ray, "Affective Responses Mediating Acceptance of Advertising," *Journal of Consumer Research, 13* (September 1986), pp. 234–49.

28. Tim Ambler and Tom Burne, "The Impact of Affect on Memory of Advertising," *Journal of Advertising Research, 29,* no. 3 (March/April 1999), pp. 25–34; Ronald Alsop, "TV Ads That Are Likeable Get Plus Rating for Persuasiveness," *The Wall Street Journal,* February 20, 1986, p. 23.

29. Abhilasha Mehta, Advertising Attitudes and Advertising Effectiveness, *Journal of Advertising,* May-June 2000, pp. 67-72.

30. David J. Moore and William D. Harris, "Affect Intensity and the Consumer's Attitude toward High Impact Emotional Advertising Appeals," *Journal of Advertising, 25,* no. 2 (Summer 1996), pp. 37–50; Andrew A. Mitchell and Jerry C. Olson, "Are Product Attribute Beliefs the Only Mediator of Advertising Effects on Brand Attitude?" *Journal of Marketing Research, 18* (August 1981), pp. 318–32.

31. David J. Moore, William D. Harris, and Hong C. Chen, "Affect Intensity: An Individual Difference Response to Advertising Appeals," *Journal of Consumer Research, 22* (September 1995), pp. 154–64; Julie Edell and Marian C. Burke, "The Power of Feelings in Understanding Advertising Effects," *Journal of Consumer Research, 14* (December 1987), pp. 421–33.

32. Richard E. Petty and John T. Cacioppo, "Central and Peripheral Routes to Persuasion: Application to Advertising," in *Advertising and Consumer Psychology,* ed. Larry Percy and Arch Woodside (Lexington, MA: Lexington Books, 1983), pp. 3–23.

33. David A. Aaker, Rajeev Batra, and John G. Myers, *Advertising Management,* 5th ed. (Upper Saddle River, NJ: Prentice Hall, 1996).

34. Gerald J. Gorn, "The Effects of Music in Advertising on Choice: A Classical Conditioning Approach," *Journal of Marketing, 46* (Winter 1982), pp. 94–101.

35. James J. Kellaris, Anthony D. Cox, and Dena Cox, "The Effect of Background Music on Ad Processing: A Contingency Explanation," *Journal of Marketing, 57,* no. 4 (Fall 1993), p. 114.

36. Richard E. Petty, John T. Cacioppo, and David Schumann, "Central and Peripheral Routes to Advertising Effectiveness: The Moderating Role of Involvement," *Journal of Consumer Research, 10* (September 1983), pp. 135–46.

37. Demetrios Vakratsas and Tim Ambler, "How Advertising Works: What Do We

Really Know?" *Journal of Marketing, 63* (January 1999), pp. 26–43.

38. Bruce F. Hall, "A New Model for Measuring Advertising Effects," *Journal of Advertising Research, 42,* no. 2, (March/April 2002), pp. 23–31.

39. William M. Weilbacher, "Point of View: Does Advertising Cause a 'Hierarchy of Effects'?" *Journal of Advertising Research, 41,* no. 6 (November/ December 2001) pp. 19–26; William M. Weilbacher, "How Advertising Affects Consumers, *Journal of Advertising Research,* June 2003, pp.231-234.

40. Stephen D. Rappaport, "Lessons from Online Practice: New Advertising Models," *Journal of Advertising Research,* June 2007, pp. 135-141.

41. Thomas E. Barry, "In Defense of the Hierarchy of Effects: A Rejoinder to Weilbacher," *Journal of Advertising Research* (May/June 2002), pp. 44–47.

CHAPTER FIVE

1. Robert A. Kriegel, "How to Choose the Right Communications Objectives," *Business Marketing,* April 1986, pp. 94–106.

2. Donald S. Tull, "The Carry-Over Effect of Advertising," *Journal of Marketing,* April 1965, pp. 46–53.

3. Darral G. Clarke, "Econometric Measurement of the Duration of Advertising Effect on Sales," *Journal of Marketing Research, 23* (November 1976), pp. 345–57.

4. Philip Kotler, *Marketing Decision Making: A Model Building Approach* (New York: Holt, Rinehart & Winston, 1971), ch. 5.

5. Russell H. Colley, *Defining Advertising Goals for Measured Advertising Results* (New York: Association of National Advertisers, 1961).

6. Don E. Schultz, Dennis Martin, and William Brown, *Strategic Advertising Campaigns,* 2nd ed. (Lincolnwood, IL: Crain Books, 1984).

7. Courtland I. Bovee and William F. Arens, *Advertising,* 3rd ed. (Burr Ridge, IL: Richard D. Irwin, 1989).

8. Stewart H. Britt, "Are So-Called Successful Advertising Campaigns Really Successful?" *Journal of Advertising Research, 9,* no. 2 (1969), pp. 3–9.

9. Steven W. Hartley and Charles H. Patti, "Evaluating Business-to-Business Advertising: A Comparison of Objectives and Results," *Journal of Advertising Research, 28* (April/May 1988), pp. 21–27.

10. Ibid., p. 25.

11. Study cited in Robert F. Lauterborn, "How to Know If Your Advertising Is Working," *Journal of Advertising Research, 25* (February/March 1985), pp. RC 9–11.

12. Kristin Laird, "Canadian Blood Services Gets Personal," *Marketing Magazine,* May 5 2009.

579

Endnotes

13. Chris Powell, "*Globe* Targets Circulation Gains," *Marketing Magazine*, February 2, 2004.
14. Brian Wansink and Michael Ray, "Estimating an Advertisement's Impact on One's Consumption of a Brand," *Journal of Advertising Research*, November-December 2000.
15. Angela Scardillo, "Making Milk COOL," *Marketing Magazine*, August 11, 2003.
16. Nick Krewen, "Prairie Dairy Milks Teen Media," *Strategy*, December 2009, p. 9.
17. Paul Ferris, "CTC Hits the Road with Toyota," *Marketing Magazine*, September 15, 2003.
18. Carey Toane, "CTC Sells Stay-cations," *Strategy*, June 2009, p. 6.
19. Paul Ferris, "Ditching the Minivans," *Marketing Magazine*, March 15, 2004.
20. Danny Kucharsky, "French Transit Ads Tell Traffic Truths," *Marketing Magazine*, February 9, 2004.
21. Frank Dennis, "Selling Hidden Brands," *Marketing Magazine*, May 10, 2004.
22. Eve Lazarus, "Taking on Goliath," *Marketing Magazine*, March 22, 2002.
23. Brent Cuthbertson and Grant Stockwell, "That Rings a Bell," *Marketing Magazine*, October 20, 2003.
24. Dave Scholz and Gilbert Paquette, "The Impact of Auto Advertising," *Marketing Magazine*, June 30, 2003.
25. Lesley Young, "It Pays to Get Aggressive," *Marketing Magazine*, February 12, 2001.

CHAPTER SIX

1. *Ayer's Dictionary of Advertising Terms* (Philadelphia: Ayers Press, 1976).
2. Eve Lazarus, "Happy Planet Takes a Shot at Energy Drinks," *Marketing Magazine*, May 29, 2009.
3. "WestJet Fuels Up Advertising Effort," *Marketing Magazine*, March 2001; "Flying the Cluttered Skies," *Marketing Magazine*, April 9, 2001.
4. http://cassies.ca/caselibrary/winners/2006pdfs/_546WestJet_Web_DR.pdf
5. Chris Sorensen, "Westjet's Big Plans to Conquer Air Canada and Then the World," *Maclean's*, May 27, 2010.
6. Carey Toane, "Airlines," *Strategy*, March 2009, p. 52.
7. Jonathan Paul, "Dentsu's Min Ryuck: Driving Interactive Digital," *Strategy*, June 2009, p. 24.
8. Charles Blankson, Stavros P. Kalafatis, Julian Ming-Sung, and Costas Hadjicharalambous, "Impact of Positioning Strategies on Corporate Performance," *Journal of Advertising Research*, March 2008; Charles Blankson and Stavros P. Kalafatis, "Congruence between Positioning and Brand Advertising," *Journal of Advertising Research*, March 2007.
9. Davis A. Aaker and John G. Myers, *Advertising Management*, 3rd ed.

10. Jack Trout and Al Ries, "Positioning Cuts through Chaos in the Marketplace," *Advertising Age*, May 1, 1972, pp. 51–53.
11. http://cassies.ca/caselibrary/winners/2006pdfs/_546WestJet_Web_DR.pdf
12. Carey Toane, "Airlines," *Strategy*, March 2009, p. 52.
13. Larry Percy and Richard Elliot, *Strategic Advertising Management*, 2nd ed. (Oxford University Press, 2004); Orville Walker Jr., John Mullins, Harper Boyd Jr., and Jean-Claude Larreche, *Marketing Strategy: A Decision-Focused Approach*, 8th ed. (McGraw-Hill Irwin, 2006).
14. Based on case study available at www.cassies.ca.
15. Based on case study available at www.cassies.ca.
16. Lesley Young, "Harvey's Keeps an Eye on the Grill," *Marketing Magazine*, September 29, 2003.
17. Emily Spensieri, "A Slow, Soft Touch," *Marketing Magazine*, June 5, 2006.
18. Jonathan Paul, "Dentsu's Min Ryuck: Driving Interactive Digital," *Strategy*, June 2009, p. 24.
19. Russ Martin, "Nutella Launches Better Breakfast Challenge," *Marketing Magazine*, May 13, 2009.
20. Brian Wansink and Jennifer Marie Gilmore, "New Uses That Revitalize Old Brnds," *Journal of Advertising Research*, April 1999.
21. Kristin Laird, "Reitman's Beats Haute Couture Again," *Marketing Magazine*, May 5, 2009.
22. Based on case study available at www.cassies.ca.
23. Matt Semansky, "Yves Rocher Plants New Brand, Store, Concept in Montreal," *Marketing Magazine*, May 22, 2009.
24. Theresa Wood, "Lay's Calls on Local Spuds," *Strategy*, March 2009, p. 17.
25. Jonathan Paul, "Wanna Talk About it?" *Strategy*, January 2009, p. 23.
26. Jennifer Wells, "Brock Offers a Lesson in Boldness," *The Globe and Mail*, April 17, 2009, p. B5.
27. For a review of multiattribute models, see William L. Wilkie and Edgar A. Pessemier, "Issues in Marketing's Use of Multiattribute Models," *Journal of Marketing Research*, 10 (November 1983), pp. 428–41.
28. Joel Rubinson and Markus Pfeiffer, "Brand Key Performance Indicators as a Force for Brand Equity Management," *Journal of Advertising Research*, June 2005.
29. Based on case study available at www.cassies.ca.
30. Based on case study available at www.cassies.ca.

31. Lesley Young, "An Order of Fries, with Attitude," *Marketing Magazine*, November 17, 2003.
32. Lesley Young, "Wireless Marketers Unleash Hounds," *Marketing Magazine*, December 8, 2003.
33. Norma Ramage, "WestJet Finds a Competitive Niche," *Marketing Magazine*, July 28, 2003.
34. Jeff Robillard and Phil Copithorne, "Big Idea Fits in Small Space," *Marketing Magazine*, February 23, 2004.
35. George Walton, "Appealingly Local," *Marketing Magazine*, May 5, 2003.
36. Michelle Warren, "*Fubar* Guys Light Up Anti-Smoking Ads," *Marketing Magazine*, January 19, 2004.
37. Based on case study available at www.cassies.ca.
38. Based on case study available at www.cassies.ca.
39. Based on case study available at www.cassies.ca.
40. Based on case study available at www.cassies.ca.
41. Based on case study available at www.cassies.ca.
42. Based on case study available at www.cassies.ca.
43. Based on case study available at www.cassies.ca.
44. Based on case study available at www.cassies.ca.
45. Based on case study available at www.cassies.ca.

CHAPTER SEVEN

1. Mary Teresa Bitti, "Future Ad Execs?" *National Post*, April 14, 2009, p. FP14.
2. Jaafar El-Murad and Douglas C. West, "The Definition and Measurement of Creativity: What Do We Know?" *Journal of Advertising Research*, June 2004.
3. Sheila L. Sasser and Scott Koslow, "Desperately Seeking Advertising Creativity," *Journal of Advertising*, Winter 2008, 37(4).
4. Leonard N. Reid, Karen Whitehall, and Denise E. DeLorme, "Top-Level Agency Creatives Look at Advertising Creativity Then and Now," *Journal of Advertising*, Summer 1998, 27(2).
5. Anonymous, "Envisioning the Future of Advertising Creativity Research," *Journal of Advertising*, Winter 2008.
6. Daniel W. Baack, Rick T. Wilson, and Brian D. Till, "Creativity and Memory Effects," *Journal of Advertising*, Winter 2008 37(4); Brian D. Till and Daniel Baack, "Recall and Persuasion," *Journal of Advertising*, Fall 2005 34(3).
7. Elizabeth C. Hirschman, "Role-Based Models of Advertising Creation and Production," *Journal of Advertising*, 18, no. 4 (1989), pp. 42–53.
8. Ibid., p. 51.
9. Edith G. Smit, Lex Van Meurs, and Peter C. Neijens, "Effects of Advertising Likeability: A 10-Year Perspective,"

Journal of Advertising Research, March 2006

10. Karolien Poel and Siegfried Dewitte, "Getting a Line on Print Ads," *Journal of Advertising,* Winter 2008, 37(4).

11. Micael Dahlen, Sara Rosengren, and Fredrick Torn, "Advertising Creativity Matters," *Journal of Advertising Research,* September 2008

12. Charles Young, "Creative Differences between Copywriters and Art Directors," *Journal of Advertising Research,* June 2000.

13. Alisa White and Bruce L. Smith, "Assessing Advertising Creativity Using the Creative Product Semantic Scale," *Journal of Advertising Research,* December 2001; Douglas C. West, Arthur J. Kover, and Alber Caruana, "Practioner and Customer Views of Advertising Creativity," *Journal of Advertising,* Winter 2008.

14. Nicolas Massey, "Answer a Higher Calling," *Marketing Magazine,* March 22, 2004.

15. For an interesting discussion on the embellishment of advertising messages, see William M. Weilbacher, *Advertising,* 2nd ed. (New York: Macmillan, 1984), pp. 180–82.

16. David Ogilvy, *Confessions of an Advertising Man* (New York: Atheneum, 1963); and Hanley Norins, *The Compleat Copywriter* (New York: McGraw-Hill, 1966).

17. Hank Sneiden, *Advertising Pure and Simple* (New York: ANACOM, 1977).

18. Scott Koslow, Sheila L. Sasser, and Edward A. Riordan, "Do Marketers Get the Advertising They Need or the Advertising They Deserve?" *Journal of Advertising,* Fall 2006.

19. www.matsterthelongtrip.com.

20. James Webb Young, *A Technique for Producing Ideas,* 3rd ed. (Chicago: Crain Books, 1975), p. 42.

21. W. Glenn Griffin, "Development Models of the Creative Process," *Journal of Advertising,* Winter 2008.

22. Jon Steel, *Truth, Lies & Advertising: The Art of Account Planning* (Wiley, 1998).

23. Sandra E. Moriarty, *Creative Advertising: Theory and Practice* (Englewood Cliffs, NJ: Prentice Hall, 1986).

24. Bruce MacDonald, "The Art of the Brief," *Marketing Magazine,* October 27, 2003.

25. John O'Toole, *The Trouble with Advertising,* 2nd ed. (New York: Random House, 1985), p. 131.

26. Rosser Reeves, *Reality in Advertising* (New York: Knopf, 1961), pp. 47, 48.

27. Michael McCarthy, "New Theme for Reebok," *USA TODAY,* February 10, 2005, p. 5B.

28. Susan E. Morgan and Tome Reichert, "The Message Is in the Metaphor: Assessing the Comprehension of Metaphors in Advertisements," *Journal*

of Advertising, Winter 1999 28(4); Barbara J. Phillips and Edward F. McQuarrie, "Impact of Advertising Metaphors on Consumer Belief," *Journal of Advertising,* Spring 2009, 38(1).

29. Martin Mayer, *Madison Avenue, U.S.A.* (New York: Pocket Books, 1958).

30. Pamela Parker, "IBM Campaign Introduces Company's 'Other Side,'" www.clickz.com/news, April 11, 2005.

31. Jack Trout and Al Ries, "The Positioning Era Cometh," *Advertising Age,* April 24, 1972, pp. 35–38; May 1, 1972, pp. 51–54; May 8, 1972, pp. 114–16.

32. Ingrid Button, "Turning the Export Ship Around," *Marketing Magazine,* August 27, 2001.

33. Lara Mills, "Campaigns with Legs," *Marketing Magazine,* May 15, 2000.

34. Danny Kucharsky, "Pepsi Guys Star in Quebec Ads," *Marketing Magazine,* March 17, 2003.

35. Matt Semansky, "Koodo Ditches Spandex for New Language," *Marketing Magazine,* March 16, 2009.

36. Lara Mills, "Campaigns with Legs," *Marketing Magazine,* May 15, 2000.

37. Emily Wexler, "Labatt's Kristen Morrow: Beer Drinkers' Best Bud", *Strategy,* July 2009, p. 10.

38. Carey Toane, "Creating a New Connection," *Strategy,* January 2009, p. 30.

39. Michael Adams, *Fire and Ice* (Penguin, 2003).

40. Nancy Evans and Bruce Maclellan, "The Risk of Frost Bite," *Marketing Magazine,* June 30, 2003.

41. David Macdonald and Michael Adams, "We Are What We Drive," *Marketing Magazine,* March 15, 2004.

42. Stan Sutter, "Canada's Ad Renascence," *Marketing Magazine,* March 29, 2004.

43. Stan Sutter, "Vive la Difference," *Marketing Magazine,* January 26, 2004.

44. Chris Daniels, "Canucks vs. Yanks," *Marketing Magazine,* May 22, 2000.

45. *Marketing Magazine,* "Cannes-ada," July 3, 2000; "Cannes 2001," July 2, 2001; "Cannes Ad Festival Can be a Real Eye-Opener for Marketers," July 2, 2001; "The Bashful Beaver," November 26, 2001; "More Canuck Work Entered at Cannes," May 29, 2002; Jim McElgunn, "Canucks at Cannes," July 1, 2002; Angela Kryhul, "Where Big Ideas Rule," June 30, 2003; "Canada Arrives at Cannes," July 12, 2004.

46. Sandra E. Moriarty, *Creative Advertising: Theory and Practice,* 2nd ed. (Englewoods Cliffs, NJ: Prentice Hall, 1991), p. 76.

47. William Wells, John Burnett, and Sandra Moriarty, *Advertising* (Englewood Cliffs, NJ: Prentice Hall, 1989), p. 330.

48. William M. Weilbacher, *Advertising,* 2nd ed. (New York: Macmillan, 1984), p. 197.

49. William L. Wilkie and Paul W. Farris, "Comparative Advertising: Problems and Potential," *Journal of Marketing, 39* (1975), pp. 7–15.

50. For a review of comparative advertising studies, see Cornelia Pechmann and David W. Stewart, "The Psychology of Comparative Advertising," in *Attention, Attitude and Affect in Response to Advertising,* ed. E. M. Clark, T. C. Brock, and D. W. Stewart (Hillsdale, NJ: Lawrence Erlbaum, 1994), pp. 79–96; and Thomas S. Barry, "Comparative Advertising: What Have We Learned in Two Decades?" *Journal of Advertising Research, 33,* no. 2 (1993), pp. 19–29.

51. Stuart J. Agres, "Emotion in Advertising: An Agency Point of View," in *Emotion in Advertising: Theoretical and Practical Explanations,* ed. Stuart J. Agres, Julie A. Edell, and Tony M. Dubitsky (Westport, CT: Quorom Books, 1991).

52. Francois Lacoursiere, "La Vie en Bleu," *Marketing Magazine,* February 2, 2004.

53. Edward Kamp and Deborah J. Macinnis, "Characteristics of Portrayed Emotions in Commercials: When Does What Is Shown in Ads Affect Viewers?" *Journal of Advertising Research,* November/ December 1995, pp. 19–28.

54. Kristin Laird, "Women Feel Good in Lusty Ads for Second Clothing," *Marketing Magazine,* November 25, 2009.

55. For a review of research on the effect of mood states on consumer behaviour, see Meryl Paula Gardner, "Mood States and Consumer Behavior: A Critical Review," *Journal of Consumer Research, 12,* no. 3 (December 1985), pp. 281–300.

56. Cathy Madison, "Researchers Work Advertising into an Emotional State," *Adweek,* November 5, 1990, p. 30.

57. Joanne Caza, "From Destination to Journey," *Marketing Magazine,* September 8, 2003.

58. Michael L. Ray and William L. Wilkie, "Fear: The Potential of an Appeal Neglected by Marketing," *Journal of Marketing, 34* (January 1970), pp. 54–62.

59. Brian Sternthal and C. Samuel Craig, "Fear Appeals Revisited and Revised," *Journal of Consumer Research, 1* (December 1974), pp. 22–34.

60. Punam Anand Keller and Lauren Goldberg Block, "Increasing the Persuasiveness of Fear Appeals: The Effect of Arousal and Elaboration," *Journal of Consumer Research, 22,* no. 4 (March 1996), pp. 448–60.

61. John F. Tanner, Jr., James B. Hunt, and David R. Eppright, "The Protection Motivation Model: A Normative Mode of Fear Appeals," *Journal of Marketing, 55* (July 1991), pp. 36–45.

62. Ibid.

Endnotes

63. Herbert Jack Rotfeld, "The Textbook Effect: Conventional Wisdom, Myth and Error in Marketing," *Journal of Marketing, 64* (April 2000), pp. 122–27.

64. Hollie Shaw, "Sell It with a Laugh," *National Post,* March 27, 2009, p. FP12.

65. For a discussion of the use of humour in advertising, see C. Samuel Craig and Brian Sternthal, "Humor in Advertising," *Journal of Marketing, 37* (October 1973), pp. 12–18.

66. Harlan E. Spotts, Marc G. Weinberger, and Amy L. Parsons, "Assessing the Use and Impact of Humour on Advertising effectiveness: A Contingency Approach," *Journal of Advertising,* Fall 1997 26(3).

67. Yong Zhang, "Response to Humorous Advertising: The Moderating Effect of Need for Cognition," *Journal of Advertising, 25,* no. 1 (Spring 1996), pp. 15–32; Marc G. Weinberger and Charles S. Gulas, "The Impact of Humor in Advertising: A Review," *Journal of Advertising, 21* (December 1992), pp. 35–59.

68. Marc G. Weinberger and Leland Campbell, "The Use of Humor in Radio Advertising," *Journal of Advertising Research, 31* (December/ January 1990–91), pp. 44–52.

69. Thomas J. Madden and Marc C. Weinberger, "Humor in Advertising: A Practitioner View," *Journal of Advertising Research, 24,* no. 4 (August/September 1984), pp. 23–26.

70. David Ogilvy and Joel Raphaelson, "Research on Advertising Techniques That Work and Don't Work," *Harvard Business Review,* July/August 1982, p. 18.

71. *Topline,* no. 4 (September 1989), McCann-Erickson, New York.

72. Media Innovation Awards, *Marketing Magazine,* November 5, 2003.

73. Herbert C. Kelman, "Processes of Opinion Change," *Public Opinion Quarterly, 25* (Spring 1961), pp. 57–78.

74. William J. McGuire, "The Nature of Attitudes and Attitude Change," in *Handbook of Social Psychology,* 2nd ed., ed. G. Lindzey and E. Aronson (Cambridge, MA: Addison-Wesley, 1969), pp. 135–214; and Daniel J. O'Keefe, "The Persuasive Effects of Delaying Identification of High- and Low-Credibility Communicators: A Meta-Analytic Review," *Central States Speech Journal, 38* (1987), pp. 63–72.

75. Roobina Ohanian, "The Impact of Celebrity Spokespersons' Image on Consumers' Intention to Purchase," *Journal of Advertising Research,* February/March 1991, pp. 46–54.

76. Erick Reidenback and Robert Pitts, "Not All CEOs Are Created Equal as Advertising Spokespersons: Evaluating the Effective CEO Spokesperson," *Journal of Advertising, 20,* no. 3 (1986), pp. 35–50; Roger Kerin and Thomas

E. Barry, "The CEO Spokesperson in Consumer Advertising: An Experimental Investigation," in *Current Issues in Research in Advertising,* ed. J. H. Leigh and C. R. Martin (Ann Arbor: University of Michigan, 1981), pp. 135–48; and J. Poindexter, "Voices of Authority," *Psychology Today,* August 1983.

77. A. Eagly and S. Chaiken, "An Attribution Analysis of the Effect of Communicator Characteristics on Opinion Change," *Journal of Personality and Social Psychology, 32* (1975), pp. 136–44.

78. For a review of these studies, see Brian Sternthal, Lynn Phillips, and Ruby Dholakia, "The Persuasive Effect of Source Credibility: A Situational Analysis," *Public Opinion Quarterly, 42* (Fall 1978), pp. 285–314.

79. Brian Sternthal, Ruby Dholakia, and Clark Leavitt, "The Persuasive Effects of Source Credibility: Tests of Cognitive Response," *Journal of Consumer Research, 4,* no. 4 (March 1978), pp. 252–60; and Robert R. Harmon and Kenneth A. Coney, "The Persuasive Effects of Source Credibility in Buy and Lease Situations," *Journal of Marketing Research, 19* (May 1982), pp. 255–60.

80. For a review, see Noel Capon and James Hulbert, "The Sleeper Effect: An Awakening," *Public Opinion Quarterly, 37* (1973), pp. 333–58.

81. Darlene B. Hannah and Brian Sternthal, "Detecting and Explaining the Sleeper Effect," *Journal of Consumer Research, 11,* no. 2 (September 1984), pp. 632–42.

82. H. C. Triandis, *Attitudes and Attitude Change* (New York: Wiley, 1971).

83. J. Mills and J. Jellison, "Effect on Opinion Change Similarity between the Communicator and the Audience He Addresses," *Journal of Personality and Social Psychology, 9,* no. 2 (1969), pp. 153–56.

84. Ben Kaplan, "A&W Guys Are the New Apple Guys," *National Post,* November 19, 2009, p. AL1.

85. Matt Semansky, "Harry Rosen Keeps It Real," *Marketing Magazine,* February 11, 2009.

86. Lise Laguerre, "It's Respect in Either Language," *Marketing Magazine,* May 6, 2002.

87. Louisa Flinn, "Kings of the Road," *Marketing Magazine,* February 16, 2004.

88. B. Zafer Erdogan, Michael J. Baker, and Stephen Tagg, "Selecting Celebrity Endorsers: The Practioner's Perspective," *Journal of Advertising Research,* June 2001; B. Zafer Erdogan and Tanya Drollinger, "Endorsement Practice: How Agencies Select Spokespeople," *Journal of Advertising Research,* December 2008.

89. Jason Stein, "Inside Chrysler's Celine Dion Advertising Disaster," www.adage.com, November 24, 2003.

90. Valerie Folkes, "Recent Attribution Research in Consumer Behavior: A Review and New Directions," *Journal of Consumer Research, 14* (March 1988), pp. 548–65; John C. Mowen and Stephen W. Brown, "On Explaining and Predicting the Effectiveness of Celebrity Endorsers," in *Advances in Consumer Research,* vol. 8 (Ann Arbor, MI: Association for Consumer Research, 1981), pp. 437–41.

91. Charles Atkin and M. Block, "Effectiveness of Celebrity Endorsers," *Journal of Advertising Research, 23,* no. 1 (February/March 1983), pp. 57–61.

92. Michael A. Kamins, "An Investigation into the 'Match-Up' Hypothesis in Celebrity Advertising," *Journal of Advertising, 19,* no. 1 (1990), pp. 4–13.

93. Grant McCracken, "Who Is the Celebrity Endorser? Cultural Foundations of the Endorsement Process," *Journal of Consumer Research, 16,* no. 3 (December 1989), pp. 310–21.

94. Ibid., p. 315.

95. B. Zafer Erdogan, Michael J. Baker, and Stephen Tagg, "Selecting Celebrity Endorsers: The Practitioner's Perspective," *Journal of Advertising Research, 41,* no. 43 (May/June 2001), pp. 39–48.

96. Matt Semansky, "Brand Nash," *Marketing Magazine,* September 14, 2009.

97. For an excellent review of these studies, see Marilyn Y. Jones, Andrea J. S. Stanaland, and Betsy D. Gelb, "Beefcake and Cheesecake: Insights for Advertisers," *Journal of Advertising, 27,* no. 2 (Summer 1998), pp. 32–51; and W. B. Joseph, "The Credibility of Physically Attractive Communicators," *Journal of Advertising, 11,* no. 3 (1982), pp. 13–23.

98. Michael Solomon, Richard Ashmore, and Laura Longo, "The Beauty Match-Up Hypothesis: Congruence between Types of Beauty and Product Images in Advertising," *Journal of Advertising, 21,* no. 4, pp. 23–34; M. J. Baker and Gilbert A. Churchill, Jr., "The Impact of Physically Attractive Models on Advertising Evaluations," *Journal of Marketing Research, 14* (November 1977), pp. 538–55.

99. Robert W. Chestnut, C. C. La Chance, and A. Lubitz, "The Decorative Female Model: Sexual Stimuli and the Recognition of the Advertisements," *Journal of Advertising, 6* (Fall 1977), pp. 11–14; and Leonard N. Reid and Lawrence C. Soley, "Decorative Models and Readership of Magazine Ads," *Journal of Advertising Research, 23,* no. 2 (April/May 1983), pp. 27–32.

100. Amanda B. Bower, "Highly Attractive Models in Advertising and the

Women Who Loathe Them: The Implications of Negative Affect for Spokesperson Effectiveness," *Journal of Advertising, 30,* no. 3 (Fall 2001), pp. 51–63; Amanda B. Bower and Stacy Landreth, "Is Beauty Best? Highly Versus Normally Attractive Models in Advertising," *Journal of Advertising, 30,* no. 1, pp. 1–12.

101. Jack Neff, "In Dove Ads, Normal Is the New Beautiful," *Advertising Age,* September 27, 2004, pp. 1, 80.

102. Michelle Jeffers, "Behind Dove's 'Real Beauty,'" *Adweek,* September 12, 2005, pp. 34–35.

CHAPTER EIGHT

1. Gerald J. Gorn and Charles B. Weinberg, "The Impact of Comparative Advertising on Perception and Attitude: Some Positive Findings," *Journal of Consumer Research, 11*(2) September 1984.

2. "If You Don't Like This Ad, You're Simply Not Subaru Material," *National Post,* November 20, 2009, FP10.

3. Norma Ramage, "Toyota Owners Drive Prairie Effort, *Marketing Magazine,* March 17, 2003.

4. Bob Garfield, "Listerine Eschews 'Creativity' for an Ad That Actually Works," *Advertising Age,* September 20, 2004, p. 57.

5. Jeff Chatterton, "A Whole New Ball Game," *Marketing Magazine,* November 10, 2003.

6. Judith A. Garretson and Scot Burton, "The Role of Spokescharacters as Advertisement and Package Cues in Integrated Marketing Communications," *Journal of Marketing, 69*(October) 2005.

7. Angela Kryhul, "The Great Canadian Icon," *Marketing Magazine,* June 26, 2000.

8. Barbara B. Stern, "Classical and Vignette Television Advertising: Structural Models, Formal Analysis, and Consumer Effects," *Journal of Consumer Research, 20,* no. 4 (March 1994), pp. 601–15; and John Deighton, Daniel Romer, and Josh McQueen, "Using Drama to Persuade," *Journal of Consumer Research, 15,* no. 3 (December 1989), pp. 335–43.

9. Karen Howe and Ian Mcintosh, "A Clever Parody," *Marketing Magazine,* January 12, 2004.

10. Herbert E. Krugman, "On Application of Learning Theory to TV Copy Testing," *Public Opinion Quarterly, 26* (1962), pp. 626–39.

11. William E. Baker, Heather Honea, and Cristel Antonia Russell, "Do Not Wait to Reveal the Brand Name: The Effect of Brand-Name Placement on Television Advertising Effectiveness," *Journal of Advertising,* Fall 2004 33(3).

12. C. I. Hovland and W. Mandell, "An Experimental Comparison of Conclusion Drawing by the Communicator and by the Audience," *Journal of Abnormal and Social Psychology, 47* (July 1952), pp. 581–88.

13. Alan G. Sawyer and Daniel J. Howard, "Effects of Omitting Conclusions in Advertisements to Involved and Uninvolved Audiences," *Journal of Marketing Research, 28* (November 1991), pp. 467–74.

14. George E. Belch, "The Effects of Message Modality on One- and Two-Sided Advertising Messages," in *Advances in Consumer Research, 10,* ed. Richard P. Bagozzi and Alice M. Tybout (Ann Arbor, MI: Association for Consumer Research, 1983), pp. 21–26.

15. Robert E. Settle and Linda L. Golden, "Attribution Theory and Advertiser Credibility," *Journal of Marketing Research, 11* (May 1974), pp. 181–85; and Edmund J. Faison, "Effectiveness of One-Sided and Two-Sided Mass Communications in Advertising," *Public Opinion Quarterly, 25* (Fall 1961), pp. 468–69.

16. "Campaigns with Legs," *Marketing Magazine,* May 15, 2000.

17. Ibid.

18. Alan G. Sawyer, "The Effects of Repetition of Refutational and Supportive Advertising Appeals," *Journal of Marketing Research, 10* (February 1973), pp. 23–37; and George J. Szybillo and Richard Heslin, "Resistance to Persuasion: Inoculation Theory in a Marketing Context," *Journal of Marketing Research, 10* (November 1973), pp. 396–403.

19. Andrew A. Mitchell, "The Effect of Verbal and Visual Components of Advertisements on Brand Attitudes and Attitude toward the Advertisement," *Journal of Consumer Research, 13* (June 1986), pp. 12–24; and Julie A. Edell and Richard Staelin, "The Information Processing of Pictures in Advertisements," *Journal of Consumer Research, 10,* no. 1 (June 1983), pp. 45–60; Elizabeth C. Hirschmann, "The Effects of Verbal and Pictorial Advertising Stimuli on Aesthetic, Utilitarian and Familiarity Perceptions," *Journal of Advertising, 15,* no. 2 (1986), pp. 27–34.

20. Jolita Kisielius and Brian Sternthal, "Detecting and Explaining Vividness Effects in Attitudinal Judgments," *Journal of Marketing Research, 21,* no. 1 (1984), pp. 54–64.

21. H. Rao Unnava and Robert E. Burnkrant, "An Imagery-Processing View of the Role of Pictures in Print Advertisements," *Journal of Marketing Research, 28* (May 1991), pp. 226–31.

22. Susan E. Heckler and Terry L. Childers, "The Role of Expectancy and Relevancy in Memory for Verbal and Visual Information: What Is Incongruency?" *Journal of Consumer Research, 18,* no. 4 (March 1992), pp. 475–92.

23. Michael J. Houston, Terry L. Childers, and Susan E. Heckler, "Picture–Word Consistency and the Elaborative Processing of Advertisements," *Journal of Marketing Research,* November 1987, pp. 359–69.

24. Hollie Shaw, "The Elephant in the Room," *National Post,* December 18, 2009, p. FP10.

25. William F. Arens, *Contemporary Advertising,* 6th ed. (Burr Ridge, IL: Irwin/McGraw-Hill, 1998), p. 284.

26. W. Keith Hafer and Gordon E. White, *Advertising Writing,* 3rd ed. (St. Paul, MN: West Publishing, 1989), p. 98.

27. Michelle Warren, "Press and Poster," *Marketing Magazine,* March 24, 2003.

28. Surendra N. Singh, V. Parker Lessig, Dongwook Kim, Reetina Gupta, and Mary Ann Hocutt, "Does Your Ad Have Too Many Pictures?" *Journal of Advertising Research,* January-April 2000.

29. Janet Kestin, "Reality Rules," *Marketing Magazine,* February 26, 2001.

30. Hollie Shaw, "It's a New Reality," *National Post,* May 15, 2009, p. FP10.

31. Matt Semansky, "Kokanee Says It's Time to Move Beyond Ranger," *Marketing Magazine,* May 28, 2009.

32. Linda M. Scott, "Understanding Jingles and Needledrop: A Rhetorical Approach to Music in Advertising," *Journal of Consumer Research, 17,* no. 2 (September 1990), pp. 223–36.

33. Ibid., p. 223.

34. Russell I. Haley, Jack Richardson, and Beth Baldwin, "The Effects of Nonverbal Communications in Television Advertising," *Journal of Advertising Research, 24,* no. 4, pp. 11–18.

35. Gerald J. Gorn, "The Effects of Music in Advertising on Choice Behavior: A Classical Conditioning Approach," *Journal of Marketing, 46* (Winter 1982), pp. 94–100.

36. "Follow the Bouncing Ball to P.E.I.," *Marketing Magazine,* March 22, 2004.

37. Matt Semansky, "Delissio Touts the Multiple Advantages of Garlic," *Marketing Magazine,* June 4, 2009.

38. Angela Kryhul, "Name Your Tune," *Marketing Magazine,* October 14, 2002.

39. Jeromy Lloyd, "Swiss Chalet Blasts Back from the Past," *Marketing Magazine,* September 23, 2009.

40. Chris Powell, "Astral Media Expands Its Audio Identity," *Marketing Magazine,* April 09.

41. Richard Vaughn, "How Advertising Works: A Planning Model," *Journal of Advertising Research, 20,* no. 5 (October 1980), pp. 27–33.

42. Richard Vaughn, "How Advertising Works: A Planning Model Revisited," *Journal of Advertising Research, 26,* no. 1 (February/March 1986), pp. 57–66.

43. Christopher P. Puto and William D. Wells, "Informational and

Transformational Advertising: The Different Effects of Time," in *Advances in Consumer Research, 11,* ed. Thomas C. Kinnear (Ann Arbor, MI: Association for Consumer Research, 1984), p. 638.

44. www.cassies.ca.

CHAPTER NINE

1. Mary Tolan, "Holidays Are Here and So Is Ad Puzzle," *Advertising Age,* November 16, 1998, p. 36.

2. Ibid.

3. Laura Bird, "Loved the Ad. May (or May Not) Buy the Product," *The Wall Street Journal,* April 7, 1994, p. B1.

4. "What Is Good Creative?" *Topline,* no. 41 (New York: McCollum Spielman Worldwide, 1994), p. 4.

5. James R. Hagerty, "Tests Lead Lowe's to Revamp Strategy," *The Wall Street Journal,* March 11, 1999, p. B18.

6. John M. Caffyn, "Telepex Testing of TV Commercials," *Journal of Advertising Research, 5,* no. 2 (June 1965), pp. 29–37; Thomas J. Reynolds and Charles Gengler, "A Strategic Framework for Assessing Advertising: The Animatic vs. Finished Issue," *Journal of Advertising Research,* October/ November 1991, pp. 61–71; Nigel A. Brown and Ronald Gatty, "Rough vs. Finished TV Commercials in Telepex Tests," *Journal of Advertising Research, 7,* no. 4 (December 1967), p. 21.

7. Charles H. Sandage, Vernon Fryburger, and Kim Rotzoll, *Advertising Theory and Practice,* 10th ed. (Burr Ridge, IL: Richard D. Irwin, 1979).

8. Lyman E. Ostlund, "Advertising Copy Testing: A Review of Current Practices, Problems and Prospects," *Current Issues and Research in Advertising,* 1978, pp. 87–105.

9. Jack B. Haskins, "Factual Recall as a Measure of Advertising Effectiveness," *Journal of Advertising Research, 4,* no. 1 (March 1964), pp. 2–7.

10. John Philip Jones and Margaret H. Blair, "Examining 'Conventional Wisdoms' about Advertising Effects with Evidence from Independent Sources," *Journal of Advertising Research,* November/December 1996, pp. 37–52.

11. Paul J. Watson and Robert J. Gatchel, "Autonomic Measures of Advertising," *Journal of Advertising Research, 19* (June 1979), pp. 15–26.

12. Priscilla A. LaBarbera and Joel D. Tucciarone, "GSR Reconsidered: A Behavior-based Approach to Evaluating and Improving the Sales Potency of Advertising," *Journal of Advertising Research,* September/ October 1995, pp. 33–40.

13. Flemming Hansen, "Hemispheric Lateralization: Implications for Understanding Consumer Behavior," *Journal of Consumer Research, 8* (1988), pp. 23–36.

14. Kevin Lane Keller, Susan E. Heckler, and Michael J. Houston, "The Effects of Brand Name Suggestiveness on Advertising Recall," *Journal of Marketing,* January 1998, pp. 48–57.

15. Jan Stapel, "Recall and Recognition: A Very Close Relationship," *Journal of Advertising Research,* July/August 1998, pp. 41–45.

16. Hubert A. Zielske, "Does Day-after Recall Penalize 'Feeling Ads'?" *Journal of Advertising Research, 22,* no. 1 (1982), pp. 19–22.

17. Arthur J. Kover, "Why Copywriters Don't Like Advertising Research— And What Kind of Research Might They Accept," *Journal of Advertising Research,* March/April 1996, pp. RC8– RC10; Gary Levin, "Emotion Guides BBDO's Ad Tests," *Advertising Age,* January 29, 1990, p. 12.

18. Terry Haller, "Day-after Recall to Persist Despite JWT Study; Other Criteria Looming," *Marketing News,* May 18, 1979, p. 4.

19. Dave Kruegel, "Television Advertising Effectiveness and Research Innovations," *Journal of Consumer Marketing, 5,* no. 3 (Summer 1988), pp. 43–52.

20. John Philip Jones, "Single-source Research Begins to Fulfill Its Promise," *Journal of Advertising Research,* May/ June 1995, pp. 9–16.

21. Gary Levin, "Tracing Ads' Impact," *Advertising Age,* November 12, 1990, p. 49.

22. Jeffrey L. Seglin, "The New Era of Ad Measurement," *Adweek's Marketing Week,* January 23, 1988, p. 24.

23. James F. Donius, "Marketing Tracking: A Strategic Reassessment and Planning Tool," *Journal of Advertising Research, 25,* no. 1 (February/March 1985), pp. 15–19.

24. "21 Ad Agencies Endorse Copy-Testing Principles," *Marketing News, 15,* no. 17 (February 19, 1982), p. 1.

25. Ibid.

26. Russell I. Haley and Allan L. Baldinger, "The ARF Copy Research Validity Project," *Journal of Advertising Research,* April/May 1991, pp. 11–32.

CHAPTER TEN

1. William A. Cook and Vijay S. Talluri, "How the Pursuit of ROMI Is Changing Marketing Management," *Journal of Advertising Research,* September 2004; Joan Fitzgerald, "Evaluating Return on Investment of Multimedia Advertising with a Single-Source Panel: A Retail Case Study," *Journal of Advertising,* September 2004.

2. Bruce Grondin, "Building North–South Links," *Marketing Magazine,* March 15, 2004.

3. Chris Powell, "Talking Heads," *Marketing Magazine,* March 23, 2009.

4. Jennifer Wells, "Finding the There, There," *The Globe and Mail,* January 23, 2009, p. B6.

5. Carey Toane, "Integrated," *Strategy,* June 2009, p. 51.

6. Mary Teresa Bitti, "Manage Your Message," *National Post,* July 7, 2009, FP7.

7. Chris Powell, "Youth Confound Traditional Media," *Marketing Magazine,* March 1, 2004.

8. Lesley Young, "Primus Takes Aim at Cable, Telcos," *Marketing Magazine,* January 19, 2004.

9. Chuck Ross, "Study Finds for Continuity vs. Flights," *Advertising Age,* April 19, 1999, p. 2.

10. Lesley Young, "Campbell Warms Up to Bad Weather," *Marketing Magazine,* February 16, 2004.

11. Michael J. Naples, *Effective Frequency: The Relationship between Frequency and Advertising Effectiveness* (New York: Association of National Advertisers, 1979).

12. Joseph W. Ostrow, "Setting Frequency Levels: An Art or a Science?" *Journal of Advertising Research, 24* (August/ September 1984), pp. 9–11.

13. Joseph W. Ostrow, "What Level Frequency?" *Advertising Age,* November 1981, pp. 13–18.

14. Jack Myers, "More Is Indeed Better," *Media Week,* September 6, 1993, pp. 14–18; Jim Surmanek, "One-Hit or Miss: Is a Frequency of One Frequently Wrong?" *Advertising Age,* November 27, 1995, p. 46.

15. Ostrow, "What Level Frequency?"

16. Hugh M. Cannon, John D. Leckenby, and Avery Abernethy, "Beyond Effective Frequency: Evaluating Media Schedules Using Frequency Value Planning," *Journal of Advertising Research,* November-December 2002.

17. William Havlena, Robert Cardarelli, and Michelle De Montigny, "Quantifying the Isolated and Synergistic Effects of Exposure Frequency for TV, Print, and Internet Advertising," *Journal of Advertising Research,* September 2007.

18. David A. Aaker and John G. Myers, *Advertising Management,* 3rd ed. (Englewood Cliffs, NJ: Prentice Hall, 1987), p. 474.

19. Joel N. Axelrod, "Induced Moods and Attitudes toward Products," *Journal of Advertising Research, 3* (June 1963), pp. 19–24; Lauren E. Crane, "How Product, Appeal, and Program Affect Attitudes toward Commercials," *Journal of Advertising Research, 4* (March 1964), p. 15.

20. Nick Allen, "Microsoft Wants Out of the Family," *National Post,* October 28, 2009, p. A1; "Microsoft Pulls Out of *Family Guy* Sponsorship," *Marketing Magazine,* October 28, 2009.

21. Max Kilger and Ellen Romer, "Do Measures of Media Engagement

Correlate with Product Purchase Likelihood?" *Journal of Advertising Research*, September 2007.

22. Kazuya Kusumot, "Affinity-based Media Selection: Magazine Selection for Brand Message Absorption," *Journal of Advertising Research*, July-August 2002.

23. *McGraw-Hill Lap Report* no. 3151 (New York: McGraw-Hill, 1988); Alan D. Fletcher, *Target Marketing through the Yellow Pages* (Troy, MI: Yellow Pages Publishers Association, 1991), p. 23.

24. George S. Low and Jakki Mohr, "Setting Advertising and Promotion Budgets in Multi-Brand Companies," *Journal of Advertising Research*, January/February 1999, pp. 667–78.

25. Jody Harri and Kimberly A. Taylor, "The Case for Greater Agency Involvement in Strategic Partnerships," *Journal of Advertising Research*, December 2003.

26. Frank M. Bass, "A Simultaneous Equation Regression Study of Advertising and Sales of Cigarettes," *Journal of Marketing Research, 6*, no. 3 (August 1969), p. 291; David A. Aaker and James M. Carman, "Are You Overadvertising?" *Journal of Advertising Research, 22*, no. 4 (August/September 1982), pp. 57–70.

27. Julian A. Simon and Johan Arndt, "The Shape of the Advertising Response Function," *Journal of Advertising Research, 20*, no. 4 (1980), pp. 11–28.

28. Paul B. Luchsinger, Vernan S. Mullen, and Paul T. Jannuzzo, "How Many Advertising Dollars Are Enough?" *Media Decisions, 12* (1977), p. 59.

29. Paul W. Farris, *Determinants of Advertising Intensity: A Review of the Marketing Literature* (Report no. 77–109, Marketing Science Institute, Cambridge, MA, 1977).

30. Melvin E. Salveson, "Management's Criteria for Advertising Effectiveness" (Proceedings 5th Annual Conference, Advertising Research Foundation, New York, 1959), p. 25.

31. Robert Settle and Pamela Alreck, "Positive Moves for Negative Times," *Marketing Communications*, January 1988, pp. 19–23.

32. Boonghee Yoo and Rujirutana Mandhachitara, "Estimating Advertising Effects on Sales in a Competitive Setting," *Journal of Advertising Research, 43*(3), 2003, pp. 310–320.

33. James O. Peckham, "Can We Relate Advertising Dollars to Market Share Objectives?" in *How Much to Spend for Advertising*, ed. M. A. McNiven (New York: Association of National Advertisers, 1969), p. 30.

34. *Strategy Magazine*, April 2006.

35. Demetrios Vakratsas and Zhenfeng Ma, "A Look at the Long-Run Effectiveness of Multimedia Advertising and Its Implications for Budget Allocation Decisions," *Journal of Advertising Research*, June 2005.

36. David Berkowitz, Arthur Allaway, and Giles d'Souza, "The Impact of Differential Lag Effects on the Allocation of Advertising Budgets across Media," *Journal of Advertising Research*, March/April 2001.

37. John P. Jones, "Ad Spending: Maintaining Market Share," *Harvard Business Review*, January/February 1990, pp. 38–42; James C. Schroer, "Ad Spending: Growing Market Share," *Harvard Business Review*, January/February 1990, pp. 44–48.

38. Randall S. Brown, "Estimating Advantages to Large-Scale Advertising," *Review of Economics and Statistics, 60* (August 1978), pp. 428–37.

39. Kent M. Lancaster, "Are There Scale Economies in Advertising?" *Journal of Business, 59*, no. 3 (1986), pp. 509–26.

40. Johan Arndt and Julian Simon, "Advertising and Economics of Scale: Critical Comments on the Evidence," *Journal of Industrial Economics, 32*, no. 2 (December 1983), pp. 229–41; Aaker and Carman, "Are You Overadvertising?"

41. Mary Welch, "Upbeat Marketers Wield Bigger Budgets, Shift Marketing Mix," *Business Marketing*, February 1993, p. 23.

42. George S. Low and Jakki J. Mohr, "The Budget Allocation between Advertising and Sales Promotion: Understanding the Decision Process," 1991 AMA Educators' Proceedings, Chicago, Summer 1991, pp. 448–57.

CHAPTER ELEVEN

1. Television Bureau of Canada website (www.tvb.ca).

2. Radio Marketing Bureau, The 2009 Foundation Study, rmb.ca.

3. Stephen Stanley and Carey Toane, "Subaru: DDB's Sumos Get Sexy," *Marketing Magazine*, June 2009, p. 50.

4. "Making the Most of Magazines," *Marketing Magazine*, October 15, 2001.

5. Kate Lynch and Horst Stipp, "Examination of Qualitative Viewing Factors of Optimal Advertising Strategies," *Journal of Advertising Research*, May-June 1999.

6. Stephen Stanley and Carey Toane, "NFLD Tourism: Target Truly Transports You," *Marketing Magazine*, June 2009, p. 50.

7. Laura Petrecca, "4A's: Production Costs for TV Spots Up by 6%," *Advertising Age*, August 18, 1997, p. 30.

8. TV BASICS 2009-2010, Television Bureau of Canada, tvb.ca.

9. Joe Flint, "Commercial Clutter on TV Networks Rises to Record," *The Wall Street Journal*, March 2, 2000, p. B18.

10. Lex van Meurs, "Zapp! A Study on Switching Behavior during Commercial Breaks," *Journal of Advertising Research*, January/February 1998, pp. 43–53; John J. Cronin, "In-Home Observations of Commercial Zapping Behavior," *Journal of Current Issues and Research in Advertising, 17*, no. 2 (Fall 1995), pp. 69–75.

11. Cronin, "In-Home Observations of Commercial Zapping Behavior."

12. Paul Surgi Speck and Michael T. Elliot, "Predictors of Advertising Avoidance in Print and Broadcast Media," *Journal of Advertising* Fall 1997 26(3).

13. Carrie Heeter and Bradley S. Greenberg, "Profiling the Zappers," *Journal of Advertising Research*, April/May 1985, pp. 9–12; Fred S. Zufryden, James H. Pedrick, and Avu Sandaralingham, "Zapping and Its Impact on Brand Purchase Behavior," *Journal of Advertising Research, 33* (January/February 1993), pp. 58–66; and Patricia Orsini, "Zapping: A Man's World," Spring Television Report, *Adweek's Marketing Week*, April 8, 1991, p. 3.

14. Lex van Meurs, "Zapp! A Study on Switching Behavior during Commercial Breaks," *Journal of Advertising Research*, January/February 1998, pp. 43–53.

15. Alan Ching Biu Tse and Rub P w. Lee, "Zapping Behaviour during Commercial Breaks," *Journal of Advertising Research, 41*(3) May/June 2001.

16. Christopher Kelly, "What They Want, When They Want It," *Marketing Magazine*, May 5, 2003.

17. John J. Cronin and Nancy Menelly, "Discrimination vs. Avoidance: 'Zipping' of Television Commercials," *Journal of Advertising, 21*, no. 2(June 1992), pp. 1–7.

18. Television Bureau of Canada website (www.tvb.ca).

19. Kirsten Chase, "Confessions of a PVR User," *Marketing Magazine*, March 26, 2007; Chris Powell, "PVRs: Canadians vs. Americans," *Marketing Magazine*, March 26, 2007; Pierre Delagrave, "Dawn of the Ad Zapper," *Marketing Magazine*, February 20, 2006.

20. Television Bureau of Canada website (www.tvb.ca).

21. Kenneth C. Wilbur, "How the Digital Video Recorder (DVR) Changes Traditional Television Advertising," *Journal of Advertising, 37*(1) Spring 2008.

22. Cristel Antonia Russell and Christopher P. Puto, "Rethinking Television Audience Measures: An Exploration into the Construct of Audience Connectedness," *Marketing Letters, 10*(4) 1999.

23. Linda F. Alwitt and Parul R. Prabhaker, "Identifying Who Dislikes Television Advertising: Not by Demographics Alone," *Journal of Advertising Research, 32*, no. 5 (1992), pp. 30–42.

24. Banwari Mittal, "Public Assessment of TV Advertising: Faint Praise and Harsh Criticism," *Journal of Advertising Research* no. 34, 1 (1994), pp. 35–53; Ernest F. Larkin, "Consumer Perceptions of the Media and Their Advertising Content," *Journal of Advertising, 8* (1979), pp. 5–7.
25. Lucy L. Henke, "Young Children's Perceptions of Cigarette Brand Advertising Symbols: Awareness, Affect, and Target Market Identification," *Journal of Advertising, 24,* no. 4 (Winter 1995), pp. 13–28.
26. Rick White and Mary Kreuk, "Money Show Management," *Marketing Magazine,* May 3, 2004.
27. Kristin Laird, "Brick Puts Red Baron on TV for First Time," *Marketing Magazine,* January 5, 2010.
28. Television Bureau of Canada website (www.tvb.ca).
29. Ibid.
30. Chris Daniels, "Shift Disturbers," *Marketing Magazine,* April 30, 2007.
31. Tim Wilson, "Give Digital a Chance," *Marketing Magazine,* March 29, 2004.
32. Chris Powell, "Follow the Viewer," *Marketing Magazine,* May 17, 2004.
33. Robert J. Kent, "Second-by-Second Looks at the Television Commercial Audience," *Journal of Advertising Research,* January-February 2002.
34. Television Bureau of Canada website (www.tvb.ca).
35. Suein L. Hwang, "Old Media Get a Web Windfall," *The Wall Street Journal,* September 17, 1999, p. B1.
36. Verne Gay, "Image Transfer: Radio Ads Make Aural History," *Advertising Age,* January 24, 1985, p. 1.
37. Avery Abernethy, "Differences Between Advertising and Program Exposure for Car Radio Listening," *Journal of Advertising Research, 31,* no. 2 (April/May 1991), pp. 33–42.
38. Foundation Research Study 2007-2009 accessed on RMB website (rmb.ca)
39. Ibid.

CHAPTER TWELVE
1. Herbert E. Krugman, "The Measurement of Advertising Involvement," *Public Opinion Quarterly, 30* (Winter 1966–67), pp. 583–96.
2. Magazinescanada.ca.
3. Maureen Cavan, "Building Our Own," *Marketing Magazine,* April 14, 2003.
4. Chris Powell, "A Pro-Barf Buy," *Marketing Magazine,* April 5, 2004; Eve Lazarus, "The Luxe Approach," *Marketing Magazine,* March 29, 2004.
5. Chris Powell, "*Hello!*'s Rising Star," *Marketing Magazine,* April 6, 2009.
6. Chris Powell, "La Difference," *Marketing Magazine,* May 10, 2004.
7. Consumer Magazine Fact Book 2009, Magazines Canada.
8. Ibid.

9. Chris Powell, "*Maclean's* Opens Up for Audi," *Marketing Magazine,* April 1, 2009.
10. Jonathan Paul, "Cundari's Camo *Vice* Cover Ad," *Strategy,* June 2009, p. 47.
11. Mary Pompili and Janet Eger, "Power Tools," *Marketing Magazine,* April 19, 2004.
12. Study cited in Jim Surmanek, *Media Planning: A Practical Guide* (Lincolnwood, IL: Crain Books, 1985).
13. Effect of Size, Color and Position on Number of Responses to Recruitment Advertising, LAP Report no. 3116, McGraw-Hill Research, New York.
14. Paul-Mark Rendon, "Osprey Takes Flight," *Marketing Magazine,* August 11, 2003.
15. David Chilton, "The Daily News," *Marketing Magazine,* March 13, 2006.
16. Norma Ramage, "Frisky Business," *Marketing Magazine,* May 3, 2004.
17. Kristin Laird, "Molson Is in the Fridge for Christmas Promo," *Marketing Magazine,* December 11, 2009.
18. Randy Stein, "The Intimate Medium," *Marketing Magazine,* August 11, 2003.
19. Chris Powell, "Cheery of Evolution," *Marketing Magazine,* November 20, 2006.
20. Chris Powell, "When Push Comes to Shove It," *Marketing Magazine,* March 15, 2004.

CHAPTER THIRTEEN
1. *Adweek,* August 25, 1997, p. 3.
2. Mukesh Bhargava and Naveen Donthu, "Sales Response to Outdoor Advertising," *Journal of Advertising Research,* August 1999, pp. 7–18.
3. Charles R. Taylor, George R. Franke, and Hae-Kyong Bang, "Use and Effectiveness of Billboards," *Journal of Advertising, 35*(4), Winter 2006, p. 21.
4. Lex Van Meurs and Mandy Aristoff, "Split-Second Recognition: What Makes Outdoor Advertising Work?" *Journal of Advertising Research,* March 2009, pp. 82-92.
5. Chris Powell, "Hip to Be Square," *Marketing Magazine,* March 10, 2003.
6. Hollie Shaw, "Driving the Message," *National Post,* March 20, 2009, p. FP12.
7. Tom Shepansky, "The Exotic Tuna," *Marketing Magazine,* March 10, 2003.
8. Day in the Life Study accessed at omaccanada.ca.
9. Danny Kucharsky, "Outdoor's Measurement Challenge," *Marketing Magazine,* May 17, 2004.
10. David Chilton, "Eying Outdoors," *Marketing Magazine,* October 26, 2006.
11. Sally Basmajian, "Walking the Talk," *Marketing Magazine,* September 15, 2003.
12. "Cinema Advertising Comes of Age," *Marketing Magazine,* May 6, 2002.
13. Joanna Phillips and Stephanie M. Noble, "Simply Captivating: Understanding Consumers' Attitudes

toward the Cinema as an Advertising Medium," *Journal of Advertising, 36*(10), Spring 2007, p. 81.
14. Jeromy Lloyd, "Toyota's Cinema Spot 20 Years in the Making," *Marketing Magazine,* December 22, 2009.
15. Rick T. Wilson and Brian D. Till, "Airport Advertising Effectiveness," *Journal of Advertising, 37*(1), Spring 2008, pp. 59-72.
16. Jonathan Paul, "Lexus RX's Touch Screen Touchdown at Airpot," *Strategy,* June 2009, p. 22.
17. Michael A. Belch and Don Sciglimpaglia, "Viewers' Evaluations of Cinema Advertising," Proceedings of the American Institute for Decision Sciences, March 1979, pp. 39–43.
18. "Catch a Commercial at the Movies," *Center for Media Research,* October 29, 2007.
19. Phillips and Noble, "Simply Captivating."
20. Promotional Products Association International (Irving, TX), 1996.
21. 2003 Promotional Products Industry Sales Volume Study, Promotional Products Association of Canada, May 2003.
22. Mark Freed, "Trinkets to Treasure," *Marketing Magazine,* May 8, 2006; Norma Range, "Treasured Trinkets," *Marketing Magazine,* August 28, 2006.
23. George L. Herpel and Steve Slack, *Specialty Advertising: New Dimensions in Creative Marketing* (Irving, TX: Specialty Advertising Association, 1983), pp. 76, 79–80.
24. Ibid., p. 78.
25. M. J. Caballero and J. B. Hunt, *Smilin' Jack: Measuring Goodwill,* unpublished research report from the Center for Professional Selling, Baylor University, 1989; M. J. Cooper and J. B. Hunt, *How Specialty Advertising Affects Goodwill,* research report of Specialty Advertising Association International (now PPAI), Irving, TX, 1992.
26. Herpel and Slack, *Specialty Advertising,* p. 75.
27. Shahnaz Mahmud, "Branded Content, Mobile to Grow," *Adweek,* August 8, 2007.
28. Michael Belch and Cristel A. Russell, "A Managerial Investigation into the Product Placement Industry," *Journal of Advertising Research,* March 2005, pp. 73–92.
29. Philip J. Hart, "Product Placement for Dummies," *Marketing Magazine,* May 5, 2003; Paul-Mark Rendon, "Casting Call," *Marketing Magazine,* May 5, 2003.
30. Eve Lazarus, "Keep It Real," *Marketing Magazine,* March 13, 2006.
31. Philip J. Hart, "Product Placement for Dummies," *Marketing Magazine,* May 5, 2003.
32. Hart; Danny Kucharsky, "A New Brand of Show," *Marketing Magazine,* May 5, 2003; Paul-Mark Rendon, "Casting

Call," *Marketing Magazine,* May 5, 2003; Rosanne Caron, "On the Right Track," *Marketing Magazine,* July 14, 2003.

33. Philip J. Hart, "Product Placement for Dummies," *Marketing Magazine,* May 5, 2003.

34. Wahjudi Harsono and Elizabeth Kan, "Reaching the Target," *Marketing Magazine,* May 5, 2003.

35. Danny Kucharsky, "A New Brand of Show," *Marketing Magazine,* May 5, 2003.

36. Danny Kucharsky, "Rona Wants to Build a Stronger Image," *Marketing Magazine,* March 24, 2003.

37. John Intini, "Will & Grace Loved Their *Maclean's,*" *Maclean's,* June 26, 2006; Keith McArthur, "No, Those Casino Rama Ads Aren't Running in NYC," *The Globe and Mail,* March 15, 2006.

38. Paul-Mark Rendon, "Casting Call," *Marketing Magazine,* May 5, 2003.

39. Pola Gupta and Kenneth Lord, "Product Placement in Movies: The Effect of Prominence and Mode on Audience Recall," *Journal of Current Issues and Research in Advertising, 20,* no. 1 (Spring 1998), pp. 1–29.

40. Pola B. Gupta and Stephen J. Gould, "Consumers' Perceptions of the Ethics and Acceptability of Product Placements in Movies: Product Category and Individual Differences," *Journal of Current Issues and Research in Advertising, 19,* no. 1 (Spring 1997), pp. 40–49.

CHAPTER FOURTEEN

1. Louis J. Haugh, "Defining and Redefining," *Advertising Age,* February 14, 1983, p. M44.

2. Scott A. Nielsen, John Quelch, and Caroline Henderson, "Consumer Promotions and the Acceleration of Product Purchases," in *Research on Sales Promotion: Collected Papers,* ed. Katherine E. Jocz (Cambridge, MA: Marketing Science Institute, 1984).

3. J. Jeffrey Inman and Leigh McAlister, "Do Coupon Expiration Dates Affect Consumer Behavior?" *Journal of Marketing Research, 31,* August 1994, pp. 423–28.

4. "Slow + Steady: Promo's Exclusive Annual Report of the U.S. Promotion Industry," *Promo,* April 2002.

5. Betsy Spethman, "Sudden Impact," *Promo,* April 1999, pp. 42–48; Betsy Spethman, "Is Advertising Dead?" *Promo,* September 1998, pp. 32–36.

6. Wayne Karl, "The Cup Runneth Over," *Marketing Magazine,* August 27, 2007.

7. Brent Armstrong, "The First Meal's Not Enough," *Marketing Magazine,* September 10, 2001.

8. *The Effects of Promotion Stimuli on Consumer Purchase Behavior* (Glenview, IL: FSI Council, 1999).

9. Richard Sale, "Evaluation in Evolution," *Promo,* September 1998, pp. 63–68.

10. "It's Elementary," *Marketing Magazine,* December 3, 2001.

11. R. M. Prentice, "How to Split Your Marketing Funds Between Advertising and Promotion Dollars," *Advertising Age,* January 10, 1977, pp. 41–42, 44.

12. Betsy Spethmann, "Money and Power," *Brandweek,* March 15, 1993, p. 21.

13. Adapted from Terrence A. Shimp, *Advertising, Promotion, and Supplemental Aspect of Integrated Marketing Communication,* 4th ed. (Fort Worth, TX: Dryden Press, 1997), p. 487.

14. Brian C. Deslauries and Peter B. Everett, "The Effects of Intermittent and Continuous Token Reinforcement on Bus Ridership," *Journal of Applied Psychology, 62* (August 1977), pp. 369–75.

15. Michael L. Rothschild and William C. Gaidis, "Behavioural Learning Theory: Its Relevance to Marketing and Promotions," *Journal of Marketing Research, 45,* no. 2 (Spring 1981), pp. 70–78.

16. "Hostess' Heroes," *Marketing Magazine,* August 6, 2001.

17. Kristin Laird, "McDonald's Serves UP Fresh, Free Coffee for All," *Marketing Magazine,* April 20, 2009.

18. Jonathan Paul, "HarperCollins Opens Eyes and Ears," *Strategy,* November 2009, p. 80.

19. "Trial and Conversion VI: Consumers' Reactions to Samples and Demonstrations," Promotional Marketing Association, Inc. 2002.

20. Lesley Young, "Marketing Direct Briefs," *Marketing Magazine,* November 3, 2003.

21. Jerry Langton, "Economics of the Humble Coupon," *Toronto Star,* July 7, 2008.

22. J. Jeffrey Inman and Leigh McAlister, "Do Coupon Expiration Dates Affect Consumer Behavior?"

23. Wayne Mouland, "Choosing the Right Face Value," *Marketing Magazine,* May 10, 2004.

24. www.Newswire.ca, press release from i-com.com, July 31, 2008.

25. Lesley Young, "Stores Remain Wary of Web Coupons," *Marketing Magazine,* September 29, 2003.

26. "Cereal Killer," *Marketing Magazine,* May 14, 2001.

27. Michelle Halpern, "Labatt's Big PROMO! Score," *Marketing Magazine,* October 6, 2003.

28. "Doughboy Promo Pops Off the Shelf," *Marketing Magazine,* January 14, 2002.

29. Wayne Mouland, "Sweeping Up Additional Sales," *Marketing Magazine,* October 6, 2003.

30. "P&G and MuchMusic Head to the Prom," *Marketing Magazine,* February 23, 2001; "Much, P&G Team Up to Target Teens," *Marketing Magazine,* March 5, 2001.

31. Paul-Mark Rendon, "Axe Seeks Best Mating Calls," *Marketing Magazine,* July 28, 2003.

32. Bob Woods, "Picking a Winner," *Promo,* August 1998, pp. 57–62.

33. Bruce Hawley, "More Than Just O.K.," *Marketing Magazine,* July 28, 2003.

34. Maxine S. Lans, "Legal Hurdles Big Part of Promotions Game," *Marketing News,* October 24, 1994, pp. 15–16.

35. Survey by Oxtoby-Smith, Inc., "Many Consumers View Rebates."

36. Peter Tat, William A. Cunningham III, and Emin Babakus, "Consumer Perceptions of Rebates," *Journal of Advertising Research,* August/September 1988, pp. 45–50.

37. Martha Graves, "Mail-In Rebates Stirring Shopper, Retailer Backlash," *Los Angeles Times,* January 11, 1989, Pt. IV, p. 1.

38. Edward A. Blair and E. Lair Landon, "The Effects of Reference Prices in Retail Advertisements," *Journal of Marketing, 45,* no. 2 (Spring 1981), pp. 61–69.

39. Kristin Laird, "Milestone's Wants to Make Dates," *Marketing Magazine,* April 28, 2009.

40. James Adams, "Who Gets the Biggest Piece of the Digital Pie?" *The Globe and Mail,* February 28, 2009.

41. R. J. Igneizi, "WD-40@50," *The San Diego Union-Tribune,* November 10, 2003, pp. D1, 4.

42. Betsy Spethmann, "Switching Loyalty," *Promo,* July 2002, pp. 40–45.

43. Kathleen M. Joyce, "Keeping the Faith," *Promo's 12th Annual Source Book 2005,* p. 24.

44. Eve Lazarus, "GAP Turns Upside Down for New Loyalty Program," *Marketing Magazine,* November 6, 2009; Kristin Laird, "Canadian Tire Putting New Money into Loyalty Program," *Marketing Magazine,* December 2, 2009; Emily Wexler, "Club Sobeys Hits a Million," *Strategy,* January 2009, p. 6.

45. Paul-Mark Rendon, "Aveeno Smoothes the Slopes," *Marketing Magazine,* February 16, 2004.

46. Paul-Mark Rendon, "Coffee-Mate Gets Street Smart," *Marketing Magazine,* February 23, 2004.

47. Chris Powell, "Rich Media," *Marketing Magazine,* June 25, 2007.

48. Frank Green, "Battling for Shelf Control," *San Diego Union,* November 19, 1996, pp. C1, 6, 7.

49. Paul N. Bloom, Gregory T. Gundlach, and Joseph P. Cannon, "Slotting Allowances and Fees: Schools of Thought and Views of Practicing Managers," *Journal of Marketing, 64,* April 2000, pp. 92–108.

50. Melissa Campanelli, "What's in Store for EDLP?" *Sales & Marketing Management,* August 1993, pp. 56–59; "Procter & Gamble Hits Back," *Business*

Endnotes

Week, July 19, 1993, pp. 20–22; and Amy Barone and Laurel Wentz, "Artzt Steering Barilla into EDLP Strategy," *Advertising Age,* February 26, 1996, p. 10.

51. NCH Reporter, no. 1 (Nielsen Clearing House, 1983).

52. Cynthia Rigg, "Hard Times Means Growth for Co-op Ads," *Advertising Age,* November 12, 1990, p. 24.

53. Michelle Warren, "P&G Celebrates Small Communities with Nice'n Easy Skating Tour," *Marketing Magazine,* February 2, 2004.

54. Srinath Gopalakrishna, Gary L. Lilien, Jerome D. Williams, and Ian K. Sequeria, "Do Trade Shows Pay Off?" *Journal of Marketing, 59,* July 1995, pp. 75–83.

55. Edwin L. Artzt, "The Lifeblood of Brands," *Advertising Age,* November 4, 1991, p. 32.

56. Jack Neff, "The New Brand Management," *Advertising Age,* November 8, 1999, pp. S2, 18; Benson P. Shapiro, "Improved Distribution with Your Promotional Mix," *Harvard Business Review,* March/April 1977, p. 116; and Roger A. Strang, "Sales Promotion—Fast Growth, Faulty Management," *Harvard Business Review,* July/August 1976, p. 119.

57. Priya Raghubir and Kim Corfman, "When Do Price Promotions Affect Pretrial Brand Evaluations?" *Journal of Marketing Research, 36* (May 1999), pp. 211–22.

58. Alan G. Sawyer and Peter H. Dickson, "Psychological Perspectives on Consumer Response to Sales Promotion," in *Research on Sales Promotion: Collected Papers,* ed. Katherine E. Jocz (Cambridge, MA: Marketing Science Institute, 1984).

59. William E. Myers, "Trying to Get Out of the Discounting Box," *Adweek,* November 11, 1985, p. 2.

60. Leigh McAlister, "Managing the Dynamics of Promotional Change," in *Looking at the Retail Kaleidoscope,* Forum IX (Stamford, CT: Donnelley Marketing, April 1988).

61. "Promotions Blemish Cosmetic Industry," *Advertising Age,* May 10, 1984, pp. 22–23, 26.

62. Elizabeth Gardener and Minakshi Trivedi, "A Communications Framework to Evaluate Sales Promotion Strategies," *Journal of Advertising Research,* May/June 1998, pp. 67–71.

CHAPTER FIFTEEN

1. Raymond Simon, *Public Relations, Concept and Practices,* 2nd ed. (Columbus, OH: Grid Publishing, 1980), p. 8.

2. Scott M. Cutlip, Allen H. Center, and Glen M. Broom, *Effective Public Relations,* 8th ed. (Upper Saddle River, N.J.: Prentice Hall, 2000).

3. Richard E. Rotman, "When Worlds Combine," *Marketing Magazine,* September 29, 2003.

4. William N. Curry, "PR Isn't Marketing," *Advertising Age,* December 18, 1991, p. 18.

5. Martha M. Lauzen, "Imperialism and Encroachment in Public Relations," *Public Relations Review, 17*(3) (Fall 1991), pp. 245–55.

6. Cutlip, Center, and Broom, *Effective Public Relations.*

7. Simon, *Public Relations,* p. 164.

8. Karin Scott, "Beyond Press Coverage," *Marketing Magazine,* June 16, 2003.

9. Thomas L. Harris, "How MPR Adds Value to Integrated Marketing Communications," *Public Relations Quarterly,* Summer 1993, pp. 13–18.

10. http://www.ikea.com/ms/en_CA/ about_ikea/press_room/press_release/ national/sleep_newsrelease.html.

11. Jonathan Paul, "Childlike Fascination Insightful for Honda," *Strategy,* May 2009, p. 19.

12. Raymond Simon, *Public Relations, Concepts and Practices,* 3rd ed. (New York: John Wiley & Sons, 1984), p. 291.

13. Walter K. Lindenmann, "An Effectiveness Yardstick to Measure Public Relations Success," *Public Relations Quarterly, 38,* no. 1 (Spring 1993), pp. 7–10.

14. Deborah Holloway, "How to Select a Measurement System That's Right for You," *Public Relations Quarterly, 37,* no. 3 (Fall 1992), pp. 15–18.

15. Julie Rusciolelli, "PR Discovers Metrics," *Marketing Magazine,* March 29, 2004.

16. Linda Smith, "When the Trust Begins to Rust," *Marketing Magazine,* March 1, 2004.

17. *Marketing Magazine,* May 18, 2009.

18. Matt Semansky, "Google Debuts in the Top Spot on the 2009 Marketing/ Leger Corporate Reputation," May 18, 2009.

19. Dave Scholz, "It's Hard Out There for a Reputation," *Marketing Magazine,* May 14, 2007.

20. Dave Scholz, "Damage Control," *Marketing Magazine,* May 18, 2009; Carey Toane, "Food/Grocery," *Strategy,* March 2009, p. 54.

21. David Ebner, "Coke Will Use the Olympics to Launch Its Latest Environmental Push," *The Globe and Mail,* June 10, 2009, B1; Carey Toane, "Coke Turns Green for 2010 Olympics," *Strategy,* May 2009, p. 8.

22. Hollie Shaw, "HBC Goes for Gold Yet Again," *National Post,* October 2, p. FP10.

23. Kristin Laird, "IBM's Smart Conversation with CBC, CANWEST," *Marketing Magazine,* September 15, 2009.

24. Prakash Sethi, *Advertising and Large Corporations* (Lexington, MA: Lexington Books, 1977), pp. 7–8.

25. Harvey Meyer, "When the Cause Is Just," *Journal of Business Strategy,* November/December 1999, pp. 27–31.

26. Michelle Warren, "Cause Commotion," *Marketing Magazine,* October 6, 2003.

27. Emily Wexler, "Virgin Re*Generates," *Strategy,* January 2009, p. 8.

28. Carey Tonae, "Brilliant!" *Strategy,* January 2009, p. 7.

29. Kristin Laird, "Kraft Has a Recipe for Joy," *Marketing Magazine,* December 18, 2009.

30. Emily Wexler, "Indigo Fights Illiteracy with Squirrel Power," *Strategy,* November 2009, p. 90.

31. Kristin Laird, "Cadbury Builds Bikes for Africa," *Marketing Magazine,* April 17, 2009; Emily Wexler, "Cadbury Bikes to Africa," *Strategy,* May 2009, p. 6.

32. Kristin Laird, "Canadian Tire Jumpstarts Fundraiser," *Marketing Magazine,* May 26, 2009.

33. Harvey Meyer, "When the Cause Is Just," p. 28.

34. Michelle Warren, "Cause Commotion."

35. Sarah Dobson, "The Hucksters Are Gone," *Marketing Magazine,* April 5, 2004.

36. www.sponsorshipmarketing.ca press release.

37. Hollie Shaw, "Carpetbragging," *National Post,* September 18, 2009, FP12.

38. Michelle Warren, "The Sporting Life," *Marketing Magazine,* February 23, 2004.

39. Mark Harrison, "Own Alone," *Marketing Magazine,* February 23, 2004.

40. Dan Cimoroni, "Don't Just Wish Upon a Star," *Marketing Magazine,* February 23, 2004.

41. Sarah Dobson, "The Measurement Question," *Marketing Magazine,* December 4, 2006.

42. Chris Daniels, "Show Time," *Marketing Magazine,* January 16, 2006.

43. "The 'Bush Leagues,'" *Marketing Magazine,* May 14, 2001.

44. Chris Daniels, "Take It Down a Notch," *Marketing Magazine,* December 4, 2006.

45. Bettina Cornwell and Isabelle Maignan, "An International Review of Sponsorship Research," *Journal of Advertising,* March 1998.

46. Michel Tuan Pham, "The Evaluation of Sponsorship Effectiveness: A Model and Some Methodological Considerations," *Gestion 2000,* pp. 47–65.

47. Sandra Iacobelli, "Harder-Working Sponsorships," *Marketing Magazine,* October 6, 2003.

48. Ian Malcolm, "Made to Measure," *Marketing Magazine,* February 23, 2004.

49. Sarah Dobson, "The Measurement Question," *Marketing Magazine,* December 4, 2006.

50. Arlene Lebovic, "A Eureka Moment," *Marketing Magazine,* September 18, 2006.

CHAPTER SIXTEEN

1. Peter D. Bennett, ed., *Dictionary of Marketing Terms* (Chicago: American Marketing Association, 1988), p. 58.
2. "A Potent New Tool for Selling: Database Marketing," *BusinessWeek,* September 5, 1994, pp. 56–59.
3. Herbert Kanzenstein and William S. Sachs, *Direct Marketing,* 2nd ed. (New York: Macmillan, 1992).
4. The Goldstein Group, "Acquisition Marketing in a Multi-Channel World: The Resiliant Principles of Successful Direct Mail." Report on Canada Post Website.
5. Ibid.
6. Marketing Research Fact Sheet, from Canada Post website, based on their Canada Facts study done every two years (approx).
7. Cleveland Horton, "Porsche 300,000: The New Elite," *Advertising Age,* February 5, 1990, p. 8.
8. Goldstein Group, "Acquisition Marketing in a Multi-Channel World."
9. Michelle Warren, "Counting on Catalogues," March 6, 2006.
10. Lesley Young, "Home Depot Unveils 'Dream Book'," *Marketing Magazine,* October 20, 2003.
11. Lesley Young, "Campbell Evolves from 'Soup to Food' with New Direct Campaigns," *Marketing Magazine,* November 3, 2003.
12. Mandeep Singh, Siva K. Balasubramanian, and Goutan Chakraborty, "A Comparative Analysis of Three Communication Formats: Advertising, Infomercial, and Direct Experience," *Journal of Advertising,* 29(4), Winter 2000.
13. Profiling study by Naveen Donthu and David Gilliland.
14. Lesley Young, "HBC Custom Magazine *Living Spree* to Track Readers' Shopping Habits," *Marketing Magazine,* August 11, 2003.
15. Tom Eisenhart, "Tele-media: Marketing's New Dimension," *Business Marketing,* February 1991, pp. 50–53.
16. Direct Marketing Association 2000.
17. *Canadian Marketing Association 2005 Fact Book,* 2005.
18. Michelle Warren, "Sprint Grows Up," *Marketing Magazine,* April 19, 2004.
19. "Bear Market," *Direct,* December 1999, p. 1+.
20. Goldstein Group, "Acquisition Marketing in a Multi-Channel World."

CHAPTER SEVENTEEN

1. Chang_Hoan Cho and HyoungKoo Khang, "The State of Internet-Related Research in Communications, Marketing, and Advertising: 1994-3003," *Journal of Advertising,* 35(3) Fall 2006, p. 143–163

2. Juran Kim and Sally J. McMillan, "Evaluation of Internet Advertising Research," *Journal of Advertising,* 37(1), Spring 2008, pp. 99-112.
3. http://www.statcan.ca, online data tables.
4. "Canadians Getting More News from the Web: Survey," *Marketing Magazine,* May 20, 2009.
5. Cate Riegner, "Word of Mouth on the Web: The Impact of Web 2.0 on Consumer Purchase Decisions," *Journal of Advertising Research,* December 2007.
6. David A. Aaker, "Fast Brand Building in Slow-Growth Markets," *Strategy and Business,* third quarter 2002, pp. 48–57.
7. Mike Sharma, "If Not Online, Where Are You?" *Marketing Magazine,* June 5, 2006.
8. Nigel Hollis, "Ten Years of Learning on How Online Advertising Builds Brands," *Journal of Advertising Research,* June 2005, pp. 255-268.
9. Mathew Ingram, "Catering to Web-savvy Moms," *The Globe and Mail,* Jan 18, 2007; Stuart Elliott, "Online, P&G Gets a Little Crazy," *The New York Times,* December 14, 2006; Diane Francis, "P&G's Army of 'Moms'," *National Post,* July 7, 2006.
10. Grace J. Johnson, Gordon C. Bruner II, and Anand Kumar, "Interactivity and Its Facets Revisited," *Journal of Advertising,* 35(4), Winter 2006, pp. 35-52.
11. Ibid.
12. Maria Sicilia, Salvador Ruiz, and Jose L. Munuera, "Effects of Interactivity in a Web Site," *Journal of Advertising,* Fall 2005, 34(3), pp. 31-45; Alex Wang, "Advertising Engagement: A Driver of Message Involvement on Message Effects," *Journal of Advertising Research,* December 2006, pp. 355-368.
13. Qimei Chen and William Wells, "Attitude toward the Site," *Journal of Advertising Research,* March-September 1999, pp. 27-38; Qimei Chen, Sandra J. Clifford, and William Wells, "Attitude toward the Site II: New Information," *Journal of Advertising Research,* March-April 2002.
14. Gary L. Geissler, George M. Zinkhan, and Richard T. Watson, "The Influence of Home Page Complexity on Consumer Attention, Attitudes, and Purchase Intent," *Journal of Advertising,* 3(2), Summer 2006, p. 69.
15. Micael Dahlen, Alexandra Rasch, and Sara Rosengren, "Love at First Site? A Study of Website Advertising Effectiveness," *Journal of Advertising Research,* March 2003, pp. 25-33.
16. Julie S. Stevenson, Gordon Bruner II, and Anand Kumar, "Webpage Background and Viewer Attitudes," *Journal of Advertising Research,* January-April 2000, pp. 29-34;

Gordon Bruner II and Anand Kumar, "Web Commercials and Advertising Hierarchy-of-Effects," *Journal of Advertising Research,* January-April 2000, pp. 35-42.
17. Jeromy Lloyd, "Bolder Man Is Bull's Eye for Kraft," *Marketing Magazine,* June 1, 2009.
18. Joe Plummer, Steve Rapparport, Taddy Hall, Robert Barocci, *The Online Advertising Playbook, 2007* (John Wiley & Sons, Hoboken, NJ).
19. Chris Gaither, "Yahoo to Sell 'Contextual' Website Ads," *Los Angeles Times,* August 3, 2005, p. C2.
20. Rob Gerlsbeck, "The Next Prime Time," *Marketing Magazine,* May 8, 2006.
21. Interactive Advertising Bureau of Canada, Canadian Advertising Revenue Survey, www.iabcanada.com.
22. Anonymous, "Great Canadian Online Disconnect," *National Post,* September 26, p. FP1.
23. Ibid.
24. Wendy Davis, "Banner Ads Are Alive—Though Not Clicking," *Marketing Week,* January 29, 2004, p. 37.
25. Tessa Wegert, "The Ad Banner Turns 10," www.clickz.com, November 4, 2004, pp. 1–2.
26. Chang-Hoan Cho, Jung-Gyo Lee, and Marye Tharp, "Different Forced-Exposure Levels to Banner Advertisements," *Journal of Advertising Research,* July-August 2001, pp. 45-56.
27. Prem N. Shamdasani, Andrea J. S. Stanaland, Juliana Tan, "Location, Location, Location: Insights for Advertising Placement on the Web," *Journal of Advertising Research,* July-August 2001, pp. 7-21; Wenyu Dou, Randy Lim, and Sixian Yang, "How Smart Are 'Smart Banners'?" July-August 2001, pp. 31-43.
28. Micael Dahlen, "Banner Advertisement through a New Lens," *Journal of Advertising Research,* July-August 2001, pp. 21-30.
29. Kelli S. Burns and Richard J. Lutz, "The Function of Format: Consumer Responses to Six On-line Advertising Formats", *Journal of Advertising,* 35(1) Spring 2006, pp. 53-63; Robert S. Moore, Claire Allison Stammerjohan, and Robin A. Coulter, "Banner Advertiser-Web Site Context Conguity and Color Effects on Attention and Attitudes," *Journal of Advertising,* 34(2) Summer 2005, pp. 71-84; Ritu Lohtia, Naveen Donthu, and Edmund K. Hershberger, "The Impact of Content and Design Elements on Banner Advertising Click-thorugh Rates," *Journal of Advertising,* December 2003, pp. 410-418.
30. Peter J. Danaher and Guy W. Mullarkey, "Factors Affecting Online Advertising Recall: A study of Students," *Journal of Advertising Research,* September 2003, pp. 252-267; Idil Yaveroglu and Naveen

589

Endnotes

Donthu, "Advertising Repetition and Placement Issues in On-Line Environment," *Journal of Advertising, 37*(2), Summer 2008, pp. 31-43.

31. Jonathan Paul, "ICE Widget Activates Ads," *Strategy,* February 2009, p. 26.

32. Tessa Wegert, "Consumers Unhappy with Web Site Simply Go Away," www.CenterforMediaResearch.com, August 23, 2005, pp. 1–2.

33. Steven M. Edwards, Hairong Li, and Joo-Hyun Lee, "Forced Exposure and Psychological Reactance: Antecedents and Consequences of the Perceived Intrusiveness of Pop-Up Ads," *Journal of Advertising, 31*(3), Fall 2002, pp. 83-95.

34. Chris Daniels, "Off to a Flying Start," *Marketing Magazine,* February 3, 2003.

35. Jessica E. Vascellaro, "Yahoo Set to Aid Marketers with New Online Ad Tools," *Globe and Mail,* February 24, 2009, p. B12.

36. "Getting Search Right," *Marketing Magazine,* March 1, 2010.

37. Chris Powell, "Online TV Accounts for 1.6% of Canadian TV Ad Spend: Study," *Marketing Magazine,* April 8, 2009.

38. Danny Kucharsky, "Ads On Demand," *Marketing Magazine,* May 15, 2006.

39. Chris Powell, "Broadband or Bust," *Marketing Magazine,* June 19, 2006.

40. Jeff Leiper, "The Battle for Internet TV," *Marketing Magazine,* February 27, 2006.

41. Daniel M. Haygood, "A Status Report on Podcast Advertising," *Journal of Advertising Research,* December 2007, pp. 518-523.

42. Chris Sherman, "What Is RSS, and Why Should You Care?" www.search-enginewatch.com, August 30, 2005, pp. 1–4.

43. Michelle Warren, "Blogger Knows Best," *Marketing Magazine,* April 6, 2009.

44. Simon Houpt, "For Popular Bloggers, Some Things Come for Free," *The Globe and Mail,* October 9, 2009, p. B5.

45. David Ebner, "EA Makes Bet on Social Media Game," *The Globe and Mail,* November 10, 2009, p. B6.

46. Jonathan Paul, "RPGx Look for Brands to Play With," *Strategy,* April 2009, p. 33.

47. Theresa Wood, "Microsoft & Ubisoft Grab Game Makers," *Strategy,* March 2009.

48. Jeromy Lloyd, "Nissan Decides to Augment Reality," *Marketing Magazine,* April 23, 2009.

49. Kristin Laird, "Chasing Koodo's Gingerbread Man," *Marketing Magazine,* December 10, 2009.

50. Nick Barbuto, "Virtual Thirst," *Marketing Magazine,* January 16, 2006.

51. Sarah Dobson, "Taking the High Road," *Marketing Magazine,* April 7, 2003.

52. Basil Katz, "Email Newsletters Aim for Men's Inbox, Wallet," *National Post,* September 11, 2009, p. FP10.

53. Brett A.S. Martin, Joel Van Durme, Mika Raulas, and Marko Merisavo, "E-mail Advertising: Exploratory Insights From Finland," *Journal of Advertising Research,* September 2003, pp. 293-300.

54. David Chilton, "Spreading the Message," *Marketing Magazine,* March 6, 2006.

55. Joseph E. Phelps, Regina Lewis, Lynne Mobilio, David Perry, and Niranjan Raman, "Viral Marketing or Electronic Word-of-Mouth Advertising: Examining Consumer Responses and Motivations to Pass Along Email," *Journal of Advertising Research,* December 2004, pp. 333-348.

56. Alexandra Lopez-Pacheco, "Nirvan Is the Exception," *National Post,* July 14, p. FP7.

57. Ibid.

58. Gary Schwartz, "Mobile Marketing 101," *Marketing Magazine,* July 14, 2003.

59. Ibid.

60. Sarah Dobson, "Mobile Matters," *Marketing Magazine,* October 9, 2006.

61. Michelle Halpern, "Friends and Their Phones," *Marketing Magazine,* January 30, 2006.

62. Sarah Dobson, "Mobile Matters," *Marketing Magazine,* October 9, 2006.

63. Paul-Mark Rendon, "Does Text Sell?" *Marketing Magazine,* April 26, 2004.

64. Jeromy Lloyd, "Txting Out an SOS," *Marketing Magazine,* May 18, 2009.

65. Jacque Natel and Yasha Sekhavat, "The Impact of SMS Advertising on Members of a Virtual Community," *Journal of Advertising Research,* September 2008, pp. 363-374.

66. Simon Houpt, "Why Click When You Can Scan Your Way to Ad Messages?" *The Globe and Mail,* October 16, 2009, p. B8.

67. Michelle Halpern, "Shows On the Go," *Marketing Magazine,* February 6, 2006.

68. Chris Daniels, "Tiny Screen, Huge Potential," *Marketing Magazine,* May 15, 2006.

69. Michelle Halpern, "Shows On the Go."

70. Jonathan Paul, "Mobile 2.0 Gets Upgraded," *Strategy,* January, 2009, p. 26.

71. Katie Bailey, "Canadians Not So Smart About Smartphones," MediainCanada.com, April 2010.

72. Matt Hartley, "The Mobile Revolution: So Fast You May Not Notice," *The Globe and Mail,* May 21, 2009, p. A3.

73. Jeromy Lloyd, "Gone Mobile," *Marketing Magazine,* March 1, 2010.

74. "Mobile Applications: The Next Big Thing in Mobile Marketing?" http://www.mobiadnews.com/?p=3172.

75. Subdh Bhat, Michael Bevans, and Sanjit Sengupta, "Measuring Users' Web Activity to Evaluate and Enhance Advertising Effectiveness," *Journal of Advertising, 31*(3), Fall 2002, p. 97.

76. Alexa Bezjian-Avery, "New Media Interactive Advertising vs. Traditional Advertising," *Journal of Advertising Research,* August 1998, pp. 23–32; Qimel Chen and William D. Wells, "Attitude toward the Site," *Journal of Advertising Research,* September 1999, pp. 27–38; Kim Bartel Sheehan and Sally J. McMillan, "Response Variation in E-Mail Surveys," *Journal of Advertising Research,* July 1999, pp. 45–54; and John Eighmey, "Profiling User Responses to Commercial Websites," *Journal of Advertising Research,* May 1997, pp. 59–66.

77. "Measurement Guidelines and Measurement Certification," www.iab.net, 2006.

78. Melita Kuburas and Carey Toane, "Ben & Jerry's," *Strategy,* June 2009, p. 7.

79. Katie Bailey, "Banff Goes Nuts with Crasher Squirrel," *Strategy,* October 2009, p. 9.

80. Matt Semansky, "Silk Seeks Smiles for New Campaign," *Marketing Magazine,* April 21, 2009.

81. Hollie Shaw, "Doing Digital Right," *National Post,* May 8, 2009, p. FP9.

82. Anonymous, "Internet Marketing: Daunting," *National Post,* November 11, 2009, p. FP3.

83. Sung-Joon Yoon and Joo-Ho Kim, "Is the Internet More Effective Than Traditional Media? Factors Affecting the Choice of Media," *Journal of Advertising Research,* December 2001.

84. Katherine Gallagher, K. Dale Foster, and Jeffrey Parsons, "The Medium Is Not the Message: Advertising Effectiveness and Content Evaluation in Print and on the Web," *Journal of Advertising Research,* July-August 2001; Katherine Gallagher, Jeffrey Parsons, and K. Dale Foster, "A Tale of Two Studies: Replicating 'Advertising Effectiveness and Content Evaluation in Print and on the Web'," *Journal of Advertising Research,* July-August 2001.

85. Johanna S. Ilfeld and Russell S. Winer, "Generating Website Traffic," *Journal of Advertising Research,* October 2002.

86. Yumiin Chang and Esther Thorson, "Television and Web Advertising Synergies," *Journal of Advertising, 33*(2), Summer 2004, pp. 75-84.

87. Ali M. Kanso and Richard Alan Nelson, "Internet and Magazine Advertising: Integrated Partnerships or Not?" *Journal of Advertising Research,* December 2004.

88. Jonathan Paul, "*The Score* Draft Pick: Gillette," *Strategy,* October 2009, p. 8.

89. Robert Davis and Laszlo Sajtos, "Measuring Consumer Interactivity in Response to Campaigns Coupling Mobile and Television Media," *Journal of Advertising Research,* September 2008; Randolph J. Trappey III and Arch

G. Woodside, "Consumer Responses to Interactive Advertising Campaigns Coupling Short-Message-Service Direct Marketing and TV Commercials," *Journal of Advertising Research,* December 2005.

CHAPTER EIGHTEEN

1. Robert L. Heilbroner, "Demand for the Supply Side," *New York Review of Books, 38* (June 11, 1981), p. 40.
2. "CRTC Keeps Hands Off New Media," *Calgary Sun,* June 5, 2009.
3. Chris Powell, "The Inventory Debate," *Marketing Magazine,* January 26, 2004.
4. Brenda Pritchard and Susan Vogt, *Advertising and Marketing Law in Canada* (LexisNexis, Butterworths, 2006).
5. A Guide to the Amendments of the *Competition Act,* Competition Bureau Canada, April 22, 2009.
6. Hollie Shaw, "Bogus Ads," *National Post,* May 22, 2009, p. FP12.
7. "Fanning the Embers," *Marketing Magazine,* September 10, 2001.
8. Canadian Code of Advertising Standards Interpretation Guidelines, http://www.adstandards.com/en/ASCLibrary/interpretation Guidelines.pdf.
9. http://www.adstandards.com/en/childrensinitiative/yearOne ComplianceReport.pdf.
10. Jeromy Lloyd, "Hot Water," *Marketing Magazine,* April 20, 2009.
11. Jeromy Lloyd, "Shell Advertorials Spurn Complaint to Ad Standards Council," *Marketing Magazine,* February 11, 2010.
12. Matt Semanksy, "Bell Ignores ASC Ruling," *Marketing Magazine,* February 23, 2009.
13. http://adstandards.com/en/standards/complaints_report/2001ascReport En.pdf, accessed December 12, 2007.
14. http://www.adstandards.com/en/-standards/adComplaintsReports.asp?perio dquarter=1&periodyear=2007, accessed December 12, 2007.
15. David Brown, "Kia Gets the Goat," *Marketing Magazine,* February 27, 2007.
16. http://www.adstandards.com/en/Standards/adComplaintsReports.asp?periodquarter=2&periodyear=2007.
17. http://www.adstandards.com/en/standards/adComplaintsReports.asp?periodquarter=2&periodyear=2008
18. Ibid.
19. Eric N. Berkowitz, Roger A. Kerin, Steven W. Hartley, William Rudedius, et al., *Marketing,* 5th ed. (Burr Ridge, IL: Irwin/McGraw-Hill, 1997), p. 102.
20. Stephanie O'Donohoe, "Attitudes to Advertising: A Review of British and American Research," *International Journal of Advertising, 14* (1995), pp. 245–61.
21. Banwari Mittal, "Public Assessment of TV Advertising: Faint Praise and Harsh

22. Sharon Shavitt, Pamela Lowery, and James Haefner, "Public Attitudes toward Advertising; More Favorable Than You Might Think," *Journal of Advertising Research,* July/August 1998, pp. 7–22.
23. Gita Venkataramini Johar, "Consumer Involvement and Deception from Implied Advertising Claims," *Journal of Marketing Research, 32* (August 1995), pp. 267–79; J. Edward Russo, Barbara L. Metcalf, and Debra Stephens, "Identifying Misleading Advertising," *Journal of Consumer Research, 8* (September 1981), pp. 119–31.
24. Ivan L. Preston, *The Great American Blow-Up: Puffery in Advertising and Selling* (Madison: University of Wisconsin Press, 1975), p. 3.
25. David Menzies, "Carlsberg Conspiracy," *Marketing Magazine,* March 29, 2004.
26. Shelby D. Hunt, "Informational vs. Persuasive Advertising: An Appraisal," *Journal of Advertising,* Summer 1976, pp. 5–8.
27. Banwari Mittal, "Public Assessment of TV Advertising: Faint Praise and Harsh Criticism"; J. C. Andrews, "The Dimensionality of Beliefs toward Advertising in General," *Journal of Advertising, 18,* no. 1 (1989), pp. 26–35; Ron Alsop, "Advertisers Find the Climate Less Hostile Outside the U.S.," *The Wall Street Journal,* December 10, 1987, p. 29; Sharon Shavitt, Pamela Lowery, and James Haefner, "Public Attitudes toward Advertising; More Favorable Than You Might Think," *Journal of Advertising Research,* July/August 1998, pp. 7–22.
28. David A. Aaker and Donald E. Bruzzone, "Causes of Irritation in Advertising," *Journal of Marketing,* Spring 1985, p. 47–57.
29. Stephen A. Greyser, "Irritation in Advertising," *Journal of Advertising Research, 13* (February 1973), pp. 3–10.
30. For an interesting analysis of an interpretation of this ad from a literary theory perspective see Aaron C. Ahuvia, "Social Criticism of Advertising: On the Role of Literary Theory and the Use of Data," *Journal of Advertising, 27,* no. 1 (Spring 1998), pp. 143–62.
31. James B. Arndorfer, "Skyy Hit the Limit with Racy Ad: Critics," *Advertising Age,* February 7, 2005, p. 6.
32. Tim Nudd, "Does Sex Really Sell?" *Adweek,* October 17, 2005, pp. 14–17.
33. Scott Ward, Daniel B. Wackman, and Ellen Wartella, *How Children Learn to Buy: The Development of Consumer Information Processing Skills* (Beverly Hills, CA: Sage, 1979).
34. Thomas S. Robertson and John R. Rossiter, "Children and Commercial Persuasion: An Attribution Theory

Analysis," *Journal of Consumer Research, 1,* no. 1 (June 1974), pp. 13–20; and Scott Ward and Daniel B. Wackman, "Children's Information Processing of Television Advertising," in *New Models for Communications Research,* ed. G. Kline and P. Clark (Beverly Hills, CA: Sage, 1974), pp. 81–119.
35. Merrie Brucks, Gary M. Armstrong, and Marvin E. Goldberg, "Children's Use of Cognitive Defenses against Television Advertising: A Cognitive Response Approach," *Journal of Consumer Research, 14,* no. 4 (March 1988), pp. 471–82.
36. For a discussion on consumer socialization, see Scott Ward, "Consumer Socialization," *Journal of Consumer Research, 1,* no. 2 (September 1974), pp. 1–14.
37. Tamara F. Mangleburg and Terry Bristol, "Socialization and Adolescents' Skepticism toward Advertising," *Journal of Advertising, 27,* no. 3 (Fall 1998), pp. 11–21.
38. Robert E. Hite and Randy Eck, "Advertising to Children: Attitudes of Business vs. Consumers," *Journal of Advertising Research,* October/November 1987, pp. 40–53; Ann D. Walsh, Russell N. Laczniak, and Les Carlson, "Mother's Preferences for Regulating Children's Television," *Journal of Advertising, 27,* no. 3 (Fall 1998), pp. 23–36.
39. Paul-Mark Rendon, "Cherry's Bubba's Out, Says ASC," *Marketing Magazine,* September 22, 2003.
40. John K. Galbraith, *The New Industrial State* (Boston: Houghton Mifflin, 1967), cited in Richard W. Pollay, "The Distorted Mirror: Reflections on the Unintended Consequences of Advertising," *Journal of Marketing,* August 1986, p. 25.
41. Raymond A. Bauer and Stephen A. Greyser, "The Dialogue That Never Happens," *Harvard Business Review,* January/February 1969, pp. 122–28.
42. Morris B. Holbrook, "Mirror Mirror On the Wall, What's Unfair in the Reflections on Advertising," *Journal of Marketing, 5* (July 1987), pp. 95–103; and Theodore Levitt, "The Morality of Advertising," *Harvard Business Review,* July/August 1970, pp. 84–92.
43. Stephen Fox, *The Mirror Makers: A History of American Advertising and Its Creators* (New York: Morrow, 1984), p. 330.
44. Richard W. Pollay, "The Distorted Mirror: Reflections on the Unintended Consequences of Advertising," *Journal of Marketing, 50* (April 1986), p. 33.
45. Jules Backman, "Is Advertising Wasteful?" *Journal of Marketing, 32* (January 1968), pp. 2–8.
46. Hunt, "Informational vs. Persuasive Advertising."
47. Ibid., p. 6.

Endnotes

48. Alice E. Courtney and Thomas W. Whipple, *Sex Stereotyping in Advertising* (Lexington, MA: Lexington Books, 1984).

49. Daniel J. Brett and Joanne Cantor, "The Portrayal of Men and Women in U.S. Television Commercials: A Recent Content Analysis and Trends of 15 Years," *Sex Roles, 18,* no. 9/10 (1998), pp. 595–608; John B. Ford and Michael La Tour, "Contemporary Perspectives of Female Role Portrayals in Advertising," *Journal of Current Issues and Research in Advertising, 28,* no. 1 (1996), pp. 81–93.

50. Beverly A. Browne, "Gender Stereotypes in Advertising on Children's Television in the 1990s: A Cross-National Analysis," *Journal of Advertising, 27,* no. 1 (Spring 1998), pp. 83–96.

51. Richard H. Kolbe, "Gender Roles in Children's Advertising: A Longitudinal Content Analysis," in *Current Issues and Research in Advertising,* ed. James H. Leigh and Claude R. Martin, Jr. (Ann Arbor: University of Michigan, 1990), pp. 197–206.

52. Steven M. Kates and Glenda Shaw-Garlock, "The Ever Entangling Web: A Study of Ideologies and Discourses in Advertising to Women," *Journal of Advertising, 28,* no. 2 (Summer 1999), pp. 33–49.

53. Basil Englis, Michael Solomon, and Richard Ashmore, "Beauty before the Eyes of Beholders: The Cultural Encoding of Beauty Types in Magazine Advertising and Music Television," *Journal of Advertising,* June 1994, pp. 49–64.

54. www.adstandards.com/en/consumer complaints/2009adcomplaintsreport.pdf.

55. Nathalie Atkinson, "Picture-Perfect Manipulation," *National Post,* October 10, p. A3.

56. Kristin Laird, "Loblaw Stands by Sexy Joe Fresh Underwear Flyer," *Marketing Magazine,* April 7, 2009; Kelly Egan, "Sexualized Ads Signal Disturbing Trend," *Ottawa Citizen,* April 3, 2009,

57. Jeromy Lloyd, "Shell Advertorials Spurn Complaint to Ad Standards Council," *Marketing Magazine,* February 11, 2010

58. James Stearns, Lynette S. Unger, and Steven G. Luebkeman, "The Portrayal of Blacks in Magazine and Television Advertising," in *AMA Educator's Proceedings,* ed. Susan P. Douglas and Michael R. Solomon (Chicago: American Marketing Association, 1987).

59. Robert E. Wilkes and Humberto Valencia, "Hispanics and Blacks in Television Commercials," *Journal of Advertising, 18,* no. 1 (1989), pp. 19–26.

60. Julia Bristor, Renee Gravois Lee, and Michelle Hunt, "Race and Ideology: African American Images in Television Advertising," *Journal of Public Policy and Marketing, 14* (Spring 1995), pp. 48–59.

61. Corliss Green, "Ethnic Evaluations of Advertising: Interaction Effects of Strength of Ethnic Identification, Media Placement, and Degree of Racial Composition," *Journal of Advertising, 28,* no. 1 (Spring 1999), pp. 49–64.

62. Charles R. Taylor and Barbara B. Stern, "Asian-Americans: Television Advertising and the 'Model Minority' Stereotype," *Journal of Advertising, 26,* no. 2 (Summer 1997), pp. 47–61.

63. Jo Marney, "Counting Ethnic Canadians In," *Marketing Magazine,* June 4, 2001.

64. Lou Puim, "How Wal-Mart Learned Diversity," *Marketing Magazine,* January 23, 2006.

65. Jef I. Richards and John H. Murphy, II, "Economic Censorship and Free Speech: The Circle of Communication between Advertisers, Media and Consumers," *Journal of Current Issues and Research in Advertising, 18,* no. 1 (Spring 1996), pp. 21–33.

66. Lawrence C. Soley and Robert L. Craig, "Advertising Pressure on Newspapers: A Survey," *Journal of Advertising,* December 1992, pp. 1–10.

67. Soley and Craig, "Advertising Pressure on Newspapers."

68. Randy W. Elder, Ruth A. Shults, David A. Sleet, James L. Nichols, Robert S. Thompson, and Warda Rajab, "Effectiveness of Mass Media Campaigns for Reducing Drinking and Driving and Alcohol-Involved Crashes," *American Journal of Preventative Medicine, 27*(1), 2004.

69. Kristin Laird, "LCBO Is Deflating Elephants," *Marketing Magazine,* December 9, 2009.

70. For a discussion of monopolies in the cereal industry, see Paul N. Bloom, "The Cereal Industry: Monopolists or Super Marketers?" *MSU Business Topics,* Summer 1978, pp. 41–49.

71. Lester G. Telser, "Advertising and Competition," *Journal of Political Economy,* December 1964, pp. 537–62.

72. Robert D. Buzzell, Bradley T. Gale, and Ralph G. M. Sultan, "Market Share—A Key to Profitability," *Harvard Business Review,* January/February 1975, pp. 97–106.

73. Robert D. Buzzell and Paul W. Farris, *Advertising Cost in Consumer Goods Industries,* Marketing Science Institute, Report no. 76, August 1976, p. 111; and Paul W. Farris and David J. Reibstein, "How Prices, Ad Expenditures, and Profits Are Linked," *Harvard Business Review,* November/ December 1979, pp. 173–84.

74. Paul W. Farris and Mark S. Albion, "The Impact of Advertising on the Price of Consumer Products," *Journal of Marketing 44*(3), Summer 1980, pp. 17–35.

75. Ibid.

76. Lee Benham, "The Effect of Advertising on the Price of Eyeglasses," *Journal of Law and Economics, 15* (October 1972), pp. 337–52.

77. Robert L. Steiner, "Does Advertising Lower Consumer Price?" *Journal of Marketing, 37,* no. 4 (October 1973), pp. 19–26.

78. Farris and Albion, "The Impact of Advertising," p. 30.

79. James M. Ferguson, "Comments On 'The Impact of Advertising on the Price of Consumer Products,'" *Journal of Marketing, 46,* no. 1 (Winter 1982), pp. 102–5.

80. Farris and Albion, "The Impact of Advertising."

592

CREDITS AND ACKNOWLEDGMENTS

Credits and Acknowledgments

Apple Computer, Inc.; p. 209: Photo: P. Demarchelier for TAG Heuer; CP/Halifax Daily News/Jeff Harper; p. 211: Courtesy of PowerBar; p. 212: Courtesy of Unilever.

CHAPTER 8

p. 217: The Canadian Press/Christof Stache; p. 218: Courtesy of Hitachi America Ltd.; p. 219: Courtesy of Eagle One Industries, an operating unit of Valvoline, a division of Ashland, Inc. Eagle One, Nanowax, and Valvoline are trademarks owned by Ashland, Inc.; Courtesy of Church & Dwight Co., Inc.; p. 220: Used with permission from Pennzoil/Quaker State Company; Courtesy of Pfizer Consumer Healthcare. Pfizer Inc.; p. 221: Used with permission of Procter & Gamble. Photography by Ondrea Barbe; p. 223: Courtesy of DaimlerChrysler Corporation; Courtesy of bebe; p. 224: Eaton Corporation. All rights reserved 2005; p. 226: Courtesy of White Wave, Inc.; p. 227: Courtesy of Novartis Consumer Health Canada Inc.; p. 228: GE Appliances/MABE Canada; p. 229: Courtesy Volkswagen of America; p. 230: Used with permission of Procter & Gamble; p. 237: www.tourismkelowna. com; p. 238: Courtesy of Skyy Spirits, LLC; p. 240: © New York Fries; Used with permission of BMO Financial Group; p. 241: Used with permission of Ferrero.

CHAPTER 9

p. 247: JFB/Stone+/Getty Images; p. 248: AP/Wide World Photos/PRNewsPhoto/Multi-Color Corporation; p. 255: Tetra Images/Getty Images; p. 262: Kieth Brofsky/Photodisc/Getty Images; p. 267: Courtesy of Ipsos-ASI, Inc.; p. 268: Courtesy of Decision Analyst, Inc.

CHAPTER 10

p. 275: © Getty Images.

CHAPTER 11

p. 319: Used with permission of Corus Entertainment; p. 321: Courtesy of Hitachi America, Limited and Lambesis; p. 339: 2000-2001 BBM Television Data Book. Television Summer Drop-off. Used with permission.

CHAPTER 12

p. 349: The Canadian Press/Adrian Wyld; p. 352: Used with permission of Intel and Cohn & Wolfe; p. 353: Courtesy of Under Armour Inc.; p. 354: Andrew Zuckerman/Wired; Harry Magazine cover courtesy of Harry Rosen Inc.; p. 355: Courtesy of Lenovo Canada; p. 357: Cover, Chatelaine, December 2010 is owned by and used with permission of Rogers Publishing Ltd. All rights reserved., Courtesy of Heineken Breweries; p. 358: Toronto Life, August 2010. Printed with permission; p. 359: Courtesy Hyundai Motor

America; Courtesy V & S Vin and Spirit AB. Imported by the Absolut Spirits Co., New York, NY.

CHAPTER 13

p. 383: The Canadian Press/Francis Vachon; p. 386: Andrew Simpson; Courtesy of Outdoor Advertising Association of America; p. Photo Courtesy of Toshiba; p. 393: Courtesy of Outdoor Advertising Association of America; p. 394: Courtesy of Outdoor Advertising Association of America; p. 396: Cover: Courtesy of Bearskin Airlines Photo Credit: Shannon Lepere Photography; p. 406: AP/World Wide Photos; p. 409: Courtesy of Activision; p. 411: AP/Wide World Photos.

CHAPTER 14

p. 419: Jamie McCarthy/Getty Images; p. 420: Courtesy of Aspen Marketing Services; p. 421: CP/Patrick Doyle; p. 422: © 2006 Kellogg North America Company. The copyright in and to the images is and shall remain the sole property of Kellogg North American Company; p. 423: Courtesy of Wal-Mart, Inc.; p. 424: Use of the ARM & HAMMER, ARM & HAMMER logo, distinctive trade dress and other content of the Arm & Hammer web site is with the express permission of Church & Dwight Co., Inc., Princeton, New Jersey © Church & Dwight Co.; p. 430: ArmorAll Products Corporation; p. 434: © McGraw-Hill Companies/Jill Braaten, photographer; p. 435: Courtesy of ValPak Direct Marketing Systems, Inc.; AP/Wide World Photos/PR NewsFoto; p. 438: Used with permission of General Motors Corp; p. 439: Used with permission from Pennzoil/Quaker State Company; p. 440: ArmorAll Products Corporation; p. 441: KAO Brands Company; Courtesy of WD-40 Company; p. 442: Courtesy of AST; p. 447: Courtesy of Wilson Sporting Goods Co. and Great North Corporation-Display Group; p. 449: Courtesy of Bridgestone Golf, Inc.; Courtesy of Intel Corporation; p. 452: Courtesy of MasterCard.

CHAPTER 15

p. 459: Jeff Vinnic/kGetty Images; p. 461: The Canadian Press/Nathan Denette; p. 462: Gone Wild/Getty Images; p. 465: McGraw-Hill Ryerson; Courtesy of BP; p. 466: Courtesy of Syngenta; p. 472: Courtesy of Eward Jones Investments; p. 473: Courtesy of the General Mills archives; p. 475: Courtesy Tyco International; p. 476: Grant Thornton brand-building advertising; WHIRLPOOL is a registered trademark of Whirlpool., U.S.A. © 2005 Whirlpool Corporation. All rights reserved. HABITAT FOR HUMANITY is a registered trademark of Habitat for Humanity International, Inc.

CHAPTER 16

p. 487: © Jason Isley - Scubazoo/CORBIS; p. 489: Courtesy of Tourism Saskatchewan, www.sasktourism.com; p. 491: Courtesy of Costco; p. © Tracy Leonard, Shoppers Optimum and Shoppers Optimum Card are trademarks of 911979 Alberta Ltd., used under license.; p. 493: Used with permission of Rogers; p. 494: Courtesy of Porsche Cars North America, Inc.; p. 495: Shoppers Optimum and Shoppers Optimum Card are trademarks of 911979 Alberta Ltd., used under license.; p. 496: © Mercedes-Benz USA, LLC. Courtesy of DaimlerChrysler AG; p. 497: AP/Wide World Photos/PRNewsPhoto/Executive Visions Inc.; p. 498: Used by permission of Lenox, Inc.

CHAPTER 17

p. 507: Photo Courtesy of Molson Coors Canada; p. 512: "SNAPPLE is a registered trademark of Snapple Beverage Corp. Used with permission. All rights reserved."; Reprinted Courtesy of Caterpillar Inc.; p. 513: The Procter & Gamble Company; p. 515: Used by permission of Unilever Canada.; p. 516: p. 519: p. 521: © 2008 Google; p. 523: Ryan McVay/Getty Images; p. 526: Courtesy of Facebook; p. 527: Habbo Hotel screenshot courtesy of Sulake Corporation; p. 528: © ChryslerLLC. Used with permission; Ben & Jerry's Homemade, Inc.; p. 529: Vicky Kasala/Getty Images; Road Runner Sports - World's Largest Running Store.

CHAPTER 18

p. 543: The Canadian Press/Francis Vachon; p. 544: Courtesy Benetton Cosmetics Corporation. Photo by O. Toscani; p. 549: Used by permission of Advertising Standard Canada; p. 550: © Davide Campari-Milano S.P.A. All rights Reserved; p. 553: Used by permission of Advertising Standard Canada: p. 557: © Tim Boyle/Getty Images; p. 558: Courtesy Airwalk; Courtesy of Skyy Spirits, LLC; p. 559: Concept: O. Toscani. Courtesy of United Colors of Benetton; p. 560: Courtesy of United Colors of Benetton; p. 561: AP/World Wide Photos/PR Newswire; p. 562: © American Association of Advertising Agencies; p. 564: Courtesy of Network Solutions. © Copyright 2005 Network Solutions. All rights reserved; p. 565: Courtesy of Unilever; p. 566: Courtesy IKEA and Deutsch Inc.; p. 567: Courtesy International Advertising Association; p. 568: D. Falconer/PhotoLink; p. 569: Courtesy of the Procter & Gamble Company; p. 572: © American Association of Advertising Agencies.

594

NAME AND COMPANY INDEX

A

A Channel, 326
A&E, 546
A&W Restaurants, 182, 207, 221
Aaker, David, 153, 513
ABC Canada Literacy Foundation, 477
ABC Network, 327, 471
Abernethy, Avery, 340
Absolut, 179, 182, 359, 417
AC Nielsen, 267, 405
Academy Awards, 329, 477
Access, 326
Acura, 90
Adams, Deborah, 564
Adams, Michael, 193
Adidas/Adidas Canada, 83, 443
Advantage Bars, 197
Advertising Age, 184, 461
Advertising Control for Television (ACT), 259
Advertising Research Foundation, 271, 516
Advertising Standards Canada, 131, 222, 524, 564
Advertising Standards Council, 545, 547–554, 557, 560
Adweek, 184
Aeroplan, 442
Agency.com, 56
Air Canada, 6, 8, 88, 151–154, 166, 173, 343, 394
Air Miles, 529
Air Farce, 168
Airwalk, 558
Aislin, 168
Alberta Beef, 353
Alberta Securities Commission, 82
Alberta Weekly Newspapers Association, 372
Albion, Mark, 570–571
Allard Johnson, 42
Allport, Gordon, 72
Alpine Canada Alpin (ACA), 481
Altius Sport, 42
Altoids, 202
AMA. See American Marketing Association
Ambler, 115
American Association of Advertising Agencies (AAAA), 17, 562, 573
American Eagle, 73
American Express Co., 10, 204
American Greetings, 477
American Marketing Association (AMA), 4, 22
Anaheim Ducks, 421
Anand-Keller, Punam, 200
Anderson DDB, 42
Anheuser-Busch InBev, 233, 301
Apple Computer, 53, 402, 497
Aquafina, 153
Arbitron, 536
Archdiocese of Montreal, 369
Architectural Digest, 295
Arm & Hammer, 424
Armani, 352
Armor All, 430
Armstrong, 196

Armstrong, Lance, 210–211
Armstrong Partnership, 452
Arpin, Dominic, 275
ARTV, 333
Ashley Madison Agency, 543
Aspen Marketing Services, 420
Association of Canadian Advertisers (ACA), 49, 334, 556–557
Association of National Advertisers, 129
Association of Quebec Advertising Agencies, 194
AST Dew Tour, 442
Astral Media, 234, 337, 543
Astral Media Outdoor, 385, 389, 391
Astral Media Radio, 543
Astral TV, 275
AT&T/AT&T Canada, 230
Atelier America, 471
Athletics World, 83
Atkins, 197
Atlantic Community Newspapers Association, 372
Audi, 90, 198, 361, 532
Audit Bureau of Circulation, 363, 372, 536
Auto Trader, 553
Aveeno, 239–240, 443–444
Axe, 438

B

B.C. Dairy Foundation, 35, 137
B!G Awards, 281
Banff Lake Louise Tourism, 538
Bank of Montreal, 8
Bank of Nova Scotia, 8
Barrett, Dave, 208
Barry, Thomas, 116
Barrymore, Drew, 109
Bauer, Raymond, 561
Bay, The, 72, 503
Baylor University, 405
BBDO, 42, 265, 384
BBDO Toronto, 3
BBM Analytics, 336
BCAA Insurance, 47
BCE Inc., 8
Bear Mountain Resort, 496
bebe, 223
Becel, 158, 231, 329, 476, 477, 539, 568
BehaviorScan, 267
Belairdirect, 368, 539
Bell Canada, 8, 54, 140, 149, 344, 529, 551
Bell Mobility, 83, 140, 166, 531
Bell Sympatico, 520
Bell World, 140
Belle magazine, 352
Ben & Jerry's, 528, 538
Benetton, 40, 544, 558–560
Benham, Lee, 571
Bennett, Peter, 488
Bentley, 497
Bessies, 195
Better Business Bureau, 550
Big Brothers/Big Sisters, 478
Bits & Bites, 221

Black & Decker, 159
Black's, 232
BlackBerry, 8
Blair, 260
Blitz Direct, 42
Block, L.G., 200
Bloom Digital, 42
Bloom, Paul, 446
BMO Financial Group, 8, 58, 481
BMW, 6, 179, 312
Bob and Margaret, 407
Boeing, 198
Bombardier Inc., 8
Book of Lists, The, 492
Boot, Suni, 349
Bos, 487
Bosh, Chris, 3
Boston Pizza, 337
Bourne, Shae-Lynn, 450
BP (British Petroleum), 465
Brainwave Science, 262
Brand Finance Canada, 6
BrandSpark, 131
Brandweek, 58, 184
Brasseur, Isabelle, 450
Bravo!, 333
Brick Brewing Co., 329
Bridgestone Golf, 449
Bristol, Terry, 560
British Airways, 56
British Columbia & Yukon Community Newspapers Association, 372
British Columbia Automobile Association, 208
Broadband Network, 521–522
Broadcast Code for Advertising to Children (Children's Code), 547, 554, 560
Broadcasting Act, 545
Brock University, 161
Broil King, 10
Broom, Glen M., 461
Browning, Kurt, 450
Bruce Mau, 42
Bryan Mills Iradesso, 42
Buckley's Mixture, 226, 227
Bud Light, 80, 192, 301
Bud Light Institute, 196
Budget, 53
Budweiser, 233
Bull's-Eye, 516
Bureau of Broadcast Measurement of Canada (BBM), 325, 332, 334–336, 338, 342, 394
Burger King, 80, 388
Burke Day-After Recall Test, 265
Burnett, Leo, 189, 573
Business Edge, 367
Business News Network, 333
Business Publications Audit, 363

C

CAA Magazine, 351
Cacioppo, John, 125
Cadbury North America, 383, 478
Cadbury's Cocoa Partnership, 478
Calgary Stampede, 481
Campaign for Real Beauty, 129, 184, 212, 565

Campari, 550
Campbell Company of Canada, 497
Campbell's Soup, 289
Canada AM, 329
Canada Post, 8, 492, 493, 494
Canadian Advertising Foundation (CAF), 491
Canadian Advertising Rates and Data (CARD), 299, 342, 350, 352–353, 358, 365, 372
Canadian Advertising Research Foundation (CARF), 375
Canadian Architect, 354
Canadian Association of Advertisers, 545
Canadian Association of Broadcasters, 334, 546, 554
Canadian Beef, 142
Canadian Blood Services, 135
Canadian Breast Cancer Foundation, 476–477, 483
Canadian Broadcasting Corporation (CBC), 8, 12, 326–328, 332, 408, 420–421, 459, 475, 479, 521, 548
Canadian Broadcasting Standards Council, 550
Canadian Business, 354
Canadian Cancer Society, 493
Canadian Children's Food & Beverage Advertising Initiative, 548, 549, 560
Canadian Circulations Audit Board, 363
Canadian Code of Advertising Standards, 548–549
Canadian Community Newspapers Association (CCNA), 372–373
Canadian Cosmetic, Toiletry and Fragrance Association, 554
Canadian Football League (CFL), 102
Canadian Geographic, 361
Canadian Grocer, 354
Canadian House & Home, 48, 91
Canadian Idol, 20
Canadian Imperial Bank of Commerce. See CIBC
Canadian Lawyer, 354
Canadian Living magazine, 281, 297, 319, 351, 357, 483
Canadian Magazine Publishers, 355
Canadian Marketing Association (CMA), 35, 466, 491, 492
Canadian Newspaper Association, 195
Canadian Opera Company, 481
Canadian Out-of-Home Measurement Bureau (COMB), 387–389
Canadian Parks and Wilderness Society, 459
Canadian Radio-television and Telecommunications Commission (CRTC), 323, 331, 407, 544, 545–546, 550, 553–554, 560

Canadian Sea Turtle Network (CSTN), 487
Canadian Standards Association, 549
Canadian Television Network (CTV), 14, 90, 100, 326–329, 332, 521–522
Canadian Tire, 8, 43, 91, 442, 474, 478, 496
Canadian Tourism Commission, 35, 138
Canadian Wireless Telecommunications Association (CWTA), 531
Canadian Women's Foundation's Economic Development Fund, 21
Canal D, 333
Canal Vie, 333
Cannes Advertising Festival, 95, 565
Cannes Film Festival, 99
Cannes International Advertising Film Festival, 195
Cannon, Joseph, 446
Canon, 209
CanWest, 281, 326, 331, 332, 367, 408, 475, 551
Capital C, 3, 162, 281
Capital One, 88
Captain High Liner, 221
Carat Canada, 247
Carling, 43, 533
Carlsberg, 157, 555–556
CARP News. See FiftyPlus magazine
CASSIES, 194–195
Caterpillar, 512
CBC. See Canadian Broadcasting Corporation (CBC)
CBC Newsworld, 333
CBS Network, 327
CBS Outdoor, 385, 389, 391, 395
Census Canada, 566
Center, Allen H., 461
CFL. See Canadian Football League
Chanel, 533
Chang, Howard, 349
Change, 131
Chatelaine magazine, 296, 297, 351, 357, 358, 495
Cheese Whiz, 408
Cheerios, 72
Cherry, Don, 560
Chevrolet, 157
Children's Miracle Network, 450
Chill Magazine, 352
Chouinard, Josée, 450
Chrysler Corporation, 195, 209, 528. See also DaimlerChrysler
CHUM, 341, 522, 532
CIBC (Canadian Imperial Bank of Commerce), 8, 161, 483, 568
Cineplex Odeon Entertainment, 417
Cisco Systems, 12, 43, 459, 465
CityFlitz, 386
CityTV, 326
Claritas, 83
Clark, Glenn, 208
Clark, Heather, 530
Clorox, 221
Clover Leaf, 386
Club Sobeys, 442
CMG, 42
CN Tower, 8
Coach, 97, 98, 150
Coastal Contacts, 518

Cobra Golf, 197
Coca-Cola Company, 101, 135, 141, 437, 475
Code for Broadcast Advertising of Alcoholic Beverages, 553–554
Coffee Crisp, 88
Coffee-Mate, 444
Cogeco, 43
Colgate-Palmolive, 188
Colgate Total, 188
Colley, Russell, 129
Columbia Sportswear Company, 67, 68
ComBase, 375
Comedy Network, The, 333
Competition Act, 544, 546
Competition Bureau, 545, 546, 549
comScore, 436
Confessions of an Advertising Man (Ogilvy), 188
Connors, Stompin' Tom, 232
Le conseil des norms, 550
Consumer Drug Advertising Guidelines, 554
Consumer Protection Act of Quebec, 547
Consumer Response Council, 550
Consumer Reports magazine, 69
Consumerqueen.com, 436
Contagious Magazine, 180
Converse, 73
Coopersmith, Ryan, 3
Coors, 53
Coors Light, 6, 507
Coppertone, 443
Coppertone Sun Protection Patrol, 443
Corfman, Kim, 453
Corner Gas, 408
Corus Television, 319, 332
Cosmopolitan, 355
Cosmopolitan TV, 319
Cossette, 41, 42
Cossette Communication Group, 482
Costco, 491
Country Music Television, 333
Couponclick.ca, 436
Coupons.com, 435
Cover Girl, 109, 438
CP24, 326, 333
Craig, Robert, 566
Crankworx, 481
Crash and Burn, 162
Crescendo Rising Crust Pizza, 167–168
Crest, 141
Critical Mass, 42
Crosby, Sidney, 72, 189, 208, 209
CRTC. See Canadian Radio-television and Telecommunications Commission
CSI, 297
CTV. See Canadian Television Network
CTV.ca, 14
CTV NewsNet, 100, 333
Cube, 162
Curry, William N., 461
Cutlip, Scott M., 451

D

D'Angelo, Frank, 206
DaimlerChrysler, 424, 528
Dairy Farmers of Canada, 43
Dairy Queen, 552
Dairyland, 140

Danone, 89, 207–208
Dare Simple Pleasures, 319
DAS, 42
DDB Canada, 35, 42, 43, 196
DDB Echology, 42
Degree deodorant, 194
DeGroote School of Business, 178
DejaView, 333
Delissio, 168, 232
Dell Computer, 14
Denny's Restaurants, 421
Dentyne, 383
Dickson, Peter, 454
Dictionary of Marketing Terms (Bennett), 488
Diet Pepsi, 195
Dion, Celine, 209
Direct Mail List Rates and Data, 492
Discovery Kids, 319
Discovery Network/Channel, 333, 393–394, 500
DIY Network, 332
Dole, 12
Dollars & Sense, 329
Doner, 275
Doritos, 3
DoritosGuru.ca, 3
Double Blue, 436
Dove, 43, 129, 184, 196, 205, 212, 357, 370, 495, 514–515, 522, 564, 565
Dove Optimum Rewards, 495
Dow, Hugh, 196
Dr. Pepper, 53, 301
Draft FCB, 42
Dubow, Joel, 260
Dufferin Research, 524
Dundas Square, 383, 385–386
Dunn and Bradstreet, 492
Durfy, Sean, 217
Dusk, 332

E

E!, 328
EA, 526
Eagle One, 218, 219
Eaton Centre, 385
Echo, 160
Eddie Bauer, 496
Edward Jones, 472
Effem, 431
Ehm, Erica, 524
Eisenhart, Tom, 498
Eisler, Lloyd, 450
Elle Canada, 319, 360
eMarketer, 536
Endless Vacation, 355
Energie, 275
Energizer, 71
Energizer Bunny, 71
Environics, 83, 193
Equestrian, 481
Esquire, 360
Esso, 480
eTalk Daily, 477
Etc.tv, 233
Ethos, 42
Evian, 182
Exclaim!, 356, 481
Extra Awards, 195

F

Fab Shop program, 459
Facebook, 3, 15, 524–526
Fairchild Television, 333
Familiprix, 195
Family Channel, The, 333
Family Guy, 296
Family Literacy Day, 477

Famous, 351
Farris, Paul, 570–571
Fashion, 360
Fashion Shops, 362
Fashion Television, 532
Ferguson, James, 571
Fido, 166, 443, 481, 534
FiftyPlus magazine, 357
Figure Skating Canada, 481
Financial Post, 475
Fine Living Canada, 332
Five Alive, 169–170
Fjord Interactive, 42
Flare, 360, 361, 364
Fleishman-Hillard Canada, 3, 42, 474
FLO, 462
Flyp Media, 360
Food & Drink, 351, 352
Food and Drugs Act and Regulations, 554
Food Banks Canada, 477
Food Network, The, 333
Foote, Cone & Belding, 235
Ford Motor Company, 124, 125, 140, 312, 535, 552
Ford of Canada, 46, 552
Forrester Research, 324
Fortune 500, 492
Fortune magazine, 360
4Refuel, 286
Fox Television, 327
Fox, Stephen, 562
Frito-Lay. See Hostess Frito-Lay
Fubar, 167
Fuel Industries, 526
Fusion Alliance Marketing, 42, 482
Future Shop, 548

G

Galbraith, John Kenneth, 561
Gallup and Robinson, 264–265
Gap, The, 81, 82, 442, 490, 496–497
Gardener, Elizabeth, 455
Garnier, 503
Gatchel, Robert, 260
Gatorade, 168–169, 209, 421
Gaz Métro, 199
General Electric (GE), 228
General Mills, 435–436, 472, 473
General Mills Canada, 437
General Motors (GM), 405, 406, 463, 481
GGRP, 487
Gillette Co., 41
Global News, 475
Global Television Network, 327–328, 332, 407
Globalive, 514
Globe and Mail, The, 136, 297, 366, 367, 377, 550–551
Glow magazine, 495
GM Canada, 407, 463
Godes, David, 99
Golf Pride, 224
Golf Town, 349
Good Times, 319
Good Year Tires, 224
Google, 474, 517, 519, 520, 521, 538
Gorn, Gerald, 114
Gould, Stephen, 410
Gould/Pace University, 405
GQ magazine, 360
Grand Prix, 195
Green, Corliss L., 566
Grey Advertising, 42, 487, 520
Greyser, Stephen, 561

Grip Limited, 54, 196
Grolsch, 88, 157
GroupM, 42
Gucci, 6
Guide to Food Labelling and Advertising, 554
Guidelines for Cosmetic Advertising and Labelling Claims, 554
Guinness, 14
Guitar Hero, 409
Gundlach, Gregory, 446
Gupta, Pola, 410

H
H.J. Heinz Co., 80, 108
Habbo Hotel, 527
Haefner, James, 555
Halo, 80
Hallmark, 189, 190
Happy Planet, 150
Harbinger Communications, 564
Harper, Stephen, 262
HarperCollins, 429
Harris, Thomas L., 467
Harris/Telmar, 375
Harry magazine, 352, 354
Harry Rosen, 207, 352
Harvard Business Review, 313
Harvey's, 6, 158, 163–165
Hasbro, 435
Haskins, Jack, 260
Hawkins, Scott, 108
Hayek, Salma, 550
HBC (Hudson's Bay Company), 352, 442, 475, 498
HBC Rewards, 498
Head and Shoulders, 166
Health Canada, 544, 546, 554
Heart and Stroke Foundation, 28, 329, 476, 477
Heart, The, 477
Heart Truth campaign, 477
Heavy Construction magazine, 354
Heckler, Susan, 264
Heinz. See H.J. Heinz Co.
Hellman's, 43, 281
Hello!, 356
Henderson Bas, 42, 530
Herbal Essences, 130
Hervieux, Marc, 337
Hewlett-Packard, 469
HGTV, 332, 333
Hill & Knowlton, 42
Hirschman, Elizabeth, 180
Historia, 333
History Television, 332, 333
Hitachi, 105, 218, 320, 321
Hoch, Stephen, 108
Hockey Canada, 481
Hockey Hall of Fame, 480
Hockey News, The, 357, 362
Hockey Night in Canada, 280, 329, 420–421, 459
Holt Renfrew, 362, 480
Holt's magazine, 362
Home Depot, 312, 496
Homemakers magazine, 319, 483
Honda Motor Co./Honda Canada, 83, 90, 169, 417, 468, 477
Hostess Frito-Lay, 3, 428
Hour, The, 459
House Beautiful, 295
Houston, Michael, 264
Hudson's Bay Company. See HBC
Hueber, Graham, 470
Hugo Boss, 352
Hunt, Shelby, 562
Hutchinson, Craig, 18

Hydro Quebec, 199
Hyundai, 90, 358, 359

I
IBM, 51, 190, 475
Identics, 42
IKEA, 6, 467, 496, 566
IKEA Canada, 467
IMS, 375
In Style, 355
In Touch Weekly, 355
Indigo, 478
Industry Canada, 546
Info Canada, 492
Information Resources Inc., 267
ING Direct, 530
ING Investment Management, 535
Inman and McAlister, 432
Institute of Communications and Advertising (ICA), 40, 50, 51, 184, 194
Institute of Marriage and Family, 543
Intel Corporation, 140, 449
Interact Direct Marketing, 496
Interactive Advertising Bureau of Canada, 517, 533–535, 537–538
International Advertising Association, 567–568, 572
International Communications Group, 294
Internet Advertising Bureau, 536
Internet Protocol Television (IPTV), 522
Interpublic, 41, 42
Intrawest, 503, 531
iPod, 84
Ipsos-ASI, 247, 258, 264, 266–267
Ipsos Reid, 262, 301, 436, 478

J
J.D. Power & Associates, 472
Jackson-Triggs, 13
James Ready Beer, 337
Janssen-Ortho, 531
Jeep, 223, 312
Jennings, Peter, 471
Jergens, 164, 208
Joe Fresh, 564
Joe's Jeans, 6
Johnnie Walker, 48
Jones, 260
Jones, John, 313
Joshua Perets, 73
Journal of Advertising Research, 513
Juicy Fruit, 170–171
Jumpstart, 478
Juniper Park, 281
Jupiter MediaMetrics, 536
Just for Laughs, 201–202
JWT (J. Walter Thompson), 41, 42, 183
JWT Sauce, 42

K
Kamp, Edward, 200
Kantar, 42
Karacters, 35
Kates, Steven, 563
Keg Steakhouse, 5
Kellaris, James J., 114
Keller, Kevin, 264
Kellogg Company, 189, 434
Kellogg's, 422, 427, 434
Ketchum Effectiveness Yardstick (KEY), 470
Ketchum Public Relations, 42, 469–470

Kia/Kia Canada, 177, 552
Kidthink, 35
Kim, Tanya, 477
Kinder Surprise, 77
Kit-Kat, 137
KitchenAid, 476
Kivilo, Alar, 320
Knorr, 193, 490, 493
Kokanee, 6, 231, 556
Koo Creative, 42
Koodo, 192, 526
Kool-Aid, 221
Kraft Canada, 63, 167–168, 192, 474, 479
Kraft Dinner, 63
Kraft-General Foods, 221, 477
Kraft Hockeyville, 479–480
Kraft Peanut Butter, 63
Krugman, Herbert, 108

L
L'Oréal Canada, 20, 21, 109
La Fête de la Pub, 195
LaBarbera, Priscilla, 260
Labatt Blue, 87, 512
Labatt Breweries of Canada, 6, 54, 80, 233, 436, 531, 532, 555–556, 570
Lamar Transit, 389
Lambesis, 238
Lancôme, 114
Land's End, 159, 490
LaPointe, Kirk, 370
Lavidge, Robert, 104, 131–132
Lavo, 131
Lay's, 161, 219, 220, 281, 337, 420–421
Le Grand blond avec un show surnois, 407
Lee Valley Tools, 496
Legends of Hockey, 480
Leger Marketing, 474
Lemar, 395
Lenovo, 354, 355
Leo Burnett, 41, 42
Leo Burnett Agency, 180, 189, 265
Les Jutra, 477
Lever Pond's of Canada, 193
Levi Strauss & Co., 58, 481, 530
Lexus, 90, 352, 360, 399
LG Electronics, 136, 417
Library and Archives Canada, 370
Lifestyle, 498
Liking, Rob, 10
Lindenmann, Walter, 469
Link, 262
LinkedIn, 524
Lions awards, 195
Lipton, 161
Liquor Control Board of Ontario, 227
Listerine, 166, 171–172, 195, 220
Little Boy Games, 522
Liu, Lucy, 189
Loblaw Companies Ltd., 8, 17, 18
Loblaws, 8, 18, 206, 450, 564
Local 416, 444
Long and Strong, 503
Looking Glass Foundation, 337
Lorain, Sophie, 207–208
Lord, Kenneth, 410
Lotus HAL, 469
Loulou, 362
Love of Reading Foundation, 478
Low, George, 299, 315
Lowe Roche, 42
Lowery, Pamela, 555
Lowes, 252
Lucky, 362
Lysyj, Lesya, 383

M
Ma Maison Rona, 407
MacInnis, Deborah J., 200
MacLaren McCann, 42
MacLaren Momentum, 42
MacLaren MRM, 42
Maclean's, 280, 299, 358, 361–362
Magazine Impact Research Service (MIRS), 264–265
Magnet Search, 42
Major League Baseball (MLB), 204
Mangleburg, Tamara, 560
Manitoba Community Newspapers Association, 372
Manning, Eli, 139
Mansbridge One on One, 475
Manulife Financial Corp., 8
Maple Leaf Foods Inc., 461, 474
Maple Lodge Farms, 23
Marcelle, 207
March of Dimes, 5
Marketing Magazine, 41, 42, 58, 63, 184, 195, 367, 474
MarketSource, 267
Marks Work Wearhouse, 86
Marriott International, 182
Mars Corporation, 431
Martha Stewart Living, 355
Marvel comics, 428
Maserati, 7, 496
Maslow, Abraham, 67, 562
MasterCard, 452
MasterCard International, 204
Matta, Tony, 3
Maxim, 355
Maxwell House, 63
Maybelline, 82
Maytag, 189, 221
Mazda, 275
Mazlin, Diane, 99
McAlister, 432
McCain Foods, 167–168
McCain, Michael, 461
McCann-Erickson Worldwide, 203, 204
McCollum Spielman Worldwide (MSW), 252, 259
McCracken, Grant, 210, 211
McDonald's Restaurants, 127, 172, 189, 196, 429, 435, 438, 465, 523
McGee, Christine, 344
McGill University Alumni, 499
McGuire, William, 104
McMaster University, 178
MDC Partners, 41, 42
Mediabrands Canada, 196, 349
Media Company, The, 247
Media Experts, 349
Media Merchants of Vancouver, 388
MediaBrands, 42
MediaCom, 247
Mediaweek, 325
Melitta Coffee, 29
Men's Health, 355
Mentadent, 219
Mercedes-Benz, 200, 352
Mercedes-Benz Canada, 200
Messier, Mark, 421
Metro, 366, 370
Metromedia, 394
Metromedia Plus, 389, 395
Meunier, Claude, 191
Microsoft Corp., 72, 80, 217, 296, 497, 522, 526
Miles Thirst, 527
Milestone's, 441

Millward Brown, 258, 262, 513
Mini, 173, 232
The Mirror Makers: A History of American Advertising and Its Creators (Fox), 562
Mittal, Banwari, 555
Moen, 66
Mohr, Jakki, 299, 315
Molson Breweries, 368, 507, 560, 570
Molson Canadian, 87, 195, 507, 512, 525–526, 531
Molson Canadian Amphitheatre, 526
Molson-Coors, 6
Molson Dry, 507
Molson Export, 191
Montblanc, 5
Montreal Canadiens, 8
Montreal Gazette, 168
Montreal Scope, 358
Moore's Clothing for Men, 171
Moosehead Breweries, 58, 555–556
More, 319
Moriarty, Sandra, 184
Motor Trend, 69, 472
Motorola Electronics, 209
Motts Fruitsations, 164
Mountain Dew, 442
Mountain Equipment Co-op (MEC), 459
Movie Channel, The, 331
Movie Entertainment, 351
Movie Network. See The Movie Network
Mr. Sub, 53
MRI, 536
MS&L, 42
MSN Canada, 513
MSNSpaces, 524
MTV, 73
Much On Demand, 443
MuchMoreMusic, 333
MuchMusic, 3, 333, 438, 522, 532
Musique Plus, 275, 438
Myers Reports, 293
Myers, John, 153, 293, 294
MySpace, 524
Mystery, 333

N

Nabob, 72
NanoWax, 218, 219
NASCAR, 252
Nash, Steve, 211
National Ballet of Canada, 88
National Basketball Association (NBA), 211
National Geographic, 16, 355, 487
National Geographic Society, 491
National Hockey League (NHL), 189, 204, 420–421, 479–481
National Hockey League Alumni, 480
National Hockey League Players Association, 479–481
National Post, 295, 297, 366, 376, 377
Nature Valley, 520
NBC Network, 327
Nestea, 97, 98, 142
Nestlé, 166, 550–551
Nestlé Canada, 58
Netherlands Institute of Public Opinion, 265
Network Solutions, 563, 564
Neutrogena, 198, 199

New York Fries, 85, 166, 239–240
NEWAD, 389, 397, 443
Newspaper Audience Databank Inc. (NADbank), 372–375
NHL. See National Hockey League
Nice'n Easy, 450
Nichol, Dave, 18
Nielsen Media Research, 308, 310, 333–334, 436
Nielsen Net Ratings, 536
Nike, 84, 97, 204–205, 223, 402, 480, 520
Nintendo, 180
Nissan, 21, 162, 191, 281, 526, 531
No Frills, 18
Nolin BBDO, 388
Nordica, 352
Northstar, 42
Northwestern University, 17
Nova Scotia Office of Health Promotion, 167
Novell, 465
Nubody's Fitness, 493
Nucleus, 42
Nutella, 241
Nuvo magazine, 356

O

O, The Oprah Magazine, 355
O'Toole, John, 188
O.K. Tire, 438–439
OBN, 389
Ogilvy, 43, 281
Ogilvy & Mather, 41, 42, 196, 262, 565
OgilvyAction, 42
OgilvyOne, 42
Ogilvy, David, 188, 203
Ohanian, Roobina, 205–206
Olay Ribbons, 230
Old Navy, 301
Olson, Jerry, 72
Olympic Games, 459, 475
OMD Canada, 3, 42
Omnicom, 41, 42
Ontario Community Newspapers Association, 372
Ontario Milk Producer magazine, 353
Ontario Produce Farmer magazine, 353
OpenRoad Auto Group, 90
Optimum, 42
Oral B, 65
Orser, Brian, 450
Osprey Media Group, 366
Ostlund, Lyman, 260
Ostrow, Joseph, 292, 294
Ottawa Citizen, 370
Ottawa Senators, 421
Oulton, Joe, 337
Out-of-Home Marketing Association (OMAC), 389–391, 394, 399
Outdoor Advertising Consumer Exposure Study (OACES), 391

P

P&G Canada, 19
Page, Graham, 262
Palm, 66
Palm + Havas, 95
Palmer, Frank, 196
Panasonic, 474
Parent, Jeff, 21
Parissa Wax Strips, 388

Patak Taste of India, 4
Pattison Outdoor, 385, 387, 389, 391, 397
PBS, 327
Peckham, James O., 310, 311
Peek Freans, 424, 425
Pennzoil, 439
People magazine, 355
PepsiCo., 80, 153, 191–192, 195, 420–421, 442, 538
Percy, Larry, 86–89, 115, 117, 118, 134, 165, 236–238, 270
Perrier, 443
Perron, Marie-Claude, 275
Peter, J. Paul, 72
Petro-Canada, 8
Petty, Richard, 112
PGA, 204
Pharmaprix^{MD}, 495
Philadelphia cream cheese, 192
Philips Electronics, 132, 133, 141
PhotoLife, 356
Pillsbury, 437
Ping, 72
Playland, 182
Pogo, 48, 79, 80
Point of Purchase Advertising Institute (POPAI), 447
Pollay, Richard, 562
Polo Ralph Lauren, 564
Porsche Cars North America, Inc., 67, 68, 100, 494, 496
Porter Airlines, 88–89, 152
Porter Noveli, 42
Powerade, 169, 480
PowerBar, 211
PowerWise, 123
Prada, 6
Prairie Milk Marketing Partnership, 138
Premium Plus, 63
President's Choice, 474
Primus, 288
Print Measurement Bureau (PMB), 364, 566
PRIZM$_{NE}$, 83
PRIZM C2, 83
Process Equipment and Control News, 354
Procter & Gamble, 19, 38, 109, 189, 301, 438, 447, 450, 455, 513, 532, 570
Promotion Decisions Inc., 421
Promotional Marketing Association, 429
Promotional Products Association of Canada, 466
Promotional Products Association International (PPAI), 401
Promotional Products Professionals of Canada (PPPC), 401
Protocol, 55
Provincial Business Directory, 492
Proximity, 3, 41
Public Relations on the Internet (Holtz),
Publicis Canada/Worldwide, 42
Publicité Club de Montréal, 194

Q

Quatre Saisons, 327–328
Quebec Community Newspapers Association, 372
Quebec Federation of Milk Producers, 195, 388
Quipp, Jeff, 521

R

Radar, 42
Radiate, 42
Radio Advertising Bureau, 339
Radio-Canada, 326–328, 521
Radio Marketing Bureau (RMB), 342
Radio Shack, 83
Raghubir, Priya, 453
Raphaelson, Joel, 203
Rapp Collins Worldwide, 42
Ray, Michael, 106, 107, 203
RBC Financial Group, 8, 131, 168, 192–193, 221
RDI, 333
RDS, 333
Reach 400 Max, 407
Reactine, 531
Reader's Digest, 295, 351
Reality in Advertising (Reeves), 188
Red Baron, 329
Red Bull, 150
Red Bull Crashed Ice, 443
Red Dress Fashion Show, 477
Redworks, 42
Reebok, 189
Reeves, Rosser, 188
Reitmans, 43, 160
Relay, 324
Report on Business magazine, 367
Report on Business Television, 329, 333
Res Publica, 42
Research in Motion, 8
Residence Inn, 182
Rethink, 182, 196, 388
Rice Krispies, 5
Richard Manville Research, 405
Richards, Lauren, 48
Rickards, 157
Ries, Al, 153, 189
Ripley, M. Louise, 39
Rivet, 42
Ritz, 63
RMG Connect, 42
Road & Track magazine, 69
RoadRunner Sports, 529
Rocket XL, 42
Roddick, Andy, 189
Rogers, 6, 8, 144–145, 149, 493, 534, 551, 569
Rogers Cup, 481
Rogers Media, 360
Rogers SportsNet, 333
Rogers Wireless, 230, 367
Rogers@Home, 144
Rona, 407, 459
Ronald McDonald, 221
Roper ASW, 263
Rossignol, 352
Rossiter, John, 86–89, 115, 117, 118, 134, 165, 236–238, 270
Rotfeld, Herbert, 201
Royal Bank of Canada. See RBC Financial Group
Royal Vancouver Yacht Club, 499
Run for the Cure, 483, 568
RunTO, 480

S

Saatchi & Saatchi, 42
Salomon, 352
Salveson, Melvin, 306
Samplesaint.com, 436
Samsung Electronics, 421
Saskatchewan Weekly Newspapers Association, 372
Save.ca, 435
Sawyer, Alan, 454

Scantrack, 267
Schick Canada, 158
Schreiber and Associates, 404
Schroer, James, 313
Schultz, Don, 17
Score Television Network, The, 333
Scotiabank, 329
Scott, Linda, 232
Sears, 72
Series+, 333
Science World, 182
Scope, 171
Scotiabank, 8, 170, 417
Scott, Linda, 232
Scream, 332
Seadoo, 6
Seagram, 266–267, 270
Search Engine People, 521
Sears, 490, 496, 503
Second Clothing, 200
Segal, 42
Seiko, 139
Senses, 101
7-Eleven, 531
Shade Brigade, 109
Sharapova, Maria, 209
Shavitt, Sharon, 555
Shaw-Garlock, Glenda, 563
Shell Canada, 128, 551
Sheng, Sui, 48
Shoppers Drug Mart, 53, 109, 450, 474, 495
Shoppers Optimum, 495
Shopping Channel. See The Shopping Channel (TSC)
Shopping Clin d'oeil, 362
SHOPTV Canada, 326
Showcase, 333
Showcase Action, 333
Showcase Diva, 332, 333
Shreddies, 5, 43, 63, 195
Sid Lee, 443
Sierra Club Canada, 551
Silk Canada, 538
Silk Soymilk, 226
Simon, Andrew, 35
6 Degrees, 42
Ski Canada, 352
Skiing, 295
Skyy Spirits, 558
Skyy Vodka, 238
Sleep Country Canada, 344
SMRB, 536
Snapple, 512
Snowfest, 444
Snuggie, 35, 219
Sobeys, 442
Soley, Lawrence, 566
Solo Mobile, 182
Sonicare, 141
Sony Corp., 465, 474
Space, 333
Special K, 48
Spider-Man, 526–527
SponsorScope, 482
Sponsorship Marketing Council of Canada, 479
Sports Illustrated, 355
Sprint Canada, 499
Sprite, 312, 527
Sprize, 442
St. Huberts, 221
Stanley Cup, 420–421
Staples, 301, 474
Star Académie, 20
Starch Ad Readership Report, 263–264

Starcom MediaVest Group (SMG), 42, 48
Starweek, 351
Statistics Canada, 375, 492, 512
Steel, Jon, 183
Steiner, Gary, 104, 131–132
Steiner, Robert, 571
Stella Artois, 532
Steve Nash Foundation, 211
Stevens, Penny, 349
Stevenson, Fiona, 109
Stojko, Elvis, 450
Strateco-Blitz, 42
Strategic Business Insights, 82
Strategic Planning Institute, 8
Strategy magazine, 35, 43, 48, 184, 195, 281, 459, 487, 522
Style at Home, 91
Su, Kim Ssang,
Subaru, 35, 107, 194, 219, 322
Sudler & Hennessy, 42
SUN TV, 326
Sun-Rype, 76
Sunkist, 307
Sunlight, 195
Sunsilk, 423
Super Bowl, 233
Supernatural, 332
Surmanek, Jim, 294,
Survivor, 297
Suzuki, David, 123
Swiffer, 48
Swiss Chalet, 6, 232
Swiss Water Decaffeinated Coffee Company, 139–140
Sympatico. See Bell Sympatico
Syngenta, 466, 487
Szego, Michael, 262

T

Tabi/Tabi International, 483
TAG Heuer, 41, 209
Talk Broadband, 288
Tango, 153
Target Marketing and Communications, 487
Tassimo, 48
Taxi, 43, 196, 222, 388, 522
TBWA Worldwide, 42, 182
TD Bank Financial Group, 8
Team Sports Radio Network, 341
Ted Bates agency, 188
Tele-Quebec, 326–328
Telecommunications Act of 1993, 545
Telelatino, 333
Teletoon, 221, 333, 428
Television Bureau of Canada (TVB), 195, 336, 342
Television Quatre Saisons, 326–328
Telser, Lester, 570
Telus/Telus Mobility, 22, 149, 181, 192, 212, 367, 530–531
Telus World Ski and Snowboard Festival, 481
Temptations, 431
Testostérone, 407
The Movie Channel, 331
The Nature of Things, 475
The Score, 532, 539
The Shopping Channel (TSC), 497–498
The Sports Network. See TSN
Thermasilk, 312
This Hour Has 22 Minutes, 168
Tide, 90, 248
Tim Hortons, 8, 12, 232, 474

Tim Hortons Children's Foundation, 474
Time/Time Canada, 266, 360
Time, Inc., 266, 270
Titan 360, 389
TiVo, 324
TNS Canadian Facts, 69, 519
Top Drawer Creative, 349
Toronto District School Board, 548
Toronto Hydro Telecom, 43
Toronto International Film Festival, 13, 480
Toronto Life, 358
Toronto Maple Leafs, 8
Toronto Raptors, 3
Toronto Star, 295, 312
Toronto Transit Commission (TTC), 543
Tourism Kelowna, 27
Tourism Yukon, 496
Toyota Canada, 131, 219, 463
Toyota Motor Company, 22, 88, 90, 138, 156, 160, 169, 299, 343, 398, 463, 474
Trade Show Bureau, 451
Tragos, Bill, 182
Transcontinental, 319
Transformers: Revenge of the Fallen, 388
Travel, 295
Travel Alberta, 388, 517
Treehouse, 319, 333
Tribal, 35
Tribute, 351
Trident, 171
Trivedi, Minakshi, 455
Trojan, 222
Tropicana, 70
Trout, Jack, 153, 189
Truth, Lies & Advertising: The Art of Account Planning (Steel), 183
TSN, 331, 333, 443
Tucciarone, Joel, 260
TV5, 333
TVTropolis, 333
TV/A, 327–328
24, 177
24 hours, 366
Twinings, 79
Twitter, 524
Tyco, 475

U

U.S. Organic Orange Growers, 167
Ubisoft, 526
Ultra Tide, 110–111
Under Armor, 352, 353
Unilever, 51, 98–99, 212, 262, 477, 491, 535, 543
Union Station, 388
United Way, 5, 343, 370, 568
Universal Studios, 535

V

V-8, 156
Vachon, 548
Vakratsas, 115
Valpak, 435
Valvoline, 161
Vancouver Magazine, 358
Vancouver Sun, 370
Vander Zalm, Bill, 208
Vaughn, Richard, 235, 236
Varvatos, John, 73
Venture Communications, 388
Veritas, 42
Verkade, Gabriel, 495

Versace, 6
Via Rail, 8, 159
Viagra, 43, 222
Vice magazine, 356, 361
Victoria's Secret, 491, 502
Vim, 262
Virgin Mobile, 477
Virgin Radio, 543
Visa, 29, 107, 204
Vision TV, 333
Viva, 319
Vocalpoint, 513
Volkswagen, 95, 222, 229
Volkswagen Jetta, 229
Volvo, 444, 523
Volvo Cars of Canada, 444
Vonk, Nancy, 196
VRAK TV, 333

W

W Movie, 319
W Network, 319, 333
W.K. Buckley Limited, 226
Walmart, 131, 301, 423, 566
Warner Music, 531
Watson, Paul, 260
WD-40 Fan Club, 441
Weather Network, 196, 289, 333
Weilbacher, William, 115, 197
Wendy's, 136
West Valley Market, 388
Western Union, 91
West49, 73
WestJet, 5, 53, 151–154, 166, 173, 217, 343
Weston, Galen, 18
Westworld, 351
What!, 356
What's Cooking magazine, 351
Whirlpool, 51, 476
Whiskas, 431
Whistler Ski Resort, 503
White Swan, 163
Wilson, 447
Wind Mobile, 514
Windows Live, 524
Windows 7, 296, 522
Wired magazine, 354
Wish, 91
Women's Health, 355
Women's World, 355
Wonder, 164
World News Tonight, 471
WPP, 42
Wrigley Canada, 481
Wunderman, 42

X

Xbox 360, 80

Y

Yahoo!, 517, 521
Yoo and Mandhachitara, 308
Young and Rubicam, 42, 53, 289
Young, James Webb, 183
YouTube, 3, 15, 522
YTV, 221, 319, 333
Yummy Mummy Club, 524
Yves Rocher, 160, 496

Z

Zehrs, 18
Zellers, 450
Zenith, 42
ZenithOptimedia, 349
Zig, 42, 262
Zinc Research, 524
Zoom Media, 389, 397
Ztele, 333

SUBJECT INDEX

A

ability, 113
absolute cost
  definition, 296
  magazine advertising, 361
  newspaper advertising, 370–371
  outdoor media, 392
  place-based media, 399
  product placement, 409
  promotional products marketing media, 404
  radio advertising, 338
  television advertising, 323
  transit media, 396
acceleration tool, 418
account executive, 46
account planners, 45
account planning, 45, 183–184
account services, 46
account-specific marketing, 423
accountability, 17, 422
ACT theatre methodology, 259
action, 129
activities, interests, and opinions (AIOs), 82
actual state, 65
ad execution-related thoughts, 111
advertiser control, 567–568
advertisers, 15–16
advertising, 4, 6, 7, 9–11
  advocacy, 476
  bad taste, 557–559
  business-to-business, 11
  carryover effect, 126
  cause-related, 476–479
  children and, 559–560
  classifications of, 11
  classified, 368
  communication task, 129
  consumer manipulation and, 562–563
  consumer markets, 11
  cooperative, 448–449
  corporate. See corporate advertising
  creative strategy. See creative strategy
  creative tactics. See creative tactics
  deceptive, 555–557
  definition, 11
  demonstration, 218–219
  direct-response advertising, 13, 497
  display, 367–368
  economic effects of, 568–573
  ethical effects of, 555–560
  features of, 9–10
  feedback, measurement of, 101
  general, 368
  image, 188–189, 475–476
  importance of, 10
  in-flight, 394
  information, and, 572–573
  Internet companies, by, 517–526
  limits, 545
  local, 11, 368
  magazines. See magazine advertising

market power, and, 571–572
market type, and, 5
materialism and, 561–562
media and, 566–568
media strategy, 29
movement away from, 19
mystery ads, 204
national, 11, 368
nature and purpose, 10
network, 326–328
newspaper, 367–368
nonpersonal component, 12
offensive, 557–559
paid component, 11–12
primary demand, 11
print. See print advertising
professional, 11
radio. See radio advertising
reminder, 71
retail, 11
search engine, 520–524
selective demand, 11
slice-of-life, 220
social benefit and, 568
social effects of, 560–568
special, 368
specialty, 401
sponsorship, 328–329, 520
spot, 328
stereotyping and, 563–566
subliminal perception, 71
teaser, 204
television. See television advertising
tobacco, 546–547
trade, 11, 419
transit, 393
untruthful, 555–557
virtual, 407
advertising agencies, 16, 38–54
  account services, 46
  accountability, 50
  agency-client partnership, 58–59
  compensation, 47–54
  creative boutiques, 46–47
  creative services, 42–44
  definition, 16
  evaluation of, 51–52
  family tree, 41, 42
  financial audit, 51
  full-service, 42–46
  IMC services. See IMC services
  in-house agency, 38–40
  industry, 41
  long-term relationships, 59
  losing clients, 52–54
  management issues. See management issues
  marketing services, 44–45
  media buying services, 47
  option, 40
  qualitative audit, 51
  responsibility for IMC, 57–58
  services offered, 56–57
  specialized services, 54–56
  subsidiaries, as, 55, 57
  superagencies, 41
advertising appeal, 197–199
advertising campaign, 187

advertising creativity. See also creative strategy; creative tactics
  definition, 178–179
  importance of, 179–181
  objections to testing, 250
  perspectives on, 180
advertising effectiveness
  avoiding costly mistakes, 248
  budgeting decisions, 248
  costs of measurement, 249
  creative strategy decisions, 250
  creative theme/idea, 250
  decisions for measurement, 250–253
  essentials of effective testing, 270–271
  evaluating alternative strategies, 248–249
  field tests, 253
  framework, 116
  increasing advertising efficiency, 249
  laboratory tests, 252
  measurement debate, 248–250
  measurement methods. See measurement methods
  media decisions, 250
  objections of creative specialists, 250
  PACT (Positioning Advertising Copy Testing), 269–271
  posttests, 251, 252, 263–268
  pretests, 251–252
  program for measuring, 268–271
  promotional tools, 251–252
  reasons for measurement, 248–249
  reasons for non-measurement, 249–250
  research problems, 249
  response model, 115–116
  testing bias, 252
  what to test, 249, 250–251
  when to test, 251–252
  where to test, 252–253
advertising manager, 36–37
advertising regulations
  Advertising Standards Council, Canada, in, 547–554
  Competition Act, 546
  CRTC (Canadian Radiotelevision and Telecommunications Commission), 545–546
  Internet, 545
  Quebec regulations on children's advertising, 547
  tobacco advertising, 546–547
Advertising Standards Council
  alcohol, 553–554
  Canadian Code of Advertising Standards, 548–549
  children's advertising, 554
  clearance process, 553–554
  complaints for debate, 552–553
  complaints process, 550–551
  complaints report, 551–552
  cosmetics, 554
  food, 554

  Gender Portrayal Guidelines, 550
  non-prescription drugs, 554
advertising units, 295
advocacy advertising, 476
affect, 115
affect referral decision rule, 74, 115
affective stage, 104
affective strategy, 236
affiliates, 326, 327
affordable method, 305–306
agate line, 376
agencies. See advertising agencies
agency compensation
  commission system, 47–49
  cost-plus system, 50
  fee arrangement systems, 49–50
  fee-commission combination, 49
  fixed-fee method, 49
  incentive-based system, 50–51
  negotiated commission, 49
  percentage charges, 50
agency of record (AOR), 53
agents, 99
AIDA model, 103–104
airline transit media, 398–399
alcohol, 545, 553–554
alpha activity, 261
alternative evaluation
  bundles of attributes, 72
  evaluative criteria, 71–72
  evoked set, 71
  functional benefits, 72
  functional consequences, 72
  implications, 114–115
  reminder advertising, 71
  top-of-mind awareness, 71
alternative response hierarchies
  dissonance/attribution model, 106–107
  implications of, 108–109
  low-involvement hierarchy, 108
  standard learning model, 106
alternative strategies, 248–249
animatic, 186
animation, 220–221
applications, 533
arbitrary allocation, 306
art department, 43
aspirational reference group, 77
association tests, 185
associative process, 114
attention
  magazine advertising, 361
  newspaper advertising, 371
  outdoor media, 391
  place-based media, 400
  product placement, 410
  promotional products marketing media, 404
  radio advertising, 340
  television advertising, 321–322
  transit media, 397
attentiveness, 295
attitude toward the ad, 111–112
attitudes, 72, 112
  brand attitude, 118, 141
  change strategies, 163–165
  elaboration likelihood, 112
  importance of, 69
  influence on, 163–164

multiattribute attitude model, 163
salient beliefs, 162
study of, 70
target audience brand attitude, 162–165
attractiveness
described, 206
familiarity, 206, 208
identification, 206–207
likability, 206, 207–208
similarity, 206, 207
attributes
add new belief, 164
influence belief, 163–164
influence belief of competitor brand, 164–165
influence importance, 164
attribution theory, 454
audience
airline transit media, 399
external, 464
internal, 464
Internet marketing, 533–534
magazine readership, 364
media publicity, 472
options, 86–89
share of, 336
target, 79, 129–130, 168–171, 464–466
target audience coverage, 285–287
target audience decision, 78–89
total, 364
audience contact, 19–20
audience measurement
audience measures, 335–336
average quarter-hour (AQH) figures, 342
average quarter-hour rating (AQH RTG), 342
average quarter-hour share (AQH SHR), 342
cume, 342
diary, 334–335
Internet, 533–534
magazine advertising, 364
newspaper advertising, 374–375
outdoor media, 387–391
portable people meter (PPM), 334–335
product placements, 410
program rating, 335–336
promotional products marketing media, 404–405
radio, 342
ratings point, 335–336
reporting, 336
resources, 342
share of audience, 336
technology, 336
television, 334–336
audio messages, 234
audio portion of commercial, 231–232
audiotex, 498
average frequency, 294
average quarter-hour (AQH) figures, 342
average quarter-hour rating (AQH RTG), 342
average quarter-hour share (AQH SHR), 342
awareness, 129, 512

B

backlit posters, 385
bad taste advertising, 557–559
banner ads, 518–519

barrier to entry, 569
behavioural learning theory
continuous reinforcement schedule, 427
intermittent reinforcement schedule, 427
operant conditioning, 426
partial reinforcement schedule, 427
reinforcement, 427
schedules of reinforcement, 427
shaping, 427
behavioural objectives
IMC plan, 28
options for, 134–138
public relations plan, 466
purchase-related behaviour, 136–137
repeat consumption, 137–138
repeat purchase, 128, 135–136
sales growth, 126–128
trial purchase, 128, 134–135
behavioural stage, 105
behavioural targeting, 516
behaviouristic segmentation
definition, 84
loyalty, 84
situation, 85
usage rate, 84–85
user status, 84
beliefs, 162–163
benchmark measures, 130
benefit segmentation, 85
Bessies, 195
billboards, 385
bleed pages, 359
blocking chart, 299–300
blog, 523–524
body copy, 229–230
bonus packs, 440
bottom-up budgeting, 305
objective and task method, 309–310
payout plan, 310–311
bounce-back coupons, 434
brain waves, 261
brand, 6
levels of relationships with, 203–204
brand attitude, 118, 141, 279
media objectives, 279
persuasion, 163–165
target audience, 162–165
brand attitude model, 163
brand-attitude grid tactics, 237–241
brand awareness, 118, 140, 279
brand awareness tactics, 236–237
brand benefit, 160–162
brand comparisons, 219
Brand Development Index (BDI), 287, 288
brand equity, 7, 424–425, 453–455
brand history, 295
brand identification, 6
brand image, 188–189, 512–513
brand-loyal customers, 86, 168–169
brand loyalty, 74, 295, 421, 527, 569
brand management systems, 39
brand manager, 37
brand names, 6
positioning by, 159
brand position, 153, 155–156, 480–481
brand positioning strategy assessment, 155

brand benefit, 160–162
brand-loyal customers, 168–169, 170
brand position, 153, 155–156
brand switchers, 169, 170–171
buyer decisions, 173
central positioning, 160
by competitor, 155
competitor's position, 155
consumer purchase motive, 165–167
corporate brands, 173
decision-making, 158
decision process, 154–157
definition, 153
determining, 156
differential advantage, 159–162, 168
encouraging retailers to display brands, 445
extensions, 172–173
illustration by attributes, 154
illustration by benefits, 154
intellectual stimulation, 171–172
implementing, 156
maintain trade support for established brands, 444–445
market definition, 158–159, 167–168
market partition, 154–155
market position, 158–159
monitoring, 157
monitoring position, 159
multiple target audiences, 172–173
new category users, 169–170
options, 154–157
position by brand name, 159
position by end benefit, 158–159
position by product category, 159
position by usage situation, 159
price/quality, by, 159
problem-solution, 171
process, 154–158
product attributes and benefits, by, 151
product class, by, 166–167
product life cycle, 160
product user, by, 160–161
purchase motivation, 171–172
repositioning, 167–172
salient attributes, 153
salient benefits, 154
target audience, 162–165, 168–171
use or application, by, 159
user positioning, 160–162
brand proliferation, 421–422
brand purchase facilitation, 142
brand purchase intention, 118, 141–142
brand re-trial objective, 135
brand re-trial purchase, 135
brand relationships, 203–204
brand repeat purchase, 279
brand repositioning strategy, 167–172
differential advantage, 168
market definition, 167–168
new target audience, 168–171
purchase motivation, 171–172
brand share, 295
brand-switching objectives, 135
brand-switching purchase, 135
brand trial, 135, 279
brand trial objective, 135

brand trial purchase, 134–135
branding, 6
broadcast advertisements
posttesting, 265–268
pretesting finished, 258–261
tracking, 267–268
Broadcast Code for Advertising to Children, 547, 554
broadcast media
direct-response advertising, 497
infomercials, 497
short-term programs, 497
teleshopping, 497–498
television spots, 497
Broadcasting Act of 1991, 545
budget. See media budget
budget allocation, 451–452
budgeting decisions, 37
bulletins, 385
bundles of attributes, 72
Burke Day-After Recall Test, 265
business advertising, 11
business organizations, 466
business publications, 353–354
business-to-business advertising, 11
buyer decision stages, 173
buying allowances, 446
buzz marketing, 99

C

cable television, 330
call centres, 13
campaign theme, 191
Canadian Advertising Rates and Data (CARD), 350–354
Canadian Code of Advertising Standards, 548–549
Canadian creative themes, 193–195
importance of, 193–194
successful, 194–195
Cannes, 195
carryover effect, 126
CASSIES, 194–195
catalogues, 496–497
Category Development Index (CDI), 287–288
category need, 118, 138–140, 279
category trial objectives, 135
category trial purchase, 135
cause-related marketing, 476–479
celebrity endorsements, 208–210
meaning movement and endorsement process, 210
meaning of, 210–211
overexposure, 209
overshadowing the product, 209
target audience's receptivity, 210
Census Agglomeration (CA), 375
Census Metropolitan Area (CMA), 375
Census Subdivisions (CSD), 375
central positioning, 160
central route to persuasion, 113
centralized system
administration, 37
advertising department under, 36
advertising manager, 36–37
budgeting, 37
coordination with other departments, 37
coordination with outside agencies and services, 37
execution, 37
planning, 37

channels, 99–100
    definition, 99
    direct, 9
    indirect, 9
    personal, 100
    nonpersonal, 100–101
children
    advertising to, 548, 559–560
    consumer socialization
        process, 554
    Quebec regulations, 547
cinema advertisements, 398
circulation
    magazines, 363
    newspapers, 372–373
city zone, 373
civic organizations, 466
classical conditioning, 114
classified advertising, 368
clearance service, 553–554
client/agency policies, 314
clients, 15–16
clipping service, 308
clutter
    Internet marketing, 537
    magazine advertising, 362
    media factor, 295
    media publicity, 472
    movie theatre advertising,
        371–372
    outdoor media, 392
    place-based media, 401
    product placement, 409
    promotional products
        marketing media, 404
    radio advertising, 341
    television advertising, 323–324
    transit media, 397
Code for Broadcast Advertising
    of Alcoholic Beverages,
    553–554
cognition, 115
cognitive dissonance, 75
cognitive processing of
    communications
    cognitive response approach,
        110–112
    elaboration likelihood model,
        112–115
cognitive response approach
    ad execution-related thoughts,
        111
    attitude toward the ad, 111–112
    counterarguments, 110–111
    model, 110
    product/message thoughts,
        110–111
    source bolsters, 111
    source derogations, 111
    source-oriented thoughts, 111
    support arguments, 111
cognitive responses
    definition, 110
    direct marketing, 500
    magazine advertising, 358–359
    newspaper advertising, 370
    outdoor media, 392
    place-based media, 399–400
    product placement, 410
    promotional products
        marketing media, 403
    radio advertising, 339
    television advertising, 320
    transit media, 396
cognitive stage, 104
collateral services, 16
column width, 376
ComBase, 375
commercial testing, 254, 256

commercials
    audio element, 231–232
    infomercials, 331, 497, 545
    jingles, 232
    needledrop, 232
    planning, 231
    posttests, 252–253
    production, 232–233
    script, 232–233
    split-30s, 323–324
    three phases of production, 234
    video element, 231
    voiceover, 231
commission system, 47–49
common ground, 100
communication. See also
        communication objectives
    approved objectives, and, 124
    cognitive processing, 110–112
    definition, 96
    distribution, 9
    effects, 133
    marketing, 4–9
    nonpersonal channels, 99–100
    objectives, 124
    personal channels, 99
    price, 7–9
    product, 5–7
    task, 130
    word-of-mouth, 99
communication effects, 118–119
    application, 138–142
    brand attitude, 118, 141
    brand awareness, 118, 140
    brand purchase intention,
        118, 141
    category need, 118, 138–140
    cross-media optimization
        studies, 534–535
    Internet measures, 534–535
    online measuring, 535
    planning implications, 118–119
    purchase facilitation, 118, 142
    recall and retention, 535
    surveys, 535
    tracking, 535
    types of, 118, 138
communication effects
    hierarchy, 132
communication effects
    pyramid, 133
    setting objectives using, 134
communication objectives
    assessment of DAGMAR, 129
    basis of, 128
    benchmark measures, 130
    for buyer decision stages,
        142–144
    characteristics, 128
    communication task, 129
    comprehensive response model
        applications, 131–134
    concrete, measurable tasks, 130
    Defining Advertising Goals
        for Measured Advertising
        Results, 129–131
    definition, 28, 128
    degree of change sought, 130
    IMC approach, 136
    options for, 138–142
    public relations plan, 466–467
    target audience, 129–130
    time period, 130–131
    translation from general
        marketing goals, 128
    website, 511–513
communication process models
    basic model of communication,
        96–103
    channel, 99–100

cognitive processing of
        communications, 110–115
    decoding, 100
    encoding, 97
    feedback, 101
    field of experience, 100
    message, 97–98
    noise, 101
    receiver, 100
    response, 101
    response process, 103–109
    semiotics, 97–98
    source, 96
communication task, 129
community involvement, 471
community members, 465
community newspapers, 366
commuter transit media
    exterior posters, 393
    interior door cards, 393
    interior transit cards, 393
    limitations of, 396–397
    station posters, 393
    strengths of, 395–396
    subway online, 394
    transit shelters, 394
comparison execution style, 219
comparative appeal, 197–198
compensation. See agency
        compensation
competitive advantage, 423
competitive analysis, 160–161
competitive parity method,
        308–309
competitors
    barrier to entry, 569
    consumers' perceptions of, 166
    economic effect on, 569–570
    economies of scale, 570
    identification of, 154–155
    influence attribute belief of,
        164–165
    positioning, and, 155
    positions of, 155
    sales promotions, and, 423
complaint process, 550–551
complaints for debate, 552–553
complaints report, 551–552
comprehension, 129
comprehension and reaction
    tests, 256
comprehensive measures, 266
comprehensive response model
    applications, 131–134
conative stage, 105
concave-downward function
    model, 303
concept testing, 251, 253–254
concrete, measurable tasks, 130
conclusion drawing, 225–226
conditional response, 114
conditioned stimulus, 114
consistency
    across executions, 192
    across media, 192
    across products, 192–193
    across promotional tools, 192
    across time, 191–192
    creative theme, 191–193
consumer, 78
consumer adoption of technology
    and media, 22
consumer behaviour
    decision-making. See consumer
        decision-making process
    definition, 64
    environmental influences, 426
    influence on purchase
        behaviour, 66
    novelty-seeking behaviour, 65

consumer choice, 569
consumer complaints, 550
consumer credit cards, 497
consumer decision-making
        process
    affect referral decision rule, 74
    alternative evaluation, 71–72
    assessing, 143
    attitudes, 72, 162–165
    brand loyalty, 74
    cognitive dissonance, 75
    consumer behaviour, 54
    consumer motivation, 66–67
    consumer perception, 69–71
    evaluative criteria, 71–72
    external search, 68
    functional consequences, 72
    group, 77–78
    heuristics, 74
    information search, 68–69
    integration processes, 74
    internal search, 68
    model, 64
    need recognition, 64–66
    perception, 69–71
    postpurchase evaluation, 74–75
    purchase decision, 73–74
    roles in family of, 78
    satisfaction, 75
    types, 76
    variations in process, 76–89
Consumer Drug Advertising
    Guidelines, 554
consumer franchise-building
    (CFB) promotions, 425
consumer juries, 256–257
consumer magazines, 350–352
Consumer Protection Act of
    Quebec, 547
consumer purchase motives
    importance of, 165
    informational motives, 165, 166
    transformational motives, 165,
        166–167
    types, 165
consumer sales promotion
    bonus packs, 440
    brand equity, 424
    brand equity building,
        424–425
    consumption, increase in, 424
    contests, 437–439
    coupons, 431–435
    definition, 12, 419
    distribution, 428
    event marketing, 442–444
    event sponsorship, 442
    franchise-building
        characteristic, 425
    frequency programs, 441–442
    game, 437
    geographic markets, application
        across, 427–428
    incentive characteristics,
        426–427
    incentive, value of, 428
    incentives, 426
    nonfranchise-building
        characteristic, 425–426
    objectives of, 423–425
    premiums, 435–437
    price-off deals, 440–441
    product lines, application
        across, 427
    rebates, 439–440
    refunds, 439–440
    repeat purchase, 424
    repeat purchase objective, 424
    samples, 429–431
    sampling, 429–431

shift of marketing dollars to, 20
strategy decisions, 425–428
strategy options, 425, 428–444
support of IMC program, 426
sweepstakes, 437–439
tactical decisions, 428
tactics decisions, 428
target, 10
techniques and tools, 426, 427
timing, 428
trial purchase objective, 423–424
consumer socialization process, 560
consumers, 77
advertising to, 11
competitors, perceptions of,166
declining brand loyalty, 421
dissatisfaction, 65
economic effect on choice, 569
fragmentation of consumer market, 421–422
lifetime value of, 22
listening to, 248–249
manipulation of, 562–563
motivations, 66–67
outdoor media, and, 384
perceptions, 15–16, 69–71
perspective, 26
point of view, 20–21
preferences, 170
public relations plan, and, 465
receptivity to magazine advertising, 361
technology and media, adoption of, 22
content sponsorship, 520
contests
consumer sales promotion, 437–438
definition, 437
game, 437
limitations, 438–439
strengths, 438
vs. sweepstakes, 437–438
trade sales promotion, 449–450
contextual targeting, 516–517
contiguity, 114
continuity, 289, 290
continuity programs, 441–442
continuous reinforcement schedule, 427
control, 252
controlled-circulation basis, 363
conviction, 129
cooperative advertising
definition, 448
horizontal, 449
ingredient-sponsored, 449
vertical, 448
copy platform, 186–187
copy testing, 258, 266, 269
copywriters, 42–43
corporate advertising, 473–482
advocacy advertising, 476
brand activities, 481–482
brand positioning, 480–481
cause-related marketing, 476–479
control of message, 473
controversy, 476
corporate reputation, 473–475
definition, 473
effectiveness, measurement of, 482
ethics, 480
event sponsorship, 479–480
exposure methods, 482
financial support, generation of, 476

general image/positioning ads, 475
image advertising, 475–476
limitations, 481
positioning, 475
questionable effectiveness, 482
recruitment, 475–476
sponsorship, 479–482
target audience exposure, 481
target audience fit, 481
television sponsorships, 475
tracking measures, 482
corporate brands, 173
corporate identification effect, 473
corporate leaders, 206
corporate name, 6
corporate reputations, 473–475
Corporate Social Responsibility Annual Report, 26
cosmetics, 554
cost efficiency
magazine advertising, 361
newspaper advertising, 370–371
outdoor media, 391
place-based media, 399
product placement, 409
promotional products marketing media, 404
radio advertising, 338
television advertising, 321
transit media, 396
cost estimates
absolute cost, 296
cost per ratings point (CPRP), 297–298
cost per thousand (CPM), 296–297
pass-along rate, 298–299
readers per copy, 298
relative cost, 296
target CPM (TCPM), 298
cost per ratings point (CPRP), 297–298
cost per point (CPP), 297
cost per thousand (CPM), 296–297
cost-plus system, 50
costs
commuter transit media, 396
couponing, 432–433
direct marketing, 500
Internet marketing, 537
magazine advertising, 361
measurement of advertising effectiveness, and, 249
media publicity, 472
outdoor media, 391, 392
place-based media, 399
products, 570–571
promotional products marketing media, 404
radio advertising, 338
television advertising, 321, 323
counterarguments, 110–111
coupons
bounce-back, 434
calculating costs, 432
cross-ruff, 434
direct mail, in, 433–434
distribution, 433–435
freestanding inserts, 433
in-store couponing, 434–435
inside package, 434
instant, 434
Internet, on, 435
limitations, 432–433
magazines, in, 434
misredemption, 433

newspapers, in, 434
online, 435
origins, 431
on packages, 434
redemption rates, 433
strengths, 431–432
coverage
definition, 280
geographic, 287–288
marketing, 286
outdoor media, 391
target audience, 285–287
television advertising, 322
waste, 286, 392, 396
creative boutiques, 46–47
creative brief, 45
creative challenge, 182–183
creative evaluation, 241–343
creative execution, 191, 192, 204
creative execution style
animation, 220–221
comparison, 219
definition, 218
demonstration, 218–219
dramatization, 223–224
factual messages, 218
humour, 224
imagery, 221–223
personality symbol, 221
scientific/technical evidence, 218
slice-of-life executions, 220
straight-sell execution, 218
testimonial, 219
creative factors, 295
creative personnel, 185–186
creative process, 173
research in, 184–186
creative services, 42–44
creative space buys, 359
creative strategy, 29, 178
See also advertising creativity
account planning, 183–184
animatic, 186
Canadian themes, 193–195
challenges, 182–183
consistency, 192–193
copy platform, 186–187
creative personnel, 185–186
creative process, 183
creative theme/ideal, 187–195
described, 29
focus groups, 185
general preplanning input, 184
illumination, 183
incubation, 183
key decisions, 250
message appeals, 195–205
planning, 181–187
preparation, 183
product/service-specific preplanning input, 184
in public relations plan, 468
research, 184
source of message appeal, 205–212
storyboards, 185
verification, 183
creative tactics, 178
audio messages, 234
brand attitude grid tactics, 237–239
brand awareness tactics, 236–237
creative execution style, 218–224
design elements, 227–234
evaluation of creative designs, 241–243
FCB planning model, 235–236

framework, 235–241
high involvement-informational, 240
high involvement-transformational, 241
importance of, 218
low involvement-informational, 239
low involvement-transformational, 239
message structure, 224–227
for print advertising, 228–231
R&P planning model, 236–241
video messages, 231–233
creative theme, 187–195
advertising campaign, 187
big ideas, 187–188
campaign theme, 191
Canadian, 193–195
consistency of, 191–193
image advertising, 188–189
inherent drama, 189
origin of, 187–191
positioning, 189, 191
sales promotion, 187, 452
unique selling proposition (USP), 188
creativity
advertising, 179
definition, 178,
television advertising, 320
magazine advertising, 358–359
newspaper advertising, 370
Internet marketing, 537
credibility
corporate leaders, 206
definition, 205
expertise, application of, 205–206
internalization, 205
limitations of credible sources, 206
news media options, 471–472
public relations, 13
sleeper effect, 206
source, 205–206
trustworthiness, 206
cross-media optimization studies, 534–535
cross-ruff coupon, 434
cross-sell, 491
cultural anthropology, 98
culture, 83
cume, 342
customer groups, 86–87
customer relationship management (CRM), 491
customers, 465

D

DAGMAR, 129–131
daily newspapers, 365–366
database
cross-sell, 491
customer relationship management, 491
definition, 489
developing, 489–492
effectiveness, 492
functions, 490–491
market segment selection, 490
repeat purchases stimulation, 490–491
sources of information, 492
using information, 489–491
database marketing, 489
day-after recall scores, 260
day-after recall tests, 265–266
dayparts, 329

decentralized system
  brand management systems, 39
  brand manager, 37
  described, 37–38
deceptive advertising, 555–557
decision maker, 78
decision rules, 74
declining brand loyalty, 421
decoding, 100–101
decorative models, 211–212
Defining Advertising Goals
  for Measured Advertising
  Results (DAGMAR), 129–131
demographic segmentation, 82
demographic selectivity, 357
demonstration advertising,
  218–219
departmental system, 46
design, 5
design elements
  audio messages, 234
  evaluation of, 241–243
  IMC tools, 227–234
  print messages, 228–231
  video messages, 231–234
diagnostic measures, 258
diary, 334–335
differential advantage, 159–162,
  168
differentiation, 569
direct broadcast satellite (DBS)
  services, 330
direct channels, 9
direct headlines, 229
direct mail
  advertising dollars and, 494
  coupons, and, 433–434
  direct-response media, 494, 496
  junk mail, 500
  mailing list, 496
direct marketing
  accuracy, 501
  cognitive responses, 500
  costs, 500
  database development, 489–492
  decision-making process,
    501–502
  definition, 13, 488
  direct-response advertising, 13
  direct-response media, 488
  e-mail, 529–530
  effectiveness, 499
  emotional responses, 500
  evaluation of, 499–501
  flexibility, 500
  frequency, 500
  IMC planning, 501–503
  IMC tools, 502–503
  Internet marketing
    communications, 529–533
  limitations, 500–501
  measures of effectiveness, 499
  media image, 500
  mobile, 530–533
  objectives, 493–494
  personalization, 500
  program plan. See direct-
    marketing program plan
  reach, 501
  scheduling flexibility, 500
  segmentation, 499
  segmentation capabilities, 499
  selective exposure, 501
  strengths, 499–500
  target audience coverage, 501
  target audience selectivity, 499
  target audiences, 492–493
  telemarketing, 13
  timing, 501
  tools, 13

direct-marketing program plan
  audiotex, 498
  broadcast media, 497–498
  catalogues, 496–497
  database, 489–492
  direct mail, 433, 494, 496
  direct-marketing objectives,
    493–494
  direct-response advertising, 497
  e-mail marketing, 529–530
  infomercials, 497
  mailing lists, 496
  media, 494–499
  one-step approach, 494
  print media, 498
  target audiences, 492–493
  telemarketing, 498
  telemedia, 498
  teleshopping, 497–498
  two-step approach, 494
direct response advertising,
  13, 497
direct-response agencies, 55
direct-response media
  broadcast media, 497–498
  catalogues, 496–497
  definition, 488
  direct mail, 494, 496
  mailing list, 496
  one-step approach, 494
  print media, 498
  telemarketing, 498–499
  two-step approach, 494
direct sampling, 429–431
direct source, 205
display advertising, 367–368
display/sponsorship, 533
displays, 447–448
dissatisfaction, 65
dissociative groups, 77
dissonance/attribution model,
  106–107
distribution
  communicating, 9
  consumer sales promotion,
    of, 428
  coupons, 433–435
  decisions, and IMC, 5
  marketing channels, 5, 9
  new products, 444
  promotional strategy, 12
  resellers, 5
diverting, 447
door-to-door sampling, 430
dramatization, 223–224
drugs, 545
dummy advertising vehicles,
  258
duplicated reach, 290

E
e-mail, 529–530
e-mail marketing, 529–530
economic censorship, 566–567
economic effects of advertising
  barrier to entry, 569
  competition, 569–570
  consumer choice, 569
  differentiation, 569
  economies of scale, 570
  information, and advertising,
    572–573
  market power, 571–572
  price, 570–571
  product cost, 570–571
  summary of, 571–573
economies of scale, 313, 570
editorial environment, 295
educators, 466
effective reach, 293

effectiveness
  advertising. See advertising
    effectiveness
  corporate advertising, 482
  difficulty measuring, 282
  direct-marketing, 499
  Internet, 533–536
  public relations, 468–469
  sales promotion, 455
elaboration, 112
elaboration likelihood model
  (ELM)
  ability, 113
  central route to persuasion, 113
  classical conditioning, 114
  conditioned response, 114
  conditioned stimulus, 114
  description of, 112–113
  explanation for, 114
  implications of, 114–115
  motivation, 113
  peripheral route to persuasion,
    113
  simplified model, 112
electrodermal response, 260
electroencephalographic (EEG)
  measures, 261
emotional appeals, 199–200,
  203–205
  combined rational and,
    203–205
  bases for, 199
emotional bonding, 203–204
emotional integration, 200
emotional responses
  direct marketing, 500
  magazine advertising, 358–359
  newspaper advertising, 371
  outdoor media, 391
  place-based media, 399–400
  product placement, 409
  promotional products
    marketing media, 404
  radio advertising, 339
  television advertising, 320
  transit media, 396
employees of firm, 464
encoding, 97
endorsement, 472
environmental influences
  culture, 83
  social class, 84
  subcultures, 83
esteem needs, 67
ethics
  advertising in bad taste,
    557–559
  children's advertising, 559–560
  corporate advertising, and, 480
  deceptive advertising, 555–557
  definition, 555
  fear appeals, 557
  gender stereotyping, and,
    563–564
  misleading ads, 555–557
  offensive advertising, 557–559
  puffery, 555
  sexual appeals, 557–558
  shock appeals, 558–559
  untruthful advertising, 555–557
  visible minorities, and,
    564, 566
ethnic publications, 352–353
ethnography, 98
evaluation guidelines, 242–243
evaluation of creative designs,
  241–243
evaluative criteria, 71–72
event marketing, 442–444
event sampling, 430, 450

event sponsorship, 442, 443,
  450, 479
events, 450
everyday low pricing (EDLP), 447
evoked set, 71
exchange, 4
exclusives, 471
executions, consistency across,
  192
experience, 115
expertise, 205–206
exposure, 534
exposure methods, 482
extended problem solving, 76
exterior posters, 393
external analysis, 26–28
external audiences, 464
external audits, 469
external search, 68
Extra Awards, 195
eye movement research, 261,
  390–391
eye tracking, 261, 390–391

F
factual messages, 218
false ads, 545, 546, 555
false claiming, 263–264
familiarity, 206, 208
farm publications, 353
favourable brand switchers,
  86, 169
favourable price appeal, 198
FCB planning model, 235–236
fear appeals, 200–201, 557
feature appeal, 197
fee arrangement systems, 49–50
fee-commission combination, 49
feedback, 101
field of experience, 100
field tests, 253
financial audit, 51
financial groups, 466
fixed-fee method, 49
Flesch formula, 258
flexibility
  direct marketing, 500
  magazine advertising, 362
  newspaper advertising, 369
  outdoor media, 391
  place-based media, 401
  product placement, 410
  promotional products
    marketing media, 404
  radio advertising, 339
  television advertising, 322
  transit media, 396
flighting, 289, 290
focus groups, 185, 253–254
food, 554
Food and Drugs Act and
  Regulations, The, 554
foreign publications, 354–355
forward buying, 447
four Ps, 5
fragmentation, 340
franchise-building promotions,
  425
free premiums, 435
freestanding inserts (FSIs), 433
frequency
  average, 294
  commuter transit media, 396
  definition, 280
  direct marketing, 500
  effects of, 292
  establishing levels of, 291–292
  factors, 295
  gross ratings points (GRP), 292
  level needed, 291–292

magazine advertising, 361–362
media publicity, 473
newspaper, 368–369
outdoor media, 391
place-based media, 401
product placement, 408
promotional products marketing media, 403
radio advertising, 338
vs. reach, 290–294
representation of, 291
television advertising, 322
transit media, 396
frequency programs, 441–442
full-service agencies
account executive, 46
account planners, 45
account services, 46
art department, 43
copywriters, 42–43
creative brief, 45
creative services, 42
definition, 42
departmental system, 46
group system, 46
layout, 43
management, 46
marketing services, 44–45
media department, 45
organizational chart, 44
production department, 44
research department, 44–45
storyboard, 43
structure, 44
traffic department, 44
functional benefits, 72
functional consequences, 72
functional magnetic resonance imaging (fMRI), 261

G

galvanic skin response, 260
game, 437
gatefolds, 359
Gender Portrayal Guidelines, 550
general advertising, 368
general image/positioning ads, 475
general preplanning input, 184
geographic coverage
magazine advertising, 358
media strategy, 287–288
newspaper advertising, 369
outdoor media, 391
place-based media, 401
product placement, 409
promotional products marketing media, 404
radio advertising, 338–339
television advertising, 322
transit media, 396
geographic segmentation, 82
geographic selectivity, 371
geographic targeting, 517
goodwill, 465
governments, 466
gross ratings points (GRP), 292
group decision making, 77–78
group system, 46
GRP showing, 391
Guide to Food Labelling and Advertising, 554
Guidelines for Cosmetic Advertising and Labelling, 554

H

habit formation strategy, 236
halo effect, 257

headlines
definition, 228
direct, 229
functions of, 228
indirect, 229
segmentation and, 228
subheads, 229
types of, 229
hemispheric lateralization, 261
heuristics, 74, 183
hierarchy models of communication response
implications, 104–105
types of, 103–104
hierarchy of effects model, 104
hierarchy of needs, 67
high elaboration, 112
high involvement decision, 237
high involvement media, 350
high involvement-informational creative tactics, 240
high involvement-transformational creative tactics, 241
horizontal cooperative advertising, 449
humour
appeals, 201–202
conclusions of study on, 202
creative execution style, and, 224

I

ideal state, 65
identification, 206–207
illumination, 183
image advertising
advocacy, 476
creative theme, 188–189
definition, 475
financial support, 476
positioning, 475
recruitment, 475–476
television sponsorship, 475
image sell, 295
image transfer, 339
imagery executions, 221–223
IMC planning
agency relationships, 56–59
brand positioning extensions, 172–173
budget allocation, 311–315
guidelines for creative evaluation, 241–243
message and source combinations, 212–213
objectives for buyer decision stages, 142–145
organization of text, 30–31
program for measuring effectiveness, 268–271
response model for decision making, 115–119
strategic use of broadcast media, 343–345
strategic use of direct marketing, 501–503
strategic use of Internet media, 538–539
strategic use of out-of-home media and support media, 410–413
strategic use of PR, 482–483
strategic use of print media, 377–379
strategic use of sales promotion, 451–455
target audience profile, 89–91

IMC services
benefits of, 56–57
disadvantages of, 57
expansion into, 57–58
responsibility for IMC, 57–58
IMC tools, 312–313
direct marketing and, 502–503
in-depth interviews, 185
in-flight advertising, 394
in-house agency, 38–40
in-store couponing, 434–435
in-store sampling, 430
inbound telemarketing, 498
incentive characteristics, 426–427
incentive-based system, 50–51
incentives, 418, 428, 449–450
incomplete satisfaction motives, 166
inconsistent terminologies, 282
incubation, 183
index number, 286
indirect channels, 9
indirect headlines, 229
indirect methods, 261
indirect source, 205
influencer, 78
infomercials, 331, 497, 545
information
and advertising, 572–573
disseminating, 512
insufficient, 280–282
interpreting, 70
retaining, 71
selecting, 70
information-persuasion dichotomy, 562
information processing model, 104
information provider, 78
information search, 68–69
informational creative tactics, 239, 240
informational motives, 165, 166
informative strategy, 235–236
ingredient-sponsored cooperative advertising, 449
inherent drama, 189
initiator, 78
ink-jet imaging, 357–358
innovation adoption model, 104
innovative marketing practices, 20–21
inquiry tests, 263
inserts, 359, 368
instant coupons, 434
insufficient information, 280–282
integrated marketing communications (IMC)
assessment of situation, 25–28
audience contacts, 19–20
behavioural objectives, 28, 134–138
brand equity, 453–455
budget allocation, 311–315, 451–452
characteristics of, 17–18
client/agency policies, 314
communication objectives, 28, 138–142
consumer adoption of technology and media, 22
consumer's point of view, 20–21
control of plan, 29–30
creative themes, 452
decision-making process, 501–502
definition, 17
design elements, 227–234
direct marketing, 502–503

distribution decisions, 5
evolution of, 17
external analysis, 26–28
growth, reasons for, 17–19
implementation of plan, 29–30
importance of, 19–23
innovative marketing practices, 20
internal analysis, 25–26
Internet marketing, and, 14–15
magazines, 377–378
management approach, 23, 117–119
market share goals, 313–314
marketing objectives, 28
marketing plan, 23–25
media support, 452–453
message and source combination, 212–213
model, 24, 25
new generation marketing approach, 17–19
newspapers, 379
objectives. See objectives
organizational characteristics, 315
out-of-home media, 411–412
participants, 15–16
permanent change, as, 19
planning efficiency and effectiveness, 23
planning for, 23–30
price decisions, 5
product decisions, 5
program development, 28–29
promotional budget, 28–29
promotional management, 23
promotional strategy, 8
radio advertising, 344–345
relationship marketing, 21–22
renewed perspective, 17–19
responsibility for, 57–58
services. See IMC services
strategic use of direct marketing, 501–503
strategic use of Internet media, 538–539
strategic use of out-of-home and support media, 410–413
strategic use of print media, 377–379
strategic use of public relations, 482–483
strategic use of sales promotion, 451–455
support media, 412–413
technology and media, consumer adoption of, 22
television advertising, 343
theoretical debate, 116
integrated services. See IMC services
integration processes, 74
intellectual stimulation, 171–172
intellectual stimulation or mastery motives, 167
interactive agencies, 56
interactive games, 526
interactive media, 14
interior door cards, 393
interior transit cards, 393
intermittent reinforcement schedule, 427
internal analysis, 25–26
internal audiences, 464
internal audits, 469
internal search, 68
internalization, 205

Internet
  advertising by Internet
      companies, 517–526
  advertising research, 254, 255
  consumers and, 20
  defining the Internet, 508
  definition, 508
  direct marketing on, 529–533
  electronic teleshopping,
      497–498
  microsites, 173
  public relations on, 527–528
  regulations, 545
  sales promotion on, 526–527
  sampling, 431
  usage, 508–511
  World Wide Web, 508
Internet marketing, 14–15
  advertising regulation, 545
  audience characteristics,
      533–534
  behaviour message, 536
  clutter, 537
  communication effects,
      534–535
  control for selective exposure,
      537
  costs, 537
  coupons, 435
  creativity and, 537
  evaluation of, 536–538
  exposure, 534
  integrated marketing
      communications, and,
      538–539
  interactive media, 14
  involvement, 537
  limitations, 537–538
  measuring effectiveness of,
      533–536
  media image, 537–538
  processing, 534
  processing time, 537
  reach, 537
  sources of measurement
      data, 536
  speed, 515
  strengths, 536–537
  target audience coverage, 537
  target audience selectivity,
      536–537
  target marketing, 516–517
  website promotion, 14
Internet marketing
      communications
  banner ads, 518–519
  brand image, 512–513
  content sponsorship, 520
  direct marketing, 529–533
  e-mail, 529–530
  information dissemination, 512
  interactive games, 526
  interstitials, 520
  links, 520
  mobile, 530–533
  paid search, 520–524
  personalization, 520
  pop-unders, 519
  pop-ups, 519
  public relations, 527–528
  push technologies, 520
  sales promotion, 526–527
  social media, 524–526
  sponsorship, 520
  Web participants, 508–510
  webcasting technologies, 520
  website communication
      objectives, 511–513
Internet media options, 516–533
  advertising, 517–526

  behavioural targeting, 516
  contextual targeting, 516–517
  direct marketing, 529–533
  geographic targeting, 517
  public relations, 527–528
  sales promotion, 526–527
  site-loyalty targeting, 517
  target audiences, 516–517
  time of day targeting, 517
Internet newspapers, 366–367
interstitials, 520
interviewer sensitivities, 264
interviews, 471
introductory allowances, 446
investors, 465
involvement
  Internet marketing, 537
  outdoor media, 393
  place-based media, 400
  product placement, 409
  promotional products
      marketing media, 404
  radio advertising, 341
  television advertising, 325
  transit media, 397
island ads, 372

J

jingles, 232
junk mail, 500

K

Ketchum Effectiveness Yardstick
    (KEY), 470

L

laboratory tests, 252
layout, 43, 230–231
learning. See consumer behaviour
likability, 180, 206, 207–208
limited problem solving, 76
links, 520
listener attention, 340
local advertising, 11, 368
location sampling, 430–431
logo, 6
low-credibility sources, 206
low elaboration, 112
low involvement decision, 237
low-involvement hierarchy, 108
low involvement-informational
    creative tactics, 239
low involvement-transformational
    creative tactics, 239
loyalty, 84
loyalty programs, 426, 441–442

M

magazine advertising
  absolute cost, 361
  attention, 361
  audience measurement, 364
  bleed pages, 359
  business publications, 353–354
  buying space, 363–364
  circulation, 363
  classification of magazines,
      350–354
  clutter, 362
  competition, 354–355
  consumer magazines, 350–352
  consumer receptivity and
      involvement, 361
  controlled-circulation basis,
      363
  cost efficiency, 361
  costs, 361
  coupons, 434
  creative space buys, 359
  creativity, 358–359

  demographic selectivity, 357
  ethnic publications, 352–353
  farm publications, 353
  flexibility, 362
  foreign publications, 354–355
  frequency, 361–362
  gatefolds, 359
  geographic coverage, 358
  ink-jet imaging, 357–358
  inserts, 359
  lead time, 362
  limitations, 361–362
  media image, 360–361
  pass-along readership, 363
  permanence, 360
  PMB study, 364
  prestige, 360–361
  processing time, 359–360
  rates, 365
  reach, 361–362
  reader involvement, 359–360
  readership, 363–364
  reproduction quality, 371
  scheduling flexibility, 362
  selective binding, 357
  selective exposure, 361
  selectivity, 355–358
  strategic use of print media,
      377–378
  strengths of, 355–361
  target audience coverage, 362
  total audience, 364
  variety of magazines, 350
Magazine Impact Research
    Service (MIRS), 264–265
mail, sampling through, 430
mailing list, 496
mall intercepts, 254
mall posters, 398
management by objectives, 469
management issues
  advertising agency decision,
      38–40
  advertising agency option, 40
  creative boutiques, 46–47
  full-service agencies, 42–46
  in-house agency option, 38–40
  media buying services, 47
managerial approaches in budget
    setting
  affordable method, 305–306
  arbitrary allocation, 306
  bottom-up budgeting, 305
  client/agency policies, 314
  clipping service, 308
  competitive parity method,
      308–309
  factors influencing budget
      decision, 300–301
  market potential, 287–288, 313
  market share goals, 313–314
  market size, 313
  objective and task method,
      309–310
  organizational characteristics,
      315
  payout plan, 310–311
  percentage-of-sales method,
      306–307
  ROI budgeting method, 309
  top-down budgeting, 305
marginal analysis, 302
market analysis
  competitive analysis, 160–161
  market opportunities, 282
  strategic marketing plan, 150
market definition, 158–159,
    167–168
market opportunities, 282
market partition 154–155

  market position, 151
  market positioning strategy,
      150–152
  market potential, 287–288, 313
  market power, 571–572
  market segmentation. See
      segmentation
  market share goals, 313–314
  market size, 313
  market testing of ads
    comprehensive posttest
        measures, 266
    day-after recall tests, 260
    false claiming, 263–264
    Gallup & Robinson Magazine
        Impact Research Service,
        265
    inquiry tests, 263
    interviewer sensitivities, 264
    posttests of broadcast
        commercials, 265–268
    posttests of print ads,
        263–265
    recall tests, 264–265
    recognition tests, 263–264
    reliability of recognition
        scores, 264
    single-source tracking
        methods, 267
    split-run tests, 263
    Starch recognition method,
        263–264
    test marketing, 266–267
    tracking print/broadcast ads,
        267–268
  market threats, 282
  marketer-controlled sources, 68
  marketer-induced need
      recognition, 65–66
  marketing
    account-specific, 423
    cause-related, 476
    database, 489
    decisions, 5
    definition, 4, 22
    direct, 13
    e-mail, 529–530
    event, 442–444
    exchange, 4
    function, 4–5
    Internet. See Internet marketing
    objectives, 28
    promotional products, 401–405
    relationship, 21–22
  marketing and promotions
      process model, 79
  marketing channels, 9
  marketing communication
    distribution, 9
    integrated. See integrated
        marketing communications
    marketing, 4–5
    price, 7–9
    product, 5–7
  marketing coverage, 286
  marketing decisions, 5
  marketing factors, 295
  marketing function, 4–5
  marketing mix, elements of, 5
  marketing objectives
    carryover effect, 126
    choice of type of, 125–126
    definition, 125
    IMC plan, 28
    sales objectives, 126
    statement of, 125–126
  marketing plan, 23–25
    definition, 23
    elements in, 23–24
    review of, 23–25

marketing planning process, 78–80
marketing program development
  branding, 7
  distribution decisions, 5, 9
  IMC decisions, 23–25
  packaging, 6–7
  price decisions, 5, 7–9
  product decisions, 5–7
  promotion and, 29
marketing public relations (MPR), 467
marketing research. See also effectiveness
  association tests, 185
  creative strategy, 184
  emotional bonding, 203–204
  in-depth interviews, 185
  focus groups, 185, 253–254
  methods, 185
  motivation, 66–67
  projective techniques, 185
marketing services, 44–46
marketing strategy. See marketing program development
mass media, 100
materialism, 561–562
meaning transfer model, 210–211
measurement data, 536
measurement methods
  alpha activity, 261
  behaviour, 536
  brain waves, 261
  commercial testing, 254, 256
  comprehension and reaction tests, 256
  concept testing, 251, 253–254
  consumer juries, 256–257
  copy testing, 258, 266, 269
  day-after recall scores, 260
  diagnostic measures, 258
  dummy advertising vehicles, 258
  electrodermal response, 260
  electroencephalographic (EEG) measures, 261
  eye tracking, 261
  field tests, 253
  finished broadcast ads, 258–261
  finished print messages, 257–258
  Flesch formula, 258
  functional magnetic resonance imaging (fMRI), 261
  galvanic skin response, 260
  halo effect, 257
  hemispheric lateralization, 261
  indirect methods, 261
  laboratory tests, 252
  market testing of ads, 263–268
  on-air tests, 260
  physiological measures, 260–261
  portfolio tests, 257–258
  positron emission tomography (PET), 261
  posttests, 251, 252, 263–268
  pretests, 251–252, 257–261
  pupillometrics, 260
  readability tests, 258
  rough testing, 254, 256
  theatre testing, 258–260
measurement of effectiveness. See effectiveness
media
  availability of, 282
  commissions from, 47–49
  consistency across, 192
  high-involvement, 350
  interactive, 14

number used, 295
public relations plan, and, 465–466
sampling through, 430
target audience profile for, 90–91
media-usage characteristics, 284
media budget
  absolute cost, 296
  affordable method, 305–306
  allocation, 311–315, 451–452
  arbitrary allocation, 306
  bottom-up budgeting, 305
  client/agency policies, 314
  clipping service, 308
  competitive parity method, 308–309
  concave-downward function model, 303
  cost per ratings point (CPRP), 297–298
  cost per point (CPP), 297
  cost per thousand (CPM), 296–297
  economies of scale, 313
  factors influencing budget decision, 304
  function of, 300
  IMC tools, 312–313
  managerial approaches, 305–311
  marginal analysis, 302
  market share goals, 313–314
  objective and task method, 309–310
  organizational characteristics, 315
  overview, 300–301
  pass-along rate, 298–299
  payout plan, 310–311
  percentage-of-sales method, 306–307
  readers per copy, 298
  relative cost, 296
  ROI budgeting method, 309
  S-shaped response curve, 303
  sales response models, 303–304
  size of, 302
  target CPM (TCPM), 298
  theoretical approaches, 301–304
  top-down budgeting, 305
media buying services, 47
media characteristics, 284–285
media class, 280
media decisions, 250–251
media department, 45
media engagement, 296
media factors, 295
media image
  direct marketing, 500
  Internet marketing, 537–538
  magazine advertising, 360–361
  newspaper advertising, 369
  outdoor media, 392
  place-based media, 400
  product placement, 410
  promotional products marketing media, 404
  radio advertising, 339
  television advertising, 322, 325–326
  transit media, 396
media mix, 283–285
media objectives, 279–280
  brand attitude, 279
  brand awareness, 279
  brand repeat purchase, 279
  brand trial, 279
  category need, 279

definition, 276
media planning, and, 279–280
media organizations, 16
media planners, 282
media planning, 276–282
  activities involved in developing, 278
  challenges of, 280–282
  coverage, 280
  definition, 276
  effectiveness, difficulty of measurement, 282
  flexibility, 282
  frequency, 280
  inconsistent terminologies, 282
  insufficient information, 280–282
  media class, 280
  media objectives, 276, 279–280
  media options, 276
  media plan, 279
  media strategy, and, 280
  media vehicle, 280
  medium, 280
  overview, 276–279
  reach, 280
media publicity
  community involvement, 471
  definition, 469
  exclusives, 471
  interviews, 471
  limitations, 473
  media options, 470–471
  press conferences, 471
  press releases, 471
  strength, 471–473
media strategy, 29, 276, 280, 283–294
  Brand Development Index (BDI), 287, 288
  Category Development Index (CDI), 287–288
  continuity, 289, 290
  decisions, 283–294
  described, 29, 280
  direct marketing, 494–499
  flighting, 289, 290
  frequency, 290–294
  geographic coverage, 287–288
  gross ratings points (GRP), 292
  index number, 286
  media mix, 283–285
  media planning, and, 280
  pulsing, 289, 290
  reach, 290–294
  scheduling, 289–290
  target audience coverage, 285–287
  waste coverage, 286
media support, 452–453
media tactics, 276, 280
media tactics decisions, 294–300
  blocking chart, 299–300
  media vehicle, 294–296
  relative cost estimates, 296–299
media vehicle, 280, 282, 294–296
media, the
  advertising, and, 566–568
  mass media, 100
  public relations plan, and, 465–566
medium, 280
message
  communication effects of, 118–119
  communication process model, in, 97–99
  definition, 97
  development, 29
  factual, 218

one-sided, 226
processing, 117–118
public relations plan, in, 467–468
refutational, 226
semiotics, 97–98
sidedness, 226
target audience profile for, 89–90
two-sided, 226
verbal, 226–227
visual, 226–227
message appeals
  advertising appeal, 197
  comparative appeal, 197–198
  creative execution, 191, 192, 204
  definition, 195
  emotional appeals, 199–200, 203–205
  favourable price appeal, 198
  fear appeals, 200–201
  feature appeal, 197
  humour appeals, 201–202
  news appeals, 198
  product/service popularity appeals, 198
  rational appeals, 196–199, 203–205
  reminder appeal, 198–199
  sexual appeals, 557–558
  shock appeals, 558–559
  source of, 205–212
message complexity, 295
message factors, 295
message structure
  conclusion drawing, 225–226
  message sidedness, 226
  one-sided message, 226
  order of presentation, 224–225
  presentation and, 224
  primacy effect, 224
  recency effect, 224
  refutation, 226
  two-sided message, 226
  verbal message, 226–227
  visual message, 226–227
message uniquenesss, 295
message variation, 295
metatags, 521
microsites, 173
Millennials, 3
mindscribing, 183
misleading ads, 545, 555–557
mixed approach-avoidance motives, 166
mnemonics, 71
mobile advertising
  display/sponsorship, 533
  mobile applications, 533
  mobile content, 532–533
  mobile search, 533
  short-message service (SMS), 530–532
mobile applications, 533
mobile content, 532–533
mobile search, 533
mobile signage, 386
motivation
  elaboration likelihood, 113
  hierarchy of needs, 67
  marketing research, 66–67
  purchase, 171–172
motives
  consumer purchase, 165–167
  definition, 66
  incomplete satisfaction, 166
  informational, 165, 166
  intellectual stimulation or mastery, 167

motives (*continued*)
mixed approach-avoidance, 166
normal depletion, 166
problem avoidance, 166
problem removal, 166
sensory gratification, 166–167
social approval, 167
transformational, 165, 166–167
movie theatres, 398
limitations, 398
multiattribute attitude model,163
multimedia messaging service (MMS), 532–533
multiple methods, 431
music, 232
mystery ads, 204

N
NADbank, 374–375
national advertising, 11, 368
national newspapers, 366
need recognition
actual state, 65
cause of, 65
definition, 64
dissatisfaction, 65
ideal state, 65
marketer-induced, 65–66
new needs/wants, 65
new products, 66
out of stock products, 65
related products/purchases, 65
sources of, 65–66
needledrop, 232
negotiated commission, 49
network advertising, 326–328
network radio, 341
new campaigns, 295
new category users, 87–88, 169–170
new products
distribution, 444
need recognition, and, 66
news appeals, 198
news media options
accuracy, 473
audience reach, 472
brand weakness, 473
clutter, 472
community involvement, 471
corporate identification effect, 473
cost, 472
credibility, 471–472
endorsement, 472
exclusives, 471
frequency potential, 473
image building, 472
interviews, 471
limitations, 473
message consistency, 473
press conferences, 471
press release, 471
strengths, 471–473
telephone press conferences, 471
timing, 473
newspaper advertising
absolute cost, 370–371
agate line, 376
attention, 371
audience measurement, 374–375
buying space, 372–377
circulation, 372–373
city zone, 373
classified advertising, 368
clutter, 371–372
cognitive responses, 370
column width, 376

ComBase, 375
community newspapers, 366
cost efficiency, 370–371
coupons, 434
daily newspapers, 365–366
display advertising, 367–368
emotional responses, 371
extensive penetration, 368–369
flexibility, 369
frequency, 368–369
future of, 377
general advertising, 368
geographic coverage, 369
geographic selectivity, 371
Internet newspapers, 366–367
island ads, 372
limitations, 371–372
local advertising, 368
media image, 369
NADbank, 374–375
national advertising, 368
national newspapers, 366
newspapers, types of, 365–367
open-rate structure, 377
poor reproduction, 371
preferred position rate, 377
preprinted inserts, 368
processing time, 369
rates, 376–377
reach, 368–369
reader involvement and acceptance, 369
readership, 373–374
retail trading zone, 373
run of paper (ROP), 377
scheduling flexibility, 369
selective exposure, 371
selectivity, lack of, 371
services offered, 370–371
short life span, 371
special ads and inserts, 368
special-audience newspapers, 367
strategic use of print media, 379
strengths of, 368–371
supplements, 367
target audience coverage, 371
target audience selectivity, 371
types of, 367–368
Next*Print, 259
Next*TV, 266
noise, 101
non-customer groups, 87–89
non-prescription drugs, 554
nonfranchise-building (non-FB) promotions, 425–426
nonpersonal channels, 99–100
normal depletion motives, 166
novelty-seeking behaviour, 65

O
objective and task method, 309–310
objectives
behavioural objectives. See behavioural objectives
brand re-trial objective, 135
brand trial objective, 135
brand-switching objectives, 135
buyer decision stages, 142–145
category trial objectives, 135
communication objectives. See communication objectives
communications and, 124
consumer sales promotion, 423–425
decision making and, 124–125
direct marketing, 493–494
evaluation of results, 125

isolating, 309
marketing objectives, 28, 125–126, 127
measurement of results, 125
media, 279–280
media budget, and, planning and, 28, 124–125
reevaluating, 310
repeat-consumption objective, 137
repeat-purchase objective, 135–136
sales objective debate, 126
setting IMC objectives, 134–142
setting objectives, 124–129
types of, 125–126
value of, 124–125
off-invoice allowance, 446
offensive advertising, 557–559
on-air tests, 260
on-package sampling, 430
one-sided message, 226
one-step approach, 494
online commercials, 521
online measuring, 535
open-rate structure, 377
operant conditioning, 426
order of presentation, 224–225
organization
advertising manager, 36–37
brand management systems, 39
brand manager, 37
centralized system, 36–37
characteristics, 315
decentralized system, 37–38
out-of-home media
other brand loyals, 88–89, 170
other brand switchers, 88, 170–171
out of stock products, 65
out-of-home media
definition, 384
movie theatres, 398
new options in, 384
outdoor media, 384–393
pervasiveness of, 384
place-based media, 397–401
strategic use of, 411–412
transit media, 393–397
types, 384
outbound telemarketing, 498
outdoor media, 384–393
See also out-of-home media
absolute cost, 392
attention, 391
audience measurement, 387–391
awareness and, 385
backlit posters, 385
bulletins, 385
clutter, 392
cognitive responses, 392
COMB, 387–389
consumers' view of, 389–390
cost efficiency, 391
coverage, 391
creativity, 388
effectiveness, 389
efficiency, 391
emotional responses, 391
frequency, 391
geographic coverage, 391
geographic flexibility, 391
GRP showing, 391
involvement, 393
limitations, 392–393
media image, 392
mobile signage, 386
OMAC, 389–391
operators, 385

options, 384–387
posters, 385
processing time, 392
reach, 391
schedule, 387
scheduling flexibility, 391
selective exposure, 391
spectaculars, 385
street-level posters, 385
strengths of, 391
superboards, 385
target audience coverage, 392
transit-shelter posters, 385
overexposure, 209

P
packaging, 6–7, 434
PACT (Positioning Advertising Copy Testing), 269–271
criteria for effective research, 269–270
definition, 269
guidelines for effective testing, 270–271
principles, 269
paid search
blogs, 523–524
definition, 520
online commercials, 521
podcasting, 522–523
Really Simple Syndication (RSS), 523
video on demand, 521–522
partial reinforcement schedule, 427
participants in promotional process
advertising agencies, 16
clients, 15–16
collateral services, 16
media organizations, 16
specialized marketing communications services, 16
pass-along rate, 298–299
pass-along readership, 363
payout plan, 310–311
people meter, 334–335
percentage charges, 50
percentage of projected future sales, 307
percentage-of-sales method, 306–307
perception
definition, 69
information interpretation, 70
information retention, 71
information selection, 70
mnemonics, and, 71
selective, 69
selective attention, 70
selective comprehension, 70
selective exposure, 70
selective retention, 71
sensation, 69–70
source of message appeal, and, 205–212
subliminal, 71
perceptual map, 152
Performance by Results (PBR) system, 50–51
peripheral cues, 113
peripheral route to persuasion, 113
personal channels, 99
personal experience, 68
personal selling, 15
personal sources, 68
personal video recorders (PVRs), 324–325
personality, 83

personality symbol, 221
personalization
  direct marketing, 500
  Internet marketing
    communications, 520
persuasion
  brand attitude, 163–165
  central route to, 113
  peripheral route to, 113
physiological measures
  alpha activity, 261
  brain waves, 261
  electrodermal response, 260
  electroencephalographic (EEG)
    measures, 261
  eye tracking, 261
  galvanic skin response, 260
  hemispheric lateralization, 261
  indirect methods, 261
  pupillometrics, 260
physiological needs, 67
PIMS (Profit Impact of Marketing
  Studies), 7–8
place, 5
place-based media
  absolute cost, 399
  attention, 400
  clutter, 401
  cognitive responses, 399–400
  cost efficiency, 399
  emotional responses, 399–400
  flexibility, 401
  frequency, 401
  geographic coverage, 401
  involvement, 400
  limitations, 400–401
  mall poster, 398
  media image, 400
  movie theatres, 398
  operators, 397
  options, 397–399
  processing time, 401
  reach, 401
  scheduling flexibility, 401
  selective exposure, 400
  strengths of, 399–400
  target audience coverage, 401
  target audience selectivity, 399
planning efficiency and
  effectiveness, 23
PMB study, 364
podcasting, 522–523
point-of-purchase displays,
  447–448
pop-unders, 519
pop-ups, 519
portable people meter (PPM),
  334–335
portfolio tests, 257–258
positioning, 150–157, 189, 191
  brand name, 159
  brand positioning strategy,
    152–154
  brand positioning strategy
    decision process, 154–157
  central, 160
  creative theme, 189, 191
  definition, 150
  end benefit, 158–159
  image advertising, 475
  market positioning strategy,
    150–152
  product category, 159
  usage situation, 159
  user, 160–162
positron emission tomography
  (PET), 261
posters, 385
  backlit, 385
  exterior, 393

mall, 398
  station, 394
  street-level, 385
postpurchase dissonance,
  106–107
postpurchase evaluation, 74–75
posttests
  broadcast commercials,
    265–268
  classification of, 251
  comprehensive measures, 266
  day-after recall tests, 265–266
  definition, 251
  described, 252
  inquiry tests, 263
  print ads, 263–265
  recall tests, 264–265
  recognition tests, 263–264
  single-source tracking methods,
    267
  split-run tests, 263
  test marketing, 266–267
  tracking print/broadcast ads,
    267–268
  tracking studies, 267–268
preferred position rate, 377
premiums
  definition, 435
  free, 435
  limitations, 437
  self-liquidating, 437
  strengths, 435–437
preparation, 183
preprinted inserts, 368
presentation, order of, 224–225
press conferences, 471
press release, 471
pretests
  advantages of, 252
  classification of, 251
  day-after recall scores, 260
  definition, 251
  described, 251
  diagnostic measures, 258
  disadvantages of, 252
  dummy advertising vehicles,
    258
  finished ads, 257–261
  finished broadcast ads, 258–261
  finished print messages,
    257–258
  Flesch formula, 258
  on-air tests, 260
  physiological measures,
    260–261
  portfolio tests, 257
  readability tests, 258
  theatre tests, 258–260
price, 5
  communicating, 7–9
  decisions, and IMC, 5
  definition, 7
  economic effects on, 570–571
  positioning by.
price-based heuristics, 74
price-off deals, 440–441
price planning, 7
primacy effect, 224
primary demand advertising, 11
print advertising. See also
  magazine advertising
  body copy, 229–230
  creative tactics for, 228–231
  headlines, 228–229
  layout, 230–231
  magazines, 362
  posttesting, 263–265
  pretesting finished, 257–258
  tracking, 267–268
  visual elements, 230

print media
  direct marketing, and, 498
  direct-response media, 498
  magazines, 377–378
  newspapers, 379
print test, 257
PRIZM$_{NE}$, 83
problem-solution, 171
problem avoidance motives, 166
problem removal motives, 166
processing, 534
processing time
  Internet marketing, 537
  magazine advertising, 359–360
  newspaper advertising, 369
  outdoor media, 392
  place-based media, 401
  product placement, 410
  promotional products
    marketing media, 404
  radio advertising, 339
  television advertising, 323
  transit media, 395
product class, 166
product decisions, 5
product manager, 37
product/message thoughts,
  110–111
product placement
  absolute cost, 409
  attention, 410
  audience measurement, 410
  clutter, 409
  cognitive responses, 410
  cost efficiency, 408
  decisions, 405–408
  described, 405
  emotional responses, 409
  expenditures on, 406
  frequency, 408
  geographic coverage, 409
  involvement, 409
  issues related to, 407
  limitations, 409–410
  media image, 410
  processing time, 410
  reach, 408
  scheduling flexibility, 410
  selective exposure, 409
  strengths, 408–409
  target audience coverage, 410
  target audience selectivity, 410
  virtual ads, 407
product/service popularity
  appeals, 198
product/service-specific
  preplanning input, 184
product symbolism, 6
production department, 44
products, 4, 5
  attributes and benefits, 151
  branding, 6
  bundles of attributes, as, 72
  communicating, 5–7
  consistency across, 192–193
  cost of, 570–571
  new, 66
  out of stock, 65
  overshadowing, 209
  packaging, 6–7
  related, 65
  salient attributes, 153
  salient beliefs, 162
  salient benefits, 154
professional advertising, 11
Profit Impact of Marketing
  Strategies (PIMS), 7–8
program rating, 292, 335–336
programs, 329–330
projective techniques, 185

promotion, 5, 9
  brand positioning strategy,
    152–157
  definition, 9
  marketing strategy, and, 29
  vs. sales promotion, 12
promotion-based heuristics, 74
promotional allowances, 446
promotional budget, 28
promotional management, 23
promotional mix
  advertising, 9–10
  coordination of elements, 9
  definition, 9
  direct marketing, 13
  Internet marketing, 14–15
  participants in promotional
    process, 15–16
  personal selling, 15
  public relations, 12–13
  sales promotion, 12
  tools of, 9
promotional plan, 17, 30
promotional products marketing
  media
  absolute cost, 404
  attention, 404
  audience measurement,
    404–405
  clutter, 404
  cognitive responses, 403
  cost efficiency, 404
  coverage, 403, 404
  definition, 401
  frequency, 403
  geographic coverage, 404
  involvement, 404
  limitations, 404
  media image, 404
  processing time, 404
  reach, 404
  research, 404–405
  scheduling flexibility, 404
  selective exposure, 404
  specialty advertising, 401
  strengths, 403–404
  strengths of, 403–404
  target audience coverage, 403
  target audience selectivity, 403
  trends, 402
promotional pull strategy,
  419–420
promotional push strategy, 419
promotional sensitivity, 421
promotional strategy, 25
promotional tools
  consistency across, 192
  testing, 250–251
psychographic segmentation
  culture, 83
  definition, 82
  personality, 83
  social class, 84
  values and lifestyle, 82–83
public relations
  advantages of, 13
  classes of relationships,
    460–461
  corporate advertising. See
    corporate advertising
  criteria for measuring the
    effectiveness of, 469
  definition, 12, 460
  effectiveness, 468–469
  exclusives, 471
  historic role, 467
  IMC planning, 482–483
  Internet marketing
    communications, 527–528
  interviews, 471

public relations (continued)
  Ketchum Effectiveness
    Yardstick, 470
  marketing public relations
    functions, 467
  media publicity. See media
    publicity
  new role, 460–461
  news media options, 468–469
  press conferences, 471
  press release, 471
  publicity, 12–13, 461–462
  video news release (VNR),
    462
public relations firm, 55
public relations plan
  behavioural objectives, 466
  business organizations, 466
  civic organizations, 466
  communication objectives,
    466–467
  community members, 465
  creative strategy, 468
  customers, 465
  delivery, 468
  educators, 466
  effectiveness, 468–469
  employees of firm, 464
  external audiences, 464
  financial groups, 466
  governments, 466
  internal audiences, 464
  investors, 465
  marketing public relations
    (MPR), 467
  media, 465–466
  message focus, 467–468
  relevant target audiences,
    464–466
  shareholders, 465
  situation analysis, 463–464
  strategy, 467–468
  suppliers, 465
  tactics, 468
public service announcement, 10
public sources, 68
publicity, 12–13, 461–462
puffery, 555
pulsing, 289, 290
pupillometrics, 260
purchase
  brand-switching, 135
  brand re-trial, 135
  brand trial, 134–135
  category trial, 135
  related, 65
  repeat, 135–136
purchase cycles, 295
purchase decision, 73–74
purchase facilitation, 118, 142
purchase intention, 73, 118
purchase motivation, 171–172
purchase motives
  consumer, 165–167
  importance of, 165
purchase-related behaviour,
  136–137
purchase situation, 85
purchasing agent, 78
push money, 449
push technologies, 520

Q
qualitative audit, 51
qualitative research, 184–185
quality, positioning by, 159
quantitative benchmarks, 130
Quebec regulations on children's
  advertising, 547

R
R&P perspective
  behavioural objectives,
    134–138
  brand attitude, 141
  brand awareness, 140
  brand purchase facilitation, 142
  brand purchase intention, 141
  category need, 138–140
  communication objectives,
    138–142
  purchase-related behaviour,
    136–137
  repeat consumption, 137–138
  repeat purchase, 135–136
  trial, 134–135
R&P planning model
  brand attitude grid tactics,
    237–241
  brand awareness tactics,
    236–237
  high involvement-informational
    creative tactics, 240
  high involvement-
    transformational creative
    tactics, 241
  low involvement-informational
    creative tactics, 239
  low involvement-
    transformational creative
    tactics, 239
radio advertising
  absolute cost, 338
  amount of processing time, 339
  audience measurement, 342
  average quarter-hour (AQH)
    figure, 342
  average quarter-hour rating
    (AQH RTG), 342
  average quarter-hour share
    (AQH SHR), 342
  buying radio time, 341
  clutter, 341
  cost, 338
  cost efficiency, 338
  creative limitations, 339
  creativity for cognitive
    responses, 339
  creativity for emotional
    responses, 339
  cume, 342
  efficiency, 338
  flexibility, 339
  fragmentation, 340
  frequency, 338
  geographic coverage, 338–339
  image transfer, 339
  integrated marketing
    opportunities, 344–345
  involvement, 341
  limitations, 339–341
  listener attention, 340
  media image, 339
  mental imagery, 339
  network radio, 341
  reach, 338
  research data, 342
  scheduling flexibility, 339
  selective exposure, 340
  selectivity, 340
  spot radio, 341
  strategic use of broadcast
    media, 344
  strengths of, 338–339
  target audience coverage, 340
  target audience selectivity, 338
  time classifications, 341–342
random samples, 258
ratings point, 335–336

rational appeals, 196–197
  combined emotional and,
    203–205
reach
  amount of, 290–291
  commuter transit media, 395
  definition, 280
  direct marketing, 501
  duplicated, 290
  effective, 293–294
  establishing levels of, 290–291
  vs. frequency, 290–294
  gross ratings points (GRP), 292
  Internet marketing, 537
  magazine advertising, 361–362
  newspaper advertising,
    368–369
  outdoor media, 391
  place-based media, 401
  product placement, 408
  promotional products
    marketing media, 404
  radio advertising, 338
  representation of, 291
  television advertising, 322
  transit media, 395
  unduplicated, 291
reach program rating, 292
readability tests, 258
reader involvement
  magazine advertising, 359–360
  newspaper advertising, 369
readers per copy, 298
readership
  magazines, 363–364
  newspapers, 373–374
  pass-along, 363
  total, 364
Really Simple Syndication
  (RSS), 523
realism, 252
rebates, 439–440
recall and retention, 535
recall tests, 264–265
receiver, 100–101
recency effect, 224
recognition method, 263
recognition tests, 263–264
recruitment, 475–476
reference group, 77
refunds, 439–440
refutation, 226
regulations. See advertising
  regulations
reinforcement, 427
related products/purchases, 65
relationship marketing, 21–22
relative cost, 296
reminder advertising, 71
reminder appeal, 198–199
repeat consumption, 137–138
repeat-consumption objective,
  137
repeat exposures, 295
repeat purchase, 128, 135–136,
  424
repeat-purchase objectives,
  135–136
repetition, 114
repositioning, 167–172
research, 184
  creative process, 184–186
  eye movement, 261, 390–391
  Internet advertising, 254, 255
  marketing. See marketing
    research
  motivation, 66–67
  promotional products, 404–405
research department, 44–45

research problems, 249
response, 101
response process
  affective stage, 104
  AIDA model, 103–104
  alternative response
    hierarchies, 106–109
  behavioural stage, 105
  cognitive stage, 104
  conative stage, 105
  decision making, 115–119
  dissonance/attribution model,
    106–107
  hierarchy of effects model, 104
  information processing model,
    104
  innovation adoption model,
    104
  low-involvement hierarchy, 108
  models of, 103
  standard learning model, 106
  traditional response hierarchy
    models, 103–105
retail advertising, 11
retail inventory building, 445
retail trading zone, 373
retailers' power, 422–423
return on investment (ROI), 309
RFM scoring method, 492
ROI budgeting method, 309
rough testing, 254, 256
routine problem solving, 76
RSS (Really Simple Syndication),
  523
run of paper (ROP), 377

S
S-shaped response curve, 303
safety needs, 67
sales promotion
  acceleration tool, 418
  account-specific marketing, 423
  bonus packs, 440
  brand equity, 453
  brand proliferation, 421–422
  budget allocation, 451–452
  characteristics of, 418
  competition, 423
  consumer. See consumer sales
    promotion
  contests, 437–438, 449–450
  cooperative advertising,
    448–449
  coupons, 431–435
  creative themes, 452
  declining brand loyalty, 421
  definition, 12, 418
  displays, 447–448
  event marketing, 442–443
  event sponsorship, 443–444
  events, 450
  extra incentive, 418
  fragmentation of consumer
    market, 422–423
  frequency programs, 441–442
  growth of, 420–423
  IMC issues, 451–455
  incentives, 428, 449–450
  increased accountability, 422
  increased promotional
    sensitivity, 421
  inducement, 418
  Internet marketing
    communications, 526–527
  measuring effectiveness, 455
  media support, 452–453
  operant conditioning, 426
  plan. See consumer sales
    promotion

planning, 418–423
point-of-purchase displays, 447–448
premiums, 435–437
price-off deals, 440–441
vs. promotion, 12
promotional pull strategy, 419–420
promotional push strategy, 419
push money, 449
reaching specific target audience, 421
rebates, 439–440
refunds, 439–440
retailers' power, 422–423
sales training programs, 450–451
sampling, 429–431
schedules of reinforcement, 427
short-term focus, 422
spiffs, 449
strategic importance, 420–421
strategic role, 453
sweepstakes, 437–438
trade. See trade sales promotion
trade advertising, 419
trade allowances, 445–447
trade shows, 451
trap, 454
types of, 418–420
sales promotion agencies, 54
sales promotion trap, 454
sales response models, 303–304
sales training programs, 450–451
salient attributes, 153
salient beliefs, 162
salient benefits, 154
sampling
creative approaches, 430–431
definition, 429
direct, 430
door-to-door, 430
event, 430
in-store, 430
Internet, 431
limitations, 429–430
location, 430–431
methods, 430–431
multiple methods, 431
on-package, 430
strengths, 429
through mail, 430
through media, 430
satisfaction, 75
scatter market, 328
schedules of reinforcement, 427
scheduling, 289–290, 295
scheduling flexibility
direct marketing, 500
magazine advertising, 362
newspaper advertising, 369
outdoor media, 391
place-based media, 401
product placement, 410
promotional products marketing media, 404
radio advertising, 339
television advertising, 322
transit media, 396
scientific/technical evidence, 218
script, 232–233
search engine advertising, 520–524
segmentation
applicability of approach, 80
bases for, 80–85
behaviouristic, 84–85

benefit, 85
demographic, 82
direct marketing,
examples of variables, 81
geographic, 82
headlines and, 228
psychographic, 82–84
selective attention, 70
selective binding, 357
selective comprehension, 70
selective demand advertising, 11
selective exposure
definition, 70
direct marketing, 501
Internet marketing, 537
magazine advertising, 361
newspaper advertising, 371
outdoor media, 391
place-based media, 400
product placement, 409
promotional products marketing media, 404
radio advertising, 340
television advertising, 324–325
transit media, 396
selective perception, 69, 107
selective retention, 71
selectivity
commuter transit media, 396
demographic, 357
geographic, 371
magazine advertising, 355–356
newspaper advertising, 371
promotional products marketing media, 404
radio advertising, 340
television advertising, 323
self-actualization needs, 67
self-liquidating premiums, 437
self-satisfaction strategy, 236
semiotics, 97–98
sensation, 69–70
sensory gratification motives, 166–167
sex role stereotypes, 563–564
sexual appeals, 557–558
shaping, 427
share of audience, 336
share of voice, 295, 313
shareholders, 465
shock appeals, 558–559
short-message service (SMS), 530–532
short-term programs, 497
signal substitution, 545
similarity, 206, 207
simultaneous substitution, 331
single-source tracking methods, 267
site-loyalty targeting, 517
situation analysis, 27, 463–464
situations, 85
sleeper effect, 206
slice-of-life executions, 220
slotting allowances, 446
social approval motives, 167
social class, 84
social effects of advertising
manipulation of consumers, 562–563
materialism, 561–562
media, the, 566–568
stereotyping, 563–566
summary of, 568
visible minorities, portrayal of, 564, 566
women, portrayal of, 563–564
social/love and belonging needs, 67

social media, 15, 524–526
sound, 234
source
bolsters, 111
definition, 96, 205
derogations, 111
direct, 205
indirect, 205
low-credibility, 206
message, 96–97
power, 205
source of message appeal
attractiveness, 206–212
celebrity endorsements, 208–211
characteristics, 205–212
compliance, 205
credibility, 205–206
decorative models, 211–212
definition, 205
direct source, 205
familiarity, 206, 208
indirect source, 205
likability, 206, 207–208
perceptions, 208
similarity, 206, 207
source power, 205
source-oriented thoughts, 111
spam, 529
special advertisements, 368
special-audience newspapers, 367
special interest group complaints, 550
specialized marketing communications services, 16
specialized services
direct-response agencies, 55
interactive agencies, 56
public relations firm, 55
sales promotion agencies, 54
specialty advertising, 401
specialty networks, 331–334
specialty television advertising, 330–334
spectaculars, 385
spiffs, 449
split-30s, 323–324
split-run tests, 263
sponsorship
brand activities, 481–482
brand positioning, 480–481
content, 520
corporate advertising, 479–482
event, 479
exposure methods, 482
Internet advertising, 520
measuring effectiveness, 482
target audience exposure, 481
target audience fit, 481
television advertising, 328–329
tracking measures, 482
types, 480
sponsorships, 520
spot advertising, 328
spot radio, 341
standard learning model, 106
Starch recognition method, 263–264
station posters, 394
station reps, 328
stereotyping, 563–566
stockholders, 476
stocking allowances, 446
storyboard, 43, 185, 186, 233
straight-sell execution, 218
strategic marketing plan, 150
street money, 446
street-level posters, 385
subcultures, 83

subheads, 229
subliminal perception, 71
subway online, 394
super-bus, 394
superagencies, 41
superboards, 385
superstations, 330
suppliers, 465
support arguments, 111
support media
definition, 384
product placements, 405–410
promotional products marketing media, 401–405
strategic use of, 412–413
surveys, 535
sweepstakes
definition, 437
game, 438
limitations, 438–439
strengths, 438
vs. contests, 437–438
symbols, 6

T
target audience, 79
brand attitude, 162–165
communication objectives, 129–130
corporate advertising, 481
direct marketing, 492–493
Internet, 516–517
marketing factor, 295
multiple, 172–173
new, 168–171
place-based media, 401
public relations plan, 464–466
reaching specific, 421, 516–517
receptivity, 210
target audience coverage
direct marketing, 499–501
Internet marketing, 537
magazine advertising, 362
media strategy decisions, 285–287
newspaper advertising, 371
outdoor media, 392
place-based media, 401
product placement, 410
promotional products marketing media, 403
radio advertising, 340
television advertising, 320–321
transit media, 396
target audience decision, 78–89
market segmentation, 80–85
marketing planning process, 78–80
target audience options, 86–89
target market selection, 85–86
target audience options, 86–89
customer groups, 86–87
non-customer groups, 87–89
target audience profile, 89–91
target audience selectivity
direct marketing, 499
Internet marketing, 536–537
magazine advertising, 355–358
newspaper advertising, 371
outdoor media, 392
place-based media, 399
product placement, 410
promotional products marketing media, 403
radio advertising, 338
television advertising, 323
transit media, 396
target CPM (TCPM), 298
target market, 79

611